The Shaping Of America Program

The Shaping Of America

RICHARD O. CURRY, University of Connecticut, Storrs, Connecticut

JOHN G. SPROAT, Lake Forest College, Lake Forest, Illinois

KENYON C. CRAMER, Hawken School, Lyndhurst, Ohio

Encounters with America's History
DeAnne Sobul, formerly of the Los Angeles Public Schools
Los Angeles, California

Audio-Visual Kit
Elmer W. Ruhnke ⎫ Baldwin High School
John Roy Elden ⎭ Baldwin, New York

Teaching Strategies
William N. Murphy, Hanover Junior-Senior High School
Hanover, New Hampshire

Tests
Leanne Corbi, Cuyahoga Falls High School
Cuyahoga Falls, Ohio

Art Consultant: Billie Greene, Atlanta Public Schools, Atlanta, Georgia
Literature Consultant: Alene Axelrad, Bellaire High School, Houston, Texas
Editorial Consultant: Stephen H. Bronz

The Shaping Of America

Richard O. Curry

John G. Sproat

Kenyon C. Cramer

Holt, Rinehart and Winston, Inc.

New York   Toronto   London   Sydney

ISBN: 0-03-084489-4
12345 032 987654321

Richard O. Curry is Professor of United States History at the University of Connecticut and has taught at the University of Pittsburgh and Pennsylvania State University. He received his B. A. and M. A. degrees from Marshall University and his Ph.D. degree from the University of Pennsylvania. In addition to publishing articles in historical journals, including *Civil War History* and the *Journal of Negro History*, Dr. Curry is the author of *A House Divided: A Study of Statehood Politics and the Copperhead Movement*. He has edited and co-edited several books, among them *The Abolitionists*. Dr. Curry is a past Fellow of the Society of Religion in Higher Education and the National Endowment for the Humanities and has served as Associate Director of the NDEA Institutes in United States History.

John G. Sproat is Professor of History and Chairman of the History Department of Lake Forest College. He has taught in colleges and universities both in the United States and Europe, including Michigan State University, Williams College, University College, Cambridge, and as a Fulbright lecturer at the University of Hamburg. Dr. Sproat received his B. A. degree from San Jose State College and his M. A. and Ph.D. degrees from the University of California at Berkeley. He is author of *The Best Men: Liberal Reformers in the Gilded Age*, and in addition to publishing articles in such journals as *Social Education* and *Journal of Southern History*, he has contributed to several collections of essays, including *Main Problems in American History*.

Kenyon C. Cramer is Chairman of the History Department of Hawken School, where he teaches courses in American history and the humanities. Mr. Cramer also taught for several years at Shaker Heights High School and was a lecturer at Case Institute of Technology and Western Reserve University. He received his B. A. degree from Oberlin College and was a John Hay Fellow at Harvard University. He is the editor of *The Causes of War*, volume one in the *Problems in American History* series..

Each part of *The Shaping of America* reflects the style and historical interpretations of its author: Introductory chapter and Parts 1 and 2—Richard O. Curry; Part 3—Kenyon C. Cramer; Parts 4 and 5—John G. Sproat.

Title page: *View of St. Louis* (detail), Leon Pomarede, *c.* 1832
Cartography by Goushā

ACKNOWLEDGMENTS

Grateful acknowledgment is given to the following publishers for permission to reprint copyrighted materials. This list is continued on pages 790 and 791. Art acknowledgments appear on pages 792-794.

AMERICAN HERITAGE PUBLISHING CO., INC., for "Murder Most Foul," from *Murder Most Foul* by Archie Robertson. Copyright © 1964 by American Heritage Publishing Co., Inc.

CONTENTS

ART PORTFOLIOS

LIFE PORTFOLIOS

MAPS

CHARTS

FEATURES

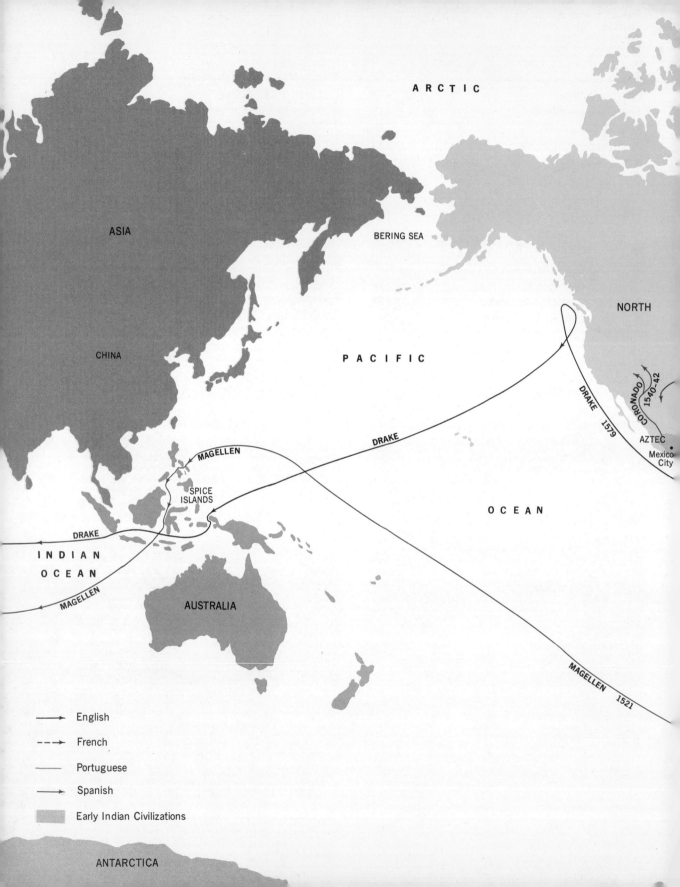

ARCTIC

ASIA

BERING SEA

NORTH

CHINA

PACIFIC

DRAKE 1579

CORONADO 1540-42

DRAKE

AZTEC

Mexico City

MAGELLEN

SPICE ISLANDS

OCEAN

DRAKE

INDIAN OCEAN

MAGELLEN

AUSTRALIA

MAGELLEN 1521

→ English

--→ French

— Portuguese

→ Spanish

Early Indian Civilizations

ANTARCTICA

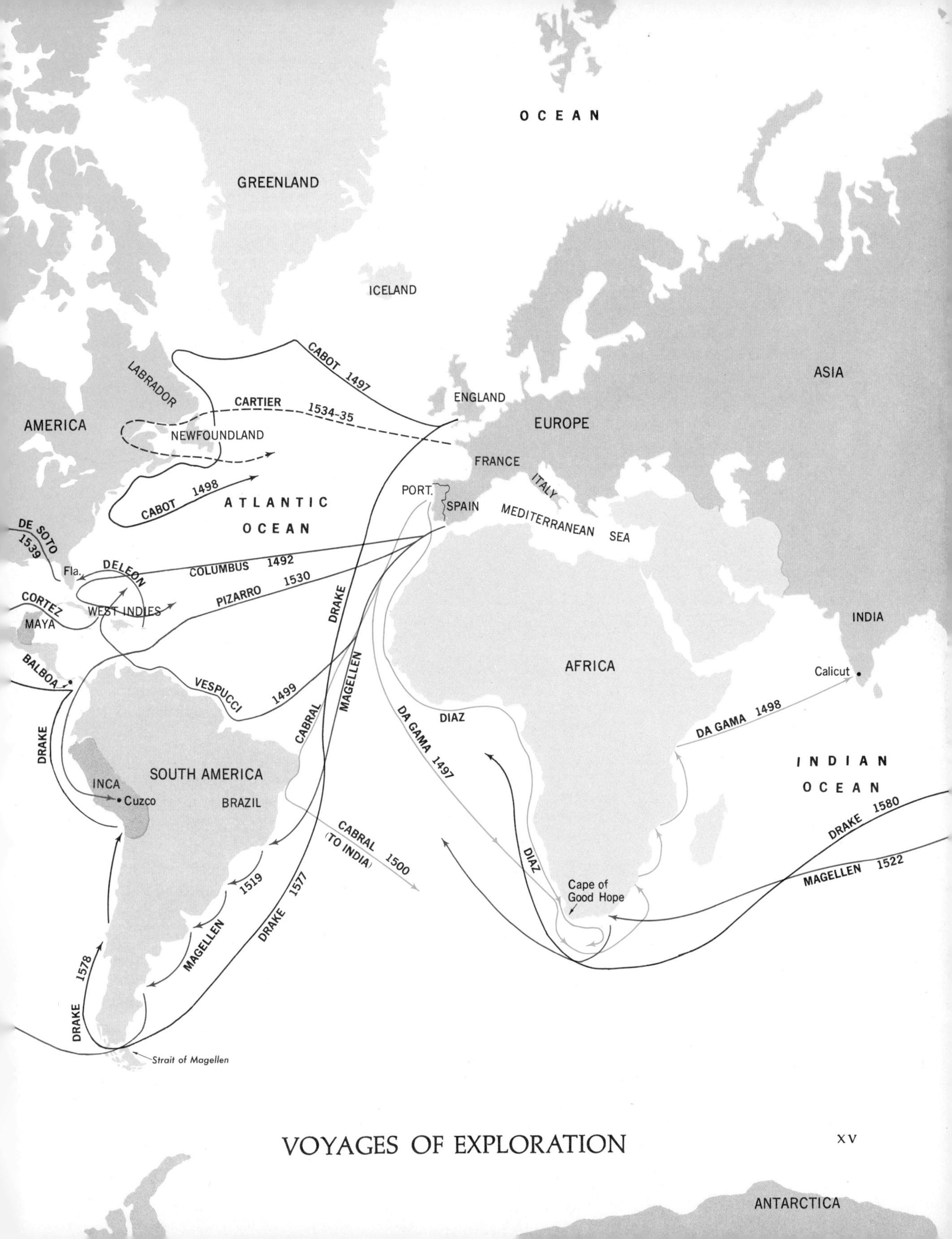

OCEAN

GREENLAND

ICELAND

ASIA

LABRADOR

CABOT 1497

CARTIER 1534-35

ENGLAND

EUROPE

AMERICA

NEWFOUNDLAND

FRANCE

ITALY

CABOT 1498

ATLANTIC
OCEAN

PORT.

SPAIN

MEDITERRANEAN   SEA

DE SOTO
1539

DELEON

COLUMBUS 1492

Fla.

CORTEZ

PIZARRO 1530

INDIA

MAYA

WEST INDIES

DRAKE

AFRICA

Calicut •

BALBOA

VESPUCCI

1499

DA GAMA 1498

DRAKE

CABRAL

MAGELLEN

DIAZ

INDIAN
OCEAN

INCA

SOUTH AMERICA

DA GAMA 1497

• Cuzco

DRAKE 1580

BRAZIL

CABRAL 1500
(TO INDIA)

DIAZ

MAGELLEN 1522

1519

Cape of
Good Hope

MAGELLEN

DRAKE 1577

DRAKE

1578

Strait of Magellen

VOYAGES OF EXPLORATION

XV

ANTARCTICA

TO THE READER

THE SHAPING OF AMERICA has been developed to meet the needs of those students who are inquiring into this nation's history—not just its political and military aspects, but its social, cultural, and economic aspects as well. It is designed for those who want to understand the nature of history itself—that history involves the constant interpretation and reinterpretation of evidence by scholars who do not share the same point of view and who often disagree. A history text cannot be considered "a closed book," for its contents are constantly open to question, disagreement, and critical evaluation.

This text seeks to serve the needs of history and of history students through the use of a variety of study aids, sources, types of evidence, and points of view. A brief description of the various elements in the text should alert the reader to what constitutes this variety.

Leading off the text is an *introduction* that presents a survey of the European backgrounds for the discovery, exploration, and settlement of America. The map on pages xiv–xv provides a graphic presentation of the voyages of exploration. The book is then divided into five *parts,* each one dealing with a period in America's history. Each part contains a series of from three to nine chapters.

All *chapters* begin with an introduction that places the people and events in it in their place and time in history. There follow a few questions to keep in mind while reading the chapter. From there the chapter divides into from three to six *sections*—each one a self-contained reading assignment. Each of these also begins with three or four questions; with these questions in mind, the reader searches out evidence within the section that helps him to discover its major themes.

The section contains not only the narrative, but other elements as well. It may contain one of the sixty or so *features,* which generally fall into three categories—explanations of basic economic concepts, contemporary or firsthand accounts of events, or interpretations that conflict with those presented in the text. Or it may contain one of the fifty or so *maps* that help the reader to locate people or events in their geographic surroundings; if it is a war map, it is generally accompanied by a commentary outlining the progression of the decisive battles. The section might also contain one of the more than thirty *charts*—presenting graphic summaries of material in the narrative or providing new data.

Many sections include one- or two-page *picture groupings* that provide more evidence about the subjects under inquiry. Sixteen color *portfolios* are spotted throughout the book. Eight of them show examples of representative American art of various periods, and the other eight show what life looked like at certain times in America's history.

Finally, each chapter culminates with a *conclusion* in which the author evaluates the events or offers an interpretation of the evidence presented in the chapter. *End-of-chapter questions* follow to help the reader to recall and to organize what he has learned. The chapter concludes with an *annotated bibliography* for the reader who wants to expand his knowledge or pursue a special interest.

The last element in the book is a *reference section* containing an atlas of the United States, information about its Presidents, and a detailed index.

EUROPE EXPANDS INTO THE NEW WORLD

For thirty-three days the three small caravels flying the banner of Spain under the command of Christopher Columbus had struggled westward across the Atlantic. Then, early on the morning of October 12, 1492, a sailor spotted land, a small island in the Bahamas, in the West Indies. The next morning Columbus stepped ashore on the heavily wooded island, which he claimed for Spain and gave the name San Salvador—"Holy Savior." Columbus later noted in his journal that the people of the island "could be subjected and made to do all that one wished." But Columbus had no time to reflect on this terrible forecast of the fate of the American Indian. His own quest for wealth and glory absorbed him completely. "I intend to go," he wrote in his journal, "and see if I can find the island of Japan."

The momentous voyage of Columbus was part of the great European explorations that began in the early fifteenth century, as Europe emerged from the Middle Ages. These explorations were undertaken for several reasons. First was the desire to find new trade routes to the wealth of the Orient. The East was the source of exotic products highly valued by Europeans—spices (used mostly to kill the taste of spoiled meat), perfumes, silks, carpets, precious stones, and even opium, the only drug then known to kill pain.

Throughout the Middle Ages, Europe had traded with the East, but eastern goods were costly because the combined land and sea routes were long, complicated, and hazardous. Moreover, eastern trade was in the hands of Italian and Arab merchants and passed through Italian cities like Venice and Pisa. European merchants were naturally anxious to break this monopoly. To Europeans, then, direct trade with the Orient offered the possibility of cheaper goods and high profits.

Yet, trade and profit were not the only motives that impelled Europeans to set out in new directions. Many were driven by a sense of adventure, and many others were influenced by missionary zeal. Most Europeans in the fifteenth and sixteenth centuries were extremely pious, and the Church demanded a unified Christian world, promising that those who served the needs of the Church would gain God's favor. Christianizing the world was one way to gain God's favor; hence, many explorers saw themselves as soldiers under the banner of Christ.

In addition, drastic changes in the political, religious, and economic order of Europe began to take place around the middle of the fifteenth century. Powerful monarchies were gradually destroying the old feudal order; new economic forces—collectively known as the Commercial Revolution—disrupted traditional patterns of trade and commerce; and the Protestant Reformation not only changed the way men thought about God but also shattered the peace of Europe. By the end of the sixteenth century, Europe was a collection of strong states which quarreled with one another over religion and territory. To the new monarchs of Europe, who financed the voyages of exploration, the New World offered possible solutions to the tremendous social, political, economic, and religious problems of Europe itself.

Emergence Of Strong National Monarchies

War was the common experience of Europeans of the Middle Ages. The Crusades against the Moslems had stretched over two centuries and were closely followed by the Hundred Years' War between France and England which ended in 1456. England, exhausted from the war, was soon torn by civil strife between contenders for the throne; and a devastated France was ruled by powerful nobles who disregarded their feeble monarchs and often entered into alliances against them.

In England this chaotic situation changed in the latter part of the fifteenth century, when Henry Tudor gained the throne and suppressed the feuding nobles. Henry had the support of a rising middle class of merchants and gentry who were becoming more and more involved in international trade. Weary of war, they were willing to pay the taxes necessary for peace and order. The Tudor kings wisely encouraged commerce, and the taxes they collected helped the monarchy flourish.

At the same time in France, King Louis XI also gained middle-class support and consolidated his power at the expense of the rebellious nobles by skillfully arranged marriages and political intrigue. For centuries, Spain had been a collection of rival northern kingdoms warring against the Moors, the Moslems who had swept across North Africa and into Spain in the eighth century. The two most powerful monarchs in Spain were Isabella of Castile and Ferdinand of Aragon. Their marriage in 1468 helped unify Spain, and their combined strength had by the end of the fifteenth century driven the Moors from the country. Spain was further unified by its Catholic religion, which had for centuries brought Spanish Christians together under its banner to fight the Moors.

In order to keep and extend the absolute power they wanted, the monarchs of Europe needed money, and what they could raise in taxes and a variety of royal fees was never enough. One possible source of revenue was the wealth to be gained from voyages of discovery. In sponsoring these adventures, the kings arranged for the profits to flow into the royal treasury. The wealth that Spain extracted from its New World empire enabled that nation to dominate Europe for nearly a century.

Unfortunately for the French and English kings, their explorers failed to discover great wealth, and confronted by burgeoning Spanish power and plagued by internal difficulties, France and England lagged behind Spain in building overseas empires. Ultimately, however, France and England would challenge Spanish supremacy, both in Europe and the New World.

The Protestant Reformation

While the spiritual ideal of the Christian Church was the salvation of men's souls, Christianity had slowly developed over the centuries into a highly complex institution whose basic secular aim was religious unity. And yet unity had never really been achieved. In the eleventh century, the eastern branch of the Church refused to accept the authority of the Pope in Rome and broke away. The western, or Roman, branch of the Church also had a long history of heresies and schisms, or divisions, which weakened its authority. The fourteenth-century English reformer John Wycliffe and the Bohemian Jan Hus both attacked Church authority, and Hus's followers led violent revolts against Rome in the fifteenth century.

Moreover, as the power of national monarchs increased, the authority of the Church and its leadership declined. In the mid-1400's, France denied the Pope the power to appoint high church officials in France, and England followed suit. Although the majority of Europeans still accepted the spiritual authority of the Church, its temporal power was being questioned.

Then, in the early sixteenth century, the unity of the Church was shattered beyond repair when a German monk and teacher named Martin Luther defied the authority of the Pope and attacked the teachings of the Church, thus setting in motion the Protestant Reformation. "All Germany is in commotion," a churchman wrote to the Pope in 1520. "Nine out of every ten cry 'Luther' and the tenth, if he does not care for what Luther says, at least cries, 'Death to the court of Rome!'"

Protestants objected not only to the teachings of the Church but they also believed that the Church was both too wealthy and too wordly. The Papal court was a luxurious center of artistic and literary culture, not all of it sacred. It was also a center of political intrigue. Initially, Luther's attack on the Church had centered around the Church's sale of indulgences, a guarantee by the Church that in the afterlife sinners could escape God's wrath. Luther and his followers condemned this sale of Divine grace. Luther also objected to the Catholic theory of the eucharist, or communion, and to the use of Latin in the mass.

Had the Protestant revolt been confined to Germany, it might have been crushed like earlier schisms and heresies. But Martin Luther, in attacking the power of the Papacy, articulated the ideas and feelings of thousands of people all over Europe. Attacks on the Church increased, and Protestantism spread to Scandinavia, France,

Switzerland, Holland, Scotland, and ultimately, to England.

Much of the popularity of the Reformation can be traced to the role of the vernacular, the language of the man in the street. The invention of movable type by Gutenburg in 1455 made possible the large-scale production of cheaply priced literature. In an age when religion was basic to man's understanding of his world and destiny, the early literature was almost entirely theological. By 1500, pamphlets and books in the native tongues of Europe were common. This led to a demand for English, French, and German Bibles, for religious services in the languages of the people, and increased the interest of ordinary people in religious issues.

As the Reformation spread across Europe, demands were voiced insisting that the Church be radically altered. Some groups were content simply to deny the authority of Rome, leaving the old doctrines nearly intact. Others, especially the followers of the Frenchman John Calvin, created an entirely new approach to worship, church organization, and theology.

Calvinists contended that the elaborate ceremonies of the Church obscured the real meaning of Christianity. They also denied that the Church government should be vested in bishops, cardinals, and the Pope, pushing to its logical conclusion the basic idea that inspired Protestants, that of the priesthood of all believers. According to Calvinists, all men who dedicated the work of their hands to God were engaged in a "divine calling." This being so, monks and bishops were not merely unnecessary, they were an affront to God.

Disputes among Protestants on these matters were inevitable. The Lutherans, who were confined mainly to Germany and the Scandinavian countries, retained bishops, as did the Anglican Church, which grew up in England, thus incurring the wrath of Calvinists. Calvinists in turn questioned the efficacy of Baptism, which scandalized the Anglicans.

Almost from its inception, the Reformation inspired warfare in Europe. In fact, a continuous war interrupted by temporary treaties kept the continent in turmoil from the 1540's through the 1690's. The theological and institutional unity of Christendom would never be restored.

War in the Middle Ages, while chaotic and sometimes devastating, was carried on primarily by the nobility and small bands of retainers. Even the great Crusading armies had been mere collections of nobles and their followers. The general populace was scarcely involved. Warfare had been waged for dynastic reasons or simple plunder, and the passions of the mass of people had never been aroused.

But the religious wars launched by the new national monarchs touched the deepest convictions of men. As the monarchs demanded strict conformity to the accepted state church, Europeans developed religious loyalties and a new sense of national identity which combined love of God with hatred of foreigners and religious dissenters. In these wars the whole nation was involved, and armies grew in size and weapons in destructiveness.

The financial and military burden fell upon the new national monarchies, while the personal burden fell most heavily upon tens of thousands of people who would not conform to established state religions, whether Anglican, Lutheran, or Roman Catholic. As the religious disruptions continued, fortunately for the dissenters the New World offered an alternative to persecution because of religious and political beliefs.

The Rise Of Atlantic Commerce

In the Middle Ages, the trade routes were dominated by the Mediterranean, and international trade was financed largely by great banking families in Italy and Germany who loaned money to merchants at exhorbitant rates. In order to free themselves from the bankers, merchants during the fifteenth century began to form *joint stock companies.* Merchants of moderate means joined together to finance a venture, and shared in the risks and the profits. The new capital made available through this innovation stimulated a considerable expansion of European industry.

Then in 1497, the Portuguese sailed around the tip of Africa and on to India, opening up a direct water route to the East. At the same time, Spain was beginning to explore the westward route to the Orient across the Atlantic. The Mediterranean monopoly of trade was over. Portugal and Spain were followed in turn by the French, the English, and the Dutch, all of whom sponsored exploring expeditions across the Atlantic in search of new routes to the East to tap its wealth and open up new markets for European products.

Along with the expansion of international trade and the growth of industry in Europe a new theory of wealth called *mercantilism* began to evolve. The full development of this theory would not come until the seventeenth century, but its main outlines were clear by 1550.

The primary objective of mercantilism was to create economic self-sufficiency for a nation. The importance of accumulating precious metals was stressed. Spain, of course, acquired huge quantities of gold and silver from its empire in the New World. England and France, however, did not control gold mines in the New World, and they had to depend upon the expansion of trade and industry to earn gold and to prevent it from being spent on acquiring raw materials. In order to do this, a nation had to keep its balance of trade perpetually favorable by exporting more goods than it imported. Only essential raw materials that could not be obtained at home were to be imported, and these were then converted into finished products to be sold abroad.

Ultimately, European nations established colonies to serve both as sources of raw materials and as markets for the manufactured products of the mother country. Moreover, colonial trade with rival nations was limited to products not considered essential to the home economy. Theoretically, these products were to be shipped first to the mother country before going on to foreign ports. Kings could then exact taxes and duties, and merchants and shippers at home could profit by serving as middlemen. Furthermore, colonies were not allowed to engage in manufacturing enterprises that would compete with those at home. Under the mercantile system, the welfare of the mother country, not the colonies, was the primary consideration.

All European nations passed legislation incorporating mercantile principles, but enforcement was not always easy or possible. Individuals and nations violated these laws whenever it suited their purposes. In order to protect commerce and to prevent smuggling, large navies became a national necessity. One historian has summarized the rationale behind mercantilism: "Each nation tried to establish a monopoly for itself; and each nation sought to defy the monopoly pretensions of the others."

The emergence of modern Europe was characterized by great political, religious, and economic changes, and as Europe expanded, the New World began to assume tremendous significance for the Old. By 1550, exploration was directed by centralized monarchies seeking new sources of revenue. The wealth of the New World must be used to solve the religious, political, and economic problems of Europe. The New World, however, was not the East. It was the continents of North and South America which were discovered, conquered, and exploited by European nations.

Early Voyages Of Discovery

Portugal was the first European nation to systematically begin exploration. Under the direction of Prince Henry—called Henry the Navigator—Portuguese sailors began exploring the west coast of Africa as early as 1420. For half a century, Portuguese mariners worked their way down the coast until in 1484 Bartholomew Diaz had reached the southern tip of Africa. Then, in 1497, the Portuguese trading empire was launched when Vasco da Gama rounded Africa and sailed on to India.

By that time Spain had already begun exploring the westward route to the East. The first reports of Columbus indicated that he had found the East Indies, and he assumed that Japan lay not far beyond. In the fifteenth century, such a view was typical, since most Europeans believed that the world was much smaller than it actually is. In 1492, a global map drawn by Martin Behaim, a German geographer, located Japan more or less where Columbus had discovered the West Indies.

After Columbus's epic voyage, geographical knowledge grew rapidly. In 1496, King Henry VII of England commissioned John Cabot to search the North Atlantic for a suitable route to the East. Cabot touched on Labrador and probably Newfoundland. He did not find a route to the East, but he did confirm the fact that the ocean off the North American continent abounded in cod fish.

It was the exploration of the Central and South American coasts, however, that finally convinced Europe that old geographical speculations were wrong. Columbus returned three times to the New World. In addition to planting the first Spanish colony in Haiti, he explored most of the Caribbean islands, the coasts of Venezuela, Panama, and Honduras. Brazil was accidentally discovered by the Portuguese when in 1500 a fleet bound for India under the command of Pedro Alvarez Cabral lost its way in the Atlantic and landed on Brazil's coast.

The voyages of Amerigo Vespucci, who published a set of letters describing his travels to Central America, Guiana, and Brazil, were also of major importance. The German geographer Martin Waldseemuller reprinted these letters in 1507, and suggested that the new World be named after Amerigo. This fact in itself indicates the tremendous excitement the voyages of discovery created all over Europe. The great American continents were named by a German after an Italian who sailed under the flags of Spain and Portugal!

Exploration under the Spanish flag now proceeded swiftly. In 1513, Ponce de Leon landed in Florida, and Vasco de Balboa crossed the Isthmus of Panama and sighted the Pacific Ocean. Then, in 1519, Ferdinand Magellan sailed around the tip of South America and circumnavigated the globe. These early voyages demonstrated beyond dispute that America was not the East, and that Spain had lost to Portugal the great race for discovering the easiest trade route to the Indies. The westward route to the East was too arduous to be utilized extensively. Yet, in 1519, another event occurred which suddenly elevated America to singular importance in the eyes of Europeans. The Spanish adventurer Hernando Cortez discovered large quantities of gold in Mexico.

The Spanish Empire

In the early years of the sixteenth century, few Spaniards came to America with the idea of establishing permanent colonies. Finding new trade routes to the East, not the founding of an American empire, had been the object of the early voyages of discovery. Most of those Spaniards who did man the Caribbean outposts in the New World were old soldiers seeking adventure after the Moorish wars had ended. They were tough, hard to govern, and incurably romantic.

One such adventurer was Hernando Cortez who set out from Cuba in 1519 to raid the coast of Mexico. Marching inland from the coast, Cortez overran the Indian empire of the Aztecs, and razed their capital, Mexico City, to the ground. In the process, he acquired the fabulously rich gold mines of Mexico for the king of Spain. Cortez's first act was to send his grateful sovereign a shipload of the precious metal.

Because of Cortez's exploits, all Spain was aroused by the prospect of empire. Soon after, in the 1530's, Francisco Pizarro conquered the Inca empire of Peru, giving Spain still more wealth in the form of silver.

The mad scramble for gold and silver and land continued as expeditions wandered across the face of North America. In 1539, Hernando de Soto landed in Florida and marched north in search of a mysterious city called Apalache. He wandered across Georgia, Alabama, and Mississippi, and although he discovered the Mississippi River, he died convinced that he had seen nothing of great consequence. Francisco de Coronado trekked across the southwestern part of the United States in search of the fabled land of Cibola, with its seven golden cities. But Cibola, like Apalache, did not exist.

Meanwhile, Spain began to face the task of running an empire. It was a stupendous undertaking. For one thing, the *conquistadores,* as these adventurers were called, however heroic, were poor governors. They quarreled violently among themselves, reduced Peru to a permanent state of civil war, brutalized the Indians, ignored the king's demands for money, and displayed a remarkable lack of interest in converting the Indians to Christianity. Moreover, the oceans were unsafe, as Pirates swarmed over the Caribbean. Since the New World was also suitable for agricultural production, the Spaniards began to import black slaves, whom they purchased from the Portuguese, to work the land. The Spanish conquistadores gave little thought to their rights.

By 1550, chaos and confusion in Spain's overseas empire were replaced by a highly centralized government. Every detail of life and trade in America was regulated as minutely as it was in Spain. The king's overseas dominions were, in effect, separate kingdoms, and these were ruled by various councils based in Spain and staffed with lawyers who regulated trade, appointed all colonial officials, passed all laws that were to be enforced in the colonies, and acted as a court of appeals.

In America, the empire was carved into several large provinces governed by viceroys who exercised supreme military and civil authority. The viceroys were aided by local councils which exercised both legislative and judicial functions. All Spanish officials from the viceroys to local mayors represented the king, not the people. In the New World, Spain created an elaborate, rigid, nearly unworkable system of government that was unresponsive to the needs or the desires of the settlers.

In addition to creating a highly centralized bureaucracy, the Spanish monarchy exercised almost absolute power over the Spanish Church in America. The kings appointed the bishops, authorized missionary enterprises, and determined the amount of temporal power the Church could exercise over the natives. The monarchy also collected fees from the New World churches and decided how the money was to be spent.

Nevertheless, it was the Church that insisted that both blacks and Indians had souls, and the monarchy cooperated by demanding their conversion and by creating laws protecting black marriages, religious rights, and working conditions. This was small compensation for the degrading conditions and the harsh labor, but they were greater privileges than were later accorded to slaves in North America. Even these laws, inadequate as they were, were often difficult to enforce. The huge array of colonial officials and the cumbersome machinery of the courts offered many opportunities for corruption and abuses. Yet, the Spanish empire accomplished the one great task the kings had set for it. It provided the monarchy with stupendous quantities of gold and silver.

Gold from the New World financed an immense military machine. Spanish rulers regarded themselves as defenders of Roman Catholic orthodoxy, and Spanish armies trooped over Europe fighting Protestants in the Netherlands, Italy, and Germany. Spain was also embroiled in endless wars with France.

Unfortunately for Spain, none of the wealth acquired from the New World was put to any productive use at home. Spain virtually ignored agricultural improvements and failed to develop industries that would have increased its economic self-sufficiency. Instead, the nation exported large quantities of gold and silver to other European nations to purchase foodstuffs, textiles, and military equipment. By 1700, Spain had the greatest land and sea empire in the world, but was rapidly depleting its economic resources. Spain soon lost its position of world power, but its lavish expenditures during the sixteenth century astonished the rulers of England and France. If the Spanish monarchy could tap such incredible sources of wealth in the New World, why was it not possible for them?

France In The New World

Throughout most of the sixteenth century, in spite of their interest in the New World, France and England were unable to sponsor serious colonizing enterprises. Neither nation had the time nor the capital and both nations were involved in expensive foreign wars and confronted by serious internal difficulties.

France was shattered by civil wars involving intricate dynastic struggles to seize the throne combined with religious conflicts between French Protestants—called Huguenots—and Catholics. Peace was eventually restored, but not until the close of the century when King Henry IV secured the throne and issued the Edict of Nantes, which assured a measure of toleration to the Huguenots.

These disorders so absorbed France that it could do little more than send out privateers to plunder Spanish treasure fleets, expand the fishing industry off Nova Scotia and Newfoundland, and charter voyages of exploration. In three separate voyages, from 1534 through 1541, Jacques Cartier explored the Gulf of St. Lawrence and the St. Lawrence River. He discovered that Canada was not the eastern tip of Asia, as the French king thought, and that the St. Lawrence River was not a passageway to the Orient. Cartier established a small colony a few miles from present-day Quebec, but the settlers soon returned to France, discouraged by their failure to find gold.

By the beginning of the seventeenth century, when France had settled its internal disorders, it was able to begin serious colonization in the New World. While the Spanish empire was carved by conquistadores out of the remnants of Indian empires, and was governed by lawyers for the benefit of the king, the French empire in North America was created from the wilderness by fur traders and governed by profiteers for their own benefit.

Settling at Quebec in 1608, the French were soon drawn into the wars which raged between the Iroquois and the Huron Indians. By forming an alliance with the Hurons, the French eventually secured mastery over Canada, or New France as it was called, and the Ohio Valley, the region between the Ohio and Mississippi rivers. The right to govern Canada, as well as a monopoly of its extremely valuable fur trade, was granted by France to various promoters, who, interested only in the profits from the fur trade, discouraged settlement. Other than traders and trappers, the most important group of Frenchmen who settled in Canada were the missionaries, who came to convert the Indians. They performed many valuable services, including the negotiation of treaties with the Indians, whom they often protected from exploitation by unscrupulous traders. In general, the French treated the Indians fairly well, neither reducing them to serfdom as the Spanish did, nor exterminating them as the English were inclined to do.

Because the promoters in New France were more interested in the profits from the fur trade, early attempts to colonize failed. By 1663, only 3,000 French settlers and traders lived in the New World, compared to 200,000 Spaniards and 70,000 Englishmen. If France was to maintain its position in America, it was essential to rectify the imbalance.

Assuming direct control, the French government set up a confusing system, headed by a governor, usually a general, whose responsibility was limited to military and diplomatic affairs. Beneath him was a royal official who directed the colony's economic development and actually had greater power than the governor. In addition, a Superior Council, many of whose members were appointed by the king, advised the governor. Since much of the authority overlapped, conflict was inevitable, and jealousy, suspicion, and corruption were rife.

Moreover, a large group of people who might have helped New France prosper were not allowed to settle there. In 1698, the king revoked the Edict of Nantes, and 200,000 Huguenots were driven into exile. Denied permission to emigrate to New France, large numbers of Huguenots settled in the growing English colonies.

Another factor which also inhibited the development of Canada was France's attempt to transfer the feudal land system to the New World. Farming the land as a serf for a nobleman was a most uninviting prospect for potential settlers. By 1750, when the English colonies contained over a million inhabitants, the population of New France had reached only 55,000. The French empire in North America remained a fur trading enterprise which was profitable to a few, useless to the king, and vulnerable to English plans for conquest.

England On The Eve Of Colonization

For several reasons the most enduring and successful empire in the New World was established by England, the smallest and poorest of the new monarchies. During the sixteenth century, England suffered severe social and economic dislocations that produced widespread poverty and unemployment among the lower classes. England also experienced protracted religious quarrels. After breaking with the Catholic Church in 1559, the nation continued to be disrupted by conflict between the established Anglican Church and the dissenters, or Puritans, who objected to its beliefs and practices. Finally, reflective Englishmen, concerned about England's economy, concluded that overseas colonies could provide solutions to far-reaching social, economic, and international problems.

For nearly two centuries, England had exported wool to Flanders, in what is now Belgium. The trade was so profitable that more and more land was "enclosed" or appropriated, to raise sheep. As less land became available for agriculture, many yeomen—small farmers and landholders—and tenant farmers were forced off the land. Moreover, England's population during the sixteenth century increased from three million to over four million. By the end of the century, England contained countless thousands of beggars and vagabonds who faced a hopeless future and whose plight threatened society itself.

Some of the distress was relieved when England began to develop its own weaving industry and also established its own overseas trading companies. England also restricted imports by placing high taxes on foreign goods. The merchant fleets from Flanders and Venice that once visited England were replaced by English trading companies. The English monarch wanted English goods carried in English ships.

England also aided its shipping interests by granting charters to joint stock companies. Amassing enough money to carry out large-scale trade was difficult, and although England had a number of rich men, none was wealthy enough to assume all the risks in a vast trading enterprise. Not only did a joint stock company solve this problem but provided additional security in that the government charters granted foreign monopolies to English merchants and permitted them to regulate their own affairs without constant interference from the government.

Several of these companies were formed in the sixteenth century, the first of which, the Muscovy Company, traded with Russia. The Levant Company was formed to trade with the Middle East and free England from dependence on Italian middlemen. The Guinea Company attempted to break the Spanish and Portuguese monopoly of the African slave trade, and the East India Company challenged the Portuguese monopoly in the Orient.

Spain was disturbed by this explosion of mercantile activity, which included not only legitimate trading companies but more dubious ventures as well, which were supported by the monarch, Queen Elizabeth I.

England's dashing privateers—men like Sir Francis Drake and Sir John Hawkins—not only plundered Spanish treasure ships from the New World but did so under the charter of a company whose main stockholder was the queen. One of Drake's most famous exploits was his voyage of 1577–1579, during which he combined piracy and exploration. After capturing several Spanish treasure ships off the coast of South America, he sailed to California, claiming it for England, and then capped his exploits by circumnavigating the globe.

This increasing commercial rivalry and the piracy of the English privateers added fuel to England's long-standing religious and diplomatic quarrels with Spain. For years, Protestant England and Catholic Spain had been embroiled in conflict over the Spanish monarch's attempt to bring Protestant Europe back into the Catholic fold. Most of the conflict revolved around the Protestant Netherlands, which had revolted against Spain and which had England's support. Finally, when England destroyed Spain's "invincible Armada," it became Europe's foremost naval power, a supremacy which contributed mightily to England's success as a trading and colonizing power.

Although England did not establish a successful colony in the New World until 1607, the government had sponsored some voyages of exploration beginning in 1497 when Cabot had explored the northern coast of America. England continued to be interested in exploration in the New World, hoping to find a northwest passage to the Orient or wealth in gold and silver. A northwest passage particularly excited Sir Humphrey Gilbert, whose pamphlet, *A Discourse of Discovery for a New Passage to Cathay*, intrigued a generation of English mariners.

Gilbert himself perished on his second voyage of exploration in 1583 when he attempted to found a colony in Newfoundland. However, Gilbert's half-brother, Sir Walter Raleigh, continued his explorations. Raleigh sent several expeditions to explore the east coast of North America, which he called Virginia, in honor of the unmarried Queen Elizabeth. Raleigh's famous colony, the Lost Colony of Roanoke, off the coast of North Carolina, vanished without a trace around 1588. Nevertheless, his efforts continued to keep alive the idea that England could gain profits by colonizing the New World.

In the 1580's, many thoughtful Englishmen began to publish treatises urging the government to sponsor the settlement of North America. Richard Hakluyt, a clergyman, was the most influential of the publicists, and his paper, "A Discourse on the Western Planting" (1584), was a classic statement of mercantile principles.

England, Hakluyt reasoned, was at war, and was likely to be so with either France or Spain for many years. North American colonies would not only provide naval bases from which Spanish trade could be attacked, but would also check further Spanish expansion. North America also contained vast quantities of "pitch, tar, hemp, and all things incident for a navy royal," and these supplies would reduce the monarchy's dependence upon a tightfisted Parliament in providing for military needs.

Military considerations were meant to appeal to a queen caught up in the toils of war, but Hakluyt's economic arguments were more important in the long run. He pointed out that since the New World could supply many commodities, including salt, tropical fruits, wine, and iron, which England imported from Spain and other countries, colonies would not only increase England's self-sufficiency, but would also injure the economies of her chief European rivals. Equally important, long European wars seriously disrupted English trade and commerce, and the New World would contain settlers and also natives to whom English merchants could sell manufactured products. Moreover, trade with America would provide steady employment for English seamen who normally were left idle half the year because of short European voyages.

Colonies, Hakluyt argued, had still another value. They would reduce unemployment and alleviate the burden placed upon society by the masses of poor evicted from the land. In fact, colonies would transform starving English vagabonds, slum dwellers, and petty criminals into prosperous American farmers. The views of Hakluyt and other writers did not fall upon deaf ears. In 1603, when the war with Spain finally ended, English companies, encouraged by the

monarchy, were ready to send out settlers to establish an empire in North America.

In addition, in sixteenth-century England, religion was as important as finance. The established state church, whose head was the monarch, required all Englishmen to be members and obey its doctrines. Although Anglican churchmen received their powers from England's Parliament and their offices from the monarch, the English church resembled the Roman Catholic Church in its organizational structure and many of its practices.

Numbers of English dissenters, influenced by the teachings of John Calvin, dissented from the practices and teachings of the Anglican Church. While most of these Puritans did not object to the existence of a state church, they complained that the Anglican Church was riddled with Roman Catholic practices and governed by what they considered sinful men. According to Puritans, God bestowed grace only upon an "elect" few who were predestined to receive salvation and were entitled to govern his church. More extreme Puritans, called Separatists, insisted that church membership be limited to the elect and denied the authority of the government in church affairs.

Queen Elizabeth, distracted by war and bored with theological wrangling, generally ignored the conflict between the Anglicans and the Puritans. But her successor, James I, who believed he ruled by Divine right, considered Puritans an affront not only to God, but to himself. Although James did not expel Puritans from England, they came under heavy attack, and eventually many left to colonize the New World.

Thus, by the first decade of the seventeenth century, several groups of Englishmen, for different reasons, concluded that the establishment of colonies in North America could solve many of England's problems. The government could rid itself of landless farmers, beggars, and petty criminals; England could become rich and powerful from the profits of colonial trade; and Puritans could worship God as they pleased. Throughout the seventeenth century, thousands of Englishmen migrated from the Old World to the New. These settlers carried with them English attitudes, ideas, and even some English institutions. Yet, much of the social and political structure of the England they left behind could not be adapted to a new society carved out of the wilderness.

Perhaps the most striking feature of English society and politics in the seventeenth century was the power of the aristocracy. An aristocrat, or peer, who sat in the House of Lords, the upper house of the English Parliament, was not simply a rich man with influence. His role in government was hereditary, as was his wealth, derived primarily from large landholdings. And he exercised enormous influence over the local neighborhood where he lived.

Beneath the aristocrats was a fairly large group of moderately wealthy landholders, the gentry, whose ancient lineage entitled them to the name of "gentlemen." John Winthrop, who emigrated to America and became governor of the Massachusetts Bay Colony, came from this class. But the largest group of Englishmen who migrated to America were yeomen, who regarded the gentry and the aristocracy with deference, since aristocrats and gentlemen dominated political, religious, and economic life. The average Englishman who came to America had lived his entire life in a highly institutionalized society dominated by hereditary classes. He had little conception of a different way of life, and certainly had never heard of, nor agitated for, democracy.

Old and familiar institutions regulated the Englishman's existence. The omnipresent church, presided over by the local bishop, exacted from him its tithes, or fees, and punished him if he violated church teachings. A cumbersome court system meted out severe punishment to debtors and criminals. In seventeenth-century England the death penalty was handed down for crimes ranging from blasphemy to witchcraft to highway robbery. In the administration of everyday affairs, however, the local justice of the peace was the most important official the average Englishman encountered.

Almost always a member of the gentry, the justice of the peace was in charge of roads and poorhouses, regulated the markets, made sure soldiers received their pensions, that the aged and indigent were provided for, and collected taxes. Parliament may have enacted the laws, but the justice of the peace enforced them. Thus, Englishmen were accustomed to a high degree of local government control.

The Englishman who came to America, then, was leaving behind a highly stratified society, elaborately organized and minutely governed. But in America none of these things existed. He was faced with the task of importing his traditional social order into the New World, or devising a new social order by which his life might be governed.

Part 1

Establishing
A New Nation

Van Bergen Overmantle, (detail) anonymous, *c.* 1700

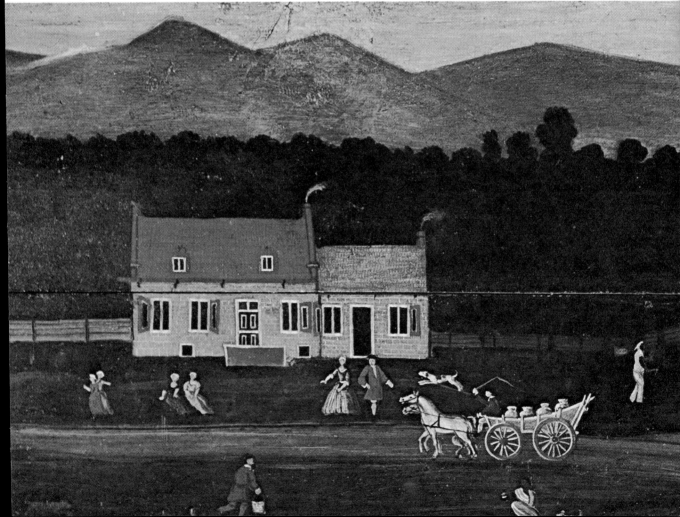

His Majesty's American Subjects

The voyagers who set out for America in the seventeenth century had different reasons for making the perilous trip. Those from England and Europe came willingly, seeking riches from the new land, economic opportunity, or escape from religious persecution. Those from Africa were brought unwillingly, as slaves.

The earliest and most influential colonists were the English. To fortify themselves for an uncertain future in an unknown land, they brought not only material supplies but also the familiar elements of their English heritage—their law, government, political philosophy, and even place names. Their aim was to create a "new England" out of the wilderness.

But the wilderness had a power of its own. Its harshness imposed certain limitations on the settlers, yet at the same time it freed them from some of the restrictions of English life. Forced by circumstances, they improvised new patterns of economic, political, and social life. In the process they themselves were changed. In his poem *Western Star*, Stephen Vincent Benet expresses what was happening to the settlers: "And those who came were resolved to be Englishmen/Gone to world's end, but English every one/And they ate the white corn-kernels, parched in the sun/And they knew it not, but they'd not be English again." As you read about the colonists' attempts to tame the wilderness, keep these questions in mind:

1. What kind of people settled the colony of Virginia, and what problems did they face?
2. What was the impact of religion on the settlement of New England?
3. Why did the proprietary form of government fail in the Middle and Southern colonies?
4. What kind of control did Great Britain exert over the colonies?
5. In what ways did colonial society differ from English society? In what ways were they similar?

1 Settlers Gain A Foothold In Virginia

1. What were the problems the settlers faced in colonizing Jamestown?

2. What types of settlers came to Jamestown and what were their reasons for coming?

3. Why were blacks denied the status of indentured servants and considered slaves?

4. Is it possible to identify stages of colonial development in the growth of the Virginia colony? If so, what are they?

Virginia was founded as a business enterprise in 1607 by the Virginia Company, a joint stock company with two branches—the Plymouth Company, based in Plymouth, England, and the London Company. James I had granted a charter to these companies that gave them permission to establish colonies in America. The charter also spelled out how the settlers would be governed (see chart, page 15).

It was the London Company that backed the expedition to Virginia. Although according to the terms of the charter the main purpose of the colony was to convert the Indians to Christianity, the shrewd investors were more interested in gold than in Indians. When the company dispatched three ships carrying one hundred men to the New World, it expected the colony they would establish to yield a profit.

Grave problems arise. From the time the settlers landed in the spring of 1607, the colony was beset by difficulties. Unfortunately, the inexperienced colonists chose an unhealthy, swampy area in which to plant their settlement, Jamestown. Influenced by tales of fantastic wealth, they spent much of their time searching for gold and silver instead of planting the crops necessary to carry them through the winter. Many of the settlers died from disease, especially malaria, inflicted by swarms of deadly mosquitoes which thrived in the region around Jamestown. Within six months, nearly half of the original colonists had perished. Additional colonists who were sent out by the company were no better prepared to survive in the wilderness.

The terrible struggle for survival was made even more difficult by constant quarreling among the early leaders of the colony. Their greed, jealousy, and lust for power clearly shows that they had neither the talent nor the temperament to carve a new civilization from the wilderness. For a time, Captain John Smith, a soldier and adventurer, provided able leadership. In 1608 he saved the colony from starvation and possible extinction by forcing the settlers to plant crops and by arranging a trade agreement with Powhatan, chief of all the Indian tribes in the Chesapeake region.

Unfortunately, Smith was severely injured in 1609 and was forced to return to England. The situation reached its lowest ebb in the winter of 1609–10, called the "Starving Time," in which three quarters of the settlers were wiped out by famine and disease. When spring came, the discouraged colonists were ready to quit Virginia. But by then a governor, Lord De La Warre, arrived with fresh supplies and three hundred new settlers. Once more the colony was saved.

The situation brightens. In 1612, two developments occurred which not only guaranteed survival, but eventually brought economic prosperity to Virginia. John Rolfe's marriage to Pocahontas, Powhatan's daughter, ensured peace with the Indians for nearly a decade, and Rolfe's development of a mild blend of tobacco resulted in the creation of a successful tobacco trade with Europe. At first, some Englishmen, including James I, expressed doubt about the morality and profitability of the new import. The king expressed his disapproval in *A Counterblaste To Tobacco*, and one member of the company sneered that England could not "build an Empire on Smoake." When it became apparent that England could collect taxes on tobacco, the headstrong monarch dropped his objections. As production increased, it became obvious that "this precious stinke" would provide the basis for Virginia's economic development.

The company institutes reforms. To encourage further growth of the colony, the company decided to make it more appealing to settlers and investors. The directors inaugurated a system of private land ownership. Until 1618, the company had retained sole possession of the colony's land, but a chronic shortage of settlers led the company to offer fifty acres of land to any resident who

13

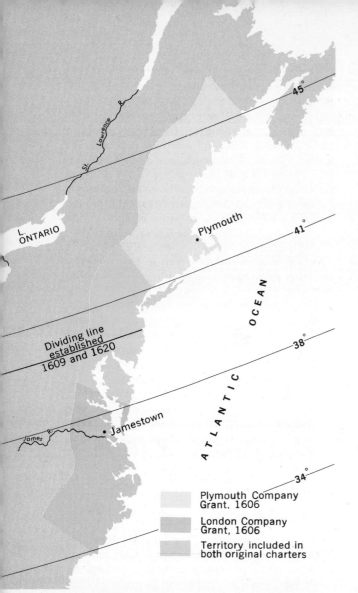

VIRGINIA LAND GRANTS

elect members to the House of Burgesses, thus establishing the first representative assembly in the New World. The company also assured the colonists that they would be governed by the common law of England, with its provision for trial by jury.

By 1622, the company seemed to be on the verge of economic success when disaster struck once again. Indians attacked the colony in force, killing more than three hundred settlers. This onslaught not only destroyed the company's plans for economic development, but also helped convince James I that the London Company was incapable of governing the colony.

The company's charter was revoked in 1624, and Virginia became the first royal colony in America. No basic governmental changes were made except that now the king, instead of the company, appointed the governor and his council. At first, Virginians were not certain that the monarchy would permit the House of Burgesses to continue passing laws, but in 1639 King Charles I confirmed its right to meet.

Social and political development. The typical seventeenth-century Virginian was a self-sufficient yeoman farmer who owned from one hundred to three hundred acres. Although these small farmers grew a variety of crops, the Virginia economy was dominated by tobacco. Because crude agricultural methods rapidly depleted the soil, eventually only those who owned large plantations, some of which exceeded five thousand acres, could profitably engage in tobacco cultivation.

The best land lay near the rivers that flowed into the Chesapeake Bay. This land was prized not only for its fertility, but for the direct access it provided to merchant vessels. The policy of building large plantations along the rivers made towns unnecessary; the plantation fed itself and produced most of its own tools and furnishings. Aside from the governmental center at Williamsburg and the tobacco port of Norfolk, no cities of any size were founded in colonial Virginia.

By the end of the seventeenth century, a society had evolved in the Old Dominion, as Virginia came to be called, that was dominated both socially and politically by a few wealthy landowning families. Although some were self-made men, many of the "First Families of Virginia" were

would pay the cost of transporting one new settler to Virginia. This practice, known as the "head right" system, resulted in the establishment of large plantations farmed by *indentured servants,* who worked from four to seven years to repay their sponsor for their passage. At the end of their terms of service, these indentured servants were entitled to fifty acres of land.

The company initiated another reform when it decided to liberalize the colony's political system. In 1619, landowners were granted the right to

COLONIAL GOVERNMENTS

Charter	Governor	Councillors (Upper House)	Assembly (Lower House)
Royal	Appointed by Crown	Appointed by Crown	Elected by freemen
Proprietary	Proprietor or his appointee	Appointed by proprietor	Elected by freemen
Corporate Non-self governing	Appointed by company directors	Appointed by company directors	Elected by freemen
Self-governing	Elected by freemen	Elected by freemen	Elected by freemen

descended from the younger sons of English merchants and gentry whose future was brighter in Virginia than at home. Among these families were the Byrds and Burwells, Ludwells and Lees, Randolphs and Washingtons. They had arrived between 1660 and 1680 and had risen swiftly to the top of the social order.

This landed gentry had the money as well as the free time required to play an active role in politics. More important, however, the English tradition of rule by aristocracy and gentry carried over into Virginia. Most colonial Virginians believed that those who had the greatest economic stake in the colony should govern it. Control of politics by a landowning *oligarchy* (rule by a few) was not achieved, however, until after a rebellion against the autocratic regime of Governor William Berkeley in 1676.

Bacon's rebellion. Sir William Berkeley conducted governmental affairs in a high-handed and arbitrary manner. No new elections for Burgesses were called during the final sixteen years of his rule. The same men gathered at Jamestown every year to pass laws, and Berkeley bought most of them off. He rewarded his friends with lucrative offices, granted them extensive lands, and invited them to participate in the monopoly over the fur trade. Since he controlled the fur trade with the Indians, Berkeley ignored the demands of frontiersmen for protection from Indian raids.

Dissatisfaction with Berkeley's rule finally led to revolt in 1676, when Nathaniel Bacon, who though a member of the governor's council,

despised him, raised an army and deposed the governor. Although the revolt was swiftly suppressed and Berkeley was returned to power, it had not been in vain. The king was moved to institute a number of reforms: elections to the House of Burgesses were to be held every two years, and greater powers, including the collection of taxes, were given to the county governments, which were dominated by the great landowners. Bacon's rebellion, therefore, marked the end of government by the royal governor and his cronies and the beginning of an era of political domination by a wealthy, landed oligarchy.

Slavery in the colonial south. The African slave trade, opened by Spanish and Portuguese merchants in the sixteenth century, attracted European rivals, especially the Dutch. The Europeans established posts along the west coast of Africa and purchased black slaves from African kings who, in turn, captured or bought them from interior tribes. For three centuries gangs of Africans were herded to the coast, packed into small merchant vessels, and shipped across the Atlantic to Brazil, Central America, and the West Indies.

Of fifteen million Africans seized, some estimates declare, nearly one-third died on the march to the coast, in the pestiferous camps of the traders, and in the Middle Passage, as the voyage to the New World was called. Once in the West Indies the slaves were "broken." They were subjected to brutal treatment in the hope of making them docile, frightened, and forgetful of their African heritage and independence. On the

15

whole, this systematic brutalization was successful; most black men, on the surface at least, accepted their condition and did as they were told. The alternative was death.

The first Africans to arrive in Virginia, brought by Dutch traders in 1619, were regarded as indentured servants rather than slaves. For at least twenty years thereafter, black workers were freed after completing their terms of labor and received the fifty acres of land to which servants were entitled. Beginning around 1640, however, Virginia gradually began to enact laws restricting the African's freedom. By 1700, blacks in all southern colonies had been systematically deprived of their freedom and legal rights. In fact, slaves were considered chattel property, not human beings.

Slaves could not sue in court, nor could they serve as witnesses against white men. Slave marriages were neither recognized by law nor solemnized by the churches. In theory, slave masters were forbidden to murder or mutilate their "property," but a cruel master or overseer who

chose to do either was rarely brought to justice. Slaves could be bought and sold like cattle, and their children could be sold away from them.

Chattel slavery as practiced in British America had no precedent in English law or moral codes. Some historians argue that economic forces account for the enslavement of the African, that increasing tobacco production made a large labor force necessary. But blacks did not, in the seventeenth century, constitute more than 10 percent of the population. The black slave became a significant economic factor only in the eighteenth century, well after the legal codes enslaving blacks were established.

But slavery was more than simply a labor system. It was, in essence, a system of social control based on racial prejudice whereby elaborate legal and institutional arrangements were created to assure absolute domination of one race by another. Although Africans came from a complex and highly artistic culture, it was one that Englishmen could not easily understand. Throughout

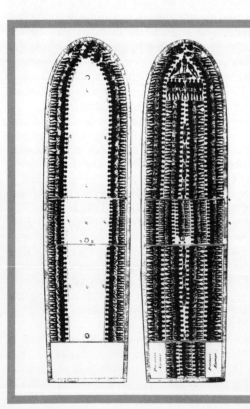

GUSTAVUS VASA

This diagram of the floor plan of a slave ship shows how Africans were packed into the hold for transport to America. One African who made such a trip was Gustavus Vasa, captured as a child in West Africa. In the following excerpt, he describes the "Middle Passage."

"The closeness of the place . . . added to the number in the ship, which was so crowded that each had scarcely room to turn himself, almost suffocated us . . . . the air soon became unfit for respiration from a variety of loathsome smells, and brought on a sickness among the slaves, of which many died. . . . This wretched situation was again aggravated by the galling of the chains . . . and the filth of the necessary tubs, into which the children often fell and were almost suffocated. The shrieks of the women and the groans of the dying rendered the whole a scene of horror almost inconceivable. . . . One day . . . two of my wearied countrymen who were chained together . . . jumped into the sea: immediately another quite dejected fellow . . . followed their example . . . two of the wretches were drowned, but they [the ship's crew] got the other and afterwards flogged him unmercifully for thus attempting to prefer death to slavery."

recorded history, people have assumed that individuals of differing ethnic, religious, and cultural backgrounds are inferior and potentially dangerous. The African with his dark skin, non-Christian religions, and exotic homeland seemed to the Englishman particularly strange. How could he be assimilated into an English culture and society?

This conviction that the African was different from the Englishman led swiftly to the false conviction that the black man was inferior, incapable of adapting to the civilization of the white man. He was also dangerous to the unity of the colony for the same reason. Slowly, a system of slavery emerged as the only way in which blacks could be controlled and made useful to the economy and society of Virginia. The origin of slavery lies in race prejudice, a conviction that white men are culturally, religiously, and economically superior to black men.

The African, although terrorized by the horrors of the Middle Passage and broken in spirit by the brutal treatment meted out to him, still desired freedom and eagerly grasped it whenever he could. In colonial America, however, the black slave could not easily escape. Not only did the slave seeking freedom run the risk of being captured, beaten, or killed, he literally had no place to go. Few white men were able to live alone in the wilderness; for the African, rigidly policed and cut off from his own people, it was virtually impossible.

2 "Saints In The Wilderness" Colonize New England

1. Why were Puritan settlers referred to as "Saints in the Wilderness"?

2. In what ways did the church influence colonial society in New England?

3. What are the strengths and weaknesses of a church-oriented civil government similar to that in colonial New England?

4. What factors accounted for the decline of Puritanism in New England?

Plymouth Plantation, the first permanent colony in New England, was established in 1620 by a small group of English Puritans called Separatists. Like all Puritans, the Separatists were influenced by the theology of John Calvin, which taught that human nature was corrupt and that most men were predestined by an angry God to suffer damnation for their sins. Only the elect, the few chosen by God, could hope for eternal life.

English law required all Englishmen to be members of the Church of England, the established state church. However, Anglican rituals and theology conflicted with Puritan beliefs. In order to stay within the law, most Puritans professed to be loyal members of the established church, hoping that in time they could persuade the government to reform the church along Calvinistic lines. The Separatists refused to make this compromise. They denounced the English government for meddling in religious affairs, and fled to Holland.

The founding of Plymouth. After a few years in Holland, the Pilgrims, as this group of Separatists is commonly called, secured a land grant from the Plymouth branch of the Virginia Company and emigrated to America. Originally, they intended to settle near the mouth of the Hudson River, at that time claimed as part of Virginia. The prevailing winds, however, carried their tiny ship, the *Mayflower*, to Cape Cod. Realizing that their landfall lay well outside the Virginia Company's jurisdiction, the leaders concluded they would not have to conform to their charter. Therefore, they drew up the famous Mayflower Compact, in which they promised "in the presence of God and one . . . another" to organize a government and to obey the laws it passed.

During the first terrible winter, 50 of the original 101 Pilgrims perished. The remnant established the most liberal government to be formed in the colonies, with few restrictions on voting. But a liberal government did not insure that the colony would grow. There were few Separatists to swell the population, and trade was insignificant. In 1691, Plymouth Colony was annexed to its mighty neighbor, Massachusetts Bay.

Arrival of the Puritans. In 1629, the colony of Massachusetts Bay was founded by Puritans determined to create a religious utopia. John Winthrop, their first governor, declared, "We

FOUNDING OF THE COLONIES

Colony	Date Settled	Government Charter
Virginia	1607	Corporate until 1624 / Royal after 1624
Massachusetts		
Plymouth	1620	Self-governing corporate
Massachusetts Bay	1629	Self-governing corporate / Massachusetts colonies merged 1691 / Royal charter after 1691
Rhode Island	1636–44	Self-governing (no charter)
Maine	1622	Proprietary / Part of Massachusetts 1677–1820
New Hampshire	1622	Proprietary until 1641 / Part of Massachusetts 1641–1680 / Royal after 1680
Connecticut		
Hartford	1636	Self-governing (no charter)
New Haven	1639	Self-governing (no charter)
		Connecticut colonies merged 1662, self-governing corporate charter
Delaware	1638	Proprietary until 1682 / Part of Pennsylvania 1682–1703 / Self-governing after 1703
Maryland	1634	Proprietary until 1691 / Royal from 1691–1715 Proprietary after 1715
New York	1624 (Dutch) 1664 (English)	Colony of Dutch West India Company until 1664 Proprietary until 1685 / Royal after 1685
New Jersey	1664	Proprietary until 1702 / Royal after 1702
North Carolina	1663	Proprietary until 1729 / Royal after 1729
South Carolina	1670	Proprietary after 1729 / Royal after 1729
Pennsylvania	1682	Proprietary
Georgia	1730	Proprietary until 1752 / Royal after 1752

shall be as a City upon a Hill, the eyes of the World upon us." In fifteen years over 30,000 Englishmen had gone to Massachusetts, driven by political, economic, and religious forces.

The charter granted to the Massachusetts Bay Company did not stipulate, as did most other charters, that the company's headquarters be located in England. John Winthrop and ten other rich Puritan leaders purchased the company's stock, placed its charter aboard ship, and sailed to America, where they intended to govern the colony without interference from the king, Anglican bishops, or English investors. This brilliant coup coincided with a massive attack against the Puritans in England. Puritan ministers were purged from the Church of England, and Puritan leaders were driven from the government. England became too dangerous for many Puritans.

Although thousands of early settlers left England for political and religious reasons, thousands more came in search of economic opportunities. High taxes and the collapse of the cloth industry in eastern and southern England during the 1620's caused much suffering. England "grows weary of her inhabitants," Winthrop lamented. "All towns complain of the burdens of their poor."

A Bible commonwealth. The leaders of the New England colonies firmly believed that God had commanded the settlement of New England as part of His plan for the reformation of a sinful world. The grave magistrates who made the laws and the fiery ministers who propagated the faith insisted that salvation was the only proper business of man.

On the surface, the government of Massachusetts Bay appeared to be more liberal than that of many other colonies. The voters of Massachusetts elected the governor and his council, and the members of the assembly, who sat together as the General Court. Until 1691, however, only adult male church members could vote for these colonial lawmakers. Some historians have estimated that not more than one-fourth of the adult population ever became full-fledged members of Puritan congregations, and thus voters.

According to Puritan theology, only "God's Elect," that is, those who had been "saved" by God's grace through a conversion experience— could become church members. Puritans learned from childhood that God had chosen, or predestined, a few persons for salvation, and one of the difficult tasks of a Puritan church was to decide who was saved. All who claimed to have received God's grace through conversion were questioned at great length by the congregation. Many people did not have the nerve to undergo this ordeal, and others were rejected because they were found to have doubts about their salvation. Those whose testimony convinced the congregation that they had truly received saving grace were counted among God's "visible saints," invited to join a church, and thus given the right to vote.

The Bay colony was not a *theocracy* (rule by the clergy), although church and state were closely connected. Ministers were often consulted about governmental affairs and were responsible for disciplining churches and individuals who violated Puritan beliefs. Everyone was required to attend church whether or not he was saved. Those who refused to accept theology or failed to live moral lives incurred the wrath of God as interpreted by the ministers, and the wrath of the General Court as decided by the magistrates.

"Troublers of Zion." "The devil," Governor Winthrop lamented, "will never cease to disturb our peace, and [will] raise up instruments one after the other." Not the least of these instruments, according to Puritans, was Roger Williams. When Williams first arrived in Boston in 1631, he was warmly welcomed by the Puritans because of his towering reputation for learning, eloquence, and religious zeal. But it soon became apparent that Williams had dangerous ideas.

Williams took the unpopular position that the Indians ought to be paid for their land. He also denounced the Puritans for not abandoning the legal fiction that they were loyal members of the Church of England. And he mortally offended the leaders of Massachusetts Bay when he denied the General Court's right to interfere in the affairs of local churches. In 1635 Williams was banished from Massachusetts. He fled to Rhode Island, where he established a government based on separation of church and state and toleration for all believers except Roman Catholics.

The fiery Anne Hutchinson was another famous heretic who was expelled from the Bay colony. She claimed to have received a direct revelation from God, a statement that scandalized most Puritans. God's will, the Puritans believed, was revealed solely through the Scriptures. The ministers had interpreted the Bible to their own satisfaction, and they wanted everyone else to accept their judgment without question. Otherwise, religious orthodoxy, the very purpose for establishing the colony, could not be maintained. Anyone who challenged Puritan ideals had to be eliminated. As one Puritan put it, other Christians "shall have free liberty to keep away from us, and such as will come [must] be gone as fast as they can, the sooner the better."

Occasionally, Puritans relied on the hangman's

rope to enforce religious purity. In 1692 mass hysteria gripped Massachusetts with the terrible news from Salem Village that there were witches in Essex County. The belief in witches—persons who made a pact with the Devil—was not peculiar to New England. In Europe, this superstition had claimed the lives of thousands of innocent victims. In Massachusetts Bay, twenty people, accused by three hysterical teen-age girls, were executed. Some three hundred more citizens were in jail awaiting trials when the frenzy began to subside. The ministers finally realized that convictions were being obtained without the proper evidence, and the governor halted this grim episode.

The expansion of New England. The Puritans spread rapidly across New England. Religious conflicts in the Bay colony produced a sizable number of refugees, most of whom fled to Rhode Island. Economic opportunities also induced thousands of people to seek their fortunes elsewhere. Narragansett Bay in Rhode Island, with its excellent anchorages, was destined to become a major center of maritime commerce. The extensive pine forests of New Hampshire and Maine provided tar, turpentine, pitch, and masts. By 1660, New England had become the center of an American shipbuilding industry which built nearly one-third of all the vessels used in the British empire.

Connecticut was settled by two different groups of Puritans. One group, led by Thomas Hooker, traveled in 1636 to the Connecticut Valley, which rapidly became the fur-trading center of New England. In 1639, a band of Puritans from London, dominated by the Reverend John Davenport, founded a colony at New Haven. It hoped to rival Boston as a center of maritime commerce, but it succeeded only in surpassing Boston in the rigor of its Puritanism. In 1662, the king issued a charter combining the towns of the Connecticut Valley and New Haven into the single colony of Connecticut.

New England society. The settlement of New England was a result of social planning. The New England town, which was chartered by the colony's representative assembly and run under its close supervision, was settled primarily by family groups. The town was the basic unit of local government and the primary instrument of social control. No town could be organized until a church, which had to have a nucleus of at least seven members, had been formed.

A town was normally governed by a group of selectmen, chosen by the adult male "freemen," or property holders. Even in Massachusetts, religious qualifications were not required for membership in the town meeting and election of town officials. Called upon to regulate nearly every aspect of human life, the freemen in their town meetings constituted a large populace accustomed to self-government, touchy about their rights, and highly skilled in political argument.

Education was extremely important to the Puritans. In 1636, they founded Harvard College, "dreading to leave an illiterate Ministry to the Churches, when our present Ministers shall lie in the Dust." The role of the college in preserving religious orthodoxy was so crucial that when the prominent minister Cotton Mather and others decided that Harvard was showing signs of liberalizing its theology, they founded Yale in 1701. The Puritans were convinced that a learned ministry was essential if sermons, the heart of Puritan religious services, were to be kept at a high standard of theological subtlety. This conviction also required that the congregation be sufficiently educated to follow the difficult arguments of the sermons.

All New England towns were required to maintain common schools. Puritan children were not only expected to learn the "three R's," but also to master the *New England Primer,* a handbook of Puritan theology and ethics. A system of apprenticeship was a crucial part of the educational system. In addition to teaching practical trades, master craftsmen taught young men to read and write and were held responsible for their apprentices' moral behavior. Above all, the masters were ordered to see that the apprentices attended church and understood the sermons. Those preparing for college attended grammar schools, where they were drilled in the Greek and Latin classics.

The whole society, from the duties assumed by town meetings to the regulations for education, had two great aims: to preserve order in a wilderness where men might easily abandon civilized habits, and to serve the churches.

The decline of Puritanism. After 1675, the harsh and rigid social order established by the Puritans began to decline. For one thing, the number of highly emotional conversion experiences decreased, and fewer people became church members. Perhaps the descendants of the early Puritans found three-hour sermons boring. Perhaps they thought the examination of candidates for church membership too rigorous. Whatever the reason, the ministers were convinced that New Englanders of the third and fourth generation were simply more sinful than their fathers.

As Boston's trade expanded, luxuries became common, and the port attracted people who cared little for Puritan goals and rules. Cotton Mather was appalled by this change; unless the people repented, Mather warned to no avail, God would punish New England. As Mather had prophesied, disaster struck, but not in the form of a plague or a swarm of locusts. It was planned and carried out by the English government.

Since the 1660's the English government had become increasingly irritated by the failure of the New England colonies to obey several laws passed by Parliament to regulate the commerce of the British empire. Moreover, by 1680, a rich merchant class had emerged in Boston which was not interested in theology, but in the West Indies trade. They resented being excluded from political life and believed that a royal government would serve their interests better than the Puritan magistrates. In 1684 came the startling news that the Crown had revoked the Massachusetts charter and that Sir Edmund Andros was on his way to govern all New England in the name of the king.

The Puritan state thus perished; church members would never again monopolize offices and restrict the franchise to themselves. New England would no longer be a religious experiment on the fringes of the wilderness, but part of a vast international empire shaped and ruled from London. But the Puritans left their indelible imprint. The organization of society in small, self-governing towns; the importance of public education; the Puritan conviction that moral behavior should be decreed by civil law; and the quality of fierce independence in religious matters all were basic elements of the heritage bequeathed by the Puritans.

3 Proprietors Establish The Middle And Southern Colonies

1. What were the characteristics of a proprietary colony? Why were proprietary colonies unworkable?

2. Why were American colonies willing to become royal colonies rather than remain proprietary colonies?

3. What were the similarities and the differences in the New England colonies, the Middle colonies, and the Southern colonies?

4. What signs are visible which would indicate that there would be continuing problems between Britain and America?

The English government, ill prepared to assume the task of creating and governing colonies during the seventeenth century, left the settlement of the new world in private hands. In addition to granting charters for corporate colonies, the government also encouraged the establishment of proprietary colonies. A proprietor was granted a large tract of territory by the king, with the right to collect rents from settlers, sell estates to speculators, and govern the colony almost as he saw fit. Normally, proprietors were important English politicians who had done some favor for the king and received part of America in return.

Proprietorships are created. The first proprietary colony was Maryland, granted by Charles I to Cecil Calvert, Lord Baltimore, in 1632. Baltimore's motive in establishing a colony in the Chesapeake area was religious. The Calverts had become Roman Catholics in 1625, and they hoped that Maryland would become a haven for English and Irish Catholics who suffered persecution at home. Baltimore hoped to make money by selling Manors—estates of two thousand or more acres—and by collecting quitrents, a fee paid by all landowners to the proprietor. All proprietors used this form of taxation, generally without much success and always accompanied by bitter disputes with the colonists.

The second proprietary colony was New York, carved out of the area that had originally been the Dutch colony of New Netherland. Established in 1621 by the Dutch West India Company, New Netherland had been plagued with troubles from the beginning. Settlers were unwilling to leave the rich farms of Holland. Moreover, in order to attract investors, the best land had been divided into gigantic estates called patroonships—or. , belonging to the Van Rensselaer family, had over two hundred thousand acres—and the patroon charged rents and fees for hunting and for grinding grain at his mill. Few Dutch burghers were attracted by the idea of being tenants.

Englishmen from New England, however, were attracted to Long Island, and they demanded representative government of the kind they had enjoyed in New England. The autocratic Dutch governor, Peter Stuyvesant, flatly declared, "We derive our authority from God and the Company, not from a few ignorant subjects." The restive English urged King Charles II, engaged in a furious war with Holland for control of the seas, to capture the colony. Charles readily complied, and in 1664, England wrested New Netherland from the Dutch. The king then presented the entire colony to his brother James, Duke of York, to hold as a proprietary colony.

As proprietor, James proved to be no reformer; he refused to permit representative government, confirmed the land titles of the Dutch patroons, and created many new manors which he gave to his friends. He was so generous to his friends, in fact, that he gave two of them, Lord John Berkeley and Sir George Carteret, the whole of New Jersey, which had been part of New Netherland.

For ten years the two New Jersey proprietors quarreled bitterly with New York over boundary lines, over who had governmental authority in New Jersey, and over the collection of quitrents which the settlers showed no disposition to pay. Berkeley became so discouraged that he sold out to a group of Quakers who continued the endless disputes about the specific powers of the proprietors. In 1680, Carteret's heirs sold his share to another group of Quakers. The normally peaceful Quaker proprietors were so embroiled in arguments over land boundaries that the colony was finally divided in two and an arbitrator was called in. Not even the worthy William Penn could untangle the confusion of New Jersey, but the

prospect of a Quaker proprietary colony excited him.

The Society of Friends, popularly called Quakers, believed that God speaks directly to man, revealing Himself through an "Inner Light," not through churchmen, sermons, or sacraments, and this doctrine infuriated English bishops. Moreover, Quakers refused to show deference to aristocrats, to fight in wars, and to take oaths in courts, and this alarmed the English government. Quaker beliefs and practices challenged every custom Englishmen lived by.

William Penn looked upon America as a promised land where his fellow Quakers might find peace and where an intense religious life might be cultivated. He would provide religious toleration, avoiding the strife and injustice which had marked the Puritan commonwealths in New England. Fired with the dream of beginning a "Holy Experiment," Penn persuaded the king to give him a huge grant of land in 1681 in payment for a debt the king owed his deceased father.

Penn's policy of religious toleration attracted not only English and Welsh Quakers, but also thousands of religious dissenters from Germany and France. His generous real-estate terms—extremely low costs and rentals—made possible the migration of thousands of other colonists. By 1686, nearly ten thousand people had settled in Pennsylvania.

Of all the dreams which led men to invest in the New World, the objectives of the Carolina proprietors were surely the strangest. In 1663, the Carolinas were granted to eight noblemen who sought to create a perfect feudal society in the wilderness! The proprietors not only intended that the Carolinas be ruled by a hereditary nobility, but also planned to reduce about two-fifths of the farmers to the status of serfs who would work the estates of the newly created aristocracy. The remaining settlers would be tenant or yeoman farmers who would pay quitrents to the proprietors.

The last proprietary colony was Georgia, granted in 1730 to a group of philanthropists led by General James Oglethorpe. Whereas most colonies were created for the benefit of the proprietor, Georgia was meant to be a refuge for the debtors who rotted in English jails. The Georgia proprietors, however, in common with all proprietary

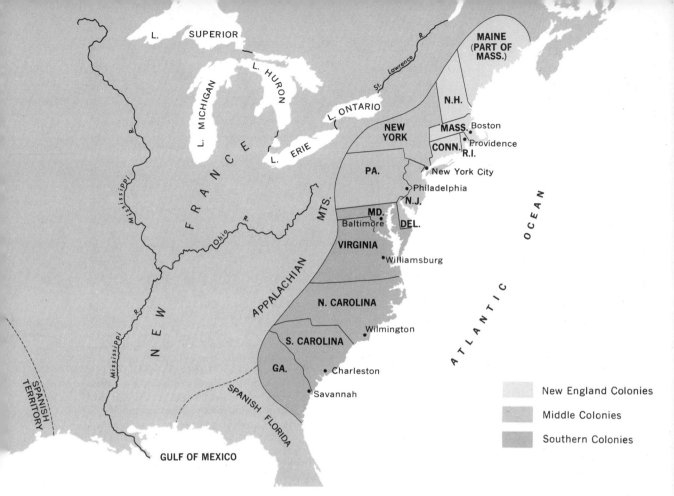

THE THIRTEEN COLONIES, 1750

governments, were determined to rule without consulting their subjects.

Proprietary colonies fail. Proprietary colonies soon revealed a serious defect. The interests of the proprietors and those of the settlers differed. The proprietor looked upon his colony as a vast estate, a profit-making enterprise of which he was the absolute master. The settlers resented his claims to complete authority over government, his economic privileges, and his political and religious views. Between proprietor and settler opened a vast gulf, disputes so deep and furious that stable government in most of the proprietary colonies was impossible.

Economic grievances caused many of the settlers to refuse to pay quitrents or to ignore the proprietor's authority. In New York, small farmers opposed the policy of granting most of the available land in great manorial estates, slowly forcing small farmers into becoming tenants. In the Carolinas the proprietors constantly attempted to evict squatters from their lands. And Georgians complained that the proprietors were not only stingy about land grants, but also maintained a monopoly of the warehouses and stores where settlers had to purchase supplies.

These economic discontents added fuel to the deep discord over the nature of proprietary government. The settlers wanted representative governments more responsive to their needs; almost all proprietors resisted this demand for self-government. In New York, for example, James stoutly resisted demands for a representative assembly. After twelve years of agitation, he finally allowed an assembly to meet. When it drew up a charter insisting that the assembly,

Facing the vast wilderness of the New World and turning it into a place of work and worship and trade were the tasks that greeted the colonists. The engraving above was made in 1733 for a book written to attract new settlers to Georgia; it purports to show the actual founding of the colony. The colonial wheelwright at the left and the Virginia tobacco traders and slaves below show some of the kinds of work being done in the colonies; shipping, the ministry, and farming engaged many thousands of other colonists. Baltimore was on its way to becoming a major seaport in 1752, as the sketch at the top right shows. Though it was not done at that time, it is based on the artist's "certain recollection and that of other aged persons well acquainted with" the city of that date. The *Wesley Chapel on John Street* (center right), painted in 1768 by an unknown artist, gives a good idea of what New York City looked like; and *The Plantation* (below right), though not painted until 1825, is still a reliable rendering of what a plantation of the 1750's encompassed—the main house, slave cabins, a warehouse and work buildings, and a water mill, all of them convenient to shipping.

25

rather than the proprietor, was entitled to exercise supreme legislative authority, James ignored it.

In the Carolinas the resistance to proprietary political authority was more violent. So effectively did North Carolinians resist that none of the governors sent out by the proprietors between 1664 and 1689 lasted long enough to establish effective government. Some governors were deposed, some were jailed and exiled, and one was forbidden even to land by the cantankerous colonists.

In South Carolina open defiance led to the deposing of one governor and the virtual ignoring of others. The greatest dispute between South Carolinians and their proprietors laid bare the defects of the whole proprietary system. The people wanted vigorous support against the Indians, but the proprietors, seeing no profit in an Indian war, persistantly refused to help. In short, the people came to feel that the proprietors cared only about their own profits, and not about the safety and profits of the colonists.

Religious disputes also wracked the proprietary colonies. Dutch reformed and Puritan churches in New York were convinced that the Church of England meant to outlaw them, and dissenters were angered by taxation to support Anglican ministers. In South Carolina, a similar attempt to force Puritans and Baptists to pay salaries to priests of the Church of England resulted in riots.

The scene of the deepest religious strife was Maryland. By 1650, Protestants greatly outnumbered Catholics. In an attempt to avoid religious turmoil, Lord Baltimore issued the Act of Religious Toleration of 1649, which declared that anyone who professed the divinity of Jesus Christ should be allowed to worship as he pleased. But this act was unsatisfactory to the Protestant majority, which overthrew the proprietary government in 1652. When the Baltimores were reinstated by Charles II, nervous Protestants continued to spread rumors that the proprietor was in league with Jesuits and Indians to destroy Protestantism and that he even invited the French or Spanish to seize the colony.

Rebellions destroy proprietary rule. These grievances produced rebellions which either ended or greatly altered proprietary rule. In England, when James became king in 1685, he made it clear that he wished to revise to his advantage the House of Commons, making it more willing to grant the Crown money and power. He stationed troops near London and began to appoint Roman Catholics to command them. James himself married a Catholic, and his son would be a Catholic king. This was horrifying to Englishmen, who regarded Catholicism as one of the greatest dangers in the world.

James's high handed policies were extended to America, where the king sought to centralize administration and reduce the colonies to absolute control by the Crown. The New England colonies were stripped of their charters and united to New York and New Jersey. Called the Dominion of New England, this new entity was governed by Sir Edmund Andros, who exemplified the tyranny Englishmen feared so much. He tried to void all land titles, impose quitrents, and collect deed fees. He decreed new taxes, refused to call assemblies, forced Puritan churches to allow the Church of England to use their meetinghouses, and, as a crowning blow, prohibited town meetings. Colonists became convinced that a Catholic-led plot to enslave them and destroy Protestantism was afoot.

In the spring of 1688, outraged Englishmen revolted, drove out James, and persuaded King William and Queen Mary of Holland to accept the English throne. The new monarchs agreed to a Bill of Rights which provided that the king could not suspend laws passed by Parliament, that no tax could be levied without Parliamentary consent, and that persons could not be arrested without due process of law. Protestant dissenters were to be free to practice their religion, and the monarchy must ever be Protestant.

These events stimulated rebellions in America. In Boston, Andros was arrested, and the New England colonies resumed their representative governments. In New York, a merchant named Jacob Leisler seized power, repealed the economic monopolies imposed by James, and created a legislative assembly. In Maryland, armed Protestants proclaimed the end to proprietary rule. All of these colonies, except Connecticut and Rhode Island, became royal colonies, as the people demanded, each with an elected legislature.

The other proprietary colonies were doomed.

New Jersey's endlessly quarreling proprietors reduced the colony to such confusion that the royal government ended their rule in 1702. In 1719, South Carolinians exiled the proprietary governor and refused to admit another. By 1729, both colonies had accepted royal governments. The proprietors of Georgia, unable to control the turbulent frontiersmen, surrendered their charter to the Crown in 1752.

While the Penns still retained control of Pennsylvania, the nature of the government was altered. The governor's council, for example, was denied any role in legislation, and the lower counties of Pennsylvania were permitted to form a separate colony called Delaware with their own representative assembly. Thus, the system of government by private individuals was replaced by imperial control and, more importantly, by the guarantee of representative government given by the British government.

4 Britain Seeks To Strengthen And Expand Its Empire

1. Why was Britain's administration of colonial American affairs so poor?

2. What were the points of conflict between Britain and France during the first half of the eighteenth century?

3. To what extent were the Americans capable of defending themselves against the French and the Indians?

From the time of its earliest ventures in colonization, England intended its empire to be an economic union in which the colonies shipped raw materials to England in return for manufactured articles. In theory, neither colonies nor mother country would need to rely on foreigners for anything.

Economic regulations. To make sure that these principles of mercantilism were carried out, Parliament passed, starting in 1660, a number of laws which are collectively referred to as Navigation Laws. First, Parliament decreed that all ships

TARIFFS

A tariff, or customs duty, is a tax a government places on goods imported from or exported to foreign countries. The tax is paid to the government by the merchant, who then passes it on to his customers in the form of higher prices.

Basically, there are two types of tariffs. A *revenue* tariff is designed only to provide additional income for the government. In enacting a revenue tariff, a government does not usually want to discourage its citizens from buying foreign goods or from selling goods to foreign countries. So, revenue tariffs are kept low. A *protective* tariff is placed on foreign goods which compete with domestically produced goods. When a government enacts a protective tariff, it wants to discourage its citizens from buying foreign goods or from selling goods to foreign countries. So, the rates of a protective tariff are usually high—or at least high enough so that consumers will get a better price by buying domestically produced articles.

In colonial times, Britain's aim was to make its empire into an economic union, independent of the rest of the world. In order to achieve such a goal, the British government had to pass many protective tariffs.

engaged in the imperial trade must be owned by citizens of England or of the colonies. This prevented Dutch and French ships from transporting goods within the empire. Second, certain commodities were *enumerated*, meaning that some articles, notably tobacco, cotton, indigo, rice, molasses, beaver furs, and naval stores could be shipped from the colonies only to England.

Third, foreign countries were not allowed to trade directly with the American colonies. Foreign goods had to be shipped first to England and transferred to English or colonial vessels. Finally, at the time of the transfer, the English collected a tax, called a *duty* or *tariff* (see feature above), on the goods. England sought to stimulate certain types of production and discourage others. The British government sought to encourage the colonies to produce naval stores; for example, pitch, masts, tar, hemp, and turpentine were subsidized by the government. On the other hand, Americans were forbidden in 1732 to export hats, and iron production was placed under similar restrictions in 1750.

Most Americans regarded these laws, with the exception of the Iron and Hat Acts, as beneficial. Foreign competition was eliminated, and the colonial shipbuilding industry was aided by the law banning foreign ships from the imperial trade. However, American wheat and fish could be sent directly to southern Europe because of a special loophole in the law.

What made the empire so satisfactory to Americans was the fact that its laws were rarely enforced with rigor. Smuggling was rife and uncontrolled. During the French and Indian War (pages 30, 31, 32), many colonial merchants calmly went on trading with the enemy. On paper, the economic regulations governing the colonies seemed thorough, minute, and even irritating, but Parliament had not been able to devise a governmental system capable of enforcing its rules and regulations.

Governing the empire. The responsibility of governing the British empire lay in the hands of a number of committees and boards in London, subject to the ultimate authority of the Privy Council (the king's advisers) and the Cabinet. The most active department concerned with the colonies was the Board of Trade, which formulated economic policies, sent instructions to the royal governors, and reviewed the laws passed by colonial assemblies to make sure they did not violate British law. The Treasury Board collected the customs duties. None of the members of these boards bothered to visit the colonies, and often they failed to consult each other or the Cabinet official responsible for colonies—the Secretary of State for the Southern Department, who also conducted all foreign relations with Mediterranean nations!

To enforce the edicts of these officials and carry out the Navigation Acts, royal governors were sent out to preside over the colonies (except Connecticut and Rhode Island, which had been

TRADE RESTRICTIONS

Act	Provisions
Navigation Acts 1650, 1651, 1660–61, 1696	Colonial trade limited to English and colonial ships. European goods required to pass through England. Tobacco, cotton, indigo, and other colonial goods could be sent only to England.
Woolen Act 1699	No export of wool or wool cloth from colonies.
Hat Act 1732	No export of colonial-made hats.
Molasses Act 1733	Colonies required to pay high duty on foreign sugar, molasses, and rum.
Iron Act 1750	No new iron plants allowed in colonies. No duty on iron imported from England into colonies.

accorded the privilege of electing their own governors, and Pennsylvania and Delaware, where the Penn family appointed the governor). These men were usually British politicians who hoped to make a fortune out of the numerous fees owed to a royal governor. Many did not even trouble themselves to cross the Atlantic, sending instead a deputy governor to collect the salary and fees. Those who did come found that no real civil service existed to aid them. The governor was assisted by a council, made up of wealthy colonial merchants and planters who often disagreed with him. As a result, the most crucial men in the government of the empire were either indifferent to the task of keeping the colonies in line or simply incapable of doing so.

In brief, the empire was badly run because the British government never created a centralized authority to rule the colonies. Deeply involved in their own political maneuverings, British politicians had little time to devote to American affairs. Moreover, through most of the eighteenth century, Britain was engaged in wars with France which distracted it from the task of giving its colonial empire a vigorous government.

Struggle for a continent. From 1690 to 1815, Britain and France were rivals for power on the continent of Europe. Britain was determined to check the expansion of an aggressive France; for 125 years there were wars or preparations for war between Britain and a perennial French-Spanish alliance. The New World was an obvious prize in this contest.

Even without the rivalries in Europe, however, France and Britain were bound to come into conflict in America. Both nations claimed the Ohio River Valley basin, but France had only a tiny population with which to occupy its lands. The population of the British colonies grew from 250,000 in 1700 to 1,200,000 in 1750, and this population explosion led to a drive for western lands. The enormously profitable fur trade of the Ohio Valley quickly attracted British trappers and traders. In addition, both France and Britain claimed Nova Scotia, an important rendezvous for the fishing industry.

To these economic factors must be added religious rivalry. Catholic France seemed a religious menace, especially to New England's Protestant ministers, who believed that the wars with the French in the New World were not simply brutal struggles in the forests waged for land and furs, but holy wars against the pope.

A crucial element in British and French plans for trade and settlement in the Ohio Valley was the attitude of the Indians, whom the French made great efforts to befriend. The British settlers had attempted to drive the tribes westward or exterminate them. Consequently, most of the Indians cooperated with the French. One tribe, the Iroquois, sided with the British. As the French advanced their fur operations into the Ohio and Illinois valleys, they encroached upon hunting preserves claimed by the Iroquois. The British and Dutch fur-traders at Albany took advantage of this situation and formed with the Iroquois a military alliance.

The struggle raged on and off in both Europe and North America. War followed war (see chart above), but little was actually settled by the belligerents. By 1748, after more than fifty years of intermittent wars, only Novia Scotia and an ill-defined area around Hudson Bay had come into British hands. Frustrated Americans were convinced that the wars had been in vain.

WARS BETWEEN BRITAIN AND FRANCE 1689–1763	
In America	**In Europe**
King William's War 1689–1697	War of the League of Augsburg 1689–1697
Queen Anne's War 1702–1713	War of the Spanish Succession 1702–1713
King George's War 1744–1748	War of the Austrian Succession 1740–1748
French and Indian War 1754–1763	Seven Years' War 1756–1763

British defeat. But still the wars did not end. The struggle for control over the Ohio Valley was now joined by two groups determined to oust all rivals. French merchants in Montreal had gained control of the fur trade and the monopoly right to supply the Indians with goods. British traders rushed in to underbid them.

More important than these traders were the colonial land companies. Pennsylvania had already staked out a claim in the Ohio country and bought it from the Iroquois. The same land, and more besides, was claimed by the Ohio Company, which was controlled by a group of Virginia planters, including Lawrence and Augustine Washington and the colony's governor, Robert Dinwiddie. Competition between the economic elites of Montreal and Virginia rapidly brought on a crisis.

The French acted first, constructing a line of forts between Lake Erie and the Allegheny River and destroying two British trading stations. Governor Dinwiddie of Virginia countered by sending a small force to erect a fort at the forks of the Ohio, where the Allegheny and Monongahela rivers meet to form the Ohio. The French drove the Virginians away, built Fort Duquesne, and captured a relief column led by George Wash-

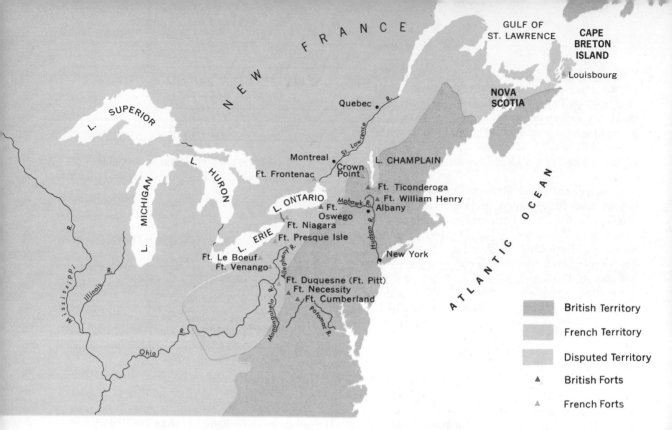

British Territory
French Territory
Disputed Territory
▲ British Forts
▲ French Forts

THE FRENCH AND INDIAN WAR, 1754–1763

ington in July, 1754. Virginia and French Canada were at war (see map above).

Meanwhile, the British government was trying to work out a reasonable colonial defense policy that would place the burden on the colonists. Great Britain was preoccupied with European diplomacy and battlefields. Beyond this, it had to protect its West Indian colonies, preserve the slave trade, and even compete with France in India. It had few troops to spare for America, and the colonies, it hoped, would protect themselves.

The colonists had proven singularly incapable of doing so, because the colonies refused to cooperate with each other. New England bitterly resented the refusal of New York to join its efforts; New York castigated New Jersey for its failure to supply troops. The Carolinas were angered by the near-neutrality of Virginia, before 1754, and everyone, including many inhabitants of Pennsylvania, was irritated by the pacifism of the Quakers. In the face of this, Great Britain called a conference of delegates from colonial assemblies to meet at Albany for the purpose of creating a unified command in case of another war.

When the Albany Congress met—minus Virginia and New Jersey, who refused to send delegates—in September 1753, Benjamin Franklin presented a plan to unite the colonies. It called for a President-General to be appointed by the king and for a legislative Grand Council made up of delegates appointed by the assemblies of the colonies proportioned according to population and wealth. The Union would control Indian affairs, raise and direct its own army and navy, and have the right to requisition money from the various colonies for this purpose. When the Albany Plan of Union was presented to the various colonial assemblies, it was either rejected or ignored. Some colonies disapproved of the tax feature, and others refused to surrender control over the Indian trade.

The failure of the Albany Plan of Union made it clear to Britain that it would bear the main burden of defending its colonies and conquering

Canada. The first phase of the war, lasting from 1755 to 1757, was a series of disasters for the British. The French and their Indian allies, the Delaware, trapped and routed an army under General James Braddock, who hoped to capture Fort Duquesne. In New York the great French commander the Marquis de Montcalm seized Fort Oswego, exposing the Mohawk Valley to invasion, and captured Fort William Henry, threatening Albany. The frontiers of Pennsylvania, New York, and New Hampshire were savagely raided by Indians.

British victory. The victories of the French had tremendous repercussions in Britain. Prime Minister William Pitt, who believed that a commercial empire was the basis of Great Britain's future wealth, took over direction of the war. He was more interested in acquiring French colonies than in defeating French armies in Europe. Pitt promptly dispatched fifteen thousand soldiers to

NORTH AMERICA IN 1763

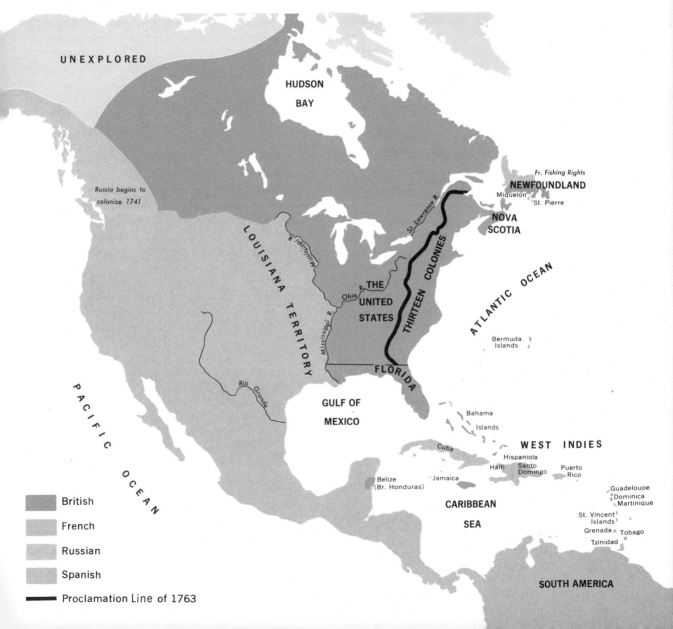

UNEXPLORED

HUDSON BAY

Russia begins to colonize 1741

Fr. Fishing Rights
NEWFOUNDLAND
Miquelon
St. Pierre

NOVA SCOTIA

St. Lawrence R.

LOUISIANA TERRITORY

Mississippi R.

Ohio R.

THE UNITED STATES

THIRTEEN COLONIES

ATLANTIC OCEAN

Mississippi R.

Bermuda Islands

FLORIDA

Rio Grande

GULF OF MEXICO

Bahama Islands

Cuba

WEST INDIES

Hispaniola
Haiti
Santo Domingo
Puerto Rico

Belize (Br. Honduras)

Jamaica

Guadeloupe
Dominica
Martinique

CARIBBEAN SEA

St. Vincent Islands
Grenada
Tobago
Trinidad

PACIFIC OCEAN

SOUTH AMERICA

British

French

Russian

Spanish

Proclamation Line of 1763

America, commanded by Lord Jeffrey Amherst and General James Wolfe. He induced the colonial assemblies to stop quarreling over taxes by promising them a subsidy of over a million pounds. Lastly, Pitt had a careful military plan which was carried out almost without a hitch.

First, Montcalm must be either defeated or immobilized. General James Abercromby, with six thousand British regulars and six thousand colonial militia, assaulted Fort Ticonderoga. Although Abercromby was repulsed with hideous losses, Montcalm was tied down in the fort. In August 1758, a small colonial force took Fort Frontenac, breaking French communications between Montreal and the Ohio Valley. The isolated Fort Duquesne soon fell to the British and was renamed Fort Pitt. While these operations were breaking the French hold on the Ohio Valley, Amherst and Wolfe captured Louisbourg, on Cape Breton Island.

In 1759, the campaigns were aimed at reducing the major French bases—Fort Niagara, Quebec, and Montreal. Niagara fell without difficulty, and Amherst marched toward Montreal, seizing Ticonderoga and Crown Point. He met little resistance because Montcalm was forced to rush back to Quebec to meet the major British offensive. When the Marquis arrived at the city, Wolfe had already laid it under siege. On the night of September 12, Wolfe led his troops up the massive heights of Quebec by an unguarded path. The next morning the British totally defeated the French; both Wolfe and Montcalm were killed. A year later, Amherst rode into Montreal.

The war dragged on for two more years, with Britain victorious everywhere—French India, Spanish Cuba, and the French West Indies were all added to the empire. Not everyone was as pleased with the war as Pitt. The new king, George III, wanted peace, and was willing to give back many of the conquests to achieve it. For two years British politicians argued about whether they should give up Canada or the French West Indies. In the end, the British West Indies sugar planters, fearing the competition of the newly acquired islands, persuaded the government to give back the French West Indies and retain Canada. Spain, because it was an ally of France, was forced to give Florida to the British, who then returned Cuba to Spanish rule.

The struggle was over, and the British and the Americans could rest secure in the knowledge that they had driven their French antagonists from the North American continent.

5 A Distinctly American Society Emerges

1. How was American society different from British society in the eighteenth century?

2. What classes made up American colonial society, and which groups composed each class?

3. How did society differ in the New England colonies, the Middle colonies, and the South?

British travelers in the colonies were often startled by the discovery that the American colonists were different from the inhabitants of the mother country. An Anglican clergyman found it "singularly peculiar" that "the lower classes of people are impertinently curious and inquisitive." Equally strange to British ears was the variety of foreign tongues. In 1744, an astonished Scottish doctor found himself dining in Philadelphia

. . . with a very mixed company of different nations and religions. There were Scots, English, Dutch, Germans and Irish; there were Roman Catholics, Anglicans, Presbyterians, Quakers, Methodists, Seventh day men, Moravians, Anabaptists, and one Jew.

If some British visitors were astonished by social conditions in America, they also saw much to admire. They noted that the lower- and middle-class colonists ate better food and lived in better houses than did their counterparts in Great Britain. Colonial cities were not disfigured by the hordes of beggars that disgraced London. Americans, then as now, lived in the midst of plenty, even though not everyone shared in the abundance of the land.

A French immigrant named Michel Guillaume Jean de Crèvecoeur put his finger on a basic difference when he pointed out that American society

Mrs. Freake and Baby Mary, anonymous, c. 1674

Sea Captains Carousing in Surinam, John Greenwood, *c.* 1758

Isaac Royall and Family, Robert Feke, 1741

Art in colonial America had to develop in the face of conditions that were not friendly to it. The great wealth which often produces patrons to support and encourage artists did not exist. The business of the colonials was establishing themselves and their new nation, and they had little time to appreciate or support art.

Among the earliest colonial artists to emerge were the limners, as self-taught portrait painters were called. They traveled about the country, hiring out their abilities to family heads who wanted their wives or children painted. The painting on page 33 is a good example of the limner's art; in it the figures are stiff, the faces are in a three-quarter pose, and neither the arms nor the body position shows any foreshortening.

Portraiture continued to be the main type of colonial painting through the eighteenth century, although there was some landscape painting as well, generally by folk artists. One painting that does not fall into either category appears top left; it is one of the few examples of genre painting—the picturing of daily life—produced during colonial times. The artist was not technically accomplished, but he painted some original and highly satiric works that departed from the typically staid pictures of the period. The picture bottom left, a group portrait done some seventy years after the limner's portrait, shows an improvement in technique, but still suffers from a certain stiffness and lack of facial differentiation. Yet it has a grace about it.

Colonial architecture borrowed heavily from European models. The painting below, the Old State House in Boston, built in 1748, reflects the British Georgian style.

Old State House, Boston, *1801*, J. B. Marston

Gravestone of Colonel John Hathorne, Salem, Massachusetts, 1717

Sculpture in colonial America was predominantly a folk art, and it had a distinctly utilitarian basis. Ships' figureheads, gravestones, weathervanes, and symbols for advertising to a semi-literate people all needed to be carved. Among the earliest carvings were gravestones. The stone above was carved to mark the grave of Colonel John Hathorne, a judge at the Salem witch trials in 1692 and an ancestor of author Nathaniel Hawthorne. The skull in the ornamentation that surrounds the lettering is crudely drawn, but the sculptor uses it to achieve a properly sombre tone. The metal sculptor who created the copper weathervane at the left had a cheerier task. The rooster was the most common subject for weathervane carvers, but Indians, horses, and even grasshoppers were also used during the eighteenth century. They were sturdily built; often they stood upon cast iron legs. But copper was used for the upper parts because it could be hammered easily to show considerable detail.

Weathervane of an Indian Archer,
Shem Drowne, c. 1700

. . . is not composed, as in Europe, of great lords who possess everything, and a herd of people who have nothing. Here are no aristocratical families, no court, no kings, no bishops, no ecclesiastical dominion . . . no great manufactures employing thousands, no great refinements of luxury. The rich and the poor are not so far removed from each other as they are in Europe.

Crèvecoeur's analysis of American society was somewhat oversimplified, but it was a generally accurate capsule survey of the major differences which distinguished the American colonies from England.

The upper class. While there was no aristocracy in America, there was an upper class which dominated the economy and exercised political power. The nature of this wealthy group differed from region to region. In the North three groups comprised the ruling class. New York was governed by the great manorial landholders of the Hudson River Valley, who often had important import-export businesses in the city of New York. Other northern cities were dominated by a merchant class whose shipping firms controlled much of the American economy.

Professional men—ministers and lawyers— were also part of the colonial elite. Lawyers were crucial to a society in which land titles were so important. Ministers, often the best-paid men in town, not only shaped religious life, but also conveyed from their pulpits political theories and moral teachings. In rural towns, the ministers were the chief introducers of new ideas.

South Carolina and Virginia were ruled by a closely intermarried class of great planters. Many lived in large, graciously decorated houses, rode in magnificent coaches (George Washington's cost over three hundred pounds, which was three times the yearly salary of a New England minister), dressed themselves and their wives in the best silk clothing England could provide, entertained sumptuously, and had sufficient time to cultivate the fine arts and study political philosophy. Their land holdings were enormous. Washington, for example, owned ten thousand acres, the Carter family thirty thousand. Moreover, both Washington and the Carters owned hundreds of slaves.

Unlike British aristocrats, who rarely concerned themselves with the management of their estates, southern planters were hard-working businessmen. They were up at dawn to supervise work on their crops of tobacco or rice; they arranged to feed and care for their slaves; and they repaired and improved their plantations. They negotiated with British merchants in regard to crop shipments; they kept track of the price of slaves in Virginia and the price of tobacco in London. They worried about the weather, about their speculations in frontier lands, and about the economic policies of the British government.

Lawyers, merchants, and planters, most of them college graduates, provided the majority of representatives who served in colonial assemblies, on governor's councils, or as county judges. Office holders and representatives had to possess considerable property in order to stand for election, and the royal government in Britain insisted that councillors and judges be men of substance.

"The middling sorts of people." Beneath the class of merchants and landowners stood the middle class, the great mass of skilled artisans and almost self-sufficient small farmers. Most of these middle-class colonials were farmers who owned between fifty and two hundred acres of land. Although they depended on Britain for ironwares, and a few pieces of "parlor furniture," they were otherwise free from dependence on foreign goods. They grew wheat, tobacco, rice, and indigo for the British market, and they distilled most of the rum New England made world-famous. In the South, these middle-class farmers owned most of the land and most of the slaves, even though individual holdings were small.

In the five colonial cities—Boston, Newport, New York, Philadelphia, and Charleston—skilled cabinetmakers, metalworkers, retail shopkeepers, shipwrights, printers, and clerks in mercantile houses made up the majority of the population. Like the farmers, they owned property and invested their small profits in trading ventures. In colonial America a merchant ship might have ten, twenty, or more owners who pooled their capital and shared risks in overseas trade.

The middle class depended on the imperial trade nearly as much as the great planters and merchants. They believed that their economic interests were similar to those of the upper classes. Consequently, there was little economic "class warfare" in America. The middle class as a whole was respectable and hardworking, driven by the desire for profits and economic security; they lent to colonial society a high degree of conservatism which Europeans regarded as the strongest feature of the American social order.

"The poorer sorts of people." The vast majority of immigrants arrived in the colonies as indentured servants. Some of them entered service voluntarily, in order to leave their homeland and begin anew in the colonies. Others entered service involuntarily—convicts, kidnapped children, and debtors were often bought by enterprising ships captains and sold into service in the colonies. In the eighteenth century over fifty thousand convicts were shipped to the colonies by British authorities, who were anxious to relieve social pressure and reduce prison costs at home. Convicts were required to serve terms as indentured servants from periods ranging from seven to fourteen years. They made poor workers, and colonial assemblies often protested the practice of bringing them in, but to no avail.

For people other than convicts, terms of indenture varied—seven years in New England, and four in other colonies was usually the case. At the end of their terms of indentured service, servants were provided with tools, clothing, and in theory at least, enough money to buy land. Nearly 70 percent of all eighteenth-century Americans were "graduates" of the indenture system.

Benjamin Franklin approved of this system and lauded its virtues:

A little money saved of the good wages they receive . . . while they work for others, enables them to buy the land and begin their Plantation, in which they are assisted by the good will of their neighbors and some credit. Multitudes of poor people from England, Ireland, Scotland and Germany have by this means in a few years become wealthy farmers.

But there was a hitch in this arrangement which Franklin failed to mention. The best land, closest to rivers and ports, was already taken. Only in the West was sufficient land available to satisfy the tremendous demand. Released servants, especially Scots and Irish, poured into frontier areas, and traveled the Great Wagon Road from Pennsylvania to Georgia.

These frontiersmen, although they always asserted their tough individualism, were, in fact, dependent upon the rest of society. Their tools, weapons, and household utensils were supplied by the more settled communities. Their rights to settle on the lands they explored had to be determined by the courts and legislatures in the eastern parts of the colonies, and they often could not afford the lawyers' fees required to give them clear title to the land they occupied. Moreover they found it difficult to transport agricultural produce to markets. As a result of these conditions, most frontiersmen lived in squalor.

Another group of poor people were the old, the sick, and the handicapped. Most elderly persons lived with their children, but in every area, large numbers of people were totally dependent upon society for life itself. A number of different ways were devised to handle such "welfare cases," all of them organized by local units of government. In New England, for example, every year the town agreed to pay families for taking in and caring for the old, the handicapped, and the needy.

Blacks in the colonies. By 1760, about 325,000 Africans lived in America, nearly all of them slaves. The discipline imposed upon the slave was extremely harsh, and sometimes fatal. Equally as degrading as brutality were the squalid conditions under which most slaves lived. Slaves had a poor diet, consisting primarily of fish and corn meal; they lived in miserable cabins, and were exposed to the elements and disease-bearing insects. The death toll was high, particularly in the South Carolina rice swamps.

It is true that many masters were personally kind to their slaves, but no amount of good treatment could compensate for depriving men of what they needed most: a sense of dignity and worth. In the South, it was remarked by travelers and placidly assumed by the upper classes that the poor—both black and white—were "lazy." In fact, the laziness was likely to be the result of debilitating diseases and parasites that were rife in the South. The poor often suffered from diseases such as pellagra, and, because they went barefoot, were subject to hookworm infestation from the soil.

In eighteenth-century America the few blacks who were freed made important contributions to society, and several excelled. For example Benjamin Banneker, an excellent mathematician, and Phyllis Wheatley, the famous Boston poetess of the 1770's, clearly challenged the unenlightened whites who doubted the black man's capacity for intellectual achievement.

Variety. America was a land of distinctive societies. New England, the Middle Colonies, the South, and the thin line of settlements merging into the forests of the West each presented different characteristics.

New England was the most homogenous of the colonial societies. Discouraged by reports of Puritan intolerance and the lack of cheap land, European immigrants avoided New England. The people there were almost entirely of British stock, had the same religious institutions, and shared a history of suspicion of British authority. New England was a society of tightly knit small towns, and social control was basically assured by community opinion. Men in New England might quarrel furiously about theology and sue each other with amazing frequency over land claims, but morality, manners, and dress were uniformly agreed upon and enforced.

If community was the essence of New England, individualism was the prime characteristic of the South. With few towns and a weak established church (Anglican), the southerner had few institutional restraints to govern his behavior. Law enforcement, especially the control of slaves, tended to be informal. That is, southerners relied on posses rather than the town constables and sheriffs who enforced the law in the North. This engendered a tendency to ignore the legal codes by which societies normally govern themselves. The upper classes, however, sought to conform to the ideal of the British gentleman—grave, reserved, excessively formal, polite, and hospitable.

The Middle Colonies were characterized principally by their diversity. Englishmen, Dutchmen, and Germans, Quakers, Protestants, Catholics, and Jews generally managed to live together in harmony. Living in these colonies induced a certain sophistication, an ability to get along with strangers, that neither New England or the South ever mastered.

Social mobility. The social order in eighteenth-century America was marked by mobility as well as geographical variety. Class boundaries, with the important exception of the racial line between white and black people, were easy to cross. There were no legal barriers, no hereditary aristocracies to slam the door in the face of talent. This condition alone made for a general conviction among the colonials that theirs was a good society. Benjamin Franklin, who rose from newsboy to printer, and thence to philosopher and statesman, was the American success story par excellence.

The importance of this easy upward mobility was not merely economic. It ensured that new political leaders appeared, as the newly rich sought and achieved political power. Many leaders of the American Revolution were men of this type. John Adams, the son of a farmer, became a successful lawyer and an outstanding politician. This fluidity of class lines, combined with a willingness to move about the country, astonished Europeans. Nothing in America seemed settled and ordered to foreigners, who were used to the rigid class distinctions and geographical rootedness of European communities.

6 Americans Adopt New Patterns Of Thought

1. What important changes took place in religious thought and practice in colonial America between the seventeenth and eighteenth centuries?

2. What important changes took place in political thought and practice in colonial America between the seventeenth and eighteenth centuries?

3. Why did these changes in religion and politics occur at this particular time in America?

4. Were similar influences involved in the political and religious trends in eighteenth-century America? If so, what were they?

The values of seventeenth-century Americans were diverse. Different ethnic origins, religious beliefs, political systems, and environmental conditions combined to produce distinctive societies in New England, the Middle Colonies, and the South. As time wore on, basic intellectual changes occurred which helped to make eighteenth-century American society markedly different from that of the seventeenth. Eighteenth-century Americans did not think or behave precisely the same way as their forebears.

Religious changes. The most striking social and intellectual changes in eighteenth-century America occurred in religious thought and practice. In New England, the old Puritan order, with its heavy emphasis on theology and conformity, began to decline toward the end of the seventeenth century. By the middle of the eighteenth century, orthodox Puritanism was virtually dead, and was replaced by a form of Christianity involving emotionalism and toleration. Religious experience became more intense, a matter of personal emotional involvement; and the cause of religious freedom made rapid progress. The greatest outward manifestation of change in religious thought and feeling at this time was the Great Awakening.

The Great Awakening. In part, the origins of the Great Awakening in America can be traced to England. During the 1730's the Anglican Church was confronted by a serious revolt in its own ranks called *Wesleyanism* or *Methodism.* John Wesley agreed with the basic tenet of Anglican theology: that all men could be saved. But Wesley advocated simplicity of ritual and the importance of making emotional appeals to sinful men. In 1740, Wesley's brilliant collaborator George Whitefield came to America.

Whitefield found the colonies stirring with religious unrest. Some Puritan ministers had already opened church membership to all comers, eliminating the tough examinations the early Puritans had imposed. In 1735, Minister Jonathan Edwards noted of his townsmen in Northampton, Massachusetts, "All seemed to be seized with a deep concern about their eternal salvation." So deep was the concern, so frustrated were people with the dull sermons of their ministers, that they sought some assurance that God loved them and that they could be saved. Whitefield provided an answer.

His tour of the colonies was a missionary triumph. He preached dramatically, flailing his arms, bursting into tears as he described Hell, smiling rapturously as he foretold the joys of Heaven. He taught that man could merit salvation by hating sin and by so strongly desiring Grace that God would send it. Thus, all men could not only be saved, but they could also work for their own salvation. In short, Whitefield preached that the ideas of predestination and the elect were dead.

This simple doctrine was easy to preach; it did not involve an elaborate theology. The minister had only to terrify his congregation by defining, with grim precision, the torments of sinners in hell, and then beg the sinners to seek the aid of Christ to prevent such a fiery future. The response of the people to the new doctrines and exciting preaching was tremendous. People wept, shouted, ran about the meeting house, rolled in the aisles, sang, and confessed their sins with gusto. So many people joined churches and so many laymen began to preach without authorization that the movement was called the Great Awakening.

Orthodox ministers denounced the emotionalism of the sermons, the hysteria of the communicants, and the shocking idea that everyone could be saved. As a result, splits often occurred in the churches, especially after Whitefield explained that some ministers, "stony of heart," were not themselves "saved." The noisy services and the idea that a man could do something to earn salvation were especially popular on the frontier and among the lower classes. New denominations appeared and grew rapidly; the Baptists in New England, for example, increased from six churches to over three hundred in a few years.

Natural religion. The upper classes, the lawyers, merchants, and great planters, like Washington, were not affected by the uproar caused by the Great Awakening. Just as the doctrines of evangelical religion had come from England, so another conception of religion was exported to the colonies, the idea of natural religion. This new theory argued that religion existed to promote virtue, which could be understood and achieved by human effort without the aid of divine grace.

Deism, the most extreme form of natural religion, regarded Jesus as a good man to be emulated, but not as a divine person to be worshiped. Heaven and hell were ignored and miracles were denied. Deists sought to understand how God wanted men to behave, rather than what He wanted them to believe. The behavior they advocated was, in fact, traditional Christian morality, based on the Ten Commandments. To explain the necessity of this morality for men, Deists emphasized that it would bring order and harmony to society.

Natural religion was not a sect but an attitude. It was skeptical of theology and dubious about the literal accuracy of the Bible, and it sought to make toleration a part of the fundamental law of society. Adherents of natural religion emphasized reason and law. Just as the English scientist Sir Isaac Newton could define the laws of gravity and motion, they believed that philosophers and statesmen could define God's rules for human society. It followed that men so convinced would give a good deal of thought to the way in which an orderly society was to be maintained without God's direct intervention. In short, they paid close attention to secular political theory.

Political ideas and practice. As already emphasized, the revolution of 1688 in England strengthened representative government both in that country, where Parliament became the ultimate source of political authority, and in the colonies, where representative institutions were restored to the New England colonies whose charters had been revoked by James.

Colonial Americans recognized the supremacy of Parliament when it came to purely imperial concerns, such as navigation laws or declarations of war and peace. But from an early date, they denied the right of Parliament to interfere in their internal affairs.

Colonial Americans derived their political philosophy primarily from their English heritage and their own experience. English theorists and philosophers, especially John Locke, Richard Harrington, John Trenchard, Thomas Gordon, and Algernon Sydney, were widely read in the American colonies, and many of their ideas became integral parts of American social and political theory. The works of Locke, especially his *Second Treatise of Civil Government* and his *Letter on Toleration,* and the best selling political essays, *Cato's Letters,* by Trenchard and Gordon, were most often quoted.

These English thinkers examined and elaborated upon the social-compact theory of government. This theory held that before the organization of society, men lived in a natural state in which they had unlimited freedom. Unfortunately, in the natural state, the strong preyed on the weak, and no man's property was safe. Therefore, men agreed to form a society in order to protect themselves, but in doing so, they voluntarily surrendered much of their freedom. Even so, certain "natural rights" could not be surrendered, especially the right to life and the right to amass and dispose of property.

These rights were considered inherent in the nature of man and could not be granted or revoked by government. Government, then, must exist and be maintained only by consent of the governed. Individuals would express their consent through their representative institutions and through permitting the king to exercise executive power.

According to the social-compact theory, in addition to natural rights, men are entitled to enjoy civil rights or liberties. These liberties are part of the social compact by which society is created, and serve to protect the individual from the exercise of arbitrary power by the state. Freedom of the press, religious toleration, trial by jury, taxation only by the consent of elected representatives, and *habeas corpus* (a writ forbidding illegal imprisonment) were all defined as liberties which could not be revoked.

To Americans this theory had a familiar ring. They were convinced that *Cato's Letters* and the political theories of Locke were not merely abstract speculation about the nature of political authority, but descriptions of their own political systems. For example, when Andrew Hamilton of Philadelphia defended John Peter Zenger in a case involving freedom of the press in 1735, he drew heavily upon the principles expressed in *Cato's Letters.*

Zenger, a New York newspaper editor, had written an article severely criticizing the governor of New York. According to the prosecution, Zenger's attack was "seditious libel," a vicious attempt to undermine the foundations of government itself. Under British law, the trial judge could determine whether or not the words Zenger used were libelous. The jury's only function was to determine whether or not Zenger had actually printed the article.

Hamilton managed to convince the court that the jury had the right to determine whether or not a libel had occurred. Hamilton further insisted that if the printed items were true, they could be considered neither libelous nor seditious. Although Zenger was acquitted, his trial did not establish a new legal precedent. Other editors could still be prosecuted for editorial attacks on governmental officials. Yet Zenger's acquittal was important, as the case made other governors more cautious in their attempts to restrain a critical press. In fact, most royal governors during the eighteenth century were more cautious than the British government intended them to be.

Growth of the assemblies' power. The most notable fact of colonial political life during the first sixty years of the eighteenth century was the growth of the power of the representative assemblies. The assemblies were determined to reduce the power of royal governors by refusing to pay uncooperative governors their salaries. Since most governors were not wealthy, they acquiesced in the expansion of the power of the assemblies.

As time passed, the colonial legislatures demanded and got the right to appoint military officers, treasurers, tax collectors, and agents to deal with the Indians. They also established committees to supervise the expenditures of funds to determine tax rates. They did not succeed in abridging the right of the governors to appoint judges, but their right to appropriate funds to pay the judges' salaries provided protection from arbitrary judicial decisions.

In addition to curbing the power of royal officials, members of colonial assemblies utilized their influence to enrich themselves and their allies. In nearly all colonial assemblies, rival political factions competed for such things as offices, monopolies over timber rights, titles to western lands, and licenses to trade with the Indians. Moreover, almost every colonial legislature was deeply concerned by the issue of paper money. In the colonies a chronic shortage of gold and silver existed, since colonists had to use it to pay for British manufactured goods. In order to relieve the currency shortage, colonial legislatures advanced numerous banking schemes involving paper money designed for use as currency at home. All such plans were vetoed by the British government, and became a source of friction

CURRENCY FOR THE NATION

One of the most crucial economic problems the American colonies faced was finding enough money to carry on profitable trade. The problem of establishing and maintaining a uniform and stable medium of exchange, or currency, is one that has recurred several times in the histories of most nations. In America, the problem was not solved in colonial times, and has continued to be a difficulty.

Throughout history, people have used various commodities as currency. In general, if a commodity was rare enough to be considered valuable, but still obtainable, it was a good candidate for a medium of exchange. At some times in some places, diamonds, ivory, and furs have all been used as currency. Gradually, more and more places came to accept gold or silver as their medium of exchange. Metals could easily be made into coins of different sizes and weights and thus of different values. And coins were certainly a more convenient, portable form of currency than furs or elephant tusks.

Eventually, however, people found that gold and silver were not perfect currencies. In any quantity metal coins are heavy and not easily portable. And, as trade increased, there were not enough coins, or *specie currency*, to cover all the transactions. This was the major money problem faced by the American colonies.

People began to look for a substitute currency, and soon paper money came into use. Each piece of paper money represented, or was *backed* by, a certain amount of gold or silver. In theory, the government had to exchange the paper money for specie if the holder demanded. In fact few people in few places demand metal in exchange for their paper money. This is because they have faith that their paper money is generally accepted—that they can use it in their transactions and others will accept it at its *face* value, that is, the nominal value which appears on a piece of money. It is this acceptance that makes a nation's currency stable.

between the colonies and the mother country.

Another issue which absorbed the energy of colonial legislators was the problem of western representation. As settlement expanded westward, the people in these newly settled areas unsuccessfully demanded *proportional representation* in their colonial assemblies (representation in a legislature according to population). Legislators from eastern counties of the colonies refused to relinquish their power and influence in the assembly.

Westerners were confronted by higher tax rates, exploited by exorbitant legal fees, required to travel long distances to secure a hearing in court, short-changed on appropriations for internal improvements, and enraged by the failure of legislatures to protect the frontier against Indian attacks. It was not until the American Revolution, when colonial assemblies were faced by the necessity to unify ranks to defeat the British, that the western areas of most colonies were finally given adequate representation.

During the eighteenth century, suffrage in the colonies was limited to property owners. Property qualifications varied from colony to colony, but they were low enough to permit nearly 65 percent of the adult male white population over twenty-one to vote. The poor were not represented, but then, colonial Americans reasoned, neither did they pay property taxes.

By 1750, therefore, the assemblies embodied all the attributes of self-government. They had the power over the purse, had whittled down the power of royal governors, debated the problems of western representation, determined voting qualifications, and played a major role in Indian relations and the disposal of western lands. By 1763, when Great Britain was free to reorganize its empire, it found itself dealing with colonial lawmakers who had been working out their own policies for half a century. They considered themselves accountable only to their constituents and were determined to resist any interference in their domestic affairs by Parliament.

■ CONCLUSION

The dreams and expectations of the men who founded the thirteen colonies were not realized.

The Virginia and New England companies made no money for their stockholders, and a feudal society was not established in the Carolinas. The Puritan state perished, and the philanthropists of Georgia were defeated. America had proved to be the graveyard of utopias.

The new ideas and new institutions the colonists had developed made America radically different from England, and the difference was a source of conflict. By English standards, American society was unstable. Class lines in the colonies were not fixed, and geographical mobility was common. Immigrants who poured in had little loyalty to England, and along the frontier, government scarcely existed.

Moreover, American ideas tended to undermine the values of English tradition and authority. The colonists' concepts of religious toleration down-graded the importance of closely knit, state-related churches and emphasized the freedom of the individual. Having adopted the political theory of John Locke, Americans believed, and their leaders acted on this belief, that no society can exist and no laws can be passed without the consent of the governed.

When, in 1763, Britain became the dominant imperial power in North America, it viewed with alarm the growing symptoms of American self-determination. And Britain set about to strengthen its authority over the colonies.

■ QUESTIONS

1. Why was colonization undertaken in America, and why did the immigrants come to America?

2. Did the founders of the American colonies realize their expectations? Explain your answer?

3. What similarities existed throughout colonial American society?

4. What sectional differences existed in colonial American society?

5. How did life in America differ from life in Europe? What accounted for these differences?

6. Which differences caused friction between America and Britain? Why?

7. What were the strong European influences which affected America?

8. Why did an independent American spirit arise in America?

9. Is it possible to perceive stages of colonial development in America? If so, what are they? If not, why?

10. What similarities exist between American colonial society and contemporary American society in terms of class structure?

◼ BIBLIOGRAPHY

POMFRET, JOHN E., AND FLOYD M. SHUMWAY, *Founding the American Colonies, 1583–1660*, New American Nation Series, Harper & Row. Various publishers have produced series of books which are intended to survey the periods of American history from discovery to the present. This book is a recent addition to one of those series, and its wealth of information plus useful bibliography will help students understand the period of early settlement. Throughout the year students may want to refer to the appropriate book in the history series for background information.

BRADFORD, WILLIAM, *Of Plymouth Plantation 1620–1647*, ed. by Samuel Eliot Morison, Knopf.

BYRD, WILLIAM, *The Great American Gentleman, the Diary of William Byrd of Westover in Virginia*, ed. by Louis B. Wright and Marion Tinling, Putnam's (Capricorn Books).

SEWALL, SAMUEL, *The Diary of Samuel Sewall*, ed. and abr. by Harvey Wish, Putnam's (Capricorn Books).

Students should always be encouraged to go to original sources when trying to understand a period. Bradford's book concerns the early years of the Plymouth colony which he led. Byrd's diary describes daily life as he experienced it in Virginia between the years 1709 and 1712. Sewall's diary provides insight into the life of a Massachusetts merchant community leader and religious zealot whose life spanned the seventeenth and eighteenth centuries. Although some useful information may be gained from the books, students should remember that the authors were unusual people and not necessarily typical of most colonists.

PARKMAN, FRANCIS, *LaSalle and the Discovery of the Great West*, New American Library (Signet Books).

PRESCOTT, WILLIAM, *The Conquest of Peru*, ed. and abr. by Victor W. Von Hagen, New American Library (Mentor Books).

These two nineteenth-century historians represent a school of American historians who emphasized literary style when writing history. Their works are excellent, and students should not be limited to the two examples mentioned above.

DEMOS, JOHN, *Little Commonwealth: Family Life in Plymouth Colony*, Oxford University Press. In a short, readable account, the author shows how a historian can gain more understanding of a well-worn subject by using new methods. He is very interested in the physical features of Plymouth, and uses archeological techniques to assist him. He examines both houses and clothing and then applies psychological concepts to explain the behavior of the settlers.

HAGAN, WILLIAM T., *American Indians*, U. of Chicago Press. This is probably the best general account for high school students of the Indians in America. Since white contact with the Indians is very important throughout our history and particularly today, students are encouraged to have this book available for reference during the year.

KATZ, WILLIAM LOREN, *Eyewitness: The Negro in American History*, Pitman. This book is recognized by many as the best history of Black America. It combines original sources with a narrative account to present a detailed picture of blacks in America. Students should also have this book available for reference through the year.

The American Revolution Creates A New Political Order

Britain's victory over France in 1763 had given Britain a vast North American empire, and Britain was determined to tighten its imperial control. Through the years when British authority was weak, the colonists had grown accustomed to making their own decisions. When Parliament began to impose unwanted restrictions on their economic and political freedom, the colonists were angered. Jealous of their liberties, politically self-reliant, Americans refused to accept Britain's claim that Parliament had supreme jurisdiction over the internal affairs of the colonies.

Many on both sides of the Atlantic tried to mediate the conflict, but the lines of disagreement became increasingly clear-cut. On one side was a group of British leaders determined that the colonies should follow policies that benefited the British empire as a whole. On the other side was a group of American colonists equally determined to follow policies that they considered best for their welfare.

What was not clear-cut at the beginning was the depth of feeling. No one knew to what lengths the British would go to force compliance or how far the colonists would go to retain control of their own destinies. As the conflict deepened, it remained to be seen how many would join a war for national independence. Here are some questions to consider as you read about the growing conflict and its outcome:

1. What measures did Great Britain take to strengthen its authority over the colonies?
2. How did the colonists resist?
3. Why did Americans increasingly favor independence?
4. In what ways did the Revolution change American life?

1 The Empire Faces A Crisis

1. What problems confronted Britain following the conclusion of the French and Indian War?

2. What steps did Grenville and Townshend take to relieve these problems? Why did the colonists resist these steps?

3. To what extent were the British or Americans unreasonable in their handling of Anglo-American relations?

4. Were there any acceptable alternatives to the British and American steps taken during the crisis over imperial control? If so, what were they?

In 1763 the British government was confronted by several difficulties. It was faced with the task of administering the newly won portions of the North American empire, liquidating a huge national debt incurred during its series of wars, and strengthening the feeble enforcement of British authority within the colonies. Lord George Grenville, the new prime minister, was called upon to solve these problems. An able financier, Grenville was, nevertheless, ignorant of the realities of colonial politics.

Reorganizing the western lands. Grenville first tried to formulate a governmental policy for the Ohio Valley that would win the loyalty of the Indians to the British Crown and convince the French Canadians that British rule would be beneficial. The only way to do this, Grenville reasoned, was to allow Canadian fur-traders to continue to profit from the Indian trade and to protect the suspicious Indians from the steady westward expansion of colonial Americans.

Accordingly, he drew up the Proclamation of 1763, ordering American frontiersmen not to settle beyond the crest of the Allegheny Mountains, regulating the fur trade by Crown-appointed Indian agents, and placing the entire Ohio Valley under the jurisdiction of the commander-in-chief of the British army in North America. The proclamation also declared that the British government alone could make land grants in the West—and only to veterans of the French and Indian War.

The Proclamation of 1763 was intended only as a temporary measure to placate the Canadians and the Indians. However, several of the colonies insisted that their charters (although vaguely worded) entitled them to large areas of land in the Ohio Valley, and they feared that the British government was determined to deny their claims. The proclamation enraged colonial land companies which had been formed by leading colonists to exploit the fur trade and to speculate in land. Many colonial ministers also feared that this "promised land" was to be abandoned to "pagan" Indians and French Jesuit missionaries.

Thus the Proclamation of 1763 aroused the anger of nearly the entire colonial upper class. Moreover, the proclamation ordered the withdrawal of colonists who had already settled in the western areas. These frontiersmen not only ignored the order but pressed on into what is now eastern Kentucky and Tennessee.

Strengthening British authority. Ignoring colonial protests against his western-lands policy, Grenville persuaded Parliament to enact the rest of his plan for reorganizing the empire. His policies were shaped by two crucial considerations. First, British finances were severely strained by the wars with France, during which Britain had accumulated a staggering national debt. Overburdened British taxpayers demanded relief. Instead, Grenville could only offer more expenditures, required by his second consideration, the needs of defense.

As early as 1760 the British government had concluded that Anglo-French rivalry would be permanent and that a large standing army had to be maintained. The British people, however, were traditionally suspicious of standing armies and were flatly opposed to paying for one. From Grenville's point of view, stationing an army in North America not only would allay their fears, but also would provide an ideal base from which to attack the French West Indies and the Spanish colonies in case of war. Equally important, the American colonies sorely needed protection from Indian attacks along the frontier. This need was dramatized in 1763 when an Indian confederation led by the Ottawa chief Pontiac waged war to prevent colonial expansion into the Ohio Valley.

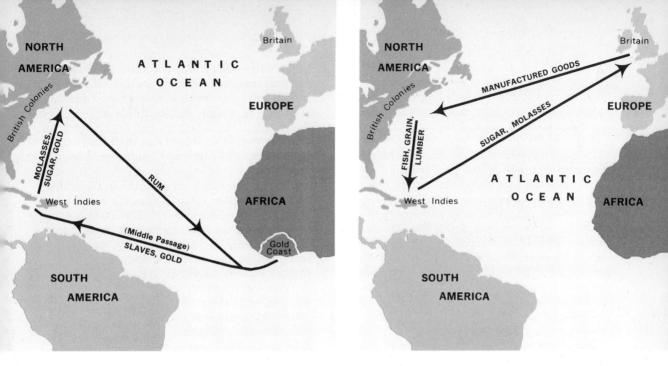

TRIANGULAR TRADE ROUTES

Because the colonies had an unfavorable balance of trade with Britain, they had a constant need for specie to pay for imported British goods. To obtain specie, colonial merchants developed trade through various triangular trade routes, many of which violated the Navigation Acts since they involved direct trade with foreign nations. One popular route took colonial-made rum to West Africa where it was exchanged for slaves—as well as gold. The slaves were then taken to the West Indies and sold for sugar, molasses, and gold. The molasses and sugar were shipped to the colonies and distilled into rum. Another profitable route took colonial fish, grain, and lumber to the West Indies. Here they were exchanged for sugar and molasses, which then went to Britain to be exchanged for manufactured goods needed in the colonies.

Grenville believed that the colonies ought to pay half the cost of maintaining an army, and he recognized that they could not play their expected part in his plans until colonial policy was changed from the previous British neglect to strong control by the government. Like other British politicians, Grenville was shocked that American merchants had traded with the enemy during the war, ignored the Navigation Acts, and engaged in massive smuggling. In order to solve these problems, he framed four laws (see chart, page 49).

In 1764 Parliament passed the Sugar Act which lowered the duty on sugar but imposed new duties on many other products. In addition, the act provided for rigid enforcement. Although New England merchants could afford the new duties, they claimed that the Sugar Act would ruin trade.

Their protests, however, failed to gain the support of the other colonies. Colonists had always conceded that Parliament could levy customs duties for the regulation of trade.

To insure rigid enforcement of the Sugar Act, Parliament not only increased the number of customs officers in the colonies, but also decreed that half the value of a cargo seized from a convicted smuggler would be awarded to the arresting officer. Furthermore, trials of colonial merchants and ship captains accused of smuggling were to be conducted by naval vice-admiralty courts, which did not use juries.

Parliament also passed the Currency Act of 1764, which forbade colonial assemblies to issue paper currency. The Quartering and Stamp Acts of 1765 completed Grenville's new policy. The

47

Quartering Act required colonial legislatures, governors, and sheriffs to provide the army with housing, rum and beer, beds, cooking utensils, salt, candles, and other commodities. The Stamp Act levied taxes on newspapers, legal documents, advertisements, playing cards, even college diplomas, all of which had to display the stamp certifying that the tax had been paid.

Grenville felt that his legislative program was both moderate and reasonable. Britain had spent an enormous amount of money compared to that spent by the colonies to defeat the French and had sent a large army to police the colonial frontiers. Moreover, Britain had reduced the sugar duties, and although the stamp tax was unprecedented in the colonies, such taxes were customary in Britain. Grenville, however, failed to consult the colonies, and scarcely warned them of his plans.

The colonists resist. The Stamp Act stirred up violent opposition. In Boston, mobs surged through the streets and wrecked the home of Lieutenant Governor Thomas Hutchinson. Newly appointed tax collectors were hanged in effigy, tarred and feathered, and forced to resign. Ships bringing the cursed stamps from Britain were not permitted to unload, and colonial lawyers and printers refused to use them. The response of colonial merchants, however, hurt Britain more than this furious mob action. In the leading ports, colonists agreed not to import any goods from Britain until the law was repealed, and within a few months British trade had declined disastrously.

Resistance to the Stamp Act was led by the colonial assemblies. First came the famous Virginia Resolutions of May 1765, which maintained that Virginians, under the terms of their original charter, possessed all the rights of Englishmen, one of the most important of which was that no man shall be taxed without the consent of his elected representatives. Throughout the colonies, similar arguments appeared in pamphlets and newspapers declaring that since colonists were not represented in Parliament by representatives they had elected, Parliament had no right to levy direct taxes against them.

Britain replied that every citizen of the empire, whether he voted or not, was "virtually" represented in Parliament. The House of Commons, the British asserted, was not a collection of delegates representing specific geographical areas but a body whose members represented and legislated for all people in the British empire. The Americans contended that members of Commons acted according to the wishes of British voters, who were not concerned with the colonists' problems.

These arguments were restated in the resolutions of the Stamp Act Congress, which met in New York in October 1765. This congress, the first sign of colonial unity against the authority of Parliament, declared that "the only representatives of the people of these colonies are persons chosen therein by themselves, and that no taxes ever have been, or can be constitutionally imposed on them but by their respective legislatures." It also insisted that vice-admiralty courts, without juries, "have a manifest tendency to subvert the rights and liberties of the colonists."

Parliament finally repealed the Stamp Act, but not solely because of American protests. British merchants, faced with economic ruin because of the colonists' nonimportation agreements, forced its repeal in March 1766. At the same time, however, Parliament issued the Declaratory Act in which it bluntly asserted its claim of legislative supremacy over the colonies.

The crisis deepens. After the repeal of the Stamp Act, Grenville was forced to resign. The most powerful figure to emerge in the British government was Charles Townshend, chancellor of the Exchequer (Treasury), who fully agreed with Grenville that American colonists must help support the army. Since Americans admitted that Parliament had the right to impose customs duties on the colonies, Townshend persuaded Parliament, in 1767, to place duties on glass, lead, paint, paper, and tea. Americans were almost totally dependent upon Britain for the first four items, and colonial women were nearly addicted to tea.

The Townshend duties also provided for rigorous enforcement through *writs,* or search warrants, that gave little protection to citizens. In addition, part of the income derived from the duties was to be used to pay the salaries of royal governors and judges in the colonies. This provision was designed, of course, to undermine the financial power traditionally exercised by colonial assemblies over recalcitrant British officials. Fi-

THE GRENVILLE AND TOWNSHEND ACTS

Law	Provision	Colonial Reaction
Grenville Acts Sugar Act (1764)	Reduced duties on foreign molasses. Increased duties on foreign sugar. Placed new duties on foreign goods shipped from Britain to colonies.	
Currency Act (1764)	Forbade colonies to issue paper money. Required colonial tax payments in gold or silver coin.	
Quartering Act (1765)	Required colonies to quarter and supply British troops.	January 1766. New York Assembly refused to cooperate. Finally agreed to comply in June 1767. January 1770. New York citizens battled soldiers.
Stamp Act (1765)	Taxed newspapers, almanacs, legal documents, pamphlets, diplomas, licenses, ads, insurance policies, playing cards, dice.	May 1765. Virginia resolutions passed, claiming colonists had rights of Englishmen, including no taxation without representation. 1765. Sons of Liberty formed to organize resistance to Stamp Act. October 1765. Stamp Act Congress. Meeting of colonies passed Declaration of Rights and Grievances reaffirming no taxation without representation. Claimed that only colonial legislatures could tax colonies and asked for repeal of Stamp Act. Non-importation. New York, Philadelphia, and Boston merchants agreed not to buy European goods until Stamp Act was repealed.
Townshend Acts **(1767)**	New duties on imported glass, lead, paints, paper, tea Legalized *writs of assistance* (general search warrants) allowing British officials to search any colonial property at any time. Provided that part of collected duties were to be used to pay salaries of colonial governors and judges.	November 1767. John Dickinson published his "Farmer's Letters," which denied right of Britain to tax colonies solely to raise revenue. February 1768. "Massachusetts Circular Letter," by Samuel Adams, informed other colonies that Massachusetts denounced idea of taxation without representation, criticized attempt to make colonial officials independent of people, and asked other colonies for suggestions. 1767–1769. Non-importation. Merchants agreed not to import goods listed in Townshend Acts until the acts were revoked.

nally, the New York assembly, which had refused to supply the troops under the Quartering Act, was forbidden by Parliament to meet.

Again, colonists vigorously protested. John Dickinson of Pennsylvania published a series of twelve "Farmer's Letters," adding a new twist to colonial arguments against imperial control. Americans, Dickinson said, were obliged to accept duties intended to regulate trade and discourage French or Dutch imports. But the purpose of the Townshend duties, he pointed out, was to raise a revenue. Since these duties were nothing more than taxes in disguise, they were illegal and therefore not binding. Finally, Dickinson declared that Parliament could not suspend the New York legislature, since one independent legislature could not depose another.

In Massachusetts, the legislature sent a circular letter containing Dickinson's arguments to all other colonial assemblies. Boston merchants once again announced a nonimportation agreement, and customs officials were threatened. The Boston town meeting called for a provincial convention to decide on a proper course of action.

Britain responded swiftly and drastically to these challenges to parliamentary authority by ordering four regiments of the army to Boston to protect royal officials. And in 1769, Parliament resolved that the Massachusetts circular letter was of an "unwarrantable and dangerous nature, calculated to inflame the minds of his Majesty's subjects in other colonies, tending to create unlawful combination, repugnant to the laws of Great Britain, and subversive of the constitution." In addition, Parliament condemned the election of delegates to the Massachusetts Provincial Convention as "audacious usurpations of the powers of government." These harsh words reveal how deep the crisis had become.

In Boston, words finally gave way to violence. For months, Bostonians had antagonized the British soldiers quartered among them, and Samuel Adams, a rising leader in the resistance movement, filled the newspapers with savage denunciations of the standing army. On the night of March 5, 1770, these passions boiled over into a riot. Intimidated by the uproar of the crowd, the troops fired into its midst, killing five.

The "Boston Massacre" symbolized the failure of British policy. In April 1770, all the Townshend duties except that on tea were removed. Lord Frederick North, who now became prime minister, persuaded Parliament to retain the tea tax as a reminder of its right to tax the colonies. For the time being, the colonies had successfully resisted British policy without a major conflict. Thus the lines of the dispute were drawn. Parliament asserted its dominion over the entire empire, including, through the Declaratory Act, its right to impose taxes of any kind upon the colonies. The colonists, especially in the resolutions of the Stamp Act Congress, denied this and declared their own assemblies supreme legislators for the American colonies.

2 The Colonies Revolt

1. What were the causes of the American Revolution? Was there a primary cause? If so, what was it?

2. What steps did Britain take in response to the Boston Tea Party? How did America respond to Britain's actions?

3. Beginning with the earliest signs of independence, what were the events and circumstances which led up to the first shots at Lexington and Concord on April 19, 1775?

4. Why did the moderates lose out to the radicals in 1775?

For nearly two years after the repeal of the Townshend Acts, an uneasy peace existed in the colonies. The more radical leaders of colonial resistance, especially Samuel Adams, urged that the nonimportation agreements remain in force until the remaining duty on tea was withdrawn. Colonial merchants, however, were tired of endless crises and the disruption of commerce. They renewed trade with Britain and also continued to smuggle tea from Holland. But a new confrontation between the colonies and the mother country was brewing.

Organized resistance. In 1770, Samuel Adams concluded that resistance to the endless attempts of Britain to tax Americans must be organized more effectively. He noted that it had proven difficult to enforce the nonimportation agreements and even more difficult to mobilize the great mass of small farmers behind the revolutionary efforts of the city mobs and the merchants. A rumor that the British government intended to weaken the power of the Massachusetts legislature by paying the governor and judges directly from the British treasury provided Adams with the ammunition he needed.

Under his direction, a large number of Committees of Correspondence were organized to distribute propaganda, pass along information about British intentions, and stimulate the populace to opposition. The idea quickly spread to other colonies. Thomas Jefferson and Patrick Henry convinced the Virginia House of Burgesses to follow Massachusetts' lead. In addition, the shrewd Virginians urged the establishment of committees to keep the colonial assemblies in constant communication with one another "to produce a unity of action." By late spring of 1773, nearly every colony had a network of Committees of Correspondence ready to stir up popular passions, mobilize mobs, even take over the local governments. When war came, these committees not only provided effective revolutionary leaders, but actually exercised governmental power at the town and county levels.

Meanwhile, in England Lord North was confronted by a difficult problem: the British East India Company was bankrupt. In an effort to help the company sell its huge stocks of tea, North gave it a monopoly on the sale of tea in America, allowing the company agents to handle the tea supply for the colonies. Much to the surprise of the British, the colonists not only resented the monopoly, but also were still angry over paying customs duties on tea—even though the price was lower than that of tea smuggled from Holland.

In Boston, resentment resulted in the famous Boston Tea Party of December 17, 1773, when Samuel Adams roused his followers and, dressed as Mohawk Indians, they dumped 340 chests of tea into the harbor. In New York, the patriotic organization called the Sons of Liberty followed suit in April 1774. Philadelphians forced the tea ships to return to Britain, while in Charleston, colonists seized the cargoes, stored them in warehouses, and later used them to help finance the Revolution.

The Intolerable Acts. The British government responded to the tea crisis in drastic fashion. Parliament passed a series of Coercive Acts, known in America as the Intolerable Acts. The Boston Port Act closed the harbor to shipping until the tea that had been destroyed was paid for. Boston Harbor was blockaded by a British fleet, and additional troops were rushed to the city. Equally severe was the Massachusetts Government Act of May 1774, which prohibited town meetings without the governor's consent and gave him the sole right to appoint judges and administrative officials. Above all, the act decreed that the governor rather than the legislature would choose the members of the council. A new quartering act was approved, and Parliament decided that British officials accused of crimes were to be tried in England, not Massachusetts. To complete the humiliation of Massachusetts, General Thomas Gage, commander-in-chief of the British army in North America was appointed governor.

The Intolerable Acts were soon supplemented by the Quebec Act, which placed the Ohio Valley under the jurisdiction of the Province of Quebec. Besides rousing fears of "popery" among New Englanders because of the act's acceptance of the Roman Catholic church, the Quebec Act made it clear to colonial assemblies that the British government would not recognize their claims to western lands.

The response of the colonists to these acts astounded the British government, which assumed that by limiting coercion to Massachusetts, Britain would split the resistance movement and retain the loyalty of the other colonies. Instead, the Committees of Correspondence not only organized an effective relief system to feed the blockaded Bostonians, but originated and popularized a demand calling for an intercolonial congress to oppose arbitrary British rule.

The First Continental Congress. In September 1774, fifty-six delegates from twelve colonies arrived in Philadelphia to attend the First Continental Congress. Among the colonial leaders present were John Adams and Samuel Adams from Massachusetts; George Washington, Patrick

INTOLERABLE ACTS AND QUEBEC ACT, 1774

Law	Provision	Colonial Reaction
Intolerable Acts Boston Port Bill	Closed Boston Harbor, which could be reopened when colonists paid for their destruction of the tea.	September and October 1774. The Continental Congress endorsed the Suffolk Resolves, passed by towns in Massachusetts. The Resolves declared the Intolerable Acts unconstitutional and not to be obeyed. They urged Massachusetts to withhold taxes from the royal government until the acts were repealed, advised the people to form a militia, and recommended economic sanctions against Britain.
Administration of Justice Act	Provided that British officials in Massachusetts who were charged with crimes could be tried in England.	
Massachusetts Government Act	Provided for many Massachusetts government officials to be appointed by the King rather than elected by freemen. Prohibited town meetings without the governor's approval. Required the colonists to quarter British officials sent to enforce the law.	
Quebec Act (Passed while Continental Congress in session)	Extended the boundary of British Canada to the Ohio River into the area already claimed by Virginia, Connecticut, and Massachusetts. The act provided for a highly centralized government under the British Crown.	Declaration and Resolves. Denounced the Intolerable Acts and the Quebec Act, criticized British tax measures since 1763. They listed the rights of the colonists, including "life, liberty, and property," and pledged economic sanctions against Britain until the acts were repealed. A Continental Association was formed to stop imports from Britain, discontinue the slave trade, embargo exports to Britain, and institute nonconsumption of British goods.

Henry, and Richard Henry Lee from Virginia; Roger Sherman from Connecticut; John Jay from New York; and John Dickinson from Pennsylvania.

After weeks of debate and deliberation, the Congress finally issued a Declaration of Rights and Grievances bluntly denying Parliament's power to tax the colonies or interfere in their internal affairs. The Congress also insisted that stationing troops in a colony in peacetime without the consent of its assembly violated the British constitution. To force repeal of the Intolerable Acts, the Continental Congress created an "association" intended to prohibit all trade with Great Britain.

While the First Continental Congress was still in session, King George III wrote to Lord North, "The die is now cast. The Colonies must either submit or triumph." While many people on both sides of the Atlantic shared His Majesty's opinion, others were still hopeful that the differences between Britain and its colonies could be settled.

Moderates at the Continental Congress had proposed a modified version of the old Albany Plan of Union as a means of reconciliation. Under this plan, laws passed by an American grand council, to be appointed by assemblies, were to be approved by Parliament, and those of Parliament affecting the colonies were to be approved by the American council. But Samuel Adams, who now privately yearned for independence, rallied the radicals in Congress to defeat this plan. In Britain, former prime minister William Pitt attempted, without success, to induce Parliament to withdraw the troops from Boston. The moderates on both sides had clearly lost control of the situation.

British rule ends. The American Revolution began quietly and was well under way even before the meeting of the First Continental Congress. In May 1774, eighty-nine members of the Virginia House of Burgesses met in Williamsburg and called for a provincial congress without the consent of the royal governor. By the end of the summer, illegal congresses in New Hampshire, Pennsylvania, Maryland, and North Carolina began to govern these colonies in defiance of British authority.

In Massachusetts, when General Gage refused to call the newly elected assembly into session, its members, meeting in Harvard College, announced that Gage had ceased to exercise lawful authority and appointed their own treasurer to collect taxes. Similar developments soon eliminated the authority of royal officials in New Jersey and South Carolina. In the face of such opposition, six of nine royal governors fled immediately, and Dunmore of Virginia and Wright of Georgia were defied. The authority of the British empire had been overthrown without violence or bloodshed.

The remaining royal governor in the colonies was Gage of Massachusetts, and he was under tremendous pressure. The militia of Massachusetts was zealously stockpiling ammunition and supplies; Tories, or supporters of the Crown, were being attacked, and many were driven into Boston to the protection of the British army.

In September 1774, Gage sent a detachment of troops to seize a supply of gunpowder at Cambridge, but thousands of militiamen threatened to open fire against the British troops if they again attempted to move through the New England countryside. Several months later, in March 1775, Gage dispatched 200 troops to Salem to confiscate the militia's military stores. At Salem the way was obstructed by a raised drawbridge over a river outside the town. Moreover, a number of militiamen were rapidly assembling on the other side. War was avoided by a comic compromise whereby the British were permitted to cross the bridge, make an about-face, and march emptyhanded back to Boston. As they filed away, the British regimental band played a tune called "The World Turned Upside Down."

The government in London demanded that Gage stamp out colonial resistance, and he had come to the conclusion that only a demonstration of force could repair the crumbling authority and dignity of the royal government. He decided to send an expedition to destroy a militia supply depot at Concord.

The beginning of hostilities. Late on the night of April 18, 1775, eight hundred British soldiers marched out of Boston hoping to surprise the militia. The efficient spy system established by the revolutionary Committees of Safety quickly detected the movement, and Paul Revere and William Dawes soon sped away on their dramatic "midnight rides." When the British army marched into Lexington, it discovered about seventy men of Captain Thomas Parker's Minuteman company stretched in a ragged line across the common.

Historians cannot decide who fired the first shot, but the point is moot. The British had orders not to retreat, and Parker had declared, "If they mean to have a war, let it begin here." One tremendous volley by the British regulars swept the militia aside, killing seven of them, and the British continued to Concord. After destroying some cannon carriages and supplies of flour, the British were stunned to discover that one of their detachments had been attacked and routed. Some thirty towns in eastern Massachusetts mobilized nearly 3,700 militiamen who sniped away at the retreating British from behind trees and walls. By nightfall, after suffering heavy casualties, the British were back in Boston, and colonial militiamen had surrounded the city. The rebellion had begun (see battle maps, page 64).

3 Rebellion Leads To Independence

1. Why did Americans finally seek independence from Britain in 1776?

2. What reasons did Thomas Paine give in *Common Sense* which supported American independence? In what ways were these ideas new, and in what ways a repetition of past arguments?

3. What reasons were given in the Declaration of Independence for severing American ties with Britain? Do you think these reasons were justified by previous events of the period?

When the Second Continental Congress assembled in Philadelphia on May 10, 1775, Thomas Jefferson, Benjamin Franklin, and John Hancock added their immense prestige to the gathering. As its first act, the new Congress authorized the raising of an army and appointed George Washington its commander-in-chief. Washington, nominated by John Adams in order to bind the South to the revolutionary cause, declared to the delegates, "I will enter upon the momentous duty and exert every power I possess in your service, and for the support of the glorious cause." But what was the glorious cause? Did the delegates in Congress, or for that matter, did the American people want independence or reconciliation with Britain?

Congress petitions Parliament. The Continental Congress drew up two documents which were meant to test the policies of the British government. The first, the Olive Branch Petition, was drafted by John Dickinson. It declared that while the colonies could not comply with the idea of parliamentary supremacy, they were still loyal to the Crown. Furthermore, the petition urged George III to use his influence to repeal the Intolerable Acts.

The second document, "A Declaration setting forth the Causes and Necessity of Taking Up Arms," stated that the British government was engaged in a plot to destroy American liberties through unconstitutional taxes, and protested the "unprovoked assault" on the innocent citizens of Lexington. The declaration concluded:

We have counted the cost of this contest, and find nothing so dreadful as voluntary slavery. Honour, justice, and humanity forbid us tamely to surrender that freedom which we received from our gallant ancestors, and which our innocent posterity have a right to receive from us.

The response of the royal government to these statements was "A Proclamation for Suppressing Rebellion and Sedition," declaring that the colonists were rebels, and that no loyal British subject was to assist them. Thus, for more than a year— from April 1775 to July 1776—the war waged by the colonies was not a struggle for independence, but a revolt aimed at securing their liberties within the empire.

A war of rebellion. After Lexington and Concord, the British had swiftly dispatched three experienced generals, Sir William Howe, Henry Clinton, and John Burgoyne, with ten thousand soldiers to Boston. Even these reinforcements, however, were not enough to break the siege which sixteen thousand colonial militiamen had clamped on the city.

Then, in June, the Americans foolishly fortified Breed's Hill on the Charlestown peninsula. The British could have easily landed behind them, but General Howe chose to demonstrate to the colonial "peasantry" the grim effectiveness of the royal army's bayonet charge. His demonstration backfired; concealed American marksmen inflicted one thousand casualties on the British before Howe's troops could capture the hill, which had no strategic significance. This battle, called the Battle of Bunker Hill, had tremendous effects: not only did it encourage the colonists in their fight, but never again during the war would a British general send his meticulously drilled regiments against Americans in such entrenched positions.

In July of 1775 George Washington took command of the armed mob which Congress called an army. The siege of Boston dragged on for months until a dark night in March 1776, when Washington suddenly planted artillery on Dorchester Heights commanding Boston Harbor.

Thoroughly outmaneuvered and intimidated, the British army evacuated the city, sailing away to Halifax, Nova Scotia.

The victory at Boston, however, was balanced for the Americans by a shattering defeat in Canada. Hoping to rally French Canadians to the cause of rebellion, two American armies set out to conquer the province of Quebec. One captured Montreal and moved down the St. Lawrence Valley to the city of Quebec, joining there the troops of Benedict Arnold who had struggled with great suffering through the wilderness of Maine. On New Year's Eve, 1775, the Americans assaulted the massive fortress city, but were bloodily repulsed. For several months the remnants of the American army camped on the Plains of Abraham, dying of hunger and cold until British reinforcements drove them out of Canada. This disastrous campaign not only cost five thousand casualties, but also proved beyond any doubt that French Canadians would not join the revolutionary effort.

Changing American attitudes. American attitudes toward continued participation in the British empire underwent a slow change toward the end of 1775. Up to that point a majority of Americans opposed any thought of independence. The North Carolina legislature resolved in September that reconciliation with Britain was the aim, and the provincial congresses of Maryland, Pennsylvania, New Jersey, and New York instructed their delegates to the Continental Congress to oppose any move for independence.

By January 1776, this mood of conciliation toward Britain and confusion about colonial objectives had changed. It was partly the result of British policy, and partly the work of revolutionaries committed to breaking the imperial tie. In late September of 1775, it became known that the British government had refused to discuss Dickinson's Olive Branch Petition, and the king's proclamation declaring the colonies to be in revolt had arrived. This was followed by an act of Parliament cutting off the colonies from all trade with the empire, placing America under military rule, and instructing the British navy to capture and confiscate all American vessels. Throughout the colonies, the rumor also spread, finally confirmed in May 1776, that Britain was trying to hire as mercenaries German or Russian troops to quash the rebellious colonies.

The increasing harshness of British measures coincided with increasing radicalism in America. The Adamses of Massachusetts had long favored independence; by January, the relatively conservative George Washington was urging it in his private letters.

It was in that month that one of the most influential writings of the revolutionary era appeared—Thomas Paine's *Common Sense*. The real villain in the imperial dispute, Paine wrote, was not Parliament, but the king himself, and Paine asserted that a monarchy was not a fit government for Americans. In urging complete independence, Paine pointed out the advantage of being free to trade with the whole of Europe. He also concluded that Britain could never defeat the colonies in a protracted war. The capstone of Paine's argument, summing up fifty years of American familiarity with John Locke's thought, was the assertion that genuine government derives from the consent of the governed. "A government of our own," he declared, "is our natural right." At least one hundred thousand copies of this fiery pamphlet were distributed throughout the colonies and helped to arouse popular support for independence.

Independence is declared. During the spring of 1776, these forces shaped the attitudes of the provincial congresses of the colonies. In April, North Carolina informed her delegates that if a majority of Congress favored independence they should agree. On May 10, the Massachusetts Provincial Congress urged the towns of the Commonwealth to vote (at their annual meetings) on the question of independence, which they enthusiastically endorsed. Five days later the Virginia House of Burgesses made the decisive move, instructing its delegates to the Continental Congress to demand American independence from Britain.

Congress itself had already taken a momentous step. Early in May it advised the colonies to develop new constitutions on the ground that "it appears absolutely irreconcilable to reason and good conscience for the people to take the oath necessary for the support of any government under the Crown of Great Britain."

A SOCIETY of PATRIOTIC LADIE·S,

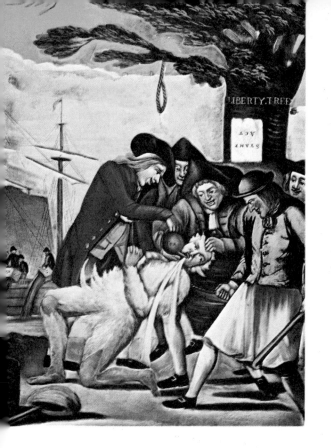

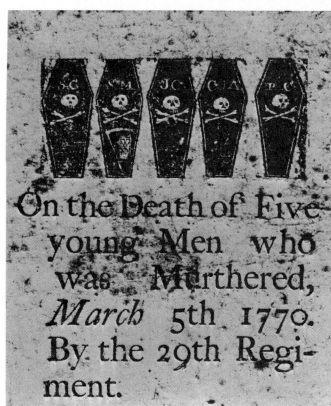

On the Death of Five young Men who was Murthered, March 5th 1770. By the 29th Regiment.

Resistance to British rule took many forms in the years preceding the outbreak of full revolution. In 1775, two years after the Boston Tea Party, the Patriotic Ladies of North Carolina, at the far left, decided to show their sympathy with the cause by signing a pledge to drink tea no more. The Bostonians above left also used tea to defy the British; having tarred and feathered the hated tax collector, they proceed to force tea down his throat. The unfortunate tax man frequently served as the recipient of this brand of colonial outrage at British laws. Anti-British propaganda was another device the colonists used. The broadside above was executed by Paul Revere to remind the colonists of the Boston Massacre. The five coffins he drew show the initials of the five men who fell that day—Samuel Gray, Samuel Maverick, James Caldwell, Crispus Attucks, and Patrick Carr. The boycott was still another device, as the notice at the left shows. If a militant colonial group, such as the Sons and Daughters of Liberty, felt that a merchant's sympathies lay with the British, they would discourage other colonists from dealing with him.

The Virginia instructions were carried out by Richard Henry Lee, who on June 7 introduced a motion, seconded by John Adams, "that these United Colonies are, and of right ought to be, free and independent states." While Congress debated the motion, Thomas Jefferson, Benjamin Franklin, Robert R. Livingston, John Adams, and Roger Sherman settled down to draw up a declaration explaining it. Lee and Adams also worked to win over the more cautious delegates. Finally, on July 2, 1776, Congress voted unanimously for independence.

The Declaration of Independence. Written principally by Thomas Jefferson, the Declaration of Independence, which was addressed to "the opinions of mankind," sought to explain why a new nation should appear "among the powers of the earth." In the first place, it asserted that the colonies were entitled to be independent by "the laws of nature and nature's God," who had endowed men with natural rights, including "life, liberty, and the pursuit of happiness." Governments, stated the Declaration, have the chief task of preserving these rights, and they are given power to do so by the governed. When any government fails to protect these rights, the governed are justified in replacing it.

The rest of the Declaration is an elaborate attempt to prove that the British government not only failed to preserve natural rights, but actually attempted to destroy them. In a sense, the Declaration is a work of historical analysis, a chronicle of imperial relations since 1760, meant to demonstrate Britain's contempt for the rights of American legislatures and the health of American society. Partly persuaded by Paine, partly as a literary device, Jefferson blamed the king of England rather than Parliament for "repeated injuries and usurpations, all having in direct object the establishment of an absolute tyranny over these states."

The objections fall naturally into three categories: the relationship between the royal officials and the assemblies, the acts of Parliament, and the response of the royal government to American protests. Royal governors continuously interfered with freedom of the assemblies, the Declaration asserts, by vetoing laws, refusing to enlarge the basis of representation, dissolving an assembly before it could act, and refusing to permit new elections. Worse, the royal government oppressed the people by making them quarter troops in peacetime, by sending a swarm of bureaucrats to America, and by hindering free immigration. Many of these complaints were exaggerations, but all had some basis in fact.

Less dubious were the allegations against Parliament: taxation without consent, denial of trial by jury, revocation of charters, suspension of legislatures. Jefferson asserted that the whole point of these laws was to reduce the colonies to the status of Quebec, which had no representative institutions. In short, they were part of a plot to destroy liberty. When Americans protested, the Declaration complained, the response of the king was to ignore humble petitions and wage war, using mercenaries and Indians to terrorize the people. "A prince whose character is thus marked by every act which may define a tyrant is unfit to be the ruler of a free people."

Thus, Americans applied the philosophy of Locke to the specific conditions of their time. Government, the Declaration asserted, must adhere to certain principles and observe certain limitations. If it violates the very basis of government by flouting the principle that it can act only with the consent of a majority of the people, the people are justified in overturning it. The phrases "Liberty" and "the pursuit of Happiness" were not vague abstractions to Jefferson. They involved a specific set of guarantees, including taxation only by the consent of elected representatives, trial by jury, the right to petition for redress of grievances, and freedom from the presence of standing armies used for police duties without the express consent of elected lawmakers.

So deeply had these ideas become a part of American ideology during the eighteenth century, and especially during the revolutionary agitation between 1765 and 1776, that Congress scarcely debated the document. It summed up perfectly the meaning of the resolutions and pamphlets, the petitions and declarations they had hurled for ten years at an uncomprehending royal government. On July 4, 1776, Congress adopted the Declaration of Independence as the official explanation of its actions. The rebellion had become a war for national independence.

THE DECLARATION OF INDEPENDENCE

July 4, 1776

PREAMBLE

When, in the course of human events, it becomes necessary for one people to dissolve the political bands which have connected them with another, and to assume, among the powers of the earth, the separate and equal station to which the laws of nature and of nature's God entitle them, a decent respect to the opinions of mankind requires that they should declare the causes which impel them to the separation.

NEW PRINCIPLES OF GOVERNMENT

We hold these truths to be self-evident: that all men are created equal, that they are endowed by their Creator with certain unalienable rights, that among these are life, liberty, and the pursuit of happiness.

That, to secure these rights, governments are instituted among men, deriving their just powers from the consent of the governed;

That whenever any form of government becomes destructive of these ends, it is the right of the people to alter or to abolish it, and to institute new government, laying its foundation on such principles, and organizing its powers in such form, as to them shall seem most likely to effect their safety and happiness. Prudence, indeed, will dictate that governments long established should not be changed for light and transient causes; and accordingly all experience hath shown that mankind are more disposed to suffer while evils are sufferable, than to right themselves by abolishing the forms to which they are accustomed. But when a long train of abuses and usurpations, pursuing invariably the same object, evinces a design to reduce them under absolute despotism, it is their right, it is their duty, to throw off such government, and to provide new guards for their future security.

REASONS FOR SEPARATION

Such has been the patient sufferance of these colonies; and such is now the necessity which constrains them to alter their former systems of government. The history of the present king of Great Britain is a history of repeated injuries and usurpations, all having in direct object the establishment of an absolute tyranny over these states. To prove this, let facts be submitted to a candid world.

He has refused his assent to laws the most wholesome and necessary for the public good.

He has forbidden his governors to pass laws of immediate and pressing importance, unless suspended in their operation till his assent should be obtained; and when so suspended, he has utterly neglected to attend to them.

He has refused to pass other laws for the accommodation of large districts of people, unless those people would relinquish the right of representation in the legislature, a right inestimable to them, and formidable to tyrants only.

He has called together legislative bodies at places unusual, uncomfortable, and distant from the depository of their public records, for the sole purpose of fatiguing them into compliance with his measures.

He has dissolved representative houses repeatedly, for opposing, with manly firmness, his invasions on the rights of the people.

He has refused, for a long time after such dissolutions, to cause others to be elected; whereby the legislative powers, incapable of annihilation, have returned to the people at large for their exercise; the state remaining, in the mean time, exposed to all the dangers of invasion from without and convulsions within.

He has endeavored to prevent the population of these states; for that purpose obstructing the laws of naturalization of foreigners, refusing to pass others to encourage their migration hither, and raising the conditions of new appropriations of lands.

He has obstructed the administration of justice, by refusing his assent to laws for establishing judiciary powers.

He has made judges dependent on his will alone for the tenure of their offices, and the amount and payment of their salaries.

He has erected a multitude of new offices, and sent hither swarms of officers to harass our people and eat out their substance.

He has kept among us, in times of peace, standing armies, without the consent of our legislature.

He has affected to render the military independent of, and superior to, the civil power.

He has combined with others to subject us to a jurisdiction foreign to our constitution and unacknowledged by our laws, giving his assent to their acts of pretended legislation:

For quartering large bodies of armed troops among us;

For protecting them, by a mock trial, from punishment for any murders which they should commit on the inhabitants of these states;

For cutting off our trade with all parts of the world;

For imposing taxes on us without our consent;

For depriving us, in many cases, of the benefits of trial by jury;

For transporting us beyond seas, to be tried for pretended offenses;

For abolishing the free system of English laws in a neighboring province, establishing therein an arbitrary government, and enlarging its boundaries, so as to render it at once an example and fit instrument for introducing the same absolute rule into these colonies;

For taking away our charters, abolishing our most valuable laws, and altering, fundamentally, the forms of our governments;

For suspending our own legislature, and declaring themselves invested with power to legislate for us in all cases whatsoever.

He has abdicated government here, by declaring us out of his protection and waging war against us.

He has plundered our seas, ravaged our coasts, burned our towns, and destroyed the lives of our people.

He is at this time transporting large armies of foreign mercenaries to complete the works of death, desolation, and tyranny already begun with circumstances of cruelty and perfidy scarcely paralleled in the most barbarous ages, and totally unworthy the head of a civilized nation.

He has constrained our fellow-citizens, taken captive on the high seas, to bear arms against their country, to become the executioners of their friends and brethren, or to fall themselves by their hands.

He has excited domestic insurrections among us, and has endeavored to bring on the inhabitants of our frontiers the merciless Indian savages, whose known rule of warfare is an undistinguished destruction of all ages, sexes, and conditions.

In every stage of these oppressions we have petitioned for redress in the most humble terms; our repeated petitions have been answered only by repeated injury. A prince whose character is thus marked by every act which may define a tyrant is unfit to be the ruler of a free people.

Nor have we been wanting in attention to our British brethren. We have warned them, from time to time, of attempts by their legislature to extend an unwarrantable jurisdiction over us. We have reminded them of the circumstances of our emigration and settlement here. We have appealed to their native justice and magnanimity; and we have conjured them, by the ties of our common kindred, to disavow these usurpations, which would inevitably interrupt our connections and correspondence. They, too, have been deaf to the voice of justice and of consanguinity. We must, therefore, acquiesce in the necessity which denounces our separation, and hold them, as we hold the rest of mankind, enemies in war, in peace, friends.

A FORMAL DECLARATION OF WAR

We, therefore, the representatives of the United States of America, in General Congress assembled, appealing to the Supreme Judge of the world for the rectitude of our intentions, do, in the name and by authority of the good people of these colonies, solemnly publish and declare, that these united colonies are, and of right ought to be, free and independent states; that they are absolved from all allegiance to the British crown, and that all political connection between them and the state of Great Britain is, and ought to be, totally dissolved; and that, as free and independent states, they have full power to levy war, conclude peace, contract alliances, establish commerce, and to do all other acts and things which independent states may of right do. And, for the support of this declaration, with a firm reliance on the protection of Divine Providence, we mutually pledge to each other our lives, our fortunes, and our sacred honor.

John Hancock (MASSACHUSETTS)

NORTH CAROLINA

William Hooper
Joseph Hewes
John Penn

SOUTH CAROLINA

Edward Rutledge
Thomas Heyward, Jr.
Thomas Lynch, Jr.
Arthur Middleton

GEORGIA

Button Gwinnett
Lyman Hall
George Walton

MARYLAND

Samuel Chase
William Paca
Thomas Stone
Charles Carroll
   of Carrollton

VIRGINIA

George Wythe
Richard Henry Lee
Thomas Jefferson
Benjamin Harrison
Thomas Nelson, Jr.
Francis Lightfoot Lee
Carter Braxton

PENNSYLVANIA

Robert Morris
Benjamin Rush
Benjamin Franklin
John Morton
John Clymer
James Smith
George Taylor
James Wilson
George Ross

DELAWARE

Caesar Rodney
George Read
Thomas McKean

NEW YORK

William Floyd
Philip Livingston
Francis Lewis
Lewis Morris

NEW JERSEY

Richard Stockton
John Witherspoon
Francis Hopkinson
John Hart
Abraham Clark

NEW HAMPSHIRE

Josiah Bartlett
William Whipple
Matthew Thornton

MASSACHUSETTS

Samuel Adams
John Adams
Robert Treat Paine
Elbridge Gerry

RHODE ISLAND

Stephen Hopkins
William Ellery

CONNECTICUT

Roger Sherman
Samuel Huntington
William Williams
Oliver Wolcott

4 Americans Win The War

1. What were the advantages and disadvantages of the British in fighting the Revolutionary war?

2. What were the advantages and disadvantages of the Americans in fighting the Revolutionary war?

3. What were the most important factors which accounted for American success in the war?

4. What military strategies were proposed by the opposing commanders, and what were their strengths and weaknesses? What alternatives would you have suggested if you had been commander? Why?

George Washington was under no illusions about the difficulties he faced. The British possessed important military advantages. In Canada they had a base from which to invade the northern colonies, and from Florida they could attack the South. The Royal Navy was strong enough to protect British transport and supply ships from the hundreds of American privateers which swarmed across the oceans. The king's ships blockaded American ports, and under their escort, General Howe, now British commander-in-chief, could strike at any point on the east coast.

The opposing forces. The British army was a superbly equipped, harshly disciplined force. The infantrymen were magnificent soldiers; at the Battle of Bunker Hill, 40 percent of them were shot down, but the rest rallied and took the hill. Their officers, especially the generals, were almost all seasoned veterans of the European wars, who outmaneuvered the Americans in battle after battle. In addition, the British were supported by thirty thousand Hessian mercenaries who were not the clumsy oafs many historians have caricatured. Hessian Jägers (which means "hunters"), for example, proved to be expert marksmen and superb forest fighters.

In comparison, the American army seemed feeble. The militiamen were an unreliable force who all too often fled at the first shot or abandoned the army during the winter, and they were not always good marksmen. The regular troops, called the Continental Line, eventually were a match for the British in a formal battle, but there were never many of these. Although Anthony Wayne, Daniel Morgan, and Nathaniel Greene ultimately proved to be brilliant generals, many American officers were completely ignorant of the art of war. Supplies were always scarce, and there was so little money to pay the troops that in 1780 many of them mutinied. The small Continental navy, despite the heroic exploits of John Paul Jones and John Barry, was blown off the ocean by 1779.

American advantages. Nevertheless, the Americans had two key advantages. The country was a wilderness, with poor roads, few cities, and a widely scattered population. Hence, the war was a guerrilla war, with the British easily occupying the cities but unable to pacify the countryside. The militia might never stand up to a bayonet charge, but it could cut off supply trains, ambush patrols, and thus control the wilderness. Washington rarely won a pitched battle, but he was able to keep his army together, constantly threatening the British and preventing them from establishing firm control over the land. As General Greene explained, "We fight, get beat, rise, and fight again."

The second advantage followed from the first. Washington needed only to survive and other factors would impede and eventually wreck the British war effort. British opinion was divided, and after 1777, vocal elements in Parliament demanded an end to the frustrating war. British armies were dependent upon 3,000-mile supply lines and upon orders (which often arrived too late) from political leaders ignorant of American terrain and conditions. When France joined the war in 1778 (page 63), Britain with a vast empire to protect and fearing invasion of the home islands, was forced to weaken and eventually end her military effort to retake the colonies.

Stalemate. In the summer of 1776, thirty thousand British soldiers under Howe poured ashore on Long Island, defeated Washington (who had moved down from Boston), and captured New York City. By December, Washington's now dwindling army had retreated across New Jersey to the safety of the Pennsylvania side of the

Delaware River. A panic-stricken Congress fled from Philadelphia to Baltimore.

Howe, following the customary rules of European warfare, withdrew the bulk of his forces to winter camp in New York, leaving small detachments comfortably bedded down in New Jersey. On December 25, Washington led his shivering army across the Delaware and surprised and routed the Hessians at Trenton, capturing one thousand. A week later, Washington destroyed a British force at Princeton and fortified a strong position in the hills of Morristown. These brilliant maneuvers forced the British to abandon New Jersey. The campaign was thus a stalemate; Howe occupied New York, but the American army was still intact.

The year of miracles. In 1777, the British suffered a military disaster which had far-reaching diplomatic consequences and which proved to be the turning point of the war. General John Burgoyne had convinced the Secretary of State for America, Lord George Germain, that the Hudson Valley was the key to victory. Burgoyne's plan was that he would march from Canada to Albany, joining Howe, who would sweep up the Hudson from New York, thereby cutting New England off from the rest of the colonies. Sir William Howe had a different scheme entirely. He thought that if he captured the rebel capital of Philadelphia, the Americans would be so disheartened that they would sue for peace. Germain, in effect, approved both plans and sent such confusing orders to Howe that the commander-in-chief never understood that he must cooperate with Burgoyne.

Militarily, Howe's campaign was successful. Sailing up the Chesapeake Bay, his army landed south of Philadelphia and smashed Washington's forces at the Battle of Brandywine. In September the British staged a triumphal march into Philadelphia. Contrary to Howe's expectations, however, Congress, which had returned to the city, merely moved again, this time to Lancaster, Pennsylvania, and continued its proceedings as if nothing had happened. Washington's troops entrenched themselves on the steep hills of Valley Forge, which Howe was afraid to attack.

Howe's pointless occupation of Philadelphia left the northern American army free to deal with Burgoyne, who, encumbered by an enormous baggage train, moved slowly south through the forests of northern New York. At the same time, a force of British, Indians, and Tories commanded by Colonel Barry St. Leger was marching from Lake Ontario down the Mohawk Valley to meet Burgoyne at Albany. In early August of 1777, both British armies suffered serious setbacks.

St. Leger, who was halted at Fort Stanwix in central New York State, was surprised by a force under Benedict Arnold. Arnold fooled the Indians into believing that he led a mighty army. The Indians and Tories fled, and the rest of St. Leger's forces retreated. Meanwhile, Burgoyne, whose supplies had run out, sent an expedition of Hessians into Bennington, Vermont, in search of grain and cattle. On August 15 it was annihilated by a militia force. A month later, Burgoyne, still pushing southward, came upon the northern American army near Saratoga, New York. Burgoyne attacked, but in two bloody battles, his troops, floundering hopelessly in the tangled woods, were ripped apart. On October 17, Burgoyne's army, surrounded and starving, with Howe's expected expedition nowhere in sight, surrendered.

France joins the Americans. The destruction of Burgoyne's army resulted in a diplomatic triumph for the Americans. France had been delighted when the colonies revolted against its traditional enemy, Britain. From the beginning of the war, the French government secretly sent supplies and encouraged officers, such as the Marquis de Lafayette, to join the American army. But France would not offer open support until it was sure the Americans could win. Burgoyne's defeat convinced the French foreign minister, Vergennes, that by entering the war France had an opportunity to revenge the humiliating defeat of 1763. Distracted by the war in America, Britain would not be able to resist French attacks in India and the West Indies. For Americans, French support meant loans, troops, and the power of the French navy. On February 6, 1778, France and the United States concluded a treaty of alliance.

The news of the French alliance greatly heartened American forces, especially Washington's army at Valley Forge. Freezing and nearly starving, ravaged by disease and plagued by short supplies, the men at Valley Forge suffered through the grim winter of 1777–78. For the first time,

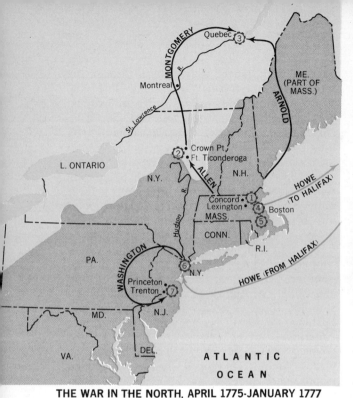

THE WAR IN THE NORTH, APRIL 1775-JANUARY 1777

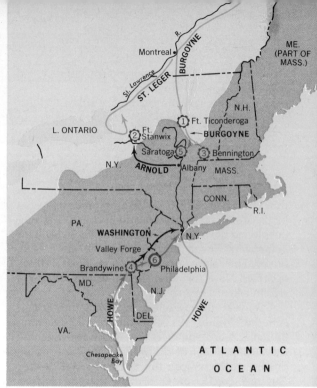

THE WAR IN THE NORTH, JULY 1777-JUNE 1778

THE AMERICAN REVOLUTION

Colonies	→ American Moves
Other British possessions.	→ British Moves
⬡	Battle Sites

THE WAR IN THE SOUTH, DECEMBER 1778-MARCH 1781

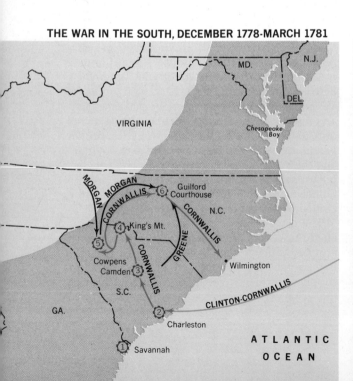

SIEGE OF YORKTOWN, JUNE 1781-OCTOBER 1781

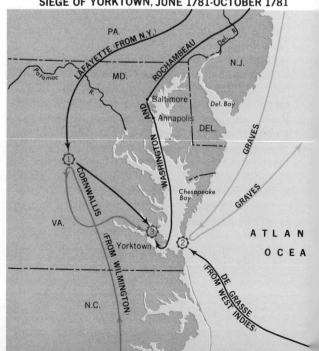

THE AMERICAN REVOLUTION

THE WAR IN THE NORTH, 1775-1777

① **April 19, 1775. Lexington and Concord.** Militiamen at Lexington fail to stop British from reaching Concord, where they seize American military stores.

② **May 10 and 12, 1775. Ft. Ticonderoga and Crown Point.** Americans under Ethan Allen capture the forts.

③ **Sept. 12-Dec. 31, 1775. Quebec.** Two-pronged attack by American forces (Arnold from Maine and Montgomery from Crown Pt.) is repulsed.

④ **June 17, 1775. Bunker Hill.** British force Americans to withdraw. British suffer heavy losses.

⑤ **May 1775-March 1776. Boston.** Americans force British to vacuate Port of Boston.

⑥ **August 27, 1776. Long Island.** British under General Howe capture New York City. Washington retreats to Pennsylvania.

⑦ **Dec. 25, 1776 and Jan. 2, 1777. Trenton and Princeton.** Washington crosses the Delaware, captures Trenton and Princeton, forcing British to withdraw from New Jersey.

THE WAR IN THE NORTH, 1777-1778

① **July 5, 1777. Ft. Ticonderoga.** Burgoyne, moving from Quebec to Albany, recaptures the fort.

② **Aug. 6, 1777, Ft. Stanwix.** British, led by St. Leger, heading for Albany, are defeated by Americans under Benedict Arnold.

③ **Aug. 16, 1777. Bennington.** Hessian troops under Burgoyne's command are ambushed by Americans.

④ **Sept. 11, 1777. Brandywine.** Howe sails up Chesapeake Bay to Pennsylvania and defeats Washington. Howe occupies Philadelphia and Washington retreats to Valley Forge.

⑤ **Oct. 17, 1777. Saratoga.** Burgoyne, still pushing toward Albany, is defeated by Americans, halting the invasion of Albany.

⑥ **June 18, 1778. Evacuation of Philadelphia.** Howe's army, now under Clinton's command, abandons Philadelphia and withdraws to New York. Washington pursues him and camps just north of New York City.

THE WAR IN THE SOUTH, 1778-1781

① **Dec. 29, 1778. Savannah.** British capture the city with little resistance.

② **May 12, 1780. Charleston.** British under Generals Clinton and Cornwallis, take Charleston. Clinton leaves Cornwallis in charge.

③ **August 16, 1780. Camden.** Cornwallis defeats Americans under General Gates.

④ **Oct. 7, 1780. King's Mountain.** Left wing of Cornwallis' army is wiped out by Kentucky and Tennessee riflemen.

⑤ **Jan. 17, 1781. Cowpens.** Cornwallis dispatches Tarleton to Cowpens where he is defeated by Americans under General Morgan.

⑥ **March 15, 1781. Guilford Court House.** Cornwallis pursues Morgan to North Carolina. There, Morgan and Greene lead joint attack against Cornwallis. Americans are defeated but British suffer heavy casualties and withdraw to Wilmington.

SIEGE OF YORKTOWN, JUNE-OCTOBER, 1781

① **June 1781.** Lafayette engages Cornwallis in central Virginia. Cornwallis retreats to Yorktown with Lafayette in pursuit.

② **Sept. 5-10, 1781.** British fleet under Admiral Graves is defeated at the mouth of Chesapeake Bay by the French fleet under de Grasse. Graves retreats to New York.

③ **Sept. 14-Oct. 19, 1781. Siege of Yorktown.** Combined troops of Washington and Rochambeau, having moved southward from New York, sail down the Chesapeake (with the aid of the French fleet) and begin the siege of Yorktown. On October 19, Cornwallis surrenders.

FINANCING THE REVOLUTION

How was the revolutionary, young American government to pay the enormous cost of a rebellion against the established government of Britain? The Continental Army had to feed and equip its soldiers, and food, shelter, and salaries were continuing expenses. To meet these financial demands, the American government tried several measures. First, the government sold bonds, at home and abroad, particularly to the French and the Dutch. (A bond is an agreement by which a group or individual loans the government a specified amount of money. The government agrees to pay the money back, plus interest, at a later date.) Very little money was raised this way since few Americans had the currency to buy bonds, and with the exception of Dutch bankers, there was little faith in the ability of the government to honor its debts.

Sometimes, the government requisitioned goods directly and in exchange gave citizens certificates of indebtedness called Continental certificates. It also requisitioned money from the states according to their estimated populations. But the government had no power to tax the people. Because money was scarce, no state contributed more than a small part of its share.

In desperation, the national government tried to raise funds by issuing paper money; many of the states also issued their own currency. Most of this paper money was not backed by specie. As the war continued and other fundraising methods failed, more and more paper money was issued, until each individual paper bill was worth only a fraction of its face value. By 1780, Congress decided to stop issuing paper money and take existing paper money out of circulation. The states were ordered to accept Continental currency, the paper money issued by the Continental Congress, at the rate of forty paper dollars to one silver dollar, and then send the paper money to Congress to be destroyed. If the money was not turned in for taxes at a fortieth of its face value, it would be declared utterly worthless—thus the phrase "Not worth a Continental."

however, they began to receive regular and proper military training. Under the direction of the Prussian officer Baron Von Steuben, they finally emerged from their ordeal a well-disciplined fighting force.

In the spring of 1778, the British forces in Philadelphia, now under the command of Sir Henry Clinton, were ordered to abandon the city. Followed by Washington, Clinton's forces crawled wearily across New Jersey and into New York to assume the defensive. Washington's army, camped above New York City, was too weak to attack, but it prevented British forces from moving up the Hudson. In effect, the British had given up the war in the North.

Decision in the South. Clinton, aware that a large number of colonists in the Carolinas and Georgia sympathized with the British, and convinced that the conquest of Virginia would demoralize the Americans, decided to shift the war to the South. In 1779–80, a powerful British offensive captured Savannah and forced five thousand American soldiers to surrender Charleston. From these bases, British forces under General George Cornwallis quickly subdued Georgia and South Carolina.

Three factors, however, combined to frustrate further British gains. As Cornwallis marched toward North Carolina, guerrilla bands emerged from the swamps and destroyed his supply lines. In October 1780, the left wing of Cornwallis' army was wiped out at King's Mountain, in South Carolina, by Kentucky and Tennessee riflemen. Finally, the scattered patriots were rallied by the most brilliant American commander of the war, Nathaniel Greene.

In the campaign that followed, Greene wore down the British army by luring it into long, fruitless marches away from its supply bases. In battle, Greene sought not to win, an impossibility with his undisciplined forces, but to inflict so many casualties on the British that they could not win. Cornwallis, realizing that victory was impossible, withdrew to the security of the coast and allowed Greene to destroy British forts and outposts in the Carolinas. By the fall of 1781, the British retained only Charleston and Savannah.

The American victory at Yorktown. With his southern strategy a failure, Clinton decided on a last desperate gamble, and ordered Cornwallis to

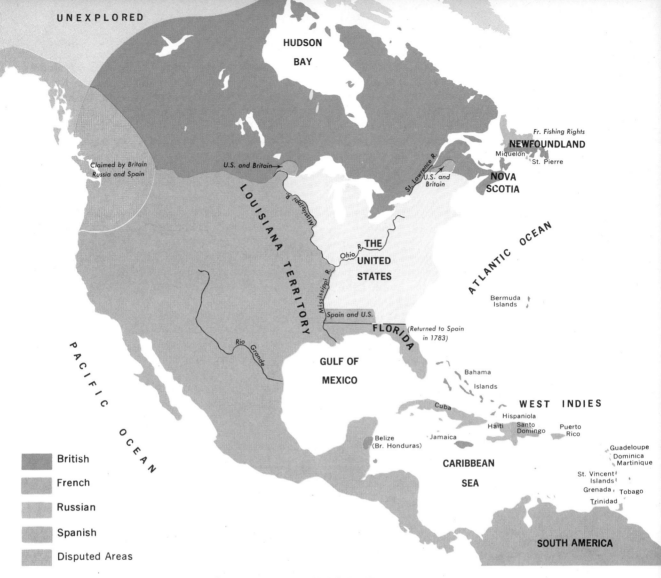

UNEXPLORED

HUDSON BAY

Fr. Fishing Rights
NEWFOUNDLAND
Miquelon
St. Pierre

Claimed by Britain
Russia and Spain

U.S. and Britain →

St. Lawrence R.

U.S. and
Britain

NOVA
SCOTIA

LOUISIANA TERRITORY

Mississippi R.

U.S. and Britain →

ATLANTIC OCEAN

Ohio R.

THE
UNITED
STATES

Mississippi R.

Bermuda
Islands

Spain and U.S.

FLORIDA

(Returned to Spain
in 1783)

Rio Grande

GULF OF
MEXICO

Bahama
Islands

PACIFIC OCEAN

WEST INDIES

Cuba

Hispaniola
Haiti Santo
Domingo

Puerto
Rico

Belize
(Br. Honduras)

Jamaica

Guadeloupe
Dominica
Martinique

CARIBBEAN

SEA

St. Vincent
Islands
Grenada Tobago
Trinidad

British

French

Russian

Spanish

Disputed Areas

SOUTH AMERICA

NORTH AMERICA IN 1783

Virginia. Washington sent the Marquis de Lafayette, with a sizable contingent of the now well-trained Continental Line, south to stop the latest British threat. Cornwallis prudently retired to Yorktown, Virginia, and urged Clinton to send reinforcements from New York.

Almost at the same time, Washington, who had been joined by six thousand French regulars under the French commander General Jean Rochambeau, learned that a French fleet commanded by Admiral de Grasse was sailing for the Chesapeake Bay. Washington instantly saw his opportunity. After convincing Clinton that he was about to assault New York, Washington led his American-French army by forced marches to Virginia. Arriving at Yorktown in September 1781, he found that the French fleet had beaten off the British fleet. Cornwallis was trapped.

The siege of Yorktown ended on October 17, 1781, with the surrender of Cornwallis' entire army. Officially, the war continued two more years, but the British now recognized the futility of attempting to conquer the colonies. Lord North, when he heard the news of Yorktown, summed up the attitude of the British government and people by crying out, "Oh, God, it is all over!"

Peace is signed. The surrender at Yorktown convinced many influential Englishmen that the long, financially exhausting war must end. By this time the conflict had become worldwide in scope, raging from Gibraltar to India. Over the king's objections, the British government opened negotiations in Paris with the American peace commissioners Benjamin Franklin, John Adams, and John Jay. In the peace treaty of 1783, the Americans gained a brilliant diplomatic triumph.

The British were willing to recognize the independence of the American states, but they were not willing to release the Ohio Valley to the new nation nor grant Americans the same fishing rights in Newfoundland they had enjoyed as colonists. Ultimately, the British did grant fishing rights in Canadian waters and were forced, by the sheer tenacity of the American negotiators, to give up the Ohio Valley, extending the boundaries of the United States to the Mississippi River (see map, page 798). The treaty was ratified in 1784, and the United States of America took its place, as the Declaration of Independence had promised, "among the powers of the earth."

5 The Revolution Brings Internal Changes

1. Why did some Americans remain loyal to the king?

2. How was the American social structure changed as a result of the war? Were these changes significant enough to indicate a revolutionary change in the American social order?

3. What changes occurred in the American political order as a result of the war? Were these changes fundamental enough to indicate an American revolution?

How "revolutionary" was the American Revolution? Did this great struggle produce fundamental changes in the internal structure of American society? Unlike the French Revolution of the late eighteenth century, and the Russian Revolution in the early twentieth century, the American Revolution was not directed by one social class against another. Consequently, America never witnessed the widespread and systematic terror that destroyed the upper class of France and both the upper and middle classes of Russia. The men who led the American Revolution—Washington, Jefferson, Franklin, John Adams, Samuel Adams, and Patrick Henry—were not seeking to alter the structure of society; therefore, the American Revolution was not a broad social revolution. It did, however, involve a bitter civil war between the revolutionaries and the colonists who remained loyal to Britain—the Tories.

Treatment of the Tories. Samuel Adams wrote of the Tories that "more is to be apprehended from the secret machinations of these rascally people than from the open violence of British and Hessian soldiers. . . ." They served the king as spies and propagandists; twenty-five thousand of them joined the British armies, and many thousands more, especially in the South, formed guerrilla bands. Although John Adams' estimate that nearly one-third of the population was Tory was probably exaggerated, their total was enormous. When the British army evacuated America in 1783, eighty thousand Tories sailed with it.

All segments of American society contained people loyal to the king. Many small tenant farmers in upstate New York, who hated their patriot manorial lords, were Tories. Frontiersmen in North and South Carolina, who had long resented the political domination of their colonies by rich eastern supporters of the revolution, supported the royal cause. Most ministers of the Anglican church, many merchants with close economic ties to Britain, nearly all the former officeholders under the royal governments of the colonies, and over half the population of New York supported the British government.

To deal with this enormous threat, the new state legislatures quickly acted upon the advice of the Second Continental Congress that all Tories be declared traitors and severely punished. All the states drew up oaths of allegiance, and most state legislatures made loyalism to Britain a crime punishable by jail or exile.

Raising the Liberty Pole, John McRae, 1875

America's revolution started not with the first shot fired but with the colonials' coming more and more to the conclusion that they were a people fit to determine their own destinies in the land that they had settled. The hopefulness and jubilance of setting up a liberty pole marked what must have been to them a coming of age as a people and a nation. Once their decision had been made, the battle was joined, and new troops had to be mustered. Since the army relied on enlistment and not on the draft, patriotism and a spirit of adventure had to be appealed to, and they had quite a drawing power. Enlistment figures for the Continental Army and state militias vary from about 185,000 to 400,000. The weapons of war were in short supply, even though civilians built factories for their manufacture and weapons were imported from Europe.

Army Recruiting Poster

TO ALL BRAVE, HEALTHY, ABLE BODIED, AND WELL DISPOSED YOUNG MEN,
IN THIS NEIGHBOURHOOD, WHO HAVE ANY INCLINATION TO JOIN THE TROOPS, NOW RAISING UNDER
GENERAL WASHINGTON,
FOR THE DEFENCE OF THE
LIBERTIES AND INDEPENDENCE
OF THE UNITED STATES,
Against the hostile designs of foreign enemies,

TAKE NOTICE,

THAT *Middlesex* County, attendance will be given by Lieutenant *Keating* Battalion of the 11th regiment of infantry, commanded by Lieutenant Colonel Aaron Ogden, for the purpose of receiving the enrollment of such youth of SPIRIT, as may be willing to enter into this HONOURABLE service.

The ENCOURAGEMENT at this time, to enlist, is truly liberal and generous, namely, a bounty of TWELVE dollars, an annual and fully sufficient supply of good and handsome cloathing, a daily allowance of a large and ample ration of provisions, together with SIXTY dollars a year in GOLD and SILVER money on account of pay, the whole of which the soldier may lay up for himself and friends, as all articles proper for his subsistance and comfort are provided by law, without any expence to him.

Those who may favour this recruiting party with their attendance as above, will have an opportunity of hearing and seeing in a more particular manner, the great advantages which these brave men will have, who shall embrace this opportunity of spending a few happy years in viewing the different parts of this beautiful continent, in the honourable and truly respectable character of a soldier, after which, he may, if he pleases return home to his friends, with his pockets FULL of money and his head COVERED with laurels.

GOD SAVE THE UNITED STATES.

The Battle of Princeton, January 3, 1777, William Mercer, *c.* 1790

Battle Between the Serapis *and the* Bonhomme Richard, *September 1779*

The British, on the other hand, never had more than 45,000 fighting men in North America, although they were joined by about 30,000 mercenaries, 50,000 Loyalists, and at times an unreckoned number of Indians.

Battles raged on land in the colonies themselves and on sea, both near the colonies and far distant. As the war went on, the American army became a stronger fighting force, and a new American navy was developed. Among the battles in which the new army was victorious was that at Princeton. The picture of that fighting which appears on the preceding page was painted by the deaf-mute son of a participant there. Notice how he renders the sound of the exploding cannon in a visual way. Probably the most famous naval hero to emerge was John Paul Jones, who was captain of the "Bonhomme Richard," pictured in battle on the preceding page. Although he forced the "Serapis" to strike her colors and was able to board her in triumph, his ship had sustained the more telling damage, and as he stood on the deck of the "Serapis," he watched his ship sink.

Life away from the battle areas went on as best it could. Since the colonies were basically agricultural, the loss of farmers to the service was keenly felt. Those at home yearned to have the men back to put in new crops, and those farmers in service yearned to get back to do the planting. Many of them enlisted for only short terms so that they could do just that. Some of them even deserted to get back.

Finally after years of struggle, the war came to an end with Cornwallis' surrender at Yorktown. John Trumbull, an artist who had actually fought in the Revolutionary War, captured that memorable day years later in the monumental work which he reproduced in the Capitol rotunda in Washington.

Surrender of Lord Cornwallis, John Trumbull, *c.* 1824

In November 1777, Congress urged the states to seize and sell Tory lands. Among the huge landholdings promptly confiscated were the great manors of the Johnson, De Lancy, and Phillipse families of New York, amounting to more than three hundred thousand acres. The vast holdings of the Penn family were seized by Pennsylvania; Virginia sold the estates of Washington's neighbor, Lord Fairfax; and the Georgia revolutionaries had the pleasure of dividing up the lands of their royal governor. In North Carolina, the entire upper half of the state was happily taken from its British owners, the Grenville family. Much of this land was broken into small parcels and sold to the poorer and middle classes. To an extent, then, the Revolution did help to equalize landed wealth.

Beginning of opposition to slavery. While the Revolution left the class and economic relationships of society virtually intact, some changes did occur. In Virginia, for example, Jefferson persuaded the House of Burgesses to eliminate the laws of *primogeniture* (which limited inheritance to the eldest son) and *entailment* (forbidding an estate owner to dispose of any part of an estate). The abolition of these British laws for keeping landed wealth in the hands of the aristocracy had no far-reaching practical importance, however, because they had never been widely practiced in colonial America.

Far more significantly, the Revolution produced the first important challenge to the institution of slavery in America. With the exception of Georgia and South Carolina, the states offered freedom to slaves who served in the army. During the Revolution nearly 5,000 blacks fought in the Continental army and the militia. The British widely advertised that slaves who voluntarily entered their lines would receive their freedom, and more than 25,000 took advantage of the offer.

Of greater importance for the future was the belief of many American leaders, especially Washington and Jefferson, that slavery was incompatible with the principles of republican government. As a result, the issue of the abolition of slavery became a familiar topic of debate, although virtually nothing was done about it in the South except that Virginia and North Carolina prohibited the further importation of slaves.

AN ENGLISHMAN VIEWS THE NEW NATION

Even after the Americans had won their war for independence, many people doubted the ability of the new nation to survive. Although loyalists may have fled, most remained confident that they would shortly be able to return if they so wished. And not all of the Americans who had fought for independence were fully convinced of the permanence of their new nation. Many people in Europe and in America agreed with Josiah Tucker, an English clergyman, who near the end of the Revolution wrote:

"As to the future Grandeur of *America*, and its being a rising Empire under *one Head*, whether Republican or Monarchical, it is one of the idlest and most visionary Notions that was ever conceived even by Writers of Romance. . . . The *Americans* will have no *Center of Union* among them, and no *Common Interest* to pursue, when the Power and Government of England are finally removed. Moreover, when the Intersections and Divisions of their Country by great Bays of the Sea and by vast Rivers, Lakes, and Ridges of Mountains—and, above all, when those immense inland Regions beyond the Back Settlements, which are still unexplored, are taken into the Account, they form the highest Probability that the *Americans* never can be united . . . . under any species of Government whatever. Their fate seems to be—A DISUNITED PEOPLE, till the End of Time."

In the North every state either abolished slavery outright or enacted general emancipation laws between 1776 and 1804. In Massachusetts, for example, the Supreme Judicial Court declared that slavery was incompatible with the first article of the state constitution which proclaimed that "all men are born free and equal."

Slaves were not numerous in the North, however, and despite emancipation in the North, by 1790, only 60,000 free blacks lived in America compared to 680,000 slaves. Although the failure of the Revolutionary generation to resolve the issue of slavery was tragic, the seeds of militant northern opposition to slavery had been planted. During the Revolution, two abolitionist societies were created, one in Philadelphia and one in New York City.

The creation of political order. Although the Revolution involved mass confiscation of the property of Tories and saw the beginning of opposition to slavery, it left the social order basically intact. In what sense, then, did a revolution take place? Part of the answer may be found by looking at the new political order which emerged in America during the war.

Americans, from the time they found themselves in disputes with Englishmen over the power of Parliament, emphasized that their charters had extended to them the rights of Englishmen. This belief that written documents were the basis of their governments, and the rights those governments were expected to protect, underlay the political ideas that Americans advanced early in the war. Society, Locke said, had developed from a state of Nature, in which no government existed, into a Social Compact. Americans argued, as Patrick Henry put it, "We are in a state of Nature, Sir," because the authority of Britain had dissolved. It was necessary for Americans to enter into social compacts, and they insisted that these compacts be written down in a constitution.

When the Continental Congress advised the colonies, in May 1776, to create governments, they set out to write constitutions that would solve four basic problems. First, how should the representation of the people be established and what power should these representatives have? Second, what power should the executive branch—the governor—exercise? Third, how should power be divided among the branches of government? And fourth, what special rights did people retain against the possible abuses of power by government officials? Different states provided different answers. The Revolution was a period of experimentation in formulating constitutions.

State constitutions. Pennsylvania insisted that since all men were equal before the law, they need be represented only by a legislature of one house. The influence of tradition showed here, since Pennsylvania had a *unicameral* (one-house) legislature in the colonial period. All other states felt that an upper house, which they expected would represent the wealthier citizens, was desirable. All the states except South Carolina greatly expanded the representation of their western counties, and all gave their lower house of representatives far greater powers than they had exercised under the royal governments.

Since Americans were suspicious of the power a strong executive might use to curtail their rights, a governor's power was drastically reduced from the authority which royal governors, as representatives of the king, had been granted. The governor of North Carolina became a mere figurehead. Pennsylvania and New Hampshire replaced the governor with an executive committee, believing that such a "plural executive" was unlikely to become tyrannical. In most states the governor could not summon or suspend the legislature, had no veto over its acts, had a short term of office, and could be impeached and removed from office.

In the Revolutionary state constitutions, power was not carefully divided between the executive, legislative, and judicial branches of government. The legislatures held virtually supreme powers. Not only were the powers of the governor generally weak, but the judiciary was under the thumb of the legislature, which either directly appointed or consented to the appointment of judges, paid their salaries, could determine their powers, and could remove them.

An important tendency toward wider participation in political life appeared in the new states. The Revolutionary houses of representatives were chosen by a larger electorate than during the colonial period. In Massachusetts, Delaware, Pennsylvania, and Georgia, payment of taxes, no matter how small, replaced the old property qualifications for voting. New Hampshire required only a small poll tax. The other states retained the colonial property qualifications, which, in fact, disenfranchised only about one quarter of the free adult white males.

Bills of rights. To many citizens of these new states, the crucial feature of their constitutions was the bill of rights. A bill of rights was intended to say what government cannot do, what rights belong to the people and cannot be invaded or abolished by law. In effect these Americans were trying to put Locke's conceptions of Natural Law into man-made law. Locke had said that under the Natural Law of Liberty no man could be dominated by the arbitrary will of another. The bills of rights in the several state constitutions were meant to spell out the details of this theory.

Virginia led the way, adopting a bill of rights written by George Mason in June 1776. Trial by jury, freedom from taxation by unrepresentative governments, and immunity from cruel punishments, excessive bail, and delayed trials were guaranteed to all citizens. Freedom of the press, the right to bear arms (the Virginia Bill of Rights specifically declared that standing armies were "dangerous to liberty"), and freedom from domination by a hereditary nobility were proclaimed in all the state constitutions, indicating the radical difference between political institutions in America and Europe.

Religion proved a difficult problem, for religious tolerance was not accepted everywhere. Virginia's bill of rights insisted that "all men are equally entitled to the free exercise of religion, according to the dictates of conscience." On the other hand, the Massachusetts Constitution of 1780, written by John Adams, permitted tax support for ministers, compulsory church attendance, and whatever laws the General Court of Massachusetts deemed best in the interest of public worship.

These state constitutions, despite some differences and even peculiar clauses, were all attempts to solve the greatest problem posed to man: how can a people establish a just government, responsive to their needs and wishes and protective of their rights? The world had never witnessed such an attempt to create a new political order. The answer to the problem of justice under government given by Americans of 1776 was to limit the power of the government over the citizen by weakening executive authority, broadening the basis of representation, and, above all, by defining the inalienable liberties of free men in bills of rights. This achievement was the true American Revolution.

■ CONCLUSION

What had begun as a quarrel over the source of authority within the British empire became a struggle for American independence. In the end that struggle led Americans into a search for a new form of government. They redefined the powers and limits of government and created a new political order which embodied the rights and liberties they had learned to cherish.

In fighting the war for independence, Americans had found a common cause, and many had acquired a sense of national unity. Leaders from different states, with different economic interests and social backgrounds, had discovered a greater loyalty than the narrow regard for the exclusive rights of their individual states. Patrick Henry defined this new attitude when in 1774 he declared to the Continental Congress, "The distinction between Virginians, Pennsylvanians, New Yorkers and New England are no more. I am not a Virginian, but an American."

Beneath this discovery of common interests, however, lay a serious unresolved problem. The Revolutionary leaders feared centralized power. The form of government they created placed enormous powers in the representative assemblies of the states, while leaving the national government as little more than a coordinating committee. Such a government could not hold together thirteen colonies used to going their separate ways. Having declared and won their independence, Americans now had to create a form of government that could make it last.

■ QUESTIONS

1. How did Britain's victory over France in 1763 affect the relationship between Britain and its American colonies?

2. What steps did Britain take to tighten imperial control over the American colonies from 1763 to 1775? How successful was Britain in its efforts?

3. What were the causes of the American Revolution, and what was the primary cause if one existed?

4. Do you think the reasons for American rebellion, as stated in the Declaration of Independence, were adequate and accurate? Explain your answer.

5. Could the American Revolution have been averted? Explain your answer. What alternatives were available to Britain and the colonies?

6. To what extent were the Americans unified in their responses to British policies leading up to and including the Revolutionary war?

7. How did the colonists become more American, more unified, as a result of the revolutionary experience?

8. Why did America win the Revolution?

9. How did the Americans wish to be governed?

10. Did the revolutionary process in America pass through identifiable stages? If so, identify the stages. If not, explain your answer.

■ BIBLIOGRAPHY

FRANKLIN, BENJAMIN, *Autobiography and Selected Writings*, ed. by Dixon Wecter and Larzer Ziff, Holt, Rinehart & Winston. Despite the continual appearance of new books on the colonial period, students would do well to begin with Benjamin Franklin and meet the man whom many consider the epitome of the American colonial. His account of the first fifty-one years of his life is readable and the source of many quotable passages on colonial life and thought.

PECKHAM, HOWARD H., *The Colonial Wars, 1689–1762*, U. of Chicago Press. To review the period leading up to the hostilities with England, students may consult this military history. It is a readable account, and may be particularly attractive to those boys who yearn for a little more action than the usual survey.

GIPSON, LAWRENCE HENRY, *The Coming of the Revolution, 1763–1775*, Harper & Row (Torchbooks). To parallel the development in the text of the crisis in the empire, students should read Gipson's scholarly appraisal of that topic. The book is not necessarily easy reading, but it should be used as a reference tool or for those students who want to consider the subject in more depth.

MORGAN, EDMUND S., *The Birth of the Republic, 1763–1789*, U. of Chicago Press. This book completes the period by bringing the reader through the Revolution and Confederation periods to the ratification of the Constitution. The book is relatively brief, and it has been used successfully at both the junior and senior high school levels.

ROBERTS, KENNETH, *Oliver Wiswell*, Fawcett (Premier Books). For a change of pace students are strongly encouraged to sample the historical novels of Kenneth Roberts. Contrary to some novelists who use historical themes, Roberts is especially careful of his historical detail. Sometimes the romantic interests which are added to the stories are weak, but the historical drama is excellent. This book is particularly provocative since it is a sympathetic view of Tories during the Revolution.

MORISON, SAMUEL ELIOT, *John Paul Jones: A Sailor's Biography*, Little, Brown. More adventure can be found in Morison's Pulitzer Prize-winning account of John Paul Jones. The author combines extensive research, a fluid style, and a love of the sea and sailing in this absorbing biography.

BRINTON, CRANE, *Anatomy of Revolution*, Random House (Vintage Books). This book demonstrates the comparative approach to history through analysis of four revolutions—the American, English, French, and Russian. Although the American Revolution receives the least treatment of the four, students can find a helpful discussion of definitions at the beginning of the book and an excellent summary of a model for revolution at the end.

BECKER, CARL LOTUS, *The Declaration of Independence: A Study in the History of Political Ideas*, Random House (Vintage Books). The author closely analyzed the various evolving drafts of the Declaration of Independence, which allowed him to provide an excellent interpretation of the document, its authors, and its signers. Although originally published in 1909, this book is still strongly recommended.

SOBUL, DE ANNE, *Encounters with America's History*, Holt, Rinehart & Winston. An early draft of the Declaration of Independence contained a mention of the evil of slavery, but it was stricken in later versions. The first of five inquiry-oriented problems in this book asks the question why was it stricken, and the student works through a series of documents and other source materials to answer the question for himself.

The Creation Of The Federal Union

The thirteen separate colonies were now united into one independent nation. But the United States was so weak, militarily and economically, that European powers doubted whether it would survive. Spain and Great Britain in particular stood to gain if the new nation faltered. In addition to the threats from abroad, the nation faced economic chaos at home, caused by war debts, heavy taxation, and business depression.

The country obviously needed many things to strengthen its domestic and international position—sound currency, stable government, strong leadership, and firm diplomacy. But above all it needed a sense of national unity. Unless the American people were willing to put the national good above the interests of their several states, the nation would disintegrate into what George Washington warned against: "Thirteen sovereignties pulling against each other."

For the fifty years following independence, the American people were engaged in a search for national unity. The most severe challenge facing the new nation was the divisive tendencies that threatened to disrupt the still tenuous bonds of unity. The American people had united *against* a common enemy to achieve their independence; now an even greater task lay ahead—to unite *for* a common future. As you read about the struggle to achieve national unity, these are some questions to keep in mind:

1. What were the failings of the Articles of Confederation?
2. How did the Constitution strengthen the national government?
3. What contributions did the Federalists make toward national unity?
4. Why did the nation enter an "Era of Good Feelings" after the War of 1812?

1 Government Falters Under The Articles Of Confederation

1. Why were the Articles of Confederation acceptable to most Americans when they were adopted?

2. What were some of the successes of the Confederation government? What were some of its failures?

3. What were the provisions of the Northwest Ordinance of 1787? Why were the provisions of this ordinance acceptable to at least nine states?

4. How adequate were the Articles of Confederation for the needs of the new nation?

In 1777, the Second Continental Congress formed a national government when it adopted the Articles of Confederation and Perpetual Union. Under the Articles the states retained their "sovereignty, freedom and independence." In establishing a government that emphasized the rights of states, Congress was reflecting its fear of centralized power. The leaders of the American Revolution, convinced that a corrupt executive branch of the British government had plotted the destruction of American liberties, sought to create a government which reduced the executive power to a minimum.

The frame of government. The Articles of Confederation did not create an independent Presidency or a federal judiciary; Congress was the sole instrument of national government. In Congress each state was entitled to one vote, and the votes of nine of the thirteen delegations— which were chosen by legislatures of the various states—were necessary to enact the most important resolutions, such as declarations of war, treaties, and military expenditures.

Achieving a three-fourths majority in Congress was difficult at best, and in many instances crippled the ability of Congress to govern effectively. Moreover, Congress was not even empowered to legislate on such important issues as regulating trade between the states or with foreign nations, setting tariffs, or levying taxes. Without these powers, Congress could only ask state governments to provide it with the necessary funds, and if state legislatures refused to make appropriations, as they often did, Congress had no way to force them to do so.

Moreover, the absence of a national judiciary made it virtually impossible for Congress to resolve disputes between the states, or to enforce its decisions in those areas where it was specifically authorized to act. By the mid-1780's, many American leaders were advocating constitutional changes to strengthen the government and enable it to deal more effectively with its domestic and international problems, including western expansion, foreign relations, and finance.

Congress organizes the western lands. Since the United States was an agricultural nation, its future lay in opening up the western lands. Yet the region was also a source of discord, for eastern states had numerous conflicting claims to western lands (see map, opposite page). States with charter claims to western territories planned to sell these lands to pay off their debts and reduce taxes.

States that had no claims to the Ohio Valley demanded that this area be placed under the jurisdiction of Congress. Unless this was done, land speculators in states without claims would find it nearly impossible to purchase large tracts of land in the West. In fact, Maryland refused to join the Confederation unless the western lands were surrendered to Congress. By 1781, however, states with land claims had surrendered them, and the Ohio Valley became a national domain.

The Land Ordinance of 1785. To develop and settle the West and to govern it, Congress devised a system that was set forth in two *ordinances*, or laws. The Land Ordinance of 1785 provided for the sale and orderly survey of the Ohio Valley (see diagram, page 80). A carefully surveyed frontier was designed to prevent squatting and avoid disputes over deeds. Congress also hoped that the low prices and relatively small parcels of land would attract small farmers.

Soon, however, land speculators, seeking to buy great tracts of western land, descended on Congress. The most persistent was a New England organization called the Ohio Company, which shrewdly included several Congressmen among its shareholders. The company wanted to buy one and a half million acres (about the area of the state of Delaware) at ten cents an acre, and also wanted

WESTERN LAND CLAIMS

BRITISH AMERICA

Claimed by Britain

L. SUPERIOR

MAINE
(PART OF MASS.)

VIRGINIA

L. HURON

N.Y.

N.H.

L. MICHIGAN

L. ONTARIO

MASS.

VA. AND MASS.

N.Y. AND MASS.

NEW YORK

CONN. R.I.

L. ERIE

VA. AND CONN.

CONN.

R.

PENNSYLVANIA

N.J.

Mississippi

Ohio R.

MD.

DEL.

VIRGINIA

VIRGINIA

Spanish Louisiana

NORTH CAROLINA

N. CAROLINA

NORTH CAROLINA

S. CAROLINA

SOUTH CAROLINA

R.

GEORGIA AND S. CAROLINA

GEORGIA

SOUTH CAROLINA

ATLANTIC OCEAN

Mississippi

Claimed by Spain and Ga.

Boundary dispute resolved by Pinckney Treaty of 1795

Spanish Florida

NORTHWEST TERRITORY
(with present-day state boundaries)

MINN.

L. SUPERIOR

MICH.

L. HURON

WIS.

L. MICHIGAN

R.

Mississippi

L. ERIE

ILL.

IND.

OHIO

Ohio R.

States

Disputed areas with foreign nations

Lands claimed by states

Northwest Territory

an option for an additional five million acres. Congress, desperate for money, agreed to the company's terms.

The Northwest Ordinance of 1787. Government for the West was provided by the Northwest Ordinance of 1787. The Ohio Valley region, established as the Northwest Territory, was to be divided into not less than three nor more than five territories. During its early years, each territory would be administered by a governor, a secretary, and three judges appointed by Congress. When a territory contained five thousand voters, it could organize a representative assembly and send a delegate to Congress. When the total population reached sixty thousand, a territorial convention was entitled to frame a state constitution and apply to Congress for admission into the Union. Thus, the United States would not have "colonies," but new additions to the federal government.

The Northwest Ordinance also provided for religious freedom and urged the establishment of educational institutions. In addition, it set forth such legal safeguards as *habeas corpus*, trial by jury, proportional representation, the inviolability of private contracts, and the prohibition of "cruel or unusual punishments." Such guarantees foreshadowed the Bill of Rights.

Another important provision of the ordinance was the prohibition of slavery in the Northwest Territory, establishing the precedent that Congress could determine the future of slavery in the West. The ordinance did stipulate, however, that fugitive slaves who entered the region must be returned to their masters. In 1787, the slavery issue provoked little controversy. Slavery was not profitable in most southern states, and many American leaders were convinced that it would gradually die out. Moreover, most late eighteenth-century Americans were more concerned with maintaining the fragile national unity than with abolishing slavery. In establishing a western policy, Congress ended the disputes over claims to the Ohio Valley and planned for the orderly

THE LAND ORDINANCE OF 1785: A TOWNSHIP SURVEY

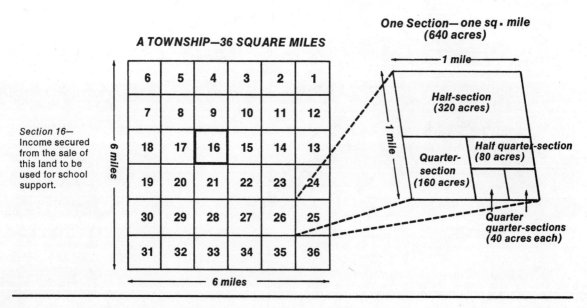

One Section—one sq . mile
(640 acres)

A TOWNSHIP—36 SQUARE MILES

Section 16—Income secured from the sale of this land to be used for school support.

1 mile

Half-section (320 acres)

Quarter-section (160 acres)

Half quarter-section (80 acres)

Quarter quarter-sections (40 acres each)

6 miles

expansion of the new nation. But problems remained, for other nations were also interested in exploiting the American West.

Diplomacy under the Confederation. American foreign policy during the mid-1780's was based upon two necessities—trade and security. American merchants hoped to resume their traditional pre-Revolution trade with British ports of the West Indies, and the more than seventy-five thousand pioneers who had settled in eastern Kentucky and Tennessee hoped to ship their products down the Mississippi River through Spanish-controlled territory to New Orleans. When Congress, therefore, attempted to secure commercial treaties with Great Britain and Spain, the negotiations were complicated by ominous security problems. Nations like Britain and Spain expected the American Confederation, with its weak government and almost nonexistent army, to collapse, and they paid little attention to its authority.

According to the peace treaty of 1783, several British garrisons south of the Great Lakes were to withdraw to Canada; Britain, however, ordered them to remain, primarily to retain control of the lucrative trade with the Indians and possibly to seize the Northwest Territory if the American government collapsed. Western settlers, who believed that the British supplied arms to the Indians and encouraged attacks along the frontier, demanded the removal of the British forts. The British ignored the protests of John Adams, the American minister to Britain, and Congress did not have the power to compel British withdrawal. Adams also failed to negotiate a commercial treaty allowing American ships to trade in the West Indies; the British refused to enter into a treaty with a nation that could not enforce it.

Spain, which feared the expansion of the new nation, also had ambitions in the West. It disputed the southern boundary lines established by the treaty of 1783 and plotted to detach settlers in Kentucky and Tennessee from the Confederation. Spain denied American barges the right to float produce down the Mississippi to New Orleans and also supplied Indian tribes with arms, keeping the southern frontier in a constant state of warfare.

John Jay, the secretary of foreign affairs, played into Spain's hands when in 1785 he negotiated a treaty in which the United States would stop using the Mississippi for twenty-five years in return for favorable trade arrangements in the Spanish West Indies. This scheme, which would have benefitted merchants in New York (Jay's home state) and New England, so infuriated the West that Congress hastily rejected it. Many westerners were convinced that the government was ignoring their needs.

The diplomacy of the Confederation, then, was unsuccessful. Unless the United States could establish firm control over its western lands and secure more favorable trade arrangements with Britain and Spain, its economic prospects and national future appeared bleak. It is small wonder that George Washington exclaimed, "How then can we fail in a little time, becoming the sport of European politics and the victims of our own folly."

Problems of finances. Congress had hoped to pay the expenses of the national government by selling western land. Prospective settlers, however, would buy land only if Congress could remove the British, defeat the Indians, and secure permission from Spain to ship produce down the Mississippi. In addition, financial affairs were further complicated by the refusal of state governments to permit Congress to levy a tariff to help pay the nation's bills.

By 1786, the foreign debt amounted to $10 million, a huge amount for a new nation with no reliable source of income. In that year, Congress was not even able to pay the interest owed to France. However, Dutch bankers, who considered the western lands excellent security, were still willing to extend loans to America. Congress always managed to pay interest owed to them. Congress also had inherited a large domestic debt from the American Revolution, how large no one knew exactly. Much of the debt was in the form of certificates used to pay the army. They were meant to be redeemed by Congress in specie, but the Confederation government never had enough gold and silver to pay the holders. As a result, the value of the certificates fell sharply, and they were bought up by speculators, who then demanded that Congress pay its obligations.

To the national debt was added that of the state governments, which was in the form of bonds sold by the states to finance the Revolution. The states made tremendous efforts to reduce their own debts, and in so doing, they generally cut down or ignored altogether requests from Congress for money. The only way the states could raise money to pay off these debts was by imposing tariffs on interstate commerce or by property taxes, which were to be paid in specie. Throughout the 1780's, property taxes rose steadily, and farmers whose land was being taxed to pay off the debt saw their cash going to support the merchants and lawyers who held the bonds. Many farmers had to mortgage their lands, and their creditors demanded regular payments.

In 1786, the financial burden became too great for the farmers of western Massachusetts to bear, and they rebelled. Led by Daniel Shays, a group of farmers closed the state courts and marched on the arsenal at Springfield. There they were defeated by the state militia, and Shays's Rebellion collapsed. Discontent continued to smoulder, however, and in other states the plight of the farmer was equally grim. And property holders were terrified that a civil war might be in the making.

Demands for change. Today it is easy to understand the confusion of the Confederation period. Some historians have emphasized the chaos, the failures in diplomacy and finance, the threats of secession in the West, and the tumult of Shays's Rebellion, calling the years between 1783 and 1787 a "critical period," fraught with national humiliation and anarchy. Others have pointed out that in many ways the Confederation did succeed. Under this weak system of government, the Revolutionary War was fought and won. Certainly the land ordinances were products of sound statesmanship. The intrigues of Britain and Spain in the West never affected the large majority of the people. Shays's Rebellion, these historians argue, was not a revolution, but an isolated outbreak.

By 1786, however, some Americans strongly felt that the Confederation had been a disaster. For years, Alexander Hamilton, a former aide-de-camp to Washington and a prominent New York politician, had been convinced that the Confederation had brought the United States "to the last stage of national nothingness." The voice that resounded most clearly for change was that of George Washington. "If the powers of Congress are inadequate," he declared, "amend or alter them, but do not let us sink into the lowest state of humiliation and contempt, and become a byword in all the earth."

In every state, groups of men, called nationalists, worked to create a strong government. They were horrified by the possibility of more outbreaks similar to Shays's revolt. They were angered by the maneuvers of Britain and Spain in the West, alarmed by the inability of Congress to establish sound finances, and disturbed by its failure to work out a commercial treaty with Britain. Above all, they feared that America might collapse into thirteen feeble, jealous, and quarrelsome republics—their greatest fear was disunion.

2 The Constitution Strengthens The Union

1. What were the major issues separating the delegates attending the Constitutional Convention, and how were these issues resolved?

2. Why did the anti-Federalists oppose the Constitution?

3. What were the arguments given by the Federalists in support of the Constitution?

4. How did the Federalists secure the ratification of the Constitution?

Perhaps the chief defect of the Confederation was the disunity among the states caused by economic quarrels. New York, for example, levied heavy duties on goods shipped to other states via New York City's harbor; Virginia and Maryland quarreled over maritime control of the Chesapeake Bay and the Potomac River. These interstate disputes made it clear to many that the Articles of Confederation were inadequate, and that a stronger national government was essential.

Decision to act. In January 1786, nationalists

led by James Madison convinced the Virginia legislature that all thirteen states, with their different tariffs and their maritime disputes, must establish a standardized commercial policy. Virginia then called for a convention of all states to meet at Annapolis, Maryland, to discuss the regulation of commerce. When the convention met in September, James Madison and Alexander Hamilton persuaded the delegates that the root of the problem was Congress' lack of power to create a common commercial policy. The delegates unanimously adopted a blunt resolution stating that "there are important defects in the system of Federal Government...." The Annapolis Convention suggested that Congress call a general meeting of the states "to devise such further provisions as shall appear ... necessary to render the constitution of the Federal Government adequate to the exigencies of the Union." Congress agreed, and in February 1787, sent out a call for a convention to meet in Philadelphia in May to amend the Articles of Confederation.

The states responded in various ways. Rhode Island, prospering at this time, flatly refused to participate. New Hampshire, apathetic toward national issues, did not bother to choose a delegation until June. Governor George Clinton of New York, unwilling to surrender his state's economic independence, was hostile to any move designed to strengthen the federal government. He sent a delegation composed of men committed to the principle of *states' rights,* that is, the theory that the sovereignty of states is more important than the power of a national government. The other states responded favorably, although Maryland and Delaware, concerned for the equality of small states with larger, forbade their delegations to agree to any alteration of the system of one vote for each state in Congress.

The Constitutional Convention meets. When Thomas Jefferson, then the American ambassador to France, saw the list of the fifty-five men who attended the Constitutional Convention, he wrote to John Adams, "It is an assembly of demigods!" While the delegates were not godlike, they were a remarkably seasoned group of political thinkers, men who combined an acute knowledge of constitutional theory with practical experience in government.

Three of the delegates had participated in the Stamp Act Congress, and eight had signed the Declaration of Independence. Forty-two had served in Congress, and thirty had fought under George Washington in the Revolution. Nearly half the delegates had helped to write state constitutions. In short, they had experienced the growing pains of the Republic, and were well aware that something was radically wrong with the Articles of Confederation.

Many of the delegates arrived in Philadelphia believing that their task was merely to correct some of the defects of the Articles. The nationalists electrified the Convention on May 29 when they presented a plan for an entirely new government. Written by James Madison, the "Virginia Plan" flatly repudiated the Confederation concept of government. It called for a Congress with the power not only to levy taxes, but also to nullify state laws contrary to a federal constitution. According to Madison's plan, Congress would consist of two houses, one of whose members would be elected by the people of each state and one whose members would be appointed by state legislatures. Representation in Congress would be in proportion to "the number of free inhabitants" in each state, which would give large states more power in Congress. The Virginia Plan also gave Congress the authority to elect separate executive and judicial branches.

While the delegates failed to adopt the Virginia Plan, the convention did adopt a resolution repudiating the Articles of Confederation and declared "that a *national* government ought to be established consisting of a *supreme* legislative, executive and judiciary." It soon became clear that three vital issues were to be bitterly disputed— representation, the powers of the executive branch, and slavery.

The structure of Congress. The most important question concerned the nature and structure of Congress. Was it to be a powerful body which had national authority and was based on proportional representation, or was Congress to continue as it was under the Confederation? William Paterson of New Jersey introduced his own plan, which would preserve the one state, one vote structure, although it would give Congress more power to regulate commerce and raise money.

The New Jersey Plan, he argued, would maintain the equality of the states.

This difficult issue was resolved by Roger Sherman of Connecticut. Under the terms of the Connecticut Compromise the upper house of Congress, or the Senate, retained the Confederation principle of equal representation for each state; representation in the lower house, or House of Representatives, was to be determined by population. Senators were to be chosen by state legislatures, representatives by direct popular vote. According to this compromise, the nationalists secured a legislative body directly representing the people, and the advocates of states' rights were satisfied in their belief that senators would faithfully defend the interests of the state governments.

The powers of the Presidency. The second great problem faced by the convention dealt with the nature and powers of the Presidency. The nationalists favored a strong executive branch, with a popularly elected President exercising the right to veto congressional legislation. On the other hand, states' rights advocates, who regarded Congress as the most important part of the national government, wanted a weak executive. To prevent too great a concentration of power, Paterson's New Jersey Plan suggested that executive powers be exercised by a committee elected by Congress and subject to dismissal by a majority vote of state governors.

In the convention, the nationalists won the debate with relative ease, adopting a recommendation of a special "committee on detail." The committee proposed that the President be chosen by a special group of electors in each state who could either be appointed by the state legislature or elected by the people. The President was to have the power of veto (but Congress could override his veto by a two-thirds majority) and he was to be commander-in-chief of the army and navy.

The status of slaves. The third major convention dispute related to the status of slaves. The southern delegates advocated two contradictory principles. When representation in the House of Representatives was being considered, they insisted that blacks were human beings and ought to be counted in apportioning delegates. When

it was suggested, however, that taxes be levied by Congress according to population, southerners contended that slaves were not human beings, but property.

The compromise on this issue clearly revealed that a majority of northern delegates were not prepared to jeopardize the creation of a viable national union by demanding the abolition of slavery. The convention decided that both taxes and representation in the House would be apportioned among the states on the basis of all adult free males plus three-fifths of "all other persons." With these major stumbling blocks removed, the Constitution was signed on September 17, 1787, and sent to Congress for transmission to special state conventions for ratification. The future of the United States was now in the hands of its people.

Opposition to the Constitution. Nationalists, now called Federalists, watched in alarm as opposition to the new Constitution gathered swiftly. In every state, Anti-Federalists, as opponents of the Constitution were called, included famous and powerful men: Samuel Adams and John Hancock of Massachusetts, Governor Clinton of New York, Patrick Henry of Virginia, all opposed ratification. Some Anti-Federalists argued that if the Constitution was ratified, a strong national government, dominated by small groups of dangerous politicians, would control the destinies of the American people. Had the United States thrown off British tyranny merely to create an American version of the British Parliament?

Other critics were confused by the Constitution's phraseology. The government it envisioned appeared to be neither a confederation nor a highly centralized government patterned on European models. Precisely what did such phrases as "We the people," "The general welfare," and "necessary and proper" mean? Until such vague concepts, which might be used to undermine the power of the states, were carefully defined and limited, Anti-Federalists were not willing to support ratification.

Finally, all opponents of the Constitution objected to the absence of a Bill of Rights. The Anti-Federalists regarded themselves as the defenders of the principles for which the Revolution had been fought. Basic to their understanding of politics was a conviction that governmental power, always exercised by corrupt men, is dangerous; citizens must be protected against the government's tendency to destroy liberty. This could be done in two ways. First, the structure of government could be made weak, as under the Articles of Confederation. Second, citizens could be protected by a Bill of Rights, which legally restricted the activities of government, forbidding it to hamper the free exercise of certain natural rights (the "inalienable rights" mentioned in the Declaration of Independence).

Federalists defend the Constitution. The Federalists, led by Washington, Madison, and Hamilton, conducted a well-organized campaign of promotion and politics. Most newspapers favored the Constitution, and the wealthy and educated part of the populace, seeking financial stability and social order, poured out letters and pamphlets supporting it. *The Federalist Papers,* written as newspaper columns by Madison, Hamilton, and John Jay, were the most famous of these defenses of the Constitution.

Government, the Federalists insisted, must be so constructed that it can both protect the commerce and security of the nation and at the same time preserve political and human rights. The great danger to republican government comes from selfish factions which attempt to manipulate it for their own ends. Such a possibility, the Federalists maintained, could not occur under the Constitution. A system of checks and balances carefully divided power between the executive, legislative, and judicial branches of the government and made it virtually impossible for any small faction to gain control. The greatest defense of liberty, the Federalists continued, was not a Bill of Rights, but a frame of government designed to prevent the abuse of power.

In addition to being accomplished political theorists, the Federalists were also shrewd politicians. They recognized that Massachusetts, Virginia, and New York were the most crucial states. Not only were these the largest states, but they dominated geographical regions. If New York or Virginia refused to join the Union, it would be split in two. Moreover, these states dominated the economy of the United States, and without them the Union would founder in financial chaos.

In Massachusetts, the Federalists convinced John Hancock to support the Constitution by promising him the Vice-Presidency. Samuel Adams gave his support when Federalists promised to secure a Bill of Rights. In the Massachusetts ratifying convention, the support of Hancock and Adams proved crucial.

The Constitution is ratified. When Massachusetts finally ratified in 1788, five states had already approved the new Constitution, and others followed. In June of 1788, New Hampshire proudly became the ninth state to ratify, thus putting the Constitution into operation.

The Union would collapse, however, unless Virginia and New York joined. The ratifying conventions of both states were dominated by Anti-Federalists because powerful state leaders—especially Patrick Henry of Virginia and Governor George Clinton of New York—dominated the rural areas. And traditionally, rural areas supported a states' rights, anti "big government," philosophy. The state political leaders furiously resisted any increase in federal power. The Federalists, however, advanced one basic argument the Anti-Federalists could not counter: what would become of the states of Virginia and New York without a union?

In the Old Dominion, James Madison and young John Marshall, later chief justice of the United States, debated sharply with Patrick Henry on the basic issue: "Union or no Union." Confronted by such a stark choice, Virginia narrowly voted to accept the Constitution. In New York, Alexander Hamilton argued that New York would be isolated and discriminated against by a hostile Constitutional government. Hamilton suggested that the City of New York, which favored ratification, might withdraw from the state and join the new nation. On July 26, by another close vote, New York joined the Union.

The Constitution was completed with the addition of the first ten amendments, the Bill of Rights. Many states had made their ratification conditional upon such amendments, and among the first acts of the new Congress was the passage of the Bill of Rights in September 1789. When the Bill of Rights was ratified by the states in 1791, Rhode Island and North Carolina joined the new nation.

The Constitution
Of The United States

(Each part of the Constitution is printed with a commentary in bold face. Portions with lines through them have gone out of date or have been changed by amendment.)

■ PREAMBLE

We the People of the United States, in Order to form a more perfect Union, establish Justice, insure domestic Tranquility, provide for the common defence, promote the general Welfare, and secure the Blessings of Liberty to ourselves and our Posterity, do ordain and establish this CONSTITUTION for the United States of America.

The Preamble is an introduction which explains the purposes of the Constitution. It has no legal force.

■ ARTICLE 1. THE LEGISLATIVE BRANCH

SECTION 1. CONGRESS

All legislative Powers herein granted shall be vested in a Congress of the United States, which shall consist of a Senate and House of Representatives.

***The law-making body.* All federal laws are to be made by the Congress, which consists of two houses—the Senate and the House of Representatives.**

SECTION 2. THE HOUSE OF REPRESENTATIVES

1. The House of Representatives shall be composed of Members chosen every second Year by the People of the several States, and the Electors in each State shall have the Qualifications requisite for Electors of the most numerous Branch of the State Legislature.

***Election of members.* Members of the House of Representatives serve two-year terms. The term *electors* is here used to refer to voters. Voters in each state who are eligible to vote for members of the state's largest legislative branch may vote for members of the national House of Representatives.**

2. No Person shall be a Representative who shall not have attained to the Age of twenty-five Years, and been seven Years a Citizen of the United States, and who shall not, when elected, be an Inhabitant of that State in which he shall be chosen.

***Qualifications for Representatives.* A representative, must live within the state from which he is elected. Political custom also requires the representative to live within the district from which he is elected. In 1842, Congress passed a law requiring all members of the House of Representatives to be chosen by districts within each state.**

3. Representatives and direct Taxes shall be apportioned among the several States which may be included within this Union, according to their respective Numbers, ~~which shall be determined by adding to the whole Number of free Persons, including those bound to Service for a Term of Years, and excluding Indians not taxed, three fifths of all other persons~~. The actual Enumeration shall be made within three Years after the first Meeting of the Congress of the United States, and within every subsequent Term of ten Years, in such Manner as they shall by Law direct. The Number of Representatives shall not exceed one for every thirty thousand, but each State shall have at Least one Representative; ~~and until such enumeration shall be made, the State of New Hampshire shall be entitled to choose three, Massachusetts, eight, Rhode Island and Providence Plantations, one, Connecticut, five, New York, six, New Jersey, four, Pennsylvania, eight, Delaware, one, Maryland, six, Virginia, ten, North Carolina, five, South Carolina, five, and Georgia, three.~~

***Representation and taxation.* A census is to be taken every ten years in order to determine the number of representatives. Every representative must represent at least 30,000 people, but each state must have at least one representative. In order to prevent the House of Representatives from growing too large, Congress in 1929 limited the membership of the House to 435. In order to find out approximately how many people**

each representative represents, simply divide 435 into the total population of the United States.

Direct taxes, those which the citizen pays directly to the national government, are also to be apportioned according to the population of the states. But Congress has not levied a direct tax outside the District of Columbia since the Civil War with the important exception of the income tax. The Sixteenth Amendment (1913) permits this tax to be levied on individual incomes rather than basing it upon the populations of the states.

"Three fifths of all other Persons" refers to black slaves. The Fourteenth Amendment (1868) provides that all the people of a state, except for Indians not taxed, shall be counted in full in order to decide how many representatives that state may have.

4. When vacancies happen in the Representation from any State, the Executive Authority thereof shall issue Writs of Election to fill such Vacancies.

Filling vacancies. If a member of the House of Representatives dies or resigns, the voters of the state are guaranteed the right to choose his successor.

5. The House of Representatives shall choose their Speaker and other Officers; and shall have the sole Power of Impeachment.

Choosing a Speaker; impeachment. The Speaker is always a member of the House of Representatives, although the Constitution does not say that he must be.

"To impeach" means to bring an accusation against someone, in this case, an official of the United States—the President, the Vice President, a cabinet official, or a federal judge. Members of Congress may not be impeached since they have their own methods of censuring their members. Only the House of Representatives has the right to "impeach." The Senate tries all impeachment cases.

SECTION 3. THE SENATE

1. The Senate of the United States shall be composed of two Senators from each State, chosen by the Legislature thereof, for six Years, and each Senator shall have one Vote.

Number of senators, term, and vote. The Seventeenth Amendment (1913) gave the voters the right to elect their senators directly.

2. Immediately after they shall be assembled in Consequence of the first Election, they shall be divided as equally as may be into three Classes. The Seats of the Senators of the first Class shall be vacated at the Expiration of the second Year, of the second Class at the Expiration of the fourth Year, and of the third Class at the Expiration of the sixth Year, so that one-third may be chosen every second Year; and if Vacancies happen by Resignation, or otherwise, during the Recess of the Legislature of any State, the Executive thereof may make temporary Appointments until the next Meeting of the Legislature, which shall then fill the Vacancies.

Staggering senatorial elections. The first senators chosen are to divide themselves into three groups. The first group is to serve two years, the second four years, and the third six years. The purpose of this was to start the staggered system of electing one-third of the members of the Senate every two years. This would mean that there would always be an experienced group of men in the Senate. This original provision is now obsolete, and each senator serves a term of six years.

3. No person shall be a Senator who shall not have attained to the Age of thirty Years, and been nine Years a Citizen of the United States, and who shall not, when elected, be an Inhabitant of that State for which he shall be chosen.

Qualifications for senators. Compare this clause to SECTION 2, Clause 2.

4. The Vice President of the United States shall be President of the Senate, but shall have no Vote, unless they be equally divided.

The Senate president. Presiding over the Senate is the only Vice Presidential duty specified in the Constitution. He votes only to break a tie.

5. The Senate shall choose their other Officers, and also a President pro tempore, in the absence of the Vice President, or when he shall exercise the Office of President of the United States.

Choosing other Senate officers. If the Vice President is absent or has become President, the Senate chooses a president pro tempore (temporary). By custom, the president pro tempore is usually the ranking (greatest number of years in the Senate) member of the majority party. Like the House, the Senate may select its own officers.

6. The Senate shall have the sole Power to try all Impeachments. When sitting for that Purpose, they

shall be on Oath or Affirmation. When the President of the United States is tried, the Chief Justice shall preside; And no Person shall be convicted without the Concurrence of two thirds of the Members present.

Impeachment trials. **Only the Senate may try impeachment cases (see commentary for SECTION 2, Clause 5). As president of the Senate, the Vice President presides at all impeachment trials other than that of a President, at which the Chief Justice of the Supreme Court presides. The Vice President is exempted from presiding at such a trial to avoid the possibility that his own self interest might prevent him from conducting the trial fairly. In order to convict an impeached official, two-thirds of the senators present must vote guilty.**

7. Judgment in Cases of Impeachment shall not extend further than to removal from Office, and disqualification to hold and enjoy any Office of honor, Trust, or Profit under the United States: but the Party convicted shall nevertheless be liable and subject to Indictment, Trial, Judgment and Punishment, according to Law.

Penalty for conviction. **If the Senate finds an official guilty, it may only remove him from office and prevent him from holding any other federal office.**

SECTION 4. ELECTION AND MEETING
OF CONGRESS

1. The Times, Places and Manner of holding Elections for Senators and Representatives, shall be prescribed in each State by the Legislature thereof; but the Congress may at any time by Law make or alter such Regulations, except as to the Places of choosing Senators.

Congressional elections. **Congress has called nearly all federal elections for the first Tuesday after the first Monday in November, in the even-numbered years. Alaska is allowed to hold certain elections in October.**

2. The Congress shall assemble at least once in every Year, and such Meeting shall be on the first Monday in December, unless they shall by Law appoint a different Day.

Meetings of Congress. **The Twentieth Amendment (1933) changed the time to January 3.**

SECTION 5. CONGRESSIONAL ORGANIZATION
AND RULES

1. Each house shall be the Judge of the Elections, Returns and Qualifications of its own Members, and

a Majority of each shall constitute a Quorum to do Business; but a smaller Number may adjourn from day to day, and may be authorized to compel the Attendance of absent Members, in such Manner, and under such Penalties as each House may provide.

Seating new members; quorums. **Either the House or Senate may refuse to seat a new member-elect. Although the Constitution states that a majority of the members, or *quorum*, must be present in order to carry on business, business is frequently carried on without a quorum and can continue to be carried on as long as no member objects. Each house can compel the attendance of its members when their presence is needed.**

2. Each House may determine the Rules of its Proceedings, punish its Members for disorderly Behavior, and, with the Concurrence of two-thirds, expel a Member.

3. Each House shall keep a Journal of its Proceedings, and from time to time publish the same excepting such Parts as may in their Judgment require Secrecy; and the Yeas and Nays of the Members of either House on any question shall, at the desire of one-fifth of those Present, be entered on the Journal.

Records of congressional meetings. **Each house must keep a record of its proceedings. The *Congressional Record* is published for every day Congress is in session and records the actions of both houses. Members may vote to omit certain things from the *Record*. The vote of each member on a particular question—whether yes or no—is put into the *Record* if one-fifth of the members present want this to be done. The *Record* allows voters to see how their congressmen voted on any given bill.**

4. Neither House, during the Session of Congress, shall, without the Consent of the other, adjourn for more than three days, nor to any other Place than that in which the two Houses shall be sitting.

Adjournment. **Once Congress has met, the House and Senate must remain at work until both agree on a time to adjourn. Since they work closely together, they must both work in the same locality.**

SECTION 6. CONGRESSIONAL PRIVILEGES
AND RESTRICTIONS

1. The Senators and representatives shall receive a Compensation for their Services to be ascertained by Law, and paid out of the Treasury of the United States.

They shall in all Cases, except Treason, Felony and Breach of the peace, be privileged from Arrest during their Attendance at the Session of their respective Houses, and in going to and returning from the same; and for any Speech or Debate in either House, they shall not be questioned in any other Place.

Pay and privileges. **Members of Congress may not be arrested while attending a session, or while coming from or going to such a session, except for treason, breaking the peace, or a serious crime. This exemption from arrest has little importance today, although it may save a congressman now and then from a minor traffic ticket. The framers of the Constitution had in mind cases in Great Britain and the American colonies when legislators were arrested simply to keep them from performing their duties. The phrase "they shall not be questioned in any other Place" means that congressmen cannot be sued for libel or slander while they are debating in either house. The purpose of this provision is to give members of Congress the greatest possible freedom of debate. These privileges, called *congressional immunity*, are meant to give congressmen freedom in carrying out their duties.**

2. No Senator or Representative shall, during the Time for which he was elected, be appointed to any civil Office under the Authority of the United States, which shall have been created, or the Emoluments whereof shall have been increased, during such time; and no Person holding any Office under the United States, shall be a Member of either House during his Continuance in Office.

Restrictions. **If Congress creates a new office or raises the salary of an old one, no member of Congress may fill that office until his term expires. This provision prevents congressmen from voting themselves into higher-paying jobs. Nor can a congressman hold a position in either the executive or judicial branches.**

SECTION 7. HOW BILLS BECOME LAWS

1. All Bills for raising Revenue shall originate in the House of Representatives; but the Senate may propose or concur with Amendments as on other Bills.

Tax bills. **Most bills can be started in either the Senate or the House of Representatives. However, bills for raising money by taxes may be started only in the House. This provision has little practical importance, however, since the Senate may amend such bills.**

2. Every Bill which shall have passed the House of Representatives and the Senate, shall, before it becomes a Law, be presented to the President of the United States; If he approve he shall sign it, but if not he shall return it, with his Objections to that House in which it shall have originated, who shall enter the Objections at large on their Journal, and proceed to reconsider it. If after such Reconsideration two thirds of that House shall agree to pass the Bill it shall be sent, together with the Objections, to the other House, by which it shall likewise be reconsidered, and if approved by two thirds of that House, it shall become a Law. But in all such Cases the Votes of both Houses shall be determined by Yeas and Nays, and the Names of the Persons voting for and against the Bill shall be entered on the Journal of each House respectively. If any Bill shall not be returned by the President within ten Days (Sundays excepted) after it shall have been presented to him, the Same shall be a Law, in like Manner as if he had signed it, unless the Congress by their Adjournment prevent its Return, in which Case it shall not be a Law.

How a bill is passed or vetoed. **When both the Senate and the House of Representatives have voted in favor of a bill, it is sent to the President of the United States. If he is in favor of the bill, he signs it and the bill then becomes law. But if the President opposes the bill, he *vetoes* it, that is he refuses to sign it. The President then sends the bill back to the house where it started, usually with a written message stating his objections to the bill. If the two houses pass the bill by a two-thirds margin, they can *override* the President's veto. That is, the bill becomes law without the President's approval. But if they fail to pass the bill by the two-thirds margin in both houses, the President's veto is *sustained* and the bill does not become law. In such cases, the vote of each member of Congress must be recorded. (In actual practice, when the President vetoes a bill, it is usually killed. Overriding the President's veto is usually difficult since it is very hard to obtain the necessary two-thirds vote.)**

When the President receives a bill passed by both houses and keeps it for ten days (not counting Sundays) without either signing it or vetoing it, it becomes an official law. But if Congress adjourns within the ten-day period, it does not become law. This is called the *pocket veto* and is designed to protect the President against having to consider a large number of bills at the end of the session. A bill so vetoed

BRANCHES OF THE FEDERAL GOVERNMENT

LEGISLATIVE BRANCH

Senate
Standing Committees
Aeronautical and Space Sciences
Agriculture and Forestry
Appropriations
Armed Services
Banking and Currency
Commerce
District of Columbia
Finance
Foreign Relations
Government Operations
Interior and Insular Affairs
Judiciary
Labor and Public Welfare
Post Office and Civil Service
Public Works
Rules and Administration

House of Representatives
Standing Committees
Agriculture
Appropriations
Armed Services
Banking and Currency
District of Columbia
Education and Labor
Foreign Affairs
Government Operations
House Administration
Interior and Insular Affairs
Internal Security

Rules
Science and Astronautics
Standards of Official Conduct
Veterans Affairs
Ways and Means
Interstate and Foreign Commerce
Judiciary
Merchant Marine and Fisheries
Post Office and Civil Service
Public Works

EXECUTIVE BRANCH

Executive Departments
Agriculture
Commerce
Defense
Health, Education and Welfare
Housing and Urban Development
Interior
Justice
Labor
Post Office
State
Transportation
Treasury

Administrative Conference of the
  United States
American Battle Monuments
  Commission
Appalachian Regional Commission
Atomic Energy Commission
Canal Zone Government
Civil Aeronautics Board
Commission of Fine Arts
Delaware River Basin Commission
District of Columbia
Equal Employment Opportunity
  Commission
Export-Import Bank of the
  United States
Farm Credit Administration
Federal Coal Mine Safety Board
  of Review
Federal Communications Commission

The Executive Office
The White House Office
Bureau of the Budget
Council of Economic Advisors
Council for Urban Affairs
National Security Council
National Aeronautics and
  Space Council

National Council for Marine
  Resources and Engineering
  Development
Office of Emergency Preparedness
Office of Science and Technology
Office of the Special Representative
  for Trade Negotiations
Office of Intergovernmental Relations

Independent Agencies
Federal Deposit Insurance Corporation
Federal Home Loan Bank Board
Federal Maritime Commission
Federal Mediation and Conciliation
  Service
Federal Power Commission
Federal Reserve System, Board of
  Governors of the
Federal Trade Commission
Foreign Claims Settlement Commission
  of the United States
Foreign Trade Zones Board
General Services Administration
Indian Claims Commission
Interstate Commerce Commission
National Aeronautics and Space
  Administration
National Foundation on the Arts
  and the Humanities

National Labor Relations Board
National Mediation Board
National Science Foundation
Panama Canal Company
Railroad Retirement Board
Renegotiation Board
Securities and Exchange Commission
Selective Service System
Small Business Administration
Smithsonian Institution
Subversive Activities Control Board
Tax Court of the United States
Tennessee Valley Authority
United States Arms Control
  and Disarmament Agency
United States Civil Service Commission
United States Information Agency
United States Tariff Commission
Veterans Administration

JUDICIAL BRANCH
The Supreme Court of the United States

Lower Courts
Circuit Courts of Appeals
  of the United States
District Courts of the United States

Special Courts
United States Court of Claims
United States Court of Customs
  and Patent Appeals

United States Customs Court
Territorial Courts
United States Court of Military Appeals

cannot be overridden; it must be introduced all over again in the next session of Congress.

The Presidential veto is an important check of the executive branch of the government over the legislative branch. Congress checks the President on the rare occasions when it overrides a veto.

3. Presidential approval or veto. Every Order, Resolution, or Vote to which the Concurrence of the Senate and House of Representatives may be necessary (except on a question of Adjournment) shall be presented to the President of the United States; and before the Same shall take Effect, shall be approved by him, or being disapproved by him, shall be repassed by two thirds of the Senate and House of Representatives, according to the Rules and Limitations prescribed in the Case of a Bill.

Other acts of Congress. Congress does not need Presidential approval to propose an amendment to the Constitution.

SECTION 8. POWER GIVEN TO CONGRESS

The Congress shall have Power
1. To lay and collect Taxes, Duties, Imposts and Excises, to pay the Debts and provide for the common Defence and general Welfare of the United States; but all Duties, Imposts and Excises shall be uniform throughout the United States;

To levy taxes. **Congress has the power to levy taxes to pay the nation's debts, to provide for national defense, and to provide for general welfare of the people. All federal taxes must be equal in various parts of the country.**

2. To borrow Money on the Credit of the United States;
To borrow money. The Constitution sets no limit on the amount Congress can borrow—Congress itself sets the national debt.

3. To regulate Commerce with foreign Nations, and among the several States, and with the Indian Tribes;

To regulate commerce. **Congress has the power to regulate trade with foreign nations. It also has direct control over interestate commerce; among its powers it can regulate transportation, radio and television broadcasting, and the stock markets.**

4. To establish a uniform Rule of Naturalization, and uniform Laws on the subject of Bankruptcies throughout the United States;

To make laws about naturalization and bankruptcy. **Congress can decide how immigrants become citizens. It can also make laws about procedures involved in business failures.**

5. To coin Money, regulate the Value thereof, and of foreign Coin, and fix the Standard of Weights and Measures;

To coin money and fix weights and measures. **Congress can mint coins, print paper money, and set the value of both American money and foreign currency within this country. It can also set standard measurements for the nation.**

6. To provide for the Punishment of counterfeiting the Securities and current Coin of the United States;

To punish counterfeiters. **Congress can make laws fixing the punishment for counterfeiting currency, bonds, or stamps.**

7. To establish Post Offices and post Roads;

To build post offices and roads. **Congress can grant money to states for road construction. It also uses this clause to aid railroads, shipping lines, and airlines.**

8. To promote the Progress of Science and useful Arts, by securing for limited Times to Authors and Inventors the exclusive Right to their respective Writings and Discoveries;

To govern patents and copyrights. **Congress can pass patent and copyright laws to give the sole rights to inventors and artists for their works for a number of years. Anyone who uses patented inventions or copyrighted material without permission may be punished.**

9. To constitute Tribunals inferior to the supreme Court;

To establish lower federal courts. **All federal courts except the Supreme Court are established by acts of Congress.**

10. To define and Punish Piracies and Felonies committed on the high Seas, and Offenses against the Law of Nations;

To regulate crimes at sea and against international laws. **Congress can decide what acts committed on American ships are crimes and how such acts should be punished. It can also decide the punishment for American citizens who break international laws.**

11. To declare War, ~~grant Letters of Marque and Reprisal,~~ and make Rules concerning Captures on Land and Water;

To declare war. **Only Congress may declare war. However, American forces have engaged in combat in some instances without a congressional declaration of war, for example, in the Vietnam war. *Letters of marque and reprisal* refers to permission granted to American merchant ships to attack enemy ships, a practice common in early wars.**

12. To raise and support Armies, but no Appropriation of Money to that Use shall be for a longer Term than two Years;

To raise and support armies. **All money for the army comes from Congress. However, Congress may not grant money to the army for longer than a two-year period. This is to make sure that civilians (nonmilitary people) will have financial control over the army.**

13. To provide and maintain a Navy;

To raise and support a navy. **There is no two-year limit on naval appropriations because the navy was not considered a threat to liberty.**

14. To make Rules for the Government and Regulation of the land and naval Forces;

To regulate the armed forces. **Such rules now include the Air Force. Since Congress can create the armed forces, it is necessary to give it the power to make rules for the services.**

15. To provide for calling forth the Militia to execute the Laws of the Union, suppress Insurrections, and repel Invasions;

To call out the militia. **Congress can call into federal service the state militia forces (citizen-soldiers now referred to as the National Guard) to enforce federal laws and defend life and property. Congress can empower the President to call out the militia, but only for the reasons named here.**

16. To provide for organizing, arming, and disciplining the Militia, and for governing such Part of them as may be employed in the Service of the United States, reserving to the States respectively, the Appointment of the Officers, and the Authority of training the Militia according to the discipline prescribed by Congress;

To regulate the militia. **The states may appoint the officers for the militia, but Congress establishes rules for training the militia.**

17. To exercise exclusive Legislation in all Cases whatsoever, over such District (not exceeding ten Miles square) as may, by Cession of particular States, and the acceptance of Congress, become the Seat of the Government of the United States, and to exercise like Authority over all Places purchased by the Consent of the Legislature of the State in which the Same shall be, for the Erection of Forts, Magazines, Arsenals, dock-Yards, and other needful Buildings;

To govern the federal capital. **Congress makes all laws for the capital. District of Columbia officials are appointed by Congress and people in the district do not have the right to elect the officials of their local government. For many years people in the District have fought for "Home Rule"—the right to govern themselves through their elected officials. This fight has not been successful although the Twenty-third Amendment (1961) gives people in the District the right to vote in Presidential elections.**

18. —And
To make all Laws which shall be necessary and proper for carrying into Execution the foregoing Powers, and all other Powers vested by this Constitution in the Government of the United States, or in any Department or Officer thereof.

To exercise its powers. **Congress can make laws which are needed to carry out the powers the Constitution has given it. Of course, these laws are subject to review by the judicial branch. Because this paragraph has been stretched to cover so many acts of Congress, it is called the *elastic clause.***

SECTION 9. POWERS DENIED TO THE CONGRESS

1. ~~The Migration or Importation of such Persons as any of the States now existing shall think proper to admit, shall not be prohibited by the Congress prior to the Year one thousand eight hundred and eight, but a tax or duty may be imposed on such Importation, not exceeding ten dollars for each Person.~~

Importation of slaves. **Congress could not prohibit the importation of slaves before 1808.**

2. The Privilege of the Writ of Habeas Corpus shall not be suspended, unless when in Cases of Rebellion or Invasion the public Safety may require it.

DISTRIBUTION OF GOVERNMENT POWERS

Federal Government	State Government	Both
Regulate interstate and foreign commerce	Regulate voting laws and procedures	Collect taxes
Make citizenship laws	Establish and maintain public education	Borrow money
Coin money	Make marriage and divorce laws	Set criminal laws
Set weights and measures	Make corporation laws	Charter banks
Run postal system	Make traffic laws	Take property for public purposes (eminent domain)
Regulate copyrights and patents	Regulate intrastate commerce	
Establish lower courts	Grant return of criminals and suspects	
Declare war		
Establish and support armed forces		

Habeus Corpus. **A writ of** *habeus corpus* **is an order demanding that a person who is arrested be brought before a court so a judge can decide if he is being held lawfully. Congress may not suspend this right except in cases of rebellion or grave national danger.**

3. No Bill of Attainder or ex post facto Law shall be passed.

Bills of attainder and ex post facto laws. **A bill of attainder is a law that declares someone guilty of a crime and orders him punished without a trial. An ex post facto law declares an act a crime after it has been committed.**

4. No capitation or other direct Tax shall be laid, unless in Proportion to the Census or Enumeration herein before directed to be taken.

Direct Taxes. **Congress must divide direct taxes among the states according to their populations. The Sixteenth Amendment (1913) makes it possible for Congress to levy a tax on individual incomes without regard to state population.**

5. No Tax or Duty shall be laid on Articles exported from any State.

No tariffs on exports. **Congress can tax imports, but not exports.**

6. No Preference shall be given by any Regulation of Commerce or Revenue to the Ports of one State over those of another: nor shall Vessels bound to, or from, one State, be obliged to enter, clear, or pay Duties in another.

No favored ports. **No port in any state is to have preference over any other. Ships going from state to state may not be taxed by Congress.**

7. No Money shall be drawn from the Treasury, but in Consequence of Appropriations made by Law; and a regular Statement and Account of the Receipts and Expenditures of all public Money shall be published from time to time.

Public spending. **Only Congress can grant permission for money to be spent from the Treasury. Congress must publish statements from time to time showing how much money was paid out and how much was taken in.**

8. No Title of Nobility shall be granted by the United States: And no Person holding any Office of Profit or Trust under them, shall, without the Consent of the Congress, accept of any present, Emolument, Office, or Title, of any kind whatever, from any King, Prince, or foreign State.

Titles of nobility; favors from foreign governments. **This clause prohibits the establishment of a noble class and discourages the possibility of American officials being bribed by foreign governments.**

SECTION 10. POWERS DENIED TO STATES

1. No State shall enter into any Treaty, Alliance, or Confederation; grant Letters of Marque and Reprisal; coin Money; emit Bills of Credit; make any Thing but gold and silver Coin a Tender in Payment of Debts; pass any Bill of Attainder, ex post facto Law, or Law

impairing the Obligation of Contracts, or grant any Title of Nobility.

Powers forbidden the states. No states may make treaties or issue letters of marque and reprisal (see SECTION 8, Clause 11). States are forbidden to issue money. They cannot pass bills of attainder or ex post facto laws (see SECTION 9, Clause 3). States may not pass laws that would destroy the legal contracts which individuals make with each other, nor can they grant titles of nobility.

2. No State shall, without the Consent of Congress, lay any Imposts or Duties on Imports or Exports, except what may be absolutely necessary for executing its inspection Laws: and the net Produce of all Duties and Imposts, laid by any State on Imports or Exports, shall be for the Use of the Treasury of the United States and all such Laws shall be subject to the Revision and Control of the Congress.

Import and export taxes. States cannot interfere with commerce by taxing goods, although they may charge fees for inspecting such goods. Any such inspection fees must be paid into the Treasury of the United States. Also, all duties and taxes on imports and exports must be paid into the Treasury of the United States. Therefore all tariff revenue goes to the national government and not to the states.

3. No State shall, without the Consent of Congress, lay any Duty of Tonnage, keep Troops, or Ships of War in time of Peace, enter into any Agreement or Compact with another State, or with a foreign Power, or engage in War, unless actually invaded, or in such imminent Danger as will not admit of Delay.

Further limits on states' powers. These further restrictions are laid upon the states to strengthen the authority of the United States government.

■ **ARTICLE 2. THE EXECUTIVE BRANCH**

SECTION 1. PRESIDENT AND VICE PRESIDENT

1. The executive Power shall be vested in a President of the United States of America. He shall hold his Office during the Term of four Years, and, together with the Vice President, chosen for the same Term, be elected, as follows.

Term of office. This clause gives executive power to a President of the United States who is to serve for a term of four years.

2. Each State shall appoint, in such Manner as the Legislature thereof may direct, a Number of Electors, equal to the whole number of Senators and Representatives to which the State may be entitled in the Congress; but no Senator or Representative, or Person holding an Office of Trust or Profit under the United States, shall be appointed an Elector.

3. The Electors shall meet in their respective States, and vote by Ballot for two persons, of whom one at least shall not be an Inhabitant of the same State with themselves. And they shall make a List of all the Persons voted for, and of the Number of Votes for each; which List they shall sign and certify, and transmit sealed to the Seat of the Government of the United States, directed to the President of the Senate. The President of the Senate shall, in the Presence of the Senate and House of Representatives, open all the Certificates, and the Votes shall then be counted. The Person having the greatest number of Votes shall be the President, if such Number be a Majority of the whole Number of Electors appointed; and if there be more than one who have such Majority, and have an Equal Number of Votes, then the House of Representatives shall immediately choose by Ballot one of them for President; and if no Person have a Majority, then from the five highest on the List the said House shall in like Manner choose the President, but in choosing the President, the Votes shall be taken by States, the Representation from each State having one Vote; A quorum for this Purpose shall consist of a Member or Members from two-thirds of the States, and a Majority of all the States shall be necessary to a Choice. In every Case, after the Choice of the President, the Person having the greatest Number of Votes of the Electors shall be the Vice President. But if there should remain two or more who have equal Votes, the Senate shall choose from them by Ballot the Vice President.

The electoral system. The people are not permitted to elect the President directly. Instead, a special group of electors is to elect the chief executive. Originally, the state legislatures chose the electors, but since 1828 they have generally been nominated by the political parties and elected by the people. The electors from all the states make up the electoral college, though they never meet as a single group. Each state has as many electors as it has senators and representatives. Thus, states with larger populations have more votes in the election of the President. No member of Congress or office-holder of the United States may be an elector.

This system provided that each elector vote for two candidates, with the man receiving the largest number of votes (providing it was a majority) becoming President and the runner-up becoming Vice President. However, in 1800 the two top candidates tied, making it necessary for the House to choose the President. The Twelfth Amendment (1804) was passed to make it impossible for the same situation to recur.

4. The Congress may determine the Time of choosing the Electors, and the Day on which they shall give their Votes; which Day shall be the same throughout the United States.

Dates for choosing electors and for electors to vote. **Congress has ordered electors to be chosen on the first Monday after the first Tuesday in November.**

5. No Person except a natural born Citizen, or a Citizen of the United States, at the time of the Adoption of this Constitution, shall be eligible to the Office of President; neither shall any Person be eligible to that Office who shall not have attained to the Age of thirty-five Years, and been fourteen Years a Resident within the United States.

Qualifications for President. **To become President, one must be a citizen of the United States by birth, must be at least thirty-five years old, and must have lived in the United States at least fourteen years.**

6. In Case of the Removal of the President from Office, or of his Death, Resignation, or Inability to discharge the Powers and Duties of the said office, the same shall devolve on the Vice President, and the Congress may by Law provide for the Case of Removal, Death, Resignation or Inability, both of the President and Vice President, declaring what Officer shall then act as President, and such Officer shall act accordingly, until the Disability be removed, or a President shall be elected.

Filling a Presidential vacancy. **If the Presidency becomes vacant, the Vice President takes over the office. Congress may decide by law who will become President when neither the President nor the Vice President is able to serve. In the present succession law, the Speaker of the House is next in line and the president pro tempore of the Senate follows.**

The Twenty-fifth Amendment (1967) has been

passed to deal further with problems surrounding the inability of a President to discharge his duties.

7. The President shall, at stated Times, receive for his Services, a Compensation, which shall neither be increased nor diminished during the Period for which he shall have been elected, and he shall not receive within that Period any other Emolument from the United States, or any of them.

Presidential salary. **The President's salary may not be increased during his term of office, and he may receive no form of payment from the states other than his stated salary. In 1969, the President's annual salary was set at $200,000.**

8. Before he enter on the Execution of his Office, he shall take the following Oath or Affirmation:—"I do solemnly swear (or affirm) that I will faithfully execute the Office of President of the United States, and will to the best of my Ability, preserve, protect, and defend the Constitution of the United States."

SECTION 2. POWERS OF THE PRESIDENT

1. The President shall be Commander in Chief of the Army and Navy of the United States, and of the Militia of the several States, when called into the actual Service of the United States; he may require the Opinion, in writing, of the principal Officer in each of the executive Departments, upon any subject relating to the Duties of their respective Offices, and he shall have Power to grant Reprieves and Pardons for Offenses against the United States, except in Cases of Impeachment.

Presidential powers. **The President, who cannot be a member of the military, heads the country's armed forces. He can ask the heads of executive departments for written opinions about matters related to their departments. This clause provides a Constitutional basis for the Cabinet. The President can postpone the execution of a sentence or remit a penalty in cases involving federal law.**

2. He shall have Power, by and with the Advice and Consent of the Senate, to make Treaties, provided two-thirds of the Senators present concur; and he shall nominate, and by and with the Advice and Consent of the Senate, shall appoint Ambassadors, other public Ministers and Consuls, Judges of the Supreme Court, and all other Officers of the United States, whose Appointments are not herein otherwise provided for, and which shall be established by Law: but the Con-

gress may by Law vest the Appointment of such inferior Officers, as they think proper, in the President alone, in the Courts of Law, or in the Heads of Departments.

Treaties and appointments. **The President can make treaties with foreign countries but such treaties must be approved by two-thirds of those present at a session of the Senate. Note that this is a power given to the Senate, but not to the House, and is also a part of the checks and balances system.**

The Senate must also approve the appointment of American foreign representatives abroad, judges of the Supreme Court, and any other government officials not already provided for in the Constitution. However, Congress may make laws allowing either the President, the courts, or heads of departments, to appoint minor government officials.

3. The President shall have Power to fill up all Vacancies that may happen during the Recess of the Senate by granting Commissions which expire at the End of their next Session.

Temporary appointments. **If vacancies occur in appointive federal offices when the Senate is not in session, the President may make temporary appointments.**

SECTION 3. DUTIES OF THE PRESIDENT

He shall from time to time give the Congress Information of the State of the Union, and recommend to their Consideration such Measures as he shall judge necessary and expedient; he may, on extraordinary Occasions, convene both Houses, or either of them, and in Case of Disagreement between them, with Respect to the Time of Adjournment, he may adjourn them to such Time as he shall think proper; he shall receive Ambassadors and other public Ministers; he shall take Care that the Laws be faithfully executed, and shall Commission all the Officers of the United States.

Presidential duties. **The President must give the Congress information about the condition of the country. It has become customary for the President to deliver a "State of the Union" message to the Congress every January. If the need arises, the President may call either or both houses of the Congress into special session. The President has the power to end a session of Congress if the two houses cannot agree on an adjournment date. The President is to receive foreign representatives, see that the laws of**

the federal government are carried out, and commission all officers of the United States armed forces.

SECTION 4. IMPEACHMENT

The President, Vice President and all civil Officers of the United States, shall be removed from Office on Impeachment for, and Conviction of, Treason, Bribery, or other high Crimes and Misdemeanors.

Removing government officials. **The procedures for removal from office are explained in Article 1, SECTION 2, Clause 5 and SECTION 3, Clauses 6 and 7.**

▪ ARTICLE 3. THE JUDICIAL BRANCH

SECTION 1. FEDERAL COURTS

The judicial Power of the United States shall be vested in one supreme Court, and in such inferior courts as the Congress may from time to time ordain and establish. The Judges, both of the supreme and inferior Courts, shall hold their Offices during good Behavior, and shall, at stated Times, receive for their Services, a Compensation which shall not be diminished during their Continuance in Office.

Judicial power. **The Constitution creates a Supreme Court and permits Congress to set up other federal courts, including district courts and courts of appeals. Federal judges are appointed by the President with the approval of the Senate. They hold their jobs for life, and their pay may not be lowered while they are in office.**

SECTION 2. FEDERAL JUDICIAL JURISDICTION

1. The judicial Power shall extend to all Cases, in Law and Equity, arising under this Constitution, the Laws of the United States and Treaties made, or which shall be made, under their Authority;—to all Cases affecting Ambassadors, other public Ministers and Consuls;—to all Cases of admiralty and maritime Jurisdiction;—to Controversies to which the United States shall be a Party;—to Controversies between two or more States; between a State and Citizens of another State;— between Citizens of different States;—between Citizens of the same State claiming Lands under Grants of different States, and between a State, or the Citizens thereof, and foreign States, Citizens or Subjects.

Jurisdiction. **Here are listed the kinds of cases to be handled by the federal courts. State courts normally deal with state and local law, while federal courts usually are concerned with federal law. A few cases**

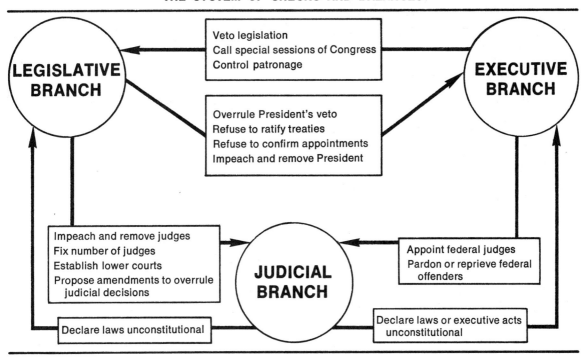

The System of Checks and Balances

LEGISLATIVE BRANCH

Veto legislation
Call special sessions of Congress
Control patronage

Overrule President's veto
Refuse to ratify treaties
Refuse to confirm appointments
Impeach and remove President

EXECUTIVE BRANCH

Impeach and remove judges
Fix number of judges
Establish lower courts
Propose amendments to overrule
    judicial decisions

JUDICIAL BRANCH

Appoint federal judges
Pardon or reprieve federal
    offenders

Declare laws unconstitutional

Declare laws or executive acts
unconstitutional

---

may be handled in either a state or a federal court. The Eleventh Amendment (1798) was passed to eliminate the provision that is crossed out.

2. In all Cases affecting Ambassadors, other public Ministers and Consuls, and those in which a State shall be Party, the supreme Court shall have original Jurisdiction. In all the other Cases before mentioned, the supreme Court shall have appellate Jurisdiction, both as to Law and Fact, with such Exceptions, and under such Regulations as Congress shall make.

Supreme Court cases. Original jurisdiction refers to the first court empowered to try a case. Actually, very few cases come directly to the Supreme Court. Most federal court cases begin in the district courts. They may be appealed to the Federal Courts of Appeal and finally carried up to the Supreme Court. *Appellate jurisdiction* refers to the right to try cases carried by appeal from lower courts. Most cases reaching the Supreme Court are taken to it on appeal. This clause gives the Supreme Court original jurisdiction in cases involving foreign representatives, or in cases in which a state is a party.

3. The trial of all Crimes, except in Cases of Impeachment, shall be by Jury; and such Trial shall be held in the State where the said Crimes shall have been committed; but when not committed within any State, the Trial shall be at such Place or Places as the Congress may by Law have directed.

Trials for federal crimes. Except for impeachment cases, anyone accused of a federal crime has the right to a trial by jury. The trial must be held in the state where the crime was committed. If a crime was not committed in any state—for example, at sea—Congress can decide where the trial shall be held. The district courts are the only federal courts which regularly use the jury system.

SECTION 3. TREASON

1. Treason against the United States, shall consist only in levying War against them, or in adhering to their Enemies, giving them Aid and Comfort. No Person shall be convicted of Treason unless on the Testimony of two Witnesses to the same overt Act, or on Confession in open Court.

Treason is defined as waging war against the United States or aiding the nation's enemies. No one can be found guilty of treason unless two witnesses testify that he committed the act or he confesses in court.

2. The Congress shall have power to declare the Punishment of Treason, but no Attainder of Treason shall work Corruption of Blood, or Forfeiture except during the Life of the Person attainted.

Punishment for treason. Congress has the power to fix punishment for treason. But the families and descendants of a person found guilty of treason cannot be punished for his crime.

■ ARTICLE 4. INTERSTATE RELATIONS

SECTION 1. OFFICIAL ACTS

Full Faith and Credit shall be given in each State to the public acts, Records, and judicial Proceedings of every other State. And the Congress may by general Laws prescribe the Manner in which such Acts, Records and Proceedings shall be proved, and the Effect thereof.

Reciprocal recognition. Each state must respect the laws, records, and court decisions of other states. If this were not the case, a person might move to another state to avoid legal punishment in the first state. The "full faith and credit" clause avoids much of the confusion arising from different state regulations.

SECTION 2. MUTUAL DUTIES OF STATES

1. The Citizens of each State shall be entitled to all Privileges and Immunities of Citizens in the several States.

Privileges of citizens. This clause gives a person moving into a state the same rights which the state gives to its own citizens. The state may still require a person to meet its own residence requirements for voting and holding office.

2. A person charged in any State with Treason, Felony, or other Crime, who shall flee from Justice, and be found in another State, shall on Demand of the executive Authority of the State from which he fled, be delivered up, to be removed to the State having Jurisdiction of the Crime.

Extradition. If a suspect flees to another state, the governor of the state where the crime was committed may request that he be returned. Sending escaped

suspects back for trial or punishment is called *extradition.* In the vast majority of cases, the suspected criminal's return is automatic, but in a very few cases state governors have refused to return the fugitives.

3. ~~No person held to Service or Labour in one State, under the Laws thereof, escaping into another, shall, in Consequence of any Law or Regulation therein, be discharged from such Service or Labour, but shall be delivered up on Claim of the Party to whom such Service or Labour may be due.~~

Fugitive slaves. This clause provided the Constitutional basis for slave owners to have their escaped slaves returned to them. The Thirteenth Amendment (1865) ended slavery, making this clause obsolete.

SECTION 3. NEW STATES AND TERRITORIES.

1. New States may be admitted by the Congress into this Union; but no new States shall be formed or erected within the Jurisdiction of any other State; nor any State be formed by the Junction of two or more States, or Parts of States, without the Consent of the Legislatures of the States concerned as well as of the Congress.

Admission of new states. Congress has the right to admit new states into the Union, but no new state can be created by dividing an already existing state, or by joining two or more states or parts of states, unless both the state legislatures of the states concerned and Congress approve.

2. The Congress shall have Power to dispose of and make all needful Rules and Regulations respecting the Territory or other Property belonging to the United States; and nothing in this Constitution shall be so construed as to Prejudice any Claims of the United States, or of any particular State.

Federal territories and properties. Congress may govern and make regulations for the territories and properties of the United States. *Territories* here refers to lands not under the control of any state.

SECTION 4. FEDERAL GUARANTEES TO
THE STATES

The United States shall guarantee to every State in this Union a Republican Form of Government, and shall protect each of them against Invasion; and on Application of the Legislature, or of the Executive (when the Legislature cannot be convened) against domestic Violence.

Protection for States. In practice, Congress determines whether a state has a republican form of government. The Constitution also requires the federal government to protect a state against invasion, and upon request of the proper state authorities to protect it against rioting and violence. Sometimes Presidents have ordered federal intervention without the state's request when federal laws were being violated.

ARTICLE 5. AMENDING THE CONSTITUTION

The Congress, whenever two thirds of both Houses shall deem it necessary, shall propose Amendments to the Constitution, or, on the Application of the Legislatures of two-thirds of the several States, shall call a Convention for proposing Amendments, which, in either Case, shall be valid to all Intents and Purposes, as Part of this Constitution, when ratified by the Legislatures of three-fourths of the several States, or by Conventions in three-fourths thereof, as the one or the other Mode of Ratification may be proposed by the Congress; Provided that no Amendment which may be made prior to the Year One thousand eight hundred and eight shall in any Manner affect the first and fourth Clauses in the Ninth Section of the first Article; and that no State, without its Consent, shall be deprived of its equal Suffrage in the Senate.

Proposing and passing amendments. By a two-thirds vote of both houses, Congress can propose an amendment. Or if two-thirds of the state legislatures request it, Congress is to call a convention to propose an amendment. So far, all amendments have been proposed by Congress. An amendment must be approved by three-fourths of the state legislatures or by conventions in three fourths of the states.

The provision that has been crossed out forbade an amendment before 1808 that would allow Congress to end the importation of slaves. Except for a state's right to have equal representation in the Senate, any part of the Constitution can be amended.

ARTICLE 6. THE SUPREMACY OF THE CONSTITUTION

1. All Debts contracted and Engagements entered into, before the Adoption of this Constitution, shall be as valid against the United States under this Constitution, as under the Confederation.

Standing debts and agreements. All debts and treaties made under the Articles of Confederation are recognized by the United States.

2. This Constitution, and the Laws of the United States which shall be made in Pursuance thereof; and all Treaties made, or which shall be made, under the Authority of the United States, shall be the supreme Law of the Land; and the Judges in every State shall be bound thereby, any Thing in the Constitution or Laws of any State to the Contrary notwithstanding.

The supreme law of the land. This is the famous "Supremacy" clause, one of the most important in the Constitution. The Constitution, federal laws, and treaties are supreme over other law. All state judges are bound to recognize this. Thus, in cases of a conflict between state laws and one of these three supreme kinds of law, the latter must be obeyed. While the federal government has limited power, whenever it does have power, it is supreme.

3. The Senators and Representatives before mentioned, and the Members of the several State Legislatures, and all executive and judicial Officers, both of the United States and of the several States, shall be bound by Oath or Affirmation, to support this Constitution; but no religious Test shall ever be required as a Qualification to any Office or public Trust under the United States.

Oaths of office. All the officials listed must pledge themselves to support the Constitution. But such a pledge, or oath, cannot include any religious test or requirement that a person belong to a particular religious faith.

ARTICLE 7. RATIFYING THE CONSTITUTION

The Ratification of the Conventions of nine States, shall be sufficient for the Establishment of this Constitution between the States so ratifying the Same.

The approval of nine states was necessary for the Constitution to go into effect. The Constitution was signed by thirty-nine men on September 17, 1787. Within nine months, nine states had approved the Constitution. By the middle of 1790, all of the thirteen original states had voted their approval of the Constitution.

Amendments To The Constitution

The first ten amendments constitute the Bill of Rights. Because many Americans did not feel that the original Constitution sufficiently protected the people's liberties, the first Congress proposed these amendments, and in 1791 they became an official part of the Constitution.

■ AMENDMENT 1 (1791) FREEDOM OF RELIGION, SPEECH, PRESS, ASSEMBLY, AND PETITION

Congress shall make no law respecting an establishment of religion, or prohibiting the free exercise thereof; or abridging the freedom of speech, or of the press; or the right of the people peaceably to assemble, and to petition the Government for a redress of grievances.

Congress may not establish a national religion, or restrict people's freedom in their religious beliefs. Congress may not limit freedom of speech and press. (This is not an absolutely unlimited freedom. There are laws against slander and libel, and the government has imposed limitations on speech and press during wartime.) The people may peaceably assemble and hold meetings, and they have the right to ask their government to correct their grievances.

■ AMENDMENT 2 (1791) RIGHT TO BEAR ARMS

A well regulated Militia, being necessary to the security of a free State, the right of the people to keep and bear Arms, shall not be infringed.

The federal government may not interfere with the rights of the states to arm and drill their militia, but this does not mean that the right of citizens to own guns and other weapons cannot be regulated by the states.

■ AMENDMENT 3 (1791) HOUSING TROOPS

No Soldier shall, in time of peace be quartered in any house, without the consent of the Owner, nor in time of war, but in a manner to be prescribed by law.

This amendment was put into the Bill of Rights because of the British policy of quartering their troops in the houses of Americans. No one may be compelled to give board and room to soldiers during peace time, or even in wartime except under laws passed by Congress.

■ AMENDMENT 4 (1791) SEARCHES AND SEIZURES

The right of the people to be secure in their persons, houses, papers, and effects, against unreasonable searches and seizures, shall not be violated; and no Warrants shall issue but upon probable cause, supported by Oath or affirmation, and particularly describing the place to be searched, and the persons or things to be seized.

This amendment is a result of the British practice of issuing blanket search warrants—Writs of Assistance—permitting officers to search any house at any time. This amendment provides that a federal officer must obtain an official order from a judge—a search warrant—before he may search a house, seize a person's papers, or arrest a person. No judge may issue such warrants unless he is certain that they are necessary in order to apprehend criminals or prevent crime.

■ AMENDMENT 5 (1791) LIFE, LIBERTY, AND PROPERTY

No person shall be held to answer for a capital, or otherwise infamous crime, unless on a presentment or indictment of a Grand Jury, except in cases arising in the land or naval forces, or in the Militia, when in actual service in time of War or public danger; nor shall any person be subject for the same offense to be twice put in jeopardy of life or limb, nor shall be compelled in any criminal case to be a witness against himself, nor be deprived of life, liberty, or property, without due process of law; nor shall private property be taken for public use, without just compensation.

In a federal court no person can be held for a serious crime unless indicted, or charged, by a grand jury. A grand jury is a group of 23 persons who hear in secret the charges against the accused and then decide whether or not the person should be tried in court. Twice put in jeopardy, or double jeopardy, means that no person can be tried twice in federal courts for the same crime.

No person can be forced to give evidence against himself that will help prove his guilt. This provision goes back to earlier history when persons were tortured in order to make them confess. This clause allows a person on trial to refuse to answer questions when he fears that his answers might convict him of the crime.

"Due process of law," has become quite complicated, but the framers probably wished here to guarantee legal procedures for a person accused of a crime. The taking of private property for public use is called the right of "eminent domain." The government cannot take such property without giving the owner a fair price for his property—which price is determined by a court.

▪ AMENDMENT 6 (1791) RIGHT TO A SPEEDY, FAIR TRIAL

In all criminal prosecutions, the accused shall enjoy the right to a speedy and public trial, by an impartial jury of the State and district wherein the crime shall have been committed, which district shall have been previously ascertained by law, and to be informed of the nature and cause of the accusation; to be confronted with the witnesses against him; to have compulsory process for obtaining witnesses in his favor, and to have the Assistance of Counsel for his defense.

These rules are designed to achieve a fair trial. A person has the right to a prompt and public trial—not a secret one. He has the right to trial by jury in the state and district where the crime was committed. He must be told the nature of his crime and he must be

given a chance to see and hear witnesses against him. Witnesses in his favor may be compelled to come to court to give their evidence. Also, every person accused of a crime in a federal court is entitled to be represented by a lawyer.

▪ AMENDMENT 7 (1791) CIVIL SUITS

In suits at common law, where the value in controversy shall exceed twenty dollars, the right by trial jury shall be preserved, and no fact tried by a jury, shall be otherwise reexamined in any court of the United States, than according to rules of the common law.

If a sum of money larger than $20 is involved in an injury or damage suit, the persons may insist on a jury trial.

▪ AMENDMENT 8 (1791) BAILS, FINES, AND PUNISHMENTS

Excessive bail shall not be required, nor excessive fines imposed, nor cruel and unusual punishments inflicted.

A person accused of a crime may be released from prison until his trial if he pays a sum of money, called *bail*, to the court. The money is returned to him if he comes to trial as ordered. Federal courts must not charge "unreasonable" amounts for bail. Also there shall be no excessive fines or unusually cruel punishments inflicted. The Supreme Court is the final court of judgment in deciding just what "excessive," "cruel," and "unusual" mean in specific cases.

▪ AMENDMENT 9 (1791) RIGHTS NOT ENUMERATED

The enumeration in the Constitution, of certain rights, shall not be constructed to deny or disparage others retained by the people.

All rights not listed in the Constitution are retained by the people.

▪ AMENDMENT 10 (1791) POWERS NOT DELEGATED

The powers not delegated to the United States by the Constitution, nor prohibited by it to the States, are reserved to the States respectively, or to the people.

Powers not given to the United States or forbidden the states in the Constitution, are reserved to the states or to the people.

◼ AMENDMENT 11 (1791) SUITS AGAINST STATES

The Judicial power of the United States shall not be construed to extend to any suit in law or equity, commenced or prosecuted against one of the United States by Citizens of another State, or by citizens or Subjects of any Foreign State.

No federal court can try any case in which a state government is being sued by a citizen of another state or of a foreign country. The trial must be held in the state being sued. This amendment was added because many states were afraid that damage suits against them from Revolutionary War days and since that time would go against them if tried in federal courts.

◼ AMENDMENT 12 (1804) ELECTING THE PRESIDENT AND VICE PRESIDENT

The Electors shall meet in their respective states and vote by ballot for President and Vice President, one of whom, at least, shall not be an inhabitant of the same state with themselves; they shall name in their ballots the person voted for as President and in distinct ballots the person voted for as Vice President, and they shall make distinct lists of all persons voted for as President, and of all persons voted for as Vice President, and of the number of votes for each, which lists they shall sign and certify, and transmit sealed to the seat of the government of the United States, directed to the President of the Senate;—The President of the Senate shall, in the presence of the Senate and House of Representatives, open all the certificates and the votes shall then be counted;—The person having the greatest number of votes for President, shall be the President, if such number be a majority of the whole number of Electors appointed; and if no person have such majority, then from the persons having the highest numbers not exceeding three on the list of those voted for as President, the House of Representatives shall choose immediately, by ballot, the President. But in choosing the President, the votes shall be taken by states, the representation from each state having one vote; a quorum for this purpose shall consist of a member or members from two-thirds of the states, and a majority of all the states shall be necessary to a choice. And if the House of Representatives shall not choose a President whenever the right of choice shall devolve upon them, before the fourth day of March next following, then the Vice President shall act as President, as in the case of the death or other constitutional disability of the President. The person having the greatest number of votes as Vice President shall, be the Vice President, if such number be a majority of the whole number of Electors appointed, and if no person have a majority, then, from the two highest numbers on the list, the Senate shall choose the Vice President; a quorum for the purpose shall consist of two-thirds of the whole number of Senators, and a majority of the whole number shall be necessary to a choice. But no person constitutionally ineligible to the office of President shall be eligible to that of Vice President of the United States.

This Amendment replaces Article 2, SECTION 1, Clause 3 under which the electors voted for President and Vice President without showing which person they wanted for each office. A serious problem arose in the Presidential election of 1800 because the two top candidates tied. This amendment was passed to prevent such confusion.

The election of the President and Vice President today is somewhat different from the Twelfth Amendment procedure, which goes as follows: Electors of each state meet and vote for President and Vice President. (This is just a formality now since separate electors represent the two major parties, and if a Presidential candidate gets a majority of the popular votes in the state, he also gets all the electors' votes.) Either the Presidential or Vice Presidential candidate must live outside the elector's own state. The electors cast two ballots, one for President and one for Vice President. The lists from each state are sent to the United States Senate, and the votes are counted in the presence of the entire Congress. The Presidential candidate with the majority of electoral votes for that office wins the office. If no candidate has a majority, the House of Representatives chooses the President from among the three highest candidates. If no President has been chosen by the House by the date for his duties to begin, the Vice President who has been elected acts as President.

The Vice Presidential candidate with the majority becomes Vice President. If none has a majority, the

Senate chooses from the candidates with the largest votes. It should be noted that when the House votes for the President, each state has one vote, and that if there is a Senate vote to name the Vice President, at least two-thirds of the senators must be present, and the candidate must have a majority of their votes to be named.

This amendment still does not permit the people to vote directly for the President or Vice President.

■ AMENDMENT 13 (1865) ABOLITION OF SLAVERY

Section 1. Neither slavery nor involuntary servitude, except as a punishment for crime whereof the party shall have been duly convicted, shall exist within the United States, or any place subject to their jurisdiction.

Slavery is forbidden in the United States and in all its lands.

Section 2. Congress shall have power to enforce this article by appropriate legislation.

Congress feared that President Andrew Johnson would not enforce this amendment.

■ AMENDMENT 14 (1868) CITIZENSHIP

Section 1. All persons born or naturalized in the United States and subject to the jurisdiction thereof, are citizens of the United States and of the State wherein they reside. No State shall make or enforce any law which shall abridge the privileges or immunities of citizens of the United States; nor shall any State deprive any person of life, liberty, or property, without due process of law; nor deny to any person within its jurisdiction the equal protection of the laws.

Citizenship is defined for the first time. All persons born or naturalized in the United States and who are under its laws are citizens—both of the United States and the states in which they live. No state may take away a person's life, liberty, or property except according to law. The main purpose for this amendment was to give the blacks equal rights. The last clause of this section has been the legal basis upon which many civil rights cases have been argued.

Section 2. Representatives shall be apportioned among the several States according to their respective numbers, counting the whole number of persons in each state, excluding Indians not taxed. But when the right to vote at any election for the choice of electors for President and Vice President of the United States, Representatives in Congress, the Executive and Judicial officers of a State, or the members of the Legislature thereof, is denied to any of the male inhabitants of such State, being twenty-one years of age and citizens of the United States, or in any way abridged, except for participation in rebellion, or other crime, the basis of representation therein shall be reduced in the proportion which the number of such male citizens shall bear to the whole number of male citizens twenty-one years of age in such State.

This section eliminated the three-fifths clause of the Constitution. A black henceforth was to be counted as one person, like any other citizen, in determining the number of Representatives. It further provides that if any state prevents its eligible citizens from voting, its membership in the House of Representatives is to be cut down accordingly. This penalty has never been imposed on any state.

Section 3. No person shall be a Senator or Representative in Congress, or elector of President and Vice President, or hold any office, civil or military, under the United States, or under any State, who, having previously taken an oath, as a member of Congress, or as an officer of the United States, or as a member of any State legislature, or as an executive or judicial officer of any State, to support the Constitution of the United States, shall have engaged in insurrection or rebellion against the same, or given aid or comfort to the enemies thereof. But Congress may, by vote of two-thirds of each House, remove such disability.

No person can become an official of the federal government or a state government if he has held such an office and then rebelled against the federal government. Large numbers of southern leaders were prevented from holding office by this section. Congress did not restore these privileges entirely until 1898.

Section 4. The validity of the public debt of the United States, authorized by law, including debts incurred for payment of pensions and bounties for services in suppressing insurrection or rebellion, shall not be questioned. But neither the United States nor any State shall assume or pay any debt or obligation incurred in aid of insurrection or rebellion against the United States, or any claim for the loss or emancipation of any slave; but all such debts, obligations and claims shall be held illegal and void.

Here the Constitution upholds the legality of the debt of the United States government but wipes out the debts created by the rebellion against the United States.

Section 5. The Congress shall have power to enforce, by appropriate legislation, the provisions of this article.

■ AMENDMENT 15 (1870) RIGHT TO VOTE

Section 1. The right of citizens of the United States to vote shall not be denied or abridged by the United States or by any State on account of race, color, or previous condition of servitude.

Neither the United States nor any state may prevent a citizen from voting because of his race, color, or because he was once a slave. Despite this Constitutional amendment, many states have found ways to keep blacks from voting.

Section 2. The Congress shall have power to enforce this article by appropriate legislation.

■ AMENDMENT 16 (1913) INCOME TAX

The Congress shall have power to lay and collect taxes on incomes, from whatever source derived, without apportionment among the several States, and without regard to any census or enumeration.

This amendment permits Congress to tax individual incomes without basing the tax on state populations.

■ AMENDMENT 17 (1913) ELECTING SENATORS

Section 1. The Senate of the United States shall be composed of two Senators from each State, elected by the people thereof, for six years, and each Senator shall have one vote. The electors in each State shall have the qualifications requisite for electors of the most numerous branch of the State legislatures.

This amendment gives the people the right to elect their senators directly. Before this senators were elected by the state legislatures.

Section 2. When vacancies happen in the representation of any State in the Senate, the executive authority of such State shall issue writs of election to fill such vacancies: Provided, That the legislature of any State may empower the executive thereof to make temporary appointments until the people fill the vacancies by election as the legislature may direct.

If a senator dies, resigns, or is removed from office during his term, the governor of the state may issue orders for the election of his successor. Usually, the legislature gives the governor the right to appoint a temporary successor until the next election.

Section 3. This amendment shall not be so construed as to affect the election or term of any Senator chosen before it becomes valid as part of the Constitution.

■ AMENDMENT 18 (1919) PROHIBITION

Section 1. After one year from the ratification of this article the manufacture, sale, or transportation of intoxicating liquors within, the importation thereof into, or the exportation thereof from the United States and all territory subject to the jurisdiction thereof for beverage purpose is hereby prohibited.

Section 2. The Congress and the several states shall have concurrent power to enforce this article by appropriate legislation.

Section 3. This article shall be inoperative unless it shall have been ratified as an amendment to the Constitution by the legislature of the several states, as provided in the Constitution, within seven years from the date of the submission hereof to the states by the Congress.

This amendment forbade the manufacture, sale, or shipment of intoxicating beverages, and gave Congress and the states the right to pass laws to enforce it. It was repealed by the Twenty-first Amendment (1933).

■ AMENDMENT 19 (1920) WOMEN'S SUFFRAGE

Section 1. The right of the citizens of the United States to vote shall not be denied or abridged by the United States or by any State on account of sex.

Neither the federal nor state governments can bar women from voting.

Section 2. Congress shall have power to enforce this article by appropriate legislation.

AMENDMENT 20 (1933) "LAME DUCK" AMENDMENT

Section 1. The terms of the President and Vice President shall end at noon on the 20th day of January, and the terms of Senators and Representatives at noon on the 3rd day of January, of the years in which such terms would have ended if this article had not been ratified; and the terms of their successors shall then begin.

The Twentieth, or "Lame Duck" Amendment, requires the new President to take office January 20 instead of March 4. Newly elected senators and representatives shall take office January 3 instead of in December of the year following the election—thirteen months after the election.

The period between the election and the actual taking up of the duties of the office has often been one of hesitation and confusion. Thus, the term *lame duck* has been applied to it.

Section 2. The Congress shall assemble at least once in every year, and such meeting shall begin at noon on the 3rd day of January, unless they shall by law appoint a different day.

This changes the date given in ARTICLE I SECTION 4, Clause 2.

Section 3. If, at the time fixed for the beginning of the term of the President, the President elect shall have died, the Vice President elect shall become President. If a President shall not have been chosen before the time fixed for the beginning of his term, or if the President elect shall have failed to qualify, then the Vice President elect shall act as President until a President shall have qualified; and the Congress may by law provide for the case wherein neither a President elect nor a Vice President elect shall have qualified, declaring who shall then act as President, or the manner in which one who is to act shall be selected, and such person shall act accordingly until a President or Vice President shall have qualified.

If the person elected as President dies before he can take office, the person elected as Vice President shall become President. If no President has been chosen by January 3, or if the President who has been chosen does not qualify to hold office, the person chosen as Vice President will act as President until a President has qualified.

Congress may make laws stating who shall act as President, or how an acting President shall be chosen, in case neither the President elect nor the Vice President elect qualifies for office. Whoever is chosen will act as President until a President or Vice President has qualified.

Section 4. The Congress may by law provide for the case of the death of any of the persons from whom the House of Representatives may choose a President whenever the right of choice shall have developed upon them, and for the case of the death of any of the persons from whom the Senate may choose a Vice President whenever the right of choice shall have devolved upon them.

Congress can decide what will happen if the President or Vice President chosen by Congress dies before taking office. Congress has not yet exercised this power.

Section 5. ~~Sections 1 and 2 shall take effect on the 15th day of October following the ratification of this article.~~

Section 6. ~~This article shall be inoperative unless it shall have been ratified as an amendment to the Constitution by the legislatures of three-fourths of the several States within seven years from the date of its submission.~~

AMENDMENT 21 (1933) REPEAL OF PROHIBITION

Section 1. The eighteenth article of amendment to the Constitution of the United States is hereby repealed.

This amendment repeals the Eighteenth Amendment.

Section 2. The transportation or importation into any State, Territory, or Possession of the United States for delivery or use therein of intoxicating liquors, in violation of the laws thereof, is hereby prohibited.

Transporting liquor into a "dry" state is forbidden.

Section 3. ~~This article shall be inoperative unless it shall have been ratified as an amendment to the Constitution by conventions in the several States, as provided in the Constitution, within seven years from the date of the submission hereof to the States by the Congress.~~

AMENDMENT 22 (1951) LIMIT ON PRESIDENTIAL TERMS

Section 1. No person shall be elected to the office of the President more than twice, and no person who has held the office of President, or acted as President, for more than two years of a term to which some other person was elected President shall be elected to the office of the President more than once. But this Article shall not apply to any person holding the office of President when this Article was proposed by the Congress, and shall not prevent any person who may be holding the office of President, or acting as President, during the term within which this Article becomes operative from holding the office of President or acting as President during the remainder of such term.

This is the "no third term" amendment. It was passed because many people feared that Franklin D. Roosevelt's four terms set a dangerous precedent. The amendment also says that anyone who serves less than two years of another person's term can be elected twice.

Section 2. This article shall be inoperative unless it shall have been ratified as an amendment to the Constitution by the legislatures of three-fourths of the several States within seven years from the date of its submission to the States by the Congress.

AMENDMENT 23 (1961) SUFFRAGE FOR WASHINGTON, D. C.

Section 1. The District constituting the seat of Government of the United States shall appoint in such manner as the Congress may direct:

A number of electors of President and Vice President equal to the whole number of Senators and Representatives in Congress to which the District would be entitled if it were a State, but in no event more than the least populous State; they shall be in addition to those appointed by the States, but they shall be considered, for the purposes of the election of President and Vice President, to be electors appointed by a State; and they shall meet in the District and perform such duties as provided by the twelfth article of amendment.

This amendment gives the residents of Washington, D. C., the right to vote for President and Vice President through electors. However, they still cannot elect local officials.

Section 2. The Congress shall have power to enforce this article by appropriate legislation.

AMENDMENT 24 (1964) POLL TAXES

Section 1. The right of citizens of the United States to vote in any primary or other election for President or Vice President, for electors for President or Vice President, or for Senator or Representative in Congress, shall not be denied or abridged by the United States or any state by reason of failure to pay any poll tax or other tax.

When this amendment was passed, a few states still used the poll tax to discourage black people from voting.

Section 2. The Congress shall have the power to enforce this article by appropriate legislation.

AMENDMENT 25 (1967) PRESIDENTIAL DISABILITY

Section 1. In case of the removal of the President from office or his death or resignation, the Vice President shall become President.

The Vice President becomes President when the President dies, resigns, or is removed.

Section 2. Whenever there is a vacancy in the office of the Vice President, the President shall nominate a Vice President who shall take the office upon confirmation by a majority vote of both houses of Congress.

This clause was designed to insure that the United States will always have a Vice President.

Section 3. Whenever the President transmits to the President pro tempore of the Senate and the Speaker of the House of Representatives his written declaration that he is unable to discharge the powers and duties of his office, and until he transmits to them a written declaration to the contrary, such powers and duties shall be discharged by the Vice President as Acting President.

The Vice President can act as President if the President notifies Congress he cannot do his job.

Section 4. Whenever the Vice President and a majority of either the principal officers of the executive departments or of such other body as Congress may by law provide, transmit to the President pro tempore of the Senate and the Speaker of the House of Representatives their written declaration that the President is unable to discharge the powers and duties of his office, the Vice President shall immediately assume the powers and duties of the office as Acting President.

Thereafter, when the President transmits to the President pro tempore of the Senate and the Speaker of the House of Representatives his written declaration that no inability exists, he shall resume the powers and duties of his office unless the Vice President and a majority of either the principal officers of the executive department or of such other body as Congress may by law provide, transmit within four days to the President pro tempore of the Senate and the Speaker of the House of Representatives their written declaration that the President is unable to discharge the powers and duties of his office. Thereupon Congress shall decide the issue, assembling within 48 hours for that purpose if not in session. If the Congress, within 21 days after receipt of the latter written declaration, or, if Congress is not in session, within 21 days after Congress is required to assemble, determines by two-thirds vote of both houses that the President is unable to discharge the powers and duties of his office, the Vice President shall continue to discharge the same as Acting President; otherwise, the President shall resume the powers and duties of his office.

If the Vice President and a majority of the Cabinet notify Congress that the President is unable to do his job, the Vice President can act as President, even if the President himself does not notify Congress of his disability.

■ AMENDMENT 26 (1971) LOWERING THE VOTING AGE

Section 1. The right of citizens of the United States, who are eighteen years of age or older, to vote shall not be denied or abridged by the United States or by any State on account of age.

Section 2. The Congress shall have power to enforce this article by appropriate legislation.

3 The Federalists Bring Order To The New Government

1. How did the positions of Alexander Hamilton and Thomas Jefferson differ regarding the proper function of the American government?

2. What were the goals of American foreign policy, and how effective was the government in meeting these goals?

3. What factors led to the formation of early political parties?

4. What were the accomplishments of the administrations of Washington and Adams?

When George Washington was inaugurated as President on April 30, 1789, he was confronted by enormous problems in finance and diplomacy. Alexander Hamilton, secretary of the Treasury, had to bring order to the chaotic situation posed by the mass of debts left over from the Revolution. Secretary of State Thomas Jefferson inherited the failure of the Confederation to remove Spanish and British threats to the West.

These problems were facets of the greatest task facing the new government, that of insuring national unity. The search for policies that would best promote unity soon led to bitter quarreling between the followers of Hamilton and Jefferson. These brilliant men based their measures on very different philosophies of government and society. Washington's administration was characterized by a series of political disputes that raised basic questions about the nature of American government.

Hamilton's economic program. Alexander Hamilton was convinced that the Republic could survive only if the states were subordinated to the federal government, and if the government gained the support of merchants, wealthy planters, and financiers. These men, Hamilton believed, would be attracted to the new government if economic policies that promoted their interests were adopted. Thus, his legislative program was designed to give the federal government a vigorous role in the economy by placing the full authority of the government behind the banking system and by extending special benefits to merchants and manufacturers.

On January 14, 1791, Hamilton unveiled the first part of his program, in which he proposed to reorganize the entire foreign and domestic debt of the United States. First, he attacked the problem of the Continental certificates and bonds that Congress had issued during the Revolution. He proposed to redeem them at their original, or face, value with interest-bearing bonds. Second, he insisted that the federal government assume all state debts. Most of the certificates and many of the state bonds were held by speculators, merchants, bankers, and Congressmen who had purchased them during periods of economic depression from their original owners for as little as one-tenth of their face value.

James Madison and Thomas Jefferson vigorously opposed Hamilton's plan. They complained that citizens, forced to sell their certificates during hard times, would not receive their just rewards. Moreover, they saw no valid reason for the federal government to assume debts that the states were capable of paying themselves. Hamilton candidly replied that the assumption of state debts would help to stabilize the national government since former state bondholders would henceforth look upon the federal government as a major source of profit and financial stability.

The second part of Hamilton's program called for the creation of a national bank. (see feature, opposite page). Because it could lend money to merchants and financiers, such a bank would stimulate economic growth. It would provide a sound currency and promote general financial stability. More important, in Hamilton's view, the bank would be another means by which the national government would be strengthened. In addition, Hamilton proposed protective tariffs and subsidies to industries to encourage economic growth.

Jefferson was appalled by Hamilton's bank proposal. He declared that the purpose of a written constitution was to clearly define and limit the activities of the federal government. Insisting upon a "strict," or literal, interpretation of the Constitution, he believed that since the Constitution did not specifically authorize the establishment of a national bank, its creation would be unconstitutional. Jefferson argued on the basis of the Tenth Amendment, which reserved for "the states respectively or to the people" all powers not granted directly to the federal government.

Jefferson's greatest objection, however, was based on his belief that republican government could be maintained only in a society of relatively equal, economically independent farmers. He viewed the growth of an urbanized, industrial society in the United States as a danger wherein financiers and politicians would dominate the lives of a poorly paid urban *proletariat,* or working class. According to Jefferson, the policies of Hamilton all pointed toward the creation of an undemocratic social order.

Despite Jefferson's opposition, the law creating the national bank was passed. In retrospect, Hamilton's program was essential to the economic stability of the young nation. Investors now had faith in the government's financial integrity and stability. Under the Bank of the United States, new banks sprang up, greatly increasing the money available for capital investment.

Maintaining internal order. It was essential for the new government to bring order and peace to the frontier and maintain its authority there. The years of Indian warfare which had slowed settlement in the Northwest Territory finally came to an end in 1794 when the tribes north of the Ohio River were crushed. The Indians gave up most of what is now southern Ohio, opening up vast tracts of land for settlement.

In 1794, the government also faced a revolt of frontiersmen against a tax placed on whiskey. One of Hamilton's early proposals to bring in revenue was a whiskey tax, which was also designed to show the government's power to reach into the frontier. Westerners complained bitterly. Since roads were poor, whiskey was the most easily transported product westerners sent to market; whiskey also served as currency in the West. When farmers in western Pennsylvania talked wildly of declaring their independence and raised a military force, the government sent out the militia, and the "Whiskey Rebellion" collapsed.

Aims of American foreign policy. The primary aim of American foreign policy from 1789 until the early twentieth century was to avoid involvement in European wars. American neutrality often proved difficult to maintain, however, especially

THE FIRST BANK OF THE UNITED STATES

With the establishment of the new government, the need for a sound monetary system was recognized. The Constitution prohibited the states from minting coins or printing paper money, reserving those powers for the federal government. Once the Constitution went into effect, people were unable to obtain money from the states and, not being provided with enough by the federal government (it had not yet begun to print money or mint coins), they turned to private banks for bank notes, which they used as paper money. Secretary Hamilton was not satisfied to leave the supply of bank notes entirely to private institutions. Thus, he submitted his plan for a national bank.

The First Bank of the United States, chartered in 1791, had a capital stock (the stock issued to its stockholders for money) of $10 million. One-fifth ($2 million) of the stock was bought by the government; the remaining stock was sold to the public. The bank was authorized to issue bank notes up to the amount of its capital stock ($10 million) and these notes circulated freely all over the country. It also served as the government's financial agent—holding government funds, assisting in tax collection, selling government bonds, and loaning the government money.

The bank's most valuable service was its function as a sort of "central bank": As depository for government funds, all debts to the government were paid to the bank, mostly with state and private bank notes. The bank could exert control over those state and private banks by immediately *redeeming,* or exchanging, those notes for specie, and thereby exhausting those banks' supply of specie. This restricted the amount of notes state and private banks could then issue (with any specie backing). Conversely, when the nation was in need of paper money, the bank could ease the pressure by refraining from redeeming its state and private bank notes.

from 1789 to 1815, when the United States attempted to steer a neutral path between the rival maritime policies of Britain and France during the wars following the French Revolution. In addition, American leaders quarreled furiously over the policies that would best achieve neutrality.

Many Americans, including Jefferson, welcomed the French Revolution. In its early stages, it seemed to be an extension of the idea of the American Revolution. Others, such as Hamilton, were horrified by its bloody excesses and shocked by its assaults on religion and the social hierarchy. To this ideological conflict were added important political and economic considerations. Hamilton believed that America's future prosperity lay in reestablishing close trade ties with Britain and the British West Indies. Yet, Americans had a traditional hatred of Britain; they also had a treaty with France and a desire to trade in the French West Indies. When Britain and France declared war in 1793, the conflicts in American society over the direction of foreign policy became acute.

In addition to neutrality, two other goals also shaped the foreign policies of Washington's administration: British withdrawal of their forts in the Northwest Territory; and trading rights at New Orleans, along with a settlement of the southern boundary with Spain. What made all of these objectives so difficult to obtain was the fact that the United States had very little military strength with which to support her demands.

Relations with foreign powers. In 1794, John Jay was sent to London to negotiate a commercial treaty with Britain and settle outstanding differences between the two nations. Jay was to induce the British to withdraw from their forts in the Northwest Territory. In addition, he was to persuade Britain to respect American neutral rights and halt the practice of seizing American ships and *impressing,* or forcing, American sailors into the British navy.

Completed late in 1794, Jay's Treaty fell short of American expectations. Britain was to abandon its forts in the Northwest Territory, provided it was permitted to continue the fur trade. And small American vessels were allowed to trade in the British West Indies, although the British restricted the right of Americans to carry goods from the West Indies to other parts of the British empire. The treaty, however, did nothing to halt British

seizure of American ships or the impressment of sailors.

Popular opposition to Jay's Treaty was severe. The South was angered at the refusal of the British to compensate slave owners for the loss of slaves during the Revolution. Shipping interests blamed Jay for Britain's refusal to stop seizing American ships. Washington, however, was convinced that nothing more could be gained from Britain by a militarily weak United States, and he signed the treaty. Pinckney's Treaty with Spain in 1795 was more successful. Spain, again aligned with France, and fearful of a United States alliance with Britain, agreed to let Americans establish warehouses at New Orleans, and finally accepted the 31st parallel as the southern boundary of the United States (see map, page 798).

The treaties, however, had not solved the problem of American neutrality. Britain still seized American ships trading with France and impressed American seamen. Protests were unavailing, and France, angry because the United States had not sent it aid, also began to seize American ships.

In 1797, when the new President, John Adams, attempted to secure French recognition of American neutral rights, the French foreign minister demanded a bribe from the American delegation. Outraged at this treatment, Congress broke off trade with France, repudiated the treaty of 1778, and authorized the capture of French ships. A two-year undeclared naval war followed.

Federalists, urged on by Alexander Hamilton, demanded war; the supporters of Jefferson argued that war was unnecessary. Both sides exaggerated the threat of war and the danger of French policy, and John Adams, despite demands from his own party, wisely continued to seek peace. Another delegation to France was received by Napoleon Bonaparte, the new dictator, who was quite willing to settle the difficulties between the two nations.

Although during the 1790's, the United States achieved important diplomatic successes, Federalist foreign policy had a divisive effect. The quarrels over Jay's Treaty and the war scare of 1798 convinced Hamiltonians that pro-French factions sought to undermine peaceful commercial relations with Britain. Jeffersonians were just as stoutly convinced that the Federalist administration was eager for war with revolutionary France.

The Alien and Sedition Acts. As the nation divided bitterly over questions of economic and foreign policy, the threat of war with France convinced many Federalists that sinister conspiracies threatened to overthrow the government. Believing that opposition to the policies of President Adams was not merely wrong but treasonable, they made no distinction between loyal opposition to governmental policies and disloyal attempts to overthrow the government. In 1798, through the Alien and Sedition Acts, the Federalists unwisely attempted to crush all political opposition.

The Alien Act allowed the President to expel "dangerous" foreigners by an *executive decree,* that is, without having to follow established judicial procedures. The Naturalization Act, part of the Alien Act, increased the period required to gain citizenship from five to fourteen years, an attempt to lessen the influence of French and anti-British Irish immigrants. Finally, the Sedition Act, whose aim was to silence all antiadministration newspapers made it a crime to criticize the President or Congress.

Jefferson's supporters, appalled by this display of hysteria and intolerance, raged against the "Federalist Reign of Terror." Some of his supporters, who had begun to call themselves Democratic-Republicans, responded with a series of resolutions passed by the legislatures of Kentucky and Virginia. The resolutions (written secretly by Jefferson and Madison) declared that the Alien and Sedition Acts were unconstitutional and *null and void,* that is, without force or validity, in Kentucky and Virginia. Jefferson explained that in his view the Union was simply a compact voluntarily agreed to by the states, and since the states had created the Constitution, they had the sole right to interpret it.

This states' rights theory was not accepted by other state legislatures, and Kentucky and Virginia did not act upon the resolutions. But the Democratic-Republicans began to organize for the election of 1800, fully convinced that Federalist excesses would give them victory.

The emergence of political parties. As opposition to Federalist policies mounted, Americans found themselves confronted by an unprece-

dented situation—the emergence of political parties. This was regarded, at first, as dangerous to governmental stability. Madison had written in the *Federalist Papers* that "Factions" were the greatest danger to law, order, and the preservation of liberty, and Washington's Farewell Address contained grim warnings against "the baneful effects of the spirit of party."

But when Jefferson and Hamilton disagreed so completely, they attracted allies, organized newspapers, and began to establish societies and clubs for the purpose of swaying voters. These grew into political parties. Unlike factions, political parties were meant to be permanent, national in scope, and above all, ideological; they embodied the clashing political philosophies of Hamilton and Jefferson.

Thus in 1800 the country was fundamentally divided, and many Americans predicted that the outcome of the election would determine the nation's future. The campaign itself was vicious. Federalists falsely claimed that the Democratic-Republican candidate, Thomas Jefferson, was an atheist, a supporter of the Reign of Terror during the French Revolution, and a scheming politician who advocated a dangerous states' rights philosophy. The Democratic-Republicans countered by claiming that the Federalist candidate, John Adams, was a monarchist, an English stooge, and a tyrant who wanted to destroy the Bill of Rights. While such accusations and fears were groundless, they do represent not only the viciousness of partisan politics, but also the tendency of Americans in times of national crisis to think in conspiratorial terms. This tendency obscures the real issues that divide parties, sections, and classes by appealing to passions and irrationality based on fear.

Jefferson won the election of 1800; twelve years of Federalist rule ended in defeat. But the Federalists had made many contributions toward creating a stable government. They established the major governmental offices, proved the government's authority in the West, opened the Mississippi to American commerce, and forced France to abandon its attacks on American shipping. Equally important, the Federalists had created an orderly economic system which established the government's credit at home and abroad, proving Hamilton's assertion that commerce was the basis of prosperity and that the national government must win the confidence of its merchants and bankers.

Perhaps the most important achievement of the Federalist period, however, was their acceptance of defeat in 1800. Americans had demonstrated that no matter how bitter their political disputes, they were firmly committed to the idea that change should occur through established procedures rather than revolution.

4 America Expands And Goes To War

1. What were the advantages and disadvantages of acquiring the Louisiana Territory?

2. What program was followed by Jefferson and Madison in maintaining American relations with other countries?

3. Why did America go to war with Britain in 1812?

4. How were the Jefferson and Madison administrations similar to those of Washington and Adams, and how were they different?

Thomas Jefferson was aware that he must dispel the bitterness left by the campaign of 1800. Federalists feared that he would strip the national government of its hard-won power, destroy the Bank of the United States, irreparably damage British-American relations, and usher in a new and dangerous age of French egalitarianism. Such fears were groundless.

In his first inaugural address Jefferson tried to allay unwarranted fears aroused by the bitter election campaign by explaining that he planned no revolution. "We are all Federalists, we are all Republicans," he proclaimed. Jefferson, who believed that the chief value of government was to serve as "a mild and safe corrective of abuses," promised that his administration would be based upon principles of moderation. He was convinced the power of government should be limited, and

he looked forward to presiding over "a wise and frugal government which shall restrain men from injuring one another, and shall leave them otherwise free to regulate their own pursuits in industry and improvement. . . ."

The one great object of American society, Jefferson believed, was to produce virtuous men who could be trusted to govern themselves. Such men would naturally be small farmers and sturdy independent yeomen, who would maintain America as Jefferson had known it in the eighteenth century—a nation dominated by an agricultural middle class. In place of merchants and planters, Jefferson hoped to see America governed by "an aristocracy of talent and virtue."

Conflicts over western expansion. Jefferson's belief that virtue and prosperity must rest upon a solid mass of yeoman farmers convinced him that the future of the nation lay in the West. By 1801, American traders were again forbidden to use warehouses in New Orleans because Spain had ceded to France the entire Louisiana Territory (see map, page 798). Jefferson was determined to solve this problem by annexing New Orleans even if he had to make an alliance with Britain. To his astonishment, in 1803, France offered to sell the whole Louisiana Territory for only $15 million. Napoleon knew he could not hold the territory against a determined British attack. Moreover, the possibility of gaining the United States as an ally contributed to his decision.

When the Louisiana Purchase treaty was presented to Jefferson, he faced a dilemma, for the Constitution said nothing about the acquisition of territory. Informed that Napoleon was impatient, Jefferson abandoned his principle of strict Constitutional interpretation. The opportunity to acquire a million and a half square miles of magnificent farmland convinced Jefferson that in politics practicality must often replace theory.

The West in American history has always had a double image. It has served as the symbol of the nation's desire to create what Jefferson called "an empire of Liberty" in the wilderness. And its wealth not only assured growth of national power but contributed to individual success. Yet the West has also been a source of contention, alarm, and fear.

The Louisiana Purchase precipitated bitter political conflicts during the administrations of

Jefferson and his successor James Madison. The eastern states, especially New England, feared that Louisiana eventually would be carved into agricultural states which would weaken New England's influence in Congress. Some New England Federalists began to talk seriously of withdrawing from the Union and forming a New England Confederation.

More dangerous than separatist tendencies in New England was the bizarre attempt of Aaron Burr, Jefferson's first Vice-President, to detach Louisiana from the Union, mobilize an army, and invade Mexico. Although this enterprise was broken up, and Burr was arrested, Jefferson was alarmed by the number of Burr's supporters. Burr's fantastic scheme and the rumblings of some New England Federalists revealed that the indivisibility of the Union was not universally accepted.

Politics under Jefferson. Jefferson's domestic policies had the dual aim of crushing the Federalists and at the same time maintaining national unity. He had the hated whiskey excise tax re-pealed, and he allowed the Alien and Sedition Acts to expire. The Bank of the United States was maintained until its charter expired in 1811. Jefferson reduced the national debt from $83 million to $57 million. Jefferson's cautious policies pleased the Federalists, but deprived them of political ammunition.

One issue, however, went beyond politics and touched upon the Constitutional fabric of the nation itself. Jefferson was angered by Adams's last-minute appointment of numerous Federalists to federal judgeships the night before his term as President expired. These "Midnight Judges" included the Chief Justice, John Marshall. Jefferson had long disliked the Federalist incumbents on the bench. Not only had they upheld the Alien and Sedition Acts, but also one of them, Samuel Chase, used his position to deliver intemperate attacks on Jefferson and his party. As a result, the Democratic-Republicans in Congress tried to impeach Chase as the first step in a full-scale purge of the Supreme Court. The move failed, however, and from then on, federal judges

---

THE MARSHALL COURT — IMPORTANT DECISIONS

Marbury v. Madison (1803). The court refused to grant Marbury official papers (a *writ of mandamus*) to force Secretary of State Madison to confirm Marbury's appointment as a judge. The court said that the law empowering it to issue such writs was unconstitutional. The case established the principle of judicial review—that the Supreme Court is the final interpreter of a law's Constitutionality.

Fletcher v. Peck (1810). Georgia state legislators had been involved in fraudulent land-grant deals, and succeeding legislators tried to invalidate the grants. The court upheld the original grants, ruling that they were contracts. This was the first time the court ruled a state law unconstitutional.

Martin v. Hunter's Lessee (1816). A Virginia court refused to let an Englishman inherit land in Virginia. The court upheld his rights, setting the precedent that state-court rulings are subject to review when Constitutional issues are involved.

McCulloch v. Maryland (1819). Maryland taxed the Baltimore branch of the Bank of the United States heavily. McCulloch, a bank officer, refused to pay, and the court upheld the Constitutionality of the bank, ruling that no state could interfere with government business.

Dartmouth College Case (1819). New Hampshire revised the college charter and placed it under state control. The court ruled that the charter was a private contract and could not be changed without the consent of both parties, setting the precedent against state interference with private contracts.

Gibbons v. Ogden (1824). New York granted Ogden a monopoly for steam commerce on the Hudson River. The court ruled against the state, setting the precedent that the federal government has sole jurisdiction over interstate and foreign commerce.

were relatively free from partisan political interference.

Several early precedents were established by the Marshall Court. The most important was *Marbury* v. *Madison,* in which the Court explicitly declared the right of *judicial review,* that is, its right to determine the constitutionality of laws passed by Congress. This decision became the basis of the now accepted theory that the Supreme Court has final authority to interpret the meaning of the Constitution.

The trials of neutrality. Neutrality during wartime is difficult for commercial nations like the United States to maintain. Trade is the essence of prosperity, and war anywhere on the globe will interfere with trade. Immediately upon assuming office, Jefferson faced the problem of the Barbary pirates, who for years had captured American ships trading in the Mediterranean. Rather than send tribute to the pirates, Jefferson sent the navy. In 1805, the pirates of Tripoli backed down, and the value of a strong navy was clearly demonstrated. Nevertheless both Jefferson and Madison deprived the army and navy of funds. The fear of standing military forces, and the conviction that armies and navies are dangerous to liberty, proved decisive in American political thought at the very moment the United States found its trade threatened by the Napoleonic Wars in Europe.

When Napoleon began his conquest of Europe in 1803, Britain proceeded to sweep French shipping from the oceans. The United States declared its neutrality and insisted that its ships had the right to carry goods to all warring nations. Neither Napoleon nor Britain accepted this position. In 1806, the French emperor threatened to seize any neutral vessel trading with Britain, and the British countered by declaring that France was blockaded. Within a year, nearly fifteen hundred American ships had been seized by Britain and France, and Britain clearly intended to continue impressing American sailors.

Then in 1807, a British frigate attacked an American frigate and killed or wounded twenty-one Americans and impressed four sailors. Many Americans clamored for war, but instead Jefferson asked Congress to enact an *embargo,* or order prohibiting all foreign trade. The embargo, which caused complete economic stagnation, was an unqualified disaster. Both New England merchants and southern planters suffered serious economic losses and demanded repeal. Responding to popular pressure, Congress repealed the embargo and passed instead the Nonintercourse Act, allowing trade with all nations except France and Britain.

In 1810, under the new President, James Madison, the Nonintercourse Act was replaced by Madison's own plan, called Macon's Bill Number Two. The United States would stop trading with Britain if France agreed to respect American maritime rights, or with France if Britain would agree. But the plan failed. Although Napoleon agreed, and American trade with Britain was cut off, France continued to seize American shipping. And Britain still refused to withdraw its orders to seize neutral ships. By 1812, Americans had become so angry at British naval policy that Madison, convinced at last that no peaceful policy would force Britain to respect American rights, asked Congress to declare war.

Sentiment for war was strong, especially in the South and the West. Despite losses, huge profits were being made by New England merchants and shippers. They refused to concede that their trade was seriously impaired by the British navy. And New England knew that a war would be disastrous for its commerce. But American pride had been injured. New men in Congress, like Henry Clay of Kentucky and John C. Calhoun of South Carolina, had grown up in an independent America, and they felt humiliated by the impressment of American seamen. In addition, they believed that British agents had stirred up the Indians who attacked along the frontier in 1811. A third factor motivated southern and western congressmen: they believed that war would enable the United States to annex Canada and Florida.

The War of 1812. The war of 1812 was pointless. By the time hostilities began, the British had actually repealed their orders to seize neutral ships, although they indicated that impressment would still continue. New England Federalists, convinced that the war was needless, refused to participate. The regular army, about seven thousand ill-prepared men, was scattered along the frontier. And the navy, though well-trained and equipped, was no match for the much larger British fleet, which blockaded American ports (see battle map, page 116).

When the war was not going well for the Americans during the first half of 1813, an artist sought to raise American spirits by depicting the young nation as a hornet, smaller than the British peacock, but still able to deal him a damaging blow. But in actual battle, the Americans were not always so successful. Below, the American ship *Chesapeake* meets its adversary, the British *Shannon*, just off Boston on June 1, 1813. The two ships crashed together, and the crews went into hand to hand combat on the decks and in the riggings. Both crews suffered heavy casualties, and the British finally won. Nevertheless, the battle gave the American navy one of its traditions. As the *Chesapeake's* captain, James Lawrence, lay mortally wounded on the deck, he shouted to his men, "Don't give up the ship!"

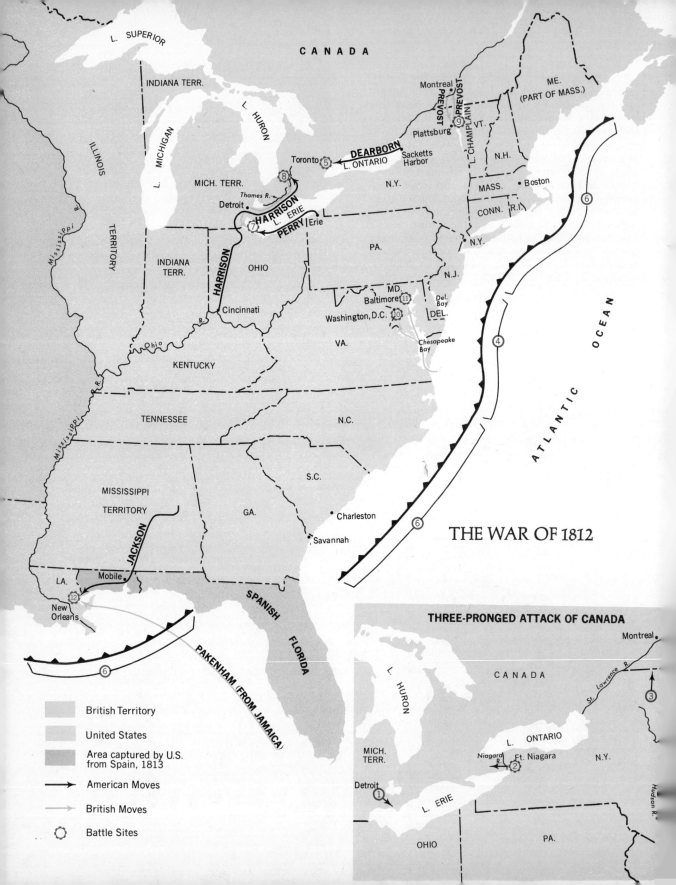

L. SUPERIOR

CANADA

INDIANA TERR.

L. HURON

Montreal
PREVOST
PREVOST
ME.
(PART OF MASS.)

L. MICHIGAN

Plattsburg
L. CHAMPLAIN
VT.

Toronto
DEARBORN
Sacketts
Harbor
N.H.

ILLINOIS

MICH. TERR.
Thames R.
Detroit
HARRISON
L. ERIE
PERRY Erie

L. ONTARIO
N.Y.

MASS.
Boston

CONN.
R.I.

TERRITORY

INDIANA
TERR.

OHIO

HARRISON

N.Y.

PA.

N.J.

ATLANTIC OCEAN

Cincinnati

MD.
Baltimore
Washington, D.C.

Del.
Bay
DEL.

Ohio R.

KENTUCKY

VA.

Chesapeake
Bay

TENNESSEE

N.C.

THE WAR OF 1812

MISSISSIPPI
TERRITORY

S.C.

GA.

Charleston

Savannah

JACKSON

Mobile
LA.
New
Orleans

SPANISH
FLORIDA

PAKENHAM (FROM JAMAICA)

British Territory

United States

Area captured by U.S.
from Spain, 1813

American Moves

British Moves

Battle Sites

THREE-PRONGED ATTACK OF CANADA

Montreal

L. HURON

CANADA

St. Lawrence R.

MICH.
TERR.

L. ONTARIO

Niagara
R.
Ft. Niagara

N.Y.

Detroit

L. ERIE

Hudson R.

OHIO

PA.

THE WAR OF 1812

④ **Dec. 26, 1812. British Blockade.** Chesapeake and Delaware Bays are shut off from commerce.

⑤ **April 27, 1813. Toronto.** Combined naval and military expedition under General Henry Dearborn raids Toronto. American troops burn the city's public buildings before withdrawing.

⑥ **May 26, 1813 and April 25, 1814.** British blockade is extended from New Orleans to New England.

⑦ **Sept. 10, 1813. Lake Erie.** Oliver Perry decisively defeats a British fleet, forcing the British to abandon Detroit.

⑧ **Oct. 5, 1813. Thames River.** General William Henry Harrison pursues British retreating from Detroit and defeats them at the Thames River.

⑨ **Sept. 11, 1814. Lake Champlain.** Thomas Macdonough defeats a British fleet and gains control of the entire lake. British, under Prevost, waiting on shore are forced to return to Montreal.

⑩ **Aug. 24-25, 1814. Washington.** British sail up Chesapeake Bay, and meeting token resistance at Bladenburg, outside the city, enter Washington, burning public buildings before they withdraw.

⑪ **Sept. 12-14, 1814. Baltimore.** British sail up from the Potomac River to Baltimore. At Ft. McHenry, outside the city, they meet strong resistance. After unsuccessfully bombarding Ft. McHenry, the British withdraw.

⑫ **Jan. 8, 1815. New Orleans.** British forces are decisively defeated by Andrew Jackson's troops.

A series of disasters followed. In 1812, the Americans surrendered Detroit and were defeated at the Niagara River; Indians terrorized the Ohio frontier; and numerous attempts to march on Montreal ended in failure. By the middle of 1813, the American position in the West was precarious. Fortunately, a decisive naval victory by Commodore Oliver H. Perry on Lake Erie, combined with a victory over the Indians and their British allies near Toronto saved the West. But Canada could not be taken, and in 1814, the Americans abandoned their plans to conquer Canada.

The American navy performed brilliantly for a time, but by 1814 it was unable to penetrate the British blockade, and trade fell by 90 percent. Moreover, by 1814 Napoleon had been defeated in Europe, and the British were now ready to send troops to put down the impudent Yankees. A large British army arrived in Canada to invade from the north, and a smaller British force prepared to attack Washington and Baltimore in the south.

As the war dragged into 1814, New Englanders, whose trade was being ruined by the blockade, became increasingly bitter, and even talked of secession. Opposition finally erupted at the end of 1814, when delegates from New England convened at Hartford, Connecticut. Although a majority of the delegates were opposed to secession, they did condemn the war and adopted a series of states' rights resolutions that would have resulted in more power for New England in the national government. Before the resolutions could be presented to Congress, however, the war was over. Nevertheless, New England's hostility showed how divisive the war had become.

Although the first two years of the war had been humiliating for the Americans, the last year proved embarrassing to the British. In the North a British fleet was destroyed on Lake Champlain, and an invading army from Canada retreated. In the South, although the British penetrated Washington and burned government buildings, they were unable to take Baltimore. The final battle was fought at New Orleans, where militia under Andrew Jackson repulsed several British assaults. After suffering severe losses, the British withdrew.

Paradoxically, this most dramatic battle of a meaningless war was fought two weeks after the signing of a peace treaty at Ghent, Belgium, in

1814, which restored the situation as it had been before the war. Now that the Napoleonic Wars were over, Americans saw no point in continuing the debate on impressment. And the British, after learning that their armies had failed to achieve their objectives, withdrew their own conditions for peace. If the treaty settled none of the issues over which the war had been fought, it did insure peace in the future. The Treaty of Ghent arranged for commissions to be set up in the future to settle the vaguely defined border between the United States and Canada.

The administration of Thomas Jefferson had opened with the President preaching national unity and envisioning the creation of a great empire in the West; that of his successor, James Madison, ended with the country disunited and exhausted by war. Yet the American Constitutional system, as fragile as it seemed to many Americans, had survived. In fact, there finally emerged from the chaos and strife created by the War of 1812 an unprecedented sense of national unity. For a few years after the war, Americans were able to rejoice in the birth of an "era of good feelings."

5 The Nation Enjoys An Era Of Good Feelings

1. What were the parts of the American System, and how did they tend to encourage nationalistic tendencies?

2. How did the decisions of the Supreme Court strengthen the powers of the federal government?

3. What were the provisions of the Monroe Doctrine, and why did John Quincy Adams encourage its pronouncement?

4. What issues tended to divide the United States in the 1820's? Why did these issues arise?

The national unity of the United States from 1815 to 1820 was due in part to the virtual demise of the Federalist party. James Monroe, who succeeded Madison in 1816, was elected twice with only token opposition from Federalists and presided over a one-party government. The greatest source of unity, however, was the modification, if not the total abandonment, of Jeffersonian ideals after the War of 1812. The Democratic-Republican party virtually adopted the Federalist platform in economic and foreign policy.

Henry Clay later called the result the "American System," a policy of vigorous government participation in the economy through the Bank of the United States, high tariffs to protect and encourage the growth of industry, and government subsidies for roads, canals, and turnpikes. Clay's followers, initially joined by John C. Calhoun of South Carolina, were fervid nationalists who agreed with Alexander Hamilton that the development of manufacturing would ensure continued prosperity.

Nationalist economic policy. The national government's more active role in economic affairs was a response to the British policy of dumping manufactured goods on the American market. By underselling American producers they hoped to stifle the infant textile industry which had begun earlier in New England. To protect American industry, Congress, in 1816, passed a tariff placing such high duties on British cotton goods that American firms soon dominated the home market.

In the same year, Congress rechartered the Bank of the United States for a period of twenty years. Modeled on the first bank, the Second Bank of the United States served as the sole depository of government funds, regulated the financial policies of state banks, extended loans, and issued bank notes which served as a national currency. Because the United States was a developing nation, it faced a chronic shortage of investment capital. By extending loans to investors and to banks, the national bank could increase the amount of capital available. And its regulatory powers over state banks helped to stabilize the currency and increased the confidence of business in the stability of the monetary system.

Good transportation was also important for the orderly development of the American economy. The primitive eighteenth-century roads had to be replaced by new turnpikes and canals capable of transporting goods in large quantities. However, little came of Calhoun's demand to "bind this

The Era of Good Feelings saw the almost complete abandonment of Jefferson's economic ideas and the adoption of the financial philosophy of Alexander Hamilton. In order to stimulate American economic growth, the national government instituted a policy of protective tariffs. Most leaders believed that protective tariffs were important for several reasons. High tariffs would protect domestic industries, especially "infant industries," from foreign competition, thus providing workers with jobs and keeping wages high. High tariff rates would also help to develop American self-sufficiency, which was felt to be particularly important in wartime. (War was much on the minds of Americans, since they had just come through the War of 1812.) Finally, protective tariffs would provide added income for the government.

Opponents of protective tariffs argue that high rates allow domestic producers to monopolize the market and artifically raise prices. They also claim that high tariffs encourage inefficiency and inferior products by eliminating foreign competition. Further, they argue that high rates hurt a nation's exports because other nations will retaliate by placing high tariffs on goods they import.

republic together with a perfect system of roads and canals." Presidents Madison and Monroe, after agreeing to the construction of the National Road (see map, page 152), began to doubt, as had Jefferson, the Constitutionality of such direct action by the federal government. Nevertheless, some progress was made by both private investment and public expenditure. The intervention of the federal government in economic affairs had been remarkable for its time.

Role of the Supreme Court. The emerging nationalism was expressed in several Supreme Court decisions, under Chief Justice John Marshall, which clearly placed the authority of the federal government above that of the states in some crucial areas. In *Fletcher* v. *Peck* (1810) the Court asserted its right to determine the Constitutionality of state laws. In *McCulloch* v. *Maryland* (1819), Marshall declared that the Bank of the United States was Constitutional and that state governments could not tax a federal corporation. In *Gibbons* v. *Ogden* (1824), Marshall ruled that only Congress, not the states, could regulate commerce between the states. All of these decisions made clear the meaning of Article VI of the Constitution: "This Constitution, and the Laws which shall be made in pursuance thereof . . . shall be the supreme law of the land. . . ."

Diplomacy of the period. American foreign policy from 1815 to 1828 reverted to its traditional course of avoiding conflict with European nations, a course disastrously interrupted by the War of 1812. However, a new militancy marked the American diplomacy of this period, especially under Monroe's secretary of state, John Quincy Adams. To Adams, foreign policy had one great goal besides neutrality—territorial consolidation by the United States on the North American continent. He believed that the United States must expand to its "natural Boundaries," by which he meant the whole of North America. He was also convinced that European powers would continuously seek to weaken the United States if they remained on its borders.

Andrew Jackson, the hero of the Battle of New Orleans, provided Adams with his opportunity to acquire Florida. The Seminole Indians, stirred up by British agents and protected by Spanish officials in Florida, attacked American settlers in Alabama. Jackson promptly chased the Indians into Florida and seized Pensacola. When Spain protested, Adams defended Jackson and demanded that Spain apologize for the Indian raid. In 1819, convinced that it could not hold Florida against American incursions, Spain sold it to the United States for $5 million. In the same treaty, the Adams-Onis Treaty, the boundary between the Louisiana Territory and Mexico was defined (see map, page 798). The United States gave up its claim to Texas, and more important, Spain relinquished its claims to the Oregon Territory. The United States had reached the Pacific.

Meanwhile, American relations with Britain were devoted to defining the border between the United States and Canada. The Maine-Quebec boundary was not settled until 1842, but great success was achieved in the West. The Rush-

Bagot agreement (1817) demilitarized the Great Lakes, and the following year a joint commission agreed upon a boundary line between Canada and the United States. Britain, however, also laid claim to Oregon where fur companies had built trading posts. Thus, the two nations decided, for the time being, to share the Oregon region (see map, page 798). However, Russia, hoping to expand southward from Alaska (which it owned until 1867), claimed the Pacific Coast north of the 51st parallel, which included most of Oregon.

The Monroe Doctrine. At the same time, revolutions were occurring in Latin America and Spain. European powers not only cooperated in crushing the Spanish revolution, but also considered joint intervention in Latin America. Both Great Britain and the United States, who cherished republican principles and the prospect of trade with Spain's former dependencies, were alarmed. Great Britain suggested that the two nations issue a joint declaration opposing foreign intervention in Latin America.

John Quincy Adams, unlike some American officials, was not impressed by the British offer. He believed that the British were interested in acquiring Cuba, and he was as much concerned about British and Russian claims to Oregon as he was about the threat of European intervention in Latin America. As a result of Adams's advice, President Monroe included in his state of the Union message in December 1823 what has come to be called the Monroe Doctrine. It declared that any further European encroachment or colonization in the Western Hemisphere would be considered hostile to the best interests of the United States. At the time, Europeans generally ignored the Monroe Doctrine. The British navy was far more influential in preventing European intervention in Latin America than Monroe's declaration. In time, however, the Monroe doctrine became a fixture of American foreign policy.

Rise of political tensions. The Era of Good Feelings, marked by party harmony and a feeling of national unity, was short-lived. The nation soon experienced new tensions resulting from economic depression, the entry of new states into the Union, and the issue of slavery expansion.

The years after 1815 were characterized by rapid economic growth, which has occurred in American society after every war. By 1819, the market was glutted with goods, and state banks had made too many speculative loans. The Bank of the United States, in an effort to control the increasingly disorderly economy, refused to make new loans and also raised its interest rates. Investors were so unnerved by this strict policy that a financial panic occurred. People blamed the Bank of the United States for the ensuing depression, which struck the West most severely. Since the bank was controlled by easterners, rich merchants, and bankers, it was a convenient target for aspiring western politicians.

Moreover, western politicians were obliged to win the support of the ever-increasing number of farmers migrating westward, and in time the national leaders of the Democratic-Republican party were forced to heed the voice of the newly created states. Indiana entered the Union in 1816, followed by Mississippi (1817), Illinois (1818), and Alabama (1819). Congressmen from these states not only were inclined to attack the bank but soon began to question protective tariffs. Their states had little industry that needed protection, and the tariff kept prices high on goods they had to buy. On the other hand, many westerners wanted the price of land reduced and also federal spending for internal improvements.

Another issue, rarely discussed before 1819, suddenly appeared on the national scene with explosive force. When in that year Missouri applied for admission into the Union, a New York congressman, James Tallmadge, proposed that slavery be outlawed in the new state. The Senate rejected the Tallmadge Plan, but the House of Representatives supported it. Northern senators and congressmen were well aware that the admission of Missouri as a slave state would give the South virtual control of the Senate, a supremacy most northerners were not prepared to accept.

In 1820, Henry Clay managed to devise an acceptable compromise. Missouri was admitted as a slave state, but Maine came in as a free state to maintain the sectional balance of power. Then, in an attempt to avoid future conflict on the slavery issue, the Missouri Compromise outlawed slavery in the remaining territory north of the parallel 36°30'. Sectional peace on this issue had been restored temporarily, but the angry debates signaled the end of the Era of Good Feelings.

ART IN THE FEDERALIST PERIOD

Thomas and Sarah Mifflin, John Singleton Copley, 1773

Toward the end of the eighteenth century, American painting, still predominated by portraiture, rose to a new height of professional competence. Part of the reason for the advance was the talent of John Singleton Copley, an artist whose career spanned the colonial and federalist periods. The painting on the preceding page shows his skill as a draftsman and his realistic approach to his subjects.

Unlike their earlier, self-taught counterparts, Copley and several other American artists of the period went to Europe to study. Perhaps the most influential of these painters was Benjamin West, whose painting bottom right is unfinished because the British commissioners refused to pose. He had moved to London from Pennsylvania, and there several other American painters studied with him, three of whom are represented in these pages—Charles Willson Peale, Gilbert Stuart, and John Trumbull. Having taken advantage of the superior art facilities in Europe, they were able to paint in what was called "the grand style" and were able to raise American painting to the level of European painting of the time. They were also able to expand the range of American painting to go beyond portraiture. New types of painting came to enrich the American art scene—historical, genre, allegorical, and landscape painting among them.

The Artist in His Museum, Charles Willson Peale, 1823

Portrait of Thomas Jefferson, Gilbert Stuart, 1799

Portrait of Alexander Hamilton,
John Trumbull, after 1804

American Commissioners,
Benjamin West, 1783

Fourth of July in Centre Square, John Lewis Krimmel, 1810–12

The genre painting above shows examples of the architecture and sculpture of the period, both of which reflect heavy Greek and Roman influences. The noble building with the Greek portal and the Roman dome was designed by architect Benjamin Latrobe. In the fountain is a water nymph carved in the Grecian style by sculptor William Rush. And the allegorical painting below, illustrating a Bible story, shows a distinct Renaissance influence.

Elijah in the Desert, Washington Allston, 1818

Political realignment. Growing sectional tensions over slavery and economic issues disrupted the Democratic-Republican party in 1824. Since the second Presidential election, it had been customary for the most powerful party leaders in Congress to form a *caucus*, or meeting of party leaders, to nominate candidates for President and Vice President. The secretary of state was the logical choice after a President had served two terms—both Madison and Monroe had been nominated this way.

In 1824, however, four major candidates refused to support the caucus nominee, William H. Crawford of Georgia. Kentucky championed Henry Clay, the nationalist spokesman of the West. Tennessee nominated Andrew Jackson, also a westerner and a national military hero. South Carolina advocated its own native son, John C. Calhoun, who would best defend southern interests. Calhoun, however, agreed to run for Vice President with Jackson, fully expecting to be Jackson's heir apparent after he stepped down from the Presidency. New England favored John Quincy Adams, a brilliant architect of foreign policy but a cold and tactless man.

In the election that followed, Jackson won more electoral and popular votes than any other candidate, but he lacked a majority in the electoral college, and the election was thrown into the House of Representatives. Adams was finally elected after Clay gave him his support. The grateful President promptly chose Clay as his secretary of state. As President, Adams was thwarted at every turn. Like Clay, he passionately believed in the American System, but virtually all of his nationalistic proposals for federal intervention in the economy were so severely challenged that his program was doomed to failure. In addition, the circumstances under which he achieved the Presidency convinced many voters that Adams and Clay had made a "corrupt bargain."

Disunited, filled with angry rumors and speculation, the United States slowly drifted away from the political and economic nationalism so ardently championed by leaders such as Alexander Hamilton, John Quincy Adams, and Henry Clay. The nation had experienced the first phase of the political conflicts that would lead to the reemergence of a two-party system.

EXPLORING NEW LANDS

During the early days of the Republic, explorers were sent out by the new government to study the extent and features of the vast lands to the west. Two of the most memorable of these daring men were Merriwether Lewis and William Clark, who set out in mid-May of 1804. Of the many tense situations the two men described in their journals, perhaps the most potentially damaging one occurred one year into the trip, when it appeared that the year may have all been for nothing. Lewis, not known for his excellence in spelling, describes the incident involving a pirogue, a dugout canoe:

". . . It happened unfortunately for us this evening that Charbono was at the helm of this perogue . . . [he] . . . is perhaps the most timid waterman in the world. . . . In this perogue were embarked our papers, instruments, books, medicine, a great part of our merchandize and in short almost every article indispensibly necessary to further the views, or insure the success of the enterprize in which we are now launched to the distance of 2200 miles. . . . the perogue was under sail when a sudon squawl of wind struck her . . . and instantly upset the perogue . . . Such was their confusion and consternation at this moment that they suffered the perogue to lye on her side for half a minute before they took the sail in, the perogue then wrighted but had filled within an inch of the gunwals. Charbono still crying to his god for mercy, had not yet recollected the rudder, nor could the repeated orders of the bowsman, Cruzat, bring him to his recollection untill he threatened to shoot him instantly if he did not take hold of the rudder . . . The waves by this time were running high but . . . Cruzat saved her. He ordered 2 of the men to throw out the water . . . while himself and two others rowed her ashore, where she arrived scarcely above the water. We now took every article out of her and lay them to drane as well as we could for the evening. . . ."

■ CONCLUSION

The concept of national unity, so crucial in the thinking of the Founding Fathers, proved difficult to realize in fact. Instead of harmony, American political life was characterized by disputes so profound they led to the formation of political parties. The attempts of Alexander Hamilton to create national unity through a national economy vigorously regulated by the government and strongly supported by commercial interests was challenged by the conviction of Jefferson and Madison that the "government which governs least governs best." This basic philosophical division over the nature of government would characterize almost every period of American history that followed.

The Founding Fathers saw the essential problems of the nation as Constitutional and political. Problems of finance, diplomacy, and civil liberties dominated their thinking. Hence, they practically ignored other forces that were stirring. The nation was growing, and the westerner was becoming a political force. More Americans were voting, and through their participation in the political process, the country was becoming more democratic. A new America was emerging—competitive, enterprising, egalitarian—and was on the verge of a new era, the age of Jackson.

■ QUESTIONS

1. What were the problems in the western part of the United States facing the Washington administration when the Constitution took effect in 1789? How successful was the new government in handling these problems? What were the problems in the same area in 1828?

2. What were the economic problems facing the United States in 1789? What steps were taken to correct these problems? How effective were the measures taken? What were the economic problems facing the United States in 1828?

3. What were the diplomatic problems facing the United States in 1789? What steps were taken to correct these problems? How effective were the measures taken? What were the diplomatic problems facing the United States in 1828?

4. How would you grade the leaders of the United States from 1789 to 1828 on their attempt to establish national unity? What did they do to encourage unity? What should they have done? How would you evaluate the degree of unity during the period from 1789 to 1828?

5. What was the theory of government advocated by Alexander Hamilton and his supporters? What was the theory of government advocated by Thomas Jefferson and his supporters? Was the government from 1789 to 1828 more Hamiltonian or Jeffersonian? Explain your answer.

■ BIBLIOGRAPHY

JENSEN, MERRILL, *The New Nation: A History of the United States During the Confederation, 1781–1789*, Random House (Vintage Books).

CUNLIFFE, MARCUS, *The Nation Takes Shape: 1789–1837*, U. of Chicago Press.

These two interpretive accounts provide excellent background and impressive analysis by recognized scholars in the field.

HAMILTON, ALEXANDER, JAMES MADISON, AND JOHN JAY, *The Federalist Papers*, ed. by Clinton Rossiter, New American Library (Mentor Books). These collected essays are perhaps the most outstanding American contribution to political theory. Written to encourage the ratification of the Constitution, they are exceptional in their insight into the political process.

LEWIS, MERIWETHER, AND WILLIAM CLARK, *Journals of Lewis and Clark*, intro. by Bernard DeVoto, Houghton Mifflin (Sentry Editions). At the present time in America's development when we are so concerned with the environment, students should read about the American West as explored by Lewis and Clark. They describe the Great Plains, Northern Rockies, and Pacific Northwest before settlement by the whites.

MALONE, DUMAS, *Jefferson the President: First Term 1801–1805*, Little, Brown. This biography is particularly good since it provides a new, fresh appraisal of Jefferson's administration and shows how Jefferson was able to secure the goals of the Revolution as he perceived them.

PERKINS, DEXTER, *A History of the Monroe Doctrine*, Little, Brown. The Monroe Doctrine reappears continually in American history, and students should note this book for future reference.

MOORE, GLOVER, *The Missouri Compromise 1819–1821*, University Press of Kentucky. An important outcome of this period was the Missouri Compromise, and students who may want to know more about this agreement should consult Moore's book. It is a factual, relatively complete handling of the topic.

Part 2

The New Nation And Its Crises

Second Street North from Market Street with Christ Church. Philadelphia, William Birch and Son, 1799

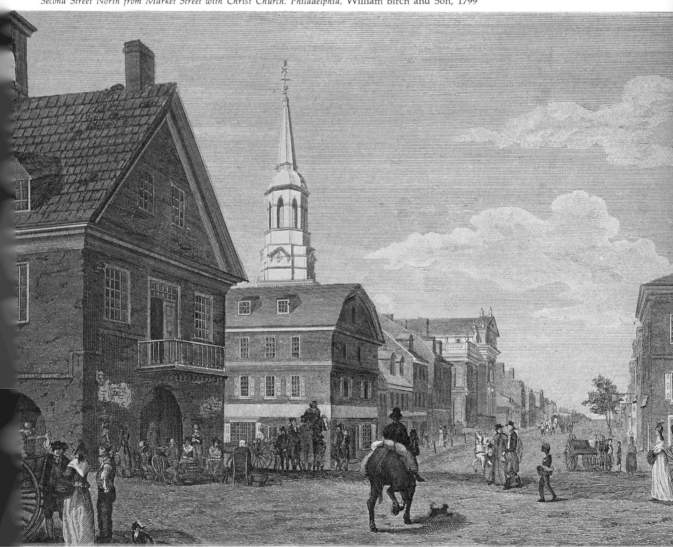

CHAPTER FOUR/1828–1844

The Jacksonian Era

The era in American history named after Andrew Jackson was one of the most critical in the nation's history. It was an age of transition and conflict. In one sense it was the "era of the common man" in politics. The rapid expansion of suffrage and the enactment of political reforms since the Revolution made politics in America more democratic than in any other nation. These advances toward a more democratic political order were accompanied by far-reaching social and economic changes and by the re-emergence of the two-party system.

Differing widely in philosophy, the two parties battled over fundamental economic and political issues. The Jacksonian Democrats adhered to the Jeffersonian concepts of states' rights and opposition to centralization of government. Their opponents championed the economic and political doctrines of the old Federalist party. At stake were questions of public lands, the tariff, internal improvments, finance, and most important, the role of the federal government. In addition, sectional conflicts and the old fears of national disunity were revived. The outcome of the struggle between Jacksonian Democrats and their opponents would determine the economic and political direction the nation was to take. As you analyze the events of the Jacksonian era, here are some questions to keep in mind:

1. In what ways did politics become more democratic in Jackson's time?
2. How did Jackson's background and personality affect his policies as President?
3. How did the theory of nullification threaten the Union?
4. Why was the Bank of the United States such a divisive issue?
5. How did the two-party system reemerge?

1 Political Democracy Advances In America

1. To what extent was political democracy extended during the period from 1780 to 1840?

2. Why was suffrage extended during this period?

3. What changes in the election process developed during this period to indicate a greater "professionalization" of American political life?

4. What do you think are the characteristics of a desirable political democracy?

By 1828, far-reaching political changes had occurred in the United States which made the American political system more democratic than it had been at the time of the American Revolution. One indicator of the level of political democracy is the right to vote. Between 1780 and 1824, restrictions on suffrage were removed in most states. After 1824 significant restrictions were retained only in Virginia, Louisiana, Mississippi, and Rhode Island. By 1856, white male suffrage existed throughout the United States.

Extension of suffrage. On the eve of the Revolution, the colonies had virtually achieved self-government based on representative institutions. Yet, American society at that time cannot be described as democratic. Large numbers of Americans were disenfranchised through property qualifications for voting, and small groups of wealthy men controlled the colonial assemblies. The American Revolution, however, was a major catalyst in starting the inexorable transition in American society away from the politics of elitism and toward political democracy. "In one sense," historian J. R. Pole writes, "this great transition *was* the American Revolution." Revolutionary leaders won the support of disenfranchised Americans in the struggle for independence. In so doing, however, they aroused a democratic spirit among the people that could not be denied once independence was achieved.

Of the original thirteen states, five (Pennsylvania, North Carolina, Delaware, New Hamp-

shire, and Georgia) adopted constitutions substituting tax payment for property qualifications. Since taxation in the 1780's was based primarily upon property holdings, universal adult male suffrage did not follow immediately. But the principle of divorcing suffrage from property holding had far-reaching implications for the future. During the early national period the expansion of economic opportunities combined with the states' need for revenue other than land taxes effectively broadened suffrage. Equally important, the emergence of national political parties in the 1790's led many politicians to advocate suffrage extension in order to find new sources of support. Jefferson's party, the Democratic-Republican, led the way in demanding suffrage extension. After 1800, however, the Federalists adopted the same tactics in an effort to retain their position. As a result, in many states the poll tax—an individual tax of a fixed amount—came to be the only tax required for voting.

Expansion of the frontier. Another factor which helps to explain the advance of democracy was the expansion of the frontier. Of the eight states admitted into the Union between 1796 and 1821, five permitted adult male suffrage, while three required moderate taxes or militia service, and sometimes both. As historian Chilton Williamson observes, this partially reflects the incorporation of the "democratic ideas which had been the conscious inheritance of the American people since the Revolution."

But Williamson goes on to point out that practical factors were at work on the frontier as well as in the East. For example, Congress, in establishing governments for new territories, abolished property qualifications out of necessity. In the early years of settlement, interminable delays in securing bona fide land titles would have disenfranchised the vast majority of the settlers if property qualifications had been maintained. As a result, suffrage in the territories was usually based on either taxpaying or militia service.

Political activity in early nineteenth-century America was generally colorful. In his painting *Election Day at the State House, Philadelphia, 1816*, on the following pages, John Lewis Krimmel captured the excitement of election day.

129

131

Voters in the territories naturally incorporated liberal suffrage provisions in their state constitutions when applying to Congress for admission into the Union.

Social and economic mobility. In analyzing the advance of democracy in America, J. R. Pole emphasizes the importance of social and economic mobility in challenging the wealthier groups and promoting democracy. The opening up of new areas of economic opportunities and the expansion of the frontier, with its demands for extended suffrage and equal representation, threatened the power of the privileged classes in the East. And in the West, social and economic mobility made it impossible to establish entrenched privileged groups.

Thus, democracy in America, both in the East and on the frontier, advanced for several reasons. It was an extension of the Revolutionary inheritance. And it was also the result of political and practical considerations and an increasing economic and social mobility.

Changes in American politics. Other political reforms also had occurred. By 1828, in all states except South Carolina and Delaware, Presidential electors were chosen by popular vote rather than state legislatures—a more democratic procedure. In addition, the caucus system of party leaders in Congress selecting Presidential candidates was replaced by nominations by state legislatures, and in 1832 by the national nominating convention. Finally, by 1840, the voters rather than the legislatures elected the governor and the judges in most states.

It must be remembered, however, that these reforms applied only to white men. Despite vigorous agitation from the 1830's onward, women made little progress in their quest for suffrage until the twentieth century. And free blacks were disenfranchised in every northern state except Maine, New Hampshire, Vermont, and Massachusetts. The fact that only 7 percent of the northern free black population lived in these four states may account for the fact that they were not deprived of their right to vote.

Despite these inequities, the advent of universal white male suffrage was destined to revolutionize American political life. Between 1824 and 1828, the number of eligible voters who cast ballots doubled; by 1840 the number was two and a half times as large as it had been in 1828. In part, this increased voter participation was a reflection of democratic reforms that had occurred since the Revolution. Historians have noted, however, that eligibility to vote and the actual exercise of that vote are two different things. The fact that the number of eligible voters who cast ballots in 1840 was two and a half times the number in 1828 clearly reveals that the increased political consciousness of the "common man" was nearly as great a change in the nature of American politics as extended suffrage and electoral reforms. Thus, the dramatic upsurge in voter participation in political life was at once a reflection of and a catalyst for far-reaching changes in political organization in the 1820's and 1830's.

During this period, the two-party system re-emerged in America. This, combined with universal white male suffrage in most states, caused politics to become more professionalized at every level—local, state, and national. In an effort to win over the increasingly large numbers of voters, politicians created efficient organizations, or "machines," which used both paid and volunteer workers. Although such devices as mass rallies, torch-light parades, barbecues, and emotional appeals existed in earlier times, in Jackson's era they began to be used more professionally and more effectively. The dispensing of patronage for loyal party service (for example, government jobs and printing contracts) was designed to marshal support for candidates whose personal popularity often exceeded their qualifications for office.

Although American political life was being revolutionized, some historians have maintained that the extent of political democracy during the Jacksonian era has been exaggerated. Edward Pessen, a leading Jacksonian scholar, argues that in many ways Jacksonian America "was neither an age of egalitarianism nor of the common man." He observes that shrewd politicians publicly praised the virtues of democracy but retained "tight control over nominations and policymaking." And, as a rule, political leaders and candidates were recruited from the wealthier segment of society. In essence, democratic innovations could be reduced to token importance, and large numbers of voters could be manipulated just as easily as a handful.

It is true that many politicians of the Jacksonian

period did not have the public interest at heart and often used the new democratic forms for their own special ends. It is also true that advances in democracy do not necessarily mean that ideal or complete democracy has been achieved. Democratic procedures can be manipulated to serve special interests, and no period of American history has been free of those who will use democratic forms to suit their own private goals. Contemporary American political life is far more democratic than it was in Jackson's time; yet, damagoguery, patronage, the misuse of party machinery, fraud and corruption, still exist.

2 Jackson Takes Over The White House

1. What were the characteristics of the Presidential campaign of 1828?

2. What were the strengths and weaknesses of Andrew Jackson as a Presidential candidate in 1828? What were his views of the Presidency once he was elected to office?

3. Why were the Cherokee Indians removed from their lands? Do you think their removal was justified?

4. What are the advantages and disadvantages of replacing incumbents in government positions with loyal party members?

In 1824, when John Quincy Adams became President, the Democratic-Republicans had split into two factions. The faction led by Adams and Henry Clay, which was strongest in the Northeast, took the name National Republicans. Their opponents, who called themselves Democrats, were led by Andrew Jackson and John Calhoun, and their support was centered in the West, in New York, and the South. As the election of 1828 approached, the Democrats, with Jackson and Calhoun as their candidates, were ready to challenge the National Republicans.

The election of 1828. Important issues were at stake in the election—the tariff, public lands, internal improvements, Indian affairs. The principles of Adams and the National Republicans were clear. They advocated measures that would promote rapid development of the national economy and strengthen the influence of the federal government. If the position of Adams was clear on national issues, that of General Jackson was not. His managers deliberately obscured the real issues and waged a campaign that showed little respect for the intelligence of the American voter.

Jackson was pictured as a man of the people who would champion the rights of the masses against the aristocratic principles of President Adams. Much was made of the "corrupt bargain" charge which had been leveled at Adams and Clay following Adams's election in 1824 (page 125). Clay, as the ardent champion of the "American System," had naturally supported Adams. But the fact that Adams had then appointed Clay secretary of state placed both men in the position of being falsely accused of corruption.

In fact, the campaign of 1828 was one of the most unprincipled ever waged in the nation— one that helped set the tone for future electoral campaigns in which real issues were avoided in favor of slanderous attacks against the moral principles of the rival candidates. Jackson, for example, was accused of being a murderer and an adulterer. The murder charges stemmed from duels he had fought and from his Florida expedition in 1819 during which he hanged two British citizens for inciting the Indians. As for the adultery charge, Jackson and his wife had married believing that her divorce from her first husband was legally final. When the mistake was cleared up, they went through a wedding ceremony a second time. Adams himself never approved of his supporters' tactics. But Jackson's partisans, in retaliation, falsely accused Adams of having attempted to provide the Czar of Russia with the favors of a young American servant girl when Adams was the American ambassador to Russia.

When this scurrilous campaign was over, Jackson emerged with a smashing victory in the electoral college, 178 to 83. In terms of popular votes the election was much closer, 640,000 to 508,000. Jackson carried the West and the South; Adams's strength was confined primarily to New England.

Jackson's qualities. Jackson's major assets as a Presidential candidate stemmed from his reputation as a military hero and a self-made man. He was indeed born in a log cabin in the backcountry of North Carolina in 1767. In early manhood, after receiving an elementary education confined primarily to "the three R's" and some rudimentary legal training, Jackson moved to Nashville, Tennessee, where he earned a reputation as a lawyer, Indian fighter, public prosecutor, and judge. He also served briefly in Congress in 1797 before resigning because of temporary financial difficulties. In time, Jackson became a wealthy slaveholder, land speculator, and breeder of race horses. He owned not only one plantation near Nashville where he built a magnificent manor house—The Hermitage—but another in Alabama as well.

Critics have argued that Jackson's wealth and his involvement in Tennessee politics, in which he usually aligned himself with the interests of the creditor class, hardly entitles him to his reputation as the "champion of the common man." Yet it must be remembered that to a majority of early nineteenth-century Americans, equality meant equality of opportunity, not of conditions. And Jackson, who had been born in humble circumstances and had managed to rise in economic status through his own efforts, possessed those qualities which Americans admired. Indeed, many hoped to emulate Jackson's example. These qualities, combined with his military reputation, appealed to enough workingmen, small farmers, and small businessmen who wanted to become *entrepreneurs*, or business promoters, to make Jackson President.

Moreover, Jackson's own vagueness on many public issues during the campaign enabled his political managers to represent "Old Hickory" * as being all things to all people. For example, his statements that he opposed excessively high tariffs but also recognized that some industries must receive reasonable protection were vague enough to be interpreted in various ways. By such imprecise statements on the tariff he was pictured as a low tariff man to the South but a pro-tariff man to the Northeast and portions of the West. Jackson was also a southerner by birth and a slave owner by choice, which was sufficient evidence to convince a majority of southerners that he would oppose massive federal support of the economy or any other program that would tend to expand the power of the national government at the expense of the states.

Jackson's views of the Presidency. Although Jackson's position on political issues was frequently obscure during the campaign, he clarified his ideas once he succeeded Adams in the White House. Most earlier Presidents played a fairly passive role in the nation's political process—confining themselves primarily to enforcing the laws passed by Congress. Jackson, however, was determined to transform the Presidency into a powerful and independent instrument of government.

He looked upon Congress as a stronghold of special privilege dominated by self-seeking politicians who often passed laws inimical to the public interest but beneficial to their own. As the first popularly elected President and the only public official elected by all the people, he thought of himself as the embodiment and chief interpreter of what he termed the "will of the people." During his two terms in office, Jackson vetoed twelve bills; all the Presidents before him had vetoed only nine among them. Naturally, Jackson's unparalleled assertion of Presidential authority in determining national policy was attacked by his enemies, who called him a "tyrant."

The "Spoils System." In addition to expanding the powers of the Presidency, Jackson strongly advocated the principle of "rotation" in public office. He believed that men who stayed in office too long tended to lose sight of the public welfare. In his first annual message to Congress, he declared:

[in a democracy] no one man has any more intrinsic right to official station than another. The duties of all public officers are . . . so plain and simple that men of intelligence may readily qualify themselves for its performance.

To Jackson, the administrative aspects of government depended on personal qualities of officeholders rather than on well-established procedure. Jackson recommended that Congress pass a law limiting service in most public offices to four years. The only exceptions Jackson sug-

---

*Jackson earned his nickname during the War of 1812 when he led an expedition into Mississippi. His courage and toughness made him the idol of his troops, who called him "Old Hickory."

gested were judges, cabinet officers, and diplomatic officials whose expertise and experience were crucial. Congress, however, failed to follow the President's direction.

To many of Jackson's followers, the principle of rotation meant simply: "To the victors belong the spoils," a phrase used by William L. Marcy, a prominent New York Democrat, in a Senate speech. Jackson himself, however, steadfastly refused to sanction wholesale removal of officeholders for political reasons alone. He replaced only about 20 percent of the federal officeholders who served under Adams. Many of them were dismissed for dishonesty or incompetence, although in some cases Jackson replaced political opponents with less qualified men. Thus, while Jackson's name is commonly associated with the creation of the spoils system, he does not entirely deserve the criticism. He did set the precedent, but it was developed by his successors, who exercised little of the restraint he himself demonstrated.

Jackson and states' rights. Jackson was a strong President, but he did not attempt to use his power to expand the authority of the federal government at the expense of the states. In December 1829, he declared to Congress:

> The great mass of legislation relating to our internal affairs was intended to be left where the Federal Convention found it—in the State governments. . . . This is not the reflection of a day, but belongs to the most deeply rooted convictions of my mind.

Despite this warning to Congress, Jackson was not always consistent in applying this principle. In vetoing federal funds to aid in construction of the Maysville Road in Kentucky (1830), he vigorously asserted his opposition to federal support of internal improvements as unconstitutional. Such improvements, he maintained, should be financed by the states. Yet, Jackson signed more measures for federal support of internal improvements than did Adams. Because of this, his critics dismiss his states' rights pronouncements as hypocritical rhetoric.

Such criticism does not do justice to Jackson's basic political beliefs. Certainly, Jackson, like all Presidents, was many times governed by political considerations. The Maysville road, for example, was a pet project of his opponent Henry Clay.

More important than the fact that he approved some federally sponsored internal improvements was his refusal on the basis of principle to approve large-scale federal spending for any purpose.

Removal of the Indians. Less defensible was Jackson's use of states' rights arguments to permit the state of Georgia to relocate the Cherokee Indians. The question of Indian removal had come up during Adams's administration, and had originally involved the Creek Indians. In 1826, the governor of Georgia had ordered the lands belonging to the Creek Indians surveyed and sold to white planters. President Adams had threatened to use federal troops, if necessary, to protect the Indians from exploitation. A confrontation between federal and state troops was avoided when the Creeks reluctantly agreed to surrender their lands and migrate west across the Mississippi.

The Cherokee nation was not so easily removed as the Creeks. In 1827, the Cherokees, a progressive people well adapted to farming life, decided to establish an independent state and apply for admission into the Union. Georgia officials responded by ordering the seizure of all Cherokee lands, which the Cherokees believed were protected by treaty. The controversy finally reached the Supreme Court, and in 1832, in the case of *Worcester* v. *Georgia,* Chief Justice John Marshall declared that "the laws of Georgia can have no force" in the lands belonging to the Cherokees.

After this decision was handed down, Jackson was reported to have remarked: "John Marshall has made his decision, now let him enforce it." Some historians have suggested that Jackson's position, in this instance, was dictated by his own hatred of Indians, dating from his military days, and his unwillingness to antagonize the South, rather than by his convictions about states' rights.

Jackson was well aware that popular sentiment supported removal of the Indians. In any case, he disregarded the Supreme Court, supported the sovereignty of the states in dealing with their own "domestic affairs," and even declared that removal was the best possible solution for the Indians themselves. The forcible seizure of the Cherokee lands and their removal west of the Mississippi was a dark moment in American history. Nearly one-fourth of the Cherokee nation

The forcible removal of the Cherokee nation from their lands in Georgia so that their homes and farms could be taken over by white men was unfortunately just one in a long series of such incidents, but it was a particularly dramatic episode. One of the Cherokee chiefs who protested the removal bitterly was Coowescoowe, at the right. Actually he was only part Cherokee, on his mother's side; his father was a Scot, and Coowescoowe's other name was John Ross. Though he fought removal tenaciously, he finally had to give in and lead his tribe on "The Trail of Tears"—the terrible march west of the Mississippi in 1838 and 1839. His portrait, *Chief John Ross*, was painted by John Neagle in 1846. Although *The Trail of Tears* below, by John Lindneux, was not painted until a century after the event, it captures the deep sadness that the defeated and uprooted Cherokee must have felt during their long and, for many, fatal journey.

died on its trek westward, in what the Indians came to call "The Trail of Tears."

The Cherokees were not the only Indians to suffer during this period. In the early 1830's, during the brief Black Hawk War, hundreds of Sac and Fox Indians in Illinois were needlessly slaughtered by state militia and federal troops. The Indians had moved east across the Mississippi River to plant crops, and the whites, interpreting this as a potential threat, attacked. Moreover, in Florida, between 1835 and 1842, federal troops carried on a war of extermination against the Seminole Indians who resisted removal.

If Jackson's position on federal-state relationships was based at times on his shrewd political sense as well as his own personal convictions, it was, nevertheless, plain that he was determined to uphold what he considered to be the "legitimate spheres of state sovereignties." And he did so despite his willingness to make minor concessions on some issues if it served to strengthen his own influence and that of the Democratic party. However, when the issue of states' rights was carried to such extremes that it posed a threat to the maintenance of the Union, Jackson's stand was unmistakably clear—"I will die with the Union."

3 Nullification Threatens The Union

1. What were the positions of the North, the South, and the West regarding the tariff issue? How did their positions differ?

2. Why did South Carolina react so strongly to the tariff issue in 1828?

3. What were the positions of the North, the South, and the West regarding western land policy? How did their positions differ?

4. What steps did South Carolina take in handling the tariff issue, and what was Jackson's response? Do you think this was a wise course of action for the President to follow?

In 1832, a crisis developed that raised the specter of secession. The issue began with the tariff, and it had come about even before Jackson's election. The question of tariffs was becoming an important one in the expanding American economy. As northern industry developed, manufacturers wanted higher tariffs on imported goods to protect their industries. Many westerners, in turn, wanted higher duties on raw materials to protect their agricultural products. The South vigorously opposed tariffs; southern cotton needed no protection, there was little southern manufacturing to protect, and high tariffs raised the cost of manufactured goods for the South.

Southern opposition to the tariff. In these sectional conflicts, Jackson's supporters in Congress thought they saw a chance to promote his election. In 1828, they proposed a tariff to place high duties on raw materials, which would please the West, but not on manufactured goods, which the North wanted. Jackson's supporters actually did not want the bill to be passed; it was simply a scheme to get Jackson elected. They reasoned that since the bill did not protect manufacturing, northern interests would join with the South in defeating it. This would please the South, and at the same time, Jackson supporters in the North and the West could still vote *for* the tariff and claim credit for supporting it even though it failed. The scheme backfired, however. New England protectionists, determined to keep the principle of protection at all costs, joined with westerners to pass the bill, which came to be called the "tariff of abominations" by its critics. In fact, the bill had little, if any, effect on the election of Jackson, but it did have repercussions in the South.

The South was infuriated by the tariff, and many southern leaders advocated resistance. South Carolina was especially enraged. John C. Calhoun wrote a tract (published anonymously), *The South Carolina Exposition and Protest* (1828). Calhoun declared that if a majority in Congress passed legislation which seriously injured the interests of any state, that state had the right to declare the law null and void. Despite southern anger over the tariff, the South in general opposed nullification as the solution to the problem. Why then did South Carolina react so militantly to the issue? According to historian William Freehling, it was a combination of factors which at the time were more deeply felt in South Carolina than in other southern states.

South Carolina's economy was declining in the 1820's. That state had been one of the first to expand its cotton-planting lands, but now, after a generation of prosperity, its soil was depleted and prices were low. Some states such as Virginia and North Carolina had suffered depressions in the past and were more willing than South Carolina to accept the hard times of the 1820's. In contrast, other regions such as Alabama, Mississippi, and Louisiana were benefitting during this period from the westward expansion of their cotton-planting lands.

Another factor was the unity that existed in the 1820's between the planters of South Carolina's coastal region and the farmers of the inland area. In other states of the South, these groups were either in conflict or had little or no communication. Freehling concludes that "South Carolina's combination of internal unity . . . and new experience with economic depression was unique in the South in the 1820's and 1830's."

South Carolinians blamed their plight almost entirely upon the tariff, however, and they expected Jackson, once elected, to recommend an immediate reduction in the tariff schedules. But Jackson kept the tariff, because the revenues provided a huge treasury surplus with which he could reduce the national debt. The President predicted that the debt would be paid off within two or three years. At that time, Congress could reduce the tariff levels. Unwilling to accept such assurances, South Carolina politicians hoped to attract support for immediate tariff reductions from western congressmen if southerners in turn agreed to support land policies designed to promote rapid western expansion.

The issue of western expansion. As noted in Chapter 3, New England had consistently opposed western expansion. Many New Englanders resented the relative decline of their own influence in Congress as the expanding West gained political power. In addition, New England spokesmen looked upon expansion as an economic threat. They feared that a liberal western land policy would cause mass migration of New Englanders to the frontier, producing a labor shortage which would drive up wages.

Moreover, New Englanders noted that so much income was being received from the sale of western land that the national debt would eventually be abolished from this source alone. When this occurred, one of New England's prime arguments in favor of high tariff levels—that revenue was needed to reduce the national debt—would no longer be valid.

Desperately trying to protect their diminishing power, New Englanders resorted to the proposal to close the West to further settlement. In 1830, Senator Samuel A. Foote of Connecticut called for an end to western land surveys and demanded that sales be limited to land already placed upon the market by the government. His proposal provided the opportunity for the South and the West to join forces.

Foote's resolution was bitterly denounced by Senator Thomas Hart Benton of Missouri. Benton not only demanded that additional territory be opened, but called upon Congress to lower the price of land. He also championed "squatters' rights." Most settlers in the West did not bother to purchase land. They simply marched into the wilderness and settled, occupying land to which they had no legal title. Benton demanded that these individuals be given the right to buy this land at the minimum price of $1.25 an acre. Benton also advocated the principle of "graduation," proposing that government lands which did not sell within a reasonable length of time be reduced in price. Eventually, if there were no takers even at reduced prices, the lands were to be given away.

The Webster-Hayne debates. Following Benton's speech, Senator Robert Y. Hayne of South Carolina declared that the South would gladly support the western position on public lands if the West would vote for a low tariff. In his proposal, Hayne not only attacked the tariff, but also raised the question of nullification. In response to this issue, Daniel Webster, the shrewd and eloquent senator from Massachusetts, replied to both Benton and Hayne, in what has come to be called the Webster-Hayne debates.

In his opening speech, Webster delivered a ringing attack on the South and the concept of states' rights. As Webster had anticipated, Hayne fell into his trap. The South Carolina senator vigorously began to defend Calhoun's doctrine of

ANDREW JACKSON

What kind of man was Andrew Jackson? The question has long fascinated historians. In the following excerpt from his biography of Jackson, the historian John Spencer Basset describes something of Jackson's character.

". . .His enemies hated him and rarely saw his good qualities; his friends loved him and reluctantly admitted his failings; and in a sense each was right. Some of the good things he did are excellent and some of the bad things are wretched. His puzzling personality defies clear analysis, but we must admit that he was a remarkable man. He lacked much through the want of an education, and he acquired much through apparent accident, but it was only his strong character which turned deficiency and opportunity alike to his purpose and made his will the strongest influence in his country in his time.

"The secret of his power was his adjustment to the period in which he lived. Other men excelled him in experience, wisdom, and balanced judgment; but the American democrats of the day admired neither of these qualities. They honored courage, strength, and directness. They could tolerate ignorance but not hesitancy. Jackson was the best embodiment of their desires. . . .

"Jackson accepted democracy with relentless logic. Some others believed that wise leaders could best determine the policies of government, but he more than any one else of his day threw the task of judging upon the common man. And this he did without cant and in entire sincerity. . . . 'You know I never despair,' he said; 'I have confidence in the virtue and good sense of the people. . . .'

"Much has been said about his honesty. . . . Most of Jackson's contemporaries were as honest as he, but he excelled them in candor. . . . He was apt to speak his mind clearly, although he could on occasion. . . . be as diplomatic as a delicate case demanded."

nullification, declaring that a state had the right to nullify an act of Congress, if it felt it was a violation of its sovereignty. The Senate debates then shifted away from the issues of the tariff and western lands and focused attention on the nature of the federal Union.

In a series of brilliant speeches, Webster suggested that Hayne's views bordered on treason. He argued further that only the Supreme Court was entitled to determine the Constitutionality of laws passed by Congress. If this position was not accepted in all sections of the country, Webster warned, the nation would be plunged into fratricidal strife that would drench American soil with blood. "Liberty and Union," Webster declared, "now and forever, one and inseparable."

Popular reaction in the North and West was highly favorable to Webster's position. The result was that political ties between the Northeast and the West were strengthened, and the South's bid for western support failed.

Predictably, Jackson also made the Union cause his own. At a Jefferson birthday dinner attended by Vice-President Calhoun and other leading Democrats, Old Hickory looked Calhoun squarely in the eye and proposed a toast: "Our Union—it must be preserved!" Undaunted, Calhoun calmly replied: "The Union—next to our liberty most dear. May we always remember that it can only be preserved by distributing equally the benefits and burdens of the Union."

Rift between Jackson and Calhoun. In the following months, relations between Jackson and Calhoun deteriorated, and Calhoun's hopes of becoming Jackson's heir apparent vanished. The question of nullification was the major issue dividing them; nevertheless, personal conflicts also contributed to their growing hostility.

Early in 1830, Jackson discovered that, when Calhoun had been Monroe's secretary of war, he had recommended that Jackson be disciplined for his expedition against the Florida Indians. Jackson, who had believed Calhoun had supported his Indian campaign, was furious and now demanded an explanation. Unable to give a satisfactory answer, Calhoun accused Martin Van Buren, Jackson's secretary of state, of conspiring to turn the President against him. Angered by Calhoun's charges, Jackson denounced his Vice-President as a character assassin: "I have no hesitation," he declared, "in saying that Calhoun is one of the most hypocritical and unprincipled villains in the United States."

Calhoun's charges against Van Buren were not entirely unfounded. The secretary of state was a shrewd politican (one of his nicknames was "the Little Magician") and a powerful influence in New York State politics. Now he was Jackson's close adviser, and he had Presidential ambitions of his own. When Cabinet dissension erupted over slander surrounding the wife of John Eaton, secretary of war, Van Buren sided with Jackson, who vigorously defended Mrs. Eaton's reputation. Then Van Buren offered to resign, calculating that his resignation would allow Jackson to reorganize the Cabinet and eliminate Calhoun's supporters. The President not only accepted Van Buren's resignation, but also demanded that the entire Cabinet resign.

In part, Jackson's motives were personal. He was enraged because Cabinet members and their wives had vilified Mrs. Eaton. More important, he used the attacks on Van Buren and Mrs. Eaton to justify the replacement of Calhoun's supporters in the Cabinet with men whose loyalty to him was unquestioned. Now the break between Jackson and Calhoun was complete, and Van Buren's shrewd maneuvering had strengthened the ties between him and the President.

Crisis over nullification. Despite the rupture between Jackson and Calhoun, the President was not unsympathetic to southern demands for tariff reform. In his message to Congress in 1831, Jackson observed that since the national debt had virtually been retired, Congress ought to revise the tariff downward. In part, this message was designed to placate the South. But this was not the only purpose, since a low tariff, except for products seriously threatened by foreign competition, was perfectly consistent with Jackson's earlier pronouncements.

In 1832, Congress responded to Jackson's recommendations by passing a tariff bill that lowered duties on many items. South Carolina bitterly denounced it, however, since the tariff did not reduce duties to levels South Carolina considered acceptable. The state legislature condemned the tariff and called for a convention to consider nullification. Calhoun resigned as Vice-President and returned to South Carolina to lead the nulli-

fication forces. Once in session, the convention voted overwhelmingly to adopt a Nullification Ordinance declaring the tariffs of both 1828 and 1832 null and void. It instructed the state legislature not to permit the collection of customs duties in South Carolina after February 1, 1833, and also warned the government that any attempt to collect the duties would be followed by secession.

Jackson reacted decisively but cautiously. In his carefully worded Nullification Proclamation (December 10, 1832), he declared that the doctrine of state sovereignty was fatal to the existence of the Union and warned that he was willing to use force to collect customs duties and suppress rebellion. At the same time he urged conciliation and appealed to the national pride of the people of South Carolina. His proclamation aroused a fever of patriotic support around the country. In February 1833, Congress passed the Force Act, which authorized the President to do whatever was necessary to preserve the integrity of the Union. In the meantime, Henry Clay introduced a new tariff bill.

Finally, on March 2, 1833, Jackson signed both the Force Act and Clay's compromise tariff, which reduced duties over a ten-year period to levels that South Carolinians considered reasonable. Even Calhoun, who had been elected senator upon his return to South Carolina, voted for the compromise. Soon thereafter, the South Carolina convention repealed the Nullification Ordinance, although it did declare the Force Act null and void. Jackson wisely overlooked this new act of defiance, recognizing it as nothing more than an empty gesture.

Thus an early crisis that threated to disrupt the Union ended in conciliation and moderation. But the issues behind the confrontation transcended the immediate question of the tariff. Historian Charles M. Wiltse has observed that South Carolinians, by the spring of 1833, were no longer interested in debating whether the tariff was right or wrong "but whether the Federal Government had the power to impose it." The crisis passed, but, Wiltse notes, that the Nullification controversy

. . . fixed the lines of cleavage between North and South, and prepared the ideological basis both for the ultimate withdrawl of the South from the Union and for the coercion of the seceding states.

4 Jackson Wars With The Bank Of The United States

1. What were the advantages and disadvantages of the Second Bank of the United States?

2. How did Jackson regard the Second Bank of the United States, and what led him to believe as he did?

3. What were the causes of the Panic of 1837?

4. How would you evaluate Jackson and the handling of financial affairs during his administration? What did he do that was right and what did he do that was wrong? What alternatives might he have pursued?

Another crisis in Jackson's administration was created by his opposition to the Second Bank of the United States. This crisis, no less than the one over nullification, aroused both passionate support for Old Hickory and fervent denunciations of him. At stake were not only the fiscal policies of the federal government, but also the personal fortunes of thousands of small farmers, businessmen, merchants, professional men, and workingmen, as well as those of wealthier segments of society.

Critics of the bank. When the Second Bank of the United States was chartered in 1816 for a period of twenty years, it was given enormous power over the currency and credit of the entire nation (page 118). As a central bank it was especially useful in times of expansion and of industrial development because it provided a uniform, stable, and honest system of finanical operations and because it acted to check overexpansion of state banks. Despite the claim that it was a monopoly, it held only one-third of the nation's total bank deposits and handled only one-fifth of the nation's loans. It was, however, the dominant bank.

Opposition to the bank had existed since its establishment and had risen and fallen with economic conditions. But during the 1820's, as the bank became more successful in its operations, opposition to it hardened. The bank's foes opposed its chartered privileges and its control by a few wealthy men—most of its investors were in the bank's home city of Philadelphia, in other Eastern cities, and in Europe. Its foes also feared its potential power to corrupt political life, since it extended loans and favors to legislators and other influential people. Many of its critics claimed, as had Jefferson, that the bank was unconstitutional (although the Supreme Court had ruled to the contrary in 1819).

Much of the opposition to the bank came from bankers themselves. Eastern bankers objected to the concentration of money and power in one city—Philadelphia (the bank was often characterized as the "Monster of Chestnut Street"). Bankers of New York City's Wall Street especially wanted banking profits to flow into New York, which was rapidly becoming the nation's financial capital. Western and southern bankers particularly disliked the bank's strict credit and monetary policies which restrained their expansion, and they resented "eastern" control.

Westerners—small businessmen, farmers, land speculators—were strong in their opposition to the national bank because it kept state banks from giving them more credit and money to buy land and to expand. The majority of westerners, including bankers, were "cheap money" men. They wanted more paper money in circulation, looser credit, and higher prices—in effect, more inflationary policies.

In opposition to these inflationary policies were the "hard money" men, mostly eastern industrialists, merchants, businessmen, and professional men. They agreed on the need for a stable, uniform currency such as the bank provided, but they generally wanted less paper money in circulation and also opposed the bank because of its unique powers. Among the hard money group were most workingmen, who opposed banks generally as monopolies and who wanted to be paid in hard cash instead of what they considered worthless paper money. Indeed, unscrupulous employers often paid their workers in depreciated bank notes.

Thus, when Jackson decided to destroy the bank he drew support from diverse groups. Small businessmen, farmers, land speculators, and some bankers who wanted an inflationary economy to ease credit restrictions and expand business opportunities were behind him. Eastern capitalists and businessmen who resented the bank's privileged economic position, and workingmen who opposed paper money in any form, supported Jackson. Obviously, once the bank was dead, the cheap and hard money men would fight each other with as much vigor as they had the Second Bank of the United States.

Jackson's opposition. Much of the antagonism toward the bank centered on its president, Nicholas Biddle, who had become its head in 1823. A member of a wealthy Philadelphia family, Biddle, and two other stockholders who cooperated with him, owned a majority of the bank's stock. He thus exercised absolute control over the bank's operating policies. For the most part Biddle, who was intelligent and industrious, acted responsibly, and certainly under his direction the bank prospered. However, "Czar Nicholas" (as his enemies called him) was not known for his tact or modesty. He was inclined to boast, perhaps not entirely inaccurately, that he had more power than the President of the United States.

Jackson opposed the bank on principle, believing that no institution in a democratic society should be allowed to exercise unlimited power. Furthermore, he himself was a hard money man, suspicious of banks and paper notes in general. In fact, Jackson's opposition to a national bank dated back to 1797 when, as a congressman from Tennessee, he was especially critical of Hamilton's financial program, particularly the creation of a national bank.

Moreover, in 1797, Jackson suffered severe financial reverses which he ascribed solely to the overissue of notes of the First Bank of the United States. Thus, Jackson's strict constructionist principles, combined with his early financial reverses and his ignorance of economic principles, had made him a hard money man. He did not appreciate the fact that sound banking principles were essential to the orderly development of the nation's economy. As he remarked to Nicholas Biddle in 1828: "I do not dislike your Bank any more than all banks."

Nevertheless, Jackson's first steps were marked by caution. Old Hickory was fully aware that many of his political backers favored some type of central bank—though not necessarily Biddle's. As a result, Jackson recommended to Congress in his annual messages of 1829, 1830, and 1831 that the bank be abolished, to be replaced by a government-owned central bank that would exercise far less power over the economy than Biddle's institution.

Biddle challenges Jackson. Biddle himself had no desire to become involved in politics. In 1832, however, convinced that Jackson intended to destroy the bank at all costs, and encouraged by Henry Clay, Jackson's political rival, he decided to force the issue by asking Congress to renew the bank's charter four years before it was due to expire. In explaining his decision, Biddle wrote:

For myself I do not care a straw for him [Jackson] and his political rivals . . . but if he means to wage war upon the bank—if he pursues us till we turn and stand at bay, why then—he may perhaps awaken a spirit which it is wisest not to force into offensive defense.

Because of differences between cheap money and hard money men in his own party, and because he was aware that the bank was a powerful institution with powerful men among its supporters, Jackson let it be known as the Presidential election of 1832 approached that he was willing to compromise. If Biddle were willing to accept changes that would permit a degree of governmental control over the bank's operations, Jackson was prepared to recommend renewal of its charter.

Biddle, however, was in no mood to compromise. He misinterpreted Jackson's willingness to bargain as a sign of weakness. Biddle knew that enough congressmen supported the bank to pass a bill renewing its charter. He was also aware that Jackson was prepared to veto any bill that did not include the changes he had demanded. But Biddle was convinced that the bank could muster the two-thirds majority necessary to override the President's veto and that as a result of the veto Jackson would be defeated by Henry Clay in the upcoming election. Clay shared Biddle's optimism, informing him that "The friends of the Bank expect the application [for renewal] to be made." Thus Biddle made his decision. He submitted a request asking Congress to renew the bank's charter, subject to no changes whatsoever.

Senator Willie P. Mangum of North Carolina, one of the bank's supporters, was convinced that Biddle had committed a supreme act of folly. Mangum predicted that in the coming "trial of strength between Gen Jackson and the Bank . . . the Bank will go down—For Gen J's popularity is of *a sort* not to be shaken at present."

Mangum proved to be absolutely correct in his judgment. Jackson vetoed the bank bill. His veto message, delivered in July, 1832, was a masterpiece of political strategy. He focused on the issues that all foes of the bank could agree on, attacking the bank on the grounds that it was a monopoly incompatible with democratic institutions. He claimed that it was a dangerous central-ization of national power at the expense of the states, and he called it unconstitutional. And he argued, perhaps most effectively, that the bank was a tool of the "rich and powerful" against the poor.

His political rhetoric was extremely persuasive, and served as well to mask the serious divisions within his own party. During the election campaign in which the bank veto was his chief platform, Jackson remarked to his nephew: "The veto works well. . . . Instead of crushing me as was expected and intended, it will crush the Bank." And he was right. In the election, he defeated Clay handily. As Mangum had predicted, Jackson's popularity was unshakable.

Results of Jackson's victory. Having won the election, and aware of popular support behind him, Jackson was determined to abolish the bank long before its charter expired in 1836. Jackson began by asking that all government funds be withdrawn from the national bank and placed in selected state banks. In September 1833, the secretary of the Treasury ordered all government funds to be placed in state banks selected by the government. In fact, government funds were not suddenly withdrawn from the bank; they were allowed to become depleted and no further funds were deposited.

Nicholas Biddle's bank may have been dying, but it was not yet dead. He ordered a curtailment of all further loans by the bank and required payment on a number of outstanding loans. This move to tighten credit and get funds back into the bank caused extreme hardship among much of the business community. Biddle hoped his measures would bring enough pressure on Jackson to force him to reconsider his position. However, Biddle's strategy backfired once again. In the popular view, his actions confirmed Jackson's charges that the bank was a dangerous and irresponsible institution. Business leaders blamed Biddle rather than Jackson for their difficulties, and finally he was forced to abandon his tactics.

The bank war looms large in the history of Jackson's administration. But as historian Carl N. Degler has pointedly observed, it was considered by Jackson and his advisers as little more than "a skirmish in the broader war upon the banking and currency system of the time."

Andrew Jackson's considerable height, shock of white hair, quick temper, and colorful personality made him a cartoonist's dream, and during his public life, cartoonists made great use of him, in both flattering and unflattering ways. The political cartoon at the right, drawn for a tract circulated during the vicious 1828 campaign, warns that Jackson may very well turn against his supporters, once he is successfully in the White House and no longer in need of their help. The tract was entitled "A Mirror for Politicians." The cartoon below also registers anti-Jackson feeling—this time during the 1832 campaign. It shows Henry Clay in the lead in the race against Jackson, whose veto of the renewal of the bank charter is about to cause him to stumble and thus most certainly lose. The results of both elections showed that neither cartoonist had chosen the winning side.

"Jackson is to be President, and you will be HANGED."

Race over Uncle Sam's Course
4ᵗʰ March 1833

First of all, Jackson selected seven "pet banks" (ultimately the number was increased to nearly one-hundred) in which to deposit all government funds. In order to qualify for government deposits, the pet banks were obliged to stop issuing notes of small denominations. This regulation was designed to decrease the amount of paper money in circulation. In short, Jackson hoped to create a uniform and stable currency that would eventually force the nation's banks to virtually adopt a hard money monetary system.

Before this new system could effectively be put into operation, however, state banks, no longer circumscribed by the regulatory functions of the Second Bank of the United States, flooded the country with depreciated bank notes. Inflation ran rampant. Between January 1835 and December 1836, the number of bank notes increased from $82 million to $120 million. Much of this depreciated currency was invested in government land. Alarmed by this state of affairs, Jackson attempted to stem the inflationary tide by issuing his Specie Circular of 1836, which stipulated that government lands must thereafter be paid for in gold or silver. This decision was a severe jolt to the nation's credit system and forced thousands of speculators and scores of western banks into bankruptcy.

Moreover, economic hardship in Great Britian was forcing British investors who had helped to finance numerous internal-improvement ventures in the United States—canals, railroads, turnpikes—to cash in their American securities. The result was that gold and silver which was badly needed to stabilize the American economy was drained away to England. All of this, plus a decline in the demand for American products in Europe, helped to bring about the panic of 1837—a severe economic depression whose effects were to be felt in the United States until the mid-1840's.

In the end, Jackson, by his successful war on the Second Bank of the United States, succeeded only in contributing to the vicious cycle of "boom and bust" which he opposed and feared. Jackson cannot be faulted for objecting to the monopoly features of the national bank. But the "cure" he prescribed proved far worse than the "disease" itself.

5 The Whigs Challenge The Democrats

1. What were the positions of the Whig and Democratic parties concerning the major issues in 1836?

2. What were the strengths and weaknesses of the Independent Treasury system?

3. How did the Whig Party secure victory in the election of 1840?

4. What policies were pursued by Tyler once he became President?

The Whig party was formally organized in 1834, when the National Republicans joined forces with thousands of southern nullifiers and former Jacksonians who opposed the compromise tariff of 1833 and the destruction of the Second Bank of the United States. The only common denominator which bound all these elements of the Whig coalition together was their hatred of Andrew Jackson. In fact, in 1841, most nullifiers returned to the Democrats because they did not believe in Whig economic policy. The name Whig was chosen in an effort to persuade American voters that Andrew Jackson was a tyrant. In Great Britian the Whig party historically had opposed the Tories, the friends of the king. Thus, the American Whigs believed that their party label would enable then to capitalize on the idea that they opposed the dictatorial policies of "King Andrew I."

Philosophies of the opposing parties. The Whig party's stand on national issues was markedly different from that of the Democrats. In the economic sphere, the Whigs, like the National Republicans, were committed to a high tariff, not only to protect industry, but also to provide funds to run the federal government. Whigs also advocated a national bank and federally sponsored internal improvements.

In addition, they supported the distribution of the national treasury surplus to the states. This measure was designed not only to promote internal improvements, but also to justify maintaining a high tariff. The Whigs feared that as government revenue increased from the sale of western lands, the Democrats would maintain that there was sufficient income to run the government, and they would reduce the tariff levels. If the surplus revenue was distributed to the states, however, the government would then need the revenues from a high tariff.

Finally, in 1841, the Whigs supported *preemption,* or the safeguarding of squatters' rights to land, a measure also vigorously advocated by western Democrats. Most Whigs were committed to the idea of positive government—the principle of using the national government as an instrument to promote economic growth and development.

During Jackson's two terms as President, the Democrats also developed a fairly coherent political philosophy. The Democrats were far less inclined to support massive federal spending than the Whigs. Where the Whigs emphasized national development, the Democrats consistently placed the burden of economic growth upon private individuals and the states. On the tariff issue, the Jacksonians were not opposed to the principle of protection, but they were not prepared to protect as many commodities nor to impose duties as high as the Whigs demanded.

The Democrats were more consistent in opposing special privileges and monopolies than the Whigs. Ultimately, the Democrats adopted the position that government and private enterprise ought to be divorced, and that the national government should not grant any special privileges to anyone. This concept that the federal government should not intervene in the national economy is the principle of *laissez faire,* which means literally, "let people do as they please."

On the state level, this principle was reflected in the passage of general incorporation laws, which permitted an individual or group of individuals who had sufficient capital to set up businesses without securing special charters from the state legislature. These laws prevented established businessmen from using their political influence in the state legislatures to stifle potential competition by blocking new applications for corporate charters. In some states, however, as historian Edward Pessen points out, Democrat-dominated legislatures did indeed sometimes grant monopolies to favored individuals as readily as the

Whigs. On balance, however, Democrats were far more inclined to liberalize economic opportunities than their opponents.

Outside the economic sphere, Whigs tended to be somewhat more liberal than the Democrats. The Whigs were not so hostile to the Indians as the Democrats, and they were not inclined to be as sympathetic to slavery. Northern Whigs were, as a rule, adamantly opposed to further territorial expansion, which would involve the question of slavery expansion, a policy ardently supported by most Democrats. In part, Whig opposition to expansion was based on political grounds, but so-called Conscience Whigs acted from moral conviction as well.

The election of 1836. In 1836 the Whigs were in no position to successfully challenge the victorious Democrats. Martin Van Buren, Jackson's handpicked successor, occupied a commanding position. Prosperity was still in full swing, and Jackson's handling of the nullification crisis and the national bank issue gave the Democratic party a strong edge with the electorate.

In the face of the popular support for Jackson's policies, the Whigs decided that no single candidate could defeat Van Buren. Hence they ran four candidates, each of whom was intended to appeal to regional rather than national constituents. In this way the Whigs hoped to split the popular vote so many ways that the election would be thrown into the House of Representatives, where they might have a chance to win the Presidency. Among the four Whig candidates were Daniel Webster of Massachusetts and the popular military hero General William Henry Harrison of Ohio.

The Whig strategy failed, however. Van Buren won a decisive victory in the electoral college, although in popular votes the election was close. Harrison was Van Buren's closest competitor in the electoral college. Thus, "Old Tippecanoe" (as Harrison was called because of his victory over the Indians at the Tippecanoe River in 1811) was looked upon as the Whig party's major hope in the election of 1840.

Van Buren's policies. Less than three months after Van Buren was inaugurated, the nation was paralyzed by the panic of 1837. Partially as a result of Jackson's fiscal policies, hundreds of banks and businesses failed, states defaulted on the payment of their debts, and thousands of unemployed workers suffered severe privations. Severe riots even occurred in New York and Philadelphia. Although Van Buren called a special session of Congress, it was only to recommend that the government borrow $10 million to see it through the crisis.

Conceivably, a Whig President might have attempted some positive action such as advocating federal spending for internal improvements in an effort to stimulate the economy. But Van Buren, an ardent Jacksonian, declared: "The less government interferes with private propety the better for the general prosperity." This was good Jacksonian rhetoric, but it was irrelevant in an emergency situation. In fairness to Van Buren, however, no machinery for government action or tradition of intervention existed. (None was to exist until the Great Depression of 1929, nearly one hundred years later.)

The only major legislative accomplishment achieved by Van Buren was the creation of the so-called Independent Treasury, or subtreasury, system, which replaced the pet bank scheme. Not only did Van Buren adhere to Jackson's hard money philosophy, he pushed it to an extreme. The subtreasury system completely divorced governmental finance from private banking. All government funds were withdrawn from state banks and placed in government vaults, making government funds no longer available for loans. Whenever government obligations came due, funds were simply withdrawn from the vaults to meet them.

With this system, financial reform was left up to the states, many of which did adopt measures designed to prevent the overissue of state bank notes. State laws demanding that banks keep a reasonable ratio between their reserve specie and the notes in circulation did give a certain amount of stability and uniformity to the nation's currency.

The subtreasury system made economic recovery even more difficult. The refusal of the government to loan its funds, accompanied by the withdrawal of British capital investments during the panic, dried up important sources of capital—always short in a developing nation, as the United States was at the time. In addition, Van Buren's policies had important political repercussions.

The Whigs, of course, were infuriated, and more importantly, many Democrats were alienated. The subtreasury system did please those Democrats who favored a complete return to a hard-money economy. But many state bankers and businessmen, while they had opposed a strong national bank, did not want a complete divorce of government and banking. They needed government loans for expansion and investment. Thus, Van Buren's policies did nothing to alleviate the panic and even drove many Democrats into Whig ranks.

The election of 1840. As the election of 1840 approached, the Whigs were jubilant. They not only had a prime issue—the depression—but they also had an attractive and popular candidate, General Harrison. Most important of all, the Whigs used the same tactics against Van Buren that the Democrats had used so successfully against John Quincy Adams in 1828. Avoiding the issues, Whig politicians pictured Harrison, scion of a wealthy Virginia family, as a humble man of the people. And they used the log cabin and hard cider as symbols against the opulence, extravagance, and aristocratic pretensions of "Van, Van, a used up man," as one of the campaign slogans described him.

In fact, Van Buren's orgins were far more humble than Harrison's. The Whigs were simply capitalizing on the tactics the Jacksonians had used so effectively in 1828. They believed that elections were won by concentrating on personalities rather than principles, and they did not even adopt a platform in this campaign. Moreover, the Whigs nominated John Tyler of Virginia for Vice-President in an effort to attract the southern anti-Jackson vote. Like Calhoun, Tyler was a former states' rights Democrat who joined the Whigs only because of his hatred of Andrew Jackson.

In the election, "Old Tippecanoe" defeated the "Little Magician" in the electoral college, 234 to 60. In popular votes, however, Harrison's majority was razor thin, 1,275,000 to 1,129,000. One of the most significant aspects of this Presidential election was the marked increase in voter turnout.

The number of eligible voters who cast ballots in 1840 was two and a half times the number who had voted in 1828.

John Tyler becomes President. Although the Whigs had avoided issues during the campaign, Daniel Webster and Henry Clay expected that once in office they would push through Congress a comprehensive Whig program to reverse the trends of the Jackson-Van Buren era. Unfortunately for the Whigs, President Harrison died of pneumonia a month after his inauguration. John Tyler was now President, setting a precedent by becoming the first Vice-President to assume the full powers of the Presidency. Having expected to dominate the policies of the administration, Whig leaders soon regretted that they had supported Tyler for the Vice-Presidency.

With Tyler's blessing, Congress did pass the Pre-emption Act of 1841, an extremely popular measure in the West. Any squatter could now buy 160 acres of government land at $1.25 an acre before new areas were placed on the open market. Tyler, however, refused to go along with the whole of the Whig program. As far as his principles were concerned, he was a southern states' rights Democrat.

The Whig majority in Congress did pass a bill raising tariff duties to the levels established in 1832. Clay, however, was also determined to get through a measure distributing federal surplus revenues to the states, and he wanted to include such a provision in the tariff law. Tyler took the position, popular with southern Democrats, that he would not consider such a provision unless the bill declared that distribution would cease when the tariff exceeded a certain level. Twice, the Whigs passed a distribution bill regardless of increases in the tariff rates. Twice, Tyler vetoed it, serving notice that Congress could choose either distribution or a high tariff. Under no circumstances would he permit a law that included both.

On the issue of banking, Tyler allowed the repeal of the subtreasury system, but he vetoed a bill rechartering the Bank of the United States. His refusal to support a new bank bill robbed the Whigs of what they considered the legitimate fruits of their victory. Infuriated, Whigs leaders read the President out of the party, and with the exception of Secretary of State Daniel Webster, the Cabinet resigned. All but two members of Tyler's new Cabinet were southerners with strong states' rights views. Webster was involved in negotiations with the British over the northeastern American-Canadian boundary. But once a treaty (the Webster-Ashburton treaty) was ratified in 1842, Webster also stepped down. His place was taken by John C. Calhoun.

For the Whigs, the Tyler administration was one of conflict and frustration, and in the final analysis, even their modest successes came to nought. The next administration, which was Democratic, reinstituted the subtreasury system and passed a low tariff. More important, new issues were coming to the fore which overshadowed such traditional controversies as the tariff and public finance. The United States was entering an era of territorial expansion.

■ **CONCLUSION**

The era of the common man in politics brought about some enduring changes in American political life. The reforms established in the age of Jackson laid the foundation for continuing advances in American democracy. And, although many were still excluded from the democratic process, the principles established during this period helped pave the way for the eventual enfranchisement of all Americans. Accompanying these advances toward a more democratic political order was the reemergence of the two-party system. Out of the division of Jefferson's old party, the Democrats and the Whigs were formed.

In economic terms, the Jacksonians were the foes of entrenched monopoly and special privilege, refusing to sanction large-scale government intervention into the economy. They developed the old Jeffersonian concept of the least government as the best government into the principle of laissez faire. Jacksonian ideas of unregulated capitalism, competition, and the doctrine of "rugged individualism"—that all men should have the opportunity to rise through their own effort and industry without the help of government—set the tone of American economic development down to the 1860's. But the nation's economy changed tremendously after the Civil War, and the individualism and economic liberalism of the Jacksonians proved inadequate to meet these changes. In the long run, laissez faire encouraged the very forces it was intended to oppose.

■ QUESTIONS

1. What evidence is there that the Presidency of Andrew Jackson encouraged the extension of political democracy?

2. What position did the North take on the issues of public lands, tariffs, internal improvements, finance, and the role of the government in general?

3. What position did the South take on the issues of public lands, tariffs, internal improvements, finance, and the role of the government in general?

4. What position did the West take on the issues of public lands, tariffs, internal improvements, finance, and the role of the government in general?

5. Why did the positions of the West, the South, and the North differ on these issues?

6. Which two sections of the country had the most in common and were most likely to join together in a common legislative program? Explain your answer.

7. How did the position of the Whig party and the Democratic party differ regarding the issues of public lands, tariffs, internal improvements, finance, and the role of government in general?

8. What were the characteristics of political campaigns between 1824 and 1840, and how do they compare to today's campaigns?

9. How effective were the measures taken to control the economic growth of the country? Explain your answer.

■ BIBLIOGRAPHY

BUGG, JAMES L., JR., ed., *Jacksonian Democracy: Myth or Reality*, American Problem Studies Series, Holt, Rinehart & Winston. There are many series of books whose purpose is to provide different viewpoints on important topics in American history. This book includes excerpts from the most important books on the nature of Jacksonian Democracy. Students may read this collection to get a general idea of the conflict of interpretation and then go to the complete works of the authors mentioned.

TAYLOR, GEORGE R., ed., *Jackson Versus Biddle: The Struggle over the Second Bank of the United States*, Problems in American Civilization, Heath. This is another example of a book from a problems series which students may use to gain perspective on a particular issue. Frequently such a book serves as a good starting point for a research paper assignment.

HOFSTADTER, RICHARD, *The American Political Tradition and the Men Who Made It*, Random House (Vintage Books). The essay on Andrew Jackson is one of a number of short essays by Hofstadter on important figures in American political history. The book covers most of the outstanding political leaders of our country in a readable, insightful manner.

JAMES, MARQUIS, *Andrew Jackson: Portrait of a President*, Grosset & Dunlap (Universal Library). As a Pulitzer Prize winner in the field of biography, this book may be singled out for its style and research. If this volume is enjoyed, the reader should also look at the author's other volume on Jackson and his biography of Sam Houston.

CLARK, THOMAS D., *The Rampaging Frontier: Manners and Humors of Pioneer Days in the South and Middle West*, Indiana U. Press. There was more to life in the Jacksonian Era than politicking, speculation, and sectional crises. Students can read this book to get a better idea of what it was really like for the so-called average man in America's past. A wide range of social customs are discussed to amuse and inform the reader.

SYDNOR, CHARLES S. *The Development of Southern Sectionalism 1819–1848*, History of the South, Vol. 5, La. State U. Press. In this text chapter, students see the general emergence of sectional conflict in America. In this book, Sydnor concentrates upon the South as a section, and provides a detailed examination of one part of the over-all trend.

GUNDERSON, ROBERT G., *The Log-Cabin Campaign*, University Press of Kentucky. If one wants to compare the campaign of "Tippecanoe and Tyler too" with current elections, the Gunderson book provides a wealth of information on the earlier campaign. Not only does the author consider the noise and pretension, but he also examines the serious consequences for American government.

The Creation Of Economic Sections

In the early nineteenth century, the United States consisted of a string of seaboard states inhabited by some eight million farmers, small businessmen, artisans, and slaves. Economic changes in the new nation were becoming perceptible, and some of them were noted by the French writer and visitor to America Alexis de Tocqueville: "No people in the world has made such rapid progress in trade and manufacturing as the Americans," he marveled. Furthermore, the nation was moving westward. "It seldom happens that an American farmer settles for good upon the land he occupies . . . he brings land into tillage in order to sell it again. . . ." The South was growing, too, for "every year a swarm of the inhabitants of the North arrive . . . and settle in the parts where the cotton-plant and the sugarcane grow. . . ."

What Tocqueville was witnessing was the growth of three economic sections—the North, the West, and the South. Although each section developed differently, a crucial influence for all was the Industrial Revolution, the tremendous increase in the production and distribution of manufactured goods that began in England and soon spread to the United States. The United States was ripe for industrialism—it had raw materials, cheap labor, ample sources of power, and growing markets. Furthermore, the American people soon displayed their genius for technology. As you trace the rise of economic sections from 1815 to 1860, keep these questions in mind:

1. How did the rise of manufacturing affect the North? What changes did it produce in life there?
2. What was the impact of the Industrial Revolution on the agricultural West?
3. Why did the South develop a slave economy?

1 The North Becomes An Industrial Region

1. What were the factors which characterized the Industrial Revolution in the North between 1815 and 1860? How did these factors contribute to industrial growth?

2. What was urban life like in America during the first half of the nineteenth century?

3. How did the government's policy of laissez faire affect the growth of industry and American life?

The revolution in manufacturing began during the eighteenth century in the British textile industry with the invention of new spinning and weaving machines. Soon steam power was developed, new ways were found to cast and use iron, and mills and factories sprang up. These technological advances began to reach the United States around the end of the eighteenth century in the textile industry of the Northeast.

Shortly after the American Revolution, some machinery was being used in American mills; at his inauguration, George Washington wore a brown suit made from wool produced by America's first large woolen mill in Hartford, Connecticut. But the revolution in American manufacturing began in the cotton-textile industry.

In 1790, Samuel Slater, an English weaver, brought his knowledge of British cotton-spinning machinery to Rhode Island, where he established a cotton-yarn mill. Slater's mill used waterpower, and the narrow swift streams of New England were an ideal source. Other cotton-spinning mills sprang up rapidly in the Northeast. These early mills were small operations and used machinery only to spin yarn, which was woven by hand. The mills, however, were the first step in the development of new ways to organize production.

The factory system. Much of eighteenth-century American manufacturing was characterized by "cottage industry"—that is, whole families working in their homes for an employer who supplied the raw materials. Most products—shoes, clothing, utensils—were laboriously handcrafted. Quality was frequently high, but productivity and profits were low. Moreover, this kind of production served a limited local market. Although handcrafting continued, especially on the frontier, it was overtaken by an entirely new mode of production—the factory.

In 1814, in Waltham, Massachusetts, a group of Boston investors built a completely mechanized factory. The Boston Manufacturing Company, as it was called, took in raw cotton and turned out uniformly woven cloth. All the steps in producing cloth were done under one roof by an assembly line. Instead of handcrafting the whole product, a laborer now tended a machine that made only part of it. This specialization, or division of labor, is the basis of the factory system.

The advantages of the factory system were quickly apparent to entrepreneurs, who extended it to the woolen industry. Soon, the textile industry began to expand at a spectacular rate. In 1820, there were about two hundred cotton mills and one hundred woolen mills in the country. By 1840, there were more than twelve hundred cotton mills and fourteen hundred woolen mills; and by 1860, textiles accounted for nearly $200 million annually.

Expanding production. Around 1798, Eli Whitney, a young Connecticut inventor, hit upon the idea of creating interchangeable, uniform parts in the manufacture of guns. Whitney made the several different parts of a musket by machines, each machine cutting thousands of identical pieces which could then easily be assembled into a finished product. Whitney's mass-production system, which spread rapidly to other industries, was the beginning of the machine-tool industry (machines making other machines).

The development of mass production and the establishment of a machine-tool industry served the needs of the expanding textile industry. By 1840, ready-made clothes were being turned out by a full-fledged garment industry, which received a further impetus in the 1850's with the invention of the sewing machine.

The demand for mass-produced manufactured goods—from machine tools to guns, from agricultural machinery to potbellied stoves—spurred the development of the iron and mining industries. In the period from 1820 to 1860, for example, production of pig iron increased fortyfold and that of anthracite coal over 2,500 times. The

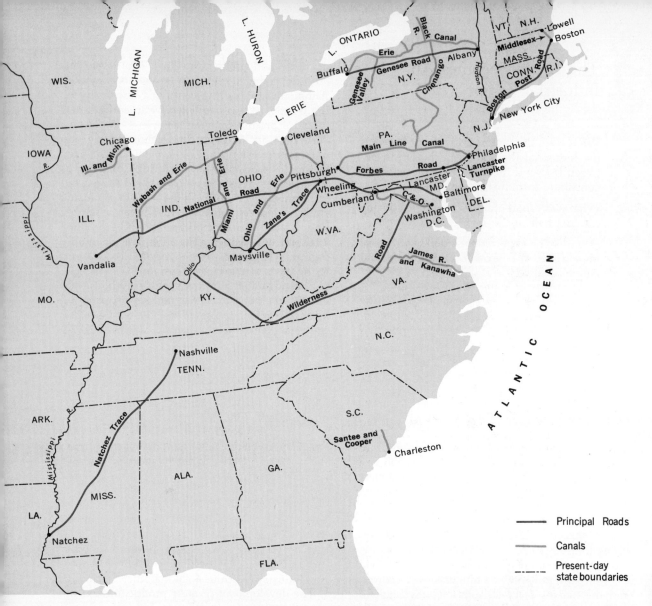

EARLY CANALS AND ROADS, 1785–1860

importance of this tremendously expanded production to the national economy can be seen by comparing the value of manufactured goods and agricultural products. In 1840, agricultural products were valued at $1 billion and manufactures at $485 million. By 1860, the value of agricultural commodities and manufactured goods had each risen to $2 billion.

Transportation. The factory system and mass

production made it possible for manufacturing to be concentrated in a few areas. These producing outlets needed an expanded transportation network to distribute goods and enlarge their market.

The transportation system was created in three phases. Through 1830, large sums were invested in ten thousand miles of turnpikes—toll roads supported by fees from users. Turnpikes were then succeeded by the canals, which not only

152

linked industrial centers of the Northeast with great shipping terminals, but also laced the Midwest and connected the Ohio Valley with the East. The textile mills of the Merrimac Valley in Massachusetts shipped their products down the Middlesex Canal to Boston, while the products of Pennsylvania's iron furnaces and coal mines traveled along the great Pennsylvania Main Line Canal stretching from Philadelphia to Pittsburgh.

Although canals continued to be important arteries of commerce, they were soon challenged by the railroads. In 1829, the first commercial railroad, a thirteen-mile stretch of the Baltimore and Ohio, opened for business. Expansion continued at a steady pace until the 1850's, during which a phenomenal outburst of construction connected Chicago, St. Louis, Memphis, and New Orleans to the East (see map, page 318).

Finance. Unprecedented sums of money were needed to finance the transportation system and the growing factories. In general, the canals and railroads were built with state and municipal loans and through investments by British bankers. Factories were financed almost entirely by domestic savings.

Governments played an important role in the expanding industries. State governments gave charters to corporations for the purpose of constructing roads and bridges and establishing banks. Generally, these early charters established monopolies, especially over transportation routes, and often granted state-owned lands or special tax-exemptions to the corporation. In chartering banks and insurance companies, state governments helped create the institutions necessary to finance industry. Most textile mills, for example, were started privately through loans from banks. Insurance companies also helped finance industry by investing in corporation stocks and bonds.

Many roads, canals, and railroads were also financed directly by governments. At a cost of $7 million, the federal government built the National Road from Maryland to Wheeling, West Virginia. It was state governments, however, that lavished financial aid on transportation companies. New York State underwrote the Erie Canal, and Pennsylvania spent nearly $32 million on the Main Line Canal. In all, the states invested almost $150 million on canal construction, while private investors spent $40 million.

Railroads, too, were financed by a mixture of public and private funds, although the role of state governments in financing railroads was less important than it had been in canal construction. State governments did purchase railroad bonds, and both state governments and the national government granted huge tracts of land to railroad corporations. But it was foreign investors who bought nearly half the railroad securities.

The relative decline in state participation in railroad financing was the beginning of a trend that became more accentuated as the century progressed. In the 1840's, political and industrial leaders called for an end to governmental regulation and financing of economic ventures. Under this developing doctrine of laissez faire, the federal government ceased intervening directly in the economy. Moreover, monopolistic corporation charters were attacked as unfair privileges incompatible with democracy. And state governments rapidly gave up the practice of issuing charters. Finally, as trade and production increased, so did profits available for new investments. By the 1840's, there was less need for government financing.

The doctrine of laissez faire was a crucial part of the development of modern American capitalism. For the remainder of the nineteenth century, capital would be amassed and invested almost entirely through private interests, and the economy would proceed according to its own standards, unregulated by government.

The labor force. In addition to technology and capital, the expanding industries needed labor. The workmen who operated the machines and built the canals and railroads came from the New England countryside and Europe. Overpopulation because of a high birthrate, and the fact that the best land for farming had already been divided up in the Northeast drove thousands of New Englanders into industry. And immigration, which steadily increased from 1820 to 1840, swelled into a flood in the 1840's and 1850's. Two million Irish, driven from their lands by agricultural disasters, emigrated to America. One and a half million Germans, also hit by agricultural disasters and political upheavals, left their lands.

Because of this constantly expanding labor force, wages, though higher in America than in Europe, remained fairly low and static. To protect

A FACTORY IN WALTHAM

Most observers of life among New England factory workers in the mid-nineteenth century were horrified by the conditions they saw. But Harriet Martineau, an English social observer who visited a Waltham factory in the 1830's, saw things differently:

". . . The establishment is for the spinning and weaving of cotton. . . . Five hundred persons were employed at the time of my visit. The girls earn two, and some three, dollars a week, besides their board. The little children earn one dollar a week. Most of the girls live in the houses provided by the corporation, which accommodate from six to eight each. When sisters come to the mill, it is a common practice for them to bring their mother to keep house for them and some of their companions in a dwelling built by their own earnings. In this case, they save enough out of their board to clothe themselves, and have two or three dollars a week to spare. Some have thus cleared off mortgages from their fathers' farms; others have educated the hope of the family at college; and many are rapidly accumulating an independence. I saw a whole street of houses built with the earnings of the girls; some with piazzas, and green venetian blinds; and all neat and sufficiently spacious.

"The factory people built the church, which stands conspicuous on the green in the midst of the place. The minister's salary (eight hundred dollars last year) is raised by a tax on the pews. The corporation gave them a building for a lyceum, which they have furnished with a good library, and where they have lectures every winter. . . . The girls have, in many instances, private libraries. . . .

"The people work about seventy hours per week. . . . The time of work varies with the length of the days, the wages continuing the same. All look like well-dressed young ladies. The health is good; or rather . . . it is no worse than it is elsewhere."

themselves from exploitation and also to protect their skills against the new machines, workers began to form societies early in the nineteenth century. Most of these early organizations were craft unions, that is, unions of artisans rather than industrial workers of the factories, mills, and mines.

In addition to working for higher wages and shorter hours, the early unions advocated public funds for education and agitated for the end of debtors' prison. Less admirable were their attempts to restrict immigration, a reflection of the native workers' fear of competition from immigrant workers, especially the many Irish laborers. This economic competition boiled over into religious hatred for Roman Catholicism, and in the 1850's, many native workers supported the anti-Catholic Know-Nothing party (pages 218, 219).

The early unions had a difficult struggle to persuade society that unions were legitimate. The courts usually ruled that strikes were illegal; hence, unions were denounced as unlawful conspiracies. This theory was broken in 1842 when the Massachusetts Supreme Court ruled that workers did have a right to organize, strike, and strive for the *closed shop* (the requirement that all workers in a company join a union). Important as this ruling was, other state courts ignored it.

The early unions were craft unions. The creation of strong industrial unions prior to the Civil War was almost impossible because of the conditions under which most industrial workers lived. No paid union organizers existed, and in the textile mills, for example, nearly half the workers were women and children, incapable of forming a union. Male industrial workers were sometimes housed in company-built tenements, bought their food on credit from a company-owned store, and could easily be fired and replaced by the ever-growing masses of unskilled workers.

Increasing urbanization. The growing factories and mills and mines, the expanding trade and commerce, the influx of masses of immigrants all contributed to the tremendous growth of cities in the years before the Civil War. The population during this period began to shift from the countryside to the cities. In 1820, a mere 6 percent of the population lived in urban centers of more than twenty-five hundred people. By 1860, this figure had jumped to 19 percent. With expansion, the

POPULATION GROWTH OF PRINCIPAL UNITED STATES CITIES
(The ten largest cities as of 1860)

City	1810	1820	1830	1840	1850	1860
Baltimore	35,585	62,738	80,625	102,313	169,054	212,418
Boston	33,250	43,298	61,392	101,383	136,881	177,840
Buffalo	1,508	2,095	8,653	18,213	42,261	81,129
Chicago	—	—	—	4,853	29,963	109,260
Cincinnati	2,540	9,642	24,831	46,338	115,437	161,044
New Orleans	17,242	27,176	46,310	92,193	116,378	168,675
New York City*	96,373	123,706	202,589	312,710	515,547	813,669
Philadelphia	91,874	112,772	161,410	220,423	340,045	565,529
Pittsburgh	4,768	7,248	12,568	21,115	46,601	77,923
St. Louis	1,600	4,508	5,852	16,469	77,860	160,773

*Only includes population of Manhattan. The Bronx, Brooklyn, Queens, and Richmond were incorporated into the City of Greater New York in 1898.

nature of the city began to change. By 1850, suburbs were springing up to shelter the middle class from the miseries of urban life, and by then these miseries were in full flower.

Slums proliferated as hordes of newcomers, mostly poor, pressed into the cities. In Boston, for example, instances occurred in which as many as thirty people were crowded into one cellar. Housing inspection was nonexistent, and no one suggested that the government should erect low-cost housing. Police forces, recently organized, were unable to keep public order. Not only did crime make the streets unsafe, but rioting was common. So great was the influx of people, so rapid the growth of cities that urban services were severely strained. The prevailing philosophy of laissez faire insisted that these services be privately provided, but private agencies were unable to meet the burden.

The conditions under which the increasing numbers of urban poor lived and worked were symptoms of an important social development. America was becoming a nation characterized by growing inequalities. The nation was getting richer, but a class system was emerging in which the wealth was being monopolized by the few. The Industrial Revolution created a tremendous disparity between the rich and the poor, who, increasingly, were forming a huge lower class.

2 The West Trades In Agriculture

1. Why did people move westward from 1810 to 1860?

2. What were the stages through which the settlement of the West passed?

3. How did the federal government encourage the development of the West?

4. Would the West be more inclined to favor a loose confederation of states emphasizing states' rights or a national state exercising strong positive control over its citizens and their economic activity? Why do you think so?

Between 1815 and 1860, millions of Americans poured across the Appalachian Mountains, moving westward. Some moved north of the Ohio River into the Northwest Territory; others moved south of the Ohio into the lower Mississippi Valley. Many settled on the edge of the Great Plains while still others struck out for Oregon and California in the Far West (see map, page 198). The Great Plains were bypassed and were not settled until after the Civil War.

In 1810, only one-seventh of the population lived west of the Appalachians; by 1860 half the people of the nation earned their livelihoods in the Northwest Territory and the lower Mississippi Valley. This enormous migration was not merely the result of the pull of fertile lands. It was also set in motion by a decline in the profitability of agriculture in the East.

Migration. The West was settled primarily by Americans who had been displaced by declining economic conditions in the North and South. The southern Piedmont region, the plateau between the coastal plain and the Appalachians, had been a fertile area in colonial times. Its soil now depleted and its economic prospects dimmed by the lack of good transportation routes to the coast, farmers by the thousands left and headed west.

These people wandered through Kentucky, crossed the Ohio River, and settled in large numbers in Ohio, Indiana, Illinois, and Missouri. Abraham Lincoln's family was typical of these pioneering farmers, moving from Virginia to Kentucky in 1782, from Kentucky to Indiana around 1816, and finally to Illinois in 1830. Other southerners headed for the lower Mississippi Valley into the "Black Belt." This was an incredibly rich crescent of black loam, twenty to fifty miles wide, running from Georgia across mid-Alabama into northeastern Mississippi (see map, page 166).

New Englanders moved in whole colonies across New York State and created new towns in Ohio, Indiana, and Illinois. This process was hastened not only by overpopulation in New England, but also by the decline in agriculture in the Northeast. During the 1840's, European immigrants—Irish, German, and some Scandinavians—also added to the westward movement. By 1850, one of every seven persons in the old Northwest was foreign-born. Large numbers of Germans and Swedes, for example, settled in the new states of Minnesota and Wisconsin where land was cheap.

Patterns of settlement. The first and perhaps most adventurous pioneers to seek wealth in the West were the fur trappers. As early as 1795, when Congress set up a system of trading posts to regulate the fur trade in the Northwest Territory, trappers had swarmed into the area. By the early 1800's, they were crossing the Mississippi and striking out over the Great Plains for the forests and rivers of the Rocky Mountains and Oregon, ranging far ahead of the farmers who were pushing westward. By the 1840's, the great fur resources were nearly exhausted, but the trappers and traders had helped to open up much the West and to prepare the way for settlement of the Far West (Chapter 7).

Behind the trappers and traders came a wave of land speculators. Land speculation, a traditional occupation in America, underwent an important change in the nineteenth century. In colonial times and for several years following the Revolution, land speculation had been the prerogative of the rich, but after the War of 1812, the pattern changed. This change was partly because the federal government limited the amount of land any man or group could purchase. From then on, settlers themselves became speculators. The first wave of farmers bought the land cheaply, cleared it, threw up a rude cabin, and produced several crops. Then they would sell the improved farm for a good profit to more permanent settlers and move off to the advancing frontier to repeat the process.

A later wave of settlers included laborers, often immigrants, who helped build roads and canals in the 1830's. And from 1840 to 1860, factory workers flooded into the West to work in the growing western cities.

The role of government. The federal government played an important role in aiding western development. First, the government removed the Indians, the greatest obstacle preventing land-hungry people from occupying the soil. The Indians were removed by a variety of tactics—persuasion, outright fraud, and when all else failed, extermination.

Before 1825, the Indians, especially in the Northwest Territory, had been driven slowly westward after several military defeats. In 1825, the government decided to negotiate with the various groups that remained east of the Mississippi. As already shown, the Creeks agreed to move westward, but the Cherokees of Georgia, after a series of legal maneuvers, were forcibly driven west and their ancestral lands divided up among the settlers.

The federal government also played a crucial role in regulating land policy. It guaranteed land

LIFE IN THE EMERGING NATION

Broadway from Astor House, August Kollner, 1850

Everyone Worked at Bishop Hill, Olof Krans, c. 1900

Life in the United States bustled along from 1815 to 1860. Cities grew, more and more lands were turned into productive farms, and trade and transportation burgeoned. The cities offered fine churches, shops and restaurants, hotels, enclosed horse-drawn carriages, and theaters and music halls. Life in rural areas was perhaps quieter and the pleasures

The Quilting Party, anonymous, 1854

Lawrence Wharf, New London, Connecticut, *c. 1850*

were simpler. The scene top left shows farmers at work on an Illinois prairie. Below it, country folk amuse themselves at a quilting bee.

A country flanked by great oceans and blessed with plenty of inland waters put them to good use. The seas gave ready access to foreign ports, and the waters within encouraged domestic travel and trade.

View of St. Louis, Leon Pomarede, 1835

159

After the Sale: Slaves Going South from Richmond, Eyre Crowe, 1853

Slavery still marked the land, although the importation of slaves had ended in 1808. Slaves were of great value in the cotton fields of the South, for there "cotton was king."

The Cotton Bureau at New Orleans, Edgar Degas, 1873

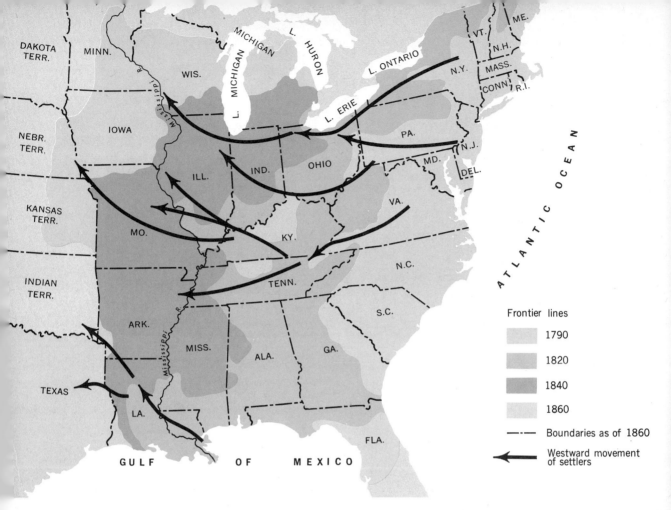

WESTERN MIGRATION OF SETTLERS, 1790–1860

titles and passed laws which benefitted small farmers with little or no capital. The Land Act of 1820, for example, provided for 80-acre tracts to be sold at $1.25 an acre, payable in gold or silver. This helped to prevent land speculators from buying large blocs of land on credit. And in 1841, the Pre-emption Act opened up more land.

An expanding transportation system was particularly important in the development of the West. And government financing helped transportation to grow. As early as 1803, the federal government, by purchasing Louisiana, had made it possible for western farmers to ship their produce down the Mississippi to New Orleans for transshipment to the East. The Erie Canal, completed in 1825, linked the Great Lakes area to the

port of New York, and transportation costs were slashed dramatically. For example, the cost of shipping one ton of produce from Ohio to New York declined from nearly $100 to $15.

The success of the Erie Canal sparked a canal-building boom, which was heavily financed by state governments. The expansion of canal construction was also spurred by the invention of a practical steamboat by Robert Fulton in 1807. By 1820, steam navigation was common in the East and was growing in the West. In 1815 the steamboat *Enterprize* chugged upriver from New Orleans to Pittsburgh. Five years later seventy steamboats were plying western rivers, and by 1860, the number had increased to nearly eight hundred. The opening of this great water transportation

161

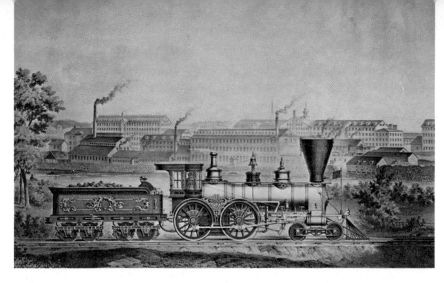

A rapidly expanding nation needs transportation to bind it together, and fortunately, the United States was able to develop it. Stagecoach service was established along the newly built turnpikes (above left), and railroads were built to carry both goods and people. The locomotive above was one of the early "American-type" wood burners built in the 1850's. The completion of the Erie Canal in 1825 (lower left) made possible inland flatboat shipping over a large area of the Northeast and had a tremendous impact on its development. In New Orleans' harbor, as shown below in an engraving made around 1850, every kind of water transportation is in evidence—flatboats, sailboats, rowboats, and the newly developed steamboat.

network, later supplemented by the railroads, made possible the economic development of the West.

Western farming. As the nation's economy developed into regions of specialized production, the West became the meat and grain center. Wheat, which was easy to grow and could be ground into flour for easy shipment, was the main cash crop. Initially, western wheat was shipped down the Mississippi to New Orleans, but the Erie Canal drastically altered the importance and direction of this trade. Increasingly, western wheat found its major market in the Northeast, especially in New York.

Corn, cattle, and pork were also important western products. Since corn was too bulky to ship in large quantities, much of it was fed to hogs and poultry, and by 1860, western pork dominated both the eastern and southern markets. Western cattle supplied the voracious slaughterhouses of growing cities like Chicago and Cincinnati. And the rapid expansion of the railroads in the 1850's opened up new markets for western cattle in the Northeast.

Western farmers were agrarian capitalists, producing meat and grain for a national and even an international market. While profits from western agriculture were large and the crops increasingly essential to the national economy, the actual return to the farmer was small. Between the farmer and the consumer stood an array of middlemen: millers, meat processors, barge and railway companies, wholesale distributors. It was to the advantage of these middlemen to keep the initial prices for products low and profits from their own activities high. Millions of individual farmers could not control the amount of produce reaching the market, hence they could not control the price.

Commerical farming in the West, unlike the subsistence farming of the old colonial frontier, led to the formation of other economic activities. The country store was a crucial institution in most communities, serving as a local bank and extending credit to farmers during the growing season, before they could sell their crops for money. Regular banks preferred to lend money on farm mortgages, and, above all, for canal and railroad construction.

The great expansion of the farming frontier coincided with a series of improvements in agricultural methods called the Agricultural Revolution. Improved fertilizers, the development of scientific stock-breeding, and the creation of societies to educate the farmer all added to the improvement of the American farm.

Most important, however, was the introduction of farm machinery, which transformed agriculture as technology had transformed industry (see chart, page 182). The invention of the cast-iron plow (1820) and John Deere's steel plow (1837) enabled the farmer to break the tough prairie sod. The mechanical reaper invented in 1834 by Cyrus McCormick could harvest ten times as much wheat as a farmer equipped with a scythe. And in 1847, Hiram Pitt and his brother John began mass-producing a threshing machine which separated wheat from chaff, previously a time-consuming and wasteful process.

These inventions made possible the farming of large acreages and were especially important in a region always short on both labor and the hard cash to pay hired hands in large numbers.

Equally important was the fact that these machines were mass-produced in the new cities mushrooming in the West. Chicago became the world's leading manufacturer of threshers and reapers. Chicago was also, by 1850, the nation's largest railroad center. Cincinnati, also a trading center, was so vital to the meat-processing industry that it was known as Porkopolis. The growth of these cities, centers of manufacturing and terminals for shipping crops and meat to the East, was a dazzling development that had great political as well as economic consequences.

The development of the West was crucial to the Industrial Revolution. Urban growth was made possible by the creation of this vast food-producing region which was tied to the urban centers by railroads and canals. Now, it was possible to assemble and feed the great pool of labor needed by industry. Since the rapid expansion of the West was shaped in great part by the federal government, westerners were keenly aware of their role in the national economy and their dependence on the national government. Thus the West had no desire to champion the doctrine of states' rights so prevalent in the South.

3 Cotton Rules The South

1. How did the dominance of cotton production affect the southern economy and way of life?

2. What was the class structure of southern society?

3. What were the characteristics of slavery? Is there evidence that blacks resisted slavery? If so, what is the evidence?

4. How did slavery affect white southern society?

The South, by virtue of its institutions and the way they affected the character of its people, differed greatly from the rest of the country. In time, these differences would seem so great to southerners that they played a significant role in bringing on the Civil War. The roots of southern distinctiveness lay in the South's economy and its social structure.

The South's economy was dominated by the production of cotton. Almost exclusively agricultural, the South had no major cities beyond the cotton-exporting centers of New Orleans and Savannah, and the small manufacturing center of Richmond. This rural society was ruled politically and economically by an elite of the largest plantation owners. Slavery, which southerners called "the peculiar institution," not only united all whites, rich and poor alike, in a passionate defense of the harsh slave codes which regulated the life of blacks, but also determined the southern role in national politics.

Cotton shapes the southern economy. In 1857, Senator James Hammond of South Carolina exultantly told the United States Senate, "Cotton is King." By that date, cotton accounted for 70 percent of the value of all American exports to Europe. The Industrial Revolution in America was financed in good part by the earnings of northern merchants in the cotton trade.

The invention of the cotton gin in 1793 by Eli Whitney literally created an industry. Before the cotton gin, only the long-staple cotton of the coastal areas, the seeds of which were easily separated from the boll, could be grown profitably. But the long-staple plants were delicate, unable to survive in most southern soil. Short-staple cotton could grow almost anywhere, but it was difficult to clean. By hand, a slave could clean the seeds from only one pound of short-staple cotton a day; with Whitney's machine, he could easily clean fifty pounds a day.

The economic feasibility of cotton turned the westward movement in the South into a land rush (see map, page 166). Speculators poured into western Georgia, Alabama, and Mississippi after the War of 1812, when the federal government "persuaded" the Indians to deed over their lands to the white man. Wealthy planters from the seaboard states, often accompanied by gangs of slaves, quickly bought up large plantations, thus monopolizing the best lands and preserving their domination of society.

Even so, cheap land was so readily available that relatively poor men, like Andrew Jackson, could buy plantations and join the planter aristocracy. Although unscientific farming methods rapidly depleted the soil, thousands of miles of cheap land still beckoned, and the cotton frontier rolled on. The most productive land was the Black Belt, and this fertile strip of land became the heart of the southern economy. By 1860, cotton growing had expanded west of the Mississippi, and one-quarter of the South's cotton was grown there.

Vast amounts of capital and 60 percent of the slaves were employed in the production of cotton. By 1860, the South grew two-thirds of the world's supply of cotton. The planter shipped his crop by flat boat to New Orleans, Savannah, or Mobile, and consigned it to cotton "factors," businessmen who acted as sales agents and bankers. About half the crop was shipped to Liverpool, England, by way of New York, for the British textile mills. The remainder went to New England.

The profits from the cotton trade were enormous, but only half of the return benefitted the planter. More than 40 percent of the profits flowed into the pockets of northern merchants who owned the cargo ships. Southerners resented this loss of income, as well as their dependence on the North for manufactured goods. The South, however, did not diversify its agriculture nor

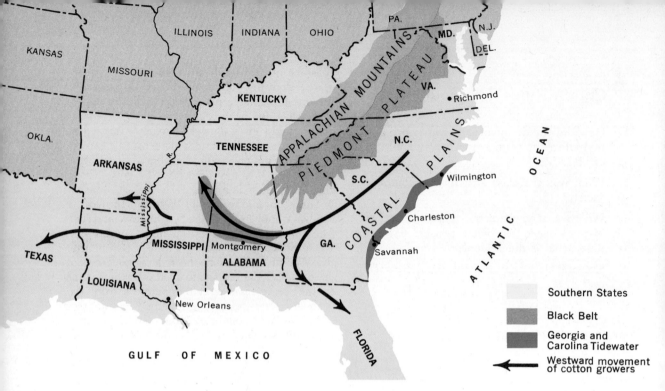

THE EXPANDING SOUTH, 1790–1860

create industry. Its capital flowed into land speculation and the purchase of slaves. The dominance of cotton production thus had extremely serious effects on the South.

Structure of southern society. The pre-Civil War, or antebellum, South was characterized by an elaborate class structure. At the top of society stood the planter. In 1850, about 2,700 great planters owned more than 100 slaves each, and another 50,000 planters each had between 50 and 100 slaves. These men, especially the tiny elite, ruled the South. Not only did they dominate its politics, but they also determined the South's ideals, its unhesitating defense of slavery and states' rights, and its commitment to an agrarian way of life.

The aim of these great planters was self-sufficiency; almost half of their land, for example, was used to raise corn and peas. Few of the planters succeeded in being self-sufficient, however, and fewer still lived in the luxury that romantic myth associates with them. The cost of slaves and northern manufactured goods was so great that only a minority of southern planters had sufficient capital to build the columned man-

sions of popular fiction. The average plantation was a few hundred acres worked by a gang of between 20 and 50 slaves. Perhaps 100,000 such large farms produced three-quarters of the cotton crop.

Beneath this minority was the great mass of southern farmers, 75 percent of whom owned no slaves and produced little cotton. As suppliers of staples such as pork and corn to the plantations, the farmers were tied to the plantation economy. They accepted the planters' leadership not only because they were dependent upon the planters economically, but also because they agreed with them on nearly every issue, especially the necessity of slavery. Indeed, the average southern farmer hoped eventually to own slaves himself.

Also dependent upon the plantation system were the professional classes and businessmen, such as the cotton factors and slave traders. Lawyers adopted the Constitutional views of the planters, the belief in a rigid maintenance of states' rights. Some southern doctors wrote treatises arguing the biological inferiority of blacks, and both college professors and newspaper editors wrote long-winded defenses of slavery.

At the bottom of white society stood that sub-merged class most often called by the term said to have been coined by slaves, "poor white trash." Their poverty stemmed from the exhausted soil of the Piedmont region, where most of them lived. They had been left behind in the great westward migration. Unable to sell and get enough capital to start anew, and plagued by diseases, they were too weak to compete economically. Perhaps half a million strong, the poor whites had little in common with other groups in southern society except that fear and contempt for the blacks which underlay the southerner's conviction about his economy and society.

Free blacks. More than 250,000 free blacks, living largely in Virginia, Maryland, and North Carolina, constituted a massive paradox in southern society. Their very existence denied the myths many southerners had invented to justify the treatment of the slaves. Refuting the theory that the black was too unintelligent and lazy to function outside of slavery were the black artisans, preachers, and teachers found in almost every southern town.

The liberty of free blacks was severely restricted, however, especially after 1831. Georgia actually tried to outlaw free blacks, and all southern states denied them the vote, a place in the militia, the right to testify in court and sit on juries, the right to assemble in large numbers, and equal access to education. Similar restrictions on the free blacks were also common in the northern states. Racism was not exclusively a southern phenomenon; it poisoned the North as well. But in the South it lay at the basis of the South's most distinctive feature and greatest problem—slavery.

Slavery. Economically, slavery was an agrarian labor system which southerners believed was uniquely suited to the plantation system. The bulk of slaves were unskilled field hands who normally worked in gangs directed by a driver, himself a trusted slave, under the grim and unrelenting supervision of an overseer. On smaller plantations worked by fewer than ten slaves, there was no overseer, and the master himself directed the slaves and worked alongside them. Large plantations also kept domestic slaves—cooks, maids, butlers, coachmen—who were often educated and trusted, and rarely beaten.

THE UNDERGROUND RAILROAD

Probably the term "Underground Railroad" came into use sometime after 1831, along with steam railroads. But real railroads were almost never used in escapes—in the Underground Railroad ordinary railroad terms had new meanings. "Conductors" on the Railroad carried their "passengers" in wagons. They found their way by scanning landmarks—rivers, mountains, and sometimes on cloudy nights, they pointed their way northward by feeling the moss on trees. Underground Railroad "stations" were only about ten to twenty miles apart. There, fugitives were hidden to wait until dark to continue their journey.

The historian John Hope Franklin describes in part the operations of the Underground Railroad:

". . . All, or almost all, of the operations took place at night, for that was the only time when the fugitive and his helpers felt even partially secure. Slaves prepared to make their escape by taking supplies from their masters and, if it was felt necessary, by disguising themselves. Those of fair complexion frequently passed as white persons and sometimes posed as their own masters. . . . There are several cases on record where fugitives were provided at crucial moments with white babies in order to make their claims of being nurses appear more convincing. . . ."

Living conditions of the slave varied widely, depending partly upon the whim of the overseer and owner, partly upon the economic condition of the plantation. On very small cotton plantations, the owner himself lived in a crude cabin with few luxuries; the distance between his living style and that of his slaves was not great. In general, however, most slaves lived in unheated cabins, were given shoes and rudimentary clothing, and were allowed to cultivate small vegetable gardens.

While numerous instances of outstanding kindness or grotesque cruelty are recorded, the average slave experienced neither. The overseer or owner carried a whip, which he was quick to use on malingerers, runaways, and "saboteurs." Every black child learned this harsh lesson, and this fear was generally sufficient to maintain order.

Worse than physical hardship was the denial of human personality, the bland assumption of black inferiority. Southern whites tried to persuade themselves that the system was kindly and beneficial. They argued that the slaves were happy, touchingly loyal to their masters, and not bright enough to desire a free society or to survive in one. Having argued this, southerners then established throughout the South a vigilante system to prevent such good people from revolting.

Slaves did revolt, however. One of the most violent slave uprisings occurred on the night of August 22, 1831, when a Virginia slave preacher named Nat Turner roused his followers to rebellion. Raging through dozens of plantations, the militant slaves killed fifty or sixty whites, mostly women and children, within twenty-four hours. This outbreak was bloodily suppressed, but the rebellion threw the South into a frenzy of fear and hatred. Numerous laws were passed restricting the movements of slaves, forbidding them to receive an education, and limiting religious activity.

Some historians have noted that in the antebellum South, aside from Turner's revolt and acts of violence on individual plantations, slaves did not openly challenge the system. Yet, the black man did resist. Possibly fifteen thousand—the number is impossible to determine—fled to the North, many by means of the Underground Railroad. Most of them escaped from the border states of Kentucky, Missouri, Maryland, and Delaware. Slaves from states such as Mississippi, Georgia, Louisiana, and Texas, in the lower South, unable to reach the North, sometimes fled for a brief period to escape work, sometimes in a desperate search for families from whom they had been forcibly separated.

The laziness and low productivity southerners often commented on were probably deliberate "slowdowns," if they were not attributable to disease. Equipment was often destroyed, and sometimes brutal overseers were murdered. The slaves' resistance or flight, the southern slave codes, vigilante patrols, and the general fear of

a slave insurrection all stand as grim testimony to the fact that the black man desired his freedom.

Perhaps the most unsavory aspect of slavery, even in the eyes of most southern gentlemen, was the slave trade. This traffic in human lives was managed by firms which purchased slaves in Virginia and the Carolinas and exported them to meet the inexhaustible demand from the lower South. In addition, a lively smuggling trade existed after the importation of slaves was forbidden in 1808. Upper-class southerners regarded the slave auctioneer as a social pariah—until he retired with his huge profits and became a gentleman planter.

As already noted, slavery was not simply a labor system; it was a form of social control based on race prejudice. Capital which might have been spent on scientific agriculture and mechanization, as in the West and North, was tied up in a labor system noted for the low productivity of its workers compared to the wage laborer of the North. The system was psychologically ruinous—it brutalized and frightened the white masters, and it degraded and dehumanized the blacks. Where the black man was free he was industrious and intelligent; where he was enslaved, he was usually passive, uncooperative, and resentful.

Above all, the system was a challenge to the doctrine "that all men are created free and equal." It was inevitable that an institution so at variance with American political theory would be challenged politically. Equally, it was inevitable that the southerner, convinced of the necessity of slavery, impelled by racial fears and hatreds, would resist.

The South, then, was not merely a region with curious variations in social and political institutions; it was a distinct civilization. With its one-crop economy, its plantations worked by slaves, its society dominated by an elite few, southern civilization saw itself as a new version of Greece and Rome, which southerners believed had similar social systems. If its social structure was unique and its political views shaped by the necessity of defending its "peculiar institution," the South was not independent. It was part of a national economy, dependent on the North and West for goods and foodstuffs, relying on northern merchants to transport the cotton crop to market. This lay at the root of the South's dilemma: how long could it maintain its unique institutions and still remain in the Union?

CONCLUSION

By 1860, the United States spanned the continent; its population was 32 million; and its economy had developed rapidly under the impact of industrialization. The tremendous economic expansion in the years before the Civil War created not only economic sections, but a national economy as well. A transportation revolution bound the nation together economically. The West and the South depended upon the North for manufactured goods; the South looked to the West for grain and meat; the manufacturing North was dependent upon southern cotton and western agriculture.

However, the creation of a national economy did not result in the growth of nationalistic feelings. Other forces were also at work. The doctrine of laissez faire, by insisting that government refrain from intervening in or attempting to regulate the economy, placed a premium on local initiative and individualism, weakening the bonds of national unity. Equally important, each section of the country had specific economic and political interests to defend, and conflicts over these issues produced sectional antagonisms that could not be easily resolved. As time passed, thoughtful observers began to question whether the bonds that held the Union together were strong enough to resist the forces that had the potential to destroy it.

QUESTIONS

1. What sectional factors tended to bind the American nation together? How did the economic growth of the period from 1815 to 1860 encourage this unity?

2. What sectional factors worked against national unity and encouraged regional loyalties?

3. How did the government's policy of laissez faire encourage sectionalism and discourage nationalism?

4. To what extent were the innovations of the Industrial or Agricultural revolutions experienced in each section of the country?

5. What were the social and economic gains and losses to the American people which accompanied the rapid economic growth of the first half of the nineteenth century?

BIBLIOGRAPHY

GREEN, CONSTANCE MCL., *Eli Whitney and the Birth of American Technology*, Library of American Biography, Little, Brown. Although Whitney is usually remembered for his invention of the cotton gin, he had a far greater role in the growth of American technology. His efficient production of arms for the American government by the use of interchangeable parts had far-reaching significance.

HIDY, RALPH W., AND PAUL E. CAWEIN, *The Formative Era of American Enterprise: The Virginia Company; Boston Merchants and the Puritan Ethic; and the Factory System*, Case Studies in Business History and Economic Concepts, Heath. Economists and business historians have attempted to make the understanding of economic concepts more meaningful to high school students by incorporating them in case studies of specific American businesses. Particular attention is drawn to the section on the factory system in this book.

ELKINS, STANLEY M., *Slavery: A Problem in American Institutional and Intellectual Life*, U. of Chicago Press. The author uses concepts from the field of psychology to understand the slave personality, and he draws upon comparisons with other restrictive societies such as the concentration camp of World War II to explain slave behavior.

DOUGLASS, FREDERICK, *Narrative of the Life of Frederick Douglass an American Slave*, New American Library (Signet Books). To understand the role of the black in the antebellum period, one must meet Frederick Douglass, and there is no better way to do this than to let Douglass speak for himself, taking his reader back with the slaves of the South and the escape to the North.

DUFF, JOHN B. AND PETER M. MITCHELL, *The Nat Turner Rebellion: The Historic Event and the Modern Controversy*, Harper & Row. This book considers literature, history, and the contemporary scene in the light of the Nat Turner Rebellion. There are excerpts from the original account and from a recent popular account. Students may want to use this book to generalize on the extent of interpretation permitted in reporting the past.

CHAPTER SIX/1815–1860

The American Character

Human societies are governed not only by political, social, and economic forces, but also by values—that is, by standards of thought and conduct, by what people believe, and by what they hope to attain. In fact, values, or the search for values, often determine the type of political, social, and economic organizations people and nations live by. This is especially true during periods of rapid change when individuals and groups within nations attempt to defend or redefine the standards by which they live.

Such a period occurred in America between 1815 and 1860. These were the years when the West was expanding, cities were growing, political life was becoming more democratic, and industrialization was transforming the national economy. These changes combined to produce a period of intellectual and social ferment that was to have an enduring impact upon the development of American society. Diversity in thought, religion, and politics characterized society during this period. Established ideas were challenged by new and diverse points of view. Although there were many contradictory elements, American social, political, and intellectual life was dominated by four major trends: individualism, romanticism, evangelicalism, and reform. As you read about these trends, consider these questions:

1. How were the changing American values reflected in literature and philosophy?
2. What were the distinctly American elements of the national culture?
3. How did the rise of evangelicalism affect established religion?
4. What social problems did reformers tackle during this period? What were the results of their work?

1 Literature And Philosophy Reflect American Values

1. How did the Transcendentalist philosophy define the concept of democracy?

2. What were the characteristics of Romanticism, and how did they appear in American literature?

3. How did the works of Hawthorne, Melville, and Poe compare with other writers of the period?

4. How did Romanticism encourage a distinctive southern culture?

During the 1820's and 1830's, with the rise of mass politics based upon universal white male suffrage, American politicians, poets, novelists, philosophers, and historians tried to define the meaning and implications of the concept of democracy. Clearly it was a difficult task. Democracy implied more than the election of officials by popular vote; it suggested that the common man had the ability to govern.

Concepts of democracy. Two theories of the nature of democracy emerged in the 1830's—the concept of the General Will and the concept of Individualism. The idea of the General Will was expressed by the nineteenth-century historian and statesman George Bancroft. Bancroft held that "all great noble institutions of the world have come from popular efforts." This was so, he thought, because the masses have a common mind or spirit at which they arrive by intuition. "The Spirit of God," declared Bancroft, "breathes through the combined intelligence of the people."

The theory of the General Will, however, had several defects. One European observer of American society, the French writer Alexis de Tocqueville, regarded the American belief in the wisdom of popular opinion as dangerous. Tocqueville believed that it would lead to the tyranny of the majority over the minority.

Many American thinkers shared Tocqueville's fears and believed in the doctrine of Individualism—that the conscience and needs of the individual should take precedence over the demands made by a majority of the community. The New England essayist and philosopher Henry David Thoreau summed up this concept:

I think we should be men first and subjects afterward. It is not desirable to cultivate a respect for the law, so much as for the right. The obligation which I have a right to assume is to do at any time what I think right.

Although Tocqueville feared the tyranny of the majority in a democratic society, he nevertheless believed that excessive individualism, such as that expressed by Thoreau, was equally hazardous. Such a doctrine, Tocqueville noted, would result in men no longer being "bound together by ideas, but by [economic] interests." And human opinions he wrote, would be "reduced to a sort of intellectual dust, scattered on every side, unable to collect, unable to cohere."

With some exceptions, American thinkers during the early and mid-nineteenth century placed greater value upon the concept of Individualism than on that of the General Will. In fact, much of America's social and intellectual history during the first half of the nineteenth century may be characterized in terms of variations on the theme of Individualism. How could Americans create a distinctive national culture where community interests often clashed with individual freedom of conscience and action? The dilemma posed by Tocqueville has been debated by Americans throughout their history, and it has never been resolved.

Transcendentalism. At the beginning of the nineteenth century, Deists had organized the Unitarian church. This denomination preached a life of temperance and respectability, of calmness and dignity, a doctrine that appealed primarily to the upper classes in New England, especially in the Boston area. By the 1830's, however, many young Unitarians, including the writers Ralph Waldo Emerson and Henry David Thoreau, had concluded that their religion was "corpse-cold." These Unitarians felt that it exalted reason over the emotions, emphasizing pious platitudes and formal practices. It lacked imagination and intellectual excitement. It did not come to terms with man's individuality, or his relationship to Nature and the mysteries of the universe. The rebellion against Unitarianism was called Transcendentalism. It emphasized a mystical, intuitive approach to life in which man could "transcend" or go beyond the limitations of reason by faith in himself and belief in the goodness of the universe.

Man, Emerson argued, is not simply a creature of society, bound to observe customs and traditions inherited from his forebears. The most important and the most exciting aspect of man, Emerson believed, is his individuality—his ability to mold his own character and to develop the capacity for self-reliance. This individuality can be fully realized only when man is in communion with Nature, of which he is a part. Man's soul is part of the soul of Nature, or what Emerson called the Oversoul. By contemplating both himself and the natural world around him, man most fully understands his place in the universe. This doctrine made churches unnecessary and insisted that most human activities—business and politics in particular—distracted man and prevented him from involving himself in Nature.

Thoreau carried this idea to its ultimate conclusion by rejecting society and living for a year in isolation at Walden Pond near Concord, Massachusetts. Thoreau despised the world of cities and commerce. In the forest, in continuous interaction with Nature, he felt that man finds peace, simplicity, and contentment, and his life is no longer spent making money or producing artificial luxuries. Man is happiest when he seeks not to conquer Nature, but to live within it.

The transcendental emphasis on individualism and self-reliance was celebrated in the poetry of Walt Whitman, whose best-known work was *Leaves of Grass* (1855). In one of his poems, "Song of Myself," Whitman lyrically proclaimed that all men were united through Nature.

> I celebrate myself, and sing myself
> And what I assume you shall assume
> For every atom belonging to me as good belongs
>   to you.

The Transcendentalists tried to solve the problem posed by the idea of democracy by declaring that every man was an individual but was united into a common whole with his fellow men because all were a part of Nature.

A national literature. American writers in the first half of the nineteenth century were searching for new models of progress. Their traditions, literary modes, and philosophical ideals had come from Europe. They now began to demand a national literature, using native themes and settings, emphasizing purely American speech patterns, and expressing uniquely American philosophical ideas. Yet, from Europe, Americans adopted the major ideas of romanticism, which they found in the novels of Sir Walter Scott, the poetry of Goethe, and the philosophy of Thomas Carlyle. Romanticism emphasized the emotions over reason, urged the use of historical materials in literature, and celebrated the individual's struggle against society. At the same time, the romanticists made a mystique out of nationalism, emphasizing the cultural uniqueness of each people.

Thus, from European romantics, American writers partially derived the idea that they ought to create a national literature based on American rather than European themes. Noah Webster, whose famous dictionary included peculiarly American words, declared that "America must be as independent in *literature* as she is in *politics*."

In the years 1815 to 1860, a notable group of writers—poets, novelists, historians—sought to create a literature using American historical materials and American geographical and social settings. Most idealized the past, glorified the virtues of individualism, emphasized the wilderness as a factor shaping the American character, and sought to portray the Indian as a "noble savage." The stress many American writers placed upon nature, self-reliance, democracy, and individualism blended with both the laissez faire political doctrines of Jacksonian Democracy and the moral values taught by Emerson and Thoreau.

The novelist James Fenimore Cooper based many of his books on the French and Indian War and the American Revolution. In his series of novels, *The Leatherstocking Tales* (1823–41) he contrasted the freedom and innocence of his hero, the frontiersman Natty Bumppo, with the materialism and commercial competitiveness of the city. Idealizing men of the wilderness—both Indian and white—Cooper presented the frontier experience as crucial in the shaping of American attitudes.

Historians also catered to the need of the American people to find in their history inspiring examples and directions for the future. It was history which could keep alive the great memories of the Puritans' early struggles, the wars against the French and, above all, the ideas of the Founding Fathers. George Bancroft, whose great ten-volume *History of the United States* appeared between 1834 and 1875, regarded history as a great moral struggle between wicked aristocrats and kings and good common people. God, he insisted,

had destined the American people to create a civilization based upon the supreme value of democracy.

Poetry also reflected American themes. Walt Whitman was the poet of democracy, a passionate believer in the vitality and goodness of American life. He was unique in celebrating the city, and his poetry is vivid with the conviction that ordinary people and settings would help produce specifically American poetry rather than pale imitations of European works. The New England poet John Greenleaf Whittier wrote the beautiful lyrics of "Snow Bound" (1866) in praise of New England life. An ardent abolitionist, he also produced reams of poems denouncing slavery.

Hawthorne, Melville, Poe. American literature reached its most profound insights into the human condition in the novels of Nathaniel Hawthorne and Herman Melville. These writers dealt with Americans caught in a struggle between individual values and the demands of society, a struggle in which the individual generally loses. Injecting into American literature a note of pessimism and tragedy, they rejected the normally optimistic tone of American writers and their uncritical glorification of the past.

In *The Scarlet Letter* (1850), a novel about adultery in Puritan New England, Hawthorne deals with the consequences of sin within the structure of society and, perhaps more importantly, within the conscience of the individual. Hawthorne's bitter satire on the Transcendentalists, *The Blithedale Romance* (1852), turns into a tragedy when the individualist heroine commits suicide.

Herman Melville, who had been a sailor, used the sea as a background for much of his work. In his novel *White Jacket* (1850), he exposed the brutality of life aboard American warships. But it was in *Moby Dick* (1851) that Melville created the greatest romantic hero in American fiction, Captain Ahab. Ahab's obsessive search for the great white whale symbolizes man's unsuccessful attempt to cope with the problem of evil in the universe.

One of the most imaginative writers of this period was Edgar Allan Poe—literary critic, poet, short-story writer, and master of the detective story and tales of horror. Poe portrayed the bizarre, the fanciful, and even the nightmarish in much of his work. In stories like "The Black Cat,"

"The Pit and the Pendulum," "The Premature Burial," he explores the evil in human nature. Poe's characters do not live in the self-reliant world of early nineteenth-century America; he did not attempt to comment on this world.

The South embraces romanticism. The South created a distinctive culture. Romanticism, especially the medieval world portrayed in the novels of Sir Walter Scott, appealed to southerners. A society resting on slavery appeared comparable to medieval European society based on serfdom. The upper classes in the South easily identified with the noble knights, the fair maidens, and the military feats glorified by Scott.

The southern gentleman exulted in his own code of honor, in which the duel replaced the medieval joust. He romanticized southern history, insisting that his Virginia forebears were Cavaliers, the aristocratic supporters of King Charles I. He delighted in the romances of the South Carolina planter William Gilmore Simms, whose works glorified the South in the American Revolution. Above all, the southerner found in his role of lordly gentleman a perfect defense of the institution of slavery.

One of the major spokesmen for the southern way of life was George Fitzhugh, whose book *Cannibals All* (1857) was virtually a handbook for slaveowners. Every great civilization, Fitzhugh wrote, rested upon a system of slavery. Civilization was the work of the leisured upper classes, and the southern gentleman was in the process of creating a civilization marked by elegant architecture, exquisite manners, and an advanced social and political philosophy. Armed with this vision of itself, the southern upper class ruthlessly stamped out any competing ideas. A society emerged which admired war and violence; a truculent and touchy upper class in the South stood ready to spring to arms at the slightest challenge.

In its own way the South was deeply affected by both romanticism and individualism—concepts and attitudes which left their indelible imprint elsewhere in American society. But in the South these attitudes and concepts were so closely tied to the defense of slavery that any parallels one might legitimately draw between northern and southern modes of thought were far outweighed by irreconcilable differences.

2 A Popular American Culture Develops

1. How was popular culture of the period from 1820 to 1860 transmitted to the people?

2. How did American painters of this period portray American national life?

3. What are the characteristics of the Hudson River School, genre painting, and folk art. How do they differ from one another?

4. What are the characteristics of Greek and Gothic architecture, and what accounted for their popularity in America?

Jacksonian Democracy changed American life politically, economically, and culturally as well. Imbued with the democratic ideal that each man was the equal of his neighbor, Americans began to thirst after the "culture" that had been the sole province of the wellborn few in the early years of the republic.

Rise of mass culture. The beginnings of industrialization not only raised the general standard of living but also made it possible to produce large quantities of books, magazines, and newspapers at low cost. By 1859, there were more than two thousand booksellers in the country, and a fifty-volume set of the works of Sir Walter Scott sold for only $27.50. In 1833, the first penny newspaper, the New York *Sun*, was published, joined two years later by the New York *Herald*. Both papers featured sensational news to attract readers. Magazines such as *Godey's Lady's Book* brought the latest word on Paris fashions and middle-class morals to American women.

However, if culture began to be spread more widely, it was also spread more thinly. A whole crop of moralistic, sentimental "domestic" novels flourished. A typical example was *The Lamplighter* (1854) by Marria Cummins, the heartrending story of Little Gerty, an orphan saved from a dire fate by Trueman Flint, a kindly lamplighter. In *The Anatomy of American Popular Culture*, Carl Bode calls these novels the "great-grandmothers" of modern soap operas. Among poets, the most popular and commercially successful was Lydia

The legitimate theater relied heavily on the plays of Shakespeare during the 1800's. Above, a performance of *Julius Caesar* featured three actors from the famous Booth acting family. Shown here are three of the sons of Junius Brutus Booth, a popular British Shakespearean actor who emigrated to the United States in 1821. They are John Wilkes as Marc Antony, Edwin as Brutus, and Junius, Jr. as Cassius. The most prominent, Edwin, was to remain a well-loved actor until his death near the end of the century. His brother John did not share the same fate; he was to die in 1865 after assassinating Abraham Lincoln. At the right is a song sheet of the period, a sentimental song that Stephen Collins Foster wrote in 1854. He wrote a total of about two hundred songs, of which fifty or so became popular, but he died penniless, in part because he sold them so cheaply.

Huntley Sigourney, who wrote sweet and sentimental verses celebrating mother love and romanticizing historical incidents.

Music, too, was reaching the people. By the 1850's, opera was presented regularly in New York, Boston, Philadelphia, Chicago, and New Orleans. Talented musicians, largely German immigrants, performed in orchestra and band concerts. At the same time, all America was singing these maudlin lyrics by Henry Russell: "I love it, I love it and cannot tear/ My soul from a Mother's Old Arm Chair."

These contrasts between "high" and "low" culture can be found easily in any subsequent era, but it was at this time that a mass culture first became apparent. Whatever reservations might be made about the level of popular culture, there is no doubt that Americans were determined to have it. All over the country, civic leaders aspired to build playhouses, libraries, museums, and auditoriums as measures of their city's cultural achievements. By the 1850's, there were nearly one thousand libraries in the country, with a total of nearly eight million books, a substantial increase over the previous decade. In 1854, two major libraries were opened—the Boston Public Library and the Astor Public Library in New York. Historical societies were founded to preserve the traces of an already disappearing past.

Performers on tour. The spread of culture over the country was facilitated not only by improved mass cummunication, but also by transportation advances. European musical stars followed their successes at home with an American tour. These performers were regarded by American audiences somewhat as curiosities, admired more for their technical virtuosity than for their musicianship.

Crowds turned out to cheer such luminaries as the singer Jenny Lind ("the Swedish nightingale"), the dancer Fanny Elssler ("the divine Fanny"), and the flashy Norwegian violinist Ole Bull. Many of these stars were brought to this country by P. T. Barnum, the flamboyant showman.

Famous European actors toured as well. The Irish actor Tyrone Power (great-grandfather of the movie actor Tyrone Power) recorded in a diary his enthusiastic receptions in Savannah, Baltimore, and New Orleans. Popular American actors, such as Edwin Booth, Fanny Kemble, and William Macready, also toured the major cities, attracting large audiences. Lesser-known troupes of players performed Shakespeare and melodramas to eager audiences in small towns.

Minstrel shows. Among the most popular traveling companies were the minstrel shows, which flourished between 1850 and 1870. Largely a white man's production, with white actors made up in blackface, the minstrel shows used many songs, dances, and musical instruments that originated with the plantation slaves. The typical minstrel show was divided into two parts, the first a lively, continuous program and the second a collection of variety acts. The performers sat in a semicircle, with the "interlocutor," or master of ceremonies, in the center flanked by two "end men."

Today much of the minstrel show humor seems pointless and vulgar, and the entire concept a degrading caricature of black culture. However, the minstrel show was a distinctly American form of entertainment, immensely popular in its time. And many of its songs have survived to become part of the American musical tradition.

One of America's most popular composers, Stephen Foster, wrote his most famous songs— "Old Folks at Home," "My Old Kentucky Home," "Oh, Susanna," and "Camptown Races"—for minstrel shows. Raised in Pittsburgh and Cincinnati (and not in the Deep South he idealized in his songs), Foster combined the European art song with the lively vitality of frontier and plantation music. Torn between writing for "polite" audiences and creating his own versions of slave melodies, he finally chose the latter. "I have concluded . . . to pursue the Ethiopian business [minstrel songs] without fear or shame," he wrote in 1852. Had he not, he would scarcely be known today.

American painting. Before the 1830's, an American who visited a museum was likely to see Indian relics, mastodon bones, and curiosities such as an eight-footed pig, with perhaps a painting or two thrown in for good measure. However, interest in art generally, and in American painting specifically, increased rapidly over the next decades.

One enticement was the chance of winning a painting in a lottery. An ingenious scheme was presented to the American public by the American Art-Union. For $5, a person could become a

ART IN THE EMERGING NATION

Kaaterskill Falls, Thomas Cole, 1827

A Long Speech, George Catlin, c. 1850

The Verdict of the People, George Caleb Bingham, 1855

As the federalist period drew to a close, American artists looked less to European influences and more to subject matter and inspiration from their own land. The pervading national spirit of self-reliance, individualism, and democracy was ever present in the artist's work. A growing sense of nationalism attracted the artist to subjects like the common man, the frontier, the natural beauty and natural resources of his own land, all of which lend themselves to romanticism. American landscape painting truly came into its own. Members of the "Hudson River School" created breathtaking panoramas to celebrate the American wilderness, like the painting by the school's founder, Thomas Cole, on page 177.

Genre painting too came into its own, as the paintings on these pages show. The genre painters were not only able to capture the look and feel of everyday life in America, they were also able to infuse their paintings with humor and sometimes satire. At the left, the artist makes a little fun of the long-winded powwows that Indians—his favorite subjects—frequently held. In it the chief has spoken so long that the braves are now covered over with snow. The other genre painters whose works are shown here were also most adept at drawing their subject matter from the ordinary of the time and imbuing it with great vitality. The drama of election day and the serenity of the fishing scene are brilliantly conveyed.

Eel Spearing at Setauket, William Sidney Mount, 1845

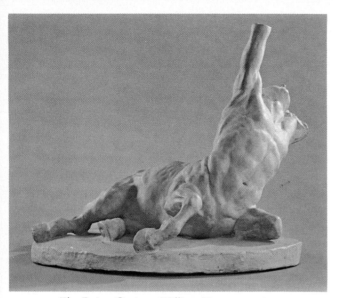

The Dying Centaur, William Rimmer, c. 1871

During this period, sculpture ranked especially high in public esteem—between 1830 and 1850 even higher than painting. Most of the important sculptors of the time studied, and sometimes settled, in Italy, where they received generous commissions. One who neither studied in Italy nor grew affluent on commissions created the sculpture at the left. For years he struggled against poverty and indifference, and his struggle seems to show in this work.

The Greco-Roman influence on architecture seemed to give way to a Gothic revival, that is, to the style of the Middle Ages. Probably the finest example of this architectural revival is the Trinity Church below, executed by Richard Upjohn and completed in 1849. All of its details seem to work together to create a continuous sweep up toward its towering spire.

Bird's Eye View of Trinity Church, New York, John Forsyth and E. W. Nimee, 1847

"member" of the Art-Union. He would then receive an engraving of an art work by an American artist, and in addition a chance to win one of a number of original works if his number were drawn at an annual lottery. The proceeds of the subscription were used to purchase the paintings from the artists.

In 1849, more than sixteen thousand people subscribed and half a million viewed the paintings at the Art-Union's gallery in New York. Although the Art-Union did little to encourage innovators or to improve public taste in art, it did provide a substantial means of support for serious painters and acquainted thousands of their countrymen with their work. The lottery was declared illegal by a New York court in 1851, but similar unions were founded in other states in the next few years.

Among the most popular painters whose works were purchased by the Art-Union were members of the Hudson River School. These artists found their fulfillment of the romantic ideal in the American wilderness. Turning away from portraiture, which had been the prevailing eighteenth-century style, they painted vast and realistic panoramas of natural landscapes. Although many of their works did picture the Hudson River Valley and the adjacent Catskill Mountains, these painters also painted scenes in other parts of the country.

Nature-oriented writers of the times urged them on. The poet William Cullen Bryant is in fact one of the *Kindred Spirits* portrayed in Asher Durand's painting of that name (1849). Standing with Bryant on a rock ledge overlooking a Catskill gorge is Thomas Cole, Durand's art teacher and a founder of the Hudson River School.

The opening of the West provided inspiration for many painters. Albert Bierstadt, a member of the Hudson River School, painted the Rocky Mountains in all their grandeur. Alfred Miller recorded the Old West, particularly Fort Laramie, in the Wyoming territory, in a series of watercolor sketches. Responding to the same lure but painting in a different style, George Catlin traveled and lived among various Indian tribes for eight years. "The history and customs of such a people," he wrote, "are themes worthy of the lifetime of one man." Sensing that the Indian cultures were doomed, he preserved a valuable historic and artistic record of their peak.

"Genre" paintings, that is, pictures that tell a story, were also prominent. William Sydney Mount stated the genre painter's philosophy: "Paint pictures that will take with the public—never paint for the few, but the many." Mount had the talent to produce pictures that were more than "pretty," as many of his colleagues did not. He chose as his theme the people and activities of a rural Long Island village. George Caleb Bingham, an outstanding genre painter, portrayed the rowdy and vigorous activities of the Missouri River boatmen.

Folk artists of all kinds flourished in this period before industrialization and mechanization had taken full root. These "grass-roots" painters, as art historian Alexander Eliot calls them, painted portraits, landscapes, still lifes, memorials to dead relatives, and historical and contemporary scenes. Their best efforts, many of them anonymous, have a simple and direct appeal that more than compensates for their technical inadequacies.

One folk artist who was neither anonymous nor inexpert was Edward Hicks. A Quaker preacher haunted by the words of the Biblical prophet Isaiah ("And the wolf shall lie down with the lamb . . . and a little child shall lead them"), Hicks painted at least sixty and perhaps as many as one hundred versions of *The Peaceable Kingdom*. In these paintings, children and animals are frozen into attitudes of trust and serenity, staring hypnotically at the viewer. In the backgrounds are realistic historical scenes and lettering.

American architecture. The romantic yearning for the remote in time and place found expression in various forms of architectural revivalism. The most prominent was the Greek revival style. The classic symmetry of the columns and porticos of ancient Greek temples were well suited, thought the Americans, to the growing need for dignified civic buildings. (The Greeks in the 1830's were also fighting for their independence from Turkey, a symbolism that no doubt influenced the Americans.) Soon every American city—large, small, and middling—had one or more public buildings in the Greek style. Some private homes, mainly row houses in New York and Boston, were also built in this style.

In the South, particularly in the wealthy cotton-growing areas of the lower Mississippi Valley, Greek architecture was adapted to the life style of the plantation owners. The wealthiest of these men could afford to build large and gracious mansions and to maintain them in elegant style with slave labor. The prevailing southern romantic attitudes were clearly expressed in the columned temples that served as homes for the rich.

By the 1840's, however, the landscape architect Andrew Jackson Downing was happy to proclaim that "the Greek temple disease has passed the crisis." The next revival to dominate architecture was Gothic. The pointed windows, towers, spires, vaults, and other castlelike features were remi-

niscent of German architecture of the thirteenth and fourteenth centuries. Used in many types of buildings, Gothic was especially well suited to church construction. Some of the best examples are Richard Upjohn's Trinity Church, and James Renwick's Grace Church and St. Patrick's Cathedral, all in New York City.

Gothic architecture was particularly susceptible to distortion and exaggeration. Mark Twain described the not uncommon sham-medievalism of the state capitol at Baton Rouge, Louisiana: "A white-washed castle with turrets and things . . . materials all ungenuine within and without, pretending to be what they are not."

The vocal opponent of the Greek style, Andrew Jackson Downing, had said, "A dwelling house should look like a dwelling house, not a Greek temple." What he thought a dwelling house should look like was a cottage in the Gothic style, painted in subdued colors. He looked forward to a time when "smiling lawns and tasteful cottages begin to embellish the country." "Carpenter Gothic" his buildings came to be called, and his book *The Architecture of Country Houses* (1850) served as a guide for designers all over the country. Scarcely any of Downing's buildings stand today, but his influence was felt for generations in another field. He was among the first to emphasize the importance of landscaping for both private homes and public places.

Although technological advances were made during this period, the emphasis on the picturesque and the exotic often obscured form and function. The architect Alexander Jackson Davis listed in his diary in 1867 the many styles in which he was competent: "American Log Cabin, Farm House, English cottage, Collegiate Gothic, Manor house, French suburban, Switz cottage, Lombard Italian, Tuscan from Pliny's villa at Ostia, Ancient Etruscan, Suburban Greek, Oriental Moorish, and Castellated." At this point, writes Oliver Larkin in *Art and Life in America*, "the architect's dream had become a nightmare." Not until the late nineteenth century would there be a renaissance of architecture (Chapter 14).

Thus, nationalism, romanticism, and an attitude of optimism pervaded literature and the arts in the antebellum period, and these themes were reflected in the religious, social, and reform movements of the times as well.

DEVELOPMENTS IN SCIENCE AND TECHNOLOGY

Date	Inventor	Contribution
1783	John Stevens	multi-tubular steam engine
1791	John Fitch	first steamboat
1793	Eli Whitney	cotton gin
1793	Thomas Jefferson	moldboard plow
1797	Charles Newbold	cast-iron plow
1798	Eli Whitney	jig for guiding tools
1799	Eliakim Spooner	seeding machine
1807	Robert Fulton	first successful steamboat
1819	Jethrow Wood	cast-iron three-piece plow
1825	John Stevens	multi-tubular boiler locomotive
1830	Peter Cooper	first American locomotive
1834	Cyrus McCormick	mechanical reaper
1834	Thomas Davenport	electric motor
1837	John Deere	steel plow
1839	Thomas Davenport	electric printing press
1839	Charles Goodyear	vulcanization of rubber
1842	Dr. Crawford Long	first use of ether as anesthetic
1844	Samuel F. B. Morse	telegraph
1847	Elias Howe	sewing machine
1847	Hiram and John Pitts	threshing machine
1852	Elisha Otis	electric elevator
1856	William Kelley	modern steelmaking process
1859	Edwin Drake	oil drilling process

3 Evangelicalism And Unorthodoxy Transform Religion

1. Why did religious piety decline in America after 1770?

2. What were the characteristics of evangelicalism which accounted for its success?

3. How did evangelicalism affect the established churches?

4. What were some of the common characteristics of the Shakers, the Mormons, and members of the Oneida Community?

At the beginning of the nineteenth century, Protestant ministers were alarmed by the decline of religious piety in America. Church attendance, the ministers announced, had declined dramatically since the 1770's. Ministers themselves were no longer respected as they had been, and atheism appeared to be flourishing.

Protestant ministers felt that the greatest danger to the churches lay in the West and in the cities. The frontier continually moved faster than the churches. Kentucky, Tennessee, and Ohio had no established churches and only a few ministers. Worse than the slow pace of church recruitment, as far as Protestants were concerned, was the startling progress of the Roman Catholic Church. By 1808, a bishopric had been established at Bardstown, Kentucky, and Jesuit missionaries were preaching all over the frontier.

Protestant clergymen were virtually unanimous in their conviction that drastic measures were needed. Yet, Protestant churches were sharply divided along class lines. The Episcopal church and the ultra-liberal Unitarian church appealed primarily to the upper classes. Decorous, serene, they cared little for the problems of those living either on the harsh frontier or in the poorer parts of the growing towns.

As cities grew steadily between 1790 and 1860, the older Protestant denominations—the Methodists, Bapists, Presbyterians—were unable to convert the new urban masses. Many of the newcomers from Europe, of course, were Roman Catholics, and they remained loyal to their traditional faith. But the greatest group of migrants to the city in the early part of the nineteenth century came from the American countryside. These people had abandoned their traditional allegiance to the Protestant churches, and no sermon, apparently, could compete effectively with the diversions or problems of urban life.

The rise of evangelicalism. As Eastern ministers worried about the low state of religious zeal in America, a dramatic revival was under way in the West. In 1800, a Presbyterian minister named James McGready gathered numerous backwoods families at a camp meeting (an open-air religious service), and with his fiery preaching aroused them to a pitch of religious enthusiasm. The next year some twenty thousand people assembled at Cane Ridge, Kentucky, and participated in an even more spectacular revival. The western ministers had found a means of reaching the apathetic.

Their secret lay in combining emotional preaching with the pressure of public opinion. They would single out notorious sinners and urge the crowd to pray for them, while at the same time describing the peace of mind and the joy in repentance and conversion. On numerous occasions, repentance and conversion were accompanied by extremely emotional experiences. As sinners became convinced that the Holy Spirit had entered their bodies, they would often burst into joyous laughter, roll on the ground, sing, or dance. On the frontier, being a Christian was no humdrum business; it provided excitement and emotional release. This emotional approach to preaching, based on the idea that a desire for salvation may be aroused in the congregation, was called evangelicalism.

Evangelicalism was particularly suited to the frontier. Many families lived in isolation, and their lives were often a desperate struggle for existence. Revival meetings became anxiously awaited social occasions. The revival also appealed to frontiersmen because it offered spiritual certitude. Life on the frontier was not only harsh, but also insecure. Indian attacks were a constant threat; the weather was unpredictable; disease often decimated whole families or neighborhoods. Moreover, in the early decades of the nineteenth century, none of the familiar institutions of the

East—church, town, government—were present to give people a sense of security. Revivals of religion brought in their wake accepted standards of belief and behavior—a degree of certainty in a perilous world.

Revivalism spread along the frontier, with notable successes being achieved in upstate New York, an area inhabited principally by New England emigrants. Under the leadership of Charles G. Finney, the revival movement in the Mohawk Valley was so sweeping and so intense that the area became known as the Burned Over district. Besides being a magnetic preacher, Finney was also a major theologian who provided the revival movement with a new goal.

In his sermons and his *Lectures on Revivals of Religion* (1835), Finney argued that God freely offers grace to all people, not just a Puritan elect. This new doctrine was in keeping with the democratic and highly individualistic impulses of the common man. Moreover, the idea that God wishes all men to receive His grace convinced Finney that a preacher's business was to convert the whole community, indeed the entire world.

To accomplish this, Finney sought to intensify the conversion experience. When he arrived in a town he asked merchants to close shop. He kept people in church all day and well into the night singing, praying, and listening to emotion-laden appeals to accept God's grace. He refused to stop until the entire community had embraced "a new life in the Spirit."

Many ministers disapproved of Finney's methods and ideas. In the East, more conservative theologians clung to the Puritan doctrine of the elect, while others denounced the carnival-like atmosphere of the revival, which struck them as vulgar. They also feared that such rural excitements would repel the dignified upper classes and seem comic rather than miraculous to the urban poor. They could not have been more mistaken. The revival stirred the cities as it had the frontier and village, and for the same reasons. The revival church of the emerging slums was an important

J. M. Burbank depicted a revival meeting in early America in his watercolor *Religious Camp Meeting* (opposite), which shows the impact of the preacher's words upon his congregation.

social center, a place where workingmen and clerks could forget their grinding routine and be lifted above the meanness of everyday life.

Evangelicalism changes the churches. One important development associated with the growth of revivalism was a tendency among many laymen to ignore denominational controls. Democratic Christians, impatient with theological debate, also resented the attempts of churches to set standards of dogma (belief) and doctrine (teachings about the practical application of belief). Hundreds of splinter groups sprang up, each professing some doctrine peculiar to itself. Some Christians even rejected all traditionally organized churches, insisting that God converted each man individually and that this conversion was the only significant religious experience.

More important than the creation of new sects, however, was the declining significance of theological subtleties and denominational loyalties. Except over the politically and socially explosive issue of slavery, the Protestant churches shared a common ideological outlook. A key point was the democratic nature of evangelical Protestantism. This emphasis on individualism was accompanied by a relative lack of interest in the precise nature of a person's theological beliefs; the unity of American Protestant Christianity was achieved at the expense of exact doctrines and religious practices. This, however, was the source of its greatest strength. This sense of unity enabled ministers and laymen from numerous churches to pool their resources and create many interdenominational organizations designed to convert the godless.

In 1810, New England ministers formed the American Board of Commissioners of the Foreign Missions, which sent missionaries to India and China. Clergymen of all denominations also supported the American Colonization Society, formed in 1816, which not only sent emancipated slaves to Africa, but also tried to convert Africans.

The frontier and the cities, however, continued to be the primary battlefield in the evangelical war against sin. The American Home Missions Society, organized in 1826, financed the activities of itinerant revivalists on the frontier. The pressing need for religious education was met by a variety of interdenominational agencies. The American Educational Society, established in 1815, encouraged schools to preach godliness and the Protestant ethic. (The Catholic Church responded to this evangelizing of schools by creating its own parochial school system.) The American Sunday School Union prepared plans of study, sent out organizers, and channeled funds to churches to provide the younger generation with proper religious training.

Noting that Bibles were a rarity on the frontier, the American Bible Society, established in 1816, flooded the country with low-cost editions of the Scriptures. More important was the American Tract Society, established in 1825, which reprinted sermons and moralistic essays on such subjects as temperance, gambling, deathbed confessions, Sabbath observance, thrift, and licentious behavior. By 1860, the society had distributed over fifteen million such tracts all over the country. Important also were denominational colleges, of which more than five hundred were established between 1815 and 1860. Over one hundred of these survive today. These colleges were to provide a steady flow of ministers and create a curriculum avowedly based on the Bible and which would enforce its religious ideals. By 1820, evangelical Protestantism had become a vast and energetic crusade to cleanse American society.

The growth of unorthodox sects. The decline of formal theology and denominational controls during the pre–Civil War period encouraged the growth of unorthodox religious beliefs and practices. Among the most important were the Shakers, the Mormons, and the Oneida community.

The Shakers were millennialists, that is, they believed that the Second Coming of Christ was imminent. Founded in the 1780's by an English woman, Ann Lee, they prepared themselves for the event by living godly lives. For the Shakers this meant not only the rejection of marriage, but the practice of celibacy. By the 1830's, more than twenty Shaker communities existed, mostly in New England, with over six thousand members. They were especially good artisans, and produced fine furniture, valued today for its simplicity and excellent design. The Shakers were admired for their kindness, geniality, and hospitality. Since they had no children, however, and as they attracted fewer and fewer converts as the years passed, the Shaker communities declined.

One of the most controversial socio-religious experiments of this period was the Oneida community. It was established in central New York State in 1848 by John Humphrey Noyes, a former Yale Divinity student and Congregationalist minister. Noyes too was a millennialist, but unlike the Shakers, he preached that the Second Coming of Christ had occurred in A.D. 70, when Jerusalem was burned. Noyes's belief that the Second Coming of Christ had already occurred led him to declare that he was therefore "perfect."

Noyes and his followers succeeded in living in peace and harmony and economic prosperity at Oneida for thirty-one years. At its peak the community included three hundred people. Members of the group practiced "complex marriage," that is, each man was considered married to each woman. Although most Americans condemned this practice, members of the community had fewer nervous disorders and produced fewer congenital idiots than members of society at large. As a result of social, religious, and legal pressures the community was forced to abandon its system of complex marriage in 1879. Nevertheless, its industries continued to thrive, producing animal traps used all over the world, exquisite silk products, and the justly famed Oneida silver.

The largest and most successful unorthodox religious sect established during the antebellum period was the Mormon Church, or the Church of Jesus Christ of Latter-Day Saints. Its founder, Joseph Smith, was a religious enthusiast from Palmyra in western New York, part of the Burned Over district. Smith declared that he had received direct revelations from God's angel, Moroni, which enabled him to discover several golden tablets containing strange symbols. With the aid of a pair of "magic spectacles," Smith translated these symbols and compiled the Book of Mormon, according to which God would return to America and establish His kingdom on earth.

The Mormons attracted thousands of converts. The sect, however, was persecuted, partly because of its unorthodox ideas, and partly because it attacked slavery. The Mormons were forced to abandon settlements in New York, Ohio, Missouri, and Illinois. Smith then received a new revelation which he said told him to establish polygamy, that is, the practice of one man having many wives. Smith himself took at least twenty-five wives. Outraged by this teaching, an angry mob murdered Smith in Illinois in 1844.

Directed by their new leader, Brigham Young, the Mormons set out across the Great Plains, hoping to establish a community in the West. In 1847, they arrived at the edge of the Great Salt Lake in Utah and there they founded Salt Lake City, which they called Zion. The Mormons mastered desert farming, and their community flourished. They created an elaborate welfare system, with common storehouses for the needy and a fund to pay for the travel expenses of Mormon immigrants from Europe. By the late nineteenth century, they were forced to abandon polygamy, but the Mormon religion still remains the dominant religious, social, and political force in Utah.

The emergence of political democracy and the breakdown of denominational controls in American society during the early part of the nineteenth century contributed to the growth of these unorthodox sects. But most of these sects did not have a great impact. Evangelical revivalism, which transformed the major denominations, such as the Congregationalists, Methodists, and Baptists made a more lasting impression upon society.

4 Reformers Change American Society

1. What were some of the problems considered by social reformers? What methods did they use to solve these problems?

2. Why was there large-scale interest in educational reform, and what changes in education were completed during this period?

3. How successful were reformers in removing the restrictions placed upon women's rights?

4. Why were people particularly interested in humanitarian reform during this specific period?

The period between 1830 and 1860 was the first great era of social reform in American history. Evangelical moral reformers directed their energies against gambling, drinking, prostitution, and what they considered licentious behavior. Many reformers, however, broadened their scope to include such pressing problems as slavery, abolition of debtors' prison, general prison reform, women's rights, public education, and help for the physically and mentally handicapped.

Evangelical moralists approached their crusade in a highly individualistic manner, viewing social problems solely in terms of individual sin. They did not consider that environmental factors—the often tedious life of the frontier, the long working hours for laborers, with low pay and little hope of advancement—caused men to turn to drink. Nor did they ask whether slum life, poverty, the lack of meaningful marriage opportunities, caused numerous young women to turn to prostitution.

This is not to say that these reformers were not earnest in their concern about such problems or that they should be condemned for failing to utilize twentieth-century concepts that did not exist during this period. Nevertheless, it is important to recognize that moral reformers did not understand and therefore did not concern themselves with the causes of social maladies. Rather they confined their activities to condemning the maladies themselves as evils which could be overcome by individual repentance from sin. As the abolitionist William Lloyd Garrison phrased it, social problems were not matters "of laws to be passed or steps to be taken, but of *error* to be rooted out and *repentance* to be exacted."

The temperance crusade. Americans in the early nineteenth century consumed vast quantities of alcohol. The magnitude of the problem is indicated by a police report from New York City in 1852 showing that of 180,000 arrests more than 140,000 were for offenses connected with drinking. Reformers, however, did not look for the root causes of this problem. Instead, they condemned drinking as a sin and attempted to use moral persuasion to reform the "sinner."

One method of persuasion was antiliquor propaganda in the form of tracts which vividly described the evils of liquor. The American Temperance Union, founded in 1826, distributed countless thousands of these tracts throughout the country. In addition, public lectures and religious revivals urged drunkards to repent and sign the "cold water" pledge. In fact, reformed drunkards were often the most effective speakers. John B. Gough, a member of the Washington, D.C., temperance society, lectured all over the east coast during the 1830's. He stirred thousands by his dramatic description of the seven wasted years he spent in the company of "demon rum." Invariably, Gough would end his exhortation with a ringing appeal to his audience: "Crawl from the slimy ooze, ye drowned drunkards and speak out against the drink."

By 1840, nearly three thousand local temperance societies with close to one million members had been organized. Ultimately, however, these organizations concluded that moral persuasion alone was not sufficient to accomplish their goal, and they turned to political action. In 1846, after an energetic campaign by Mayor Neal Dow of Portland, Maine passed the first antiliquor law. Within twelve years, ten other states had followed suit. However, loopholes in the laws, political opposition, and the determination of people to drink made the laws unenforceable. By 1865, only six states retained antiliquor laws, and even these were repealed shortly thereafter.

The temperance movement failed to accomplish its objective, but interest in temperance remained strong. The societies kept up their work, which finally culminated in the Prohibition Amendment (the Eighteenth) in 1920 (Chapter 20).

Advances in education. As late as 1830, no state had established a public, tax-supported school system. Formal education was usually available only for the children of the wealthy, who went to private schools or were tutored at home. Other children sometimes learned the rudiments of reading, writing, and arithmetic from relatives or perhaps a Sunday school teacher.

But there was a large-scale interest in educational reform from many sources and for different reasons. Horace Mann, the leading exponent of public education in Massachusetts, believed that education would prevent the development of class conflict caused by the social and economic inequities created by the Industrial Revolution. As Mann stated: "Now surely nothing but universal education can counterwork this tendency to the domination of capital and servility of labor." As long as the masses remained ignorant, Mann believed they would be dependent upon capitalists. But, with an education, no class of "intelligent and practical men" could remain permanently poor.

Still other reformers believed that the masses of immigrants must be indoctrinated to accept "the American way of life." The evangelist Lyman Beecher declared that education for immigrants who were "extensively infected with infidelity and Rationalism" was absolutely essential. When they learned English, they could read the Bible and be made aware that a "land of liberty is not a place to indulge in irreligion and licence." Thus, to Beecher, education was a means of social control. The attitudes of workingmen themselves were especially important. Working-class parents were strongly motivated to support public education by a desire to provide their children with better opportunities than they had.

Through political pressure and persuasion, educational reformers made considerable progress in the years from 1830 to 1860. By the 1850's the principle of tax-supported elementary schools had been accepted by all the states. Unfortunately, funds were limited and the quality of instruction was poor. In 1860 only one in six children of elementary school age in the North and West were enrolled in public schools; in the South the ratio was one in seven. By 1860, public high schools existed in some states. In that year, New York had twenty-two "free academies" (high schools), while Massachusetts had nearly one hundred. About three hundred existed elsewhere in the nation.

A number of other educational innovations were begun during this period. Oberlin College in Ohio pioneered in coeducational instruction, opening its doors to women in 1837. Women's seminaries were also founded, including Mount Holyoke in Massachusetts, which later became a major women's college. Moreover, more than a dozen state universities were established during this period. A few law and medical schools were opened, and Harvard, Yale, West Point, and Rensselaer Polytechnic Institute gave specialized training in engineering.

There were also attempts to give adults educational opportunities. Libraries and scores of mutual improvement societies called lyceums were established. The first lyceum was founded in Millbury, Massachusetts, in 1826, and by 1831, more than a thousand existed throughout the country. Establishing lecture circuits, the lyceums enabled thousands to hear prominent American and European speakers.

Women's rights. Another major reform movement that emerged during the 1830's was the cause of women's rights. Traditionally, a woman's place was in the home, and women had few legal rights. They could not vote, and although single women could hold property, when they married, title to their property went to their husbands. In addition, women were rarely permitted to have any advanced formal education. If they came from socially prominent families, they were sometimes sent to female seminaries to learn the social graces.

When women began to revolt, they defied the tradition that frowned on women speaking in public or even offering prayers in church. Many women, including Lucretia Mott, Lydia Maria Child, and Elizabeth Cady Stanton actively supported other reform movements. They wrote and lectured on temperance and slavery as well as women's rights. In 1848, the first Women's Rights Convention was held at Seneca Falls, New York, where delegates adopted resolutions paraphrasing the Declaration of Independence, maintaining that "all men and women are created equal." The convention further declared that the history of man "is a history of repeated injuries and usurpations on the part of man towards woman, having in direct object the establishment of an absolute tyranny over her."

Before the Civil War, agitation for women's rights led to laws in some states giving women control over their property and the right to divorce cruel or irresponsible husbands. And one profession at least was open to them—a career in elementary education. A few women also managed to excel in areas traditionally confined to men: Dr. Elizabeth Blackwell became America's first female physician; and Margaret Fuller edited the transcendentalist journal *The Dial* and was for a short time literary editor of the New York *Herald*

Tribune. While women failed to achieve many of their goals during this period, they did inaugurate a movement that continued into the twentieth century.

Humanitarian reform. Many reformers were also active in helping the mentally and physically handicapped. Dorothea Dix, a New England schoolteacher, pioneered in behalf of the insane and the mentally retarded. Based on her personal investigations in jails and poorhouses in Massachusetts, Miss Dix wrote a *Memorial to the Legislature of Massachusetts* (1843). She described in stark and vivid terms the maltreatment inflicted on inmates in asylums:

> The condition of human beings, reduced to the extremest states of degradation and misery, cannot be exhibited in softened language. . . . I proceed . . . to call your attention to the *present* state of insane persons confined within this Commonwealth in *cages, closets, cellars, stalls, pens! Chained, naked, beaten with rods,* and *lashed* into obedience.

As a result of Miss Dix's untiring efforts in exposing such conditions, most states took measures to ensure the better care and treatment of the mentally ill.

In working with the physically handicapped, Thomas Hopkins Gallaudet established the first free institute for deaf-mutes in Hartford, Connecticut. In Boston, Dr. Samuel Gridley Howe, who became a famous abolitionist, founded the Perkins Institute, creating a sensation in medical circles when he communicated with a blind deaf-mute. Howe was also instrumental in founding the Massachusetts School for the mentally retarded, and he devised a *Reader for the Blind,* a book printed in raised letters. Eventually, this system was replaced by Braille, which uses raised dots.

During this period, imprisonment for debt was abolished in most states, and equally important was the beginning of general prison reform. In the prisons of the time, first offenders were often confined in the same quarters with hardened criminals and the insane. In Connecticut, many prisoners were kept in an abandoned mine shaft where they were treated brutally, fed inadequately, and rarely allowed to exercise in the sunlight.

Prison reforms of this period, however, seem

NEW HARMONY, INDIANA

The Scottish industrialist Robert Owen purchased New Harmony from a group of German religious utopians. These origins of Owen's famous community are somewhat ironic, as Owen himself openly called all religions "superstitions." He paid for the land and facilities with part of his personal fortune: accounts of the price vary from $50,000 to $190,000. In any case, he could well afford it, and he probably got a bargain.

Without setting up any plan of organization for the new community, Owen immediately began to publicize it. Soon, more than a thousand people had moved in. In a speech to the new settlers, Owen declared, "I am come to this country to introduce an entire new state of society, to change it from an ignorant, selfish system to an enlightened social system which shall gradually unite all interests into one, and remove all causes for contests between individuals."

Owen's ideas were grandiose, but his plans never quite kept pace with his speeches. Things might have run smoothly if he had remained in New Harmony to direct operations, but he was frequently away. Without his leadership, and without a workable day-to-day plan, discontent quickly spread throughout New Harmony. In a letter to a friend, one member of the community wrote, "The idle and industrious are neither of them satisfied, the one contending that they do enough for their allowance, the other thinking themselves entitled to more." And lack of organization led to failures in farming, also. The community failed to produce enough vegetables to last through the first winter, and food had to be bought from the outside.

New Harmony was plagued by similar difficulties throughout the two short years of its existence, and as a utopian community, it must be counted a failure. Nevertheless, it left a legacy. Among the innovations credited to New Harmony are the first kindergarten in America, the first trade school, the first free library, and the first community-supported free school.

harsh by modern standards. In New York, prisoners worked during the day, separated from one another, and were placed in solitary confinement at night. The theory was that separation would prevent hardened criminals from corrupting the young and that solitary confinement would give the prisoner ample time to meditate and repent of his sins. Moral and religious instruction were sometimes provided. In practice, solitary confinement drove many to the brink of insanity.

Despite this kind of treatment, Alexis de Tocqueville and other European observers claimed that conditions in American prisons were far better than those in Europe. Not until the twentieth century, however, would more effective methods of rehabilitating criminals be discovered. And even now, American prisons fall short of being model institutions where rehabilitation rather than punishment is the goal.

Secular utopias. Most American reformers approached social issues in terms of individuals. They did not deal with or theorize about the effects of environmental conditions, such as the Industrial Revolution, in molding human behavior. However, European critics, who had more experience with the disruptive effects of industrialization, did influence American reformers.

In America, criticism of capitalism came primarily from the British industrialist Robert Owen and the followers of the French social theorist Charles Fourier. Owen and the Fourierists were so disillusioned with industrial capitalism, which they considered exploitative and degrading to the individual, that they planned cooperative communities as an alternative way of life.

Owen established a community at New Harmony, Indiana, which lasted from 1825 to 1827. The Fourierists founded several communities, the most famous of which was Brook Farm in West Roxbury, Massachusetts. These experiments in communal living failed and were not taken seriously by most Americans. However, as writer Gilbert Seldes points out, Owen and the Fourierists had recognized that the nation was destined to plunge "headlong into the factory system which was presently to become pestilential almost beyond our power to imagine." Not until the twentieth century did reform movements emerge that were able to correct the most glaring abuses of industrialization.

5 Abolitionists Fight Slavery

1. What steps had been taken before 1830 to abolish slavery in America?

2. How did the abolition movement of the 1830's differ from the earlier antislavery tradition?

3. To what extent were black Americans involved in the abolition movement?

4. What caused the crisis over strategy and tactics within the abolition movement, and what was the outcome of the crisis within the movement?

The abolitionist crusade against slavery, which began during the 1830's, was the most militant, controversial, and politically divisive social movement which had occurred up to that time in the nation's history. To be sure, opposition to slavery in American society was nothing new. One of the results of the American Revolution was the abolition of slavery or the passage of gradual emancipation laws in every northern state by 1804. Moreover, Congress had excluded slavery from the Northwest Territory in 1787, outlawed the slave trade in 1808, and barred slavery north of the parallel 36° 30′ in 1820. Thus, the abolitionist movement of the 1830's may be considered a logical culmination of an earlier antislavery tradition. But it was also more than that.

Rise of the abolition movement. Most antislavery groups in the late eighteenth and early nineteenth centuries had favored gradual emancipation and advocated indirect methods in attacking slavery. For example, they urged that freed slaves be returned to colonies in Africa and opposed the geographical expansion of slavery. The abolitionists, however, were different—they were militant antislavery radicals who condemned slavery on moral and religious grounds.

Most early abolitionists were evangelical Protestants who participated in the many moral and humanitarian reform movements already discussed. In their view, slavery, like alcohol, was sinful and had to be eradicated. Thus, such abolitionist groups as the American Anti-Slavery Society, formed in Philadelphia in 1833, hoped to convince individual slaveholders that they must admit their guilt, repent, and voluntarily free their slaves.

During this period, abolitionists did not attempt to attack slavery by organizing a political party; moral persuasion, not political coercion, was the chief weapon in their arsenal. The one striking exception to this occurred in 1836 when abolitionist societies flooded Congress with petitions demanding the abolition of slavery in the District of Columbia. Leaders of both parties persuaded the House of Representatives to pass a *gag rule* (shelving petitions without debate) which effectively barred discussion of the issue in the national legislature.

Prominent abolitionists. Traditionally, historians have dated the beginning of the abolitionist crusade with the publication on January 1, 1831, of William Lloyd Garrison's Boston newspaper *The Liberator.* In his first editorial, Garrison bodly declared:

I shall strenuously contend for the immediate enfranchisement of our slave population. . . . I will be as harsh as truth and as uncompromising as justice. . . . I am in earnest—I will not equivocate—I will not excuse—I will not retreat a single inch—and *I will be heard.*

Garrison was undeniably an important figure in the movement, and New England was an important center of abolitionist activity. Nevertheless, Garrison did not dominate the movement, and New England was only one of several important geographical centers of abolitionism. New York City, the Burned Over district of western New York, and the vicinity of present-day Cleveland, Ohio, all produced significant numbers of abolitionists. In New York City, the most prominent leaders were the wealthy silk merchants Arthur and Lewis Tappan. In western New York and Ohio, among the leading abolitionist organizers were Theodore Dwight Weld, Gerrit Smith, and Elizur Wright.

Although these men and many others were abolitionist leaders in western New York and Ohio, most were either born in New England or had New England backgrounds. Some historians have argued that abolitionism was primarily a product and extension of New England influences. It was not only New Englanders, however, who contributed to the growth and development of the abolition movement. Quaker influence was also strong, especially in the Philadelphia area. And southern "exiles," including the sisters Angelina and Sarah Grimké of South Carolina and James Gillespie Birney, a former slaveholder from a prominent Kentucky family, are only three of a number of leading abolitionists who were forced to leave the South because of their opposition to slavery.

Opposition to abolitionists. During the 1830's, abolitionists were nearly universally condemned in the North by groups and individuals who felt no moral urgency over slavery and who feared that controversy over the slavery question could lead to disunion. Abolitionists were not only denounced, but they were also openly threatened or assaulted.

In 1835, Garrison was dragged through the streets of Boston with a rope around his waist. In Canterbury, Connecticut, Prudence Crandall, who opened a private integrated school, was forced to close down because of the racist convictions of a majority of the townspeople. In Philadelphia, Pennsylvania Hall was specially built to hold abolitionist meetings because officials and many church leaders were reluctant to turn over their facilities for such purposes. Only five days after the hall was completed, a mob burned it to the ground. In Alton, Illinois, Elijah Lovejoy, a fiery abolitionist editor who refused to cease publication, was murdered by a group of vigilantes.

In the decades after the 1830's, however, northern attitudes toward abolitionist agitators began to change. As the United States increased its territory, a furor over slavery expansion developed. This, combined with years of abolitionist agitation, brought an end to mob violence against them.

Black abolitionists. Free blacks and escaped slaves contributed greatly to the abolitionist movement. Many free blacks were active in the work of antislavery societies. When the American Anti-Slavery Society was formed, three black men, Robert Purvis and James McCrummell, well-to-do Philadelphians, and James G. Barbadoes, a clothing-store owner from Boston, helped draw up its declaration of intentions. These three men were also appointed to the society's board of managers, along with John B. Vashon, a Pittsburgh barber, Peter Williams, pastor of an Episcopal church in New York, and Abraham D. Shadd, an agent for Garrison's *The Liberator*. Blacks also participated in the formation of numerous affiliates of the American Anti-Slavery Society, among them societies in Boston and New York.

Comparatively few northerners, including most abolitionists, ever had direct contact with slavery. Hence, most northerners received their impressions of slavery from the lectures and writings of escaped slaves. Among the ablest speakers and authors of the movement were William Wells Brown and Frederick Douglass.

Brown, who had escaped from Kentucky, lectured extensively in New York and Massachusetts in the 1840's. One of the most active men in the movement, he was also interested in women's suffrage, temperance, and prison reform. Brown was a prolific writer. In addition to an account of his own life, *Narrative of William W. Brown, a Fugitive Slave* (1847), he was the author of novels, dramas, histories, and travel literature. He also compiled *The Anti-Slavery Harp*, the best of the antislavery song books.

The most eloquent of all antislavery speakers was Frederick Douglass. Escaping from Maryland in 1838, Douglass settled in New Bedford, Massachusetts, where he became a lecturer for the Massachusetts Anti-Slavery Society. In addressing a meeting of the society in 1842, Douglass displayed his famous oratorical style: "I appear before the immense assembly this evening as a thief and a robber. I stole this head, these limbs, this body from my master, and ran off with them." Douglass also founded an abolitionist journal, the *North Star*, and was the author of *Narrative of the Life of Frederick Douglass* (1845), a best seller on two continents.

The work of men like Brown and Douglass was influential in rousing antislavery sentiment in the North. Still, despite changing northern attitudes, the North in general did not think of blacks as equals. This prejudice existed even among some abolitionists. For example, the women's antislavery society of New York would not admit black members. And a Philadelphia group declared that

OW SLAVERY HONORS OUR COUNTRY'S FLAG.

THE DESPERATION OF A MOTHER.

Rise, Sons of Africa! 6s & 4s.

1. Ye who in bondage pine, Shut out from light divine,
2. Shout! for the hour draws nigh, That gives you liberty;

3. The night—the long dark night Of infamy and slight,

4 Speed, speed the hour, O Lord, Speak, and at thy dread word,

Bereft of hope! Whose limbs are worn with chains, Whose tears be-
And, from the dust— So long your vile embrace— Up - ris - ing,

Shame and disgrace, Of slavery—worse than e'er Rome's slaves were

Fetters shall fall From every limb—the strong No more the

dew our plains, Whose blood our glory stains, In gloom who grope!
take your place Among earth's noblest race, 'Tis right and just.

doom'd to bear, Horrid beyond compare—Recedes apace.

weak shall wrong, But Liberty's song Be sung by all.

The abolition movement had about it a distinct air of evangelicalism, and the antislavery press, active from the 1820's until the Civil War, certainly reflected this spirit. Publications like the *Anti-Slavery Almanac* presented woodblock prints showing the evils of slavery in highly dramatic terms. These evils could hardly have been shown more stirringly than they are in the two *Almanac* prints above; they use both motherhood and the American flag to drive home the point. But the antislavery press did not rely solely on graphics to propagate its ideas. News stories, memoirs of runaway slaves, sermons and addresses— all of these were printed to convert people to the antislavery cause. So were hymns; the one on the right appeared in an abolitionist publication called the *Anti-Slavery Offering and Picknick*, and its singing must have had a powerful effect on believer and unbeliever alike.

while it would admit blacks, it would not encourage social relationships between blacks and whites. However, this did not reflect the attitudes of a majority of white abolitionists, who were far ahead of their time in their commitment not only to the abolition of slavery, but also to black equality.

Division among the abolitionists. By the end of the 1830's, many abolitionist leaders realized that moral pressure as a weapon against slavery was not going to work. Southerners had made it clear that they considered the idea of emancipation preposterous. The apparent failure of moral force, combined with other factors, led to a crisis over strategy and tactics with the movement itself.

A majority of the abolitionists concluded that it was time to form a political party, and in 1840 the Liberty party was organized. Garrison and his followers, however, bitterly opposed direct political action. In order to succeed in politics, the Garrisonians reasoned, abolitionists would be forced to compromise their principles, a policy unacceptable to Garrisonians. Instead, Garrison believed the abolitionists should increase their efforts to radicalize northern public opinion. Only then could they reasonably expect to have a decisive effect on national politics. Nevertheless, they should at no time participate in politics; their major function should be that of agitators, trying to force politicians to take increasingly radical positions against slavery.

Garrison's views on politics, which were rejected by a majority of abolitionists, contributed to an irreparable division in their ranks in 1840. His political views, however, were only one factor among many that caused the split. For example, most political abolitionists opposed the admission of women into the American Anti-Slavery Society. They reasoned that women's rights was an extraneous issue, unrelated to the abolition of slavery, which might alienate potential converts to their cause. Garrison vehemently attacked this position. Human equality, regardless of sex or race, was his ideal.

Many abolitionists were also alienated by Garrison's espousal of the doctrine of "no human government." Garrison's point was that human nature was corrupt. In his view the only hope for organizing a just society lay in the complete moral regeneration of mankind. Only then could men,

acting under the influence of divine guidance, create a just society. Garrison was a thorough-going philosophical radical who attacked nearly all American traditions and institutions (including the churches) as corrupt. He urged "true Christians" to secede from corrupt churches, and he characterized the Constitution as a covenant with hell.

Garrison's opponents maintained that he was an anarchist, completely out of touch with reality. They believed that most American social institutions were basically just and that if only slavery could be eradicated, a good society would not be difficult to achieve. To be sure, Garrison had perfectionist standards which no human society has yet been able to attain. To admit this, however, is far different from dismissing Garrison as a mindless fanatic whose thought was devoid of meaningful social commentary, as many historians have done.

Impact of the abolitionist movement. Far from persuading the South that slavery had to be eradicated, abolitionist agitation helped to harden southern attitudes and placed southerners on the defensive. The most moderate abolitionists aroused fear and suspicion in the South, but the extreme views of men like Garrison in particular enraged southerners. Soon after Garrison began publishing *The Liberator*, the South condemned it as incendiary and banned it. In fact, many southerners tried to connect Nat Turner's insurrection in 1831 with the publication of *The Liberator*.

Moreover, during the 1840's and 1850's, abolitionists accused the South not only of engaging in a great slave-power conspiracy to spread slavery throughout the nation, but also of conspiring with northern capitalists to enslave all workers, white and black. Such extreme charges had little foundation, but they helped to intensify southern feelings and make southerners more aggressive in their defense of slavery.

Events in the 1840's and 1850's brought about a change in northern attitudes toward slavery and slavery expansion. Northerners became increasingly antislavery and increasingly less willing to compromise on the issue. While it is true that during these years abolitionists helped to influence northern attitudes, it is impossible to measure the precise influence they had in polarizing northern opinion.

CONCLUSION

As the American mind took shape in the forty-five years before the Civil War, a series of contradictions emerged. Americans cherished individualism, yet many attempted community reforms. They were boundlessly optimistic about their economy and society, yet their major novelists emphasized the struggle of the innocent individual with the malign forces of social control and evil in the universe. Rejoicing in democracy, Americans nevertheless had difficulty defining the degree to which the individual was subject to the demands of the community. Some Americans also looked upon slavery, alcohol, and infidelity as major evils, yet distrusted the institutions which might correct these evils. Evangelical reformers insisted that social reform must follow from converting individual sinners, but humanitarian reformers hoped to create institutions that would counteract social wrongs.

These often contradictory attitudes about goals, and the means of achieving these goals, affected politics throughout the early national period. Conflicting views as to the nature of the American political system and the role of government in economic development were expressed in such issues as tariff, finance, and internal improvements. The attempts of Americans to cope with the issues of territorial expansion, slavery, and slavery in the territories was marked by contradictory beliefs and increasingly irreconcilable political positions.

QUESTIONS

1. In what areas of American life were there attempts to promote reform through individual conversion, and in what areas were there attempts at community reform? How successful were the attempts in these areas?

2. To what extent was the American character portrayed optimistically between 1820 and 1860, and to what extent was this a pessimistic portrayal?

3. How did some Americans emphasize the importance of individualized responses to American life, and how did others stress the group reactions?

4. What factors might explain the extent of contradictory attitudes which existed in America between 1820 and 1860?

5. How does a discussion of the American character relate to the political and economic history of the period?

6. To what extent was this period one which glorified the image of the common man? Explain your answer.

7. In what ways were sectional attitudes encouraged by intellectual and social developments of the period?

8. How successful was America in creating a distinctive national culture where community interests could be reconciled with individual freedom of conscience and action? Explain your answer.

BIBLIOGRAPHY

DE TOCQUEVILLE, ALEXIS, *Democracy in America*, 2 vols., ed. by Phillip Bradley, trans. by Henry Reeve, Random House (Vintage Books). As the years pass, it seems that the observations made by Tocqueville after his visit to the United States in 1831 become more and more relevant, and quotes from him are frequently used to explain American political behavior.

TROLLOPE, FRANCES, *Domestic Manners of the Americans in the First Half of the 19th Century*, ed., by Donald Smalley, Random House (Vintage Books). Mrs. Trollope was another visitor to the United States, and although she confined her remarks to the more everyday aspects of American life, she is still very useful in understanding nineteenth-century America.

TYLER, ALICE FELT, *Freedom's Ferment: Phases of American Social History from the Revolution to the Outbreak of the Civil War*, Harper & Row (Torchbooks). Students may want to consult this book for a general background to the social history of the period. The many reform movements are discussed along with utopian communities, romanticism, and Transcendentalism.

LARKIN, OLIVER W., *Art and Life in America*, Holt, Rinehart & Winston. This is one of many books on the history of art in America. Students may use it throughout the year when studying the interplay of painting, sculpture, and architecture with political, economic, and social behavior of Americans. It is fully illustrated to complement the text.

HAWTHORNE, NATHANIEL, *Blithedale Romance*, Dell. Hawthorne knew the operation of the Brook Farm communal experience from firsthand contact. In this intriguing novel, he assesses the experiment and provides insight into its difficulties.

Expansion And Slavery

By the 1820's and 1830's, Americans moving west had already crossed the Mississippi River. Ahead of them lay the Great Plains and the Rocky Mountains and beyond these barriers the Far West. In the Pacific Northwest was the Oregon Territory, a vast area whose northern boundary extended to Alaska. South of Oregon stretched Mexico's province of California, the New Mexico Territory, and Texas.

Many Americans looked eagerly at these territories and yearned to extend the United States to the Pacific. Their feelings were summed up in the phrase "Manifest Destiny," first used by the expansionist writer John L. O'Sullivan. He declared that nothing should be allowed to thwart "the fulfillment of our manifest destiny to overspread the continent allotted by Providence for the free development of our yearly multiplying millions."

Americans who agreed with this philosophy were imbued with a profound sense of mission, a feeling that they were ordained by God to spread upon the North American continent the blessings of their institutions and their democracy. This philosophy was also a rationalization for more selfish motives: the agricultural and commercial gains promised by the fertile valleys and beckoning harbors of Oregon and California, and the fear that other powers might seize these lands.

Territorial expansion, however, would bring the United States into conflict with other nations. Even more serious, it would raise the question of whether slavery should be allowed to expand into the new lands. Each step taken toward achieving Manifest Destiny was a step away from national unity. As you read about American expansion, keep these questions in mind:

1. What factors drove American settlers westward to California, Oregon, New Mexico, and Texas?
2. Why did the United States go to war with Mexico?
3. How did the Compromise of 1850 attempt to solve the dispute over the expansion of slavery into new territories?

1 Americans Reach Toward The Pacific

1. Why did Americans move westward into Oregon, California, New Mexico, and Texas?

2. What were the sources of friction between the Americans in Texas and the Mexican government?

3. Why was the admission of Texas into the Union a controversial issue?

4. What factors contributed to the amicable settlement of the Oregon boundary dispute?

While some Americans were preaching Manifest Destiny, thousands of others were putting it into action. The first adventurers to penetrate the far western wilderness were the fur trappers. These "Mountain Men," with their knowledge of the region and their explorations, helped open the way for the pioneers who followed. Economic decline in the East after the panic of 1837 and the lure of fertile western lands urged Americans to push into the Oregon Territory. Year after year, wagon trains of settlers, gripped by the "Oregon Fever," rolled into the territory. By 1846, more than five thousand Americans had settled in Oregon, mostly in the rich Willamette Valley.

California, thinly populated and poorly controlled by Mexico, also beckoned Americans, although they did not arrive in great numbers until the gold strike of 1848. Nevertheless, the resources of California were highly publicized. Its magnificent harbors of San Francisco and San Diego had long been stopping places for American ships, and these ports, potentially valuable prizes for the development of the Oriental trade, were coveted by American businessmen.

In the Southwest, American interest centered in the profitable trade carried on at Santa Fe in the New Mexico Territory. Each year an American trading caravan moved down the Santa Fe trail to trade for furs and valuable Mexican silver. In Texas, American settlement had begun in the early 1820's, and settlers poured in as the cotton frontier moved westward.

Expansion brings conflict. The American surge westward revived the dispute with Great Britain over the Oregon Territory. As early as 1818, the two nations had agreed to a joint occupation of the territory for ten years, an agreement which was then re-negotiated to allow either nation to terminate the arrangement with a year's notice. By 1844, however, the increasing number of Americans in the territory were demanding from the government recognition and protection. Pressure was growing to find a permanent solution so Congress could extend its jurisdiction over Oregon. Conflict in the Far West with Britain was matched by conflict in the Southwest with Mexico over Texas.

The Texas question. As part of the Adams-Onis Treaty of 1819 with Spain, the United States had abandoned its claim that Texas was part of the Louisiana Purchase, and American settlers were discouraged from entering the area. Soon after Mexico won its independence from Spain in 1821, however, the Mexican government invited American settlers to migrate to Texas, an area inhabited only by scattered Indian tribes. The Mexican government made large land grants to American promoters called *empresarios*, who easily convinced settlers of the advantages of cultivating cotton on the fertile coastal plain.

The first American *empresario* was Moses Austin, who received a large land grant from Spanish officials in Mexico but died before he could take advantage of it. Soon after the Mexican Revolution, his holdings were transferred to his son Stephen, who directed the first significant migration of Americans into Texas. In the years that followed, numerous other grants were made to enterprising settlers. By 1830, nearly thirty-two thousand Americans, including around two thousand slaves, had settled in the region.

But the Americans were not ideal subjects, from the Mexican point of view. They refused to become Roman Catholics, as they had originally agreed to do. Mostly southern and slave-owning, they violated Mexico's prohibition against the slave trade, and they were unwilling to pay the taxes the Mexican government so desperately needed. As tensions rose, Mexico stationed troops in Texas, forbade further American immigration, and abolished slavery. Defying the Mexican authorities, the settlers revolted in 1836, declaring

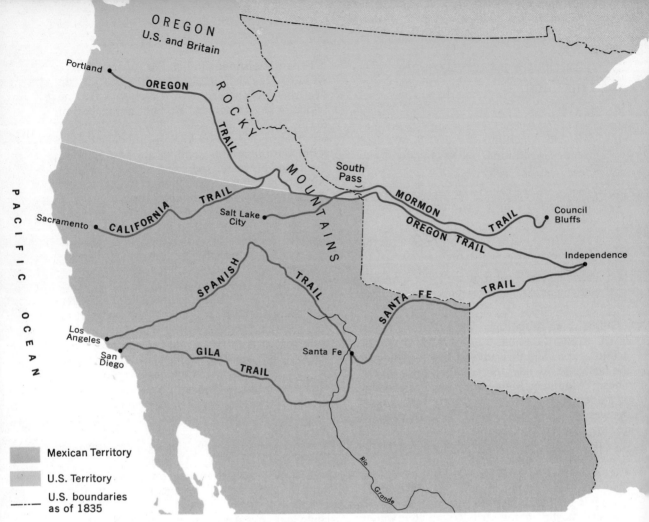

TRAILS TO THE FAR WEST

themselves an independent state—the Lone Star Republic—and electing Sam Houston their president.

Texas becomes a republic. The Mexican dictator, Santa Anna, determined to crush the revolution, led an army northward. After a bitter struggle, the Mexican forces captured the Alamo, an abandoned mission at San Antonio held by 187 Americans. All the defenders of the Alamo, including Davy Crockett and the legendary Jim Bowie (designer of the Bowie knife), were killed. Another small Texas garrison at Goliad was also wiped out by Mexican troops.

In April 1836, however, General Houston's outnumbered army decisively defeated Santa Anna's forces at the battle of San Jacinto, near present-day Houston, and captured Santa Anna. Although Mexico never officially recognized Santa Anna's agreement to renounce its sovereignty over the Lone Star Republic, Mexico was too weak to challenge the independence of Texas. Even so, the Texans did not want independence; President Houston formally applied for admission into the Union.

Controversy over annexation. Fearing war with Mexico, as well as rising antislavery sentiment in the North, neither President Jackson nor President Van Buren had been willing to deal with the issue. But President Tyler was concerned over the possibility of a permanent alliance between Texas and Great Britain if immediate steps were not taken to assure annexation.

198

Texas, independent since 1836, had petitioned the United States for admission into the Union, only to be rebuffed. American expansionists feared that if the United States refused to annex the Lone Star Republic, Texas would be forced to ally itself politically with Great Britain, America's chief commercial rival in the Western Hemisphere. Texas, they reasoned, not only would be a major source of cotton for British textile mills, but also eventually would become a prime market for British manufactured goods.

Moreover, southerners feared that Texans might be forced to abolish slavery in order to persuade Britain to guarantee Texas' sovereignty and to sign commercial agreements with her. The British Foreign Secretary, Lord Aberdeen, admitted to John C. Calhoun in 1844 that "with regard to Texas, we avow that we wish to see slavery abolished there, as elsewhere. . . ." But he assured Calhoun that the British Government had no intention of taking any measures to achieve this objective. The "governments of the slaveholding states may be assured," Aberdeen wrote, that "we shall neither openly nor secretly resort to any measures which can tend to disturb their internal tranquility. . . ."

Neither Calhoun, who became secretary of state in early 1844, nor President Tyler were calmed by such assurances, and the President instructed Calhoun to negotiate a treaty of annexation with the Texans. Unfortunately, Calhoun stressed publicly that one of the major purposes in acquiring Texas was to extend slavery. His statements created such a furor in the North that the Senate refused to ratify the treaty of annexation. The Presidential election of 1844, however, was to dramatically change the situation.

The election of 1844. Many times, politicians, in order to succeed, must be able to judge public sentiment accurately on issues that cannot be avoided. The Presidential election of 1844 is an outstanding example of the failure of major party leaders to assess correctly the public temper. As the election approached, it was widely assumed in both parties that Martin Van Buren and Henry Clay would be the standard bearers for the Democrats and the Whigs respectively. Both Van Buren and Clay agreed before the nominating conventions met that they would not make expansion—especially the annexation of Texas—

and with it the slavery question, a campaign issue. Clay received his party's nomination as expected, but Van Buren did not.

Van Buren, antiexpansion and antislavery, entered the convention with well over half the delegates committed to him. His stand on expansion and slavery, however, had alienated many westerners and southerners, and his opponents succeeded in establishing a rule requiring a two-thirds vote for nomination. Had Van Buren been willing to reverse his position on the Texas question, he might have carried the day. But he refused.

The delegates, who were in an expansionist mood, nominated the relatively obscure James K. Polk of Tennessee, the first "dark-horse" candidate in American history. Polk, a strong Jacksonian Democrat who had served as Speaker of the House and as governor of Tennessee, was an ardent expansionist and thoroughly committed to the Democratic platform. As adopted, the platform called for the reannexation of Texas and the reoccupation of Oregon, the implication being that the United States had always owned these regions.

Henry Clay, sensing that he had miscalculated on the Texas question, reversed himself, declaring that he would favor the admission of Texas if it could be accomplished "without dishonor, without war, with the common consent of the Union, and upon just and fair terms." In all probability, Clay would have been better advised to remain silent, for his statements straddled the issue, satisfying neither the expansionists nor the antislavery voters.

The election was extremely close. Polk received 170 electoral votes to Clay's 105; in popular votes Polk's majority was a mere 38,000. The key was New York State, which Clay lost by only 5,000 popular votes. The abolitionist Liberty party in that state, formed in 1840, nominated its own candidate, who, most historians agree, took votes away from Clay rather than Polk. Whether or not Clay would have retained enough antislavery support to defeat Polk if he had not compromised on the Texas issue is open to speculation. It is certain, however, that this small minority played a crucial role in electing Polk.

Polk's election settled the issue of Texas annexation. On the eve of his inauguration, Con-

Manifest Destiny meant people on the move—to California, to Texas, to Oregon. The painting above, by Oriana Day, done during the great surge westward, is entitled *Mission San Carlos del Rio Carmelo*. This mission, founded at Carmel in 1770, was one of the twenty-one that Spanish Franciscans established in California by the 1820's. They were the centers of communal life; the friars ran them, and Indians worked the mission lands. By 1846, these lands would be sold off to new settlers. By 1849, Texas had gone from being a republic to being a state, and San Antonio was a thriving place, as the painting above right shows. In that year W. G. M. Samuel showed it as he saw it in his *Main Plaza, San Antonio, Texas*. His style is primitive, but he does succeed in recording a wide variety of activities that were typical of a growing Texas town at this time. The trip to reach the West was a long and hard one, and the settlers did well to travel in groups. The *Oregon Trail*, below right, by William Henry Jackson, was not painted until 1929, but it is an accurate depiction of what the trail looked like during the 1840's. Independence Rock appears in the background; it was a landmark that wagon trains looked for on the journey, since it lay next to the Sweetwater River, the only safe water for fifty miles west of Casper, Wyoming. It was a good place to camp, rest, and replenish the water supply.

200

West Side Main Plaza, San Antonio, Texas 1849 — WGM Samuel

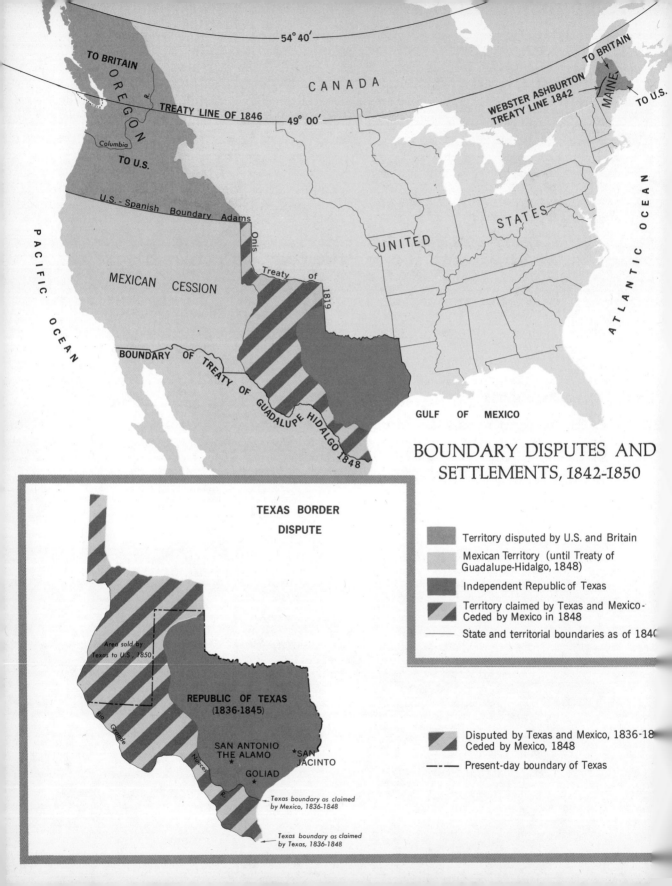

BOUNDARY DISPUTES AND SETTLEMENTS, 1842-1850

54° 40'

TO BRITAIN

OREGON

TREATY LINE OF 1846

49° 00'

CANADA

Columbia R.

TO U.S.

WEBSTER ASHBURTON
TREATY LINE 1842

TO BRITAIN

MAINE

TO U.S.

U.S. - Spanish Boundary Adams

Onis

Treaty of 1819

UNITED STATES

PACIFIC OCEAN

MEXICAN CESSION

BOUNDARY OF TREATY OF GUADALUPE HIDALGO 1848

GULF OF MEXICO

ATLANTIC OCEAN

Legend

	Territory disputed by U.S. and Britain
	Mexican Territory (until Treaty of Guadalupe-Hidalgo, 1848)
	Independent Republic of Texas
	Territory claimed by Texas and Mexico- Ceded by Mexico in 1848
	State and territorial boundaries as of 1840

TEXAS BORDER DISPUTE

Area sold by Texas to U.S. 1850

Rio Grande

Nueces R.

REPUBLIC OF TEXAS
(1836-1845)

SAN ANTONIO
THE ALAMO
★

★SAN JACINTO

GOLIAD
★

R.

Texas boundary as claimed
by Mexico, 1836-1848

Texas boundary as claimed
by Texas, 1836-1848

	Disputed by Texas and Mexico, 1836-18 Ceded by Mexico, 1848
	Present-day boundary of Texas

gress passed a resolution to admit Texas to the Union. When the admission became official in December 1845, Mexico, in protest, broke off diplomatic relations with the United States.

Settling the Oregon controversy. In 1844 the Democrats advocated the acquisition of the entire Oregon Territory, whose northern boundary extended to the 54th parallel (see map, opposite page). In his inaugural address, Polk declared: "Our title to the country of Oregon is 'clear and unquestionable,' and already are our people preparing to perfect that title by occupying it with their wives and children." A few months later in his first annual message to Congress, in terms recalling the language of the Monroe Doctrine, Polk forcefully declared that the United States would refuse to permit interference by Great Britain on the Texas issue. The President boldly asserted that "the people of *this continent* alone have the right to decide their own destiny." Despite the narrowness of his victory, Polk interpreted his election as a mandate for territorial expansion.

While Polk was determined to have the Oregon Territory, he was not nearly as aggressive in action as he was in his public pronouncements. He hoped to settle the dispute peacefully, and he was willing to accept the Oregon boundary at the 49th parallel—that is, the present boundary of the United States. Polk opened negotiations with the British, and in June 1846, the two nations signed a treaty formally establishing the 49th parallel as the permanent boundary between the United States and Canada. The Senate quickly ratified the agreement, although some senators complained that the United States should have held out for the 54th parallel. Such a demand would have been unrealistic, however, since British acceptance represented a significant concession on their part.

In 1846, less than a thousand British subjects lived in the Oregon Territory compared to more than five thousand Americans, and more Americans were obviously going to follow. In addition, the fur trade, Britain's primary interest in the Oregon country, was becoming less profitable as the fur resources declined, and Britain was not willing to risk a war over an area in which its vital interests were not involved.

Other factors also contributed to a spirit of conciliation—the goodwill created by the Webster-Ashburton treaty of 1842 (settling the northeastern boundary between Canada and the United States); the amicable settlement of other minor difficulties along the Canadian-American frontier during the early 1840's; and the passage of the low Walker tariff of 1846, which enlarged the American market for British goods. Moreover, the Americans had granted the British navigation rights on the Columbia River, and abandoned all claims to Vancouver Island. Finally, Polk had no desire to jeopardize Anglo-American relations at a time when the United States was at war with Mexico.

2 The United States Goes To War With Mexico

1. What grounds did the United States have for declaring war against Mexico? Do you think these reasons were sufficient to justify declaring war?

2. What was Polk's strategy in waging the war with Mexico?

3. To what extent was the Treaty of Guadalupe Hidalgo a reasonable settlement of the Mexican War?

While Polk was negotiating for Oregon, conflict with Mexico was deepening. Polk was determined to extend America's boundary in the Southwest as well as the Northwest. And in the fall of 1845, he dispatched an emissary, John Slidell, to Mexico City to open negotiations for the purchase of Mexican lands in the West. Slidell was authorized to offer $5 million for the New Mexico Territory and $25 million for California, Polk's primary objective. Resentful over the loss of Texas and hostile to American ambitions in the West, Mexico refused even to receive Slidell.

Preparations for war. Polk had hoped to obtain Mexican territory peaceably, by purchase, but he was resolved to go to war if he had to. After Mexico severed diplomatic relations, Polk had ordered an army under General Zachary Taylor south to the Nueces River in case of a Mexican attack. The area between the Nueces and the Rio Grande (see map, page 202) was disputed territory, with both Texas and Mexico claiming it. In fact, Texas had never exercised proper governmental control beyond the Nueces, and Mexico had a far better claim to the area. Early in 1846, however, when it became clear that Slidell had failed, Polk ordered Taylor's army to proceed south to the Rio Grande.

As far as Polk was concerned, the American boundary lay at the Rio Grande, and in ordering Taylor's advance, Polk showed he was looking for trouble. For months Polk awaited an incident that would justify hostilities against the Mexicans. When nothing occurred, he began to prepare a message to Congress asking for a declaration of war. Polk's grounds were that Mexico had failed to pay claims owed to American citizens who had lost property in Mexican revolts (Mexico had in fact paid some of the claims) and that the refusal of the Mexican government to receive Slidell constituted a grave insult to America's national honor.

Before this message was sent to Congress, news arrived that a Mexican force had crossed the Rio Grande and attacked American forces, killing about fifty soldiers. Elated, Polk revised his war message and piously declared:

The cup of forbearance has been exhausted. After reiterated menaces, Mexico has passed the boundary of the United States, has invaded her territory and shed American blood upon the American soil.

Congress, accepting Polk's view that the Rio Grande was the legal boundary between the United States and Mexico, voted overwhelmingly to declare war on May 13, 1846.

Conquest of New Mexico and California. The Mexican War was short and decisive. Polk, an excellent military strategist, planned most of the campaigns, attacking along three fronts (see battle map, page 205). He believed that if troops occupied northeastern Mexico, the New Mexico Territory, and California, the Mexican government would agree to a settlement on American terms. Plagued by political and financial instability caused by civil wars and an underdeveloped economy, Mexico was militarily weak. It did not have the resources necessary to reconquer Texas or to protect California and New Mexico from American aggression. For example, Mexico's military expenditures in 1845 were $21 million, while the income of its national government was only $10 million!

Polk's first objective was the city of Monterrey, south of the Rio Grande River. General Taylor, known affectionately by his soldiers as "Old Rough and Ready," dislodged the enemy from the city in September 1846. Although Taylor was hailed as a hero throughout the nation, his victory was not as decisive as Polk had anticipated. The Mexican army was not annihilated, and was allowed to withdraw in good order. Moreover, Taylor was a Whig, and Polk feared that, like other military heroes before him, Taylor might capitalize upon his reputation to run for the Presidency. Thus, Polk decided that Taylor was not the man to lead an invading army south toward Mexico City. In fairness to Polk, however, it would have been militarily difficult for anyone to invade by this route. The terrain between Monterrey and Mexico City was extremely rugged and presented serious supply problems.

Meanwhile, an American army commanded by Colonel Stephen W. Kearney had marched into New Mexico and occupied the trading center of Santa Fe without opposition. Leaving a small detachment to occupy Santa Fe, Kearney dispatched more than half of his troops south to join Taylor at Monterrey and marched with the rest of his force to assist in the conquest of California. In 1846 California's population consisted of about 7,000 Mexicans, 700 Americans and about 24,000 Indians. The Americans—farmers, ranchers, traders—were eager to be free of Mexican domination.

Even before hostilities with Mexico began, the explorer John C. Frémont, a captain in the United States Army, had entered the region with other army personnel, ostensibly to conduct a topographical survey. Frémont, by talking openly of the eventual annexation of California to the United States, alienated Mexican officials, and he was asked to withdraw. He did so, but only to the Oregon border.

When war broke out, his party reentered California. Along with Commodores R. F. Stockton and John D. Sloat of the United States Navy, Frémont and his men helped the American settlers stage a revolt, called the "Bear Flag Revolt."

① **Aug. 18, 1846. Santa Fe.** Colonel Stephen Kearny takes Santa Fe. Leaving a small occupying force, he proceeds to California.

② **Sept. 24, 1846. Monterrey.** General Taylor captures the city, forcing the Mexicans to withdraw.

③ **Jan. 10, 1847. Conquest of California.** After the "Bear Flag Revolt" begins (July 7, 1846), Sloat captures Monterey and Kearny takes San Diego. The conquest is complete when Fremont, Kearny, and Stockton take Los Angeles.

④ **Feb. 27, 1847. Buena Vista.** After taking Buena Vista, Taylor repulses an attack by Santa Anna.

⑤ **March 27, 1847. Veracruz.** General Winfield Scott lands at Veracruz and takes the city.

⑥ **April 18, 1847. Cerro Gordo.** Scott's troops proceed to Mexico City. At Cerro Gordo Scott outmaneuvers the Mexicans, forcing them to withdraw.

⑦ **Sept. 14, 1847. Mexico City.** At the outskirts of Mexico City, Scott defeats the Mexicans at Churubusco and Molina del Rey. After storming Chapultepec Heights, Scott takes the city.

THE MEXICAN WAR

As a result, the American settlers declared their independence from Mexico. When Kearney arrived in California, he brought all revolutionary and American military forces under his command. By the autumn of 1846, the conquest of California was almost completed, and the settlers abandoned their plans for independence by demanding annexation to the United States.

Invasion of Mexico. These early campaigns accomplished all of Polk's objectives, but the Mexicans, motivated by strong pride, refused to negotiate a peace settlement. Polk then arranged for General Santa Anna, who was in exile in Cuba in 1846, to return to Mexico City. Santa Anna had given Polk assurances that when he returned to power he would agree to a settlement along the lines the Americans demanded. Once in power, however, Santa Anna repudiated his bargain and urged further resistance to the Americans. When Polk heard this, he and Winfield Scott, the commanding general of the United States Army, planned a campaign to capture Mexico City. They reasoned that with the capital city in American hands the Mexicans would have to negotiate.

Since Polk had decided not to send Taylor's army southward from Monterrey, he dispatched an army commanded by Scott himself to the coastal city of Veracruz. Landing at Veracruz, Scott captured the city after a three-week siege, and prepared for the 260-mile march inland to Mexico City. Learning of the Americans' strategy, Santa Anna marched north to attack Taylor's forces, part of which had been ordered to join Scott in Veracruz. After eliminating Taylor, Santa Anna then planned to march south and meet the new threat posed by Scott. In February 1847, Santa Anna attacked Taylor's outnumbered army at Buena Vista. Although he inflicted heavy casualties, the Mexican general did not achieve a victory, and he withdrew.

In the meantime, "Old Fuss and Feathers," as Scott was called, began the long march inland, traveling the same route as had the Spanish conqueror Hernando Cortes three hundred years earlier. This campaign was one of the most brilliant in American military history. At the heavily fortified mountain pass of Cerro Gordo, Scott managed to outflank the Mexican army and force it to withdraw. Especially prominent in this action were Captain Robert E. Lee, Captain George B. McClellan, and Lieutenant Ulysses S. Grant. Among other things, the Mexican War provided

In 1846, President Polk sent out the call for 50,000 men to fight in the war against Mexico. One young man who answered this call was an adventurous sixteen-year-old from Boston named Sam Chamberlain. He served first as a volunteer infantryman and then as a regular dragoon, or cavalryman. Though he was neither a professional writer nor artist, he did write and illustrate his own personal war history. In the picture at the right, *The Devil's Pass*, he shows a column of dragoons moving through the pass as two Mexican soldiers conceal themselves in the rocks while they watch the troop's progress. Below, another artist recorded what he thought the seige of the Mexican port city of Veracruz must have looked like. For three days during March 1847, the city was bombarded by 200 United States Navy ships and by American gun emplacements ashore. After three weeks, the city finally fell to General Winfield Scott.

combat experience for the generals who would command both the Union and Confederate armies during the Civil War.

After the action at Cerro Gordo, Scott's army met no further resistance until it reached the approaches to Mexico City. At Cherubusco, the Americans lost nearly one-seventh of their fighting force. The Mexican losses were even greater, and three thousand prisoners were taken, including eight generals. After the American army defeated the Mexicans at Molina del Rey and after it successfully stormed the Mexican fortress on the heights at Chapultepec, the Mexicans offered no further opposition. On September 14, 1847, the American army marched into Mexico City.

The Treaty of Guadalupe-Hidalgo. Polk, anticipating victory, had sent the chief clerk of the State Department, Nicholas Trist, to accompany Scott's army into the Mexican capital. Trist's instructions for negotiating a peace treaty were almost identical to those given to Slidell earlier. Impatient at the delay, however, the President recalled Trist at the very moment he was entering meaningful negotiations with the new Mexican government. With Scott's blessing, Trist ignored Polk's directive and concluded the Treaty of Guadalupe-Hidalgo in February 1848. By its terms the United States agreed to pay the Mexican government $15 million for New Mexico and California (an area called the Mexican Cession) and to assume responsibility for debts totaling $3.25 million owed by Mexico to American citizens.

When the treaty arrived in Washington, Polk was furious because Trist had defied him. The President had been considering annexing Mexican territory without payment, and many of his advisers had been giving serious thought to the possibility of annexing all of Mexico. But Polk was under pressure, both from northern Whigs who were extremely critical of the war, and from a majority of southerners of both parties who opposed the annexation of all of Mexico.

Most southerners were convinced that Mexico would not lend itself to the expansion of slavery. A few northern Whigs who had originally opposed the war agreed with southern reasoning that Mexico would not be suited to slavery. These Whigs now demanded total annexation on the grounds that Mexico would eventually enter the Union as one or more free states. Polk, realizing that further delay could serve only to intensify the political controversies caused by the war, accepted the treaty and submitted it to the Senate, which voted 38 to 14 in favor of ratification.

The United States had completed its march to the Pacific, adding 500,000 square miles of territory at a cost of 12,900 American lives and nearly $20 million. Of the men who died, 1,721 were killed in battle or died from their wounds; the remainder died from other causes, primarily disease. Another cost, however, could not be measured—the strain placed on an already tenuous national unity.

3 The Mexican War Leaves A Bitter Heritage

1. How successful a President was James K. Polk?

2. How did the Mexican War encourage sectional conflict?

3. What were the sectional issues in 1850?

4. What roles did Henry Clay, John C. Calhoun, and Daniel Webster play in the resolution of sectional difficulties in 1850? To what extent do their efforts indicate statesmanship?

James K. Polk was one of the most successful of all American Presidents in the sense that while in office he accomplished nearly every objective he aimed for. In addition to settling the Oregon controversy and acquiring New Mexico and California, Polk's administration reinstituted the Independent Treasury System and lowered the tariff.

Before leaving office, Polk also turned his attention to new fields of possible expansion. Although he attempted to buy Cuba from Spain and failed, he was successful in negotiating a treaty with Colombia granting the United States rights to build a canal across the Isthmus of Panama, then a part of Colombia. When Great Britain objected because such a move threatened its ambitions in the Caribbean, the two nations agreed (in the Clayton-Bulwer Treaty of 1850) that any canal built would be an international waterway. No canal was built then, but American interest in the Caribbean had been established.

In the 1840's, vast new lands were added to the United States. But America's aggressive expansion sowed the seeds that led to secession and four years of civil war. The Mexican War reopened the question of the status of slavery in the territories, an issue that had been smoldering for years.

Opposition to the war. Despite the patriotic fervor stirred up by supporters of the war, the nation was by no means unanimously in favor of it. From the beginning, the war was unpopular in the northeastern and Middle Atlantic states; nearly 90 percent of the fifty thousand volunteers who were recruited came from the South and the Middle West. Northern abolitionists condemned the war from the outset, although a few ultimately did demand the annexation of all of Mexico, believing that her economy and land would never support slavery.

One antislavery idealist who bitterly opposed the war was the essayist Henry David Thoreau. In protest Thoreau in 1845 refused to pay his poll tax and spent a night in jail. Later, in his essay "Civil Disobedience" (1849), he condemned slavery and the war:

> . . . when a sixth of the population of a nation which has undertaken to be the refuge of liberty are slaves, and a whole country [Mexico] is unjustly overrun and conquered by a foreign army, and subjected to military law, I think that it is not too soon for honest men to rebel and revolutionize. . . . This people must cease to hold slaves, and to make war on Mexico, though it cost them their existence as a people.

More important, at the early stage of the sectional controversy, northern Whigs bitterly denounced the war—some on moral grounds, others for political reasons. They viewed the conflict as part of a "great slave power conspiracy" to increase the political power of the South. Even so, most Whigs voted for military appropriations, fearing that if they did not, they might be discredited politically.

Some opposition to the war was even voiced by southern Democrats, including John C. Calhoun. Calhoun and his followers vigorously supported the annexation of Texas, but opposed the acquisition of New Mexico and California precisely because they feared that the political repercussions of further expansion would threaten the stability of the Union. They too were convinced that most of the new territory was not conducive to the expansion of slavery.

Open political conflict began during the early stages of the war itself. In August 1846, David Wilmot, an anti-slavery Democrat from Pennsylvania, introduced an amendment to a war appropriations bill advocating that slavery be barred forever in all territories acquired from Mexico. Although the Wilmot Proviso was defeated in Congress, it created a tremendous and lasting furor. Southern politicians bitterly attacked the Wilmot Proviso, claiming that the new territorial acquisitions belonged to all the states and arguing (despite the precedents provided by the Northwest Ordinance of 1787 and the Missouri Compromise) that Congress did not have the authority to legislate on the subject of slavery expansion.

The election of 1848. Worried politicians, especially in the Democratic party, began to devise possible solutions to resolve the impasse. James Buchanan of Pennsylvania, Polk's secretary of state and a strong contender for the Democratic nomination for the Presidency, suggested extending the Missouri Compromise line—36° 30'—westward to the Pacific. The formula finally adopted by the Democrats was the doctrine of "squatter sovereignty" (later called "popular sovereignty") which was first proposed by Governor Lewis Cass of Michigan.

This doctrine was a clever idea indeed, as it attempted to take the question of slavery expansion out of national politics by advocating that the future of slavery ought to be decided by the people of California, Oregon, and New Mexico themselves. In this way the issue could be neutralized, at least for the time being. Cass was rewarded for his ingenuity by being nominated for the Presidency.

The Whigs, unable to agree on a platform, reverted to the tactics so effectively utilized in the election of 1840. Ignoring issues, they nominated General Taylor for the Presidency, a man whose military exploits were well known but whose political views were not. A third party, the new Free Soil party, made up of former Liberty party supporters and antislavery Whigs and Democrats who vehemently opposed slavery expansion, appealed to voters who could not tolerate either

One man who spoke out against the conquest of Mexico was Senator Thomas Corwin of Ohio. In February 1847, he denounced the motives of the Polk administration in invading Mexico:

"Sir, look at this pretense of want of room. With twenty million people you have about one thousand million acres of land, inviting settlement by every conceivable argument . . . and allowing every man to squat where he pleases. But the Senator from Michigan says we will be two hundred millions in a few years, and we want room. If I were a Mexican I would tell you, 'Have you not room in your own country to bury your dead men? If you come into mine we will greet you with bloody hands and welcome you to hospitable graves.'

". . . We ought to have the Bay of San Francisco. Why? Because it is the best harbor on the Pacific! . . . I never yet heard a thief arraigned for stealing a horse plead that it was the best horse that he could find in the country. We want California? What for? . . . the Senator from South Carolina . . . says you cannot keep our people from going there. . . . Sir, it is not meet that our old flag should throw its protecting folds over expeditions for lucre or for land. But you still say you want room for your people. . . ."

major party. It nominated Martin Van Buren for President, and ran on a platform endorsing the Wilmot Proviso, free homesteads, and also a high tariff.

Taylor won a narrow victory, receiving 1,360,000 popular votes to Cass's 1,222,000. In the electoral college his margin was 163 to 127. Although Van Buren won no electoral votes, he did receive a respectable 300,000 popular votes. Moreover, the Free Soilers succeeded in electing ten congressmen. As it had been in 1844, New York was the pivotal state in the election. Van Buren's strength in New York may well have taken enough votes away from Cass to provide Taylor with his margin of victory.

Conflict over slavery expansion. Although Taylor avoided the issue of slavery expansion in the campaign, once in office he had to face it. He proposed that California and New Mexico bypass territorial status and be admitted immediately into the Union as states. Taylor reasoned that since the right of a state to determine the status of slavery within its own boundaries was not questioned, the issue would not come before Congress.

In terms of eligibility for statehood, California presented no problem. In 1848, gold was discovered at Sutter's Mill in the Sacramento Valley. News of the strike brought thousands of adventurers. They traveled over land, or across the Isthmus of Panama, or around the tip of South America in search of wealth. Some, of course, struck it rich, but most were disappointed and soon turned to other pursuits, especially farming. By 1850, the population was nearly 100,000, and the people were clamoring for statehood.

Congress, especially the southern representatives, was unwilling to accept Taylor's proposal. In 1849, the South was able to maintain its position in Congress only because the Union was comprised of fifteen slave and fifteen free states. The admission of California, and possibly New Mexico, as free states would upset the sectional balance of power in the Senate—a prospect that southerners found unacceptable.

In addition, other issues confronting Congress caused fear and uncertainty in the South. Northern antislavery advocates were demanding the abolition of slavery in the District of Columbia, and a number of northern states had passed personal liberty laws which prevented state authorities from helping federal agents recapture fugitive slaves. To further complicate the issues, Texans were angry because the federal government, during the Mexican War, had assigned to New Mexico part of the territory Texas claimed for itself. The Texans also wanted the national government to assume the debts Texas had amassed in its war for independence.

The Compromise of 1850. In an attempt to restore harmony, Henry Clay, in January 1850, introduced in the Senate an omnibus bill designed to resolve all the major issues dividing the nation. Clay, seventy-three years old, and having lost all hopes of attaining the Presidency, now had only one major ambition—to preserve the Union.

Clay's bill made six basic proposals. (1) He called for the admission of California into the Union as a free state. (2) He advocated the division of New Mexico into two territories, New Mexico and Utah, and recommended that the slavery question be resolved by popular sovereignty. (3) He proposed that Texas be compensated for its loss of territory to New Mexico by the assumption of its state debt, which amounted to $10 million. (4) He recommended the abolition of the slave trade in the District of Columbia but not of slavery itself without the consent of Maryland (out of whose territory the District had been created) and the residents of the District. (5) He suggested that the Fugitive Slave Law of 1793 be replaced by a much more stringent measure. (6) He declared that Congress should go on record as opposing federal interference with the domestic slave trade between the states.

Clay's bill triggered an angry debate which lasted for months. Northern antislavery politicians, including William H. Seward of New York, Charles Sumner of Massachussets, and Joshua Giddings of Ohio, attacked the compromise, bitterly denouncing northern subservience to the "slave power." In one speech, Seward declared that there was a "higher law" than the Constitution, the "law of God," in whose eyes slavery was an abomination. Southern opposition to the bill was no less extreme, and many southern senators talked of secession. Then, early in March, John C. Calhoun argued the position of the South before the Senate.

Calhoun, extremely ill and with less than a month to live, had prepared a speech which one of his colleagues delivered for him. It was Calhoun's last major public declaration. He denounced Clay's compromise proposals as totally inadequate to preserve the Union. He then demanded major Constitutional changes, the most important of which was the creation of a dual Presidency: that is, two Presidents, one northern and one southern, each of whom could exercise veto power over congressional legislation.

Furthermore, he declared, the North must agree to stop stirring up the slavery question, and guarantee the South equal access to the territories. If the North was not willing to accept these demands, Calhoun wrote, "let the States . . . agree to separate. . . . If you are not willing we should part in peace, tell us so, and we shall know what to do."

Shaken by Calhoun's intransigence, Daniel Webster, old and weary at age sixty-nine, rose in the Senate to make the last of his great addresses, the "Seventh of March Speech." He spoke, he said, not "as a Massachusetts man, nor as a Northern man, but as an American." Like Clay, his only ambition now was to preserve the Union. He argued that the debate over slavery in the territories was devoid of real meaning, for slavery in the new acquisitions was excluded by the "law of nature—of physical geography."

Webster then pleaded with his colleagues to exercise tact and discretion, and work to restore the harmony essential to preserve the Union:

Never did there devolve on any generation of men, higher trusts than now devolve upon us for the preservation of this Constitution and the harmony and peace of all those destined to live under it. Let us make our generation one of the strongest and brightest links in that golden chain which is destined, I fully believe, to grapple the people of all the States to this Constitution, for ages to come.

Webster's support of the compromise and his pleas for conciliation were attacked bitterly by antislavery idealists in the North, and he was portrayed as a man who had sold his soul to the Devil.

As the debates dragged on into the summer of 1850, Clay, exhausted by his labors, left Washington to rest. At this point, Senator Stephen A. Douglas, the "Little Giant" from Illinois, took command. Douglas proposed a separate vote for each measure in Clay's bill—a strategy that worked. In its final form the Compromise of 1850 included nearly every one of Clay's measures. California was admitted as a free state; slavery in the Utah and New Mexico territories was to be resolved by popular sovereignty; Texas received the $10 million compensation; the slave trade, but not slavery, was abolished in the District of Columbia; and a more stringent fugitive slave law was passed.

President Taylor had not been pleased with Clay's compromise proposals, insisting that California be admitted as a free state before any other legislation was passed—a position the South would not accept. Taylor died suddenly in July 1850, however, and he was succeeded by Millard

Fillmore of New York, who signed the compromise bills into law. Thus ended the first major political crisis caused by the Mexican War. The Union had been preserved, and by adopting the principle of popular sovereignty, Congress had removed the extremely dangerous question of slavery in the territories from the realm of national politics. Or so it seemed at the time.

CONCLUSION

In his inaugural address of 1845, President Polk confidently declared, "[I believe] that our system may be safely extended to the utmost bounds of our territorial limits, and that as it shall be extended, the bonds of our Union, so far from being weakened, will become stronger." Despite Polk's confidence, and despite the talk of mission, the spread of democracy, and the economic necessity of expansion, the triumph of Manifest Destiny during the 1840's served primarily to emphasize a most serious flaw in the American political system.

Expansionism demonstrated far more effectively than controversy over such questions as the tariff and western lands ever could that the United States was not yet a nation. It was a federal republic in which regional and sectional loyalties took precedence over the idea of national interests. The conflict over slavery in the territories, which ended with the adoption of the Compromise of 1850, revealed just how delicate the threads of Union actually were. This tenuous bond would be stretched to the breaking point in the decade to come.

QUESTIONS

1. Why did America believe that it should extend its borders to the Pacific Ocean? Were its reasons justifiable? Explain your answer.

2. How did the acquisition of new territories influence sectional controversies?

3. How did American leaders propose to handle the issue of slavery expansion into the newly acquired lands?

4. What were the causes of the Texas War for Independence? Were the Texans justified in revolting? Explain your answer.

5. What were the causes of the Mexican War? Were the American justified in declaring war against Mexico? Explain your answer.

6. Was James K. Polk a great American President? Explain your answer.

BIBLIOGRAPHY

COIT, MARGARET L., *John C. Calhoun*, Houghton Mifflin (Sentry Editions).

CURRENT, RICHARD N., *Daniel Webster and the Rise of National Conservatism*, Library of American Biography, Little, Brown.

EATON, CLEMENT, *Henry Clay and the Art of American Politics*, Library of American Biography, Little, Brown. The national government of the period was dominated by Congress and Congress was dominated by Clay, Calhoun, and Webster. These biographies of the three men are very well-written accounts and provide a necessary handle for understanding the growing conflicts of sectionalism and the dimensions of compromise.

MORISON, SAMUEL ELIOT, et al, *Dissent in Three American Wars*, Harvard U. Press. Dissent in a time of war is a very relevant topic for Americans, and three Harvard professors—Morison, Frederick Merk, and Frank Freidel—examine the issue during the War of 1812, the Mexican War, and the Spanish-American War.

THOREAU, HENRY DAVID, *Walden and the Famous Essay on Civil Disobedience*, New American Library (Signet Books). Perhaps America's most famous dissenter was Thoreau, who in protest over the Mexican War refused to pay his poll tax and was jailed. This edition presents both his essay on civil disobedience and his comments on life at Walden Pond, which have meaning for today's ecology-minded student.

BILLINGTON, RAY ALLEN, *The Far Western Frontier, 1830–1860*, Harper & Row (Torchbooks). Billington's book is recognized by many as the best survey of the western migration during the first half of the nineteenth century. The book provides an excellent framework for understanding Manifest Destiny, the frontier, and economic expansion along the Santa Fe trail and into the California Gold Rush territory.

DE VOTO, BERNARD, *The Year of Decision, 1846*, Houghton Mifflin (Sentry Editions). De Voto was a firm believer that a history book should be readable, and the reader profits from this outlook in the author's many books. As a pivotal year in American history, 1846 is closely researched and well reported by De Voto.

The Coming Of The Civil War

From its beginnings the United States had experienced sectional conflicts. Issues such as western lands, the tariff, finance, and internal improvements had always aroused controversy. Despite sectional differences, however, Americans had been able to resolve these issues through compromise. Even the explosive question of slavery expansion had been settled in the past without violence. Yet, in the 1850's, a decade characterized by violence, the North and the South failed to reconcile their differences peaceably.

The question of slavery expansion was not resolved by the Compromise of 1850, which provided only a temporary respite. Unlike the Northwest Ordinance of 1787 and the Missouri Compromise, the settlement of 1850 did not limit slavery to specific areas. As long as the status of slavery in the territories was not clearly defined, sectional antagonisms would continue to smolder. But Congress, unable to agree upon a suitable formula, simply agreed not to debate this controversial issue. As the nation expanded, attempts to bypass the question of slavery in the territories did not work. The issue became so explosive that from the middle of the decade on, it complicated virtually all questions of domestic and foreign policy. One by one, events unfolded that led to extremism and violence. As you follow the deepening conflict, look for the answers to these questions:

1. What events aggravated sectional tensions in the early 1850's?
2. Why did violence erupt in Kansas, and what was the outcome?
3. What was the effect of the Dred Scott decision on antislavery forces?
4. How did sectional conflict affect the political parties?
5. How do the various historical interpretations of the causes of the Civil War differ from one another?

1 The Nation Maintains An Uneasy Compromise

1. What were the results of the passage of the Fugitive Slave Law?

2. How great an impact did Harriet Beecher Stowe's novel *Uncle Tom's Cabin* have on the American public?

3. What was the position of the two major parties on the issue of slavery in the territories in the election of 1852?

4. How successful was the foreign policy of Franklin Pierce?

Between 1850 and 1854, most Americans accepted the terms of the Compromise of 1850. Nevertheless, antislavery agitation in the North continued. Abolitionists and Conscience Whigs were especially critical of the terms of the Fugitive Slave Law which denied alleged fugitives jury trials and did not permit them to testify in their own behalf. The word of a slave owner or his agent was all the so-called evidence required to establish guilt. Fearing strict enforcement, nearly three thousand blacks living in the North fled to Canada within three months after the law was passed. Historian Benjamin Quarles estimates that by 1860 the number reached over fifteen thousand. Most were fugitive slaves, but a sizable (though undetermined) number of free blacks also left the country.

Resistance to the Fugitive Slave Law. In many Northern states, outraged citizens, both black and white, resisted enforcement of the law, and several attempts to rescue captured fugitives succeeded. In February 1851, for instance, a group of nearly fifty Boston blacks freed Fred Wilkens and rushed him to safety in Canada. In Syracuse, New York, a group of blacks and whites rescued William Henry from federal custody; in Christiana, Pennsylvania, a slaveowner pursuing a runaway slave was killed and his son wounded by a band of fugitive slaves and free blacks. Before they could be arrested, the entire group escaped to Canada.

Not all fugitives were so fortunate. In 1854, Anthony Burns from Virginia was captured in Boston and returned to slavery by federal authorities. Burns's seizure so infuriated the Massachusetts legislature that it passed a personal-liberty law which virtually made the Fugitive Slave Law unenforceable in the state. In fact, during the 1850's, ten northern states passed personal-liberty laws which declared that state officials were not obliged to assist federal officers in their attempts to enforce the Fugitive Slave Law. Eventually, the Supreme Court intervened, declaring Wisconsin's personal-liberty law unconstitutional in 1859. Authorities in Wisconsin and other northern states, however, simply ignored the Court's decision.

Uncle Tom's Cabin. As important as the fugitive slave law in arousing northern antislavery sentiment during the early 1850's was Harriet Beecher Stowe's novel *Uncle Tom's Cabin* (1852). Although northerners had no direct knowledge of slavery, some had read narratives of fugitive slaves which were published in the North from the 1830's onward. Others were acquainted with Theodore Dwight Weld's savage indictment, *American Slavery As It Is: Testimony of a Thousand Witnesses* (1839). Weld included in his account the personal narratives of former slaveholders, the slave codes, newspaper items—all pointing to the barbaric treatment of slaves.

But no book attacking the evils of slavery created as much of a sensation as Mrs. Stowe's novel. During its first year of publication, the book sold more than three-hundred-thousand copies in the United States, and by 1860 sales had reached one million. These are startling figures, even for the twentieth century, when the American population is nearly seven times larger than it was in 1852. Mrs. Stowe took much of her material from Weld, and while *Uncle Tom's Cabin* cannot be described as a literary masterpiece, it is a devastating indictment of man's inhumanity to man which stirred the northern conscience.

For a few months after its publication, the book was sold in the South, but in 1853 it was banned in every southern state. The depth of southern feeling against Mrs. Stowe was reflected in an editorial in *The Southern Literary Messenger*, which condemned the novel as "a criminal prostitution of the high function of the imagination" and characterized Mrs. Stowe as a female "eaten up with fanaticism, festering with the malignant virus

UNCLE TOM'S CABIN

In this engraving from an original edition of *Uncle Tom's Cabin,* Eliza tells Uncle Tom she is about to flee north to the Ohio River and freedom. The following excerpt from the book describes Eliza's flight across the ice-choked river.

"In that dizzy moment her feet to her scarce seemed to touch the ground, and a moment brought her to the water's edge. Right on behind they came; and, nerved with strength such as God gives only to the desperate, with one wild cry and flying leap, she vaulted sheer over the turbid current by the shore, on to the raft of ice beyond. It was a desperate leap. . . .

"The huge green fragment of ice on which she alighted pitched and creaked as her weight came on it, but she stayed there not a moment. With wild cries and desperate energy she leaped to another and still another cake;— stumbling—leaping—slipping—springing upwards again! Her shoes are gone—her stockings cut from her feet— while blood marked every step; but she saw nothing, felt nothing, till dimly, as in a dream, she saw the Ohio side, and a man helping her up the bank."

of abolitionism." One anonymous southerner even sent Mrs. Stowe a package containing a black man's ear. Years later, President Lincoln, on meeting Mrs. Stowe for the first time, remarked: "So this is the little lady who wrote the book that made this great war." Lincoln was exaggerating, of course, but his comment reflects the tremendous influence of this novel in converting thousands in the North to an antislavery position.

The election of 1852. Despite the rising passions, national leaders of both the Democratic and Whig parties were determined not to tangle with the issue of slavery in the territories. In 1852, both parties adopted platforms pledging strict adherence to the Compromise of 1850. However, a sizable minority of northern Conscience Whigs refused to remain silent. Although they were not in a commanding position within the party, their outspoken condemnation of slavery weakened the Whigs.

After a long convention struggle, the Whigs nominated the Mexican War hero General Winfield Scott for President on the fifty-third ballot. Scott was an available candidate—that is, a man who had not been personally involved in recent political controversies. Adopting the same strategy, the Democrats nominated Franklin Pierce, an affable and noncontroversial New Hampshire politician, who had served in Congress and had also been a general in the Mexican War. Pierce carried the electoral college by the resounding majority of 254 to 42, losing only Kentucky, Tennessee, Massachusetts, and Vermont. In popular votes, however, the election was much closer; Pierce polled 1,601,274 votes as compared to 1,386,580 for Scott.

The Democratic party, the northern and southern wings of which were united in their support of the Compromise of 1850, was placed in a strong position. Divisions over slavery in the Whig party, however, did not augur well for its future. It was clear to many political observers that further agitation over the expansion of slavery would prevent future cooperation between northern and southern Whig leaders. If that occured, the Whig party would be destroyed.

Pierce's foreign policy. Franklin Pierce entered the White House in March 1853, in a confident mood. Thus far, antislavery sentiment in the North had succeeded only in weakening the Whig party and strengthening the Democrats. Democratic unity could be maintained, Pierce and his advisers reasoned, if northern proslavery Democrats continued their policy of supporting and placating the South on all issues relating to slavery and slavery expansion. In his inaugural address, Pierce pledged strict adherence to the compromise measures adopted in 1850, emphasizing that careful attention must be given to "the rights of the South" by vigorous enforcement of the Fugitive Slave Law.

In addition, Pierce strongly advocated further territorial expansion and increased political and economic influence in the Caribbean area, Canada, and the Far East. In part, Pierce's foreign policy represented a continuation of the aggressive expansionism (both economic and territorial) pursued by Polk and earlier Presidents.

In the economic sphere, the extension of America's influence was remarkably successful during Pierce's administration. In 1854, Commodore Matthew Perry succeeded in negotiating a treaty with Japan which opened that nation to American trade and commerce. In the same year, the United States also negotiated a reciprocity treaty with Canada which opened American markets to Canadian products, especially timber, farm produce, and fish. In return, Americans were granted fishing rights in Canadian waters and unlimited navigation rights on the St. Lawrence River and the Great Lakes. Although Great Britain retained political control of Canada, the treaty virtually amounted to an economic union with the United States, as Canadians were almost totally dependent upon American markets for their prosperity.

The aggressiveness of Pierce's foreign policy was most pronounced in its plans for territorial expansion. In 1854, the United States successfully negotiated the Gadsden Purchase from Mexico (see map, page 798), acquiring 45,535 square miles of territory in order to facilitate the construction of a transcontinental railroad to California via a southern route. The attempts of the Pierce administration to acquire Hawaii and Cuba, however, ended in failure. Secretary of State William L. Marcy negotiated an annexation treaty with Hawaii, but the Senate refused to ratify it on the grounds that acquiring these islands was not essential for either American prosperity or national security. Nevertheless, American business interests dominated the islands' economic and political life, and astute contemporary observers correctly predicted that the United States would eventually annex Hawaii.

Controversy over Cuba. Far more significant in its impact on the internal politics of the United States than any other issues of foreign affairs was the aggressive policy pursued by the Pierce administration in regard to Cuba. The attempt to gain Cuba produced an explosive political situation which aggravated sectional tensions, for it enabled northern antislavery advocates to charge that American designs on Cuba were part of a great slave power conspiracy to add new slave states to the Union.

In 1854, under instructions from the secretary of state, the American ambassadors to Spain, France, and Great Britain met in Ostend, Belgium, to discuss ways by which the United States might detach Cuba from Spain. They drew up a series of recommendations, known as the "Ostend Manifesto," which declared that if Spain refused to sell Cuba, the United States, "by every law, human and divine," would "be justified in wresting it from Spain if we possess the power." When the contents of the Ostend document were made public, such a furor resulted that the administration was forced to abandon its plans.

It is highly improbable that a gigantic slave power conspiracy actually existed. Yet, the Democratic party was undeniably sympathetic to the South. In addition, northern fears of proslavery expansionism were accentuated in the early 1850's by an unsuccessful expedition against Cuba from American territory by a Venezuelan general. An American adventurer, William Walker also established a short-lived military dictatorship in Nicaragua before being deposed and executed. Although the federal government did not sponsor these expeditions, neither did it take effective action to prevent them. Little wonder that northern antislavery people suspected the worst.

If the Pierce administration had hoped to unite the American people by pursuing an aggressive foreign policy, it misread the mood of a majority of northerners on the question of slavery expansion. It is doubtful that northern public opinion would have tolerated the acquisition of Cuba under any circumstances. Northern feelings on the slavery issue were made clear in 1854 when the issue of slavery expansion in the territories was reopened by the passage of the Kansas-Nebraska Bill.

2 The Kansas-Nebraska Act Brings Violence

1. Why did Senator Stephen Douglas propose the Kansas-Nebraska Bill?

2. How workable was the doctrine of popular sovereignty in the territories on the slavery issue?

3. What were the political repercussions of the Kansas-Nebraska Act?

4. What does the Sumner-Brooks affair and the conflict in Kansas illustrate about the state of sectional sentiments in the 1850's?

As already noted, sectional tensions were aggravated during the early 1850's by enforcement of the Fugitive Slave Law, by the publication of *Uncle Tom's Cabin,* and by an expansionist foreign policy, particularly over the issue of Cuba. Nevertheless, after the Compromise of 1850, the question of slavery expansion in the territories was not an issue in Congress until 1854, when Stephen A. Douglas introduced the Kansas-Nebraska Bill.

The Kansas-Nebraska Act. Ironically, Douglas, who was chairman of the Senate's Committee on Territories, had no intention of reintroducing the slavery question when he drafted the original bill. A prime advocate of western expansion, Douglas was not only anxious to organize the territories for settlement, but also wanted to construct one or more transcontinental railroads—by northern, central, or southern routes. When Congress rejected the idea of building more than one route,

Douglas hoped to get a central line through the Nebraska Territory.

Anticipating southern objections to the organization of a territory that eventually would become a free state (Nebraska was north of the Missouri Compromise line), Douglas inserted a phrase in the bill calling for popular sovereignty on the issue of slavery. By so doing, Douglas assumed, without explicitly saying so, that the Compromise of 1850 (which provided for popular sovereignty in New Mexico and Utah) had replaced the Missouri Compromise as the guide in determining the status of slavery in new territories. Even so, southerners demanded that a specific provision be included repealing the Missouri Compromise. After some hesitation, Douglas agreed.

In addition, southern senators also demanded that Nebraska be divided into two territories. Again, Douglas agreed. The northern part, which was much larger, continued to be called Nebraska; the smaller southern area became Kansas.

Douglas believed that the status of slavery in Kansas and Nebraska would be determined by economic criteria. He declared that whenever a territory's "climate, soil, and productions" made slavery profitable, it would be legalized by the inhabitants; otherwise, it would not be adopted. "You come right back to the principle of dollars and cents," he concluded. Douglas could not comprehend why anyone would object to the passage of the Kansas-Nebraska Bill. From Douglas's point of view, the principle of popular sovereignty had saved the Union in 1850, and its inclusion in the Kansas-Nebraska Bill was simply a logical extension of the same principle.

Douglas believed that he had paved the way for western expansion and the construction of a transcontinental railroad. He reasoned that the Kansas-Nebraska Bill had strengthened his position in the North and also made him an acceptable Presidential candidate in the South, since popular sovereignty recognized the theoretical rights of slaveholders in these territories.

The final vote on the bill, however, showed how badly Douglas has misjudged the situation. All but two southern Democrats and a majority of southern Whigs voted for it; all the northern Whigs and nearly half of the northern Democrats voted against it. Not only had Douglas been mis-

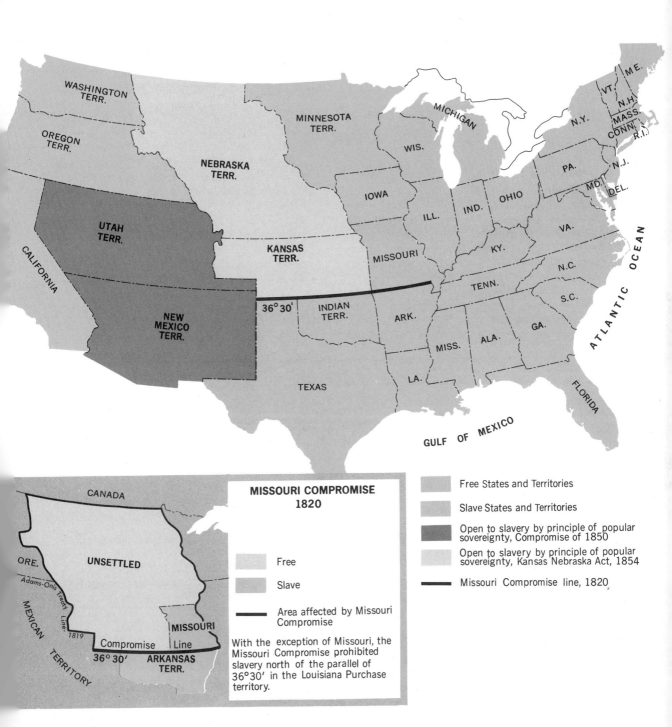

MISSOURI COMPROMISE 1820

Free

Slave

Area affected by Missouri Compromise

With the exception of Missouri, the Missouri Compromise prohibited slavery north of the parallel of 36°30′ in the Louisiana Purchase territory.

Free States and Territories

Slave States and Territories

Open to slavery by principle of popular sovereignty, Compromise of 1850

Open to slavery by principle of popular sovereignty, Kansas Nebraska Act, 1854

Missouri Compromise line, 1820

NEW TERRITORIES OPEN TO SLAVERY, 1854

taken about the aims of southern extremists in regard to Kansas, but he had also completely misread northern sentiment on the possibility of further slavery expansion. Douglas may have been prepared for criticism but not the political turmoil which the passage of the act produced in the North. The Kansas-Nebraska Act destroyed the Whig party, shook the Democratic party to its very foundations, and unleashed a train of violent events.

Two new parties emerge. The period following the passage of the Kansas-Nebraska Act was marked by party realignment. Within a few months, two new political parties appeared—the Republican party and the American party, which was better known as the "Know-Nothing" party because of the frequent refusal of its members to discuss their principles openly.

The Republicans, a coalition of northern Whigs, "anti-Nebraska" Democrats, and former supporters of the Free Soil party, were a purely sectional party whose major platform was the free

soil doctrine opposing slavery expansion. On the other hand, the Know-Nothing party attracted voters in all sections, including southern Whigs as well as some northern Whigs and anti-Nebraska Democrats. Although national in scope, the Know-Nothing appeal was based upon nativist principles, or *nativism*, which favored native-born Americans over immigrants, fearing that the newcomers posed a threat.

In part the Know-Nothing movement was a result of the irrational fears created by the migration of hundreds of thousands of Irish and Germans to the United States during the 1840's and 1850's. One Know-Nothing journal editorialized that immigration was making the United States "the sewer of the world." Most of these immigrants were Roman Catholics, and many Americans associated Catholicism with political despotism, since many Catholic countries were governed by absolute monarchs. Hence, many American Protestants tended to look upon foreigners as dangerous subversives whose very

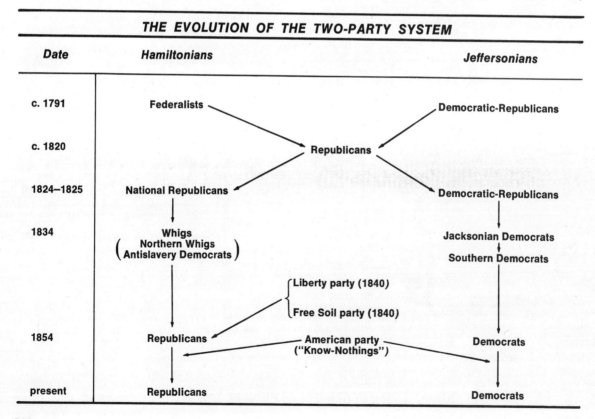

THE EVOLUTION OF THE TWO-PARTY SYSTEM

Date	Hamiltonians		Jeffersonians
c. 1791	Federalists		Democratic-Republicans
c. 1820		Republicans	
1824–1825	National Republicans		Democratic-Republicans
1834	Whigs (Northern Whigs / Antislavery Democrats)		Jacksonian Democrats / Southern Democrats
		Liberty party (1840) / Free Soil party (1840)	
1854	Republicans	American party ("Know-Nothings")	Democrats
present	Republicans		Democrats

presence was a threat to American institutions. In addition, immigrants were often willing to work for lower wages than native-born Americans. Thus, prejudice, fear, and economic competition convinced many that foreign influences had to be resisted.

Many Americans were appalled by the intolerance of the Know-Nothings. Abraham Lincoln best summarized the feelings of those who opposed Know-Nothing bigotry when as a Whig he campaigned against the party in Illinois in 1854. Lincoln observed that

As a nation we began by declaring that "all men are created equal." We now practically read it, "all men are created equal except Negroes." When Know-Nothings control, it will read: "All men are created equal except Negroes, foreigners and Catholics."

In 1854, however, the Know-Nothings, who advocated the exclusion of aliens from public office and the increase of residence requirements for citizenship, were far more successful than the Republicans in appealing to the voters. Then within a year, the Know-Nothing tide receded. The party's appeal was weakened by violence directed against Catholics, Jews, and foreigners in several cities including Cincinnati, Chicago, and New York. Equally important, the northern and southern wings of the party divided over the issue of slavery. In 1855 the vast majority of southern Know-Nothings joined the Democratic party, whereas most northerners ended up in the Republican camp.

Conflict in Kansas. One of the consequences of the Kansas-Nebraska Act was to make Kansas itself a bloody battleground. The opening of the Kansas territory in 1854 set off a fierce contest between proslavery forces and antislavery forces, called Free-Soilers, to determine whether Kansas was to be slave or free. When the New England Emigrant Aid Society began to raise $5 million to send northern settlers to Kansas, fear spread throughout the South.

Alarmists raised the specter of thousands of abolitionists descending upon the plains of Kansas, robbing the South of the possibility of adding a new slave state to the Union. As a result, many southern communities and organizations armed and equipped their sons to settle in Kansas.

Southern fears increased when it was reported that the Yankee settlers were heavily armed, especially with Sharp's repeating rifles, popularly known as "Beecher's Bibles." They were named after the Reverend Henry Ward Beecher, brother of Harriet Beecher Stowe, whose congregation donated rifles and money to the Emigrant Aid Society.

Despite exaggerated fears, not more than two thousand settlers were actually sent to Kansas by the New England Emigrant Aid Society, and few southerners brought slaves with them into the territory. The uncertainties of transplanting slavery into a territory whose future was to be determined by popular sovereignty was a risk most slaveholders were unwilling to take. In the long run most settlers in Kansas came from the Ohio Valley. Nevertheless, the conflict over Kansas played a crucial role in widening sectional cleavages and preparing the way for war.

In March 1855, Andrew Reeder, Kansas' first territorial governor, called for elections to the new territorial legislature. On election day, proslavery advocates from Missouri crossed over into Kansas and voted. One well-armed group was led by Senator David Atchison, who said, "There are eleven hundred coming over from Platte County Missouri to vote, and if that ain't enough we can send five thousand—enough to kill every . . . damned abolitionist in the territory."

In the elections, the Free-Soil settlers cast 791 votes, compared to 5,427 proslavery votes. According to historian Allan Nevins, 4,908 of these votes were illegal, cast by proslavery men from Missouri. Governor Reeder, who knew that fraud had occurred, disqualified nearly one-third of the proslavery members "elected." But even Reeder was not aware until too late that *most* of the ballots cast for proslavery delegates were fraudulent. When Reeder explained the situation to the President, Pierce refused to challenge the results. Instead, he removed Reeder from office.

Meanwhile in Kansas, the proslavery territorial legislature not only legalized slavery but limited officeholding to proslavery men. The Free-Soilers, most of whom lived near the town of Lawrence, declared that they would not obey the dictates of the proslavery legislature. They then drew up and ratified a Free-Soil constitution, which they sent to Washington for approval by Congress. Pierce not only refused to intervene in behalf of the antislavery settlers, but declared that the proslavery legislature was the legal government of Kansas and branded the Free-Soil government as revolutionary. Resistance to the proslavery legislature, he warned, would be treated as "treasonable insurrection."

"Bleeding Kansas." While Congress fruitlessly debated the issue, the situation in Kansas worsened. In May 1856, a federal posse descended on Lawrence to arrest the officials of the Free-Soil government for treason. The posse degenerated into a mob which burned and looted. Although no one was killed, the so-called sack of Lawrence had immediate and grave consequences.

A violent abolitionist and Free-Soiler named John Brown had recently settled in Kansas to fight the proslavery forces. Brown, who considered himself an agent of the Almighty, set out to avenge the Lawrence raid. A few days later, Brown and a small band hacked to death five unarmed southern sympathizers. The Pottawatomie Massacre, as Brown's attack was called, inaugurated a guerrilla war in which over two hundred people died. President Pierce sent in federal troops to restore order, but the last acts of the drama in "bleeding Kansas" remained to be played.

The Sumner-Brooks affair. Another major consequence of violence and corruption in Kansas was a vitriolic speech by Senator Charles Sumner of Massachusetts. During the same week as the sack of Lawrence and John Brown's attack, Sumner described the situation in Kansas as the "rape of a virgin territory, compelling it to the hateful embrace of Slavery; and it may be clearly traced to a depraved longing for a new slave state . . ." These were harsh words, indeed, but impersonal. Sumner, however, also singled out for personal abuse Andrew P. Butler, an elderly senator from South Carolina who was absent from the chamber. Following Sumner's speech, he was approached by Preston Brooks, a congressman from South Carolina and a nephew of Butler, who attacked Sumner, seriously injuring him.

Brooks was censured by the House of Representatives, and in defiance, he resigned. His congressional district then reelected him to the House. In the North, Brooks was bitterly denounced. The Massachusetts legislature, as a sign of its indignation, refused to replace Sumner, although he was to be incapacitated for over three years. The consequences of the Kansas-Nebraska Act—the demise of the Whig party, violence and guerrilla war on the Kansas plains, the Sumner-Brooks affair—were all ominous signs of the growing inability of North and South to resolve their differences peaceably. As Senator Butler remarked: "Really it [the Union] is broken already; for the spirit which cherished it has been extinguished."

3 **President Buchanan Pursues A Disastrous Policy**

1. What did the election of 1856 indicate about the future direction of American party politics?

2. What were the legal arguments on both sides in the Dred Scott case? Why did the Supreme Court render the decision it did?

3. What impact did the Dred Scott decision have on the nation?

4. In what ways did President Buchanan's position regarding the admission of Kansas represent a disastrous blunder?

By 1856, Know-Nothing influence had declined, and the Presidential election appeared to be a battle between the Democrats and the Republicans. A Democratic victory seemed likely, since only 149 votes were necessary for a majority in the electoral college, and the slave states had a solid bloc of 120 electoral votes. Yet, the northern Democrats had lost support as a result of policies in Kansas. Many party leaders feared the potential strength of the Republican coalition in the free states.

The election of 1856. In their party platform in 1856, the Democrats called for overseas expansion, free trade, and popular sovereignty in the territories. After a long struggle, they chose James Buchanan of Pennsylvania as their Presidential candidate. Buchanan, who had served in

Congress and as a diplomat (he was one of the authors of the Ostend Manifesto), was not as divisive a candidate as Douglas or Pierce; in addition, Pennsylvania had 27 electoral votes, second only to New York's 35.

The Republicans also bypassed prominent but controversial party leaders such as William H. Seward of New York and Salmon P. Chase of Ohio. They nominated instead the dashing and popular John C. Frémont, the explorer who had taken part in the California revolt during the Mexican War. The Republican party, a coalition of northern Whigs, anti-Nebraska Democrats, and Free-Soilers, by 1856 also included many former members of the Know-Nothing party. The only common denominator of the Republican party was its opposition to slavery expansion, which was expressed in the major plank in the party's platform.

The Republicans declared that Congress exercised sovereign power over the organization and government of the territories, "and that in the exercise of this power, it is both the right and imperative duty of Congress to prohibit in the Territories those twin relics of barbarism—Polygamy [a reference to the Mormons in Utah] and Slavery." Concentrating on the slavery issue, the Republicans did not adopt economic planks such as a high tariff, nationally sponsored internal improvements, and homestead legislation—issues that they would use with great effectiveness four years later.

Even though the Republicans campaigned on only one issue and Buchanan did win, Frémont carried eleven of sixteen northern states and ran an extremely close second to Buchanan in Pennsylvania and Indiana. In popular votes Buchanan received 1,838,169 to 1,341,364 for Frémont. The electoral votes were 174 for Buchanan to 114 for Frémont, while the Know-Nothing candidate, former President Millard Fillmore, took Maryland's eight votes. However, the combined popular vote of Frémont and Fillmore exceeded that of Buchanan.

Had the Know-Nothing party combined forces with the Republicans in 1856 (as indeed most Know-Nothings did in 1860), Frémont would have won. As Allan Nevins has observed:

The three Northern States that had given Buchanan his victory, Pennsylvania, Illinois, and Indiana, were all moving inexorably toward the Republican column; and the prospect loomed that in the next election the North would be solidly Republican, and could then carry the Presidency without a single Southern vote.

Many southern politicians, even at this time, threatened disunion if and when the Republicans succeeded in winning a national election.

The Dred Scott case. Two days after Buchanan was inaugurated, the Supreme Court announced its decision in the Dred Scott case, one of the most controversial and momentous decisions in the nation's history. The legal maneuvering involved in this case was exceedingly complex, but the major issue that the Court was called upon to decide was the status of slavery in the territories.

Scott, the slave of an army surgeon from Missouri, Dr. John Emerson, had in the 1830's traveled with Emerson to Illinois and the Wisconsin territory. After Emerson's death in 1846, Scott sued for his freedom in the Missouri courts. He claimed that he was entitled to be free because he had lived in Illinois and Wisconsin, which were north of the Missouri Compromise line. Scott won his case in Missouri's lower courts, only to have the decision reversed by the state supreme court. It maintained that when Scott voluntarily returned to Missouri with Emerson, he automatically became a slave again.

There matters stood until 1853 when control of Emerson's estate went to his widow's brother, J. F. A. Sanford of New York. Scott's lawyer then brought suit for Scott's freedom in the federal courts against Sanford on the grounds of diverse citizenship—that is, a citizen of one state is entitled under the Constitution to bring suit against a citizen of another state in the federal courts. The federal court upheld the decision of the Missouri Supreme Court, paving the way for an appeal by Scott's lawyer to the United States Supreme Court.

The Dred Scott decision. At first, a majority of the Supreme Court judges were inclined only to accept the decisions of the lower courts, thus avoiding the need to make any pronouncement on the issue of slavery in the territories. At least one, and possibly two factors, however, changed the outlook of a majority of the Supreme Court justices.

First, it was widely believed that Justices Benjamin R. Curtis and John McLean were prepared

Charles River Bridge v. Warren Bridge (1837). The Charles River Bridge Company had a charter to operate a toll bridge over the Charles River, and it sued when Massachusetts gave a charter to the Warren Bridge Company to build a toll-free bridge, claiming that the new charter was invalid. The court ruled that the toll-free bridge was allowed since contracts have no implied rights, and ambiguous clauses must be decided in the public's favor.

License Cases (1847). In three cases of states taxing liquor from out of state, the court ruled that the taxes were legal since the state has the right to regulate interstate commerce when it does not interfere with federal laws.

Luther v. Borden (1849). When rebels in Rhode Island set up a new state government, the state declared martial law. The rebels claimed that the law was void because their government was the only lawful one. The court ruled that in cases of armed conflict within a state, only the President can decide which government is lawful.

Passenger Cases (1849). The court ruled that head taxes placed on aliens by New York and Massachusetts were illegal since the power to regulate foreign commerce belongs solely to Congress.

Dred Scott v. Sanford (1857). The court ruled that blacks were not national citizens and that slavery could not be excluded in the territories, declaring the Missouri Compromise unconstitutional.

Ableman v. Booth (1858). When a Wisconsin court released an abolitionist convicted of violating the Fugitive Slave Law, the court ruled that no state court can interfere with a federal law.

Ex Parte Merryman (1861). John Merryman, a Baltimore secessionist who had been put in a military prison, was granted a writ of *habeas corpus* by the Supreme Court. When the military commander denied the writ, the court declared that only Congress has the power to suspend *habeas corpus*.

---

to write dissenting opinions, arguing not only that Scott was entitled to his freedom because of his residence in the North, but also that Congress had exclusive jurisdiction over the status of slavery in the territories. Thus, the seven Democratic judges on the Court (five of whom were southerners) may have felt it crucial to refute these views by writing their own opinions.

Second, and more important, Buchanan used his influence to persuade the Court to render a decision on the issue of slavery in the territories. The President publicly denied in his inaugural address that he knew in advance what the Court's decision would be, but the evidence that he did intervene is irrefutable. Justice Grier, in replying to a letter he received from the President on the matter, stated: "We fully appreciate and concur in your views as to the desirableness . . . of having an expression of the opinion of the Court on this troublesome question." As historian Roy F. Nichols has demonstrated, Buchanan "practically participated in their deliberations and influenced their judgment."

The Court's decision, given in March 1857, with Justices Curtis and McLean dissenting, was highly favorable to the South. Not only did the Court deny Scott his freedom, declaring that blacks were not citizens and therefore could not sue in federal courts, but it also went on to state that slavery could not be excluded from the territories. In other words, the Missouri Compromise of 1820 was declared unconstitutional.

Justice Curtis, in a vigorous dissenting opinion, pointed out the historical inaccuracies of Chief Justice Roger B. Taney's declaration that the founding fathers had not intended blacks to receive national citizenship. Black men had in fact voted and exercised all the rights of national citizenship in several New England states. Moreover, according to the Constitution, citizens of a state were automatically entitled to national citizenship; many blacks, therefore, were and always had been citizens.

Curtis also pointed out that Congress had exercised control over the status of slavery in the territories from the very beginning of the nation's history, as exemplified by the Northwest Ordinance of 1787 and the Missouri Compromise of 1820. Equally important, congressional jurisdiction had been accepted by all branches of the government and all sections of the country throughout most of the nation's history. Curtis argued that the Supreme Court's decision completely disregarded past precedents and experience. Thus, he reasoned that the Court's majority had arrived at an illogical and dubious conclusion. Nevertheless it was the conclusion that counted, despite the inconsistencies and erroneous suppositions involved in reaching it.

In the North, the furor caused by the Dred Scott decision was nearly as great as that aroused by the passage of the Kansas-Nebraska Act. Republican party leaders declared that they would not accept it as conclusive, and vowed that when they came into power, they would appoint enough new Supreme Court judges with antislavery opinions to reverse it. If Republicans were outraged by the decision, northern Democrats, especially those who advocated popular sovereignty, were placed in an awkward position. Southerners concluded that the Court had not only declared Republican opposition to slavery in the territories unconstitutional, but had also decided that popular sovereignty was no longer legal.

The Lecompton Constitution. Despite widespread disagreement in both the Republican and the Democratic parties, Buchanan accepted the Dred Scott decision as a final solution to the difficulties presented by the issue of slavery expansion. The President then tried to resolve the practical difficulties created by the explosive situation in Kansas. However, Buchanan's approach to the question was no more realistic than that of his predecessor Franklin Pierce. Buchanan's policies not only further alienated the Free-Soilers in Kansas, but also brought about additional defections in the Democratic party.

The President was determined to have Kansas admitted to the Union as quickly as possible, and he instructed the territorial governor to call for the election of delegates to a constitutional convention. But Buchanan's strategy backfired. The Kansas Free-Soilers boycotted the elections, and, as a result, proslavery forces dominated the convention. Meeting in Lecompton, Kansas, the convention drew up the Lecompton Constitution, which legalized slavery. The constitution was then submitted to the people, and with the Free-Soilers again abstaining from voting, it was adopted. When Buchanan learned this, he claimed that since the Free-Soilers refused to participate in the elections they had no legitimate grievances. Soon thereafter, the President demanded that Congress admit Kansas into the Union as a slave state.

Meanwhile, the governor of Kansas called for elections to the new territorial legislature. This time the Free-Soilers turned out in force and won an overwhelming majority of seats. The Free-Soil legislature then resubmitted the Lecompton Constitution to the Kansas electorate, which voted to repeal it by a majority of nearly 10,000 votes. Despite this, Buchanan, under extreme pressure from his southern backers, persisted in his demand that Congress admit Kansas as a slave state. "Seldom in the history of the nation." Allan Nevins observes, "has a President made so disastrous a blunder."

In the Senate, the Lecompton Bill, as Buchanan's proposal was called, passed easily, but it met serious opposition in the House of Representatives. In an attempt to push the bill through Congress, Buchanan even tried to force Douglas to support his position. At a long and bitter meeting, Buchanan threatened Douglas with political reprisals if he failed to fall into line. Douglas responded by declaring, "Mr. President, I wish *you* to remember that General Jackson is dead," a reference to Andrew Jackson's assertion of Presidential power. Douglas then used his considerable influence to persuade western Democrats in the House to vote against the bill. It was finally killed by a coalition of western Democrats, Republicans, and anti-Nebraska Know-Nothings.

In part, Douglas refused to support Buchanan because he believed that the events in Kansas were a travesty of his concept of popular sovereignty. Primarily his position was based on political considerations. Public opinion in Illinois vigorously opposed the admission of Kansas under the Lecompton Constitution; and in 1858 Douglas was up for reelection.

Ultimately, Congress passed a compromise measure, under the terms of which the Lecompton Constitution would once again be submitted to the Kansas electorate. If they accepted it, the state would receive a sizable federal land grant, and be

The American party, or Know-Nothings, had a rather brief period as an organized party, but during its life it had many committed members. It even had a song written for it, as the song sheet on the right shows. The only Presidential election in which the Know-Nothings ran their own candidate was in 1856. The cartoon below was published during that campaign, and it attacks the Democratic platform. Because the Democratic party favored popular sovereignty at the time, four of its leading members—Senator Stephen Douglas, President Franklin Pierce, Presidential candidate James Buchanan, and Senator Lewis Cass are shown attempting to force slavery down the throat of an unwilling Kansas Free-Soiler.

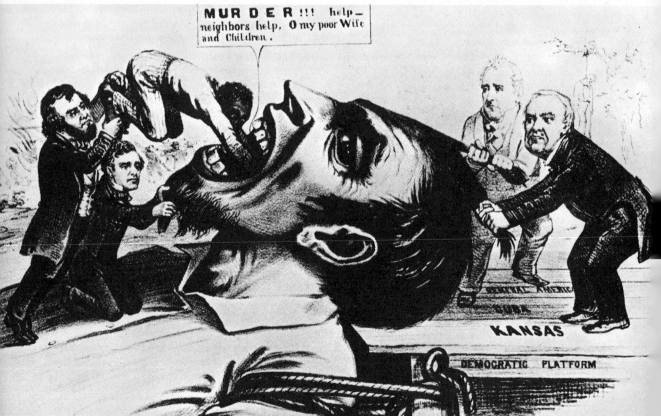

admitted into the Union. If they voted it down, statehood for Kansas would not again be considered by Congress until its population reached 93,600. Predictably, the Free-Soil majority in Kansas once again decisively rejected the Lecompton Constitution, and Kansas did not enter the Union until 1861, when it was admitted as a free state.

By stubbornly refusing to accept political realities in Kansas, Buchanan succeeded only in intensifying sectional hostilities and in further dividing the Democratic party. Moreover, he made it extremely difficult for any future Democratic Presidential candidate to heal the party's wounds and lead a united party in the Presidential election of 1860. In fact, the Democratic party, by 1858, was on the verge of disintegration. Thus, the Republicans had good reason for facing the future with optimism.

4 America Heads Toward Disunion

1. What were the causes and effects of the panic of 1857?

2. In what ways did the Lincoln-Douglas debates alter the political situation in the United States?

3. Do you think John Brown was justified in resorting to violence and illegal measures to achieve his goals?

4. How did Brown's raid affect the nation?

During the 1850's, few social, political, or economic issues lacked sectional overtones. Even the panic of 1857, which was caused by domestic and international economic forces, added fuel to the sectional fires that raged virtually uncontrolled in the United States from 1854 onward.

The panic of 1857. One of the major causes of the panic was the Crimean War in Europe, during which investments on the Continent became more profitable than in the United States.

When many Europeans who had invested in American industries and transportation cashed in their American holdings, banks were forced to pay off in gold, thus creating a specie shortage in the United States. And, in order to meet these financial obligations, banks called in many outstanding domestic loans, which brought about business failures and widespread unemployment in the Northeast.

Equally important, the Crimean War had stimulated the European demand for American agricultural products. When the war was over, the demand declined sharply, primarily affecting farmers in the Middle West. The decreasing demand for American agricultural products also brought an end to a western land boom, triggered in part by the temporary expansion of agricultural trade with Europe. In addition, overexpansion in railroad building absorbed millions of dollars in investment without producing enough profits to sustain growth and development.

Unlike the Northeast and the Middle West, the South was not seriously affected by the panic. The South was a producer of staples, in which capital investments were not as great as in northern industry and transportation. And even though a decline in prices lessened profits for the South, it did not suffer the severe economic reverses of the North. But the panic did affect the attitude of the South toward its own position. As Roy F. Nichols has observed, the panic instilled in many southern political leaders a false sense of their economic independence, which had important political overtones. Nichols comments that to many southerners the panic clearly demonstrated that

> The South was stable, impervious to business fluctuation, her wealth and prosperity secure. The South was necessary to the North, but the North contributed little to the South. Cotton was King! The South therefore could contemplate independence with great confidence, could be careless in its [political] demands [on the North] with slight fear of evil consequences.

In the North, on the other hand, many business leaders believed that since the southern economy was not seriously affected, the panic must have been caused by a low tariff which was beneficial to the South. This oversimplified view was reinforced by the fact that the Democratic majority in Congress had passed the lowest tariff in the nation's history in 1857.

The Lincoln-Douglas debates. Important as economic forces were in contributing to sectional conflict, the questions of slavery and slavery expansion still occupied center stage. After the struggle over the Lecompton Constitution, the next important development occurred in Illinois in 1858.

When Senator Douglas returned to Illinois to campaign for reelection to the Senate, he was challenged to a series of debates by his Republican opponent, Abraham Lincoln. Except for having served one term as a Whig congressman during the 1840's, Lincoln had not been an active participant in national affairs, although he was well known in Illinois. Although Douglas was one of the most forceful and eloquent speakers of his day, Lincoln was himself a shrewd and gifted orator.

Lincoln had made his views on slavery known when he accepted the nomination for senator. In what came to be called his "House Divided" speech, Lincoln declared, "'A house divided against itself cannot stand.' I believe this government cannot permanently endure half slave and half free." Lincoln, however, was not an abolitionist; neither he nor any other Republican politician advocated interference with slavery in the South. But Lincoln was opposed to the expansion of slavery under any circumstances, and he vigorously condemned both the Dred Scott decision and the doctrine of popular sovereignty. In Lincoln's view, slavery must be contained because it was morally wrong, economically inefficient, and politically divisive.

Such a position may not appear to be radical today. At the time, however, the Constitution recognized the legality of slavery. And short of a Constitutional amendment abolishing slavery, or a revolution (neither of which seemed likely), opposition to further expansion of slavery was the most advanced political position any major candidate could then take within the American Constitutional system.

The high point of the Lincoln-Douglas debates was reached at Freeport, Illinois, when Lincoln asked Douglas a crucial and embarrassing question. In light of the Dred Scott decision, Lincoln queried, "Can the people of a United States Ter-

ritory in any lawful way . . . exclude slavery from its limits prior to the formation of a State constitution?"

If Douglas answered yes he would incur the wrath of southern Democrats, who contended that the Dred Scott decision had once and for all made it unconstitutional for Congress—and hence a territorial legislature, which was a creature of Congress—to exclude slavery from the territories. Yet, if he said no, he would publicly repudiate his own doctrine of popular sovereignty, which Democrats had used so effectively since 1850. It was a doctrine that had satisfied northern Democrats that the territories would eventually become free states and at the same time allowed them to recognize the theoretical right of slaveholders to settle in the territories. This principle united the northern and southern wings of the party and enabled them to avoid conflict on such an explosive and divisive issue.

Douglas's reply at Freeport was ingeniously devised, considering the circumstances. Slavery, he answered, could not be excluded from the territories by Congress. Even so, since the Supreme Court's decision had not clearly defined the duties of a territorial legislature, such a body could either pass laws to protect slavery or could refuse to enact a slave code. If a territorial legislature refused to pass laws protecting slavery, few slaveholders would risk the consequences of settling in such a territory.

Douglas's reply, which became known as the Freeport Doctrine, seemed a clever answer to a shrewd question. He had retained the support of his northern followers (which did result in his reelection to the Senate) and he had not repudiated the Dred Scott decision. Nevertheless, Douglas was well aware that his answer lost him support in the South. Leading southern politicians were furious because he had not endorsed the South's interpretation of the Dred Scott ruling. Moreover, the Freeport Doctrine further divided the already disunited Democratic party. As for Lincoln, he emerged from the debates with a national reputation and became a prime candidate for the Republican Presidential nomination in 1860.

For Douglas to win the Democratic Presidential nomination in 1860, he had to find a way to regain southern support. He believed that if northern

Democrats adopted the southern position they would lose the election; thus he refused to abandon the doctrine of popular sovereignty. Hoping to convince southerners to modify their position, Douglas reasserted the doctrine in an article in *Harper's New Monthly Magazine* in 1859.

Douglas argued again that popular sovereignty was still a viable political position, since the Dred Scott ruling had not defined the powers of territorial legislatures, only those of Congress in the territories. If and when the Supreme Court made a decision on this subject, Douglas declared, he would abide by its ruling. Historian Robert R. Russel points out that Douglas's interpretation of the Dred Scott case was reasonable and defensible: the problem was would the South accept it. If not, the chances of the Democratic party remaining united in the face of the Republican threat in 1860 were dim indeed.

John Brown's raid on Harpers Ferry. In 1859, while both Democratic and Republican leaders were working out their strategy for the coming Presidential compaign, electrifying news startled the nation. On October 16, John Brown, the chief architect of the Pottawatomie Massacre, had descended on Harpers Ferry, Virginia, with eighteen men, capturing the federal arsenal and killing five people. Buchanan rushed a force of Marines, commanded by Colonel Robert E. Lee, to Harpers Ferry. After a two-day siege, in which ten of Brown's followers were killed, Brown was captured and turned over to Virginia authorities.

As details of the raid became public, it was learned that Brown had hoped to stir up a slave insurrection in Virginia and then wage a war of liberation from the mountains. A cache of nearly four hundred rifles and revolvers and nearly a thousand pikes was discovered on a nearby Maryland farm, and, in addition, authorities seized dozens of Brown's letters which revealed that he had received encouragement and material aid from several prominent northern abolitionists. Among these were the so-called Secret Six—Dr. Samuel Gridley Howe, Theodore Parker, Gerrit Smith, Thomas Wentworth Higginson, George L. Stearns, and Franklin B. Sanborn. None of these men knew the time or place that Brown would strike, nevertheless, they were well aware that he planned to take violent action.

John Brown himself, after Governor Henry Wise of Virginia decided he was sane, went to trial for murder and treason against the state of Virginia. Throughout his trial, in which he behaved with restraint and dignity, Brown consistently maintained that his only purpose had been to free the oppressed. He was found guilty, and on December 2, 1859, was hanged, thus assuring his martyrdom.

Reaction to Brown's raid. At first, reaction in both the North and the South tended to be that Brown's raid was the isolated and criminal act of a deranged man. Republican leaders went to great lengths to condemn the raid. Senator Henry Wilson of Massachusetts was so disturbed upon hearing the news that he commented: "Brown's invasion has thrown us, who were in a splendid position, into a defensive position. If we are defeated next year we shall owe it to that foolish and insane movement of Brown's." In Virginia, Governor Wise himself had at first dismissed the raid as an isolated event with no particular political significance. He had considered simply declaring Brown insane and committing him to an asylum.

But the relative calm that had characterized the initial reactions to Brown's act soon gave way to intense feelings. In the South, the incident conjured up visions of slave insurrections and "Black Republicans" destroying slavery at all costs. C. Vann Woodward notes that "the South had been living in a crisis atmosphere for a long time. It was a society living in the grip of an insecurity complex, a tension resulting from both rational and irrational fears." In a similar vein, Roy F. Nichols concludes that Brown's raid was enough to convince many southerners that Brown was "in the pay of the Republican Party." Southerners believed, writes Nichols, that northerners "were plotting slave uprisings in the South, and if the Republicans came into power they would send other John Browns into slave territory to rouse Negroes to arson, rapine, and murder."

Such fears may have been irrational, but they were not dispelled by the attitudes of some northerners. Although most Republican politicians continued to denounce Brown's raid, prominent northern abolitionists, including Emerson, Thoreau, and the militant Boston reformer Wendell Phillips, used the event to heap invectives upon the South and slavery.

John Brown was brought to trial for treason and murder in Charlestown, Virginia, in November 1859. Most witnesses agree that at his trial he behaved with great dignity. Even a southern observer at his trial remarked that his "bearing was admirable."

Throughout the trial Brown defended himself. At the beginning of his trial, however, Brown was asked whether he had any legal counsel or if he wanted counsel. Following is his answer:

"Virginians, I did not ask for quarter at the time I was taken; I did not ask to have my life spared. The Governor of the State of Virginia tendered me his assurance that I should have a fair trial, but under no circumstances will I be able to attend to my trial. I have no counsel, I have not been able to advise with any one. I know nothing about the feelings of my fellow prisoners, and am utterly unable in any way to attend to my own defense.

"My memory don't serve me. My health is insufficient, though improving. If a fair trial is to be allowed us there are mitigating circumstances that I would urge in our favor, but if we are to be tried by a mere form, a trial for execution, you might spare yourselves the trouble. I am ready for my fate; I do not ask a trial. I beg for no mockery of a trial, no insult, nothing but that which conscience gives or cowardice would drive you to practice. I ask again to be excused from the mockery of a trial. I do not know what the special design of the examination is; I do not know what is to be the benefit of it to the Commonwealth. I have now little further to ask, other than that I may not be foolishly insulted, as only cowardly barbarians insult those who fall into their power."

Brown himself was characterized as a martyr by many abolitionists, who wrote and spoke in vindication of his cause. In a speech in Concord, Massachusetts, just before Brown was executed, Thoreau eulogized Brown:

I am here to plead his cause with you. I plead not for his life, but for his character, his immortal life; and so it becomes your cause wholly, and is not his in the least. Some eighteen hundred years ago Christ was crucified; this morning, perchance, Captain Brown was hung. These are two ends of a chain which is not without its links. He is not Old Brown any longer; he is an angel of light. I see now that it was necessary that the bravest and humanest man in all the country should be hung. Perhaps he saw it himself. I *almost fear* that I may yet hear of his deliverance, doubting that if a prolonged life, if *any* life, can do as much good as his death.

As C. Vann Woodward points out, Brown became "a symbol of the moral order and social purpose" of many abolitionists who were beginning to reject their pacifist principles in favor of violence if necessary to purge the nation of its sins.

Although abolitionist views did not represent majority opinion in the North, numerous southern leaders interpreted them as such. As the election of 1860 approached, southern leaders, especially those in the lower South, warned that if a Republican were elected in 1860, they intended to secede from the Union and establish a new southern nation.

5 The South Leaves The Union

1. What were the provisions of the Republican platform in 1860? How did it differ from their platform of 1856? To what can these differences be attributed?

2. For what reasons and on what basis did the states of the lower South secede? Do you think these reasons were justified?

3. At what point had the situation deteriorated so far as to make war inevitable?

4. What measures could national leaders have taken to save the Union prior to the outbreak of hostilities? At what point would they have had to take these measures?

The election of 1860 was perhaps the most crucial in the nation's history. Although the Republicans as yet had no effective national party machinery, their strength in the North had increased substantially since 1856, aided in part by growing dissension between the northern and southern factions of the Democratic party. When dissension split the party into two factions, the only hope of preventing a Republican victory lay in the possibility that the Republicans would not receive a majority in the electoral college. If that happened, the election would be decided, as it had been in 1824, by the House of Representatives.

The Republican position on slavery. The Republican National Convention met in Chicago in May 1860. William H. Seward of New York was the leading contender for the nomination. But because he had espoused the "higher law" doctrine during the debates leading up to the Compromise of 1850 (page 210), he appeared to be more radical than he actually was. As a result, on the third ballot, the convention delegates turned to Abraham Lincoln, in part because he was a less controversial figure than Seward. The Republican delegates also believed that Lincoln had the best chance to carry Illinois and Indiana, which the Republicans had lost in 1856. The Republican platform of 1860, however, was far more comprehensive and far more radical on the slavery issue than the platform had been four years earlier.

In the economic sphere, the platform called for a high tariff, homestead legislation, and nationally sponsored internal improvements, including a transcontinental railroad. These planks, none of which had been included in the 1856 platform, were designed to appeal to dissatisfied economic interest groups who might hesitate to support the Republican party if opposition to slavery expansion was its only campaign pledge.

In 1856, the Republicans had declared that Congress had the power to regulate and the duty to exclude slavery in the territories. In 1860, however, they asserted that the Fifth Amendment automatically outlawed slavery in the territories. The platform completely denied "the authority of Congress, of a territorial legislature, or of any individuals, to give legal existence to slavery in any territory of the United States." It further declared that the Dred Scott decision was "a dangerous political heresy, at variance with the explicit provisions [of the Constitution]. . . ." As Robert R. Russel has pointed out, the Republican position in 1856 was not without historical precedent, for Congress had indeed excluded slavery from the territories in 1787 and again in 1820. The position taken by the Republicans in 1860, however, was not only a "more intransigent" one, but had absolutely no basis whatsoever in the nation's previous legislative and judicial history.

Precisely why the convention adopted what Russel calls such a "historically indefensible" position has never been explained. Certainly, the Republican position reveals a growing antagonism toward the South and an absolute refusal to go along with the Dred Scott decision. Also, from a political point of view perhaps the Republican "harder line" against slavery expansion appealed to a majority of voters in the free states. In this sense, it is possible that the militant Republican position on slavery reflected a rising antislavery sentiment. Whatever the reasons for the Republican stand, Lincoln himself did not subscribe to this more radical view. As Russel observes, Lincoln had consistently "advised acquiescence in the Dred Scott decision (understanding it as he did to protect slavery in the territories) until it should be overruled by a more responsible court." (In his inaugural address in 1861, Lincoln repudiated this plank of the platform.)

The Democratic party is shattered. The Democratic National Convention first convened in April 1860, in Charleston, South Carolina. Douglas entered the convention as the leading candidate, with over half the delegates pledged to him. But, as the convention had done in 1844 with Van Buren, it ruled that the successful candidate had to muster a two-thirds majority, an unlikely possibility. The northern and southern wings of the party each had its own platform, and neither was prepared to yield on any major point.

The northern (or Douglas) platform reiterated Douglas's position that the Supreme Court had not yet decided the extent of the powers of a territorial legislature and that when it did northern Democrats would support its ruling. Meanwhile, popular sovereignty was still a legal and viable doctrine for resolving sectional differences.

Southern Democrats were not willing to accept the Douglas platform. They stuck to the position they had maintained all along—that the Dred Scott ruling had resolved the issue of slavery in the territories once and for all.

Not only did the southern platform deny the right of Congress or territorial legislatures to impair the personal or property rights of citizens, it also declared "that it is the duty of the Federal Government in all its departments, to protect, *when necessary*, the rights of persons and property in the Territories." As Russel observes:

The Southern platform thus *did not* demand the passage of a congressional slave code for the territories, as has so often been carelessly asserted. It *did* contain a resolution which would justify making a demand for a congressional slave code *if* and *when* such a code should seem *necessary*.

Even so, the northern and southern platforms were poles apart. When the northern Democrats finally adopted the Douglas platform in Charleston, delegates from eight states in the South withdrew. The convention was then adjourned until June, when it reconvened in Baltimore. It was clear to everyone that unless the party could unite, the Republicans would probably win the election. Southern delegates, however, would not accept Douglas as the party's candidate and again they withdrew, this time to Annapolis, Maryland, where they nominated John C. Breckenridge of Kentucky for President on their own platform.

The split in Democratic ranks created a fourth party, the Constitutional Union party, whose strength was concentrated in the border states, where the Whig tradition was still strong. The party adopted no platform, simply pledging itself to uphold the United States Constitution. John Bell of Tennessee was nominated for President.

It seemed possible that with four parties in the field, the election might be thrown into the House of Representatives; but that was not to be the case. When the election was over, Lincoln had swept the North and the West. Breckenridge took the South, with the exception of Virginia, which went to Bell, and two of the border states. Bell also carried two of the border states while Douglas took one, Missouri. Lincoln, however, won the Presidency by only 40 percent of the popular vote. Equally important, the Republicans did not command a majority in Congress. Clearly, they were in no position to threaten the South, even if they had been inclined to do so.

The lower South secedes. As a result of the election, the seven states of the lower South—South Carolina, Alabama, Georgia, Mississippi, Louisiana, Texas, and Florida—were no longer willing to remain in the Union. According to southern political theory, which stemmed in part from the Virginia and Kentucky resolutions of 1798 (page 111) and the nullification crisis of 1833 (page 140), the United States was a confederation of sovereign states which were legally entitled to withdraw from the Union if, in their judgment, their rights or security were threatened.

On December 20, 1860, South Carolina, after calling a special convention whose members voted unanimously to secede, withdrew from the Union. The other six states of the lower South followed South Carolina, and in February 1861, delegates from all seven states met in Montgomery, Alabama, and established a new nation—the Confederate States of America.

The Confederate states systematically took control of all federal property and installations in their territory with two important exceptions—Fort Sumter, in the harbor of Charleston, and Fort Pickens, in the harbor off Pensacola, Florida. President Buchanan took no steps that might lead to open hostilities, and worked closely with congressional leaders, hoping to arrange compromise solutions that would persuade the Confederate states to return to the Union.

On the other hand, Confederate authorities tried to pressure Buchanan into surrendering Forts Sumter and Pickens. The President steadfastly refused; he was determined to maintain these installations as symbols of federal authority.

Attempts at compromise. Meanwhile, in Congress, feverish attempts were made to formulate

These photographs of Lincoln cover a span of only eight years, beginning in 1857 with the famous "tousled hair" pose (top left). The burden of leadership was beginning to reveal itself in the portrait at top right, taken in 1860. At bottom, Lincoln poses with his son Tad in 1864, and the final portrait shows a careworn President four days before his assassination.

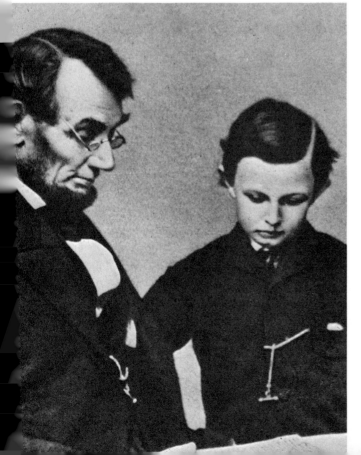

The Confederacy

States seceded before fall of Ft. Sumter

States seceded after fall of Ft. Sumter

Union States

Slave states remaining in Union

Territories adhering to Confederacy

Territories under Union control

Dates indicate date of secession

ALIGNMENT OF STATES AND TERRITORIES, 1861

acceptable compromise proposals. Senator John J. Crittenden of Kentucky proposed three Constitutional amendments, the most important of which would have guaranteed the existence of slavery in the South in perpetuity and would have extended the Missouri Compromise line of 36° 30' to the Pacific.

Southerners from states of the upper South—Virginia, North Carolina, Arkansas, Tennessee—which had not yet seceded, indicated their willingness to accept these proposals if the Republicans would do so. Several moderate Republicans agreed tentatively, subject to the approval of the President-elect, who indicated he would support a Constitutional amendment guaranteeing the security of slavery in the South. But Lincoln refused to endorse the idea of extending the Missouri Compromise line.

Lincoln argued that such an agreement would encourage imperialistic southern ventures in the Caribbean and Central America in an effort to add new slave states to the Union. Privately, he wrote to one congressman:

Prevent as far as possible, any of our friends from demoralizing themselves and our cause by entertaining propositions of any sort on 'slavery extension.' There is no possible compromise upon it which but puts us under again and leaves us all our work to do over again. On that point hold firm, as with a chain of steel.

Lincoln was well aware that any such compromise, which would have violated the Republican platform, might well destroy the party. Many antislavery radicals made it clear that they were prepared to withdraw from the Republican coalition and start a new antislavery coalition if the party failed to live up to its campaign pledges.

In addition, Lincoln overestimated the strength of Unionist sentiment in the lower South. He believed that secession was little more than a threat by southern extremists to gain unrealistic concessions and that once it became clear that the Republicans would not yield, the lower South would voluntarily return to the Union. After all, he reasoned, the Democrats would still have a majority in Congress, and for the time being at least, a majority on the Supreme Court was favorable to southern interests.

In Lincoln's first inaugural address, he made a stirring appeal to the states of the lower South to return to the Union. He called upon the "mystic chords of memory, stretching from every battle-field, and patriot grave, to every living heart and hearthstone, all over this broad land," and expressed the hope that such sentiments "will yet swell the chorus of Union." In addition, he said:

I have no purpose, directly or indirectly, to interfere with the institution of slavery in the States where it exists. I believe I have no lawful right to do so, and I have no inclination to do so. . . . In your hands, my dissatisfied fellow countrymen, and not in mine, is the momentous issue of civil war. The government will not assail you. You can have no conflict, without being yourselves the aggressors.

The war begins. Almost immediately after assuming office, however, Lincoln had to face the fact that Fort Sumter and Fort Pickens could not hold out indefinitely without fresh provisions. Like President Buchanan, Lincoln was determined to hold both forts. After one unsuccessful relief expedition to Fort Pickens, Lincoln ordered an expedition to Fort Sumter. Although he realized that Confederate batteries might fire upon Union ships, thus touching off a war, he nevertheless believed that the loss of Fort Sumter, even by default, would mean virtual acquiescence in secession. Lincoln reasoned that if the Confederates allowed Sumter to be reprovisioned, Union authority would be maintained in the South, and war might yet be avoided through negotiation.

If the Confederates attacked the relief expedition, however, the onus for starting the war would rest upon the South. In the end, the Confederates were not willing to tolerate Union troops in Charleston harbor, and on April 12, 1861, at 4:30 A.M. Confederate batteries opened fire on Fort Sumter. After a forty-hour bombardment, Union forces evacuated the fort. The first act in the gigantic struggle that was destined to last four long years had taken place. War had come at last.

6 Historians Interpret The Causes Of The Civil War

1. What makes the study of historical forces which produce change such a difficult operation?

2. To what factors do each of the various schools of historical thought attribute the causes of the Civil War?

3. What is the position of Stanley Elkins on the causes of the Civil War?

4. What are the strengths and weaknesses of each of these interpretations of the causes of the Civil War?

"If the search for the causes of a crisis such as the Civil War is one of the most absorbing historical problems," writes historian Kenneth M. Stampp, "it is also one of the most exasperating." What Stampp means is that the study of history is not an exact science. The forces that produce change, conflict, and war cannot be measured with mathematical precision. A historian who records or interprets human events is a fallible human being whose outlook is determined by many factors: the climate of public opinion during the era in which he writes, his social and educational background, his own values and experiences, the availability of evidence, and his ability to understand and analyze it.

In this section we shall consider the findings and conclusions of representative writers of three major schools of twentieth-century historical thought, as well as the views of a few historians who do not fit into any particular school. Only a few of the ideas expressed by these historians are new (the participants in the sectional crises of the 1850's and the war voiced strikingly similar opinions). Nevertheless, we shall try not only to differentiate between diverse points of view, but also to assess the merits of each.

The economic determinists. Charles A. Beard, writing in the 1920's and 1930's, was perhaps the most influential writer among the economic determinists who saw the war as an "irrepressible conflict" in which northern capitalism inevitably triumphed over southern agrarianism. Beard was a social reformer whose views were influenced by the politics of the Progressive era during the early 1900's (Chapter 17).

He was disturbed that the rapid industrialization of the United States after 1865 had produced grave social injustices that the national government did little to correct. In Beard's view, politics and wealth were controlled by an economic elite which had gained and consolidated its power at the expense of farmers, laborers, businessmen, and the professional middle class. Beard reasoned that if this economic determinism were true of the Progressive era, it must also have been true of earlier periods of American history.

In *The Rise of American Civilization* (1927), written in collaboration with his wife, Beard portrayed the Civil War as a "social cataclysm in which capitalists, laborers, and farmers of the North and West drove from power in the national government the planting aristocracy of the South." Prior to 1860, the planter aristocracy, with the support of the farmers of the North and West, controlled the national government. But by 1860, the capitalists of the North and the farmers of the North and West had joined forces.

According to Beard, the basis of this alliance was strictly economic. As evidence of this, he cited the Republican platform of 1860 (page 229), which proposed measures the southern-planter aristocracy had opposed for years. Thus, Beard concluded, war between these conflicting economic systems was inevitable. After the war, however, northern farmers and laborers had cause to regret their alliance with capitalists, for they came to suffer serious economic reverses at capitalist hands. But in 1860, all northern economic interest groups believed they were acting in their own self-interest.

As for slavery, Beard discussed it in economic rather than moral terms, concluding that the ethics of slavery was not a basic issue in the years before the war. In addition to Beard, the works of historian Vernon L. Parrington and some of the writings of another historian, Louis M. Hacker, present similar theories.

The revisionists. Economic interpretations of the causes of the Civil War remained influential during the 1930's and 1940's. However, during the 1930's another school of thought emerged—the revisionist interpretation, which looked upon the Civil War as a "repressible conflict" caused by blundering politicians and mindless fanatics. The principal architects of revisionism were James G. Randall and Avery O. Craven.

The revisionists were profoundly influenced by events of the post-World War I era. People became disillusioned with war as a means of settling international disagreements. In revisionist writing, the disillusionment with war as a positive force was combined with the ideas of the Viennese psychiatrist Sigmund Freud, who argued that men often acted from irrational, and indeed, subconscious forces. Randall wrote that "the desire for war is artificial, unnatural and abnormal." Similarly, Craven believed that the differences between nations are never so great that ideological or moral issues have to produce conflict. The causes of war cannot be discovered, Craven concluded, if historians "omit the element of abnormality, or bogus leadership or inordinate ambition for conquest. . . ."

Applying this thesis to the Civil War, both Randall and Craven contended that blundering politicians, fanatical abolitionists, and southern extremists, or "fire eaters," produced mass hysteria. Thus, economic, social, or political differences did not produce war in 1861, but only provided "the materials with which passions worked." Slavery, Randall declared, was utterly insignificant as a moral issue and as a major cause of the Civil War.

Both Craven and Randall were critical of southern extremists, but they particularly condemned such northern antislavery radicals as William Lloyd Garrison and John Brown. Craven remarked that "Garrison . . . if living today could profitably consult a psychiatrist." Influenced by Freudian concepts, Craven characterized Garrison as a social outcast, deprived of childhood opportunities, whose life "would have probably been spent in protesting even if slavery had never existed." Yet, said Craven, the militant antislavery doctrines of one individual would gradually "seep into the subconscious of a whole people." As for John Brown, Randall believed that if he were not actually insane, at the very least he was an obsessed, unbalanced fanatic.

Moral urgency of the slavery issue. During the 1940's, another group of historians, rejecting the views of economic determinists and revisionists, revived the traditional antebellum thesis that the moral urgency of the slavery question was the primary cause of the Civil War. The rise of modern totalitarianism in the 1930's and its defeat in World War II convinced a number of historians that democratic nations must sometimes meet aggression with force if they are to survive. In part, the views of such liberal northern historians as Bernard de Voto, Arthur Schlesinger Jr., and Russell B. Nye on the causes of the Civil War also reflected their own involvement in the civil rights movement, which was beginning to reemerge as a major issue in American eyes.

De Voto rejected the ideas of revisionist historians as a "regression, a deterioration of general ideas in American history." Schlesinger was even more outspoken. He declared:

. . . when a society based on bond slavery acts to eliminate criticism of its peculiar institution, it outlaws what a believer in democracy can only regard as the abiding values of man. A society closed in the defense of evil institutions thus creates moral differences [between itself and the society outside it] far too profound to be solved by compromise. Because the Revisionists felt no moral urgency themselves, they deplored as fanatics those who did feel it, or brushed aside their feelings as the artificial products of emotional propaganda.

Schlesinger concluded by pointing out that an absolute standard for judging institutions does not always exist, but that certainly human slavery was "one of the few issues of whose evil we can be sure." Slaveholders refused to compromise; war then was inevitable.

Russell B. Nye reformulated the abolitionist argument that the South was an aggressive slavocracy conspiring "to destroy civil liberties, control the policies of the federal government, and complete the formation of a nationwide ruling aristocracy based on a slave economy."

Nye conceded that no highly organized, deliberately planned conspiracy existed; the South was never so completely united in purpose. Nevertheless, claims Nye, the abolitionist charges were essentially correct. What, asks Nye, could have been more natural or more dangerous than a union between slaveholders and unscrupulous northern capitalists? And he concluded that the results of the Dred Scott decision "clinched the evidence," because the "slave power" had crossed the Mason-Dixon line, bent on extending slavery throughout the United States and even into the Caribbean and Central America.

Sinister as this purpose was, Nye maintains that the aim of the slavocracy was not merely to perpetuate black slavery, for human bondage was not just a matter of race, but a condition by which the strong enslaved the weak. He agrees with the abolitionist charge that there was a real danger that slavery would be extended to the white labor force. For the first time in the history of the American republic, an impasse had been reached, and slavery had to be destroyed if liberty was to be preserved.

Other interpretations. As we have seen, a majority of twentieth-century historians writing from the 1920's on were inclined toward *monistic* interpretations—that is, they emphasized one major factor, while excluding or downgrading the importance of other influences. As already noted, the arguments of most twentieth-century historians differed very little from those of the actual participants in the Civil War.

A few prominent historians, such as Arthur C. Cole and Carl Russell Fish, rejected the monistic approach. They argued that the North and South were separate and distinctive civilizations, and not one factor, but a combination of forces—social, economic, moral, and political—made conflict inevitable. Nevertheless, such attempts to combine conflicting points of view were not unanimously accepted in historical circles. One notable exception, however, was the publication in 1959 of Stanley Elkins's controversial and innovative *Slavery: A Problem in American Institutional and Intellectual Life.*

First of all, Elkins expressed his belief that war came in 1861 because of "the estrangement of the North and South over slavery." But did the moral urgency of the slavery question make the Civil

War inevitable? Elkins answers no. Was it the result of fear, hatred, and hysteria aroused by the extreme doctrines of abolitionists and southern "fire eaters?" Again Elkins answers no. In fact, Elkins contends that a healthy society needs, indeed must have, its moral passion and fanaticism if meaningful social change is to occur. If this is true, what fatal flaw existed in American society to prevent a peaceable transition from slavery to freedom?

Elkins believes that the political and institutional structure of American society, which placed a premium upon states' rights and individual enterprise was at fault. In other words, the absence of strong national institutions prevented politicians and reformers from treating slavery as a national problem, and "blocked off all concrete approaches to problems of society." If politics, reform, law, religion, and financial power had been rooted along national or inter-sectional lines, sufficient power might have been mustered "to resist a sectional movement." In the end the issue of slavery could be resolved only by secession and war.

Elkins is not a determinist in the sense of Charles A. Beard or members of the moral-urgency school of historians. Nevertheless, considering the lack of national institutional arrangements at that time in the nation's history, Elkins concludes that although war was not preordained, ultimately it became unavoidable.

Evaluating the theories. In attempting to evaluate the validity of the conclusions of the various interpretive schools of thought, there are three important points to keep in mind. First, a distinction must be made between the causes of sectional conflict and the causes of secession and war. Second, monistic interpretations of history are often valid, but only up to a point. Human motivation is far too complex to be explained solely in economic, political, social, ideological, or psychological terms. Third, there are still many unanswered questions about the causes of the Civil War.

The economic determinists rightly point out that sectional differences over such issues as the tariff, internal improvements, and western lands produced conflict. That these issues alone "inevitably" led to war is extremely doubtful. The sections of the country had succeeded in resolving

their differences on economic questions on numerous occasions without violence. Moreover, economic determinists seem to have confused results with causes: the fact that industrial capitalism emerged from the war in a commanding position does not prove that the war itself was caused by economic forces.

Revisionist historians also have a valid point. The politics of the 1850's were indeed characterized by unparalleled extremism, violence, and high emotionalism. Yet, Craven and Randall deal with these forces as if they were generated in a vacuum, and as if all men who opposed slavery on moral grounds were social misfits or unbalanced fanatics, which they were not. Schlesinger, de Voto, and others of the moral-urgency theory quite properly criticized the revisionist historians for their failure to see that in a society professing democratic ideals, opposition to slavery was not abnormal. Does this mean, however, that the moral urgency of the slavery question made war inevitable?

Stanley Elkins correctly emphasized that all human societies have often resolved (or failed to resolve) serious economic, moral, and ideological problems without resorting to war. Elkins's thesis is indeed a brilliant attempt at bringing together all these ideas. While admitting that moral, economic, and political differences were important in precipitating the crisis, he correctly observes that most previous historians had failed to appreciate the importance of the institutional environment in which passions worked.

Yet, no historian can maintain beyond reasonable doubt that strong national institutions would have guaranteed a peaceable transition from slavery to freedom. Certainly Great Britain, with its much-vaunted institutional structure, was not able to resolve its relations with Ireland by peaceable means. In the end, violence won Ireland its independence.

It is a valid generalization (although there are important exceptions) that most historians in the 1960's and early 1970's are convinced that if slavery had not existed, the Civil War would not have occurred. But none has explained precisely why, during the 1840's and 1850's, Americans were unable to resolve their differences over slavery and slavery expansion, as they had done in 1787 and again in 1820. Equally important, during the 1830's abolitionists were mobbed on numerous occasions in the North; and yet, in striking contrast was the fierce northern resistance to the Fugitive Slave Law during the 1850's!

Why had attitudes changed so much? This is one of the most crucial unanswered questions historians must probe in depth. Of equal importance, why did the South secede, especially when Lincoln's election represented no immediate threat to the South or slavery? And why did the North fight to preserve the Union rather than allow peaceful secession? Historians have offered many different answers to these last two critical questions. But so far no definitive answers have been given. Perhaps none will ever be found. But, as Kenneth M. Stampp says:

. . . the prospect of a continuing debate, however much it may annoy those who find it disagreeable to live with uncertainties, offers the best promise that research and writing in this period of American history will continue to have vitality.

■ CONCLUSION

The firing on Fort Sumter in April 1861, was the culmination of nearly ten years of increasing violence. Following the passage of the Kansas-Nebraska Act in 1854—the most crucial year of the decade—the United States seemed inexorably propelled toward secession and Civil War. The resulting furor over the Kansas-Nebraska Act destroyed the Whig party and inaugurated fierce guerrilla warfare in Kansas. The North, infuriated by the Dred Scott decision, refused to accept it as a final solution to the question of slavery in the territories. And the South adamantly rejected the doctrine of popular sovereignty, the principle which had held northern and southern Democrats together. Finally, the Democratic party was hopelessly shattered, and the Republicans came into power.

As already noted, Americans had always in the past been able to compromise the many political and economic issues that aroused sectional conflict, including the issue of slavery. What, then, made the politics of the 1850's so distinctive was the inability of political leaders and the people to resolve their conflicts. For the first time, Americans had been confronted by a problem so deep and divisive that they could not find a solution except through civil war.

■ QUESTIONS

1. What issues separated the North and South in the 1850's?

2. What incidents enflamed sectional feeling in the decade prior to the Civil War?

3. What changes in the political structure of America occurred between the election of Franklin Pierce and that of Abraham Lincoln?

4. What arguments can be presented to show that the Civil War was or was not inevitable?

5. How have the causes of the Civil War been explained by leading historians?

6. Why were political leaders in the 1850's unable to resolve the conflicts facing the nation?

■ BIBLIOGRAPHY

STOWE, HARRIET BEECHER, *Uncle Tom's Cabin: or Life Among the Lowly,* Collier. This book touched off bitter controversy in the North and South, and it should be considered as a valuable social document and be read to see what caused such extreme reactions.

MCKETRICK, ERIC L., ed., *Slavery Defended: The Views of the Old South,* Prentice-Hall (Spectrum Books). To understand the position of the South prior to the Civil War, students can study the views of the major apologists for slavery included in this volume.

GENOVESE, EUGENE D., *The World the Slaveholders Made: Two Essays in Interpretation,* Pantheon. The author is one of the few Marxist historians in the United States today, and his controversial views may be of interest to students.

ROZWENC, EDWIN D., ed., *Causes of the American Civil War,* Problems in American Civilization, Heath. Especially designed for high school students, this edition has many useful and varied articles on causation.

CUBAN, LARRY, ed., *The Negro in America,* Scott Foresman. This excellent book provides exceptional understanding of the black's role in America, not only in the nineteenth century, but also through to the present.

BOTKIN, B. A., *Lay My Burden Down: A Folk History of Slavery,* U. of Chicago Press. Before the last of the ex-slaves died, researchers in the twentieth century tried to capture their personal reminiscences of slavery and emancipation through individual interviews. This book gives a glimpse of slave life and folklore as the ex-slaves remembered it, rather than as contemporary commentators might try to reconstruct it.

NYE, RUSSELL B., *William Lloyd Garrison and the Humanitarian Reformers*, Library of American Biography, Little, Brown. Although there were many important abolitionists and the reform movement reached beyond the slavery issue, it is most often that one associates reform with abolition and abolition with Garrison. Nye, however, is able to put Garrison in perspective, and through this readable biography one meets many leaders and their wide ranging interests.

MCCLOSKEY, ROBERT G., *The American Supreme Court*, U. of Chicago Press. McCloskey presents a good interpretation of the Dred Scott case, particularly as it relates to the role of the Supreme Court in American life. The book itself is a history of the Supreme Court, and students should refer frequently to it as other important judicial issues are discussed in the text.

The Civil War

On July 4, 1861, Abraham Lincoln declared in an address to Congress: "Our popular government has often been called an experiment. Two points in it . . . have already [been] settled—the successful *establishing*, and the successful *administering* of it. One still remains—its successful *maintenance* against a formidable internal attempt to overthrow it." He then asked for $400 million and 400,000 volunteers to suppress the rebellion.

Unlike many of his more optimistic countrymen, Lincoln did not expect the war to be over in six months. The North was faced with imposing problems. Raising, training, and equipping a fighting force from inexperienced volunteers and finding effective military leadership would take time. And the navy—virtually nonexistent in 1861—had to be reshaped into a strong blockade force. Although northern industrial capacity was superior, enormous problems were involved in organizing this industrial machine and bringing it to bear against the South.

In addition, it was uncertain what the attitude of Europe would be. European nations were aware that the United States, if it remained united, was destined to be a major power in world affairs. They might intervene, seizing this chance to disrupt and weaken the country. Also, the possibility that Britain, dependent on southern cotton, might intervene in favor of the South, was a cause of concern.

Another important factor was the strength of northern unity. Many expected a short war. Should the conflict be prolonged, disillusionment and war-weariness might cause the North to falter. In addition, northerners did not agree on whether it was to be a war for union alone or for the destruction of slavery as well. Most northern Democrats opposed fighting an antislavery war, while many Republicans wanted to transform the war into an antislavery crusade. Although the initial northern response was unity to preserve the Union, potentially divisive forces existed. It remained to be seen whether the Lincoln administration could successfully cope with them. In tracing the course of the Civil War, keep these questions in mind:

1. At the outset, what were the strengths and weaknesses of the North? of the Confederacy?
2. Why did the early campaigns end in a stalemate?
3. What controversial political and economic actions were taken by Lincoln in the course of the war?
4. Why was the North finally victorious?

1 The South Faces Northern Strength

1. How realistic were the hopes of northern and southern leaders relative to the course and duration of the war?

2. Why were the border states valuable to the North?

3. What advantages did the North have at the beginning of the war? What advantages did the South have?

4. What problems did the Confederacy face in 1861?

On April 15, 1861, only three days after the Confederates fired their first shots at Fort Sumter, Lincoln called upon loyal governors to provide 75,000 ninety-day volunteers "to maintain the honor, the integrity and the existence of our national Union." Within a month, the President increased the size of the regular army, requested 42,000 three-year volunteers for Federal service, and ordered a blockade of the ports of all states in rebellion.

The lines are drawn. The states in the upper South condemned the President's decision to use force to maintain the Union and joined the Confederacy. When Virginia seceded, Richmond became the new capital of the Confederacy. In the border slave states of Missouri, Kentucky, Maryland, and Delaware, the people were divided in outlook, but Unionist sentiment prevailed. Moreover, the western counties of Virginia repudiated secession, organized a provisional government, and launched a movement for statehood which culminated in 1863 in the admission of the new state of West Virginia into the Union.

The manpower resources and the strategic value of the border states were of the utmost importance. The city of Baltimore was a vital transportation center which connected Washington with the Northeast and was also the eastern terminus of the Baltimore and Ohio Railroad. The B & O crossed Maryland and western Virginia, providing the only direct link between Washington and the Midwest. In addition, the occupation of western Virginia was necessary to protect the Ohio River Valley, and to guard the western flank of Union armies operating in Virginia's Shenandoah Valley. Kentucky and Missouri not only served as buffer zones between the Confederacy and the Union states, but were also important bases of operations for invading the heartland of the Confederacy via the Mississippi, Tennessee, and Cumberland River valleys.

In the early months of the war, Kentucky, torn between its loyalty to the Union and its cultural and economic ties with the South, attempted to remain neutral. Although neutrality could not be maintained indefinitely, Lincoln respected Kentucky's position for the time being. He believed that time and circumstances would lead the state to declare unequivocally for the Union. In addition, Lincoln feared that any abrupt move would strengthen secessionists in the state. Lincoln's policy of "watchful waiting" paid off. When a Confederate army violated Kentucky's "neutrality" in September 1861, by occupying the town of Columbus in the western part of the state, Kentuckians rallied to the Union banner in overwhelming numbers. Ultimately, Kentucky provided nearly 100,000 men for Federal service, compared to only 25,000 for the Confederate army.

In Maryland, western Virginia, and Missouri, however, Lincoln chose to use military force to assure Union control. In Missouri, Union forces disarmed pro-Confederate units of the state militia, drove the pro-southern governor into exile, and set up a military district. In western Virginia, an army of 30,000 Ohio volunteers, commanded by General George B. McClellan, easily routed smaller Confederate forces and took the region. In Baltimore, after a pro-Confederate mob fired on Massachusetts troops en route to Washington, Lincoln ordered Federal troops to use all necessary means, including "the bombardment of their cities," and the suspension of *habeas corpus*, to maintain control of Maryland.

Throughout the summer of 1861, persons suspected of traitorous activities were arbitrarily arrested. During the autumn congressional elections, Union troops rigorously policed the polls, preventing suspected southern sympathizers from voting. Such acts may have been unnecessary, for the voters of Maryland cast their ballots for unconditional Union candidates by large majorities.

Northern advantages. Holding the border states for the Union was one critical advantage which gave the government cause for confidence in the early stages of the war. Another was the fact that northern military potential far outweighed that of the Confederacy. The loyal states contained a population of some 23 million; the South had only 9 million people, of whom nearly 4 million were slaves of doubtful loyalty. Moreover, the North possessed nearly 80 percent of the nation's manufacturing plants, the vast majority of its skilled workers and mineral resources, and an extensive railway network which permitted the rapid transport of troops and supplies between the eastern and western military theatres.

Northern superiority could not be brought to bear immediately, however. Mobilizing a nation for war required time. In 1861, the North was little more than a giant in swaddling clothes. In addition, most northern generals in the early years of the war were no match for their southern counterparts. The Confederacy made a fortunate choice of military leaders; in the North it was a kind of process of trial and error before any great Union generals emerged.

Northern commanders in the eastern theatre of war proved to be either overcautious or incompetent. And the defensive nature of the war fought by the South gave southern generals an advantage. Some historians refer also to the existence of a military tradition in the South, and relatively speaking, a greater interest in military training than in the North. Even Union naval power, which eventually provided an effective blockade of southern ports and permitted large-scale army and navy operations against Confederate forces in the Mississippi Valley, was virtually nonexistent in 1861.

Confederate problems. In the early stages of the war, the South was able to confront northern manpower and firepower on the battlefield on virtually equal terms. The Confederates gained large quantities of munitions by seizing Federal arsenals in the South, and for a brief time, additional arms were acquired from Europe.

Besides, the South was not required to conquer the North in order to maintain its independence. It needed only to defend successfully its own soil against invading armies. Confederate leaders believed that by inflicting heavy casualties on northern armies, the South could make the price of victory higher than the North was willing to pay. The Confederates believed that the war would be short, ending in peace negotiations that would recognize southern independence. Early Confederate victories, engineered by such brilliant generals as Robert E. Lee and Thomas J. "Stonewall" Jackson, contributed greatly to the Confederates' unrealistic evaluations of their own strength.

In addition, southern leaders not only expected Great Britain to recognize their independence, but also believed that because of British dependence

In 1863, the war was still going fairly well for the South, and a proud General Robert E. Lee found time to pose for the full-length photograph at the right. It was taken around the time that Lee had successfully repulsed another attempt on the part of the Union to capture the Confederate capital of Richmond. The painting below shows several other talented southern military leaders surrounding the President of the Confederate States of America, Jefferson Davis. Entitled *Equestrian Group of Confederate Officers*, this picture was an imaginary scene created by an unknown artist. The leaders he gathered together on canvas are General Pierre G. T. Beauregard and General Thomas J. "Stonewall' Jackson, to the left of Davis, and General J. E. B. Stuart and General Joseph E. Johnston to the right. Two of these generals, Stuart and Jackson, would not survive the war; Stuart was felled by Union fire and Jackson shot by his own men, who mistook him at nighttime for the enemy.

on southern cotton, Britain would eventually intervene in the war on the South's behalf. One Confederate governor astonished British officials when he declared: "A failure of our cotton crop for three years would be a far greater calamity to England than three years' war with the greatest power on earth." It is true that Britain imported 75 percent of its cotton from the South, and in time, cotton shortages did create economic distress in Britain; however, the South's reliance on the power of "King Cotton" proved to be an illusion (page 254).

As the war progressed, it became increasingly clear that the South could not survive a long war of attrition. Confederate soldiers fought magnificently, but mounting casualties, the ultimate failure of cotton diplomacy, and dire shortages of clothing, food, medicine, and weapons brought about by the successful Union blockade slowly weakened the South's capacity to fight. Yet, critical shortages of men and materiel were not the only handicaps under which the Confederacy labored.

Conflicts within the Confederacy. Jefferson Davis, President of the Confederacy, was not an ideal war leader. He quarreled continuously with members of his cabinet (seventeen different men occupied six cabinet positions in four years), with members of the Confederate Congress, and with the governors of the southern states. Moreover, Davis, who had served in the Mexican War, fancied himself a military strategist. He often interfered, with disastrous results, in the conduct of military operations.

Davis made his most serious error, however, right at the beginning of the war. Acting on the theory that cotton shortages would force British intervention, Davis sanctioned an embargo on the shipment of cotton to Europe at a time when the Union blockade could not prevent such shipments. Sale of southern cotton in Europe during the early part of the war would have provided millions of dollars in foreign exchange, badly needed to purchase supplies and establish the Confederate government's credit abroad. By the time it became clear that the self-imposed cotton embargo was a blunder, the Union blockade was capable of preventing large-scale shipments to Europe.

Despite his handicaps, however, Davis was by no means primarily responsible for the failure of the Confederate government to exercise effective leadership. Historian Frank L. Owsley has concluded that the Confederacy died from "states' rights disease"—that is, the political theory the southern states used to justify secession became a serious liability during wartime. The Confederate Constitution explicitly recognized state sovereignty. This provision proved to be a major obstacle for Davis, since many southern governors placed a higher premium on maintaining state sovereignty than on winning the war. Davis, for instance, was widely denounced throughout the South when he suspended *habeas corpus* and attempted to restrict travel within the Confederacy.

The most serious problem caused by states' right disease, however, was the failure of southern governors to enforce the Confederate Conscription Act of 1862. When the number of Confederate volunteers declined sharply after the first few months of the war, the Confederate Congress made military service mandatory for all white males between the ages of eighteen and forty-five. Governor Joseph Brown of Georgia not only refused to allow Confederate authorities to enforce the draft in his state, but also on more than one occasion ordered Georgia troops away from battlefronts to harvest crops or to defend their "native land" from possible invasion.

At one point, Brown even informed the Confederate secretary of war that the Georgia state army "was an organization of gallant, fearless men, ready to defend the state against usurpation of power [by the Richmond government] as well as invasions of the enemy." He even implied that Georgia would be justified in seceding from the Confederacy because of the "centralizing tendencies" of the Davis administration.

In addition to "states' rights disease," the Confederacy died from a number of other factors—not the least of which was northern power. But it cannot be denied that the short-sighted views of southern governors like Brown, who carried the doctrine of states' rights to its logical but disastrous extreme, helped to undermine the Confederate war effort. With the problems the Confederacy faced, it is remarkable that it was able to wage war effectively for nearly four years.

2 No Victor Emerges In The Early Campaigns

1. Why were Union operations in the East unsuccessful during the first two years of the war?

2. What significant victories were won by the Union forces in the West during this period? Why were they important to the northern cause?

3. Which generals emerged as successful strategists and executors of plans in the early years of the war? Why were they successful?

On June 29, 1861, Lincoln ordered General Irvin McDowell to attack Confederate forces concentrated at Bull Run Creek near Manassas Junction, Virginia, an important railroad center about thirty miles southwest of Washington. McDowell's army, the Army of the Potomac, was formed in the summer of 1861 and composed primarily of untrained volunteers. The Army of the Potomac, with headquarters in Washington, would carry out offensive operations in Virginia throughout the war.

Initial northern strategy. Both McDowell and General Winfield Scott, the commander-in-chief, opposed Lincoln's plan, arguing that an advance by an army of nearly 38,000 untrained volunteers invited disaster. Scott, in fact, did not want to launch offensive operations in Virginia at all. He urged the President to raise and equip a well-trained army of 300,000 men whose primary objective would be to capture the Mississippi Valley. Scott reasoned that control of this vital artery of commerce, in conjunction with an effective naval blockade, would cut the Confederacy in two and squeeze it into submission.

Lincoln recognized the merits of Scott's "Anaconda Plan" (named for the Anaconda python, a snake that crushes its victims to death), but the President was under terrific pressure from the northern press and Washington politicians to act immediately. Besides, the Confederates had only 22,000 men at Manassas Junction, and they were no better trained than the Union volunteers.

Lincoln believed that the Confederate army could be outflanked and forced to retreat.

On July 21, 1861, the Army of the Potomac clashed with Confederate forces in the First Battle of Bull Run (see battle maps, page 246). McDowell's army seemed to be near victory when Confederate reinforcements arrived. The Union army began to withdraw. What began as an orderly retreat soon gave way to panic, and the green northern forces disintegrated into a confused mob, stampeding back to Washington.

The Union defeat at Bull Run created jubilation throughout the South and despair in the North. Lincoln, however, was not easily shaken by adversity. On the day after the battle, he announced that immediate steps would be taken to strengthen the Union blockade and to organize military campaigns to attack the enemy on three fronts—Virginia, east Tennessee, and the Mississippi Valley.

In 1861, most northern strategists believed that their major military objective in the East was to take the Confederate capital, not to destroy Confederate armies. The theory was that the capture of Richmond and the occupation of sizeable portions of Confederate territory would demoralize the South. Hence, between 1861 and 1863, the Army of the Potomac launched four offensive operations against Virginia. And each time faulty strategy or heavy casualties caused Union generals to retreat.

Moreover, in the first years of the war, Union offensives were not well coordinated. When the Army of the Potomac suffered defeat in northern Virginia, weeks or months would pass before it was ready to resume the attack. This allowed the Confederates to divert thousands of troops to counter Union offensives in the West until Richmond once again was threatened. This situation changed when Ulysses S. Grant became commander-in-chief in 1864. Until then, however, Confederate forces in the East, under Robert E. Lee, inflicted staggering setbacks on a succession of Union generals.

The Peninsula Campaign. Following the Battle of Bull Run, Lincoln removed General McDowell and replaced him with General McClellan. McClellan was a vain and arrogant young man who held all his superiors in contempt, including the President himself. Lincoln, aware of McClellan's feelings, once remarked: "I will hold McClellan's horse if he will bring us victory." Unfortunately, McClellan was not the man for the job.

Although he was an excellent administrator who organized the Army of the Potomac into an efficient fighting force, he was an overcautious, timid commander. Fearful of failure, he consistently exaggerated the enemy's strength and underestimated his own. Not until early April 1862, after months of delay, was he ready to take his army into the field.

While McClellan was preparing his army, the North had been thrown into near panic by a Confederate attempt to break the blockade. On March 8, the ironclad warship *Virginia* slipped out from Norfolk into Hampton Roads, Virginia. Constructed on the hull of an abandoned Union ship (the *Merrimac*), this iron monster, with a ram attached to her, created havoc among the Union's wooden blockade ships. The next day when the *Virginia* went out to finish the job she was confronted by a Union ironclad—the *Monitor*—built in a New York shipyard while the Confederates were reconverting the *Merrimac* into the *Virginia*. In a two-hour battle, the ironclads fought to a draw, and the *Virginia* retreated to Norfolk. (She was finally scuttled by the Confederates when Union forces took Norfolk in May.)

Overnight, the nature of naval warfare had been revolutionized; wooden ships had now become obsolete. Unfortunately for the South, it did not have the resources to build other ironclads. The North did, however, and used them very effectively in the naval blockade of the South and in the western campaigns, especially in the Mississippi Valley.

A month after the battle of the ironclads, McClellan transported his army of more than 100,000 men to the peninsula between the York and James rivers in Virginia and prepared to march on Richmond. His overall strategy in the Peninsula Campaign was sound. Landing his army on the peninsula omitted a march through rugged terrain, eliminating problems of fatigue and supply and the possibility of severe opposition during an overland march. It was McClellan's execution of the plan, not the plan itself, that was the major weakness.

Moving cautiously up the peninsula, the Union army met only light resistance. Finally, on May 31, the Confederates engaged McClellan about five miles east of Richmond in the Battle of Seven Pines. The attack was repulsed, and the Confederates under Robert E. Lee waited nearly a month for McClellan to attack. But the Union general, convinced that his army was outnumbered, wired Lincoln that he would not attack until he received reinforcements. Actually, the reverse was true. Lee was never able to muster more than 90,000 soldiers to defend Richmond.

Lee believed that his only chance lay in inflicting heavy losses on McClellan and forcing him to retreat. Well aware of McClellan's overcautious tendencies, Lee took the chance that he would not counterattack. On June 26, at the opening of the Seven Days' Battle, Lee attacked and was bloodily repulsed. McClellan was now in an excellent position to take Richmond. The Union commander, however, still convinced he was badly outnumbered, would not advance. Instead, not having received the requested reinforcements, McClellan ordered a retreat.

As McClellan retreated toward the James River, Lee attacked. Twice, the Union army inflicted heavy losses on the Confederates. Still McClellan retreated, leaving the field to the astonished Confederates. Finally, in mid-July, the Army of the Potomac evacuated the peninsula and returned to Washington. By refusing to assume the offensive and eventually leaving the peninsula, McClellan lost a golden opportunity to deal the Confederates a crippling blow. He won all the battles but lost the campaign by default.

Union disasters in the East. Instead of relieving McClellan of command, Lincoln simply created a new army, the Army of Northern Virginia, under the command of General John Pope. In August Pope boldly advanced toward Richmond, and fell into a carefully laid trap near Manassas Junction. After suffering some 16,000 casualties at the Second Battle of Bull Run, Pope retreated to Washington. He was relieved of command, and his army was disbanded.

Then, in September, Lee astonished the North by launching an invasion of Maryland. Hoping to weaken northern morale, he also believed that a Confederate victory on northern soil would hasten British recognition of the Confederacy. And he expected to capture large quantities of badly needed arms and supplies. Lee reasoned

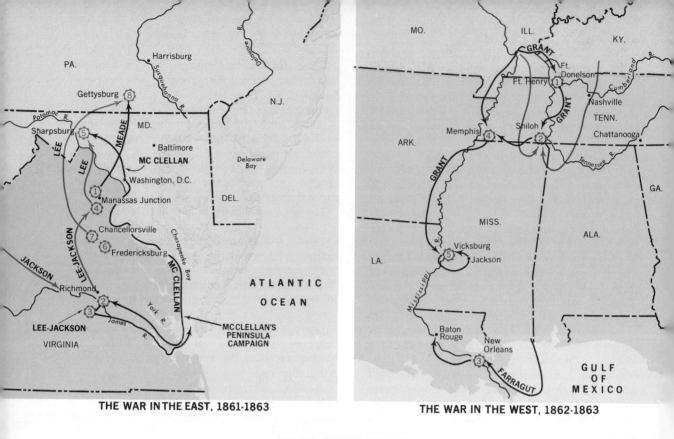

THE WAR IN THE EAST, 1861-1863

THE WAR IN THE WEST, 1862-1863

THE CIVIL WAR

▨ Confederate States	→ Confederate Moves
▨ Union States	→ Union Moves
	⬡ Battle Sites

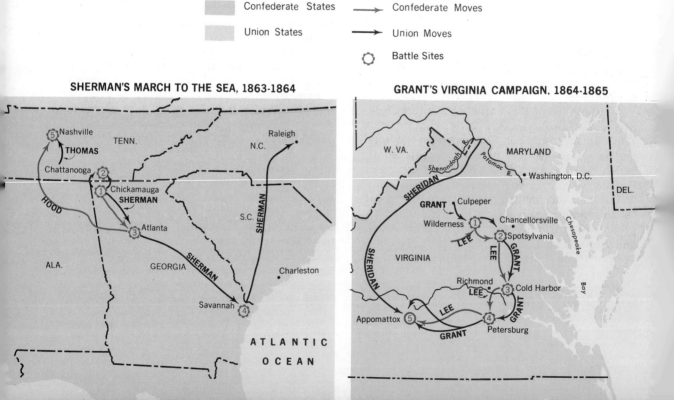

SHERMAN'S MARCH TO THE SEA, 1863-1864

GRANT'S VIRGINIA CAMPAIGN, 1864-1865

THE CIVIL WAR

THE WAR IN THE EAST, 1861-1863

① **July 21, 1861. Bull Run.** Union forces advance on Confederates at Manassas Junction. Union attack fails. Union army retreats to Washington.

② **May 31, 1862. Seven Pines.** Union army, under General McClellan, advancing to Richmond (Peninsula Campaign) is attacked by Confederates 5 miles outside the city. Both sides suffer losses.

③ **June 26-July 2, 1862. Seven Days' Battle.** Confederates under Lee and Jackson repeatedly assault McClellen's troops, forcing them to retreat. Union's attempt to take Richmond is thwarted and Peninsula Campaign fails.

④ **Aug. 29-30, 1862. Second Bull Run.** Union army tries to reach Richmond by land. At Manassas Junction Union army is defeated by Lee and Jackson and retreats to Washington.

⑤ **Sept. 17, 1862. Antietem Creek.** Lee advances to Maryland (planning to invade Pennsylvania) and is caught by McClellen near Sharpsburg. Lee's invasion plan is thwarted and he withdraws to Virginia.

⑥ **Dec. 13, 1862. Fredericksburg.** Attempting to move on Richmond via Fredericksburg, Union forces are defeated in a series of attacks on Lee's men.

⑦ **May 2-4, 1863. Chancellorsville.** In another attempt to take Richmond, Union troops fail to break Lee's lines.

⑧ **July 1-4, 1863. Gettysburg.** Attempting to invade the North, Lee advances to Pennsylvania. At Gettysburg he is forced into battle by General Meade. Lee is defeated and retreats to Virginia.

THE WAR IN THE WEST, 1862-1863

① **Feb. 1862. Fts. Donelson and Henry.** Union troops capture Ft. Donelson and Ft. Henry.

② **April 6-7, 1862. Shiloh.** Confederates attack Grant at Shiloh, taking him by surprise. After a day of fighting Grant receives reinforcements and Confederates are forced to withdraw.

③ **April 26, 1862. New Orleans.** Union Admiral Farragut takes New Orleans and proceeds up the Mississippi River, capturing Baton Rouge.

④ **June 6, 1862. Memphis.** A Union fleet defeats a Confederate fleet and takes the city, leaving the upper Mississippi in Union hands.

⑤ **July 4, 1863. Vicksburg.** Grant moves down the Mississippi, and, after many unsuccessful assaults on the city, takes Vicksburg, putting the entire Mississippi River in Union control.

SHERMAN'S MARCH TO THE SEA, 1863-1864

① **Sept. 19-20, 1863. Chickamauga.** Union Generals Rosencrans and Thomas maneuver Confederates out of Chattanooga and pursue them into Georgia. The armies clash at Chickamauga, where Confederates crack Union lines. Union forces retire to Chattanooga and Confederates beseige the city.

② **Nov. 23-25, 1863. Chattanooga.** Grant (with the armies of Hooker, Thomas, and Sherman) drives the Confederates back into Georgia.

③ **Sept. 2, 1864. Atlanta.** Sherman invades Georgia, with Confederates in pursuit. Hood evacuates Atlanta and Sherman takes the city.

④ **Nov. 14-15, 1864. Nashville.** Hood pursues Thomas into Tennessee. At Nashville, the Union army virtually destroys Hood's forces.

⑤ **Dec. 22, 1864. Savannah.** Sherman takes Savannah, and marches up through the Carolinas.

GRANT'S VIRGINIA CAMPAIGN, 1864-1865

① **May 5-6, 1864. The Wilderness.** Lee outmaneuvers Grant, but battle is indecisive.

② **May 8-12, 1864. Spotsylvania.** Grant meets Lee in another indecisive battle.

③ **June 1-3, 1864. Cold Harbor.** Grant assaults Lee's army and is bloodily repulsed.

④ **June 15-18, 1864. Petersburg.** Failing to take the city, Grant begins a 9-month siege. Unable to lift the siege, Lee withdraws in March, 1865.

⑤ **April 9, 1865. Appomattox.** Surrounded by Union troops, Lee surrenders to Grant.

247

that McClellan's army "will not be prepared for offensive operations—or he will not think it so—for three or four weeks." However, learning the details of Lee's plans, McClellan for once advanced rapidly. On September 17, 1862, along Antietam Creek, near Sharpsburg, Maryland, he hurled 70,000 men against Lee's army of 40,000.

The Confederates held their ground, inflicting 12,500 casualties on the Union army; Lee's own losses during this bloodiest day of battle in the entire war were 13,500. Characteristically, McClellan again refused to order a final assault, which almost certainly would have crushed Lee's gallant troops. Content with having repelled Lee's invasion, McClellan allowed the Confederates to withdraw across the Potomac into Virginia. When the Union general failed to comply with Lincoln's order to cut off Lee's retreat, an angry and disillusioned President relieved McClellan of command.

To replace McClellan, Lincoln chose General Ambrose Burnside. Doubting his own ability for supreme command, Burnside accepted reluctantly. Once again the Army of the Potomac moved south toward Richmond. In mid-December, at Fredericksburg, Burnside hurled his troops against Lee's nearly impregnable positions. The result was another terrible slaughter, and the Army of the Potomac reeled back toward Washington.

The President next chose Joseph "Fighting Joe" Hooker, who boasted, "My plans are perfect. May God have mercy on General Lee, for I will have none." By late April 1863, with an army of nearly 150,000 men, Hooker moved south. Early in May, Lee's outnumbered army met his at Chancellorsville, and in a three-day battle inflicted 17,000 casualties on the Union forces. Had Hooker thrown in his reserves against Lee's troops, the Union forces might have won, but he lost his nerve and ordered a retreat.

When Lincoln learned of the defeat he cried out, "My God! My God! What will the country say? What *will* the country say?" Yet, at Chancellorsville, the Confederates too had suffered. They lost one of their most brilliant generals, Stonewall Jackson, accidentally killed by one of his own men. A military genius of the first rank, his death alone was a disastrous blow to Confederate hopes for ultimate victory. By the spring of 1863,

the war in the East had resulted only in a bloody stalemate, and the end was nowhere in sight.

Victory in the West. While General Lee was thwarting Union commanders in the East, Union army and naval forces operating in Kentucky and Tennessee won a series of victories that opened the Mississippi Valley to conquest. Early in 1862, Union forces drove the Confederates from western Kentucky and captured the key Confederate positions of Fort Henry on the Tennessee River and Fort Donelson on the Cumberland River. These expeditions were carried out by a combined land and naval force under the command of General Ulysses S. Grant and Commodore Andrew H. Foote.

The strategic importance of these victories cannot be exaggerated. Western Tennessee had been reconquered, and Union forces were now in a position to carry the war into the lower reaches of the Mississippi Valley. Once the lower Mississippi Valley was taken, the Confederacy would be cut in two—a devastating blow to southern hopes of final victory.

More immediately, the Union victories forced the Confederate army in northern Tennessee to abandon its positions around Nashville and retreat south toward Mississippi. Grant, with an army of 45,000 men moved in pursuit. In early April 1862, Grant halted at Shiloh, Tennessee, to await reinforcements. There, at dawn, on April 6, a Confederate army completely surprised the Union forces. During the first day's battle, Grant's army was severely pressed. On the following day, however, reinforcements arrived and the Union army rallied. The Confederate forces, their commander killed in the battle, retreated into Mississippi.

Two weeks after Shiloh, Admiral David G. Farragut's naval squadron captured New Orleans, the Confederacy's largest city and principal seaport. Soon thereafter, Baton Rouge was taken, and in June, Memphis fell to another naval squadron. Thus, by the summer of 1862, the Confederacy was reeling from a series of staggering defeats in the West. The remaining Confederate stronghold in the West was Vicksburg, Mississippi. Its capture would cut the Confederates off from men and supplies from Louisiana, Texas, and Arkansas, and prevent shipment of supplies from Europe via Mexico. Vicksburg, however, would not fall

Matthew Brady was a prominent photographer prior to the Civil War. When the war began, he and his assistants traveled with the Union armies, becoming probably the first combat photographers. One of them, Alexander Gardner, was at the Battle of Antietam in September 1862, and took the photo at right of Lincoln talking with General George B. McClellen following that battle. The photo below left of General Ulysses S. Grant, his wife, and youngest son Jesse was taken by Brady or one of his assistants much later in the war, shortly before the end. Grant's family had come to visit him at Appomatox Manor, City Point, Virginia. General William T. Sherman sat for a Brady portrait in 1864 (bottom right), the same year in which he took Atlanta and began his bloody "March to the Sea" to Savannah.

easily. The Union offensive bogged down, and Confederate commanders were able to seize the initiative in the West. The final outcome of this gigantic struggle was still in doubt.

3 The North Debates Political And Economic Issues

1. Why did Lincoln wait until 1863 to issue the Emancipation Proclamation?

2. What role did blacks play in the Civil War?

3. On what grounds did northern Democrats object to Lincoln's domestic policies and his conduct of the war?

4. What problems were encountered by the Union in recruiting troops during the war?

Not until January 1, 1863, did President Lincoln officially declare that the destruction of slavery was an object of the war. In 1861, such a declaration would have alienated the border states and also hundreds of thousands of northern Democrats and Republicans alike who favored the Union but were not prepared to fight an antislavery war. Because of such attitudes, Lincoln exercised great caution in dealing with slavery.

Steps toward emancipation. When General John C. Frémont, commander of the Department of Missouri, issued a declaration in September 1861, granting freedom to all slaves in his military district, Lincoln repudiated the decree. The President was disturbed by Frémont's attempt to undermine his own power as commander-in-chief and more important, Lincoln was unwilling to risk jeopardizing Unionist sentiment in the border states. As one prominent Kentuckian informed the President: "There is not a day to lose in disavowing emancipation or Kentucky is gone over the mill dam."

Lincoln, however, did take some action against slavery before issuing the Emancipation Proclamation. In early 1862, with his approval, Congress outlawed slavery in the territories and provided for gradual emancipation in the District of Co-lumbia that would compensate owners for their slaves. In addition, Lincoln negotiated a treaty with Great Britain pledging American naval support in suppressing the African slave trade. By July 1862, however, Lincoln became convinced that in order to maintain his leadership of the Republican party, he had to take more decisive action.

In that month the Republican-dominated Congress challenged Lincoln's leadership by passing a sweeping act granting freedom to all slaves of masters engaged in rebellion. Lincoln secured a modification of the bill, and in its final form, the act applied only to slaves of rebels duly convicted in a court of law. Moreover, it could be applied only at the discretion of the President. Nevertheless, congressional pressure led Lincoln to prepare a preliminary draft of the Emancipation Proclamation and present it to his Cabinet. While it was approved unanimously, Lincoln accepted the advice of Secretary of State William Seward to await a Union military victory before issuing it, so that it might have the greatest possible psychological effect.

Meanwhile, the New York newspaper editor Horace Greeley, unaware of Lincoln's plans, wrote an editorial entitled "The Prayer of Twenty Millions." Since slavery was the major cause of the war, Greeley declared, it was "preposterous and futile" not to take more decisive steps to destroy it. In his reply to Greeley, the President took the opportunity to explain his war aims. Lincoln had often expressed his own *personal* wish that all men everywhere could be free." As President, however, he attempted to occupy a middle ground between conservative Unionists and radical antislavery idealists.

Lincoln did not expect to create a consensus in the North. He fully expected severe criticism from the antislavery radicals in his own party and conservative northern Democrats. What Lincoln hoped to prevent was the fragmentation of northern political opinion to the point where irreconcilable differences on slavery would seriously jeopardize the war effort. Slavery, Lincoln believed, was destined to die "by mere friction and abrasion—by the mere incidents of war." He therefore appealed constantly to the American people for unity, based on the Jacksonian dictum that "the Union must and shall be preserved."

Only from this vantage point can Lincoln's reply to Greeley be understood:

My paramount object in this struggle *is* to save the Union, and is *not* either to save or destroy slavery. If I could save the Union without freeing *any* slave I would do it; and if I could save it by freeing some and leaving others alone I would also do that. What I do about slavery . . . I do because I believe it helps to save the Union; and what I forebear, I forebear because I do *not* believe it would help save the Union.

The Emancipation Proclamation. Lincoln's letter to Greeley was actually an attempt to prepare the American people for the most dramatic pronouncement of the war. On September 22, 1862, only five days after the Union victory at Antietam, the President issued his preliminary emancipation proclamation. Unless the rebels laid down their arms before January 1, 1863, the President declared, he would issue a final proclamation declaring all slaves in those areas of the South still under Confederate control "forever free." As Lincoln was well aware, the Confederacy had no intention of giving up its struggle for independence. Offering the South the opportunity to do so, however, permitted him to emphasize once again, for the benefit of his Democratic critics, that the preservation of the Union, not the destruction of slavery itself, was his objective.

Between September and the January deadline, however, Republicans suffered a severe political setback when Democrats made major gains in local and congressional elections (page 252). Many antislavery radicals began to fear that because of these Republican defeats Lincoln would not issue the final decree. But the President did not falter; he signed the Emancipation Proclamation as scheduled, describing it as a "fit and necessary war measure," and an "act of justice, warranted by the Constitution upon [grounds] of military necessity."

Most Democrats were outraged, and many Republicans caustically pointed out that the proclamation applied only to areas under Confederate control—which was true—areas in which it could not be enforced. Although Lincoln did specifically exempt the border states and certain areas in the South that were already under the control of Union forces, he nevertheless had clearly committed the nation to the destruction of slavery. It was now up to the force of Union arms to see the task through.

Black soldiers. A relatively little-known provision of the Emancipation Proclamation was Lincoln's announcement that black soldiers would now be recruited into the Union army. As the poet Henry Wadsworth Longfellow wrote after watching a regiment of black soldiers parade in Boston: "An imposing sight, with something wild and strange about it, like a dream. At last the North consents to let the Negro fight for freedom." And black soldiers did indeed fight with distinction, taking part in 449 separate actions during the war.

At first, because of widespread doubts that blacks would fight well, it was planned to use them as garrison and supply troops. However, the valor of black soldiers in such battles as Port Hudson and Milliken's Bend in Louisiana and Fort Wagner in South Carolina dispelled such fears. In commenting on the battle of Milliken's Bend, Assistant Secretary of War Charles Dana wrote that "the bravery of the blacks in the battle . . . completely revolutionized the sentiment of the army with regard to the employment of negro troops." At Fort Wagner, in July 1863, a black regiment, the 54th Massachusetts, distinguished itself by leading a charge and fighting tenaciously. Although the attack ultimately failed, the battle was widely hailed throughout the North for the courage the 54th had shown against overwhelming odds.

By 1865, approximately 186,000 black soldiers were serving in the Union army. Of this number nearly 38,000—or more than 10 percent of all Union war deaths—were either killed in battle or died from wounds and disease. In spite of their sacrifices and the respect and admiration they won, black soldiers were still discriminated against. Their units were segregated, and most of their officers were white. At first they were paid only half as much as white soldiers; when this was rectified in 1864, they were still not given back pay. And not until the end of the war did black soldiers receive bounties (payments to enlist or reenlist) as white soldiers did.

The Confederacy, of course, bitterly resented the use of black troops against the South. As the result of a Confederate order that black soldiers be treated as rebellious slaves, some captured troops were executed. Finally in 1864, the Confederacy agreed to treat black captives like other prisoners of war.

Democratic opposition. The elections in the fall of 1862 had given the Democrats control of the legislatures of several key midwestern states and the governorships of the crucial states of Ohio and New York. Moreover, in the House of Representatives, Democratic victories had reduced the Republican majority to only nine votes. Although the bitter opposition of most northern Democrats to Lincoln's emancipation policies contributed to these dramatic Democratic gains, other issues were also involved.

Democrats were infuriated by the arbitrary arrest of conservative Democrats unfairly charged with disloyalty, and by the suspension of *habeas corpus* in Maryland and elsewhere. Occasionally, Democratic newspapers that criticized the war policies of the government were suppressed. And Republican newspapers often charged that Democrats were traitorous "Copperheads" (a reference to the copperhead snake, which strikes without warning) who wanted the South to win its independence.

The vast majority of Democrats undeniably favored the preservation of the Union. The Democratic slogan, however, "The Constitution As It Is, And The Union As It Was," indicated that the Democratic party wanted to restore the old Federal Union as it existed in 1860. Such a position was totally unacceptable to the abolitionists and antislavery radicals in Congress who looked upon the Civil War as a long-awaited opportunity to destroy slavery. If slavery was not destroyed, most radicals believed, the Union was not worth preserving. Considering that radicals and Democrats held such divergent views, it is surprising that political partisanship did not impede Lincoln's conduct of the war more than it actually did.

Economic issues also roused the objections of Democrats. As already noted, the Republican platform of 1860 had called for a high tariff, homestead legislation, federally sponsored internal improvements—measures traditionally opposed by the Democratic party, both North and South. With the secession of the South, however, the Republicans had a majority in Congress, and they proceeded to pass several economic measures benefitting the West and the Northeast.

FINANCING THE CIVIL WAR

The North used three principal means of raising money: taxation, the sale of bonds, and the issuance of paper money called greenbacks, which were unbacked by specie. In 1861, the government levied the nation's first income tax—a 3 percent duty on incomes over $800. Later in the war, the rates were increased. A tax was also placed on such items as tobacco and alcohol. Tariff rates were raised in 1861 and again in 1864. Over the course of the war, the North raised about $667 million in taxes.

About $450 million was issued in greenbacks. Without specie backing, however, the value of greenbacks was determined only by faith in the North's credit. Their value fluctuated with the success or failure of the Union armies. At one point, inflation was so severe that each greenback dollar was worth only 35 cents. Most of the North's revenue was raised through bond sales—more than $2.6 billion.

The South relied primarily on the same three money-raising schemes as the North, but ran into much more financial difficulty. Over the course of the war, the South had only $27 million in specie.

In 1861, the Confederate government levied a property tax, but because most southerners objected to such a tax, it was not successful. A measure which required farmers to contribute 10 percent of their produce to the government was of little help either.

Bond issues by the Confederate government did not sell well, because the people had no money. The Confederacy also issued bonds payable in goods such as food and cotton to supply the army. Bonds, including those sold in Europe, raised about $15 million.

Finally, the South issued about $1 billion in Confederate notes—unbacked paper money. But this currency soon became wildly inflated, and by 1863, a barrel of flour sold for $300. At the end of the war, each Confederate dollar was worth only 1.6 cents.

In 1862, Congress enacted the Morrill Tariff, the highest yet to protect American manufacturers. A transcontinental railroad bill (1862) gave large land grants and generous financial subsidies to the Union Pacific, the Central Pacific, and other railway corporations. The Homestead Act (1862) gave, after five years, 160 acres of land to a settler who farmed and improved it, and the Morrill Land Grant Act (1862) gave land to states and territories to support colleges. In addition, Congress passed several measures to help finance the war effort.

These measures were less controversial than issues involving slavery and the suppression of civil liberties during wartime. Nevertheless, overall Republican policies convinced hundreds of thousands of states' rights northern Democrats that Lincoln was a dictator. They believed that the tendencies of the Republican party to centralize power in the national government threatened to destroy traditional and deeply cherished values long held by the Democratic party.

Recruiting soldiers. Although the Union government had a much larger manpower reservoir from which to recruit volunteers, some states, by 1863, were not filling the quotas established by the government. In order to encourage men to volunteer or reenlist, bounties were offered by the Federal government and local governments. In some parts of Illinois, for example, a volunteer was entitled to bounties that exceeded $1,000. Hundreds of men volunteered, collected their bounties, deserted, and then enlisted again under an assumed name in another district or state. Severe penalties, including death in some instances, did little to stop abuses of this system.

Finally, in 1863, because of the failure of the bounty system and the decline in the number of volunteers, Congress passed the Union Conscription Act. Unfortunately, it contained discriminatory features which benefitted the wealthy. Men who had been drafted were allowed to escape military service by hiring a substitute or by paying the government $300. Many poor Americans and newly arrived immigrants who could afford to do neither bitterly resented the draft act, complaining that the Civil War had become "a rich man's war and a poor man's fight." Bloody rioting over the draft erupted in several cities, notably in New York in July 1863.

Many of the early victims of the New York riots were free blacks. Poor workingmen, many of them Irish immigrants, feared the economic competition of the freemen, and vented their wrath against them. In the end, however, the rioters themselves became the chief victims. In three days of savage fighting, hundreds of whites were killed or wounded by New York police and Federal troops before order was restored.

4 The Northern Cause Gains Momentum

1. What role did Great Britain play during the Civil War? Why was Britain's position important?

2. How significant was the Battle of Gettysburg to the outcome of the war?

3. How important were the Union victories at Vicksburg and Chattanooga?

In the first two years of the war, one of the South's greatest hopes and one of the North's greatest fears was the possibility of British intervention. The Confederates believed British dependence on southern cotton would force Britain to break the Union blockade of southern ports. When this happened, southerners reasoned, war between the United States and Britain would break out, thus assuring the independence of the Confederacy. As it turned out, two crises threatened to rupture British relations with the Union during the war, but neither had anything to do with cotton.

Problems with Britain. The first confrontation, known as the *Trent* affair, occured in late 1861 when a Union naval captain illegally removed two Confederate envoys, James M. Mason and John Slidell, from the British mail steamer *Trent* en route to England. International law did allow American vessels to search neutral ships and seize war contraband—arms and munitions. Mason and Slidell, however, could hardly be classified as contraband, and Britain was highly incensed by this violation of its maritime rights. Britain readied a naval squadron, bolstered Canada's defenses, and sent the United States government an ultimatum demanding the release of the two men. The Lincoln administration wisely complied and assured the British prime minister that the United States had intended no insult to Britain's national honor.

The second crisis between Britain and the United States was also a maritime dispute. A number of commerce raiders, among them the *Alabama*, the *Shenandoah*, and the *Florida*, had been delivered in 1862 to Confederate authorities by a British shipbuilding firm. These raiders wreaked havoc upon northern shipping. In fact, Confederate naval vessels destroyed approximately 250 Union merchantmen during the war. The *Alabama* alone, before she was finally sunk in 1864, destroyed more than 50 ships.

Then in 1863, the American ambassador to Great Britain discovered that ironclads for the Confederate navy were being built in Britain. When the ambassador pointed out to the British government that delivery of these vessels would mean war, Britain put a stop to shipbuilding for the Confederacy. Thus, if Britain had wanted war with the United States, either the *Trent* affair or the crisis over the ironclads could have been used to provoke hostilities. In each instance, however, Britain chose a conciliatory course—much to the distress of Confederate officials, who were slow to realize that "King Cotton Diplomacy" (as Frank L. Owsley phrased it) was destined to have no effect on British foreign policy.

Cotton undeniably was important to the British economy. Before the war ended, nearly five million British workers were severely affected by cotton shortages. Great Britain acquired only about 25 percent of its normal cotton needs from India, Brazil, Egypt, and Algeria; the rest came from the states of the Confederacy. Then why did the Confederacy's "King Cotton Diplomacy" fail to influence British foreign policy?

For one thing, British cloth manufacturers had huge stockpiles of cotton on hand when the Civil War began. Shortages, therefore, did not begin to affect the British economy until late 1862. For another, the decline of the cotton industry in Britain was partially offset by expansion in the manufacture of woolen and linen goods. The Union also purchased large quantities of arms, munitions, and other manufactured products from Britain, and Britain purchased large amounts of Union wheat.

Even more important from the British point of view was the question of Canada. To defend Canada from any Union attacks would be costly; also, to strengthen Canada, Britain would have to weaken the British military position in Europe. This discouraged Britain, since serious problems were developing on the Continent which might lead the British to war in Europe. Equally important, during the War of 1812, American privateers had destroyed or captured more than two thousand British merchant ships, and Britain was unwilling to risk such losses in another confrontation with the United States.

In addition, since Confederate commerce destroyers such as the *Alabama* were inflicting heavy losses upon the United States merchant marine, Britain's chief rival in world trade, Britain stood to benefit economically from the misfortunes of its leading competitor. In fact, during the war the American maritime industry suffered losses from which it never fully recovered. After the war an international arbitration commission awarded the United States $15.5 million in damages from the British government in the so-called *Alabama* claims, far less than what the Americans demanded for the damage that the British-built Confederate raiders had inflicted.

Both Confederate optimism and northern fears about British intervention proved in the end to be groundless. One contingency, however, might have induced Britain to intervene: the failure of Union armies to win decisively on the battlefield. As the war entered its third year without significant Union victories, it is possible that Britain would have used diplomatic and military resources to force a settlement favorable to the Confederacy. In late 1862, some members of the British government had taken the position that the North could not win militarily and that to protect Britain's economic relations with the South, intervention was necessary.

Although such proposals were put aside, it was clear that unless the Union won a decided advantage, the interventionist view would gain strength in Britain. Both militarily and diplomatically, 1863 was destined to be the year of decision.

Gettysburg. Despite their proven superiority in Virginia, the Confederates' military prospects were not promising elsewhere by late spring of 1863. In the West, Grant was about to begin his campaign against Vicksburg, and in Tennessee another Union army was threatening Chattanooga, whose capture would open the way for a Union invasion of Georgia and Alabama. Some Confederate leaders urged that part of Lee's army be sent to Tennessee to prevent the loss of Chattanooga and to force Grant to delay or abandon his campaign against Vicksburg.

General Lee, however, had other ideas. He believed that his Army of Northern Virginia ought to seize the initiative by invading the North once again. A successful campaign, Lee contended, would provide his army with badly needed supplies and would relieve pressure on Chattanooga and Vicksburg by forcing the Union army to transfer troops from the west. More important, Lee believed that a major Confederate victory on northern soil would produce shock waves in both Europe and the North. It might lead European nations to recognize the Confederacy's independence; and conceivably, a war-weary North, despairing of victory, might induce the Lincoln administration to agree to a negotiated peace settlement.

In early June, with an army of approximately sixty thousand men, Lee began his march north across Maryland toward the Pennsylvania capital of Harrisburg, on the Susquehanna River. By the end of June, the Confederate army, which had been followed on its march by a Union force, was in southern Pennsylvania. Then, on July 1, near the small town of Gettysburg, Union and Confederate forces clashed.

The Union army, now commanded by General George Meade, occupied excellent defensive positions on high ground just south of Gettysburg and defied Lee to attack such well-fortified entrenchments. To the horror of some of Lee's generals, he chose to do precisely that. On July 2, Lee ordered attacks on both Union flanks. Despite savage fighting and heavy casualties on both sides, the Confederates failed to dislodge the seasoned Union forces. Still Lee persisted, and on

THE RED BADGE OF COURAGE

Stephen Crane's novel *The Red Badge of Courage* is about a battle in the Civil War and a young Union soldier who takes part in that battle. In the following excerpt, the young man's regiment has just repulsed an attack, and there is a lull in the battle:

"Some in the regiment began to whoop frenziedly. Many were silent. Apparently they were trying to contemplate themselves.

"After the fever had left his veins, the youth thought that at last he was going to suffocate. He became aware of the foul atmosphere in which he had been struggling. He was grimy and dripping like a laborer in a foundry. He grasped his canteen and took a long swallow of the warmed water. . . .

"The youth turned to look behind him and off to the right and off to the left. He experienced the joy of a man who at last finds leisure in which to look about him.

"Under foot there were a few ghastly forms motionless. They lay twisted in fantastic contortions. Arms were bent and heads were turned in incredible ways. It seemed that the dead men must have fallen from some great height to get into such positions. They looked to be dumped out upon the ground from the sky. . . .

"A small procession of wounded men were going drearily toward the rear. It was a flow of blood from the torn body of the brigade.

"To the right and to the left were the dark lines of other troops. Far in front he thought he could see lighter masses protruding in points from the forest. They were suggestive of unnumbered thousands. . . .

"As he listened to the din from the hillside . . . and to the lesser clamors which came from many directions, it occurred to him that they were fighting, too, over there, and over there, and over there. Heretofore he had supposed that all the battle was directly under his nose."

July 3, he ordered the now famous "Pickett's charge" against the Union center on a rising stretch of ground called Cemetery Ridge.

Anticipating this maneuver, Meade had strengthened his center with additional troops and artillery. Pickett's division had to cross nearly a mile of open ground before reaching the base of Cemetery Ridge. The Union forces shrewdly permitted the Confederates to advance for nearly half a mile before opening fire. Only a few Confederates reached the crest of Cemetery Ridge before being killed or hurled back. Nearly half of Pickett's division was either killed or wounded, and the rest straggled back to their own lines. Assuming full responsibility for the disaster, Lee mourned: "I thought my men were invincible."

Lee then tried to rally his shattered army, anticipating a Union counterattack. Such an attack had a fair chance of annihilating the Confederates and ending the war in the East in 1863. Meade, however, like McClellan before him, failed to exploit the opportunity, and Lee was permitted to retreat back into northern Virginia.

The fall of Vicksburg. In 1862, Union forces in the West had gained control of New Orleans, Baton Rouge, and the upper reaches of the Mississippi Valley. Only Vicksburg, the last Confederate citadel in the Mississippi Valley, remained to prevent Union forces from controlling the entire Mississippi Valley and cutting the Confederacy in two. As Lincoln expressed his disappointment over Meade's failure to exploit fully his victory at Gettysburg, word came that Grant had taken Vicksburg. Even at that time, Grant's Vicksburg campaign was recognized as a dazzling achievement.

The Confederates considered Vicksburg, high on the bluffs overlooking the Mississippi, an impregnable fortress. Because of rugged terrain, all efforts to take it from the north and east had failed; the only feasible approach was from the south. With the support of Union gunboats, Grant established a base some forty miles south of Vicksburg and prepared to march north on the city. If he delayed too long, however, superior but scattered Confederate forces would have time to concentrate against him.

Traditionally, advancing armies were followed by huge supply trains, but Grant, in a daring and unprecedented move, cut his lines of communication and ordered his troops to live off the land as they advanced. Grant's decision to move quickly and cut loose from his base was virtually unparalleled in the history of warfare, and allowed him to neutralize potentially superior forces. The commander of Vicksburg, instead of combining forces with a Confederate army east of the city, vainly attacked Grant's nonexistent supply line. Thus, Grant was able to position himself between the two forces and deal with each separately. By the end of May, Grant had fought his way to Vicksburg, and after a harrowing forty-seven-day siege, the city surrendered on July 4.

Final victory in the West. Because of his brilliant campaigns, Grant was placed in command of all Union forces in the West. Now that the Mississippi Valley was secure, Union strategy was to dislodge the Confederates from eastern Tennessee and open up the way to drive through the deep South. In the fall of 1863, Grant moved into Tennessee and completely crushed Confederate resistance in the West at the battle of Chattanooga.

In September, a Union force, after suffering defeat at the battle of Chickamauga, was besieged in Chattanooga. Arriving in October, Grant ordered reinforcements and began the assault on the strongly entrenched Confederate forces around the heights of the city. Finally, at the end of November, a part of Grant's army, acting without orders, stormed the precipitous heights of Missionary Ridge, one of the most astonishing feats of the war. To the amazement of both Grant and the Confederate commander, Union troops carried the heights while veteran Confederate soldiers fled in panic.

By the end of 1863, the tide of war had definitely turned. After Gettysburg, Lee would never again be able to launch offensive operations in the North. And Union objectives in Tennessee and the Mississippi Valley had been achieved. The Confederacy was finally cut in two with the loss of Vicksburg, and the fall of Chattanooga had opened the gateway from which to carry the war into Alabama and Georgia. As 1864 approached, the triumph of Union military force appeared to be a certainty.

5 The Confederacy Collapses

1. What was Grant's strategy to end the war? How was it different from that of previous Union commanders?

2. Why was Lincoln successful in gaining re-election in 1864?

3. How did Grant, Sherman, and Sheridan destroy the Confederacy?

The primary military objective of most Union generals in the early years of the war was to capture Richmond rather than to destroy Lee's army. Certainly, the fall of the Confederate capital would have been a blow to southern morale; in addition, the South's largest munitions factory, the Tredegar Iron Works, was in Richmond. Nevertheless, by not destroying Lee's army, Union forces had been driven from northern Virginia time after time.

Grant takes command. Through trial and error, Lincoln had mastered the fundamentals of sound military strategy, and he appointed Grant commander-in-chief of all Union forces in 1864 for two reasons. First, Grant appeared to be the only Union commander capable of successfully planning and directing military strategy on a national scale. And second, Grant, like Lincoln, recognized that the destruction of Lee's armies, not the capture of Richmond, was the key to victory.

Although Grant suffered heavy casualties in 1864, he refused to retreat. Instead he called for reinforcements and maintained unrelenting pressure on Lee. In short, Grant used northern superiority in manpower and materiel to its greatest advantage, offsetting Lee's advantage of conducting defensive operations on familiar terrain. Grant clearly understood that while Lee was capable of winning individual battles, he had neither a sufficient number of troops nor the necessary supplies to resist continuous pressure from a numerically superior and better equipped army over a long period of time.

By the middle of March 1864, Grant had planned the military strategy destined to end the war. He decided to remain with the Army of the Potomac and push into Virginia, engaging Lee in constant battle. Meanwhile, the army under General William Tecumseh Sherman, still in Tennessee, was to march south to Atlanta, inflicting, as Grant ordered, "all the damage you can against their war resources. . . ." Moreover, while Grant was operating against Lee in northern Virginia, another Union army under General Phillip Sheridan was dispatched to the Shenandoah Valley.

One of Sheridan's objectives was to defend Washington from possible attack by a small Confederate army stationed in the valley. More important, Grant ordered Sheridan to burn and destroy crops and farm equipment so that the Shenandoah region, the breadbasket for Lee's army, would be useless. "Eat out Virginia clean and clear," Grant wrote, "so that crows flying over it for the balance of the season will have to carry their own provender [food]." Although these operations, combined with an ever-tightening naval blockade, marked the beginning of the end for the Confederacy, nearly a year's hard fighting still remained, including some of the most savage of the war.

Grant moves south. Grant began his advance against Lee in late March 1864. Lee, outnumbered two to one, did not challenge Grant's advance until the Union army reached an area near Chancellorsville called the Wilderness. In this thick, almost impenetrable forest, Lee stood and fought, inflicting 18,000 casualties upon Grant's army. Unlike earlier Union generals, however, Grant refused to retreat. He regrouped his army, called for reinforcements, and forced Lee to withdraw to the vicinity of Spotsylvania Court House. There the two armies once again fought to a standstill.

Although the losses on both sides were heavy, Grant pressed on, pushing Lee southward to strong defensive positions at Cold Harbor, near Richmond. After being repulsed at Cold Harbor with appalling losses, Grant decided to bypass Richmond and try to take Petersburg, an important rail center several miles south of the Confederate capital. The fall of Petersburg would isolate Richmond and force Lee's army to abandon its well-entrenched fortifications around

Richmond and fight in open country. The end of the war in Virginia appeared to be in sight. Unfortunately, some of Grant's subordinates hesitated to attack just long enough to permit Lee to rush enough reinforcements to Petersburg to prevent its capture. The Confederates held their positions at Petersburg, and Grant put the city under siege.

In a month's savage fighting, Grant's army had advanced sixty miles, fought four major battles, and kept constant pressure upon the Confederates. Yet, he had failed in his major objective: the destruction of Lee's army. True, Lee's force had suffered nearly 40,000 casualties, but Union losses exceeded 55,000. Many northerners, horrified by such staggering casualties and by the lack of decisive results, began to question whether the Union could be preserved by military force.

The election of 1864. In June, Lincoln easily won renomination for the Presidency. As his running mate, he shrewdly chose a Democrat, Andrew Johnson of Tennessee. A staunch supporter of the war, Johnson had served in Congress, was former governor of Tennessee, and had been military governor of that state since 1862. Attempts by militant antislavery radicals to replace Lincoln were accurately described by Lincoln's supporters as a "grand fizzle." Yet, Lincoln and his party (the Republicans called themselves the Union party in 1864) had valid reasons to fear that the Democrats, who had made large gains in the elections two years earlier, were capable of sweeping the national elections in 1864.

In 1862, the Democrats were able to capitalize on Lincoln's war policies and the economic legislation passed by the Republican majority in Congress. In 1864, the Democrats expected to use not only these issues to good advantage, but also the conscription acts, the draft riots, and Grant's failure to end the war. By August 1864, Horace Greeley wrote privately to a friend: "Mr. Lincoln is already beaten. He cannot be elected." Greeley's views were shared not only by thousands of Republicans, but also by the President himself. "It seems exceedingly probable," Lincoln wrote, "that this administration will not be reelected."

Thus, the Democratic National Convention met in Chicago in August 1864, confident of victory. The Democratic platform openly declared that the war was a failure, and advocated immediate steps to arrange a negotiated peace with the South. Contrary to traditional interpretations, the Democrats did not advocate a negotiated peace which recognized the independence of the Confederacy, but rather a negotiated peace on the basis of Union. Nevertheless, the Republicans shrewdly distorted the Democratic platform by arguing that the Democrats were prepared to end the war by recognizing southern independence. As a consequence, General McClellan, the Democratic Presidential nominee, was repeatedly asked to clarify the so-called peace plank.

In reality, the basic difference dividing the Democrats and the Republicans centered on the issue of slavery. Its destruction had became a formal war aim of the Republican party when Lincoln signed the final Emancipation Proclamation. The Democrats, however, were perfectly willing to restore the Union with slavery intact, and attempted on this basis to persuade the South to return voluntarily to the Union in 1864.

Then suddenly war weariness in the North and nagging doubts about the capability of the Union army began to disappear. Although Grant's offensive in Virginia had bogged down at Petersburg, General Sherman had reached his objective in Georgia. In September, he cabled the President: "Atlanta is ours and fairly won." Sherman's capture of Atlanta—in conjunction with Admiral Farragut's seizure of Mobile Bay a month earlier, closing the Gulf coast to blockade runners, and Sheridan's decisive victory in the Shenandoah Valley—further elated the North. These military successes were prime factors in turning the political tide in Lincoln's favor. In popular votes, Lincoln's margin of victory was less than half a million, but in the electoral college he won by the overwhelming majority of 212 to 21.

The last days of the Confederacy. After the fall of Atlanta, Sherman rested his army and contemplated his next move. The Confederate commander in Georgia, having failed to halt Sherman's advance, moved his army back toward Tennessee, confident that Sherman would follow in order to protect Chattanooga. Sherman, however, was not deceived. Dispatching part of his forces north to counter the Confederate offensive, he himself requested permission from Grant to begin his march across Georgia from Atlanta to the sea:

Unless we can repopulate Georgia, it is useless for us to occupy it; but the utter destruction of its roads, houses and people, will cripple their military resources. . . . I can make this march and make Georgia howl!"

Cutting his lines of communication with his base, and living off the land as he advanced, Sherman moved virtually unopposed on a front fifty miles wide and three hundred miles long. He reached Savannah shortly before Christmas. On Christmas Eve, the President received welcome news from the dramatic and ebullient Sherman: "I beg to present you as a Christmas gift the City of Savannah." Meanwhile, in Tennessee, the Union force sent by Sherman virtually annihilated the Confederate army near Nashville, reducing it to a disorganized mob which fled in panic. Effective Confederate resistance in the West had been crushed.

The war now moved to a swift and dramatic conclusion. Leaving Savannah, Sherman marched northward through the Carolinas, meeting only token opposition. In March 1865, Union forces captured Mobile, Selma, and Montgomery in Alabama. And General Sheridan, after completing mopping-up operations in the Shenandoah Valley, joined Grant for the final push on Lee's army. Although Lee realized that the end was near, he made one last effort to free himself from Grant's clutches. Abandoning Petersburg and Richmond, Lee moved westward, hoping to join with a Confederate force in North Carolina. But Grant moved swiftly, blocking Lee's escape routes.

Finally on April 9, 1865, Lee surrendered to Grant at Appomattox Court House in southwestern Virginia. On April 12, Lee's army marched out to lay down its arms. One Union officer later described the scene: "Not a sound of trumpet more, nor roll of drum, nor a cheer nor word nor whisper of vain-glory . . . but an awed silence rather, and breath-taking, as if it were the passing of the dead." Although some Confederate units did not surrender until a few days or even weeks later, the war itself ended at Appomattox. Then, tragically, on the evening of April 14, at the hour of vindication and triumph, Abraham Lincoln was fatally shot at Ford's Theater in Washington by a crazed pro-southern actor

named John Wilkes Booth. The President died the next morning, without ever regaining consciousness.

CONCLUSION

In 1861 not even the most pessimistic observer could have foreseen the hundreds of thousands of lives and the billions of dollars that the war would cost the nation. Before Lee finally surrendered in April 1865, more than 600,000 Americans from a total population of 32 million had lost their lives in battle or from disease. Nearly one of every five northern soldiers and one of every four southern soldiers died; tens of thousands more were maimed, hopelessly crippled, or sick in mind and spirit. Many innocent civilians likewise suffered from the violence and savagery of war. Although the cost was high, the Union had been preserved. The doctrine of secession had been totally discredited, and slavery, a curse to both white and black, had been destroyed.

But the Union victory created as many problems as it solved. At the war's end it remained to be seen what peace conditions would be imposed on the South. The victors were not agreed on what course of action they should take to restore the Confederate states to the Union. Some northerners advocated harsh peace conditions; others a more lenient settlement. Equally important was the status of the former slaves. Although blacks were now free, they were not yet citizens, and it was doubtful that southerners would be willing to accept blacks on an equal basis. The role of blacks in American society remained to be defined. The racial aspects of the years following the Civil War were fraught with significance for the future development of American democracy. And the physical scars of war were destined to heal far more rapidly than the social and psychological scars.

QUESTIONS

1. What were the advantages and disadvantages of the North and the South at the outset of the Civil War? How successful was each side in exploiting these advantages?

2. What were the military strategies of the North and the South in conducting the war? How effective were the two sides in carrying them out?

3. Why was the Confederacy able to wage a four-year war despite its limitations and the strength of the Union forces?

4. To what extent was the North united behind the war effort, and what accounted for any friction?

5. How effective was Lincoln as a war-time President? Explain your answer.

6. What role was played by black Americans in the war?

7. What were the immediate results of the Union victory? What were the probable future consequences?

8. What were the costs of the Civil War to the nation?

9. Considering the costs, was a war designed to preserve the Union and end slavery worth fighting? Why or why not?

▪ BIBLIOGRAPHY

CATTON, BRUCE, *This Hallowed Ground*, Pocket Books. Bruce Catton emerged during the Civil War Centennial as the most popular historian of the Civil War period. He has been able to take an enormous amount of detail and transform it into an exceptional narrative prose. This book covers the Civil War from the Union Army's point of view. He has written numerous other books and articles on the Civil War which also stand highly recommended.

DOWDEY, CLIFFORD, *The Land They Fought For: The South as the Confederacy, 1832–1865*, Doubleday. As Catton has written from the northern point of view, Dowdey writes with a southern perspective. For the complete picture, students should read both versions.

SANDBURG, CARL, *Abraham Lincoln: The Prairie Years and The War Years*, 3 vols., Dell. Abraham Lincoln is an obvious American folk hero, and there are numerous interpretations of his life. In this book, Sandburg combined a warm empathy for the man with a fine literary style to produce a classic study of Lincoln.

FREEMAN, DOUGLAS SOUTHALL, *Lee of Virginia*, Scribners. For the South, Lee was the venerated hero of the Civil War and Freeman is his able biographer. He has immersed himself in the life of Lee as a sympathetic observer and produced a multi-volumed account of Lee. This shortened version is aimed at students in grades seven to eleven and gives the reader a good introduction to Robert E. Lee.

DONALD, DAVID, ed., *Why the North Won the Civil War*, Collier.

——, *Lincoln Reconsidered: Essays on the Civil War Era*, Random House (Vintage Books).

In these two volumes the author and various contributors provide new and interesting insights into the Civil War period. They are good sources for the student who wants to go beyond the general narrative accounts and the laudatory biographies.

FRANKLIN, JOHN HOPE, ed., *The Emancipation Proclamation*, Doubleday (Anchor Books). This is an excellent historical study of the Emancipation Proclamation by a recognized authority in the field. Students may use the book for reference or as an excellent beginning to a research project on the circumstances surrounding Lincoln's decision to go ahead with Emancipation.

CHESTNUT, MARY BOYKIN, *A Diary From Dixie*, ed. by Ben A. Williams, Houghton Mifflin (Sentry Editions). As the Civil War progressed, life in the South became more and more strained. In this diary the author provides a firsthand account of both the leaders of the Confederacy and the southern noncombatants in their reactions to the war.

LIFE DURING THE CIVIL WAR

Equipment, W. L. Sheppard, *c.* 1900

COME AND JOIN US BROTHERS.
PUBLISHED BY THE SUPERVISORY COMMITTEE FOR RECRUITING COLORED REGIMENTS
1210 CHESTNUT ST. PHILADELPHIA.

Union Recruiting Poster

Philadelphia Servicemen's Center

Union Cartridge Factory

As the Civil War began, there was a certain exhilaration in the country, in the North and in the South, for both sides felt their cause was just and worthy of their best men and efforts. Volunteers joined up and civilians encouraged and supported them. All hoped for an early end to it. But as the war wore on, the horrible realities of it became all too apparent to soldiers and civilians alike. Many men did not want to go, and when a draft was legislated to make up for the lack of volunteers, violent resistance resulted in several Union cities. The hoped-for end finally came after four years of bloody combat, horrendous loss of life, and seemingly permanent scars on the national unity.

New York City Draft Riots, July 1863

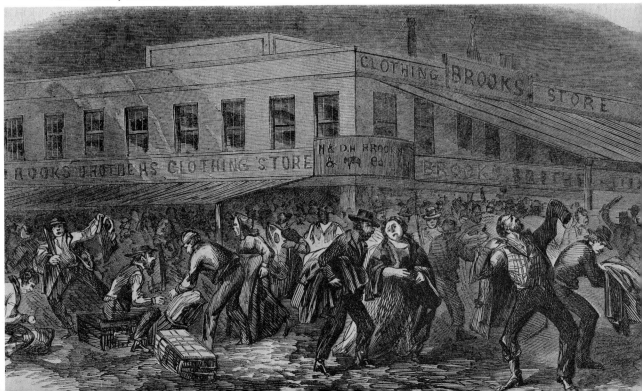

Cavalry Charge near Rappahonnock Station, Va., Edwin Forbes, 1864

Prisoners from the Front, Winslow Homer, c. 1866

Reconstruction

Northern travelers who went South in the weeks and months immediately following the war commented at great length upon the physical devastation suffered by the Confederacy. One such visitor was Carl M. Schurz, a leader in the antislavery fight and a former Union general. In writing about South Carolina, Schurz observed that the interior "looked for many miles like a broad black streak of ruin and desolation—the fences all gone; lonesome smoke stacks, surrounded by dark heaps of ashes and cinders, marking the spots where human habitations had stood; the fields along the road wildly overgrown by weeds, with here and there a sickly looking patch of cotton or corn cultivated by negro squatters. . . ."

Large sections of Richmond, Atlanta, Columbia, South Carolina, and other cities lay in ruins. Two-thirds of the South's railroads had been destroyed. Fields lay fallow, and thousands of people, white as well as black, were in dire need of relief. However, the physical scars caused by war would disappear far more rapidly than the social and political issues created by the South's defeat and the liberation of nearly four million slaves. The future status of the former slaves—the freedmen—and the conditions that would be imposed on the vanquished Confederates had been debated in the North long before the war ended. Just how the South would be restored to the Union was a politically divisive issue that aroused sharp controversy within Republican ranks. When Lee surrendered in the spring of 1865, it was by no means clear what precise direction postwar politics would take. As you analyze the policies of Reconstruction that followed the Civil War, here are some questions to guide you:

1. What were the Presidential plans for Reconstruction? Why did Congress oppose them?
2. What policies did Congress enforce in the South?
3. What was the position of black men in the South?
4. How was white supremacy restored?

1 Presidential Reconstruction Arouses Controversy

1. What was Lincoln's plan for Reconstruction?

2. Why did many members of the Republican party oppose Lincoln's plan?

3. Why was President Andrew Johnson a disappointment to Republican congressional leaders?

4. How did the newly formed governments in the South react toward the freedmen?

Historians have long been impressed by Lincoln's skillful handling of the great many political, military, diplomatic, and economic problems involved in winning the Civil War. Lincoln also devoted considerable time to the question of Reconstruction—that is, restoring the rebellious states to their place in the Union.

Lincoln's plan. Lincoln himself favored a lenient peace settlement. As early as 1862, he had recognized the legality of provisional governments in those parts of Tennessee, Louisiana, and Arkansas conquered by the Union army. The following year he issued a "Proclamation of Amnesty and Reconstruction."

This decree stated that when 10 percent of the people in any Confederate state who had been eligible to vote in 1860 promised "henceforth [to] faithfully support, protect and defend the Constitution of the United States" and accept all Presidential decrees and congressional acts relating to slavery, they would be permitted to organize a government and elect representatives to Congress. Lincoln, however, did not extend amnesty to high-ranking Confederate leaders or to former United States congressmen, judges, and military officers who supported the rebellion. These men could not participate in politics.

Congressional opposition. Lincoln's "ten per cent plan" aroused widespread opposition within the ranks of his own party. In July 1864, Congress passed the Wade-Davis Bill which declared that Congress, not the President, was entitled to determine the conditions under which the Con-

federate states could be readmitted into the Union. The Wade-Davis Bill also demanded a stronger loyalty oath than the President prescribed, and provided for the immediate abolition of slavery.

Lincoln disposed of the Wade-Davis Bill with a "pocket veto"; that is, he used a Constitutional provision by which a President neither returns a bill nor signs it if it is passed within the final ten days of a congressional session (Article I, Section 7 of the Constitution, page 89). He then publicly announced his reasons for failing to sign the measure, stating that slavery could be legally abolished only by a Constitutional amendment, not by Congress. In addition, the President declared that he was not willing to commit himself to any one plan of Reconstruction, although he agreed that if any southern state preferred the congressional plan to his own, he would take immediate steps to implement it.

The antislavery radicals in Congress were enraged by Lincoln's action. Obviously, no southerner would voluntarily submit to the harsher Reconstruction terms proposed by the Wade-Davis Bill. The radicals responded to Lincoln's position by issuing the "Wade-Davis Manifesto" which bluntly declared that the President must "confine himself to his executive duties—to obey and execute, not make the laws . . . and leave political reorganization to Congress."

In one sense, the Wade-Davis Bill represented an attempt by Congress to regain the policy-making powers which Lincoln had assumed during the war. With the exception of Andrew Jackson's Presidency, Congress had usually exercised greater governmental power than the President. In another sense the bill reflected the fears of many Republicans that Lincoln was planning to readmit the South without exacting conditions that would assume future loyalty.

Division in the Republican party. To be sure, the Republican congressmen who opposed Lincoln's Reconstruction policies acted from a variety of motives. Some were sincerely concerned about the fate of the freedmen, the former slaves whom Lincoln appeared willing to abandon; others were more interested in the potential political power freedmen represented.

Many Republicans believed that the early return of rebels to Congress would not only jeopardize the power of the Republican party, but would also undermine the Union cause. On the other hand, if the freedmen were enfranchised and their civil rights protected, a strong Republican party could be built in the South. Finally, some Republicans feared that a successful coalition of former Rebels and conservative northern Democrats would lead to the repeal of such economic measures as the Morrill Tariff and the Banking Acts passed by the Republicans during the war.

Lincoln had a different view of the national scene. He was aware that many former Whigs in the South believed in economic principles similar to those of the Republican party. Once slavery was dead and a lenient peace imposed, the Republicans conceivably could win their allegiance. Lincoln also believed that a harsh peace settlement would weaken, not strengthen, the Republican party's chances of broadening its national appeal.

One thing is clear: the Republican party was badly divided on the issues presented by Reconstruction. In his message to Congress on December 6, 1864, Lincoln stated that "the time may come—probably will come—when . . . more rigorous measures than heretofore shall be adopted." Shortly before his death, Lincoln also announced that he favored the enfranchisement of "very intelligent" blacks and all those who had served in the Union army. As historian Kenneth M. Stampp interprets it:

The President thus seemed to be wavering slightly. He may well have been near to deciding to seek some kind of accommodation with Congress to avoid a disastrous rupture in the Republican Party.

This is a question, however, that can never be fully answered, for the President was assassinated before the debates over Reconstruction policies reached their critical stage.

Andrew Johnson takes command. Vice-President Andrew Johnson of Tennessee had been the only southern senator who refused to resign his seat and support the rebellion. He had also served the Union cause well as military governor of Tennessee before becoming Vice-President. Johnson, who had risen from poverty, was noted for his hatred of the South's planter aristocracy, and he laid the blame for secession on this group.

"You know perfectly well," he told a delegation of Virginians, "it was the wealthy men of the South who dragooned the people into secession." And, in 1865, Johnson declared that the prewar leaders of the South "must be conquered and a new set of men brought forward who are to vitalize and develop the Union feeling in the South." These new leaders, Johnson believed, would be the small southern farmers, the "peasantry and yeomanry of the South," as he put it.

Antislavery radicals, some of whom privately viewed Lincoln's death as "a godsend to the country," clearly expected Johnson as President to cooperate with them in imposing a harsh peace settlement on the South. "Johnson, we have faith in you," Benjamin Wade, the radical senator from Ohio, and author of the Wade-Davis Bill, exclaimed, "By the Gods, there will be no trouble now in running the government."

Never were congressional leaders more mistaken in judging the character and ideas of an American President. Andrew Johnson had no intention of cooperating with Congress. Nor was he prepared to impose a harsh peace on the South. Johnson held to the theory that while secession was illegal, the South had not really seceded but had only been out of its proper relationship to the Union. Furthermore, as a former slave owner, a believer in the superiority of whites, and a states' rights Democrat, Johnson felt that the future status of the freedmen was the business of the southern states. He did not favor federal intervention to aid blacks.

Johnson's plan of Reconstruction. At Lincoln's death, Congress was not in session and was not to reconvene until December 1865. Not only did Johnson refuse to call a special session of Congress, but he also declared that Reconstruction was his responsibility alone. At the same time he extended amnesty to a large number of former Confederates, although like Lincoln, he did not include high-ranking civil and military officials.

After issuing his amnesty decrees, Johnson set about to form new governments in the Confederate states. Provisional governors were appointed, constitutional conventions were called, and elections were held for state and national offices. The only conditions the President demanded from the newly formed governments were ratification of the Thirteenth Amendment abolishing slavery,

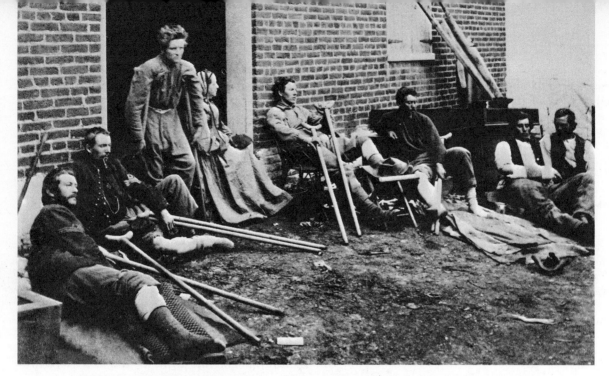

Statistics concerning war casualties or property destruction cannot tell the story of war's devastation that these pictures can. Above, Union soldiers, their wounds all too obvious, recuperate at Fredericksburg, Virginia in 1864. Below, in the same year, Corey Street in another Virginia city, Richmond, was photographed.

repudiation of Confederate war debts, and repeal of the secession ordinances.

In extending amnesty to former Confederates, Johnson went a step further than Lincoln's plan and required that large-property holders apply to him directly for pardons. This provision reflected Johnson's hatred and resentment of the southern aristocracy. Moreover, he fully expected the small southern farmers, whose cause he so ardently championed, to seize political power. Johnson, however, was wrong in believing that the aristocracy had been discredited in the eyes of humble southern whites. Most of them did not share Johnson's hatred of the southern aristocracy, and in the elections they voted overwhelmingly for the very leaders Johnson had excluded from his amnesty.

Instead of admitting failure and repudiating his policies (thus giving Congress an opportunity to take command), Johnson began issuing pardons by the hundreds to former prominent Confederates, thus allowing them to legally take the offices to which they had been elected. Soon, the President was defending the men he had resolved to punish. As Kenneth M. Stampp has observed:

No longer did Johnson speak of punishing traitors and making treason odious; rather, he said: "I did not expect to keep out all who were excluded from the amnesty . . . but I intended they should sue for pardon, and so realize the enormity of their crimes." The pardons flowed from the President's office to men who realized nothing of the sort; to men who accepted him now, humbled themselves before him . . . and captured his governments in the South.

By December 1865, Reconstruction—Johnson style—had been completed. Southern senators and representatives had arrived in Washington to take their seats in Congress. The southern congressional delegations included four Confederate generals, five colonels, several members of the Confederate Congress, and Alexander H. Stephens, former Vice-President of the Confederacy.

Johnson had tried to present the Republican party with an accomplished fact, but there was a fatal flaw in his plan. Congress was the sole judge of the qualifications of its own members, and when it convened in December, the Republicans refused to seat southern delegates. Most Republicans were outraged by the election of so many high officials of the Confederacy to national

office. Moreover, resenting Johnson's assertion of executive supremacy, Congress then proceeded on its own to investigate conditions in the South. Equally important, most Republicans were concerned about the treatment of freedmen by the southern state governments.

The Black Codes. The newly formed governments in the South not only denied the freedmen citizenship and the right to vote, but had passed a series of acts known as the Black Codes. These acts convinced many northerners that the South intended to reenslave the blacks. Some of the codes were harsher than others, but all were designed to maintain white supremacy and guarantee southern planters a stable supply of agricultural workers.

In South Carolina, for instance, unless a freedman could pay $100 for a license, an enormous sum in those days, he could not work except as an agricultural laborer. Moreover, freedmen who could not prove that they were gainfully employed could be arrested for vagrancy and their labor then auctioned off to employers. In Louisiana, all black agricultural workers were required to make labor contracts with employers for a year. If a worker ran away for any reason, he was subject to imprisonment until he agreed to return to work. Provisions such as these virtually negated the freedmen's new rights to own property, to sue and be sued, and to serve as witnesses in court when at least one of the parties involved was black.

Historian Rembert Patrick has observed that

While the black codes did not father Congressional Reconstruction, they become a powerful weapon in the arsenal of Congressmen desiring to discredit Presidential Reconstruction and win national support for Congressional policies.

Even so, in December 1865 and in early 1866, many moderate Republican congressmen hesitated to break openly with the President. Had Andrew Johnson been willing to compromise by guaranteeing federal protection for the freedmen's civil rights (not necessarily including suffrage), an irreparable breach between the President and Congress might have been avoided. The ability to compromise, however, was not part of Johnson's personality. Because of his intransigence, most moderate Republicans joined forces in 1866

with the antislavery radicals in Congress. Together they were able to repudiate Presidential
policies and impose their own terms on the South.

2 Congress Opposes Andrew Johnson

1. What political mistakes did Johnson make in 1865 and 1866?

2. What was the philosophy of Thaddeus Stevens and the radical Republicans on Reconstruction, and how did they justify it?

3. What were the provisions of the Fourteenth Amendment, and how was it used by the Republicans to their political advantage?

4. Why did the Republican party gain a sweeping victory in the elections of 1866?

The confrontation between Johnson and Congress began early in 1866 when the President
vetoed an act extending the powers of the Freedmen's Bureau, created by Congress early in 1865
to give temporary aid to freedmen. The bureau,
which was part of the War Department, provided
rations, medical treatment, and schooling, and
supervised labor contracts between freedmen and
planters. The new act would have extended the
life of the bureau indefinitely and would have
authorized it to use military courts to try all cases
of discrimination against freedmen because of
race, color, or previous condition of servitude.

Johnson's veto. The Freedman's Bureau Bill
reflected congressional determination to undermine the enforcement of the Black Codes. Johnson assured Congress that he too had "the
strongest desire to secure to the freedmen the full
enjoyment of their freedom and property and
their . . . equality in making [labor] contracts."
Nevertheless, in his veto message he declared that
portions of the bill were unconstitutional. Since
the authority of the United States government in
the South had been restored, the use of military
courts (which did not provide for trial by jury)
in peacetime violated the Constitutional guarantee
of trial by jury.

THE FREEDMEN

David Macrae was a Scottish writer who
toured the South in 1867, talking with black and
white southerners about their new lives. The
following excerpts are taken from his book, *The
Americans at Home.*

"I was glad to find the condition and prospects
of the emancipated slaves better than the reports . . . had led me to expect. We are often
told that the Negroes are poorer now and less
happy than they were in slavery. . . .

"That many of them are poorer is beyond a
doubt. But this was exactly what had to be
looked for at first, even by those who fought
for emancipation. . . .

". . . the government had to establish a bureau for the issue of supplies to keep many of
the freed Negroes from starving. But I was assured by the [Freedmen's] Bureau officers,
wherever I went, that things were righting
themselves, that the Negroes were finding employment, and that the number needing government aid was rapidly diminishing. . . .

"When the war closed in 1865 and the gates
of the South were thrown open, the extraordinary spectacle was beheld of an ignorant and
enslaved race springing to its feet after a bondage of 200 years, and with its first free breath
crying for the means of education. In immediate
response to this cry, the Freedmen's Bureau . . . and various other societies began to
scatter their teachers over the vast area of the
South. . . .

". . . I visited a large number of these Negro
schools and was amazed and delighted. The day
schools were crowded for the most part
with . . . boys and girls who were wonderfully
eager over their lessons and seemed to have a
real delight in schoolwork. . . .

"An odd feature in some of these day schools
is the presence of . . . men and women who are
either too old or infirm to work or else are out
of employment at the time. I have seen three
generations sitting on the same bench, spelling
the same lesson. . . ."

Johnson presented his case ably; but his intemperate public attacks on several members of Congress helped to destroy what remaining confidence moderate Republicans had in him. He denounced a congressional Reconstruction committee as "an irresponsible central directory" among whose members were a number of traitors with revolutionary aims that exceeded the original objects of the war. "You ask me who they are?" Johnson declared in one public address, "I say Thaddeus Stevens of Pennsylvania is one; I say Mr. [Charles] Sumner of the Senate is another; and [the abolitionist] Wendell Phillips is another." Johnson even hinted that Stevens was plotting his assassination.

As far as Andrew Johnson was concerned, Reconstruction was over. He had restored the southern states to their proper place in the Union, and these states were now entitled to representation in Congress. To deny this fact was an act of legislative tyranny. Johnson's version of what the American governmental system was and ought to be was the old Federal Union as it existed in 1860 (with the sole exception that slavery could not be resurrected). According to Johnson, any attempt by Congress to impose further conditions, such as federal guarantees to protect the rights of freedmen, was a "revolutionary" act that violated the Constitution and traditional American concepts of government. Although Johnson's veto was sustained, it was the President's first and last victory over the Republican majority in Congress.

Congressional Reconstruction begins. On March 13, 1866, Congress passed a civil rights bill which provided the first definition of national citizenship in American history. Disregarding the Dred Scott precedent (which had denied citizenship to free blacks), the Civil Rights Act of 1866 declared that freedmen were national citizens entitled "to full and equal benefit of the laws" that were "enjoyed by white citizens" throughout the nation. But Johnson would not accept it. Despite repeated efforts by moderate Republicans to persuade him to sign the bill, the President vetoed it. It was, he declared, unconstitutional. He argued that the bill was an unwarranted expansion of federal power at the expense of the states, and also that it was unwise to allow four million blacks to become citizens without a period of probation.

Offended by Johnson's arrogance, his unwillingness to compromise, and his impassioned personal attacks on many congressional leaders, this time enough moderate Republicans joined forces with the radicals to override the President's veto. Then in July, Congress passed a revised version of the Freedmen's Bureau Bill. Again Johnson vetoed the measure, and again his veto was overridden. In effect, Congress and the President were now at war. Nevertheless, although Republicans agreed in opposing the President's policies they could not agree on a positive Reconstruction program.

Congressional theories. Northern radicals such as Stevens and Sumner agreed with Johnson that secession was illegal, but they had long denounced the Presidential theory that the South had not actually seceded. Sumner declared that the southern states, by passing secession ordinances, had committed "state suicide," and thereby reverted to the status of territories over which Congress was entitled to exercise jurisdiction.

Thaddeus Stevens's "conquered province" theory was even more far-reaching in its implication. Congress, Stevens declared, had the right to remold completely the social and economic institutions of the South. In discussing how the South should be treated, Stevens stated:

The whole fabric of southern society *must* be changed and never can it be done if this opportunity is lost. How can Republican institutions, free schools, free social intercourse exist in a mingled community of nabobs [wealthy men] and serfs? . . . If the South is ever to be made a safe Republic, let her lands be cultivated by the toil of the owners, or the free labor of intelligent citizens. This must be done even though it drive her nobility into exile.

Stevens went on to say that by the exile of 70,000 white families, millions of acres would become available for distribution. In answering his critics on the question of exile, Stevens pointed to the fact that Lincoln himself had at one point favored colonizing the freedmen abroad. "Far easier and more beneficial to exile 70,000 proud, bloated, and defiant rebels," Stevens replied, "than to expatriate 4,000,000 laborers, native to their soil and loyal to their government."

Had the ideas of Stevens and Sumner been adopted, even in part, congressional Reconstruction would deserve to be characterized as "radical." The fact that such ideas were never considered seriously by the Republican majority clearly shows that the term *radical*, so often used by historians of the Reconstruction era, has very limited application.

Another theory, put forth by Representative Samuel Shellabarger of Ohio, was designed to accommodate moderate Republicans, without whose support no plan of congressional Reconstruction could be implemented. Shellabarger's idea offered Congress several choices it could act upon, depending on the circumstances. For instance, Congress could recognize the southern state governments already in existence, it could try to work out a compromise with the President, or it could initiate entirely new programs. In effect, Shellabarger advocated a "wait and see" policy before the Republican party committed itself irrevocably to any one course of action. Future congressional action would depend as much upon the attitudes and actions of Johnson and the southerners themselves as it did upon Congress.

The Fourteenth Amendment. In the summer and fall of 1866, the conflict between President Johnson and Congress rapidly reached its climax. Shortly after passing the Freedmen's Bureau Bill over Johnson's veto, Congress drew up the Fourteenth Amendment and submitted it to the states for ratification.

In part, the Fourteenth Amendment was intended to make the Civil Rights Act of 1866 an irrevocable part of the nation's fundamental law. Without the Fourteenth Amendment, there was nothing to prevent a future Congress from repealing the Civil Rights Act or a hostile Supreme Court from declaring it unconstitutional. Only a Constitutional amendment declaring freedmen national citizens who could not be denied "life, liberty or property" by any state "without due process of law" could adequately define the freedmen's status in American society.

Nevertheless, the Republican majority was not willing at this point to make universal manhood suffrage obligatory. Racism was widespread in the North, and most politicians feared the effects of such a proposal on northern voters. On the other hand, the death of slavery meant that southern states would eventually increase the size of their delegations in Congress by counting all blacks for representational purposes, instead of the 60 percent provided by the original three-fifths compromise in 1787 (page 84).

In order to force its conditions upon the South and at the same time avoid the race issue in the North, the Fourteenth Amendment merely stated that if any state deprived its national citizens of the right to vote that state would lose seats in Congress. The logic behind this provision was simple. The vast majority of freedmen lived in the South; hence, if northern states refused to comply with these terms their representation in Congress would not be reduced. In fact, between 1865 and 1868 fourteen northern states refused to grant black suffrage.

Another provision of the Fourteenth Amendment disenfranchised thousands of leading former Confederates and stipulated that these political restrictions could not be removed without the vote of two-thirds of Congress. The Fourteenth Amendment therefore was not only an attempt to ensure civil liberties (short of suffrage) for freedmen, but also a political ploy by Republicans to strengthen the party's position in Congress without having to risk the wrath of race-conscious northern voters who opposed universal manhood suffrage.

On submitting the Fourteenth Amendment to the states, Republican leaders announced that the South must ratify it before Congress would even consider seating southern delegations. The President vigorously denounced the amendment and advised the southern states to reject it. Tennessee ratified the amendment and its representatives were admitted to Congress. The remaining ten states of the Confederacy followed the President's advice. As a result Tennessee was the only Confederate state to escape congressional Reconstruction.

Elections of 1866. In part, Johnson refused to compromise with Congress because of his inflexible commitment to strict states' rights principles of government. At the same time, he was convinced that a majority of the American people would vindicate his policies and principles in the congressional elections of 1866. At the end of August, Johnson began to campaign for congressional candidates who favored his policy. He made a "swing around the circle" of large cities—

north to New York, west to Chicago, south to St. Louis, and then to Washington. The tour was a failure.

The President's abusive campaign style had served him well in his rapid rise to prominence in rural Tennessee politics, but his emotional and extremely personal attacks on the motives and loyalty of his opponents did not work for him now. In addition, his apparent approval of the handling of violent race riots which broke out in New Orleans and Memphis, in which scores of blacks were killed or injured, hurt his cause. All of this, combined with his rejection of any compromise with Congress and the South's adamant refusal to accept the Fourteenth Amendment, alienated moderate and even conservative Republicans. And Johnson needed their support if his policies were to win approval by northern voters.

The Republicans swept the state and congressional elections of 1866, winning every northern governorship at stake and more than a two-thirds majority in Congress. Presidential Reconstruction as carried out by Andrew Johnson had been repudiated, and Congress now proceeded to formulate a program of its own.

3 Congressional Reconstruction Becomes Law

1. What steps did Congress take to bring about Reconstruction in the South?

2. For what reasons, alleged and actual, did Congress seek to remove Johnson from office? What was the essence of Johnson's defense?

3. How did the election of Grant in 1868 demonstrate the significance of the role of blacks and congressional Reconstruction policies in promoting Republican victories?

4. How have historians differed as to why the Fifteenth Amendment was ratified? What effects did the amendment have?

Before enacting its own plan of Reconstruction, Congress passed three laws, all of doubtful Constitutionality, attempting to limit or circumvent Johnson's power. First, it passed a bill, over Johnson's veto, calling Congress into special session on March 4, 1867. Ordinarily, Congress would have adjourned in March and would not have reconvened until December. Congressional leaders, however, feared the consequence of allowing the President a free hand over an extended period of time.

Second, Congress passed the Tenure of Office Act designed to prevent the President from removing Cabinet officers without the Senate's permission. The third act was an army appropriations bill, which included a provision limiting Johnson's power as commander-in-chief: the President could not issue any military orders except those approved by the commanding general of the army, Ulysses S. Grant.

Congressional Reconstruction. Having taken steps to limit the President's executive authority, Congress then passed the First Military Reconstruction Act. The southern state governments organized under Johnson's policy were repudiated, and the South was divided into five military districts, each commanded by a high-ranking army officer. The Reconstruction Act also authorized the suspension of *habeas corpus* and the trial of civilians by military courts if deemed necessary by the district commanders. To reorganize the state governments, the commanders were to enroll all eligible voters, including freedmen, who would then be permitted to elect members to state constitutional conventions. Once the new constitutions were completed and ratified, elections would be held for state and national officials.

Finally, after the new state governments ratified the Fourteenth Amendment, their representatives would be seated in Congress. In time Congress also passed three other Reconstruction acts, but these merely elaborated upon or corrected deficiencies in the original bill. By the beginning of 1868, six states had complied with congressional conditions and were readmitted into the Union. Virginia, Mississippi, Texas, and Georgia were readmitted in 1870.

Congress and the Supreme Court. Andrew Johnson was an exceedingly contentious and

Post-Civil War cartoonists caught the bitterness that Reconstruction engendered in both North and South. The cartoon below appeared in 1880 in *Puck*, a magazine with decidedly Democratic leanings. In the cartoon, the "Solid South" is forced to carry the burden of carpetbag rule, symbolized by U. S. Grant, well armed, riding on the back of the beleaguered South, which is held in chains by the troops who are needed to protect the oppressive rule. *Harper's Weekly*, a magazine that began publishing in 1857, carried many cartoons dealing with Reconstruction. The one on the near right, which appeared in the January 9, 1875, issue, purports to show the fate that awaits the black man if his protector, the Union soldier, ceases to occupy the South. The ones at the far right and bottom right, both of which appeared during the election of 1876, were prompted by each political party's accusation that the other was intimidating the newly enfranchised black man and forcing him to vote for its candidates. In one, Union troops force him to vote Republican, and in the other, southerners force him to vote Democratic.

THE "STRONG" GOVERNMENT 1869—1877.

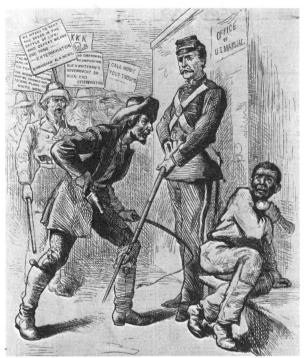

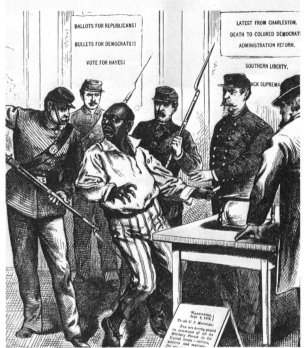

stubborn man: he was not subdued by the Republican victories in 1866 nor was he intimidated by the Reconstruction legislation in 1867. In fact, on various occasions, he confidently predicted that the Supreme Court would declare the Republican program null and void, especially the provision of the Reconstruction Act which allowed the suspension of *habeas corpus* and authorized civilian trials in military courts.

Johnson's optimism was based on an 1866 decision of the Supreme Court. That ruling had declared that outside a theater of military operations and where the civil courts were functioning, *habeas corpus* could not be suspended and civilians could not be tried by military courts. This decision had caused widespread alarm in Republican ranks, for if the Supreme Court followed this precedent, it could declare portions of the Reconstruction Act unconstitutional. To prevent this possibility, Congress passed, over the President's veto, a bill forbidding the Court to hear any appeals on cases of *habeas corpus*. In this instance the Court accepted the supremacy of Congress, which had once again imposed its will over that of the President.

Impeachment proceedings begin. The next aim of congressional Republicans was to remove Johnson from office through impeachment proceedings (Article 2, Section 4 of the Constitution, page 96). The President, who had no intention of bowing to Congress, declared that he "would be compelled to stand on his rights, and maintain them, regardless of consequences." Johnson did not specify precisely what rights he had in mind, but many Republicans interpreted this message as an ominous threat to congressional policies.

The President had already issued an executive order limiting the powers of military governors in the South and had replaced a number of "radical" commanders with generals whose political inclinations made them hostile or indifferent to congressional measures. In addition, Johnson had tried to replace Secretary of War Edwin M. Stanton in August 1867, with General Grant. When the Senate refused to confirm Grant's appointment, the general withdrew his name and Stanton retained his office. Johnson was furious over Grant's decision, because he had planned, with Grant's help, to test the Constitutionality of the Tenure of Office Act.

As a result of the President's obstructionist tactics, many Republicans wanted to impeach him in December 1867. A committee was appointed to investigate this possibility, but all charges were dropped when the House of Representatives, which initiates impeachment proceedings, decided that "there is not a particle of evidence before us which would be received by any court in the land." However, when in February 1868, Johnson once again defied Congress by attempting to replace Stanton, Republicans were so outraged that the House adopted a resolution indicting the President, and appointed a committee to prepare the articles of impeachment.

In early March, eleven articles of impeachment were adopted, the first nine of which referred to Johnson's violation of the Tenure of Office Act and alleged violations of his powers as commander-in-chief. The tenth article constituted the heart of the congressional position. It accused Johnson of being "unmindful of the high duties of his office . . . and of the harmony and courtesies which ought to exist and be maintained between the executive and legislative branches of the government." By making "certain intemperate, inflammatory, and scandalous harangues," and uttering "loud threats and bitter menaces," the President had attempted "to bring into disgrace, ridicule, hatred, contempt and reproach the Congress of the United States." The eleventh article was simply a summary of the other ten charges.

The President's trial. Under the Constitution, the trial of a President is conducted by the Senate. The chief justice of the Supreme Court presides, and a two-thirds majority vote is required for conviction. When the trial began on March 5, the prosecutors argued that the President was guilty of "high crimes and misdemeanors" within the meaning specified by the Constitution. They further argued that the Senate did not have to have the kind of evidence required by a court of law to convict him. All the Senate had to determine, they declared, was that Johnson was no "longer fit to retain the office of President." According to this argument, impeachment was a political process, not a judicial one.

Johnson's lawyers easily demolished the charges against the President (who did not appear at the trial). First of all, they pointed out that in trying to remove Stanton, the President was not even technically guilty of violating the Tenure of Office Act. That act stated that Cabinet officers were only entitled to serve during the term of the President who appointed them—and Stanton had been appointed by Lincoln.

They further argued that there was no evidence against Johnson of a crime or misdemeanor, and hence his conviction would be political rather than judicial. If this were to occur, no President would be safe from legislative tyranny whenever a majority of Congress was of the opposition party. Despite extreme party pressure, seven Republican senators joined with twelve Democrats to acquit the President; the vote was only one short of the two-thirds majority required for conviction. Thus ended one of the most controversial episodes in American history.

The election of 1868. In the state elections of 1867, the Republican party had suffered some setbacks. The Democrats hopefully interpreted these gains as a sign that congressional Reconstruction would not be sustained by northern voters in the national elections of 1868. As their nominee, the Democrats chose a northerner, former governor of New York Horatio Seymour. The Democratic platform denounced congressional Reconstruction as "unconstitutional, revolutionary, and void." It also advocated abolition of the Freedmen's Bureau, amnesty for all former Confederates, and the early restoration of the South to the Union. The Democrats also called for inflation to provide economic relief for western farmers. Moreover, during the campaign, the Democrats tried to exploit the race issue by appealing to northern fears and prejudice.

To counter the potential Democratic threat, the Republicans nominated Ulysses S. Grant and played down the issue of black suffrage in the North. The Republican platform bluntly declared that

The guaranty by Congress of equal suffrage to all loyal men at the South was demanded by every consideration of public safety, of gratitude, and of justice, and must be maintained; while the question of suffrage in all the loyal Northern States properly belongs to the people of those States.

As C. Vann Woodward writes, "Thus Negro disfranchisement was assured in the North," along with enfranchisement in the South.

The Republicans also promised pensions for war widows and jobs for Union army veterans, justified Andrew Johnson's impeachment trial, and guaranteed payment of the national debt. This last pledge was put in such ambiguous terms, however, that it could be interpreted favorably by both inflationist and anti-inflationist Democrats. Republicans also emphasized that congressional Reconstruction was necessary to guarantee the future loyalty of the South.

On economic issues, therefore, the position of both parties was vague. Reconstruction issues, however, were more clearcut, despite the failure of the Republicans to face the "specter" of black suffrage in the North. In terms of popular votes, the election was extremely close. Grant received over 450,000 black votes in the South, the only reason he won a popular majority. In the electoral college, Grant's victory was far more decisive, 214 to 80. He won the electoral votes of all the six southern states that had been readmitted. Republicans were in control in the South and blacks were voting. Taking no chances, Republicans mustered as much southern support as possible.

The Fifteenth Amendment. In 1869, the Fifteenth Amendment, declaring that "The right of citizens of the United States to vote shall not be denied or abridged by the United States or by any State on account of race, color, or previous conditions of servitude," was passed by Congress. It was ratified on March 30, 1870. The amendment, however, did not give blacks unqualified suffrage. As Senator Oliver P. Morton of Indiana observed, the Fifteenth Amendment "leaves the whole power in the state as it exists, now, except that colored men shall not be disenfranchised for the three reasons of race, color, or previous condition of slavery."

The idealistic radical minority in the Republican party who wanted to take the control of suffrage qualifications away from the states and place it in the hands of Congress was sorely disappointed. Unless Congress could establish and enforce suffrage regulation, the radicals argued, blacks could be deprived of the right to vote by any number of devices—literacy tests, property qualifications, poll taxes, elaborate registration procedures. In fact, if not in theory, the Fifteenth Amendment did not far surpass the provisions of the Fourteenth Amendment.

Historian William Gillette has suggested that the real object of the amendment was to secure the permanent enfranchisement of black voters in the North. In several northern states, Gillette argues, Republican and Democratic strength was so evenly matched that black votes might well mean the difference between victory and defeat. Gillette's interpretation has been vigorously challenged by historians John and LaWanda Cox. The Coxes argue that the number of potential black voters was not sufficiently large in most closely contested election districts to affect the outcome. Moreover, they contend that the political risks involved in enfranchising black voters in the North were far greater than the benefits, because of the danger of alienating thousands of race-conscious northern voters. Finally, they suggest that more idealism was present in Republican ranks than has been recognized.

Whatever the motivations of the men who framed the Fifteenth Amendment, it *did* have the effect of guaranteeing black suffrage in most northern states and *did not* bolster the freedmen and the Republican party in the South. Ultimately, southern white supremacists successfully defied the enforcement of the Fifteenth Amendment. Neither Congress nor President Grant was willing to take the stringent measures necessary to protect blacks' civil and political rights.

4 Republican Rule Brings Changes To The South

1. What political role did blacks play in the Republican governments of the South?

2. In what ways is the stereotyped view of radical rule in the South accurate, and in what ways is it inaccurate?

3. What evidence is there that political corruption was a national phenomenon during the Reconstruction period?

4. What advancements were achieved during the period of Republican control in the South?

Congressional Reconstruction in the South did not come to an end until 1877, when federal troops were withdrawn from Louisiana, Florida, and South Carolina. Nevertheless, in the other states of the Confederacy, conservative southern Democrats succeeded in overthrowing Republican rule and restoring white supremacy earlier. For example, as early as 1870 Virginia and North Carolina were restored to Democratic rule, or "redeemed," as white supremacists phrased it. Congressional policies, therefore, had relatively little impact on these states. As a rule, Republican domination lasted longest in those states of the lower South where the black population was extremely large.

Southern Republicans. Only about 20 percent of all whites in the South supported the Republican party, most of whose leadership was provided by native-born southerners (disparagingly referred to as "scalawags" by southern Democrats) and a relatively small group of Northerners called "carpetbaggers." (Most northerners who settled in the South after the war were either Union soldiers, teachers, Freedmen's Bureau agents, clergymen, or entrepreneurs with capital to invest.)

Blacks too supported the Republican party and held office in Republican governments in the South. But they were not always represented in proportion to their numbers. In Mississippi, where blacks outnumbered whites, only 40 of 115 members of the state legislature were blacks. And in Florida, where blacks comprised 45 percent of the population only 19 of 76 legislators were black. Only in the South Carolina legislature did the blacks outnumber the whites. Even in this state, white Republicans controlled the state senate, the governorship, the state supreme court, and most other important offices.

Many southern Unionists, those who had supported the North, especially in eastern Tennessee, western North Carolina, northern Alabama, and other nonslaveholding regions which had opposed secession, had very little use for the Democratic party. Before the war, the nonslaveholding areas of the South had been underrepresented in southern legislatures. In addition, the people of these areas paid higher taxes, received inadequate sums for internal improvements, and in most instances, no money at all for public education.

Although many white Republicans were nearly as prejudiced against the blacks as were the Democrats, they were willing to cooperate with the freedmen in order to secure governmental reforms. As one observer declared:

There is some amount of squirming about the privileges extended to the recent slaves, but time will overcome all this as there is no Union man who does not infinitely more fear and dread the domination of recent Rebels than that of recent slaves.

The Republican party in the South also drew some support from upper-class whites who had been Whigs before the war and who favored the economic principles of the Republican party. Some of these men supported national subsidies for internal improvements, especially railroads, while others wanted high protective tariffs— measures which the Democratic party traditionally had opposed. For example, James L. Alcorn, the successful Republican candidate for governor of Mississippi in 1869, had been a prominent Whig planter during the prewar period. Even General James A. Longstreet, one of Lee's leading corps commanders, joined the Republican party. After the war, Longstreet was a cotton factor and was also in the insurance business in New Orleans.

If blacks did not dominate the Republican party in the South, many freedmen and northern-born blacks did hold important positions under Republican administrations. In Louisiana, Pinckney B. S. Pinchback, Oscar J. Dunn, and C. C. Antoine held the office of lieutenant-governor. In South Carolina, Alonzo J. Ransier and Richard H. Gleaves were elected to the same office, and both Samuel J. Lee and Robert B. Elliott served capably as Speaker of the House of Representatives. In Florida, Jonathan Gibbs had a distinguished career as superintendent of public instruction. Altogether, eight black men held this position in various states during the Reconstruction period.

Between 1869 and 1901, twenty southern blacks served in Congress. One of these men was Senator Blanche K. Bruce of Mississippi. Bruce was born into slavery in Virginia, but eventually escaped. After studying for several years in the North, he settled in Mississippi and entered politics. Before his election to the Senate, he served

SOUTHERN WHITES DURING RECONSTRUCTION

Below are excerpts from the diary of Eliza Frances Andrews, daughter of a Georgia plantation owner, who recorded her impressions of Reconstruction. They were written in June, 1865.

"It seems strange to think how we laugh and jest now over things that we would once have thought it impossible to live through. We are all poor together, and nobody is ashamed of it. We live from hand to mouth like beggars. Father has sent to Augusta for a supply of groceries, but it will probably be a week or more before they get here, and in the meantime, all the sugar and coffee we have is what Uncle Osborne brings in. He hires himself out by the day and takes his wages in whatever provisions we need most, and hands them to father when he comes home at night. He is such a good carpenter that he is always in demand, and the Yankees themselves sometimes hire him. Father says that except Big Henry and Long Dick and old Uncle Jacob, he is the most valuable Negro he ever owned.

"The next war . . ., I think, will be against the Negroes, who are already becoming discontented with freedom, so different from what they were taught to expect. Instead of wealth and idleness it has brought them idleness, indeed, but starvation and misery with it. There is no employment for the thousands that are flocking from the plantations to the towns, and no support for those who cannot or will not work. . . . A race war is sure to come, sooner or later, and we shall have only the Yankees to thank for it. They are sowing the wind, but they will leave us to reap the whirlwind. . . . No matter what laws they make in his favor, nor how high a prop they build under him, the Negro is obliged, sooner or later, to find his level, but we shall be ruined in the process. Eventually the Negro race will be either exterminated or reduced to some system of apprenticeship embodying the best features of slavery, but this generation will not live to see it."

successively as a tax collector, county sheriff, and superintendent of public instruction.

Stereotype of "radical" rule. The characterizations just drawn of the composition of the Republican party in the South clashes sharply with the traditional stereotype created by southern redeemers, those men who restored Democratic rule to the South. This stereotype, which was widely accepted by historians until recent years, paints a bleak picture of Republican rule. According to this picture, scalawags and carpetbaggers were "the merest trash that could be collected in a civilized community," as a Nashville newspaper phrased it. Nearly all were considered to be unprincipled adventurers bent on stealing and plundering and using the freedmen as dupes in their quest for power and profit. In fact, one northern conservative described Republican administrations in the South as nothing more than "barbarism overwhelming civilization by force."

Like most stereotypes, this one has some basis in fact. Some blacks, carpetbaggers, and scalawags were interested only in enriching themselves at public expense. In South Carolina, the administrations of the scalawag Franklin J. Moses, Jr. and the carpetbagger Robert K. Scott were undoubtedly the most corrupt in that state's history. In Louisiana, Governor Henry C. Warmouth was so blatantly crooked that he was impeached, convicted, and removed from office less than six weeks before his term expired.

Bribery or graft in the awarding of franchises and of printing and construction contracts, in the collection of taxes, and in the manipulation of school funds accounted for much of the corruption that occurred under Republican administrations. The largest single source of illegal income, however, came from the manipulation of railroad bonds by corrupt legislators, officials, and promoters. Millions were added to the bonded indebtedness of most southern states by unscrupulous promoters who were more interested in speculation than in rebuilding the South's badly damaged transportation system. Nevertheless, in the end, the speculators, not the taxpayers, lost out; most southern states simply repudiated the railroad debts incurred by the speculators.

Political corruption. Placing exaggerated emphasis on corruption in the South, however, while ignoring other factors, completely distorts the total picture. Many of the redeemers themselves, once they returned to power, were as corrupt as their predecessors. And in the North, political machines such as that of "Boss" Tweed in New York City (Chapter 14) mercilessly bilked the public. In fact, Tweed's machine stole more money than all corrupt officials in southern Republican governments combined. The most shocking scandals of the period, however, grew out of the Grant administration itself. These make the financial manipulations of some southern Republicans seem like petty thievery by comparison.

Under Grant, the abuse of patronage (the "spoils system") was probably the most flagrant of any administration in American history. While Grant was personally honest, many of his appointees and close associates took advantage of their office to grow wealthy at the taxpayer's expense. Grant's personal secretary was implicated in the "Whiskey Ring" scandal which defrauded the government of millions of dollars in taxes.

Both the secretary of war and Grant's brother were accused of involvement in frauds connected with Indian affairs, and the ambassador to Great Britain used his position to operate a gold-mine swindle. The secretary of the navy grew unaccountably wealthy while in office, and the secretary of the Treasury was forced to resign because of another scandal over the collection of taxes. Perhaps the most notorious was the affair of the Credit Mobilier company (Chapter 11), which involved a number of congressmen who accepted bribes offered by the company to forestall a congressional investigation.

In effect, corruption was a national phenomenon and cannot be viewed as an outgrowth of congressional Reconstruction policies in the South. Overall, corruption in Republican governments in the South was not as widespread as it was in the North. What is more important, however, is the fact that southern Republican governments instituted several political and social reforms of lasting benefit to the South.

Achievements of Republican rule. First, the

constitutions drawn up by southern Republican conventions were more democratic than the ones they replaced. They provided for universal manhood suffrage, eliminated property qualifications for voting, gave western areas of southern states more equitable representation, and abolished debtors prisons. Furthermore, Republican administrations provided more social services for the southern people than they had received before the war. For the first time in southern history, state legislatures passed laws creating public school systems, giving financial assistance to orphans and indigent persons, and establishing asylums for the mentally and physically handicapped.

Following Reconstruction, few of these reforms, which had been inaugurated in most northern states during Jackson's time, were abolished. For example, South Carolina did not make any changes or modifications in its "radical" constitution until the mid-1890's. Yet, attacks on the South Carolina constitutional convention were common. One critic complained that it was dominated by "Sixty-odd Negroes, many of them ignorant and depraved, together with fifty white men, outcasts of Northern society, and Southern renegades, betrayers of race and country." Thus, in South Carolina it was not the new constitution that bothered most whites, but the fact that black men helped to frame it.

On balance, the governments of Republican regimes were enlightened, and black Americans performed creditably in responsible public positions whenever given the opportunity. Black legislators showed little malice toward former Confederates. The vast majority of blacks did not favor Confederate disenfranchisement, and they consistently opposed confiscating the property of former rebels. Unfortunately, such feelings were not reciprocated. The color of a man's skin or his ethnic background, not his native ability or real contributions to society, was the major criterion by which most nineteenth-century Americans judged an individual's worth. The position taken by a state Democratic convention in Louisiana was typical: "We hold this to be a government of White People, made and to be perpetuated for the exclusive benefit of the White Race. . . ."

5 White Supremacy Is Restored

1. What role was played by economic pressure and violence in restoring rule by the white supremacists in the South?

2. What attempts were made by the federal government to protect the rights of the blacks? How successful were these attempts?

3. Why were northern Republicans increasingly more willing to abandon southern blacks?

4. What was the Compromise of 1877, and how did it bring an end to the Reconstruction period?

William W. Davis, a Reconstruction historian, has aptly observed: "The [N]egro was first freed, then enfranchised, and then launched into practical politics, and then mercilessly beaten into . . . subjection." For an understanding of how this process occurred, two related questions need to be answered. Why were Republican regimes overthrown in the South, and why did the federal government allow blacks to be disenfranchised and reduced to peonage by southern conservatives?

In the first place, very little of congressional Reconstruction was radical. Proposals by militant antislavery idealists that the government confiscate enough land to make freedmen independent farmers were never considered seriously by the Republican majority in Congress. Congress did enact a southern homestead law in 1866, but few blacks had the resources to take advantage of its provisions, and national authorities made no attempt to aid them.

Even the Freedmen's Bureau, which had done excellent work in providing educational opportunities and much-needed relief, was eventually abolished by Congress. Although the bureau remained in existence until 1874, its activities had virtually ceased after 1870. Thus, the failure of Congress to buttress the black man's political rights by providing a measure of economic security enabled southern white planters to intimidate black voters.

Violence and terrorism. Because economic pressures alone were not decisive enough in intimidating black voters, white supremacists resorted to violence and terrorism to prevent blacks from going to the polls. In states like North Carolina, Arkansas, and Tennessee, the black population was in the minority. There the terrorist tactics of southern redeemers belonging to organizations such as the Ku Klux Klan, the Knights of the White Camellia, the White Brotherhood, and the Pale Faces enabled white supremacists to regain political control by the early 1870's. Hooded riders burned Freedmen's Bureau schools and black churches, and shot, lynched, or maimed their victims. In addition, southern Democratic newspapers constantly preached the gospel of white supremacy—at times provoking race riots which took scores of lives.

Generally, in such states of the lower South as Florida, Louisiana, South Carolina, and Mississippi, where the blacks comprised 45 to 55 percent of the population, the Republican party was more firmly entrenched. Even in these states, however, Republicans could not indefinitely resist the tactics of overt terrorism against blacks and southern white Republicans. In Mississippi, in 1875, for instance, Democrats resorted to a campaign of massive violence and intimidation, known as the "Mississippi Plan," and restored white supremacy.

Attempts at enforcement. For a time, the national government tried to protect southern Republicans from violence and abuse. In 1870, Congress passed two Force Acts to strengthen the Fifteenth Amendment. Anyone convicted of violating the voting rights of blacks under the Fifteenth Amendment could be fined or imprisoned. The next year, Congress passed the Ku Klux Act, another force bill, which imposed even heavier penalties on anyone found guilty "of depriving any person or any class of persons of the equal protection of the laws, or of equal privileges or immunities under the laws." On one occasion President Grant even suspended *habeas corpus* in several South Carolina counties. Numerous arrests were made and dozens of people were convicted, fined, and imprisoned.

Unfortunately, neither Grant nor congressional Republicans were consistent in upholding the rights of blacks. Never, at any time, did Congress appropriate sufficient funds to enable enforcement officials to carry out their duties properly. Nor, as a rule, did Grant utilize federal troops in large enough numbers to cope with the imposing problems presented by enforcement. For example, only 185 federal troops were stationed in all of Tennessee during the congressional elections of 1874, and this number was reduced to 50 after the Presidential election of 1876.

Even when federal attorneys made indictments, convictions in most instances were difficult to win. In Gibson County, Tennessee, for example, nearly one hundred self-appointed vigilantes dragged sixteen blacks from a local jail and killed five of them. When a federal grand jury indicted fifty-three men for the crime, no convictions were obtained. Eyewitnesses, fearful for their own lives, refused to testify.

The Supreme Court intervenes. The Force Acts were far more comprehensive in asserting federal supremacy over voting rights in the states than the Fifteenth Amendment, despite the failure of the government to implement them. As already noted, when the Fifteenth Amendment was passed, militant Republicans observed that it did not give unqualified suffrage to blacks; and attempts by militant Republicans to make the amendment more stringent failed. By the mid-1870's, the worst fears of the radical Republican minority were realized. In the Supreme Court case of *United States* v. *Reese* (1876), the Court declared some of the more crucial provisions of the Force Acts unconstitutional.

In the Reese case, Chief Justice Morison Waite stated that the Fifteenth Amendment "did not confer the right to vote on anyone"; it merely prohibited the states from disqualifying voters on racial grounds. And the language of the Force Acts, he declared, was broad enough to allow federal enforcement officers to undermine state control over suffrage qualifications in any and all circumstances, racial or otherwise, where blacks were involved.

Considering the phraseology of the Fifteenth Amendment, the Reese decision was understandable, but it was a devastating blow, nevertheless. Federal attorneys now found it exceedingly difficult to prove that such devices as poll taxes, literacy tests, property qualifications, and elaborate registration procedures were adopted solely for the purpose of discriminating against black voters.

Changing attitudes in the North. By the mid-1870's, therefore, the Court had abandoned the passive role it adopted in 1867 when Congress had withdrawn the Court's jurisdiction in *habeas corpus* cases. Yet, the role of the Court, however crucial in itself, was welcomed by an increasing number of northern Republicans who were now willing to abandon the black man in order to achieve sectional harmony.

In part, the flaws in the congressional Reconstruction program, which ultimately proved to be fatal, can be explained by the existence of unenlightened racial attitudes in the North. The Fourteenth and Fifteenth amendments obviously were framed with a great deal of caution. More important, very few Republicans were committed wholeheartedly to the ideal of racial equality. For many, congressional Resonstruction had been a means by which to punish the South, guarantee its future loyalty, and perpetuate the ascendancy of the Republican party. By the mid-1870's it was clear that the Republican party had consolidated its position in the North and could win national elections without depending upon black votes in the South. Thus, many "practical Republicans," as Kenneth M. Stampp calls them, were willing to abandon the blacks to the less-than-tender mercies of southern white conservatives.

In addition, northern business interests in the mid-1860's had feared the prospect of the South's return to Congress unless harsh conditions were imposed. Now they believed that the death of slavery and the destruction of the South's resources had created a favorable climate of opinion for northern investors. One entrepreneur explained the situation:

What the South needs now is capital to develop her resources, but this she cannot obtain till confidence in her state governments can be restored, and this will never be done by federal bayonets. . . . We have tried this long enough. Now let the South alone.

Sentiments such as these, combined with growing dissatisfaction with corruption in the

A FREEDMAN'S LIFE

Whylie Nealy was a former slave who served with the Union forces. He describes what his life was like after he was mustered out of the army:

"I stayed in camp till my sisters found a cabin to move in. Everybody got rations issued out. It was a hard time. The Yankees promised a lot and wasn't as good as the old masters. All dey wanted was to be waited on, too. The colored folks was freed when the Yankees took all the stock and cattle and rations. Everybody had to leave and let the government issue them rations. Everybody was proud to be free. They shouted and sung. . . .

"After I was mustered out I stayed around the camps and went to my sister's cabin till we left there. Made anything we could pick up. Men came in there getting people to go to work for them. Some folks went to Chicago. A heap of the slaves went to the Northern cities. Colonel Stocker, a officer in the Yankee army, got us to come to a farm in Arkansas. We wanted to stay together is why we all went on the farm. . . .

"Colonel Stocker is mighty well known in St. Francis County. He brought lots of families, brought me and my brother, my two brothers and a nephew. . . . Colonel Stocker promised to pay six dollars a month and feed us. When Christmas come he said all I was due was twelve dollars and forty-five cents. We made a good crop. That wasn't it. Been there since May. Had to stay till got all the train and boat fare paid. There wasn't no difference in that and slavery 'cept they couldn't sell us. . . .

"The first votin' I ever heard of was in Grant's election. Both black and white voted. I voted Republican for Grant. Lots of the Southern soldiers was franchised and couldn't vote. Just the private soldiers could vote at all. I don't know why it was. I was a slave for thirteen years from birth. Every slave could vote after freedom. . . ."

Grant regime, produced a split in Republican ranks in 1872. Meeting in Cincinnati, the dissidents, who called themselves Liberal Republicans, adopted a platform advocating civil service reform to stop the abuses of patronage, and sectional reconciliation. The Liberals pledged "exact and equal justice to all, of whatever nativity, race, color, or persuasion, religious or political." At the same time, they demanded the removal of all federal troops from the South. According to the Liberals, impartial suffrage administered by state governments held greater promise for the protection of the rights of blacks than national intervention. Precisely how and why was a question the platform did not attempt to answer.

In the election that followed, Grant easily defeated Horace Greeley, the Democratic as well as the Liberal Republican nominee. Grant carried every northern state. As a result of his decisive victory, the Liberal Republican movement collapsed. Grant, however, did not interpret the election returns as a mandate to enforce rigorously congressional Reconstruction policies in the South. In fact, national intervention in the South was virtually over.

The Compromise of 1877. The panic of 1873, which plunged the nation into a major depression, in conjunction with the scandals of the Grant regime, helped the Democratic party to win control of both houses of Congress in 1874. Democrats confidently looked forward to success in the Presidential election of 1876. In that year, the Democratic candidate was the reform governor of New York, Samuel J. Tilden. The Republicans nominated the former Union general and governor of Ohio Rutherford B. Hayes. The election was extremely close, and neither candidate received a majority in the electoral college. The votes of three southern states—Louisiana, Florida, and South Carolina—were claimed by both parties.

The situation was so confused that a deadlock might have continued indefinitely had not both parties agreed to turn the problem over to a special electoral commission of senators, representatives, and Supreme Court justices. There were seven Republicans, seven Democrats, and one neutral member. But he was replaced by a Republican, and the commission voted for Hayes. His "election" was acceptable to southern Democrats in return for a number of concessions.

First, Hayes agreed to keep his campaign pledge to withdraw all remaining federal troops from the South. Second, the Republicans promised to appropriate large sums of money for internal improvements in the South, especially for the construction of railroads. Many influential southerners who joined the Democratic party during the Reconstruction era had been Whigs before the war. These former Whig-Democrats believed that they had more to gain economically from a Republican regime under Hayes than they did from Tilden, a northern states' rights Democrat opposed to large-scale government spending.

Ultimately, the economic part of the bargain would not be fulfilled. Nevertheless, the original agreement had played a vital role in helping to end one of the most baffling deadlocks in American political history. Shortly after taking office, President Hayes made good on his pledge and removed the remaining federal troops from the South. As expected, the Republican regimes in Florida, Louisiana, and South Carolina collapsed. Officially, congressional Reconstruction in the South was now over.

■ CONCLUSION

In a sense, the period of congressional Reconstruction in the South can be termed a success. The states of the Confederacy had been readmitted to the Union in an orderly fashion. More important, the Fourteenth and Fifteenth amendments had been passed, thus laying the basis for the civil rights movement of the twentieth century. In addition, many enduring reforms in southern states were instituted by Republican state governments.

In terms of full equality for blacks, however, congressional Reconstruction was a failure. As carried out by Congress, Reconstruction was not radical. White southerners were not disenfranchised for any length of time, and property was not confiscated. The freedmen were not given land or educational opportunities; in fact, after 1877, they were entirely abandoned to their own devices.

By that time, the Republican party had discovered that it no longer needed black support to maintain itself politically. Republicans also feared northern white backlash if they attempted to take the right to establish suffrage qualifications away from the states and put it in the hands of Congress. Moreover, for Republicans to enforce black rights vigorously would have required the use of massive federal power. This concept was alien to most nineteenth-century Americans, who still held to the traditional fears of centralized power. In the end, the Compromise of 1877 was widely hailed in white America.

Only a few idealists continued to agitate for equal rights. One of these, former Governor Daniel H. Chamberlain of South Carolina, wrote an epitaph to the Republican abandonment of the freedmen that would not be fully appreciated until the middle of the twentieth century. In discussing President Hayes's southern policy, Chamberlain declared:

[It] consists in the abandonment of the Southern Republicans, and especially the colored race, to the control and rule not only of the Democratic party, but of that class at the South which regarded slavery as a Divine Institution, which waged four years of destructive war for its perpetuation, which steadily opposed citizenship and suffrage for the Negro—in a word, a class . . . opposed to every step and feature of what Republicans call our national progress since 1860.

■ QUESTIONS

1. What plans for Reconstruction were put forward at the conclusion of the Civil War?

2. Why did President Johnson and Congress conflict over Reconstruction policy?

3. Was the impeachment of President Johnson justified on judicial grounds? Explain your answer.

4. What new provisions were added to the Constitution by the Fourteenth and Fifteenth amendments? How effective were these amendments in securing black rights in the South?

5. What changes did Republican rule bring to the South?

6. How accurate is the stereotyped view of Republican rule in the South?

7. What examples of political corruption can be found in the Reconstruction era in the South, in northern cities, and in the federal government.

8. Why did the federal government allow blacks to be disenfranchised and reduced to peonage by Southern conservatives?

9. In what sense can the period of congressional Reconstruction be termed both a success and a failure?

■ BIBLIOGRAPHY

KENNEDY, JOHN F., *Profiles in Courage*, Harper & Row. This collection of essays by a President of the United States has been highly acclaimed and has enjoyed continual success. The chapter on the impeachment of Andrew Johnson is particularly good, but the student will want to go on and read about the many other Americans who demonstrated courage in the face of adversity.

SOBUL, DE ANNE, *Encounters with America's History*, Holt, Rinehart & Winston. The impeachment of Andrew Johnson is a famous and controversial episode in American history, and the second inquiry-oriented problem in this book deals with it in depth. It asks the question why were impeachment proceedings brought against Johnson, and then presents the student with a series of first-person accounts and other source materials from which he can draw an answer.

BRODIE, FAWN, *Thaddeus Stevens: Scourge of the South*, Norton. In many ways Stevens reflected the severe stance of the radical Republicans who wanted to apply harsh terms to the defeated South. The author tries to understand the motivation of the man and presents a good character study through the application of psychological principles.

FRANKLIN, JOHN HOPE, *Reconstruction after the Civil War*, U. of Chicago Press.
BUCK, PAUL H., *The Road to Reunion, 1865–1900*, Little, Brown.
These books combine to give the reader an excellent survey of the post-war period. Buck received a Pulitzer Prize for his study of the economic, social, and cultural forces, upset by the war, and finally brought back together in a new pattern of unity. Franklin's book presents a balanced account of the Reconstruction in the South. He indicates both the strengths and weaknesses of Reconstruction governments and shows that corruption was not limited to the South during this period.

FAST, HOWARD, *Freedom Road*, Crown. This excellent historical novel stays very close to accepted interpretations of Reconstruction in the South. The plot deals with emancipated blacks who try to respond constructively to their new lives but fail as the South reverts back to earlier conditions, and the bigotry of the Ku Klux Klan asserts itself.

MYERS, GUSTAVUS, *History of Bigotry in the United States*, ed. by Henry M. Christman, Putnam's (Capricorn Books). There has been a strain of bigotry which has run through American life from the first settlements to the present day. The white bigots who attacked the blacks during Reconstruction are considered in this book, but these attacks are treated as just a part of a much larger theme. Students should refer to this book at numerous times during the course of the year.

MANDELBAUM, SEYMOUR, *Boss Tweed's New York*, Wiley. The Tweed Ring in New York City has been the epitome of municipal corruption. The new demands put upon city government were not able to be met, and greedy men were ready to take advantage of the situation for personal gain. Thus it becomes quickly clear in this book that corruption was not limited to the South during the period following the war.

Part 3

The Rise Of Industrial America

Bird's Eye View of the Great Suspension Bridge, anonymous, 1883

The Settlement Of The Last West

After the Civil War, the Last West, an area larger than all the territory settled since 1607, underwent a rapid and revolutionary transformation. The westward movement had advanced to the first tier of states west of the Mississippi by the 1840's. There it stopped and jumped fifteen hundred miles to the Pacific coast. The reason was geographical. The Great Plains, which most Americans regarded as a desert wasteland, appeared to be an impossible barrier. Yet, from 1865 to 1890, the settlement of this region was so rapid that most of it was carved into states of the Union.

This remarkable transformation occurred as a result of many forces. Eastern industrial growth stimulated the development of western natural resources. Railroad builders dreamed dreams of connecting east coast to west. Mining strikes enticed prospectors to come west and make their fortunes. The cattle industry drew investors, would-be ranchers, and cowboys to help it meet the food needs of a growing population. Finally, the prospect of new farmlands encouraged settlers from both the eastern states and Europe.

The story of the Last West took place in the midst of some of the most unusual and magnificent scenery on the North American continent. The distinctive color and flavor of this story has made a permanent imprint upon the American mind. As you read about the Last West, keep these questions in mind:

1. What was the impact of each of the various forces upon western growth?
2. What effects did the West have on those who settled it?
3. How important was the settlement of the Last West in the shaping of the American nation and character?

1 The Great Plains Present A Barrier To Settlement

1. What environmental factors did the settlers face on the Great Plains? How did these factors work against them? Which of them would you point to as having the most retarding effect on settlement?

2. How were the Indians able to adapt to the Great Plains environment, which the settlers found so formidable?

3. What does this section tell you about the settlers' attitudes toward the Indians? Why do you think they held these attitudes?

During the first half of the nineteenth century, most Americans regarded the Last West as the Great American Desert. California-bound pioneers often preferred the nineteen thousand-mile sea voyage around South America or the arduous trip across the Isthmus of Panama, to the wagon trek across this forbidding country. The desert image was so fixed in the American mind that Secretary of War Jefferson Davis was able to persuade Congress in 1855 to spend $30,000 for the purchase of seventy-five camels. The army wanted to use these animals to explore the Southwest, on the theory that camels could go much longer without water than horses or mules. But when the United States Army's First (and only) Camel Corps was actually brought out to west Texas and California, the experiment failed. Its lack of success was due more to human mishandling of the camels than to their own deficiencies.

Historians define the Last West as an area roughly between the 98th and the 118th or 120th meridians (see map, page 290). The western part of the Last West was a huge area of high plateaus and mountains extending from the Rocky Mountains to the Pacific slope. Lack of rainfall makes this region unsuited to agriculture even today, and the area remains one of the most thinly populated in the United States. But it was extremely important for its mineral resources, which created a mining frontier in the West.

The eastern part of the Last West was the Great Plains. This area presented the first great obstacle to the westward march of the American frontier. The Plains area had three ominous physical characterics—it was flat, treeless, and semi-arid.* The American pioneer, accustomed to well-watered, timbered, and irregularly level country, stopped at the edge of the Plains. Walter Webb, in his classic book *The Great Plains* (1931) put it this way:

East of the Mississippi civilization stood on three legs—land, water, and timber; west of the Mississippi, not one but two of these legs were withdrawn—water and timber—and civilization was left on one leg—land. It is small wonder that it toppled over in temporary failure.

Plant and animal life. The dominant vegetation of the Plains was grass, which varied in height according to rainfall. The sod was extremely tough and often broke the conventional plows which were suitable in the east. Western animals like the antelope, jackrabbit, and coyote were wonderfully adapted to the environment because they required little water and could forage great distances.

The most numerous animal of the Plains was the buffalo. Many accounts tell of the incredible size of the buffalo herds. The Spanish explorer Coronado, the first European to see the Great Plains, in 1541, wrote to the King of Spain: "It is impossible to number them, for while I was journeying through these plains . . . there was not a day that I lost sight of them." Three centuries later, an army captain, Benjamin Bonneville, reported: "As far as the eye could see the country seemed absolutely blacked by innumerable herds."

Lack of water and timber. The lack of water and timber on the Plains was a serious obstacle to farmers. Settlers who pushed farther out into the Plains in years of relatively good rainfall were forced back again by succeeding dry periods. The treeless land did not even provide building materials for houses and barns. The first pioneers frequently built sod houses with sod walls and a center ridgepole from which rails were laid to

---

*Under 20 inches annual rainfall, which is insufficient for ordinary agriculture.

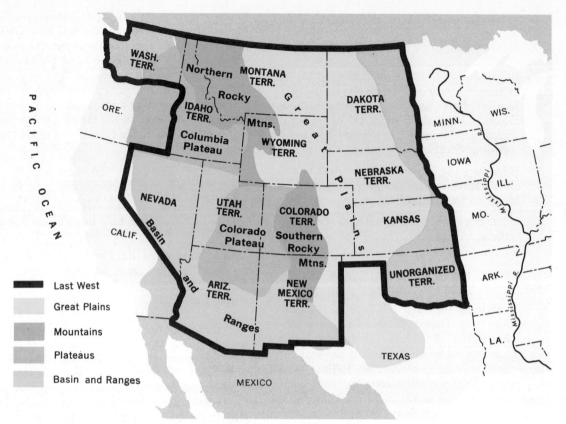

THE LAST WEST, 1866

the walls and covered with any available material to keep the roof dirt from falling through the rafters. Used temporarily until the farmer could afford to bring lumber in, these houses were dark and damp, but at least had the advantage of economy. A Kansas farmer in 1877 calculated that the cost of his sod house came to $10.05.

Adverse climate and insects. Plains weather and insects were hazards for the pioneer. The Great Plains has the most severe heat and cold in the United States, and an almost constant wind which blows harder and more consistently than anywhere else except the seashore. The word *blizzard* was first applied by O. C. Bates, an Iowa editor, to a storm in 1870. In the ferocity of a prairie blizzard, with its snow, high winds, and numbing cold, a man could get lost trying to go from the house to the barn, and anyone lost in a Plains blizzard faced almost certain death.

Even more menacing were the grasshopper invasions in which the grasshoppers came in clouds, darkening the sun, pelting houses like hailstones, and eating everything that grew. They even consumed curtains in the windows, and left, as it was said, "nothing but the mortgage." A farmer in the mid-1870's described one of these nightmares: "Vast hordes, myriads. In a week, grain, fields, gardens, shrubs, vines, had been eaten down to the ground or to the bark. Nothing could be done. You sat by and watched everything go."

Such catastrophes and the depressing effect of the flat, treeless prairie, especially on the women, are vividly described in Ole Rölvaag's novel of the northern plains, *Giants in the Earth* (1927). Through the mind of Beret, a sensitive Norwegian woman who was overcome by the land, Rölvaag describes the Dakota plains:

In a certain sense, she had to admit to herself, it was lovely up here. The broad expanse stretching away endlessly in every direction, seemed almost like the ocean. . . . It reminded her strongly of the sea, and yet it was different. . . . This formless prairie had no heart that beat, no waves that sang, no soul that could be touched . . . or cared. . . .

The infinitude surrounding her on every hand might not have been so oppressive . . . had it not been for the deep silence, which lay heavier than in a church. . . . How *could* existence go on, she thought, desperately? If life is to thrive and endure, it must at least have something to hide behind! . . .

Not for a generation did Americans find solutions to the problems of surviving and making a living under these conditions.

Plains Indians. If the land was uninviting, the Plains Indians were positively frightening. No single stereotype of the American Indian is possible because there were so many different tribes and cultures. The primitive Diggers of California and the Hopi and Zuni Pueblo Indians of the Southwest gave the white man little trouble. But the Plains Indians, the Indians of the western tradition, were quite another matter. They were fierce, determined warriors who fought bitterly for their land against the invaders.

There were approximately two hundred thousand Indians in the Great Plains after the Civil War. They were divided into many tribes: the Blackfoot, Crow, Cheyenne, Mandan, Arikara, and Sioux of the north; the Pawnee, Omaha, Oto, and Kansa of the central region; the Comanche and Apache of the Southwest, and many smaller groups. These tribes differed in language and customs but they all had a fairly uniform stone-age culture based on stone implements and tools. They had acquired the horse and nearly all of them were nomadic rather than agricultural.

Historians now generally believe that the Plains tribes got their first horses from the early Spanish settlements in what are now New Mexico and Arizona. The horse gave the tribesmen much greater mobility and enabled them to hunt buffalo more easily and to become formidable warriors. The buffalo represented life itself to the Indians, providing them with food, shelter, clothing, and fuel. The migrations of the buffalo herds determined where the Indians lived, and the horse gave them the ability to follow these migrations.

Nearly all the Plains Indians were superb horsemen. George Catlin, the painter of the Plains Indians, marveled at the skill of the Comanches:

I am ready, without hesitation, to pronounce the Comanches the most extraordinary horsemen that I have ever seen . . . [They] are heavy and ungraceful on their feet, but the moment they mount their horses, they seem at once metamorphosed [transposed].

With his short bow and quiver of one hundred arrows, the Comanche warrior could shoot his arrows with startling accuracy and enough force to run through a buffalo's hide. He used a tough buffalo-hide shield that could deflect a bullet, and his war arrows were fitted with heads that came off in the wound when the shaft was withdrawn. With the aid of a loose sling, Comanches and other Plains Indians could hang at the side of the horse, shoot under the neck with astonishing rapidity, and execute intricate cavalry maneuvers.

Western pioneers regarded these Indians as savages fit only for extermination or pacification. They believed that the tribesmen's habits of life marked them as clearly inferior. For the most part, they hated and feared them because of their obstinate resistance to settlement. The Indians could be cruel and deceitful in defending their lands, but the record shows that they did not surpass the invaders in these qualities. In the conflict with the red man, the newcomers often revealed their own savage tendencies.

2 Frontiersmen And Indians Clash

1. What were the causes of the barbarous clashes between the Indians and the settlers and the army? How do you think each side justified its actions?

2. What role did the federal government play in the conflict? What phases did the government policy take? From the policies the federal government developed toward the Indians, what conclusions can you draw about its attitude toward the Indians?

3. Why did Indian resistance finally collapse? Do you think any other ways of dealing with the Indians could have been found?

Before the 1850's, contacts between the pioneers and Indians in the West had been relatively peaceful. But in the 1850's, the Indians watched with dismay as their lands were invaded by thousands of new settlers. Indiscriminate raiding and killing began on both sides. Frontiersmen began to ask for protection against the Indians, and in 1851 the federal government adopted a policy of "concentration," whereby the Indians would be restricted to certain designated areas and promised their safety by the United States government.

But the Indians soon learned the bitter lesson that such promises were not kept. It was a pattern of American history repeating itself in the West, a formula by which new settlers, lured by land or mineral wealth, pushed into territories despite solemn treaties, and the government found that it could not protect the Indians against its own citizens.

Resistance and retaliation. During the Civil War most of the regular army troops were withdrawn from posts in Indian territory. Encouraged by this withdrawal and by their own grievances, the Sioux, in 1862, began a campaign of violence in Minnesota which was unequaled in the entire history of the West. Sioux warriors pillaged, raped, and murdered along two hundred miles of the Minnesota frontier, killing about five hundred settlers. Retribution was swift and decisive. Thirty-eight Indians were hanged, Sioux land was confiscated, and remnants of the tribe were moved elsewhere.

In 1858 and 1859, gold was discovered on Pikes Peak near Denver in present-day Colorado. The Pikes Peak Gold Rush sent thousands of prospectors racing for the Colorado territory. Just ten years before, the government and the Arapaho and the Cheyenne Indians had reached an agreement that this region would belong to the tribes forever. Now, government officials attempted to force the Indians to give up their claims to the area. Bitter young braves began to raid isolated ranches and stagecoach stations. They murdered one family within twenty miles of Denver. The four victims' festering bodies were drawn through the streets of Denver as a stark example of Indian cruelty.

In the autumn of 1864, a band of Cheyenne under Black Kettle made their winter camp on Sand Creek in eastern Colorado. Here, in November 1864, Colorado militiamen led by Colonel J. M. Chivington, a one-time Methodist minister, perpetrated the Sand Hill Massacre. Ignoring Black Kettle's attempts to surrender, Chivington's men killed more than 150 Indians, mostly women, children, and old people.

As atrocities bred new atrocities, the government decided in 1867 to review its Indian policy. Eastern humanitarians clashed with westerners as to the best line of action. Sympathy for the Indian seemed to be proportional to the distance from him. A new "reservation" policy was finally adopted which forced the Indians to abandon their old way of life and live on government reservations. At a time when the government was trying to expand the rights of blacks in the South, it was restricting the freedom of Indians in the West.

The new reservation policy did not end Indian warfare. From 1869 to 1874, there were more than two hundred battles, and countless smaller skirmishes. General Philip Sheridan explained the Indian resistance:

We took away their country, and their means of support, broke up their mode of living, their habits of life, introduced disease and decay among them, and it was for this and against this that they made war. Could anyone expect less?

But General William T. Sherman, the commanding general of the army, ordered Sheridan to fight all hostile Indians until "they are obliterated or beg for mercy."

Custer's last stand. The Sioux erupted again in 1875, enraged by the invasion of railroad crews of the Northern Pacific Railroad and miners seeking gold in the Black Hills of the Dakota Territory. Sioux chiefs Sitting Bull, Rain-in-the-Face, and Crazy Horse gathered over 3,000 Sioux and Cheyenne, possibly the largest Indian force ever assembled. At the Battle of the Little Big Horn in southern Montana on June 25, 1876, General George Armstrong Custer and 231 men were completely wiped out.

Custer's Last Stand, the most famous battle of the Indian Wars, was a tragedy of overconfidence and fumbling strategy on the part of Custer's Seventh Cavalry. The nation was shocked by the defeat when the news was reported back East on the one-hundredth anniversary of the Declaration of Independence. But in the end it was the Indians who lost. Facing starvation, they surrendered the next autumn.

The last great battles. One of the most remarkable sagas of the western Indians concerned the hitherto peaceful Nez Percé Indians of present-day Idaho. When settlers encroached upon their land, the government sought to remove these Indians to a new reservation. The Nez Percé resisted and in 1877 their leader, Chief Joseph, led his people on a desperate march to Canada. Three American armies pursued the once proud nation for twelve hundred miles and finally forced the Indians to surrender just before they reached their Canadian haven.

The decade of the 1880's saw the last of the great Indian battles. In the Southwest, the Apaches continued their hopeless fight until 1886, when their famous leader Geronimo was captured. The final incident of the Indian wars was the tragic Battle of Wounded Knee, fought in 1890 in South Dakota. Custer's old Seventh Cavalry gained a revenge of sorts when it set upon a remnant group of Sioux, killing more than two hundred, sixty-two of them women and children. With eight thousand soldiers at his command, General Nelson A. Miles forced the remaining Sioux to give up and move to reservations. The Indian resistance was over.

Final defeat. One might well ask how a handful of stone-age Indians, without unity or central leadership, could hold off veteran United States armed forces for more than twenty-five years. The explanation lies in the nature of guerrilla warfare, the vastness of the country, and the mobility and determination of the Indians. Sherman himself testified that fifty Indians could sometimes checkmate three thousand soldiers. Conquering the Indians was expensive; it was estimated that the cost of killing one Indian came to about $1 million. The fact that it was cheaper to feed them than to kill them was one of the reasons for the reservation policy.

The destruction of the buffalo was the decisive factor in the Indians' defeat. As long as the Indian could hunt buffalo, he had food, clothing, and shelter. But the white intruders hunted buffalo in a different way. At first they looked upon buffalo hunting as a sport; railroads ran hunting excursions and even permitted firing from the cars. "Buffalo Bill" Cody became the most famous of the professional hunters. Sport changed to business enterprise in 1871 when a method was discovered to make commercial use of buffalo hides. In the next three years, about nine million buffalo were slaughtered for the eastern market. By 1878, the immense southern herd was virtually wiped out, and by 1893, the American buffalo was nearly extinct. When the buffalo was destroyed, the Plains Indians were forced to submit to reservation life.

The government's Indian policy. The administration of Indian affairs is a sad page in American history. The reservation program, operated by the Bureau of Indian Affairs of the Interior Department, might have worked if the Indians had been allowed to maintain their customs and if it had been well administered. But in an era noted for its corruption, Congressman James A. Garfield charged in 1869: "No branch of the national government is so spotted with fraud, so tainted with corruption, so utterly unworthy of a free enlightened government as this Indian Bureau."

As the Indians moved to reservations, the Indian agent became well known to them. Unfortunately, these agents were frequently corrupt and inefficient. Spoiled beef, moldy flour, and motheaten blankets were the fairly common fare of the reservation Indian. Even honest agents were usually totally ignorant of Indian culture, and agents were rarely both honest and efficient.

Repeated injustices and reports of an alarming decline of Indian population gradually awakened the American conscience. Helen Hunt Jackson, the Massachusetts author of children's books, wrote a sentimental but essentially fair indictment of government policy in *A Century of Dishonor* (1881). This book and her novel *Ramona* (1884), a kind of *Uncle Tom's Cabin* for the Indian, publicized the Indian cause as never before. Reformist organizations were started and missionary and education work begun in an effort to help the Indians.

A new Indian policy. Congress finally adopted a policy of "severalty," which meant that the Indians would be set up as individual farmers and would adopt the white man's ways. Congress put this policy of forced assimilation into practice

AN ARAPAHO BOYHOOD

Moving to a reservation was an experience thousands of Indians were forced to share. In 1952, one man, Carl Sweezy, whose Arapaho name was "Black," recalled his experience as a boy:

"My people, the Arapaho, are scattered now. There are fewer than one thousand of us who are full bloods now living in Oklahoma, and many of us who are left do not know our language or our old ways and our old songs and stories. . . .

We had everything to learn about the white man's road. We had come to a country that was new to us, where wind and rain and rivers and heat and cold and even some of the plants and animals were different from what we had always known. We had to learn to live by farming instead of by hunting and trading; we had to learn from people who did not speak our language or try to learn it, except for a few words, though they expected us to learn theirs. We had to learn to cut our hair short, and to wear close-fitting clothes made of dull-colored cloth, and to live in houses, though we knew that our long braids of hair and embroidered robes and moccasins and tall, round lodges were more beautiful. . . .

". . . more than ever, we needed to carry out our old religious ceremonies, and more than ever the government was determined to make us discontinue them. . . . It was then that our chief, Left Hand, went to the agent, Major Stouch, to give him a better understanding of our plight. Left Hand, an orator and a leader in all things, made him see that our Man-Above and his God were the same, and that we differed only in the way we worshipped. 'Our way,' he said, 'has come down to us through many generations, and is the only way we know. Among white people, there are many ways of worshipping, and many kinds of belief about God. They are all tolerated, but our way is not tolerated. . . .'"

by the Dawes Severalty Act of 1887. The act provided for the dissolving of the Indian tribes and the division of tribal lands among individual Indians—160 acres to each family head and 80 acres to each single person. To protect the Indian against the loss of his land, the allotments were to be held in trust for twenty-five years. Any Indian who took up such an allotment, separated himself from his tribe, and "adopted the habits of civilized life," was given United States citizenship.

In a day when little was known about cultural anthropology, nearly all Indian reformers felt that the Dawes Act was the best solution, although a few were skeptical. Henry Dawes, the Massachusetts senator who sponsored the bill, defended it lamely as the only way to prevent the Indians from losing all of their land. When President Cleveland signed the bill, he agreed with Dawes that the "hunger and thirst of the white man for the Indian's land is almost equal to his hunger and thirst after righteousness." As for the Indians, they were decidedly cool to the act. Accustomed to a communal type of land ownership, they had little notion of the concept of private ownership of land and could not even visualize what 160 acres was. (It is one-half mile square.)

The weaknesses of the Dawes Act soon became evident. Some of the allotted land did not have adequate rainfall for agriculture. Despite the clause in the act protecting Indian ownership, white ingenuity managed to "graft" the Indians out of desirable holdings. By 1934, 86 million of the 138 million acres assigned under the Dawes Act had passed into white men's hands. William T. Hagan, an Indian scholar, observed that

. . . had it not resembled what had been happening for three centuries whenever Indian property aroused white cupidity [greed], one would have thought that some tragic deterioration of the American character had taken place.

Hagan added that while severalty may not have "civilized" the Indian, it definitely corrupted most of the white men who had anything to do with it.

Few Indians did well by the severalty policy. Tearing the Indian from his old ways only resulted in rootlessness and loss of pride, and left the reservation Indian a pathetic figure. Finally, in 1934, the United States government reversed the principle of the Dawes Act and adopted a policy of encouraging tribal ownership of land and tribal customs. By that time, however, the damage done to the American Indian was beyond repair.

Minority group treatment. The Indians were not the only group in this country that suffered in the late nineteenth-century. Minority groups in general did not fare well during that period. When the early concern for the rights of the black man ended with the failure of Reconstruction, blacks were driven deeper into segregation and second-class citizenship. Resentment against the Chinese on the West Coast was part of a growing hostility toward all immigrant groups. The attitude in the West toward the "savage" Indian was simply the most callous reflection of a general attitude toward minorities. In historian John A. Garraty's summation:

Black man, red man, or white; aboriginal inhabitant or recent arrival; savage, husbandman, or city worker— anyone who blocked the ambitions of his more powerful fellows received short shrift in post–Civil War America.

The conquest of the western Indians may be instructive in terms of ever-current problems in the relationship between technologically superior people and more primitive ones. Was there a realistic alternative to the treatment of the Indians? Roy Harvey Pearce gives one answer in his book *The Savages of America* (1965) by quoting a bluff westerner in Herman Mellville's novel *The Confidence Man* (1857): ". . . Indian-hating still exists; and, no doubt, will continue to exist as long as Indians do." Pearce adds that perhaps there will always be somebody to be subdued— men to play the part of Indians and so to be judged savages who stand in the way of civilization. In this view, the fate of Indians was, and forever will be, inevitable.

But in *The Confidence Man*, Melville expressed his concern about a world of solitary, dehumanized Indian haters. He wrote of the common humanity of all people. The typical nineteenth-century American westerner, however, would have dismissed such notions, in the words of a Wyoming editor, as "mawkish sentimentalism, unworthy of the age."

3 Miners And Cattlemen Push Back The Frontier

1. What were the causes of violence in both mining and cattle frontiers? Do you think these causes have been eliminated today?

2. In what ways did the mining and cattle frontiers influence the national scene?

3. What parallels may be drawn between the growth and development of the mining frontier and the cattle frontier? What stages did each go through? What environmental and economic factors caused each stage?

4. How do you account for the romantic myth that has evolved around the life of the cowboy?

Gold, silver, and other ores were scattered through the Rockies from Canada to Arizona. From the mid-1850's to about 1880, western miners penetrated remote areas as they rushed from strike to strike, creating towns of from five thousand to ten thousand almost overnight. Lust for the precious metals was a disease from which many never recovered. Australians, Europeans, Latin-Americans, and Orientals joined Americans in pursuing the pot of gold at the foot of the rainbow.

The first and most colorful stage of the mining frontier was that of the individual prospector using the simple tools of "placer mining." All a man needed was a shovel to throw the "pay dirt" into a pan, or cradle, and a little water in which to swirl the dirt so that the grains of gold would separate to the bottom. Often a mountainside would be swarming with sweating prospectors digging holes in their search for a rich vein. Surface pickings soon ran out, and while often plenty of gold or silver remained, it was buried deep in the mountain or locked in quartz rock which required heavy machinery for tunneling and crushing.

Mining strikes. The Pikes Peak Gold Rush of 1859 attracted over fifty thousand prospectors within months—"yonder-siders" from California and greenhorns from points east and around the

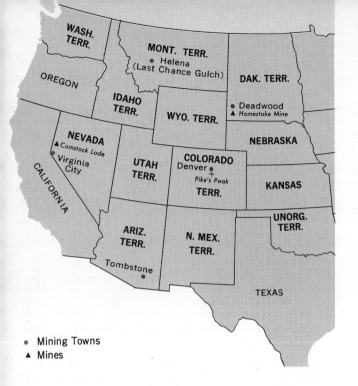

WASH.
TERR.

OREGON

MONT. TERR.
• Helena
(Last Chance Gulch)

DAK. TERR.

IDAHO
TERR.

WYO. TERR.

• Deadwood
▲ Homestake Mine

NEVADA
▲ Comstock Lode
• Virginia
City

NEBRASKA

UTAH
TERR.

COLORADO
Denver •
✝ Pike's Peak
TERR.

KANSAS

CALIFORNIA

ARIZ.
TERR.

N. MEX.
TERR.

UNORG.
TERR.

Tombstone
•

TEXAS

• Mining Towns
▲ Mines

MINING TOWNS OF THE
LAST WEST, 1880

world. Wagons crossing the Plains carried "Pikes Peak or Bust" in crude lettering on their canvas sides. Unfortunately, there was little gold in the region, and returning wagons read "Busted B'Gosh." But some of the gold-seekers stayed to lay the groundwork for Colorado's future, which was to be built on farming and grazing as well as mining. The rapid growth of Denver as a commercial center spurred the admission of Colorado to the Union in 1876 as the "Centennial State."

The most spectacular of all the mining strikes occurred in western Nevada in 1859 with the discovery of the Comstock Lode. Within a few months, nearly twenty thousand people swarmed into Virginia City, perched over a mile high on Davidson Mountain. The Comstock Lode, the richest deposit of gold and silver ever found, yielded nearly $15 million in the next four years, practically all of it in placer pickings. In a period of twenty years, incredible Comstock yielded $306 million in precious metals, of which 45 percent was in gold and 55 percent in silver.

In 1861, while other Americans were taking up arms in the Civil War, miners responded to the cry of "Gold!" on the reservation of the Nez Percé Indians in present-day Idaho. Two years later the Idaho Territory was created, with Boise at the center. The cry of "Gold!" rang out again in 1864 at Last Chance Gulch (present-day Helena) in the Montana Territory, and thousands flocked there.

Gold and silver strikes occurred in Arizona and New Mexico in 1862, and by 1863, Arizona was organized into a territory. A silver strike there created the town of Tombstone, one of the most violent towns of the era. In 1875, the famous Black Hills gold strike occurred in the Dakota Territory. Thousands of gold seekers with visions of quick riches dared to face the fierce Sioux in order to reach the strike. Deadwood Gulch in the Black Hills was reputed to exceed Tombstone as the wildest and toughest town in the West.

Mining town life. Life in these western mining towns almost defies description. Mark Twain in *Roughing It* (1872) told of buggies waiting a half hour to cross a principal street in Virginia City, so great was the press of people.

Joy sat on every countenance, and there was a glad, almost fierce, intensity in every eye, that told of money-getting schemes that were seething in every brain and the high hope that held sway in every heart.

Many discovered that the best way to make money was to mine the miners by supplying them with their needs at fabulous prices. Saloons abounded, and in the Denver region they served a whiskey called Taos Lightning, of which settlers said: "No one indulging in it ever lived long enough to become an addict."

Law was casual to say the least. In Virginia City lawsuits over conflicting claims, judges were considered dishonest only if they sold out to *both* sides. When a cutthroat named Sam Brown was shot by a man he had bullied, a Nevada coroner's jury gave a verdict that has become a classic: "It served him right." One astonished man wrote home to San Francisco from Virginia City:

California in '49 was a kind of vestibule of Hell, but Nevada may be considered the throne room of Pluto himself. I have seen more rascality in my forty-day sojourn in this wilderness . . . than in a thirteen-year experience in our not squeamishly moral state of California.

LIFE AMONG THE WESTERN INDIANS

The Rocky Mountains (detail), Albert Bierstadt, 1863

The Buffalo Dance, Charles Wimar, 1860

For centuries the Indians of the Plains had lived out their nomadic lives amid the wild scenery of the Last West. Albert Bierstadt traveled out west at about the middle of the nineteenth century and captured some of the scenic grandeur on canvas, like his painting on the preceding page. Other painters like Wimar and Catlin recorded aspects of Indian daily life, like those shown on this page. Because of the buffalo's great importance to

Sioux Indians Moving Their Tents, George Catlin, c. 1830

Buffalo Hides, Dodge City, 1874

The Battle of Little Big Horn, Kicking Bear, *c.* 1898

Ration Day at the Pine Ridge Agency, South Dakota, 1891

Indian life, he was the center of some of their ceremonies. But the newcomers to the land did not share the Indian's respect for and reliance on the buffalo. The massive slaughter for the quick dollar was the order of the day, and the Indians resisted. One of their most famous attempts to resist occurred at Little Big Horn. A Sioux Indian artist recreated the scene on the preceding page. But finally the battles ended, and the noble savage was reduced to reservation life. Now instead of hunting the buffalo for his food, clothing, and housing needs, and roaming the Plains at will, he stood in line and waited for the government to furnish what he needed and stayed in the confines of the reservation, often under the watchful military eye.

Hostile Indian Encampment, South Dakota, 1891

Mining becomes big business. The individual prospectors who made the original discoveries and provided all the color of the mining frontier almost never got rich. Corporation stockholders and big business promoters from the cities got most of the profits. After the mid-1870's, big corporations increasingly dominated western mining. They had the large capital resources which were necessary for profitable operations once the surface pickings had been taken. Western mining responded to the demands of eastern industrial growth. Copper mining in Montana and lead production in Colorado and Idaho developed in response to the need for copper wiring and lead for electric storage batteries. Individuals were hypnotized by gold and silver, but corporations with heavy machinery could make millions on other metals.

Mining spurs political organization. The mining frontier of the Last West had national, as well as local, consequences. The gold and silver helped finance the Civil War and postwar enterprises. Mining clearly speeded the process of political organization in the West, which brought western influence into national politics. For instance, Nevada became a state in 1864, sooner than its population warranted, as a political move to gain three electoral votes for Lincoln in the election of 1864.

In 1889, North and South Dakota, Montana, and Washington became states; and Wyoming and Idaho followed the next year. The Mormon state of Utah was denied admittance until 1896, when its leaders convinced Washington that the Mormon practice of polygamy had been abandoned.

Beginnings of the cattle industry. The cattle frontier was another western phenomenon founded on the persistent yearning for quick profits. It had its beginnings in the Nueces River Valley in lower Texas where, in 1865, millions of Texas longhorns, descendants of Spanish cattle, ran wild. Once steers in Texas were rounded up, they could be bought for $3 to $4 per head; these same cattle would bring up to $40 per head in eastern markets. Between southern Texas and the railheads lay the lush grass of the Plains, open range which was free to anyone who could make use of it. The attempt to connect the $4 Texas longhorn with the $40 market created the cattle-man's frontier, with its famous Long Drive and round-up, its wild cow towns and the legendary cowboy.

The Long Drive. The Long Drive was the immediate solution for getting the cattle to the nearest railhead. Drives from Texas began in earnest after the Civil War. Each herd of a thousand or more cattle was driven by six to eight cowboys, all adept horsemen, using the lasso and techniques learned from the Mexican *vaqueros*, the first cowboys. Each drive had a chuck wagon carrying food and equipment with a cook in charge. The longhorns, a cantankerous breed, were usually strung along a mile of trail. Two hours before sunup, the cook routed out the cowboys and the day began; at noon there was a halt for a meal, then the cattle were driven until nightfall. The herd could make ten to fifteen miles a day if nothing went wrong. The cattle were watched carefully at night, and two cowboys usually took the night watches, often singing plaintive songs to lull the animals.

The dangers of such a drive were numerous and unpredictable. Stampedes were a constant menace; the touchy herd could be set off by any unusual sound or smell, not to mention the lightning and thunder of prairie storms, or the deliberate efforts of Indians and rustlers. Whatever started them, the cattle reacted, as one old-timer put it, with "one jump to their feet and their second jump to hell." The cowboys then had the frantic and extremely dangerous task of stopping the mad rush and getting the herd back under control. The first cattle drives headed for Sedalia, Missouri, ran into irate Missouri farmers who feared the infection of Texas fever into their own cattle, and often battled with the drovers, shot at cattle, or stampeded the herds.

The rise of cattle towns. Abilene, Kansas, was the first important railhead, but with the march of the railroads across the plains, cattle towns shifted farther west to Ellsworth, Newton, and Dodge City in Kansas, Ogallala in Nebraska, and Cheyenne in Wyoming (see map, page 304).

The cow towns gained a reputation as places of unbridled corruption equaling the Deadwoods and Tombstones of the mining frontier. Usually they were drab villages, with dusty streets and a line of ramshackle saloons, dance halls, and gambling houses. But when the cowboys came

301

Gold and cattle drew adventurous types to the West. Above, cowboys of the period hit the trail to drive cattle to market. Below, in a photo taken in 1889, three old timers wash and pan for gold in Rockerville, Dakota; one wonders how long they have been following gold strikes and if they have ever struck it rich. The primitive conditions of the newly emerging cattle and mining towns are evident top right—Helena, Montana, as it looked in 1872. But the West was not all work. Bottom right, an audience in Cheyenne, Wyoming, watches a variety show entertainment, as shown in *Frank Leslie's Illustrated Newspaper* in 1877.

302

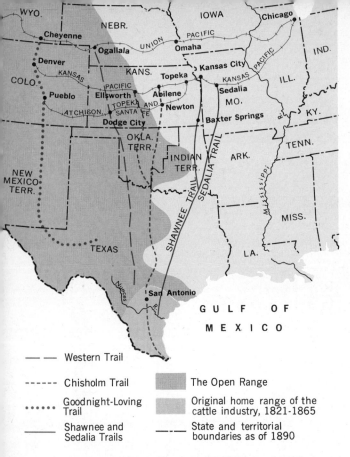

—— Western Trail

------ Chisholm Trail

••••• Goodnight-Loving
Trail

——— Shawnee and
Sedalia Trails

▓▓ The Open Range

▓▓ Original home range of the
cattle industry, 1821-1865

—·— State and territorial
boundaries as of 1890

CATTLE TRAILS AND
RAILHEADS, 1865–1890

in after a Long Drive with their six-shooters blazing, local citizens ran for cover. Saloons, faro dealers, and dance halls flourished; and chance shootings were so common nobody bothered to punish offenders. Dodge City had twenty-five murders in its first year in the cattle business. A western story tells of a drunken cowboy who boarded a train and demanded a ticket to Hell; the conductor gave him one for Dodge City.

The cattle industry grows. The Long Drive was economically practical for only a short time. The hazards were great, the longhorns lost weight en route, and Kansas and Missouri farmers became increasingly hostile to the drives because of the fever which the Texas cattle carried to their own herds. When it was discovered that cattle could survive over the winter on ranges farther north, it became feasible to raise herds on ranches nearer the railroads.

As ranching replaced the Long Drive, expensive Hereford and Black Angus bulls were imported to build up herds which had little resemblance to their tough, scrawny longhorn ancestors. From Kansas, cattle ranching spread into Wyoming and the northern plains. When railroads pushed into Texas, the Texas Panhandle was carved into enormous ranches, some so large it was said ranchers rode a hundred miles from their homes to reach the front gate.

By 1880, the cattle industry was established throughout the Great Plains and the buffalo had been replaced by millions of whitefaced longhorns from Texas to the Canadian border. The Plains had found a profitable business, and during the great beef bonanza, from about 1865 to the mid-1880's, "Grass was King." The grass was lush and free, and all a man had to do was acquire a small herd, set it out to graze, and sit back and watch it grow. Stories of easy money in cattle-raising, and books like James S. Brisbin's *The Beef Bonanza; or How to Get Rich on the Plains* (1882), aroused the same kind of speculative excitement found in the mining areas. Men with capital—easterners, Englishmen, Scots, and Canadians—came to the Great Plains to become ranchers. One of these greenhorns was a young New Yorker, Theodore Roosevelt, who had come west to hunt buffalo, liked the country, and bought a small herd of cattle in the Dakota Badlands.

The roundup. Since grazing lands were not fenced in, it was necessary periodically to separate each rancher's herd. The famous western roundup was developed to accomplish this task. Each spring and fall, ranchers gathered at a central spot and set up a camp. Then the cowboys drove the herds toward camp and began separating the cattle of various owners. Each owner used a special brand, burned into the animal with a red-hot branding iron, in order to identify his stock. Some of these brands became as famous as the baronial emblems of other days.

During the roundup, cowboys were in their saddles twelve to fifteen hours a day. Thousands of bellowing cows, blazing branding fires, scattered chuck wagons and scores of mounted cowboys, all hazy with dust and drenched by the brilliant prairie sun, made the cattle roundup one of the most fascinating institutions of western life.

Cowboy life. The cowboy has been greatly

distorted in legend, word, movie, and television. A veteran of the cow country was once asked to define a cowboy. After a considerable pause, he answered: "A cowboy is a man with guts and a horse." He was a product of his environment and his job. His leather chaps, ten-gallon hat, jingling spurs, gloves, neckerchief, and even his vest, were all suited to his job. He worked hard, and often there was little glamour connected with it. Pictures of real cowboys always bring a shock to Americans conditioned by cowboy movie heroes.

But while it is difficult to characterize the entire breed, the cowboy was always an expert horseman, often a young daredevil, resourceful and courageous, usually deferent in his behavior toward women, and possessed with an attitude of "studied disregard for authority." Despite his mythical fame, he, like the mining prospector, profited little from the cattle industry. His songs became famous, and one of these laments shows his unwillingness to be bridled even in death:

> When my old soul hunts range and rest
> Beyond the last divide,
> Just plant me in some stretch of West
> That's sunny, lone, and wide.
> Let cattle rub my tombstone down
> And coyotes mourn their kin,
> Let hawses paw and tromp the moun'
> But don't you fence it in.

The cowboy was the symbol of the open range, but by 1880 the days of the open range were nearly over. With the rush of thousands into the cattle business during the bonanza years of the 1880's, ranches became overstocked, and too many cattle brought prices down. Competition and declining prices forced ranchers to combine into stock-breeder associations to eliminate competition and control production.

The tragically severe winter of 1886-87 killed thousands of cattle and ended the open-range phase of the cattle industry. Ranchers began to fence with the newly invented barbed wire, limit their herds, improve breeding, and guarantee winter food by growing hay. Old-timers regretted these changes and the coming of farmers (nesters) and sheepherders. Violent range wars sometimes erupted as cattlemen fought against farmers, sheepherders, and fence-cutting rustlers. As the cattle frontier became a big business, its most colorful phase passed from the scene.

4 A Great Era Of Railroading Begins In The West

1. How would you characterize the role of the federal and state governments in the development and building of the transcontinental railroads?

2. What were the most important factors in the construction of the transcontinental railroads?

3. What factors contributed to the waste and general corruption that characterized the Railroad Era?

4. How did the railroads affect the settlement and development of the West?

Railroad building had a crucial impact on the development of the Last West. Between 1870 and 1880, railroad track mileage more than doubled in the two tiers of states and territories west of the Mississippi, and doubled again the following decade. By 1890, Iowa, Kansas, and Texas each had greater railroad mileage than all of New England. But it was the transcontinental railroads that struck the imagination of the nation.

Government aid to railroads. To help private railroad companies finance these huge enterprises, the federal government adopted a policy of granting them land and direct loans. Beginning with the historic land grant to the Illinois Central in 1850, the railroads received a total of over 130 million acres, most of which went to the transcontinentals. The government also made direct loans of almost $65 million, nearly all of which went to the Union Pacific and Central Pacific roads.

In addition, there were state land grants to railroads totalling nearly 49 million acres plus cash loans by state and local governments. If one adds the federal and state land grants, the total is larger than the land area of France, England, and Italy combined, or is greater than eight times the size of the state of Ohio. The government was so eager to assist western railroad building that it granted the railroads one-fourth of the total area of Minnesota and Washington, one-fifth of

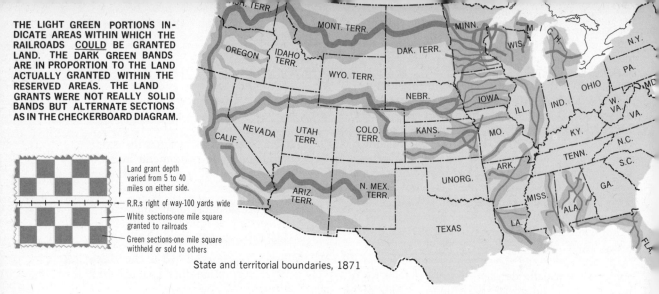

THE LIGHT GREEN PORTIONS IN-
DICATE AREAS WITHIN WHICH THE
RAILROADS COULD BE GRANTED
LAND. THE DARK GREEN BANDS
ARE IN PROPORTION TO THE LAND
ACTUALLY GRANTED WITHIN THE
RESERVED AREAS. THE LAND
GRANTS WERE NOT REALLY SOLID
BANDS BUT ALTERNATE SECTIONS
AS IN THE CHECKERBOARD DIAGRAM.

Land grant depth
varied from 5 to 40
miles on either side.

R.R.s right of way-100 yards wide
White sections-one mile square
granted to railroads
Green sections-one mile square
withheld or sold to others

State and territorial boundaries, 1871

FEDERAL LAND GRANTS TO RAILROADS

Wisconsin, Iowa, Kansas, North Dakota, and Montana, one-seventh of Nebraska, one eighth of California, and one-ninth of Louisiana.

The first Pacific Railway Act of 1862 set the pattern for these grants and fulfilled the Republican party's promise to see that a railroad to the Pacific was built. The act gave the builders of the Union Pacific and Central Pacific railroads five square miles of land on each side of the railroad line for each mile of track laid. The land was given in alternating sections in a checkerboard, one section representing railroad property and the section next to it government property.

A second Pacific Railway Act of 1864 generously doubled these figures, giving the railroads twenty square miles of land for each mile of track. The railroads were expected to sell some of their land to raise money for railroad development. However, adjacent government land was not opened to homesteaders on the theory that this would depress the price of the railroad land. The act also gave the roads direct loans which varied from $16,000 per mile for construction over level country to $48,000 per mile over mountains. For one railroad, settlers were barred from an area 100 miles wide from Lake Superior to the Pacific.

There has been a continuing controversy among historians and railroad officials about the fairness of these grants. Some kind of government aid was necessary, since private citizens could not be induced to invest sufficient funds in lines crossing undeveloped wastes which would bring no immediate profits. The mere totaling of land grants may create a false impression. Large as they were, the land grants to railroads made up only about 8 percent of the public domain, and less than 8 percent of the total track mileage in the United States was constructed with land-grant aid. Land-grant railroads were required to carry government freight at reduced rates and the direct loans were eventually paid off.

Yet, the grants were huge and it was unfortunate that Congress did not exercise more control in the use of federal aid. The railroad operators, more interested in private gain than public welfare, diverted much of the aid into their own pockets. Instead of hiring construction companies to build the roads, they formed their own construction companies. As directors of the construction companies, they charged their own railroads exhorbitant rates; and as directors of the railroads they were glad to pay these high rates, since the profits went to themselves. Capital supplied by the government was turned into construction profits, and public money made private fortunes. Another difficulty was that loans and lands were granted by the government only as track was completed, which made speed imperative. The result was poorly built roads, nearly all of which had to be rebuilt within fifteen years.

Constructing the transcontinentals. The laxity of government control over its funds resulted in the infamous Credit Mobilier scandal of the first transcontinental railroad (page 280). Credit Mobilier was the name of the construction company of the Union Pacific, which was to build the eastern half of the road. Credit Mobilier, owned by the directors of the Union Pacific, earned enormous profits. When Congress threatened to investigate its operations in 1868, Oakes Ames, a Massachusetts congressman and stockholder in the company, prevented the inquiry by distributing over three hundred shares of Credit Mobilier stock to key congressmen and government officials.

Ames was censured by the House of Representatives, but such was the character of the age that many congressmen could see nothing wrong in what Ames had done. Never was bribery of the national government carried out on such a scale. Credit Mobilier spent $400,000 for this purpose, and from 1875 to 1878, the Central Pacific Railroad spent $500,000 each year for "public relations," a thin disguise for exerting pressure on legislators.

The actual building of the first transcontinental is a mixed story of fraud and grandeur. The Central Pacific, building eastward from Sacramento, California, was to join the Union Pacific, building westward from Omaha, Nebraska. Such was the race across the Plains that at one time as many as ten thousand ex-soldiers, ex-convicts, and Irish immigrants brought in from New York worked for the Union Pacific, grading, laying track, and building bridges. Occasionally attacked by Indians, workmen threw down their picks and shovels to use their carbines and revolvers. Supplies were brought along the track as it was completed, and base camps, or "hells on wheels," moved west with construction.

While the Union Pacific was building over the level ground of the Plains, the Central Pacific had to inch along through the mighty Sierra Mountains. The Central Pacific was controlled by the famous "Big Four"—Collis Huntington, Leland Stanford, Mark Hopkins, and Charles Crocker—but it was Crocker, who learned by "on the job training," who was in charge of construction operations.

Labor was scarce until Crocker tried Chinese laborers, who averaged about 110 pounds per man. To skeptics who doubted that these Chinese could do such strenuous work, Crocker roared: "They built the Great Wall of China, didn't they?" The Chinese turned out to be excellent workers, and soon Crocker had nearly six thousand of them swarming over the mountainside. There is one unforgettable picture of these Chinese hacking away at the hard granite of the Sierra spine with hand picks, advancing only a few inches per day in the construction of the Summit Tunnel.

There was enormous waste as Crocker drove his men toward the east slope of the Sierra Mountains and level ground. Huge snowsheds were built over the track to keep out winter snows and allow the men to work. After three years of incredible labor, Crocker and his sweating gangs got out of the mountains into flat country. With speed a necessity, Crocker drove his men to lay 362 miles of track in the last half of 1868.

Meantime, the Union Pacific had pushed into Utah, and while Congress debated where the roads would join, the two companies had passed each other and rival gangs were laying parallel track! The Irish and the Chinese looked down on each other's ability to lay track, and there were a few practical jokes. The Chinese "accidentally" rolled huge boulders down on the Irish. The Irishmen retaliated by laying dynamite blasts rather far off their line, and according to one inflated account, "a thousand graders looked on in innocent wonderment as the earth parted and the Chinese, horses, wheelbarrows, and picks fountained upward."

The nation is linked. Finally, Congress decided that the rails should join at Promontory, Utah, fifty miles northwest of Ogden. Five saloons were quickly erected to take care of a crowd of about five hundred which gathered on May 10, 1869, to witness the historic event. At eleven in the morning, the Central Pacific's *Jupiter* and the Union Pacific's *No. 119* clanked their noses together.

A California gold spike was to be driven into the connecting tie. Leland Stanford, the president of the Central Pacific, and Thomas C. Durant, the chief figure in the Union Pacific management, got down to the business of driving home the last spike. Much to the delight of professionals who had driven spikes all the way from Omaha to the Pacific, both men missed on the first try. As the spike was finally driven home, telegraph operators flashed the news to the nation, and among other celebrations, the famed Liberty Bell was rung in Philadelphia. After seven years of frantic labor which overcame great obstacles, East and West were joined, and the country thrilled to the symbolic importance of the event. The Far West had truly become a part of the United States.

Within the next twenty-five years, four more transcontinentals were built. The Southern Pacific-Texas and Pacific Line, connecting Texas with the West Coast, was finished in 1882. The Atchison, Topeka and Sante Fe, usually called the Sante Fe, running from Kansas City to Los Angeles, was finished in 1883. The Northern Pacific, running from Duluth, Minnesota, to Portland, Oregon, was completed in 1883. The Great Northern Railroad, built by James J. Hill, the outstanding railroad man in the West, was completed in 1893.

Hill, a Scottish steamboatman from Canada, had long dreamed of colonizing the Northwest, and he was able, without land grants, to complete a 2,775 mile line from St. Paul, Minnesota, to Puget Sound in Washington. Hill's Great Northern Railroad was well built, soundly financed, and better integrated into the economy of the region it served than any of the other transcontinentals. Called "The Empire Builder," Hill organized parties of settlers and helped them get started. The Great Northern was the only transcontinental that did not go bankrupt when a panic hit the nation in 1893.

Railroads were a major factor in the settling of the Last West. Although their rates were often high, they sped Texas-raised cattle to market, made accessible the valuable minerals of western mines, and made it possible for the prairie farmer to exist. The shift of the wheat industry westward into the Great Plains could not have occurred without the railroads. In a truly striking way, the rapid settlement and the rise of agricultural output in the trans-Mississippi West was due to the railroads.

5 Farmers Adapt To The Plains Environment

1. What inducements might have convinced you to settle in the Great Plains if you were an immigrant? an easterner?

2. What effect did the Homestead Act have on farming? on the Indians? Why did the act prove to be such a disappointment?

3. How did the western farmer overcome the formidable obstacles of the Great Plains?

4. How did commercialization and the rise of industry affect the farmer during this period?

A western cattleman once complained in the 1880's:

These fellows from Ohio, Indiana, and other northern and western states, the 'bone and sinew of the country' as politicians call them—have made farms, enclosed pastures, and fenced water holes until you can't rest; and I say D—n such bone and sinew.

Farmers, the most permanent settlers of the Last West, were not only settling the Plains in large numbers, but were also participating in a "revolution" in American agriculture. The revolution applied to all American farming, but it was especially applicable to the West.

In the thirty years after 1870, an incredible area of new land was put to farming, practically all of it in the West. More new land was put under cultivation from 1870 to 1900 than had been farmed in the entire country since 1607! This truly remarkable fact was made possible by the revolution in farm machinery. The result was an immense outpouring of increased agricultural production.

New farms for settlers. The Homestead Act of 1862 (page 252) made it possible for any citizen (or alien who intended to become a citizen) to claim 160 acres of public land, and after building on it and living on it for five years, to gain outright ownership. Or, the homesteader could buy his land for $1.25 an acre six months after filing his claim. Intended as a democratic measure giving a free farm to any American who wanted one, the act proved disappointing in practice. The basic difficulty was that it was poorly suited to western farming conditions. Conditioned by the size of eastern farms, the sponsors of the act thought of covering the West with 160-acre farms, but for cattle or grain production, 160 acres was too small. Moreover, farming requires capital, and many prospective homesteaders lacked the funds to transport their families west and buy expensive machinery before the farm began to pay off.

The idealism of the Homestead Act overlooked the land speculator and promoter. Since it was possible for a homesteader to buy his land at $1.25 per acre after six months, speculators and corporations sometimes created "dummy" homesteaders, and bought valuable land at a low price, using the dummy names. There were many other cases of homestead fraud. One story tells of a man who claimed to have shown his intent to homestead by erecting a "twelve by four-teen" house on his land. On investigation, the house turned out to be "twelve by fourteen *inches.*"

In view of the large railroad land grants, it is not surprising that for every settler who got his land free under the Homestead Act, five or six times as many bought their land from private parties. The railroads, alone, sold more land, at an average of $5 per acre, than was taken up under the Homestead Act.

Expansion of the farming frontier. Railroad land promotion was an important by-product of the land-grant policy. Advertising their land as "Better than a Homestead," railroad land agents scoured Europe and England as well as the United States for prospective settlers. This overseas recruiting accounts in some part for the large numbers of Swedes, Norwegians, Germans, and Irish who came to farmlands on the Plains.

Though many immigrants did come to the Plains, most of the farm settlers came there from states just east of the advancing frontier. In the 1870's, all but two of the states just west of the Mississippi lost population as some of their people moved farther west. In that single decade, an area equal to Great Britain and France combined was added to the nation's cultivated area, most of it in the second tier of states west of the Mississippi. As the farming frontier moved into

the Dakotas, "bonanza farms" appeared, huge wheat-growing ventures with expensive machinery and heavy capital investment, a spectacular but not a typical kind of western farm.

In the Southwest, as settlers began to edge out into the semiarid country, land-hungry pioneers began to besiege Congress with demands that the Indians be thrown out of the Oklahoma region and the land opened for homesteading. Congress yielded, and on April 22, 1889, opened up some 20 million acres of the Oklahoma District under the terms of the Homestead Act. At noon on that day, approximately 100,000 eager "Boomers" lined up on the northern border, while federal troops tried to prevent "Sooners" from jumping the gun.

At twelve noon, a mass of humanity in wagons, trains, and every other conceivable form of transportation, rushed in to stake their claims. By that night, Oklahoma City had a population of 10,000 tent-dwellers and Guthrie had a population of 15,000, a result of what surely must be one of the most remarkable examples of land hunger in all history. An even more dramatic rush occurred in September 1893, when a much larger section, the Cherokee Outlet, was opened and the earlier rush was reenacted. By 1906, the Oklahoma Territory had 500,000 people in addition to scattered remnants of Indian tribes.

Surmounting obstacles to farming. Gradually the western farmer learned to deal with the problems of the Plains. Since there was no wood, he frequently had to live in sod houses. Without wood, he had to face the problem of fencing, so essential to farming. The difficulty was solved by the invention of barbed wire. Patented by Joseph Glidden of Illinois in 1874, it was soon mass-produced to meet the hungry demand of western farmers. Open-range cattlemen resented fencing bitterly, and one of them remarked that he hoped the "man who invented barbed wire had it all around him in a ball and the ball rolled to hell."

Soft eastern winter wheat could not be grown on the northern Plains because the severe winters killed the seed before it sprouted. After trial and error, farmers found that a "hard" variety grown in northern Europe was suitable to the northern Plains, while the hard-kerneled "Turkey Red" wheat from the Crimea in southern Russia was

THE GROWTH OF THE LAST WEST

Year	Population
1860	327,401
1870	840,913
1880	2,275,001
1890	4,860,171
1900	6,240,662
1910	9,476,769

ideal for Kansas and Nebraska. But neither variety could be grown profitably until a new milling process was developed. Using methods introduced from Europe, the mills of Minneapolis, St. Louis, and Kansas City were ready to produce vast quantities of the "New Process" white flour by 1881.

The lack of water was a crucial problem for the Great Plains farmer. It was partly solved by windmills, which could harness the perpetual winds to bring water up from deep wells. But windmills were expensive, and only wealthy farmers could afford them. Western farmers developed a technique of "dry farming"—deep plowing to bring moisture to the surface and pulverizing the topsoil in order to slow down evaporation of the soil underneath. This was temporarily helpful, but it also contributed to western "dust bowls" of the future; strong Plains winds blew the finely harrowed topsoil into the next county and state.

Not the least of the problems the western farmer faced was the loneliness and isolation of farm life. To try to deal with this problem, Oliver H. Kelly, a clerk in the Department of Agriculture, organized the National Grange of the Patrons of Husbandry in 1867. The Grange, as it was called, was an attempt to provide farmers and their families with social and educational activities. Its growth was rapid, particularly in the midwestern states. By 1875, there were 20,000

local branches around the country, claiming a total membership of about 800,000 Grangers.

Developments in farm machinery caused a revolution in agricultural production. A far better plow was needed to break the tough plains sod, and by 1877, James Oliver of Indiana had perfected the modern steel plow, one of the most important of the new farm improvements. New harrows and seed drills were developed, but the most spectacular advance in farm machinery came in wheat production. The reaper was improved, and in 1878 a mechanical twine-binder was invented which tied up the cut bundles. Threshing machines went through a series of improvements, and eventually reapers and threshers were combined in a single machine, the combine, which did the entire harvesting operation from cutting to bagging the grain.

These machines brought a spectacular increase in farm productivity. A government expert testified in 1901 that, if done by hand, harvesting a bushel of wheat took two and a half hours of human labor, but with the combine, the same work took only four minutes. Where one man could farm only 7.5 acres by old methods, he could farm 135 acres with new machinery.

Farm production soars. The result was a flood of food products and raw materials pouring from the bounty of the American farms. Wheat production increased from 152 million bushels in 1866 to 676 million by 1898; corn output increased even faster; and even cotton, so heavily damaged by the Civil War, made startling advances. So great was the torrent of production that ever-expanding American markets could not absorb it all and the surplus spilled over to the world. By 1900, the United States exported 34 percent of its wheat and 66 percent of its cotton; in all, it exported about 25 percent of its total agricultural production. The effect of these exports on some European countries was disastrous. Wheat prices declined in Germany and Sweden, for example, and caused many ruined farmers to emigrate to the land that was the source of their misery.

Fundamental changes were also taking place in the farmer's way of doing business. In early days he had been almost completely self-sufficient. But by 1900 most American farmers had given up producing their own food, clothing, and

Many newcomers to the Plains, like the family above, dug dwellings out of the sides of hills and shored them up with sod walls. This hardy family posed in front of their home in Nebraska in 1892. Once they had a roof over their heads (even a dirt one), they could turn to farming the rich soil, after they had broken through the tough sod that covered it. As the picture below shows, men, women, animals, and machinery were all needed to accomplish the task.

other necessities and were instead raising one or two cash crops and buying what they needed. This change had been going on for some years before the Civil War, but it was speeded up in the postwar era. While the farmer benefitted somewhat from the variety and cheapness of goods created by the industrial system, commercialization made him a mere cog in the national and world market. As such he had virtually no control over the price of his product and was exposed to every shock of a remote price system. After 1870, commercial farming began to limit seriously the farmer's independence and security.

▪ CONCLUSION

For many years historians have debated the relative importance of environment and tradition in American history. The eminent historian Frederick Jackson Turner believed that the total American frontier experience, of which the Last West was but the final stage, was a dominant force in the creation of a particular American kind of democracy and individualism. Turner and Walter Webb may have overstated the importance of the environment, but the settling of the Last West did change institutions, patterns of life, and to some extent, attitudes and personalities. At the same time, the materialistic spirit of the entire country, and many old traditions, can be seen as clearly in the West as in the East. When the frontier West came to an end, roughly in the 1890's, the Last West became more a part of the nation.

There is an important American tradition which claims the moral superiority of the West in contrast to the corrupt East. Many Americans believed that the West with its broad prairies and majestic mountains would somehow renew the American spirit of democracy and equality. But the story of the Last West put that tradition to a severe test, for the reality did not match the dream. Sod houses, grasshoppers, high railroad rates, and uncertain prices were hardly utopian. Farm disillusionment during these years was to bring bitterness and revolt at the end of the century.

But the old romantic idea that American history is to be fulfilled in the West still persists. With the spectacular growth of western population and influence in the twentieth century, some contemporary historians see in the West the full blossoming of trends begun in the East. They would have us look to the West for America's future as we have looked to the East for America's past. But whatever may be the future role of the West, the American people continue to be fascinated by the Last West. In its setting of heroic size and sculptured beauty, the Wild, Wild West had a flair, a style, which seems to have an inexhaustible appeal to the American mind.

The Last West cannot be understood if it is considered in isolation from the rest of the country. Eastern markets and industrial growth were bound up with western development. Important and colorful as western history is, the industrialization of the East was to have a more profound effect upon the daily lives of every American.

▪ QUESTIONS

1. How did the ranchers, miners, farmers, and railroaders become involved with and affected by one another in making the history of the Last West?

2. How do the separate histories of each of these groups compare with and parallel each other? Is it possible to formulate generalizations regarding their parallel roles in the development of the West? If so, give some examples.

3. Explain the role technological advancements and innovative techniques played in the settlement of the Last West.

4. Is lawlessness, massacres by both whites and Indians, competitive struggles between power-hungry and land-hungry groups, political corruption, and shameful treatment of the Indians the inevitable price of progress, civilization, and modernization? Explain your answer.

5. In addition to the Indians and white men, what other interest groups came into conflict with each other when they sought to protect and expand their special interests during this period? What accounted for the conflict between them?

6. In terms of environmental forces, how did the Great Plains differ from other areas of the earlier American frontier? In what ways were the Plains similar?

7. Explain the effect of the Homestead Act on each of the following: farming; the cattle industry; the Indians.

8. What impression has the frontier experience made on American life? How do you account for this?

9. How do you account for the poor treatment and general attitude of whites toward Indians?

10. What do historians mean when they say that the frontier had closed by about 1900? What are the implications of this statement? Were there no new frontiers after 1900? Explain.

■ BIBLIOGRAPHY

FOGEL, ROBERT W., *Railroads and American Economic Growth: Essays in Econometric History*, Johns Hopkins. Fogel's book is highly important for its use of statistical and econometric techniques. The book is not easy reading for the general student, but the better reader with, or without, a strong mathematical background should be interested. Quantification in history is becoming more and more evident, and students will eventually have to come to terms with this method. This book is a serious challenge to the importance of the role of railroads in America as a stimulant for the general national industrialization.

DOBIE, J. FRANK, *The Longhorns*, Grosset & Dunlap (Universal Library). Dobie is one of the highly regarded authors of the American West. In this book he traces the rise and decline of the longhorn with the colorful institutions that characterized the ranching frontier.

WEBB, WALTER PRESCOTT, *The Great Plains*, Grosset & Dunlap (Universal Library). Any study of the Great Plains should begin with Webb's book. Although published in the thirties, it is still the best account of the Plains and the various societies it supported. Some of his interpretations have come into question, but the bulk of his study remains.

CLEMENS, SAMUEL (Mark Twain), *Life on the Mississippi*, New American Library (Signet Books). There is no better place to turn for a clearer picture of the riverboat era and the mighty Mississippi than to Mark Twain. Students should not be limited to the early stages of Twain's career, but should also look at his later writings of social criticism.

GARLAND, HAMLIN, *Boy Life on the Prairie*, U. of Nebraska Press (Bison Books).
———, *Main-Travelled Roads*, New American Library (Signet Books).
Garland's first volume is basically an autobiography of his childhood in Iowa after the Civil War. The second volume is a collection of short stories which provide considerable insight into the life of the midwestern farmer.

TURNER, FREDERICK JACKSON. *Frontier and Section: Selected Essays of Frederick Jackson Turner*, Prentice Hall (Spectrum Books). Throughout our lives we have been living with the idea that the western frontier shaped the American mind and American democratic institutions. Despite very serious challenges to this idea, most people still accept it as true, and it was Turner who is usually credited as the historian who spread the idea through his students and eventually to a receptive public. This book contains essays which outline the famous Turner thesis.

SMITH, HENRY NASH, *Virgin Land: The American West as Symbol and Myth*, Random House (Vintage Books). Smith examines the idea of the frontier and the West in literature and folklore. The book is difficult reading, but it is an important interpretation of the western hero and western rural virtues.

JACKSON, HELEN HUNT, *A Century of Dishonor: The Early Crusade for Indian Reform*, ed. by Andrew F. Rolle, Harper & Row (Torchbooks). This book has been regarded as the "Uncle Tom's Cabin" of the movement for Indian rights. While concern for the American Indian is clear today, it would be well to go back to this pioneering work and then try to identify the cause for the extended delay between identification of the problem and attempts at solution.

GRINNELL, GEORGE BIRD, *By Cheyenne Campfires*, Yale University Press. As an ethnologist and the major authority on the Cheyenne, Grinnell lets the reader see the clearest picture of Cheyenne life before their restriction to reservations and domination by white culture. It is a good study of the everyday life of the Cheyenne as well as early American history.

CHAPTER TWELVE/1865–1890

The Rise Of Industrialism

The settlement of the Last West in such a remarkably short time could not have taken place without the widespread industrialization that was occurring in the United States at the same time. Many nations industrialized in the last half of the nineteenth century, but none matched the United States in the total volume of industrial production. Economic historians mark the beginning of our industrial growth in the 1830's and 1840's, but its effects were most deeply felt in the years from 1865 to 1914.

Unquestionably, American industrial expansion was the most significant development in American life in the half century after Appomattox. It created vast changes—in the work people did, in how they did it, in where they lived, and in how they lived. In the years that followed this great expansion, few things in the United States would be the same as they were before. No other single force touched life as thoroughly or changed the face of the country as completely. It is little wonder then that one American historian has called this movement the Second American Revolution. As you read about it and try to analyze it, keep these questions in mind:

1. Why did it come, and why so predominantly, to the United States?
2. How did the railroads contribute to American economic growth?
3. Why did industry tend toward monopoly?
4. What was the role of the famous captains of industry?

1 American Industries Flourish

1. What economic factors must be considered when predicting economic success?

2. Why did industrialization occur so dramatically in the United States?

3. Do you think the United States still has the same opportunities for economic success as it did in the period from 1865 to 1914?

The census of 1890 revealed that for the first time the value of manufactured products was greater than that of agricultural commodities. The United States, which in 1860 ranked fifth among the nations in the value of its manufactured products, was first by 1894. By that time, it produced half as much as all of Europe put together. It is estimated that the total value of all the goods and services produced in this country increased from about $16 billion in 1860 to $88 billion in 1900. By 1914, when the United States was beginning to take an active role in world affairs, it had become the greatest industrial power on earth.

The essence of this remarkable expansion was the use of machines to increase production. Today, economists use the term *productivity* (output per man per hour) to measure the productive performance of a nation or industry. A truly dynamic or revolutionary rise in production comes, not from the mere increase in population, but from the greater productive output of each worker. The value of manufactured goods in the United States rose nearly twelve times from 1860 to 1914, while the population increased only three times. The dynamic factor in the American production achievement was the ability to produce more goods in less time with less effort—through machines.

The United States had always had a labor shortage and, therefore, it had always welcomed the machine. Americans were traditionally tinkerers and inventors. Europeans led in pure science, but Americans were more skillful in practical application. An Englishman, Michael Faraday, did the most important theoretical work in electricity, but Thomas Edison devised a practical light bulb. Gottlieb Daimler, a German, invented the internal combustion engine, but Henry Ford made the Model T automobile and sold 15 million of them. American inventors of this era also developed the typewriter, the telephone, the electric dynamo, and the airplane—all of which have profoundly affected the lives of people around the world.

The clerk of the United States Patent Office in 1838 thought all the important inventions had been developed, but in 1909 the Patent Office issued over 37,000 patents in one year, more than all the patents registered before 1860. "Machinery is the new Messiah," cried Henry Ford, himself a born tinkerer and one of the most ingenious American users of the machine.

Foreign capital. European capital was of vital importance to American industrialization. Capital, or accumulated savings, was necessary for the building and operation of large industrial enterprises. As an underdeveloped country short of capital, the United States benefitted substantially from foreign investments, especially during the early stages of industrial growth. The availability of the accumulated savings of Europe made it easier for the United States to industrialize than it has been for the Soviet Union and China in the twentieth century.

As industrial profits rose, American industry was able to supply more of its own capital needs and even accumulate a surplus for foreign investment. By 1914, $2.5 billion of American surplus savings had been invested in business ventures in foreign countries.

Natural resources. No explanation of America's industrialization is adequate if it does not emphasize the vast richness of the nation's resources. No amount of machinery and ingenuity can overcome a lack of coal, iron, and other resources. In mineral wealth, so essential to industrialization, nature's bounty was especially lavish. The United States' coal resources were unequaled, and there was iron ore in abundance; the famed Mesabi range in eastern Minnesota was a veritable mountain of iron. There were extensive deposits of other metals—copper, zinc, silver, gold, and above all, there was "black gold"—petroleum.

The nation possessed rich agricultural lands and forests for the lumber industry. The climate was varied and invigorating. The United States was uniquely favored with the resources needed for industrial growth, and led the world in many resources, although its land area constituted only 6 percent of the world's total.

Expanding markets. A great industrial expansion must have an expanding market—people to buy what is being produced—and it must have workers to fill up the factories and the farms. The increase in the American population from 31 million in 1860 to over 95 million in 1914 was, in itself, an enormous stimulus to industrial production. The swelling tide of immigrants (some 23 million of them arrived during this era) added immensely to the American labor force, since a large proportion of the new arrivals were men of working age.

Wages increased and, in striking contrast to recent history, the purchasing power of the dollar went up, at least until 1898. Best estimates indicate that the dollar of 1860 was worth about $1.50 in 1890. With increased population, increased purchasing power, and a large free market (in contrast to European tariff barriers), American consumers in 1893 were able to absorb 93 percent of the nation's manufactured goods.

It has long been customary to say that the Civil War was a major factor in stimulating the industrial boom of the late nineteenth century. But Thomas Cochran, an economic historian, argues convincingly that the Civil War actually retarded growth in certain industries. He shows that of the decades between 1840 and 1900, economic growth was lowest in the 1860's, the war decade. Reminding us of the great destruction and waste of war, he demonstrates that production in pig iron, railroad track, and building construction declined during the war. The problem is not yet settled; enormous federal expenditures in shoes, food, clothing, and munitions stimulated those industries. But the historian can no longer state positively that the Civil War was a major stimulus to economic growth.

Favorable government attitudes. The results of the war did provide a stimulus in a political sense. The victorious Republican party, with no southern opposition to tariffs and business subsidies, was eager to promote business expansion. The

A BUSINESSMAN'S PHILOSOPHY

Andrew Carnegie, in his autobiography, chronicled his remarkable career as an entrepreneur, and also expressed his philosophy of business:

"I never was quite reconciled to working for other people. At the most, the railway officer [he had been an official in the Pennsylvania Railroad Company] has to look forward to the enjoyment of a stated salary, and he has a great many people to please; even if he gets to be president, he has sometimes a board of directors who cannot know what is best to be done; and even if this board be satisfied, he has a board of stockholders to criticize him, and as the property is not his own he cannot manage it as he pleases.

"I always liked the idea of being my own master, of manufacturing something and giving employment to many men. There is only one thing to think of manufacturing if you are a Pittsburgher, for Pittsburgh even then had asserted her supremacy as the 'Iron City'. . . .

"Always we are hoping that we need expand no farther; yet ever we are finding that to stop expanding would be to fall behind; and even today the successive improvements and inventions follow each other so rapidly that we see just as much yet to be done as ever. . . ."

prevailing laissez faire atmosphere of the American political system was ideal for industrial growth of an individualistic, free enterprise kind. Not only did business benefit from the warm, sympathetic attitude of government, but government directly aided business through tariffs and through spectacular railroad land grants.

Industrial leaders. Who were the men who controlled industry during this period of great expansion—the great industrial barons, the go-getting businessmen who are trademarks in American history but who were never so prominent as in this era? We have usually thought of them in "rags to riches" terms—poor farm boys or penniless immigrants who rose to great wealth.

Such cases did exist, but recent studies of the entrepreneur as a group alter the general picture. One study of one hundred industrial leaders of the 1870's comes to this conclusion about the typical industrial leader:

American by birth, of a New England father, English in national origin, Congregational, Presbyterian, or Episcopal in religion, urban in early environment, he was rather born and bred in an atmosphere in which business and a relatively high social standing were intimately associated with his family life. Only at about 18 did he take his first regular job, prepared to rise from it, moreover, not only by a rigorous apprenticeship begun when he was virtually a child, but by an academic education well above average for the time.

The one personality trait that nearly all industrial leaders had in common was a tremendous capacity for work and a narrow, but single-minded absorption in their work. Most of them wanted to be rich, but sheer greed does not wholly explain their motivation. To beat a competitor, to bring order to a chaotic industry, to make a better product or a new product—these aims frequently drove them more than money. Their methods were ruthless and often dishonest, but they made a fundamental contribution to rising standards of living by introducing new technology and by demonstrating exceptional organizational ability.

Attitudes of the populace. The spirit of the whole people must be taken into account, although it is difficult to analyze. Other cultures have been content to remain nonproductive and static. Why did these Americans work so hard for material success and betterment? Their Puritan past had emphasized hard work, thrift, and self-control. The frontier environment encouraged self-reliance and a willingness to try new methods. The United States had a dynamic, free, individualistic society, in contrast to some of the more settled countries of Europe, and in this society men seemed to feel that they had a duty to better themselves.

Whatever it was, the generation which accomplished the revolution liked to call it "character" or "hustle." With the bloody Civil War over at last, future prospects were bathed in a rosy glow of optimism. A famous New York lawyer of the day, Charles O'Conor, caught the mood:

In old worn-out, king-ridden Europe men must stay where they are born. But in America, a man is accounted a failure, and certainly ought to be, who had not risen above his father's station in life.

The United States was extremely fortunate in the combination of factors which gave it leadership in the industrial movement. The country's relationship to Europe, its resources, people, and historical setting were all more favorable than in any other land. But because of its great land area, it required one remaining essential factor—an effective transportation system.

2 Railroads Become America's First Big Business

1. In what ways did the growth of railroads affect the course of American history?

2. Why do you think abuses and corruption were a common factor in railroad growth and expansion?

3. To what degree may an individual have free use of his property? When is it reasonable that limitations be imposed by an outside body?

Economist Walt W. Rostow has argued that nations experience a "take-off" in their economic growth, that is, a revolutionary jump in productive capacity due to a decisive new stimulus. The railroad, Rostow believes, has been the most important initiator of take-offs in many countries. In the United States, he says, "it was decisive."

In 1865 there were 35,000 miles of railroad track in the United States, an impressive achievement in itself. By 1914 the railroad network had reached an all-time high of 254,000 miles, more than in all of Europe including Russia. A staggering total of 73,000 miles was added in the decade of the 1880's alone. Henry Adams, an American historian writing at the time, stated that the railroads were the "one active interest, to which all others were subservient, and which absorbed the energies of some sixty million

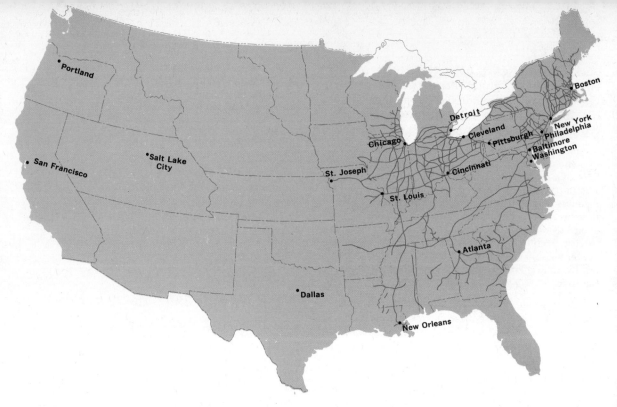

RAILROADS IN OPERATION, 1860

people." In ballad, song, and legend, the Iron Horse won a permanent place in American folklore.

Building this vast network required an enormous outlay of capital. In Europe the governments of the various countries generally took the responsibility for building and operating their railroads, but in the United States, the job was done essentially by private enterprise with some government help. In the three decades following the Civil War, the financial operations of the railroads probably had a greater effect on the economy than did those of the federal government.

Stimulus to settlement and industry. The importance of the railroads in opening the West has already been seen. Railroads began to have an important influence in the 1850's, particularly as a stimulus to the settlement of the states carved out of the Northwest Territory. Historian Allen Nevins concluded that the "Northwest Surge" was the most decisive event for the future of all the developments of the critical 1850's. Most

agricultural products of the Mississippi valley had traveled east through New Orleans, but by 1860 Chicago had replaced New Orleans as the shipping center of the West. It had become, in poet Carl Sandburg's words, "Player with Railroads and the Nation's Freight Handler."

As the nation's leading business enterprise, the railroads were a powerful stimulus to other industries. The railroads created the first need for large-scale iron and steel production. By 1880, three-fourths of the steel produced in the United States went into rails. The railroads also intensified the demand for coal, a demand which expanded in proportion to railroad growth. Railroads became large users of machine tools, copper, glass, rubber, and oils.

The railroad's achievement in reducing transportation costs and providing rapid service was profoundly significant. By 1885, the average American railroad could carry a ton of goods one mile for less than one cent. The importance of this in terms of reducing the haulage costs of large industrial operations can hardly be over-

RAILROADS IN OPERATION, 1895

Map legend:
- Major Western Railroads
- Pennsylvania Railroad
- New York Central Railroad
- Baltimore and Ohio Railroad
- Southern Railroad
- Erie Railroad

estimated. Coal and iron might be found within a few miles of each other, yet no steel mill would be possible without cheap transportation. Railroads, running the year around, reduced the time for a trip from New York to Chicago to three days. Only with cheap, rapid, and reliable transportation could mass production in heavy industries be developed.

Consolidation of railroads. After the Civil War, the eastern railroads helped create a national system by filling in the gaps in the existing network. Hundreds of small lines had been built to serve only local areas. The South had four hundred railroad companies which averaged only about forty miles each. Gradually, through consolidation, nearly two-thirds of the country's railroads were brought under the control of a few large companies. By 1890, the Pennsylvania Railroad was a combination of seventy-three smaller companies. Four dominant systems emerged—the New York Central, the Pennsylvania, the Erie, and the Baltimore and Ohio—all connecting eastern ports with the West.

Cornelius Vanderbilt was the dominant figure in the New York Central. Aggressive, arrogant, and clever, he never read a book until after his seventieth year. Beginning as a Staten Island ferryman, he eventually acquired a steamship line and the enduring name "Commodore." At the ripe age of sixty-six, he gave up his steamship interests and began a new career in railroads. After taking control of the New York Central, the "Commodore" and his son William extended their lines to St. Louis and Chicago. Ruthless competitors, the Vanderbilts built a sound, efficient, and profitable system. Cornelius left an inheritance of $75 million at his death in 1877, a fortune which his son enlarged to $200 million by the time of his own death in 1885.

The Central was known for its somber black locomotives and for the uninhibited language of the Vanderbilts. When cautioned about the doubtful legality of one of his ventures, the "Commodore" is supposed to have snarled: "Law! What do I care about law. Hain't I got the power?" A reporter once asked William Vanderbilt his opinion concerning public reaction to a Central policy. His famous reply, "The public be damned," symbolized for many the arrogant attitude of the railroad kings.

The colorful Vanderbilts have somewhat obscured the impressive story of the Central's chief rival, the Pennsylvania Railroad. The "Pennsy," under the able guidance of J. Edgar Thompson and Thomas Scott, became one of the best run and most profitable roads in the nation. It was the only American railroad which never failed to pay its regular dividend. As a carrier of coal, steel, oil, lumber, beef, and grain, it became the greatest system in terms of freight tonnage. The final step in its expansion came in 1910 with the building of a tunnel under the Hudson River to carry its lines into New York, one of the greatest engineering achievements of its time.

The Erie Railroad linked New York City with the Great Lakes and later with Cleveland and St. Louis. The Baltimore and Ohio ran from Baltimore to Chicago, St. Louis, and Philadelphia, but was never able to gain access to New York. By 1890, the South had increased its trackage to fifty thousand miles, and its numerous short lines were successfully consolidated in the decade following. The Southern Railway, organized in 1893, was the largest system in the South.

Railroad abuses in this period. Impressive gains were made in railroad efficiency and safety, but railroad financing was frenzied and corrupt. "Railroaded through" became part of the national vocabulary to describe doing something with undue speed and deception. Most railroad builders were in business for private gain rather than public interest. Speculators like Daniel Drew, Jim Fisk, and Jay Gould were notorious for "milking a railroad"—getting the maximum profits for themselves while allowing the property to fall into disrepair. Historian Leland Baldwin describes Gould:

[He was] probably as sinister and cold blooded a leech as ever fastened himself on the American financial structure. He bought only to wreck, and reorganized only to suck out the last delicious drops. . . .

Crooked stock manipulation was possible because the public was willing to supply money to the railroads in the form of stocks and bonds. Dishonest promoters used inside information to buy stock at a low price and sell at a high price. Others issued stock to themselves, then sold it to the gullible public and pocketed the cash. Railroads were notorious for issuing watered stock, that is, stock which far exceeded the actual value of the railroad property. This put a heavy burden on the roads to make profits so that they could pay dividends on the stock. They were frequently unable to pay dividends because heavy borrowing from the public resulted in a chronic indebtedness and a shaky financial structure.

The struggle for profits led to vicious and ruinous competition. In order to increase the volume of their business, railroads over-expanded and built too much track for the needs of the time. Sometimes a railroad company would build a parallel line just to harass a competitor. Fantastic *rebates*, secret rates below the published figures, were offered to attract large shippers. Outrageously high rates were charged, even over short distances, where there was no competition. But when competition did exist, as it often did on long runs, railroad companies charged very low rates in order to compete. Thus, a tub of butter could be sent from Chicago to New York for thirty cents while the rate for the same tub shipped to New York from no more than 165 miles away could be seventy-five cents.

A call for regulation. Western farmers were especially bitter about these long haul-short haul abuses because they desperately needed to use the railroads, and the lack of railroad competition in the West led to high shipping rates. These farmers, especially those organized in the Granger movement, began to demand that the government regulate the railroads in order to correct these abuses.

But the demand for railroad regulation was not exclusively a farmer's movement. In some urban areas, merchants, industrialists, and shippers were more prominent in their agitation for regulation than farmers. All resented the uncertainties and discrimination of rates as well as the long and short haul differences. Many Americans resented the size and power of the railroads and their influence over national and state legislatures. On one occasion a member of the Pennsylvania legislature was reported to have said: "Mr. Speaker, I move we adjourn unless the Penn-

Although the railroads did a great deal to open up the West to settlement, trade, and industry, they did not necessarily do much to promote comfort. The engraving above, entitled *The Modern Ship of the Plains*, appeared in *Harper's Weekly* in 1886 and shows rather primitive conditions—though not as primitive as those on board the earlier ship of the Plains, the covered wagon. This engraving appeared about twenty years after the railroads first began advertising for passengers and freight for the West. The ad at the right appeared in 1867, and it offers passengers crossing the Plains a luxury the riders above seem to lack—"Pullman's Palace Sleeping Cars on All Night Trains."

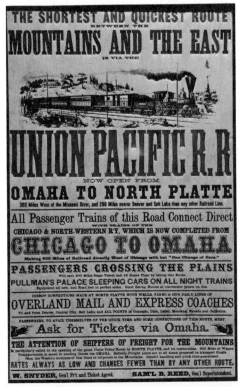

321

sylvania Railroad has some more business for us to transact."

State governments took the initiative. The New England states set up railroad commissions, but the most famous state regulation came with the "Granger Laws" in about a dozen midwestern states, resulting from farm pressure. In general, these laws established regulatory commissions, forbade abuses, and attempted to establish reasonable rates.

Railroads fought this legislation vigorously and ignored the laws on the grounds that they were unconstitutional. Citing the Dartmouth College decision (page 113), railroad lawyers argued that the states had violated the original charters of the railroads. But in 1876 in *Munn* v. *Illinois,* the Supreme Court upheld the Constitutionality of an Illinois law which had fixed the maximum rates railroads could charge for storing grain. The court declared that when property is "affected with a public interest" it "must submit to control by the public for the common good." The Munn case set an important legal precedent for regulation. However, in the 1886 *Wabash* case (*Wabash, St. Louis and Pacific Railway Company* v. *Illinois*), the court held an Illinois law invalid because the railroad involved was engaged in interstate commerce. If the traffic was interstate in character, states could not regulate it.

The Interstate Commerce Act. With effective state action nullified, attention turned to the national Congress. A Senate investigating committee fortified the public clamor by strongly recommending regulation. The passage of the Interstate Commerce Act of 1887 was a landmark in American legislative history. The act provided for "just and reasonable" charges, forbade a higher charge for a short haul than for a long, made rebates illegal, and ordered that all rates and fares be publicly posted.

The administration of the law was placed in the hands of an Interstate Commerce Commission of five members, which was given the power to hear complaints, call witnesses, and issue decisions. If the ICC decided that a railroad company was violating the law, it was required to take the question to the federal circuit court. This requirement seriously weakened the commission because it made its role subordinate to that of the courts whose rulings were nearly always favorable to the railroad companies. The Interstate Commerce Commission was not an effective regulatory agency until it was later strengthened by additional legislation.

The Interstate Commerce Act was hardly a victory of the people against the railroads. Even the sponsor of the bill described it as "conservative legislation" made to look like a reform measure. From the railroad point of view, the act satisfied public agitation without really regulating. Yet, in the long run, the act was an important break in the dominant laissez-faire beliefs of the day. For the first time, the United States government had assumed the right to regulate a major business. The Interstate Commerce Act marked the beginning of federal regulation of business through the regulatory commission, a device used many times since the historic precedent of 1887.

The railroads continued on their merry way after the ICC Act until a severe economic depression, the panic of 1893, brought a number of them down to ruin. To secure funds for reorganization, the bankrupt roads turned to bankers, and to none more frequently than J. Pierpont Morgan, the nation's leading banker.

A veritable rock of stability and financial power, Morgan had a passion for order and a distaste for wasteful competition. In reorganizing some of the largest railroad systems in the country, the House of Morgan usually reduced the large debt, consolidated small lines into larger systems, and put some of its own men on the boards of directors of various railroads to give the Morgan interests some degree of control over them. Morgan and his associates charged high fees for their services, but they helped to bring stability to the industry.

The railroads, America's first big business, were a major influence in the developing economy. They served as "take-off" initiators, opened new areas for settlement, provided cheap, reliable transportation, and stimulated other industries. From the 1850's to the 1880's, American railroads stimulated economic growth far more than did any other industry. Meantime, rising new industries were beginning to adopt and modify patterns that were started by the railroads. From the 1880's on, other industries began to replace railroads as prime promoters of change in the American economy.

3 Industrial Empire Builders And Innovators Emerge

1. What were the primary characteristics of industry during the period from 1865 to 1914?

2. What type of men were most successful in industry from 1865 to 1914?

3. Do you think the same type of men would be successful today?

One of the emerging, dynamic industries was the iron and steel business. Technological advances, notably the Bessemer and open-hearth processes, made it possible to produce large quantities of steel cheaply. The rich iron deposits in upper Michigan and eastern Minnesota were developed as soon as railroads were extended into these areas. Steel, like other industries, needed men to organize and promote its expansion. Andrew Carnegie became the leading steel magnate in the late nineteenth century.

Andrew Carnegie. Andrew Carnegie was not a typical entrepreneur. He had genuine intellectual interests, wrote four books, and loved music and Shakespeare. A poor immigrant boy from Scotland, he came to America in 1848 at the age of twelve and worked up from the very bottom. He began as a bobbin boy in a cotton mill. By the time he was eighteen, he had become a telegraph clerk working for Thomas A. Scott, an official of the Pennsylvania Railroad. Carnegie worked hard, saved his money, made wise investments, and at twenty-eight had an income of about $50,000 per year.

Carnegie went into the iron and steel business and in 1875 opened his J. Edgar Thompson Steel Works, named for his chief customer, the president of the Pennsylvania Railroad. More than one thousand iron and steel companies existed in the nation in the 1880's. But, like railroads, steel manufacturing was not suited to small enterprises, and eventually a few giants controlled the business. Carnegie was a superb competitor, and in consolidating, he left a trail of ruined companies in his wake.

Carnegie had unlimited faith in America, and unlike his competitors he expanded during the depression which began in 1873. He said about his actions later:

> . . . so many of my friends needed money that they begged me to repay them [for their investments in Carnegie enterprises]. I did so and bought out five or six of them. That was what gave me my leading interest in this steel business.

He did not live lavishly from his profits, but plowed them back into the industry. He was one of the first industrialists to hire chemists and scientists to improve production. A superb salesman who benefitted from his early railroad experience, he developed what he called an "integrated" company, one which owned iron ore deposits, coal mines, limestone quarries, railroads, and a fleet of ore boats. This integration made it possible for ore mined in Minnesota on Monday to be made into steel rails in Pittsburgh by Saturday night. His rise was based on production efficiency, low labor costs, and unusually able partners. He had a cunning way of pitting his partners against each other so as to strengthen his own position in the company.

By the 1890's, Carnegie was the leading steel producer. His company made a profit of $40 million in 1890, of which Carnegie's personal share was $25 million. Fear of his great power led makers of finished products like wire and tubing to plan to band together to produce their own steel, and thus become independent of Carnegie. In retaliation, Carnegie threatened to begin producing finished products himself and drive these other producers out of business. A major war seemed imminent in the steel industry. But the Scotsman wanted to retire, and he sold out to the Morgan interests in 1901 for just under $500 million. J. P. Morgan then proceeded to organize a gigantic company, the United States Steel Corporation, with capital of $1.4 billion, the first billion-dollar corporation.

John D. Rockefeller. Machines needed oil, and as more and more of them came into use, the petroleum business grew in importance. Petroleum had often been seen, especially in western Pennsylvania, seeping to the surface of streams and springs, but nobody had known what to do with it. Enterprising salesmen bottled and sold it as a cure-all patent medicine. When it was found that petroleum could be used for lighting and that it was valuable for its by-products—paraffin, naphtha, and lubricating oil—prospectors flocked to western Pennsylvania as to a gold rush.

The first oil well was put down by Edwin L. Drake in 1859 near Titusville, Pennsylvania. Soon, forests of derricks rose in pastures and cornfields, and the area took on all the elements of a wild frontier mining region. Refineries, more profitable than wells, were established mainly in Pittsburgh and Cleveland. But soon there was too much oil, prices fluctuated wildly, and chaotic conditions prevailed.

Into this situation came the greatest consolidationist of his day—John Davison Rockefeller. He came to Cleveland as a young man, saved his money, and with a skilled oil technician, Sidney Andrews, entered the oil business at the end of the Civil War. He saw the need to bring order into the chaotic oil industry by consolidating the oil refineries. This meant eliminating competitors, which he proceeded to do with cold-blooded efficiency. He and his associates drove most of the other refineries in Cleveland to the wall, and in 1870, they organized the Standard Oil Company.

The early success of the Standard was based on its ability to make a high quality "standard" product, which did not fluctuate in quality, at a lower cost. The company charged low rates in certain areas to choke off a competitor. As the business expanded, Rockefeller took a decisive step. From the railroads that shipped Standard Oil products, he demanded and got substantial rebates, which gave him a tremendous advantage over his competitors.

In 1872, the Standard Oil Company secretly banded together with several large railroad companies to form the South Improvement Company. The purpose of this organization was to give the companies involved special shipping advantages. The scheme provided that the railroads in the Pennsylvania oilfields would (1) raise their shipping rates to companies not part of the South Improvement Company, (2) grant Standard Oil and its affiliates large rebates on their oil shipments, and (3) grant them a *drawback*, that is, a part of the rates competing oil companies paid!

The public learned of this scheme, and it had to be abandoned, but the Standard Oil Company continued to get rebates and drawbacks. Rockefeller's position became stronger, and he was able to buy out a number of competing oil companies during the panic of 1873. By 1880, Standard Oil controlled about 95 percent of the nation's oil refining business.

John D. Rockefeller spoke of consolidating the refineries in these words:

It had to come, though all we saw at the moment was the need to save ourselves from wasteful conditions . . . The day of combination is here to stay. Individualism is gone, never to return.

A devout Baptist and regular Sunday-school teacher, this shrewd, silent operator ruined competitors with pitiless skill. Intensely single-minded and diligent, Rockefeller by the late 1890's was the richest man in America. His statement "God gave me money" reflected his belief that he was a trustee of his huge fortune, over $500 million of which he gave away to various worthy projects.

Field, Sholes, and Bell. New inventions brought better communication and also created large new industries. The telegraph, introduced before the Civil War, was extended to all parts of the nation. In 1866 Cyrus Field successfully completed his transatlantic telegraph cable, making fast communication with Europe possible. In the early 1870's, Christopher L. Sholes and his associates made the first practical typewriter.

Even more significant was the invention of the telephone by Alexander Graham Bell in 1876. His "speaking telegraph," or telephone, was thought to be a toy at first, but its practical value soon became realized. The Bell Company won expensive patent suits over its rivals, and its service steadily improved. Male operators, who sometimes "cussed out" irritable customers, were replaced by the more polite "hello girls." Long distance service was added in 1884; and to expand its business, the Bell directors set up a new company, the American Telephone and Telegraph Company in 1885, a consolidation of over one hundred local conpanies. A. T. & T. dominated the business and still does. It is the world's largest corporation in terms of total assets.

Edison and Westinghouse. Economists who emphasize the importance of the innovator as a

DEVELOPMENTS IN SCIENCE AND TECHNOLOGY

Date	Inventor	Contribution
1864	George Pullman	railroad sleeping car
1866	Cyrus Field	transatlantic cable
1867	Christopher L. Sholes	typewriter
1869	George Westinghouse	air brake
1876	Alexander Graham Bell	telephone
1878	Thomas A. Edison	phonograph
1879	Thomas A. Edison	first practical incandescent light bulb
1891	Thomas A. Edison	first radio patent in the United States
1884	Ottimar Mergenthaler	linotype printing machine
1895	George B. Selden	first automobile patent
1896	C. Francis Jenkins Thomas Armat	motion-picture projector
1903	Wilbur and Orville Wright	first successful flight in a motor-powered plane
1918	Peter C. Hewitt F. B. Crocker	helicopter

promoter of growth stress the career of the inventor-entrepreneur Thomas Alva Edison. This remarkable man, who created a research laboratory at Menlo Park, New Jersey, took out over one hundred patents, including patents for the phonograph, the storage battery, the motion picture projector, and the mimeograph. His most important achievement was the discovery of the incandescent lamp, or electric light bulb.

In 1882, the Edison Illuminating Company opened a power station in New York City and began to supply current to eighty-five customers. The Edison system used direct current which could be transmitted only a mile or two. It was soon demonstrated that alternating current could be sent safely over long distances, and this encouraged George Westinghouse to organize the Westinghouse Electric Company in 1886. Edison stubbornly refused to believe that alternating current was safe, and predicted that Westinghouse would kill one of his customers. For a time the expression "to Westinghouse" meant to electrocute. But the Westinghouse system proved itself, and alternating current became standard.

The industry expanded rapidly, and in 1882 the General Electric Company was formed from the union of the Edison companies and other interests. The electrical industry was a powerful stimulant to the economy and an innovation which affected the life of every American.

Henry Ford. Of all the emerging American industries, none exploited the possibilities of mass production as effectively as the automobile industry. Henry Ford was a genuine industrial innovator. When he entered the automobile business in 1903, only the rich could afford cars. Ford proposed to mass-produce automobiles so that they could become cheap enough for nearly everyone. He believed that mass production for a broad market, plus high wages for his workers, would result in large profits for the company.

By installing ever more efficient assembly lines, Ford was able to produce a car every ninety-three minutes in 1914, and a car every ten seconds by 1925. The price of the Model T (the customer could have any color as long as it was black) went down from $850 in 1909 to $290 in 1927, when it was discontinued. In 1914, Ford established the $5-per-day wage rate, much higher than the prevailing rate in the industry.

Model T's, or Tin Lizzies, as they were called, were scattered over the land, profits rolled in, and Henry Ford became an immensely wealthy man and an American folk hero. When he became famous, his comments on a variety of social questions were widely quoted. They nearly always revealed Ford's limited social outlook in many fields. He declared he had no use for all the art in the world, and he also said that "history is bunk," a remark that has not endeared him to historians. He once placed the American Revolution in 1812 and admitted he did not understand the Constitution. The company newspaper, *The Dearborn Independent*, was anti-Semitic.

Although Ford paid high wages, he drove his men hard, tolerated no unions, employed spies to keep an eye on the workers, and enforced such rigid plant supervision that the workers devised the "Ford whisper" so they could talk without moving their lips. Ford stubbornly refused to make changes in the Model T and as a result lost his dominant position in the industry in the 1920's. But with all his shortcomings, Henry Ford was a great innovator in terms of his basic concepts of mass production, low prices, high wages, and high profits.

In these new industries, entrepreneurs like Carnegie, Edison, and Ford brought new technology to large enterprises. But technical progress did not result solely from the work of a few well-known inventors and innovators. More frequently it came from an endless series of improvements made by unknown skilled workmen, a testimony to the quality of American skilled labor. As technical progress continued, so did the trend toward powerful business combinations, which reached its highest peak at the turn of the century. The American public welcomed new technology, but its attitude toward powerful combinations became increasingly fearful and hostile.

4 Industrial Consolidation Brings Government Regulation

1. Why did industry tend toward monopolistic organizations?

2. What stages of economic growth and decline, both within a specific industry as well as on a national level, can you identify?

3. To what extent is government regulation of business desirable in a free society?

4. Do you think that because a company is big, it is necessarily bad?

During the latter half of the nineteenth century, there was a powerful, almost inevitable, tendency in the American business scene toward business consolidation. Nearly every industry began with many small, competing companies. The companies usually overexpanded, prices fell, as did profits, and business concerns found themselves enmeshed in an intense, self-defeating, competitive struggle. United action in some form was the only escape from the dilemma.

In industry after industry between 1865 and 1900, so many businesses joined together in combinations that the number of firms decreased although the value of their products increased many times. By 1900, less than 2 percent of the manufacturing companies in the nation produced nearly 50 percent of the total manufactured goods. The tendency toward consolidation was not confined to American capitalism; wherever industrialization occurred, the same trend was evident—in Japan, Germany, France, and Britain.

Pools. The *pool* was the first method American companies used to join together in order to avoid the hazards of competition. It usually took the form of an agreement among several companies in the same industry to keep prices up, divide the market, and control output. But pooling agreements were not legally binding, and members tended to violate them whenever it was in their interest to do so. Pools proved unreliable and were generally abandoned in the 1880's.

Trusts. Another way in which businessmen attempted to combine their companies in order to further their interests was through the *trust*. Corporations in related businesses combined into a trust. The stockholders of the corporations turned their stock over to a group of *trustees*, the men who would run the trust. In return, the stockholders received *trust certificates*, which earned dividends on the basis of the profits the trust made.

The idea behind forming a trust was that it could eliminate competition and earn greater profits than competing individual corporations could. With enough corporations in the trust, the trustees could control an entire industry, thereby creating a monopoly. With a monopoly, or even a near-monopoly, they gained much greater control over the prices they charged for their products. The Standard Oil Company was the first trust, but other powerful combinations like the Sugar Trust, the Whiskey Trust, and the Steel

Trust used the same type of organization. The word *trust* came to be used for any big business, regardless of its organization.

The call for regulation. Consumers and many small businesses soon raised a cry of protest against the monopolies because they felt they were being victimized by them. Consumers had to pay the high prices the monopolies charged, and small concerns were being squeezed out of competition by large consolidated firms. Both groups began to demand government control of these giants.

The consolidation movement also ran squarely against strong American traditions. The capitalistic system was supposed to operate best with free competition, which would automatically regulate prices and production. Moreover, as we saw in the national bank struggle in Jackson's day, there was a powerful American distrust of uncontrolled financial power. American democracy seemed to many to be turning into a *plutocracy*—rule by the rich for their gain, to the detriment of the public interest. A widespread feeling developed that monopolies must be checked. As Henry Demarest Lloyd, a reformer, put it: "If the tendency to combination is inevitable, control of it is imperative."

The sentiment for control became so insistent that by the late 1880's all of the major political parties included in their platforms some kind of antitrust planks. Public outrage was quickened by widely publicized abuses of big firms and by the stranglehold of companies like Standard Oil. Action came first in the states, but state action was ineffective and in some instances was promoted by the trusts themselves to forestall federal regulation.

Sponsors of federal antitrust legislation faced a perplexing Constitutional problem. The Interstate Commerce Act was clearly based on the interstate commerce power given to Congress in the Constitution; but the trusts were almost exclusively manufacturing companies operating within state boundaries. Conservatives feared that if the federal government could regulate these companies, they could regulate anything. However, John Sherman of Ohio took a broader view and argued that the interstate commerce clause of the Constitution contained the necessary authority to deal with this problem.

The Sherman Anti-Trust Act. The Sherman Anti-Trust Act was passed in 1890, unanimously in the House and with only one dissenting vote in the Senate. Its essential clause provided that all combinations and contracts "in restraint of trade or commerce among the Several States, or with foreign nations" are illegal. The purpose of the act was "to protect trade and commerce against unlawful restraints and monopolies." The attorney-general's office was empowered to bring suits against such combinations as were guilty under law, subjecting their officers to heavy fines and jail sentences. Persons injured by such combinations could sue for damages in the federal courts.

The Sherman Anti-Trust Act did not discourage consolidation. It was vague in its wording, and its precise meaning was left to the determination of the courts. Like the Interstate Commerce Act, it was ineffective until a later period. Presidents Harrison, Cleveland, and McKinley had no interest in bringing suits against trusts. Large industrial combinations simply devised new types of business organization which would make them less vulnerable to suits under the Sherman Act.

A favorite new type of organization was the *holding company*, a form of corporate organization which exists today in such giants as the United States Steel Corporation and Standard Oil of New Jersey. In the holding company, the directing corporation "holds" the controlling stock of member companies. It directs the operations of the producing companies under its wing. Thus, the United States Steel Corporation plans and controls the operations of National Tube, American Steel and Wire, and other companies which produce various kinds of steel products.

Another less formal type of consolidation was the *interlocking directorate*. Directors in one corporation often became directors in several other corporations, thus contributing to unified action and common understanding. These and other forms of industrial combination led to increasing business consolidation in spite of the Sherman Anti-Trust Act.

As Finley Peter Dunne, the political humorist, said of the Sherman Act: "What looks like a stone wall to a layman, is a triumphal arch to a corporation lawyer." Between 1898 and 1902, business

The abuses of rapidly growing and powerful industry gave cartoonists all they could want for subject matter with which to display their talents. Thomas Nast, perhaps the foremost cartoonist of the time, drew the devastating protest at the right in 1889. Note the ship named "The People" foundering at the foot of statue. Joseph Keppler drew the cartoon below in the magazine *Puck* in the same year, shortly before Congress was about to debate the Sherman Anti-Trust Bill. Note his symbol of the closed door at the Peoples' Entrance.

THE BOSSES OF THE SENATE

consolidation reached its highest peak ever; during those four years 189 new combinations were organized with a total capitalization of $4 billion. However, beginning in 1903, Congress made funds available for antitrust suits, and the Sherman Act began to be enforced somewhat more vigorously. The Northern Securities railroad combination was dissolved in 1904, and the Standard Oil Company was adjudged to be in violation of the Sherman Act in 1911.

The idea behind the Sherman Act was that the government should act to protect free competition without destroying large business organizations. It was unique among the industrial nations: no other country adopted similar legislation in this period. The Sherman Act, strengthened by later antitrust measures, attempted to revive the old American concept of free competition against the threat of huge combinations operating "in restraint of trade." Despite the difficulties in determining what "restraint of trade" meant, the Sherman Act provided the only brake against monopolistic practices in big business.

The role of banking. As with railroads, consolidation of other industries brought in banking interests who were able to gain a large measure of control over many industries. Finance capitalism was an indication of a maturing economy in which individual firms could no longer finance their operations, and banking capital had accumulated to the point where it could invest and partially control consolidated firms. It was in this phase that the House of Morgan gained an almost mythical reputation as a financial colossus.

As bankers came to have a greater role in big businesses of all kinds, a concern arose about the "money power." In the Progressive era (Chapter 17) this fear prompted the establishment in 1912 of the Pujo Committee of the House of Representatives to investigate the money trust.

The committee found that a small group of financiers "strike at the very vitals of potential competition in every industry that is under their protection." In its report on the Morgan interests, the committee discovered a great concentration of power. If all the Morgan partners in affiliated banks were lumped together, it would be found that these men held 341 directorships in 112 corporations with a total capitalization of $22 billion. While it cannot be argued that all of these

men worked closely together, a small group of men did possess very substantial control over large sectors of the national economy. As consolidation brought many small businesses into a few hands, the wealth of the nation became highly concentrated in a relatively tiny group of top business leaders.

5 The New Rich Manifest New Attitudes And Behavior

1. According to social Darwinism, will the fittest individuals emerge in positions of importance and leadership in a free and open society? Why? Do you agree with this position?

2. Do you think the rich were justified in the accumulation of enormous wealth? How would a believer in the theory of the Gospel of Wealth answer this question?

Industrialization in America brought a new class of power. Business leaders became the elite of American society, replacing the old middle class and political leaders like Clay, Webster, and Calhoun. Most of the new ruling group came to their high position quickly and with little sense of the social consequences of their great wealth. As a group they tended to regard themselves as self-made men whose business activities were identical with the good of the country.

They lived within a particular climate of attitudes and beliefs. Frederick Lewis Allen, in his biography of J. Pierpont Morgan, described the social setting of the upper-class businessman:

He [Morgan] belonged to what in Europe would be called the *haute bourgeoisie* . . . a vaguely defined group of men who had plenty of money, were engaged in large corporate business or finance, voted the Republican ticket, believed in the sanctity of property, subscribed to sedate and conservative newspapers, held a low view of most politicians and practically all Democratic politicians, and an even lower view of "labor agitators"; who belonged to the right sort of

J. P. MORGAN'S NOSE

Edward Steichen created a work of art in this photograph which illustrates the great Morgan's formidable appearance. Steichen observed that meeting Morgan's gaze was like confronting the headlights of an express train bearing down on one. Morgan hated the picture, but after critics praised it as great art, he offered to buy it for $5,000.

Many stories surround Morgan's character, behavior, and appearance. A favorite piece of Morgan folklore deals with an unfortunate ailment that afflicted him—a nose infection called rhinophyma, which gave him a markedly large nose. When Dwight Morrow, a banker and later American ambassador to Mexico, became a Morgan partner, Mrs. Morrow decided to invite the eminent man for tea. Her only worry was that her precocious daughter, Anne, might innocently make some remark about Morgan's astonishing nose. Anne was carefully drilled to say only, "Good afternoon, Mr. Morgan," and then leave.

Little Anne did perfectly, and as she left the room, Mrs. Morrow was wildly relieved. She turned to the great man. "Mr. Morgan," she said, "do you take nose in your tea"?

church (preferably the Episcopal Church, which as Clarence Day* put it was "a sect with the minimum of nonsense about it—no total immersion, no exhorters, no holy confession"); served on the boards of well-established charities, hospitals, and museums; joined reputable clubs . . . where they would be unlikely to be troubled by hearing any queer ideas; had a proper taste for good cigars and good wines; had decent manners, at least toward one another; and expected their wives to be charming and angelic, but not to know anything about their business affairs or for that matter about affairs of moment.

Morgan himself had little social traffic with artists, musicians, writers, scholars, or with professional men generally, except corporation lawyers and such architects or lawyers or physicians as he or his firm might have occasion to engage professionally. His social world was a world of business gentlemen of English descent and Protestant affiliations.

It is true that Morgan was a giant among business leaders, but many a lesser businessman

*Hero of the play *Life with Father.*

shared the same general attitudes and social atmosphere.

Social Darwinism. Charles Darwin's idea of an evolutionary struggle seemed to fit the American business battlefield perfectly. Although evolution had been discussed for many years, Darwin was the first to systematize the theory and provide factual evidence to support it.

In his great work, *The Origin of Species,* published in 1859, Darwin argued that all living animals and plants had evolved from earlier forms over millions of years, and that existing species were the result of a process of natural selection. In the constant struggle for life, those organisms which were best suited to survive were, so to speak, "selected" by nature. Their offspring carried the particular variations which enabled them to survive, and over a very long time a new species was produced.

Social Darwinism, the application of the principles of evolution to society, held that struggle was the natural state of life and that in that struggle the strong prevailed and the weak died. Businessmen found these ideas most congenial because they justified what they were doing and, better still, they had a "scientific" basis.

Most of the business elite had fought their way up through the competitive struggle of their business, and many believed that they had succeeded because of their own superior virtues—industry, thrift, piety, and brains. According to their view, people who did not succeed had some defect of character—laziness, alcoholism, immorality, or stupidity. Those who got to the top did so because of their superior survival qualities.

The leading exponent of social Darwinism was the Englishman Herbert Spencer, who had coined the expression "survival of the fittest" before Darwin's *Origin of Species* was published. Spencer believed that evolution was leading to social progress and that in the struggle for the better society, the fit must be strengthened and the weak sloughed off. So extreme was Spencer's opposition to government interference with this process that he opposed public education or even public health measures. He felt that if the poor could not survive, let them die; nature's laws are impartial and absolute.

The ablest American disciple of Spencer was William Graham Sumner, a leading sociologist and professor at Yale. Sumner believed that men became millionaires by the process of natural selection. They simply had superior qualities for the harsh struggle for survival, and their success was beneficial to society because they accumulated the capital which was vitally needed for economic growth.

Sumner regarded social planning and government regulation as futile and superficial. He had an overwhelming contempt for reformers, do-gooders, socialists, and legislation like the Sherman Anti-Trust Act. Unlike most businessmen, Sumner was consistent in that he also opposed government assistance to business. "Professor," a student once asked Sumner, "don't you believe in government aid to industries?" "No," replied the Professor, "It's root, hog, or die."

People who had never heard of Spencer or Sumner could nonetheless understand the idea of social Darwinism in a simplified form. The common faith of the day equated success with hard work, reasonable honesty, shrewdness, willingness to take a chance, and perhaps, a little luck. The optimistic and sentimental novels of Horatio Alger, so immensely popular at the time were more congenial to the popular mind than the heavily argued works of Spencer and Sumner. Alger's heroes always got to the top through pluck, hard work, honesty, and a stroke of good fortune. Alger's recognition of luck as a factor in the rise of the successful businessman was often closer to the truth than the dogmatic assertions of the social Darwinists about the superior qualities of businessmen.

The Gospel of Wealth. The Gospel of Wealth, a business creed expounded most clearly by Andrew Carnegie, was related to social Darwinism. It combined Darwinian evolution with Protestant ethics. Carnegie, in describing the duties of the wealthy, put it this way:

> First, to set an example of modest living, shunning display or extravagance; and . . . to consider all surplus revenues which come to him simply as trust funds, which he is called to administer . . . in the manner best calculated to produce the most beneficial results for the community—the man of wealth thus becoming the mere agent . . . for his poorer brethren, bringing to their service his superior wisdom, experience, and ability to administer, doing for them better than they would or could do for themselves. . . . Such in my opinion is the true Gospel concerning Wealth.

Carnegie added that "The man who dies thus rich dies disgraced."

The Gospel of Wealth implied the superiority of the wealthy, a struggle for survival in which only the shortcomings of the individual would limit his success, and no government interference except to protect property. The rich, because of their superior understanding, would decide what was best for the poor.

The philanthropic activities of some of the business leaders showed that not all of them were callous to their social responsibilities. Rockefeller gave away about $500 million to foundations, colleges, and programs for social betterment in the South. Carnegie gave away a large part of his fortune, much of it to libraries in the United States and abroad. Vanderbilt is best remembered for his contributions to Vanderbilt University; and Daniel Drew, one of the greatest fleecers of the lambs, is best known, ironically, as the founder of the Drew Theological Seminary!

Cost seemed to be no object when the newly rich sought to display their affuence. Cornelius Vanderbilt, grandson of the railroad tycoon, was particularly adept at such displays. He spent $4 million to build a seventy-room "cottage"—his summer home in Newport, Rhode Island. Completed in 1895, The Breakers, as he called it, became an incredible showplace. One of its rooms, the billiard room, appears at the right. Perhaps never before or since has the game of billiards been played in such splendor. The Bradley Martin Ball presented another opportunity for the rich to amuse themselves amid splendid surroundings. In 1897, *Harper's Weekly* carried the illustration of it below, made from sketches done at the ball. The ball made the Martins so successful at showing the extent of their wealth that their tax assessment was doubled as a result. Shortly thereafter, the family moved abroad.

Through assorted charities and good works, many of the elite satisfied themselves that they were contributing to the good of society. But many of them spent their money lavishly for their personal self-esteem and glorification.

Conspicuous displays of wealth. One of the leading economists of the time, Thorstein Veblen, was a severe critic of American capitalism. He used the term *conspicuous waste* to describe the efforts of the new rich to show off their status. The sober-minded wealthy used restraint in spending their money, but the extravagance of others turned the period into what has been called the "Great Barbecue."

Parties and dinners became more elaborate and lavish, some of them the result of a frantic effort to reach high society. A Pittsburgh millionaire sat his guests down at a table in the center of which was a large glass tank in which a female disported, lightly clad in golden fish scales. A competitor put his girl in a huge pie, out of which she bounded along with a flock of brilliantly plumed birds.

At Newport, Rhode Island, one of the summer play spots for the rich, a party was given for the pet dogs of millionaires. According to social chronicler Cleveland Amory, most of the dogs appeared in fancy dress and the menu was "stewed liver and rice, fricasse of bones, and shredded dog biscuit." Another of Newport's excesses was the "monkey dinner," at which a monkey, in full evening dress, drank too much champagne, climbed the chandelier, and pelted the guests with light bulbs.

The most notorious of all the extravagant parties was the Bradley Martin Ball of 1897, held in a period of bad times and bread lines. The Bradley Martins billed the affair as a way of helping the needy "by putting money into circulation." They rented the Waldorf-Astoria Hotel in New York City and transformed the interior into a magnificent replica of the palace at Versailles in France, using tapestries, exotic flowers, and hundreds of lights. Several hundred guests came dressed as characters from the courts of the kings and queens of France and England. The party cost $350,000 including the costumes; it was widely reported that financier August Belmont spent $10,000 on his costume—a suit of gold-inlaid armor.

This party was denounced in the press, and many conservative businessmen were alarmed by this kind of reckless display. Mark Hanna, the Cleveland industrialist, thought it was foolish and remarked that it would have served the witless Martins right if some terrorist had thrown a bomb and blown "the dancing fops and their ladies to spangles and red paste." It was much more dignified to spend one's money on a stable of horses, a private yacht, European art works, or large ornate houses. One such vast residence contained a pool, a gym, a billiard room, a private chapel with a ten-ton marble altar, a $50,000 organ, and a refrigerator large enough to hold twenty tons of beef.

Such was the fluff and gilt of the industrial age, fascinating social history in an age of widespread economic hardship and discontent. It is true that even the poor were better off than they had been previously, but the rich were more numerous and vastly wealthier than ever before. It was the great *difference* between the two that many noticed. While Andrew Carnegie was enjoying an annual personal income of something like $15 million (with no income taxes), the mass of unskilled workers in the North were receiving less than $460 a year, and in the South less than $300.

■ CONCLUSION

Some historians have referred to the entrepreneurs of the American Industrial Revolution as "Robber Barons" and have stressed their greed, their cold-blooded destruction of competitors, and such unethical practices as bribing legislatures. Their critics, for example, Matthew Josephson, have seen them as dominated by the profit motive, to the detriment of consumers and the general public. More recently, such historians as Allan Nevins and others have treated them more favorably. Nevins, in his book *John D. Rockefeller*, emphasizes Rockefeller's positive achievements: his organization of the industry, his technical innovations, and his philanthropic efforts. But to defend the entrepreneur on the grounds of the business ethics of his day is to forget the protests of their activities and to ignore the working classes. The issue is difficult to settle on moral grounds. Industrialization was achieved, but the cost was extremely high.

It may be more profitable to look at their philosophy in terms of its adequacy to the American scene. This philosophy, as we have seen, held that the rich had superior qualities, that divisions between rich and poor would always exist, and that there was nothing the state could do about it. Many Americans admired the success of the rich businessman. But when his activities seemed to foreclose the opportunity of every American to succeed, widespread dissent followed. On this point the ideals of the entrepreneurial class were at odds with the powerful American tradition of equality of opportunity.

The factor of greatest long-range importance in the era from the Civil War to World War I was the creation of higher standards of living through the use of machines. To be sure, benefits were highly concentrated in a few hands and the gains came in a wasteful, uncontrolled, ruthlessly competitive manner. Material success became the ultimate measure of human achievement, but life in the dirty, congested industrial cities made a mockery of that goal for millions. Yet, in spite of the heavy cost in human suffering and frustration, the enormous productive capacity of the new industrial system created for the first time the vision of a world without poverty and want.

But if Americans had found the means to lift burdens from men's backs, they had not yet discovered how to spread the benefits of industrialization equitably among the people. The laboring classes of the nation shared these benefits less than any other group. If the industrial movement was the Second American Revolution, a third revolution was coming which would bring more of the advantages of industrialization to the common people. That revolution was begun by reform agitation and the rise of the American labor movement.

■ QUESTIONS

1. What factors were at work in the United States that contributed to its rapid industrialization? Are all of these factors still present and to the same degree in this nation? How would you compare them then and now?

2. Do you think that railroad growth could have been accomplished if the railroad builders and consolidators were entirely free from corruption? Can you make a comparison with any currently fast-growing industry?

3. What business practices can you identify that contributed to economic growth during the Second American Revolution? How are they similar or different from business practices you can identify today?

4. Do you think that the industrial and economic growth achieved in the period from 1865 to 1914 could have been achieved without the creation of monopolies? Why or why not?

5. Is it possible to identify stages of economic growth and decline? If so, what are they?

6. What characteristics best describe the captains of industry during the late nineteenth century? Which of these characteristics are still admired and which are not? Why are some no longer admired?

7. To what can you attribute the popularity at the time of social Darwinism and the Gospel of Wealth?

■ BIBLIOGRAPHY

BUREAU OF THE CENSUS, *Historical Statistics of the United States: Colonial Times to 1957*, Government Printing Office. Although it may seem strange to recommend a book of statistics, the reader may gain some insights into American life after a few surveys and comparisons. Some students may like a good historical novel while others may prefer working with figures. With the statistics the student can develop his own hypothesis with less restriction than a student who reads a predigested text.

COCHRAN, THOMAS C., AND WILLIAM MILLER, *The Age of Enterprise: A Social History of Industrial America*, Harper & Row (Torchbooks). This is probably the best general history of industrial growth in America, and despite its early publication date, remains somewhat of a standard source. The popularity of the book stems from its ability to handle economic topics in an intelligible manner without the use of jargon and excessive tables and statistics.

ROSTOW, WALT WHITMAN, *The Stages of Economic Growth, A Non-Communist Manifesto*, Cambridge University Press. Rostow's model for economic growth is particularly interesting since it suggests a general process through which industrializing nations pass. Thus the student has a handy model to apply to both American economic development and also the growth of today's emerging nations. Certainly there are weaknesses to the theory, but it is still a valuable tool for the student who seeks a general method rather than countless thousands of vaguely related facts.

JOSEPHSON, MATTHEW, *The Robber Barons*, Harcourt Brace. Written during the depression, *The Robber Barons* has lent a label to the stereotyped view of the evil industrialist at the end of the nineteenth century. The student will probably want to read selectively because of the length of the book.

ADAMS, CHARLES FRANCIS, JR., AND HENRY ADAMS, *Chapters of Erie*, Cornell University Press. Brother Henry concentrated upon the gold conspiracy of 1869 while Charles Francis Adams Jr. was writing an exposé of the corruption of the Erie Railroad, perhaps the most manipulated corporation in our history. The investigations were typically thorough and the basic positions have remained generally unchanged through the years. The Adams's exposés set the pattern for the muckraking stories which followed later.

NEVINS, ALLAN, *John D. Rockefeller*, ed. and abr. by William Greenleaf, Scribner. For a much broader portrait of Rockefeller than that provided by Josephson the student should read this condensation of Nevins's' two-volume biography. Some scholars may argue that Nevins was too generous to Rockefeller, but the student will still find valuable insight into Rockefeller's career as industrialist and philanthropist.

LATHAM, EARL, ed., *John D. Rockefeller: Robber Baron or Industrial Statesman*, Problems in American Civilization Series, Heath. By presenting opposing points of view, Latham encourages the student to form his own opinion of Rockefeller and thus his fellow industrialists. The student should be particularly aware of the date of publication of each article and the background of the author in order to better evaluate the selection.

HOFSTADTER, RICHARD, *Social Darwinism in American Thought*, Beacon Press. This is the best discussion of the influence of Darwin's biological theory upon American social thought and behavior. The student needs to understand the theory of Social Darwinism before evaluating the behavior of nineteenth-century industrialists, and in this book he can find an intelligible explanation of the theory and application.

NORRIS, FRANK, *The Octopus*, New American Library (Signet Books). This novel is a dramatic indictment of the railroad industry as it operated in California at the end of the century. The student is bound to be moved by the corrupt business practices and the unequal distribution of wealth and privilege. Norris was an important literary muckraker and author of social protest.

HOWELLS, WILLIAM DEAN, *The Rise of Silas Lapham*, Collier. Silas Lapham is a fictionalized character who portrays the rising businessman of the nineteenth century. Although business considerations are handled, the book focuses upon the adjustment of the new rich in American society.

Labor And Immigration

The enormous industrial expansion of the United States obviously could not have taken place without a steadily expanding labor force. Such a force came from two sources—native labor from the American countryside and a large influx of immigrants, mostly eastern and southern Europeans. In the fifty years after the Civil War, labor tried to find ways to organize and to gain its fair share of the wealth that industry and machines were creating. Its efforts to achieve these ends were only partially successful, and they were accompanied by unusually turbulent and violent labor-management relations. Industrial and business managers feared the rise of labor and fought against it with all of their great resources and power.

New immigrants made up a large percentage of the working class. Both the new immigrants and the native-born laborers sought to achieve the rich material promise of American life. Both groups sometimes felt that they were "strangers in the land" because of public opposition and mistrust. But in an expanding and optimistic nation, both groups continued to believe that, in time, the blessings of the Industrial Age would come to them and their children. As you read about these people, keep these questions in mind:

1. What conditions caused workers to organize labor unions?
2. What kinds of unions did they form?
3. How successful were these unions in correcting conditions?
4. What caused great floods of immigrants to come to the New World?
5. What problems did they encounter as they sought to find the promise they thought it held?

1 Workers Organize To Protect Their Interests

1. What new forces of industrialization led to the creation of problems for the American working man? What was the nature of these problems?

2. What factors made the labor movement necessary for the well being of the working man at the turn of the century?

3. Why did groups such as farmers and businessmen regard the labor movement as un-American?

4. How do you account for the lack of success of socialism within the union movement and the basic conservatism of labor leaders?

One of the high costs of industrialization is the cost in human suffering. Many Americans in the last quarter of the nineteenth century began to be aware of the effects of industrial development upon human beings—the men who dug the coal, poured the steel, and operated the machines. The outlook was often grim.

Long hours and low wages. Many workers found it difficult to earn a decent living. At the turn of the century, industrial wages averaged between $400 and $600 a year, or about $9 a week. Prices of typical commodities were also low: beef cost 17½¢ a pound; eggs 21½¢ a dozen; shoes about $2 a pair. But while these prices were low by modern standards, they were high in relation to an average worker's income. Experts estimated that an annual income of $600 was necessary to maintain a minimum standard of living in this period. Clearly, many industrial workers were barely able to buy the necessities of life for themselves and their children.

Hours of work in the early factories tended to approximate the hours of daylight. One of labor's most persistent demands during this period was the eight-hour day, but by 1910 only about 8 percent of all workers had achieved that goal. The length of the workday did gradually decline, but by the 1880's workweeks ranging from sixty to eighty hours were still common. Work schedules were particularly heavy for trainmen, bakers, and textile workers. The workday in the North Carolina textile industry averaged over eleven hours, even for women and children, who made up over half the work force. Employers wanted to keep their expensive machinery going full-tilt when demand was high. The machine determined working conditions. The worker had to adjust to it, not the other way around.

Unsafe working conditions. Working conditions were frequently hazardous to life, limb, and health. Every year approximately sixteen or seventeen thousand operating trainmen in the railroad industry were injured. Miners faced a constant threat of devastating underground explosions, fires, and fumes. In textile mills, which employed many women and children, conditions were noisy, damp, and unhealthy. Before the passage of effective compulsory school attendance laws, beginning about 1901, child labor was common. In 1890, approximately six hundred thousand children between the ages of ten and fourteen were working in industry, often under conditions harmful to their health.

Man vs. machine. In addition to the day-by-day hardships of working conditions, there were profound psychological frustrations. Machines made work monotonous and lessened pride in workmanship. At a New York Worker's Lyceum meeting in 1880, men spoke of the "treadmill monotony of existence" and deplored "the tension resulting from the American system of seeking to increase quantity, rather than quality of products."

In industry after industry, new machines made old skills obsolete. Formerly, a good shoemaker, for example, had a solid bargaining position because his skill was valuable to his employer. But when his job could be done by a machine operated by an unskilled workman, his experience counted for little. One textile mill superintendent told in 1880 how his company avoided trouble with the skilled workers who operated spinning mules, a type of spinning machine:

The mule-spinners are a tough crowd to deal with. A few years ago they were giving trouble at this mill, so one Saturday afternoon, after they had gone home, we started right in and smashed up a roomful of mules with sledge hammers. When the men came back on Monday morning, they were astonished to find that

The rapid industrializing of the United States during the latter half of the nineteenth century and into the twentieth drew millions of workers—men, women, and children—into the factories. The photographs on these pages were all taken by Lewis W. Hine, who frequently used labor conditions for subject matter. Below, women and children work in a vegetable cannery in 1912. Note that the only man in this operation is the foreman in the background. At the right, a girl of perhaps ten years stands by her spinning machine in a textile mill in North Carolina in 1908; she was one of the approximately 75,000 workers under sixteen in the textile industry and one of the nearly two million in all industries at the time. Below right is another 1908 picture, showing men and boys at work in a glass works in Indianapolis, Indiana. Because of the heat and the need to work at great speed, work in the glass factories was particularly hard on the workers' health.

there was no work for them. That room is now full of ring frames [a new spinning machine] run by girls.

American workers began to feel a loss of identity as large industry destroyed the old personal relationship which had existed between the employer and employee in a small shop. As the worker became just another cog in the machinery, management began to regard him as merely a "commodity" of production, another cost item. Labor deeply resented being thus depersonalized. John Mitchell, head of the United Mine Workers union, protested:

Make men commodities? Labor . . . is a part of the very being of the man who sells it. The commodity sold is a human creature, whose welfare in the eye of the law should be of more importance than any mere accumulation of wealth on the part of the community.

Another psychological handicap for labor was the opposition of public opinion throughout much of this era. Most Americans were not far removed from their rural background, and the farm community was generally hostile to the aspirations of urban workers. The old Jeffersonian image of the free, independent farmer died hard.

Farmers disliked what they thought of as the slavish dependence of industrial workers on their employers. Farmers worked long hours for a small return, and it was hard for them to understand why factory employees should ask for more pay for shorter hours of work. Still a large part of the population in the late nineteenth century, the farm community tended to join businessmen and the urban middle class in regarding labor unions as radical and somehow "un-American" organizations.

Theoretical influences. Adverse working conditions made some Americans responsive to radical ideas which grew out of the European Industrial Revolution. The revolutionary theories of Karl Marx won some support in the United States. Marx believed that the total value of commodities came from the labor that produced them. Unless labor received the entire value of what it produced, it was being exploited by the capitalist managers. For Marx, economic class struggles were the central theme in history. The modern class struggle pitted the working class

(proletariat) against the capitalists (bourgeoisie). A violent revolution would finally achieve victory for the proletariat.

Marxian socialism split into many factions. Some groups, like the Fabian socialists in England, wanted to achieve socialist goals through peaceful evolution; more radical groups favored violence and militant action. In general, socialists believed that the basic means of production and distribution should be owned and controlled by society for the advantage of all, rather than by private individuals for the benefit of a few.

American socialists, like their European counterparts, agreed on objectives but differed as to the means of achieving them. Daniel DeLeon, radical leader of the American Socialist-Labor party, sought the immediate overthrow of the capitalist system in favor of a socialist state controlled by labor unions. By far the largest socialist organization in the United States was the moderate Socialist Party of America, founded in 1900 by Eugene V. Debs and others, for the purpose of achieving socialism gradually through democratic processes.

Another revolutionary theory which came from Europe was anarchism. Anarchists believed that government was the worst of all evils and must be abolished. Some anarchists opposed violence, but others favored bombings and political assassination. One of the most radical of the anarchists to come to the United States was Johann Most, a big black-bearded German who won a following among German and Polish laborers in Chicago. After Chicago police had killed several strikers on the eve of the Haymarket riot (page 343), Chicago anarchists sent out this appeal:

The masters sent out their bloodhounds—the police, they killed 6 of your brothers at McCormick's this afternoon. They killed the poor wretches because they, like you, had the courage to disobey the supreme will of your bosses . . . To arms, we call you, to arms!

This kind of call to revolution got little response from the rank and file of the American workers. The dangers of anarchism were exaggerated by the hysterical fears of newspapers and property-conscious Americans.

Socialistic ideas had a fairly strong appeal for American writers and labor sympathizers who saw no hope of ending the exploitation of labor in traditional capitalism. Edward Bellamy's socialist novel *Looking Backward* (1888), which pictured a utopian society based on equality and cooperation under a highly centralized state, was widely read. Upton Sinclair's novel *The Jungle* (1906) and Jack London's militant *The Iron Heel* (1907) urged workers to overthrow their capitalistic oppressors. Theodore Roosevelt wrote to Henry Cabot Lodge in 1906: "There has been during the last six or eight years a growth of socialistic and radical spirit among workingmen . . . ." It is estimated that in 1912, 1,141 Socialists held elective offices in the United States.

Labor's basic conservatism. Actually, while the socialist movement reflected the extent to which the interests of the workers were being ignored, it was not to be the wave of the future. When compared with labor movements in other countries, the American labor movement was basically conservative. In Japan, Italy, France, Germany, and Britain, industrial workmen displayed a strong bent toward socialism; in fact, this was the typical pattern, and the United States was the exception.

Why did American socialism have so little success in the long run, especially among labor unions? One factor seems to have been the fluid American class structure. In other industrialized nations, sharp divisions separated workers, the middle class, and the aristocracy. It was difficult, if not impossible, to move upward from one class to another. This kind of rigid class structure did not exist in the expanding, growing United States. The chance to rise from the lowest to the highest position in society was an ever-present hope, even under adverse circumstances. Also, despite the doleful list of labor's problems and difficulties, capitalism was working, however imperfectly. Workers' purchasing power increased, and living standards gradually improved.

This becomes clear when we compare American working conditions of the time with those in contemporary European countries. The Mosley Commission of British Trade Unionists, visiting the United States in 1902, was impressed by the better working conditions in American factories when contrasted to Britain's. H. G. Wells, the perceptive English novelist, commented a few years later on the "exceptional prosperity" of New York as compared to London. "Even in the congested entrances, the filthy back streets of the East Side, I find myself saying a thing remarkable, 'These people have money to spend.'"

With the exception of a few minor groups, American laborers accepted the capitalistic system and tried to make it work for their own betterment. This does not mean that American labor was passive and nonviolent; in their efforts to achieve conservative goals, they were often more militant and violent than their European fellow workers.

Labor unions have been conservative in another sense. In the longer view of history, capitalism has been the revolutionary force, changing society in many ways and freeing the worker from serfdom and from the old medieval guilds. But while the worker's status improved with capitalism, he became far less secure. In the old system he had had a fixed, although low, place in society. With industrial capitalism he might have more mobility, but against the giant corporation he was powerless. In *A Philosophy of Labor* (1951), Frank Tannenbaum writes that "the helpless individual could find neither dignity nor security in isolation." Therefore, he joined unions in order "to find himself a member of a community once again." Labor unions were therefore conservative because they looked back to the more communal past of preindustrial society.

The revolutionary forces of the Industrial Age—its giant corporations, its increasing use of machines, its tendency toward mass production—all presented new conditions and new problems for labor. The labor movement was created by industrialization in the same way, as historian Carl Degler puts it, "that a blister is the consequence of a rubbing shoe." As the blister is the body's protection against the irritation of the shoe, labor unions were the worker's protection against the consequences of industrialization.

Unions were essential because only through organization could the individual worker gain strength. A worker alone was at the mercy of his employer. But how to organize and how to stay organized were difficult problems. Of the many unions born in the late nineteenth century, few survived into the twentieth. In a day when business growth was paramount, the welfare of the workers seemed of secondary importance to many Americans.

2 In Union There Is Strength

1. What types of labor unions emerged during the latter part of the nineteenth century?

2. Why were some types of unions more successful than others?

3. Why was it difficult to organize unskilled workers?

Faced with revolutionary new problems, union leaders were uncertain about objectives and the best way to organize to achieve them. In general there were three kinds of labor organizations in the post–Civil War era. The first type was made up of loose federations of national unions which espoused programs of social reform to be achieved through political action. A second type was a federation of craft unions with much narrower and more clearly defined aims of improving wages and conditions on the job. A third and much more radical kind of labor union, and the least influential, tried to organize all workers through tactics of militancy and violence. Its ultimate aim was to overthrow the capitalistic system and replace it with a worker-controlled economy.

The National Labor Union. An example of the loose federation was the National Labor Union, founded in 1866. As industry became national in scope, unions were forced to organize on a national basis. If iron molders, for example, wanted to keep wages high in one place, they had to be concerned about maintaining iron molders' wages in other areas. Important for the future of organized labor was the growth, before and during the Civil War, of national craft unions like the machinists, printers, cigar makers, boot and shoe workers, bricklayers, and miners. The National Labor Union was a loose federation of these unions and other laboring groups, and was the first attempt to bring all labor together into one union.

The NLU was an industrial union—one which includes *all* workers in an industry regardless of their skill or occupation. Its able president,

William Sylvis, tried to bring black workers into the NLU, but northern white workers feared black competition and would not permit them to join local unions.

The policies of the NLU show the reluctance of labor to accept a permanent wage-earner status. The NLU wanted the workers to take over and direct the economy, not in a revolutionary way, but through education, politics, and producer's and consumer's *cooperatives*. Cooperatives are business organizations owned by a group of private persons which are operated without private profit for the benefit of all. For example, farmers might organize a producers' cooperative to store and market their wheat; they saved money by not having to pay commercial firms for these services. An example of a consumer's cooperative would be a grocery store owned and operated by the members. The NLU believed that such cooperatives would free the worker from industrial bondage.

The NLU also actively promoted the eight-hour day, immigration restriction, currency reform, and disposal of public lands only to actual settlers and not to speculators. In 1872 it became the National Labor Reform party and nominated a candidate for President. With his subsequent withdrawal from the race, and the loss of many of the national craft unions who opposed political action, the movement collapsed. It was able to gain the passage of the eight-hour day for federal employees, but its vague program of social reform did not meet workers' immediate needs.

Knights of Labor. Similar in its broad membership and lack of carefully developed and clearly stated goals was the Noble and Holy Order of the Knights of Labor, founded in 1869 by a Philadelphia tailor Uriah Stephens. Originally a secret organization, the Knights of Labor had one foot in the past and one in the future. Under Stephens and his successor, Terence V. Powderly, the Knights—like the NLU—rejected the idea that workers must become permanent wage earners. By pooling their resources, the Knights hoped to become capitalists themselves through the organization of cooperatives. "There is no good reason," wrote Powderly, "why labor cannot, through cooperation, own and operate mines, factories, and railroads."

Hoping to abolish the wage system, the leaders of the Knights opposed strikes as "acts of private warfare," to be used only as a last resort. Politically minded, they supported reforms that had no direct connection with working conditions, such as curbing land speculation and *nationalizing* natural resources, that is, bringing them under the control of the government.

The Knights rejected the traditional craft organization in favor of one big industrial union which would include everyone. They welcomed black workers, women, immigrants, and unskilled as well as skilled workers. Their appeal was to the most downtrodden, the people who were in greatest need of a union. At one point, blacks made up about 10 percent of the Knights' membership. The eight-hour day was a basic demand. The Knights favored it because they believed increased leisure would allow workers to develop more cultivated tastes.

The relative prosperity of the 1880's and successes in several strikes on western railroads brought the Knights an astonishing increase in membership. From a total of only 19,000 members in 1881, the Knights swelled to more than 700,000 in 1886, a phenomenal but too rapid increase for the stability of the union.

At the peak of their power, the Knights were seriously weakened by the famous Haymarket Riot in Chicago in 1886. During an anarchist demonstration against police brutality at Haymarket Square, a bomb was thrown, killing one policeman and six others. A riot followed during which six more policemen were killed and many people were injured. A jury found eight anarchists guilty, and four were hanged, although their guilt was questionable because the identity of the bomb thrower was never established.

The Knights had nothing to do with the Haymarket Riot, but they were widely blamed for it and their membership declined rapidly. The failure of subsequent strikes and of cooperative enterprises, together with the inability to hold a diverse membership together, proved fatal. The Knights disappeared as a major force in the labor movement in the early 1890's.

Fumbling and disorganized though they often were, the Knights tried to bring all working groups into one union in the democratic tradition of opportunity for all. Its industrial unionism foreshadowed that of the Congress of Industrial Organizations (CIO) in the 1930's. But strong business opposition and internal divisions within the union made it impossible for the Knights to organize unskilled workers. Their real difficulty lay in the conflict of interest between the unskilled workers and the craft unions.

The skilled workers in craft unions did not want to join with unskilled workers because they were afraid their jobs would be in danger. Employers, reluctant to fire skilled workers, were tolerant of craft unions; they had no such feelings about unskilled workers or unions they might join. Skilled craftsmen tended to look down on unskilled workmen. This feeling grew after the 1880's, when many of the unskilled were southern and eastern Europeans.

The American Federation of Labor. The American Federation of Labor, organized in Columbus, Ohio, in 1886, was a federation of craft unions—the aristocracy of labor. Rejecting the vague reformist goals of the Knights, the AFL accepted the fact that most workers would remain wage earners all their lives. Its goals were limited to "bread and butter" objectives—higher wages, shorter hours, and better working conditions. Its aim was to build a strong union of dues-paying members who would gain their ends through collective bargaining and the strike, labor's strongest weapon. In no sense a radical organization, the AFL wished to improve the status of craft workers in the competitive struggle for economic betterment.

Samuel Gompers of the cigar-makers' union was elected the first AFL president in 1886, and except for one year, he held the office until his death in 1924. An immigrant boy of Jewish-Dutch background, he started to work at ten, came to the United States at thirteen, and grew up with the trade union movement. Gompers' American experience caused him to give up his early leanings toward socialism. In an age of business, he made his union a business. Out of a total work force of blacks, native white workers, and immigrants, the AFL confined its membership to skilled workmen and the more "acceptable" elements of society. Gompers built a narrow but lasting organization whose goals were always

ORGANIZING LABOR

In his autobiography, Samuel Gompers, first president of the American Federation of Labor, tells of the efforts to organize a local cigarmakers' union in New York City in the 1870's:

"In our union meeting we talked over the problem of organization and decided we had to work out a program to meet New York difficulties. Our plan was to reach those who were otherwise ineligible, thus to supplement the International [the International Cigarmakers' Union] as well as build it up. We called shop meetings and mass meetings of cigarmakers and finally launched the United Cigarmakers. . . .

"Subsequent mass meetings . . . were unanimous in declaring that resistance must be interposed against employers who were decreasing wages, forcing the use of molds, and extending the tenement house system, and that the cigarmakers of New York and vicinity must be organized regardless of sex, nationality, or method of work. . . .

"As the tenement house system was one menace upon which all workers could unite, we concentrated our New York program upon that issue. We held agitation meetings, first in locals, and finally, a mass meeting. That mass meeting was my first public speech on labor. . . .

"Local No. 144 had many meeting places. The only rooms available in early days were meeting rooms which saloons kept for renting purposes. We first met in the Bowery . . . and various other places until we had money enough to rent offices on Eighth Street. . . .

"Our efforts to build up No. 144 were ceaseless struggles. I doubt if there is another union in the country into which so much devotion, idealism, and practical ability were poured without reservation. The men who constituted the group of active workers and who could always be relied on for any service, were brainy and resourceful. They gave tone and virility not only to their own union, but to the whole labor movement of New York and to the International Cigarmakers."

designed to gain specific, immediate ends. "First and foremost," he said, "I want to increase the workingman's welfare year by year."

Each union in the American Federation of Labor had a great deal of autonomy. Gompers' role was more like that of the Secretary-General of the United Nations than that of the President of the United States. His actions were confined to organizing, advising, and reconciling differences, but in this narrow sphere he showed unusual skill. He was not too rigid to accept industrial unions such as the United Mine Workers and the Brewery Workers. On the other hand, not all craft unions joined. The railroad brotherhoods, which tended to be conservative and exclusive, were reluctant to become part of the AFL for many years.

Gompers tried to persuade member unions to accept blacks, but with little success. Apparently feeling that insistence on this point would split the AFL, he was by 1900 allowing city federations to exclude blacks, and was even chartering separate black federations.

The ability of the AFL to adapt itself to the American scene was the secret of its success. Starting with a total membership of about 150,000, its ranks grew to 2,382,000 by 1911. The AFL was by far the strongest labor organization of this era.

Railroad brotherhoods. An unusual kind of craft unionism developed in the railroad industry. Railroad work was exceedingly dangerous, and few insurance companies would insure railroad workers because of the high risk. Primarily to protect themselves and their families, skilled railroad workers formed organizations called brotherhoods. The "Big Four" Brotherhoods—Locomotive Engineers, Conductors, Firemen, and Trainmen—were organized between 1863 and 1883. The constitutions of the brotherhoods omitted all but the vaguest references to wages, hours and other working conditions. Their members paid "premiums" rather than dues, and they were essentially insurance organizations. The Brotherhood of Railroad Trainmen, organized in 1883, had the most elaborate insurance program of all, including insurance against loss of life, as well as endowment policies that were not related to railroad accidents. The railroad brotherhoods tended to be conservative and exclusive, and they were reluctant to join other labor groups.

The radical "Wobblies." The most important radical labor union in the United States was the Industrial Workers of the World, popularly known as the "Wobblies." The IWW was organized in Chicago in 1905. In almost every way it was the direct opposite of the AFL. Under the leadership of William D. ("Big Bill") Haywood of the Western Federation of Miners, the Wobblies preached violent abolition of the state and the creation of a nationwide industrial organization run by the workers. Most IWW recruits were migratory workers, hoboes, and unskilled workers in mining, dockyards, and other rough occupations—the bottom rungs of American labor at that time. Their Chicago manifesto included these statements: "The working class and the employing class have nothing in common. . . . It is the historic mission of the working class to do away with capitalism."

In 1912 the Wobblies won one of the bloodiest strikes in labor history in the textile mills of Lawrence, Massachusetts. Later strikes were failures, however. When the United States entered World War I in 1917, there were growing pressures for conformity caused by war hysteria and exaggerated fears of radicalism. The Wobblies came under widespread harassment and the movement collapsed. Far too radical for America, the IWW was most important as a protest against the AFL's claim to speak for all American labor at a time when unskilled (and thus largely unorganized) workers were becoming a larger and larger part of the total work force.

In terms of labor tactics between 1865 and 1914, only the narrow craft-unionism of the AFL was really successful. Skilled labor always had a better bargaining position, and its unions could be more tightly organized around specific trade objectives. The obstacles against organizing the unskilled were too great: internal divisions, employer opposition, and goals too idealistic for the times. Radical unions which offered "pie in the sky" objectives could make little headway in an America where opportunity still beckoned. But as labor continued to try to make the industrial system humane as well as productive, it often found that strikes and violence were inevitable.

3 Industrial Conflicts Reveal Labor's Weakness

1. What role did the government play in labor disputes in the last quarter of the nineteenth century?

2. What tactics were used by unions and employers in labor disputes? How effective were these tactics?

3. How do you account for public opposition to the labor unions' tactics prior to 1900?

4. What progress was made by labor between the Civil War and World War I?

Labor history in the early Industrial Age is filled with violence. The depression of 1873 caused severe hardships, particularly for miners and railroad workers. Violence in the Pennsylvania coal fields was blamed on a group of Irish immigrants known as the "Molly Maguires." Sensational press stories told how members of this organization terrorized and murdered coal operators, just as Irish rebels had done to landlords in Ireland under a famed widow, Molly Maguire. Shortly after a coal strike in 1875, twenty-four men were charged with atrocities; ten of them were hanged and the others jailed.

The evidence convicting the men was supplied by a Pinkerton detective, hired by the coal company to infiltrate the ranks of the Mollies. The evidence was shaky at best, and it is now clear that the operators themselves instigated attacks on their own mines in order to provide an excuse to crush the organization.

Railroad strike of 1877. The first great national railroad strike occurred in 1877. It developed from a background of depression and the distresses of railroad workers. It began when the firemen of the Baltimore and Ohio Railroad quit work. A Baltimore *Sun* editorial of July, 1877, shows the desperation of the workers:

There is no disguising the fact that the strikers . . . have the fullest sympathy of the community. The 10 percent reduction [in pay] after two previous reductions was ill-advised. . . . The firemen have evidently worked hard and suffered much on very small pay. They are chiefly old employees, married, and having families. . . . The singular part of the disturbance is in the very active part taken by the women, the wives and mothers of the firemen. They look famished and wild, and declare for starvation rather than have their people work for reduced wages. . . . Better to starve outright, say they, than to die of slow starvation.

The strike spread to several cities, accompanied by rioting in Chicago, St. Louis, and San Francisco. For a time in midsummer 1877, two thirds of the nation's railroads were shut down. The climax came in Pittsburgh, where the conflict was so violent that President Hayes sent federal troops. Battles between troops and the strikers resulted in twenty-five deaths and scores of injuries. The widespread destruction of property that accompanied the strike turned public opinion against the strikers, and real grievances were lost in the general panic. The St. Louis *Republican* called it "a labor revolution"; and the New York *Herald-Tribune,* deploring the lawlessness of the strike, said, "The mob is a wild beast and needs to be shot down."

The Homestead strike. A serious strike occurred in the steel industry in 1892. Led by members of the Amalgamated Association of Iron, Steel, and Tin Workers, 3,800 workers struck the Carnegie Steel Works at Homestead, near Pittsburgh. Three hundred Pinkerton detectives were hired by the company to suppress the strike. When they arrived, thousands of strikers and others resisted in a bloody day-long battle which resulted in the death of nine strikers and three Pinkertons and in numerous wounded.

A week later about 4,000 state militiamen took possession of the Homestead plant. After a five-month holdout, the strike failed miserably as new immigrant strikebreakers were brought in. Less than a third of the striking workers were rehired.

The Pullman strike. One of the most famous railroad strikes was started in 1894, not by railroaders, but by factory workmen in George M. Pullman's Palace Car Company near Chicago. The Pullman employees lived in a "model" town provided by the company, which company press agents described as a beautiful place "where all that is ugly and discordant and demoralizing is eliminated." In reality, the workers had no other place to live, and the rentals for living quarters

were 25 percent higher than in nearby communities. The company apartments contained no bathtubs in most cases and provided only one water faucet for every five families.

When the depression struck in 1893, the Pullman Company laid off more than half of its nearly six thousand employees and reduced the wages of the rest from 25 to 40 percent, without reducing the rents for company apartments. One workman found that after the rent was deducted from his pay, his check amounted to two cents. While the layoffs and reduced wages caused severe hardships for the workmen, the company continued to pay regular dividends to the stockholders.

The Pullman workers organized in locals of the American Railway Union, a new industrial union formed by Eugene V. Debs. When the company refused even to discuss the workers' complaints, the ARU ordered its members not to handle Pullman cars. This action broadened the conflict from the Pullman Company to all railroads using Pullman cars. The General Managers' Association, a group of railroad executives of the twenty-four railroads entering Chicago, then ordered the discharge of any worker who "cut out" a Pullman car from any train. By the end of July 1894, the strike had become so general that nearly all midwestern railroads were affected.

Debs gained national attention through his leadership in the Pullman strike. He was an able organizer and an idealistic leader who was beloved by the workers. Debs had been an officer in one of the railroad brotherhoods, but had become disillusioned by its exclusive attitude and its unwillingness to cooperate with other railroad employees. "While there is a lower class I am in it," he said. Debs advised the strikers to avoid violence and destruction of property.

The General Managers' Association, however, brought in strikebreakers, clashes broke out, and property was destroyed. The association then asked President Cleveland to send federal troops to restore order. Governor John P. Altgeld of Illinois refused to ask for federal forces because he felt that the reports of violence had been exaggerated. But railroad officials convinced the President and his attorney-general, Richard Olney, himself a railroad lawyer and director, that federal intervention could be justified on the

The labor strife of the 1800's frequently led to terrorism and violence. One terrorist group—the Molly Maguires—used the "coffin notice" at the right to frighten those they considered their enemies. They put any "blacklegs," or strikebreakers, on notice with it, threatening them with the same evil consequences that other enemies had suffered. The scene of destruction and coercion below shows the great strike of street-railway employees in New York City in 1886. The strikers had objected to working fourteen hours a day for less than $2, and when the company owners refused to yield to their demands, "a crowd of strikers, whose number had been augmented by a brigade of street-loafers always on hand to make mischief at such times," began overturning streetcars. After 900 policeman had been called out to clear the way, the company agreed to $2 for a twelve-hour day with a half hour for dinner.

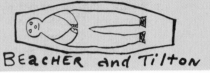

grounds of protecting the mails and maintaining interstate commerce. Cleveland is supposed to have remarked, "If it takes every dollar in the Treasury and every soldier in the United States to deliver a postal card in Chicago, that postal card should be delivered." Federal troops were sent to Chicago despite Governor Altgeld's protests.

Disorder and violence spread as angry mobs tried to prevent the movement of trains protected by the troops. Public officials and the respectable press around the country reacted hysterically to the striker's actions. The New York *Times* called Debs "an enemy of the human race," and the Chicago *Herald* referred to the gentle labor leader as a "reckless, ranting . . . impudent braggadocio. . . ." In general, the press gave the erroneous impression that Chicago was in the hands of a revolutionary mob.

The railroads finally succeeded in obtaining a federal court injunction against the workers. The injunction forbade any person from interfering with the mails or railroad transportation in interstate commerce on penalty of fine or imprisonment. Debs and other strike leaders were tried and jailed for violating the injunction. With strikers opposed by the powerful forces of the courts and federal troops, and deprived of their leadership, the strike collapsed. Debs was jailed for six months, during which time he became a socialist, convinced that labor would never make gains under the capitalistic system. Public leaders, the press, and intellectuals hailed the action of Cleveland and Olney as forestalling a "Debs Rebellion."

The Pullman strike gave new importance to the court injunction as a weapon against strikes. Also threatening to labor was the fact that the government based its request for the injunction on the Sherman Antitrust Act of 1890, arguing that the ARU was a "combination in restraint of trade." This interpretation seemed to endanger the very existence of unions. If employers could get court injunctions against strikes, labor would have little chance to achieve its demands. From the Pullman strike on, labor fought incessantly against what they called "government by injunction."

The balance sheet. These violent conflicts and many others reveal the powerful forces arrayed against organized labor. Industrial managers

LABOR TERMS

Yellow-dog contract	Contract in which worker agrees not to join a union
Blacklist	List of labor "agitators" circulated among employers
Scab	Worker who takes the place of a striker
Boycott	Refusal to use or purchase a product
Open Shop	Shop in which employment is not based on union membership
Closed Shop	Shop in which only union members are employed
Injunction	In the field of labor, a court order compelling a labor union to or restraining it from some course of action
Lockout	Refusal on the part of a company to permit its employees to work
Sabotage	Destruction of an employer's machinery or other property for the purpose of disrupting production
Industrial union	Union open to all workers, or all workers in a particular industry, skilled and unskilled
Craft union	Union whose members share a particular skill, for example, carpentry, shoemaking, and so on
Picket	Person posted by a labor union at a company to protest some company policy or action
Company town	Town in which houses, stores, and other buildings are owned by a company and rented and used by the company's workers

could use many potent weapons against the workers. The corporation could do without the worker much more easily than the worker could do without the corporation. The employer could lock his doors against striking employees and wait until they were starved into submission. He could compel his workers to sign a "yellow-dog contract," in which the workers promised not to join a union. He could circulate "blacklists" of labor agitators among other employers to prevent union members from getting jobs.

In his "company town" he could keep the workers in a perpetual state of debt by charging high rates. With the advantages of wealth, an employer could hire able lawyers, influence the press (though this was not usually necessary), and exert pressure on politicians. Many employers did not hesitate to import strike-breakers, or hire armed thugs to harass union members.

The combined pressure of management, public opinion, government, and federal courts usually constituted an overwhelming obstacle to labor gains. In spite of all the impressive-sounding union activities and the fuss and fury of strikes, labor's organizing accomplishments between 1865 and 1914 were exceedingly meager. By 1914, less than 10 percent of all American industrial workers belonged to unions.

Yet it would be a mistake to say that labor had made no progress. The Progressive era (Chapter 17) brought some advances. On the federal level, progress was made in recognizing unions and establishing shorter working hours. The Progressive era also brought reforms in state social legislation for industrial workers. Child labor laws were passed, and by 1917 most states had passed laws limiting the hours of women working in industry. Many states also passed workmen's compensation laws. Despite lax enforcement of these laws in some instances, by 1917, the industrial codes of the states were notably improved in terms of the health and safety of industrial workers. Gradually, the public was showing a greater willingness to accept unions.

These gains were extremely modest in terms of the continued long hours and low wages in the mass-production industries. There were no unions of importance in steel, automobiles, agricultural machinery, the electrical industry, public utilities, tobacco manufacturing, or meat packing.

THE OPEN-SHOP CONTROVERSY

In the early 1900's, labor and management clashed over still another issue. Unions favored the closed shop, to protect workers from cheap labor. Management favored the open shop, stressing the worker's right to choose whether or not to join a union. Finley Peter Dunne, an American humorist who wrote in an Irish brogue, commented on the situation through his character "Mr. Dooley:"

"What's all this that's in the papers about the open shop?" asked Mr. Hennessy.

"'Why, don't ye know?" said Mr. Dooley. 'Really, I'm surprized at yer ignorance, Hinnissey. What is th' open shop? Sure, 'tis where they kape the doors open to accommodate th' constant stream av min comin' in t' take jobs cheaper than th' min what has the jobs. 'Tis like this, Hinnissey: Suppose wan av these freeborn citizens is workin' in an open shop f'r th' princely wage av wan large iron dollar a day av tin hour. Along comes anither son-av-gun and he sez t' th' boss, "Oi think Oi could handle th' job nicely f'r ninety cints." "Sure," sez th' boss, and th' wan dollar man gets out into th' crool woruld t' exercise hiz inalienable roights as a freeborn American citizen an' scab on some other poor devil. An' so it goes on, Hinnessey. An' who gits the benefit? Thrue, it saves th' boss money, but he don't care no more f'r money thin he does his right eye.

"'It's all principle wid him. He hates t' see min robbed av their indipindence. They must have their indipindence, regardless av anything else.'

"'But,' said Mr. Hennessey, 'these open-shop min ye menshun say they are f'r unions if properly conducted.'

"'Shure,' said Mr. Dooley, 'if properly conducted. An' there we are: an' how would they have them conducted? No strikes, no rules, no contracts, no scales, hardly iny wages, an' dam' few mimbers.'"

The very industries that were becoming most important were little affected by union activity. These corporations were so strong financially and so stubbornly antiunion that all efforts to organize their workers failed. The most that can be said of the labor movement during this period is that it had gone through a needed trial-and-error experience which built a platform for the really powerful union growth that was to come in the 1930's.

Labor conditions were very different in 1914 from what they had been in 1865. The number of industrial workers had increased from less than 3 million in 1860 to well over 14 million by 1914. Few workers could expect to escape from the grimy cities to the more peaceful countryside. Labor was profoundly affected by the steady influx of immigrants which reached a flood-tide in the early years of the twentieth century. By World War I, immigrants constituted a majority of the industrial workers, and a new pattern of immigration had created additional problems for the labor movement.

4 Patterns Of Immigration Change

1. How did the immigrants prior to the late 1880's differ from those of succeeding years?

2. Why did immigrants in both groups migrate from their homelands?

3. Why did two-thirds of the European emigrants emigrate to the United States rather than to another country?

The exodus of discontented Europeans to other parts of the world in the nineteenth and early twentieth centuries was one of the great mass migrations of world history. Between 1820 and 1930, over 60 million people uprooted themselves from their homes in Europe and began a journey which led most of them to the New World. Over 60 percent came to the United States—the Prom-

ised Land where they hoped and expected to enjoy a better life. Most of them became laborers in American mines, factories, and farms.

The old immigration and the new. Historians divide immigration to the United States into two main periods: (1) the "old" immigration, prior to the late 1880's; and (2) the "new" immigration, from the late 1880's on. These terms are useful if one does not make the distinctions too rigid and absolute. The clearest difference between the two periods lay in the geographical areas in Europe from which the two streams came. The old immigration was largely northern and western European—German, English, Irish, Scotch-Irish, and Scandinavian. The new immigration came mostly from southern and eastern Europe—Austria-Hungary, Italy, Russia, Greece, Rumania, and Turkey.

The extent of this change can be seen by comparing the immigration of 1882 with that of 1907, the highest points of each wave. Of the 788,000 immigrants who came in 1882, 87 percent were from northern and western Europe, and only 13 percent came from southern and eastern Europe. But in 1907, when 1,285,000 immigrants arrived, only 19.3 percent were from northern Europe and the remainder came from southern and eastern Europe.

The new immigration was much larger than the old. Before 1880, annual arrivals had never totaled more than half a million, but in several years of the early 1900's, over a million immigrants arrived annually. What had been a steady stream of newcomers became a flood. In the twelve years from 1902 to 1914, more immigrants came than in the sixty years before 1880. By 1920 there were almost 14 million foreign-born persons in the United States. Adding "first generation Americans" (those with at least one foreign-born parent), the foreign stock came to nearly one quarter of the total white population.

Cultural and religious differences made it more difficult for the new immigrants to gain acceptance. Many of the older immigrants spoke English, and except for the Irish and some Germans, they were Protestants. To a considerable degree they shared the same, or similar, cultural traditions. The new immigrants spoke "strange" tongues and brought with them customs and habits that seemed outlandish to many

PATTERNS OF IMMIGRATION, 1861–1910

Date	Northwestern Europe	Southeastern Europe	Asia	Americas
1861–1870	2,031,642 (88%)	33,628 (1%)	64,630 (3%)	166,607 (7%)
1871–1880	2,070,373 (74%)	201,889 (7%)	123,823 (4%)	404,044 (14%)
1881–1890	3,778,633 (72%)	958,413 (18%)	68,380 (1%)	426,967 (8%)
1891–1900	1,643,492 (45%)	1,915,486 (51%)	71,236 (2%)	38,972 (1%)
1901–1910	1,910,032 (22%)	6,225,981 (70%)	243,567 (3%)	361,888 (4%)

1. Percentage figures represent percentage of total immigration for each time period.
2. Immigration for Africa and other places not mentioned totaled less than 1%.

native-born Americans. Immigrants from southern and eastern Europe were predominantly Catholic or Jewish, adding religious distinctions to the other differences.

Also, to a greater extent than the older immigrants, the new arrivals moved into cities rather than spreading out over the country. This fact made them even more obvious and "different" for an America which, at the turn of the century, was still strongly rural in outlook and habit. The fact that most of the new immigrants were poor and unskilled, and frequently illiterate, caused many Americans to question the traditional policy of unrestricted immigration.

Why people left home. It would be a mistake to exaggerate the differences to the point where the new immigration appears to be entirely distinct and separate from the old. The two waves of immigrants most resembled each other in their reasons for leaving home. The underlying motive for the migration of 25 million "old" and "new" immigrants between 1865 and 1914 was economic. The factors of compelling importance were the serious, sometimes desperate, conditions in their homelands, coupled with the vision of America as a haven of free land, higher wages, and better working conditions.

Fundamental industrial and agricultural upheavals were taking place all over Europe. When cheap foreign grain flooded European markets, many farmers in England, Sweden, and Germany were ruined. In central and southern Europe, the division of land into smaller and smaller plots and the absence of industrial opportunities drove peasants from the land. This was the case in the sprawling Austro-Hungarian Empire and in southern Italy, where economic distress was perhaps the worst in all Europe.

Some people have held that thousands of agents from American railroads, state immigration commissions, and steamship lines created a kind of "artificial immigration." This argument has been overstressed. There were numerous agents in foreign countries, but their activities were less a matter of stimulating immigration than of directing it. They took advantage of a movement already under way.

Also overrated has been the role of contract labor—a modern form of indentured labor, in which a prospective worker contracted with an employer to work for one year in return for his steamship passage. It has been widely assumed that between 1864, when Congress legalized contract labor, and 1885, when the Foran Act forbade it, thousands of immigrants were brought to the United States on contract to fill up the factories. Recent research has shown that contract labor was extremely rare during this period, primarily because industry had too much trouble holding the worker to his contract.

One factor of enormous importance to immigration was the introduction of steam vessels in the 1850's and 1860's, replacing sailing ships. The sea voyage, which used to take as long as three months, was now reduced to about ten days. The opening of new steamship routes also made emigration possible for the entire European continent. Steam did not make the voyage a pleasure cruise, but a congressional report of 1873 indicated that "the cruelty, ill-usage, and general discomfort of the steerage belong to the history of the past." Such reports should not hide the fact that the complete journey, from the old home to a new job and home in the United States, was a risky and often a mentally shattering experience. Historian Oscar Handlin has called it, a "brutal filter," which only the strong survived.

Although economic hardship was the basic motive for most immigrants, emigration from Russia was primarily for religious and political reasons. A strong Russian nationalist movement grew up after the assassination of Czar Alexander II in 1881. It led to a systematic and ruthless persecution of the Jews, many of whom were massacred. Poles, Lithuanians, and Russo-Germans also left, but the Jews made up the largest single group—nearly half of the total Russian emigration. Almost all Russians who came to the United States were "alien" elements of the Russian population.

Finally, there was a small but important Asian migration. About three hundred thousand Chinese came to the West Coast of the United States between 1850 and the passage of the Chinese Exclusion Act of 1882 (page 355). Economic dislocation was also the driving force behind Chinese migration. The Taiping Rebellion of 1850–64 brought widespread hardship, and the news of the inflated wages of the '49 gold rush in California touched off an exodus of Chinese to the United States. In the mid-1880's, the Japanese emperor removed the ban on Japanese emigration, and after the American annexation of Hawaii in 1898 (page 465), about ten thousand Japanese

came to the United States yearly. One of the most striking characteristics of the late nineteenth century immigration was the widening of the areas from which immigrants were coming.

The appeal of the United States. Economic dislocations in various parts of the world stimulated the immigrant flow, but the pull of the United States was an interacting force. While not all of the European exodus came to the United States, about two-thirds of it did. Immigrants came here because of the prospects of land and jobs in the factories. Proof of the economic pull can be seen in the clear relationship between the business cycle and immigration. In bad times immigration fell off, in prosperous times it increased. American industrial expansion acted as a giant magnet by its creation of countless new job opportunities.

Yet the attraction of the United States had more varied and complex origins than material factors alone. Political freedom, educational opportunities, and the avoidance of military service were other factors. Once in the United States, immigrants wrote thousands of letters back to friends and relatives in the "Old Country." These "American letters" and the stories told by returned immigrants spread the word.

The comments were not all favorable by any means, but even when uncomplimentary, they did not deter many people from coming. A British consul wrote in 1881: "There is a charm connected with the word 'America' which silences the most ordinary dictates of caution." A German, writing home to his brother, liked the equality of American life: "No one can give orders to anybody here, one is as good as another, no one takes off his hat to another as you have to do in Germany." The same theme was expressed by a Hungarian immigrant: "The President is Mister, and I am Mister too." Material satisfaction, often a subject of the "American letter," was reflected by one jubilant Pole: "We eat here every day what we get only for Easter in our country." And a Slavic woman added her bit to the general picture when she said that while American women worked hard they were not required to submit to beatings by their husbands!

But while immigrants continued to be attracted to America, many Americans were becoming increasingly less attracted by the immigrants.

5 "Strangers In The Land"

1. What hardships were faced by the newly arrived immigrants in the United States?

2. Why did a growing number of American citizens and organizations at the turn of the century favor restricting immigration?

3. How have immigrants of the period and their descendants contributed to America?

Immigration history tells a dramatic story of countless human beings uprooting themselves from their native lands in order to make a new life in an alien country. The journey from their original homes to the port city, followed by the voyage across the sea, was full of uncertainties, emotional shocks, and anxiety about their future in America. The adjustment of the newcomers to the United States was nearly always painful. The entire experience was filled with emotional tension; Oscar Handlin calls it a "prolonged state of crisis."

Entering the portal to America. Most immigrants entered the United States through New York City. A depot to receive them was established at Castle Garden in lower Manhattan Island in 1855. There they were examined to make certain they were in good health and could support themselves. After 1892, the throng of newcomers were admitted at Ellis Island in New York harbor. In time, facilities for receiving immigrants improved, but requirements for entry became more exacting. In addition to the old requirements of health and ability to work, new questions were asked the immigrants about their moral character and political convictions. It was a tense and nerve-wracking experience for the new arrivals, many of whom had learned to fear the official class in Europe. But if they passed, they could enter the Promised Land.

Sometimes there were friends, relatives, or representatives of immigrant aid societies to help the newcomer. Often, he was left to find his way alone. Frequently he became the victim of shysters and "immigrant runners" who took advantage of his ignorance to defraud him of what money he had.

His first task was to find a job and lodging for himself and his family. Most of the Irish and the "new" immigrants came from poverty areas in Europe and arrived virtually penniless. The vast majority of them had been farmers in the Old Country, but they lacked sufficient capital to start farming in America. They had been drawn to the United States by the industrial job opportunities, and most of them found employment in industries and commercial establishments in the cities. They were eager to find work at once at any rate of pay, for they could not exist without income. They supplied a pliant source of unskilled labor for the factories, railroads, and construction projects which the growing cities required.

Italian immigrants were sometimes recruited in Italy by labor bosses, called *padroni*. The *padrone* usually paid the immigrant's fare in return for a labor contract at a fixed wage. When the *padrone* arrived in the United States, his work gang was supplied to employers at a good profit for himself. After 1890, when the movement of immigrants from Italy became very large, it was no longer necessary for labor recruiters to go to Italy. The *padrone* stayed in America and served as an employment agent for newly arrived Italian immigrants. He frequently exploited them, but he also provided them with lodgings as well as work.

Immigrants provided a cheap source of labor, but their conditions of living in the ghetto slums created new problems of poverty, disease, and crime. Housing had to be cheap and near the place of work. Immigrants crowded into dilapidated old houses, shanties, or tenement apartment buildings which became breeding places for disease, degradation, and crime. Still, conditions were not hopelessly wretched and the immigrant letters, even from slums, often spoke of hope and accomplishment.

Growing uneasiness over immigration. The new southern and eastern European immigrants were very different culturally from the older immigrants. Although, proportionally, immigrants made up no greater part of the American population than before, their differences made them more noticeable. Great masses of new arrivals, filling the cities, speaking foreign tongues, and

Many immigrants could not escape crowded conditions in their homes, places of work, or schools. Above, a whole family does piecework in their small apartment around 1900. It is very possible that all of their labor earned them no more than $15 a week. Below, at about the same time, immigrants of all ages crowd together in one room to learn reading, writing, arithmetic, and the rudiments of American citizenship, all necessary to them if they were to succeed in their new lives.

following strange customs, sometimes outnumbered native Americans by a wide margin.

Returning to the United States in 1907 after a quarter-century absence, Henry James, the novelist, experienced a "sense of dispossession." Englishman H. G. Wells wrote that he could not see an American nation, but simply a welter of contending nationality groups. Little wonder, then, that many Americans feared they were being engulfed by these "foreigners" and looked back nostalgically to the more homogeneous America of earlier days.

In 1903, a tablet was affixed to the Statue of Liberty inscribed with a poem by Emma Lazarus. Its most famous lines read:

> Give me your tired, your poor,
> Your huddled masses yearning to breathe free,
> The wretched refuse of your teeming shore,
> Send these, the homeless, tempest-tost, to me:
> I lift my lamp beside the golden door!

Ironically, by this time, increasing numbers of Americans were doubting the wisdom of Emma Lazarus's poetic welcome to Europe's "huddled masses."

Beginnings of restriction. Already, legislation curbing immigration had been passed. The Chinese Exclusion Act of 1882 (periodically renewed) suspended Chinese immigration for ten years and forbade the naturalization of Chinese. A second immigration act of 1882 excluded convicts, lunatics, idiots, and other persons liable to become public charges. Neither act was meant, however, to completely repudiate the traditional "open shore" policy of relatively umlimited immigration. The Chinese were excluded because of agitation against them on the West Coast where their labor competed with that of native-born Americans. The second act was passed because immigrant regulation could be handled better by the federal government than by the states.

From the late 1880's on, however, more and more Americans came to believe that immigrants could no longer be assimilated into American society. In a poem called "Unguarded Gates," the genteel poet Thomas Bailey Aldrich expressed the fear that America was becoming "the cesspool of Europe." Aldrich was worried about the flood of strangers—Magyars, Croats and Ruthenians, Neopolitans and Sicilians, Serbs and Slovaks, Roman Catholics, Greek Orthodox, Jews, and Moslems:

> These bringing with them unknown gods and
>   rites,
> Those, tiger passions, here to stretch their claws.
> In street and alley what strange tongues are
>   loud,
> Accents of menace alien to our air,
> Voices that once the Tower of Babel knew!
> Oh Liberty, white Goddess! is it well
> To leave the gates unguarded?

The Haymarket riot of 1886 aroused general fears about wild-eyed, black-bearded foreigners who were alleged to be undermining the American system. Businessmen, who had previously welcomed immigrant labor, became more concerned about the supposed radicalism of immigrants. The American Protective Association, formed in 1887, revived the anti-Catholicism of the 1840's and 1850's, although it tolerated immigrants who were not Catholic. The American nativist movement of this era also included racists who claimed to argue scientifically that the Nordic peoples were superior to the Mediterranean peoples of southern Europe.

Madison Grant, a wealthy New Yorker, wrote a book called *The Passing of the Great Race in America* (1916), which called for the exclusion of the "new" immigration as the only way to preserve the old Nordic stock of the United States. Unless this were done, said Grant, the "great race" which possessed the qualities to make "soldiers, sailors, adventurers . . . rulers, organizers. . . ." would be replaced by "the weak, the broken and the mentally crippled of all races."

The various nativist groups finally settled on the literacy test as a means of restriction. Since it was the new immigrants who aroused the greatest fears, and since a large proportion of them were illiterate, nativists reasoned that a literacy test would bar southern and eastern Europeans without closing the doors to immigration from other areas. Literacy, it was argued, was essential for effective citizenship in a democracy.

Literacy bills, providing for a reading knowledge of some language, passed Congress but were vetoed by President Cleveland in 1897, President Taft in 1913, and President Wilson in 1915 and 1917. In his veto message, Cleveland reminded those who said that the new immigrants were undesirable that "the time is quite within memory when the same thing was said of immigrants who, with their descendants, are now numbered among our best citizens." But a literacy bill was passed over President Wilson's veto in 1917, and in the 1920's Congress passed immigrant legislation of a much more restrictive character.

Union opposition to immigration. American labor unions opposed immigration because it weakened unions and lowered wages. It was extremely difficult to convert peasant immigrants, willing to work for any wage, to the psychology and values of the union member. Corporations exploited this weakness in labor's ranks. In order to discourage unions, factory managers "judiciously mixed" different ethnic groups. A steel mill superintendent in 1875 wrote:

> We must be careful of what class of men we collect. . . . We must steer clear of Englishmen who are great sticklers for high wages, small production, and strikes. My experience has shown that Germans and Irish, Swedes and what I denominate "Buckwheats"— young American country boys—judiciously mixed, make the most effective and tractable force you can find.

Employers also used immigrants as strikebreakers, as for example, in the Homestead strike. By and large, labor unions felt that unlimited immigration handicapped their efforts to achieve higher wages, better working conditions, and recognition of the union. Many labor leaders supported the nativist American Protective Association and, in 1892, the Knights of Labor came out in favor of a general restriction of immigration.

Sometimes it was charged that immigrants were taking jobs away from the native worker. Actually, immigration allowed native workers to rise much faster than they would have otherwise. The Congressional Immigration Commission of 1907 found that in the coal industry white collar jobs were held by native Americans and "old" immigrants, while the "new" immigrants "were confined to pick mining and unskilled labor." The same was true in other industries.

As "hewers of wood and drawers of water," immigrants made an enormous contribution to American economic growth. Before the 1890's when land was still readily available, immigrants helped to settle frontier areas, as noted in the case of the Germans, Scandinavians, Irish, and Russians. But important as immigration was to agriculture, it was more significant in industry. After 1890, the typical immigrant worked in a factory or mine. In 1907, the Immigration Commission discovered that in basic industries like iron and steel, coal mining, construction work, and oil refining, foreign-born workers made up over 60 percent of the labor force. Industrial growth could not have proceeded so rapidly without this labor source.

■ CONCLUSION

One of the basic problems for immigrants was the profound sense of alienation which they felt in their new country. They naturally tended to cluster together in ethnic groups, and they tried to bring some degree of order and stability to their lives. In their ethnic, religious, and cultural organizations, they tried to recreate a sense of community which had been lost when they came to America. Although the breakdown of a sense of community has been a general factor in American history, it was felt by the immigrant with unusual sharpness. Difficulties in maintaining old cultural ways, tensions between the generations, and pressures affecting the stability of the family were painful elements in the immigrant's adjustment.

Another problem which affected immigrants and other workers alike was the kind of work which the industrial system imposed. Not only was the relationship between employer and employee impersonal, but the job itself was, in most cases, meaningless and devoid of personal satisfaction. Only rarely did the worker understand the total production process in which he was a tiny cog, less valuable often than the machine which he operated. When this factor is added to poor working conditions and the anonymity of city life, it becomes easier to comprehend the tensions and frustrations of workingmen. In all probability, the unusual violence of American labor-management relations in the fifty years following the Civil War was due as much to emotional and psychological problems as it was to low wages and long hours.

The "new" immigration in particular added a new dimension to the variety and diversity of American life. Of the three principal American religions—Protestant, Catholic, and Jewish—the last two owe much of their strength to the new immigration. New immigrants were absorbed into American culture, but differences in religion, language, foods, newspapers, theaters, music, and holidays remained. That is why some historians have objected to the term "melting pot" as implying too much fusion and homogeneity. Carl Degler used the homely term "salad bowl" as a more accurate description; although it is possible to distinguish the tomato, the lettuce, and other separate ingredients, there nevertheless remains one salad.

The American democratic experiment of making one nation out of many has brought rich variety and strength, but often at a high cost in frustration and pain. Historians usually fail to capture the tragic drama of thousands of humble people who tried to make a new life in the United States. Many failed in the "brutal filter," their lives crushed by difficulties too great to overcome. The same thing was true of native Americans who went West or migrated into cities where they became a part of the industrial labor force. Descriptions of mass migrations which emphasize only success and growth neglect the deserted villages, the abandoned farms, and the broken lives.

In the fifty years after the Civil War, the terms "labor" and "immigrant" became more and more synonymous. Although both native laborers and immigrants were to some degree "strangers in the land," greater acceptability would come in time. Better material prospects, political freedom, and educational opportunities gave both native workers and new immigrants hope for a better life. Only blacks failed to gain from the continued economic improvement that was taking place. For many white Americans and newcomers from Europe, it still seemed possible to rise from the lower rungs. Increasingly, the focus of this hoped-for improvement lay in the urban environment. Of all the social developments of this era, none was of greater importance than the rise of the city.

■ QUESTIONS

1. Why did workers organize labor unions?

2. What types of unions did they form? How successful were these unions in correcting the unfavorable conditions of industrialization?

3. What was the reaction of government, of business, of the general public toward labor's efforts to organize? Why did these groups react as they did?

4. Why did millions of immigrants leave their homelands and come to the United States?

5. In what ways were the problems facing the immigrant similiar to those of the native industrial worker?

6. What factors led to the creation of a sense of alienation by many immigrants toward their new country?

7. In what ways did the "new" immigration add a new dimension to the already diverse nature of American life?

8. Regarding the assimilation of immigrant groups into American society is the term "melting pot" or "salad bowl" a more accurate description of what has occurred? Explain.

■ BIBLIOGRAPHY

HANDLIN, OSCAR, *The Uprooted,* Grosset & Dunlap (Universal Library). *The Uprooted* is a Pulitzer Prize-winning history of the experience of immigration. The author attempts to recreate the feelings of migrants who break away from traditional cultures and experience the shock of settlement in a new society. This is a warm, human account which has appealed to many students.

GLAZER, NATHAN AND DANIEL P. MOYNIHAN, *Beyond the Melting Pot: The Negroes, Puerto Ricans, Jews, Italians, and Irish of New York City,* 2nd ed., Massachusetts Institute of Technology Press. Once the immigrant arrived in American society it was assumed that he would be absorbed into the dominant culture. This book questions the melting pot theory and examines the cultural experiences of subsequent generations of immigrants. The chapters on blacks and Puerto Ricans are particularly good, and Moynihan's chapter on the Irish has both wit and insight.

SINCLAIR, UPTON, *The Jungle,* New American Library (Signet Books). This novel is one of the most gripping accounts of the exploitation of immigrant labor and the consumer ever published, and it led to Presidential investigation and legislative reform. The horror of the meat packing industry as reported in the book was substantiated by the investigating committee. Sinclair's advocacy of socialism was not as well received by the American public as his demand for pure food laws and protection of the worker.

MORGAN, H. WAYNE, ed., *American Socialism 1900–1960*, Prentice Hall (Spectrum Books). Morgan has attempted to collect documents which indicate the spirit of the socialist movement in America and its influence upon reform in the twentieth century. He uses speeches, letters, personal testimonies, and party platforms to show how socialism related to labor, politics, special interest groups, and American history during the first half of the twentieth century.

GINGER, RAY, *Eugene V. Debs: A Biography*, Collier. Socialism in America has largely been represented in the figures of Debs, in the early years of the twentieth century, and Norman Thomas, in the years following. In this well-written biography we learn of Debs' work with the railroad unions, the IWW, and finally the Socialist party.

IMAN, RAYMOND S., AND THOMAS W. KOCH, eds., *Labor in American Society*, Scott-Foresman. This is another in the high-school series which recognizes themes in American history, and encourages the student to form his own conclusions based on the information presented in the book and his own background. The subject matter, presented in the words of the workers themselves, spans a wide range of years.

LITWACK, LEON, ed., *The American Labor Movement*, Prentice Hall (Spectrum Books). The student should consult this book for an overview of the heritage of American union labor. This is an excellent compilation of sources from labor leaders, the workers, management, and the newspapers.

DAVID, HENRY, *History of the Haymarket Affair*, Collier. Some students may prefer the depth of a case study as opposed to the survey. This book gives an in-depth analysis of the violence in Haymarket Square as a case study in American social-revolutionary and labor movements.

The Growth Of Cities

Urbanization has been a persistent theme in American history. Colonial cities began to expand and new cities began to spring up under the first impact of industrialization in the early nineteenth century. Yet, by the time of the Civil War, the United States was still primarily a nation of farmers. In 1860 only 19 percent of the population lived in urban areas; by 1910 that figure had risen to 45 percent. Within that fifty-year span the nation was fundamentally changed by a dramatic and rapid burst of urban growth. This chapter traces the outlines of that growth— first, the development of a national network of urban centers; second, the blight and corruption that attacked the expanding cities; third, early attempts at social reform; and finally, the changing urban landscape.

Underlying these tangible features of urbanization were certain general attitudes that influenced both the way the cities grew and the attempts that were made to solve their problems. Since colonial times Americans have had mixed feelings about cities. On the one hand, they have shared Jefferson's distrust of urban life and have yearned to return to the simple, often romanticized, joys of agricultural pursuits. On the other hand, they have been irresistibly lured by the cities' promises of wealth, power, and excitement.

Another conflict in attitudes arose between the prevailing rural ideals of individualism and voluntary cooperation and the urban necessity for enforced cooperation and restrictions on personal rights. The city, it was believed, would prosper most when each of its members was left free to seek his own private fortune, joining with his neighbors only when he found it to his advantage to do so. It was not apparent at the time that these values, which had proved sufficient on the rural frontier, were not suited to the new demands of city life. As you read this chapter on cities, keep these questions in mind:

1. What were the reasons for this rapid urban growth?
2. What changes did it bring?
3. What kinds of problems did it bring?
4. Who tried to solve these problems and how?
5. What can be learned from both their successes and their failures?

1 A Network Of Cities Spreads Across The Nation

1. What factors led to the growth of urban centers in the United States after the Civil War?

2. Which groups of people came to populate America's growing cities? Why did these people move into urban areas?

3. Why did the shift from rural to urban areas create a sense of rootlessness and alienation among many of the migrants to the cities?

The pace of urbanization can be measured in statistical terms of population increase in cities and the relative proportions of urban and rural population, and in human terms of the patterns of migration and the aspirations of the people. In these respects, and by every other conceivable measure, the United States underwent a period of unprecedented urbanization from 1860 to 1910.

Growth of large cities. When the first census was taken in 1790, no American city had as many as 100,000 people. By 1900 three cities—New York, Chicago, and Philadelphia—had over a million inhabitants. In fact, by 1910 nearly 5 million people lived in the five boroughs of New York City, which had been brought under one municipal government in 1898. New York had become one of the great urban centers of the world.

In some respects the growth of Chicago was even more dramatic. A small trading-post village of 12 families in 1831, by 1860 it was the eighth largest American city, with a population of 109,260. Despite a catastrophic fire in 1871, it continued to thrive. By 1910 its population exceeded 2 million people. Chicago had become America's second-largest city and the undisputed center of midwestern trade.

Although Philadelphia dropped from its earlier rank of second-largest, its population reached 1.5 million in 1910. The other major cities, in order of population in 1910, were St. Louis, Boston, Cleveland, Baltimore, Pittsburgh, Detroit, and Buffalo. Only New Orleans among the major pre–Civil War cities showed a decline, falling from fifth in 1860 to fifteenth in 1910, as railroads surpassed river commerce and as the nation moved into a pattern of east-west rather than north-south trade.

Growth of smaller cities. In addition to the giants, many smaller cities showed very large increases in population. According to census figures, the number of cities with a population over 100,000 increased from 9 to 50 in the period from 1860 to 1910, and the number with a population between 10,000 and 25,000 increased from 58 to 369. Much of the growth was in the Midwest. Cities like Omaha, Nebraska, Wichita, Kansas, Duluth and Minneapolis, Minnesota, and Kansas City, Missouri, doubled, tripled, and even quadrupled their populations.

The South as a whole did not experience urbanization to the same extent as other regions. However, Birmingham, Alabama, which had not even existed in 1870, grew to 38,000 in 1900 as a result of its growing steel industry. Atlanta, Georgia, was a city particularly favored by northern investors, and along with Nashville, Tennessee, and Louisville, Kentucky, it became part of a bustling rail network.

In the Rocky Mountains, Denver, Colorado, grew from a small mining town in 1860 to a medium-sized city by 1880 to a thriving metropolis by 1910. The Far West as a region was more urbanized than other sections because most of the people who settled there went to cities rather than to farms. Of course, the total population was not as large as in the East.

San Francisco, which was the region's earliest metropolis, maintained its rank as the largest and most important commercial city in the region, although Los Angeles, in second place, underwent several land booms in the 1880's and 1890's. Seattle and Tacoma, Washington, and Portland, Oregon, in that order, were the three largest cities of the Pacific Northwest in the 1890's. Portland overtook Tacoma in the early 1900's, and Spokane later rose to third place.

Except for a few isolated examples (notably Miami, Florida, and Tulsa, Oklahoma) every city that was destined to be of any significance at all in American life in the twentieth century had

POPULATION GROWTH OF PRINCIPAL UNITED STATES CITIES
(The 10 largest cities as of 1910)

City	1870	1880	1890	1900	1910
Baltimore	267,354	332,313	434,439	508,957	558,485
Boston	250,526	362,839	448,477	568,892	670,585
Buffalo	117,714	155,134	255,664	352,387	423,715
Chicago	298,977	503,185	1,099,850	1,698,575	2,185,283
Cleveland	92,829	160,146	261,353	384,111	560,663
Detroit	79,577	116,340	205,876	290,277	465,766
New York City*	1,478,103	1,911,698	2,507,414	3,437,202	4,766,883
Philadelphia	674,022	847,170	1,046,964	1,203,697	1,549,008
Pittsburgh	139,256	235,071	343,904	462,801	533,905
St. Louis	310,864	350,518	451,770	575,235	687,029

* Includes the five boroughs of Greater New York

become a thriving community by the end of this period. Consolidation and suburban growth have changed some of the patterns, but the present network of urban centers was largely fixed by 1910.

Reasons for urbanization. Urbanization is a complex phenomenon, and in this period it took place so rapidly and brought so many changes that it is sometimes difficult to distinguish cause from effect. The growth of particular cities (and the failure of others to grow) was a result of both national factors and specific local conditions.

On a national scale, urbanization became possible as a result of rising agricultural productivity and rapid industrialization. During this period the production of American farms increased enormously, as farming methods were transformed by inventions (Chapter 11). The variety of new machines, their widespread use, and the application of science to agriculture in the form of insecticides, fertilizers, and new plant strains made it possible for fewer farmers to produce more food. They produced enough not only to feed the expanding urban market, but also to export increasing amounts to foreign countries.

The dramatic gains made by agriculture in this period are often underestimated in view of the even more spectacular achievements made by industry. It is clear, however, that without the tremendous increase in farm productivity, potential industrial workers would not have been released to swell urban growth.

Factories were built near cities, attracting laborers and all the commerical enterprises needed to provide services for them. In older cities, established industries, such as New York's garment industry, were given further impetus and new ones were formed to diversify the economy. Chicago became the center of the meat-packing, milling, and iron industries; Pittsburgh processed steel. Manufacturing alone was not the sole cause of the growth of the largest cities, however. Cities became the focus of a complex network of financial, marketing, and economic services that were made necessary by industrialization.

Some cities were based on the processing of a particular agricultural product—beer in Milwaukee, cotton-seed oil in Memphis, or grain in Minneapolis. Others were the home of a particular industry created by an invention—cash registers in Dayton, Ohio; electrical equipment in Schenectady, New York. Specialized products were the main interest in others—furniture in Grand Rapids, Michigan; glass in Corning, New York; candy in Hershey, Pennsylvania. Raw materials or mineral discoveries accounted for the rise of other cities, although many became ghost towns once the original resources ran out. Among those which retained their position were Butte, Montana (copper) and Wilkes-Barre and Scranton, Pennsylvania (coal).

Only the development of a national railroad system made urbanization possible on such an extensive scale. The railroads linked farm and city, raw material and factory, and finished product and market. Chicago is the prime example of a city that owed its growth to the railroad. Its ten trunk lines gave it control over the huge western trade, edging out St. Louis, which was limited by its dependence on river transportation.

The railroads literally created towns along their routes. Anywhere a railroad line went, a town could be built, regardless of the natural topography or the existence of established trade patterns. In choosing where to expand into new regions, railroad officials held out for generous concessions from town governments in the forms of right-of-way grants, stock purchases, and the donation of land for station sites. The Illinois Central, for example, created the towns of Centralia, Kankakee, Champaign, and La Salle, Illinois, when it could not work out agreements with neighboring towns.

The spirit of entrepreneurship among a town's citizens was also a factor in determining which towns could attract a railroad or a new industry. Denver's leaders, for example, zealously sought a railroad, which then made it profitable for mining companies to tap valuable mineral deposits. Denver also won recognition and prestige by being chosen the site of the United States Mint. In the Pacific Northwest, the so-called Seattle Spirit was largely responsible for vigorous community support for several enterprises. Public works projects, an international exposition, and the promotion of Seattle as a jumping-off place for Alaskan gold led it to population and commercial supremacy over its rival, Tacoma.

Thus, urbanization was the result of both tangible and intangible factors—the general level of national prosperity, the expanding network of railroads, the rapid growth of industry supported by increased agricultural productivity, and finally, the particular natural resources of communities and the vigor of their business leaders.

Patterns of migration. The people who settled in the growing cities came from two main steams—foreign countries and the American countryside. Both sources of migration represented a movement from farm to city, because most immigrants came from rural areas. Chapter 13 showed that most immigrants settled in the largest cities, partly because they were too poor to buy land and partly because there were established pockets of nationality groups in the cities which they could join. In 1890 New York contained more foreign-born residents than any other city in the world; four out of five inhabitants either had been born abroad or had foreign-born parents.

The native-born migrants did not usually move directly from the farm to a big city but from the farm to a local hamlet, then to a larger town or city, perhaps to a regional city, and finally to a metropolis such as New York or Chicago. To a farm boy, village life seemed very promising; as he became disillusioned with small-town life, he sought larger and less rigid centers in which to expand his opportunities. The boy from a small town already knew that it offered little opportunity; he moved to a larger town as his first step.

Although the rural population as a whole increased as part of the total population increase (from 32 million in 1860 to 92 million in 1910), the number of people living on farms decreased in *proportion* to the total population. Some rural areas, however, showed an actual decline in population. Sixty percent of the townships in New England lost population in the 1880's; and in Ohio and Illinois, states that as a whole grew in population, over half the townships decreased in size as farmers moved to larger towns. Rural depopulation operated selectively, leaving some areas hard hit and others untouched.

Amoung the rural migrants were southern blacks. By 1890, 700,000 blacks lived in southern cities with populations over ten thousand. In border cities like Baltimore, Louisville, and Washington, from 15 to 28 percent of the population was black. The large-scale black migration to northern cities came later, however; in 1910 only about 2 percent of residents in New York and Chicago were black.

The general trend then was definitely to move from the country to the city. However, there was also some movement back to the country as farmers became disillusioned with city life and as immigrants saved enough money to buy a little land. No matter how many people moved out, though, an endless stream of newcomers seemed ready to replace them.

The lure of the city. The foreign-born came to the cities because they had no other choice. Native rural migrants moved for a variety of reasons. As agricultural mechanization increased, leaving a surplus of labor, rural dwellers drifted toward the city. Some abandoned their farms altogether because they could not compete with more mechanized producers. Others with a relatively secure but modest stake in the land sought an even greater promise of wealth in city life.

Many rural dwellers, weary of the hardships and loneliness of farm life, sought excitement and companionship in the cities. William Allen White, a Kansas newspaper editor, wrote in his autobiography of the thrill of hearing a 60-piece orchestra—"For the first time I heard tunes that I could not whistle!"—and of hearing James Whitcomb Riley recite his poetry—"It got me. I went raving mad." All in all, White concluded, "Life was certainly one round of joy in Kansas City."

And yet this abandonment of traditional rural life created a rootlessness and a feeling of alienation among many. The novelist Hamlin Garland wrote sensitively of the harshness of rural life. Nevertheless, he felt a sense of loss when he moved to the city. "No," he wrote, "I am not *entirely* content. Deep down in my consciousness is a feeling of guilt, a sense of disloyalty to my ancestors, which renders me uneasy."

The cities did promise a better life, better than the grinding toil of subsistence-farming in New England, better than the hopeless poverty of rural Europe, better even than a sure but limited success in a small midwestern town. But in many cases the promise was more attractive than the fulfillment. The people who came to the cities found that the cities were not prepared to receive them. Too often, instead of wealth, bright lights, and fame, they found only ugliness, despair, and loneliness.

2 Blight And Corruption Attack The Cities

1. What types of problems existed in American cities at the turn of the century, and what caused these problems? What improvements were made by cities during this period?

2. How would you describe life in a city slum around 1900?

3. What forms did political corruption in the cities take? Why did widespread municipal corruption develop in America?

4. How do the problems facing urban areas today compare with those present at the turn of the century?

Men and machines crowded together in the city on a scale unprecedented in America, and even in the world. Foreign visitors were impressed by the urban bustle and energy, but appalled by the congestion and intolerable living conditions. "Having seen Chicago," the English poet Rudyard Kipling wrote in 1899, "I urgently desire never to see it again."

Urbanization was occurring so rapidly that cities could not keep up with the need and demand for increased municipal services. Furthermore, there was no clear-cut chain of responsibility for providing these services. Even the concept that the government ought to provide some of these services and control the quality of those provided by private companies was not generally accepted. Financial resources were limited, and civic officials were bombarded with requests to provide both more services and lower taxes. The cities did respond to some urgent needs, but frequently in a haphazard and unplanned fashion.

Public health. Epidemics of typhoid, cholera, and yellow fever had struck American cities in earlier times, and the threat of disease hung over the rapidly expanding cities. Most cities, even in the 1870's, relied on private cesspools and privies for waste disposal. Sewage and garbage were dumped indiscriminately in the sources of drinking water. Existing sewers were totally inadequate in such large cities as New York, Chicago, and Boston.

Chicago was particularly backward. The Chicago *Times* complained in 1880: "The Chicago River stinks. The air stinks. People's clothing, permeated by the foul atmosphere, stinks. . . ." But Chicago was not unique. All the sewers of Baltimore emptied into the city's Back Basin, which the writer H. L. Mencken later described as smelling every August "like a billion polecats." Inevitably, disease struck. A cholera epidemic swept the United States in 1866. Yellow fever, carried by mosquitos that bred in the stagnant waters, was a particular scourge of southern cities; one epidemic hit Memphis in 1878, killing nearly five thousand people.

Such an overwhelming threat to the very existence of the cities could not be ignored. In the period between 1870 and 1900, for example, Boston spent a third of its budget on sanitary projects, purifying the water supply and filling in land. By the early 1890's the New York reservoir system had been expanded to give the city ample supplies of pure water, but the waste-disposal system was still inadequate. Even Chicago made substantial progress, although its problems were not really solved until well into the 1900's.

By 1910, however, the death rate in New York, Philadelphia, New Orleans, and other large cities had dropped at least a fifth. The battle against pollution was far from won, but at least the cities had been saved from total devastation by plagues.

Improvements in transportation. Transportation between cities had been improved by the expansion of railroads, but transportation within the city was slow and antiquated. Most people still walked wherever they wanted to go, and deliveries were made by horse and wagon. The streets, for the most part still unpaved, were muddy, crowded, and unsafe. The elevated steam railroad was tried in New York, Chicago, and Boston, but it proved expensive, noisy, and smoky. Although the horse-drawn streetcar was used well into the twentieth century in many cities, it was the electric trolley car, introduced by its inventor Frank Julian Sprague in 1887 in Richmond, Virginia, that transformed local transportation.

In a study of the expansion of the city of Boston from 1870 to 1900, Sam B. Warner, an urban historian, found that the "walking city" of 1850 extended about two and a half miles from the center of town. Wealthier people could live farther out and commute by steam railroads, but these were too expensive for the ordinary workingman. The horse-drawn carriage extended the limits of the city another mile and a half in the 1870's. But the electric streetcar in the 1880's and 1890's pushed the city limits two miles outward in all directions. The towns of Roxbury, West Roxbury, and Dorchester quickly became true suburbs, populated by middle-class workers seeking some semblance of rural life but linked to their jobs in the city by the streetcar.

Other municipal improvements. Although the telegraph had earlier connected cities in a national network, local communication was still haphazard. New York established free mail delivery in 1863, but it was unreliable. The telephone was the answer to the needs of businessmen. Following its introduction in 1876, the telephone was transformed from a scientific curiosity into an essential business tool by such developments as a central switchboard. New Haven, Connecticut, was the first city to establish a commercial service in 1878, and its subscribers grew rapidly from the initial 21. In Chicago alone, the number of telephones increased from 3,400 in 1881 to 10,000 in 1893, and by 1900 there 80,000 telephone subscribers throughout the country.

Another boon to business and urban life in general was electric lighting, which replaced the dim gas streetlamps and indoor kerosene lamps. Edison's incandescent bulb made all other forms of lighting obsolete. Businesses could now stay open after dark, factories could run night shifts, and evening recreational facilities increased. Wealthy city dwellers could talk to each other by telephone and move more freely from one section of the city to others. Life was pleasanter indeed for the upper classes but generally not for the poor.

Growth of slums. Slums were not new to American cities. In the 1830's, industrial workers were housed in ramshackle buildings, many of them company-built. Even the "tenement"—which originally meant any multiple dwelling and only in this period came to mean

Chicago World's Fair Poster, 1893

The Pigeons, John Sloan, 1910

Cities in the latter part of the nineteenth century attracted all manner of people, just as cities today do. Fortunately, among these were talented painters and photographers who could capture the life of the cities—its squalid as well as its handsome aspects. Probably the most frequently recorded city was New York, for in that city was the wealth to encourage artists and the subject matter to inspire them. The contemplative

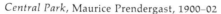

Central Park, Maurice Prendergast, 1900–02

Tenement Family, Lewis W. Hine, 1910

The Hatch Family, Eastman Johnson, 1871

The Bowery at Night, William Sonntag, 1895

and the boisterous, the poor and the rich, the immigrant and the "old family"—how they lived, what they looked like, what they did for pleasure—all have been set down on paper or canvas. As a result, contemporary society can have a view of its earlier counterpart.

Broadway North from Cortlandt St. and Maiden Lane, J. J. Fogerty, c. 1885

a dilapidated and congested building—was a standard fixture of city life. What was new in this period was the rapid spread and even more rapid decay of whole sections of the city, as middle-class people abandoned their former residential neighborhoods to incoming factories and deteriorating housing.

Zoning regulations were unknown, and the indiscriminate location of industry contributed to the blight. So did the improvement of transportation. It became easier for people to move out to the suburbs, and they were encouraged to do so to relieve congestion. Population congestion varied from section to section of the city, but in 1900 in New York's Tenth Ward (on the Lower East Side) more than seven hundred people lived on each acre. Although other cities were not quite as congested as New York, all the larger ones experienced severe problems.

Housing in the slums. Faced with the challenge of packing as many people as possible into a small area, builders resorted to ingenious (and very profitable) techniques. Building styles varied from city to city. Row houses predominated in Baltimore and Philadelphia, and "three deckers," wood structures with porches one above the other, were common in Boston, Chicago, Newark, and St. Louis.

New York had the "dumbbell" tenement, so called because the indentation at the middle combined with the indentation of the adjoining tenement to form a five-foot air shaft that gave the entire floor plan the shape of a dumbbell. Five and six stories high, these buildings were built on narrow 25-foot lots 90 feet to the rear. Three-foot hallways divided the sunless, airless flats, crowded with large families, mostly immigrants. Most landlords refused to repair or improve their property, on which they made profits of from 15 to 30 percent, and tenements quickly became vermin-infested, foul-smelling firetraps.

New York City also had what the journalist and photographer Jacob Riis described as the "color line." Landlords determined where blacks, mostly migrants from southern cities, might live. Blacks were sometimes preferred over foreign whites as tenants. One large real-estate firm reported in the *Real Estate Record* in 1889, "We find them [the blacks] cleaner and they do not destroy the property. We also get higher prices." Another firm

reported that it made an increased profit of 13.5 percent, with no investment, simply by changing from white to black tenants.

Whatever the subtleties of exploitation, all the people who lived in these buildings were kept in misery. In *How the Other Half Lives*, a vivid description of slum life in 1890, Riis took his readers on a tour of one of these dwellings on Cherry Street on Manhattan's Lower East Side:

Be a little careful please! The hall is dark and you might stumble . . . Here where the hall turns and dives into utter darkness is . . . a flight of stairs. You can feel your way if you cannot see it. Close? Yes! What would you have? All the fresh air that enters these stairs comes from the hall door that is forever slamming . . . The sinks are in the hallway, that all the tenants may have access . . . and all be poisoned alike by their summer stenches.

Under such conditions disease and crime flourished. New York had a "lung block," where tuberculosis was rampant. Three out of five babies in one Chicago district died before their first birthday. Those who survived often became, in Riis's term, "street Arabs," abandoned to a life of poverty and crime in the streets.

Even under such conditions, however, people lived, worked, and learned. Many not only survived, but became outstanding contributors to American life. In this period of dynamic economic expansion, there were many opportunities for the unskilled to learn a trade and for the skilled to improve their lot enormously. Perhaps most important, one thing the slum could not destroy was hope.

Corruption in the cities. The rapid expansion of municipal facilities—from housing to sewers to paved streets to gas lines to electric lines—created unparalleled opportunities for profit. Contracts to build all these facilities and franchises to provide these services had to be awarded. In the ensuing competition among private companies, politicians were flattered, cajoled, and bribed.

Political "rings" led by party "bosses" flourished in every major American city. James McManes, a Republican of Philadelphia, controlled the Gas Trust; and Christopher Magee of Pittsburgh made money not only from his franchises, but also from organized crime. But the most notorious "machine" was the Tweed Ring

THE BILL BUTCHERS AT THE ALBANY SLAUGHTER-HOUSE.

The "Boss" Thief—"You will keep on removing me,
but you will always put me back again—for I run your politics."

Because so many magazines were printed in New York during the late 1800's, cartoonists were familiar with city's problems and used them to comment on political corruption. The magazine *Puck* carried the cartoon above in 1880. It shows politicians—Democrats from Tammany Hall as well as Republicans—killing any bills introduced in Albany, the state capital, that might possibly benefit the citizens of New York City. The politicians are shown as the culprits in the ruin of the city. The cartoon at left points up the corruption in several cities in addition to New York—Rochester, Chicago, Milwaukee, Detroit, Pittsburgh, Memphis, Brooklyn, and St. Louis are all singled out. Uncle Sam is at the mercy of the political boss, who boldly tells him so.

in New York in the late 1860's and early 1870's. The ring was run by William Marcy Tweed, leader of the Democratic party machine ("Tammany Hall"), who had complete control of the city government.

Tweed's methods were simple and successful. Everyone who did work for the city was told to pad his bill, at first only 10 percent but finally up to 85 percent. A municipal courthouse, for example, was estimated to cost $250,000 and ended up costing $8,000,000. The difference went from the taxpayers' pockets to those of Tweed and his followers. Tweed also controlled patronage, giving city jobs to those he favored. His frauds were so outrageous that he was finally driven from power and ended his days in prison.

The deterioration of the city occurred at the same time the city was being pressed to its utmost to provide more services, a combination that provided the perfect conditions for the rise of bossism. One reason that bosses managed to stay in power was their control over the immigrant vote. Each ward in each large city had an efficient organization which befriended the newly arrived worker. Small wonder that a man new to this country, inexperienced in the procedures and concepts of democracy, should consider his vote a token appreciation for some tangible help in finding a job or a home, or advice on dealing with the authorities.

The Irish, as a group, were particularly successful in party politics in this country. Some of their success was a result of their relatively longer residence in America and some was a result of their ability to speak English. However, in *Beyond the Melting Pot* (1963), sociologists Nathan Glazer and Daniel P. Moynihan speculate that Irish political power was also based on a "merger of rural Irish custom with urban American politics."

Politics in Ireland in the eighteenth and early nineteenth centuries was, according to American standards, extremely corrupt. It was expected, if not exactly condoned, that a man's vote would be bought and sold. The Irish were also imbued with a concept of personal government; they were loyal to a particular man rather than to the man who held a particular office. At the same time, their Catholic religion and their rural social system accustomed the Irish to respect rank and authority.

HONEST GRAFT AND DISHONEST GRAFT

George Washington Plunkitt was a lifelong New York Tammany politician who was not only a power in New York City politics but a millionaire as well. Plunkitt's ideas on politics have been preserved by William L. Riordan, a reporter who interviewed Plunkitt numerous times while the politician was getting his shoes shined in the bootblack stand of the old New York County Court House. In the following excerpt, Plunkitt explains the difference that he sees between honest and dishonest graft:

"Everybody is talkin' these days about Tammany men growin' rich on graft, but nobody thinks of drawin' the distinction between honest graft and dishonest graft. There's all the difference in the world between the two. Yes, many of our men have grown rich in politics. I have myself. I've made a big fortune out of the game, and I'm gettin' richer every day, but I've not gone in for dishonest graft—blackmailin' gamblers, saloon-keepers, disorderly people, etc.— and neither has any of the men who have made big fortunes in politics.

"There's honest graft, and I'm an example of how it works. I might sum up the whole thing by sayin': 'I seen my opportunities and I took 'em.'

"Just let me explain by examples. My party's in power in the city, and it's goin' to undertake a lot of public improvements. Well, I'm tipped off, say, that they're going to lay out a new park in a certain place.

"I see my opportunity and I take it. I go to that place and I buy up all the land I can in the neighborhood. Then the board of this or that makes its plan public, and there is a rush to get my land, which nobody cared particular for before.

"Ain't it perfectly honest to charge a good price and make a profit on my investment and foresight? Of course, it is. Well, that's honest graft."

Furthermore, because of their conflict with the British, the informal government rather than the formal one was considered the legitimate source of authority. Even the poorest peasant was aware of, if not a participant in, political life. Speaking of New York City, Glazer and Moynihan say: "Instead of letting politics transform them, the Irish transformed politics, establishing a political system that from a distance seems like the social system of an Irish village writ large."

Certainly the political bosses were corrupt and certainly they enriched themselves at the expense of the taxpayer. Still, they did provide the expanding services that were being called for, and they did provide a link between the immigrant and the political and economic system.

3 Reformers Tackle City Problems

1. Which individuals and groups attempted to correct the problems of the cities? How did they approach these problems?

2. What was the Social Gospel? How was it related to urban reform movements?

3. How successful were the urban reformers of the era in dealing with the problems?

The "shame of the cities," in the descriptive phrase of the novelist and reformer Lincoln Steffens, was not limited to municipal corruption. It included child labor, inadequate recreational facilities, poor schools and medical care, intolerable housing—in short, all the needs that are usually called "general welfare."

While many people were outraged by the poverty and degradation in the city, they did not agree on what to do about it. Some believed that there was very little chance of saving the city, and that perhaps it was not worth saving. Steffens himself believed that municipal corruption was a permanent urban affliction and that perhaps only a revolutionary dictatorship could govern cities.

Some linked the troubles in the city to the "foreign element" residing there. "The city has become a serious menace to our civilization," wrote the Congregational minister Josiah Strong in 1885. He roused the fears of many Americans that urbanization—which, he warned, brought immigration, Catholicism, socialism, and other "evils"—would destroy America. Others such as the reformer and writer Henry George (page 390) believed that urban life could be reshaped, but only after a long time and a basic reappraisal of moral values. Although much antiurbanism crept into the rhetoric of commentators at the time, gradually they came to accept the city as an established part of American Life. It was no longer possible, if it ever had been, to move everyone back to the country.

Even though prophets of doom were many and eloquent, another, more practical response to urban problems was beginning to be heard. Reformers were beginning to attack many of the ills of the city on a realistic basis, by changing the environment in which men were forced to live. Their efforts were not always successful, but they established a pattern for continued involvement with the struggle against urban ills.

The response of organized religion. Religious groups played an important role in the late nineteenth-century movement toward social reform. Catholicism and Judaism responded first to the urban crisis because most of their religious adherents were first- or second-generation immigrants living in large cities.

The Catholic church, to which the large masses of Irish, Italian, and Austro-Hungarian immigrants belonged, maintained its ties with them by establishing many charitable institutions, such as hospitals and orphan asylums, and by founding local clubs or self-help societies connected with neighborhood churches. Because of their organizational ties with larger Catholic churches, the local parishes were not entirely dependent on local contributions for carrying on their programs, and thus they had an advantage over the Protestants and Jews.

Support for many urban programs lagged among priests and laymen in wealthier areas, even though the need was dramatized by Pope Leo XIII's liberal encyclical (Papal letter) issued in 1890. The encyclical supported labor unions and a decent wage and declared that "a small number of very rich men have been able to lay upon the masses of the poor a yoke little better than slavery itself."

Similarly, the Jews from various parts of central, southern, and eastern Europe founded educational groups and self-help societies. The first to come set up schools, clubs, newspapers, libraries, and other facilities to aid the new arrivals. The Baron de Hirsch Fund, established in Austria in 1891, aided Jewish refugees from Russia, first by transporting them to America and then by helping them adjust to their new environment. Many of the activities established by Jews were not religious in orientation, but stressed the common cultural heritage.

Protestantism had a far more fundamental adjustment to make to urban needs because it had traditionally been rural and individualistic in outlook. Moreover, orthodox Protestantism emphasized that poverty was a punishment for sins and wealth a reward for virtue. In "Acres of Diamonds," one of the most famous speeches of the period, the Baptist clergyman and educator Russell Conwell preached:

You have no right to be poor. It is your duty to be rich. . . . The rich have blessed the world. . . . Go through this city and your very best people are among your richest people. Owners of property are always the best citizens!

It is hardly surprising that this message did not appeal to the working class and that they drifted away from the urban churches. One worker explained to the liberal Congregationalist minister Washington Gladden why the workers did not attend church: "When we see [the employers] so full of religion on Sunday, and then grinding the faces of the poor on the other six days, we are apt to think they are insincere." As the workers left the church and as the wealthy businessmen moved to the suburbs, the number of Protestant churches in the cities declined drastically. The urban historians Charles N. Glaab and A. Theodore Brown point out that in the twenty years between 1868 and 1888, Manhattan gained 250,000 people but lost seventeen Protestant churches.

The Social Gospel. But a movement for revitalization was under way. The Social Gospel movement (Chapter 17), as it was called, stressed the application of Christian principles to contemporary problems: the improvement of man's life on earth rather than rewards in the hereafter. Sin, evils, degradation—all these existed in the cities, spokesmen of the Social Gospel admitted, but these were the result of inhuman living conditions and indifferent treatment rather than any inherent evil in the poor.

Spokesmen for the Social Gospel came from all the various Protestant denominations. Among the most prominent was Washington Gladden, who served in Massachusetts and later in Columbus, Ohio. He was particularly adept at labor-management relations. Others were R. Heber Newton, an Episcopal minister of New York, and Walter Rauschenbusch, a Baptist minister from Rochester, New York, and New York City.

Among the many services performed by the Social Gospel spokesmen was the accumulation of information about life in the slums, obtained from house-to-house surveys. These surveys were conducted primarily to obtain information that might persuade wealthy parishioners to support urban programs, but they also provided valuable statistics on health and welfare for other agencies. One concrete result of Social Gospel work was the establishment of "institutional churches," which provided lodging, adult education, reading rooms, recreation centers, and similar facilities. The institutional churches also sent volunteer workers into the streets and the tenements to help the poor.

Other religious efforts were also directed toward helping the people in the slums. For example, the Salvation Army, which began in England, also waged war on slum evils, particularly those caused by alcohol. Operating on the theory that a drowning man needs a rope, not a lecture, the Army set up kitchens and lodgings for homeless men, feeding and clothing them first and preaching to them afterward.

Many of the religiously motivated efforts reached only a few slum residents, and then provided them with the barest necessities. Nevertheless, the intense educational work these people conducted among the middle classes helped to enlighten the general public about slum conditions.

Settlement houses. In addition to the religious organizations, another form of slum agency—the settlement house—was becoming more common in the 1890's. Although these settlements were set up by private individuals, usually idealistic young people, and were supported by the funds they could raise among the rich, they too showed the influence of the Social Gospel theory and programs. Their leaders, moreover, were often motivated by religious as well as humanitarian impulses.

These institutions were modeled after an English settlement house, Toynbee House, which had been started in 1883 in London. Jane Addams, who with Ellen Gates Starr founded Hull House on Chicago's South Halsted Street, was a college student when she visited Toynbee Hall in 1889. Stanton Coit opened Neighborhood Guild, later called University Settlement, in a New York City tenement in 1886 after a similar visit. By 1895 there were over fifty settlement houses in urban neighborhoods, among them Henry Street Settlement in New York, founded by Lillian D. Wald, and Chicago Commons, organized by Professor Graham Taylor, a Social Gospel leader.

The founders of settlement houses hoped that by living with slum residents and sharing their problems, they could join together to wage a more successful attack on the indifference and corruption that permitted poor conditions to exist. Jane Addams not only started a kitchen, a kindergarten, and art and music classes at Hull House, she also campaigned for playgrounds, recognition of labor unions, and better garbage collection. She and a small woman's club committee reported over a thousand illegal sanitary hazards in a two-month period. When the corrupt Chicago officials refused to act, Miss Addams persuaded the mayor to make her a garbage inspector, and in that capacity she improved service considerably.

The settlement houses helped bridge the gap between the immigrant culture and the demands of city life. Furthermore, like the Social Gospel ministers, settlement-house leaders campaigned among the middle classes and the rich, after gathering facts about slum life to support their pleas for money. Perhaps one of their most enduring contributions was their work to convince public officials to take over successful programs. As historian Ray Ginger notes in his study of Chicago in this period:

If an enterprise proved its worth, the next step was to convince the city to enter the field. The playground, the public bath, the kindergarten—such projects instituted by Hull House were year by year taken over by the city.

Other reform efforts. Many of the settlement-house leaders and the Social Gospel ministers were also active in other reform efforts, such as working for legislation concerning housing and child welfare. In the forefront of the campaign in Illinois for a state child-labor amendment was Jane Addams. The success in Illinois in 1903 was soon followed by campaigns in other states. Also, in the field of child welfare, a notable step was taken with the establishment of special courts for juveniles. On the federal level, the Children's Bureau was established, which studied and reported on needs and programs in all aspects of child welfare.

In the field of housing, the New York Tenement Law of 1901 was a landmark. A state commission had been formed in 1900 to study the housing problem. Lawrence Veiller, a former Buildings Department inspector in New York, was named secretary, and the resulting recommendations reflected his intimate knowledge of the problem.

The 1901 law prohibited further construction of dumbbell tenements and required some improvements in those already built (however, it is interesting to note that some of these "old-law" tenements are still inhabited today). More stringent courtyard-space and fire-protection measures were provided for in this law, the first carefully drafted building code in the country. This law also was the first effectively enforced code, because it provided for a Tenement House Commission with its own corps of inspectors. By 1913, these inspectors had processed nearly half a million complaints!

Were the reformers successful? Any attempt to measure the success of the urban reformers of this period must consider the enormity of the problems they faced. Measured against the need, they were able to affect only a few areas and those only marginally. Frequently they were divided among themselves about goals and tactics; often the moralistic and superior attitudes expressed in their campaigns alienated the very people they were trying to help. They were sometimes prejudiced in their dealings with foreign-born people and did not always understand the need of immigrants to preserve elements of their culture in their new homes.

However, the reformers were struggling against formidable obstacles—entrenched landlords who profited from the miseries of the poor, corrupt municipal officials who responded only to private gain or public pressure, and the lack of understanding among the middle classes. A powerful handicap was the prevailing public opinion that a man's right to make a profit was sacred and that government ought to interfere with that right as little as possible.

The reformers did accomplish a great deal. They helped to educate the middle classes about slum life, and they established many charitable institutions that not only served the population at the time, but also served as models for future action. Their failures were useful too, for they made it clear that private energies and private funds alone could not cope with the urban crisis. To protect the general welfare, government action was necessary. That governments were often reluctant to assume this responsibility was not the fault of the reformers; that governments did take on some of the burden is to the reformers' credit.

4 City Planners Try To Change The Urban Landscape

1. How did cities tend to look at the turn of the century? In what ways did technological innovations influence the appearance of the cities?

2. What attempts were made to beautify cities and make them more livable? How successful were these attempts?

3. How did American urban architecture change between 1880 and 1910?

4. What role did city planning come to play in America around the turn of the century?

Among the least beneficial changes that industrialization brought to urban life was the nearly universal drabness created by networks of rail-

road lines connecting smoke-belching factories hard by industrial slums. Even the better sections of a city fared badly. The novelist Edith Wharton, who grew up in New York in the 1870's, described the urban landscape. In *A Backward Glance* (1934), she recalled the

. . . intolerable ugliness of New York . . . cursed with its universal chocolate-coloured coating of the most hideous stone ever quarried [brownstone], this cramped horizontal gridiron of a town without towers, porticoes, fountains or perspectives, hidebound in its deadly uniformity of mean ugliness. . .

Before the Civil War, cities had been more distinctive. For example, Charleston was noted for the gracious verandas of its homes; Savannah had attractive park squares; Baltimore and Philadelphia had rows of houses with white marble stoops. Industrialization tended to blur these distinctions and to make all cities more alike. With a few exceptions, the new midwestern cities that grew up during this period could hardly be distinguished from one another.

A composite picture of the typical American city at the end of the nineteenth century would show these characteristics: an increasingly spreadout area, with the bulk of the population and the business and commercial establishments crowded together in the center; the worst housing closest to the center, with wider rings of lower-class and middle-class housing and finally wealthy suburbs; opulent hotels and the gaudy town houses of the newly rich a few blocks away from teeming tenement blocks; and all these linked by a network of streetcar lines.

Technological changes. Technological developments influenced not only the patterns of city growth, but also the appearance of the expanding city. Where a city could not spread out easily, it was built upward. The use of cast-iron columns to support load-bearing masonry walls was pioneered by James Bogardus, making it possible to construct large, compact buildings for business and industry. Between 1850 and 1880 Bogardus built many cast-iron buildings, including warehouses, department stores, and office buildings. In a further advance, steel frames began to be used in the late 1880's.

Residential areas also grew upward. Apartment houses became socially acceptable in the 1880's, following initial fears that they would have a detrimental effect on family life. The first apartment houses were relatively modest, and often residents shared a kitchen and laundry. The first lavish apartment house was the Dakota, built in New York City in 1879. A large square building of dark yellow brick and dark stone, it is still a prime residential building on the edge of Central Park at West 72 Street.

Tall office buildings and apartment houses became feasible only when people could be transported up and down easily, a feat made possible by the application of electricity to the hydraulic elevator in the 1870's. By 1884 there were over two thousand elevators in Boston and more in New York. Chicago in particular became a city of elevators. Julian Ralph, a journalist touring Chicago in the early 1890's wrote:

In the tall buildings are the most modern and rapid elevators. . . . The slow-going stranger . . . feels himself loaded into one of those frail-looking baskets of steel netting, and the next instant the elevator-boy touches the trigger and up goes the whole load as a feather is caught up by a gale. The descent is more simple. Something lets go, and you fall from ten to twenty stories as it happens. There is sometimes a jolt, which makes the passenger seem to feel his stomach pass into his shoes, but as a rule, the mechanism and management both work marvellously towards ease and gentleness. . . .

Chicago needed so many elevators because its buildings were growing taller and taller. The rapid growth, the increasing land values, and the rebuilding efforts after the fire of 1871 leveled the city stimulated the use of new building techniques and materials. Chicago was the first city to construct skyscrapers, a kind of building described by the social critic Lewis Mumford as "the iron cage and the curtain wall." Several Chicago architects pioneered in the building of skyscrapers, among them John Root, Daniel Burnham, and William L. Jenney. The master, however, was Louis Sullivan.

Sullivan, who declared that a tall building must be a "proud and soaring thing," was a bold experimenter in the use of structural steel in skyscrapers. Sullivan's work reflected his belief in simplicity of design, his concept that the form of a building must clearly show its function. In all his work, Sullivan emphasized the relationship between architecture and the people. He wanted,

BUILDING THE BROOKLYN BRIDGE

In 1883, after sixteen years under construction, the Brooklyn Bridge connecting New York City with Long Island was opened to the public. The bridge aroused tremendous public interest partly because such a long suspension bridge was a revolutionary project and partly because of a new and almost untried technique of building underwater foundations for the bridge's towers.

The man responsible for this was Washington Roebling, chief engineer and son of the bridge's designer, who had studied the use of the pneumatic caisson in Europe. Pneumatic caissons were huge wooden crates, weighing as much as 3,000 tons and covering a half acre, which were sunk upside-down in the East River bottom and then emptied by forced-air compression. The caissons had special chambers of controlled air pressure in which the workers—the sand hogs— dug stone and sand from beneath the four cutting edges of the great box. As the men dug, the boxes sank to a position solid enough that they could be filled with concrete and the bridge's towers then erected on top of them. It was not easy to get workers to face the triple hazards of blowouts, fire, and the bends.

Sometimes openings developed at the base of the caisson, and then a blowout would occur as the air supply escaped and shot to the surface in a waterspout of mud, stone, and fish. Fires also could easily be caused by the gas burners and candles that lighted the caissons. Perhaps the most dreaded hazard was the bends, or caisson disease, caused by the high air pressure at certain depths. Many men suffered from excruciating pains and disabling cramps.

In surmounting all these difficulties, Washington Roebling completely disregarded his own health. He spent longer hours in the caissons than anyone else. During a fire in 1870, he collapsed completely, and just before the digging was completed he became seriously ill from caisson disease. Although he lived to see his work completed, he had sacrificed his health to the construction of the Brooklyn Bridge.

as he said, to make his buildings "visible parts of the social fabric, to infuse into them the true life of the people. . . ."

The "City Beautiful" movement. Much city growth was haphazard, the result of thousands of private decisions to build, buy, sell, expand, or move. What gave this era its dynamic character was the furious pace and volume of these individual transactions. What gave it its disorganized character was the fact that none of these decisions fit into any kind of overall plan. Perhaps surprisingly, the result of this chaotic real estate boom was not so much diversity as deadly conformity. Sam B. Warner's examination of 28,000 building permits in the Boston suburbs at the end of the nineteenth century showed that despite the absence of any building codes or zoning regulations, builders built very similar houses on very similar lots.

At the base of expansion was the gridiron plan: rectangular land areas divided into building lots and sold off in parcels. This plan was designed solely for the convenience of commercial and real-estate interests. It ignored such considerations as the natural landscape or the needs of human beings for open space, easy access to stores and transportation, traffic patterns, public buildings, and variety in outlook. The city, according to Lewis Mumford, was "treated not as a public institution, but as a private commercial venture to be carved up in any fashion that might increase the turnover and further the rise in land values."

Reaction to this unproductive use of land grew more vocal, culminating in what is called the "City Beautiful" movement. The movement had many aims, among them increased provision of park land, city planning, introduction of zoning regulations and building codes, and creative design of public buildings.

Park lands. Consistent with the rural ideal, Americans tried to keep some greenery in their cities. Improvement associations planted trees on their main boulevards, such as Commonwealth Avenue in Boston, Euclid Avenue in Cleveland, and Canal Street in New Orleans.

The first public park of any size was opened in Philadelphia in 1855. New York, however, took first place in creativity with the design of Central Park by Frederick Law Olmsted and Calvert Vaux in 1858. The designers wanted to keep intact the natural beauty of the 840 acres, to interfere as little as possible with the park's "easy, undulating outlines, and picturesque, rocky scenery."

Central Park was an immediate and impressive success, and Olmsted was commissioned to design parks in other cities, notably Philadelphia, Chicago, and Brooklyn, and the grounds of Stanford University in California. From 1898 to 1908 the park acreage in twenty-five cities more than doubled, although in the largest cities park areas in tenement regions were grossly inadequate. Local governments began to build playgrounds in the late 1890's and these spread rapidly.

Olmsted and other landscape architects who were contributing to the growing enthusiasm for parks saw parks as an antidote to the conditions of urban life. Olmsted told Detroit residents that parks would "divert men from unwholesome, vicious, and destructive methods and habits of seeking recreation." Whether or not Olmsted's goals for parks actually had an effect on diverting men from evil, they surely brought some natural beauty into an otherwise depressing urban scene. And the park movement as a whole, along with the tree-planting movement, did establish that the use of prime land was subject to considerations of the public welfare as well as private profit.

Changing architecture. American architecture underwent a general renaissance in the period between 1880 and 1910, coinciding with a greater civic interest in beautifying the cities. From the Civil War to the 1880's, American architecture had been largely heavy, clumsy, and unimaginative translations of the European Gothic style.

Now, however, new architects, trained abroad, began to bring fresh ideas to urban buildings. Except for Sullivan and other members of the Chicago School, these architects worked mostly in the classical tradition. Among the most successful was the New York architectural firm of McKim, Mead, and White, which designed the Boston Public Library on Copley Square in 1887. This dignified and elegant building in the Italian Renaissance style was designed with an entrance of three arches and a series of smaller arches extending across the second floor. The visitor entered through iron gates and reached the main floor by a grand staircase. Arches and columns framed a court on the interior of the building.

At far left, Trinity Church in Boston, built from 1872 to 1877, was one of the most influential buildings in the history of American architecture, and it established Henry Hobson Richardson's reputation as one of the country's most important architects. It also inaugurated the Romanesque revival in America, and stands among its most successful examples. Among the landscape architects of the time, Calvert Vaux was particularly prominent. The picture below far left, made in 1864, shows The Terrace that he designed for Central Park in New York. Later in the century, Louis Sullivan, a disciple of Richardson, designed the Wainwright Building in St. Louis (left). Completed in 1890, it became a milestone in the evolution of skyscraper design, and it fulfilled his view that a tall building should be "a proud and soaring thing." Two other admirers of Richardson, indeed they had studied with him, were Stanford White and Charles Follen McKim, who joined with a third architect to form the firm of McKim, Mead, and White. The buildings they proceeded to design contributed to the name given to the last two decades of the century— "The Age of Elegance." One of their finest creations, typical of the restrained grandeur they achieved, is the Boston Public Library (below), completed in 1895.

One of the finest achievements of the same firm was New York City's old Pennsylvania Station built in 1906 in the classical Roman style. According to architectural critics Christopher Tunnard and Henry Hope Reed, Penn Station "rivaled in scale the Baths of Caracalla of Rome." This structure also contained a grand staircase, from the top of which the traveler could look down into a great hall with its ticket counters and an information booth. A wide central corridor led to a second great space, the concourse, one level above the train platforms. Claude Bragdon, an architect who designed a railroad station himself, wrote of Penn Station that it "raised its proud head amid the pushcart architecture of that part of New York."*

Perhaps the epitome of this age of creativity was Henry Hobson Richardson. Richardson, who studied in Paris, was influenced by the heavy stone, rounded arches, and towers of the Romanesque forms. But he was not an imitator. He had the originality of mind, as Louis Sullivan said of him, to translate the spirit of his age into his buildings. "The things I want most to design," Richardson once said, "are a grain elevator and the interior of a great river steamboat."

Although he never did either of these, his libraries, railroad stations, houses, department stores, and churches reflect his originality and the native American style he developed. Characteristic of Richardson's buildings were a rich outer texture, often of rough stone or brick; the use of different materials or patterns in the surface; very high roofs, clustered windows, and deeply arched doorways. Richardson's work and his concept of architecture greatly influenced younger architects like Louis Sullivan, who, as noted, was an innovator in the development of the skyscraper.

City planning. The need for responsible city planning was becoming more obvious, and all across the nation cities were appointing commissions and boards to conduct studies and to present plans for future growth. The city-planning movement received a tremendous impetus with

*In the mid-1960's Pennsylvania Station was torn down, and a new entertainment center, Madison Square Garden, was built on the site.

the opening of the World's Columbian Exposition in Chicago in 1893. Here was a skillfully planned city, a "dream city" of the future, although the buildings were classical rather than "modern" in style. Many outstanding architects, landscape planners, engineers, and sculptors participated in the project, among them Olmsted, Daniel Burnham, Charles McKim, and Augustus Saint-Gaudens.

The "White City," as it came to be called, was an entirely new creation, and it contained all the necessary services such as transportation, sewerage, water facilities, and police and fire protection. More than 27 million people visited the Columbian Exposition in the six months it was open. A few architects, however, like Sullivan, whose Transportation Building was the only unconventional structure, opposed the classical motif of the fair. Sullivan claimed that the fair was backward-looking, and that the damages it wrought would "last half a century."

The enthusiasm generated by the "White City" and the "City Beautiful" movement in general resulted in some tangible improvements. In Washington, D.C., the McMillan Commission, headed by Senator James McMillan of Michigan and served by men of the caliber of Olmsted, Burnham, and McKim, succeeded in reviving some of the features of Major Pierre L'Enfant's 1791 design for the nation's capital. One benefit was the removal of the Pennsylvania Railroad Station from the Mall extending from the Capitol to the Lincoln Memorial.

Although these commissions and those in other cities such as Cleveland, San Francisco, and Chicago made progress, many of the grand schemes presented by such boards were laid to rest. They were considered too expensive and impractical, or perhaps most important, they conflicted with the interests of business and real estate.

Nevertheless, by the end of the period, city planning was well established as an unquestioned function of municipal governments. The general public was growing more aware that they had an interest in land use and development, and that they had to use political power to protect this interest. In spite of this, "America the Beautiful," at least as far as cities were concerned, was still a goal for the future.

CONCLUSION

By 1910 the United States was an urbanized nation. In the preceding fifty years, cities not only had grown rapidly, but also had changed dramatically. Technology changed the city's function, making it no longer just a center of commerce but now an industrial center as well. Transportation changed the city's boundaries, making it possible for people and goods to move freely in and out of ever-widening urban centers. Immigration changed the city's populations, creating conflict and competition as masses of foreign-born and natives alike sought the fulfillment of their own dreams.

This was an era of enormous vitality. The burgeoning cities contributed greatly to the nation's prosperity and were becoming centers of culture as well as of wealth. That so many new cities could be built at all in such a short time is in itself an indication of the intense energies devoted to them. These energies released destructive forces as well as creative ones, however. All the symptoms of modern urban ills were apparent in this formative period. Many of the decisions made then affect our cities' current problems—pollution, congestion, transportation, public health, education, recreation, open space, law enforcement, the assimilation of rural dwellers to city life, and discrimination.

Above all, however, is the problem faced at the turn of the century and never solved: How shall we best govern our cities? The specific problems have changed and have grown more complex, but the basic outlines were there to see in the earlier period. We have benefitted from the successes, but we are still grappling with the consequences of the failures.

QUESTIONS

1. What were the reasons for the rapid growth of cities in the late nineteenth century? What factors were now present that had not been present before?

2. How did this sudden growth affect the people involved in it? How were their ways of living changed?

3. What effects—physical, psychological, social, financial—do you think such a comparatively sudden change would have on the new urban dwellers? On the former urban dwellers whose cities were changing rapidly?

4. What specific problems did these people have to face? How well equipped were they to face them?

5. Who tried to solve these problems? How did they attempt to do it? What motivated them to try?

6. How do the problems and proposed solutions facing urban areas today compare with those present at the turn of the century?

7. What lessons can be learned from the experiences of the urban reformers of the early years of this century?

BIBLIOGRAPHY

SCHLESINGER, ARTHUR M., *The Rise of the City, 1878–1898,* Macmillan. Schlesinger is highly regarded for his ground-breaking work in the social and cultural history of the city. This book will provide an excellent background for the study of urban history at the end of the century, particularly as it relates to the character of the city and its impact upon literature, art, and education.

MAYER, HAROLD M., AND RICHARD C. WADE, with the assistance of Glen E. Holt, *Chicago: Growth of a Metropolis,* U. of Chicago Press. As Schlesinger's book was one of the first works on the city, this is one of the latest. It concentrates upon the use of visuals as historical documents which either support the conclusions of the text or encourage the student to form his own conclusions. The book should suggest to the student additional sources to consider when researching an urban topic.

STEFFENS, LINCOLN, *Shame of the Cities,* Hill and Wang (American Century Series). Steffens, one of the original muckrakers, exposed political corruption in city after city. The book is easy reading and revealing to the students, as it was relatively simple for Steffens to identify the political bosses and peddlers of influence as well as their devious practices.

RIORDON, WILLIAM L., *Plunkitt of Tammany Hall,* Dutton. This book is excellent. It is brief enough to be easily read in a short time. It raises critical issues of ethical behavior. It provides excellent insight into how to develop political leverage. And it is an excellent key to the understanding of Tammany politics in New York City.

DUNNE, FINLEY PETER, *Mr. Dooley on Ivrything and Ivrybody,* Dover. The contents of this highly quotable book are both humorous and insightful. Dunne's Mr. Dooley has become a classic comic character who commented upon a wide range of American topics extending from politics to sports to the theater. Many of his observations continue to be relevant to today's reader.

RIIS, JACOB A., *How the Other Half Lives: Studies Among the Tenements of New York,* Dover. The reader cannot remain neutral to this portrayal of slum living. As a result of Riis's efforts, public attention was focused on housing, and some changes were made. It may be instructive to compare this account with more recent reports of slum housing to see what has happened since Riis's original work.

ADDAMS, JANE, *Twenty Years at Hull House,* intro. by Henry Steele Commager, New American Library (Signet Books). This is another classic in the study of urban affairs, and particularly settlement houses. The book deals with the immigrant neighborhood served by Hull House and the specific activities of the house. It is a human, personal account of life in one part of Chicago.

ADAMS, HENRY, *The Education of Henry Adams,* Houghton Mifflin (Sentry Editions). Some have said that the history of the Adams family is the history of America. In this classic, Henry Adams provides excellent insight into the history of the Gilded Age and the maturing American society. The book is rather difficult at times, but well worth the effort, and it seems more profitable after repeated readings.

BELLAMY, EDWARD, *Looking Backward, 2000–1887,* New American Library (Signet Books). In this novel a critic of American society in the nineteenth century sees the logical extension of the growth of trusts in America to be one great trust, the United States government. This is a good example of utopian literature and should be compared with earlier agrarian models or current behavioralistic models.

Social And Cultural Trends In The Gilded Age

American cultural trends from 1865 to 1914 reflected the immense changes brought about by science, urbanization, and the complexities of industrial life. Creative thinkers rejected old ideas in education, religion, and law, and sought new answers to current problems. Writers and artists rebelled against the prevailing optimism because it did not portray the ugly realities of life which they saw around them. Not all artists fit this pattern, but a growing number of them were more inclined to see the world as it was, rather than in some idealized romantic vision.

At the same time, traditional beliefs and romantic art forms persisted. Novels and paintings of sentiment and adventure were far more popular than those of realism and pessimism. The Gilded Age, as Mark Twain called the era, produced a great many works of literature and art that were superficial, inane, and cloyingly sentimental. But it also produced writers and artists of originality and lasting influence despite its worship of money and material success.

The sharp conflict between the old ways and the new was immensely stimulating to the creative impulse. Cultural historians have begun to appreciate the groundwork which the truly original artists of the post–Civil War era laid for twentieth-century culture. Historian Lewis Mumford saw a genuine culture beginning to emerge in the Gilded Age: ". . . a Ryder, a Roebling, a Thomas Eakins, a Richardson, a Sullivan, an Adams . . . were men that any age might proudly exhibit and make use of." In art and literature, Mumford wrote, these years were "a fulfillment of the past and a starting point for the future." As you examine the cultural trends in the Gilded Age, here are some questions to guide you:

1. What changes in education were made in an attempt to meet the challenges of modern life?
2. What new intellectual concepts challenged the old ideas in religion, philosophy, and the social sciences?
3. To what extent was the trend toward realism reflected in literature, art, and music?
4. What forms of culture were popular with the general public?

1 American Education Grows And Changes

1. In what ways did public education grow and change during the Gilded Age? What caused these changes?

2. What were the ideas of John Dewey regarding public education? In what ways did his ideas influence education?

3. How did the education of blacks compare to that of white's in the Gilded Age? How did black education compare to that of women in this period?

4. In what ways did the educational program of W. E. B. DuBois differ from that of Booker T. Washington? Which program do you think was the most valid?

Cities have always been centers of literacy, culture, and education. As America became increasingly urban, public education advanced correspondingly. But in addition to growth, there was a general transformation of education at all levels.

Growth of public education. Although by the 1850's the principle of tax-supported schools was accepted by the states, the implementation of it did not become widespread until the late nineteenth and early twentieth centuries. Educational growth in terms of numbers of students and money expended from 1870 to 1910 was impressive. The total enrollment in elementary and secondary schools rose from less than 7 million in 1870 to nearly 18 million in 1910. The largest growth took place in the elementary grades, where most of the pupils were concentrated; but the growth of high schools was also impressive. By 1914, the average total schooling for Americans had risen to about six years.

Local communities were responsible for maintaining the public schools. As a result, the quantity and quality of education was extremely uneven throughout the country, depending roughly on the distribution of taxable wealth. Rural schools advanced more slowly than urban, and eastern schools were generally superior to those in the West and the South. In comparison with the North, the South had less than half the taxable wealth and a larger number of children per adult. Then too, southern states had set up separate school systems—one for whites and one for blacks—thus burdening southern school districts with the maintenance of two systems.

The two public school systems in the South were separate but never equal. The white community did not believe that blacks needed much education; furthermore, blacks paid little in taxes to support the schools. The result was that black schools were inferior in every way. Salaries for teachers in black schools were lower, the school year was not as long, and the school buildings were often rented halls or church basements. Although southern white schools were often extremely poor, they were invariably better than the black schools.

"Classical" education. Educational growth involved economic and sectional problems, but it was also concerned with the *kind* of education that would be best suited to changing conditions. Throughout the nineteenth and early twentieth centuries, the "classical" philosophy of education generally prevailed at all levels. The purpose of education in the classical view was to develop the mind and encourage aesthetic appreciation. Only the intellectually gifted were thought capable of further education. The child was supposed to adapt to the school, not the reverse.

Elementary schools rarely taught much more than the "three R's," but the classical curriculum in the upper grades and colleges consisted of mathematics, literature and the classical languages, ancient history, and moral philosophy, or ethics. There was no vocational training. Teachers needed no special "teacher-training" as long as they were scholars in their chosen fields. The ideal elements of the classical tradition of education were the gifted teacher, the classical curriculum, and an intelligent, responsive pupil.

Dewey's influence on the schools. The fact that much of this old "classical" system remains a part of American education is evidence of its great vitality. At its best it could give the student a firm background in many disciplines and enrich his approach to life's problems. But it often de-

THE MCGUFFEY READERS

School textbooks that were universally used in this period were Noah Webster's *Spellers*, the Barnes *Histories*, and, most popular of all, the McGuffey *Readers*. Before 1900, the readers had sold 100 million copies and were certainly one of the great intellectual influences on young America. The *Readers* were filled with patriotic exhortations, sentimental verse, Biblical quotations, and moral maxims. The following from McGuffey's *New Sixth Eclectic Reader* is a lesson in "falling inflection:"

FALLING INFLECTION

Rule 1.—Sentences and clauses which make complete sense in themselves, require the *falling inflection*.

Remark.—This rule is applicable, whatever may be the punctuation, and whatever other words may follow, provided they do not vary, though they may explain or strengthen, the meaning of the clause preceding.

EXAMPLES

1. By virtue we secure happiness.

2. One deed of shame is succeeded by years of penitence.

3. For thou hast said in thy heart, I will ascend into heaven: I will extend my throne above the stars of God: I will sit upon the mount of the congregation in the sides of the north.

4. The wind and the rain are over; calm is the noon of the day: the clouds are divided in heaven; over the green hills flies the inconstant sun; red through the stormy vale comes down the stream.

5. This proposition was, however, rejected, and not merely rejected, but rejected with insult.

6. There was a pause of death-like stillness, and the bold heart of MacPherson grew faint.

generated into a dull routine of excessive memorization and tyrannical teaching. It was rigid and formal, it ignored the emotional life of the child, and its curriculum was often tragically remote from life.

Darwinian evolution, the rise of science, and the revolutionary changes in American life stimulated a flood of new ideas and theories challenging the classical system. The American philosopher and educator who best expressed the ideas of the new "progressive" education was John Dewey.

Dewey illustrates the tendency of intellectuals of his day to shift away from fixed principles to specific goals based on experience. Philosophy to him was not just abstract thought but something closely related to real life. Intelligence was the "instrument" by which man could change his environment. By using his mind and the scientific method, man could attack, for example, the problem of city slums. He could investigate conditions, consider alternative remedies, and select the best line of action. In his famous *School and Society* (1899), Dewey applied his philosophic beliefs to education.

Dewey believed that industrialization created totally new problems for education. The practical education which the child had acquired in the farm family was no longer possible in the city nor applicable to urban life. The school, then, must teach the child to adapt to his environment, and, as Dewey stated:

> To do this means to make each one of our schools an embryonic community life, active with types of occupations that reflect the life of the larger society, and permeated throughout with the spirit of art, history, and science.

Dewey wanted to introduce the practical and useful arts, but not at the expense of mental discipline. "Learning by doing" meant for him not just acquiring physical skills, but gaining mental insight into the meaning of one's activities.

Dewey's program of progressive education was part of a broader program of reform, the Progressive movement (Chapter 17), in which the school was another means of changing American life. Like other reformers of his day, Dewey had a deep moral conviction that man could be improved, and that a democratic environment was best for this purpose. The teacher should not teach "values," which were always evolving, but should encourage the child to discover values for himself.

The school should be child-centered and should appeal to the child's imagination and curiosity. Dewey did not want the schools to promote the acquisitive ideals of the business culture but rather to offer a program "saturating the child with the spirit of service," and helping to promote a society "which is worthy, lovely, and harmonious." The school should be a reforming institution producing responsible citizens capable of solving the society's problems as well as a conservative institution transmitting knowledge from generation to generation.

Under the influence of Dewey and others, the modern school began to take shape. As psychologists discovered basic emotional drives which determined the child's conduct, guidance became more important than punishment and strict discipline. The curriculum of the new education offered courses in business subjects, the practical arts, and life-adjustment. Modern languages replaced Greek and Latin, ancient history was discontinued, and many of the old academic subjects, though still taught, were considerably diluted. As the schools became more "activity-minded" they became social, recreational, and community centers. Gymnasiums, athletic fields, auditoriums, shops, and social rooms became integral parts of schools concerned with the "whole" child.

Progressive education never completely dominated American public schools, but it led to their transformation. It offered a more pleasant learning situation, called attention to emotional factors in learning, and related education to life. In practice, however, Dewey's ideas were often distorted, so that reliance on children's drives sometimes led to disorganized, undisciplined classrooms. In the twentieth century, the term "progressive education" came to mean "permissive education" to many people. Nevertheless, Dewey's influence continues to this day, and most modern schools have elements of both classical and progressive education.

Changes in higher education. Higher education also changed during this era. Most American colleges in 1870 were small struggling institutions in which mediocre faculties taught in an atmosphere of intellectual stagnation. In the next few decades there was advancement in growth, curriculum, and intellectual stimulation. This change was due, in part, to a group of outstanding college presidents, of whom Charles Eliot of Harvard was most influential. Eliot dropped some of the required courses of the classical curriculum in favor of an elective system in which students could choose courses including modern languages, economics, and laboratory sciences. He also recruited men of scholarship and imagination for the faculty.

The founding of Johns Hopkins University in 1876 was a landmark in American scholarship. Its first president, Daniel Coit Gilman, modeled Hopkins on the great German universities, which stressed careful research and absolute freedom of inquiry. Gilman assembled a brilliant faculty. Within a generation after its founding, Johns Hopkins turned out a remarkable number of important scholars, including Woodrow Wilson in political science, John Dewey in philosophy, and Frederick Jackson Turner in history. The graduate program culminating in the doctoral dissertation for the PhD. degree became a model for many universities.

Financial aid to higher education. The Morrill Land Grant Act of 1862 gave public land to states in order to provide funds for the establishment of colleges. This land was not itself used for campuses; it was sold or rented by the states to provide funds for setting up colleges. Although these colleges were to emphasize agriculture and the mechanical arts, they could teach liberal-arts courses as well. Altogether, sixty-nine "land grant" institutions of higher learning were organized, among them the Universities of California, Minnesota, and Illinois, as well as Ohio State, Michigan State, and Iowa State.

Wealthy industrialists also provided funds to found new colleges or support old ones. Cornell, Stanford, Tulane, Johns Hopkins, and Vanderbilt took the names of their benefactors, and the University of Chicago received $34 million from John D. Rockefeller. Business support of higher

F.J.Webb Teacher
Rina Gadlin
Bessie Hoffman
Nettie Gadlin
Cora Sheppard
Jennie Hoffman
May Hoffman
Emma Green.
Oscar Grimes.
Lester Green.

Pleasant Ridge School

American folklore is rich with stories of walking miles to school each day in rural areas. The two photographs above, taken in the late 1800's, show the kinds of schools the story tellers walked to. At the left, a group of grade-school children play a game to celebrate the last day of school in Keota, Iowa. The group in the righthand picture represent the entire enrollment of the Pleasant Ridge School near Lancaster, Wisconsin. Below, students at Virginia's Hampton Institute are pictured in *Stairway of Treasurer's Residence. Students at Work*, a photo taken by Frances B. Johnston in 1900.

education had its drawbacks, however. At times business-minded college trustees dismissed professors whom they regarded as too radical. Thorstein Veblen, in his biting critique *The Higher Learning* (1918), charged that business ideals permeated the American university. American colleges, he said, were run by "captains of erudition" for the production of salesmen.

Higher education for women. Prior to the Civil War, women had been admitted to a few colleges like Oberlin and Antioch, but the prejudice against female college training was slow to change. Diehards clung to the notion that women were neither mentally nor physically capable of college work. College life, it was said, might destroy "the loveliness and grace and essential charm of womanhood."

Educational reformers vigorously attacked such conservative ideas. The enrollment of women in colleges gradually increased as professional job opportunities for women increased. Several women's colleges, including Vassar, Wellesley, Smith, Bryn Mawr, and Goucher, were founded after 1861. By the 1880's, most midwestern colleges admitted women on an equal basis with men. By 1901, there were 128 women's colleges in the country and women made up 25 percent of the total undergraduates.

Higher education for blacks. Blacks were excluded from most white colleges and had few schools of higher learning of their own. A second Morrill Act of 1890 provided that land-grant funds should be "equitably divided" between white and black colleges, but by 1914 no black land-grant colleges had been built. The emphasis in black colleges turned out to be vocational rather than academic. General Samuel C. Armstrong, the founder of Virginia's Hampton Institute in 1869, wanted to "lift the colored race by a practical education that shall fit them for life." Hampton taught its students respect for labor, vocational skills, and good character.

Hampton Institute's most distinguished pupil, Booker T. Washington, became the leading black spokesman for vocational education. As the first president in 1881 of Tuskegee Institute in Alabama, he taught his black students typical American middle-class values—hard work, sound morals, self-reliance, and the value of learning a trade.

Washington hoped to gain white support for black education by making the black man useful to whites as a better customer, a better citizen, and a contributing member of the economic system. Historian Merle Curti calls Washington a great American educator because of his "emphasis on the social significance of a purposeful education." But Washington's submissive attitude toward whites and his lack of militancy in the face of racial injustice brought criticism from other blacks.

William E. B. Du Bois, the first black man to earn the PhD. degree at Harvard, was Washington's best-known critic. Du Bois resembled modern civil rights leaders in his outrage at racial discrimination and his uncompromising demand for equal rights for his people. Du Bois characterized Washington's policy as follows: "When your head is in the lion's mouth, use your hand to pet him." Du Bois recognized some merit in Washington's point of view, but he rejected the idea that black education should be exclusively vocational:

So far as Mr. Washington preaches Thrift, Patience, and Industrial Training for the masses, we must hold up his hands and strive with him. . . . But so far as Mr. Washington apologizes for injustice . . . and opposes the higher training and ambition of our brighter minds—so far as he, the South, or the Nation does this—we must unceasingly and firmly oppose them.

Du Bois also criticized the academic type of black education which meekly imitated that of the white colleges. The ultimate tragedy of Washington's viewpoint was that even after accepting the American belief in hard work, self-reliance, and industrial skills, the black man was still unable to make effective progress in skilled occupations or in the development of black business establishments. These symbols of success were difficult enough for the average white man to achieve; for the black man they were virtually impossible.

American public schools in this era made impressive gains in terms of greater educational opportunities for more students. However, the overall educational scene revealed severe inequities. These unresolved, and often unrecognized, defects would have to be dealt with painfully by later generations.

2 Evolutionary Ideas Change American Thought

1. What was the impact of Charles Darwin's theory of evolution upon American thought and reform movements in the late nineteenth and early twentieth centuries?

2. What new concepts were added to the field of economics? What new perspectives were brought to the study of history? How significant were the new ideas in these fields?

3. In what way did the legal views of Oliver Wendell Homes, Jr. represent a departure from traditional legal thinking?

4. What were the principles of William James's philosophy of pragmatism?

The sharp conflict between old beliefs and the new ideas of science and industrialism resulted in one of the most intellectually creative eras in American history. In religion, philosophy, economics, law, and history, new concepts challenged the old at every point.

Many Americans of the nineteenth century had a clearly defined set of beliefs which permeated every area of life. Man was endowed with a "divine spark" which raised him above the animal world and made him capable of infinite progress. God ruled the universe as a benevolent deity and intervened directly in the affairs of men. George Bancroft, the most popular nineteenth-century American historian, believed that God had determined the course of American history. God had established certain natural laws of the universe which man should try to discover. Reasoning was a deductive process of applying eternal truths to specific situations. This world outlook was cheerful, optimistic, dynamic, and hopeful.

The human mind was regarded as a fixed structure little changed by environment. Some people were born to succeed, others to fail, because "you can't change human nature." As the Reverend Henry Ward Beecher put it, "God has intended the great to be great and the little to be little." Poverty was a sign of sin or weakness. Whether in religion, law, or any other field, the conservative viewpoint had one common characteristic. It relied on absolute ideas, which existed apart from the material world and which would be as true in the next thousand years as they were now.

The realities of the industrial world shattered this simple, comforting philosophy. In the face of class conflicts, strikes, slums, and rising crime rates, how could it be argued that history was always moving toward a better society? Were the rapid changes taking place a part of a divine plan, or were they uncontrolled and haphazard? Was truth as certain as it seemed, and was America really a land of boundless opportunities?

Darwinism. Charles Darwin's theory of evolution (page 330) was the most important single challenge to the old order. If Darwin was right, man was not a divine being, created in God's image, but just another animal. He and all other living things were products of a ruthless process dominated by the strongest and most fit. Darwin made his discovery by induction from particular facts rather than by deduction from eternal principles.

As already noted, conservatives were able to accommodate Darwin to the status quo. Herbert Spencer transferred Darwin's theory to the social scene and used the expression "survival of the fittest" to explain man and history. William Graham Sumner, a rugged character who elaborated his views in lectures, articles, and in his influential book *Folkways* (1906), argued that man was not a free agent in his actions. His behavior was determined by the forces and pressures of his own environment which were beyond his control. Therefore, he had no innate ideas and no power to change his environment.

Sumner was scornful of what he regarded as futile attempts to help the downtrodden, because the bitter struggle for survival was a fundamental law which could not be altered by man. As one of Sumner's followers explained to reformer Henry George: "You and I can do nothing at all. It's all a matter of evolution. Perhaps in four or five thousand years evolution may have carried man beyond this state of things."

Reform Darwinists. But Darwinism was a two-edged sword. Spencer and Sumner used it to defend existing conditions by arguing that evolution worked with incredible slowness.

Others, however, seized on Darwin's idea that the environment determined life. If this were true, why couldn't man use his intelligence to change the environment? They were not willing to wait four or five thousand years for the solution of pressing problems. Eric Goldman, a modern historian, has called these men "reform Darwinists."

The foremost opponent of the "conservative Darwinism" espoused by Spencer and Sumner was Lester Frank Ward, one of the founders of modern sociology. Ward accepted Darwinism, but emphasized the need for intelligent control of society by itself. In surveying human history, Ward found that advances had come not from the blind forces of the natural world, but from the human forces of invention and intelligence. Nature, he said, was uneconomical and wasteful; fruit and vegetables artificially cultivated are far superior to those which grow wild in nature. Every advance comes because of man's determination to master his environment.

An advocate of social planning and of the welfare state, Ward welcomed governmental intervention as another illustration of man's ability to control the environment. Ward's *Dynamic Sociology* (1883) was written in such a ponderous style that in six years it sold only five hundred copies. But his influence on the thinking of economic reformers began to be felt after 1900.

Economists in rebellion. One of the earliest promoters of reform Darwinism was Henry George, an amateur economist whose most notable work was *Progress and Poverty* (1879). George invoked the powerful argument of economic interpretation for the reform movement. This permitted progressive reformers to attack the rich by arguing that their "survival of the fittest" notions were simply rationalizations of greed. Reformers could put the onus of shame on their antagonists by labeling them mere money-makers who cared nothing for humanity.

In *Progress and Poverty*, George found that the answer to the paradox of great wealth and great poverty lay in the ownership of land. Speculators bought up land and sold it for a profit when it increased in value. But, George argued, the land increased in value not because of anything the owner did, but because society moved in and around it. George called this increased value of land "unearned increment." He proposed a single tax on the unearned increment so that society could benefit, and he believed that this was the only tax needed to operate the government. The single-tax idea has not taken hold in America (although it has in other countries), but George's book had an enormous influence in challenging Americans to examine old ideas about property.

One of the leading academic rebels among the economists was Thorstein Veblen, as unconventional in his personal life as he was in his thinking. Veblen was the son of Norwegian immigrants and was rasied in the isolation of a pioneer farm. He revolted against many aspects of American society, and wrote about the American way of life as if he were discussing the rituals and practices of some primitive tribe.

His best-known book, *The Theory of the Leisure Class* (1899), denied Sumner's claim that millionaires were "products of natural selection." Business enterprise, far from operating under any kind of law, was simply a chaotic clawing for profit. Millionaires were of no use to society, because their interest was solely monetary; the real contributors to industrial growth were the technicians—the builders of the industrial machine.

Veblen savagely attacked the "pecuniary" values of the rich, calling their smart clothes and well-trimmed lawns "tribal rituals." An angry moralist, Veblen used the phrase "conspicuous consumption" to describe the wasteful spending of the wealthy "kept classes." His ideas were so radical that for many years he was generally regarded as a whimsical eccentric, rather than as one of the most penetrating social and economic thinkers of this century. He urged economists to cast aside preconceptions and try to find out why man behaves as he does. He was, in his own words, "a disturber of the intellectual peace."

New interpretations of history. The impact of evolutionary ideas and the economic interpretation of society is seen clearly in the work of leading historians. In 1913, Charles A. Beard, a brilliant Columbia University professor, wrote his influential *An Economic Interpretation of the Constitution*. Beard shocked his readers by suggesting that the framers of the Constitution had advanced their own economic interests when they drew up the document. When Columbia's arch-conservative president, Nicholas Murray Butler, was

THORSTEIN VEBLEN

Thorstein Veblen, shown here in a painting by Edwin Child, was one of the most penetrating thinkers of the Gilded Age, and also one of its most nonconformist. In the following selection, Robert Heilbroner describes something of Veblen's lifestyle:

"As might be expected, he was a mass of eccentricities. He refused to have a telephone, kept his books stacked along the wall in their original packing cases, and saw no sense in daily making up the beds. . . . Lazy, he allowed the dishes to accumulate until the cupboard was bare and then washed the whole messy heap by turning the hose on them. Taciturn, he would sit for hours in silence when all his visitors were eager to hear his pronouncements. A flouter of conventions, he gave all his students the same grade, regardless of their work. . . . Curiously sadistic, he was capable of such meaningless practical jokes as borrowing a sack from a passing farmer and returning it to him with a hornet's nest inside. . . . Enigmatic, he refused to commit himself on anything. . . ."

asked, "Have you read Beard's last book?" he testily replied, "I hope so." A few years later when Beard left Columbia over an issue of academic freedom, Butler accepted his resignation with more than the usual speed. Although Beard's economic interpretation of the Constitution has been seriously questioned by later historians, he convinced many of his contemporaries of the importance of property considerations in history.

The work of Frederick Jackson Turner illustrates the tendency to stress environmental influences in history. As already noted (page 312), he believed that the influence of the frontier experience was in a large part responsible for American individualism and democracy. He hoped that the frontier experience would enable Americans to escape the social evils that plagued European civilization.

But to historian Henry Adams, grandson of John Quincy Adams, no such optimism was possible. He was sharply pessimistic, in contrast to the more traditional optimism of George Bancroft. Adams saw industrialism as retrogression, not progress. America's decline, he said, could be measured in the difference between Washington and Grant. History was little more than a chaotic struggle of forces. In "A letter to Teachers of History" (1910), he predicted collapse, war, and disintegration. Adams drew personal sustenance from the unified society of the Middle Ages. In his famous *Mont-Saint Michel and Chartres* (1913), he stressed the religious strength and unity of the medieval period, in order to contrast it to the spiritual emptiness of his own time.

Legal theory. Even in law, traditionally a conservative field, new currents were set in motion. The reaction to Charles Beard's book on the Constitution was violent because that document was held in such high reverence. Law had come to be the bulwark of private property, and all American law rested finally upon the federal Constitution. Most Americans spoke of the Constitution in tones of religious awe. A prominent

New York lawyer pictured the Constitution stretching its protective arm over the American people "like the outstretched arm of God himself." "O Marvellous Constitution," he continued, "Magic Parchment! Transforming Word! Maker, Monitor, Guardian of Mankind!"

Conservative judges saw their duty as that of logically applying fixed principles to specific cases. Oliver Wendell Holmes, Jr., one of America's most distinguished judges, challenged this notion in his *The Common Law* (1881). Law, he said, was a part of the social process and was constantly evolving. It must be related to experience and should never lag too far behind it. In a widely quoted sentence, Holmes wrote: "The life of the law has not been logic; it has been experience." Although Holmes himself disliked reformers, he believed in experimentation. There was a deep conflict in Holmes between skepticism and faith.

"The great act of faith is when a man decides that he is not God. . . . The only promising activity is to make my universe coherent and livable, not to babble about the universe."

The "pragmatic" philosophy. Among American philosophers, Holmes's good friend William James was a leading critic of those who believed in eternal and unchangeable truths. James wanted to bridge the gap between things of the mind and material things. "Granted an idea to be true," he said, "what concrete difference will its being true make in anyone's actual life?" For James, the world was open, incomplete, and always changing. Like Dewey, on whom he had a strong influence, he was concerned with the importance of actual living experience.

James's philosophy of pragmatism had two essential doctrines: (1) The meaning of an idea is only determined by its consequences, and (2) An idea is true if its consequences are satisfactory or effective, or if it fulfills a purpose. Pragmatism was a method of arriving at a relative truth, a way of moving from abstract, useless thought "towards facts, towards action and towards power." Although vulnerable to the charge that pragmatism meant anything that works, James did not mean material success. He hoped that free individuals would strive for something more in life than what he called the "Bitch-Goddess" success.

William James's "pragmatism" shows the direction of intellectual currents in America. Intellectual innovators turned away from abstract thought toward practical experience. They distrusted fixed principles and tried to relate ideas to life. They doubted but did not despair. They believed in a changing, evolutionary world in which man should try to live a life of courage and purpose, without the old faiths. The intellectual ferment of the Gilded Age produced many of the ideas that still influence modern American thought.

3 Literature Moves Toward Realism

1. How did the shift in literature from romanticism to realism reflect changes occurring in American society?

2. In what ways does the writing of the naturalists differ from that of the romantics?

3. Who were the important writers of the Gilded Age? What were their themes?

Imaginative literature provided the most sensitive mirror of a changing American society. The "Genteel Tradition" (a phrase coined by the American philosopher George Santayana) describes the prevailing literary fashion until the 1890's. Perpetuated by conservative publishers and critics, it looked upon creative writing as a means of moral improvement. Writers did not deal with the vulgarities and crudities of American life, because literature should portray life in its noblest forms. On two points the taboos were particularly strong: on sex, because a frank portrayal of sex was in bad taste, and on social conditions because a realistic treatment would end the idealization of life. Historical romances were in particular favor; people wanted to read books like Lew Wallace's *Ben Hur* (1880), which took them to faraway times and faraway places. Literature of the Genteel Tradition was romantic, sentimental, moralistic—and unrealistic.

But new pressures were mounting. The scientific outlook was spreading, religious values were losing force, and a social protest movement was rising. These pressures demanded some kind of expression. New young writers appeared, literary counterparts of the political reformers. Not all writers fit into this mold, but in general, literature became less romantic and more realistic, less optimistic and more pessimistic. Writers who sought to achieve *realism* in their works tried to describe characters and incidents as they actually were, without any idealization.

Walt Whitman. Walt Whitman had always scandalized the practitioners of the Genteel Tradition. With his "barbaric yawp" he had been the great singer for democracy and the champion of the common man. The Civil War renewed his faith in America, and in Lincoln he saw the highest potentialities of democracy. But the materialism of the Gilded Age appalled Whitman; it made society crude, cankered, and rotten. In his long poem "Passage to India" (1868), Whitman tried to recover the spirit of the past to show that materialism is not enough. He never lost his optimism completely, but it ceased to be as spontaneous as it had once been (page 173).

Emily Dickinson. While there was much of a new trend toward realism in Whitman, there is none in the poetry of Emily Dickinson. A poet or rare originality and insight, she had little concern for the social and industrial changes that were taking place around her. Miss Dickinson lived in a world of her own, and her art was that of the inner recesses of the mind.

Living almost as a recluse, she knew little but her house, her garden, and a few friends. Perhaps there had never been a poet to whom so little happened yet who felt life with such intensity. Skeptical of conventional religion, she had her own church. Though she could see life with heightened vision in bees, butterflies, and little stones, death was nearly always present:

> The bustle in a house
> The morning after death
> Is solemnest of industries
> Enacted upon earth—
> The sweeping up the heart,
> And putting love away
> We shall not want to use again
> Until eternity.

Yet no one who knew her thought of Emily Dickinson as morbidly withdrawn. One critic has remarked that her few stanzas "hold the distillation of all that it means to be human." They are her "letters to the world" which she wrote but never mailed, for it was only after her death that her complete poems were published. Van Wyck Brooks, the well-known literary critic, paid her the highest compliment: "Where others merely glowed, she was incandescent." In the New England literary tradition, she was the one authentic poetic genius of the age.

Henry James. Henry James, like Emily Dickinson, was a writer of the inner life, although unlike her, he was reared in a highly cosmopolitan atmosphere. James was born to wealth and position; his father was a noted theologian, and his brother William James was famous as a psychologist and philosopher. James was educated in Europe and by private tutors in America, but he was not happy in this country. He lived mainly in England and traveled widely in Europe, thus becoming one of America's first "expatriate" writers. Shortly before his death, he became a British subject.

Henry James produced a flood of novels, short stories, and literary criticism. He was keenly interested in the technical problems of the novel as an art form, and many of the basic principles of the modern novel originated in his work. James used the first person "point of view," in which the reader observes the action through the eyes of the characters. In James's work, the story unfolds not merely as a set of events but as the characters become more and more aware of the meaning of the events. James was also one of the first to experiment with the "stream of consciousness" style in which the thoughts and feelings of the characters are freely expressed outside the narrative sequence.

James was a realist, but his realism was psychological, not practical. Much of his writing is concerned with subtle human relationships revealed in drawing-room scenes, quiet tea parties in English manor houses, or high drama over matters of etiquette. His brother William, who always tried to write clearly and directly, once wrote to him in exasperation: "Say it out, for God's sake, and have done with it." But Henry's style was the relentless probing of moral and psychological problems through his own medium.

Although James found the United States artistically empty, it was for him still a land of innocence and promise, while Europe was beautiful but decadent. Much of James's work explores the conflict between the New World and the Old World in terms of the struggle between innocence and evil, between morality and corruption. The novel *Daisy Miller* (1878), which established his reputation, is a satirical picture of the free and natural American girl who comes to grief in Europe when she clashes with European society. A more expanded treatment of this theme is *The Portrait of a Lady* (1881), in which he describes the disillusionment of an attractive, intelligent American girl married to a charming but morally corrupt Englishman. In his later works, *The Wings of the Dove* (1902), *The Ambassadors* (1903), and *The Golden Bowl* (1904), his originality and his ability to reveal intricate personal relationships reached its peak.

Mark Twain. A greater contrast in style in two writers can scarcely be imagined than that between Henry James and Mark Twain, christened Samuel Langhorne Clemens. James was American-born, but European in taste, while Mark Twain was American to the core; James wrote about the sophisticated elite, Twain about ordinary people; James cultivated an elegant and elaborate style, Twain usually wrote in the common vernacular of the people. Yet both were great artists. Mark Twain was one of the "local color" school of writers who appeared after the Civil War, but he was far more than just a writer who wrote about a particular region or group of people.

Born in Missouri in a community but one generation removed from the frontier, Twain never entirely lost his frontier background. He traveled a good deal and saw human nature under many conditions. His *Celebrated Jumping Frog of Calaveras County and Other Sketches* (1866) brought him national attention as a humorist. *Innocents Abroad* (1869), a rollicking account of Americans traveling in Europe and the Near East, strips Europe of its pretensions and America of its hypocrisy. In *The Gilded Age* (1873), which he wrote with Charles Dudley Warner, he satirizes the corruption and materialism in American life.

Mark Twain was full of contradictions. Although he disliked the American acquisitive spirit, he was something of an entrepreneur himself, made more money than any of his contemporary authors, and hobnobbed with business tycoons. In one sense he became conservative, even business-minded; but his humor and satire were threats to everything that was respectable in the Gilded Age.

His work was the culmination of a long American tradition of expressing humor in colloquial language. In his greatest book, *Huckleberry Finn* (1884), he speaks through Huck, using the boy's crude but honest speech to describe his flight from conventional society. Complaining about the "sivilizing" Widow Douglas with whom he is forced to live, Huck says:

> She put me in them new clothes again, and I couldn't do nothing but sweat and sweat and feel all cramped up. . . . The widow rang a bell for supper and you had to come to time. When you got to the table you couldn't go right to eating but you had to wait for the widow to tuck down her head and grumble a little over the victuals though there warn't really anything the matter with them—that is, nothing only everything was cooked by itself. In a barrel of odds and ends it is different, things got mixed up and the juice kind of swaps around and things go better.

The passage clearly shows Huck's limitations, yet his life seems more vital and fresh than the flat, conventional society which he dislikes. When later in the novel the larger issues of love, loyalty, and freedom are introduced, the result is one of the great achievements of the American imagination.

In later life, financial reverses and a series of personal tragedies made Mark Twain bitter and cynical. To pay off his debts, he was forced to wander about Europe and America giving lectures. In *A Connecticut Yankee in King Arthur's Court* (1889), *Puddn'head Wilson* (1894), and *The Mysterious Stranger* (1916), published posthumously, he lost his "good humor" and life lost its buoyancy. Yet, humor was his medium and if readers are responsive to the meaning and appeal of that humor, they will recognize in his work a complex creative achievement.

William Dean Howells. Samuel Clemens's good friend William Dean Howells showed perhaps more clearly than any other writer the impact of social and economic change on literature. At first he was a leading novelist of middle-class manners, but as he grew older, he became more concerned with questions of social justice. He turned from writing about "the smiling aspects of American life" to more serious issues:

After fifty years of optimistic content with civilization and its ability to come out all right in the end, I now abhor it, and feel that it is coming out all wrong in the end unless it bases itself on real equality.

Howells thought of himself as a realist and believed writers should be faithful to their experience and to life. Although his style remained primly in the Genteel Tradition, his subject matter put him with the literary rebels of his day. In *The Rise of Silas Lapham* (1885), Lapham, the wealthy paint manufacturer, is crude but honest; in *A Hazard of New Fortunes* (1890), the millionaire Dryfoos becomes a much less honorable character. Howells's later stress on the evils of industrial capitalism and the decline of old standards of morality is emphasized in his two utopian novels, *A Traveler from Altruria* (1894) and *Through the Eye of the Needle* (1907). Howells was important not only as a critic of injustice and a masterful interpreter of the middle class, but also because he encouraged and sponsored many young writers who went far beyond his kind of realism.

Naturalist writers. Among these young rebels who appeared on the literary scene just before the turn of the century were Frank Norris, Jack London, Theodore Dreiser, and Stephen Crane. These writers not only protested against social evils, but they also found in Darwinian evolution an explanation of the social process. While the reform Darwinists saw hope in evolution, writers like London and Dreiser saw the world in terms of the survival of the fittest. Man's violent struggle for existence against the whims of fate run rampant through the works of Dreiser, Norris, and London. These writers are sometimes called "naturalists." The term *naturalism* is used to refer to realistic writing and to a philosophy which sees man tossed about by cosmic forces which he cannot control. This philosophy often led these writers to a preoccupation with tragedy and failure, creating a truly pessimistic literature.

Jack London and Frank Norris. Jack London was the most enthusiastic exponent of the struggle for survival in literature. His Wolf Larsen in *The Sea Wolf* (1904) treated his crew mercilessly because, after all, the strong must prevail over the weak. But London embraced both the utopian theories of socialism, championing the lower classes, and the ideas of the German philosopher Friedrich Nietzsche, whose concept of the "superman" embodied force and violence. Like other naturalist writers, London was never able to reconcile these contradicting philosophies.

This problem also troubled Frank Norris, whose best work, *The Octopus* (1901), was meant to be the first part of an epic which would show that "men were mere nothings" and that "force only existed." Yet *The Octopus* turned into an attack on the Southern Pacific Railroad, and ended up on a note of romantic optimism:". . . all things surely, inevitably, resistlessly work together for good."

Theodore Dreiser. Dreiser's novels were more concerned with the helplessness of man in the face of complex social forces. Much that he wrote was autobiographical—a portrayal of the hopes, frustrations, and despair of himself, his brothers and sisters, and his immigrant parents. The city was the background against which Dreiser pitted his characters. His first novel, *Sister Carrie* (1900), tells the story of a simple country girl who goes to Chicago and wins success as an actress, while her lover sinks into crime and poverty.

The shocking thing to many people about Dreiser's books was that success or failure in his novels had little to do with traditional middle class virtues—it was a matter of accident and meaningless forces. In his own mind, Dreiser did not believe that these forces were entirely uncontrollable. His later zeal for social reform shows that he felt it was possible to change the conditions which were so destructive to the lives of his fictional characters.

Stephen Crane. In his few novels and short stories, Stephen Crane expressed a similar realism and pessimism. Crane achieved a perfection of form in some of his writing, particularly in his novel *The Red Badge of Courage* (1895) (page 255), and in his short story *The Open Boat* (1898). In these works, Crane was concerned with fear as a basic motive for human conduct. Like Henry James, Crane developed a stream of consciousness style in his writing and employed a succession of bright, colorful images to convey his meaning. These images reflected Crane's belief that he "must report, with fidelity, only what his imaginative vision has verified." In this sense, Crane differed from the realists who were concerned with recording every detail. Crane was an "impressionist" who wanted "to capture the essence of an instant." His work is comparable to a "flash" series of pictures, or impressions, without explanation or subjective comment. Thus, he often failed to present complete descriptions or full accounts of dramatic scenes.

Crane was also an "objective" writer. In his novel *Maggie: A Girl of the Streets* (1893), which he published with the encouragement of William Dean Howells, he describes the violence and sordidness of the New York slums. But this work is not a plea for reform; rather it is a statement of conditions. Crane, and Dreiser, were both concerned with this technique of "keeping a distance" and avoiding the former literary tradition to sentimentalize a writer's observations. There is no moralizing in Crane's works.

Edwin Arlington Robinson. The end of the century found an authentic poetic voice in Edwin Arlington Robinson. A far more complex artist than the naturalist novelists, he was sensitive to the deep undercurrents of the American scene. Traditional in style, his mood of fortitude in the face of profound doubt was modern. Man's fate was tragic, but loyalty to some ultimate truth would reveal a gleam of light, however dim and flickering. Unsatisfied with the simple material solutions to life, Robinson pursued his art in lonely devotion, asking questions for which he had no answers, but believing nonetheless in love, loyalty, and humility. He was a poet of doubt, but not of despair. His early poem *Credo* begins in doubt:

> I cannot find my way: there is no star
> In all the shrouded heavens anywhere;

But ends in hope:

> For through it all—above, beyond it all—
> I know the far-sent message of the years,
> I feel the coming glory of the Light.

EDWIN ARLINGTON ROBINSON

Robinson began his writing in the years before World War I. Around the turn of the century he lived in poverty in New York City, where he worked at a variety of odd jobs while he wrote. In 1905, President Theodore Roosevelt, who was impressed with one of Robinson's works and who knew of the poet's difficulties, gave him a job in the New York customhouse. By 1910, Robinson had attracted a growing audience and was able to devote himself completely to writing. He became one of America's most widely read poets, and was awarded the Pulitzer Prize in 1922, 1925, and 1928.

In his early career as a poet, Robinson was a true psychologist, much like Henry James. Like James, he was concerned not with what happened but with the how and why of the mind and of human relationships. During the first half of his career, Robinson was primarily concerned with character—that of the individual and as an illustration of universal qualities. In his poem "Richard Cory," Robinson explored the contradictions of the human character:

> Whenever Richard Cory went downtown,
>   We people on the pavement looked at him:
> He was a gentleman from sole to crown,
>   Clean-favored, and imperially slim.
>
> And he was always quietly arrayed,
>   And he was always human when he talked;
> But still he fluttered pulses when he said,
>   "Good morning," and he glittered when he
>   walked.
>
> And he was rich—yes, richer than a king—
>   And admirably schooled in every grace:
> In fine, we thought that he was everything
>   To make us wish that we were in his place.
>
> So on we worked, and waited for the light,
>   And went without the meat, and cursed the
>   bread;
> And Richard Cory, one calm summer night,
>   Went home and put a bullet through his head.

4 The Arts Break With Tradition

1. In what ways were the changes taking place in American art similar to those in literature during the Gilded Age?

2. How do you explain the apparent lack of acceptance of American artists and composers during the Gilded Age?

3. Who were the primary figures in American painting, sculpture, and classical music during the period, and what was the nature of their contributions?

4. In what ways did the painting, sculpture, and classical music of the Gilded Age reflect the nature of the period?

American art of the late nineteenth century followed literature's trend toward realism. In this era European art was undergoing a revolutionary change from romanticism to realism. One important form of this realism was French Impressionism—an attempt to capture the visual impression of a fleeting moment, often using nature and outdoor scenes as subjects. Some Americans were so powerfully influenced by European painting that their art is scarcely distinguishable from it; others developed independent and characteristically American styles. In any case, American painting rose to the level of its literature for the first time in the nineteenth century.

James Whistler. Like Henry James in literature, some expatriate painters were alienated by what they regarded as the cultural poverty of American life. James A. McNeill Whistler could not even accept the fact that he had been born in the industrial town of Lowell, Massachusetts: "I shall be born when and where I want, and I do not choose to be born in Lowell."

Scorning the materialism of the middle class, Whistler became a leading exponent of the "Art for Art's Sake" school, which contended that art was independent of, and superior to, ordinary life. Subject mattered little to him; the artist's treatment was all that counted. In his most famous canvas, *Arrangement in Gray and Black* (1872; popularly known as "Whistler's Mother"), he was mainly concerned with the color and composition. How furious he would have been had he known that one day the United States Post Office would commemorate this painting on a stamp to celebrate Mother's Day!

Public reaction to Whistler's work was not enthusiastic. Upon viewing Whistler's impressionistic painting *Nocturne in Black and Gold; The Falling Rocket* (c. 1874) the famous critic John Ruskin called it "a pot of paint flung in the public's face." Whistler sued for damages and won an award of one contemptuous farthing. *Arrangement in Gray and Black* was bought by the French Government in 1891 because no one in America wanted it, even at a very low price. His works are less startling today because he helped prepare modern taste to accept artistic values in painting other than the story-telling or descriptive elements.

Cassatt and Sargent. Two other Americans who worked abroad were Mary Cassatt and John Singer Sargent, both strongly influenced by the French impressionists. Mary Cassatt developed her own individualistic style. She painted mothers and children with particular sensitivity and without sentimentality, for example, *The Bath* (1892). Her skillful drawing and composition and, above all, her radiant color gave her paintings a sense of charm and objective reality.

Sargent, like Mary Cassatt, lived abroad most of his life. As a portraitist, he had great technical ability to reproduce shape and texture, but his paintings sometimes failed to go beyond mere description. When asked if he sought the inner man behind the veil, he replied: "If there was a veil, I should paint the veil. I can only paint what I see." He was a fashionable painter; his work was nearly always brilliant, and much of it had vigor as well.

Winslow Homer. Art historians are generally agreed that the three greatest painters of the post–Civil War era were Winslow Homer, Thomas Eakins, and Albert Pinkham Ryder. Reared in Boston and Cambridge, the self-taught Homer was for many years an illustrator for *Harper's Weekly*. During the latter part of his life he lived alone in a cottage at Prout's Neck, on the Maine coast, although he took occasional trips to the Caribbean, the Adirondack Mountains, and

Quebec. Homer tried to paint his subjects as he saw them. "Whatever else you have to offer," he once remarked, "will come out anyway."

Although he first won attention for his Civil War paintings, Winslow Homer's early work, like that of Howells, was concerned with "the smiling aspects of American life." He portrayed the middle class at leisure and painted freckle-faced urchins who were the pictorial equivalents of Huck Finn and Tom Sawyer.

Homer became a very different artist in his later years. His pictures became more universal and less specific, more concerned with nature as a force than as an element in a story. He became an important technical innovator in watercolor, developing a rapid technique which rendered the impression of a momentary glance. But his greatest works were his late oil paintings, many of the sea with which he was so intimately acquainted. His sea epics show man struggling for survival against powerful natural forces.

Thomas Eakins. When someone once asked Thomas Eakins of Philadelphia whom he considered to be the greatest American painter, he replied without hesitation, "Winslow Homer." Posterity has ranked Eakins along with Homer as one of the foremost American painters. Eakins's most essential characteristic was his thorough-going realism, which perhaps explains why he was never as popular as Homer. Walt Whitman said of him, "I never knew of but one artist and that's Tom Eakins who could resist the temptation to see what they thought ought to be rather than what is." His aids were scientific: mathematics, perspective, and above all, anatomy. But his realism was more than just accurate rendering of likenesses. As he said, he never "sat down monkeylike and copied the coal scuttle."

His huge canvas *The Gross Clinic* (1875) was painted so realistically that it offended the sensibilities of the age; for example, the surgeon had blood on his hands. The medical institution which commissioned the picture refused to hang it for several years. Many of Eakins's paintings were exhibited at the Centennial Exposition in Philadelphia in 1876, but *The Gross Clinic* was considered "unfit" because of its crude realism. Subject matter aside, the painting is an effective rendering of figures in space and is interesting in terms of composition and color.

Eakins was one of the first to make sports a subject of his paintings—rowing, boxing, and wrestling. Concerned with an accurate portrayal of the nude, he used a camera to take multiple exposures of a moving figure in order to achieve greater realism in his *Swimming Hole* (1883). But his realism ran counter to the taste for prettiness and sentiment in the Gilded Age, and he fell increasingly into obscurity. In 1886, he was forced to leave his teaching position at the Pennsylvania Academy of Fine Arts because he insisted on using a nude male model in classes for young women. Many of his loyal students left with him and founded the Philadelphia Art Students League. By the time of Eakins's death in 1916, only three museums owned his work.

Albert Pinkham Ryder. Albert Pinkham Ryder, like Emily Dickinson, shows little of the general movement toward realism. Like hers, Ryder's art was the product of his inner world, little influenced by the world around him or by the paintings of others. Born into a seafaring family in New Bedford, he was romantic in temperament and responded to the mystery of the sea. In his early years, Ryder painted nature in infinite detail, as the Hudson River painters had done, but he experienced a revelation which changed his style entirely:

The old scene presented itself one day before my eyes framed in an opening between two trees. It stood out like a painted canvas—the deep blue of a midday sky—a solitary tree, brilliant with the green of early summer, a foundation of brown earth—the whole bathed in an atmosphere of golden luminosity. I threw my brushes aside; they were too small for the work in hand. I squeezed out big chunks of pure, moist color and taking my palette knife, I laid on blue, green, white and brown in great sweeping strokes. As I worked I saw that it was good and clean and strong. I saw nature springing into life upon my dead canvas. It was better than nature, for it was vibrating with the thrill of a new creation. Exultantly I painted until the sun sank below the horizon, then I raced around the fields like a colt let loose, and literally bellowed for joy.

Ryder was never bound by literal faithfulness to nature as were Homer and Eakins. The tone might be dark and sombre, the edges indistinct, but Ryder was concerned that the painting express his inner emotions about the subject. "I work altogether from my feeling for these things, I have no rule." He explained to a friend what he was trying to do:

Have you ever seen an inch worm crawl up a leaf or a twig, and then clinging to the very end, revolve in the air, feeling for something to reach something? That's like me. I am trying to find something out there beyond the place on which I have a footing.

Like Herman Melville, Ryder was fascinated by the sea. His sea paintings such as *Toilers of the Sea* (1884) reveal the triad of swelling sea, moonlit sky, and tossing sailboat. He painted romantic subjects like Macbeth and the witches, or Siegfried and the Rhine Maidens, and often his forms were hazy and indistinct. Occasionally he did a topical painting like *Death on a Pale Horse* (1910), inspired by a friend who lost his life's savings on a horse race and committed suicide. Ryder's painting was a foreshadowing of modern art in its freedom from literal representation, its relation to the unconscious mind, and its expression of ideas and emotions in abstract forms.

The "Ashcan School." There were other American painters who had little urge to find "the something out there beyond" that motivated Ryder, but were eager to paint life in the cities. Like Stephen Crane in *Maggie*, they wanted to show the slums and back alleys and the people who lived in them. Disgruntled critics labeled them the "Ashcan School." Their intellectual leader was Robert Henri, who urged his followers to immerse themselves in the teeming city atmosphere. Caught up in the Progressive movement, these painters were the reformers of the art world. John Sloan was one of the best painters of the group. His *Backyards, Greenwich Village* (1914) shows the tawdriness of the urban scene. The choice of subjects and the realistic presentation of the paintings of the Ashcan School were strong social comment on urban life.

When some of these painters exhibited their works in New York in 1908, hostile critics called them "apostles of ugliness" and denounced their paintings as "unadulterated slop." Nevertheless, the Ashcan School had considerable influence. The artists of this group encouraged experimentation and boldly asserted that ugliness and degradation were fit subjects for works of art.

George Bellows, a young disciple of Henri's, was influenced by the Ashcan School. However, unlike them, he was extremely popular, particularly for his paintings of sports. In *Stag at Sharkey's* (1909), he painted a boxing scene that combines brutality and beauty.

The break with traditional art was dramatized at the exhibition of modern European paintings held in 1913 in a New York armory. The Armory Show, which was arranged with the help of some of the Ashcan painters, shocked public and critical taste. However, it dramatically introduced modern art to America, and influenced the course of American painting.

Sculpture. American sculpture reveals similar, although somewhat less advanced, tendencies toward realism. John Quincy Adams Ward followed a native realism in his *Henry Ward Beecher* (1891), which has a burly vigor and honesty that is more attractive to twentieth-century taste than it was to his own day. More popular was Daniel Chester French, whose sculpture provided Americans with idealized symbols of the past. His two best-known works were the Minute Man at the bridge in Concord, Massachusetts, and his Lincoln of the Lincoln Memorial.

The dominant figure in American sculpture from 1880 until his death in 1907 was Augustus Saint-Gaudens. His first major work, the *Admiral Farragut Memorial* (1881) in Madison Square, New York, portrays the Admiral's face with powerful realism and gives his body a remarkable sense of potential energy. Comparable in quality is the *Shaw Memorial* (1884–97), on the edge of Boston Common opposite the State House. This Civil War monument portrays Colonel Robert Gould Shaw on horseback, accompanied by his black troops. His masterful *Adams Memorial* (1891) in Rock Creek Park in Washington, D.C., commemorates the death by suicide of the wife of his friend Henry Adams.

Music. Although American music did not achieve the levels of literature and painting, important advances were made. Europeans, particularly Germans, led in promoting orchestral music. Symphony orchestras founded in many large cities in the late nineteenth century were usually conducted and staffed by foreign musicians. In Cincinnati and later in Chicago until 1905, German-born Theodore Thomas introduced midwestern audiences to the leading foreign composers and struggled to raise the level of orchestral playing. Thomas' pioneering tours brought symphonic music to many communities that had never heard it before. Anton Dvorak, the Czech composer who visited the United States in the 1890's and wrote his *New World Symphony* (1893) on American themes, encouraged American composers to use black, Indian, and western music.

But, for the most part, European music dominated—in fact almost overwhelmed—American composers. Edward MacDowell's music was played more often than that of any other American and he was one of the first Americans to acquire fame as a composer of "serious" music. MacDowell was the musical counterpart of the Genteel writers in literature. Although he was a pleasing composer of small symphonic poems, his work was not comparable to that of European masters like Wagner, Brahms, or Debussy.

Charles Ives was a true innovator, both in his musical composition and in his use of native themes. Although his works were composed from 1895 to 1915, few of them were even performed until the middle of the twentieth century. Ives disregarded many rules of musical composition. He used old hymn tunes, camp-meeting songs, and circus-parade melodies to create music of extreme dissonance and startling new effects. Far ahead of his time, he was a rebel against Genteelism, and he hated the word *nice*. Ives's *Concord Sonata* (1901-10) is a creative attempt to make the spirit of the famous Concord transcendentalists live through music. The deeper he immersed himself in the past, the bolder became his musical forms reaching toward the future. Modern critics now recognize Charles Ives as the most original American composer of the early twentieth century.

American painters, sculptors, and composers used more American themes in their works and related them more closely to actual life. European influences were still strong, but American artists were struggling to create a native style. Music, the slowest of the arts to develop, was most dependent on European traditions. Many American artists of this period—Ryder, Eakins, and Ives are notable examples—were little appreciated in their own time. Most Americans continued to prefer romantic and sentimental art forms.

5 Popular Culture Reaches A Mass Audience

1. What forms did the popular culture of the Gilded Age take?

2. How valid is the view of many historians that the Gilded Age was a period of gross tastes?

3. What factors facilitated the spread of popular culture to mass audiences?

4. What legacy remains from the popular culture of the period?

In 1915, the critic Van Wyck Brooks used the terms "highbrow" and "lowbrow" to describe the difference between "elite" culture and the taste of the general public. Brooks felt that the gap between them was unbridgeable. A separation between the creative artists and the common people has probably existed in all cultures. Creative art often forecasts the direction toward which society is moving. But popular culture, the culture of the many, is more directly in the mainstream of life in any given period.

Popular literature. Most Americans clung to their old preferences for romantic, sentimental stories, despite the innovations in realistic literature produced by intellectuals. The popularity of romantic fiction reached monumental proportions in the late nineteenth and early twentieth centuries. While Dreiser and Crane were having difficulty getting their books published, Harold Bell Wright's sentimental and moralistic *The Winning of Barbara Worth* (1911) enthralled millions of readers. The romantic western novels of the Ohio-born dentist Zane Grey were so popular that he wrote over fifty books in the style of *Riders of the Purple Sage* (1912).

The simple but compelling books of Horatio Alger—all 135 of them—glorified the aspirations of material success. They invariably followed the rags-to-riches theme in which a poor but virtuous boy achieves success through hard work, clean living—and luck, usually in the form of a rich patron or an unexpected inheritance. Series such as *Luck and Pluck* (1869) and *Tattered Tom* (1871) inspired a generation of ambitious boys.

Arrangement in Grey and Black, No. 2: Portrait of
Thomas Carlyle, James Abbott McNeill Whistler, 1872–73

Fog Warning, Winslow Homer, 1885

Several brilliant new artists emerged as American art moved from romanticism toward realism. Among them was James McNeill Whistler, whose beautifully muted painting appears on the preceding page. His painting exemplified a turning away from a strictly literal representation of subject matter, and it introduced a more abstract style.

Still wedded to naturalism, the realistic picturing of the contemporary scene, were Winslow Homer and Thomas Eakins. Genre painting in America truly came to maturity in their work. Their native creativity shines through such paintings as those above and top right.

One painter who did not join the movement away from romanticism was Alfred Ryder, the most original romantic of his time. Literalism was of no interest to him; he was concerned with imagery and with man's inner world, his subconscious. The haunting painting bottom right is evidence of his view that "The artist should fear to become the slave of detail. He should express his thought and not the surface of it. What avails a storm-cloud accurate in form and color if the storm is not therein?"

The growing use of the city as subject matter for the artist is obvious in two of the pictures on page 404—one a warm painting and the other a sensitive photograph. In addition to showing both artists' technical skill in the use of their mediums, they also show their skill as reporters. The statue on that page is a fine example of the work of the period's most important sculptor.

Max Schmitt in a Single Scull, Thomas Eakins, 1871

The Race Track or *Death on a Pale Horse*, Albert Pinkham Ryder, 1910

Sunday, Women Drying Their Hair, John Sloan, 1912

The Flatiron Building—Evening, New York, 1905,
Edward Steichen

The Puritan, Augustus Saint-Gaudens, 1887

The public clearly liked "happy-ending" and optimistic books. In 1913, Eleanor Porter summed up the era in *Pollyanna*, a story of a good little girl who was always cheerful. *Pollyanna* and its imitators sold in the millions. Escapist literature seemed to be a tonic for the anxieties of rapid social change.

Newspapers and magazines. The spreading of popular culture was facilitated by the growth of newspapers and magazines which could now be printed cheaply enough to reach huge numbers of people. Joseph Pulitzer, the Hungarian-born newspaper publisher, was the first to reach a mass audience. By the late 1890's, Pulitzer's New York *World* had a circulation of over a million, achieving its success by the use of pictures, sensational stories of crime and corruption, comics, cartoons, and enterprising reporting. Appealing to a mixed city population, some of whom were just learning English or had just migrated from rural areas, newspapers relied less on words and more on pictures.

Publishing, like so much of American life, was becoming big business. The circulation of daily newspapers increased from about 3 million in 1870 to over 24 million by 1909. Revenue from selling more newspapers became less important than the income from advertising. By the 1890's advertising provided the major part of newspaper revenue, and its influence on American life had begun to be felt.

After the mid-1880's, magazines took on a new character. Older periodicals like *The Atlantic Montly*, *Harper's*, and *The Nation*, were dignified journals of relatively small circulation. They featured timely articles, fiction and poetry, historical and biographical material, and excellent illustrations.

The newer magazines of the 1880's and 1890's had a wider appeal. When Edward W. Bok became editor of the *Ladies' Home Journal* in 1889, he offered articles on child care, gardening, interior decorating, advice columns ("Ruth Ashmore's Side Talks with Girls"), contemporary novels by authors like Mark Twain, Rudyard Kipling, and William Dean Howells, and colored reproductions of art masterpieces. Magazines like *Cosmopolitan*, *McClure's*, and *Munsey's* reached millions of readers and became important vehicles for the reform journalism of the Progressive movement. These magazines not only catered to public tastes, but also helped create new tastes. Popularly priced at ten to fifteen cents, they featured crisp writing and "human interest" stories. Their wide distribution was made possible by new manufacturing processes and advertising revenue.

Sports. Urbanization also contributed to the rise of commerical spectator sports. Professional baseball was organized into the National and American Leagues and the world series between the winners of the two leagues had become firmly established by 1903. Boxing and horse racing fell easily into professionalism and urban promotion, although football remained an amateur college sport. The only major sport which was entirely of American origin was basketball, invented in 1891 by Dr. James Naismith, an athletic director for the International YMCA training school at Springfield, Massachusetts.

Bicycling became a craze in the 1890's. This sport helped to create better roads and the automobile industry, as well as somewhat more comfortable dress for the ladies, who were advised by L. H. Porter in 1895 that they might wear "not only skirts of short walking length, but even bloomers, without offense to feminine dignity."

Chautauqua. Popular education outside the schools spread through the country through the Chautauqua movement, founded by John H. Vincent, a Methodist minister, and Lewis Miller, an Ohio farm-machinery manufacturer. It began as a two-week summer training course for Methodist Sunday school teachers at Lake Chautauqua in western New York. The program expanded rapidly and thousands poured into the Lake Chautauqua region every summer for courses in literature, economics, and government, and lectures and musical offerings for open-air audiences. Eventually, a four-year correspondence course leading to a diploma was offered to give what Vincent called "the college outlook" for those who had not had the opportunity to go to college.

By 1900 there were about two hundred Chautauqua-type organizations in the country, offering entertainment as well as instruction. Touring Chautauqua companies brought a wide variety of musical, dramatic, and comedy programs as well as inspirational lectures to isolated

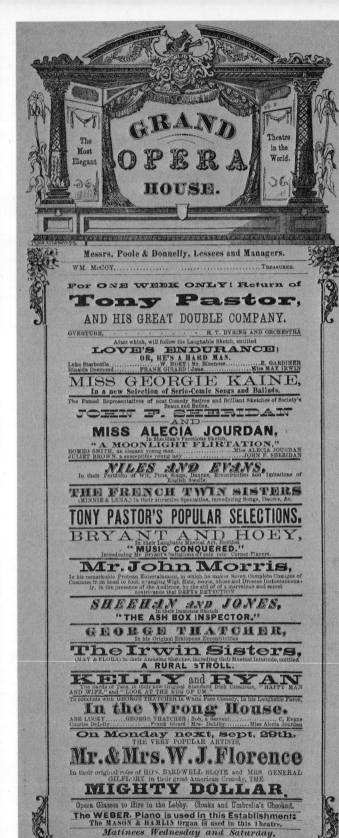

Vaudeville flourished during the late 1800's and one of its pioneers was Tony Pastor. The bill at the far left shows some of the acts with which he appeared. Sentimental songs were very popular with audiences, and a hit of 1901 was the one that appears top left. A little girl is trying to reach heaven by telephone, "for my mama's there." Melodramas like *The Concert* (below left) also played on the emotions of audiences. The scene entitled "Discord" must have brought a tear to many an eye. And for younger audiences, in search of adventure and inspiration, there were the so-called "dime novels"—story magazines like *Pluck and Luck* below.

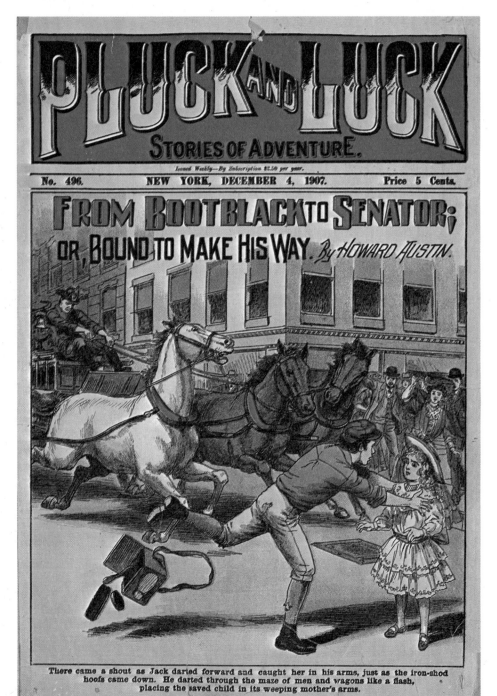

PLUCK AND LUCK
STORIES OF ADVENTURE.

Issued Weekly—By Subscription $2.50 per year.

No. 496.   NEW YORK, DECEMBER 4, 1907.   Price 5 Cents.

FROM BOOTBLACK TO SENATOR;
OR, BOUND TO MAKE HIS WAY. By HOWARD AUSTIN.

There came a shout as Jack darted forward and caught her in his arms, just as the iron-shod hoofs came down. He darted through the maze of men and wagons like a flash, placing the saved child in its weeping mother's arms.

hamlets. While the intellectual level of the Chautauqua program varied from shallow and superficial to profound and progressive, it gave thousands an excellent chance to learn about American history and the problems of their day. The Lake Chautauqua Institution in New York is still flourishing.

Popular Art. Most people could not afford original paintings, but instead bought the lithographs of Currier and Ives. These prints depicted mainly scenes of nature and outdoor recreation, as well as contemporary events, and today are valuable collector's items. In the late nineteenth century, people of modest means were able to collect inexpensive reproductions of art works.

In sculpture, the plaster group miniatures of John Rogers were enormously popular. The Rogers groups dealt with topics of human interest or historical and topical subjects. *Checkers Up at the Farm* (1875) was one of his most popular groups. While not great sculpture, it is accurate and realistic in detail. Rogers developed a flexible mold that would permit the manufacture of plaster copies of the original. Approximately one hundred thousand of these statuettes were sold, and at prices ranging from $5 to $50, to decorate middle-class homes.

In 1888, George Eastman invented the Kodak, an inexpensive small camera which opened up a new pictorial experience for thousands of people. The photography of Mathew Brady and others during the Civil War had been outstanding, but their photographs required long exposure and permitted no action shots. The Kodaks were much easier to operate and took good pictures in a split second. The new Eastman Kodak Company prospered mightily from the eager demand for its product.

Photography was not only a popular art and a commercial success; the great American photographer Alfred Stieglitz turned photography into an art form. Stieglitz's work of the 1890's has certain qualities of the "quick movement," which are like French impressionistic painting. For example, *The Terminal* (1893), by Stieglitz, recorded the frosty breath of the horses drawing the streetcar in a fascinating composition of forms and lights and darks.

Popular music. American popular music ran the gamut from hymns, ballads, Negro spirituals, and barbershop harmony, to the stirring marches of John Philip Sousa and the popular operettas of Victor Herbert. Perhaps in no other form of popular art was the sadness and dynamic beat of black American life better revealed than in "blues" and "ragtime" music. Jazz, a genuinely American art form, was to burst on the nation with greater force following World War I, but it began to have an impact in the early 1900's.

W. C. Handy wrote the famous "St. Louis Blues" in 1914, and Irving Berlin published "Alexander's Ragtime Band" and "Everybody's Doing It" in 1911. What everybody was doing was the turkey trot, and also the bunny hug and the grizzly bear. Music, catching the increased tempo of American life, moved from the stately waltz to the quick-stepping ragtime.

Theater. During the Gilded Age, serious drama was overshadowed by theater whose major aim was entertainment. Although theatrical companies with such notable actors as Edwin Booth and Richard Mansfield still drew audiences to the classics, playgoers flocked to the emotion-laden, sentimental melodramas. The theme of the melodrama was generally the triumph of rural virtue over urban evil or the dashing heroics of the "wild west."

Nearly every city in the country had a playhouse, where for 20 cents to $1.50, audiences could thrill to such favorites as *Jessie James, Only a Working Girl, The Heart of Maryland*—the latter an extremely popular play based on the old poem "Curfew Shall Not Ring Tonight." This particular play, specially written for its "star," Mrs. Leslie Carter, featured a climactic scene in which the heroine swung back and forth across the stage on the clapper of a bell to prevent its ringing and save her lover.

As audiences demanded bigger, more spectacular dramas, theaters provided earthquakes, snowstorms, train wrecks, and battles. In a hit play of the 1890's, *Blue Jeans*, a genuine buzzsaw threatened, night after night, to cut the hero in half. By 1899 stage gimmickry had progressed to the point where in a production of *Ben Hur* live horses galloped on a treadmill in a re-creation of the chariot-race scene.

Probably the most popular form of theater for the average American was vaudeville, the offspring of the old-time variety stage. Variety shows, featuring song-and-dance teams, comedians, acrobats, trained animals, had long been popular in America but were not considered "family" fare. In the 1880's, enterprising showmen like B. F. Keith of Boston, who opened the first vaudeville house in 1883, and Tony Pastor of New York made variety acts into respectable entertainment and introduced the continuous vaudeville show. Keith and his partner, Edward F. Albee, established a nationwide chain, or "circuit," of vaudeville houses. The Keith-Albee circuit and later the Orpheum circuit, whose principal showplace was the Palace Theatre in New York, brought vaudeville to millions of Americans.

Vaudeville acts varied in quality. The singing Cherry Sisters were so bad they had to perform behind a net to protect them from missiles thrown by the audience. Sharing the bill with jugglers, ventriloquists, and trained dogs were popular singers like Eva Tanguay, known as the "I Don't Care Girl," and top comedians Lew Fields and Joe Weber and the acrobatic Three Keatons, whose little boy Buster was billed as "The Human Mop." Many later stars of musical comedy and motion pictures, among them W. C. Fields, George M. Cohan, Will Rogers, began their careers in vaudeville. Although vaudeville continued to be popular into the 1920's, it was challenged early in the century by another form of entertainment—the motion picture.

The first motion pictures were actually "peep shows" in penny arcades. The viewer looked through a machine called a kinetoscope, invented by Edison about 1896, and watched little figures move against a blurred background. By 1905, images were being projected on screens in thousands of "nickelodeons" across the country. For a nickel, the moviegoer saw a film whose theme was generally some variation of the "chase."

With the *Great Train Robbery* in 1903, the idea of actually telling a story with motion pictures was introduced, and producers began turning out one-reel films with a story line. As early as 1908, the pioneer moviemaker D. W. Griffith began to use such dramatic devices as close-ups and flashbacks in the one-reelers he was producing for Biograph Studios in New York. But not until Griffith's *The Birth of a Nation* in 1915 did modern moviemaking begin (Chapter 21).

■ CONCLUSION

There was an undoubted tendency in this era toward the commercialization of popular culture. But historians have been too much inclined to see the Gilded Age as exclusively a period of excess, of grasping materialism, and of bad taste and bad art. These stereotypes have been overdrawn and overworked. It was also a period of sensitive artists, creative thinkers, and a public which was not entirely devoid of cultural interests. Mass media and mass production could create a phony "manufactured" culture, but they also offered some hope of narrowing the gap between the "elite" and the "popular" cultures.

In any case, a civilization that could produce John Dewey, Mark Twain, William James, Thorstein Veblen, Winslow Homer, Charles Ives, and others was far from a cultural wasteland. America from 1865 to 1914 was full of complexities and contradictions, but in large measure it provided opportunities for its creative artists as well as for its businessmen.

By 1914 an American cultural pattern was beginning to emerge, although diversities and contradictions remained. Artists and intellectuals had reacted creatively to the painful revolution which was taking place in American society. They scorned romantic dreams and took a hard look at the actual world. Dewey created a school for the new city; Beard revealed the self-seeking man of history; Dreiser wrote about tragedy in real cities; Eakins painted portraits that were so honest few people would buy them.

The drift of realism led toward a deeper probing of man's inner impulses and a more critical examination of American life. In their honesty and vision, the most original innovators began movements which carried far into the twentieth century. In *America's Coming of Age* (1934), Van Wyck Brooks wrote: ". . . an age of reaction is an age that stirs the few into a consciousness of themselves."

■ QUESTIONS

1. What changes occurred in American education during the Gilded Age? Why did these changes occur?

2. Which new approaches to the fields of religion, philosophy, economics, law, and history challenged the clearly defined set of beliefs that permeated every area of nineteenth century life?

3. To what extent is the intellectual ferment of the Gilded Age still influencing American thought today?

4. From a study of the Gilded Age what truth is there in the statement that "creative art often forecasts the direction toward which society is moving, but popular culture . . . is more directly in the mainstream of life in any given period."?

5. How would you evaluate the cultural legacy of this period?

■ BIBLIOGRAPHY

MCGUFFEY, ALEXANDER, *Fifth Eclectic Reader*, New American Library (Signet Books). A student may not want to study a reader, but in this case the tremendously popular *McGuffey's Reader* can shed much light on the values taught in the school. By analyzing the text, the student can make useful comparisons between education in 1900 and today.

CREMIN, LAWRENCE A., *The Transformation of the School: Progressivism in American Education, 1876–1957,* Random House (Vintage Books). For a general scholarly account of John Dewey and progressive education, the student should consult this book. It will give a good overview and place educational innovation in its historical perspective.

COMMAGER, HENRY S., *The American Mind: An Interpretation of American Thought and Character Since the 1880's*, Bantam Books. It is always a difficult exercise to try to identify general characteristics of a population. Commager does it well in this book, and the students should keep it in mind for reference to American intellectual history or the history of ideas from 1880 to the present.

SWANBERG, W. A., *Citizen Hearst*, Scribners. This biography gives the student more than information on a newspaper empire. Yellow journalism is clarified, and there is some insight into the political process. Above all it is a study of a man of conflicting moods.

BOWER, CATHERINE DRINKER, *Yankee From Olympus: Justice Holmes and His Family*, Bantam Books. Oliver Wendell Holmes, whose life spanned the Civil War and the twentieth-century Supreme Court, has been very well portrayed by the author in this biography. Bowen's numerous books are noted for their style, and this is particularly true with *Yankee from Olympus* which won a Pulitzer Prize.

FINE, SIDNEY, *Laissez-Faire and the General Welfare State: A Study of Conflict in American Thought, 1865–1901*, U. of Michigan Press (Ann Arbor Books). The limits to government involvement in American society, or the conflict between laissez faire and the welfare state, is a critical continuing issue in American history. This book does an excellent job assessing the direction taken by the government in the nineteenth century. It will help the student understand the government in the nineteenth century as well as the direction it took in the twentieth.

MUMFORD, LEWIS, *Brown Decades: A Study of the Arts of America, 1865–1895*, 2nd ed., Dover. This is a good overview of the cultural life of America during the second half of the nineteenth century. It concentrates upon graphic arts, landscape development, and architecture.

Politics Of Indifference And Rebellion

The Civil War is often used as a dividing line in American history, for perhaps no other series of events so dramatically and irrevocably altered the course of this nation's history. The country that emerged from the war was in every important way different from the one that had entered it. However, as frequently happens, there was a lag between the onset of a new period in history and the development of a framework of concepts with which to interpret it. That is, most Americans saw only growth around them and did not understand that what they were experiencing was the beginning of a new era, one in which for the first time industrialism would be dominant.

Rapidly expanding capitalism set the tone of American life, including politics. Many Americans did not question the political power of big businessmen and were concerned only with getting rich quick themselves. Others feared that the growing corruption of public officials and the concentration of the wealth of the country in the hands of a few men were undermining democracy. Governmental policies were determined by the needs of big business, which ignored the plight of farmers and workingmen. The South faced a special set of problems. It had to devise new relationships with black people, who were now free men instead of slaves; and it had to industrialize to build up its destroyed economy. The problems were great; but for the most part politicians relied on old concepts and solutions, which were to prove inadequate. Some questions that will help you understand the political problems of this era are:

1. How did business leaders influence political life?
2. What reforms were introduced in the civil service system?
3. What were the inequities of the tariff system?
4. Who were the Populists, and what did they demand?
5. How did the "free-silver" issue affect the Democratic party?
6. What problems did the South face following the end of Reconstruction?

1 Party Politics Reigns In The Gilded Age

1. What were the real problems of the industrial age, and what were the issues actually handled by Congress?

2. Why did Congress not handle the real problems of the industrial age?

3. What were the similarities and the differences between the Democratic and Republican parties? How does this comparison reflect American society at the time?

4. If you were a social reformer of the period, how would you work to bring about basic reforms?

In the Gilded Age, business leaders, not politicians, held the center of the stage. Rockefeller, Vanderbilt, and Carnegie are still familiar names, but most Americans remember very little about political figures like Presidents Garfield and Harrison or party leaders Roscoe Conkling and James G. Blaine. For the most part, businessmen themselves did not hold political office. There was no need for them to do so, since the professional politicians shared their beliefs and aspirations. Politics in the Gilded Age adapted to rising industrialism by supporting and encouraging the interests of the business community.

Politics in American society. Politics took its style from business world, where profit and material gain were the primary considerations. Older standards of public service gave way to a more acquisitive attitude. Opportunities for political graft were much greater than they had been before, since government at all levels was closely involved in the enormously expanded activities of business promotion. Many politicians came to believe that personal enrichment was the only purpose of a political career. Lord Bryce, the distinguished English historian and observer of the late nineteenth-century American scene, found the one unifying force in American politics to be "the desire for office and office *as a means of gain.*"

Politicians, however, reflected the ideals of the larger society of which they were a part. When Henry Adams said that he knew of no period in American history that was "as thoroughly ordinary," he was expressing his contempt for the scramble for profit and material gain. Yet, for most Americans, the prospects of material improvement were very real and well worth seeking. The rewards, of course, would go to the man of energy and enterprise, not to intellectuals like Adams.

Inevitably the rewards would also go to the schemer, the thief, and the reckless promoter who was little concerned with the public good. In an age of burgeoning capitalism, it is not surprising that some politicians shared the same temptations to cheat and defraud that beset other men. And yet, concentrating on the thievery of politicians disguises the fact that they also played a role, however ordinary it may seem in retrospect, in the development of industrial capitalism.

Politics also reflected some of the contradictions and inner tensions of the changing American society. Corruption and sharp business practices conflicted with the traditional belief in a strict private moral code. Opportunities for individual success were increasingly stifled by the growing concentration of business. Sharp divisions developed within the business community as the rise of giant monopolies brought a growing antagonism between small business and large business. Conflicts within and between political parties often revealed these conflicts in American society.

Party differences. Both the Democratic party and the Republican party lived on patronage and the rewards of office. The spoils system gave jobs to loyal party men, and it was a common practice to assess, or collect, regular fees from officeholders for party purposes. Business and industry spent increasingly larger sums for "favorable" legislation. No basic policy differences existed between the two parties, since both shared a common belief in the rising industrial civilization. Republicans and Democrats alike supported the idea of laissez faire—which seemed to mean that government could help business, but not workers or farmers.

The Republican party continued to receive support from the industrial North and the agri-

As criticism of the politicians holding federal offices grew, the cartoonists took to their sketching boards. In 1889, C. J. Taylor drew the cartoon at the right for *Puck.* It shows James Tanner, then the United States commissioner of pensions, showering money from the Treasury on northern Civil War veterans. His generosity with federal funds was summed up in his remark, "I am for 'the old flag and an appropriation' for every old comrade who needs it." In the days when there were such things as more money in the Treasury than the government needed, the cartoonist accuses him of wiping out any further surpluses. He later resigned his post because of the criticism he received for increasing pension payments after insufficient investigation of veterans' claims. Twenty-two years before Tanner was awarded his federal appointment during the McKinley administration, *Frank Leslie's Illustrated Newspaper* published the engraving below showing other men seeking government appointments. The scene is the lobby of the White House shortly after President Hayes' inauguration in 1877. The men wait outside his private office, where they will present their requests directly to him.

THE HORN OF PLENTY

There will be no danger of a "Surplus Issue"
in the next Presidential Campaign.

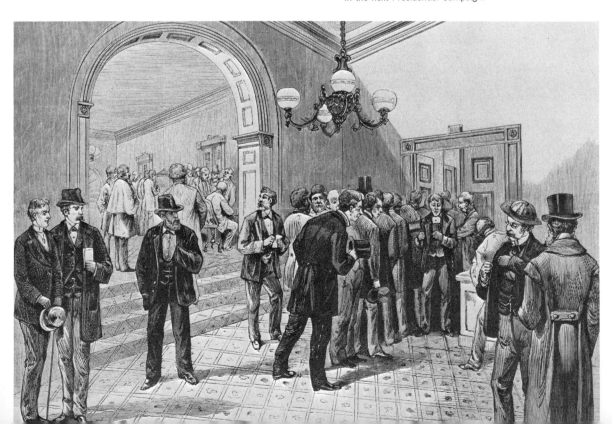

cultural West—the same coalition which had fought and won the Civil War. On the surface at least, the two parties did appear to be divided by the memories of the late war. Republican politicians never let the people forget the role of their party in the victory over the South. In every campaign they "waved the bloody shirt," an expression which meant denouncing the Democrats as rebels while praising Republican fidelity to the Union. The phrase originated in the House of Representatives when a Massachusetts congressman dramatically waved the bloody shirt of an Ohio carpetbagger who had been whipped by Mississippi terrorists.

Denouncing the Democrats in 1876, Republican orator Robert G. Ingersoll stirred up his audience until "men felt their sinew stiffen and their blood boil":

I claim that every enemy that this government has had for twenty years has been and is a Democrat. . . . Every state that seceded from this Union was a Democratic State. . . . every soldier that has a scar upon his body today carries with him a souvenir of the Democratic party; every man that shot a Union soldier was a Democrat. . . . The man who shot Abraham Lincoln was a Democrat. . . . And every man that was glad of it was a Democrat. (Loud applause)

Party divisions, however, were not based solely upon the memories of the Civil War. The Democratic party, which had been the majority party in the 1840's and 1850's, retained much of its strength in northern cities and midwestern small towns and rural areas. And after 1877, Democrats controlled the solid South. A complex and shifting balance of strength existed between the two major parties.

Although Republican Presidents occupied the White House for sixteen of the twenty-four years from 1876 to 1900, it was not a period of Republican domination. Presidential elections were close, and so was the party balance in Congress. Majorities in the House and Senate fluctuated regularly between the two parties, which concentrated their political efforts in doubtful states like New Jersey, Ohio, Connecticut, Pennsylvania, and Illinois, but especially Indiana and New York. These strategic states gained enormous bargaining power, and many of their politicians were rewarded with high offices.

From Grant to McKinley, five of the six Republican Presidential candidates came from critical midwestern states—Ohio, Indiana, and Illinois. While the Republicans almost always selected a New York Vice Presidential candidate to run with their Presidential hopeful, Democrats reversed the procedure. Democratic Presidential candidates from 1876 to 1892, with one exception, came from New York, and Vice Presidential aspirants hailed from Ohio, Indiana, and Illinois.

Declining standards. The dominance of Congress during Reconstruction continued during the following years of relatively weak chief executives. But the declining quality and close party divisions of the Congress made it ineffective in discharging its great authority. After eight years in the unruly House, George F. Hoar of Massachusetts declared that "there is nowhere responsibility for securing due attention to important measures, and no authority to decide between their different claims." With its pink and gold spittoons and perpetual odor of cheap cigars, the House was often a scene of disorder and confusion. Although somewhat more responsive to popular will than the Senate, the House was, in Woodrow Wilson's words, "a disintegrate mass of jarring elements."

A growing number of millionaire members in the Senate gave that body the reputation of a "rich man's club." Some senators represented business interests more faithfully than they did the interests of the people of their states. It should not be assumed, however, that all members of Congress were corrupt or self-seeking. Many able and conscientious men in both houses enabled Congress to carry out its minimum responsibilities.

To a remarkable degree, the two major parties avoided the real problems of the industrial age. They were primarily concerned with civil service reform, the tariff, and currency. These were important questions, but they did not strike directly at the most pressing ills of the day. Neither party seemed concerned about the alarming maldistribution of wealth. Both Democrats and Republicans ignored the plight of the urban workingman, and rarely discussed urban problems at all. Racial issues were far in the background, and the neglect of the farmer's problems became so serious that it led to a major agrarian uprising.

One explanation for the neglect of essential issues lay in the close balance between the two parties. Politicians were preoccupied with a constant clawing for office and the spoils of victory. Since both major parties were dominated by conservatives, actual differences between them were historical and sectional rather than ideological. Democrats were more inclined to favor a low-tariff policy, and Republicans were somewhat more closely aligned to business. But these differences were always blurred. Office, rather than policy, was the central objective. "What are we here for except the offices?" cried a delegate at the Republican National Convention in 1880. And when elections were close, as they always were, nobody wanted to take a stand on controversial issues.

Sectional and factional feuds within each party also interfered with legislative progress. Northern and southern Democrats were often at odds, and in the 1880's and 1890's, Democrats also split into western and eastern factions. Republicans were divided internally into various factions with colorful names like Stalwart, Half-Breed, and Mugwump.

Stalwarts, led by Senator Roscoe Conkling of New York, were blatantly for the spoils system and patronage politics. Half-Breeds, led by James G. Blaine of Maine, gave lip service to civil service reform but were only slightly less eager for the spoils of office. Mugwumps, the moderate reformers within the Republican party, espoused honesty in government and civil service reform. Stalwart Republicans were contemptuous of reformers generally, and Mugwumps in particular. One Stalwart sarcastically defined a Mugwump as a bird that sat on the fence "with his mug on one side and his wump on the other." Factional feuding absorbed much of the time and energies of party leaders.

To judge the politicians of the Gilded Age by the standards of their day, rather than by ours, it must be understood that many Americans did not believe that government ought to become involved in racial, labor, or urban problems. In an age dominated by the vision of industrial expansion, the old Jacksonian idea that government should protect the weak against the strong was temporarily sidetracked. When President Cleveland remarked that "though the people support the Government, the Government should not support the people," he was expressing the view of a majority of Americans. Politicians were not likely to adopt policies which ran counter to the wishes of their constituents.

Thomas Wolfe, a novelist of the 1920's, once referred to the procession of "gravely vacant and bewhiskered faces" which peer from the pictures of American political leaders from Lincoln to McKinley. In truth, they little understood the crucial changes which industrialization was bringing. Although not opposed to using federal power in the Hamiltonian sense—for the promotion of business growth and development—they had little vision of the use of governmental power for the welfare of all groups. As products of their age, they could not have been expected to change their habits of thought quickly. The most serious indictment against them was that they turned their backs on social distresses as acute as any in American history.

2 Civil Service Demands Attention

1. What were the deficiencies of government administration during the period from 1865 to 1876?

2. What were the problems faced by President Hayes in bringing about civil service reform? What reform steps were taken during his administration? How successful was he in bringing about civil service reform?

3. What were the provisions of the Pendleton Act? How important was Garfield's assassination in causing the passage of the Pendleton Act? How effective was the Pendleton Act in correcting the deficiencies of government administration?

4. Do you think the classification of jobs and competitive examination are the best ways of filling positions in government administration?

Civil service reform became a major political issue of the Gilded Age. The old spoils system, based on rewarding political friends with offices and contracts, was firmly entrenched by the time of the Civil War. The pressures of that war, however, had exposed serious deficiencies in government administration, and the scandals of the Grant era aroused new interest in reform. Moreover, the rapid growth of the country increased the size and complexity of government functions. The number of federal government employees rose from 53,000 in 1865 to 256,000 by 1900. There was increasing need in the various departments for skilled personnel who would not be turned out with every change in administration.

An articulate group of civil service reformers drew public attention to the corruption and inefficiency in government administration. For the most part, they were independently wealthy men who regarded spoils-minded politicians with acute distaste. Coming from a group which was often called the "Best People," they saw themselves as an elite class fit to set proper standards of political behavior. They were no more sensitive to the hardships of workers, farmers, and blacks than the general run of politicians, but they did favor honesty and efficiency in government. Their aim was to bring an end to the spoils system.

Beginning of reform. Rutherford B. Hayes took office in 1877 pledged to work for civil service reform. Like all Republican Presidents of the era, Hayes was honest and well-meaning, and he earnestly hoped to achieve a "thorough, radical and complete" reform of the spoils system. During his campaign he had remarked that if he were elected "this whole assessment business will go up 'hook, line, and sinker.'"

Hayes, however, labored under severe political handicaps. He had won a disputed election in 1876, and his enemies continued to question his right to the Presidency by calling him Ruther*fraud* Hayes and "His Fraudulency." In addition, the Democrats controlled Congress throughout most of his administration, and many members of his own party opposed him on the issue of civil service reform.

The President immediately got into trouble with the Stalwart faction of his party by naming civil-service reformer Carl Schurz as secretary of the interior. Moreover, as part of his effort to build up the Republican party in the South, Hayes appointed many southerners to government positions. The Stalwarts and their leader, Senator Conkling, felt Hayes was handing the party over to its worst enemies.

Nevertheless, Hayes vigorously attacked the corruption and inefficiency of the New York Customhouse. This was one of the richest patronage plums in the federal system, and it was in Conkling's own state. Two-thirds of the nation's imports flowed through this agency, which had daily customs collections of nearly $500,000 in the late 1860's. An investigation showed that more than a thousand employees of the agency were Conkling men, 20 percent of whom were completely unnecessary, and that the office was riddled with "ignorance, inefficiency, and corruption." Hayes replaced two directors of the customhouse and recommended a system of competitive examinations for employees.

Hayes further shocked the spoilsmen with his famous Executive Order Number 1, which banned assessment of office holders for political purposes. It also forbade federal officeholders to take part in the political activities of parties. Although this order was widely disregarded, Hayes had made a beginning in civil service reform. Greater efficiency and a lessening of political influence was achieved in federal agencies, notably in the notoriously chaotic and inefficient New York Post Office. During Hayes's term of office, a competitive examination system for jobs was also established in numerous customhouses and post offices.

Reform falters under Garfield. Before the end of his term, Hayes made it clear that he did not want another four years in the White House. "I am heartily tired of this life of bondage, responsibility, and toil," he wrote in 1879. The Republicans in 1880 selected a compromise candidate, James A. Garfield of Ohio. Garfield was put over by the Half-Breed faction of the party, and to satisfy the Stalwarts, Chester A. Arthur of New York was nominated for the Vice Presidency. Ironically Arthur was one of the officials whom Hayes had fired from the New York Customhouse. In the election of 1880, Garfield won a narrow victory over the Democratic candidate, General Winfield S. Hancock.

Garfield, the last President to be born in a log

cabin, was a big, handsome man with a fine war record and long experience in Congress. While he tried to bring the warring factions of the Rèpublican party together, he was committed to the appointment of James G. Blaine, a Half-Breed, as secretary of state. This commitment irritated Conkling and the Stalwart faction. At first, Garfield tried to please everybody, but his attitude toward the spoilsmen hardened when it was revealed that a Stalwart ring had defrauded the Post Office Department of over $4 million.

From the time he became President, Garfield was hounded by office seekers from the contending factions of his party. He confessed that he felt like "crying out in the agony of my soul against the greed for office and its consumption of my time." With some bitterness, he once asked, "What is there in this place that a man should ever want to get into it?" Garfield wanted to promote civil service reform, and he did assert his independence in some appointments. For the most part, however, he yielded to the patronage demands of the Half-Breeds.

Then, in the midst of these patronage squabbles, tragedy struck the new President, not yet four months in office. On July 2, 1881, while at the Washington railroad depot, Garfield was shot by a disappointed office seeker. The assassin, Charles Guiteau, cried out as he fired at the President, "I am a Stalwart and Arthur will be President." Guiteau was captured immediately and later tried and hanged. Garfield, who clung to life for seventy-nine days, finally died on September 19.

The Pendleton Act. Garfield's death brought about the reform in the civil service that he was unable to accomplish in life. The President's assassination by an insane office seeker gave reformers an emotion-packed issue the public could understand. Spoils-system politics was equated with murder. Goaded by an aroused populace, Congress passed the Civil Service Reform Act of 1883, popularly called the Pendleton Act. The reform bill received the active support of the new President, Chester A. Arthur, who, once in office, shed his soiled past.

The Pendleton Act established a bipartisan three-man Civil Service Commission empowered to prepare and administer competitive examinations for federal employees. The examinations

CHARLES GUITEAU

Charles Guiteau, a lawyer and self-styled evangelist who once described himself as an employee of "Jesus Christ & Co.", was a drifter and a psychopath, obsessed with delusions of persecution and dreams of glory. One of his notions was that the Republicans somehow owed him a job. In the following selection, Archie Robertson describes Guiteau's behavior leading up to his assassination of Garfield:

"His days in Washington, where he arrived on borrowed money on March 5, 1881, were discouraging and lonely, but he persisted. Once, pushing his way through a crowd of office seekers, he managed to see Garfield, who was of course courteous, and gave the President a copy of his speech. (He also sent him at least four other copies.) First, Guiteau asked for an ambassadorship; then for the consulship at Paris. In the White House he would help himself to stationery, write a note ('Can I have the Paris consulship?'), and leave it with a clerk. He also pestered Grant, Blaine, and Vice President Chester A. Arthur, and he asked many members of Congress to sign a petition on his behalf to obtain the consulship—with complete failure.

"After he was barred from the White House door sometime in May, Guiteau wrote a vaguely threatening letter to Garfield—of the kind the Secret Service would automatically be notified of today. It went unanswered. And it was, naturally, about this time that he turned against Garfield and began to brood about the President's 'removal,' as he called it. On June 8, borrowing fifteen dollars from a cousin, he purchased a .44-caliber British revolver with a white bone handle. (A cheaper model was available with a wooden handle but, he said later, he wanted one that would look well in a museum.)

"'That will make a good noise,' Guiteau told the gun-seller, who replied, 'That will kill a horse.' Guiteau, who had never fired a gun, went to some woods along the Potomac and practiced shooting at trees. Thereafter he began to haunt the President."

would test the fitness of applicants for government jobs "now classified or to be classified." Classified jobs were those which were under the competitive, merit system. The Pendleton Act itself placed only about 15,000 of the 110,000 government workers on the classified list, but it gave the President the power to extend the list. Assessment of federal officeholders for campaign purposes was also forbidden by the act.

The Pendleton Act did not completely eliminate the spoils system. In 1884, when Grover Cleveland became the first Democratic President in twenty-four years, Democrats were so hungry for offices that Cleveland was forced to remove about two-thirds of the total civil service and place Democrats in the positions. Nevertheless, this reform measure greatly improved the morale and the efficiency of the federal civil service. Succeeding Presidents enlarged the classified list until by 1914, 70 percent of all federal employees were classified.

While the Pendleton Act was one of the few significant reform measures of the Gilded Age, it had one unexpected result. With patronage funds reduced, party bosses turned more and more to big business for financial support. From 1884 on, business influence and ideals increasingly replaced those of the politician.

3 Industries Receive Tariff Protection

1. Why did the United States continue to pursue a policy of high tariffs?

2. What were some of the results of a high tariff policy in the United States?

3. What are the arguments against a high tariff as opposed to a moderate tariff?

4. Do you think a comparable argument can be made that if a laissez faire government policy is good for business nationally, then it should also be good for business internationally?

The tariff was of much greater immediate concern to American business than the civil service reform. Relatively advanced industrial nations usually favor low tariffs because they export manufactured goods they can produce so efficiently that they have little to fear from foreign competition. This was the position of Great Britain throughout most of the nineteenth century and explains its *free-trade* policy, that is, a trading system without tariff restrictions.

However, in newly developing countries, as the United States was in the nineteenth century, tariffs encourage the growth of "infant" industries by preventing cheap foreign goods from underselling them. Alexander Hamilton and Henry Clay had promoted tariffs for this reason when the United States was clearly an underdeveloped nation. After the Civil War, when America was energetically developing its vast industrial potential, high protective tariffs were pursued more vigorously than ever before. The South was no longer able to oppose tariffs effectively, and as industries grew from infancy to sturdy manhood, they intensified their pressure upon the government to support high tariffs.

Beginning of high tariffs. The Civil War marked the real beginning of the American system of *high* protective tariffs. During the war, American producers asked Congress for higher rates to offset their increased wartime tax burdens. Hurried legislation passed under war pressures raised tariff rates on dutiable goods from moderate to extremely high levels.

The Tariff Act of 1864, which remained the basic tariff for the next quarter-century, was rammed through Congress in only four days. It levied duties on 1,450 different items, but it was so hastily and unscientifically drawn up that it protected some industries that did not need protection and provided much more protection than was required in other cases. In terms of its long-range effects as a "silent subsidy" to business interests, tariff historian Frank W. Taussig has called this act "one of the most important financial measures ever passed in the United States."

After the war, the supposedly temporary tariff laws were not repealed, although the industrial taxes which had brought them into being were eliminated. Producers easily accustomed themselves to the higher prices and higher profits created by the higher tariffs. A powerful tariff *lobby*, a group representing special interests, fought attempts to lower the rates. *Logrolling* tactics, whereby one industry would support high rates for another in return for support of its tariff interests, were commonly used.

Whenever a tariff bill was before the Congress, representatives from hundreds of American business concerns swarmed into Washington to press their claims. Most effective was the threat to withhold campaign funds if the party did not support high tariffs. Typical of later years was the wartime complaint of a Congressman who favored moderate as against high rates:

What are you to do when Pennsylvania iron men and Rhode Island manufacturers . . . come down on you for higher rates, and your party colleagues tell you that if you refuse their requests the election may be lost and the cause of freedom retarded?

Opposition to high tariffs. Both political parties supported the principle of protectionism. The Democrats, who traditionally advocated low tariffs and whose business supporters came more from banking and commercial interests than manufacturing, were somewhat more inclined than Republicans to favor moderate rates. Farm groups in both parties became more and more disenchanted with high protectionism because of its exclusive benefits to industry.

High tariffs, however, came to be associated in the public mind with prosperity and economic growth. Republicans, in particular, stated again and again that tariff protection was one means which the government could employ to promote the industrial growth of the country. Significantly, in spite of dissenting voices, tariff rates from the Civil War to the end of the century went up rather than down.

A good case could be made for moderate protection. By protecting American industry from foreign competition, particularly from Britain, American business could prosper and accumulate capital for expansion. Workers, as well as industrialists, supported tariffs in the belief that the influx of cheap foreign goods would depress wages. Even tariff reformers did not propose a free-trade policy. The issue was not free-trade versus protection, but rather how much protection was needed.

Tariff moderates argued that high rates produced high prices which were passed on to the consumers. Since all Americans were consumers, they all paid a hidden tax which benefitted special interests only. As more Americans became concerned with the rise of giant industrial monopolies, it was further argued that tariffs contributed to the growth of monopolies, which had already snuffed out domestic competition, by eliminating foreign competition as well.

A new problem, strange to the present age, gave new incentive to the reduction of tariff rates. The government began to accumulate a surplus, amounting to $100 million by the early 1880's. A Treasury surplus was a problem in two ways: it withdrew needed money from the economy, and it offered an almost irresistible temptation to politicians to spend it for their own purposes. Since most of the government's revenue came from the tariff, it seemed logical to lower tariff rates. President Arthur tried to effect a moderate reduction, but tariff interests proved too strong and the high rates were maintained. It remained for Arthur's successor to cope with this issue.

Attempts to reduce the tariff. In the Presidential campaign of 1884, the Democratic nominee was Grover Cleveland, who as mayor of Buffalo and governor of New York had won a reputation for rugged honesty and independence. The Republican candidate, James G. Blaine, was a dominant figure in his party. His reputation, however, had been damaged by charges that he had sponsored favorable legislation for a railroad in which he had a personal interest. The campaign, one of the dirtiest in American history, dwelt on personalities rather than issues. Cleveland won the election, although his margin in popular votes was a scant 23,000.

Cleveland was a basically conservative man firmly wedded to laissez faire principles. But he was also stubborn and courageous, and he finally made up his mind to tackle the tariff question. He readily admitted that he knew nothing about tariffs, but he did his homework well. Warned that the issue would divide his party, he replied characteristically: "What is the use of being elected or re-elected, unless you stand for something?" By 1887, the surplus was increasing, and over four thousand separate items were under tariff protection.

GROVER THE GIANT-KILLER UNDERTAKES A BIG CONTRACT

Grover Cleveland—"I've undertaken to kill all three, and so I will if they don't kill *me!*"

In the tariff controversy, neither party favored free trade, but raising the specter of free trade was good political propaganda, as these cartoons illustrate.

THE FREE-TRADE BUGABOO

"Protection" Monopolist.—Come here, my poor friends—I'll protect you from the monster. (*Aside to his Congressional Allies:*) Whoop it up boys; make the jaws go—and we've got to keep the working man frightened.

President Cleveland devoted his entire annual message in 1887 to the tariff question. In a well-reasoned statement, he argued that existing rates were contrary to the public interest. The tariff-induced surplus withdrew money needlessly from trade and commerce and invited "schemes of public plunder." High tariffs, said the President, taxed all the people (through high prices) for the benefit of a relatively few manufacturers. He did not propose to eliminate all tariffs, nor did he believe tariff reduction would injure manufacturers. By lowering the price of American products, Cleveland suggested, American manufacturers would have a better chance to sell their goods abroad and thus help remedy periodic depressions caused by "the glutted domestic market."

In response to Cleveland's message, the Democratic House passed the Mills Bill, a moderate reduction in tariff rates. The Republican Senate, however, restored the high rates. The Senate delayed final action until the upcoming 1888 election in the hope of electing a Republican President who would be "safe" on the tariff issue. For the first time in years, the tariff became an important issue in a Presidential campaign; it was, in fact, the central issue. Cleveland was renominated by the Democrats, and the Republicans nominated Benjamin Harrison of Indiana, grandson of President William Henry Harrison. "Young Tippecanoe," as he was called, was completely colorless. Unlike Blaine, however, his integrity was unquestioned.

Harrison stood staunchly for high protection, while Cleveland defended moderate reduction along the lines of the Mills Bill. When, at one point in the campaign, it was revealed that the British minister to Washington favored Cleveland, Republicans charged that Cleveland was running for British rather than American interests. Raising the specter of "free trade," Republican campaign leaders "fried the fat" out of industrialists, who contributed a huge sum to help Harrison win. Harrison gained a narrow victory in the electoral vote, although Cleveland won the popular vote by over 90,000.

The McKinley Tariff. In 1890, the Republicans passed the McKinley Tariff Act, which rasied tariffs to new high levels. The McKinley Tariff was designed to maintain high rates and at the same time reduce revenue in order to avoid an embarrassing surplus. This was done by raising duties on some manufactured items so high that no foreign goods could come in at all, thus eliminating any revenue. High-tariff advocates abandoned the pretense of protecting "infant industries" and now openly fostered protection for mature giants. As a sop to farmers who complained that they were not protected by tariffs, a complete schedule of duties was drawn up, for the first time, on farm imports. However, since most farmers were exporters, these duties did little to help them.

The McKinley Tariff introduced the principle of tariff reciprocity, although it did so in a negative way. *Reciprocity* referred to an agreement between two nations providing for a mutual lowering of tariff barriers. The idea had developed from the belief held by many American businessmen and politicans that the domestic market was becoming saturated and that expansion of foreign trade was essential. The McKinley Tariff provided that duties on sugar, coffee, and tea, which the act had removed, could be restored if countries exporting such items to America placed "unreasonable" tariffs on American goods. Critics pointed out that this was retaliation, not reciprocity. Nonetheless a precedent for reciprocity, which became extremely important in later years, was established.

Establishment of protectionism. The unabashed espousal of protectionism, even to the point of excluding some goods, shocked tariff reformers. Cleveland denounced the act as class legislation favoring the rich. Critics made fun of the "essential" items put on the free list such as arsenic, stuffed birds, broken glass, orchids, turtles, and manufactured teeth. But whatever was said about it, none doubted that the McKinley Tariff did help reduce the surplus. The new tariff plus the extravagant spending of the Harrison administration, completely eliminated the surplus.

In the election of 1892, Cleveland defeated Harrison and again urged Congress to lower duties. Again a reform bill passed in the House was emasculated in the Senate. The final Wilson-Gorman Tariff of 1894 was such a disappointment to Cleveland that he allowed it to become law without his signature. Tariff rates were reduced slightly, but the act was barely distinguishable from the McKinley Tariff. The one novel feature of the Wilson-Gorman Act was the inclusion of a modest income tax to make up for the expected losses in revenue. Even this innovation was nullified in the next year when the Supreme Court declared the income tax unconstitutional.

Moderate protectionism for a growing industrial nation made sense. The McKinley Tariff, however, seemed to many Americans to carry protectionism beyond reasonable limits. Farmers and other depressed groups were beginning to realize that high tariffs added to the profits of big industries while raising consumer prices for everybody. Moreover, high tariff rates depressed foreign trade because other nations would not buy from the United States unless they could sell here.

Like Britain, as America became an advanced industrial power it would be required to consider lowering tariffs in the interests of selling its vast production abroad. Meanwhile, the powerful farm protest movement of the late nineteenth century took as one of its issues the inequities of a tariff system which benefitted the few as against the many.

4 The Populists Revolt

1. What occupational groups are most likely to gain from a period of inflation? From a period of deflation? Why do these groups gain?

2. What were the farmers' problems in the second half of the nineteenth century? In what way were these problems similar to the flaws in the American economy which were reflected by the Depression of 1893?

3. How did the Populists plan to correct the farmers' problems? What were the provisions of the Omaha Platform?

4. Why was the Populist party unable to attain its goals?

In the golden age of industrialization, farmers fell far behind in the struggle to gain a fair share of the nation's wealth. Their plight was basically the result of the tremendous increase in farm production (Chapter 11). Farmers watched in dismay as profits fell and costs went up. By 1889, for example, the price of corn was so low that farmers were burning it for fuel. The rise of farm mortgages was a clear indication of acute distress. As conditions worsened, farmers were forced to borrow money, offering their land as security. By the 1890's one out of every three American farms was mortgaged.

Farmers demand inflation. The years from 1865 to 1895 were years of deflation (see feature, page 142). With less and less money in circulation, the value of the dollar rose and agricultural prices fell. Creditors were paid back in dollars which were worth more than the dollars they had loaned. But for debtor farmers it was just the opposite—the dollars they paid back were of higher value and harder to acquire than the dollars they had borrowed. As debtors, farmers urged the government to put more money into circulation in order to reduce the value of the dollar and raise agricultural prices.

Sound money men—usually creditors or those on fixed incomes—backed deflation. Fearful that increasing the money supply would cheapen the dollar and destroy their wealth, they favored a stable dollar backed by bullion and redeemable in gold or silver. Following the Civil War, sound money advocates urged the government to redeem in gold the Civil War greenbacks (which had been issued without specie backing). Thus, the amount of money in circulation would be further reduced. This was accomplished in the Resumption Act of 1875, which allowed greenbacks to be redeemed when the government had built up a sufficient supply of gold.

Farmers and other debtor classes bitterly opposed the Resumption Act because it foreclosed any further greenback inflation and reduced the amount of money in circulation. A Greenback-Labor Party was formed in 1878 to fight for repeal of the act and to promote the issuance of more greenbacks. Although the party polled an astonishing 1,000,000 votes in the mid-term elections of 1878, the Resumption Act went into effect in

1879. Because the act ended all hope of expanding the currency through greenbacks, inflationists turned to a "free silver" policy. This meant unlimited government purchase and coinage of silver at a fixed price.

The silver issue. Since 1792, the United States government had used a *bimetallic* monetary standard—that is, it bought both gold and silver for coinage purposes, and the dollar was defined in terms of gold and silver. Under a *monometallic* system a government uses only one metal, gold, as a standard of value for currency. In fact, sound money men came to believe that the only way to provide for a stable currency was to adopt a single gold standard.

In 1834, the government had set the "mint ratio" value of the two metals at 16 to 1—16 ounces of silver was equal to one ounce of gold. The difficulty was that the "market ratio" between gold and silver fluctuated according to supply and demand. When, for instance, the gold strikes of 1849 increased the supply of gold, silver became dear in relation to gold. Over the years, therefore, silver miners had not offered silver to the government for coinage because they could get a better price on the commercial market. Silver dollars virtually disappeared, and with the Coinage Act of 1873, the government dropped the coinage of silver.

In the 1870's, however, the large increase in silver production in western mines lowered the commercial price of silver. By the late 1870's the commercial price had fallen below the government price. But when the silver interests tried to sell silver to the government, they found themselves shut out by the Coinage Act. Silver miners joined discontented farmers in denouncing the elimination of silver coinage.

Reflecting the intensified demand for inflating the currency through government purchase of silver, the House in 1877 voted overwhelmingly for a bill introduced by Richard "Silver Dick" Bland of Missouri calling for "free and unlimited" coinage of silver. The final Bland-Allison Act of 1878 did not provide for free coinage. It did, however, allow the Treasury to buy not less than $2 million or more than $4 million in silver per month and coin it into dollars. The act quieted silver agitation, but only temporarily.

THE GOLD STANDARD

The gold standard is a monometallic system under which the standard monetary unit of a nation is defined in terms of a fixed quantity of gold, that is, in the United States $1.00 would equal x amount of gold. An *internal*, or *unrestricted*, gold standard means that gold coins are minted and circulated as legal tender and paper money is freely redeemable in gold. In addition, gold can be freely imported and exported. Under an *international*, or *restricted*, gold standard, gold is used only as a means of making international payments. It is not coined or used as legal tender, paper money is not redeemable in gold, and it is unlawful for private individuals to hold gold.

In 1792, Congress ordered money to be minted from both gold and silver because there was not enough of either metal to meet the coinage needs. From then until 1900 the United States was officially on a bimetallic system. In practice, however, the nation did not operate on this system. Because of the law of supply and demand, the market ratio, or relative market price, of gold and silver fluctuated, and first one and then another of the metals dominated the coinage. For example, by 1834 almost no gold was in circulation; yet, by the early 1870's, silver had not circulated for many years.

This system of attempting to use both gold and silver not only contributed to an unstable monetary system, but was also a constant source of political controversy. Finally, through the Gold Standard Act of 1900, the government officially adopted the gold standard. Under this act, every dollar was backed by 100 cents worth of gold, and could be redeemed for gold. The act also provided for the unlimited coinage of gold and the unrestricted import and export of gold. The United States continued on the gold standard until 1933, when the government modified the role of gold in the nation's currency.

Rise of the Populist movement. The bitter mood of farmers was a compound of many elements. In addition to rising costs, falling prices, and railroad abuses, the farmer suffered from tax inequities. A tax system based on land and buildings rather than on dividends and income unfairly penalized farmers. High protective tariffs increased their costs and did little to protect their selling prices. Weather hazards made farming a gamble at best. Farmers also faced intangible disabilities–loneliness, drudgery, and often a profound sense of helplessness.

These elements of mood and emotion, so much a part of protest movements, found their literary expression in Hamlin Garland. His collection of short stories, *Main-Travelled Roads* (1891), tells of wasted lives and unrewarded toil. The main-traveled road of the western farmer, said Garland, was

hot and dusty in summer, and desolate and drear with mud in fall and spring, and in winter the winds sweep the snow across it. . . . Mainly it is long and wearyful, and has a dull little town at one end and a home of toil at the other. Like the main-travelled road of life it is traversed by many classes of people, but the poor and the weary predominate.

Agrarian discontent gave farmers the impetus to organize. In the 1870's, the National Grange became active in reforming railroad abuses and helped promote state "Granger Laws" to regulate grain elevators and railroad practices (Chapter 12). Although the Grange ceased to remain politically active after the late 1870's, it was the inspiration for a number of new farm organizations which mushroomed in the 1880's. By the late 1880's, these organizations had combined into two main groups—the Northern Alliance of the prairie states, and the Southern Alliance, much the larger of the two, which was loosely affiliated with a black branch, the Colored Farmers' Alliance.

Differences between these groups prevented a completely united front, but all agreed that farm prices were too low, that they were being gouged by the railroads and money-lenders, and that the money system was basically wrong. Farm groups also agreed that political action was desperately needed. Mary Ellen Lease, a rawboned Irish-woman from Kansas, expressed the general mood: "What we need to do is raise less corn and more Hell."

In July, 1892, at a meeting at Omaha, Nebraska, the various farm malcontents organized themselves into the People's, or Populist, party. (The name Populist comes from the Latin word for people, *populi.*) In a highly charged and emotional convention, the Populists adopted a platform calling for far-reaching reforms. When the platform was read, a reporter wrote that "cheers and yells . . . rose like a tornado from four thousand throats and raged without cessation for thirty-four minutes. . . ." The Populist party was the first American political party to attack seriously the problems of industrialization.

Reflecting the farmers' demands for an inflationary currency, the Omaha platform called for the free and unlimited coinage of silver at the 16 to 1 ratio. It also demanded government ownership of railroads and the telegraph and telephone systems, the establishment of postal savings banks for the "safe deposit of the earnings of the people," and a graduated income tax which would tax higher incomes more than low ones. In the interest of labor, the platform called for a shorter working day. And to give the people a greater voice in the government, it demanded the secret ballot, the initiative, and referendum, and the direct election of senators (Chapter 17).

The depression of 1893. In the midst of rising Populist agitation, a severe depression struck the country in 1893, the first since the United States had achieved full-scale industrialization. Most of the nation's railroads went bankrupt, and the stock market collapsed. The New York *Commercial and Financial Chronicle* reported in August 1893, that "mills, factories, furnaces, mines, nearly everywhere shut down in large numbers and commerce and enterprise were arrested in an extraordinary degree." More than four hundred banks and thousands of businesses failed, and about 20 percent of the total labor force was thrown out of work. In the terrible winter of 1893–94 over two and a half million workers were unemployed, and hungry tramps wandered over the countryside in search of work.

The five-year depression beginning in 1893 reflected basic flaws in the American economy.

Fierce competition forced many industries, especially railroads, to expand far beyond actual needs. As railroad companies failed, industries closely connected with railroads suffered. More than thirty steel corporations went bankrupt in the first half of 1893. The growing interdependence of the economy meant that failure in one segment inevitably affected others. The agricultural depression not only decreased farm purchasing power, but also affected railroads, farm machinery companies, and processing industries. The depression of 1893 was triggered by the withdrawal of European capital from the United States, but this would not have been sufficient to cause a major depression if the American economy had been fundamentally sound.

Many Americans were shocked and frightened by the severity of the depression and the impassioned protests which came in its wake. Alarmists believed that the revolution had begun when General Jacob S. Coxey of Massillon, Ohio, led a small "army" on a march to Washington in 1894. Coxey wanted the federal government to finance a huge road-building program to give jobs to the unemployed. When Coxey's Army arrived in Washington, however, its leaders were ignominiously arrested for walking on the Capitol lawn.

Populist influence. The disturbing depression atmosphere led many frightened Americans to view the Populists as subversive fanatics bent on destroying the capitalist system. The very manner and appearance of some of the Populist leaders was alarming. There was fiery Tom Watson of Georgia, who had a whiplash temper, and Senator William Peffer of Kansas, who looked like an avenging Hebrew prophet. Even their names were startling: "Sockless" Jerry Simpson of Kansas, Governor Davis H. "Bloody Bridles" Waite of Colorado, not to mention the "Kansas Pythoness," Mary Ellen Lease, and "Pitchfork" Ben Tillman of South Carolina.

Some Populist leaders were narrow and fanatical, others oversimplified issues, and most believed they were victims of an international gold conspiracy. They saw the country divided into two groups, one representing the money power and the other the impoverished people. Despite their excesses, however, many Populist leaders were realistic politicians and able social reformers, and a few, notably Henry Demarest Lloyd, were penetrating thinkers. The Populist program was a rational response to critical problems. The Populists objected to industrial capitalism because they felt it "dehumanized" the individual and degraded him; they did not wish to destroy the system. Breaking through the wall of laissez faire, they wanted the central government to regulate the system in order to insure equality of opportunity.

For all its intensity, Populism was strong in relatively few areas. It was centered in the South, in the midwest plains and prairies where farmers were most seriously depressed, and in the Rocky Mountain states where silver-mining companies joined the Populists for their own interests. Even in these regions, Populist influence was limited. As a party it was confined to areas where one-crop farming was the rule—mainly wheat or cotton. Populists won little support in the old Granger states of Illinois, Iowa, and Wisconsin, where farming had become more diversified and more prosperous with dairying and corn and hog production.

Populist leaders in the South who tried to unite poor whites and blacks into one political party found that they could not overcome racial barriers. Blacks generally looked to the Republican party for political leadership, while southern white Populists were Democrats. Above all, Populism was never able to attract middle class and urban labor support. Property owners were alarmed by the apparent radicalism of the Populist program, and the labor movement, so far as it existed, concluded that silver inflation would raise living costs.

At the time, however, Populist strength was widely overestimated. In Indianapolis, a rich lady surveyed the political scene and decided to take a European trip. "I am going to spend my money," she said, "before these crazy people take it." Even more rational observers were conscious of great ferment. The bitter calamities of the depression made Hamlin Garland feel that the country was approaching "a great upheaval similar to that of '61." As the election of 1896 approached, the nation was in a mood of unusual tension and apprehension.

5 Silver Becomes A Major Issue

1. What factors contributed to the gold drain in the 1890's? What affect did the gold crisis have upon the American political scene? Why did it have this affect?

2. Why was Bryan so well received by the Democratic National Convention?

3. What were the advantages and disadvantages of the Populists supporting the Democratic Presidential candidate?

4. What factors contributed to Bryan's defeat in the Presidential election of 1896? If you had been Bryan's campaign manager, what would you have done differently?

Free-silver forces had been clamoring for a more drastic silver bill ever since the Bland-Allison Act. The increasing political strength of the farmers, augmented by the admission of six new silver-producing states between 1889 and 1890 (North and South Dakota, Montana, Washington, Idaho, and Wyoming), forced the government to act. In return for silver support for the McKinley Tariff, the anti-silverites in Congress agreed to the passage of the Sherman Silver Purchase Act of 1890. The act directed the Treasury to buy 4.5 million ounces of silver each month, nearly the entire domestic production. The silver would be paid for with Treasury certificates, redeemable in either gold or silver, thereby putting new money into circulation.

Although the Sherman Act appeared to nearly double the amount of silver purchased under the Bland-Allison Act, silverites were disturbed because the Sherman Act substituted ounces for dollars. As high production lowered the price of silver, the government paid less each month for the 4.5 million ounces. In actual practice the Sherman Act proved even less inflationary than the Bland-Allison Act. Sound money men disliked silver inflation on any terms but were partially mollified by the gold backing for the Treasury certificates. The act was a half-way measure which satisfied no one.

The gold crisis. The depression that began in 1893 sharpened the clash over the silver issue, and a crisis over the government gold reserves brought it to a boiling point. Since 1875, the Treasury had maintained a gold reserve of at least $100 million for the redemption of currency. When the depression came, however, holders of greenbacks and silver certificates began to exchange their currency for gold.

President Cleveland, who had the misfortune to begin his second term with the onset of the depression, was a man of firm sound money principles. He belived that it was absolutely essential to maintain the gold reserve in order to protect the gold standard. Convinced that the Sherman Act was responsible for both the gold drain and the depression, Cleveland asked Congress to repeal the act. After a bitter struggle Congress repealed the Sherman Act in October 1893. Cleveland's triumph was a costly one which resulted in a serious split in the Democratic party.

The repeal of the Sherman Act failed to halt the depression and did not even check the fall of gold reserves. Other factors besides the redemption of Treasury certificates contributed to the gold drain. The European financial panic of 1890 caused gold withdrawals from the United States, and the McKinley Tariff brought a decline of customs receipts in gold. Although the government floated new bond issues payable in gold, as fast as it acquired gold, it had to pay it out again to frantic holders of gold and silver certificates who feared the government would soon be unable to redeem its currency.

In February 1895, with the gold reserve at $41 million and falling at the rate of $2 million a day, the Cleveland administration sought the aid of a private banking syndicate headed by J. P. Morgan and August Belmont, the American representative of European banking interests. In return for government bonds, the bankers agreed to raise $65 million in gold for the government, half of which was to be acquired in Europe. At a substantial profit to themselves, the bankers helped stem the outflow of gold to Europe.

Even J. P. Morgan, however, could not prevent nervous holders of currency from presenting it for redemption. The crisis was not finally ended until another bond sale in 1896 raised gold reserves to a safe margin. Silverites, already bitter

GROVER CLEVELAND

In his examination of the reform movement in the Gilded Age, historian John Sproat evaluates the contribution of Grover Cleveland, and concludes that Cleveland does not deserve his reputation as a champion of reform:

"Very little in Grover Cleveland's personality and background hinted that he could be the champion of anything. Unimaginative, colorless, and ill-informed, he happened on the national political scene purely by chance. . . . As a young man, he had shown little talent for his profession of law and had turned early to small-town politics. . . . Because he defied a number of his political enemies, he quickly won a reputation as a man of 'sturdy independence' and unbending integrity. Elected mayor of Buffalo in 1881, he practiced strict economy in the city's affairs and kept himself and his regime free from corruption and scandal. . . .

"As governor of New York, Cleveland displayed the same negative attitude toward the role of government that he had adopted as mayor of Buffalo. . . . With monotonous regularity, Cleveland rejected all appeals for public assistance made in the name of charity or to relieve pressing social needs. His favorite weapon was the veto; and he used it remorselessly to cut down all acts of the state legislature which trespassed his own narrowly conceived boundaries of government action. He believed that written law was the only law; thus, he interpreted the New York and Federal constitutions in the most narrow terms. Coupled with his usual refusal to act, his legalistic opinions and decisions effectively prevented the legislature from dealing with any of New York's many social and economic problems. With querulous deliberation, he scrutinized minute administrative details and legislative proposals. On one occasion he dumfounded Theodore Roosevelt by vetoing an important reform measure because the language of the bill was 'slipshod.' Because his attention seldom wavered from the papers which crossed his desk, Grover Cleveland failed utterly to comprehend the issues of the day. . . ."

over the repeal of the Sherman Act, were infuriated by Cleveland's resort to private bankers to protect the gold standard.

Division within Democratic ranks. Cleveland's monetary policy split the Democratic party wide open, with the southern and western silver factions arrayed solidly against eastern Gold Democrats. The repeal of the Sherman Act brought savage vilification of "Old Grover" across the farmlands of the West and South. To "Silver Dick" Bland, it meant the parting of the ways: "I believe I speak for the great masses of the great Mississippi Valley when I say that we will not submit to the domination of any political party . . . that lays a sacrificing hand upon silver." The disruptive forces in the Democratic party, symbolized by silver, and the Populists, were gaining strength as the election of 1896 approached.

Nomination of candidates. The 1896 Presidential election was a dramatic confrontation between middle-class conservatism and an agrarian radicalism which was blunted by its union with the Democratic party. Not since 1860 had an American election so stirred the people's emotions. The Republicans nominated William McKinley, governor of Ohio and sponsor of the McKinley Tariff. McKinley was a kindly man who was devoted from principle to the interests of the business community. His campaign was brilliantly run by Mark Hanna, the Cleveland coal and iron millionaire, who advertised the Republican candidate as "the advance agent of prosperity."

The Democratic Convention in Chicago was tumultuous and disorderly. The Cleveland Gold Democrats arrived full of fight, but were overwhelmed by the full-throated strength of the silver delegates. The platform, written largely by Governor John P. Altgeld of Illinois, called for free coinage of silver, denounced the trusts and the Supreme Court, and demanded an income tax. The convention produced one of the great dramatic moments in American political history when a handsome thirty-six-year-old former congressman from Nebraska, William Jennings Bryan, rose to address the throng.

Controlling his audience perfectly, Bryan captured the delegates with his opening words: "I come to speak to you in defense of a cause as holy as the cause of liberty—the cause of humanity." Bryan expressed the frustrations and the defiance of the plain people when he declared:

. . . we have petitioned, and our petitions have been scorned; we have entreated and our entreaties have been disregarded; we have begged, and they have mocked when our calamity came. We beg no longer; we entreat no more; we petition no more. We defy them!

Frenzied roars of applause greeted nearly every sentence as Bryan's magnificent voice, rolling on in Biblical phraseology, declaimed the struggle between the common folk and the monied interests. The delegates cheered wildly after his famous conclusion:

You come to us and tell us that the great cities are in favor of the gold standard; we reply that the great cities rest upon our broad and fertile prairies. Burn down your cities and leave our farms, and your cities will spring up again as if by magic; but destroy our farms and the grass will grow in the streets of every city in the country. . . . Having behind us the producing masses of the nation and the world, supported by the commercial interests, the laboring interests and the toilers everywhere, we will answer their demand for a gold standard by saying to them: You shall not press down upon the brow of labor this crown of thorns, you shall not crucify mankind upon a cross of gold.

Bryan was nominated as the Democratic Presidential candidate on the following day. The defiant tone of the "Cross of Gold" speech is somewhat deceptive, for Bryan was basically conservative in both his political and religious convictions. In no sense a revolutionary, he wanted fair returns for men of virtue and industry. He always opposed privilege and monopoly and had great confidence in plain, ordinary people. Known as the "Great Commoner," he was not just a spokesman for the common people—he was one of them. Bryan often oversimplified issues, but he had an intuitive grasp of the people's grievances, and his remarkable campaign awakened people to the oppressive economic inequities of the time.

The Democrats' nomination of Bryan and adoption of free silver put the Populists in a cruel quandary. Should they join the Democrats or go it on their own? Many Populists felt that fusion with the Democrats would mean giving up their party and repudiating the parts of their platform which the Democrats did not support. Others believed supporting Bryan was their only chance. One of the Populists put their dilemma clearly: "If we fuse, we are sunk; if we don't fuse, all the silver men we have will leave us for the more powerful Democrats." The Populist convention finally decided to join the Democrats and support Bryan. But as a token of their independence, they selected their own Vice Presidential candidate, Tom Watson of Georgia.

Election of 1896. Mark Hanna, playing upon the fears of rich corporation executives, milked them for unusually fat contributions. The Standard Oil Company alone contributed $250,000, almost as much as Bryan's entire campaign fund. The enormous Republican campaign chest, variously estimated at from $3.5 million to $16 million, was effectively used for speakers and publicity of all kinds. McKinley himself conducted a dignified "front porch" campaign, remaining in his home in Canton, Ohio, where he received delegations from all parts of the country. He always stressed the same theme—Republicanism was synonomous with respectability and prosperity. The blunt Hanna was more direct: "Our main issue is to elect McKinley."

Bryan's campaign was memorable. He was the first Presidential candidate to stump all sections of the country. On most of his travels he made his own arrangements, bought his own tickets, and sometimes carried his own luggage. He traveled eighteen thousand miles, made hundreds of speeches, and at times his powerful voice was reduced to a whisper. Although he did not totally neglect other issues, he hammered away on the silver question, which disturbed some of his followers. Henry Demarest Lloyd called silver "the cow-bird of the reform movement," by which he meant that silver had waited until the nest had been built and then laid its eggs in it, pushing other issues aside.

Hysteria seemed to grip many of Bryan's opponents. Some frightened Republicans got ready to leave the country if Bryan were elected. A minister called Bryan a "mouthing, slobbering demagogue whose patriotism is all in his jawbone." The New York *Tribune* said he was a "wretched rattle-pated boy . . . mouthing resounding rottenness." In reality, they had little to fear. The Populist base was too limited and

DUBIOUS.

"What awful poor wages they get in all those free silver countries, John!"
"That's so, wife, but the politicians say it will be different in America."
"I wouldn't take any chances on it, John. It's easy to lower wages and
hard to raise them. Politicians will tell you anything. We know there
was good wages when we had protection. We could never buy clothes for
the children on what they get in those free silver countries, could we?"

The controversy over silver dominated the politics
of the late 1890's, with the pro-silver forces demanding unlimited coinage of silver and the anti-silverites
contending that "free silver" would destroy the value
of the dollar. The free-silver forces in the Democratic
party were satirized in cartoons like the one above,
from the political magazine *Wasp*, in which a man
and his wife doubt the benefits of free silver for the
workingman. A special target of the anti-silver forces
was William Jennings Bryan, the man with the
"golden voice." Following Bryan's Cross of Gold
speech, he was criticized in the cartoon at right from
Judge, a magazine with Republican leanings. *Judge*
labeled him the "sacrilegious candidate" who "drags
into the dust the most sacred symbols of the Christian
world."

429

its strength exaggerated. The identification of prosperity with Republicanism was strong in the public mind. An upswing in the business cycle on the eve of the election helped McKinley. Moreover, Gold Democrats sat tight and did nothing for Bryan. Their attitude was like that of David B. Hill of New York, whose only contribution to the campaign was his well-known quip: "I am still a Democrat—very still."

McKinley won a safe, if not a landslide, victory. He carried all the Old Northwest states plus North Dakota, Minnesota, and Iowa. Bryan's failure to win labor and midwestern farm votes was decisive. The silver issue did not appeal to labor, and employer intimidation of workers was a factor in some plants. One factory owner flatly told his employees: "Men, vote as you please, but if Bryan is elected tomorrow the whistle will not blow Wednesday morning." In retrospect, Bryan's concentration on silver inflation was probably a mistake. Americans who owned stocks, bank savings, or insurance could readily understand that inflation would lower the value of their holdings. The Democratic-Populist program, responding to the needs of the most depressed part of the farming community, was too narrow to win the country.

6 A New South Emerges From Reconstruction

1. Why did most northern whites abandon racial justice and black Americans after 1877?

2. What were the obstacles facing southern agriculture in the second half of the nineteenth century? How do you think these obstacles could have been overcome?

3. What means were used to restrict the civil rights of southern blacks after 1877? How did these restrictions affect southern whites?

As noted in Chapter 10, the compromise of 1877 marked the abandonment of blacks by the Republican party. Most northern whites believed blacks were inferior and inevitably destined to play a secondary role in American life. The business-industrial community, now anxious to develop southern markets, wanted stability in race relations and reconciliation between the sections. President Hayes gave official sanction to the renunciation of the equalitarian principles of Republican Reconstruction when he said that the interests of blacks would be best protected if southern whites were "let alone by the general government." Laissez faire was to operate in race relations as well as in economic affairs.

Sharecropping. Most southern Democrats who had, as they put it, "redeemed" the South from the hated yoke of Reconstruction were businessmen and industrialists rather than planters. Their hostility toward the black man had been aroused during Reconstruction, and they meant to "keep him in his place." Economically, that place was at the bottom of the most depressed section of the nation.

Republican leaders during Reconstruction showed little concern for the enormous economic adjustment the former slave was compelled to make. After the war, most blacks had neither land nor money. At first they worked for wages, but the acute shortage of money and credit in the South forced already debt-ridden landowners to discontinue wage payments. From conditions under which blacks could not pay rent, and landowners could not pay wages, a new system called sharecropping emerged. Large plantations were divided into small farms for each black family. The owner provided housing, tools, and other supplies, while the blacks provided the labor. Usually the crop was shared equally, unless the cropper supplied some of his own tools and equipment, in which case his share was somewhat larger.

This system gave the black man greater independence and a larger share of the products of his own labor than he had ever had. Unfortunately, landowners lacked sufficient capital to make the system work. In order to acquire seed, tools, food, and other necessities for the croppers, he was forced to borrow from bankers, merchants, and storekeepers. A crop-lien method of financing was developed whereby the landowner gave the merchant a lien, that is, the landowner promised part of his forthcoming crop in return for supplies. To protect his investment, the merchant insisted upon a cash crop, usually tobacco or cotton, thus preventing crop diversification and perpetuating the evils of a one-crop system. The southern merchant was himself dependent upon northern suppliers who charged high prices because of the high risks of southern agriculture. The merchant passed on these high charges to the croppers and landowners whose liens he held.

On "settling day" the frustrated black cropper usually found that his crop was worth less than his debts. Although he was no longer a slave, his perpetual indebtedness locked him into a kind of economic peonage. White southern farmers were little better off, and many of them became farm tenants and sharecroppers. Although independent white farmers looked upon sharecropping as a black institution, they too were caught up in crop-lien financing, often mortgaging their land as well as their crops. As the price of cotton steadily declined, many of them lost everything.

The New South. The widespread problem of rootless whites who had failed in farming gave birth to the doctrine of the New South. It was to be an industrialized South in which blacks would be kept in their place raising cotton and tobacco. Whites were to find new employment in factories and mills.

In the 1880's, many southern politicians, businessmen, and newspaper editors took up the cause of industrialization with all the fervor of a religious crusade. One enthusiast exhorted the citizens of Salisbury, North Carolina: "Next to the grace of God, what Salisbury needs is a cotton mill!" A Charleston editor suggested in 1882 that importing five hundred Yankees of the right kind would "make the whole place throb with life and vivid force." Eager champions of the New South proposed to "out-Yankee the Yankee" as they preached the gospel of the hustler, the money-maker, unfettered capitalism, and the businessman's values.

The South made substantial industrial progress, particularly in the 1880's, when northern investors awakened to the possibilities of developing its coal, iron, and timber resources. Chauncey Depew, the New York railroad lawyer and politician, spoke glowingly to northern audiences about a southern "Bonanza," and coined a new slogan: "Go South, Young Man!" The rapid growth of southern railroads, spurred by huge investments from the J. P. Morgan firm, made possible the rise of other industries. Impressive gains were made in the coal and iron industry, in lumber products, and in tobacco processing.

It was the cotton mill, however, which symbolized the New South. Communities in the Carolinas, Georgia, and Alabama generated tremendous passion for "mills," motivated largely, as historian Broadus Mitchell has pointed out, by the need to absorb migrant whites who had failed at farming. By 1910, nearly half of the nation's raw cotton was processed in the South. Most of this growth came at the expense of New England mills that could not compete against cheap southern labor. As in all phases of southern life, race prejudice affected hiring policy. Since whites were preferred to blacks in factory and mill, blacks were generally limited to agriculture.

Despite industrial growth, the South remained the most rural and the poorest section in America. By 1900, southern per-capita wealth was less than half the national average. A kind of colonial status persisted, as most southern industries provided the first rough processing, after which the product was shipped North for finishing. The Northeast received the bulk of the profits from southern industries. Northern investors wanted to exploit southern raw materials, but they did not welcome competing southern manufacturing. By the end of the century, nearly 70 percent of all southerners were still engaged in agriculture; less than 4 percent were employed in manufacturing.

Southern industrial workers fared little better than farmers. Wages which were often below $2.50 for a seventy-hour work week made it necessary for all members of the family to work. It was common for women and young children to work in the southern cotton mills. Often, in mill towns and mining towns, the company owned the stores and houses, and the workers were compelled to pay high rates for food and housing. Like the sharecropper, the industrial worker often found himself trapped in a condition of constant debt.

Civil rights in the New South. The return of southern Democrats to power did not bode well for black civil rights, supposedly protected by the Fourteenth and Fifteenth Amendments. The specter of Reconstruction, which had raised some

THE NEW SOUTH, 1870–1910
(Economic Indicators)

	1870	1880	1890	1900	1910
Population	12,288,028	18,518,568	20,028,139	24,523,527	29,389,330
Production of raw cotton (in bales)*	3,011,996	5,755,359	7,472,511	9,645,974	10,594,360
Tobacco production (in pounds)	178,418,922	199,281,213	348,107,607	604,918,720	802,618,483
Persons engaged in agriculture	———	4,611,751	5,735,948	7,331,025	7,048,650
Farm acreage	189,556,302	234,919,786	256,605,867	362,036,351	354,452,860
Number of farms	885,100	1,531,077	1,836,372	2,620,391	3,097,547
Cotton manufacture (by spindles)	328,551	542,048	1,554,100	4,298,188	10,376,888
Steel production (in tons)	———	3,883	163,599	377,144	543,916
Persons engaged in manufacturing	———	500,342	827,177	1,114,570	1,292,197
Manufacturing establishments	38,759	36,938	46,455	84,257	92,184

* 1 bale of cotton = 500 pounds of cotton

blacks to positions of influence, still haunted and embittered the southern mind. Most northerners also believed blacks were not ready for full citizenship, much less social equality.

These attitudes were reflected in the decisions of the Supreme Court. By the Civil Rights Act of 1875, innkeepers, theater owners, hotel managers, and the like were required to provide equal treatment to people of all races. During the debate on the bill, a black advocate told Congress that there was "not an inn between Washington and Montgomery, a distance of more than a thousand miles, that will accommodate me to a bed or meal." But in the *Civil Rights Cases* (1883), the Supreme Court invalidated the 1875 act when it ruled that the Fourteenth Amendment restricted only state discrimination, not that of private individuals. This ruling virtually nullified the Fourteenth Amendment as a legal protector of the free and equal use of public accommodations by blacks.

In *Plessy* v. *Ferguson* (1896), the Court gave a legal basis for segregated railroad cars as long as facilities were "separate but equal." By implication, this principle also applied to schools, hospitals, rest rooms, and all other facilities, in spite of the obvious fact that such facilities were never equal. The lone dissenter in the *Plessy* case was Justice John Marshall Harlan, a Kentuckian and former slaveholder. Harlan saw the decision as a betrayal of the American ideal of freedom of citizenship:

The white race deems itself to be the dominant race in this country. . . . But in view of this Constitution, in the eyes of the law, there is in this country no superior, ruling class of citizens. There is no caste here. Our Constitution is color blind, and neither knows nor tolerates classes among citizens. . . . The law regards man as man, and takes no account of his surroundings or of his color when his civil rights as guaranteed by the supreme law of the land are involved.

Harlan predicted that the Court's decision "will, in time, prove to be quite as pernicious as the decision made by this tribunal in the Dred Scott case." Justice Harlan's gloomy forecast was to be tragically borne out in later years. At the time, however, his was decidedly a minority voice.

Segregation of blacks. As early as 1890, Mississippi was sufficiently encouraged by Supreme Court decisions to make an assault on black voting rights. The state set up three requirements for voting—a residence requirement, a poll tax, and a literacy test. Other states followed, some adding new requirements such as a good-character test. While these requirements were designed to eliminate black voting, they were often so sweeping that they disenfranchised illiterate poor whites as well. To remedy this disenfranchisement of whites, southern states passed "grandfather clauses," limiting the vote to those whose grandfathers had voted in 1860. Obviously, no southern black could qualify under this requirement. In *Williams* v. *Mississippi* (1898), the Supreme Court approved voting regulations which included the poll tax, the literacy test, and residence requirements, all designed to prevent blacks from voting.

The Populist revolt of the 1890's added to the black's plight and helped bring on segregation (sometimes called "Jim Crow") all along the line. Some southern white Populists sought black support, from those who could still vote, on the grounds that poor whites and poor blacks were in the same economic bind. Tom Watson, the Georgia Populist rebel, told black farmers that whites and blacks were being kept apart so that each might be "separately fleeced."

For a time it looked as if there might be an effective union of blacks and whites under the Populist banner. But the ruling Democratic organization and deep-seated racial antagonism proved too strong. Old-line Democratic politicians appealed successfully to the race hatred of whites. They made reckless charges that the Populist party was a black party, that it fostered black domination and meant to take the South back to the days of the carpetbagger. Such charges were fatal to the success of any party in the South and had much to do with the failure of Populism there.

The fury of pent-up hatred unleashed by southern Democratic leaders brought many kinds of reprisals against blacks. In 1892 alone, 162 blacks were lynched, and other acts of physical violence against blacks occurred with alarming frequency. For four days in 1896, white mobs roamed through the streets of Atlanta looting and murdering. Uncontrolled whites in New Orleans terrorized and looted black districts. An ugly race riot took place in Wilmington, North Carolina, in 1898, in which scores of blacks were killed and beaten by a fanatical mob. After the Populist defeat in 1896, even southern Populist leaders denounced blacks, blaming them for Populist failure.

In the last decade of the nineteenth century, southern states tightened their restrictive voting legislation. The effectiveness of such legislation is shown by Louisiana, where 130,334 black voters were registered in 1896 but only 1,342 in 1904. A flood of new laws established segregation in public transportation, housing, hosptials, rest rooms, prisons, parks, at drinking fountains, and even in cemeteries. The North accepted Jim Crow without protest, and, indeed, carried it out in its own section. Before and after the Spanish-American War of 1898, there was much talk above the Mason-Dixon line about Anglo-Saxon superiority over dark-skinned peoples. This belief tended to buttress already existing northern prejudices. The end of the Gilded Age marked the low point in the struggle for black equality.

■ CONCLUSION

The Republican party, which had supported free homesteads for farmers and black emancipation had by the 1890's become indifferent to equality for farmers and black Americans. By that decade, it was essentially the party of expanding capitalism, and its interest had shifted from Reconstruction issues to questions of tariff, sound money, and business prosperity. The Republican party had merged the interests of large and small businessmen, manufacturers and bankers, prosperous farmers and laborers, and even spoilsmen and reformers into a cohesive political force.

Returning prosperity after McKinley's victory in 1896 seemed to bear out the Republican claim that they were the party of dynamic economic expansion, although the recovery had little to do with the Republican victory. Because of crop failures in Europe, American farm prices rose. Between 1899 and 1910, farm prices rose almost 90 percent, and the farmer entered a period of relatively high income. New gold discoveries brought inflation through gold instead of silver. By the end of the decade, the silver issue was dead, and in 1900 the government adopted the gold standard. Better times stilled the farmer's militancy, and by 1900 many wondered what all the shouting had been about.

The silver issue and the Populist revolt shook the traditional laissez faire ideology of the Democratic party. The bitter struggle in Cleveland's second administration over the gold standard, and the fusion of Populists with Democrats in 1896, brought a change. Democrats had been reared on the Jeffersonian dictum "That government is best which governs least." But in the 1890's the party of Jefferson was sloughing off its old fear of centralized authority. It began to recognize the necessity of utilizing federal power to insure equality of opportunity.

The politics of the Gilded Age illustrates the difficulty of changing old habits to meet new conditions. Laissez faire principles were clearly inadequate for the needs of a complex industrial society; the politics of indifference had led only to rebellion. The problem, which still confronts political leaders, was how to achieve economic and racial equality within the urban-industrial civilization. For all its shortcomings, the Populist rebellion was the first political movement to deal seriously with the problem. Although the Populist party failed in 1896, its program succeeded. In the years from 1900 to 1914, most of the demands of the Populist platform were enacted into law. The agrarian revolt was a foreshadowing of the Progressive movement which followed.

QUESTIONS

1. What were the successes and failures of Congress from 1877 to 1900? Why did Congress not pursue a more aggressive role in confronting national problems?

2. What were the similarities and differences between the Republican and Democratic parties?

3. In what ways was the capitalistic influence demonstrated in American society? Why was Congress so responsive to the business and industrial interests?

4. What evidence is there that the Presidency was a strong (or weak) office during the period from 1877 to 1900?

5. What were the weaknesses of American society during the second half of the nineteenth century?

6. What were the problems facing the farmers? the blacks? the laborers? How did these groups intend to correct the problems?

7. What are the problems which face a third party movement in America? How can these problems be overcome?

8. To what extent was America subjected to business cycles during this period? Why did these depressions occur? What could be done to correct the situation?

9. What procedure do you think is the most appropriate to fill positions in the government administration? Explain your answer.

10. To what extent were the Populists successful in attaining their goals and to what extent were they unsuccessful? What accounted for their shortcomings?

BIBLIOGRAPHY

HOLLINGSWORTH, J. ROGERS, *The Whirligig of Politics: Democracy of Cleveland and Bryan*, U. of Chicago Press. Hollingsworth provides a history of the Democratic party extending over the period from the beginning of Cleveland's second term to 1904. This is a fine book to consult for background on the period, particularly as it relates to the monetary issue.

GLAD, PAUL W., *McKinley, Bryan, and the People*, Critical Periods of History Series, Lippincott. The campaign of 1896 was a high water mark for the Populists and the free-silver advocates. This book chronicles that election and the reasons for hard-money Republican success, Democratic failure, and Populist collapse.

HICKS, JOHN D., *The Populist Revolt: A History of the Farmers' Alliance and the People's Party*, U. of Nebraska Press (Bison Books).

TINDALL, GEORGE BROWN, ed., *A Populist Reader: Selections from the Works of American Populist Leaders*, Harper & Row (Torchbooks).

Although *The Populist Revolt* was published a number of years ago, and the author is clearly sympathetic to the Populists, relying heavily upon Populist sources, it remains the best general book on Populism. The student should begin with this book for any general questions on Populism, but for the comments of the Populists themselves, the student should consult *The Populist Reader* which provides much of the flavor of the movement.

WOODWARD, C. VAN, *Tom Watson, Agrarian Rebel,* Oxford University Press (Galaxy Books). The Populists were noted for their colorful personalities, and Watson, as represented in Van Woodward's excellent biography, is no exception. Watson is particularly interesting because he provides insight into the Populists of the South who are frequently overlooked by most historians who emphasize the Midwest. The book is also a story of tragedy as Watson becomes increasingly frustrated, bitter, and racially bigoted.

————, *The Strange Career of Jim Crow: A Brief Account of Segregation,* rev. ed., Oxford University Press (Galaxy Books). Van Woodward's account of the rise of Jim Crow has become the standard version. This book has been used successfully at the high-school level where teachers and students are trying to understand the nature of the barriers which have appeared between races.

The Progressive Movement

The American people entered the twentieth century prosperous and confident. Since the Civil War the nation had become an industrial giant and was emerging as a world power. The agrarian revolt of the late nineteenth century had subsided, and business was on the upswing. Industrialization brought many material benefits, but it had also created many problems. During the Progressive era, as the years from 1900 to the American entry into World War I in 1917 are called, reformers of many different kinds attacked these problems. They wanted to achieve social justice, political democracy, and more effective public control over big business.

Although the Progressive movement spread across the nation, it was not a single unified campaign organized by one political party or group of people. Despite their considerable differences, however, the Progressives were united in their belief that American society, though rich and bountiful, was suffering from serious ills. Moreover, they shared an optimistic faith that "reform" (differently and sometimes vaguely defined) would cure these ills. Although many of their proposals were forward-looking, they did not aim to create a new society. They wanted to restore the kind of economic individualism and political democracy that they believed had existed earlier in America. As you examine the successes and failures of the Progressive movement, these are some questions to keep in mind:

1. Who were the Progressives, and how did they reach the general public with their ideas?
2. What political reforms on the municipal and state level did the Progressives advocate?
3. How would you evaluate Theodore Roosevelt's accomplishments as a Progressive?
4. What were the differences and similarities between the ideas of Roosevelt and Woodrow Wilson?
5. How did black Americans fare under Progressivism?

1 Progressives Awaken The Conscience Of The Nation

1. Why was there such a large gap between the rich and the poor in America in 1900?

2. What were the characteristics of the Progressives? How were they similar to earlier reformers? How were they different?

3. Do you think the Progressives had a greater chance of success than earlier reformers?

4. What were the characteristics of the muckrakers?

By the early 1900's the gap between rich and poor and between powerful and powerless in this country had grown wide and deep. The very rich—perhaps 1 percent of the population—owned about seven-eighths of the wealth. They lavished their incomes (on which they did not have to pay taxes) on whims and luxuries beyond the comprehension of the average man.

Although organized labor had made some gains for skilled workers, unskilled workers still labored long hours for low wages. Women who worked were generally employed in textile mills and garment industry sweatshops where they had to endure not only long hours and low wages, but also unsafe and unsanitary working conditions. The problem was most acute in New York City, where in 1911, 148 young women were killed in a fire in the Triangle Shirtwaist Factory. Children worked alongside adults. By the early 1900's about 1.7 million children under the age of sixteen were employed in the fields and factories of the nation. Their plight moved the poet Sarah Cleghorn to write:

> The golf links lie so near the mill
> That almost every day
> The laboring children can look out
> And see the men at play.

The movement toward consolidation of businesses into trusts and monopolies that had begun in the late nineteenth century accelerated in the 1900's. As more and more bankers moved into industry, corporations grew both larger and less accessible to control by stockholders. Preeminent among the financial empires were the House of Morgan and the Rockefeller interests. "These two mammoth groups jointly constitute the heart of the business and commercial life of the nation," wrote John Moody, a financial expert, in 1904.

Urbanization had created intolerable living conditions for the poor—both native-born and immigrant. It had also created the large and powerful political "machines," which were fueled by the bribes of businessmen who wanted to win the lucrative contracts and franchises for rapidly expanding city services.

Although industrialization had given the consumer more goods to buy, he was at the mercy of the producer for the quality and safety of his purchases. Meat, milk, and other foods were processed in filthy plants. Medicines and drugs were often diluted with harmless ingredients; what was worse, they sometimes contained alcohol, cocaine, or other dangerous drugs. A syrup might soothe a baby, to be sure, but only because it contained morphine! In addition, America's seemingly boundless natural resources were being threatened. Forests were cut indiscriminately, and industrial wastes were dumped into rivers and streams. Farmlands were eroding, and wild life was being destroyed.

Predecessors of Progressives. Voices of protest had been raised against these and other abuses in the late nineteenth century. The Populist writer Henry Demarest Lloyd had attacked big business in *Wealth and Commonwealth* (1894), and various newspaper and magazine articles had also criticized conditions in government and industry.

Although Populism had mainly attracted disgruntled farmers, there is more than a grain of truth in editor William Allen White's remark that Progressivism was just Populism with the hayseed removed. Many Populist demands were incorporated into Progressive programs, for example, the graduated income tax, direct election of senators, child-labor legislation, and others. Though there are clear relationships between the two movements, Progressivism was more than rural Populism transplanted to the twentieth century.

The rise of the Progressives. Progressives were predominantly middle-class, native-born, white Protestants. Many were descended from old New England or midwestern families. They included doctors, lawyers, clergymen, merchants, small businessmen, professors, social workers, and writers. They were, in Professor George Mowry's term, the "urban gentry."

To explain why these respectable citizens took up the banner of reform, especially in a period of economic prosperity, historian Richard Hofstadter has suggested that they were the losers in a "status revolution." Formerly the most important citizens in their communities, these old families and professional groups were now less influential than the wealthier and more powerful industrialists. As Hofstadter puts it in *The Age of Reform* (1955):

In their personal careers, as in their community activities, they found themselves checked, hampered, and overridden by the agents of the new corporations, the corrupters of legislatures, the buyers of franchises, the allies of the political bosses. . . . In a strictly economic sense these men were not growing poorer as a class, but their wealth and power were being dwarfed by comparison with the new eminences of wealth and power. They were less important, and they knew it.

The presence in the Progressive movement of so many Social Gospel ministers, social workers, and literary figures gave the movement a public posture of morality and humanitarianism. Even though many of the reform movements were led by businessmen to achieve their own special interests, the philosophers of the movement expressed the goals in a larger framework of idealism.

Many of the crusades had a religious flavor reminiscent of rural evangelical Protestantism. Moral indignation not only was expressed against others, it was also expressed in terms of personal guilt. Many Progressives felt that the sorry situations they decried were their own fault. Characteristically, Lincoln Steffens dedicated his book *The Shame of the Cities* (1904), the title itself is self-accusatory, to "all the accused—to all the citizens of all the cities in the United States." To correct the evils around them, Progressives turned to familiar concepts. Says Hofstadter:

. . . the key words of Progressivism were terms like *patriotism, citizen, democracy, law, character, conscience* . . . terms redolent of the sturdy Protestant Anglo-Saxon moral and intellectual roots of the Progressive uprising.

Writing in the 1960's, historian J. Joseph Huthmacher points out that Progressives often had the support of working-class voters who were willing to support specific measures that would bring them tangible results. For example, city wards supported political reforms such as direct primary elections and direct election of senators that would give the cities a greater voice in the rural-dominated legislatures. Representatives of working-class constituencies often introduced and campaigned vigorously for social measures such as workmen's compensation, widow's pensions, wage and hour legislation, and factory and safety laws.

This cooperation did not extend to all Progressive reforms, however. Often of immigrant backgrounds, working-class populations did not want parochial schools to be closed, immigration to be restricted, or the sale of alcohol to be limited, to take a few examples of the kinds of moralistic and nativist proposals advocated by some Progressives. For their part, Progressives feared the radical element in organized labor and were either opposed to or reluctant to support reforms proposed by unions.

Progressives also received limited support from some rural areas, largely in the South and West, where Populism had been strong. These areas supported Progressive measures that would bring them benefits, such as reform of the banking and credit system and control of railroads. The basic support for the Progressives, however, came from America's small towns and medium-sized cities.

Of course, the active leaders—from the urban gentry and their working-class and rural allies— were a relatively small group of people. To achieve their goals, they needed broad support. The impetus was provided by crusading journalists known as "muckrakers."

Muckrakers expose corruption. In a speech in 1906, Theodore Roosevelt called writers who dug up "dirt" and printed it in national magazines "muckrakers." He took the term from John Bunyan's *Pilgrim's Progress* (1678), which tells of "the Man with the Muckrake, the man who could look no way but downward. . . ." Roosevelt was referring to irresponsible journalists, but most of the outstanding writers accepted the label proudly.

One of the books that sought to awaken readers to a growing class struggle in the United States was *The Silent War* by James Ames Mitchell, written in 1906. In the dedication he refers to those whose "eyes are too reverently fixed for too long a period, upon the glories of the treasure house" and who therefore "discern but vaguely the hungry toilers among the shadows in the malodorous places." To these "happy philosophers" who "continue to expound the law of the Survival of the Fittest," he dedicated his "brief tale." The picture on the left, by William Balfour Ker, illustrated that book and brings together both classes in a dramatic way. The cartoon below appeared in *Judge* in 1904. The magazine is stating that the mudslinging suffered by John D. Rockefeller, which was initiated by Ida Tarbell's series on the Standard Oil Company, should henceforth cease.

FROM THE DEPTHS

JUDGE—"BOYS, DON'T YOU THINK YOU HAVE BOTHERED THE OLD MAN JUST ABOUT ENOUGH?"

The Progressive muckrakers did not reveal any startling new themes. What distinguished them from their predecessors was the scope of their work and their audiences. The new magazines that emerged at the turn of the century sold for ten or fifteen cents a copy (compared to thirty-five cents for the old, respectable literary magazines). Their circulation ranged from 400,000 to 1 million. As the literature of exposure became a commercial success, publishers could afford to spend large amounts of money on research for muckraking articles. These articles were thus more thoroughly documented and hence more convincing.

Chief among the magazine publishers was S. S. McClure, a businessman with a keen eye to public taste. In 1902, *McClure's Magazine* began publishing Ida Tarbell's series on the Standard Oil Company. The series took her five years to research and write, and each of the fifteen installments cost an estimated $4,000. This report coldly documented the rise of the Standard Oil trust, sparing none of the sordid details.

Lincoln Steffens wrote another widely read series on "The Shame of the Cities," later published in book form. Starting with St. Louis, he gave details about the widespread graft and corruption in many American cities, including Minneapolis, New York, Philadelphia, and Pittsburgh. A third important *McClure's* writer was Ray Stannard Baker, who indicted railroad malpractices. *McClure's* success encouraged many other magazines to join in the muckraking, including *Cosmopolitan, Collier's,* and *Everybody's.*

Authors of full-length books joined the crusade. John Spargo's *Bitter Cry of the Children* (1906) exposed the appalling conditions of child labor in factories. Frank Norris's *The Octopus* (page 395) described the stranglehold of the Southern Pacific Railroad over California politics.

Most of the muckrakers, like most other Progressives, were reformers who wanted only to eliminate the evils they described. However, there were several radical writers who felt that the whole system of capitalism should be replaced. Jack London, for example, portrayed capitalism as totally vicious in his books *The Iron Heel* (page 341) and *The War of the Classes* (1905). And the eminent socialist writer Upton Sinclair set his novel *The Jungle* (page 341) in the Chicago meat-packing houses. Sinclair's main theme was a plea for socialism, but readers instead seized on a short but vivid description of the filthy conditions in slaughterhouses. A national uproar resulted in food and drug regulation and inspection. However, Sinclair felt he had failed. "I aimed at the public's heart," he wrote, "and by accident I hit it in the stomach."

The deluge of muckraking literature began to lose momentum about 1912. Much of it became repetitive, and many articles were distorted just to sell magazines. However, the best journalism of the period made a significant contribution to the Progressive movement. "To an extraordinary degree the work of the Progressive movement rested upon its journalism," writes Richard Hofstadter. "Before there could be action, there must be information and exhortation. Grievances had to be given specific objects, and these the muckraker supplied. It was muckraking that brought the diffuse malaise of the public into focus."

2 Progressives Battle For City And State Reforms

1. What were the problems that reformers tried to correct in city government? How did they intend to correct these problems? How successful were they?

2. What were the problems that reformers tried to correct in state governments? How did they intend to correct these problems? How successful were they?

3. Do you think some of the same problems still exist in state and local governments?

Municipal and state reform received a high priority in Progressive battle plans. There were three main areas of concern—political, economic, and social. Not all reformers were equally interested in all three, however. Leaders of political and economic reform tended to be businessmen who were suffering from the high and inequitable taxes that resulted from inefficient and corrupt administrations. Leaders of social-justice movements tended to be social workers, clergymen, and others directly involved in dealing with people. In some cities and states, outstanding leaders were able to bring together all the various reform elements and win enough support to institute comprehensive reform programs.

Reformers in city governments. Corruption was almost inevitable in city governments because city charters, written during the Jacksonian era, had deliberately dispersed authority and power among a mayor, a city council, and independent boards. Responsibility for mismanagement could not be placed on any one person. Instead of making cities more democratic, the charters created a power vacuum, which the political machines quickly filled. Under "The System," as Lincoln Steffens called it, outright bribery was common on the lower levels of officialdom. The police and petty politicians were linked to vice and crime. On higher levels, city officials and the political bosses who controlled them reaped huge profits from business contracts.

In 1896 and 1897, the citizens of Chicago, outraged by the revelations in W. T. Stead's book *If Christ Came to Chicago* (1893), organized into the nonpartisan Municipal Voters League. They won control of the city government and did such a good job of cleaning up City Hall that in 1903 Steffens found no evidence of large-scale corruption or machine control. Reformers in other cities also organized into good-government leagues to fight corruption. In Minneapolis the corrupt mayor and his henchmen were indicted by a grand jury and sent to prison. Reform mayors were elected in many cities to replace the discredited politicians.

Frequently the movement for municipal reform was led by a strong, colorful leader. Such a man was Tom L. Johnson of Cleveland, a successful street-railway businessman who became a reformer after reading a book by Henry George. Elected mayor of Cleveland in 1901, he demanded equal taxation and a three-cent trolley fare. Gathering around him an able group of young administrators, he set about fulfilling his campaign promises.

Johnson and his team succeeding in doubling the taxes of railroads and utility companies, which owned extensive property but under the old regime had avoided paying taxes. In his fight for a three-cent fare, Johnson had to battle not only the local traction companies, but also the state Republican machine, which controlled the state legislature and state supreme court. The court ruled that all the city charters in Ohio were illegal, and the legislature passed new statutes, weakening Cleveland's right to run its own affairs. Although Johnson did not achieve all his aims, his efficient administration gave Cleveland the reputation of being the "best-governed city in America."

Reformers soon found that it was much easier to "throw the rascals out" than to make basic changes in the political system that would prevent their return. Although reformers sought to free the cities from the control of the machine-dominated state legislatures by establishing "home rule," they had little success. Missouri, California, Washington, and Minnesota had granted home rule to the cities by the turn of the century, but only two more states with any sizable cities—Michigan and Ohio—granted this privilege between 1900 and 1914.

New forms of city government. More hope seemed to lie in establishing new systems of municipal government to replace the old mayor-council system. In 1900, in Galveston, Texas, the aftermath of a devastating hurricane provided an opportunity for reformers. When the corrupt city council could not begin the task of reconstruction, the state legislature appointed a five-member commission to run the city. The commission was so successful in rebuilding Galveston and returning its administration to fiscal economy that the plan was soon instituted in other Texas cities.

In 1907, Iowa permitted cities of over 25,000 to adopt the commission form of government. By 1910, more than one hundred cities, mainly medium-sized cities in New England, the Midwest, and the Far West, had adopted the plan. Its advocates claimed that it was a simpler, more efficient form of government. Since each commissioner was elected to oversee a particular department, such as police, public works, or sanitation, responsibility for management was more easily fixed.

From the commission plan evolved the concept of the "city manager," a professional administrator who directed the various municipal services and was responsible to the elected commission. The first city manager was appointed in Dayton, Ohio, in 1914. The advantages of having the city run by one person, interested only in competent and honest administration and not in political power, appealed to many reformers. It remains a widely practiced form of local government today.

Many of the reform administrations that swept out the old administrations were themselves voted out of office after a decade or so. Some were not able to fulfill the voters' expectations of what could be accomplished in a short time. Ties of party loyalty remained strong, even though nonpartisan elections were instituted in many cities.

Because reformers were largely interested in the economy of the cities, they failed to provide the citizens with services. For all their faults, the politicians had taken care of the people, finding them jobs, housing, legal aid, medical care, and so on. The reformers did not provide the same services, and in those days no governmental agency or private institution existed on a scale large enough to fill these needs. In addition, by the 1920's, the national interest in Progressivism had begun to wane, and reformers were no longer riding the crest.

Progressives campaign in the states. The same problems existed in the states as in the cities, except on a much larger scale. The state political machines, usually tied to the city machines, made deals with railroads, large corporations, and lobbyists. Because so many of their problems were related to the state legislatures, many of the municipal reformers worked closely with state Progressives.

In attacking abuses at the state level, Progressives championed the idea of "direct democracy." "Give the government back to the people!" they demanded. One of the most important reforms they urged was the direct primary, in which party candidates were nominated for office through special elections rather than being selected by the political bosses. By 1916, some form of direct primary had been adopted by most of the states. The demand for direct primaries stimulated the drive for the direct election of senators. By 1909, 29 states voted for senators by popular ballot, and the Seventeenth Amendment ratified in 1913,

providing for the direct election of senators, merely recognized an existing situation.

Progressives also advocated the *initiative, referendum,* and *recall*. Under the initiative, the people themselves could propose a law and force a legislature to debate it; the referendum compelled a legislature to place bills before the people so that they could accept or reject them; and recall allowed the people to remove from office an undesirable public official. Before the end of the Progressive era, several states had adopted these devices.

At the polls, people generally used ballots distributed by political parties. Because each party printed its ballot in a distinctive color and because each voter cast his vote openly, everyone could tell how his neighbor voted. Although Progressives did not initiate the idea of a secret ballot (often called the Australian ballot), they worked hard for its adoption. By 1910, most of the nation used the secret ballot in elections.

As part of the Progressive campaign in many states, women's suffrage was adopted, somewhat reluctantly in some instances. Between 1910 and 1914, seven western states granted women the right to vote, in addition to Wyoming, Utah, Colorado, and Idaho, which had already done so. The groundwork for women's suffrage had been laid many years before. However, it was during the Progressive era that the general ferment for change and the new involvement of middle-class women in political and social causes created broad enough support for this reform to succeed. In 1920, the Nineteenth Amendment ended the long and difficult struggle for the women's right to vote.

The "Wisconsin Idea." The revolution in the states was nationwide, but it was particularly strong in the Midwest, where a group of vigorous "insurgents" defeated the entrenched Republican state machines. The outstanding leader was Robert M. La Follette of Wisconsin, who instituted the most comprehensive reform program of any state at the time. He was elected governor in 1900 by opposing the politicians under the thumb of the railroad and lumber interests.

Under "Fighting Bob's" ceaseless prodding, the Wisconsin legislature enacted a direct primary law, increased taxes on railroads and corporations, passed a civil service law, a conservation bill, and a state banking control measure. La Follette also brought university professors into government ranks, either to serve on the new state regulatory commissions or to help in drafting legislation. Wisconsin under La Follette had become, as President Theodore Roosevelt later remarked, "the laboratory of democracy."

"The Wisconsin Idea," as La Follette's program was called, became a model for other states, such as Iowa under Governor Albert Cummins and Indiana under Governor Albert Beveridge. In the South, similar movements took place in Arkansas and Georgia; and in the Far West, reformers like Hiram W. Johnson of California and William S. U'Ren of Oregon won control of their state governments.

In the East, state reforms were more usually linked to large-city reform. However, Charles Evans Hughes of New York was elected governor in 1907 after he exposed the fraudulent practices of insurance companies. In New Jersey, where the alliance between corporations and the entrenched politicians (in this case Republicans) was as flagrant as any in the nation, a rebellion began within the Republican party that culminated in the election of Woodrow Wilson, a Democrat, as governor in 1911.

Evaluating reform achievements. In the long run, some of the Progressive political reforms proved disappointing. They did not destroy political machines nor did they give the people direct control of politics. Many Progressives overestimated the importance of procedures and underestimated the realities of political power. They did make some basic changes, however, such as the secret ballot and direct election of senators, reforms that certainly democratized politics.

In economic legislation, Progressives made more substantial progress, particularly toward regulating railroads and public service corporations. Also important was the movement to subject rates and services to public control and to investigate the practices of insurance and investment companies.

In the battle for social justice, many reforms were also accomplished. By 1914 every state but one had established a minimum age limit for child labor (usually fourteen), and many of them had prohibited children between the ages of

PROGRESSIVISM, LIBERAL OR CONSERVATIVE?

Among the historians who have concluded that Progressivism was essentially a conservative movement is Gabriel Kolko. He vigorously asserts that the movement was motivated by the needs of the business community:

". . . I contend that the period from approximately 1900 until the United States' intervention in the war, labeled the 'progressive' era by virtually all historians, was really an era of conservatism. Moreover, the triumph of conservatism . . . was the result not of any impersonal, mechanistic necessity but of the conscious needs and decisions of specific men and institutions.

"There were any number of options involving government and economics abstractly available to national political leaders during the period 1900–1916, and in virtually every case they chose those solutions to problems advocated by the representatives of concerned business and financial interests. Such proposals were usually motivated by the needs of the interested businesses, and political intervention into the economy was frequently merely a response to the demands of particular businessmen. In brief, conservative solutions to the emerging problems of an industrial society were almost uniformly applied. The result was a conservative triumph in the sense that there was an effort to preserve the basic social and economic relations essential to a capitalist society, an effort that was frequently consciously as well as functionally conservative. . . .

"Progressivism was initially a movement for the political rationalization of business and industrial conditions, a movement that operated on the assumption that the general welfare of the community could be best served by satisfying the concrete needs of business. But the regulation itself was invariably controlled by leaders of the regulated industry, and directed toward ends they deemed acceptable or desirable. . . ."

fourteen and sixteen from working at night or at dangerous jobs. Women in industry were also protected by state laws regulating hours and wages. Public systems of industrial accident insurance were instituted in many states between 1912 and 1916, following the revelations of many commissions that prevailing compensation systems were totally inadequate.

The battle was not won when the state legislatures had passed the laws, however, for the United States Supreme Court could declare them unconstitutional. A major victory was achieved in 1908 when the Supreme Court, overturning its traditional conservative interpretations of the rights of employers, ruled that a law passed by the state of Oregon limiting women's work to ten hours a day was Constitutional. Louis Brandeis, a successful lawyer who gave up his lucrative practice to pursue reform causes, presented an imposing array of sociological and economic facts about the harmful effects of strenuous labor on women.

Another effect of the municipal and state reform movement was that it gave the nation new leaders in Congress. La Follette, for example, was elected to the Senate in 1905. But it was Theodore Roosevelt who became the national spokesman of Progressivism, and he spoke with the authority of the President of the United States.

3 Theodore Roosevelt Speaks For Progressivism

1. How would you evaluate Roosevelt's qualifications for the Presidency?

2. What was Roosevelt's position on Progressive reform?

3. How did Roosevelt as President differ from his immediate predecessors? In what ways was his handling of the Coal Strike of 1902 different from earlier precedents?

4. What were Roosevelt's achievements as President? Do you think Roosevelt was a great Progressive reformer?

When William McKinley defeated William Jennings Bryan for the second time in 1900, McKinley's running mate was Thedore Roosevelt, governor of New York. Republican leaders had been divided about Roosevelt's selection as Vice Presidential candidate. His energetic campaigns against corruption and for social legislation had antagonized many conservative politicians. Thomas Platt, a Republican boss in New York, favored the selection because it would get Roosevelt out of the state. But Mark Hanna, McKinley's campaign manager, was worried. "Don't any of you realize," he told a group of Republicans, "that there's only one life between this madman and the White House?" That one life—McKinley's—was ended by a gunshot wound inflicted by an anarchist at the Pan-American Exposition in Buffalo, New York, on September 6, 1901. Roosevelt became president at the age of forty-three.

Roosevelt as President. Roosevelt came from an old and well-to-do New York family. He began his political career with a two-year term in the New York State legislature, and later served as a member of the Civil Service Commission. He was police commissioner of New York City and then assistant secretary of the navy. In the Spanish-American War, he fought with the famous Rough Rider cavalry regiment. After the war he was elected governor of New York in 1898.

Roosevelt was a man of tremendous energy. Hunter, rancher, historian, soldier, and politician, he was devoted to the "strenuous life." He had an uncanny knack of dramatizing everything he did. With his flashing teeth, glasses, jutting chin, and high voice expressing positive opinions about anything and everything, he became immensely popular. Children played with "Teddy" bears, and adults marveled at his dash and verve. An English visitor to the United States remarked that the two most wonderful things he had seen in America were "Niagara Falls and the President of the United States, both great wonders of nature!" Roosevelt's daughter Alice once described her father as the kind of man who wanted to be the bride at every wedding and the corpse at every funeral! Whatever one felt about Teddy's politics, no one ever claimed that he was dull.

To many of his contemporaries, Roosevelt symbolized Progressivism. He himself defined his stand as a middle ground. "We Republicans," he explained, "set out faces as resolutely against the improper corporate influence on the one hand as against demagogy and mob rule on the other." He was a strong moralist and once called the Presidency a "bully pulpit."

Roosevelt always seemed to be accomplishing far more than he actually was, which irritated some of the more advanced Progressives. La Follette complained that Roosevelt's cannonading of "rhetorical radicalism" filled the air with noise and smoke but changed little once the battle clouds had drifted by. Above all, Roosevelt believed in the possible rather than the ideal. He was a shrewd politician and bargained skillfully with the conservatives in his party in order to achieve reforms.

His strong executive leadership was stikingly demonstrated in the coal strike of 1902. In the eastern Pennsylvania anthracite mines, 140,000 workers led by John Mitchell of the United Mine Workers walked off their jobs. Poorly paid and wretchedly housed, they asked for a 20 percent pay increase, an eight-hour day, and union recognition. The mine operators stubbornly refused to negotiate; and George Baer, a company leader, is reputed to have said that labor's interests would not be protected by labor agitators, but by "the Christian men to whom God in his Infinite Wisdom has given control of the property interests of the country."

As public fears increased that there would not be enough coal to heat homes during the coming winter, Roosevelt called Mitchell and the mine operators to Washington for a conference. Mitchell agreed to arbitration, but the operators expressed resentment at "being called here to meet a criminal, even by the President of the United States." Baer was so offensive during the meeting that Roosevelt later said that if he had not been President he would have "taken him by the seat of the breeches and the nape of the neck and chucked him out of the window."

When no progress was made, the President hinted that he was prepared to send 10,000 federal troops into the coal fields to mine coal. Under this threat and with the prodding of J. P. Morgan, who had close financial ties with the mine operators, the companies agreed to allow the President to appoint an arbitration commission, provided it did not include a labor official. Roosevelt slyly appointed a former labor union leader under the title of "eminent sociologist." Ultimately the miners won a 10 percent wage increase and a nine-hour day, but they failed to gain union recognition. Only Roosevelt won a clear-cut victory. For the first time, an American President had intervened in a labor dispute as an impartial agent.

Roosevelt as a "Trust-Buster." The President shocked the business community in 1902 by instituting an antitrust suit against the Northern Securities Company. This gigantic railroad consolidation had already been criticized because it charged high rates for poor service, bankrupted railroad properties, and had been a corrupting influence on state politics. J. P. Morgan, a leader in the Northern Securities Company, hurried to Washington and, according to Roosevelt, declared, "If we have done anything wrong, send your man to my man and they can fix it up." Roosevelt was angered by Morgan's attitude and this challenge to his leadership. In 1904, by a 5 to 4 ruling, the Supreme Court ordered the Northern Securities Company broken up.

In his seven and one-half years in the White House, Roosevelt started more than forty antitrust suits, including actions against the Beef Trust, Standard Oil, and the American Tobacco Company. Although he won popular acclaim as a "trust-buster," his actual achievements were less impressive. Trusts simply re-formed in other combinations, and the movement toward consolidations of business went on.

Roosevelt did not intend to stop this trend, for he himself said, "Our aim is not to do away with corporations; on the contrary, these big aggregations are an inevitable development of modern industrialism . . . We draw the line against misconduct, not against wealth." To check on misconduct, Roosevelt prodded Congress into setting up a Bureau of Corporations to publicize the details of interstate corporations.

Legislative achievements. In his second term, Roosevelt first concentrated on railroad legislation, which he felt was a popular and politically practical objective. The courts had practically nullified the power of the Interstate Commerce Commission, rates remained high, and long- and short-haul abuses continued. The Elkins Act of

NO LACK OF BIG GAME

The President Seems to Have Scared Up
Quite a Bunch of Octopi.

"A nauseating job, but it must be done."

Cartoonists had great fun with President Theodore Roosevelt and his activities, as all these cartoons show. The one below appeared on the cover of *Puck* in 1908, after "TR" had sent a particularly strong message to a rather complacent Congress.

ROUGH ON CATS

Before and After the Current Is Turned On

1903 theoretically abolished rebates, but it failed to give the ICC power over establishing rates, which is what reformers most wanted.

Through skillful political maneuvering with the conservative wing of his party, Roosevelt managed to push through the Hepburn Act of 1906, which gave the ICC the crucial power to establish reasonable rates. Its power was extended to the regulation of sleeping car, express, and pipeline companies, and to storage, refrigeration, and terminal facilities. The Hepburn Act was the first really effective regulation of railroads by the federal government.

Roosevelt also moved to correct malpractices in the food and drug industries. While Roosevelt had been preoccupied with railroad legislation, a group of reformers led by Dr. Harvey W. Wiley, chief chemist of the Department of Agriculture, had been pressing for legislation to prohibit adulteration and misbranding of food, drugs, and beverages. Although Roosevelt had recommended the passage of a pure food and drug act in his message to Congress in 1905, he had not really become involved in the issue until he read Sinclair's *The Jungle* with its nauseating descriptions of the Chicago meat-packing plants. He appointed two of his own men to investigate, and their report comfirmed Sinclair's descriptions.

When the meat-packers refused, on Constitutional grounds, to submit to voluntary government inspection of their processing plants, Roosevelt released the report to the public. Meat sales dropped immediately, and the packers hurriedly changed their minds. A Meat Inspection Act was quickly passed by an aroused Congress, requiring enforcement of sanitary regulations in all meat-packing establishments and federal inspection of all meat shipped in interstate commerce. This act was passed as an amendment to the Pure Food and Drug Act (1906), which until then had been held up in committee. This act forbade the manufacture, sale, or transportation of adulterated or fraudulently labeled goods and drugs sold in interstate commerce.

Conservation gains a friend. An amateur naturalist and sportsman, Roosevelt felt strongly about protecting the nation's natural resources against exploitation by private interests. Nearly three-fourths of the forests had already been cut, and westerners were eager to develop the remainder for the economic benefit of the West. Roosevelt and his chief forester, Gifford Pinchot, wanted to establish great national forests. Under the Forest Reserve Act of 1891, some 47 million acres had already been set aside as national forests. Roosevelt withdrew from public sale some 150 million acres more. He also set aside large acreages of coal lands and water-power sites and created five national parks and over fifty wildlife refuges.

Roosevelt also backed Democratic Senator Francis G. Newlands' federal reclamation act of 1902, which provided that money from the sale of western lands be used for irrigation projects. Reclamation work started at once, and within four years nearly thirty different projects were under way. The Roosevelt Dam in Arizona transformed 200,000 acres of desert into rich farmland. As a result of the White House Conservation Conference, called by Roosevelt in 1908, a fifty-member national commission was appointed, headed by Gifford Pinchot. Conservation was also promoted at the state level. Of all his undertakings, conservation was Roosevelt's most enduring monument to the future.

Roosevelt gives up the Presidency. Roosevelt had pledged in 1904 not to run in 1908. Despite his popularity, he stood by his promise and chose his good friend and secretary of war, William Howard Taft, to be the party's nominee for President. The Democrats selected Bryan for the third and last time. But Roosevelt's brand of Progressivism had left Bryan without the key points of his program. After a dull campaign, Taft won by a comfortable margin. Meanwhile, Teddy went off to Africa to hunt lions. His political opponents, in a tribute to Roosevelt's aggressiveness, raised their glasses in toasts of "Health to the lions!"

Roosevelt left office with a reasonably united party and a good record of moderate reforms. He made permanent contributions to business regulation, pure food and drug laws, and conservation. He revitalized the Presidency after a period of mediocre leadership. He vindicated the national public interest over the private economic interest. A realist in politics, he was neither the "friend of the little man" of popular myth nor the power-mad fanatic his enemies portrayed.

447

4 Taft Splits With Roosevelt

1. What were Taft's qualifications for the Presidency? Do you think these were adequate for the demands of the office in 1908?

2. What were the causes of the gap between Taft and the Progressives? between Taft and Roosevelt?

3. What were the accomplishments of the Taft Administration? How did these compare to Roosevelt's accomplishments?

4. What were the provisions of Roosevelt's "New Nationalism", and how did they differ from Wilson's "New Freedom"?

Roosevelt's successor, William Howard Taft, was an able and loyal public servant. Before joining Roosevelt's cabinet as secretary of war, Taft had been a capable governor of the Philippines and administrator of the Panama Canal Zone. He was a huge man, whose weight ranged from 290 to 350 pounds, and his work habits were leisurely when compared to Roosevelt's frenetic pace. Taft disliked crowds, hated campaigning, and honestly admitted that he never wanted to be President. He lacked Roosevelt's political finesse and his zest for leadership. Moreover, he was a cautious man, more conservative in his interpretation of the President's power than Roosevelt. Mark Sullivan, a writer of the times, aptly described Taft as "a placid man in a restless time."

Taft alienates the Progressives. During the election campaign, Taft had promised to work to revise tariffs downward. Popular discontent with high tariffs had reached new peaks, especially in the midwestern states. Characteristically, Roosevelt had managed to avoid this politically explosive issue while he was in office. Although he favored lowering the tariffs, he had compromised with the conservative businessmen in the party. In exchange for their support of railroad legislation, he had not introduced tariff legislation. Taft, however, plunged ahead with tariff revision. The final bill as revised by the Senate was essentially a high tariff rather than a low tariff measure. Taft nevertheless defended the Payne-Aldrich bill in a cross-country tour as "the best tariff bill the Republicans ever passed." In so doing, he alienated the Progressives in his party.

An unfortunate controversy over conservation further widened the gap between Taft and the Progressives. Many westerners opposed Pinchot's plans for federal conservation and wanted public lands thrown open for private development. Richard Ballinger, Taft's secretary of the interior, was associated with some of these anticonservationists. Ballinger returned more than a million acres of land to the public domain on the grounds that Roosevelt had exceeded his authority in withdrawing them, and he permitted businessmen to develop Alakan coal fields. Pinchot publicly criticized Ballinger, even after Taft had accepted Ballinger's explanation. Although Taft actually favored conservation, he stubbornly refused to remove Ballinger and instead fired Pinchot from the Forest Service. From this point Taft's relations with Roosevelt began to deteriorate.

Taft's political clumsiness was shown again in the fight over the tyrannical power of the Speaker of the House, Joseph C. Cannon. Called the "Hayseed from Illinois" and "foul-mouthed Joe," Cannon had no patience with "all this babble for reform." The House rules gave the Speaker enormous power; he selected the majority members of the Rules Committee, which determined what legislation would be considered, and appointed members of other House committees.

In 1910 a group of insurgents led by George W. Norris of Nebraska won the battle against "Cannonism" by putting new rules into force. The entire House would select members of the Rules Committee, and the Speaker was excluded from membership. Taft disliked Cannon, but he refused to support the insurgents. They concluded that he was on Cannon's side, an incorrect but unavoidable conclusion under the circumstances.

Taft's political blunders obscure the real accomplishments of his administration. With his support, the Sixteenth Amendment, which legalized the income tax, was passed. Railroad legislation was strengthened by further increasing the power of the ICC. Although Taft was never called a "trust-buster," he started ninety antitrust suits in four years, compared to Roosevelt's forty-four in seven and one-half years.

Taft withdrew almost 59 million acres of coal lands from public sale, and added about 1.25 million acres to the forest reserves. A postal savings system was adopted during his term, and the government took over parcel-post mailing, which provided cheaper and better service than the private express companies had offered. Many federal jobs were added to the civil service list. The Publicity Act required political parties to disclose the amounts and sources of campaign contributions. Although it did not need Taft's support to pass, the Seventeenth Amendment, providing for direct election of senators, was ratified in 1913.

Roosevelt's "New Nationalism!" Taft's failure to hold the party together overshadowed his accomplishments. Roosevelt returned in 1910 from his African expedition and a triumphal European tour. He promised to stay out of politics and "keep my mouth shut," an impossible vow. Soon the irrepressible hunter was embarking on a nationwide speaking tour.

At Osawatomie, Kansas, in August 1910, Roosevelt announced a vigorous new Progressive program, which he called the "New Nationalism." His ideas were influenced by the Progressive writer Herbert Croly, whose book *The Promise of American Life* (1909) Roosevelt had taken to Africa with him. Croly wrote that the idea of reform could not be separated from the national idea, and praised Roosevelt for being the "first to realize that an American statesman could no longer really represent the national interest without being a reformer."

Furthermore, Croly claimed, Roosevelt had revived the Hamiltonian idea of "constructive national legislation" but had divorced it from Hamilton's goal of achieving special privileges for the rich. Jefferson, on the other hand, had promoted democracy and egalitarianism but had opposed governmental intervention in the economy. The Progressive wave of the future, said Croly, lay in the possibility of using Hamiltonian means (direct government intervention) to achieve Jeffersonian ends (democratic equality).

In his "New Nationalism," Roosevelt translated Croly's theoretical doctrines into language every-

one could understand. He called for a graduated income tax, an inheritance tax, child and women's labor laws, tariff reform, and stronger controls over corporations. Roosevelt had undoubtedly been developing his ideas for some time, but Croly's book proved a catalyst in the formation of a specific political program.

The final break with Taft. Relations between Roosevelt and Taft reached the breaking point when, soon after the "New Nationalism" speech, Taft instituted an antitrust suit against the United States Steel Corporation. Taft saw the move as just another attempt to break up a monopoly, but Roosevelt interpreted it as a personal affront.

The year before Roosevelt left office, the nation had experienced a sharp business panic, the result of overdrawn credit, excessive speculation, and the lack of a national banking system. During the recession, J. P. Morgan and his associates in the United States Steel Company, Henry Frick and Judge Elbert Gary, had sought Roosevelt's approval of their acquisition of the Tennessee Coal and Iron Company. They argued, less than candidly, that the acquisition of the company would not greatly strengthen United States States Steel but might prevent the failure of some other businesses. Roosevelt had agreed to the purchase, and naturally was angered when Taft's attorney general cited it as one of the reasons that the monopoly should be broken up. Roosevelt heatedly denied that he had been duped by the steel interests and blasted Taft's "unintelligent Toryism."

A major political battle was shaping up for the 1912 Presidential elections. The Republicans plainly faced a crisis. Progressive Republicans organized the National Progressive Republican League in 1911, presumably to support La Follette but actually hoping that Roosevelt would run. After La Follette collapsed during a speech in February, 1912, they turned to Roosevelt, who promptly announced his candidacy. At the Republican convention in Chicago, Taft's delegates controlled the key posts and were able to prevent the seating of Roosevelt's men. Taft was nominated on the first ballot. Outraged by what they considered a "steal," 344 Roosevelt men walked out.

The Bull Moose party. Roosevelt and his supporters formed a new political party. It was actually called the Progressive party but was popu-

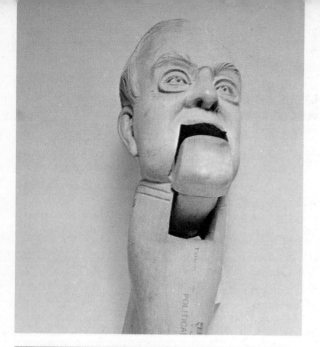

The three-way Presidential election of 1912 brought forth a particularly rich collection of campaign memorabilia. Wilson's stern jaw serves as a nut-cracker, immediately opposite. Below that is a bandana for Roosevelt supporters, complete with a campaign song. The lapel pin and the button at the bottom tout the Republican and Progressive "Bull Moose" parties respectively. The song sheet below was a martial air for Taft supporters.

larly known as the "Bull Moose party" because of Roosevelt's remark that he "felt as strong as a bull moose."

The party's convention in Chicago had elements not only of a political convention, but also of a religious revival meeting and a carnival. Singing, shouting, and stamping, the delegates interrupted Roosevelt's fiery acceptance speech time and time again with calls of "Thou Shalt Not Steal," a reference to Taft's nomination. The platform they adopted was a comprehensive list of Progressive objectives. It called for women's suffrage; initiative, referendum, and recall; social welfare legislation for women and children; workmen's compensation; limited labor injunctions; farm relief; a more elastic currency; establishment of powerful new governmental regulatory agencies. In short, it proposed to transform the federal government into a positive dynamic force for social and economic development.

Usually a hard-headed realist in politics, Roosevelt let the enthusiasm of his supporters and his own supreme self-confidence influence his decision to run against overwhelming odds. Although he split the Republican party by his candidacy, Taft's growing conservatism and his political insensitivity led Roosevelt to such a drastic step.

The election of 1912. The split in the Republican ranks was, of course, good news for the Democrats. They met in Baltimore, with Governor Woodrow Wilson of New Jersey, the favorite of eastern Progressives, and Champ Clark of Missouri, the new Speaker of the House, the choice of the old-line conservatives. The contest was long and bitter and was not decided until the forty-sixth ballot, when delegates pledged to Oscar Underwood of Alabama joined the trend to Wilson.

In addition to Taft, Roosevelt, and Wilson, a fourth candidate, Eugene V. Debs of the Socialist party, was also in the race. In fact, Debs, who favored the gradual nationalization of industry and natural resources, campaigned with more zeal than Taft.

The campaign soon settled into a debate between Wilson and Roosevelt. Although both were Progressives, they differed heatedly. Roosevelt declared that individualism was no longer an adequate goal; Progressives must turn to a strong federal government to regulate business, industry, and the workers, and to improve the condition of the great mass of the American people. Wilson, on the other hand, still believed in the laissez faire economic philosophy. Government, he thought, should remove monopolistic control from business and labor so that their potential energies would be freed for further development. This limited intervention, which Wilson called the "New Freedom," advocated the destruction of special privilege, the restoration of the free-market economy, and reliance on individual enterprise for progress.

To no one's surprise, Wilson won easily in the electoral college—435 votes to Roosevelt's 88, with Taft receiving only 8 and Debs none. National campaigns are won by state political organizations, and Roosevelt had too little time to build effective state organizations to campaign for him. The Old-Guard Republicans just sat out the election. And for the Democrats, Wilson proved to be an excellent campaigner. The combined votes of Roosevelt and Wilson proved, however, that the country overwhelmingly favored further reform.

5 Wilson Works For The New Freedom

1. What were Wilson's qualifications for the office of President?

2. How does Wilson's administration compare to that of Roosevelt and Taft? How is it different?

3. Why was Wilson successful in enacting legislation?

4. How did Wilson's approach to the tariff and banking issues reflect the theory of the "New Freedom" while his approach to antitrust legislation is strongly influenced by the "New Nationalism" philosophy? Why did Wilson make this change?

Woodrow Wilson's rise to the Presidency was unusual in American history. Until 1910, when he was already fifty-four years old, he had never held public office of any kind. Born in Virginia, the son of a Presbyterian minister, he was educated in law and political science. A college teacher for many years, he first began to achieve a national reputation as president of Princeton University. When a controversy over the control of a Graduate College at Princeton threatened his position there, he accepted the Democratic nomination for the governorship of New Jersey. Aware that Progressive support was at its peak in the state, he came out boldly for a reform program. He won an unexpected victory, and soon established his control over the state Democrats. From that position he won national leadership in 1912.

Wilson had many qualifications for the Presidency. He was well educated, intelligent, a thoughtful student of American government, and he had achieved an impressive record as governor of New Jersey. A man of firm moral convictions, he had been profoundly influenced both by his religious upbringing and by his early political indoctrination into the writings of the "Manchester School" of British economists, who advocated free trade and a minimum of government interference in the economy.

Wilson had an almost mystical belief in the essential goodness and wisdom of the American people. Arthur Schlesinger Jr. has aptly summed up the similarities and differences in the personalities of Roosevelt and Wilson:

The two men had much in common: cultivation, knowledge, literary skill, personal magnetism, relentless drive. But, where Roosevelt was unbuttoned and expansive, Wilson was reserved and cool. . . . Roosevelt's egotism overflowed his personality; Wilson's was a hard concentrate within. Roosevelt's power lay in what he did, Wilson's in what he held in reserve.

Tariff and banking reform. Wilson proved to be an extremely adept politician. His method was to formulate a legislative program and then work closely with congressional committee chairmen to implement it. The House was Democratic and contained many new men; there was a good chance of a working majority with the Republican Progressives in the Senate. Political conditions were favorable for a strong leader in the White House, and Wilson was indeed a strong leader.

The first item on Wilson's agenda was the tariff. He was determined to end the long reign of high tariffs, and the public supported him when he demanded that "everything that bears even the semblance of privilege or any kind of artificial advantage" be abolished. Wilson called Congress into special session and appeared personally to deliver his tariff recommendations.

Under his guidance the House passed the Underwood Tariff, a carefully devised measure which substantially lowered tariffs for the first time since the Civil War. When the bill ran into difficulties in the Senate, Wilson denounced the tariff lobbyists "who seek to overcome the interests of the people for their private profits." Senator La Follette and other Progressives put pressure on the reluctant senators by forcing them to reveal their personal financial interests in tariff legislation, and the bill finally was approved. To make up for the anticipated loss of revenue, the bill included a graduated income tax of 1 to 6 percent to be levied on incomes of over $4,000. This income tax measure was the first to be enacted under the Sixteenth Amendment.

The Wilson administration also placed a high priority on banking reform. The nation's obsolete banking and currency structure was hopelessly inadequate. The supply of money was insufficient and too inflexible for seasonal fluctuations. There was no way to help individual banks which were really solvent but were temporarily short of credit. As the Pujo Committee investigating the "Money Trust" had shown, the control of money and credit was concentrated in the hands of a few Wall Street firms, notably the Morgan-Rockefeller interests.

The need for banking reform was obvious to everyone, but there was no agreement on how to achieve it. Conservative Republicans wanted a strong central bank with privately controlled branches. Conservative Democrats proposed a decentralized banking system, owned and controlled by private interests but free from Wall Street control. Progressives in both parties wanted the government to own and control the banking system and the currency supply. In the end, strongly influenced by Louis Brandeis, now one of his closest advisers, Wilson came out for government control of the power to issue currency.

The Federal Reserve Act passed in 1913 was a compromise reached after a year of hot debate.

The Act set up twelve banking districts around the country, each with its own Federal Reserve Bank. All national banks were required to join the system, and state banks were free to join but were not required to do so. The Federal Reserve Banks act as "banker's banks"—that is, they loan money to member banks and control credit by raising or lowering interest rates. Credit facilities were now spread over the country instead of being concentrated in Wall Street.

Most important, the Federal Reserve system was given the power to issue a new kind of currency, called Federal Reserve notes, which could be controlled in volume as the needs of the business community required. Overseeing the entire system was the Federal Reserve Board, originally the secretary of the Treasury, the comptroller of currency, and six other Presidential appointees. A large measure of control was thus left in private hands at the local level, but there was government control and supervision at the national level.

Antitrust legislation. Tariff and banking reform were basic to the New Freedom, and Wilson succeeded in accomplishing his goals of limited intervention in these areas. However, in the third important area of legislation he tackled—antitrust legislation—Wilson turned, albeit unwillingly, toward the more advanced Progressivism advocated by Theodore Roosevelt in the New Nationalism.

Wilson's original antitrust proposals were embodied in two measures—the Clayton Antitrust Act and the Covington interstate trade commission bill. The Clayton bill outlawed a series of unfair trade practices and prohibited interlocking directorates. The Covington bill replaced Roosevelt's Bureau of Corporations with an interstate trade commission which would act as a factfinding agency for government but would have no independent regulatory authority.

These proposals were severely criticized by Progressives. Labor leaders protested the Clayton bill's failure to provide immunity from antitrust prosecution for labor unions. Progressives argued that it was futile to try to cover every unfair trade practice in a statute, as the Clayton bill attempted to do. They also scoffed at a commission with no power to regulate.

Wilson turned again to Brandeis for advice.

Brandeis proposed outlawing unfair trade practices in general terms and then creating a federal trade commission to suppress such restraints when they occurred. Since such a proposal had already been introduced in a bill by Representative Raymond Stevens of New Hampshire, Wilson threw his support to that bill and more or less ignored the Covington bill.

The Clayton bill was eventually passed in a weakened version, of which Senator James Reed of Missouri complained, "it is a sort of legislative apology to the trusts, delivered hat in hand, and accompanied by assurances that no discourtesy is intended." After a long battle, Wilson won approval of the Stevens bill, which established the Federal Trade Commission. This bill outlawed but did not attempt to define all unfair trade practices. It gave the FTC the authority to move directly against corporations accused of restraining competition. This act marked a turning point in Wilson's administration, the merging of the New Nationalism and the New Freedom.

The peak of Progressivism. The year 1916 was the high point of the Progressive era. First of all, Wilson appointed Louis Brandeis to the Supreme Court. Brandeis's advocacy of reform causes had won him many enemies in the business community; and his appointment was a victory for Progressivism, and for religious equality as well, because he was a Jew.

Then the Federal Farm Loan Act was passed, providing easier credit for farmers. The Child Labor Act of 1916 was passed after Wilson personally applied pressure on Democratic Senate leaders. For the first time, Congress used its power over interstate commerce to control conditions under which employers might operate their industries. The bill (later declared unconstitutional) forbade shipment in interstate commerce of goods produced by child labor. Congress also passed a model workmen's compensation act for federal employees, and the Adamson Act gave railroad employees the eight-hour day. Wilson also approved the principle of rational tariff protection for certain infant industries, a complete reversal of his earlier pronouncements, and an acceptance of Roosevelt's idea.

For a long time, Wilson had disappointed Progressives in refusing to support social reform

FEDERAL RESERVE POWERS

Sets the Reserve Requirement. All member banks must keep a percentage of their deposits in their district's Federal Reserve Bank. This is their "reserve" requirement. They can use the rest of their deposit money for loans and investments, but they cannot use their reserve money. The Board of Governors decides what percentage of deposits must be kept as a reserve.

Sets the Discount Rate. If a member bank wants more money (to meet a very high demand for loans, e.g.) it can borrow from its Reserve Bank. The interest rate charged by the Reserve Bank is the "discount rate." Member banks will, in turn, set their interest rate to their customers in keeping with the Federal Reserve's discount rate.

Sets the Margin Requirement. If an investor buys stock on margin, he pays partly in cash and borrows the rest (see feature, page 520). The Federal Reserve decides what percentage must be paid in cash. This is the margin requirement.

Engages in Open-Market Operations. The Federal Reserve can buy and sell government securities by dealing with private individuals and businesses on the open market.

Issues Federal Reserve Notes. The Federal Reserve issues the major part of our paper money.

HOW THE FEDERAL RESERVE INFLUENCES THE FLOW OF MONEY

When there is an: Inflationary Economy	When there is a: Deflationary Economy
The Federal Reserve can:	The Federal Reserve can:
(1) **Raise the Reserve Requirement.** If the reserve requirement is raised, member banks will have to set aside more money for reserves. Therefore they will have less money available to inject into the economy by way of loans and investments.	(1) **Lower the Reserve Requirement.** If the reserve requirement is lowered, member banks can set less money aside for reserves and will have more money to use for loans and investments, therefore putting more money in circulation.
(2) **Raise the Discount Rate.** If the discount rate is raised, the member banks, in turn, will raise their interest rates to their customers. The higher interest rate will discourage businesses and individuals from borrowing for business expansion or spending; and less money will be put in circulation.	(2) **Lower the Discount Rate.** If the discount rate is lowered, member banks can lower their interest rates on loans to their customers. Their customers (individuals and businesses) will be encouraged to borrow by the low interest rate, and more money will be put into the economy by way of bank loans.
(3) **Sell Government Securities.** If the Federal Reserve sells government stocks and bonds to businesses or individuals, it will receive payment in checks drawn on certain member banks. When the checks are cashed the reserves of those member banks will be diminished. The reserves must be replenished with money the member banks would otherwise use for loans or investments, therefore leaving the banks with less money to put into the economy.	(3) **Buy Government Securities.** If the Federal Reserve buys government securities it will pay for them with a Reserve bank check. The seller (a business or individual) will deposit the Reserve check on his account in one of the member banks. This deposit will increase the amount of money that particular member bank will have available for loans and investments, therefore increasing the amount of money it can inject into the economy.

legislation. He had blocked the AFL's campaign to obtain immunity for labor unions from application of the antitrust law for illegal strikes. He had opposed a child-labor measure in 1914 because he thought it unconstitutional, and he had refused to support a women's suffrage amendment because he thought suffrage qualifications were properly a matter for states to decide. In 1915 he had nearly vetoed La Follette's bill to enforce safety requirements on merchant vessels and to free American and foreign sailors coming into American ports from their bondage to labor contracts. How can Wilson's change of heart be explained?

Undoubtedly the political situation in 1916 influenced Wilson's policies. In order to win the election, the Democrats, normally a minority party, had to lure into their ranks some of the disenchanted Progressives. If they did not convince the Progressives that the best hope for future reform lay with the Democrats, the election would surely go to the Republicans. The best way to convince them was to pass reform measures before the election. However, it is also true that Wilson himself had changed in the Presidency. Having faced the difficult situations in the tariff, banking, and antitrust legislation, and having found the New Freedom not altogether satisfactory, he modified his views and began to accept a more active role for government.

The election of 1916. Wilson was nominated by acclamation at the Democratic National Convention in St. Louis. The Republicans in Chicago chose Charles Evans Hughes, now a Supreme Court Justice and formerly governor of New York, as their candidate. Theodore Roosevelt was nominated by the Progressive party, but he threw his support to Hughes rather than split the party again. The Progressives decided not to nominate anyone else.

The election campaign focused on domestic reform and on the growing fears of America's involvement in the war that was raging in Europe. Hughes criticized the Underwood Tariff and the Democratic conduct of foreign affairs. Wilson conducted a low-keyed campaign, and his supporters adopted the slogan "He kept us out of war."

The election was one of the closest in American history and was not decided until the final count

from California gave Wilson a slim margin of victory. The final electoral college count was 277 for Wilson and 254 for Hughes. Progressivism ended when Wilson by 1916 had carried out almost all of Roosevelt's 1912 campaign pledges.

6 Progressivism Fails To Benefit Black Americans

1. Why were black Americans generally excluded from the reforms of the Progressive Era?

2. What were some of the ways in which blacks were discriminated against during the early 1900's?

3. What were the positions advocated by various black organizations regarding the restoration and promotion of civil rights and social equality? How appropriate were these positions for the times, and how appropriate are they for today's race relations?

The black population of the United States did not participate in and did not benefit from most of the Progressive reforms achieved during the early twentieth century. The economic status of blacks improved slightly, but socially and politically they were little better off than they had been before the nation was seized by the desire for change.

Most Progressives were either prejudiced against black people or unaware of the effects and extent of discrimination against them. During the Progressive era, myths of racial superiority were widely believed. Anglo-Saxons were thought to be superior not only to blacks and Orientals, but also to Italians, Hungarians, Germans, Poles, Jews, Catholics, and every other category of national or religious group. Amidst all the ferment for reform, the special problems of black people, only fifty years released from slavery, received hardly any notice.

There were a few exceptions, of course. A small group of Progressives championed the equality of blacks. A leading figure was Oswald Garrison Villard, the liberal publisher of the *New York Evening Post* and *The Nation*, who was a grandson of the abolitionist William Lloyd Garrison. Social worker Jane Addams and journalist Jacob Riis started a Charities Publication Committee, which published a special study called "The Negro in the Cities of the North" in 1905. Muckraker Ray Stannard Baker wrote a pioneering study of racial attitudes in both North and South in his work *Following the Color Line* (1908). Several humanitarian Progressives, mainly social workers, writers, and clergymen, vigorously protested particularly outrageous incidents of racial injustice, such as the antiblack riots in Springfield, Illinois, in 1908. Nevertheless, the cause of the black American was not part of the mainstream of Progressivism.

The status of black Americans. In the early years of the century, white southerners did begin to promote public aid for black education, although the schools that were provided were far inferior to those attended by white children. Few black children had the opportunity to go beyond elementary school. In 1910, for example, only eight thousand black high-school students were enrolled in all the southern states.

Economically, blacks were kept in a subordinate status by their dependence on the sharecropping system, a less flagrant form of bondage than slavery, but equally binding. White southerners had substituted for the formal social controls of slavery a rigid caste system, and violators of the unspoken rules governing social behavior were treated harshly.

Until the Populist movement had raised the threat of possible political union between blacks and whites, blacks had enjoyed the right to vote in the South without much interference. However, after the resurgence of black political activity as both Populists and Democrats bid for their votes, blacks were removed from enfranchisement by a variety of legal requirements. Ironically as the result of a Progressive reform, the polls were finally closed to black voters. As historian C. Vann Woodward points out in *The Strange Career of Jim Crow* (1955):

But if the Negroes did learn to read, or acquire sufficient property, and remember to pay the poll tax

and to keep the receipt on file, they could even then be tripped by the final hurdle devised for them—the white primary. . . . the primary system was undoubtedly an improvement over the old convention system and did much to democratize nominations and party control. But along with the progressively inspired primary system were adopted the oppositely inspired party rules, local regulations, and in some cases state laws excluding the minority race from participation and converting the primary into a white man's club.

Although some southern Progressives achieved impressive gains against bosses and machines and trusts and railroads, and even though they helped democratize politics, their record in the field of racial equality was sorry indeed.

The North, however, was far from a shining example of equality in race relations. Fewer and fewer blacks were elected to office, even in cities like Boston, where the abolition tradition had been strong. Blacks were continually subject to discriminatory practices in hotels, restaurants, and theaters. Even though state laws forbade it, many communities set up separate schools for black students.

Policies of the federal government. On the federal level, little was done to insure equality for blacks during the Progressive era. Theodore Roosevelt was inconsistent in his attitudes, alternating between wooing black voters in the North and placating white conservatives in the South. Although he did appoint a few black men to office, his successor, President Taft, publically stated that he would not appoint any southern blacks to offices if whites objected.

During the election campaign of 1912, Wilson made vague pleas for the support of black voters, who were instinctively suspicious of a southerner. Their fears that Wilson would do little to help them proved well-founded. Under his administration, the concepts of race supremacy and segregation gained even more strength than under Roosevelt's wavering policies and Taft's insensitive ones.

Soon after his inauguration, Wilson accepted the suggestion of Oswald Garrison Villard that a commission be appointed to study the racial problem. The idea was abandoned, however, when Wilson decided he needed southern votes in Congress and could not risk losing them over the issue of race.

In 1913, with administration approval, segregation was instituted in the Post Office and Treasury departments. Workers were segregated in offices, rest rooms, and lunch rooms, and anyone who objected was fired. In the South, federal officials were given the authority to downgrade black employees. Informal segregation had existed in federal departments before, but never had it been an official policy of the United States government.

Black leaders wrote of their bitter disappointment to Wilson, and Villard and other liberal leaders raised a loud protest. As a result, the policy was reversed. Although racism was not eliminated from the federal government, its advocates were less successful after that.

Black organizations. Black people realized that white Progressivism had little to offer them. But when they looked to their own leaders for guidance, they found conflicting paths to follow. The gradualist, separatist policy of Booker T. Washington was opposed by the more militant leader William E. B. Du Bois (page 388). Du Bois's challenge to Washington's leadership took an active form in June 1905, when, with an all-black group of supporters, he founded the Niagara Movement.

Meeting at Niagara Falls on the Canadian side (hotels on the American side would not provide accommodations), the group demanded the abolition of all distinctions based on race, and called for freedom of speech, manhood suffrage, and recognition of the basic principles of human brotherhood. The following year, the movement met in Harpers Ferry, Virginia, where it drew up a resolution denouncing racial inequality. Written by Du Bois, the manifesto declared in part:

In the past year the work of the Negro hater has flourished in the land. Step by step the defenders of the rights of American citizens have retreated. The work of stealing the black man's ballot has progressed and the fifty and more representatives of stolen votes still sit in the nation's capital. . . .

Although the Niagara Movement was to be replaced by a new, more enduring organization, it was significant as the first organized attempt by blacks to protest the racial policies of white America.

In 1909, in the aftermath of the Springfield riots, a major organizational step was taken in the fight for black equality. Led by Villard, a small group which included Du Bois, founded the National Association for the Advancement of Colored People. The first chairman was Moorfield Storey, a white lawyer specializing in Constitutional law.

With the exception of Du Bois, the original founders of the NAACP were white; nevertheless blacks played a leading role from the beginning. Du Bois became editor of *Crisis*, the NAACP publication, and also its director of research. In 1916 James Weldon Johnson, a black writer, became the first executive secretary. From the start, the leaders and members of the various branches of the NAACP were black.

The NAACP program, radical for its time, hoped to destory discrimination through legislation and the courts. It scored an immediate victory by leading the protest over Wilson's segregationist policy. In 1915, the Supreme Court struck down the "grandfather clauses" that existed in several southern state constitutions (page 433). In 1917 the Court outlawed municipal residential segregation ordinances.

Most of the work of the NAACP was in attempting to break down segregation and to secure for blacks their civil rights. It had little time or resources to assist blacks in the economic or social sphere. In 1911, the National League on Urban Conditions, commonly known as the National Urban League, was founded to assist blacks in widening their economic and social opportunities. The league, with branches in many cities, set up programs which assisted blacks in getting jobs and housing and helped them to adjust to the problems of urban living.

Except for the upsurge in black organizational strength, the Progressive era was a dismal one for black Americans. In later years, more and more whites would begin to appreciate the prophetic warning of Du Bois in 1903: "The problem of the twentieth century is the problem of the color line."

■ CONCLUSION

The Progressive era came to an end when the United States entered World War I in 1917. After the war there was a return to conservatism. The temporary alliance of reform-minded groups broke apart. Many of the groups continued their agitation for reform in the 1920's, but on a separate basis. There was no national political party strong enough to unite them, and no leader of the stature of Roosevelt or Wilson to inspire them. Under the stress of war, the tensions between the groups, which had always existed, became even more disruptive. Finally, Progressives had largely achieved their stated aims by 1916, and there was no common agreement on what should come next.

Since Progressive efforts declined in the 1920's and some reforms were even reversed, it is tempting to conclude that Progressivism accomplished very little. Certainly, as we have seen, some Progressive reforms were guided by naivëte, others by narrow self-interest, and some by narrow-mindedness. Perhaps most damaging, Progressives largely ignored one entire segment of the population—black Americans. Progressive reforms did not bring a return to the simple life; if anything, the trends toward urbanization and industrialization gained more vigor.

Despite their failures, however, the Progressives did succeed in initiating some basic changes in politics and in the role of government as an active protector of the public interest. Many of their innovations paved the way for later reforms. Their vision was limited in many respects, and from a contemporary vantage point, it can be seen that they did not aim far enough and wide enough. Judged by their own goals, they succeeded; judged by the goals of future generations, they only began an important task.

■ QUESTIONS

1. Who were the Progressives, and what were the reforms they advocated? How were they different from previous reformers? Were the reforms reasonable solutions to American problems? Explain your answer.

2. How successful were the Progressives in accomplishing their purpose of reform?

3. To what extent were the muckrakers indispensable to the Progressive movement? Explain your answer.

4. How effective were Roosevelt, Taft, and Wilson in accomplishing Progressive reforms? What accounted for their individual success or lack of success?

5. What were the problems confronting America at the turn of the century? What were the problems which were characteristic of state and local governments?

6. What shifts were there in the role that government was expected to play?

7. Why did the Progressive movement cease as a strong force for reform in America?

8. Why were blacks excluded from the reforms of the period? What successes, if any, did blacks experience at the beginning of the century?

9. "The Progressive wave of the future, said Croly, lay in the possibility of using Hamiltonian methods (direct government intervention) to achieve Jeffersonian ends (democratic equality)." Evaluate this statement as a possible government philosophy in 1912.

■ BIBLIOGRAPHY

HOFSTADTER, RICHARD, *The Age of Reform: From Bryan to F.D.R.*, Random House (Vintage Books). Hofstadter has provided a readable analysis of American reform and government from the Populists through the Progressives to the New Dealers. Although some historians challenge parts of Hofstadter's work, this book remains very popular. For a slightly different view by an author who covers the same period, the student should read Eric Goldman's *Rendezvous with Destiny*.

MOWRY, GEORGE, *Theodore Roosevelt and the Progressive Movement*, American Century. Mowry has a much more limited scope of analysis than Hofstadter. Mowry's book is a standard work for the period from 1909 to 1919, with much space devoted to the campaign of 1912. As in the Hofstadter and Link books, the reading is not particularly easy, but may be read profitably by many high-school students.

LINK, ARTHUR S., *Woodrow Wilson and the Progressive Era, 1910-1917*, New American Nation Series, Harper & Row (Torchbooks). There is an ever increasing list of good books on Woodrow Wilson, and the student should not be limited to this one book. Link is recognized as the outstanding biographer of Wilson, however, and in this volume he concentrates upon Wilson's handling of domestic and foreign affairs from 1910 to 1917.

LAFOLLETTE, ROBERT M., *LaFollette's Autobiography: A Personal Narrative of Political Experience,* U. of Wisconsin Press. Although Roosevelt was a Progressive candidate and Wilson reflected Progressive reforms, the life and core of the Progressive movement can best be seen in the career of LaFollette. In addition to the three interpretations of the Progressive movement, the student should read these comments of one of the major participants in the struggle for representative democracy.

FRANKLIN, JOHN HOPE, ed., *Three Negro Classics,* Avon Books. This is a very convenient volume which should be consulted by all students since it contains classic statements by three critical figures in black history.

The three works are *Up From Slavery* by Booker T. Washington, *The Souls of Black Folks* by W.E.B. Du Bois, and *The Autobiography of an Ex-Colored Man* by James Weldon Johnson.

SOBUL, DE ANNE, *Encounters with America's History,* Holt, Rinehart & Winston. Child labor prior to and during the Progressive period was not only a common occurrence, it was encouraged—both by parents and employers. Why then did reformers finally try to regulate it and ultimately try to do away with it? The third problem in this book gives the student source material to deal with in order to answer this question for himself.

The Emergence Of The United States As A World Power

From the mid-1890's through the Progressive era many political leaders sought both reform at home and expansion abroad. Although their policies varied, Presidents Roosevelt, Taft, and Wilson thought it was beneficial to promote social and political change within the United States and at the same time to extend American influence in other areas. However, this interest in foreign affairs had not been so intense in the decades before the 1890's. As late as 1889, Henry Cabot Lodge, a Republican leader, noted that "our relations with foreign nations today fill but a slight place in American politics, and excite generally only a languid interest."

Less than ten years later, the nation was caught up in an expansionist fervor. Many factors were responsible for the change. America was becoming the dominant industrial power in the world, and businessmen believed that the expansion of foreign trade was vital for continued prosperity. The symbolic closing of the frontier, the rise of the city, and the increasing waves of immigration all signified deep changes in American life.

The world itself was drawing closer together with technological advances in transportation and communication. As all these influences were making their mark, an exhilarating new spirit of Manifest Destiny swept the nation, accompanied by a revival of the old faith that it was America's mission to spread democracy all over the world. Caught up in the excitement of the period, most people gave little thought to the consequences of the great adventure. Here are some questions to help you trace the emergence of the United States as a world power:

1. Why did the public mood favor expansionism in the 1890's?
2. How were American interests expanded in the Pacific?
3. What were the causes and results of the Spanish-American War?
4. How successful was the Open Door Policy in the Far East?
5. How was American dominance in the Caribbean assured?

1 Expansionist Sentiment Grows

1. What were some examples of American interests in expansion prior to 1890?

2. Why did the American mood become more aggressively expansionist?

3. What was the rationale for the new American Manifest Destiny? How were racist arguments used to support expansion, and how were they used to attack expansion?

4. Do you think American interest in overseas expansion was consistent with Populist and Progressive reform?

The expansionist mood of the 1890's was not entirely new. Americans had always been eager to expand their borders, and for many this was not limited to pushing westward on the frontier. Interest in Cuba existed in the early days of the Republic; and the desire for Canada, so evident in the War of 1812, persisted throughout the nineteenth century. In the 1840's and 1850's, a few Americans even wanted to take the entire Northern Hemisphere, a thirst only partially satisfied by the vast Mexican Cession of 1848. The acquisition of Oregon and California reemphasized America's interest in the Pacific and Far East, which had existed since the days of the old China trade in the late eighteenth century.

Although the Civil War diverted the expansionist fervor, a persistent thread continued. William Seward, one of the most expansionist secretaries of state, purchased Alaska from Russia in 1867 for $7.2 million, despite the jeers of critics who decried "Seward's Icebox" as a useless, frozen wasteland. The same year Seward also acquired the tiny Midway Islands in the Pacific and concluded a treaty with Denmark for the purchase of the Danish West Indies (Virgin Islands), although the Senate ultimately rejected it.

President Grant tried hard, if unsuccessfully, to persuade the Senate to annex Santo Domingo in the Caribbean in 1870. In the 1880's, James G. Blaine, as secretary of state, made a persistent effort to expand Latin-American trade through tariff reciprocity and the development of an inter-American organization which in 1910 became the Pan-American Union. But the expansionism of this period lacked widespread popular support; the nation was too busy settling the Last West and developing its industry.

In the 1890's, however, the expansionist mood changed. Not only did it become more widespread and intense, its motivation was different. An explanation of this change in attitude is essential to an understanding of the foreign outlook at the end of the century.

Economic growth. The change was due in part to America's sheer physical growth. By 1900 the United States had a greater population than any European power except Russia, and it was rapidly becoming the leader in industrial production. Foreign trade expanded rapidly as well. More manufactured goods began to be exported, accounting for an ever-growing proportion of American exports. At the same time, there was less demand for manufactured goods from abroad and a greater need for raw materials such as rubber, manganese, and tin.

As farm surpluses grew at home, agricultural prices declined, creating a demand for new markets. Although the United States continued in its traditional role as debtor to Europe, American capital began to flow toward investments in mines, industries, and railroads in Canada, Mexico, Cuba, the Caribbean, and Latin America.

These economic pressures for increased foreign trade and new markets came at a time when the European powers were also seeking new sources of raw materials and markets. The traditional imperialist powers—Great Britain, France, Russia, and Spain—were being challenged by aggressive modernizing nations such as Germany, Italy, Belgium, and later Japan. Most of Africa had already been carved up, and the lines were being drawn in Asia. Many of these nations were now looking toward Latin America, threatening American interests that had existed in this area since the Monroe Doctrine was proclaimed.

Domestic unrest. Besides pressures on the international scene, there was also unrest at home. Industrialism had fundamentally changed old patterns of life. The severe depression of 1893 and the rise of the Populist movement had challenged traditional capitalistic theories. New in-

461

GROWTH OF THE UNITED STATES, 1870–1910
(Economic Indicators)

	1870	1880	1890	1900	1910
Population	39,905,000	50,262,000	63,056,000	76,094,000	92,407,000
Railroad mileage (in operation)	52,922,000	93,262,000	199,876,000	258,784,000	351,767,000
Number of factories (includes hand and neighborhood industries)	252,148	253,852	353,864	512,339	564,810*
Persons engaged in manufacturing	2,250,000	3,170,000	4,750,000	6,340,000	8,230,000
Farm acreage	407,723,000	536,064,000	623,207,000	838,583,000	878,792,000
Persons engaged in agriculture	6,850,000	8,585,000	9,938,000	10,912,000	11,592,000
Number of farms	2,659,985	4,008,907	4,564,641	5,739,657	6,361,502
Value of exports (goods and services)	$507,000,000	$963,000,000	$960,000,000	$1.68 billion	$2.16 billion
Value of imports (goods and services)	$608,000,000	$848,000,000	$1.1 billion	$1.17 billion	$2 billion
Value of total goods and services produced	$6.71 billion	$9.18 billion	$13:5 billion	$17.3 billion	$31.6 billion

* Estimated

tellectual and artistic trends upset established standards. Writing about the unsettling effects of these changes, historian Richard Hofstadter finds that middle-class Americans experienced a "psychic crisis" in the 1890's. The developments of the 1890's came as a profound shock to Americans raised on nineteenth-century ideals that celebrated the triumph of virtue, hard work, and honesty over all evils. To restore their faith in the future, Hofstadter continues, Americans turned to exuberant patriotism, vigorous expansionism, and aggressive leadership.

Describing the American response to this decade of uncertainty, historian Frederick Merck says, "The sobering fact that the youthfulness of the nation had slipped away and needed somehow to be restored was recognized by politicians of all parties." One response was the movement for domestic reform that began with the Populists and continued through the Progressive era. An-

other response was expansionism. Albert J. Beveridge, later a leading Progressive Republican senator from Indiana, stated the case for expansionism in 1898:

American factories are making more than the American people can use; American soil is producing more than they can consume. Fate has written our policy for us; the trade of the world must and shall be ours. . . . We will establish trading-posts throughout the world as distributing points for American products. We will cover the ocean with our merchant marine. Great colonies, governing themselves, flying our flag and trading with us, will grow about our posts of trade. Our institutions will follow our flag on the wings of commerce. And American law, American order, American civilization, and the American flag will plant themselves on shores hitherto bloody and benighted. . . .

Not all politicians, not even all Republicans, shared this enthusiasm. Conservative businessmen feared that aggressive expansionism would lead to war, producing panic and depression. Many Democrats believed that it was wrong for the United States to force its power into other areas. Though the voices of opposition were never stilled, and at times became powerful in their protest, the new spirit of Manifest Destiny prevailed.

The rationale for expansionism. Writers, historians, and religious leaders provided intellectual justification for the new expansionism. Although the old Manifest Destiny had linked race with expansionism in arguments for conquering the Mexicans, the new Manifest Destiny differed because it claimed to have a scientific foundation. Darwin's idea of "survival of the fittest" in nature was applied to nations as well. The theory of "social Darwinism" (pages 330, 331) sanctioned domination of weaker nations by strong ones. Such ideas were compatible with the prevailing race prejudice in the United States. Most white Americans seriously doubted whether dark-skinned people were able to govern themselves.

One popular spokesman of this idea was John Fiske, a philosopher, historian, and lecturer. His book *American Political Ideas* (1885) extolled the superiority of the Anglo-Saxon race, which had restored order in Europe after successive waves of Germanic, Mongolian, and Moslem invaders. Although Fiske was a racist, his definition of "Anglo-Saxon" included all the various national elements which had been amalgamated in the United States. According to Fiske, the evidence of American creativity was the development of the principle of federalism in the Constitution. He considered the federal form of government the most promising government for the future of the world.

In 1885, the Congregationalist minister and promotor of missions Josiah Strong published an extraordinarily popular book called *Our Country: Its Possible Future and Its Present Crisis.* Although the main theme of his work was the need for mission funds to counteract the perils threatening the Protestant way of life in America, one chapter caught the public fancy. It stressed the mission of the Anglo-Saxon race to Christianize the world. Strong argued that Anglo-Saxons were the greatest representatives of pure Christianity and civil liberty, and from this it followed, in Strong's view, that the Anglo-Saxon was "divinely com-missioned to be, in a peculiar sense, his brother's keeper." Strong was really more of an internationalist than a nationalist; he advocated the social gospel for the world and opposed economic imperialism and selfish nationalism.

Although the writings of these and similar-minded men were used to justify expansionism, racist theories were also used by opponents of expansionism. "Inferior" peoples should not be brought under the American flag, it was claimed, because they could never master the principles of American government. The tropics, where many of these people lived, were unsuitable for the development of higher civilization. The old Manifest Destiny had been limited to areas where statehood was eventual; the United States should not undertake to govern areas where the people could never aspire to statehood.

Even among the people who used these arguments, there was no consensus. Some believed that Cubans and Mexicans could be assimilated but drew the line at Orientals, particularly mixed Orientals such as the Hawaiians. In general, then, most people believed in some form of racial superiority, but used their beliefs to justify different positions.

Far more influential on actual policy-making than any of the social Darwinists were the writings of Captain Alfred Thayer Mahan, a naval officer and historian. In his book *The Influence of Sea Power upon History, 1660–1783* (1890), Mahan traced the rise and decline of great nations and found that sea power was the key to their success. And, to be a great sea power, a nation needed bases, colonies, communications, and logistical organization. Based on these historical perspectives, Mahan declared: ". . . whether they will or no, Americans must begin to look outward. The growing production of the country demands it. An increasing volume of public sentiment demands it." A sequel published in 1892, *The Influence of Sea Power upon the French Revolution and Empire, 1793–1812,* reinforced his arguments. Both works were eagerly seized on by such advocates of naval improvements as Theodore Roosevelt and Henry Cabot Lodge.

Thus, the new Manifest Destiny came from many varied and complex sources—economic, political, and psychological. But there was another ingredient—emotion. George Kennan, a diplomat and historian, has described its strength in this way:

> ... at the bottom of it all lay something deeper, something less easy to express, probably the fact that the American people of that day, or at least many of their more influential spokesmen, simply liked the smell of empire and felt an urge to range themselves among the colonial powers of the time, to see our flag flying on distant tropical isles, to feel the thrill of foreign adventure and authority, to bask in the sunshine of recognition as one of the great imperial powers of the world.

2 Expansionism Builds Toward War

1. What developments prior to 1898 prepared the United States for its dramatic plunge into overseas expansion with the outbreak of the Spanish-American War?

2. How was the annexation of Hawaii "a consumation of the work of American missionaries, traders, whalers, sugar planters, big navyites and imperialists"? What were the reasons for and against the annexation of Hawaii?

3. What were the causes of the Venezuelan border dispute. Do you think the United States would have been justified in military intervention?

The war with Spain over Cuba in 1898 was the turning point in American foreign policy. After this time, the expansionists plunged full steam ahead, carrying along in their enthusiasm many of their former opponents. But in the decade before the war, several developments had prepared the American people for the war with Spain.

Naval buildup. The lack of interest in foreign affairs in the 1870's was symbolized by the decrepit American navy. While other nations were converting to iron steam vessels, the rotting wooden hulks of Civil War vintage made the American navy an international joke. In a book by the English author Oscar Wilde, a young American lady laments that her country has no ruins and no curiosities. An Englishman replies: "No ruins! No curiosities! You have your Navy and your manners!"

Mahan's arguments for the importance of sea power came at a time when there was already considerable agitation for naval improvements. In 1883, a naval appropriations bill was passed that provided for three new cruisers. Congress became increasingly willing to use the Treasury surpluses of the 1880's to help finance naval construction. The landmark Naval Act of 1890 authorized the building of three large battleships, the first in the nation's history.

The construction of the *Indiana, Massachusetts,* and *Oregon,* each over ten thousand tons and bristling with guns, marked a break with the past in ideas as well as technology. The new navy was expected to protect Americans in distant places as well as to guard the home shores. By the mid-1890's, the navy was ready to serve an expansion-minded nation, which turned its attention to the Pacific.

Interest in the Pacific. America's long-standing interest in the Pacific had been revitalized by the completion of the first transcontinental railroad in 1869, the purchase of Alaska, and the settlement of Oregon and California. The Samoan Islands, three thousand miles southwest of Hawaii, had long been a stopping point for American vessels plying the China trade.

In 1878, the United States signed a treaty with Samoa giving American vessels a coaling station in the harbor of Pago Pago. Great Britain and Germany were also vying for trade concessions, and an intense rivalry among the three nations developed. The situation was partially resolved in 1889 when a three-power protectorate was established over the islands. The Samoans were resentful but powerless. As one orator cried, "Who asked the Great Powers to make laws for us?" In 1899, the United States and Germany divided Samoa, with the United States acquiring the island of Tutuila with its harbor at Pago Pago. The British were compensated elsewhere.

American interest in Hawaii. More significant in terms of the United States' Pacific interest were the Hawaiian Islands, where American contact had begun in the late eighteenth century. In 1820, the first Protestant missionaries from New England arrived, followed by whalers who used the islands as a base. The missionaries were largely successful in converting the Hawaiians and in influencing their rulers. Over the years, descendants of these missionaries became the controlling force in the economy of the islands.

Other nations were also interested in Hawaii, and in the 1840's and 1850's, threats of British and French domination triggered a drive for annexation. Although two treaties of annexation were negotiated, the Senate rejected both of them, largely because they proposed the admission of Hawaii as a state. In addition, most native Hawaiians opposed annexation; the status of blacks in the United States indicated to them a general American contempt for nonwhite peoples.

Nevertheless, the growing Hawaiian sugar industry, built up by the sons of missionaries on lands donated by native princes, was binding the islands closer economically to the United States. During the Civil War and after it, high tariffs threatened to deprive the planters of their American markets. In 1875, a reciprocity treaty allowed Hawaiian sugar to enter the United States duty-free in return for Hawaii's guarantee not to make territorial concessions to any other power. This treaty irrevocably linked Hawaii's economy to the United States. In 1887, the United States gained the exclusive right to use Pearl Harbor on the island of Oahu.

By the 1890's, white Americans in Hawaii controlled about two-thirds of the land and in effect the entire islands. With the support of the strong-willed nationalistic ruler, Queen Liluokalani, resentful natives started a "Hawaii for the Hawaiians" movement. And tension was heightened by the disastrous effects of the McKinley Tariff of 1890, which wiped out the advantages Hawaiian sugar imports into the United States had had over other foreign sugar. In 1893, the queen attempted to establish a new constitution to give greater political power to Hawaiians.

In retaliation, American planters and businessmen in Hawaii began to push for annexation as the only means of protecting their property and investments. In 1893, determined to overthrow the queen, they appealed for help to the Ameri-can Minister to Hawaii, John L. Stevens. Sympathetic to the annexationists, Stevens arranged for the landing of 150 Marines, ostensibly to protect American lives and property. The queen yielded, and Stevens hastily recognized the new revolutionary regime, dominated by Americans. He proclaimed Hawaii a protectorate and advised the State Department to take the islands.

Annexation of Hawaii. The Harrison administration was inclined toward annexation. But Cleveland's administration was due to take office in just a few weeks, and Democratic opposition forced postponement of any action.

President Cleveland was a forthright man who was determined to do what he thought right. He ordered an investigating commission sent to Hawaii, and from its report he concluded that American businessmen had started the Hawaiian revolution. But undoing the wrong proved difficult. He could not restore Queen Liluokalani to the throne without using force against Americans in Hawaii, a policy sure to anger Americans at home. Instead, he denounced the American intervention and refused to consider annexation, although he did recognize the protectorate.

Annexation was postponed but not denied. The naval expansionists continued to argue that Hawaii was essential to the nation's Pacific defense and that Japan was becoming more and more interested in the islands. It was the Spanish-American War, however, that finally brought about annexation. At the outset of the war, when the United States defeated Spain in the Philippines (page 473), the annexation of Hawaii seemed not only logical but essential. In July 1898, Hawaii was bound to the United States by a treaty overwhelmingly approved in the Senate. Said President McKinley: "Annexation is not change; it is consummation." "It was indeed," comments historian Thomas Bailey, "a consummation of the work of American missionaries, traders, whalers, sugar planters, big navyites, and imperialists."

A dispute over Venezuela. As Americans argued over the annexation of Hawaii during the 1890's, a dispute with Great Britain in 1895 brought the nation to the point of war. Trouble arose in Venezuela over the long-disputed boundary line between British Guiana and Venezuela, a boundary that Venezuela had never accepted. The area in question, a region about the size of New York State, was important to Venezuela because it included the mouth of the Orinoco, the country's largest river. Gold strikes in the disputed territory in the 1870's gave the matter a new urgency.

Venezuela sought the support of the United States, asking it to invoke the Monroe Doctrine. American politicians in both parties sensed that the American public would support aggressive intervention. The chairman of the Republican National Committee urged all Republicans to take a vigorous position on the issue, and an Ohio Democratic politician wrote to President Cleveland pleading for "a little Jingo" * to help the state Democratic gubernatorial candidate.

Cleveland, who had felt he was right in refusing to annex Hawaii, believed that in the Venezuelan affair, he was right to interfere. On the basis of inadequate and inaccurate information, he decided that Britain meant to rob little Venezuela of its rightful lands. The President had just appointed a new secretary of state, Richard Olney, who had demonstrated his boldness in his handling of the Pullman strike in 1894 (page 346). Olney dispatched a note to the British in July 1895, bluntly informing them that they were violating the Monroe Doctrine:

Today the United States is practically sovereign on this continent, and its fiat is law upon the subjects to which it confines its interposition. Why? . . . It is because, in addition to all other grounds, its infinite resources combined with its isolated position render it master of the situation and practically invulnerable as against any or all other powers.

Olney then went on to threaten that if Britain refused to submit the dispute to arbitration, he would give the entire matter to Congress, which had the power to make war. His request that the British reply within four months gave the note the tone of an ultimatum. Cleveland heartily approved the message, which he called Olney's "twenty-inch gun" blast and "the best thing of its kind" he had ever read.

The British Foreign Secretary, Lord Salisbury, took his time replying. The issue, he said, was "simply the determination of the frontier of a British possession," adding that the Monroe Doctrine was not recognized in international law. Salisbury's cool answer made Cleveland fighting mad. The President submitted an angry message to Congress in December 1895, in which he recommended the appointment of an American boundary commission to decide on the correct line, after which the United States would fight to maintain it. The reaction in Britain was one of shocked dismay, but in the United States the mood was belligerent and confident. A banner headline in the New York Sun screamed, "WAR IF NECESSARY," and Theodore Roosevelt expressed the hope that "the fight will come soon."

Not all Americans wanted to go to war with Britain over Venezuela. Clergymen, businessmen, and some newspapermen, particularly Joseph Pulitzer of the New York World, spoke out for a peaceful settlement. British public opinion was appalled at the idea of war over remote Venezuela, particularly since Britain already faced trouble in South Africa, feared a rising Germany, and was threatened by an ominous diplomatic situation on the Continent. Acutely aware of its need to maintain friendly relations with the United States, Great Britain agreed after many months of negotiation to submit the dispute to United States arbitration. In October 1899, long after the war crisis had passed, the arbitration board generally confirmed that the British had been right all along and that Venezuela had inflated its demands. The Venezuelans got the mouth of the Orinoco, but most of the disputed territory was awarded to Britain.

Curiously, the affair led to an upsurge of Anglo-American friendship. The British had won their case without a major sacrifice; the United States had successfully upheld the Monroe Doctrine and had confirmed its status as the major power in the area. By itself, the Venezuelan incident was not of lasting significance. But it indicated the temper of the times. The American people could be brought to the point of war over a dispute that did not involve them directly. In 1895, the crisis was resolved peacefully; three years later another crisis led to war.

3 The United States Goes To War With Spain

1. Why did the United States support Cuba in its fight for independence and declare war against Spain?

2. What were the characteristics of yellow journalism? To what extent did the newspapers influence American attitudes toward war? To what extent was the press responsible for American involvement in Cuba?

3. What was the American strategy for war with Spain? What accounted for the success of American military efforts?

In taking a belligerent stance with Great Britain, the United States was challenging one of the major world powers. In contrast, the once-great empire of Spain had lost most of its holdings. By any standards, it was a weak power in world affairs. In 1895, the people of Cuba, one of Spain's few remaining possessions, revolted. The uprising was the latest in a series of insurrections in Cuba that had begun in the 1870's. The majority of the Cuban people lived in poverty and misery, a situation further aggravated by the worldwide depression of 1893 and the collapse of the sugar market. Since sugar was the key to Cuba's economy, the sharp decline in sugar exports caused widespread suffering. The United States tariff of 1894 also contributed to the island's economic distress by imposing duties on Cuban sugar.

The Cuban revolt. Using guerrilla tactics against the Spaniards, the Cuban rebels made hit-and-run attacks at night and melted into the population by day. They ruthlessly destroyed property, threatening American investments in Cuba estimated at some $50 million. Most of this sum was invested in sugar plantations and iron mines, although some was in tobacco, railroads, and manufactures. In addition, trade between Cuba and the United States was estimated at about $100 million annually. The rebels often forced the American property owners to pay bribes to protect their investments, using the

money to help finance the revolution. Cuban and American propaganda played down such tactics, while portraying the Spaniards as brutal tyrants.

Cuban revolutionary committees in the United States spread propaganda, raised money, and enlisted the support of many groups, including labor, the press, and religious organizations. Americans instinctively rallied to the Cuban cause, which they saw as a valiant struggle for freedom against Spanish tyranny. And, though few wanted war, until late in 1897, many favored intervention in some way not clearly defined.

The business community, and politicians closely connected with it, favored peace, not because they opposed economic expansion but because they considered war too disruptive and risky. Other political leaders took up the cry for intervention. Governor Altgeld of Illinois, a leading reformer, favored annexation. Defeated in their struggle for domestic reform, many Populists and Silver Democrats also took the opportunity to seek a new crusade abroad. However, conservative leaders in both parties were also aggressive on the Cuban question. Support for intervention in Cuba came from both parties and from all sections of the country.

Early in 1896, Spain sent General Valeriano Weyler to Cuba to stiffen resistance to the Cuban rebels. The general, known in the American press as "Butcher Weyler," established concentration camps in order to immobilize entire populations and prevent guerrilla raids. Conditions in these camps were deplorable, and thousands died of disease and starvation. Weyler's tactics and the suffering in Cuba caused widespread indignation in the United States when they were revealed in the press.

War hysteria in the press. The press, in fact, had a great deal to gain from the war. This was the era of "yellow journalism," which thrived on sex, sensationalism, and sadism but which got its name more innocently from the color of the paper on which the comic strip "Yellow Kid" was printed. Joseph Pulitzer's *New York World* and William Randolph Hearst's *New York Journal* were in fierce competition for sales and advertising. Lurid stories and screaming headlines were their weapons. The *Journal* railed against "Weyler the brute, the devastator of haciendas, the destroyer of families, and the outrager of women." The *World* was not to be outdone; its reporter on the spot described "Blood on the roadsides, blood in the fields, blood on the doorsteps, blood, blood, blood!"

When news from Cuba was short, the publishers were not deterred. Hearst sent the artist Frederick Remington to Cuba, and when Remington telegraphed, "Everything is quiet . . . There will be no war," Hearst is said to have replied, "You furnish the pictures and I'll furnish the war." However, as historian Ernest May has pointed out, "the press as a whole, not just the 'yellow press,' aided the Cuban cause." Newspaper propaganda, whether sensationalized or reasoned, merely reinforced public attitudes that had been forming for some time.

Neutrality loses ground. President Cleveland followed a cautious policy, hoping that Spain and the rebels would come to terms. He doubted the rebels' ability to form a stable government and was worried that heating up the issue would hamper American business, which was beginning to recover from the depression of 1893. When Congress called for recognition of Cuban belligerency and urged the President to seek Cuban independence, he ignored the request. Cleveland was determined to resist the clamor which he regarded as an "epidemic of insanity."

When in 1896, William McKinley became President, he was genuinely anxious to maintain peace. The business community, his most solid supporters, liked his comment, "There will be no jingo nonsense under my administration." Like Cleveland, McKinley followed a policy of neutrality and delay, hoping peace would come before his party split over the issue. His position, however, became increasingly difficult.

He offered to mediate the conflict between Spain and Cuba, but Spain rejected it. Spain did recall Weyler and promised Cuba *autonomy*, or home rule. But the rebels would accept only complete independence. The situation became more complicated when Spanish loyalists in Cuba, horrified at the prospect of being ruled by Cubans, also opposed Spain's offer. The chance of settlement without United States intervention was further reduced when loyalist rioting in Havana in January 1898 threatened American lives and property.

War comes at last. McKinley quickly dispatched the battleship *Maine* to Havana. Although the *Maine* was sent ostensibly to protect American lives and her visit was explained to Spain as a friendly gesture, the menacing white ship was an effective reminder of the powerful new United States Navy. Havana remained relatively calm until suddenly on the night of February 15, 1898, a terrific explosion blew up the *Maine*, killing 260 men of a crew of 340. The cause of the explosion has never been determined, but an excited public assumed that the Spaniards were responsible. The yellow press screamed for war. "Remember the Maine, to hell with Spain" became the new rallying cry.

Congress began war preparations, and McKinley demanded concessions from Spain which would in effect give Cuba virtual independence. Although at the last minute, Spain gave in to almost all the United States demands, it was too late. Under mounting pressure from Congress, the public, and his own party, McKinley relented. On April 11, he sent his war message to Congress, which passed its own resolutions calling for force to win Cuban independence and added an amendment (the Teller Amendment) pledging the United States not to annex Cuba.

The *Maine* disaster and other events of early 1898 inflamed public opinion, but they were not the basic causes of the war. More fundamental were factors which had operated from the beginning of the crisis: reduced trade, destruction of American property, economic expansion, military strategy, political pressures, and American ideas of justice and liberty. Old World monarchical Spain was blocking the expansion of democratic capitalism. The vague fear that some other power might take over Spain's Caribbean holdings seemed to threaten United States security.

The actual fighting began in the Pacific, in the far off Philippine Islands. Several weeks before war broke out, Assistant Secretary of the Navy Theodore Roosevelt had ordered the navy's Asiatic Squadron at Hong Kong to attack the Spanish in the Philippines if war came. On May 1, under the command of Commodore George Dewey, the Asiatic Squadron virtually destroyed the decrepit Spanish fleet in Manila Bay.

At home, rejoicing Americans gave very little thought to the implications of the victory.

LIFE AT THE TURN OF THE CENTURY

Bicycle Outing in the Gay Nineties

JUST A HARMLESS FAD

Puck Cartoon, 1906

Visitor (*in private garage*).—What's that camera on your auto for, Jim?
Enthusiastic Motorist.—Oh, it's just a little fad of mine—snapshots of the way folks look before I hit 'em. You've no idea what a zest it adds to speeding.

Telephone Advertisement, *c.* 1900

Songsheet, 1905

Life at the turn of the century reflected the new strides that technology had taken. Transportation and communication were especially affected by new discoveries and inventions. At first it was the bicycle that came in for vast improvement in manageability and safety, and a new recreational craze came into being—the cycle club. The "bicycle built for two" became a part of American folklore when it inspired a song telling Daisy that she looked "sweet upon the seat of a bicycle built for two."

The next transportation craze was for the automobile. Though the machine was in a primitive state of development and frequent breakdowns brought the admonition "Get a horse!" into American parlance, many "progress-minded" enthusiasts bought the steam- or electric-powered models that were available and took to the unpaved and often muddy roads with them. Like the bicycle before it, the motorcar also inspired the highly productive song writers of "Tin Pan Alley" to new tunes; "In My Merry Oldsmobile" became a traditional American song.

The telephone opened up a whole new world of communication and profoundly affected social and business life. Like the improvements in transportation, this improvement in communication sped up the pace of life somewhat. No longer did the businessman have to rely solely on the mails, on messenger service, or on face-to-face dealing. A phone call would now suffice for many of his transactions.

Entertainment during this period was also affected by new technology. Improved

Circus Poster, 1908

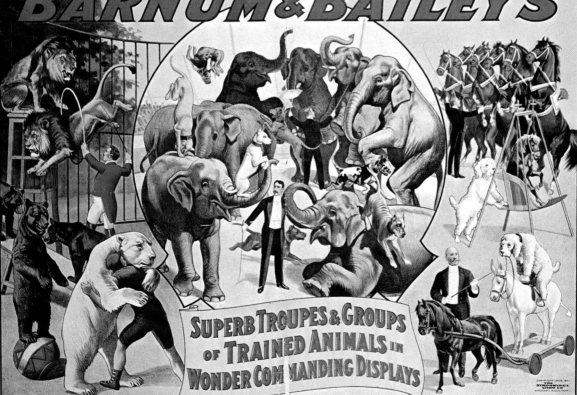

Loeb and Hollis Drug Store, Junction City, Kansas, 1902

transportation made it possible for circuses to travel all over the country, bringing tightrope walkers, trained animals, and clowns to even the smallest hamlets of rural America, as well as to the large cities.

A new center of social life appeared around this time in both small towns and city neighborhoods—the drugstore with its soda fountains offering sundaes for a dime and root beer floats for a nickel. Here people could congregate over ice cream sodas after an evening stroll or a Sunday promenade.

American buying habits underwent striking changes during this period—in large part because of the emergence of large mail-order houses. No more was the rural buyer limited to the goods at the general store or to the wares of traveling salesmen. Now a shiny new catalog would arrive in the mail, and an incredibly varied line of goods was available to the buyer, as varied as those offered to city dwellers at the large downtown stores.

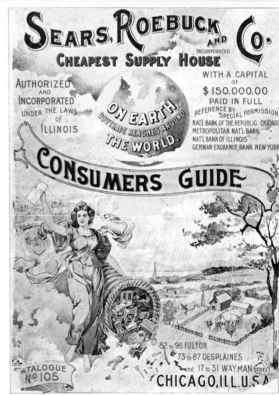

Sears, Roebuck and Company Catalog, 1897

472

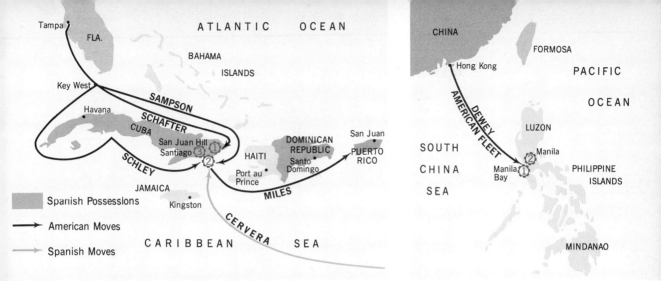

THE SPANISH AMERICAN WAR, 1898

CARIBBEAN FRONT

① **July 1, 1898. San Juan Hill.** Americans under Shafter seize the heights overlooking Santiago.

② **July 3, 1898. Santiago Harbor.** Attempting to escape from the harbor, Cervera's fleet is destroyed by American naval forces.

③ **July 17, 1898. Santiago.** American troops take Santiago. General Miles sails to Puerto Rico and occupies the island (July 25).

PACIFIC FRONT

① **May 1, 1898. Manila Bay.** Commodore Dewey, coming from Hong Kong, sails into Manila Bay and defeats the Spanish fleet.

② **August 13, 1898. Manila.** Dewey blockades the harbor and awaits more troops, which arrive in July. Americans then assault and occupy Manila.

Overnight Dewey became the man of the hour. Americans had not seen such excitement since the Civil War, and now the blue and the gray were fighting together. Dewey, however, did not have troops to occupy Manila, so he waited for an expeditionary force which reached the Philippines in July. With the help of Filipino rebels, the city was taken in August.

Fighting in the Caribbean. The Cuban phase of the war was not as immediately successful. The army, with less than 28,000 regular troops, was shockingly ill-prepared. It had no modern weapons and no adequate medical facilities or supplies (there were only heavy woolen uniforms more suitable for an Alaskan campaign). Some 182,000 volunteers joined the colors, among them the famous Rough Riders, a cavalry unit (which had no horses in Cuba) including cowboys and eastern socialites under the command of Colonel Leonard Wood and Colonel Theodore Roosevelt. The Rough Riders, less than 1,000 out of more

than 220,000 who enlisted, fought well but received a disproportionate amount of publicity.

An expeditionary force assembled at Tampa, Florida, where, because of poor management, there was wild confusion as equipment and supplies piled up in a hopeless tangle. After weeks of delay, a 17,000-man force finally left for Cuba. Landing near Santiago, the Americans met no resistance. Spanish imcompetence and lack of preparation more than matched that of the Americans (with 200,000 Spanish troops in Cuba, the Spanish command did not contest the landing). Spanish resistance was further handicapped by a sense of impending doom: even before American forces had left for Cuba, the Spanish Atlantic fleet had been bottled up in Santiago harbor by American naval forces.

The Americans pushed toward Santiago, burdened by their heavy uniforms, their rations of "embalmed beef" (spoiled meat), and their outmoded cartridges which emitted a puff of white

During the Spanish-American War, an enterprising newspaper artist, Charles J. Post, joined the New York National Guard so that he could go to Cuba in 1898 to record combat scenes in vivid water colors. Above, he shows members of his regiment eating a meal amidst their frequently flooded and mosquito-ridden tents. He also captured a rather uncharacteristically pensive Colonel Roosevelt in his rumpled army khakis (right), and the rushing of a gatling gun to relieve beleaguered Rough Riders at San Juan Hill (below).

smoke with each shot, marking a man's position. On July 1, American forces stormed San Juan Hill overlooking Santiago. After two days of grim and desperate fighting against determined Spanish resistance, the Americans won the hill. Vulnerable now to American artillery, the blockaded Spanish fleet tried to slip out of the harbor and was destroyed by an American fleet in four hours.

On July 17, Santiago surrendered, and a few days later, an American force occupied Puerto Rico. The quick Spanish surrender probably saved the American army in Cuba, which was critically weakened by heat, rains, lack of supplies, and by disease. By early August, more than 4,000 men were on the sick list.

Realities of war. The tendency of some historians to treat this war in comic-opera terms does injustice to the courage and suffering of the men who fought it. While the war made many heroes, like Theodore Roosevelt who was soon to be President, for most it was a grim and often tragic adventure. In terms of modern combat, American battle losses were small (400 men killed); however, around 500 died of malaria, dysentery, and yellow fever, and countless others were permanently disabled. A surgeon reported: "The men left in excellent spirits. Most of them return as mere shadows of their former selves. . . . Many of them are wrecks for life, others are candidates for a premature grave. . . ."

Many troops never made it to Cuba. They were left behind in training camps, for the most part the neglected victims of the disease that raged through these camps. As historian Frank Freidel points out in *The Splendid Little War* (1958), there was little glory for these men, or for the "courageous Negro troops . . . [who] had suffered so much, yet had received so little credit."

At the outset of the war, thousands of blacks had volunteered, and the regular army had four black units, all of which saw action in Cuba. Among those who stormed San Juan Hill was a black unit, the Tenth Cavalry. Of their courage, an officer later wrote, "I never saw braver men anywhere. Some of those who rushed up the hill will live in my memory forever." Although white soldiers could praise the courage of black troops, black soldiers were still not considered equal. They were confined to segregated units—on the ships to Cuba, black units were separated from others and were given the lowliest quarters. And black soldiers were commanded mainly by white officers. The black soldier's position in the army had changed little since the Civil War.

In the temporary settlement that ended the war, Spain evacuated Cuba and ceded Puerto Rico and the island of Guam (the fate of the Philippines was to be settled at the formal peace conference). The ten-week war had given the United States a new empire and in addition was immensely satisfying to the American mood. Theodore Roosevelt called it a "bully fight," and his good friend John Hay, soon to be secretary of state, wrote to Roosevelt: "It has been a splendid little war; begun with the highest motives, carried on with magnificent intelligence and spirit, favored by that fortune which loves the brave." Today Hay's statement seems unbelievably callous; but in terms of the prevailing American attitudes of supreme self-confidence, idealism, expansionism, and national destiny, it is understandable.

4 The United States Expands In The Far East

1. Why did the United States annex the Philippines? Do you think its reasons for annexation were justified?

2. What were some of the consequences of the annexation of the Philippines? Do you think annexation was a wise move for the United States to make?

3. What was the intent of American foreign policy in the Far East? How successful was that policy from 1891 to 1912? How effective were the Open Door notes?

4. What were the causes of friction between the United States and Japan? To what extent was Japan's displeasure justified?

The most perplexing question for the American commissioners at the peace conference that met in Paris was what to do about the Philippines, now that they were free from Spanish rule. At first, many felt that the Filipinos should be given their independence. But gradually opinion began to favor taking over the islands.

Debate over the Philippines. For businessmen, the Philippines were a stepping-stone to the Great China Market, a tantalizing prospect for them. Protestant missionary groups saw an opportunity to carry the gospel to the islands. Others felt that it was simply the duty and destiny of the white man to shoulder the responsibility of governing nonwhites. Poet Rudyard Kipling urged them in verse to "take up the White Man's burden," even though the rewards would be few and the criticism bitter. Kipling sent an advance copy of the poem to Theodore Roosevelt, who noted that it was "rather poor poetry but good sense from the expansionist standpoint."

President McKinley was so keenly responsive to the undercurrents of public opinion that the changes in his attitude reflect the evolution in general opinion. At first he thought that the United States should have just a coaling station in the Philippines, or at most the main island of Luzon. But he was sensitive to the commercial possibilities and alarmed that another power might take the islands.

From the response to a series of "trial balloon" speeches in the fall of 1898, he concluded that Americans liked the idea of empire. True to his devout Methodist faith, the President resorted to prayer for the final decision. The answer came to him late one night this way:

(1) that we could not give them back to Spain—that would be cowardly and dishonorable; (2) that we could not turn them over to France or Germany—our commercial rivals in the Orient—that would be bad business and discreditable; (3) that we could not leave them to themselves—they were unfit for self-government—and they would soon have anarchy and misrule over there worse than Spain's was; and (4) that there was nothing left for us to do but to take them all, and to educate the Filipinos, and uplift and civilize and Christianize them, and by God's grace do the very best we could by them, as our fellow-men for whom Christ also died. And then I went to bed, and went to sleep and slept soundly.

The statement contains all the elements of American imperialistic sentiment: a sense of moral duty, economic expansion, military rivalry, a feeling of racial superiority, and divine mission.

Reluctantly Spain agreed to give up the Philippines for $20 million. When the treaty went to the Senate for ratification, discussions there broadened into one of the great debates in American history. The anti-imperialist group crossed party lines and included such prominent Americans as former President Cleveland, William Jennings Bryan, Andrew Carnegie, Samuel Gompers, college presidents, writers and publishers, and many others. They believed that taking control of alien people was a tragic departure in American foreign policy.

Their arguments rested on morality and historic American principles. A nation founded on the idea that government exists by the consent of the governed did not have the right to subjugate 7 million Filipinos who most emphatically did not consent. Another concern was expressed by the liberal publisher E. L. Godkin when he said, "The question is what effect the imperial policy will have upon ourselves."

The imperialists, who included Theodore Roosevelt, Senators Henry Cabot Lodge, and Albert Beveridge, also used moral arguments. They believed that a major power should not shirk its responsibilities toward weaker peoples. "God has made us," said Senator Beveridge, "the trustees of the civilization of the world. . . . He has made us the master organizers . . . This is the divine mission of America. . . ."

They used practical arguments as well. If the United States did not take the islands, some other power (probably Germany) would. In addition, the Philippines would provide an important Pacific base from which the United States could develop an enormous trade with the Orient. To many imperialists, the clearer the commercial possibilities became, the less capable the Filipinos seemed of governing themselves. As the *St. Louis Post-Dispatch* later observed, "The Filipino is treacherous and deceitful. Besides, we want his country." In the end the treaty was confirmed, by a margin of two votes, and the Philippine Islands were taken.

The Filipinos, who had played an important role in the American capture of Manila and who

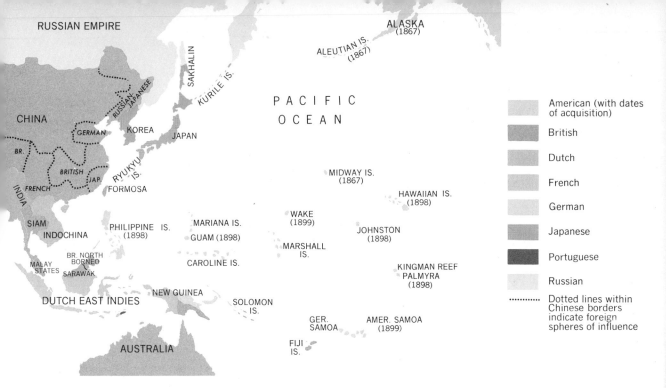

RUSSIAN EMPIRE

ALASKA
(1867)

ALEUTIAN IS.
(1867)

SAKHALIN

KURILE IS.

PACIFIC
OCEAN

CHINA

RUSSIAN-JAPANESE

GERMAN

KOREA

JAPAN

BR.

BRITISH

JAP.

RYUKYU
IS.

FORMOSA

FRENCH

INDIA

MIDWAY IS.
(1867)

HAWAIIAN IS.
(1898)

SIAM

INDOCHINA

PHILIPPINE IS.
(1898)

MARIANA IS.

GUAM (1898)

WAKE
(1899)

JOHNSTON
(1898)

MARSHALL
IS.

MALAY
STATES

BR. NORTH
BORNEO

SARAWAK

CAROLINE IS.

KINGMAN REEF
PALMYRA
(1898)

DUTCH EAST INDIES

NEW GUINEA

SOLOMON
IS.

GER.
SAMOA

AMER. SAMOA
(1899)

AUSTRALIA

FIJI
IS.

American (with dates
of acquisition)

British

Dutch

French

German

Japanese

Portuguese

Russian

Dotted lines within
Chinese borders
indicate foreign
spheres of influence

FOREIGN INTERESTS IN THE FAR EAST, 1898–1914

had been led to believe that they would be independent, had no intention of giving up without a fight. On the eve of the Senate vote on the treaty, the Filipino leader, Emilio Aguinaldo, who had formed his own government, launched a major insurrection. Seventy thousand American troops and $600 million were required to fight the Filipino rebellion, which was suppressed after nearly three years of brutal guerrilla warfare. Americans were shocked by reports that soldiers murdered and tortured Filipino prisoners and set up concentration camps as bad as Butcher Weyler's. A war that had begun to end tyranny in Cuba ended with the suppression of an alien people.

Under the leadership of William Howard Taft, governor of the islands, order was restored, and an active effort was made to include Filipinos in the government. A public school system was created, and general living conditions were improved. But these practical benefits of American control did not give Filipinos their independence, a demand which grew louder every year. Providing all these services proved more expensive than

anyone had anticipated, especially since the hopes for the Oriental market were not fulfilled. It soon became evident that the Philippines could not be defended against a major military attack. Within a few years, Theodore Roosevelt was ruefully describing the Philippines as "our Achilles' heel in the Pacific."

Opening the door in China. The Philippines were acquired at a time when the great powers were dividing China into *spheres of influence,* areas in which each nation gained special trading privileges. China's weakness had been made obvious by the disastrous Sino-Japanese War of 1894–95, and in the next few years France, Japan, Russia, and Germany scrambled for mining, railroad, and trade concessions. Britain, with 80 percent of the China trade already, feared that it might be excluded in these spheres, and in 1898 Britain tentatively inquired if the United States would join it in supporting an Open Door policy of equal trading rights for all.

Although the concept was British in origin, it suited American interests as well. It was in fact consistent with traditional American policy in the

477

THE TUG OF WAR IN THE FAR EAST

When it appeared that Russia, Germany, and France were going to partition China, the governments of Great Britain, the United States, and Japan sought to stop them. Above, *Puck* shows the tug of war that ensued in 1898, as the latter three nations tried to pull the would-be partitioners into adherence to an Open-Door Policy, in which all interested parties would share equal access to Chinese markets. Russia and Japan finally fought over conflicting interests in the Far East, but a proud Theodore Roosevelt (below left) was able to arrange a peace treaty between them. The United States, however, could not keep itself out of war in the Far East, as the battle picture below right shows. In it, in the first battle of the Filipino insurrection, native troops retreat before advancing Americans.

Far East, which had always been based on equality of trade. In 1899, Secretary of State John Hay sent notes to the German, British, Russian, French, Italian, and Japanese governments asking them to guarantee that within their respective spheres all nations would have equal trading rights. The replies were generally approving, but with reservations. Nevertheless, Hay publicly announced that the powers had given final approval.

In 1900, antiforeign feeling in China erupted in violence, as bands of Chinese, known in the West as Boxers, attacked foreigners. An international force (including American troops) was quickly dispatched to quell the rebellion. The governments showed no such haste in withdrawing their troops, and Hay was particularly concerned by Russian troops in Manchuria. He feared that the presence of armed soldiers in China would make it easy for the powers to partition the country. He therefore sent a second Open Door Note stating that it was the policy of the United States to "preserve Chinese territorial and administrative entity" and to safeguard equality of trade "with all parts of the Chinese Empire." The second Open Door Note broadened an economic concept into a political one, because Hay felt that partition would result in the exclusion of American business interests.

Hay's Open Door Notes were hailed at the time as a brilliant stroke of diplomacy which curbed the greed of the powers and protected Chinese sovereignty. Historians have long pointed out, however, that the Open Door was completely unrealistic and pretentiously moralistic because the United States did not have the means to enforce it. Hay himself said that "The talk . . . about 'our pre-eminent moral position giving us authority to dictate to the world' is mere flapdoodle." The fact that the European powers and Japan accepted the principle of Chinese sovereignty was due less to the influence of the Open Door policy than that the powers were not willing to risk a war among themselves to take China.

Nevertheless, the Open Door policy was a fundamental statement of American economic expansion and represented the new Manifest Destiny in action. If it is understood that the bedrock American interest was the spread of its great industrial power, and that preserving Chinese sovereignty was only a means to that end, then the Open Door policy stands as an important expression of twentieth-century American industrial expansion.

American-Japanese hostility. In areas of the Orient other than China, the Open Door gradually began to close. When Roosevelt became President, he was confronted with the expansionist designs of Russia and Japan, both of which wanted to extend their influence in Manchuria and Korea. Roosevelt was tempted to use force when Russia threatened to close Manchuria to American trade, but he believed that the American people would not support such a policy. Then in 1904, in a move to force Russian withdrawal from Manchuria, the Japanese attacked the Russian fleet in the Pacific. Japan won surprising victories in the Russo-Japanese War, but it was not prepared for a long conflict. In May 1905, Japan asked Roosevelt to mediate a peace between the two countries.

Although the President won the Nobel Peace Prize in 1906 for his efforts, both Japan and Russia were unhappy with the settlement. Japan gained a dominant position in Korea and southern Manchuria, but Japan resented losing the large indemnity it had requested and blamed Roosevelt for it. The Russians were embittered by what they regarded as Roosevelt's pro-Japanese sympathies. In fact, Roosevelt and much of the American public were clearly on Japan's side.

But the rise of a strong Japan posed problems, particularly in regard to the defense of the Philippines. To protect the islands, the United States, in 1905, concluded an informal agreement with Japan, the Taft-Katsura "memorandum." According to its terms, Japan renounced any aggressive intentions toward the Philippines in return for American recognition of Japan's complete control over Korea.

Japanese-American relations were seriously aggravated during this time by a growing hostility toward the Japanese on the West Coast. Japanese immigrants had been coming to the United States since the 1880's and prejudice against them had existed for years on the West Coast. Following the Russo-Japanese War, thousands of Japanese

A JAPANESE BOY IN AMERICA

Markino Yoshio came to the United States as a young boy around the turn of the century to work and study art in San Francisco. He wrote of his attempts to work and to go to school and of the prejudice he encountered:

"By the experiences day after day, I had learnt that there was nothing but domestic work left for my livelihood, because the Californians didn't recognize us as the humans and they wouldn't accept any of our brain work. I thought, 'How dreadful that is!' But I had to go through with it, for my last nickel was gone within a week and I had to get any work immediately. I decided myself that as long as I did domestic work I should persevere everything in silence. . . .

"In that way I attended to the Art School for eleven or twelve months with many intervals. . . . But as the time was passing on my suits were getting into rags, my boots worn out, and my shirts and hat getting too old to wear. Alas, I had to give up my school lessons. So I did all sorts of day-works instead of going to the school. . . . With the money I got by washing windows and scraping the steps for several months, I bought a painting box, some tubes of oil-paints, and brushes. . . . One day I went to Land's End (near Cliff House) with all my provisions to learn the sketching. Some rough boys came and destroyed all my materials. It was such a disheartening thing for me. . . .

"Once while I was passing the spare ground on the corner of Fillmore Street and Geary Street, some big fellow threw a large stone at me. It struck my head. My hat was broken and my head got hurt. I never took any notice, but walked on.

"A young lady was walking on the opposite side. She came to me and said, 'Why don't you get a policeman to prison him?'

"I said, 'No, ma'am. It is quite useless, ma'am. I tried once or twice before, but police don't take any notice of us Japanese.'

"She expressed her deep sorrow and said she would speak to her father about that."

poured into California, and Californians became fearful of the "yellow peril," as some jingoist newspapers phrased it.

In 1906 the San Francisco School Board ruled that all Oriental students must attend segregated schools. Roosevelt was able to persuade the board to change its policy in return for a promise to restrict Japanese immigration. In carrying out his end of the bargain, he negotiated a gentlemen's agreement with Japan (1907–08) in which the Japanese government agreed to restrict the emigration of unskilled laborers to the United States. The Japanese, whose national pride had swelled with their victory over Russia, were deeply resentful.

During this crisis, American sympathy for Japan changed to an attitude of fear and suspicion, and there was some talk of war in both countries. Partly as a show of force and partly to convince Congress to support his naval buildup program, Roosevelt sent the navy on a fourteen-month, 45,000-mile trip around the world. The Japanese people greeted the fleet, the second most powerful in the world by now, with great excitement and friendliness. Roosevelt later concluded that American troubles with Japan vanished "like magic." Since it is unlikely that Roosevelt would have risked the destruction of his fleet by the Japanese, it is probable that he emphasized Japanese belligerency at home to gain the new ships he wanted.

To further ease Japanese-American relations, the Root-Takahira agreement was concluded in 1908. Both countries agreed to respect each other's territorial possessions in the Pacific and to uphold the Open Door in China. In Manchuria, a balance of sorts existed between Russia and Japan, but they both wished to exclude other nations from economic penetration. There was little the United States could do to alter this situation but fight, and this it was both unwilling and unprepared to do.

Although the Open Door remained effective in China, the China market had not immediately developed as expected. Korea and Manchuria were closed. The Philippines, so eagerly sought and the subject of such controversy, had proved more of a burden than an advantage. The United States had made few friends in the Pacific, but it had made some bitter enemies.

5 The Caribbean Comes Under United States Control

1. What was the Roosevelt Corollary? Do you think the United States was justified in imposing the Roosevelt Corollary on Latin America?

2. How significant was a canal to American interests in the Caribbean? What were the advantages and disadvantages of a canal through Panama?

3. Do you think Theodore Roosevelt followed a proper course of action in the series of events leading up to the American acquisition of the Panama Canal Zone?

4. What were the political and judicial procedures established in the American territories? Do you think they were consistent with traditional American values and institutions?

American expansion in the Caribbean was far more extensive than in the Orient, not only because the Caribbean was closer, but also because the United States had already established its preeminence in the area. In Cuba, where the American army had ruled since 1898, the people were impatient for complete independence. For both economic and strategic reasons, the United States wanted to retain some control.

Both countries finally agreed to a compromise settlement. According to the Platt Amendment of 1901, Cuba was made a virtual protectorate of the United States, which was given the right to intervene to protect Cuban independence and was permitted to establish naval bases (later, Guantanamo was the principal one). Although Cubans chafed at the provisions of the Platt Amendment, they had little choice but to accept it. Troops were withdrawn in 1902, but American soldiers were sent to Cuba on several occasions to put down disorders. As one journalist quipped, "Necessity is the mother of in(ter)vention."

The Roosevelt Corollary. Roosevelt was fond of quoting the old African proverb "Speak softly and carry a big stick." The "big stick" in the Caribbean was American power, demonstrated in a second crisis in Venezuela in 1902. Venezuela had fallen into debt to both Britain and Germany, and when the two powers began to use force to collect, American public opinion turned strongly against them, particularly against the aggressive Germans. The *New York American* said it was most infuriating to see "an American republic [Venezuela] kicked and cuffed by a brace of European monarchies."

In the face of such strong sentiment, Germany and Britain agreed to arbitrate, and the crisis ended in 1903. In an effort to quiet any remaining resentment, Britain's prime minister made a most flattering suggestion:

I believe it would be a great gain to civilization if the United States of America were more actively to interest themselves in making arrangements by which these constantly recurring dificulties between European powers and certain States in South America could be avoided.

Whether influenced by this advice or not, Roosevelt followed it precisely in 1904 in a similar crisis in the Dominican Republic, whose government was unable to pay its debts to foreign powers. When these powers threatened to use force to collect their debts, Roosevelt concluded that if the United States could not allow foreign intervention (the Monroe Doctrine), it had a moral obligation to compel what he called the "wretched republics" to pay their bills. The United States would be forced, he told Congress in 1904, to the "exercise of an international police power," however reluctantly it might view the task. In the case of the Dominican Republic, the United States took over the customs system, the primary source of income, and set aside a large portion of the revenue to pay off the debts.

This new interpretation of the Monroe Doctrine, called the Roosevelt Corollary, did not seek annexation. Rather the policy was designed to prevent *foreign* interference in Latin American affairs by giving the United States the right to interfere in situations as Washington saw fit. The Roosevelt Corollary created such resentment among Latin Americans and made American interference in Latin domestic affairs such a burdensome responsibility that the corollary was officially repudiated by the State Department, but not until twenty-five years later.

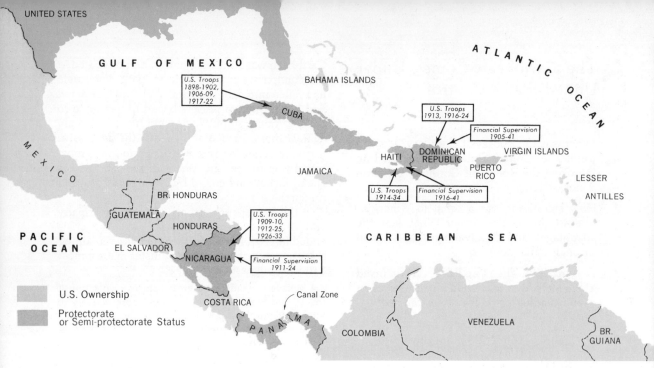

U.S. Ownership

Protectorate
or Semi-protectorate Status

UNITED STATES INTERESTS IN THE CARIBBEAN, 1898–1917

Panama and the Canal. America had a vital interest in the Caribbean for obvious economic, political, and strategic reasons. But there was another, perhaps even more important, reason. The Spanish-American War, America's growing naval power, and the expanding interests in the Pacific had renewed interest in the idea of a canal through Central America linking the Atlantic and Pacific oceans. The keystone of American policy in the Caribbean, therefore, was retaining control of the canal.

Such a canal had been proposed many times before, but now it seemed not only more important but also possible. Several obstacles had to be overcome. The first was a diplomatic hurdle. Britain, too, had been interested in a canal project and in 1850 had agreed to the Clayton-Bulwer Treaty (page 207). However, through a series of treaties negotiated after the Spanish-American War, Britain withdrew its interests in a canal, thus recognizing the United States' exclusive position in the area.

The next obstacle was the location of the canal. There were two possible routes, one through Nicaragua and one through the Isthmus of Panama, where a private French company had begun

work in the 1880's. Although the company had completed 40 percent of the work, the project fell victim to bankruptcy and disease. A new Panama Canal Company was formed out of its ruins, and it asked $109 million for its holdings.

Congress investigated both routes, and found that the Panama route was shorter, would take less time for passage through the canal, and would be less expensive to maintain. Many congressmen, however, considered the company's price inflated and favored the Nicaraguan route instead.

Fearful of losing everything, the Panama Canal Company, led by its chief engineer Philippe Bunau-Varilla, lowered its price, lobbied feverishly in Congress, and contributed to the Republican campaign fund. Then, in May 1902, a volcano erupted in Nicaragua. Bunau-Varilla shrewdly distributed to every congressman and senator an official Nicaraguan postage stamp picturing the active volcano. Despite frantic Nicaraguan denials that Nicaragua was unsafe, the maneuver worked. In 1902, Congress agreed to the Panama route at a price of $40 million for the company's holdings.

Another hurdle still remained. Panama belonged to the Republic of Colombia, and the Panama Canal Company needed Colombia's permission to sell its concessions. The United States negotiated a treaty with Colombia in 1903, but the Colombian government delayed ratification, ostensibly because the treaty was too great an infringement on its sovereignty. Actually the company's charter was due to expire within a year, and its holdings would have reverted to Colombia.

This delay, and Colombia's eventual rejection of the treaty, infuriated Roosevelt. Angrily he told John Hay: "I do not think that a lot of obstructionists should be allowed permanently to bar one of the future highways of civilization!" Panama was also disturbed by the prospect of losing the expected commercial advantages of a canal. The only way out seemed to be for Panama to secede from Colombia, a possibility that occurred to the Panamanians, to Bunau-Varilla, and to Roosevelt himself.

An uprising was planned, not in Panama, but in New York City, with Bunau-Varilla the chief organizer of a group of Panamian leaders and American army officers. Although Roosevelt was certainly not involved in the details of the plot, neither was he taken completely by surprise. Bunau-Varilla later recalled an interview he had with the President:

I . . . asked him point blank if, when the revolt broke out, an American warship would be sent to Panama to "protect American lives and interests." The President just looked at me; he said nothing. Of course, a President of the United States could not give such a commitment, especially to a foreigner and private citizen like me. But his look was enough for me. I took the gamble.

Roosevelt later gave his version of the meeting:

He was a very able fellow, and it was his business to find out what he thought our Government would do. I have no doubt that he was able to make a very accurate guess and to advise his people accordingly. In fact he would have been a very dull man had he been unable to make such a guess.

On November 2, 1903, a United States battleship arrived at Colon, Panama, and the next day the short and bloodless uprising broke out. United States naval forces prevented Colombian troops from restoring order, claiming that the troops were a threat to "free transit" of the isthmus. Only three days after the revolt, the United States recognized the newly independent nation and in the same month worked out a treaty with its government. Panama was given $10 million outright and $250,000 annually in return for a perpetual lease to a ten-mile-wide canal zone. When Roosevelt was severely criticized at home for America's role in the affair, he declared that his government had received a "mandate from civilization" to press forward with the canal.

Colombia was understandably bitter about American interference in its domestic affairs, and in 1904 it presented to the United States a statement of its grievances. As long as Roosevelt was alive, his friends were able to prevent Senate confirmation of a treaty of reparations and regret. Finally, in 1921, the United States paid Colombia $25 million in reparations. The regrets were omitted.

The canal itself opened in August 1914, ten years after construction started. Its importance to the United States and to world trade bore out Roosevelt's predictions. The circumstances of its acquisition remain an unsavory episode in American diplomatic history.

Dollar diplomacy under Taft. Taft believed that the government of a powerful industrial nation ought to assist in promoting business expansion. He and his secretary of state, Philander C. Knox, encouraged American bankers and businessmen to invest in Latin America and the Far East. The policy of the United States, said Taft, would be to "substitute dollars for bullets."

Taft's dollar diplomacy was most clearly exemplified in Nicaragua. That country's proximity to the Panama Canal made involvement there a matter of security as well as investment. In 1910, Nicaragua requested financial assistance from the United States, and with government encouragement, American bankers took over control of that country's financial affairs. When a rebellion two years later jeopardized American interests, the marines were sent to crush the revolt. During Taft's administrations, similar military interventions took place in Honduras and Haiti. It appeared that bullets were needed to support the dollars.

Wilson's Caribbean policies. Woodrow Wilson and his secretary of state, William Jennings Bryan, not only continued the previous

Certainly one of the greatest engineering feats of all times was the construction of the Panama Canal. Dynamite, air drills (above), steam shovels, dredges, and the labor of thousands of men over ten years' time joined together to make possible the linking of the Atlantic and Pacific Oceans in 1914 (below).

policies, but also intervened on a larger scale than had been contemplated by Roosevelt and Taft. The United States continued to dominate Nicaragua's financial system and also intervened in the Dominican Republic, sending in marines and establishing a military government. In Haiti, conditions were so chaotic that the United States established a tighter military and political control there than anywhere else; in the process, nearly two thousand Haitians were killed.

Having inherited a policy designed to protect the Panama Canal at all costs, Wilson found himself deeper and deeper in the tangled affairs of Latin America. Even if he had been able to extricate the United States, he might not have done so, for he believed firmly that the well-being of the Caribbean depended on American supremacy. Intervention was rationalized as a neighborly gesture from a strong power to a weak one.

Governing the new areas. Governmental arrangements had to be devised for the new areas under direct American control, whether in the Caribbean or the Pacific. The Foraker Act of 1900 gave Puerto Rico a governor appointed by the United States, an appointed upper house, and a popularly elected lower house. Observers were quick to point out that this plan was similar to the one by which Britain had ruled the American colonies. Hawaii became a territory with a governor and a territorial legislature. Guam and Samoa were put under the jurisdiction of the Navy Department.

The new American empire raised a perplexing Constitutional question. Did the Constitution follow the flag? That is, did the people living in the new possessions have the same rights as Americans living in the states? In several complex and rather confusing decisions, called the *Insular Cases* (1901–22), the Supreme Court held that there were two kinds of colonies—incorporated and unincorporated. The incorporated possessions (Hawaii and Alaska) were assumed to be a part of the United States at the time of their acquisition. They were eligible for eventual statehood and their citizens would enjoy all the rights guaranteed in the Constitution. Guam, Puerto Rico, Samoa, and the Philippines were unincorporated and not eligible for statehood. People in these possessions would enjoy life, liberty, and due process of law, but not certain procedural rights such as trial by jury. In these places, as John Hay put it, "The Constitution follows the flag but never catches up with it."

◼ CONCLUSION

The foreign policy of the United States from the mid-1890's to 1917 revealed the country's new status as a world power and its confusion about how to play the role. Reluctant to become involved in the affairs of other countries and at the same time irresistibly drawn toward political vacuums when they occurred in the Pacific and the Caribbean, political leaders exercised unprecedented powers. They did so for many reasons, and their policies were far from consistent. The underlying reasons were nearly always economic, and in some cases, strategic or political. They were formulated, however, in moral terms. It was right for the United States to intervene, it was said, because it would ultimately benefit the weaker power.

It is true that in many cases United States rule brought greater stability and internal improvements. The eradication of yellow fever in Cuba and the transformation of the Canal Zone from a disease-ridden pesthole into a community of healthy workers are but two of the more spectacular examples. Nevertheless, intervention left a legacy of bitterness among the people; and schools, roads, and telegraph lines were no substitute for freedom. Raymond Robins, a Progressive reformer, in discussing Wilson, pointed out the basic dilemma in American diplomacy:

He was willing to do anything for people except get off their backs and let them live their own lives ... He never seemed to understand there's a big difference between trying to save people and trying to help them. With luck you can help 'em—but they always save themselves.

When the War with Spain broke out, the United States had already lost its youth. By the beginning of Wilson's administration, it had lost its innocent faith in the glories of empire. But it was still unprepared for the traumatic experience that was just over the horizon—a war in Europe that threatened democracy everywhere.

■ QUESTIONS

1. Why did America become concerned with foreign affairs at the end of the nineteenth century?

2. What are the similarities and differences between American expansion at the end of the nineteenth century and the earlier period of Manifest Destiny? What were the basic policies in each case? How were these policies justified?

3. To what extent is racism evident in the formulation of American foreign policy? Explain.

4. Was it consistent for Americans to be concerned over reform within the United States at the same time the country was embarking upon an imperialistic policy? Explain your answer.

5. Was American foreign policy successful during the period from 1890 to 1916? Explain your answer. What did the United States gain and what were the problems which resulted from overseas expansion?

6. Were there any reasonable alternatives to the direction taken in the American conduct of foreign affairs? Was there a better alternative than involvement in the Spanish-American War? than annexation of the Philippines? than the landing of marines in the Caribbean republics? Explain your answers.

7. What is the most appropriate form of government for American territories? Explain your answer.

8. When, if ever, is a nation justified in sending troops to fight within the borders of another country? Justify your answer.

■ BIBLIOGRAPHY

BEMIS, SAMUEL FLAGG, *A Diplomatic History of the United States*, 5th ed., Holt, Rinehart & Winston. This is a good book for the student to have for reference on diplomatic questions. As a text it is well-written and generally complete in its coverage.

DULLES, FOSTER RHEA, *Prelude to World Power: American Diplomatic History, 1860–1900*, Macmillan. The major themes in late nineteenth-century diplomatic history are examined in this book including British-American relations, American interest in the Caribbean, the rise of the new navy, and particularly American relations with Japan and the Far East. It is a standard work by an excellent historian. The student who appreciates this book may also consult Dulles's work on the twentieth century.

KENNAN, GEORGE F., *American Diplomacy 1900–1950*, New American Library (Mentor Books). This is an excellent, brief, provocative interpretation of American foreign affairs in the twentieth century. The author has served as an American diplomat and written numerous books on foreign affairs. The book is good on the Spanish-American War and the Open Door policy, but its primary value is in raising basic issues which continually face American decision makers.

FREIDEL, FRANK, *The Splendid Little War*, Dell. The book relies heavily upon the comments of participants and reporters which are woven neatly into the narrative. It is a brief, but excellent accounting of the bloody, dirty, heroic interruption known as the Spanish-American War.

BEALE, HOWARD K., *Theodore Roosevelt and the Rise of America to World Power*, Collier. Beale's book is generally favorable to Roosevelt who saw an expanding role for the United States in world affairs. He saw the implications of international rivalries and the importance of the Far East. This is an excellent book for background on the growing international involvement of the United States.

Americans And World War I

To most Europeans in 1914, the United States was a puzzle. Here was a huge and populous nation with immense resources and growing industrial might. Like Russia, Europe's giant to the east, the United States was tied to Europe and yet not really European. Ever since the United States had acquired a coaling station at Pago Pago in 1878, American expansionist ambitions had brought it into frequent conflict with European nations. Only in 1898, however, did one of those conflicts produce war—and in that war, the anopheles mosquito proved more deadly than either the Spanish or the American army. How the makers of American foreign policy would react to a general European war was anyone's guess.

To most Americans in 1914, Europe was a mixture of elements. Many Americans, notably educated northeasterners, strongly admired European literature, art, music, and scholarship. Many others distrusted Europe as the seat of old and pointless squabbles and petty greeds. The surge of European immigration to the United States since the 1880's had deepened this distrust. Millions of non-English-speaking immigrants, crowded into city slums and patronized by machine politicians, seemed to threaten what many believed to be the American way of life. This distrust of Europe and suspicion of the new immigrants made Americans less concerned than ever with European politics.

Despite three thousand miles of ocean and the general American distaste for European quarrels, the United States found itself fighting for the first time in a European land war. World War I, bloodier than any previous war in human history, began in 1914. Yet it was not until 1917 that the United States entered the war. The complex and agonizing decision to intervene marked a basic shift in American foreign policy. And participating in the war significantly changed the American economy, society, and thought. As you read about the United States and World War I, keep these questions in mind:

1. How and why did the United States get into the war?
2. How did the war affect American society?
3. What was the American experience in Europe?
4. How did the war affect American foreign policy?

487

1 The United States Is Drawn Into War

1. What explanations have been suggested for America's entry into World War I?

2. Why was American neutrality difficult to maintain?

3. In what ways was American public opinion divided on the issue of the war prior to the United States entry?

Several of Shakespeare's tragedies include a subplot echoing the central tragedy. If World War I and its aftermath was the central tragedy for American foreign policy during the Wilson era, then Mexico provided the subplot. Most of Mexico's land was owned by a few rich landowners; most of its industry and even public utilities were owned by rich American investors. The vast majority of Mexicans were peasants who were scarcely freer than serfs.

Wilson sympathized with Mexico's difficulties, and, when a reform regime was overthrown by a military dictator, he thought he saw his chance to help. Wilson refused to recognize what he called "a government of butchers." Well-meaning but often self-righteous, Wilson said privately that he would "teach the South American republics to elect good men."

The Mexican intervention. In intervening in Mexico, Wilson, in effect, wanted to extend his New Freedom to Mexico—to promote elective democracy and restrain the political power of big business. Orderly development would also make a good climate for those American businessmen who refrained from trying to run Mexican politics. Wilson withstood the demands for full-scale war made by some Americans with large Mexican holdings and by the jingoist segment of the press. Instead, from 1913 to 1916, he doggedly tried to help Mexico achieve reform without revolution.

His efforts, however, were inept. The opponents to the dictator, led by a proud patriot named Venustiano Carranza, wanted to win their revolution without outside help. In an atmosphere of intrigue and confusion, they eventually did so, but not before Wilson twice sent troops into Mexico, almost provoking full-scale war.

Wilson unquestionably helped bring Carranza to power and thereby helped the revolution. But, with his exercise in missionary diplomacy, he caused years of Mexican resentment toward its neighbor north of the border. Wilson never seemed to understand that revolution for Mexico meant nationalism as well as reform.

The beginning of war in Europe. While Wilson was pursuing his adventures in Mexico, a far more complicated and terrible crisis exploded in Europe. On the surface, Europe was prosperous and peaceful in the first years of the twentieth century. Underneath, however, lay a tangle of rivalries and alliances. Germany, increasingly controlled by saber-rattling officers, sought to challenge British naval supremacy. France and Germany, traditional enemies, sought to keep each other from gaining supremacy on the European continent. And all three competed for colonies and trade concessions in Africa and Asia.

Even more dangerous than these rivalries was the web of alliances they produced. Fearing most of all the possibility of being alone without allies, the major European nations divided into two alliances: France, Great Britain, and Russia formed one, and Germany and Austria-Hungary dominated the other. Each nation also arranged separate alliances with smaller nations. Although the two major alliances were formed for the sake of security, their very basis threatened security.

The existence of each alliance depended on the willingness of all its members to come to the aid of any one member. Thus a dispute between any two nations could soon involve both alliances. And that is exactly what happened. On June 28, 1914, a young Serbian assassinated the heir to the Austro-Hungarian throne. Egged on by Germany, Austria-Hungary decided to take the opportunity to crush its annoying neighbor. Russia, in turn, lumbered to the aid of Serbia, a fellow Slavic nation.

Within six weeks, the system of alliances drew most of Europe into war. The German army, after cutting across neutral Belgium, was halted scarcely twenty miles from Paris in September 1914.

Then a hideous and desperate stalemate set in. Both armies spread barbed wire, set up machine guns, and dug in, beginning four deadly years of trench warfare. Winston Churchill later described it in one magnificent rolling sentence:

Governments and individuals conformed to the rhythm of the tragedy, swayed and staggered forward in helpless violence, slaughtering and squandering on ever-increasing scales, till injuries were wrought to the structure of human society which a century will not efface, and which may conceivably prove fatal to the present civilization.

American neutrality. In August 1914, Wilson asked the American people to "be impartial in thought as well as in action." Despite those words, not even Wilson could remain neutral in thought, let alone action. Like most Americans, Wilson looked upon Britain as the mother country. Since Lafayette, France had enjoyed American goodwill. And Germany, with its militarist government and ruthless invasion of neutral Belgium, seemed directly opposed to American ideals. Still, few favored giving up neutrality to help the Allies, as Great Britain, France, and Russia came to be called.

Many of those who favored more direct help to the Allies were businessmen, educators, and students in the northeast. Most were Republicans or Progressives who favored moderate reform. Britain seemed to represent all that was best and orderly. A few feared that a German victory, by sweeping the British navy from the seas, might threaten the United States. The ranks of this pro-British group included former Presidents Roosevelt and Taft, as well as passionate young men who went to war by joining one of the Allied armed forces.

Other Americans opposed an Allied victory. Millions of hard-working, well-respected German-Americans saw no conflict between American patriotism and rooting for the Central Powers—Germany and Austria-Hungary. Nor did many Irish-Americans who opposed Great Britain because Britain had ruled Ireland for centuries. Few German- or Irish-Americans expected the United States to fight the Allies. They did, however, hope to make the United States toe the line of neutrality as strictly as possible. They were joined in this desire by a large and varied group of peace advocates, some of them pacifists.

Western and southern Progressives supplied most of the peace advocates. Perhaps the most eminent was William Jennings Bryan, thrice unsuccessful candidate for President and Wilson's secretary of state. Like many leading Europeans as well as Americans, Bryan believed that international disputes could be settled by arbitration and mediation.

Bryan did his best to cool warlike feelings, and Roosevelt often did his best to inflame them, but the decisions in the end were Wilson's. In large part, Wilson's decisions revolved around the question of a neutral nation's trading rights. As Thomas Jefferson had shrewdly suggested in 1790, "The new world will fatten on the follies of the old."

Beginning in 1915, the Allies, far more dependent on imports than the Central Powers, flooded American businessmen with orders. These orders lifted the United States out of a serious recession and tied the American economy to Allied fortunes. At the same time, the British navy tried to enforce its blockade of the Central Powers by cutting off most American trade with Germany. The British, however, were careful not to be too outrageous in their violations of traditional freedom of the seas. They valued American friendship more than a total blockade, for they realized better than continental Europeans that American industry could eventually tip the balance in the war.

Submarine warfare. The German navy, in turn, tried to cut imports to Britain and France, especially from the United States. Its weapon was the submarine, which, because of its frail armor, had to strike without warning. Germany's civilian leaders tended to value American neutrality more than the blockade. Its military leadership, however, deeply frustrated by the stalemate on land, advocated submarine warfare against Allied merchant ships regardless of its effects on German-American relations.

In February 1915, Germany announced that its submarines would sink Allied ships approaching Britain. This threatened American trade, for most American exports to the Allies were carried on British ships. American passengers were threatened also, for ocean liners often carried munitions as well as travelers. On May 7, 1915, a German submarine struck the *Lusitania*, a British ocean liner, with a single torpedo. The *Lusitania* sank in eighteen minutes, carrying with it 1,198 people, including 128 Americans. The sinking jolted

American public opinion, turning it against Germany even more than had Germany's invasion of Belgium.

Wilson responded publicly by proclaiming in ringing tones: "There is such a thing as a man being too proud to fight. There is such a thing as a nation being so right that it does not need to convince others by force that it is right." Wilson protested strongly enough to Germany, however, to provoke Bryan's resignation. Bryan felt that Wilson should have protested Allied violations of international law just as vigorously.

Tension with Germany continued until May 1916, when Germany agreed, in what came to be called the *Sussex* pledge, not to sink merchant vessels without warning. Germany's military command, fond of calling the Foreign Office the *Idiotenhaus,* had been overruled—for the time being, at least. Civilian officials still had the ear of Kaiser Wilhelm II.

American preparedness. Before the *Sussex* pledge, Wilson had reacted to the crisis by strengthening the armed forces, a move long and furiously advocated by Roosevelt. Wilson still did not expect the United States to enter the war; he merely wanted it to hold a strong bargaining position when peace came. Strengthening the armed forces also gave Wilson a solid plank in his platform for the 1916 election. He shaped a second plank by shepherding through Congress a series of bills which, not by total coincidence, enacted most of the 1912 platform of the Progressive party, whose votes he needed to win. Wilson's third plank, which he personally neither used nor repudiated, was the slogan, "He kept us out of war."

Peace, preparedness, and progressivism—it was a tough platform to beat. The Republicans, seeking to win the votes of both preparedness advocates and German-Americans, ran a confused campaign. In a close vote, Wilson beat the Republican candidate, Supreme Court Justice Charles Evans Hughes.

Soon after the election, relations with Great Britain worsened. Drained by the war and exasperated by American neutrality, Britain tightened its blockade of Germany. Eager to cool Anglo-American relations, Germany took the opportunity to encourage the American mediation Wilson had often suggested. To the annoyance of the Allies, Wilson asked the two sides to state their peace terms. When each proposed terms not remotely acceptable to the other, Wilson spoke out on January 22, 1917, for "a peace without victory . . . a peace between equals." Many Americans thrilled to his words; to most Europeans, however, "peace without victory" seemed an exceedingly stingy reward for two and a half years of war.

The United States declares war. Germany, however, suddenly put an end to American neutrality. On January 31, Germany revoked the *Sussex* pledge and declared unrestricted submarine warfare. Its military leaders, winning the support of Kaiser Wilhelm, had coolly estimated that the blockade could choke the Allies before the American army could reach Europe.

In response, Wilson broke off diplomatic relations with Germany on February 3. Two more events quickened the crisis. On March 1, a clumsy German effort to form an alliance with Mexico in case of war was revealed; Mexico's sweetener was to be the recovery of Texas, New Mexico, and Arizona. Soon afterward, the Russians overthrew their czar in the March Revolution and established a provisional republic. As long as the czar ruled, it could be argued that the Allied ranks included a country as undemocratic as any of the Central Powers. With the czar overthrown, the Allied side became more attractive.

After weeks of anguish, Wilson called for a declaration of war on April 2, 1917. "The right is more precious than peace," he declared. "The world must be made safe for democracy." Thus Wilson adopted for the world the Progressive goal of creating an environment in which freedom and opportunity could flourish. Congress quickly passed the war resolution, despite the opposition of some Progressives (including Jeanette Rankin of Montana, the first congresswoman).

The Progressives—and a number of historians in the 1930's—charged that the United States went to war to defend American business and the American loans to the Allies. Certainly trade with the Allies affected German-American relations. Nonetheless, sentiment overwhelmingly favored the Allies to begin with. And, barring the complete withdrawal from trade which some peace advocates suggested, the United States had little choice but to oppose Germany.

"What Will You Give For Her?"

The Great Naval Triumph

While the Americans remained neutral from 1914 to 1917, segments of the press in the country built up anti-German feeling. Cartoons like those above played up German brutality in marching through neutral Belgium and in engaging in submarine warfare. Even so, other groups like the Woman's Peace Party of Girls below continued their efforts to keep the country out of war.

One leading adviser to Wilson—and a number of historians in the 1940's and '50's—believed that the United States went to war to keep Germany from dominating Europe and the colonial world, threatening American security. Although that may have been the result of American entry, there is little to suggest it was the cause.

Wilson himself probably provides the clearest key to American thought and action. He sympathized with the Allies and he favored democracy, but he led the nation to war over the issues of freedom of the seas and national honor. Wilson believed in the mission and the goodness of the United States; the Germans were sinking American ships and taking American lives. To Wilson these were the plainest facts of all in the unhappy spring of 1917.

2 War Changes The Nation

1. What methods were employed to organize the national economy for World War I?

2. How was the mobility of Americans affected by the war?

3. In what ways did the war influence the thinking of Americans?

4. How were those who dissented against the War treated? Why were they treated this way?

The day of the declaration of war, a top Broadway songwriter named George M. Cohan sat down at the piano in his Great Neck, Long Island, home. "All I wrote was a bugle call," he later remembered. Set to his unforgettably catchy tune were these words:

> Over there, over there, send the
>   word, send the word, over there,
> That the Yanks are coming, the
>   Yanks are coming, The drums rum-
> tumming everywhere, . . . We'll be
>   over, we're coming over, and we
> won't come back till it's over
>   over there.

With sure instinct, Cohan captured the mood of patriotism and eagerness to do the job. Singing "Over There," however, was a lot easier than getting over there. And, like it or not, the experience of war would change the United States as well as Europe.

Organizing the economy. Perhaps most obviously, the war affected the economy. To supply the Allies, let alone to equip an American army, was an enormous job. Business and labor were willing, but neither was well organized. At first hesitatingly, and then more sure-footedly, the government stepped in through dozens of new agencies.

The most powerful of these agencies was the War Industries Board, headed by Bernard Baruch, a notably successful Wall Street speculator. "The fog of a sudden and stupendous war was over this country," Baruch later recalled. "We had no experience with industrial control. Everything was improvised."

The main purpose of the War Industries Board was to increase efficiency and to set priorities by determining what products manufacturers should make and how they should make them. How much steel, for example, should go for trucks, how much for guns, and how much for non-military needs? Manned largely by up-and-coming business executives and lawyers, Baruch's staff tried to solve such tough questions through careful negotiation with industries and associations of industries. The War Industries Board was sympathetic and usually generous to big business; rarely was the ever-present threat of federal force necessary to reach an agreement. Antitrust laws were suspended and prices fixed under government supervision. Wilson's New Freedom legislation had given government a role in keeping business and the economy stable; the War Industries Board engaged in outright cooperative planning.

The results were fairly impressive. Production rose sharply and numerous bottlenecks were eliminated. Furthermore, a drive to standardize manufactured items increased efficiency. The number of colors of typewriter ribbons, for example, was cut from 150 to 5; everything from paving-bricks to baby carriages was standardized as well. Also promoting efficiency was the consolidation of the nation's railroads into a single system. Although the railroads remained officially in private hands, all were run by a federal board headed by the energetic William McAdoo, secretary of the Treasury and son-in-law of Wilson.

Perhaps the best known wartime agency was Herbert Hoover's Food Administration, which had the job of raising production and lowering the consumption of food in the United States so that more could be sent to Europe. The Fuel Administration and dozens of other agencies did similar jobs in their own special areas. Like the War Industries Board, they negotiated with associations of producers, who usually were treated quite generously. The Food Administration, for example, helped farmers by purchasing food at high prices.

Many of these agencies also worked more directly with the public. When the Food Administration campaigned for wheatless Mondays and meatless Tuesdays to conserve food, it advertised nationally. People were given a chance to participate: local chambers of commerce headed local food drives; housewives pasted food-saving posters in their kitchen windows.

Along with unprecedented centralized economic planning came a new feeling of participation. Even Calvin Coolidge, then lieutenant-governor of Massachusetts and little given to expressing emotion, caught the spirit. "The whole nation," he later wrote, seemed . . . unified and solidified and willing to make any sacrifice for the cause of liberty. . . . The entire nation awoke to a new life."

Labor and the government. As war orders flooded into the plants and prices rose, workers demanded higher pay. Hundreds of strikes resulted. Concerned with these disruptions and fearing the possible growth of the radical, antiwar Industrial Workers of the World, the Wilson Administration enlisted the cooperation of Samuel Gompers, head of the American Federation of Labor. With Gompers driving an intelligent bargain, the AFL agreed not to strike. In return, dramatically ending its hands-off labor policy, the government backed labor's right to form unions, and the eight-hour day.

This agreement was to be carried out under the supervision of the National War Labor Board, cochaired by former President Taft. The board mediated whenever possible in labor-man-agement disputes but threatened government action when necessary. The results were few strikes, good wages, and a sharp increase in AFL membership. Like many businessmen, many workers made more money during the war.

In sum, the economy was consolidated and more thoroughly organized. Big business was encouraged; so was the largest labor organization. Government played a larger part in the economy than ever before. Business executives flocked to Washington, as did larger numbers of professors, to advise the production agencies. Although many of these trends were reversed once the war ended, they proved significant precedents for the New Deal, World War II planning, and the cold-war economy of the 1950's and '60's.

Increasing mobility of Americans. War affected American society as well as the economy. As war industries grew, so did cities. An extreme example was Washington, D.C., whose population soared from about 350,000 in April, 1917, to about 526,000 a year later. This marked the turning point in Washington's change from a sleepy southern town to a busy world capital. As one older resident saw it: "Life seemed suddenly to acquire a vivid scarlet lining. . . . The one invariable rule seemed to be that every individual was found doing something he or she had never dreamed of doing before." Thousands also moved to work in steel mills in Chicago, leather factories in St. Louis, aircraft plants in Seattle, and rubber plants in Akron. The new workers came mostly from small towns and the countryside, for immigration was largely cut off by the war.

Among the Americans who moved most readily were southern blacks. Race relations during the Wilson era reached a nadir not equaled since the days of the Black Codes (Chapter 10). Southern states had just finished tidying up the laws which kept blacks from the polls, and the customs which kept blacks separate and unequal. The federal government also joined in (Chapter 16).

Drawn by jobs in war industries and the prospect of more freedom, thousands of blacks moved from their tenant fields to northern cities. It was the start of the great migration which continued through the next half century. Once the migration began, it developed a momentum of its own, as people who had migrated in turn urged their families and friends to join them. Often the

Once the United States finally entered the war, its
people went all out to get behind the war effort. Of
course, money was needed to finance the war, so great
bond-selling rallies were set up to raise funds. Enter-
tainers often provided the main attraction at these
rallies. At left, Douglas Fairbanks, Sr., a very popular
star of silent pictures at the time, uses a megaphone
to address a crowd on Wall Street. As he stands
beneath the hand of George Washington, he urges
the people to invest their money in war bonds and
thus help the boys "over there." Just as they had in
the Civil War, women came forth to take the jobs
of men who had gone off to service. In 1918, the
ladies below had learned the barbering trade and had
taken to shaving and manicuring the men who were
left at home.

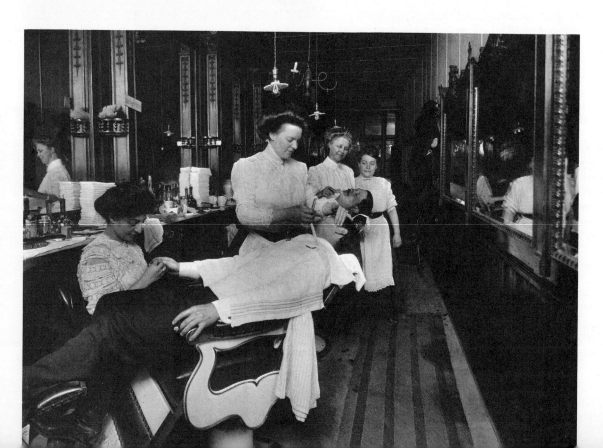

migrants were younger blacks who were intolerant of the Jim-Crow South. "The Negroes," one puzzled white observer wrote, "just quietly moved away without taking their recognized leaders into their confidence any more than they do the white people about them."

Upon arriving in the North, the black migrants rented apartments in black ghettoes like New York's Harlem and Chicago's South Side. Many found jobs that paid far better than tenant farming in the South. But they suffered the shocks of adjusting to big city life and the disappointment at finding that the North was not as free as they had hoped.

Like blacks, women received more opportunities during the war because, as men joined the army, their labor was more needed. Many women took jobs for the first time, often in factories; some moved to cities and lived on their own. "The aircraft factories . . . seem to have an especial appeal to women," observed a lady journalist. "It may be because the sewing on the delicate wings of the aircraft is something that is distinctly women's work." Politically, the women's suffrage movement, led by socially prominent militants who picketed the White House, gained rapidly.

As passage of the suffrage amendment drew near, both parties competed for the woman's vote. The Nineteenth Amendment was finally passed by Congress in June 1919, and ratified in August 1920. Proud of their new jobs, conscious of their new political power, women took a big step forward toward having their skills and intellects recognized outside of the home.

A new nationalism. The war, in fact, affected the thinking of millions of Americans. The new spirit can largely, if not wholly, be summed up in a single word: *nationalism.* Although the nationalist spirit had often surged forward before, never before had it affected so many people's lives. Millions felt a new sense of participation and of national community.

Shrewd political instinct made raising money to fight the war into a great national drive. Rather than depending solely on loans from bankers, Treasury Secretary William McAdoo promoted Liberty Bonds to be sold to the public. Their sale engaged the considerable skills of the youthful advertising industry. The Committee on Public Information, a wartime propaganda agency headed by George Creel, hired artists who produced stunning posters. Around the nation, civic groups sponsored thousands of Liberty bond parades and rallies with appearances by movie stars. Schools participated, too. In Milwaukee in April 1918, five hundred high school students marched with red, white, and blue posters with slogans like "Every quarter, every dollar, helps to make the Kaiser holler."

Along with the rise in national spirit came a desire for what was known as Americanization. The United States in 1917 had a large immigrant population and a small but much-publicized and much-feared radical labor union. Many worried that radicals would destroy the American way of life. Many also feared that the melting pot would not melt, that America would become, in the words of Theodore Roosevelt, "a polyglot boardinghouse," disunited and weak.

War itself helped shape the expression of the Americanization drive. To rally support for the war effort, the Committee on Public Information publicized the German army—"Huns," it called them—as the bloodthirsty enemy. It used pamphlets, lectures, films, posters, and advertisements to spread its message. Unavoidably, anti-German feeling soon got out of hand.

Three thousand miles from the battlefront, local superpatriots overflowed with militancy. German-Americans, most of whom rallied to the American cause once war was declared, found themselves accused of disloyalty, pressured into buying Liberty bonds, and even forced to kiss the flag. As if it would help the soldiers, people renamed sauerkraut "liberty cabbage"; some bravely burned German books. And one overexcited citizen started the rumor, reported with a straight face by the New York *Times,* that German-Americans were poisoning Red Cross bandages.

Treatment of dissenters. No large group of dissenters, like the Loyalists in the Revolutionary War, emerged during World War I. Those who did dissent, however, were treated roughly by the government as well as by local vigilante groups. The Espionage Act of June 1917, and the Sedition Act of May 1918, made the encouragement of disloyalty illegal. These vaguely-worded acts prohibited, without carefully defining, disloyal speech critical of the government, the draft, the

WAR AND CIVIL LIBERTIES

Free speech and a free press are not absolute rights in the sense that these freedoms are limited by the rights of others and by the demands of national security and public decency. When and how much these freedoms can be suspended is important in wartime, when the question arises of what is legitimate freedom of speech and press and what are disloyal or seditious statements and must be considered a threat to public safety. This question came directly before the Supreme Court for the first time after World War I, in *Schenck* v. *United States.*

During the war, Schenck had circulated among draftees a document which claimed that conscription was a violation of the Thirteenth Amendment, and exhorted conscripts to assert their opposition to the draft. Schenck was convicted of violation of the Espionage Act of 1917. He claimed his conviction was a violation of his rights under the First Amendment.

The court ruling was delivered by Justice Holmes, who applied the "clear and present danger" test to the difficult question of when a citizen's rights may be suspended.

"We admit that in many places and in ordinary times the defendants in saying all that was said in the circular would have been within their constitutional rights. But the character of every act depends upon the circumstances in which it is done. The most stringent protection of free speech would not protect a man in falsely shouting fire in a theatre and causing a panic. . . .

"The question in every case is whether the words used are used in such circumstances and are of such a nature as to create a clear and present danger that they will bring about the substantive evils that Congress has a right to prevent. It is a question of proximity and degree. When a nation is at war many things that might be said in time of peace are such a hindrance to its effort that their utterance will not be endured so long as men fight and that no court could regard them as protected by any constitutional right. . . ."

Constitution, and army and navy uniforms.

Under these acts, over fifteen hundred people, including Eugene Debs, were arrested, and dozens of magazines and newspapers were barred from the mails and thus forced out of business. Robert La Follette and the few other senators who remained peace advocates were condemned with hysterical shrillness. And the more than four hundred conscientous objectors who refused to cooperate with the draft were sent to prison, where they were often treated brutally.

Randolph Bourne, a dissenting essayist, wrote:

War determines its own end,—victory, and government crushes out automatically all forces that deflect, or threaten to deflect, energy from the path of organization to that end. All governments will act in this way, the most democratic as well as the most autocratic.

Fortunately, Bourne exaggerated the efficiency of the government, if not its will. Some government officials exercised restraint, and freedom of speech, if tarnished, survived the war. Still, the wartime civil-liberties record was miserable. Conformity of thought and action was the order of the day.

3 Americans Fight And Negotiate In Europe

1. How was the army of the United States mobilized for the War?

2. What role was played by American forces in World War I?

3. What was the essence of Wilson's program for a lasting peace embodied in the Fourteen Points? How realistic were his proposals?

4. What problems did Wilson encounter in attempting to get his peace proposals accepted? Why did these problems arise?

When the United States entered World War I, its regular army and national guard totaled 309,000 men; its air corps had 130 pilots and 55 planes considered "serviceable." Not surprisingly, the navy made its weight felt first. In April 1917,

Germany's submarine campaign threatened to starve Great Britain into surrender. Merchant ships still usually made the Atlantic crossing alone, hoping to elude the submarines. Some British officers had suggested the convoy system, by which a group of merchant ships, flanked by an escort of cruisers and destroyers, would travel together. This system was adopted, and it proved a great success; submarine damage was cut drastically.

Along with this sound advice, the navy soon sent dozens of destroyers and played a large role in keeping the Atlantic shipping lanes safe for the transportation of American soldiers and weapons to Europe.

Mobilizing an army. The regular army could provide a nucleus of officers and noncoms, but millions more soldiers were needed. To ensure an orderly flow of men into the armed forces, and to avoid disrupting vital industries, Congress passed a Selective Service Act on May 18, 1917. This first serious draft act—the Civil War draft had been an absurdity—aroused strong opposition from former peace advocates and Progressives. Speaker of the House Champ Clark informed his colleagues that his fellow Missourians saw "precious little difference between a conscript and a convict."

Nonetheless, over 9.5 million men between the ages of twenty-one and thirty (later extended to eighteen and forty-five) dutifully registered as required on June 5; 14.4 million were registered by the end of the war. Of these, 2.8 million, all unmarried, were actually drafted. Volunteers added another 2 million to the armed forces.

As bands played at the railroad stations, the new soldiers left for training camps. ("It is not that I am sorry to see my boy go" one Norfolk mother unconvincingly told a newspaperman. "These tears are tears of pride.") The recruits then spent several months in camps, where they were introduced to the undemocratic disciplines of military life. Often the training was supplemented by lectures and demonstrations by British and French officers fresh from the trenches.

As a boost to Allied and American morale, the first regiments were shipped to France in time for a parade in Paris on July 4, 1917. Brand Whitlock, once reform mayor of Toledo and then serving as an American diplomat, described the scene:

. . . The crowd swept along the street . . . from curb to curb . . . men, women, children trotting along, hot, excited, trying to keep up with the slender column of our khaki-clad regulars, who marched briskly along. French soldiers . . . trotted beside them . . . as boys trot hurrying beside a circus parade. Our soldiers were covered with flowers—and always the steady roar of the crowd and now and then cries of *Vive l'Amérique!*

That same day, at Lafayette's tomb, an American colonel announced melodramatically: "*Nous voilà,* Lafayette!—Lafayette, we are here!"

A colonel had spoken that day because General John J. Pershing, commander of the American Expeditionary Force (AEF), doubted that he could think of anything stirring to say. A solid, tough, undramatic soldier, Pershing had first attracted the eye of Theodore Roosevelt when he led black soldiers up San Juan Hill. Wilson wisely chose him as a commander who would stand up to the Allies, work well with the civilian War Department, and stay out of politics.

American troops in Europe. Part of one American division got a taste of combat in October 1917, but few Americans got to France until the following spring. Until then, to the impatience of the Allies, Pershing doggedly insisted that his soldiers be given a battlefront sector of their own, after three full months of advanced training in France. This insistence followed from Wilson's view that the United States had a unique role in the war—interested only in peace, not in victory.

The United States, in fact, called itself an Associated Power, independent of the Allies. When American soldiers did begin to arrive in numbers, the Germans were about to launch their final offensive of May 1918. After initial unsteadiness, the Americans fought well. "Most of us," one French officer noted, "were amazed by the displays on the part of the Americans of what they call, I believe, hustle." At Chateau-Thierry, Belleau Wood, and the Argonne forest, Americans won costly victories (see battle map, page 498).

Although Americans fought intensively for little more than six months, 107,500 died from battle and disease. Forty times as many Allied soldiers were killed in the war. Still, the Americans suffered more than enough to be reminded of the horror of war, which rose-clouded memories of the Civil War had tended to let them forget.

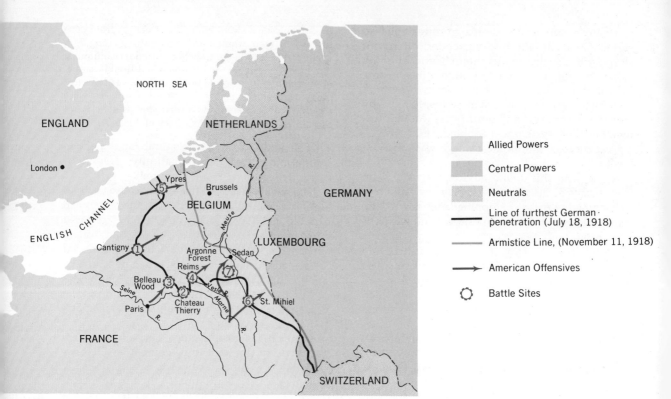

AMERICAN PARTICIPATION IN WORLD WAR I, 1918

① May 28, 1918. Cantigny. Under General John Pershing, Americans capture the town, marking the first clear-cut victory for American forces.

② June 4, 1918. Chateau-Thierry. American and French forces block a German advance just 40 miles outside of Paris.

③ June 6–July 1, 1918. Belleau Wood. Americans drive the Germans out of a strategic defense outpost.

④ July 18–August 6, 1918. The Marne. In the Second Battle of the Marne, American and French forces push the Germans back to the Vesle River. This marked the turning point of the war.

⑤ August 19–November 11, 1918. Ypres Offensive. In an offensive launched by British forces, Americans troops help push the Germans back through northern Belgium.

⑥ September 12–16, 1918. St. Mihiel. Under General Pershing, American troops, with the aid of British and French air and ground forces, capture St. Mihiel on the Meuse River. This marked the first distinctly American offensive.

⑦ September 26–November 11, 1918. Meuse-Argonne Offensive. American forces, concentrated between the Argonne Forest and the Meuse River, attack the Germans, push them east of the Meuse, and capture the heights overlooking Sedan.

The end of the war. By October 1918, the Germans were retreating and negotiating for an armistice. They had no choice: Austria-Hungary had already collapsed and the German army was mauled, the navy mutinous, and the civilian population hungry and threatening revolt. Furthermore, Germany faced the prospect of a powerful flood of fresh American soldiers, of whom 2 million were already in France. At last, at the eleventh hour of the eleventh day of the eleventh month, the armistice took effect. One American private commemorated the moment in a poem published in *The Stars and Stripes*, the AEF newspaper:

> We stood up and didn't say a word,
> It felt just like when you have dropped
>   your pack
> After a hike, and straightened out
>   your back, . . .
> [A]ll we did was stand and stare and
>   stare,
> Just stare and stand and never say
>   a word.

Proud of the soldiers, bursting with the spirit of Americanization, one American newspaper editorialized on Armistice Day that "white and black, yellow and red, Jew and Gentile, stand united as never before in the achievement of a great crusade." It sounded good, but it was not true. Black soldiers suffered systematic and continual discrimination. They were subject to the draft, but were totally barred from the elite marines and allowed in the navy only as kitchen help and servants. They were trained in segregated camps and still served in segregated units, commanded mostly by white officers.

In France, the relatively few black units trusted with combat assignments fought boldly and well; most blacks, however, worked as stevedores and on other labor details. Insults rankled, too. White officers warned French civilians to keep away from black soldiers; and *The Stars and Stripes* ran supposedly humorous Negro dialect stories. The irony of all this should have been appallingly obvious in a war fought to make the world "safe for democracy." Unfortunately it was not.

Wilson's Fourteen Points. The United States went to war over the immediate issue of freedom of the seas. But Wilson, dreading war, believed that it could be finally justified only by the higher

ALL QUIET ON THE WESTERN FRONT

World War I was seen through the eyes of a German soldier in the novel *All Quiet on the Western Front*. As the Armistice approaches, the soldier reflects on what the end of the war will bring:

"I have fourteen days' rest, because I have swallowed a bit of gas; in a little garden I sit the whole day long in the sun. The armistice is coming soon, I believe it now too. Then we will go home. . . .

"Had we returned home in 1916, out of the suffering and the strength of our experiences we might have unleashed a storm. Now if we go back we will be weary, broken, burnt out, rootless and without hope. . . .

"And men will not understand us—for the generation that grew up before us, though it has passed these years with us here, already had a home and a calling; now it will return to its old occupations, and the war will be forgotten—and the generation that has grown up after us will be strange to us and push us aside. We will be superfluous even to ourselves, we will grow older, a few will adapt themselves, some others will merely submit, and most will be bewildered. . . .

"I am very quiet. Let the months and years come, they bring me nothing more, they can bring me nothing more. I am so alone, and so without hope that I can confront them without fear. The life that has borne me through these years is still in my hands and my eyes. Whether I have subdued it, I know not. But so long as it is there it will seek its own way out, heedless of the will that is within me.

"He fell in October, 1918, on a day that was so quiet and still on the whole front, that the army report confined itself to the single sentence: All quiet on the Western Front.

"He had fallen forward and lay on the earth as though sleeping. Turning him over one saw that he could not have suffered long; his face had an expression of calm, as though almost glad the end had come."

World War I sent American troops over to Europe to fight for the first time. Not only were the surroundings new, but so were some of the weapons of war. Top left, a member of a ground crew fits bombs under the wings of a rather primitive aircraft. World War I fliers had a great glamour about them, but they also had a great casualty rate. Less glamorous but even more dangerous was the land war. The infantry gun crew, bottom left, is taking part in an advance during the battle of Belleau Wood. The denuded trees all about them show the devastating effects of artillery barrages. Finally the war ended, and those who survived it, like the members of the 369th Colored Infantry above, jubilantly sailed for home. Behind them they left the leaders of the allied countries to negotiate the peace. Below are Prime Minister Vittorio Orlando of Italy, Prime Minister David Lloyd George of Great Britain, Premier Georges Clemenceau of France, and President Woodrow Wilson of the United States.

purpose of bringing lasting peace. To this end, in an address to Congress in January 1918, he proclaimed a peace program of Fourteen Points.

Briefly, the first five points called for: (1) an end to secret alliances; (2) freedom of the seas; (3) lower trade barriers; (4) large-scale disarmament; and (5) "absolutely impartial adjustment of all colonial claims" between European powers, with some consideration even for the colonial peoples themselves. Points 6 through 13 called for national self-determination in Europe—boundary lines drawn as far as possible on the basis of nationality. Finally, point 14 proposed a league of nations to guarantee independence to all nations. The Committee on Public Information, fervently pro-Wilson, distributed millions of copies of this speech around the world. It was generally popular, even in Germany, but it met with a mixed reception among Allied governments.

On December 4, 1918, Wilson set sail for Europe, where he made a triumphal tour of Allied capitals. His official purpose was to represent the United States at the Peace Conference which would formally end World War I; his actual purpose was to represent all of humanity by persuading the Allies to accept the Fourteen Points. It was a noble but, considering the Europe of 1919, an impossible dream.

Negotiating the peace. Unlike Wilson, France sought only security against the chance of another German invasion. France could no longer count on an alliance with Russia, which had fallen to a Communist revolution in November 1917, and then signed a separate peace with Germany. Great Britain, in the eyes of the French, was a necessary but unreliable ally. What France needed was a strong non-European ally—and the United States fit the bill perfectly, if it would only be willing.

Premier Georges Clemenceau, France's representative at the peace talks, was a sharp-tongued, sharp-witted seventy-eight-year-old patriot who hated Germany. The only guarantee of peace, he believed, was a weak Germany and a strong alliance against it. Wilson's stern and lofty idealism often exasperated him. "Talk with Wilson!" Clemenceau once complained. "How can I talk to a fellow who thinks himself the first man in two thousand years to know anything about peace on earth?"

The British, represented by Prime Minister David Lloyd George, took a more fluid position. The war had strengthened the British navy and weakened the German navy. Though the British wanted revenge against Germany, they did not want to be tied too closely to the fortunes and policies of France. They believed, as the British had long believed, that peace could best be maintained by keeping as free of the European Continent as possible.

A host of less powerful claimants came to Paris as well. The Italians, who had joined the Allies in 1915, sought territory, as did the Japanese, who had joined the Allied side in order to seize Germany's colonies in the Pacific and concessions in China. Unofficial and uninvited observers tried to defend the interests of colonial peoples; these included W. E. B. Du Bois, who spoke for Africa, and a man who later took the name Ho Chi-Minh and became president of North Vietnam. A British diplomat compared the atmosphere to "that sense of riot in a parrot house." Germany, however, was not represented. That nation was to be permitted, and in effect forced, to sign the peace treaty after the victors had written it.

The Treaty of Versailles. Despite his unfamiliarity with European politics, Wilson did persuade the French and British to moderate their demands on Germany, and insisted on inclusion of a league of nations. In the final agreement, signed by the Germans on July 28, 1919, in Louis XIV's magnificent palace at Versailles, Germany lost most of its gains of the preceding fifty years. It was forced to surrender all of its colonies and some of its own territory, to permit a fifteen-year occupation of the Rhineland by the Allies, and to disarm permanently.

Germany was also forced to sign a blank check for *reparations*—compensation payments—for war damages. Still, the German nation was not dismembered. Furthermore, enforcement of most of the treaty provisions would require either the cooperation of the German government, or Allied force. Neither, in the long run, proved dependable.

With regard to Germany, the Versailles treaty fell between two stools. Had it been much harsher, Germany might have fallen to the secondary position it has occupied since World War II. Had it been milder, Germany might—though this possibility is rather remote—have reconciled its differences with France and Britain and become a friendly power. Instead, the Versailles treaty was harsh enough to embitter the Germans, whose nationalism was later whipped into a fury by an insanely brilliant and evil World War I veteran named Adolf Hitler. On the other hand, the treaty was mild enough to permit Germany to regain its power enough so that it could flaunt the treaty. World War II followed almost exactly twenty years later.

The Versailles treaty also included Wilson's charter for a League of Nations, though the French hardly counted on it to secure peace. Wilson's League, on which the United Nations later was to be patterned, was to have a permanent staff, a nine-member Council dominated by the strongest Allies and the United States, and an Assembly with representatives from all nations. Member nations would agree to submit international disputes to arbitration. Members also pledged to take whatever economic and military action the Council recommended against violators of the peace.

This League, Wilson hoped, would take the place of the entangling alliances that had brought on the war. The charter was skillfully drafted, but the power of the League rested on one factor: the willingness of the member nations to follow its direction. To Wilson's surprise the first show of reluctance came from the United States.

4 Nationalism And Disruption Follow The War

1. Why did the United States fail to ratify the Treaty of Versailles?

2. What were the causes of the race riots which followed the war?

3. What labor problems emerged in 1919?

4. Why did the hysteria of a Red scare occur after the war. What were the results of the mass fear of Communist subversion?

Just before Wilson left Paris for home, an adviser urged him "to meet the Senate in a conciliatory spirit," as he had treated the foreign representatives at the conference table. Wilson replied sharply: "I have found that one can never get anything in this life that is worthwhile without fighting for it." According to Article II, Section 2 of the Constitution, treaties must be approved by two thirds of those present of the Senate. And there lay Wilson's problem. In the elections of 1918, the Republicans had captured control of the Senate. By no means all Republicans opposed the treaty; still, for the treaty to win a two-thirds vote, Wilson would need to exercise skillful bargaining and tact.

Reactions to the treaty. A clue to how Wilson would behave had come in his choice of the delegation that accompanied him to Paris. There were no other leading national figures among them. More significant, there were no leading Republicans, even though men like Taft and Elihu Root were available and sympathetic to most of Wilson's aims. Wilson also declined to invite a Republican senator; this particularly annoyed Henry Cabot Lodge, the powerful head of the Senate Foreign Relations Committee, who keenly hated Wilson already.

On July 10, 1919, Wilson presented the treaty to the Senate with a tactless speech in which he asked: "Dare we reject [the League] and break the heart of the world?" At that point, the Senate stacked up about like this: fourteen Republicans, including Robert La Follette, opposed the League of Nations in any imaginable form. They believed that American democracy would suffer if the United States participated in any international alliance. Forty-three of the forty-seven Democrats strongly favored the treaty. Most Democrats were devoted to Wilson, who was the first President of their party since Andrew Jackson to win two consecutive elections.

Remaining were thirty-five Republicans, most of whom, led by Henry Cabot Lodge, favored strong reservations on the treaty to make doubly sure that the United States would not lose any of its independence. For the treaty to pass, nineteen of those thirty-five Republicans would have to be persuaded to vote for ratification.

Outside the Senate, first reactions to the treaty were generally favorable. To most, the League seemed a simple and inexpensive way to prevent future wars. As for the full treaty, 268 pages long, few either read or understood it. In time, oversimplifications and rumors about the treaty began to spread.

Some, including Lodge, exaggerated the extent to which the treaty undermined American independence. Representatives of American ethnic groups attacked the treaty for not promoting Irish independence from Great Britain, for not giving Italy more land from Austria-Hungary, and for treating Germany sternly. In time, the enthusiasm of the treaty's supporters ebbed; as the soldiers came home, Europe seemed further and further away. "Delay," one historian has noted, "was the great enemy of the peacemakers in America."

Rejection of the treaty. Delay was exactly the tactic Henry Cabot Lodge used. He began by reading aloud to the Foreign Relations Committee the entire 268-page treaty. This fascinating recitation took two weeks. For the next six weeks, the committee held hearings. Wilson, meanwhile, let it be known that he would accept no compromise—and most Senate Democrats would not oppose his desires.

Disheartened by the growing opposition to the treaty, Wilson decided to take his case directly to the people in a national speaking tour. A great upsurge of public opinion, he hoped, would force the senators to do their duty. It was a brave but unwise decision. The senators, most of whom would not stand for reelection until 1922 or 1924, were not likely to be budged. Furthermore, Wilson's health was poor. But he was determined: "Even though, in my condition, it might mean the giving up of my life," he told his secretary, "I will gladly make the sacrifice to save the Treaty."

Wilson left Washington by train the evening of September 3, 1919, arriving in Columbus, Ohio, for his first speech the next morning. In the next three weeks he traveled nearly eight thousand miles and gave thirty-six speeches averaging an hour each. The night of September 25, as his train headed eastward from Pueblo, Colorado, he collapsed. His train sped directly to Washington where one week later he suffered a stroke which paralyzed the left side of his face and body. Although Wilson's intellect was not affected, his emotions were. He became more stubborn and single-minded than ever.

LAFOLLETTE OPPOSES THE LEAGUE

Former governor of Wisconsin Robert M. LaFollette, who became a senator in 1906, vigorously opposed the League of Nations. He believed that the peace treaties imposed on Europe were unjust, and he protested that if the United States joined the League, it would be obliged to uphold these injustices:

". . . the little group of men who sat in secret conclave for months at Versailles were not peacemakers. They were war makers. They cut and slashed the map of the Old World in violation of the terms of the armistice. They patched up a new map of the Old World in consumation of the terms of the secret treaties the existence of which they had denied because they feared to expose the sordid aims and purposes for which men were sent to death by the tens of thousands daily. They betrayed China. They locked the chains on the subject peoples of Ireland, Egypt, and India. They partitioned territory and traded off peoples in mockery of that sanctified formula of 14 points, and made it our Nation's shame. Then, fearing the wrath of outraged peoples, knowing that their new map would be torn to rags and tatters by the conflicting warring elements which they had bound together in wanton disregard of racial animosities, they made a league of nations to stand guard over the swag!

"The Old World armies were exhausted. Their treasuries were empty. It was imperative that they should be able to draw upon the lusty man power and the rich material resources of the United States to build a military cordon around the new boundaries of the new States of the Old World.

"Senators, if we go into this thing, it means a great standing Army; it means conscription to fight in foreign wars, a blighting curse upon the family life of every American home, every hour. It means higher taxes, higher prices, harder times for the poor. It means greater discontent; a deeper, more menacing unrest. . . ."

During the next month and a half the Senate debated the treaty and proposed reservations. Some Democrats and moderate Republicans composed lists of mild reservations to offer in opposition to Lodge's harsher ones. They got little help from the treaty's chief sponsor, however. Wilson, partly incapacitated and shielded by his wife and doctors, did little except refuse to compromise. The Democrats, unwilling to break with their leader, held fast.

Lodge's reservations, qualifying American obligations to the League, were defeated by the Democrats plus thirteen of those Republicans who wanted no part of any treaty. Then the treaty without reservations—as Wilson wanted it—came to a vote. Thirty-seven Democrats and only one Republican voted aye; sixty-four votes were needed for passage. The treaty failed. (The war between the United States and the Central Powers was formally ended by a joint congressional resolution in 1921.)

Had the treaty passed, the United States might have become an active member of the League of Nations. But more likely, she would have lost interest even if she had joined. European politics excited little interest among the American people through most of the 1920's and '30's (Chapter 24). Still, the defeat was a stunning blow to those who had been moved by Wilson's idealistic leadership. A bitter man, Lodge probably did more than anyone else to defeat the treaty. But Wilson deserves a large measure of the responsibility as well, for his stubbornness helped to doom his own creation. It was a frustrating and embittering experience for nearly everyone.

Demobilizing the army. While Wilson negotiated the Versailles treaty, most of the AEF remained in France—playing poker, as Captain Harry S. Truman later remembered. On the other hand, over 200,000 soldiers attended special schools and even an AEF University was set up in France. Most of these student-soldiers studied basic reading and writing. Some American soldiers also helped the Allies occupy Germany's Rhineland. Most quickly befriended the German civilians. "The [lady's] little girl and I are buried eyebrow deep in cake and chocolate trying to eat our way out," an Illinois farmer wrote home to his wife. "She is ten years old and pretty as a picture. . . . When anyone tells you that we were

fighting the German people you tell them that I said they were mistaken as the Kaiser and his gang were the ones we were after."

During the spring and summer of 1919, most of the AEF was shipped to Boston, Hoboken, Newport News, or Charleston; deloused; paraded; and mustered out of service. By the beginning of 1920, the Army was reduced to only 130,000 men. Many of the new civilians, in addition to the 204,000 wounded, had trouble adjusting. Demobilization was rapid, and little effort was made to find the men jobs. Nor was a GI bill available like the ones which sent veterans to American colleges after later wars.

Race relations. The strains of war and demobilization showed most clearly in race relations. Even during the war, there had been one riot over job competition, in which forty blacks were killed in East St. Louis, Illinois. After the war, southern and northern whites alike reacted with hostility to the sight of black soldiers in uniform. White veterans in particular feared job competition, as well as integration of their neighborhoods by blacks overflowing swollen city ghettos. Many blacks, on the other hand, took new pride in their race and were determined to fight for their rights. Together with the general postwar anxiety, these factors led to more than twenty race riots throughout the nation in 1919.

Two of the worst riots took place in Washington, D.C., and Chicago. In Washington, the editor of the *Post*, seeking to embarrass the top command of the police force, covered normal crime as if it were a giant crime wave. The *Post* paid particular attention to alleged assaults upon whites by blacks. Combined with the general lack of interracial understanding, this sensationalist press campaign touched off a riot the night of July 19, 1919. It started when two hundred white sailors and marines on leave swept into Washington's southwest ghetto, beating up several blacks. For the following three nights, whites and blacks fought one another in and around black neighborhoods. It took marine and cavalry detachments to end the riot, which killed at least six people.

Chicago's black population had more than doubled since 1917, mostly with migrants from the south. Thus the city was already tense when, on July 27, a black swam across an unofficial racial boundary off a Lake Michigan beach. Whites stoned the black, who drowned. When the police refused to arrest the stone-throwers, blacks mobbed the police. By evening, blacks were exchanging gunfire with white police and civilians. A week-long riot had begun. Before it ended, twenty-three blacks and fifteen whites had been killed.

Labor and management clash. The truce between labor and management supervised by the National War Labor Board ended with the end of the war. Labor, suffering from continuing inflation, sought higher wages. Management, viewing its wartime labor policies as a temporary sacrifice, wanted to return to normal—which meant tightly-controlled wages and no unions, wherever possible. The result was bitter and spectacular strikes involving one out of every five workers. The most significant was in steel.

Since the bloody Homestead strike of 1892, the AFL had made no determined effort to organize the unskilled steelworkers, most of whom were eastern and southern European immigrants. During the war, the immigrant steelworkers were special targets of the Americanization campaign. By the end of the war, most proudly believed in American democracy—and wanted it extended to the steel mills, where the twelve-hour day and seven-day work week (for an average wage of only twenty-eight dollars) was standard.

In 1919, an organizing committee won widespread support with the slogan, "Eight hours and the union." Because the companies refused to recognize the new union, 250,000 steelworkers—about half the work force—went on strike on September 22, 1919. Fear of radicalism, encouraged by the press, soon turned the public against the workers. The companies also used spies and black strikebreakers to divide the strikers, and state police and special deputies to supress them.

By the time the strike ended in January 1920, twenty people, including eighteen strikers, had been killed. The strike was doomed chiefly by the federal government's refusal to intervene. Without outside help, the strikers simply lacked the power the companies had. Though the steel industry adopted the eight-hour day in 1923, unionization was postponed for two decades.

The "Red" hysteria. Both race riots and strikes were sometimes blamed on "Reds." Although the communists, in power in Russia since 1917, called for world revolution, the two American Communist parties enjoyed a total membership of only 70,000—mostly non-English-speaking immigrants. Still, the nervous public was conditioned by the wartime experience to mistake peaceful radicals for violent revolutionaries.

Fear gave way to hysteria when bombs were mailed to a number of prominent Americans in April 1919, and exploded in eight cities in June. Three months later another bomb, set off in crowded Wall Street, killed thirty-eight. The crudely planned bombings were the work of the lunatic fringe of the anarchist movement. Although neither the strikes nor the bombings were the work of the communists, the public mind fused them together into one well-coordinated giant threat.

Wilson, first preoccupied with the treaty ratification fight and then disabled by his stroke, said little. But Attorney-General A. Mitchell Palmer, formerly a leading Progressive, led a campaign against foreign-born radicals. Prejudiced against immigrants, Palmer was also politically ambitious. In November 1919 and January 1920, Palmer engineered raids of homes and meeting halls by Justice Department agents, local police, and vigilantes to seize alien communists.

The raids netted about six thousand men and women, including anarchists, communists, socialists, and nonradicals who happened to be in the wrong place at the wrong time. Some of the foreign-born were deported; most of those arrested were roughly treated before being released for lack of evidence. Not until early 1920 did the hysteria die down, as Republicans and Democrats alike realized that the radical threat had been luridly exaggerated. Still, the Palmer raids amounted to one of the worst violations of civil liberties in American history.

■ CONCLUSION

Most immediately, the United States went to war in 1917 to restore freedom of the seas. In a larger sense, it fought for national honor—a vague but powerful concept. But Wilson, wanting to justify the slaughter, proclaimed the impossible goal of making the world "safe for democracy." In effect, he hoped to teach the world, as he had tried to teach the Mexicans, "to elect good men"—and to spread his New Freedom around the world.

Because of his fervor, Wilson helped to promote a warlike spirit at home. With the Allied cause linked to making the world "safe for democracy," an expression of dissent could be seen as a blow against this noble goal—America's mission in the world. Despite Wilson's internationalist aims, the war strengthened American nationalism. Americans in 1919 were doubtful about the ability of international organizations to keep the peace. They were far more confident, as Chapter 24 will point out, of the value of pursuing economic self-interest in international relations. The flag and the dollar, rather than a League of Nations meeting in Switzerland, became the symbols of American foreign policy in the postwar era.

Looking back, some Americans remembered the war as a time of excitement, when life seemed purposeful and spirits high. But the dominant reaction was disillusionment. Roosevelt and Wilson had led Americans in a crusade to reform America; Wilson had led Americans in a crusade to reform the world. The Progressive reforms certainly improved society, but they did not transform the public spirit, as the race riots, strikes, and Red scare of 1919 demonstrated.

The war not only failed to save the world; it even failed to end the European quarrels that had been its source. Thoughtful Europeans and Americans alike were disillusioned—with the idea of progress so popular before the war, with armies, and with statesmen. Few caught that mood of disillusionment better than Ernest Hemingway in *A Farewell to Arms*, (1929), one of the best American novels about World War I. The hero of the novel says:

I was always embarrassed by the words sacred, glorious, and sacrifice and the expression in vain. I had seen nothing sacred, and the things that were glorious had no glory and the sacrifices were like the stockyards at Chicago if nothing was done with the meat except to bury it.

■ QUESTIONS

1. Why did the United States become involved in World War I? Did the United States have any alternatives to entering the war? Explain.

2. What European problems were resolved by the war? What problems were left unresolved?

3. How did the war affect American society?

4. What was the role of America in the war and the subsequent peace negotiations? If you were an American statesman, what peace proposal would you have advocated? Why?

5. What problems did the United States encounter after the war?

6. How did the war affect American foreign policy?

■ BIBLIOGRAPHY

TUCHMAN, BARBARA W., *The Guns of August,* Dell. Tuchman has received much praise for the combination of solid research and literary style she used in recreating the events surrounding the outbreak of World War I in Europe. It is a good book for leisure reading as the author takes the reader onto the battlefields of the first six weeks of the war.

REMARQUE, ERICH M., *All Quiet on the Western Front,* Fawcett (Crest Books). This novel is a classic on the futility of war. It is a moving account of life in the trenches during World War I. The student should read this book to approach an understanding of the nature of total war as the soldier frequently experiences it.

BAILEY, THOMAS A., *Woodrow Wilson and the Lost Peace,* New York Times Co. (Quadrangle Books).
————, *Woodrow Wilson and the Great Betrayal,* New York Times Co. (Quadrangle Books).
These two volumes are excellent studies of Wilson at the Versailles Peace Conference and in the battle for ratification of the peace treaty. There are numerous studies of these phases of Wilson's career. Bailey provides an exceptionally readable summary, using frequent, intriguing quotes, but the student may also consult some of the problem-centered series which present varying interpretations of the role and importance of Wilson.

TUTTLE, WILLIAM M. JR., *Race Riot: Chicago in the Red Summer of 1919.,* Studies in American Negro Life, Atheneum. Although the book focuses upon Chicago, references are made to other American cities which experienced racial rioting. In addition to examining the specific causes of the riots of 1919, the student may compare the rioting in Chicago with more recent occasions to see both the similarities and the changes which have occurred.

MURRAY, ROBERT K., *Red Scare: A Study in National Hysteria, 1919–1920*, McGraw Hill. Murray's account is a standard reference for a survey of the Red scare in America. The author investigates the propaganda and hysteria which may lead a nation into over-reaction,

a theme which is continually relevant to a democratic nation.

BRODY, DAVID, *Labor in Crisis: The Steel Strike of 1919*, Critical Periods of History Series, Lippincott. Internal disorder as indicated by the rioting and the Red scare was also evident in labor-management relations. In this well-written book, Brody indicates the causes of the dispute, the course of the strike, and the influence of the unsuccessful strike upon future labor recognition and strength.

Part 4

The Nation Becomes
A World Leader

Main Street, Gloucester, John Sloan, *c.* 1930

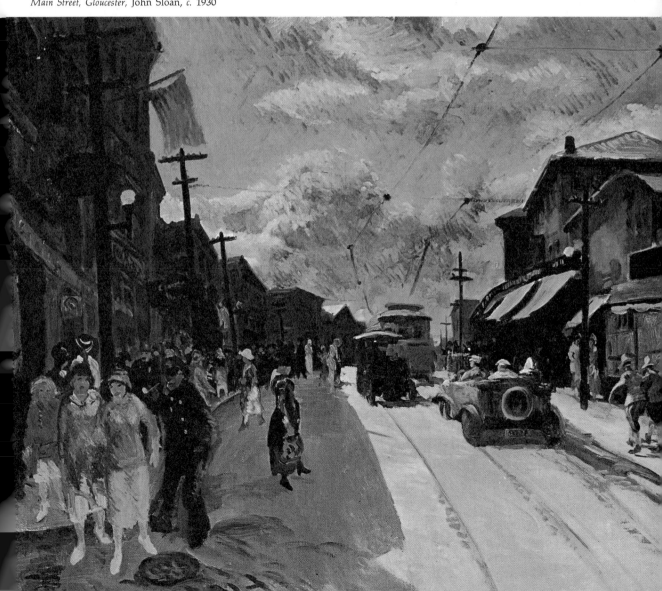

From Normality
To Depression

Perhaps because it had so little to recover from, The United States was the only belligerent nation in World War I to recover completely from the war's disruptive economic effects. A debtor nation in 1914, this nation emerged from the war as a creditor to which the rest of the world owed some $12 billion. American business and political leaders looked to the future with confidence and enthusiasm, sure that their expansive economy would continue to grow and prosper at an unprecedented rate. To be sure, they faced the sometimes painful matter of demobilization and reconversion from war to peacetime conditions; but once that hurdle was overcome, it appeared that a golden age of business lay ahead.

To a public disillusioned with the outcome of the war and cynical about foreign affairs in general, the prospect of America turning inward once again to enjoy the fruits of its own good fortune had great appeal. Historians Henry Steele Commager and Richard B. Morris have labeled the 1920's the most bleakly negative decade in our history, and the observation is an apt one in many respects. Yet, the decade was a time of optimism and excitement to many people who lived through it. How could they have guessed that the golden age would last a scant ten years and end in the shambles of the Great Depression? As you follow the movement from postwar normality to severe depression, here are some questions to guide you:

1. What economic policies did the Republicans promote?
2. Why was the prosperity of the 1920's so short-lived?
3. What was it like to be living in the United States during the Great Depression?

1 The Republicans Return To Power

1. What political scandals emerged during the Harding administration? Why were political scandals so evident at this time?

2. In what ways was Calvin Coolidge a "Puritan in Babylon?"

3. How did the election of 1928 demonstrate both continuity and a break with the past?

4. In what ways was the politics of the twenties similar to that of the Gilded Age?

Probably most ordinary Americans had mixed feelings after the war about the direction the country should take. On the one hand, they were tired of wartime restrictions and ready to return to what Senator Warren G. Harding of Ohio ungrammatically called "normalcy." Considering Wilson's repeated and often emotional appeals to their idealism during the fighting, some sort of reaction was bound to set in after the armistice. Probably, too, the people were tired of reform politics and strong Presidents. Reform tends to run in cycles and is not easily sustained for long periods. In a real sense, the postwar era was a natural time for the nation to pause and catch its breath.

On the other hand, there is no evidence that the people wanted to dismantle, or even to alter, any of the major Progressive reforms. To be sure, conservative Republicans took control of both the House and the Senate after the congressional elections of 1918 and later succeeded in undoing the tariff and tax reform of the Wilson administration. But throughout the postwar period, the voters kept enough reform-minded men in Congress to block any wholesale attempt by the Old Guard to legislate progressivism out of existence. If the voters were tired of Wilson, confused about the League, and ready for a change of some sort, they were by no means ready to repudiate everything Wilson had stood for.

Indeed, the reform spirit showed some encouraging signs of life. In 1920, Congress created the Federal Power Commission to regulate the growing electric power industry. Clearly in the best Progressive tradition was the Nineteenth Amendment, which gave women the vote. Even the ill-fated Eighteenth Amendment, which prohibited the manufacture and sale of intoxicating liquor, was hailed as a major reform, perhaps the most important since the abolition of slavery.

Still, the lure of the "good old days" was strong, for both the average citizen and the politicians. In waging a major war, the United States had engaged in large-scale economic planning. As a result, the traditional relationship between business and government changed, with government assuming new, positive functions in the economy. After the war, the demand for rapid demobilization was so great that the government simply turned over most of its new economic powers and functions to business. Neither the Republican Congress nor Wilson himself did much to check this hasty reaction.

Postwar agriculture and labor. While business in general benefitted from rapid demobilization, agriculture and labor suffered. Immediately after the armistice, the Food Administration ended its support of high food prices, and the bottom promptly dropped out of the agricultural market. By 1922, the per capita income of the farmer was only a third of what it had been in 1919. Aside from offering farmers some minimal loans, Congress and Wilson did nothing to relieve a steadily worsening situation. Labor's problems received even less sympathetic attention (Chapter 19). Even in demobilizing the armed forces, the administration followed a conservative, almost disinterested, course.

The election of 1920. To carry the limp banner of Wilsonian reform in the election of 1920, the Democrats picked the able and progressive governor of Ohio, James M. Cox. To strengthen the ticket with a "name," they chose young Franklin D. Roosevelt as his running mate. No one really expected the Democrats to win, however, for change was clearly in the air.

The election presented the Republicans with a great opportunity to give the nation dynamic new leadership, and the party had several proven leaders available for nomination. But the Old Guard bosses were not interested in the likes of a Charles Evans Hughes or a Herbert Hoover in 1920. Instead, they gave the country a pliable,

SACCO AND VANZETTI

One of the most controversial episodes in the 1920's was the trial and execution of Nicola Sacco and Bartolomeo Vanzetti. The case is still argued today, with many firmly convinced of their innocence and others just as sure of their guilt, while still others argue the fairness of the trial, which occurred in an atmosphere of fear and prejudice.

When Sacco and Vanzetti were arrested in Massachusetts in 1920 for robbery and the murder of two men, the United States was at the height of the Red scare. Although the men, both Italian immigrants, were avowed anarchists, they opposed war and violence. But they had evaded the draft in World War I, they carried leaflets attacking the government, and they possessed guns, which they claimed were for self-defense.

Neither man had a good alibi, and several witnesses placed them at the scene of the crime. Still, five men had taken part in the robbery, and the other three were not found. Also, no money was found on either Sacco or Vanzetti. Their appeal dragged on for six years, during which time a gangster confessed to the crime. But the death sentence was finally upheld, and in the face of world-wide protest, the men were executed in August, 1927.

Before his death, Sacco wrote a farewell to his son Dante in which he reaffirmed his revolutionary faith:

"Much have we suffered during this long Calvary. We protest today as we protested yesterday. We protest always for our freedom. . . .

"But remember always, Dante . . . don't you use all for yourself only, but down yourself just one step, at your side and help the weak ones that cry for help, help the prosecuted and the victim, because that are your better friends; they are the comrades that fight and fall as your father and Bartolo fought and fell yesterday for the conquest of the joy of freedom for all and the poor workers. . . ."

ineffectual member of their own clique, Senator Warren G. Harding. Probably no serious contender for the Presidency ever had fewer genuine qualifications for the office than the handsome, affable Harding. But the party leaders wanted a man they could control. To run with him, they chose the popular conservative governor of Massachusetts, Calvin Coolidge. The ticket won in a landslide, and into Washington came the men and policies that gave the twenties a peculiar flavor all its own in American political history.

The Harding administration. No man knew better than Harding how pitifully unfit he was for the office he assumed. But to handle the crucial areas of national policy, he had the good sense to pick able men. Herbert Hoover became secretary of commerce, an office he injected with new vigor. Charles Evans Hughes served with distinction as secretary of state. To head the Agriculture Department, Harding named Henry C. Wallace, a representative of the big farmers who at least knew something about farming. One of the world's richest men, Andrew W. Mellon, became secretary of the Treasury. Their presence alone saved the Harding administration from being a total disaster.

Unhappily, their influence was more than countered by the President's poker-playing, whiskey-drinking cronies. Harry Daugherty, Harding's campaign manager and a small-time lobbyist, became attorney general. A political hack of dubious reputation, Albert B. Fall, took over as secretary of the interior. Chance acquaintances, boyhood friends, and random relatives moved into such positions as head of the Veterans' Bureau, governor of the Federal Reserve Bank, and superintendent of federal prisons. The White House became the scene for activities which Theodore Roosevelt's daughter Alice Longworth described as best suited to the back room of a saloon. As for Harding himself, she concluded that he was "just a slob," not really a bad man.

Many of his friends most assuredly *were* bad men, however, as Harding learned to his sorrow. Mercifully, he died in 1923, before the public learned how shamefully his "friends" had betrayed him and while his reputation was still intact. Congressional investigators revealed that swindling in the Veterans' Bureau had cost the taxpayers millions of dollars. So blatant was the thievery in one government warehouse that goods bought with federal funds at one end of the building were promptly sold at the other end for money that went into the swindlers' pockets. The worst scandal was the Teapot Dome Affair, in which it was revealed that Secretary Fall had secretly leased government-owned oil lands in the West to private operators in return for substantial "loans." A spate of resignations, convictions, and suicides followed in the wake of the revelations. Yet, the scandals had little effect on the political fortunes of the Republican party.

Coolidge in the White House. Indeed, many people saw Calvin Coolidge as precisely the right man for the Presidency under the circumstances. Certainly the new President was a model of New England honesty and integrity. People who came into close contact with him, however, often came away more depressed than impressed by the experience. He was an austere man with few friends and a warped, almost juvenile, sense of humor. (His idea of a practical joke was to telephone the bearded, dignified Secretary Hughes at midnight to tell him the barber wanted to shave him.)

By no means a stupid man, at times Coolidge exhibited a knowledge of public affairs that impressed even cynical White House reporters. But he preferred not to say very much about anything in public and rather enjoyed his nickname of "Silent Cal." To one close observer, he was a "Puritan in Babylon," a baffling mixture of the worst and best of middle-class American qualities. The irrepressible Mrs. Longworth thought that any man so taciturn and pinched in expression must have been "weaned on a dill pickle." Totally barren of cultural or aesthetic interests, Coolidge was the perfect Philistine in the White House—dull, unimaginative, and lethargic, yet also shrewd and politically sensitive to the times.

"The man who builds a factory builds a temple, the man who works there worships there," Coolidge announced. With religious conviction, he believed that government should be run by businessmen for businessmen. He was no match for Hoover in understanding the nature of industrial capitalism in the twentieth century. His views were akin to the simple Horatio Alger legend and

crude social Darwinism of an earlier day. But by 1924 the public had come to identify prosperity with the silent man in Washington. Confident that "Coolidge prosperity" made their man unbeatable, the Republicans nominated him for a term as President in his own right.

The best the Democrats had to offer was an impeccable conservative of their own, John W. Davis, a former congressman from West Vrginia and later a lawyer in New York. But it took them 103 dreary ballots to do it, and the Democratic convention revealed a deep split in the party between urban-oriented forces and traditional Populist elements. To placate the latter, the convention named William Jennings Bryan's brother Charles to run with the urbane Davis. Politics in 1924 would have been dull business, indeed, had not Robert M. La Follette spiced up the campaign by running as the Progressive party's candidate for President.

Coolidge handily defeated his opponents in the election. Safe and traditional, his kind of political fundamentalism offered security at a time when change was rampant in other areas of American life (Chapter 21). Most voters preferred not to risk losing their "good times" by taking a chance with political change. Still, La Follette's vigorous candidacy and the 5 million votes he polled suggested that a sizable minority of the voters were still interested in liberal reform.

1928: A unique election year. Coolidge declined to run again in 1928, and so his party naturally turned to the strong man of his administration, Herbert Hoover. An outstanding engineer and able administrator, Hoover represented a forward-looking element in the Republican party. But he had strong ties with the past, too, and he epitomized the image of the self-made man. Many people were sure that if anyone could make prosperity permanent, Hoover could.

Largely on the strength of his record as governor of New York, Alfred E. Smith won the Democratic nomination in 1928. The "Happy Warrior," as he was called, was a staunch economic conservative, whose campaign manager was a General Motors executive who had voted for Coolidge four years earlier. But Smith was also a Catholic and a "city slicker," and his advocacy of repeal of the prohibition amendment made him a "wet." His candidacy was a challenge to the

In the period after World War I, the United States was headed by a succession of three Republican Presidents—Harding, Coolidge, and Hoover. The affable Harding, shown at right greeting veterans, liked occasions of this sort, where he could enjoy the privileges of the Presidency without having to worry about the burdens. To one friend he confided: "I don't know anything about this European stuff." Coolidge was shrewder, though hardly more intellectual. Below left, he poses stiffly while on a fishing expedition. The glum face is characteristic; one journalist wrote that he was always "looking down his nose to locate that evil smell which seemed forever to affront him." Hoover, below right, appears equally solemn—and no wonder. When this photograph was taken, in 1932, the country was deep in the worst depression in its history. Hoover, steadfastly opposed to federal intervention, suggested wistfully to singer Rudy Vallee: "If you can sing a song that will make people forget their troubles and the depression, I'll give you a medal."

rural, small-town values that still dominated much of the country.

Born in New York's slums, he had worked his way up in politics with the aid of Tammany Hall, the city's Democratic machine. He spoke in a rasping Lower East Side accent that many listeners to his radio speeches found strangely alien. In contrast, Hoover spoke in familiar, flat midwestern tones. Probably Smith could not have won the Presidency in 1928 under any circumstances, for prosperity alone was enough to assure Hoover's victory. But his background and religion made the campaign a vicious affair in some parts of the country. He lost so heavily that five states of the so-called Democratic Solid South went Republican. Reflecting the prejudice at the time against a Catholic in the White House, a joke had it that Smith, after his defeat, sent the Pope in Rome a one-word telegram: "Unpack!"

In another respect, the election of 1928 was unique, too. Oscar De Priest of Chicago became the first black man to be elected to Congress since 1901 and the first northern black ever to attain the distinction. His victory was a small reminder of the growing political power of urban blacks.

2 The Republicans Promote A New Economic Era

1. What was the economic philosophy of the government during the twenties?

2. How did farmers and workers fare during the twenties? How did these situations develop?

3. What position was taken by political leaders on the issue of the government's role in providing for the social welfare of the people? How did they justify that position?

4. How did Hoover hope to achieve a future which would represent progress, social justice, and order? What do you think were his chances of success?

During the 1920's, middle-class Americans attained a new social and economic status as a consequence of what historian Arthur Link calls "the flowering of American enterprise under the impact of the technological, financial, and other revolutions" of the time. Millions of people looked to the future with an expansive, almost breezy, confidence. Feeding their optimism, the leaders of the Republican party proclaimed a "New Era" in American business.

To replace the outmoded laissez faire capitalism of the nineteenth century, with its evident injustices and inequities, the "New Era" would be a time of social justice and welfare capitalism. Some visionaries spoke of the day when poverty would be abolished, wars would become obsolete, and social harmony would prevail throughout the world. The dream of a "New Era" was as utopian as any in history; but it was also perfectly in tune with liberalism and manifestly American in its assumption that society can be made perfect.

As an articulate spokesman for the "New Era," Herbert Hoover taught that American businessmen could effect a peaceful revolution in human affairs. With their superior know-how, talent for "scientific management," and dedication to serving society, they represented twentieth-century man at his best. Working within a framework of private enterprise, they would insure that enlightened self-interest guided men everywhere in the making of political and economic decisions. Strikes and labor unions would become outmoded, for the new economy would encourage cooperation among interest groups. No one would go hungry, no one would be without work, each man would prosper according to his talent and efforts. Horatio Alger had grown up and been given a college education!

At a time when businessmen were considered harbingers of the future, it was not surprising that their views should have dominated government. Most of the Harding, Coolidge, and Hoover programs were tailored specifically to encourage what businessmen called the "American Way" of unfettered private enterprise. Believing that everyone would prosper if business prospered, the Republicans did little for labor and agriculture.

Low taxes and high tariffs. After a serious postwar slump, brought about chiefly by the abrupt cutoff of heavy government wartime spending, the economy entered a new period of growth and expansion. Republican leaders set about making the recovery permanent. However much they talked of a "New Era" approach to the economy, in practice they usually turned to the tried and tested ways of their party in the past.

Secretary Mellon, for example, believed that low taxes for the rich would stimulate the capital investment needed to sustain prosperity. Thus, he reduced taxes on large incomes and corporations to a minimum, while retaining high rates for people with low incomes. By 1926, a man with a million-dollar income was paying less than a third in taxes of what he had paid in 1921. In some years, J. P. Morgan, one of the world's richest men, paid no taxes at all! Moreover, much of the money that was supposed to go into sound investments to promote economic growth actually poured into unwise speculative ventures in land and stocks. Mellon also reduced the national debt and balanced the federal budget, but he did so only by eliminating or reducing government spending in areas where it was desperately needed.

True to their past again, the Republicans raised tariffs to new highs. The Fordney-McCumber Tariff (1922) was hailed as a "scientific" approach to rate-setting, designed to equalize the costs of production abroad with those at home. A "sliding scale" of tariffs enabled rates to move up or down according to the needs of American manufacturers and without action by Congress on each move. In practice, the scale usually moved in one direction only—up. No one objected very strenuously, however, for even farmers were brought in under the tent of protection, while prosperity temporarily masked the damage the policy did to world trade.

When Congress enacted the Hawley-Smoot Tariff in 1930, raising rates to their highest point in history, a thousand professional economists urged Hoover to veto the bill. By that time the Great Depression was well under way, and they argued that the bill would further shrink foreign trade and worsen the economic crisis. But Hoover signed the bill, thereby triggering a series of retaliations against American goods by other nations and contributing to the economic demoralization that was to mark the early 1930's. Far from signifying a new economic era, Republican tariff policy was badly outdated. Because the war had devastated entire economies, the world needed economic cooperation, not traditional commercial rivalry.

HOOVER DEFENDS HIS TARIFF POLICY

In a series of speeches during the 1932 Presidential campaign, Herbert Hoover defended his support of a high tariff, pointing out its benefit to farmers:

"The very basis of safety to American agriculture is the protective tariff on farm products.

"The Republican party originated and proposes to maintain the protective tariff on agriculture products. . . . Ninety per cent of your market is at home, and I propose to reserve this market to the American farmer. . . .

". . .Except for the guardianship of the tariff, butter could be imported for 25 per cent below your prices, pork products for 30 per cent below your prices, lamb and beef products from 30 to 50 per cent below your prices. . . . Both corn and wheat could be sold in New York from the Argentine at prices below yours at this moment were it not for the tariff. . . .

"The removal of or reduction of the tariff on farm products means a flood of them into the United States from every direction, and either you would be forced to still further reduce your prices, or your products would rot on your farms. . . ."

Mr. Hoover also answered his opponents' charges that the tariff caused world-wide economic dislocation:

". . . I remind you that we levy tariffs upon only one-third of our imports. I also remind you that the actual increases made in the Smoot-Hawley Act covered only one-quarter of the dutiable imports. I may also remind you that our import trade is only one-eighth of the import trade of the world. So they would have us believe this world catastrophe . . . happened because the United States increased tariffs on one-fourth of one-third of one-eighth of the world's imports. Thus we pulled down the world, so they tell us, by increases on less than 1 per cent of the goods being imported by the world."

Business consolidation. Hoover's support of the high tariff was inconsistent with his belief in cooperation among economic units. "Progress is born of Cooperation," he asserted. He encouraged agricultural cooperatives and even labor unions of the sort that would meekly accept the dominant leadership of business. Impressed by the War Industries Board's ability to enforce cooperation during the war, he sought similar results in peacetime without government coercion.

With Hoover's blessing, businessmen formed trade associations to stabilize prices, standardize products, and restrict competition. Many industrialists welcomed the opportunity to join with their "competitors" in these associations, if only to reduce the cutthroat practices and pricing chaos that plagued the economy. But the practice virtually eliminated the free market price system, for the old "law of supply and demand" now gave way to production based on supposedly scientific methods for determining demand.

In this environment, productivity soared, with the industrial output per man-hour rising some 40 percent during the decade. Business consolidation also flourished. Factories and mines by the hundreds merged into fewer and fewer units. Large chain-type corporations swallowed up small businesses with an insatiable appetite. From about 5,000 units in 1922, the A & P food store chain burgeoned to 17,500 in 1928. Samuel Insull of Chicago built a giant pyramid of public utilities companies to the point where he literally lost track of his holdings. When Insull's empire fell, incidentally, it was the largest corporate failure in American history. By 1929, 200 large corporations controlled about half the total corporate wealth in the country, and they were all growing at a spectacular rate when the stock market crashed and brought them to a halt.

One effect of this consolidation and emphasis on efficiency was to depersonalize American business. Few people could identify the owners of the new giants, for ownership was divorced from management. Stockholders furnished the capital and theoretically "owned" the companies; but actual control rested with the big banks, insurance companies, and investment trusts that held huge blocks of stock. A new class of highly skilled, specialized, anonymous managers ran the corporations.

As historian David A. Shannon observes, systems were replacing men. Insofar as the prophets of the "New Era" encouraged this process, they did indeed help to effect a revolution in American life, though hardly the revolution Hoover had in mind. For the systematizing of business inevitably spread to other units of society—labor, agriculture, and above all, government. Doubtless, the process was a logical development of the Industrial Revolution itself; but the "bigness" that became so much a part of life in America produced social and political effects that remain with us today.

Plight of agriculture and labor. Because the farm problem was the most serious domestic problem of the decade, Republican leaders could not ignore it. When foreign markets dried up after the war and prices fell, farmers continued to produce at record rates. A huge surplus piled up, with no way to dispose of it. By 1922, agriculture was mired in a serious depression that worsened throughout the decade. In seeking relief from their troubles, the larger farm owners worked through their trade association, the Farm Bureau Federation, to gain privileges for themselves that the National Association of Manufacturers and similar groups had won for businessmen. In Congress, a "Farm Bloc" of legislators from agricultural districts advanced the interests of farmers and farm-oriented businesses.

Hoover made one serious attempt to deal with the problems of the farm surplus when he created the Federal Farm Board in 1929. In keeping with his "New Era" outlook, the board extended the trade association principle to farming by promoting cooperation, eliminating inefficient competition, and stabilizing prices. Although the board was authorized in emergencies to buy and store surpluses, it was given no means to dispose of them. Lacking the power to limit production, it failed to solve the problem of the surplus for production was the point at which the problem began. Still, the board was an important precedent for Democratic policy-makers in the next decade.

Organized labor fared badly in the twenties, partly because of government hostility, partly because its own leaders were inept. In several important decisions, the Supreme Court struck down safeguards that labor had won in the Progressive era. The Justice Department freely used

517

the injunction and antitrust laws against unions. In a major effort to drive independent unions from the factories, industry promoted a vigorous drive for the open shop.

True to his faith in cooperation, on the other hand, Hoover urged businessmen to bestow the benefits of "welfare capitalism" on their workers. To achieve social harmony, workers who joined company unions were offered profit-sharing plans, insurance programs, retirement benefits. "Welfare capitalism" benefitted only a handful of workers, to be sure; but it established some interesting precedents for future government action.

In 1924, a dismally unimaginative man, William Green, succeeded Samuel Gompers as head of the AFL. Green's cautious, conservative attitude deprived labor of the strong leadership it needed for organizing the great masses of unionless industrial workers. Union membership actually declined in the twenties. The plight of the unorganized workers was dramatized in bloody, unsuccessful strikes that swept the coal fields early in the decade and the southern textile mills a few years later.

> I'm a-going to starve,
> Everybody will,
> Cause you can't make a living
> In a cotton mill.

At Gastonia, North Carolina, a bitter struggle between resentful workers and the feudal barons who owned the mills made a mockery of the "New Era" in its last year of existence. All-out industrial warfare raged, the farthest thing from the cooperation Hoover preached.

Social welfare. The most serious flaw in the "New Era" concept was its neglect of measures to deal with the country's social ills. Both Roosevelt's New Nationalism of 1912 and Wilson's New Freedom after 1914 clearly acknowledged that government had some responsibility to insure the social welfare of the people. Progressives had started to act in such areas as workmen's compensation, sickness and unemployment insurance, child labor, minimum wages and maximum hours, and even public housing.

During the 1920's, reformers in Congress kept these ideas alive, although they were unable to translate them into laws. To Hoover, the responsibility for social welfare lay with private enterprise; government could only offer advice. He believed that enlightened business practices would accomplish what laws could never bring about. The result of government's inaction was a legislative lag of some fifteen years, leaving millions of people defenseless against the arbitrary, highly impersonal effects of modern industrial society.

In ancient Rome, the god Janus had two faces, looking in opposite directions. The Republican party in the 1920's had two faces, too. One face, epitomized best by Andrew Mellon, gazed nostalgically at the world of the nineteenth-century entrepreneurs who had created modern American capitalism. The other face was that of Herbert Hoover, who looked to a future in which a mature business system would guarantee social justice and social order. Accepting many premises of the Progressive reformers, the prophets of the "New Era" tried to prove that business could do what reformers believed only government could do. For middle-class Americans, at least, their approach functioned well when times were good, it appeared. How would it fare in a time of economic crisis?

3 "Boom And Bust"

1. How did the Model T, the Empire State Building, and the Stock Market symbolize the twenties?

2. What were the indicators of economic prosperity during the twenties? What were the indicators of economic ills?

3. What mistakes did government and business make which helped cause the depression? Do you think it realistic to fault the United States government for the failure to prevent the Depression?

4. How did Hoover attempt to correct the economic collapse. Do you think this was a reasonable approach? How successful were Hoover's attempts?

During the 1920's, Americans enjoyed the highest standard of living of any people up to that point in history. Industry turned out consumer goods in prodigious quantities at prices many people could afford—or thought they could afford. Items which once had been luxuries for the rich now came within reach of millions—homes and automobiles, radios and appliances, packaged foods and stylish clothing.

All this material prosperity had its effect on people's social and political outlook, too. Superficial class distinctions faded, as people began to think of themselves as middle class rather than as workers or tradesmen. In economic terms, the distinctions persisted; but the leveling influence of the new prosperity was strong and pervasive.

Symbols of prosperity. Nothing symbolized prosperity better than the automobile. In 1915, when Ford began to mass produce his famous Model T, only about 2.5 million automobiles rattled along America's primitive roads. By 1929, nearly 30 million were speeding over a nationwide network of paved highways. Tough, sturdy, and cheap, the Model T was a phenomenal success. By 1927, 15 million had bought it. Ford would have been content to go on producing his "Tin Lizzie" forever. But his competitors began turning out closed cars with sporty lines and comfortable seats, forcing him to discontinue his beloved T in favor of the equally successful Model A. Automobiles became a mainstay of the entire economy.

Another important measure of prosperity was construction. Home building rose to a peak in 1926, then fell off somewhat. Public building picked up the slack and soared, quite literally so in the case of the skyscraper craze. New York boasted its graceful Chrysler Building and towering 102-story Empire State Building; but other cities also refashioned their skylines with the tall new structures.

Advertising became big business and a powerful political force. Subtle appeals reshaped the buying habits of millions, orienting them toward the particular goods industry produced. "Buy Now! Pay Later!" was the theme of advertising, and credit buying quickly took over from the old, cautious "cash on the line" transactions. Easy credit was essential to the success of consumer-goods industries, for they depended on large sales volume. But it also led to overbuying among people who could not really afford the time-payment purchases they made.

Playing the market. Early in the decade, the stock market caught the public's imagination and became the popular barometer of the economy (see feature, page 520). The higher prices soared, the more investors became infected with the thought of making a "killing" on the market. Only a relatively few people actually played the market, but "margin" buying enabled many who knew nothing about the market to take the plunge with their savings. Moreover, the "easy money" policy in Washington actually encouraged speculation. Whenever the market dipped, as it frequently did, small investors on "margin" were badly hurt.

Still, only a few observers took a pessimistic view of economic conditions, and no one paid much attention to their gloomy warnings. National income soared. Corporate profits rose 80 percent. Wages climbed, though never in proper proportion to profits. In 1928, Hoover announced that "given a chance to go forward with the policies of the last eight years, and we shall soon, with the help of God, be within sight of the day when poverty will be banished from the nation." Few wise men in either party disputed his claim.

Then, on October 29, 1929, only eight months after Hoover became President, the stock market collapsed. Within a week, $60 billion in stock prices were lost and thousands of investors wiped out. Overnight, the "Big Bull Market" came to a grinding halt. Immediately, the whole economy began to creak and groan under the strain, as weaknesses in the system that prosperity had masked finally revealed themselves. By 1930, the "New Era" had become a nightmare, haunting its prophets and demoralizing the nation.

What went wrong? Why did Hoover's great dream become a nightmare? Who was to blame for this crisis that rattled the nation to its foundations? Perhaps a second look at the prosperity decade will suggest some answers to these questions.

Reasons for economic failure. For one thing, millions of people knew only unrelieved misery and insecurity during the so-called good times. Racial minorities knew almost nothing of prosperity. About 80 percent of the nation's black

BUYING AND SELLING STOCK

A share of stock represents a partial ownership in a corporation. The *face*, or actual, value of a stock varies as the assets of a company grow or diminish; a stock's value also fluctuates from day to day as public demand for the stock varies. People who own stock in a company receive annual interest called dividends on their shares. If a company pays out most of its profits to its stockholders, the dividends will be high. If a company reinvests most of its profits, the dividends will be relatively low, but the company's assets will increase and the value of each share will probably go up.

An investor usually buys stocks to earn the long-range profit from the dividends; therefore he keeps his stocks for a long time. An investor transacts his business through the stock exchange—the marketplace where stock brokers buy and sell stock. Most transactions on the stock exchange, however, are not those of investors but of speculators who buy and sell stocks to take advantage of the daily fluctuations in prices. Of the various stock manipulations that speculators employ when buying and selling stocks, the most frequently used is *margin buying,* that is, buying on credit.

The speculator pays cash for a part, or the margin, of the stock, and the broker arranges a bank loan for the rest. Such a loan is a "call loan," since the bank can call it in for repayment within twenty-four hours. If the stock's value rises and the speculator sells, he will earn a profit. If the value goes down, however, and the bank recalls the loan, he will have to sell at a loss to pay back the loan. The smaller the required margin, of course, the more stocks can be bought on credit. In the 1920's the margin requirement, which is set by the Federal Reserve, was very low, only one-tenth of a stock's value. Since the crash, however, the margin requirement has been more strictly regulated, and today it is much higher.

people lived in the rural South, where the vision of a "New Era" never penetrated at all. In 1920, 1.5 million blacks lived in the big cities; by 1930 the figure was 2.5 million. Few jobs were available to these people, and those that were paid starvation wages. For most black people, the decade was a period of bare subsistence.

In the West, 1.5 million Mexican-Americans lived in segregated poverty of the worst sort. Oriental-Americans fared somewhat better, although they too were victimized by discrimination. In the cotton states, tenancy and sharecropping reduced thousands of farmers, black and white, to conditions of misery. All told, probably a third of the entire population found the twenties to be far from a prosperity decade.

As for businessmen, many of them managed their businesses very badly indeed. Much as farmers had been doing for years, they overproduced in terms of the potential for consumption. Industrial efficiency increased markedly, but the gains were not fairly or rationally translated into lower prices, higher wages, or increased farm income. Corporate profits and stock dividends shot up out of all common-sense proportion to wages or even to the efficiency gains.

In effect, the price system failed at a time of high prosperity, an astonishing thing to happen in a business society. Instead of profits spreading throughout the economy so that people could buy more goods, they were used for speculation or to expand production still further. High dividends made industrial stocks attractive to speculators, so that by 1927 the stock market was dangerously inflated. Whether from simple greed or lack of common sense, businessmen neglected the problem of rationally distributing the gains of prosperity. Instead, they siphoned off the high profits for their own use.

Government gave them a green light, moreover. Republican tax policies encouraged speculation. The trade associations helped to cripple the free market price system. Ironically, all of business's traditional demands on government were satisfied: the budget was balanced, government spending was slashed, interest rates were kept low, trust-busting was curtailed, government activity in general was minimal. Yet the system failed. In focusing on the narrow interests of the business community, both government and busi-

JELL-O

THE KING AND QUEEN MIGHT EAT THEREOF
AND NOBLEMEN BESIDES

s good things to eat—
hat look good, taste
d are good. Whenever
e use for choice salad
good shortening or
me frying fat, you
se for Wesson Oil.

In many ways, the 1920's were the heyday of what has been called the Business Cult. The emphasis was on the self-made man, free enterprise, and salesmanship. An important component of the business world was the advertising industry, which was expanding into the new medium of radio, and benefiting too from cheap color printing and the public's interest in buying to "keep up with the Joneses." The ad for Jell-O, above, contains a not-so-subtle snob appeal: You too can dine like royalty. Maxfield Parrish, the artist, was known also for his book illustrations, posters, and murals. René Clarke painted the Wesson Oil ad at left. It was one of a series that did much to turn Americans into salad eaters. The products advertised here—an "instant" dessert and a bottled salad oil—point up another development of the period. This was the increase in canned, packaged, or otherwise prepared foods. In earlier days, housewives (or their servants) had baked their own bread, preserved their own vegetables, and made their own jams and jellies. Now all these things could be "store-bought." They were especially welcomed by working women, whose numbers grew appreciably during this period.

ness had ignored the larger, more complex interests of society as a whole. What resulted was a dangerous imbalance in the economy between business on one side and consumers, labor, and agriculture on the other. The stock market collapse did not cause the depression. Rather, it triggered a chain of events in an economy that had been ripe for a crisis for many years.

Republican leaders had encouraged the speculative boom before the depression, but they were not exclusively to blame for the system's failure. The Democrats had nothing better to offer during the twenties. More important, the imbalance developed from economic weaknesses that extended back into a century of industrial growth. In this sense, the Great Depression was long overdue when it finally came in the 1930's. Indeed, a grave economic crisis had been averted in 1914 only by the outbreak of war in Europe. Even at that early date, American industry was not providing for a rational distribution of the goods and capital it was producing. During the twenties, nobody did anything to remedy this situation.

As full-scale depression set in, the nation's leaders reacted as though the crash were merely a temporary slump. Maintain public confidence and the storm would soon pass, they advised. Let the market hit bottom, Mellon counseled, for nothing in the situation warranted pessimism. Noting that the nation had weathered some seventeen depressions in 120 years, the president of the National Association of Manufacturers concluded comfortably that there was "little on the horizon today to give us undue or great concern."

The Hoover "New Deal." But behind the mask of confidence they wore in public, the men of the "New Era" were baffled and helpless, and none more than Hoover himself. To maintain purchasing power, he asked businessmen to keep wages up voluntarily—and when wages continued to fall, he refused to let government step in to enforce his request. Rather than provide federal funds for unemployment relief, moreover, he appointed a committee to study the problem—and the committee did little more than assure the rich that they would know a "great spiritual experience" if they helped the poor.

On a more positive note, in 1932, Hoover signed the Norris-LaGuardia Act which severely curtailed the use of injunctions in labor disputes. He approved a measure to provide mortgage relief to farmers. Acknowledging finally that public works might stimulate recovery, he authorized several major construction projects, most notably Boulder (now Hoover) Dam. Reluctantly, he activated the Reconstruction Finance Corporation (RFC) and gave it authority to lend money to banks, insurance companies, and railroads. These loans were made on the theory that money pumped into the economy at the top would "trickle down" to provide benefits at all levels. In the end, too, Hoover unbalanced the federal budget and initiated a policy of *deficit financing* (borrowing money through the issuance of government bonds and thereby raising the national debt), actions which he deplored, but which he was forced to take in order to obtain revenue.

Taken together, these measures are sometimes called the "Hoover New Deal." As efforts to combat the depression, they were failures. But they provided the next administration with important precedents for the use of federal power. When Hoover unbalanced the budget, for example, he made it much easier for his successor (who, by the way, sharply criticized the action at the time) to finance the heavy spending programs of the New Deal.

As his policies failed to turn the tide, Hoover's personality became a psychological factor in the depression. His party lost heavily in the off-year elections in 1930. Opposed not only by the Democrats, but also by such old Progressive Republicans as Senators George W. Norris of Nebraska and Hiram Johnson of California, he engaged in a running conflict with Congress.

Increasingly solemn and withdrawn, Hoover became a symbol of defeat and despair to millions. The crisis seemed to bring out the dogmatic, stubborn qualities in the man, dulling his penetrating intelligence and stifling his capacity for rational analysis. He struggled manfully to combat the depression while remaining true to his innermost convictions, but it was clear that he did not understand the real nature of the crisis. As Arthur M. Schlesinger, Jr., writes, "His fault lay not in taking an optimistic line, but in bending the facts to sustain his optimism, and then in believing his own conclusions."

Judged in the context of the entire economy, the "New Era" did not function well even during prosperity. In a time of economic crisis, it failed miserably. When the Great Depression struck, the two faces of the Republican Janus became one, a face looking backward toward a past that was gone forever.

4 The Great Depression Grips The Nation

1. What statistical evidence is there of the worsening of the depression between 1929 and 1933?

2. How did the depression affect individual Americans? Which groups were hurt the most by the economic collapse? Why were these groups hurt?

3. Why did production and distribution stop during the depression when so many people were anxious to work and consume?

4. Do you think there was a serious threat to American institutions through violent change?

If one were to choose a single word to describe the Great Depression, the word would be *stagnation*. In the period from October 1929 to March 1933, the most dynamic economy in the world came close to standing still. To be sure, not everything ground to a halt. Not all businesses failed—although more than 100,000 did. Not all banks shut their doors, wiping out the savings of their depositors—although 10,000 did. Not all people were thrown out of work—although an average of 100,000 were every week. As historian Frederick Lewis Allen observes, it was sometimes oddly difficult to see the signs of depression with the casual eye. But the signs were there, and they became increasingly ominous as the months dragged by.

Cold statistics during this period tell a story of capitalism in crisis. Gross National Product (GNP), the figure by which the health of any economy is measured, plummeted from $104 billion to $32 billion. Steel production fell 75 percent, while automobile makers operated at only a fifth of their capacity. Farm income, already dismally low, was halved. As for national income in general, it went down in a spiral from $81 billion in 1929, to $68 billion the next year, to $53 billion a year later, to a bottom of $41 billion in 1932.

Cold statistics also tell a story of human despair. One quarter of the entire labor force was unemployed, which meant that about 15 million people had no earned income whatsoever. Most of them were industrial workers, whose purchasing power had kept the economy going. Without jobs they could purchase nothing but the barest necessities of life. Thirty million Americans were dependent upon public or private charity for their very existence.

Millions who managed to hang onto their jobs suffered wage cuts averaging 60 percent. Clerks worked for five dollars a week, women in some industries for ten cents an hour. Salaries fell for teachers, ministers, and almost all white-collar workers. Doctors and lawyers had difficulty collecting fees. Even the national baseball hero Babe Ruth took a heavy salary cut.

The effects of depression. It was a cruel and frustrating time, and the paradoxes of it became obvious. Why were factories lying idle when so many people wanted to work and to buy their goods. Why did purchasing power dry up in a country that was enormously wealthy? Why did industries continue paying high dividends to stockholders while they fired their workers or slashed wages? Why were people going hungry when huge stocks of food were piling up in warehouses? The tragic irony of the Great Depression was caught perfectly by the humorist Will Rogers, who noted that the United States was the only nation ever to go to the poorhouse in an automobile.

Brutally, the depression struck hardest at those who were already in difficulty. As competition for jobs became intense, racism worked to virtually exclude black people from jobs of any kind. In Mississippi, black firemen on the railroads were hounded out by murder and terror. In 1933, about 40 percent of blacks in the cities were on relief,

The Great Depression resulted in scenes quite new to American life. The Baltimore man at left, who advertised himself "for sale" in the business district, had been jobless for five months before taking this desperate step. Below, a breadline stretches across New York City's Times Square. A Broadway producer remembers: "Two or three blocks along Times Square, you'd see these men, silent, shuffling along in line. Shabby clothes, but you could see they had been pretty good clothes." Almost every large city had its "Hooverville," where the homeless unemployed scraped along on handouts and hope. The sprawling shacks at right were photographed on the outskirts of Seattle in 1933. A witness before a congressional committee on the depression testified that "the last thing I saw on the night I left Seattle was numbers of women searching for scraps of food in the refuse piles of the principal markets of the city." The aimless men below right lived in another Hooverville—this one on the Lower East Side of Manhattan.

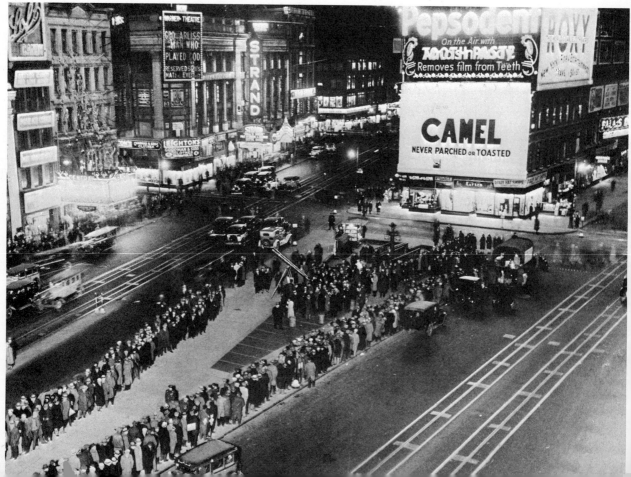

525

and in some towns the figure climbed to 80 percent. Women were squeezed out of jobs that paid anything more than starvation wages. As for tenant farmers, they left the land in droves and took to drifting about the country in search of work.

The depression further aggravated the plight of farmers from the drought-ridden "Dust Bowl" of the Great Plains. Abandoning their now useless farms, many "Okies" and "Arkies" (so called because many of them came from Oklahoma and Arkansas) sought the Promised Land in California, where they found instead prejudice and rejection. Young people just out of school often had nowhere to go except "on the road," where they led a nomadic existence.

In the congressional elections of 1930, unemployment received scant attention from the politicians. A year later things were different. Long lines of shuffling men waiting for a handout of food, jobless veterans peddling apples on street corners, and homeless people sleeping in doorways could not be ignored. Clusters of rude shacks appeared on the outskirts of every city, quickly to be dubbed "Hoovervilles." Heroic mothers fed their families on fifty cents a week or less, only, in many instances, to see them fall apart under the impact of grinding poverty. Men, women, and children scavenged in garbage dumps for bits of food, a sight that prompted one inventive business executive to propose that garbage be packaged and doled out to the poor in exchange for odd jobs! Some people actually died of starvation, while thousands were afflicted with severe malnutrition.

Men who wanted desperately to work found that no one wanted them. It was a harsh lesson to learn, for they had grown up believing that anyone who really wanted work could find it. The morale of millions was shattered by the experience. Fear spread everywhere—to the soup kitchens of the jobless, to the shabby parlor of the family whose breadwinner might lose his job tomorrow, to the offices of businessmen who saw no way out of the crisis, to the halls of government where politicians wondered how soon the unemployed would begin thinking about revolution.

Keep the people laughing, some said. Cheer them up and make them forget their troubles. To those who could afford the admission prices, the movies offered escape in gay musicals and comedies that tried to mock the depression. Popular songs reflected an ambivalence about the times. "Happy Days Are Here Again" was the tune people wanted to hear, but "Brother, Can You Spare A Dime?" somehow drowned it out.

People did their best to get along with what they had. In some areas the unemployed formed cooperative leagues to produce and sell the necessities of life, but this attempt at "self-help" foundered as the depression worsened. Jazz musicians in Harlem held "rent parties," taking over an apartment and playing for donations to pay the tenant's rent. Some people tried to move "back to the land," but they quickly discovered that life on the farm was as bad as life in the city. On a different level, twelve distinguished southerners produced a book *I'll Take My Stand* (1930), in which they argued the case for agrarianism as against industrial capitalism. Their argument came to nothing, but it reflected growing disillusion with the existing system in many quarters.

To the astonishment of many observers, communism made very little headway among the masses of unemployed workers. To be sure, class consciousness grew during the depression, but it never reached the point where great numbers of people were ready to give up capitalism and embrace communism. Moreover, organizers for the Communist party were singularly inept in their work, alienating far more prospective recruits than they attracted. By 1932 the party claimed a membership of only 12,000. The Socialists did somewhat better, their Presidential candidate in 1932, Norman Thomas, polling close to 900,000 votes. But their program was a moderate one, more in keeping with traditional politics than the proposals of the Communists.

More significant were the instances of random violence and grass-roots radicalism that spread as conditions worsened. Organized looting and mass shoplifting indicated that people were becoming desperate for food. Surly mobs gathered to prevent evictions in the cities and foreclosures on the farms. Home-grown demagogues sprang up everywhere, proposing a wondrous variety of cures for the depression. Bitterness led many people to seek scapegoats for their troubles, and they found them in Herbert Hoover and Wall

Street. So savagely and unfairly was the President attacked that long after he retired from politics, Democratic candidates for office were still running against the "Hoover Depression."

The defeat of Herbert Hoover. On occasion Hoover contributed to the destruction of his own reputation. In 1932, large numbers of unemployed veterans marched into Washington to demand payment of a bonus for their war service that Congress had promised them. Camped in shanties at Anacostia Flats, near Washington, D.C., they impressed many conservatives as the forerunners of the revolutionary mobs. In a most regrettable move, Hoover ordered the army to evict the veterans, and the country was treated to the spectacle of a pitched battle between soldiers and ex-soldiers.

Incidents such as that of the Bonus Army prompted some people to call for rule by a strong man. A national magazine put it bluntly: "Appoint a dictator!" In certain intellectual circles, too, doubts rose as to the compatibility of democracy and capitalism. A few writers went so far as to embrace communism (Chapter 23), although most of them were not so much attracted by communism's promises as they were disturbed by capitalism's failures. Growing cynicism and despair marked the national mood in 1932; yet at the time of the national election, most people seemed willing to give the political system at least one more chance. Time enough to turn to radical alternatives—even to revolution—if the system failed to produce relief.

At their nominating convention in 1932, the Republicans had no choice but to support Hoover. The President defended his policies as best he could during the ensuing campaign, arguing that further moves by the federal government would undermine traditional American liberalism and destroy private initiative. His speeches were high-minded and educational, but they were lost on the people. Hoover simply did not have the confidence of the American people, and when he went into the election, he was all but foredoomed to defeat.

In Chicago the Democrats were confident that their choice would be the next President. Al Smith wanted the nomination in order to vindicate his humiliating defeat of four years earlier. After a good bit of bargaining and dealing, however, the convention turned to the successful governor of New York, Franklin Delano Roosevelt, and gave him Speaker of the House John Nance Garner of Texas as his running mate. Among those who helped Roosevelt capture the nomination was Joseph P. Kennedy, a shrewd and successful businessman from Boston and the father of an extraordinary family that would loom large in American politics a generation hence.

The Democratic platform called for reduced government expenditures and a balanced budget; but it also noted the need for federal action to reduce the suffering of the depression and to help bring about recovery. Roosevelt broke precedent by flying to the convention to address the delegates in person, an act he told them was symbolic of his determination to strike out in new directions. "I pledge you—I pledge myself to a new deal for the American people," he vowed.

For most people the only issue in 1932 was the depression. Few voters really knew very much about Roosevelt or his plan, if any, for handling the crisis. They knew only that Hoover had failed, and they voted overwhelmingly to repudiate him and his policies. Roosevelt won with a sweeping electoral victory.

Conditions worsen. During the long interval between the election in November and the inauguration of the new President in March (the Twentieth Amendment would soon reduce this "lame duck" period by about six weeks), the economic situation became worse than ever. By February 1933, a deadly financial crisis gripped the nation, as state after state resorted to declaring a "bank holiday" (an indefinite suspension of all banking activities) in an effort to stop the massive drain on bank deposits. If the banking system failed, capitalism itself would come tumbling down in ruins. Farmers became more militant by the day, while the business community suffered an abject breakdown of morale.

As the public mood became one of desperation, the cries of the extremists became bolder and louder. Yet, revolution was not imminent in the spring of 1933. To be sure, fear and doubt prevailed across the land as Roosevelt took the oath of office on March 4. But people were ready to give the new man a chance; indeed, they were ready to follow him in any direction he chose to take them.

CONCLUSION

Although the Progressive spirit did not completely die in the 1920's, the decade really belonged to the Old Guard Republicans. Interested chiefly in advancing the interests of big business, they did their best to revive the "good old days" of prereform and prewar politics. In Harding, they gave America its most inept President; but the people liked Harding, and it was the behavior of his associates that ultmately ruined his reputation. Coolidge kept the nation "cool," as his campaign slogan promised, but only by putting on an unprecedented display of executive lethargy. Overshadowing both men, Hoover was the ablest and most imaginative Republican of his time, a visionary whose idealism softened, even if it did not actually counteract, the shortsighted selfishness of the Old Guard. But time and events proved that Hoover's noble dream was, after all, only a dream.

The stock market crash of 1929 not only led to the misery and despair of the Great Depression, but also revealed serious flaws in the economic system. An America which had enjoyed impressive prosperity in the twenties found itself, by 1930, wallowing in the worst social and economic crisis in its history. Capitalism itself was in jeopardy, ironically, because the capitalists had botched the job of managing their own system.

As the depression worsened, moreover, a disturbing number of people began to question the ability of democracy to cope with the complex problems of a modern industrial society. In 1932, it was clear that a major political change was in the offing. The only question to be answered after the election of that year was how sweeping the change would be.

QUESTIONS

1. In what ways was the political scene of the twenties similar to that of the Gilded Age?

2. What was the essence of the economic philosophy of the leaders of the Republican party in the twenties? What were the weaknesses of this philosophy?

3. What position did Hoover and other Republican leaders take on the government's role in promoting social welfare? Why did they take this position?

4. How extensive was the prosperity of the twenties? Explain your answer.

5. What elements indicated the existence of economic problems prior to the depression?

6. What steps could government leaders have taken to prevent the depression or weaken its impact? How would these steps have helped?

7. What indicators exist to prove that the depression deepened between 1929 and 1933?

8. Why did Americans starve during the depression when there were food surpluses stored in warehouses around the country?

9. What were the similarities and the differences between the Harding, Coolidge, and Hoover administrations?

10. Is it possible to refer to the twenties as a measure to evaluate the present economic health of the United States? Explain your answer.

BIBLIOGRAPHY

DOS PASSOS, JOHN, *USA*, Houghton Mifflin (Sentry Editions). The three novels, *The 42nd Parallel, Nineteen Nineteen,* and *The Big Money* are gathered together into one volume providing an excellent cross-section of American life in the first three decades of the twentieth century. The book is long and the style may be difficult for some, but with rapid reading, a unique moving picture of America emerges. The student may also choose to read selectively and profit from the excellent literary sketches of important people scattered through the story.

LEUCHTENBURG, WILLIAM, *The Perils of Prosperity 1914–1932,* U. of Chicago Press. Leuchtenburg surveys the period in a readable style which seems to be generally reflective of most of the volumes in the Chicago History of American Civilization Series. He believes that this was the period in which America tried to come to terms with the twentieth century, including the growth of the city and foreign commitment.

HICKS, JOHN D., *Republican Ascendancy 1921–1933,* New American Nation Series, Harper & Row (Torchbooks). This book concentrates upon the Republican political dominance of the twenties under Harding, Coolidge and Hoover. Since this is a detailed political analysis, the reader will find little on social, cultural, or intellectual aspects of the twenties.

SINCLAIR, ANDREW, *Era of Excess: A Social History of the Prohibition Movement,* Harper & Row (Colophon Books). Sinclair's book is more than a history of Prohibition. It is a history of an era extending from 1917 to 1933. The book is a good companion volume to the Hicks account, thus covering both the social and political history of the period.

HANDLIN, OSCAR, *Al Smith and His America,* Library of American Biography, Little Brown. The high-school student can read this excellent biography without difficulty. It deals with life in the Irish wards of New York City, state and local politics, and the rise of Al Smith to national popularity. The book examines the election of 1928 and the role of Smith's Catholic religion in accounting for his defeat.

GALBRAITH, JOHN KENNETH, *The Great Crash, 1929,* Houghton Mifflin (Sentry Editions). Galbraith is one of our best-known economists, providing excellent commentary on American civilization through well-written books. This volume examines both the influence of the crash on the American economy and the economy's influence on the crash.

Social And Cultural Trends In The Roaring Twenties

The period of the 1920's was a time of transition, when American society passed from the "good old days" of the nineteenth century into the uncertain future of the twentieth. As such, it brought profound changes in the quality of life, not only for society as a whole, but for each individual as well. But the period was not really confined to the single decade of the twenties; rather it spanned the years, roughly, from 1912 to 1930. As historian Henry F. May observes, a close look at the years before World War I reveals an almost intolerable placidity on the surface of life in America. But a probe anywhere beneath the calm surface reveals "the beginnings of the later revolution in nearly all its variety, excitement, and potential destructiveness." In particular, it reveals all the tendencies historians usually associate with the decade of the 1920's.

Yet, inevitably the Great War endowed the postwar decade with a special quality of its own. If it did nothing else, it shattered the illusion that nineteenth-century liberalism necessarily meant the triumph of reason and the inevitability of progress in human affairs. For the young, the intellectuals, the artists, for the adventurous in heart and spirit generally, the search for new attitudes, new standards, new values, became an exciting, sometimes a genuinely creative, experience. For Americans who wanted to cling to the old ways of life, it was a profoundly disturbing experience. Inevitably the advocates of the new clashed with the defenders of the old, and the collision produced effects from which the nation still suffers. As you read about the changes in American life during the 1920's, look for the answers to these questions:

1. What were the most important elements of the "social revolution"?
2. How did traditionalists respond to this decade of transition and change?
3. How did social critics view American life?
4. How was the trend toward nonconformity reflected in literature and the arts?

1 The City Challenges Traditional American Values

1. How did the new freedom of women manifest itself during the twenties?

2. What evidence is there to prove that "the city became a laboratory, in which the acids of modernity eroded the nation's traditional ideals and social stability, transforming the life style of millions of people"?

3. In what ways did radio affect American society?

4. By the 1920's what signs of a rising black awareness had appeared?

A persistent theme in American history is the conflict between rural folk and city people—the clash of "hayseeds" and "city slickers." Sometimes the issues pitting the two groups against each other have been political and economic in nature. In the early years of the twentieth century, they were overwhelmingly social and cultural. America's traditional moral attitudes and social goals had been born in agrarian soil in the eighteenth century and had flourished in the rural society of the nineteenth. As the rural majority in the population became a minority, however, the gap between the rhetoric of the old morality and the reality of modern life became all but unbridgeable. Moreover, the struggle to preserve the old ways became increasingly one-sided.

New codes of behavior. Historian David A. Shannon has suggested that the American city-dweller entered the twentieth century at least a decade or two before the rural man. By 1920, certainly, city people were fully in the mainstream of the country's future development. And while they paid lip service to the simple, old-fashioned ideals and values of the farm and village, they behaved in ways that were grimly alien to people who still lived on or near the land.

Unlike his rural fellow countryman, the city-dweller belonged to the new masses—the faceless millions of producers and consumers of the factory economy who grasped at every fad and fancy that came their way. As the center of the new mass production-mass consumption economy, the city became a laboratory in which the "acids of modernity" eroded the nation's traditional ideals and social stability, transforming the life style of millions of people.

The transformation was particularly striking in public and private morality. Changes began well before the war, when critics of Victorian morality spoke out for less restrictive and hypocritical standards. During the 1920's, the traditional moral standards crumbled, giving way to new codes of behavior that ranged from the merely permissive to the madly pleasure-seeking.

After women received the vote in 1920, they enjoyed a new freedom to realize more adequately their potential as individuals. At the same time, their emancipation contributed to the growing instability of the family, altering the traditional relationship between men and women. Women now moved into territory once generally reserved for men—big business and finance, politics and journalism, medicine and the law, even crime.

As if to advertise the freer attitudes toward personal behavior, women radically changed their appearance after the war. Out went the high-button shoes, the ungainly corsets, the long, heavy dresses of Victorian fashion. In came the costume of the flapper—short skirts, silk stockings, bobbed hair, and lipstick. As did many men, many women openly patronized the illegal speakeasies of the day, breaking the law against drinking alcoholic beverages. Many of them danced the Charleston, the Lindy, and the Black Bottom—the bold new dance steps set to the sensuous beat and wail of jazz.

To show their modernity, young people flaunted their contempt for convention, affecting an unconcerned reaction to even the most madcap behavior or boorish talk. "I'm hipped on Freud and all that," one literary heroine announced flippantly. Like many people of her generation, she had read the writings of Sigmund Freud, the Viennese physician who is known as the father of modern psychoanalysis. Few people really understood Freud's complex theories of human behavior. But the popularity of his views reflected an obsession with sex and psychology among some members of the younger generation. Quick to sense the new permissive attitudes, Hollywood and the popular press pumped out a flood of material on the "new morality."

Change engenders uncertainty. The revolution in morals effected a long overdue rejection of Victorian stuffiness and prudery, to be sure, freeing many people from old taboos and encouraging a healthy approach to the problems of human relationships. At the same time, the escape from old beliefs generated a disturbing uncertainty among middle-class people as to their social responsibilities and standards of conduct.

The problem was intensified, ironically, by the prosperity of the times. In the cities, especially, the booming economy put luxuries and services within the reach of people who had never dreamed of gaining such bounty and who were psychologically unprepared to handle it. As good disciples of the doctrine of progress, many middle-class people engaged in a frenzied rush to accumulate money and "things." In the process, too often they sacrificed their integrity to opportunism, their compassion to greed. A man's worth came to be measured by the number of cylinders in his car or the price of his cigar. Perhaps people wanted to remain true to the values and ways of their fathers, but the pace of mass society swept the old values away.

Many churches in the 1920's lacked the vitality to provide new guidelines for their flocks. For one thing, they were still reacting defensively to the onslaught of science and skepticism, which had demoralized them late in the nineteenth century. For another, religion itself all but became a business in this age of big business. As one "up-to-date" clergyman proclaimed, reading the Bible meant money in the pocket. People attended church in decreasing numbers, and some of those who continued to did so more to be seen by their friends than to be inspired by a sermon.

The advent of radio. Prosperity brought new leisure time to urban America and a wondrous variety of diversions to fill it. In 1920, station KDKA in Pittsburgh broadcast the first radio report of a national election. Four years later, a national network went into operation and the radio age began. Radio was an instrument of enormous importance in molding the mass society, for it offered the purveyors of ideas and products an instant audience of millions of people. By the end of the decade, for better or worse,

it had done much to standardize the public's taste in music, drama, literature, politics, manners, and consumer goods.

Radio also transformed sports into national entertainment. Simply by turning a dial, the average man became a part of the action as Gene Tunny upset Jack Dempsey in the prizefight of the decade; or as Helen Wills and Bill Tilden swept the tennis courts of challengers; or as Babe Ruth slugged out new home-run records each year; or as Notre Dame's "Four Horsemen" thundered over the gridiron on Saturday afternoons. The instant, intimate communication radio provided made Charles A. Lindbergh a national hero overnight in 1927, after he became the first man to complete a solo flight across the Atlantic from New York to Paris.

Nonsense and vulgarity blared from the radio, too, of course. But this was an age of "ballyhoo," when the public welcomed any diversion that offered a momentary entertainment. Endurance contests caught the popular fancy for a time—how long a man could sit on top of a flagpole or how long couples could keep dancing was of wide interest—and so did bathing-beauty contests. Whatever was new or youthful came into vogue, and for people who were caught up in the swirling prosperity of the cities, at least, the decade was a time of exuberant adolescence.

Rising black awareness. Downtown Manhattan—with its shops, restaurants, and theaters—was the center from which many new urban values and patterns flowed out to white, middle-class America. For black people, the social and cultural source was uptown, in Harlem. Since the turn of the century, blacks had been a vital part of the urban scene. By 1920, Harlem in upper Manhattan was the largest black "city" in the world. Victimized by racism in the urban North as in the rural South, however, black people shared little in the prosperity of the postwar years. Still, the decade was a time of profound changes in the social attitudes and life style of urban blacks as for urban whites.

Black people in the cities had a sharper, more aggressive awareness of racism and its socioeconomic consequences than their brothers in the rural South. Indeed, the migration of blacks to northern cities early in the century produced a new kind of black man with a new black attitude

Of the Jazz Age, one man noted that "Fitzgerald wrote it, Held drew it." The art of John Held, Jr., captured for generations to come the glamourous foolishness of the twenties. In the wry drawing at right, two women typify the divergence in life styles only then beginning to be felt. The representative of traditional, family-oriented respectability seems a bit dismayed by the easygoing nonchalance of her less conventional friend. The cartoon below takes a sly dig at the new morality—the woman, bare of knee and powdered of nose, smoking with abandon while her companion languidly siphons soda into a drink (of, undoubtedly, bootleg liquor). In drawings like this, Held immortalized the flapper, a giddy young girl who delighted in flaunting her new freedom and shocking her elders. The origin of the word is uncertain, but it is often associated with Held's numerous drawings of short-skirted girls sporting open galoshes, the buckles and tops flapping carelessly in the breeze.

URSULA: IS MY NOSE SHINY, DEARIE?
LAMBERT: NO, BUT YOUR RIGHT KNEE IS DUSTY.

533

about life. The new spirit surfaced as early as 1910, with the founding of the National Association for the Advancement of Colored People, an action which represented a definite break with the rural past of the blacks and a commitment of black people to the urban future. In 1911, it was joined by the National Urban League (page 457).

Both the NAACP and the Urban League were based in the black middle class and relied chiefly on sophisticated legal and educational tactics to achieve their goals. Over the years, they scored major victories in stripping away discriminatory laws which burdened the black man. But neither group ever captured the imagination of the masses. Their ways were too slow and deliberate for the average exploited black person. Moreover, a growing sense of race pride among young blacks resulted in an outburst of black nationalism after World War I.

Garvey's "Back-to-Africa" movement. The most spectacular manifestation of this nationalism was Marcus Garvey's Universal Negro Improvement Association, a movement which he began in his native Jamaica and then reorganized in New York City in 1916. Garvey's organization was a "Back-to-Africa" movement, which attracted upwards of a million followers in Harlem and elsewhere for a time. An avid student of African history, Garvey's goal was to reclaim Africa from the colonial powers there and turn it into a black homeland. Garvey scorned interracialism and integration, advocating what a later generation would call Black Power. "To be a Negro is no disgrace, and we of the UNIA do not want to become white," he proclaimed. "We love our race and respect and adore our mothers."

Black intellectuals, including W. E. B. Du Bois, denounced Garvey as a charlatan; but the masses took to him and poured some $80 million into his movement. As parts of his "government-in-exile," he established the African Orthodox Church, the Black Cross, the African Legion, the Black Eagle Flying Corps, and the Black Star Steamship Line. In 1925, Garvey went to jail for mail fraud and was later deported; without his magnetic leadership, his movement collapsed quickly. Probably it would have failed in any event, for the vast majority of blacks had no desire to remove themselves to Africa. But the Garvey phenomenon was the first mass move-

ment among black people to protest racial injustice in America. As another black leader at the time concluded, it was a waste in terms of money and effort, but a significant expression of "soul."

2 The Traditionalists Respond To The Challenge

1. How did rural America react to the changes in culture and society fostered by urbanization? Why did rural Americans respond this way?

2. What role did religious fundamentalism play in the culture conflict of the twenties?

3. What evidence exists of a resurgence of racism and nativism during the twenties? How does the nativism of the twenties compare with similar movements in the past? in more recent times?

4. Why was prohibition supported by traditionalist elements?

Rural America by no means rejected everything about the modern mass society of the twentieth century. Many people welcomed radio, for example, as a blessed means of bringing them out of cultural isolation or of relieving the monotony of life on the farm or in the crossroads village. Others even accepted some of the more modest changes in dress and manners after the war. To be sure, there were no flappers on the farm, and rural folk still thought of Charleston as a city in South Carolina, not as a dance step. But something of the new American life style penetrated to the most remote corners of the nation, thanks to the radio, the movies, and the bulky catalogs of the mail-order companies.

The reaction of rural Americans. It was one thing to shorten one's dresses a bit or to trade in the family carriage for a shiny black Ford Model T. It was quite another thing to accept the new morality and values of the mass society. Rural Americans disliked the *pace* of change in the world; they were baffled by the collapse of the old religious beliefs; they distrusted the wide variety of peoples who comprised the urban masses.

The more uneasy rural Americans became about the future, the more they identified the city as the source of everything that was going wrong in the country. They feared that cities spawned vice and crime, luring innocent young men and women into lives of waste and debauchery. Cities fostered class conflict and permitted all sorts of odd religious and political ideas to dilute the American way of life—a way that had stood the test of time and needed no tampering with.

In contrast to the inherent evil he saw in the cities, the rural man saw the farms and small towns—and himself—as repositories of virtue. Rural people were godly and patriotic; they saw no reason to change the old way of worshiping or to interfere with a man's public and private habits (except, perhaps his drinking and sexual behavior). In truth, of course, rural Americans recognized the lure of the cities themselves, and there was always an element of envy in their attacks on urban life. Perhaps they wanted to enjoy the freedoms urban people knew; if so, their inability to do so may have intensified their hostility to the city.

Moreover, because he was as fascinated by the idea of progress as any urbanite, the rural man found it difficult to deny his children the obvious opportunities for material success offered by the city. Even as he defended the old ways, he reluctantly sensed the drift of the future. As a wartime song had asked, "How're you gonna keep 'em down on the farm, after they've seen Paree?"

Crisis in religion. The cultural conflict centered mainly on religious matters, although it had important social and political ramifications as well. While many urban churches came to terms with the findings of science and even absorbed some of the Biblical criticism of the nineteenth century into their theology, the rural churches remained firmly fundamentalist in their approach to religion and literal in their interpretation of the Bible. Indeed, fundamentalism was their strongest appeal in rallying their people to resist modernism. Unfortunately, it also put them increasingly on the defensive, prompting them to take irrational, if not grotesque, stands on some issues which had little to do with their religion.

One issue that aroused their wrath was the teaching of evolution. Seeing Darwinian theories as totally undermining the Bible, they persuaded several states to outlaw the teaching of any view that man evolved from the lower animals. John Scopes, a young biology teacher in Tennessee, challenged his state's law and put it to a court test. In a tiny courtroom in the remote mountain town of Dayton, the fundamentalists met the modernists head-on, with a small army of newsmen and others looking on. The brilliant trial lawyer Clarence Darrow defended Scopes, while the fundamentalists called on their old champion William Jennings Bryan to make war on modernism.

The trial was entertaining for a time; but Scopes clearly had broken the law and the anti-evolutionists easily won the case. It was all really a pointless sideshow, in which, as historian William E. Leuchtenberg concludes, the arrogant provincialism of the city was arrayed against the arrogant provincialism of the country. Tennessee's law remained on the books until 1967; yet the trial had little effect on the teaching of evolution elsewhere in the country.

Resurgence of racism and nativism. Once it became apparent to all but the most fearful that a Bolshevik revolution was not imminent in the United States, the big Red scare quickly died away (Chapter 19). But as it petered out, racism and nativism became increasingly serious problems. In the first year after the war, more than eighty black people were lynched, including some veterans still in uniform. Race riots plagued the nation as a whole throughout the decade, while the persistent, vicious system of petty discrimination that blacks knew so well got worse rather than better. It was a time when many whites were hostile to anything "different" and fearful of anyone who threatened to intrude upon their comfort and security. Black demands for simple racial justice were seen as part of a modernist conspiracy against the Bible and the Constitution.

Other minorities suffered from the backlash of the white Protestant majority, too. In the pseudo-scientific jargon that sometimes passed for popular sociology early in the twentieth century, the "non-Aryan" peoples of the world were relegated to an ethnic trash heap. Only "Aryans" were deemed capable of building great civilizations and of defending them against the invasion of barbarian peoples and ideas. Thus, Jews, Catholics, eastern Europeans, and all others who failed the test of the WASP majority (the white Anglo-Saxon Protestants) joined the blacks as targets of nativist attacks. Germany was not the only western nation to breed racial and religious bigotry in the period between the wars.

The Ku Klux Klan. Nativism also reflected the troubled thinking of fundamentalists about the revolution in morals. In the labor unions, it expressed the established white worker's fear that new immigrants and blacks threatened his job. In the sedate drawing rooms of the "best people," nativist thinking focused upon the supposed threats to civil order and good government posed by untutored, "un-American" elements. Among businessmen, it was the "radicalism" of aliens that struck fear. The Ku Klux Klan was the crudest, most visible manifestation of bigotry in the 1920's, to be sure. But the same disease that infected its rural followers plagued the entire nation as well, including many members of the urban, college-educated middle and upper classes.

In effect, the Ku Klux Klan picked up where wartime hysteria and the Red scare left off. The new Klan, founded in 1915, reached a peak membership of about 5 million in 1924. It struck at blacks, Jews, Catholics, foreigners in general—and, significantly, at "loose women" and other people it considered evildoers, as well.

Klansmen went in for ritual in a big way, donning white sheets and hoods for their forays against their victims. Klan officers included an Imperial Wizard and a Grand Dragon, assisted by a wondrous and juvenile assortment of Furies, Giants, Kleagles, Terrors, Klockards, Kludds, and Klexters! In the Klan calendar, special days carried such titles as "The Dismal Day of the Weeping Week of the Hideous Month of the Year of the Klan LVII." Beyond this nonsense, the Klan was a cruel and vicious hate group, quite capable of torture and murder.

It was also a significant factor in the politics of some states for a time, and it was a staunch defender of Prohibition against those who sought to repeal the Eighteenth Amendment. In the light of its moral fundamentalism, its demise had a touch of irony. For the Klan began to fall apart in 1925, after its most talented leader went to prison for getting a young woman drunk on illegal liquor and then assaulting her.

According to its Imperial Wizard, the Klan existed for the purpose of restoring power to the "everyday, not highly educated, not overly intellectualized, but entirely unspoiled and not de-Americanized, average citizen of the old stock." To historians, it was a symptom of a widespread, deeply rooted sense of uneasiness in rural and small-town America, a basic insecurity that displayed itself in outbursts of fear and unreason.

New laws restrict immigration. The most enduring monument to the irrational moods of the 1920's is the restrictive immigration legislation of the time. In the National Origins Acts of 1921, 1924, and 1929, Congress wrote into law many of the fears and prejudices of the nativists. Instead of simply reducing immigration and putting it on a first come, first served basis, the laws set up national origins quotas, based on a tiny fraction of the foreign-born people already in the United States. The quotas overwhelmingly favored the peoples of northern Europe, all but drying up the flow from other areas. Nonwhites were excluded altogether, a provision the Japanese government interpreted for what it was—a racial insult.

The era of prohibition. Prohibition was another triumph for the fundamentalists, who saw the Eighteenth Amendment as a barrier against the erosion of old-fashioned morality in America. One historian of the times observes that it was a product of the excessive moral idealism of the Progressive era and the stress of war, and that it demonstrated the dangers of reformism run rampant. It was also a product of considerable hypocrisy among people who wanted prohibition for others, while retaining the right to drink for themselves. As the humorist Will Rogers put it, Americans voted "dry" just as long as they could stagger to the polls!

In 1919, the states ratified the Eighteenth Amendment, largely because of the successful lobbying activities of the Women's Christian Temperance Union and the Anti-Saloon League. Whereupon, Congress passed the Volstead Act, setting New Year's Day of 1920 as the last day on which Americans could legally drink alcoholic beverages of any kind.

From start to finish, Prohibition was a disaster. There were never enough federal agents available

ART IN THE ROARING TWENTIES

Chinese Restaurant, Max Weber, 1915

Modernism in American art, ushered in at about the time of the Armory Show, brought with it several new art styles. The modernists rejected the representational style of earlier art that stayed so close to visual reality. Instead they favored such styles as cubism, which attempted to show a subject from a number of points of view at one time. Two other styles which placed other considerations above visual reality were abstraction, concentrating on the artist's personal conception of his subject, and expressionism, based on the feeling the subject inspired.

One painter who had been influenced by cubism was Max Weber; his painting on the preceding page contains elements of that style. It also reflects the expressionist philosophy, since it was inspired by the feeling he had upon entering a bright restaurant from a darkened street. Another painter who used elements of cubism was John Marin (below), although he uses them in a highly modified and individual way. Using delicate water color, he breaks his subject matter into facets, but he does not distort it beyond recognition.

Charles Sheeler also made use of cubist principles. The business and industrial scene as he saw it was not distressing or exploitive; he saw it as orderly and peaceful, as a sign that man was managing nature in a rational way. The precise geometric patterns he loved so well are obvious in his painting at the right, as is his feeling that such structures have great beauty.

Maine Islands, John Marin, 1922

Offices, Charles Sheeler, 1922

Another artist who found beauty in the ordinary was Georgia O'Keeffe; she too favors clear, precise forms. Although much of her painting has been very representational, she has also produced a number of abstract works, like the painting on this page. Using a muted palette, she creates a carefully planned design that seems to hint of something mysterious behind it.

Man Ray, trained as a painter, happened on a whole new medium—later named the rayograph. He had accidentally laid some objects on light-sensitive paper, and their images were recorded on it—thus producing a sort of photograph without a camera. "Gears" is an example of the rayograph technique.

Gears, Man Ray, 1924

Abstraction, Georgia O'Keeffe, 1926

IMMIGRATION QUOTAS BASED ON THE
NATIONAL ORIGINS ACT OF 1924
(Limiting annual immigration to 2% of the foreign-born population in 1890)

Country of origin	Foreign-born residents by census of 1890	Number of Immigrants allowed entry (2% of 1890)
Great Britain (including Wales and Scotland)	1,251,402	25,028
Ireland (including Northern Ireland)	1,871,509	37,430
Scandinavia	933,249	18,665
Benelux (Belgium, Holland, Luxembourg)	107,349	2,147
Switzerland	104,069	2,081
France	113,174	2,263
Germany	2,784,894	55,698
Poland	147,440	2,949
Austria and Hungary	303,812	6,078
USSR and Baltic States	182,644	3,653
Greece and Turkey (in Europe)	3,726	75
Italy	182,580	3,652
Spain and Portugal	22,181	445

to police the personal habits of the entire nation, and enforcement proved impossible. In getting illegally what the law denied them, people went to ingenious lengths, including home manufacture of "bathtub gin" and other exotic, sometimes poisonous, potions. More important, they supported a flourishing traffic in bootleg (illegal) liquor, controlled by criminal elements. Drinking increased among women and young people; and contempt for the law was widespread. Prohibition actually encouraged the very evils it was meant to destroy.

Prohibition did not bring gangsterism to America, for organized crime flourished long before the Eighteenth Amendment. But the demand for liquor afforded criminals a vast, lucrative new field for their activities. Foremost among the bootleggers was "Scarface" Al Capone. From his Chicago headquarters, he operated an illegal business in alcohol, drugs, and gambling that grossed $60 million annually. At his command was an army of a thousand gunmen, ready to deal with the competition at any time, in any way.

From 1920 to 1927, some 250 gangsters were "rubbed out" in Chicago alone, and few of their killers were ever identified, much less prosecuted. Capone had influence in the highest echelons of business, politics, and law enforcement in Chicago. When he finally went to prison in 1931, it was on a federal conviction for income tax evasion, not for murder or bootlegging.

The fundamentalist response. The fundamentalist reaction to modernism was a symptom of a general unsettlement in America. People were weary of the Progressive reformers' zeal and disillusioned with the war and its results. Perhaps the pace of change was too rapid for people to accept all the changes that were affecting them. Certainly, the pull of the past was strong, especially on people who, for whatever reason, were excluded from the affluence and freedom of city life. The struggle of "hayseeds versus city slickers" for cultural dominance was a bitter one. In the long run, the city won the struggle in the sense that the United States is today overwhelmingly an urban nation. Yet, the rural-fundamentalist mood remains a strong and pervasive force in American life.

3 The Intellectuals Rebel

1. What evidence is there that a sense of pessimism and alienation existed among the intellectuals of the twenties? Why did this group feel alienated and pessimistic?

2. Who were the social critics of the period? What was the basis of their attack on American society?

3. How did historians and social scientists contribute to a further understanding of human behavior during the twenties?

4. How valid were the intellectuals' criticisms of American society?

An intellectual fulfills his function best when he acts as a critic of the society in which he lives. During the years before and after World War I, a vanguard of intellectuals in the United States conducted a searching critical inquiry into American civilization. Not since the 1830's and 1840's had there been anything quite like the explosion of intellectual energy that took place in these years. Not all of the fallout was of memorable quality, to be sure; but a great deal of it was. More important, the explosion itself was a sign that the skeptical tradition of doubting the absolute validity of *any* idea or value was still alive in the age of mass society.

Before 1914, the upheaval was aimed at shaking loose from the Genteel Tradition (Chapter 15), which had dictated artistic style and content for half a century. Much of the writing, fictional and analytical, was of a reflective, end-of-an-era quality, assessing the values which, for good or for ill, were already well established in American life. A note of deep despair sounded in some of it, most tellingly in the last works of Mark Twain and Henry Adams, and some assaults on the old values were notably spirited and unsparing.

On the whole, however, intellectuals remained faithful to the idea of progress. If they were beginning to doubt the effectiveness of liberal reform, they still clung to the liberal ideal of a harmonious society. Filled with youthful energy and vision, they set out to build a newer, better world—a humane, noncommercial world, in which the creative individual would challenge the bleak impersonality of the machine age. It was a "season of great beginnings" and a glorious time to be young.

The onset of pessimism. But the young intellectuals built no brave new world. Cutting into their lives with the deadly force of a bayonet, the war killed their optimism and shattered their illusions about the future. Youth triumphed after the war, to be sure; but it was youth shorn of idealism, cynical about humanity rather than compassionate, contemptuous of the past, indifferent to what lay ahead. As novelist F. Scott Fitzgerald wrote, his generation emerged from the war to find "all gods dead, all wars fought, all faiths in man shaken." The best the intellectuals could say about the war to end wars was that it had released them from the past—finally and irrevocably.

The sense of alienation from prevailing cultural values was profound. In 1922, critic Harold Stearns asked thirty outstanding intellectuals to comment on various aspects of life in this country. As gathered in his book, *Civilization in the United States: An Inquiry by Thirty Americans* (1922), their responses uniformly reflected a pessimistic, even despairing, estimate of the nation's condition. The most moving and pathetic fact of social life in America, they agreed, was the emotional and aesthetic starvation of the people, a condition they attributed to the preeminence of materialistic values in a business civilization.

For many young people, the only way to deal with America was to escape it. Some sought a way out in the extremes of pleasure seeking, an avenue epitomized in poet Edna St. Vincent Millay's line, "My candle burns at both ends." Young people poured into Greenwich Village, New York City's art quarter, lured by the notion that they could obliterate time if they lived only for the present. But for most, the bohemian life was a disillusioning experience itself. In a biting commentary on the times, one critic noted their plight:

Sons and daughters of the puritans, the rebels who flocked to Greenwich Village to find a frank and free life for the emotions and senses, felt the icy breath of the monster they were escaping. Because they could not abandon themselves to pleasure without a sense of guilt, they exaggerated the importance of pleasure, idealized it, and even sanctified it.

The burgeoning of social critics. Stearns himself and many others sought refuge abroad. Especially in Paris, Americans who had uprooted themselves from their native country found what they wanted—for a time, at least: a congenial intellectual climate, other people who shared their feelings, and a freedom and spontaneity which enabled them to do as they pleased. In the end, most of these expatriates returned home, in body if not always in spirit, usually with a fresh, uncluttered awareness of the intellectual's role in a commercial society as critic.

In rejecting past and present, the novelists and poets turned inward to explore the infinite varieties of individual human experience. As they gained an understanding of human behavior, they found themselves better able to criticize the society around them as well, and their critiques took on an innocent, almost carefree quality.

Other critics were less affected by any sense of personal despair and probed the changes that were affecting life in the United States as they actually occurred. Fortunately, America in the 1920's was prosperous enough and self-conscious enough to tolerate, even at times to welcome and reward, the most scorching criticisms. There is irony in the conclusion that the very business civilization the intellectuals loathed turned out to be a perfect target for their rebellion.

Most of the critics reached their audiences through the "highbrow" magazines and low-circulation journals of opinion of the time. In the *Nation,* Oswald Garrison Villard carried on the tradition of dissent and discriminating criticism that E. L. Godkin had established in the nineteenth century. In 1914, the *New Republic* appeared, founded by the progressive thinker Herbert Croly, to promote the concept of social planning.

By far the best social barometer of the 1920's was *Vanity Fair,* the "handbook for the sophisticates." Clever, witty, and well written, it delighted in parodying everything and everyone. More pretentiously "highbrow" was *Smart Set,* the creation of the era's two most conspicuous skep-

tics, H. L. Mencken and George Jean Nathan. As a critical commentator on literary and artistic taste, it was surpassed only by the *American Mercury,* the journal Mencken established in 1924 as his personal mouthpiece.

Mencken, Lippmann, Krutch. Mencken was a master of vilification, widely read and admired by young intellectuals and members of the "smart set." He scoffed at everything middle-class America admired, including democracy, which he likened to a zoo. In ridiculing the uncritical optimism of the "booboisie" (a name he coined to refer to the American middle class), he deliberately played up the inane, the grotesque, the barbarous. High on his list of targets were politicians, professors, and preachers, and they obligingly provided him with plenty of grist for his mill.

Mencken jolted some people into an awareness of the nation's faults, to be sure. But his own alternative to democracy was too close to fascism to have any wide appeal. His social criticism was so bleakly negative that little of it survived the decade.

Where Mencken failed as a public philosopher, Walter Lippmann succeeded brilliantly. Graduating from Harvard in 1910, Lippmann began his long career as an editor and columnist in the heyday of the Progressive movement. For a time, he was caught up in the New Nationalism and New Freedom. After the war, however, he concluded that the traditional assumptions on which American liberal democracy rested no longer had any validity.

In *Public Opinion* (1922), Lippmann noted the manner in which fragmented news and an increasingly blurred overall picture of events were forcing man to rely on casual impressions and prejudices in forming his opinions. The tendency to think in stereotypes, he observed, was crippling man's rationality; no longer could it be assumed that men would instinctively make wise laws or judicious decisions. Essential to the future health of democracy, he concluded, was a leadership of trained, informed experts to guide the actions of lawmakers and administrators.

Literary critic Joseph Wood Krutch also brooded about the qualitative changes in life that distinguished the new century from the old. In

The covers of these three magazines mirror their tone and that to which their readers aspired—slick, sophisticated, and witty. More serious journalism continued to find a market, but the clever polish of publications like these perhaps best typified the spirit of the age. *Smart Set* faded after the Nathan-Mencken era, and *Vanity Fair* was absorbed by *Vogue* in 1936. Of these three, only *Harper's Bazar*, founded in 1867, has survived. (Another "a" made it "Bazaar" in the 1930's.) The 1920's saw the first publication of three other magazines that prospered, each carving a special niche for itself: *Reader's Digest* (1921), featuring predigested articles and a message of optimism; *Time* (1923), a breezy news magazine; and the *New Yorker* (1925), whose sophistication and level of writing most closely paralleled the journals pictured here.

The Modern Temper (1929), he attributed the despair of his times to a widespread disillusionment with science. Man in the nineteenth century had hailed science as a liberator, freeing his mind from a straitjacket of outdated theology and morality. But in the process of liberation, *all* human values had been lost, and science had created nothing to replace them. Krutch observed:

Science has always promised two things not necessarily related—an increase first in our powers, second in our happiness or wisdom, and we have come to realize that it is the first and less important of the two promises that it has kept most abundantly.

Krutch saw modern man as bereft of faith even in his own nobility.

More traditionally conservative were the New Humanists, whose goal was to revive the classical idea of balance and restraint in human affairs. Irving Babbitt and Paul Elmer More spoke for this group, warning that cultural anarchy must result from the steady decline in moral and aesthetic standards. While most young intellectuals delighted in the New Humanist attack on existing society, they found it too similar to the Genteel Tradition to embrace it.

Historians and social scientists. Among historians and social scientists, the mood of cynicism and disillusion had a less searing effect. For a time, some historians engaged in a fashionable practice of "debunking" the heroes of the past by prying out their imperfections. More significant, the era saw historians break important ground in the writing of social and economic history, as in the twelve-volume *History of American Life* series (1927), edited by Arthur Meier Schlesinger and Dixon Ryan Fox.

Impressive evidence of the significant work black historians were doing came when W. E. B. Du Bois's study of the slave trade was selected to become the first volume in the new Harvard Historical Series. Black history thrust itself directly into the national consciousness in 1916, with the appearance of the *Journal of Negro History.*

Two major interpretations of American history appeared which profoundly influenced the thinking of young historians in the 1920's and after. Vernon L. Parrington appealed especially to the progressives in his three-volume *Main Currents in American Thought* (1927–1930), an interpretation of the past that emphasized Jeffersonian optimism about the judgment of the people. And in their monumental work, *The Rise of American Civilization* (page 234), Charles and Mary Beard proved that class structure, economic factors, and pressure groups are sometimes decisive factors in shaping a nation's cultural history.

Sociology took a major step forward when Robert S. and Helen M. Lynd published their pioneer social survey, *Middletown: A Study in Contemporary American Culture* (1929). Using the case-study method, the Lynds recorded the social behavior of a small city (actually Muncie, Indiana) in fascinating detail.

Franz Boas laid the foundations for a new anthropology that had momentous consequences in later years when he published his brilliant study of cultural pluralism, *Anthropology and Modern Life* (1928). Using evidence derived from his own observations of people and cultures, Boas demolished the popular notion of superior and inferior races and cultures. Cultures constantly borrowed from each other, he observed, and the diffusion produced a healthy diversity, not a sterile uniformity. Complex and contrasting cultures existed side by side on equal terms, and this cultural pluralism made it essential that men learn to tolerate ethnic and racial differences among themselves. Unfortunately, Boas's work did not appear in time to soften the harsh nativist emphasis of the new immigration laws.

As for the economists, those who were not busy giving uncritical encouragement to the business boom of the 1920's moved boldly in the direction of intelligent social planning. Thorstein Veblen continued his attacks on traditional economics, proposing to replace businessmen as leaders of the society with "technocrats," the actual organizers and managers of production. Younger economists, such as Rexford Tugwell, Wesley C. Mitchell, and Gardiner C. Means, established the "institutionalist" school, in which they used studies based on statistical surveys to point up the need for carefully controlled economic planning. Their work made little impression on political leaders at the time; but when the Great Depression struck at the end of the decade, the institutionalists were ready with new theories to fit a new situation.

4 American Writers Create A Literature Of Alienation

1. How were the activities of the writers of the twenties in keeping with the writer's traditional role in American society?

2. What was the essence of the message of the writers of the Harlem Renaissance? How did it reflect the characteristic themes of the period?

3. Who were the principal novelists of the twenties and what were their themes?

4. In what ways did the poets of the twenties break away from traditional forms and themes?

American literature in the 1920's offers an intriguing paradox. At a time when American writers were manifestly disenchanted with their country and its values, when they loathed what one of them called the "cold lethal simplicities of American business culture," they yet created a body of literature so distinguished by its vigor and aesthetic excellence that it earned for their homeland a cultural eminence the United States had never before enjoyed.

The writer in American society. The key to the paradox lies in the peculiar relationship between the artist and society throughout American history. Typically, the writer has been among the most highly individualistic of men, working independently of any school of writing and exploring only those ideas and experiences of interest to himself. For its part, society acknowledged the work of the creative writer only when it found "utility" in his work. The American artist was considered a rather expensive and frivolous luxury, and his work was more to be tolerated than to be acknowledged as a contribution to national greatness.

Estranged from society by choice and by circumstance, thus, the writer often found creative inspiration in his very alienation or in the qualities of life which produced it. Indeed, much of the enduring work in American literature ap-

peared at moments when the tension between artist and society was particularly severe. In the 1920's, for instance, writers were obsessed with themes of failure, despair, and alienation. Yet, in their blue mood they wrote brilliantly successful poetry and prose and drama.

The Harlem Renaissance. For black writers, alienation was a permanent fact of life. Bitter and cynical about the discrepancies between the rhetoric of freedom and the realities of life, they began consciously in the twenties to write about black people and their troubles. In Harlem, a literary and artistic movement of great vigor began in 1922 with the appearance of Claude McKay's book of poems *Harlem Shadows*. Defiant in spirit and fiercely race-conscious, McKay's verse set the tone of the Harlem Renaissance. Here was the cultural expression of the new nationalistic mood among urban blacks. In his novel *Fire in the Flint* (1924), Walter White penned a searing indictment of lynching; while Jean Toomer, in *Cane* (1923), depicted the black experience in terms that were both realistic and lyrical.

As for the versatile W. E. B. Du Bois, even as he was writing black history, he produced several collections of essays and poetry, notably *The Gift of Black Folk* (1924). James Weldon Johnson's classic novel *The Autobiography of an Ex-Colored Man* appeared in 1912, too early to be a part of the Renaissance, except in spirit. After the war, Johnson encouraged the angry young black poets, while also publishing his own "sermons in verse," *God's Trombones* (1927).

The giants of the Harlem Renaissance were Countee Cullen and Langston Hughes, two artists who stand in the first rank of American letters. Cullen was only twenty-two when *Color* (1925) established him as a major poet. An imaginative, sensitive artist, he was at his best when dealing with the subtle aspects of racism in delicate, gentle lyrics.

Langston Hughes, in sharp contrast, was a poet of irresistible ardor, an innovator who experimented boldly with new forms and themes all his life. His *Weary Blues* (1926) had a strong, bitter touch, and rang with the rhythms of jazz and Negro folk music. It was a promise of exciting things to come. Hughes wrote about the essence of blackness in America and bespoke the new militant spirit among urban blacks:

We younger Negro artists who create now intend to express our individual dark-skinned selves without fear or shame. If white people are pleased, we are glad. If they are not, it doesn't matter. . . . We build our temples for tomorrow, strong as we know how, and we stand on top of the mountain, free within ourselves.

Novelists of the twenties. Clearly, the writers of the Harlem Renaissance were men of the present. On the other hand, a few important figures in early twentieth-century literature wrote about an older America in which they had their roots. Some novelists, among them three gifted women, while revealing their preference for tradition, did not ignore the changes in American society.

In all of her major works, from *O Pioneers!* (1913) to *Death Comes for the Archbishop* (1927), Willa Cather celebrated the superiority of traditional values over the grasping materialism of the present. Edith Wharton wrote sympathetically of the fixed social standards of the Victorian age and the impact of the "new rich" upon those standards, as in her Pulitzer Prize novel, *The Age of Innocence* (1920). She was concerned with the change in America from an "age of innocence" to one of hard sophistication. Once a rebel against the Genteel Tradition, Ellen Glasgow ultimately found post-war America so distasteful that in *Barren Ground* (1925) she began to revise her earlier judgment of the older virtues in their favor.

Sinclair Lewis. Other writers were caught between the old and the new. Some critics thought of novelist and short story writer Sinclair Lewis as a herald of a new literature of the 1920's. He wrote scathing satires of small-town, small-city America of the times. With a sure ear and the dramatic sense of a master journalist, he captured the slipshod language, the greedy materialism, and the smug hypocrisy which he found characteristic of the middle class.

Lewis's books *Main Street* (1920) and *Babbitt* (1922) established him as one of the era's most popular novelists. Yet, he never really shook off his basic allegiance to the past; he was too caught up in the society he lampooned, too grudgingly fond of the people he caricatured to have anything very profound to say about them. *The Man Who Knew Coolidge* (1928), perhaps his most skillful work, is a superb social document on the business mind of the era; but his work in general quickly became dated.

HARLEM SHADOWS

The publication of Claude McKay's poems *Harlem Shadows* placed McKay in the front rank of American writers of the twenties. One of the best-known poems from this collection is "If We Must Die," written in response to the race riots of 1919:

If we must die, let it not be like hogs
Hunted and penned in an inglorious spot,
While round us bark the mad and hungry dogs,
Making their mock at our accursed lot.
If we must die, O let us nobly die, So that
our precious blood may not be shed
In vain; then even the monsters we defy
Shall be constrained to honor us though dead!
O Kinsmen! we must meet the common foe!
Though far outnumbered let us show us brave,
And for their thousand blows deal one death-blow!
What though before us lies the open grave?
Like men we'll face the murderous, cowardly pack,
Pressed to the wall, dying, but fighting back!

Many interpreted the poem as a militant appeal to take up arms; Senator Henry Cabot Lodge had it inserted in the Congressional Record as evidence of black radicalism. McKay commented that the poem applied universally to all who were desperate and cornered, as he felt was true of blacks in 1919. Twenty years later, at the height of World War II, when Britain was embattled and expecting a German invasion, Prime Minister Winston Churchill read the poem to the House of Commons as a call for defiance and courage in the face of a superior foe. Whether or not Churchill was aware of the author's race or defiant nationalism, he apparently agreed with McKay's interpretation of this poem.

Anderson and Dreiser. Sherwood Anderson also wrote about small-town, middle-class people; but he came far closer than Lewis to understanding the nature of their misfortunes in modern America. In *Winesburg, Ohio* (1919), he probed their minds in a fumbling, almost psychoanalytical way, depicting the frustrations and maladjustments that conditioned their behavior. Although he knew nothing about Freudian psychiatry, he concluded that at the root of their problems was their fear of expressing their sexual feelings and affections: something in American life was plainly inimical to love. In a similar, heavily naturalistic vein, Theodore Dreiser climaxed his career with *An American Tragedy* (1925). A clumsy, yet forceful and honest book, it told the story of a young man battered by powerful psychological and environmental elements in modern life.

Ernest Hemingway. In Ernest Hemingway the break with the past was sharp and clean. The most gifted and purposeful of the American expatriates in Paris, Hemingway developed a lean, hard prose style that was the complete opposite of the Genteel Tradition. In his first novel, *The Sun Also Rises* (1926), he stoically recorded the lives of people whom the war had broken. Mutilated in body or spirit, his characters shared an inability to love; and they took what they could from life in a futile, yet somehow gallant, search for diversion.

A Farewell to Arms (page 507) was both a poignant love story and a refutation of war. In the hopeless affair of a wounded young American and his English nurse, Hemingway depicted the beauty of love beside the horror of war. True to the stoic outlook, the closing pages of the novel stripped both hero and reader of any illusions about the total spiritual devastation of war and the ultimate cruelty of life.

Hemingway's impact on the younger generation was immense. His terse style became the style of the new novel. His cynical, sensual, uninvolved characters became the models for young rebels, who tried hard to talk and act as Lady Brett and Jake Barnes did in *The Sun Also Rises*. Writer Gertrude Stein once told Hemingway that he was part of a "lost generation" of postwar artists. He was not, but his work did much to inspire a cult of the Lost Generation among young writers.

F. Scott Fitzgerald. High priest of the cult and the one major writer it boasted was F. Scott Fitzgerald. Indeed Fitzgerald and his wife Zelda epitomized in their own lives the essence of the Jazz Age. Insatiable in their demands for excitement and wealth, they always seemed conscious that failure lay just ahead. So it was with Fitzgerald's characters, too. In *This Side of Paradise* (1920), *Tales of the Jazz Age* (1922), and *The Beautiful and Damned* (1922), he evoked a witty, sometimes brilliant, picture of youth in revolt against prevailing American values. All the "sad young men" in his stories wanted nothing from the shattered postwar world except pleasure. With their bright and beautiful women, they moved in a daze from party to party—parties at which critic Edmund Wilson noted, they "go off like fireworks and which are likely to leave them in pieces."

Fitzgerald's masterpiece was *The Great Gatsby* (1925), a symbolic novel in which the hero's dream of finding happiness through wealth and glamor ends in disenchantment and death. It was a tale grimly prophetic, for Fitzgerald was to find parallels to it in his own troubled future.

Poets of the twenties. If anything, the poets were even more determined than the novelists to break with tradition and to experiment with new forms and themes. To encourage them, Harriet Monroe established the magazine *Poetry* in 1912 and invited them to bombard her with new ideas. Within a few years, *Poetry* had published the early work of all those who were to become the major American poets of the next half-century.

At Chicago, the "prairie poets" wrote of things close to the people in bold, new forms. A Populist by temperament, Vachel Lindsay chanted his folk themes in rhythmic, syncopated verse. In *Spoon River Anthology* (1915), Edgar Lee Masters peered at people in small-town America and revealed the bitterness and frustrations that withered their lives. Carl Sandburg was a twentieth-century Whitman, celebrating the people of the brawling, sprawling cities in free verse and a vigorous American idiom. With a sure ear and an open heart, he was a recorder as well as a poet, capturing the many voices around him perhaps better than any other writer of his time.

Robert Frost was in a class by himself, at once a traditionalist and a modernist, a homespun New England wit and a sophisticated observer of human nature. If the cynicism of the 1920's ever touched him, it never showed in his work. His themes were invariably rural; his verse was deceptively simple; his humor was always understated; and he went entirely his own way, with no regard for fashions or "schools" of poetry. In "The Death of the Hired Man" (1914), "Mending Wall" (1914), "Birches" (1916), "Stopping by Woods on a Snowy Evening"(1923), and scores of other poems, Frost revealed his deep love of nature and his sympathetic understanding of man.

Perhaps the most highly individualistic poet was E. E. Cummings. His off-beat approach to traditional subjects and his unconventional technique, as in lines like "anyone lived in a pretty how town/(with up so floating many bells down)," mark him as a major innovator in American poetry.

For a time, Ezra Pound led a school of poetry which sought to use precise images to create a sharp, clear, new style of free verse. At the same time, he moved restlessly from country to country, seeking respite from modern civilization. Reactionary, emotionally unstable, and often deliberately obscure (as in his *Cantos*—1925–40), Pound nonetheless was a major influence in the development of modern poetry, largely because he was a bold innovator and a master of language.

The poet he most influenced was T. S. Eliot, a fellow expatriate who later became a British citizen. Like Pound, Eliot had a quarrel with modern civilization, rather than with the United States alone. In *The Waste Land* (1922), he compressed an epic into a sparse four-hundred lines, evoking a sustained, overpowering image of the emptiness and decadence of mass society. The poem was a masterpiece; and, as one historian has remarked, it became "the text of despair for a generation of intellectuals."

Eliot ultimately became a High Anglican, seeking solace for his own despair and hope for the revitalization of civilization in deep religious faith. Before he found that solace, however, he plumbed the deepest recesses of the pit in "The Hollow Men" (1925), a poem whose theme is that much of modern life is really despair.

> This is the way the world ends
> This is the way the world ends
> This is the way the world ends
> Not with a bang but a whimper.

5 The Arts Of The Eye And The Ear Flourish

1. What new styles emerged in American painting during the twenties? How did these styles differ from those of the previous decades?

2. What was the nature of Frank Lloyd Wright's contribution to architecture? Why was Wright denied recognition in the United States?

3. What led to the emergence of Jazz as an accepted musical form?

4. What were the highlights of the development of the motion picture into both a thriving industry and an art form?

Restlessness, innovation, individuality, nonconformity—the same forces that affected writers of the time also moved the major figures in the visual and performing arts. In each of the arts, some event or noticeable trend signaled a breakthrough into the modern age: in painting, the Armory Show of 1913; in architecture, the emergence of Frank Lloyd Wright; in the theater, the founding of the Provincetown Players; in music, George Gershwin's sophisticated use of the native jazz idiom; in the cinema, the bold work of David Griffith.

Painting. For American painters, the Armory Show served as a bridge to the new forms and techniques which artists abroad had been using for years. A huge exhibition of works by contemporary Europeans (Picasso, Cézanne, Van Gogh, Gauguin, Matisse, and many others), the show irritated the critics, shocked many viewers, and puzzled everyone. (Theodore Roosevelt decided that Duchamp's startling "Nude Descending a Staircase" was no better than the Navajo rug on his bathroom floor.) Not all young painters immediately rushed into abstractionism or into other radical schools of modern art; but the Armory Show was a revelation to many of them, pointing them in the direction of modernism.

Confronted by a gathering revolt against realism, the "Ashcan School" (Chapter 15) faded away by the mid-1920's. Replacing it on the frontiers of painting were such highly individualistic expressions as cubism, surrealism, and dadaism, the latter a cult of meaninglessness in art. The best of the young modernists gathered about Alfred Stieglitz, a gifted photographer, who encouraged them and hung their post-Impressionist works in his studio. His wife, Georgia O'Keefe, painted expressive landscapes, "clean-swept as though by a strong wind," as one critic remarked.

Combining representational art with strong touches of abstraction, John Marin achieved a harmony of force and stability in his seascapes. "I can have a jolly good fight going on," he wrote of his work. "There is always a fight going on where there are living human beings. But I must be able to control the fight at will with blessed equilibrium." Deeper into the reaches of abstractionism were Max Weber and Arthur Dove, both of whom openly rebelled against representational art.

Architecture. One of the true geniuses of American history and the greatest architect of the twentieth century was Frank Lloyd Wright. In the late years of the nineteenth century and early in the twentieth, Wright developed an organic architecture in harmony with his deeply felt social philosophy. A rebel against both capitalism and socialism, he craved absolute freedom of individual expression, and he found it in the kind of full-throated democracy that Walt Whitman had celebrated before the Civil War. Unwavering in his convictions, he once remarked: "You've got to have guts to be an architect! People will come to you and tell you what they want, and you will have to give them what they need."

With Henry George (page 390), he believed that at the base of all human values was the land; and in his work he sought to integrate form, materials, function, and human needs with the building site—the land itself. In the prewar years, he perfected the "prairie house," a form in which strong horizontal lines reached out to commune with the earth, even as they formed great open interiors for living, in which space flowed like water. Robie House in Chicago was a superb example of this architecture.

The timidity of the critics and the prevalence of marketplace values among builders combined to deny Wright the recognition he deserved in the United States; but elsewhere in the world he was acclaimed a genius. Indeed, young architects in Europe and Japan copied his work slavishly, while Wright himself languished at home in the 1920's, unemployed and ignored. In 1924, his great mentor, Louis Sullivan (page 376), died in penniless obscurity in a shabby Chicago hotel. Not until after World War II did the ideas of Sullivan and Wright triumph in their native land.

Theater. American drama came to life with the formation in 1915 of two theatrical companies dedicated to producing contemporary works—the Washington Square Players (later the Theater Guild) and the Provincetown Players. At about the same time, Eugene O'Neill emerged as a dramatist of great promise, and two companies readily put their stages at his disposal. O'Neill was a brooding, naturalistic explorer of the dark and violent aspects of human nature, a resourceful and inventive artist who passed restlessly through several stages of development.

In such early works as *Anna Christie* (1921) and *Desire Under the Elms* (1924), he was brutally realistic and caught up in rebellion against social injustice. But as a young artist he also experimented with expressing his views in symbolic form, as in two enormously successful plays, *The Emperor Jones* (1920) and "*The Hairy Ape*" (1922). Later in his career, he moved into a romantic phase, and his last works combined Freudian psychology with Greek tragedy. Not always aesthetic masterpieces, his plays nonetheless established a standard of excellence for the modern theater.

Elsewhere in the theater, the plays of S. N. Behrman and Philip Barry provided sophisticated comedy to Jazz Age audiences, while a black theater movement played a role in the Harlem Renaissance. In the dance, Isadora Duncan brought spontaneous emotional expression to her choreography and rightly deserved the reputation she attained as the apostle of beauty. On Broadway, Florenz Ziegfeld, Jr. staged lavish musical revues that were intended to "glorify the American girl," which they most emphatically did with the assist of some dazzling, if meager, costumes. Ziegfeld's revues also featured such great comedians as W. C. Fields, Will Rogers, Fannie Brice, and Eddie Cantor, as well as music by Irving Berlin, Jerome Kern, and other composers.

Music. With its gay, naïve, utterly unsentimental rhythms, ragtime music ushered in the Jazz Age in the years just before the war. Jazz itself was an extemporaneous, improvisational version of ragtime, a musical idiom which black people brought North as part of their cultural baggage in the wartime migration to the cities. Hundreds of unknown black musicians in such places as New Orleans had been developing its syncopated beat for years, sometimes adapting it to the kind of blues W. C. Handy wrote, more often coaxing it out of the old Negro spirituals and work songs.

In the hands of such great jazzmen as Louis Armstrong, "King" Oliver, "Jelly Roll" Morton, and Kid Ory, jazz became a sophisticated, yet, paradoxically, still wonderfully innocent, musical expression of the new era. White people flocked to Harlem and Chicago's South Side to listen and dance to it, sometimes noting from the corner of the eye the conditions under which ghetto people lived, usually oblivious to everything except the "exotic" nightclubs and the music. Pure jazz remained largely with black musicans during the twenties, although a few whites, such as trumpeter Bix Beiderbecke, kept pace with them.

To Paul Whiteman, jazz was the "folk music of the machine age." Whiteman adapted the idiom to the big dance bands and popularized it among urban whites; but in the process, he formalized and "whitened" it into something very different from the pure original. His young friend George Gershwin, a talented composer of popular music, took jazz very seriously and tried to integrate it with the symphonic form. In two classic compositions, "Rhapsody in Blue" (1924) and "An American in Paris" (1928), he came very near to achieving his high purpose. "Jazz has contributed an enduring value in America in the sense that it has expressed ourselves," he wrote in justifying his work. "It is an original American achievement which will endure, not as jazz perhaps, but which will leave its mark on future music in one form or another."

Critics in America were loath to agree with Gershwin, and it was not until the European modernists demonstrated jazz's symphonic possibilities that they accepted it as a legitimate, serious form of music. Historians have no such problem: jazz and its variations comprise the only memorable American music, serious or otherwise, of the early twentieth century.

Motion pictures. Motion pictures developed into both an art form and a thriving industry during the period. Doubtless, the most important individual in the early history of Hollywood was David W. Griffith, the man who first demonstrated the artistic possibilities of the film. *Birth of a Nation* (1915), his epic film of the Reconstruction era, was a historical and ethical disaster, ruined by crude distortions of fact and overt racism (racism for which Griffith later expressed regret). But it was a technical masterpiece and a triumph of cinema realism, full of innovation that influenced film-makers for years to come.

Griffith was the commanding figure in Hollywood until about 1920, when a new kind of producer took over the industry—the business entrepreneurs who were interested in profits, not art. During the postwar decade and after, Hollywood only rarely realized its artistic potential. Studios seldom ventured into areas of political or social consequence, preferring instead to grind out films with bland plots and stereotyped characters.

They plucked attractive young men and women out of obscurity and elevated them overnight to the status of public idols. Few of these "stars" knew anything about acting; they were merely products to be packaged and sold to the public by the studios. Showmen like Cecil B. De Mille produced garish, costly spectacles, usually based on Biblical themes, in which they fed a gullible public a mixture of piety and sex. In general, the industry aimed at reaching the lower levels of human intelligence, and it succeeded.

It also made money. At the peak of Jazz Age prosperity, probably 50 million tickets a week were sold at box offices across the country. To provide proper showrooms for Hollywood's products, theater owners transformed movie houses into palaces, palaces into cathedrals. As one historian of the industry wrote: "A routine trip to the motion-picture palace now provided a pleasure equivalent to a tour of Versailles, with the added satisfaction that audiences felt *this* palace really belonged to them." The ultimate in opulence, if not in taste, was the Roxy Theater in New York, which opened in 1927 with the fanfare of a royal coronation.

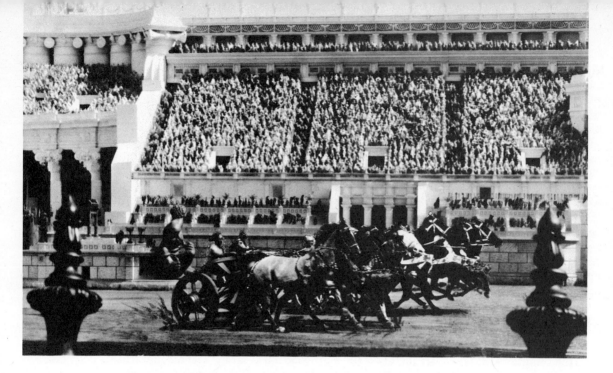

Motion pictures of the 1920's, though lacking sound and color, provided ample excitement for audiences at home and abroad. (Ninety percent of the world's movies were made in the United States.) One of the great early spectacle pictures was *Ben Hur* (1926), which starred Ramon Novarro and Francis X. Bushman. Scenes like the chariot race, above, thrilled spectators all over again when a remake was done in the 1950's. *The Sheik* (1921), below left, featured Agnes Ayres with Rudolph Valentino, the "Great Lover." Valentino, who immigrated to the United States as a gardener, enjoyed only six years of stardom before dying of peritonitis in 1926. Sobbing women stood in line for hours to view his body as it lay in state in New York City. One of the great talents of the era was Charlie Chaplin, below right, thrust into the cold in a scene from *The Gold Rush* (1925).

Not all was lost for the film as a medium of aesthetic and social expression during these years, although most of the significant work was done abroad. Some Hollywood directors fought hard to prove that films of social value could be commercial successes and make money, and King Vidor was occasionally successful. His *The Big Parade* (1925) portrayed war in bluntly realistic terms, stressing its effects on the lives of ordinary people. In an isolated masterpiece *The Crowd* (1928), Vidor probed the drabness of life in urban mass society; and he scored a major victory over commercialism in 1929 with *Hallelujah*, a film about black Americans with an all black cast.

Hollywood excelled at comedy and turned out some memorable films that still delight audiences. No subject was sacred to producer-director Mack Sennett and his stable of zany, irreverent comedians, including the Keystone Cops, Mabel Normand, and Fatty Arbuckle. Buster Keaton and Harold Lloyd developed characterizations which provoked laughter, even as they pointed to the plight of people in a mechanized society. Two of the greatest and most lovable clowns of all time were Stan Laurel and Oliver Hardy. The master of Hollywood comedy, surely, was Charlie Chaplin, whose Tramp character became a universal folk hero. In his short comedies and feature films, Chaplin superbly caricatured the dehumanizing effects of the modern world, evoking at once laughter and tears from his audiences.

CONCLUSION

"The Roaring Twenties," "The Jazz Age," "The Years of the Golden Glow," "The Day of the Flapper," "The Era of Wonderful Nonsense"—by whatever epithet they know it, millions of Americans think of the 1920's in very special terms. Some recall it with the nostalgia of the old remembering their flaming youth. Traditionalists see the twenties as an era of indiscriminate disrespect for the past, of reckless attacks on tested American values. Liberals hail it as a time of exciting new trends in all the arts—a time, moreover, when the comfortable platitudes of middle-class America came under long overdue critical examination.

Life in postwar America was exuberant or frustrating, creative or wasteful, rewarding or meaningless, depending upon one's social and economic bearings at the time. No one escaped the changes that struck at every aspect of life. Looking back, the historian sees much in those years to appall human sensibilities and grate on the national conscience. Yet, he also sees an explosion of creative energy, a strong reassertion of skepticism, and a welcome toleration of the avant-garde personality who, as one critic observes, "may not always have the right answers but sees to it that the established ones don't enjoy an undeserved long life."

QUESTIONS

1. In what ways was the decade of the twenties a time of transition, during which American society passed from the "good old days" of the nineteenth century into the uncertain future of the twentieth?

2. How significant was the role of the cities in this transition of American society? Explain.

3. What groups reacted against the social and cultural changes of the twenties and how did they react?

4. Why did intellectuals of the twenties rebel?

5. How were the views of the novelists and poets of the decade expressed in the themes and styles of their works?

6. In what ways were the changes in the visual and performing arts similar to those in poetry and prose?

7. What was the status of blacks during the twenties, and what role did they play in the intellectual and cultural movements of the period?

8. Based on your impressions of the twenties which of the following phrases do you feel accurately represents the decade: "The Roaring Twenties", "The Jazz Age", "The Era of Wonderful Nonsense", "The Era of Indiscriminate Disrespect for the Past", "The Age of Materialism", "The Era of Intolerance"? Why?

■ BIBLIOGRAPHY

ALLEN, FREDERICK LEWIS, *Only Yesterday: An Informal History of the 1920's*, Harper & Row (Perennial Library). The social and intellectual life of the twenties was a particularly exciting and frustrating phase of our history and the source of many excellent studies. Allen provides one of those studies with a very clear picture of a decade in our history. The book is particularly popular with high school students.

MOWRY, GEORGE E., ED., *The Twenties: Fords, Flappers & Fanatics*, Prentice-Hall (Spectrum Books). The intent of this volume is to show that the twenties was a decade "of amazing vitality, of social invention and change." Mowry has made an excellent selection of sources dealing with religion, marriage, moral standards, race, prohibition, and immigration. Even if the student does not read the entire book, he can find helpful articles by sampling the contents.

EDITORS OF TIME, *Time Capsule/1929: A History of the Year Condensed from the Pages of Time*, Time—Life Books. The editors of *Time* have identified particularly important years in American history and condensed the news which appeared in their magazine for that year into one representative volume. This book gives the reader a report of international and national events as well as the special departments found in the usual *Time* issue. It is a good book for students to browse through.

CHALMERS, DAVID M., *Hooded Americanism: The History of the Ku Klux Klan*, Quadrangle Books. The Ku Klux Klan and other extremist groups seem to pass through periods of popularity such as those following the Civil War, during the twenties, and during the fifties and sixties. This book documents these fluctuations and gives the reader some insight into the popularity of extremist groups.

MAY, HENRY, ED., *The Discontent of the Intellectuals: A Problem of the Twenties*, Berkeley Series in American History, Rand McNally. May's booklet is part of another important American history series with which the student should become familiar. Although the booklets are brief, the reading is important. This booklet deals with the sources of complaint during the twenties and the reasons for the degree of discontent.

HIGHAM, JOHN, *Strangers in the Land: Patterns of American Nativism, 1860–1925*, Atheneum. The book is a history of antiforeign sentiment in the United States. The student should look closely at the twentieth-century part and the final immigrant quota and exclusion acts.

GLACKENS, IRA, *William Glackens and the Ashcan Group*, Grosset & Dunlap (Universal Library). For those students who would like something a bit different, this account of Ashcan art, with its numerous illustrations, could be intriguing. The book examines the influence of Glackens and seven others, life in Greenwich Village, the nature of Ashcan art, and its ultimate influence upon twentieth-century painting.

WRIGHT, FRANK LLOYD, ed. by Frederick Gutheim, *Frank Lloyd Wright: On Architecture*, Grosset & Dunlap (Universal Library). In this book Gutheim collects some of Wright's articles and speeches which clarify Wright's conception of architecture. There is no doubt of Wright's influence, and any student with an interest in architecture or American culture should read this book.

WRIGHT, RICHARD, *Black Boy: A Record of Childhood and Youth*, Harper & Row (Perennial Classics). This is an excellent autobiographical account of Wright's boyhood in the South and his move to Chicago. It is a well-told story that gives the reader a clearer idea of what it meant to be black in the early years of the twentieth century.

The New Deal

Like the depression it sought to cure, the New Deal was rooted deeply in American history. Some of it came in response to demands that were as old as Populism, while many of its leaders were old Progressives themselves or young disciples of the Progressive approach to reform. Considering the seriousness of the crisis the New Deal had to confront, it was an inevitable development which would have come in one form or another, with or without Franklin D. Roosevelt. Propelled by a momentum of its own, it sometimes went well beyond his guidelines and in directions determined by pressures he only vaguely comprehended.

Yet the man and the program will probably always be thought of as inseparable, for the historic coincidence of the two meant that Roosevelt stamped the New Deal indelibly with the mark of his own personality and temperament. In particular, the President brought to the shaping of the New Deal his own unparalleled mastery of politics, his willingness to experiment, and his strong sense of *noblesse oblige*—the view that men of high station and wealth have an obligation to serve mankind.

Given the social and economic malaise that beset the nation in 1933, the New Deal had its work cut out for it from the start. It had to provide immediate aid to the depression's many victims. It had to generate swift recovery, if only to restore faith in the capitalistic system. It had to find ways and means of preventing future crises such as the Great Depression, or at least to cushion their effects on both people and institutions. At times, the New Deal was boldly experimental; more often, it improvised to fit the situation at hand. But it was always controversial and always inspirational. In less than half a dozen years, moreover, it changed the thinking of an entire generation of Americans about the functions and responsibilities of government. These questions will help you analyze the key features of the New Deal:

1. How were Franklin Delano Roosevelt's personality and ideas reflected in the New Deal program?
2. What measures were taken to restore financial and business stability?
3. What social welfare measures were introduced?
4. What were the political effects of the New Deal?
5. How would you evaluate the achievements and failures of the New Deal?

1 The New Deal Takes Shape Under Roosevelt

1. What tasks confronted the Roosevelt administration in 1933?

2. How could Roosevelt's background, personality, and philosophy serve to make him one of America's most memorable Presidents?

3. Who were the people that Roosevelt relied upon in preparing and implementing the New Deal? How did they differ from previous government advisers and planners?

4. How new was the New Deal?

In his inaugural address, Roosevelt spoke with a "candor and a decision," as he put it, that immediately marked the difference between him and his predecessor. The only thing the country had to fear was fear itself, he said; and he promised immediate action to restore national morale and promote recovery. By the time Congress adjourned in mid-June 1933, an avalanche of programs had poured out of Washington.

In the "Hundred Days" after the inauguration, the new administration acted in areas of banking, fiscal policy, agriculture, industrial recovery, unemployment relief, home ownership, conservation, and transportation. It moved to secure repeal of the Prohibition amendment. It established the most ambitious government project thus far in American history, the Tennessee Valley Authority (page 565). Not all of the legislation was effective, by any means, but the whirlwind of activity performed the crucial task of raising morale. Roosevelt had promised to act, and he redeemed his promise quickly and forcefully.

Roosevelt the politician. Few men have used the power of the Presidency with such skill and spirit, few have made so dramatic an impact on their times, as this extraordinary country squire from Hyde Park, New York. He served as President longer than any other man in history, in peace and in war. He created a powerful political coalition that lasted for thirty-five years. He molded the Presidency to his own terms and tried gamely to shape world affairs in the same manner. No task seemed too great a challenge to him, and he plainly relished both the office and the opportunities it afforded him to engage his antagonists at home and abroad. Little wonder he became a legend in his own time, a man acclaimed and scorned, beloved and detested. While he lived and for many years after he died, no one could be neutral about FDR.

Probably his most remarkable talent as a politician was his ability to communicate with people. Whether addressing Congress, haranguing a rally, greeting a delegation of chicken farmers, or chatting comfortably over the radio to the entire nation, Roosevelt conveyed a sense of intimacy and concern that people yearned for at the time. And this trait was the more remarkable considering his background and temperament.

Born into the Hudson River aristocracy, Roosevelt grew up in a sheltered environment. His education at the exclusive prep school Groton and at Harvard taught him less about the life of the mind than about the duties of a Christian gentleman. His strong-willed mother wanted him to settle down to manage the family estate at Hyde Park. But young Franklin had something of Theodore Roosevelt's stubbornness in him, and he decided to follow his famous relative into politics. His mother's influence stayed with him, however, constantly reminding him that he was a patrician gentleman with a special role to play in a world of imperfect men. Equally influential in his life was his wife, Anna Eleanor Roosevelt, a sensitive, imaginative woman of great charm and vitality.

In 1921, a serious attack of poliomyelitis crippled Roosevelt for life, leaving him unable to walk or stand alone. The long illness seems also to have given him a fatalistic view of life, a belief that whatever happens is inevitable and must be accepted. Certainly, Roosevelt seldom showed any conscious concern about the results of his actions. If he knew moments of emotional crisis, he kept them well hidden. At a moment's notice he could detach himself from serious affairs of state to play with his stamp collection or his dog.

It was good therapy for him, but it often irritated those who had to work with him. On balance, his breezy self-confidence was a great asset when he dealt with home-grown politicians. In the delicate art of diplomacy, it sometimes became a distinct liability.

Asked once to define his political philosophy, Roosevelt replied simply that he was a Christian and a democrat. He had no use for theories that went beyond his boyhood Episcopalianism or his honest devotion to democracy. Within the confines of traditional American politics, he was willing to try new ideas and proposals, but he was the farthest thing from a pragmatist or experimentalist in any philosophical sense. If he had a working philosophy, it was one that Benjamin Franklin would have approved: a common-sense approach to the problems of life as they arose, coupled with an instinctive unwillingness to seek any larger meaning in life beyond the truths he already knew.

He never questioned the rightness of capitalism or the superiority of the American political system. He changed both, to be sure; but his object always was to make them function so effectively that they would prevail in any contest with alien systems. A man of conservative instincts, Franklin Roosevelt shared with Jefferson a strong trust in the good sense of the people.

He was also a great showman in a profession that teemed with lively performers. His powerful torso and handsome head compensated for the lifeless legs in projecting an image of action. He got on well with reporters and was the first politician to make effective use of radio. Witty himself, he enjoyed bantering with others. He could laugh off most—but not quite all—of the hard jabs thrown at him by the opposition. Above all, he knew how to dramatize himself and his policies. But he could also be a devious, artful person, thoroughly opportunistic as to the means he used in gaining his ends. As the political historian James MacGregor Burns aptly describes him, he was both "a lion and a fox," depending upon the requirements of the occasion.

Choosing the New Deal personnel. Roosevelt was no intellectual, nor did he have an analytical mind. But he knew how to tap the minds and talents of others. From his cousin and uncle-

---

A ROOSEVELT PRESS CONFERENCE

At his press conferences, Roosevelt discontinued the practice of submitting written questions in advance, and he handled the newsmen's spontaneous questioning with a mixture of candor and humor. The following excerpt is from his first news conference:

Q: In your inaugural address . . . you said you are for sound and adequate—

THE PRESIDENT: I put it the other way around. I said 'adequate but sound.'

Q: Now that you have more time, can you define what that is?

THE PRESIDENT: No. In other words—and I should call this 'off the record' information [not for publication]—you cannot define the thing too closely one way or the other. On Friday afternoon last we undoubtedly didn't have adequate currency. No question about that. There wasn't enough circulating money to go around.

Q: I believe that (laughter). . . .

Q: . . . but you haven't defined what you think is sound, or don't you want to define that now?

THE PRESIDENT: I don't want to define 'sound' now. In other words, in its essence—this is entirely off the record—in its essence we must not put the Government any further in debt. Now the real mark of delineation between sound and unsound is when the government starts to pay its bills by starting printing presses. That is about the size of it.

Q: Couldn't you take that out and give it to us. That's a very good thing at this time.

THE PRESIDENT: I don't think so. There may be some talk about it tomorrow.

Q: When you speak of a managed currency, do you speak of a temporary proposition or a permanent system?

THE PRESIDENT: It ought to be part of the permanent system—that is off the record . . . so we don't run into this thing again.

Q: Mr. President, you said there would be two or three other subjects considered at this special session of Congress?

THE PRESIDENT: There are going to be surprises. . . .

in-law, Theodore Roosevelt, he learned about the use and abuse of power. As Wilson's assistant secretary of the navy, he learned much about reform politics. When he became governor of New York, he put university professors to work with machine politicians, treating them with genial impartiality and taking the best they had to offer. In the White House, he indulged in this indiscriminate mixing of people and ideas on a truly grand scale.

No transformation wrought by the New Deal was more sweeping than the changeover in government personnel. Washington became the nation's center of action, attracting thousands of bright young people who formerly would have gone into the business world. Economists, lawyers, social workers, union leaders, editors, and many other specialists of all kinds flocked into federal offices, where they quickly established themselves as a new breed of public servants—the New Dealers.

They quickly aroused the enmity of businessmen and older politicians; but they changed the temper of Washington, giving it the vitality it deserved as the capital city of a great nation. As historian Arthur Schlesinger, Jr. concludes, the typical New Dealer, at worst, was "an arrant sentimentalist or a cynical operator. At his best, he was the ablest, most intelligent, and most disinterested public servant the United States ever had."

Roosevelt's cabinet appointments attest his skill in drawing together diverse elements. A traditional southern Democrat, Cordell Hull, became secretary of state. The postmaster general, James A. Farley, was a skilled political manager, representing the big city machines. Frances Perkins, a New York social worker, became secretary of labor, the first woman ever to achieve a cabinet post. As secretaries of the interior and of agriculture, respectively, Roosevelt chose Harold Ickes and Henry A. Wallace, both former progressive Republicans.

Over the years, many talented men worked with FDR as personal advisers. Early in the New Deal, his "brain trust" included a conservative economist, Raymond Moley, and a radical social planner, Rexford G. Tugwell. Lawyers Adolf A. Berle, Jr., Benjamin Cohen, and Thomas G.

Corcoran were frequent visitors to the inner sanctum of the White House. No one was closer to Roosevelt than Harry Hopkins, a deceptively frail and wispy man, who entered the administration as a social worker and ultimately became the President's personal emissary to such leaders as Winston Churchill of Britain and Joseph Stalin of the Soviet Union.

In Congress, most old-time reformers became New Dealers. Senator George W. Norris of Nebraska had been a Bull Moose Republican before the war and a lonely Independent during the twenties. Now he became a New Deal stalwart and the sponsor of the Tennessee Valley Authority. In the Senate, Robert Wagner of New York represented the rising forces of organized labor, while Hugo Black of Alabama spoke for a new breed of southern whites who sought something more progressive than sterile conservatism and racism.

Elsewhere, New Dealers worked in state houses and city halls to develop local supplements to Washington's programs: Governors George Early in Pennsylvania, Frank Murphy in Michigan, and Herbert Lehman in New York, and Mayor David Lawrence in Pittsburgh, for example. Like Progressivism, the New Deal functioned at all levels of government. It moved well beyond Progressivism, however, in employing the talents of black people such as Mary McLeod Bethune and Robert C. Weaver in the administration of New Deal programs.

The roots of the New Deal. Some critics of the New Deal charged that it was an alien program, imported from Europe and subversive in its objectives. The charge is easy to refute. If the New Deal seemed "revolutionary," it was because of the breathtaking rapidity with which it was carried out. Many measures were emergency acts to deal with the economic collapse. Others were rushed through to bring government into line with the realities of economic life. Much that seemed radical to Americans in the 1930's had been accepted by conservative Englishmen for a generation.

Moreover, there is no need to look abroad for the roots of the New Deal. In such states as Wisconsin, Oregon, Massachusetts, and New York, many New Deal measures had already

Blessed with political genius and supreme self-confidence, Roosevelt dominated American life for twelve eventful years. Oliver Wendell Holmes summed him up as "a second-class intellect—but a first-class temperament." Above, he visits a CCC camp in Virginia. Among those seated with him are Secretary of the Interior Harold Ickes, third from left; Secretary of Agriculture Henry Wallace, at Roosevelt's left; and, far right, "brain truster" Rexford G. Tugwell. In his "Fireside Chats" (below left), FDR projected warmth and reassurance to a troubled people. He was an enthusiastic campaigner, showing little fatigue in spite of his handicap. Below right, at Kansas City in 1936, he talks and gestures with typical vigor.

become law by 1933: conservation, farm relief, unemployment insurance, old-age pensions. Less obvious, the trade associations of the New Era gave the New Dealers all the precedents they needed to establish controls over industrial and farm production. Relying on the type of agencies Wilson had used as war measures after 1917, the New Dealers "declared war" on the depression. Finally, the New Deal was a logical extension of the reform movement that began after the Civil War to safeguard the individual from the excesses of industrialization. The Interstate Commerce Act, the antitrust laws, the demands of the Populists, and the reforms of the Progressives, all connect with the New Deal in a historically consistent pattern.

The New Deal emerges. Bombarded from all sides with proposals for curing the depression, Roosevelt tried to harmonize the various offerings into a workable program of action. As historian David Shannon observes, he did not invent or design the New Deal, he "brokered" it, producing a complex set of compromises that constantly changed. Where possible, he relied upon traditional methods; when he deemed it necessary, he modified tradition or broke new ground. Most important, he kept his mind open to new ideas; and, if he did not always give them the attention they deserved, at least he considered them.

Certain aspects of the New Deal were clearly international in nature and will be considered in a later chapter. The major emphasis was on domestic recovery, however, and here the New Deal took several forms as it developed from 1933 to 1938. As a pragmatic response to the depression, it wrestled with the problems of unemployment relief and recovery. As a major political movement, it effected a realignment in the party system and confronted challenges from both the political right and left. As a revival of Progressivism, it produced a rich crop of reforms in a variety of areas. Probably the progressive New Deal made the most enduring impact; but the pragmatic and political New Deals were equally important at the time, not only in themselves, but also in defining the reforms and insuring their success. All three New Deals constantly overlapped and interacted with one another.

2 The Pragmatic New Deal Seeks Relief And Recovery

1. To what extent did Roosevelt reflect a clear program of priorities, and to what extent did he make a pragmatic response to the current crises?

2. What steps did Roosevelt take in the area of monetary policy to promote economic recovery? How successful were these steps?

3. How successful were Roosevelt's measures to promote industrial recovery, aid farmers, and provide relief for the jobless?

4. What was the Keynesian theory of economics? Do you think the New Deal was based upon this theory?

Roosevelt took office in the midst of a financial crisis as grave as any in the history of capitalism. Thousands of banks were closed, the gold reserve was draining away as nations and individuals demanded gold in return for their paper money, and morale in the financial community had collapsed. The President talked of attacking the crisis as he would an invading army, and some observers thought his words portended a radical alteration of the system.

In action, however, Roosevelt was a cautious commander-in-chief. True to his conservative heritage, he gave no thought to nationalizing the banks or even to tampering seriously with the existing system. Declaring a national bank holiday, he rammed through Congress in the record time of six hours an Emergency Banking Act that restored confidence in the banks and rallied the morale of the bankers. At the same time, he reiterated his commitment to economy in government and a balanced budget. Thus, he acted forcefully, while still remaining safely within the boundaries of accepted economics.

Roosevelt's monetary policy. In monetary policy, on the other hand, he ventured into new territory, frightening many businessmen and provoking the first defections from the New Deal. Like Hoover, FDR believed that business confidence was the key to recovery. In order to check the deflation and bankruptcy that plagued the economy, he set out to simultaneously increase prices and purchasing power. Thus, the New Deal embarked upon a policy of *controlled inflation*—of putting more dollars into circulation—to be achieved by manipulating the gold content of the dollar.

Roosevelt instinctively disliked the idea of tampering with the currency, but the logic of his recovery program forced him to accept it. First, in order to stop the gold drain, he took the nation off the gold standard, which meant that the government was no longer obligated to redeem paper money with gold. Second, in order to put more money into circulation, he lowered the amount of gold that backed each dollar. As a result of this move, the Treasury was empowered to issue more paper money into the economy, thus enabling people to buy more goods. In taking these steps, Roosevelt acted without regard to their effects on international trade or on the currencies of other nations. In effect, he proposed that this country "go it alone" in battling the depression.

Roosevelt's monetary policy did not produce enough buying to stimulate recovery, and its most significant result was simply to substitute a managed currency for the gold standard. In itself, this was a constructive move, for it freed the country from the old, almost mystical belief that the only money was the dollar backed by gold. Many conservatives, however, agreed with Al Smith that the new manipulated dollar was a "baloney dollar." Undersecretary of the Treasury Dean Acheson found the policy so offensive that he resigned from the administration in disgust.

Industrial and agricultural measures. In its early efforts to promote agricultural and industrial recovery, the New Deal veered away from the Populistic tradition by abandoning antimonopolism. Instead, it encouraged consolidation and tried to restrict competition. Both the National Industrial Recovery Act, or NIRA (1933), and the Agricultural Adjustment Act, or AAA (1933), rested on a theory of *planned scarcity*—a theory which assumed that restrictions on production would force a rise in prices, an increase in demand, and a revival of commerce. Together, the two measures constituted a major effort to mobilize the nation's entire productive resources against the depression.

The NIRA. Precedents for this act existed in Theodore Roosevelt's New Nationalism and in Hoover's trade associations. But the act went beyond these forebears by trying to mount a systematic attack on the depression through an integration of government, business, and labor. Its aim was to curb production in the hope that prices and wages would rise. Industries were told to draw up codes for regulating themselves in such matters as production, marketing, and pricing. One section of the act guaranteed the right of workers to bargain collectively through unions of their choice. The act provided for a National Recovery Administration (NRA) to approve and enforce the codes. To run the complex operation, Roosevelt picked General Hugh S. Johnson, a crusty old war-horse who unfortunately proved to be a poor administrator.

From the outset, the NRA suffered crippling difficulties. Businessmen who had pleaded for its establishment soon began chafing under its codes and ignoring its regulations. Labor leaders charged that NRA held down wages. Self-management proved a failure, and the blustery, profane Johnson did little to move the government into the enforcement vacuum. The NRA quickly deteriorated into an administrative tangle that no one knew how to unravel.

In 1935, the Supreme Court solved the problem by declaring the NIRA unconstitutional on the grounds that, in approving the codes, Congress had unlawfully delegated the power to legislate. Probably the NRA would not have survived in any case, for it was cumbersome and ambiguous. It was also a good example of Roosevelt's habit of "weaving together" divergent, often totally contradictory, points of view. Some New Dealers saw the NRA as the start of sustained economic planning, while others viewed it only as an expedient to be used in the emergency and then abandoned. Roosevelt supported first one view, then the other, never giving industrial recovery the firm, consistent direction it needed. The NRA helped to prevent conditions from getting worse, and it struck a blow at child labor and other industrial abuses; but it is significant chiefly as a pioneer effort at planning that failed.

NEW DEAL LEGISLATION

Emergency Banking Relief Act (3/9/33)	Regulated banking and foreign exchange. Empowered the President to take the U.S. off the gold standard.	Tennessee Valley Authority Act (5/12/33)	Created the **Tennessee Valley Authority** to develop the resources of the area.
Civilian Conservation Reforestration Relief Act (3/31/33)	Created the **Civilian Conservation Corps** to set up work camps employing young men on conservation projects.	Federal Securities Act (5/27/33)	Compelled promoters to give investors complete and truthful information about new securities.
		Home Owners' Refinancing Act (6/13/33)	Created the **Home Owners' Loan Corporation** to provide mortgage loans at low-interest rates on non-farm homes.
Agricultural Adjustment Act (5/21/33)	Created the **Agricultural Adjustment Administration** to provide farmers with subsidies for reducing crop acreage. The subsidies were to be funded by a tax on food processors. Also created the **Commodity Credit Corporation** for extending loans to farmers.	Glass-Steagall Banking Act (6/16/33)	Created the **Federal Bank Deposit Insurance Corporation** to insure individual bank deposits up to $5,000.
		National Industrial Recovery Act (6/16/33)	Created the **National Recovery Administration** to encourage business by suspending anti-trust laws, and set up fair codes of competition. Also gave labor the right of collective bargaining to be enforced by the **National Labor Board.**
Federal Emergency Relief Act (5/12/33)	Created the **Emergency Relief Administration** to grant federal money to states for direct relief. Also created the **Civil Works Administration** to employ 4 million people on federal, state, and local make-work projects. Ended 3/34.		Created the **Public Works Administration** to set up public works projects.

The AAA. Because the farmer's purchasing power was essential to recovery, no aspect of the depression demanded more forceful action than the chronic problem of agriculture. Again the New Dealers improvised, using precedents from the Populist era and the more recent Republican policies. The program they hit on satisfied no one completely, yet it somehow succeeded in generating farm recovery.

Its aim was to achieve "parity" for farmers, that is, to artificially restore their purchasing power to the level of the prewar prosperity years. Under provisions of the Agricultural Adjustment Act of 1933, an Agricultural Adjustment Administration (also AAA) was established to oversee a complex program of crop controls. Farmers were encouraged to cut production of major crops to a point where surpluses would disappear. Once the demand for farm products equaled supply, it was assumed that prices would rise and give farmers a fair return. Farming would again become a

profitable enterprise, at least for large operators.

The AAA proposed to induce production cuts simply by paying farmers to plow under their surplus crops or to let their land lie fallow. To finance this subsidy, taxes were levied on the processors of foodstuffs—who promptly passed on the burden to consumers in the form of higher food prices. In 1933 alone, a quarter of the cotton crop was plowed under and 6 million pigs were slaughtered without being sold, actions which scandalized many people but which created the desired scarcity.

In 1936, the Supreme Court invalidated several important sections of the Agricultural Adjustment Act, but the administration retained the remaining sections, and this altered act remained its basic farm policy. By 1937 farm prices were over 80 percent higher than in 1933. One secret of the AAA's success was the secretary of commerce, Henry A. Wallace. A brilliant geneticist and master of agricultural economics, he had

NEW DEAL LEGISLATION

Gold Reserve Act (1/30/34)	Empowered the President to devalue the dollar.	Social Security Act (8/14/35)	Provided for unemployment compensation and old-age and survival insurance.
Securities and Exchange Act (6/6/34)	Created the **Securities and Exchange Commission** to supervise the stock exchange.	Farm Mortgage Moratorium Act (8/29/35)	Replaced Farm Bankruptcy Act, which was declared unconstitutional.
National Housing Act (6/28/34)	Established the **Federal Housing Administration** to insure loans for construction and repair of houses and business properties.	National Housing Act (9/1/37)	Created the **U.S. Housing Authority** to lend federal funds for slum clearance and housing projects.
Farm Bankruptcy Act (6/28/34)	Enabled farmers to secure credit extensions.	Agricultural Adjustment Act (2/16/38)	Replaced first AAA which was declared unconstitutional in 1936. Provided for production quotas through soil conservation, marketing quotas, and parity payments.
Emergency Relief Appropriation Act (4/8/35)	Created the **Works Progress Administration** to provide large-scale national work programs; the **Resettlement Administration** to help resettle destitute or low-income families; the **Rural Electrification Administration** to provide isolated areas with low-cost electricity; and the **National Youth Administration** to provide jobs for youth.	Food, Drug and Cosmetic Act (6/24/38)	Prohibited misbranding and false advertising. Required food, drug, and cosmetic manufacturers to list ingredients.
National Labor Relations Act (7/5/35)	Created the **National Labor Relations Board** to arbitrate labor-management differences. Upheld the right of collective bargaining.	Fair Labor Standards Act (6/25/38)	Established minimum wages and maximum hours for workers in interstate trade. Prohibited child labor under sixteen, and restricted those under eighteen to non-hazardous occupations.

thought deeply about the farm problem and was the right man in the right job. Without him, the AAA might have gone the way of the NRA.

Still, New Deal farm policy had its faults. In reducing acreage under cultivation, the AAA forced thousands of sharecroppers and tenants off the land and into the ranks of the jobless. Throughout the New Deal period, the small farmer's condition worsened steadily. Even with the modifications in farm policy that came during and after World War II, the problem of surpluses was never solved. Most serious, perhaps, the AAA was a frank admission that the free market in agriculture had failed and that the only recourse was to create want in the midst of plenty.

Relief measures for the jobless. While setting their recovery machinery in motion, the New Dealers also had to grapple with the explosive problem of unemployment relief. Roosevelt shared Hoover's fears about the moral effect of government handouts; but he was determined

that no one should go hungry while he was President. Very quickly, he put Harry Hopkins in charge of an emergency relief program, which funneled money to the states for distribution to the jobless. Later in 1933, he created the Civil Works Administration (CWA) and put the jobless directly on the federal payroll. Hopkins had a simple theory about relief: give people work if possible, help in any case. The CWA employed 4 million persons on many projects and was the most important relief agency until the Works Progress Administration (WPA) was set up.

As a part of the NIRA, the Public Works Administration (PWA) was empowered to stimulate recovery and employment in heavy construction industries. Unfortunately, the PWA's cautious director, Secretary of the Interior Ickes, spent its money too slowly to give industry the massive boost it needed. Still, the agency provided jobs for some workers and ultimately built important public facilities, such as bridges and airports.

Roosevelt's favorite relief measure (he saw it as a reform, really) was the Civilian Conservation Corps (CCC). Organized early in 1933, the CCC provided work for thousands of young men on projects to conserve the nation's resources. The program was dramatic and popular, although it did little to reduce the unemployment rate.

In a variety of ways, the New Deal provided relief to many segments of the economy. It loaned money to farmers threatened by mortgage foreclosure and ultimately extended a similar service to homeowners. Even the old Reconstruction Finance Corporation contributed to relief. Under the direction of Jesse Jones, a conservative Texan, it bailed out railroads and businesses by the hundreds with its loans. Perhaps the most positive aspect of all this relief was that it pumped large sums of money into the economy.

Government spending. No less than Hoover, Roosevelt disliked government spending and unbalanced budgets. His aim always was to encourage private investment, hoping to create jobs and raise demand. Government spending was an expedient to be used sparingly and abandoned as quickly as possible. The theories of the noted English economist John Maynard Keynes never really got through to Roosevelt, although some of the President's advisers were Keynesians without knowing it.

To break the grip of economic stagnation, Keynes urged governments to adopt a fixed policy of heavy spending and *deficit financing*—that is, to spend more money than they received in taxes, thus unbalancing the national budget. Massive injections of public funds into the economy would compensate for a decline in private investments and spending, thereby stimulating new economic growth. Keynes was not an orthodox economist, but neither was he a socialist. Like the New Deal's pragmatic recovery program, he proposed to reinvigorate the private sector of the economy through government action.

The New Deal always spent more money than it took in, though never on the scale Keynes envisaged. Annual deficits never reached $4 billion, and federal spending never contributed more than 6 percent to the gross national product. At the first signs of recovery, moreover, Roosevelt retrenched financially, sharply reducing spending and relief. But late in 1937, the economy went

into another tailspin, dropping into a depression in some ways worse than the one Roosevelt faced when he took office. New Deal recovery programs clearly had failed to work, except in some areas of agriculture. Unemployment remained a serious problem, industries remained idle, purchasing power remained low. Under the circumstances, the New Dealers had little choice but to return to a policy of spending, particularly for relief. It was a tacit admission that Keynes was correct in his analysis of the depression.

3 The Progressive New Deal Seeks Reform

1. How did the New Deal regulate business and industry?

2. How successful were the Resettlement Administration, TVA, WPA, and the "shelterbelt" plan in conserving human and natural resources?

3. What types of programs were enacted during the thirties to promote the general welfare?

4. To what extent was the New Deal sympathetic to organized labor and minority groups?

Some historians, critical of Roosevelt's conservatism, suggest that if his initial recovery programs had succeeded, he might never have gone on to effect any significant reforms in American society. This argument overlooks several factors in Roosevelt's experience that all but insured he would become a reformer. For one thing, his political schooling took place in the Progressive era, so that he could hardly have escaped being imbued with the reforming spirit. For another, he was an *enlightened* conservative; that is, he shared Theodore Roosevelt's conviction that certain ills in society had to be corrected if only to preserve society from radical change. FDR understood that capitalism would survive only so long as people believed in its ability to provide them with a minimum of economic and social security.

Events during his Presidency helped to shape his reform views. When he took office, his chief concern was to conserve the nation's resources and to regulate the more reprehensible practices of the bankers. As the New Deal gained momentum, he began to think in terms of insuring the general welfare and of equalizing the powers of various interest groups. In the end, the New Deal created the American welfare state.

A welfare state, it should be noted carefully, is not a socialist state. Indeed, it is the antithesis of socialism in that it seeks to retain the confidence of the people in capitalism by providing them with minimal protection against economic want and social insecurity. Under the New Deal, the undisciplined laissez faire capitalism of the past gave way to welfare capitalism. Bitter opponents of the New Deal saw the change as a radical transformation, but it was hardly that. Put in historical perspective, the change was a mild one that had long since taken place in other advanced capitalistic nations.

Reforms in business. To regulate the economy, the New Deal instituted new controls on a number of businesses, including the railroads and merchant marine. Loose practices of the public utilities were outlawed or made subject to federal regulation. Companies issuing stocks and bonds were required to make full disclosures of their finances to potential investors. In 1934, Congress established the Securities and Exchange Commission (SEC) to oversee all the operations of the securities markets. Joseph P. Kennedy, father of future President John F. Kennedy and a Wall Street trader, became first chairman of the SEC in a move Roosevelt hoped would persuade brokers to accept the regulation with good grace.

As businessmen showed their unwillingness to regulate themselves under the NRA, the New Deal shifted to a more traditional antimonopoly position. Under Thurman Arnold, a former Yale law professor, the antitrust division of the Justice Department undertook the most vigorous prosecution of monopolies in American history. Yet, the New Deal never succeeded in checking the growth of monopolies, as the trend toward business consolidation continued unabated through the 1930's. And, when war broke out in Europe, Roosevelt abandoned his antitrust policy to gain business support for his defense program.

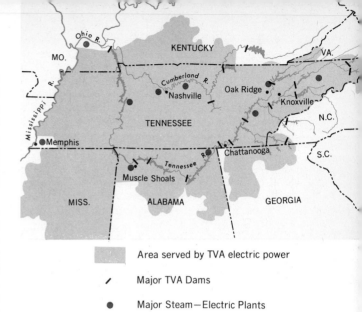

Area served by TVA electric power

Major TVA Dams

Major Steam—Electric Plants

THE TENNESSEE VALLEY AUTHORITY

Reforms to conserve resources. In the field of conservation, the New Deal made some of its boldest, most imaginative proposals. To help save the small farmer, the Resettlement Administration (RA) resettled destitute families from marginal farm lands to new acreage where they could make a fresh start. Unfortunately, neither Congress nor the President gave the RA much support, and it fell far short of its goals. Closer to Roosevelt's heart was the "shelterbelt" plan, under which great barriers of trees were planted throughout the Great Plains to curb the destructive effect of wind on the area's rich soil.

The triumph of the New Deal's conservation efforts was TVA, the Tennessee Valley Authority. TVA was a pioneering effort in regional planning, for the world as well as for the United States. The Mekong River project in Southeast Asia, the Jordan River project in Israel, and Egypt's Aswan Dam are typical of the many undertakings in other nations that are patterned after the TVA.

The project grew out of Senator George Norris's dream of saving the Tennessee Valley from exploitation by private interests and out of Roosevelt's concern for improving the lot of the rural American. In scope it was gigantic, affecting some forty thousand square miles in seven states, in one of the most poverty-ridden areas of the

565

nation. Its aim, literally, was to remake the region from a dreary economic backwater into a showcase of progressive social planning. TVA provided flood control, generated and sold electric power, and introduced new farming techniques and programs of soil conservation. Although it never fulfilled its objective of transforming the valley along rationally determined lines, it was one of the New Deal's great successes.

Conservation in the most humane sense was effected by the Works Progress Administration. In some ways the most wasteful and inefficient New Deal agency, WPA nonetheless firmly established the principle that work of any kind—even useless work—was preferable to giving a jobless person a government handout. It was a major reform in American thinking about unemployment. Under Hopkins's direction, WPA put some three million men to work doing everything from painting murals to building schools to digging useless ditches. A subsidiary agency, the National Youth Administration (NYA), aided young people in school. Its purpose was not only to give them relief, but also to keep them from flooding the job market further.

Reforms to insure general welfare. Taking up where the Progressive movement left off, the New Deal moved to protect people from economic disasters. The government insured the savings of depositors against bank failures and took some of the risk out of home-buying by loaning money to homeowners at low interest rates to help them pay off mortgages. In an ambitious attempt to replace slums with low-cost housing, Congress created the United States Housing Agency. Real estate interests saw the USHA as "socialism"; but housing was an area in which private enterprise had failed to act responsibly with the resources at its command. USHA actually provided few new housing units; and, unhappily, those it built were drab, depressing buildings that may have done more social harm than good.

A comprehensive New Deal reform was the Social Security Act of 1935. Called "the most complex measure ever considered by Congress," the act incorporated ideas that Progressives had talked of for years, as well as proposals many states had already adopted on a limited basis. In essence, it provided a system of unemployment and old-age insurance to be administered jointly by the federal and state governments. For reasons that are difficult to fathom today, the act aroused violent opposition. Some critics even saw it as a Communist plot. Actually, Social Security was a modest reform that only scratched the surface of the problems. As expanded over the years, it is easily the best known and appreciated of New Deal reforms, for it touches the lives of millions.

Reforms to equalize social power. The New Deal shifted the balance of social power in America somewhat away from business and toward farmers and workers. Roosevelt was neither antibusiness nor prolabor in any absolute sense, although he praised both workers and farmers. He believed that the system was unbalanced and that simple social justice demanded that it be put right. Moreover, because business had bungled the job and led the nation into depression, he felt that it was time to listen to other voices.

In the Wagner Act (1935), a major reform that was called "labor's bill of rights," the governmental scales were tipped in organized labor's favor for the first time in American history. The act created a National Labor Relations Board, which quickly established a new relationship between labor and management. It reaffirmed labor's gains under the NRA and enjoined employers from using "unfair labor practices" in dealing with workers. Late in the New Deal the Fair Labor Standards Act further strengthened labor's hand.

In the friendly atmosphere of these reforms, organized labor prospered and union membership swelled. But the reforms also ushered in a wave of violent industrial warfare. Bitter at Washington's new attitude toward labor, many businessmen fought the unions at every turn. Within the labor movement itself, moreover, the split between trade unionists and industrial unionists widened. As a bastion of old-fashioned trade unionism, the AFL failed to respond to the needs of workers in the basic industries.

Led by John L. Lewis of the miners, the Congress of Industrial Organizations (CIO) broke from the AFL and launched a vigorous drive to organize workers in steel, automobile, rubber, oil, and other industries. Auto workers invented the "sit-down" strike in asserting their demands, and the sight of workers refusing to leave their struck plants enraged employers.

Like Roosevelt, John L. Lewis was a man about whom few people felt indifferent. Industrialists might regard him as another Lenin or Robespierre, but in union homes, his picture often hung alongside that of FDR and a calendar print of the Last Supper. After forming the CIO in 1935, he campaigned forcefully to bring workers into it. At right, he addresses textile workers at Lawrence, Massachusetts, in 1937. That same year witnessed an outbreak of sit-down strikes, especially in the auto industry. (The United Auto Workers, also founded in 1935, joined the CIO two years later.) Organizers like Walter Reuther found willing listeners among auto workers, who had long been putting in twelve-hour days for thirty-five cents an hour. Strikers against Chrysler, below, man home-made cannons on the roof of a Detroit factory in March 1937, defying an injunction to move out. Chrysler soon recognized the union, as had General Motors earlier in the year. Ford, however, held out until 1941.

A showdown came in steel. To the CIO's surprise, the large steel companies quickly came to terms with the union. But the smaller companies ("Little Steel") put up stubborn resistance. A violent strike ensued, climaxed by the Memorial Day Massacre in 1937, when police outside the Republic Steel works in south Chicago fired into a group of peaceful pickets. In the melee, four died and eighty-four were injured. Not until 1941 did the CIO win out against "Little Steel."

For all their bitterness, business leaders ultimately had to accept the powerful new unions as spokesmen for their workers. Reconciliation was made easier, moreover, as they began to realize just how conservative the labor movement really was. And the new unions consolidated their gains and became bulwarks of capitalism.

Reforms in the tax structure. Roosevelt's tax policy disturbed businessmen almost as much as his labor policy. In 1935, the President asked Congress for a tough law to plug up the loopholes in the existing tax laws and to appreciably increase taxes on the rich and the corporations. Dubbed a "soak the rich" scheme by its enemies, the proposal was watered down in Congress to a point where it did little to redistribute the wealth. As with many New Deal measures, business was penalized more by rhetoric than by laws.

The New Deal and the minorities. Big business, big labor, and big agriculture all fared well under the New Deal. Other groups were less favored. Migrant farmers wandered westward from the wind-ravaged "Dust Bowl" of the plains, largely ignored by the government. Consumers in general paid the cost of whatever recovery came about in the form of higher prices, and no one spoke for them at Washington. In a wise reversal of past policy, Indians were allowed to hold land in communal ownership (page 295); but the New Deal did little else for the red men.

As for blacks, their experiences were varied. Many became staunch Democrats and warm admirers of Roosevelt; yet, the New Deal actually did little for them in a tangible, positive way. Roosevelt never called for civil rights legislation, nor did Congress pass any. Occasionally, he consulted with black leaders such as William H. Hastie and Robert Vann; but he never really had a "Black Cabinet," as some have suggested. Blacks suffered more from the depression than

whites and received less assistance at every level. Government agencies often tolerated rank discrimination, especially at the local level. The CCC set quotas for black applicants. As a result of some measures, black sharecroppers actually became worse off. Individually, blacks remained trapped in a snare of the white man's making.

Yet, the *general* condition of black people improved under the New Deal. The number of blacks in federal employment rose significantly. Millions benefitted from the WPA and NYA, while the Resettlement Administration made special efforts on their behalf. Moreover, Mrs. Roosevelt set an example of basic decency by displaying a total lack of color consciousness.

But the most telling advance blacks made was in expanding and consolidating their political power. They did not gain political equality, by any means. Yet, as members of Roosevelt's political coalition they gained a voice that white politicians had to heed. Early in 1941, they gave the nation a preview of a new black militancy which would emerge full-blown after the war. By threatening to march on Washington in support of their demand, they pressured Roosevelt into creating a Fair Employment Practices Commission, designed to eliminate discrimination in defense industries and government.

4 The Political New Deal Gains, Then Loses Strength

1. Why was Roosevelt able to be elected President for an unprecedented four terms?

2. What were the basic elements of the criticisms of Roosevelt and the New Deal from the conservatives and the political left? To what extent were they reasonable criticisms?

3. Why did the Supreme Court become an important political issue during Roosevelt's second term? Do you think the Supreme Court should reflect the times in its interpretation of the Constitution?

4. How effective was the New Deal in meeting the needs of the United States during the thirties?

The political success of the New Deal is attested by the fact that Roosevelt was reelected three times and retained Democratic majorities in Congress throughout his administration. In 1936, the Republicans turned from Hoover to nominate a former Progressive, Governor Alfred M. Landon of Kansas. They expected the voters to repudiate the "spendthrift" Roosevelt; but the New Deal won an overwhelming vote of confidence. Landon carried only two states, Maine and Vermont. Four years later, Roosevelt won an unprecedented third term against Wendell L. Willkie, a progressive corporation lawyer and former Democrat. In 1944, the Republicans named Thomas E. Dewey, the young, aggressive governor of New York, but he too proved no match for the champion. Roosevelt easily defeated him to win a fourth term.

Roosevelt's political success. What accounts for this extraordinary record of political mastery? Critics charged that the New Deal "bought" elections with relief checks and handouts. As one of them observed sardonically, "You can't beat Santa Claus!" To be sure, its programs involved millions of people, most of whom expressed their gratitude in the polling booths. But this simple explanation overlooks the complexity of New Deal politics.

As a strong man in a world of strong men, Roosevelt played a special political role. He was the leader of a great democracy at a time when totalitarianism threatened to destroy democracy. To millions of Americans, a vote for FDR was a vote for democracy, even before the war. Moreover, Roosevelt's personality always attracted the voters; they admired his self-confidence and enjoyed watching him outwit his opponents. He had style, an indefinable appeal and manner that gave him an enormous advantage over others in politics.

He was also something of a demagogue. To hide his confusion or uncertainty on an issue, he would sometimes oversimplify it to the point of deceiving the electorate. He and his party fashioned a new "bloody shirt" out of the depression, forever evoking a specter of ghastly consequences should the voters ever let the Republicans back in office. At the same time, the Republican party was so demoralized and discredited throughout much of the period that it had little voter appeal.

Finally, the Roosevelt coalition realigned the parties and was a new force in politics. As historian Paul K. Conkin notes, it was fragile, held together chiefly by "the glue of personality and by promises to everyone," and it lost much of its vitality after only five years. But for all its fragility, it endured as a viable political force well into the 1960's. To the traditional elements in the Democratic party—the white South, the western farmers, the city machines—the New Deal added the intellectuals, the unions, and many ethnic minorities. An electorate which had been basically Republican since the Civil War now became strongly Democratic.

By mid-decade, organized labor was regularly delivering its vote to New Deal candidates. Black America gave up its old allegiance to the party of Lincoln and became solidly Democratic. New Deal programs actually weakened the big-city machines by taking over their old "welfare" functions; yet, the Democratic hold on the cities increased as minorities flocked to the party. So many Catholics supported FDR that they affected his foreign policy during the tragic civil war that erupted in Spain in 1936. Afraid of losing the Catholic vote, he withheld American support from the anti-Church, but legitimate, loyalist government of that country.

Opposition to New Deal politics. A political movement as vigorous and wide-ranging as the New Deal inevitably aroused intense opposition. Right-wing critics charged Roosevelt with destroying free enterprise and undermining individualism. They resented the high taxes, the spending, the "socialistic" measures to regulate business. Labor's new power terrified them. Some conservatives insisted that Roosevelt had betrayed the Constitution and was intent upon making himself dictator. Hoover charged him with setting class against class, while squandering tax money. Al Smith broke with Roosevelt to lead a group of "Jeffersonian Democrats" in defense of the party's "true" principles. Business leaders galvanized their opposition in organizations such as the Liberty League, a well-financed but clumsily run propaganda group.

Stung by charges that he was a "traitor to his class," the President turned a scornful rhetoric on businessmen in the campaign of 1936. Believing that he had saved them and their system from the consequences of their own folly, he chastised them as "economic royalists" and "malefactors of great wealth." Their opposition doubtless influenced him to turn the New Deal slightly leftward during and after that election. Certainly the Republican debacle in the election left his conservative critics shattered. Significantly, however, Roosevelt never lost touch with the "economic royalists." Businessmen remained in high administration positions, their influence never really waning and actually increasing sharply after 1938.

On the left, critics characterized the New Deal as a conservative effort to save capitalism for the capitalists—which it was. They disliked its centralizing tendencies and cautious fiscal policies. They noted that no real redistribution of wealth had been effected, no sound recovery program formulated, no consistent relief policy shaped. By 1935 these charges were just true enough to make Roosevelt pay close attention to what was taking place on the left.

Most of the "thunder on the left" came from people who felt that the New Deal had failed them or who wanted a bigger piece of the economic pie. Some was clearly "crackpot" in nature, even downright dangerous. But much of it was legitimate protest, based on a reasoned evaluation of the New Deal's shortcomings.

In California, novelist Upton Sinclair proposed a cooperative effort to solve unemployment. His "End Poverty in California" movement (EPIC) skyrocketed briefly, winning him the Democratic nomination for governor before fading into thin air. Francis E. Townsend led a national movement for old-age pensions, which he proposed the federal government pay from revenues raised by a national sales tax. While his proposal was economically unsound, it highlighted a problem that needed attention. Michigan's "radio priest," Father Charles E. Coughlin, gained a huge following with his weekly broadcasts and his vague "Social Justice" movement, a form of native fascism.

The "Kingfish" of them all, as he called himself, was Huey P. Long of Louisiana. A product of poverty and deprivation himself, he gained an enormous following among rural folk with his "Share the Wealth" scheme. Long was probably the second most powerful politician in America in the early 1930's. His national organization promised to make "Every Man a King" in some not clearly specified way. An extremely effective demagogue with wide appeal, Long might have gone far in depression-ridden America had he not been assassinated in 1935. His movement lingered on, but in the hands of less skillful men, it lost its momentum.

Pressures of this sort, together with the advice of conventional liberals, induced Roosevelt to press for welfare legislation well before the election of 1936. In doing so, he disarmed the left wing in American politics, depriving it of a clear-cut program and of effective leadership. Moreover, his victory in the election naturally impressed him both as a mandate to continue his policies and as a repudiation of his critics. Ironically, as it turned out, the great electoral triumph of 1936 marked the beginning of the end for the New Deal.

For one thing, the impotence of the Republicans allowed the Democrats the luxury of squabbling among themselves, which they promptly began to do in 1937. For another, the downturn in the economy late that year put the entire Roosevelt program on the defensive. Foreign policy began to intrude more and more on the President's time, pushing domestic programs out of the limelight. Most important, Roosevelt collided head-on with the Supreme Court in a monumental struggle that shook the New Deal to its bones.

Roosevelt and the Supreme Court. It was almost inevitable that the Supreme Court should have been drawn into a confrontation with the New Deal. Many administration measures were thrown together hurriedly, with little attention to legal technicalities. Executive power increased so sharply under the New Deal (with Congress's assent), that the separation of powers was temporarily thrown out of balance. Even ardent New Dealers doubted that the Supreme Court would uphold some of their more far-reaching measures. In 1935 and 1936, the tribunal struck down one law after another in a series of decisions, several of which were unanimous, others of which revealed a 5 to 4 split among the justices. To Roosevelt, the Supreme Court seemed intent upon wrecking the entire New Deal.

Early in 1937, he sent a "bombshell" message to Congress, in which he asked authority to make a new appointment to the Supreme Court (up to

Roosevelt's policies were often attacked in newspapers, whose owners—unlike their reporters—were overwhelmingly Republican. Above, FDR resorts to his favorite magician's trick, spending. Below left, a more sympathetic view of Roosevelt's "ready remedies" shows them aiding Europe's economic health as well as that of Uncle Sam. The laboring "forgotten man," below right, thanks his benefactor.

six appointments) each time a Justice reached the age of seventy and did not retire. He justified his Judiciary Reorganization Bill on the grounds that the federal courts were overworked and needed more personnel. This may well have been the case; but it was also apparent that he was trying to put a friendly majority on the Court without actually saying so.

Roosevelt's plan raised a storm of opposition, not only among his customary enemies, but among Democrats and liberals as well. Conservative Democrats used it as an excuse to break with the New Deal, and even his loyal leaders in Congress denied him on this particular issue. The justices themselves, whether liberal or conservative, were unanimous in their resistance against Roosevelt's attack on their independence. Justice Brandeis, a lifelong liberal and the oldest member of the Court, totally rejected the President's plan. As for the Republicans, they sat back happily and let the Democrats fight among themselves over the bill. The "court-packing" scheme, as the press called it, brought Roosevelt the sharpest defeat he suffered during his long tenure. In the confusion, whatever merits the plan had were ignored.

Ironically, the Supreme Court itself took the fire out of the controversy. In approving a number of key New Deal measures, it disposed of FDR's argument that it was reactionary. Several conservative justices retired, enabling Roosevelt to get his friendly majority. Although no further New Deal legislation of significance was declared unconstitutional, Roosevelt's prestige was severely damaged.

The New Deal coalition never recovered its full effectiveness after the Court fight. To be sure, Democrats continued to win elections (though by reduced majorities), and the President's stature increased as the world situation worsened (Chapter 24). But in Congress the old conservative combination of Republicans and southern Democrats reasserted itself, effectively blocking any hope for new reforms. Persuaded that reforms run in cycles anyway, Roosevelt accepted the fact that the New Deal had run its course by 1938. He could take some satisfaction in knowing that the years since 1933 were the most politically active in the history of the Presidency.

■ CONCLUSION

What can be said in retrospect about the New Deal? Both its achievements and its shortcomings were many and substantial. Coming as it did in the midst of economic disaster, it had to move quickly and on many fronts, and it never was able to present itself in a consistent pattern. Changing conditions brought abrupt shifts in many policies, confusing people at the time and confounding historians later. Perhaps the logic of the New Deal was best expressed, long before it came, by the early nineteenth-century clergyman William Ellery Channing:

There are periods in human affairs when the principles of experience need to be modified, when hope and trust and instinct claim a share with prudence in the guidance of affairs, when in truth, *to dare* is the highest wisdom.

Yet, how daring was the New Deal? How profound were the changes it made in society and the economy? In many respects, the New Dealers displayed a basic timidity in approaching problems, particularly those involving a confrontation with the business community. They always assumed that the system needed only a few reforms to make it function perfectly. In addition, they always treated unemployment as a secondary, passing problem.

Although New Dealers talked much about redistributing the wealth on a more equitable basis, their actual efforts were ponderous and weak. They displayed a thoroughly confusing approach to the problem of monopoly, shifting from one extreme to another almost without warning. In administering their various programs, the New Dealers piled up bureau after bureau, creating administrative confusion of the worst sort in the government.

After the recession of 1937, Roosevelt and his advisers reluctantly accepted the unbalanced budget and government spending. But genuine recovery did not come until spending rose to unprecedented heights after war broke out in Europe. In his Second Inaugural Address in 1937, the President spoke of "one third of a nation ill-housed, ill-clad, ill-nourished" and promised to remedy this deplorable situation. But the New Deal itself did little of substance in these areas of deprivation, and America was still making war on poverty in the 1960's and 1970's. In this sense, the New Deal was a failure.

By the same token, the survival of capitalism in the 1970's is due largely to the rescue operation the New Deal performed in the 1930's. Merely by improving national morale, Roosevelt assured the economic system a new lease on life. The New Deal brought tangible relief and recovery to at least some farmers. It greatly improved the status of the worker and his unions, giving labor something approaching an equal voice with management in industrial relations. It revitalized much of industry by restoring popular confidence in the productive system itself. Its conservation measures salvaged whole areas of the country that had been rendered useless by past carelessness. More important, it salvaged human beings and worked hard to give people a new sense of self-respect and dignity. And, the New Deal's social security measures, inadequate though they were, guaranteed people against the worst excesses of economic disruption.

Politically, the New Deal undermined extremists on both the right and the left. Fascism and communism each had adherents in America during the 1930's, but neither system succeeded in gaining a foothold among the masses. By giving the people tangible relief, the New Deal made it unlikely that they would seek extreme solutions to their problems. Rather than look to the various "isms" of the time, people learned to look to Washington. The result was to engender among the people a new concept of government's role as the guarantor of economic stability and individual social security.

The New Deal stimulated the growth of big government, but it was not the prime factor responsible for that growth. The rise of big business made it inevitable that, one day, the countervailing power of big government, big labor, and big agriculture would come into play. Moreover, war in the twentieth century has been the great stimulus to bigness in government. Still, during the 1930's, the American people began to accept bigness as a part of their lives. They also learned how to fight economic crises, and perhaps they even learned how to avert major depressions in the future.

QUESTIONS

1. What problems confronted the Roosevelt administration in 1933?

2. How did Roosevelt's personality, style, character, and background influence his programs and actions as President?

3. In what ways was the New Deal program rooted in the American tradition?

4. What were the most striking successes of the New Deal? Explain your answer.

5. Where did the New Deal program most notably fail? Explain your answer.

6. What was the nature of the criticism of Roosevelt's policies?

7. How do you account for Roosevelt's continued political successes?

8. How profound were the economic and social changes brought about by the New Deal?

9. Which groups benefited the most and the least from New Deal policies? Why?

10. What have been the enduring influences of the New Deal on American politics, society and economy? Explain your answer.

BIBLIOGRAPHY

LEUCHTENBURG, WILLIAM E., *Franklin D. Roosevelt and the New Deal 1932–1940*, New American Nation Series, Harper & Row (Torchbooks). Any of a number of studies of Roosevelt and the New Deal may be suggested, particularly those which were written by participants in the administration. This book, however, does a good job of including much of the New Deal in a readable one-volume summary.

SCHLESINGER, ARTHUR M. JR., *The Age of Roosevelt*, 3 vols., *Crisis of the Old Order 1919–1933*, *The Coming of the New Deal*, *The Politics of Upheaval*, Houghton Mifflin (Sentry Editions). Schlesinger begins his study in the twenties and carries the ambitious narrative through the New Deal. Some historians have faulted parts of Schlesinger's emphasis, but the study still ranks as necessary reading for those who would understand the period.

ROZWENC, E. C., ED., *The New Deal: Revolution or Evolution*, rev. ed., Problems in American Civilization Series, D. C. Heath. Although we live within the shadow of the New Deal, scholars are still debating its place in

American civilization. This volume of varying viewpoints is very helpful to the student in understanding the basic arguments.

BERNSTEIN, IRVING, *Turbulent Years: A History of the American Worker 1933–1941, History of the American Worker*, vol. 2, Houghton Mifflin. The emphasis in this book is upon the worker and his response to the depression rather than a summary discussion of unions, industries, or workers in general. This is an excellent successor to Bernstein's earlier study of the worker in the twenties, *Lean Years*. The book is long, so the student will probably want to read selectively.

WILLIAMS, T. HARRY, *Huey Long*, Knopf. This is another exceptionally long work which the student may want to read selectively. It is the most recent and detailed account of one of the most controversial figures of the thirties.

WARREN, ROBERT PENN, *All the King's Men*, Random House (Modern Library). Although the author claims no intent to describe actual people in this novel, it is rather clear that the story possesses remarkable similarities to the life of Huey Long. And in Williams's biography there is nothing to deny that Warren gave a fair assessment of Long in his fictionalized character Willie Stark. The plot deals with the rise of a struggling young reformer to the governorship, but the themes are of power, reform, and corruptability.

Social And Cultural Trends In The Great Depression

Prosperity in the twenties had encouraged many people to think of themselves as "rugged individualists," beholden only to their own wits and talents for success in life. The Great Depression quickly dispelled that illusion. Americans were forced to remember that they lived in a social situation, in which the collective action of all the people was as important to their well-being as the actions of the individual. Staggered by the "hard times" and failures of the system, an entire generation turned away from the values of Horatio Alger to embrace the social and economic security that only the federal government seemed capable of providing.

Bleak and miserable as the Great Depression was for millions, it had its redeeming features. In the midst of the calamity, dynamic new forces of creativity and imagination emerged among the people. Adversity often gave birth to grim determination and a kind of sensible optimism. Not everyone felt the touch of these forces or benefitted from their effects. But it was encouraging to realize that a reservoir of talent was available that could be tapped, even in time of great trial.

Moreover, the depression was a shocking reminder that Americans were, after all, as subject to the whims of history as other peoples. The depression finally brought home the lesson that not even the powerful and distinctive United States could escape history. The effects of the crisis spread so widely that people in every section and every social class felt their impact. Routines and attitudes once taken for granted were shattered beyond repair. As the old order in politics receded before the New Deal's advances, so too the social and cultural climate changed. Here are some questions to keep in mind as you examine the social and cultural trends of the depression:

1. In what ways did American attitudes change during this period?
2. What were the influential new forces in education, religion, and the sciences?
3. How did writers and artists respond to the depression?
4. How did the depression affect popular entertainment?

575

1 The Depression Changes The Social Outlook

1. How did people's attitudes toward government change during the depression? How did the relative roles of business and labor change? Why was there no accompanying violent social upheaval?

2. To what extent did Americans turn to the extreme solutions of the right and left during the depression?

3. What were the changes in population movements both within the country and to and from the country? Why did they occur?

4. How did the depression affect the Jeffersonian ideal of an America built upon yeoman farmers?

The New Deal involved itself directly in the lives of the people, sometimes to prohibit or police certain practices, more often to provide aid and guidance. By the end of the 1930's, a profound change had taken place in public thinking about the relations between the individual and his government. Since the turn of the century, the size and cost of government at all levels had risen steadily. Urbanization, population growth, the climbing standards of living and of expectations, and the deepening involvement in world affairs all helped to account for the rise. But it took the Great Depression to dramatize for the average citizen this spectacular growth of government. Until the 1930's, Washington had been a distant entity, hardly involved in the daily routines of the individual.

Changing views toward government. During the depression, no one could be unaware of Washington. With business demoralized and local governments bankrupt, in the 1932 election the people gave the national authorities a clear mandate to relieve the misery of the depression and to rescue the general welfare. No longer was government to stand by passively while impersonal social and economic forces toyed with the lives of people. To be sure, many people grumbled about the growth of federal power or the practices of this or that bureaucratic agency—often with good reason. But the same people rarely hesitated to call on Washington for help when their own interests were threatened.

By and large, Americans learned that government can be at least a partial guarantor of economic and social security, without necessarily becoming an oppressor in the bargain. Certainly, the enhanced role of government, while changing the rules of the game somewhat, did little to inhibit private enterprise. Under the welfare state, business has enjoyed remarkably good health and almost unlimited growth.

In some quarters, the depression also awakened a compassionate idealism that was put to work on behalf of social betterment. If Roosevelt's ultimate aim was to relieve the plight of that underprivileged one-third of a nation to which he referred in 1937, the New Deal fell far short of the goal. But until the 1930's the plight itself went largely unrecognized, except by private, grossly inadequate charities. Under the New Deal it was made the responsibility of the entire nation. The fact that the problem remains with us today does not lessen the significance of the change in outlook that took place then.

Changing views of business and labor. One factor that contributed to the change was the shattering of the old image of the businessman. Once considered an infallible oracle, the businessman became an object of scorn during the worst years of the depression and for a long time after. Not until he effected the production "miracles" of World War II did he begin to recoup his good name.

In the meantime, the people turned to government experts and planners for guidance in social and economic matters. Even many businessmen willingly turned over to government some of the prerogatives which had been theirs exclusively in earlier times. It was a sign that American capitalism was maturing and coming to grips with the realities of industrialism. Representative government, acting on behalf of the people as a whole, was establishing some of the goals and priorities of the society. As one historian has noted, "the necessary evil of government had become so necessary that it had ceased to be an evil."

Labor's prestige shot up, not only at the bargaining table, but in politics and the public eye as well. By 1940, Roosevelt seldom made a significant political move without first "clearing it" with such labor leaders as Sidney Hillman. Labor's opponents charged the government with "pampering" the unions. But the advances made by union labor were, for the most part, long overdue and entirely legitimate. It was not until after World War II that some unions developed into giant entities that could rival the largest corporations in their ability to affect the economy, for good or ill.

This remarkable transformation in the relative positions of business and labor took place with very little violence and social disruption. To be sure, industrial warfare raged for a time in areas where the CIO conducted its most vigorous organizing drives. And class consciousness certainly increased during the depression years. But the United States somehow managed to escape the sustained violence, the political turmoil, and the unrelenting attacks upon fundamental institutions that plagued the nations of Europe. Indeed, the crisis ultimately brought out new strength among the people and in their institutions. Once Roosevelt managed to rally a majority of the people to his program, the possibility of a genuinely radical change all but disappeared.

"Thunder" on the left and right. Both fascism and communism posed a continuing threat, of course. In the labor movement the Communists scored some significant successes, especially in the new and inexperienced industrial unions. Communist-led protest marches and demonstrations in the largest cities continued to attract crowds, although with diminishing enthusiasm for following the Red banner. Communism's advances among the masses were superficial and temporary, as the great body of workers clung to an essentially conservative view of relations between labor and management.

The problem was more serious in Washington, where the Communist party managed to place a number of people in important government positions. Their activities became a matter of serious concern, especially as the international situation worsened, for they followed the twistings and turnings of the party leaders and willingly served the cause of the Soviet Union. When their activities were exposed publicly after World War II, the country was shocked and disgusted. Yet, considering the critical condition of capitalism during the thirties, it was reassuring that so few Americans of any class found communism an attractive alternative.

At the other end of the political spectrum, fascism also attracted a few adherents, although fewer than the leftist movements. Some of Huey Long's more flamboyant heirs developed a fascism with an American flair that exploited the anti-Semitism, or hatred of Jews, of the ignorant and the general discontent of the working class, but with little success.

At a different level, Fritz Kuhn organized the *Amerikadeutscher Volksbund* (German-American People's Federation) to exploit whatever sympathy for Nazism might exist among the German-American population. Passing himself off as the "American Führer," Kuhn boasted of his friendship with Hitler and surrounded himself with the gaudy trappings of Nazism, including "storm troopers." But "the Bund," as it was called, attracted little support among the people who he thought would answer its call—Americans of German descent. As in Europe, the fascists in the United States made anticommunism the basis of their appeals. Fortunately, most people were quick to see that fascism was every bit as repugnant as communism.

Immigration all but came to a halt during the depression, until the refugees from Nazi and other fascist tyranny began to appear in mid-decade. For a time, indeed, an embarrassing "reverse migration" took place, as some people left the United States to settle elsewhere. On one particularly revealing, though isolated, occasion, the Russians advertised in the West for 6,000 skilled workers—and more than 100,000 applications poured in from the United States alone! Doubtless, few of the applicants sympathized with communism or were especially anxious to live in the Soviet Union. For most it was a practical matter of getting a good job—anywhere.

Rural ideal vs. depression reality. Population movement within the country underwent some changes, too. For the first time in a century or more, the exodus from farm to city was reversed. Rural folk, including blacks in the South, preferred the familiar poverty of the countryside to

Farming on the Great Plains had always presented difficulties because of high winds and low annual rainfall. Since the early days, farmers there—through ignorance or indifference—had neglected to follow sound agricultural practices. They had overgrazed the land and cut down trees, so that there was little protective cover to hold the soil in place. Careless plowing heightened the danger of soil erosion. For years, small dust storms had plagued the area. Finally, in 1934, there occurred a severe drought. As a result, the high winds of that year swirled up tons of topsoil and carried them in clouds of dust as far away as the Atlantic Ocean and into the Gulf of Mexico. Millions of acres in Kansas, Oklahoma, Texas, New Mexico, and Colorado became a vast Dust Bowl, devastated and useless. Small farmers in the region had no place to turn, and thousands trekked westward to California in hopes of finding work as migrant laborers. Their plight was immortalized in John Steinbeck's novel *The Grapes of Wrath* and in numerous poignant photographs, such as these three by Dorothea Lange. Above, an abandoned farm in Dallem County, Texas (1937), is typical of the desolation. Among those who fled were the couple at upper right (shown in 1938), who stand in the shade of a billboard along U.S. 80 near El Paso, Texas. Two jalopies, lower right, are bound for Nipomo, California in 1936. One migrant spoke for many such when he said: "The country's in an uproar now—it's in bad shape. The people's all leaving the farm. You can't get anything for your work, and everything you buy costs high. Do you reckon I'd be out on the highway if I had it good at home?"

the strangeness of life in the beleaguered cities. At the same time, California's growing population indicated that not even an economic catastrophe could seriously interrupt the historic westward drift of the American people. Thousands voluntarily exiled themselves from the towns and farms of the Midwest, especially, to seek the sunny Promised Lands of the Pacific slope. Others went because they seemed to have no other choice. Among the latter were the dispossessed farmers of the Dust Bowl, whose trek John Steinbeck portrayed in epic terms in his novel *The Grapes of Wrath* (1939):

The cars of the migrant people crawled out of the side roads onto the great cross-country highway, and they took the migrant way to the West. In the daylight they scuttled like bugs to the westward; and as the dark caught them, they clustered like bugs near to shelter and to water. And because they were lonely and perplexed, because they had all come from a place of sadness and worry and defeat, and because they were all going to a new mysterious place, they huddled together, they talked together; they shared their lives, their food, and the things they hoped for in the new country.

Life for the small farmers, white and black, was especially difficult in the depression years. After living among sharecroppers in the South, James Agee described their bleak existence in a moving book *Let Us Now Praise Famous Men* (1939), a work made even more dramatic by Walker Evans's haunting photographs. Another artist to capture the rural outlook was Pare Lorentz, whose documentary films *The Plow That Broke the Plains* (1936) and *The River* (1937) are masterpieces of cinema art.

Roosevelt had a romantic, Jeffersonian notion that the real America was to be found only on the farm. Accordingly, in such agencies as the Tennessee Valley Authority and the Resettlement Administration, the New Deal sought to revitalize agriculture for cultural and sentimental reasons as well as for economic considerations. In practice, the attempt to revive the old rural values came to very little, especially when contrasted with the more tangible advances in farming. Together with the New Deal's crop-control and subsidy programs, the modernization of agriculture put the large operator at a distinct advantage over the yeoman farmer of the Jeffersonian ideal.

Moreover, for all its rural idealism, the New Deal was urban-oriented. It had to be, for the problems of the twentieth century were urban and industrial in nature. By the 1930's, over half the population lived in or near the cities. Two world's fairs during the depression—at Chicago in 1933, at New York in 1939—and an international exposition at San Francisco in 1939—dramatized the importance of the city and of urban planning in the nation's future.

More immediately, Rockefeller Center in New York, a cluster of buildings containing offices, a theater, shops, and broadcasting studios, provided a striking example of how skyscrapers could be used to create order and even a kind of beauty out of urban chaos. In the same city, the Williamsburg and Queensborough housing projects promoted new concepts in living patterns by replacing dreary slums with structures that offered people space and access to sunlight.

Paradoxes in industrial development. Most industries suffered from sharply reduced production during the depression. But the automobile factories, after an early slump, recovered quickly and experienced rising output after 1932. Gas stations multiplied everywhere, while government-sponsored road building went on as though the depression were a myth. For even the most desperate victims of the crisis, the automobile was the last personal possession to go. "I'll go without food before I'll see us give up the car," one mother declared, reflecting the accepted view of the automobile as a symbol of status and mobility. Asked why her family had a car but no bathtub, a farm wife replied: "Why, you can't go to town in a bathtub."

Going to town in the family car, especially on a Saturday night, had become part of the American way of life, not to be sacrificed even to the demands of a major depression. A man's car was his means of escaping whatever bedeviled him, a precious chariot to carry him just over the river or just beyond the next mountain to a Promised Land. When the Okies fled westward, they went not on foot, not in mule carts or even freight cars, but in their own ramshackle flivvers! Somehow, the automobile provided a man with a link to the future.

Aviation came into its own during the thirties, partly because of this same faith in the future.

In 1935, the Douglas DC-3 aircraft went into service and quickly became the workhorse of commercial flying. A year later Boeing introduced the big flying boats that made regular transoceanic service possible. In the midst of depression, with unemployment rampant and recovery still far off, the sight of the great "China Clippers" winging their way over the Pacific to the new frontiers and markets of the Far East was a portent of America's future.

2 The Depression Changes The Social Environment

1. What changes occurred in the American family during the thirties? Why did these changes occur?

2. How did the churches respond to the social and moral shifts among the people caused by the depression and the society of the thirties?

3. What were the changes which appeared in American education during the thirties? Why was there a period of liberal experimentation in education during a period of economic difficulty?

4. What was the focus of the social scientists in the thirties, and what were some of their contributions to American society? How did the focus of the physical scientists differ from that of the social scientists?

No bulwark of traditional American life underwent more wrenching changes during the depression than the family. The disaster seemed to generate a breakdown in family cohesion and a loss of old-fashioned family values. Critics of the New Deal thought the federal government, with its welfare programs and paternalistic legislation, was responsible for the transformation. But it was not the measures taken to remedy the economic crisis that altered family life, it was the economic crisis itself.

The breakdown of the family. Indeed, the breakdown started among middle-class families before World War I, long before government programs of any sort touched the structure of family life. During the depression, it hit the families of the working class, frequently shattering beyond repair the old patterns of hierarchy and authority—patterns that had been brought over from the Old World and carefully nurtured in the New.

Unable to function as the family breadwinner, the unemployed father suffered a decline in self-confidence, sometimes to the point of losing the respect of his wife and children. With parental authority undermined and mutual respect severely weakened, the family lost much of its traditional importance. Young people drifted out of the family circle to shift for themselves as best they could.

People postponed marriage, fearful that the old saying "Two can live as cheaply as one" had become "Two can't live at all unless both have jobs." Postponed marriages and an inability to support children led to a sharp drop in the birth rate. This drop, together with the fact that improved medical care led to an increase in the number of middle-aged and older people in the population, led to fears that the United States was about to become an "old-aged" nation.

Divorces declined, although desertion—the "poor man's divorce"—increased sharply. These trends were to be slowed or reversed during World War II, to be sure; but the transformation of family life was to continue well into the postwar period. The transformation would have much to do with shaping the moral climate of the 1960's and 1970's.

The rising crime rate. Somewhat surprisingly, juvenile delinquency did not become a serious problem during these years of crisis. Youngsters drifted about the land, often to be treated as vagrants or runaways. Some were involved in a rash of petty thefts and other crimes symptomatic of economic deprivation. But they made only a small contribution to the rising national crime rate, most of which was attributable to individual adult offenses and to organized crime. Moreover, young people responded readily to efforts by the New Deal to get them off the streets and into the camps of the Civilian Conservation Corp and work-relief projects of the Works Project Administration and the National Youth Administration.

Organized crime, on the other hand, challenged the best efforts of law enforcement agencies at every level of government. Racketeers moved from bootlegging into gambling, vice, and extortion. They wormed their way into organized labor, sometimes taking over entire unions to use as fronts for various criminal activities.

In the largest cities, the gang leaders linked up with corrupt politicians, unscrupulous labor leaders, and greedy businessmen to form shadowy, intricate criminal organizations, or syndicates, that reached into every facet of city life. Not even the FBI enjoyed much success in breaking up these networks. These G-men (a nickname for government men) were more successful in curbing an outbreak of bank robberies and kidnappings, crimes which made bigger headlines than the operations of the syndicates, but which were usually the work of small gangs and individuals.

New forces in religion. How did the churches respond to these social and moral shifts among the people? Oddly enough, the Social Gospel (Chapter 14) fell into disrepute, even though many clergymen were sympathetic to the New Deal's social-betterment efforts. Like other institutions, the churches were buffeted by forces that were difficult to identify, much less to understand. Congregations naturally sought traditional religious answers to the questions that disturbed them. Moreover, church leaders sensed in the economic crisis the limitations of man's best efforts to create the good society. Thus a conservative, evangelical mood swept through the entire religious establishment.

Among the rural poor, in particular, fundamentalist preachers called for a revival of belief in the unerring accuracy of the Bible in all matters. In some instances, religious fundamentalism combined with extremist political views to produce organizations of a fascist or semifascist cast such as the "Christian Front," a frankly pro-Nazi, anti-Semitic group that carried on strong-arm activities in the name of Christianity and Americanism.

In New York a black evangelist who called himself Father Divine attracted an enormous following to a cult which combined revivalist religion with shrewd commercialism in about equal proportions. Before long, Father Divine had his "Heavens" operating in many large cities, often supported by wealthy white "angels." The "refined evangelism" of the Moral Rearmament movement appealed to the pacifist instincts of many young people, until its message ("If man will be good, there will be no more wars") lost its meaning as Hitler began to rattle the sword. As always in a time of deep trouble, sects sprang up overnight, each with its own prophetic message.

Theologians undertook a profound reexamination of the relationship between man and God. Many of them concluded that liberal theology had eroded the sovereignty and traditional authority of the Almighty, and they turned back to a more conventional doctrine. Led by Reinhold Niebuhr of Union Theological Seminary, the neo-orthodox movement deeply affected the thinking of Protestants and had its counterparts among Catholics and Jews. While Niebuhr and his followers did not repudiate the practices of the Social Gospel, they rejected the optimistic, utopian, man-centered assumptions of the liberals. In his works, notably in the two-volume *The Nature and Destiny of Man* (1941, 1943), Niebuhr spoke for a conservative, more traditional, yet profoundly compassionate theology emphasizing the existential, or deeply individual, relationship of man to God.

Changes in education. If conservatism prevailed in religion, it made little headway in education. Early in the depression the schools were hard hit by lack of funds, and their recovery was a slow and painful process, especially in rural America. Yet, enrollment went up in the thirties, most markedly in the high schools and colleges.

Schools experimented with new ideas in curriculum and teaching methods, especially with the "progressive" theories of the philosopher John Dewey (Chapter 15). The demand was for "community-centered" education, in which the schools served the needs of society as well as educated the individual. In a society which put a premium on the material signs of individual success, too often this meant a kind of vocational training and "cultural attunement" that would help one to "get along" while "getting ahead."

In the racially segregated school systems of both the South and the North, the schools for blacks almost invariably were of such poor quality that black people suffered more than whites from bad education. But education for all Americans left much to be desired. Intelligence tests among soldiers during World War II revealed that an alarming number of young Americans were half-educated at best, downright illiterate at worst. In a democracy, such a condition can be disastrous, for the political process depends upon an educated electorate capable of making enlightened decisions in the best interests of the whole community. Very little was done to correct the deficiencies in education until well after the war.

The most striking development in higher education was the influx of refugee scholars from Europe. So many distinguished intellectuals sought sanctuary from Nazi brutality that the United States almost overnight became the intellectual center of Western civilization. In New York, the New School for Social Research, originally founded in 1919, became known as "refugee university" because its faculty included some 180 victims of Nazi persecution.

Students reacted to the depression much as their parents did, making the necessary adjustments and occasionally striking out in new directions. Some left school to take their chances in the shrunken labor market. Most tried to continue their education, often with the help of government relief programs. Political activity increased sharply on the campus. In 1934, students organized the American Youth Congress, which functioned, in effect, as their political lobby. Another group, the American Student Union, was boldly and loudly leftist in its orientation. Student activism clearly foreshadowed the "student power" movement of a later day and was another sign that traditional patterns of hierarchy were breaking down. Some healthy reforms resulted, including an improvement in relations between students and faculty.

The social and physical sciences. Given the evidence around them that something had gone wrong somewhere along the line in the social system, students naturally showed a lively interest in history and the social sciences. Historians responded by showing a new interest in social and cultural forces, thereby pumping fresh vitality into their accounts of the past. Among American historians, Charles Beard and Frederick Jackson Turner continued to set the pace, although younger men began to challenge their dominance. As in the Progressive era, historians sought to discover how economic factors and social patterns acted to change human institutions.

Many unemployed scholars went to work for the WPA, compiling document collections and writing local histories. Through the work of the Historical Records Survey, the country acquired a systematic inventory of its historical resources that was of immense value to scholars in many fields. In 1934, Congress provided a repository for many of these resources by creating the National Archives, an agency that was charged with accepting and preserving government records.

Sociologists found in the depression a fruitful field for research. Robert S. and Helen M. Lynd continued to examine life in a typical midwestern town, and they followed up their work *Middletown* with *Middletown in Transition* in 1937. In it they revealed the existence of unsuspected tensions in American society. Regional studies, especially of the South, broadened the perspective of all social scientists, as did the work of such black scholars as E. Franklin Frazier and Carter G. Woodson. Frazier's study *The Negro Family in the United States* (1948) confronted white America with irrefutable evidence of the grave damage slavery and racism had done to black people.

Utility and common sense were of more concern than theory among most social scientists. Economists accepted the views of John Maynard Keynes in preference to the old classical economic theories. Political scientists turned their attention to everyday problems of public administration.

One interesting development was the emergence of public-opinion polling. In 1936, the magazine *Literary Digest* predicted, on the basis of a nationwide poll it conducted, that Landon would defeat Roosevelt by a landslide in the Presidential election. When FDR swept all but two states, the magazine quietly went out of business, very nearly taking the infant "science" of polling with it! George Gallup and Elmo Roper came to the rescue with new methods of ascertaining public opinion that made their findings relatively reliable. Polling quickly became a factor of immense significance, especially in politics.

While the social scientists were busying themselves with the everyday, practical affairs of mankind, the physical scientists were conducting a quiet revolution in their laboratories. On both sides of the Atlantic, physicists probed at the structure of the atom, seeking to unlock one of nature's great secrets. Nazi persecution ultimately drove such giants of science as Albert Einstein, Enrico Fermi, Niels Bohr, Leo Szilard, and Edward Teller to the United States, where they joined such American counterparts as Ernest O. Law-

rence and Harold C. Urey. Slowly but surely, the physicists unraveled the mystery of nuclear fission. As they did so, the first faint light of a new age appeared on the horizon of history.

3 A New Intellectual Mood Emerges

1. How do the economic, political, and social characteristics of a historical period affect the intellectual life of the times?

2. How did the writers of the thirties reflect the nature of the period? What accounted for the general lack of success of writers of the twenties during the depression era?

3. What were the characteristics of the theater of the thirties? To what extent was the theater influenced by Marxian themes?

4. What contributions were made to American life by musicians during the thirties?

For a successful writer to become a bore is the most devastating thing that can happen to him. During the grim years of the depression, H. L. Mencken became a bore—a reactionary bore, whose cynical jibes at middle-class values struck precisely the wrong note at a time when people wanted to be reassured about the quality of American life. The growing social awareness left many intellectuals of the twenties stranded, without much of consequence to say in the thirties. Although he was never a bore, T. S. Eliot withdrew to the intensely spiritual world of Anglo-Catholicism and ignored the "wasteland" of modern life. Ezra Pound did his talking for Benito Mussolini, becoming an apologist for the Italian dictator's fascist tyranny.

Novelists of the Jazz Age found it difficult to cope with the changed mood of the country. F. Scott Fitzgerald sold his talents to the moviemakers in Hollywood, never fulfilling the promise of genuine genius that was so implicit in *The Great*

Gatsby. Floundering through the early 1930's, Sinclair Lewis finally caught fire again briefly when he turned his indignation against the threat of fascism in America. *It Can't Happen Here* (1935), while certainly no masterpiece of literature, sounded a much-needed alarm about the threat of home-grown totalitarianism. Hemingway, too, found in the fascist menace a theme through which he could express his compassion and idealism. In his novel *For Whom the Bell Tolls* (1940), he told a tender love story, but also dealt with the larger human tragedy of the Spanish Civil War.

Literature of social realism. Other writers became part of a new literature of social realism that emerged from the depression. Their writing was inspired in part by a humanitarian concern for social betterment, in part by a brief, essentially naïve flirtation with Marxism, and in part simply by anger at the paradox of misery in the midst of plenty. Writers of the social realist school were unsparing in their portrayal of what was wrong with the nation, but they also believed that man could change his environment and improve his society. As the fascist menace grew in the world, moreover, the intellectual community recovered its faith in America. In retrospect, the decade of the 1930's stands out as a period of *cultural nationalism*—a time when writers and critics rediscovered the positive aspects of the American experience.

John Dos Passos and John Steinbeck were the representative novelists of this new literature. Bridging the Jazz Age and the depression decade in his trilogy of novels *U.S.A.* (1937) Dos Passos presented a sweeping panorama of life in America from 1900 to 1930. Prying into every social class, dissecting a bewildering variety of real and fictional characters, he combined the disillusionment of the twenties with the social consciousness of the depression years. In his ingenious use of literary devices, he merged fiction with his own highly personal impressions of history.

Dos Passos found few redeeming features in American life. Indeed, the work was a bitter indictment of the acquisitive society; throughout, it struck a defiant note of class conflict. But Dos Passos had only a passing flirtation with Marxism. Industrial society was his real enemy, and

later in the decade he found a comfortable political faith in the traditional Jeffersonian celebration of agrarian values.

Steinbeck displayed a counter-reaction to urbanization, dealing often with the "primitive" —the poor, the simple, the oppressed, who were rooted to the land. His chronicle of the Okies, *The Grapes of Wrath,* ended on a note of optimism, affirming the triumph of the human spirit over adversity. In depicting the hardships and human tragedies of the time, the book is a graphic account of life during the depression. It endures as a social document, perhaps even more than as a work of art.

Stark realism distinguished the work of other depression writers, too. In his *Studs Lonigan* trilogy (1932–1935), James T. Farrell wrote bitterly of the manner in which city life brutalized the young. Erskine Caldwell described the deprived, often degenerate, existence of southern sharecroppers, softening the dismal picture somewhat with the bawdy humor of the region.

In *Native Son* (1940), Richard Wright told a story of unrelieved misery and despair among the blacks on Chicago's South Side. The foremost black writer of his time, Wright grew up knowing racism at its worst in both North and South. His searing prose was an early manifestation of what would later be termed "Black Power." An entire generation of young black artists grew up paying deserved homage to Wright. Another writer to capture the imagination of the younger generation was Thomas Wolfe, a tempestuous, emotional, and confused young man, whose career was cut short by an early death.

The most gifted American novelist of his time was William Faulkner, who probed deeply into the nature and meaning of social change. Taking as his theme the transformation of the Old South and the futility of the struggle to resist this change, he showed how the shattering experience of social and physical change can destroy the old values without providing new ones. In such novels as *The Sound and the Fury* (1929) and *Absalom, Absalom!* (1936), moreover, he displayed extraordinary insight into the psychological and moral problems of human relationships. Not many people read Faulkner during the depression; his intricate symbolism was too complex for readers who preferred their social realism straight and unadorned. His rewards came after World War II, in the form of public acclamation and the Nobel Prize.

Social reformism also appeared among the poets, although to a lesser extent. Carl Sandburg sang the praises of democracy in *The People, Yes* (1936), while Archibald MacLeish and Stephen Vincent Benet denounced economic exploitation and fascism. But no genuinely effective new voice was raised during the thirties. The leading poets seemed content to stay with regional themes.

Literature of escapism. Understandably, much of the popular literature was escapist in nature. Historical novels enjoyed a great vogue, for they lifted the reader out of the unhappy present and deposited him in a past which made no demands upon him. Easily the most successful novel, in terms of sales, was Margaret Mitchell's sprawling tale of the sectional conflict, *Gone With the Wind* (1936). Although it distorted history and had an ugly, subtle antiblack bias, its romantic themes and exciting characters gave readers what they wanted. Later it was made into one of the most successful motion pictures of all time.

Left-wing influences in the arts. Many writers and intellectuals during the depression showed at least a passing interest in Marxism, if only because it claimed to have the answer to capitalism's ills. Moreover, the looming menace of fascism in Europe and the Soviet Union's efforts to promote a "popular front," a coalition of all antifascist elements, stimulated some uncritical, almost romantic, thinking about the nature of communism.

In the mid-thirties, the tragic Spanish civil war seemed to prove the good sense of an alliance between democracy and communism against the right-wing dictators. As the legitimate Spanish government was assaulted first by fascists at home, then by the invading legions of Hitler and Mussolini, the only nation to offer it tangible military aid was Russia. Leftists and liberals in America enthusiastically embraced the cause of the Loyalists, and a few idealists volunteered to fight against the fascists in a "Lincoln Brigade" recruited by the Communists. For a few brief years it seemed that a "popular front" was indeed a feasible undertaking.

Disillusion began to set in when the Commu-

Entertainment in the thirties ranged from the impassioned seriousness of proletarian drama to the happy escapism of "swing" music. Above is a scene from the Group Theater's 1935 production of *Waiting for Lefty*. Elia Kazan (arms upraised) is urging cab drivers to strike without waiting for the missing Lefty. His fervent appeal brought audiences to their feet; note the standing silhouettes in the foreground. In the music of the bands of the thirties, both white and black musicians contributed to the creation of memorable sounds. "Never before in jazz," according to one critic, "were so many so good all at once." Below, at the piano with members of his band at an improvisation session is one of the best of them all—pianist, composer, and bandleader Duke Ellington.

nists in Spain showed that they were interested only in advancing their own fortunes, not in saving the republic. Then in 1939 Joseph Stalin made a cynical deal with Hitler (the Russo-German Non-Aggression Pact, Chapter 24), and all but the most gullible or hardheaded finally lost faith in the sincerity of the Soviets.

Despite the appeal of the "popular front" idea, few American writers let their work become an apology for communism. The League of American Writers, to be sure, held annual conferences to encourage the writing of "proletarian" literature, glorifying the class struggle and the downtrodden workers. But only a very few "proletarian" novels had any lasting distinction as literature, most notably Henry Roth's *Call It Sleep* (1934), a moving story describing the feelings of a Jewish boy growing up on the Lower East Side of New York. For the most part, the writing was formless political propaganda, utterly devoid of artistic quality. A handful of writers and critics joined the Communist party; but most intellectuals rebelled against subjecting their minds and talents to the dictates of any political or economic dogma.

Proletarian themes achieved more success, artistically, on the stage. Two radical dramatic companies, the Theater Union and the Group Theater, experimented freely with themes of social protest, acknowledging frankly that they were using art as a political weapon. Clifford Odets anticipated the "Living Theater" of later years by involving the audience in the action of *Waiting for Lefty* (1935), a play noteworthy also because its plot centered around a strike.

The horror and stupidity of war concerned Irwin Shaw in *Bury the Dead* (1936) and Robert Sherwood in *Idiot's Delight* (1936). Erskine Caldwell and John Steinbeck carried the depression themes of their novels over to their works for the stage. In *Dead End* (1935), Sidney Kingsley was particularly effective in depicting the vast gulf that separated the very poor from the very rich. Even comedies and lighthearted musicals usually carried some note of social concern or political satire.

The Federal Theater Project. As part of the WPA's effort to aid unemployed artists, the Federal Theater Project was an important creative force for a time. In addition to producing conventional dramas in theaters throughout the country, it accepted plays that commercial houses had rejected as too radical or innovative. One of its most imaginative efforts was the production of Shakespeare and other classics using all black companies. Orson Welles began his remarkable career in radio drama, filmmaking, and stage work as an innovator in the Federal Theater. Thousands of actors and playwrights, the mediocre as well as the gifted, were given an opportunity to use whatever talent they possessed.

Under the direction of Hallie Flanagan, a woman of wide aesthetic vision, the project experimented with a new theatrical form which it called "The Living Newspaper." Borrowing freely from all the media of communication, it combined current events, social commentary, and human interest, to give dramatic depth to contemporary social problems. It also aroused intense opposition among conservatives in Congress, who disliked such "leftist" activities. In 1939, Congress cut off the Federal Theater's appropriations and thus ended its brief but exciting life.

A musical heritage enriched. American music received a welcome lift during the thirties from two sources—the Federal Music Project and the influx of refugees from Europe. Some fifteen thousand jobless musicians went to work in the government's relief project, giving thousands of concerts and music lessons in every corner of the nation. For the first time, ordinary Americans came to know the works not only of the classical masters, but also of native composers, whose works the project introduced or popularized. To preserve the country's rich musical heritage, it also collected and recorded thousands of folk songs—the everyday tunes of the hill people, the southern blacks, the Yankee fishermen, the cowboys.

Composers still looked abroad for much of their inspiration; yet the works of Aaron Copland and Roy Harris, among others, reflected distinctive American themes, too. In the compositions of William Grant Still, the voice of the black man came through in proud and vibrant tones, sometimes brilliantly emphasizing the emotional distance between black and white. Still became the

ART IN THE GREAT DEPRESSION

Lobster Trap and Fish Tail, Alexander Calder, 1939

Dinner for Threshers (detail), Grant Wood, 1934

Just as the Armory Show had been a great impetus to artists of the twenties, so was the stock market crash an impetus to the artists of the thirties. New subject matter and a new mood characterized the art of the period, though not all of it reflected the depressed tone of the times—the delicate Calder mobile on the preceding page and the dramatic

Nighthawks, Edward Hopper, 1942

Frank Lloyd Wright house on page 592 are hardly products of social realism. But a substantial body of art did reflect the artists' turning inward on America and re-examining its institutions and values.

Regionalism, exemplified by the Grant Wood painting (top left), was built on the idea that there was a special virtue in concentrating on one's own section of this country—on maintaining an intimate association with one's roots and not losing oneself outside of it. Edward Hopper (lower left) also was affected by this philosophy, to the extent that he thought an American artist should base his art on the American scene and not on the international.

Not all artists tuned into the American scene chose such placid subjects. Jacob Lawrence painted the race riots that sometimes accompanied black migration to the North (right), and Ben Shahn captured the despondency of those victimized by injustice or by failing economic conditions (below). Walker Evans, a brilliant photographer of the period, traveled through areas of the country for the Farm Security Administration and recorded on film what he saw (page 592).

The Migration of the Negro,
Jacob Lawrence, 1940–41

Scotts Run, West Virginia, Ben Shahn, 1937

Houses, Atlanta, Georgia, Walker Evans, 1936

Falling Water, Kaufmann House, Bear Run, Pa., Frank Lloyd Wright, 1936–39

first black man to conduct a major American symphony orchestra in 1936. George Gershwin continued to pursue his goal of raising jazz to the level of the classical forms, and he finished his superb folk opera *Porgy and Bess* (1935) just two years before death ended his promising career.

Such European conductors as Leopold Stokowski and Arturo Toscanini put American symphony orchestras on a par with the world's best. Refugees also contributed much to American composing, although the full impact was not felt until after the war. Arnold Schoenberg, Paul Hindemith, and Kurt Weill continued their fresh, new work in America, influencing scores of young composers.

Jazz became "swing" in the thirties, a change that gave musicians rich new opportunities for improvisation. Benny Goodman, Glenn Miller, and Tommy Dorsey put together big bands whose performances attracted millions of avid fans. Billie Holiday, Ella Fitzgerald, and Louis Armstrong gave new distinction to the "blues," a form that became a part of every popular band's repertory.

Such artists as Chick Webb and Count Basie moved from Harlem to Broadway, bringing to white audiences the highly sophisticated jazz patterns developed by hundreds of unknown black musicians. Setting the pace in all popular music was Duke Ellington, with his haunting compositions and exciting stylistic renderings. A milestone of some sort was passed when the "King of Swing," Benny Goodman, performed in staid old Carnegie Hall with a band made up of black and white musicians.

Many of the developments in the written and performing arts were evidence that the United States was achieving cultural and intellectual maturity. To be sure, the moods of the depression were uncertain and restless. But by the end of the decade, the experimentation, the innovation, the freewheeling spirit of inquiry and skepticism, had brought out the best in the intellectuals. Their experiences in the thirties led them to uncover the country's faults, even more so than in the twenties; but it also enabled them to perceive with a clear eye the sources of the country's strength.

4 The Visual Arts Strive For Realism And Humanism

1. What were the characteristics of the visual arts during the thirties? In what ways were they similar to the literary arts and in what ways were they different?

2. In what ways did the federal government show its support or lack of support for the arts? To what extent should the federal government involve itself in supporting and promoting the arts?

3. How did the "American school" of painters differ from the "social realists"?

4. What was the direction of American architecture in the thirties, and what forces worked against architectural innovations?

As in literature, the distinctive quality in the visual arts during the depression was cultural nationalism. The problem for the painter, as for the writer, was to communicate his deep emotional responses to the human and social crises of the time. First because of the depression, later because of fascism and the approaching war, the artists turned their vision inward to rediscover the essence of America. For some, this involved a return to the traditional scenes and rural values of the past. For others, it brought out a ringing protest against the corruption of the old American Dream. A few continued to explore the intriguing frontiers of modernism and abstraction. Most artists thought that anything less than a commitment to social realism was an escape from social responsibility.

The Federal Arts Project. As the New Deal had done for the other arts, it came to the rescue of unemployed painters and sculptors. In fact, one of the most exciting developments in the thirties was the manner in which the government became the great patron of all the arts. Governmental encouragement of the arts had long been accepted as natural and desirable in Europe, but the tradition had never taken root in the United States. Historically, the American writer or painter or musician had depended upon the generosity of private sponsors, or had supported his artistic endeavors by earning his bread at some other task.

Boldly breaking with the past, the social planners of the New Deal saw no reason for artists to be treated differently from other workers. If the tailor, the bricklayer, and the salesman needed relief, so did the man who worked with a brush and an easel, or who saw beauty in a lump of raw clay. Moreover, some New Dealers hoped that the project would blossom into a Bureau of Fine Arts, to make the government's encouragement of the arts a permanent concern.

From the start, however, the whole idea of subsidizing the artist with public funds clashed not only with prevailing canons of "free enterprise," but also with a long-standing American view of art as a rather frivolous, unproductive luxury. When the time came to cut back on the New Deal's spending programs, Congress did not hesitate to chop first at the Federal Arts Project, even though the amount of money involved was very small indeed.

During the four years of its existence, the project employed thousands of artists—good and bad—in a variety of capacities. Some painted murals on the normally barren walls of public buildings and schools. Others gave free lessons or put on exhibitions. To the surprise of many, the project stirred up a widespread, if unsuspected, popular interest in the arts.

Holger Cahill, its director, believed in "imaginative realism"—freeing the artist to comment on the social scene in an intensely personal way—a view that coincided with prevailing trends among the artists themselves. Influenced strongly by such Mexican muralists as Diego Rivera, Americans used themes of social struggle and historical development to flesh out their wall paintings in post offices and courthouses. Sometimes the leftist bias in their murals was too strong for people of conservative tastes to accept, and on several occasions the works were purposely altered or actually destroyed. In most instances, the murals were allowed to stand as monuments to the social consciousness that so characterized the times.

Art as a weapon against injustice. For some artists, the social realism of the Federal Arts Project was much too tame. From 1936 to 1940,

the more avant-garde among them met annually in artist congresses, dedicated to the use of art as a weapon against the depression, fascism, and war. Shunning the themes of middle-class America, many artists chose their subjects from among the "exploited" (the blacks, the slum-dwellers, the striking workers) and the "exploiters" (the bloated capitalist, the corrupt politician, the club-swinging policeman). Sometimes their work was so blatantly contrived as to lose even its intended social impact, not to say artistic value. Yet, the acid cartoons of Art Young and the blunt caricatures of William Gropper and Joseph Hirsch, while they fell outside the realm of fine art, left a lasting imprint in the mind of the viewer.

Other social realists underscored the seamier side of life with genuine creative distinction. "I hate injustice," Ben Shahn said, discussing his approach to his work. "I guess that's about the only thing I really do hate . . . and I hope to go on hating it all my life." Shahn's realism was almost photographic in its stark detail; yet, such a work as *Vacant Lot* (1939) went well beyond technical precision in making a statement about life in the city.

So did the best work of Reginald Marsh, who wanted to do for his New York what Hogarth had done for eighteenth-century London—etch every line of its blemished face for posterity. If he fell short of his goal, his paintings *Why Not Use the "L"?* (1930) and *Negroes on Rockaway Beach* (1934) managed to capture the lonely impersonality of life in a grimy environment. Marsh once confessed that "well bred people are no fun to paint." But if the drab existence of the poor fascinated him, like many other social realists he tempered his anger with compassion for society's victims. Perhaps this was the factor that distinguished the artist from the propagandist—the ability to see in the social wreckage those human qualities which might yet salvage something for the future.

No realist had to look far to find injustice. Robert Gwathmey painted a South of segregation and brutal fact, a South he knew well as an eighth-generation Virginian. Black artists drew upon their heritage and the realities of their daily lives for self-expression and self-revelation. At Hampton Institute, Charles White's murals anticipated in paint the "Black Power" that Richard Wright foretold in prose. Horace Pippin, his right hand so badly wounded in World War I that he had to steady it with his left while he painted, paid eloquent tribute to John Brown in a series of canvases. On an intensely personal level, Jacob Lawrence painted a moving documentary on the ghetto, stressing the undertone of violence that pervades the life of the black American. Peter Blume's *The Eternal City* (1938), an essay in paint on life under Mussolini, was a powerful condemnation of fascism.

The "American school" of painters. Realism of a different sort came from the brushes of a self-proclaimed "American school" of painters. Led by Grant Wood of Iowa, Thomas Hart Benton of Missouri, and John Steuart Curry of Kansas, these regionalists painted traditional scenes with an almost photographic sharpness. Benton proclaimed their credo when he announced in 1932 that "no American art can come to those who do not live an American life, who do not have an American psychology, and who cannot find in America justification for their lives."

Hugely ambitious, Benton tried to paint everything he saw in American life, with the result that his work was often a clutter of undisciplined energy. Curry struggled with nature, sometimes coming to terms with it (as in the sweeping canvas *Wisconsin Landscape*, 1939), sometimes overwhelmed by its power (in *Hogs Killing a Rattlesnake*, 1935). His *Baptism in Kansas* (1928) was a successful commentary on rural life.

Considerably less ambitious than his fellow midwestern regionalists, Grant Wood managed to convey a sense of rural America without taking his subject altogether seriously. Indeed, there was a welcome touch of satire in his *Daughters of the American Revolution* (1932). His best-known work, *American Gothic* (1930), had a whimsical bite to it that assured it lasting popularity. Other regionalists of note were Edward Hopper, who made the Main Streets of New England his subjects, and Charles E. Burchfield, whose milieu was the fading small towns of Ohio.

Architecture. In architecture the depression years had a certain modest distinction of their own, although the period was most important as a time of preparation for a burst of activity that would follow World War II. To the United States

in the mid-thirties came the giants of European architecture, Walter Gropius and Ludwig Mies van der Rohe, hounded out of their homeland by Hitler's stupid tyranny. Both were leaders in the Bauhaus movement, which Gropius had founded in 1919. Their aim was to provide a functional architecture that fused art and life as a means of preserving man's humanity in an age of science and technology. Chicago's reputation as an architectural center was enhanced in 1937 when Gropius transferred the Bauhaus movement to that city and van der Rohe assumed a professorship at the Armour Institute there.

The impact of the movement did not become publicly evident until the economic and international situations improved sufficiently to allow men the luxury of building architectural monuments once again. Indeed, all architecture suffered during the thirties from the lull in building activity. To be sure, the federal government undertook considerable construction; but its buildings, for the most part, were either traditional neoclassic temples or timid gestures vaguely in the direction of modernism. In private building, Chicago's massive, ungainly Merchandise Mart was an example of the cluttered, eclectic style that most architects preferred.

Still, modernism was clearly on the move. In California, Richard J. Neutra established the Experimental School and designed buildings peculiarly suited to the environment of the Far West. The Rockefeller Center project, architecturally imperfect in many ways, nonetheless gave a great boost to modernism. As for Frank Lloyd Wright, he entered a new phase in his work, more brilliantly than ever fusing fantasy and engineering. Beautifully streamlined and serenely balanced in its natural setting, his masterpiece of the period was the house "Falling Water" at Bear Run, Pennsylvania. It was a perfect expression of his philosophy that man should coexist with nature in a balance which did justice to both.

As usual throughout his career, Wright proved to be too visionary for his times. It is true that artists in the thirties delved into the social condition and found a humanistic basis from which to reaffirm America's traditions and values. But at the end of the decade, the vision of the future was not an encouraging one. For if the New York World's Fair in 1939 was a preview of things to come, as its promoters insisted, its aesthetics suggested that the future would find man more than ever a slave to impersonal forces. In the "World of Tomorrow," aimless confusion prevailed over rational order, and mere man was lost in a clutter of forms and machines.

5 The Popular Taste Reflects The Need For Escape

1. What are the similarities and the differences between the popular culture of the thirties and the literary and visual arts of the same period?

2. What influence did the radio have upon American life? In what ways did radio affect newspapers?

3. How did the movies reflect the characteristics of big business? How did they meet the popular needs of the thirties?

4. How did newspapers, magazines, and sports respond to the public demand for entertainment and enlightenment?

Throughout the Great Depression, radio reached a constantly expanding audience. By 1940, nearly 54 million sets were in use, receiving broadcasts from 900 stations. Like the other media of communication, radio was big business. As such, it seldom ventured beyond the bland and mediocre in programming, for fear of alienating the advertisers who bought its time in order to peddle their wares. Doubtless its most significant function was to bring world events directly into the homes of the people. As never before in a democracy, the citizenry could judge for itself the words and deeds of the leaders.

Radio–information and entertainment. Roosevelt quickly mastered the use of radio as a political tool, bringing people seemingly into his intimate confidence with his "Fireside Chats." Techniques of campaigning changed as politicians were able to reach millions at a time with their

pitches. The rise of such demagogues as Father Coughlin and Huey Long would never have been so spectacular, perhaps would never have occurred, had it not been for the nationwide broadcasts each used so effectively.

Doubtless, too, Americans were made aware of the Nazi menace when they listened to shortwave broadcasts of Hitler's ranting speeches. If they could not understand his German words, they had no difficulty in translating the animallike roars of his party faithful. To help interpret the news, the networks provided such able commentators as Elmer Davis, Lowell Thomas, H. V. Kaltenborn, and Edward R. Murrow.

But radio diverted as well as informed. There was a touch of magic about the dial, for it could provide soothing relief or fanciful escape. One news reporter each night assured his listeners that "Ah, there's good news tonight!" even when the news was dismal. Daytime "soap operas" provided tearful, interminable "real life" dramas about people who were forever getting into scrapes or suffering from incurable diseases.

In the evenings and on Sunday afternoons, the comedians and mystery and variety shows took over. Radio produced some gifted comics, many of whom had started in vaudeville, including Jack Benny, Ed Wynn, Jack Pearl, and Edgar Bergen and Charlie McCarthy. The greatest of all was Fred Allen, a satirist whose spontaneous wit could be devastating. Allen found radio a frustrating medium, for it curbed his subject matter and forced him to cater to the lowest common denominator among his listeners.

Other stars of the time were Rudy Vallee and Bing Crosby, who turned crooning into a highly profitable business; the Lone Ranger with his faithful Indian companion Tonto; and "Jack Armstrong, the All-American Boy!" Occasionally, the networks sandwiched in a "town meeting of the air" or a symphony concert conducted by Toscanini.

A great age for movies. By 1930, the movies too were big business. Operating for the overriding purpose of making money, the studios chose their scripts carefully, doing their best to avoid controversial subject matter. Yet, the depression years proved to be a great age for the moviemakers. Sound pictures, technicolor, and other technical refinements brought the industry

THE FRED ALLEN SHOW

Fred Allen and Jack Benny delighted audiences in the 1930's with their on-radio feud. In the following scene, Allen, his wife Portland, and announcer Harry von Zell discuss an upcoming fight between Allen and Benny:

PORTLAND Are you going to train to fight Jack Benny?

ALLEN Yes, Portland, I'll have to go on a pastry diet. I'll do some soft living to get in the same condition; I don't want to take an unfair advantage. Benny's as soft as a herd of goo. . . .

HARRY What about Benny's muscles?

ALLEN His arm looks like a buggy whip with fingers. I've got veins in my nose bigger than Benny's arm. And as for those legs. I've seen better looking legs on a bridge table. . . .

PORTLAND Jack said on his program he saved your life in vaudeville. . . .

ALLEN I saved his life. I'll never forget it. Benny was out on the stage in his spangled tights playing the violin. His big number was Pony Boy. He just started to play Pony Boy when a man in the front row started to shoot.

HARRY A Westerner?

ALLEN No, a music lover. I ran out on the stage in front of Jack. I thought the star running on might save his life. In the excitement Benny stole two bows and I was shot in the chest. . . .

PORTLAND Is that when Jack gave you the transfusion?

ALLEN Yes, Portland. . . . It was the first time at a transfusion the donor ever asked for a receipt for his blood.

HARRY Did the transfusion help you?

ALLEN I had a relapse. Then as a result of the Benny transfusion I had anemia for two years. And it affected me in other ways. I couldn't get my hand in my money pocket for months. I found myself window shopping at toupee stores. It was terrible. . . .

to full maturity. Walt Disney developed the animated cartoon into an intricate technical form of great variety.

The star system made the leading players household names and created the phenomenon of fans who avidly read the movie magazines (a big business in themselves) and followed every move and mood of their idols. The list of stars was endless: Jean Harlow, Clark Gable, Shirley Temple, James Stewart, Claudette Colbert, Spencer Tracy, Bette Davis, Fredric March, to name only a few. Greta Garbo and John Barrymore became superstars and legends in their own time.

Hollywood's products ran the gamut from horror films such as *Frankenstein* (1931) and *King Kong* (1933) to memorable biographies of such figures as Disraeli, Louis Pasteur, and Emile Zola. *Little Caesar* (1930) and *Scarface* (1932) led a parade of gangster films throughout the decade, many of them glamorizing the activities of the hoodlums. Unable to avoid the depression altogether, the studios did their best to cheer up its victims and to assure them that all was well—or would soon become well. As one critic observed, lavish musicals were a nice way of "passing the time while waiting for the New Deal to get down your way." In *Stand Up and Cheer* (1934), the President appointed a secretary of amusement to help the country laugh its way out of the depression. Busby Berkeley's *Gold Diggers* series (1933, 1935, 1937) were extravagant productions with tuneful music and bevies of pretty chorus girls. The 1935 edition featured a hundred girls playing a hundred white pianos!

Comedy came of age in the movies during the thirties. Slapstick remained popular and wonderfully amusing, but a more sophisticated form of humor developed, too. Bulbous-nosed, child-hating W. C. Fields was utterly inimitable in his ability to turn an ordinary situation into a wildly funny nightmare. In Mae West's pictures, the humor was bawdy but innocent, with the heroine always ending up, as one critic noted, "wealthy, wicked, and well loved."

Charlie Chaplin's great films *City Lights* (1931) and *Modern Times* (1936) combined his often poignant humor with pointed social commentary. Comedy became anarchy in the insane films of the Marx Brothers. It was said of Groucho Marx

In the depression years, movies distracted millions of Americans from their troubles. They laughed at W. C. Fields and Mae West, shown above in *My Little Chickadee* (1940). This was the only film in which Mae West shared star billing. As a teetotaler, she strongly disapproved of Fields' well-known fondness for alcohol. (He piously advised against drinking anything stronger than gin before breakfast.) Moviegoers were fascinated by tough-talking gangsters; at left, Paul Muni and George Raft in *Scarface* (1932)—the story of Al Capone. And then there were musicals, with marvelously improbable story lines and equally fanciful dance spectaculars. The pirouetting "violinists" below graced *Gold Diggers of 1933.*

that his conversation "sees to it that no idea gets anywhere, or, if anywhere, that its destination will be of maximum unimportance to the human race." Often Groucho, Chico, and Harpo improvised as they went along, driving scriptwriters and directors to despair with their antics.

On occasion, Hollywood found it profitable to respond seriously to the problems of the day, and some of the "message" films were superior achievements. *All Quiet on the Western Front* (1930) still has few peers as a statement on the imbecility of war. Steinbeck's novel *The Grapes of Wrath* became a monumental film epic (1940) in the hands of director John Ford. *Fury* (1936) showed the ugliness and brutality of lynching, while *Black Legion* (1936) exposed the mentality of native fascists.

In considering the international scene, the movie men were reluctant to make films which might offend any nation buying their products. But by 1939, Hitler had become sufficiently menacing to warrant Hollywood's producing *Confessions of a Nazi Spy* (1939) as a straight denunciation of the totalitarians. Charlie Chaplin ridiculed Hitler and Mussolini unmercifully in his keen satire *The Great Dictator* (1939). By the time the picture was released in 1940, however, the Nazis had become the very unfunny scourges of Europe and the point was lost.

Newspapers and magazines. Newspaper reporting in the thirties raised an interesting paradox. On the one hand, the working newsmen were generally sympathetic to Roosevelt and his programs. Indeed, with some government encouragement they organized the American Newspaper Guild in 1933, the first national union of journalists. The publishers, on the other hand, joined with their fellow big businessmen in criticizing, sometimes in violently denouncing, the New Deal and the President. The result was a situation in which, as one observer noted, "the people voted with the news columns and against the editorials." One serious inroad on the press's traditional influence in politics was the growth of radio as a medium of instant communication with the people. Radio advertising, moreover, cut sharply into newspaper revenue.

A newspaper feature that radio could not match was the comic strip. Jiggs, Popeye, and the Katzenjammer Kids continued to provide laughter and color in the Sunday paper. But in the thirties they were joined by a strange band of characters who often played two interchangeable roles—one, a meek ordinary citizen, powerless to right the wrongs of society; the other, a superhuman being endowed with all sorts of special powers to overcome evil. "Superman," "Batman and Robin," "Captain Marvel," and similar heroes became so popular that comic books devoted entirely to their exploits became a flourishing business.

In magazine publishing, the most striking development was the growth of the *Reader's Digest*. Aimed at people who wanted their reading done for them first by others, then reduced to capsule form, this pocket-size magazine attained a circulation of nearly two million by 1936, then went soaring to eight million by the end of World War II. Supposedly it supplied readers with the best of magazine writing in a handy form. Often it pandered to medical sensationalism or launched "crusades" that went nowhere.

Another magazine with extraordinary appeal was *Life,* an attractive pictorial weekly founded in 1936 by Henry Luce, who already directed a large publishing empire. His *Time,* like its competitor *Newsweek,* gave readers a quick, informal, and highly distinctive summary of each week's news events.

Magazines of opinion continued to attract only a small number of readers, despite the relevance of their material to current affairs. Indeed, the five major intellectual and cultural journals, taken together, were no match in circulation for the "confession" magazine *True Story* or any of the leading movie magazines. At the same time, the *New Yorker* attracted a limited but intensely loyal group of readers, with its witty, urbane comments on the current scene.

Recreation in hard times. People took their recreation where they could during the depression. Private country clubs suffered badly; public golf links actually prospered. Forced by economic necessity to stay at home, many people turned to old, familiar parlor games for recreation. Those who could get away visited the country's national parks and forests in record numbers. Thanks to the work of the CCC, these areas were able to accommodate vastly more people than had been the case in the past. In New York City, Mayor

Fiorello LaGuardia established a model for other cities in providing free recreational facilities for all the people, as at Jones Beach and in Central Park. After the United States hosted the Winter Olympics in 1932, the sport of skiing caught on among great numbers of people.

Organized athletics suffered heavy financial losses early in the depression, as people stayed away from the games for lack of the admission price. Many colleges and universities cut back on their athletic programs, and the University of Chicago—a member of the Big Ten conference—shocked the sporting world in 1940 by dropping intercollegiate athletics altogether. Football remained popular at most institutions, however, and one of the great stars of the time was a bright young back at Colorado named "Whizzer" White, better known in later years as Justice Byron White of the United States Supreme Court. By the end of the decade, most spectator sports were doing well again.

Professional football gained in popularity, although it never threatened the primacy of baseball as the great American sport. In boxing, the sensation of the thirties was Joe Louis, the "Brown Bomber" from Detroit. Knocking out one challenger after another, he took the heavyweight championship in 1937 and held it against all comers until after the war. One of sporting's great moments came in 1938, when Louis dispatched the pride of Nazi Germany, Max Schmeling, in two minutes of the first round. Another black American to make a mockery of Hitler's absurd racial theories (page 616) was Jesse Owens, who outran the best of the "Nordic" Nazis and became the undisputed star of the 1936 Olympic Games at Berlin.

As in all periods, people found eccentric ways to amuse themselves, too. College students swallowed live goldfish, not because they were hungry, but simply to attract attention. Jitterbugging, the Big Apple, the Suzy-Q, Truckin', and the Lambeth Walk all provided young people with ways of dancing to swing music. Paradoxically, at a time when people had little money to spend on the necessities of life, gambling had widespread appeal. Churches sponsored Bingo games to raise money for parish activities. Pinball games and slot machines attracted zealous players in drugstores and bars all over the country.

And as if to prove that they were no different, really, from other generations of Americans, the people of the depression decade picked up one silly song after another, only to discard them after a few weeks of popularity. In the end, surely such songs as "Flat-Foot Floogie," "A-tisket A-tasket," and "The Music Goes 'Round and 'Round" took second place to:

> Down in de meddy by de itty bitty poo
> Fam wee itty fitty and a mama fitty foo.
> "Fim," said de mama fitty, "fim if oo tan"
> And dey fam and dey fam all over de dam.

CONCLUSION

The fact that people could be foolish in a time of adversity was a healthy sign, actually. For the coming decade of the 1940's proved that the American people had weathered the Great Depression in remarkably good fashion. Certainly, they recovered their morale and sense of national self-confidence sufficiently so that the United States could finally begin exerting the world leadership toward which it had been moving for half a century.

Much of the world succumbed to totalitarian rule during the 1930's, the system under which political opposition to the power of those who control the state was neither recognized nor tolerated. Much of Western Europe came under the heel of military dictatorship. But in the United States the people developed a new appreciation of democracy and gladly gave the system a new lease on life. With all its faults, democracy proved to be clearly preferable to the available alternatives.

Intellectually, culturally, and socially, the depression years became a period of genuine inspiration. Perhaps Ben Shahn put it best when he wrote: "I felt in complete harmony with the times. I don't think I've ever felt that way before or since."

QUESTIONS

1. What influence did the depression have upon American intellectual life of the thirties? Are there any redeeming virtues of a severe economic

crisis such as the depression? Explain your answer.

2. What was the role of the government in the support and promotion of the arts? Was this role the most appropriate one for the government to assume? Defend your answer.

3. How was social realism and cultural nationalism evident in the literary and visual arts?

4. To what extent had America attained a cultural maturity in the thirties? Explain your answer.

5. How significant was European influence upon American intellectual and cultural life?

6. What were the similarities and what were the differences between the American culture of the twenties and of the thirties?

7. To what extent were radical solutions to American problems reflected in the culture of the times? What accounted for the degree of interest?

8. In what ways was escape demonstrated in the cultural and intellectual life of the thirties?

9. Compare the popular culture of the thirties with the visual and literary arts of the same period?

▓ BIBLIOGRAPHY

ALLEN, FREDERICK LEWIS, *Since Yesterday: The 1930's in America,* Bantam Books. The book covers the period from the peak of the stock market in 1929 to Hitler's 1939 invasion of Poland in much the same way as Allen's preceding book on the twenties. This volume is not as lively as the first (which may say more for the period than the author), but its historical interpretations are better balanced. This book is a fine place to begin a social history of the thirties.

GUTHRIE, WOODY, *Bound for Glory,* New American Library (Signet Books). Guthrie's own autobiography will surely interest today's students. Few singers have had as much influence on American folk music as Woody Guthrie, who experienced the life of the wanderer during the depression and recorded his experiences in over a thousand songs. Between the book and the music, the student should get a feel for the twenties and thirties.

JONES, LEROI, *Blues People: Negro Music and White America,* Crowell (Apollo Editions). This is probably the best account of black-American music. The various black music forms are being re-discovered with maximum gain for the casual listener and the serious student who wants to know more about black America.

ELLIS, JOHN T., *American Catholicism,* 2nd ed., Chicago History of American Civilization Series, U. of Chicago Press.

GLAZER, NATHAN, *American Judaism,* Chicago History of American Civilization Series, U. of Chicago Press.

HUDSON, WINTHROP S., *American Protestantism,* Chicago History of American Civilization Series, U. of Chicago Press.

These three volumes should provide the reader with fine summaries of the three major religions in America. Monsignor Ellis is a noted Catholic historian who surveys Catholicism from the Spanish and French colonists to the present day. Hudson, another noted church historian, identifies three stages in Protestant development in America with a definite decline in Protestant influence in the twentieth century, or third stage. Glazer's book has more of a sociological orientation and concentrates upon the Jew in modern America.

The Fragile Peace

During the years of "normalcy" following World War I, the American people were much too preoccupied with their domestic concerns to give much serious thought to foreign affairs. Many were disillusioned by their experiences in the war and tried to turn their backs on the outside world. Some thought the United States had blundered tragically in entering the conflict at all, while others saw the Treaty of Versailles as a betrayal of the high ideals for which Americans had died in France. Doubtless, most people understood vaguely that the United States was now a world power. But few had any comprehension of the meaning of power or of the responsibilities which world power bestowed upon them and their government. Accustomed to living in geographic and political isolation from the rest of the world, the average American rather took his country's power for granted.

Not so the leaders at Washington. If American diplomatists were unwilling to shoulder the political responsibilities that Wilson had asked them to bear, they nonetheless understood the uses to which power could be put. Far from being a time of official withdrawal from world affairs, the postwar years saw the United States extend its economic power and moral influence into the far corners of the globe. As fascism arose in Europe and as Japan intensified its efforts to dominate East Asia, moreover, almost every event abroad confronted the statesmen and politicians in Washington with difficult, often awkward, political choices. By the mid-1930's, indeed, the major problem of the political leaders was to arouse the American people to a clear understanding of the dangers that threatened their peace and security. As you consider the diplomacy of the period between the wars, keep these questions in mind:

1. What was the impact of the Russian Revolution on American foreign policy?
2. What economic considerations influenced American diplomacy?
3. What policies did the United States follow toward Latin America? toward Asia?
4. How did the rise of totalitarianism affect America?
5. Why was America finally drawn into war?

1 Economic Considerations Shape Diplomacy In The 1920's

1. What was the basic purpose of American foreign policy during the twenties? How did programs calling for collective security through the League of Nations differ from programs supporting enlightened world leadership by America?

2. To what extent is it possible to promote American business interests and remedy possible revolutionary situations in other countries?

3. Why did the West consider it essential to crush the Bolsheviks in Russia?

4. What was the goal of American policy toward the Soviet Union? Do you think this was both a reasonable and desirable goal? What were the means used to secure that goal? Do you think these means were appropriate?

Few events in modern history have had such an enormous impact on international relations as the triumph of revolutionary communism, or Bolshevism, in Russia. Even before World War I ground to a close, the rising Red glow in Eastern Europe began to haunt the politicians in Washington and every capital in western Europe. As Herbert Hoover noted about the gathering of the diplomats at Versailles after the armistice: "Communist Russia was a specter which wandered into the Peace Conference almost daily."

Conditions in much of Europe, as well as throughout the colonial world, were so chaotic just after the war that they provided a fertile breeding ground for new revolutions—revolutions which the diplomats feared would spread Bolshevism around the globe. "Bolshevism must be suppressed," Wilson's secretary of state, Robert Lansing, asserted, and his words became a keynote in United States and western European diplomacy from 1918 on.

The threat of communism. Why did the West consider it essential to crush the Bolsheviks?

Primarily, because communism threatened to disrupt the long-established patterns of economic and political behavior that were associated with capitalism and liberal democracy. Utopian in its aims and evangelical in its motivation, revolutionary communism appealed to those peoples who had been exploited, mistreated, or bypassed by the Industrial Revolution, both in the modern nations and in the colonial territories. It professed to offer a shortcut to modernism and a system in which exploitation would have no part, once the exploiters themselves were destroyed.

To a world emerging from one of history's most horrible and senseless wars, moreover, the Marxist prophets insisted that a Communist world would be a warless world. If men had no reason to exploit and brutalize one another, they argued, all of society's coercive instruments and institutions—chiefly, the state itself—would disappear. Once the working class gained power, all men would be workers and there would be no need for authority and hierarchy in society. But the workers could take power only by destroying the existing system through revolutionary action and overthrowing the ruling class.

To the leaders of capitalism in the West, communism was a menace of ominous proportions. The liberal ideal had always been a society in which order and progress were carefully balanced, in which the essential harmony among various interest groups and individuals would prevail over such artificial disruptions as class conflict and even strikes.

But communism raised class warfare to the level of an inevitable turn of history, thereby threatening to saddle mankind with perpetual disorder. Men would become slaves to a utopian dogma, while the individual would be reduced to nothing. If the Bolsheviks were not suppressed, the leaders of the capitalist nations warned, western civilization itself would not survive. Thus, they decided that there could be no compromise with radicalism.

During the twenties, American policy-makers searched for a "road away from revolution." Recognizing that wars bred social unrest and that unrest could flare into revolution, they determined to put an end to major conflicts among nations. Proponents of the League of Nations argued that only an international organization dedicated to collective security could preserve the peace.

Opponents of the League insisted that the United States, with its enormous economic power and moral influence, could by itself provide the enlightened leadership that would persuade other nations to pursue peaceful policies. In the process, moreover, America's vital interests and internal security would be safeguarded from contamination by outside influences. Whereas Wilson believed that the United States should take the political initiative in bringing order to the postwar world (as through the League), the Republican leaders in the twenties decided in favor of an economic initiative which would serve the same purpose.

Economic basis of American policy. Not that the Republicans were unwilling to use political leverage to achieve their goals under certain conditions. As President Coolidge noted, intervention in the internal affairs of another nation was perfectly justifiable in order to "discourage revolution," much as a policeman was justified in discouraging a crime about to be committed. But such leaders as Herbert Hoover and Charles Evans Hughes believed that intervention of the political sort should be used only as a last resort. They preferred a policy which would prevent revolutions from ever becoming an imminent threat, and they relied upon the economic power of the United States to achieve that end.

In this respect, it is significant that Hoover entered the Harding-Coolidge Cabinet with the understanding that, as secretary of commerce, he would have a major voice in foreign policy. Developments throughout the world, he insisted, had an immediate, crucial bearing upon economic conditions at home.

Indeed, with almost all business and political leaders, Hoover was convinced that a steady, appreciable expansion of commerce abroad was essential to the health of American capitalism. During the twenties, some economic growth resulted from the rising standard of living at home. But the chief stimulus to capital growth came from expanding markets overseas.

As early as 1915, Harding (then a senator) had warned the National Association of Manufacturers that the postwar period would see "a struggle for commercial and industrial supremacy such as the world has never witnessed." He added that "if this land of ours desires to maintain its eminence, it must be prepared for that struggle." It was one of the few perceptive public statements Harding ever made. In effect, his warning meant that if capitalism was to survive, the United States had to take the lead over the other industrial nations in opening new markets, new sources of raw materials, and new opportunities for investment.

During the war and postwar years, an extraordinary expansion of American economic power took place precisely along these lines. The United States became a creditor nation for the first time in its history. It assumed first place among the industrial nations. It gained lucrative new markets everywhere in the world—in Latin America, in China, in Southeast Asia, in the Middle East, in Europe. The tremendous economic surge more than ever convinced the country's leaders that prosperity had to be maintained not only for the well-being of the American people, but also for forestalling revolution elsewhere in the world.

Moreover, American leaders naturally assumed that American economic expansion would bring benefits to less fortunate peoples in the world. There was nothing hypocritical in their assumption, for it was as old as America itself. Peoples everywhere, it was argued, admired the American system and would welcome its extension to their own lands. Democracy, it was assumed, would follow economic penetration as surely as day follows night. Thus, it was frustrating and sometimes embittering for Americans to discover that their good motives were not always reciprocated by gratitude.

As a further safeguard against revolution and as a guarantee against wars, American diplomacy sought to arrange an informal "concert of power" among the industrial nations. In Europe, the United States worked to bring Germany back into the family of nations, while American dollars sought to effect economic recovery in the wartorn nations. A stable Germany working in cooperation with a prosperous France and Great Britain was to provide a bulwark against the spread of communism into western Europe. A stable Europe would give American investors the opportunity to develop such backward areas as the Balkans.

The Russian Revolution resulted in the victory of communism in the Soviet Union. Above, revolutionary troops storm the Winter Palace of the czar in Petrograd (now Leningrad) in 1917. These events filled many Americans with foreboding, and some talked of "shooting Bolshevism out of Russia." President Wilson shared the anti-Soviet feeling of his countrymen, but was cautious about direct intervention. In 1918, however, he landed troops in Siberia, ostensibly to protect some Czech Allied soldiers there but actually to support "White" generals fighting the "Red" (Bolshevik) regime in a civil war. Below, American units march through Khabarovsk in 1919. When the Whites were defeated, American troops sailed for home with little to show for their efforts.

605

In the Far East, the problem was to check Japan's expansion on the Asian mainland, while bringing the Chinese revolution (page 608) to some stable, reasonable conclusion, lest the great potential markets of the area be lost. American diplomats assumed that the other industrial nations were interested in checking revolution and in promoting a rational development of the world's resources. Accordingly, they relied on a mainstay of American foreign policy, the Open Door principle, to hold the "concert of power" together and bring about international order. Not only in Asia, but everywhere in the world, the doors of trade were to be opened to all nations on an equal basis. American businessmen were entirely confident that in such a situation their own interests and the nation's would be well served.

Relations with the Soviet Union. Western leaders (including the Americans) were somewhat confused as to the best way of dealing with the Soviet Union. On the one hand, their fear of communism led them to exaggerate that nation's actual strength in the world. On the other hand, they found it difficult to believe that communism could really work. Given the right kind of encouragement and aid, surely the people would overthrow the Bolsheviks; perhaps the revolution would simply collapse of its own weight, considering its inefficiency and reliance upon repression. The problem was to quarantine the "disease" of communism until it could be eliminated in some fashion or other, but also to make certain that the process of elimination did not trigger a new war.

Thus, the Western powers treated the Soviet Union as a pariah nation, beyond the limits of respectability. They drafted the Treaty of Versailles without consulting the Soviet Union and excluded it from the League of Nations. For their part, the Soviet leaders repudiated their nation's war debts to the Western powers, scorned the thought of participating in a "bourgeois" peace settlement, and promoted revolution wherever they could in the West.

The American approach to the Soviet Union ranged from suspicion to open hostility. Wilson withheld diplomatic recognition of the new regime, implying that it was illegitimate and temporary only. More important, he joined the Allies in 1918 in a bold attempt to keep Russia in the war and to aid the anti-Bolshevik forces which were fighting a civil war against the Red Army. American troops occupied positions in northern Russia and actually fought several engagements with Communist forces before Wilson withdrew them in 1920. Probably the President regretted ever sending them in the first place, for he clearly preferred to use economic and moral pressure against the Communists. Accordingly, he replaced the troops with an economic blockade of the Soviet Union.

Ironically, the pressure to improve relations with the Soviet regime came from farmers and businessmen in the United States. Plagued with surpluses during the agricultural depression of 1921, they began to see the Soviet Union as a possible market for their goods. The farm bloc clamored to give "food relief" to the Russian people, while Hoover (who was secretary of commerce by then) concluded that economic relations of a limited sort with the Communists might result in the "Americanization" of their economy. In the end, some $78 million in food relief was extended to the Soviets. Far from helping to "Americanize" the Russian economy, the aid bolstered the Soviet regime and saved millions of Russians from starvation.

Throughout the 1920's elements in the business community pressured Washington to recognize the Soviet Union and open full-scale commercial relations with that country. The Republican leaders responded by encouraging business to seek markets in Russia, and by 1930, the volume of trade between the two nations exceeded twice the prewar figure. Yet, recognition was a touchy moral and political question and the Republicans were loath to confront it openly. The situation was a dangerous and abnormal one, and Senator William Borah of Idaho pointed to the incongruity in it: "So long as you have a hundred and fifty million people outlawed in a sense, it necessarily follows that you cannot have peace." In a real sense, it can be seen now, the seeds of the cold war between the Soviet Union and the West were planted at the moment World War I came to a close. For even in those early years, the hostility between the two systems conditioned almost every move made by both Russian and American diplomats.

This, then, was the framework in which diplomacy operated during the twenties. As Secretary of State Hughes put it, the United States sought "to establish a *Pax Americana* maintained not by arms but by mutual respect and good will and the tranquilizing processes of reason." The dream of the diplomats, in its way, was as noble as that of the business leaders who fashioned the new economic era in domestic affairs. It also proved to be as fragile.

2 Republicans Try To Maintain International Order

1. What were the political and economic realities of postwar Europe with which the United States had to deal?

2. How did the issues of high American tariffs, the repayment of war debts, and the fear of communism complicate American foreign policy?

3. What were the political and economic realities concerning the Far East with which the United States had to deal in the postwar period?

4. What is "non-political" diplomacy as practiced by the United States? How effective was "non-political" diplomacy?

As they assumed power in 1921, Republican policy-makers were confronted with certain conditions which almost immediately forced them to modify their plans. Ideals came into conflict with reality, with the result that American diplomacy during the twenties often moved in different directions at the same time.

For one thing, the historic position of the Republicans on the tariff hampered the diplomats' plans to promote the recovery of wartorn Europe. Britain, especially, desperately needed to increase its overseas trade so as to reduce its national debt and put its economy on a sound basis. But the Fordney-McCumber Tariff (page 516) all but shut off the American market for British and European goods, while the vigorous competition of American businessmen in Latin America and Asia cut deeply into markets the Allied nations had traditionally controlled. Moreover, Europe staggered under a huge burden of war debts to the United States. Unless the burden could be reduced, there was no hope of stabilizing the European economies.

War debts and reparations. With considerable justification, the Allies claimed that they had fought this country's war against Germany, as well as their own, in the years before America entered the conflict directly. The war debts, they argued, should be considered a part of America's contribution to the Allied effort. But Washington insisted that the money be repaid promptly in gold. As President Coolidge remarked flatly: "They hired the money, didn't they? Let them pay it back."

Where were the Allies to find the money? As they saw it, the only answer was to transfer the burden of the debt to defeated Germany in the form of reparations for war damages. In 1921 a Reparations Commission controlled by Britain and France fixed the claims against Germany at $33 billion, a ridiculously high figure that the Germans could not possibly meet if they were to stabilize their own economy. But the Allies insisted on payment, and the German economy went into a tailspin.

Deeply concerned about Europe's economic health, Washington tried to solve the war debts–reparations problem with the Dawes Plan (1923). Germany's annual payments to the Allies were reduced, while short-term loans from the United States stimulated temporary economic recovery in Germany and enabled that nation to resume reparations payments. In turn, the Allies made payments on their debts to the United States with the same funds! As one historian noted, "the money that came to the United States from the Allies was only rounding a circle to the point of its origin."

America's eagerness to extend credit to Germany was a symptom of the speculative fever that gripped investors during the twenties. The effort to promote lasting recovery in Europe failed, and it was only a matter of time before the whole flimsy structure came tumbling down. When the crash came in 1929, the United States worsened the situation with the Hawley-Smoot Tariff (page 516), which precipitated a trade war and ended all hope for international economic cooperation. To be sure, the goal of American diplomacy was a sound and stable Europe that would resist political extremism and cooperate economically with the United States, but the conduct of diplomacy produced far different results.

Nonpolitical diplomacy. One reason for this failure was Washington's reluctance to become involved in solving Europe's political problems, especially those which the Treaty of Versailles had spawned or aggravated. In remaking the map of Europe, the peacemakers had chopped up the old Austrian and Turkish empires into several new, polyglot nations, and had stripped Germany of entire provinces along its borders. In so doing, they reopened ethnic and territorial disputes of the sort that had produced war many times in the past. The situation demanded close, constant attention; yet, Republican policy-makers refused to confront it on political grounds, relying instead upon economic and moral diplomacy to produce stability in Europe.

As for the League of Nations, the United States established semiofficial relations with its subsidiary agencies and gave up the pretense that the League did not exist. Yet, Washington carefully avoided involvement in the League's political functions, in keeping with a determination to conduct foreign policy without interference from outside influences.

The crowning folly of this "nonpolitical" diplomacy was the Kellogg-Briand Pact of 1928 (the Pact of Paris). This extraordinary document pledged its signers (sixty-two nations) to "outlaw war" as an instrument of national policy. It reflected the strength of the peace movement at home and was consistent with the American aim of preventing a new world war. But it contained no *political* provision for the enforcement of its lofty pledge, relying instead upon "moral pres-

sure." In short, it was a useless piece of paper. Its only effect was to contribute to the complacency with which many people in the western democracies watched the rise of political extremism in central Europe.

American policy in Asia. Several factors limited American policy in Asia. On the one hand, the United States regarded Japan as a bulwark against Communist expansion in Asia and as a potential force for stability in the area. At the same time, Japan was an aggressive competitor in seeking control of Asia's vast markets. If Japan extended its influence on the mainland too far, conceivably it might exclude American commerce altogether from a region this country's leaders viewed as a trade frontier of the future.

During the 1920's, moreover, conditions in China once again commanded the attention of American policy-makers. In 1911, that giant nation had undergone a revolution which toppled the empire and replaced it with the Chinese Republic, a government the United States had gladly recognized. Plagued by internal turmoil and constant pressure from the Japanese and Russians along its borders, however, the Republic never gained control of all China, nor did it establish conditions of genuine political stability.

After World War I, the Chinese revolution erupted again, becoming militantly anti-foreign and anti-imperialist. Led by Sun Yat-sen (and later by his successor, Chiang Kai-shek), the Kuomintang, or Nationalist party, stabilized much of the country and demanded the end of all colonial privileges in China. Although most Americans were sympathetic to the revolution, the policy-makers in Washington disliked the militancy of the Nationalists. Unless the situation in Asia could be stabilized quickly, they feared, the Chinese upheaval might become the nightmare in Asia that the Russian Revolution had become in Europe.

The Washington Naval Conference. Complicating the problem was the threat of a naval race among the Pacific powers, especially Japan, Britain, and the United States. Certain that a costly ship-building competition would increase international tension, the Harding administration took steps to divert Japan, in particular, from engaging in such folly. In 1921, Secretary of

The following description of American foreign relations during the 1920's is from a recent Czechoslovakian textbook, which presents a Marxist interpretation of events:

". . . The League of Nations was founded at the initiative of the President of the United States, Woodrow Wilson. The American imperialists, who during the war greatly increased their industrial production and at the same time became the creditors of a majority of the other capitalist countries, initially believed that they might use the League of Nations for the realization of their plans for world domination. Their capitalist competitors in France and in England, basing their strength on huge colonial armies, were too strong so that . . . they were in a position to entirely destroy American plans for domination of the League of Nations. For this reason the United States finally did not even join the League of Nations, and made an attempt to strengthen its international position in a different manner.

"The conference [the Washington Naval Conference] . . . provided evidence of the growing strength of American imperialism. At this conference, the United States dictated the abolition of the English-Japanese alliance, which threatened it in the area of the Pacific Ocean, and secured in China the same privileges as those [of other] Great Powers which had penetrated China much earlier. Last but not least, the United States managed to secure the recognition of naval parity with England so that the monopolistic priority of England on the seas ended.

"The Washington system supplemented the Versailles system. Under these two systems the world was again divided in keeping with the comparative strength of the [various] capitalist countries. Not even these systems were capable of permanently eliminating the conflicts among the imperialist Great Powers and among the minor capitalist states."

States Hughes called the powers together for the Washington Naval Conference.

On paper, the conference was a success for American diplomacy. It reduced the size of existing navies and established a 5:5:3 ratio among the powers for capital ships (battleships, chiefly) in the Pacific. Japan was allowed 3 battleships to each 5 for Britain and the United States.

But the naval agreement had serious flaws and provided only a temporary solution to the problem of armaments. It failed to consider such new warships as submarines and cruisers, and it touched only briefly on the question of aircraft carriers. Its formula for naval strength predictably aroused the anger of Japan's militarists, who contemptuously referred to 5:5:3 as "Rolls Royce: Rolls Royce : Ford"! Naval disarmament failed in this period between the wars chiefly because the powers, including the United States, were not really willing to give up their modern, effective naval units.

The conference also reaffirmed the Open Door regarding China's territorial integrity and equal access of all nations to China's markets. But it provided no machinery for enforcing the policy, leaving the Open Door as difficult to defend as ever. In addition, when the United States, Britain, France, and Japan agreed to respect one another's possessions in the Pacific, the Japanese took the statement as tacit admission by the other powers that they had a "special position" in Korea and northern Manchuria, areas which they already effectively controlled.

Still, the Washington Conference briefly improved relations between Japan and the United States. Then, in 1924, Congress nullified whatever good the diplomats had accomplished by passing immigration laws excluding Orientals from the United States. Japan's militarists used the resulting uproar in Asia to set their country on a collision course with the Americans. Moreover, as in Europe, Republican tariff policy in Asia worked to defeat the purposes of Republican diplomacy. Shut out of American markets, the Japanese concluded that they must seek markets elsewhere using whatever methods proved effective.

Hoover-Stimson Doctrine. In 1931–32, the Manchurian Crisis revealed the emptiness of the Washington Conference. Under Chiang Kai-shek, the Chinese Nationalists tried to oust both the Soviet Union and Japan from northern Manchuria, a historic province of China. The Soviets reacted swiftly and decisively, defeating the Chinese before the rest of the world realized what was happening. Japan, on the other hand, invaded southern Manchuria, knowing that the action would precipitate a protracted struggle with China. In 1932, Japan finally incorporated all its holdings in Manchuria into the puppet state of Manchukuo and defied the world to alter the situation.

Secretary of State Henry L. Stimson realized at once that the American position in Asia was threatened. He wanted to impose strict *sanctions* on Japan, that is, to bring legal and economic pressure on it to cease its aggression. It was a bold proposal, and some historians believe that if such tough action had been taken in 1932, the two countries might never have started down the road to Pearl Harbor. Others argue that the United States had neither the military power nor the will to impose such a policy and see it through to completion. In any case, President Hoover decided that moral pressure alone would force Japan to back down.

The Hoover-Stimson Doctrine of 1932, usually called the Stimson Doctrine, declared that this country would not recognize actions (such as the Japanese invasion) impairing the sovereignty of China and the integrity of the Open Door. After a period of indecision, the League of Nations said essentially the same thing. Neither statement had the slightest effect upon Japan except to bring about its withdrawal from the League. Once again, the unwillingness of the United States to confront the *political* implications of its economic and moral diplomacy contributed to the breakdown of the international order it sought to maintain.

Growth of American investments. Overseas investments by Americans climbed from $94 million in 1919 to $602 million a decade later. In 1923, American businessmen gained access to the Black Sea-Turkey area and penetrated the economies of the Balkan nations in eastern Europe. In the Middle East, the State Department encouraged American oil companies to develop the resources of Saudi Arabia, while Britain and France were persuaded to accept the Open Door in the Arab lands they controlled. American business showed only slight interest in developing resources in Africa at the time, although Liberia's rubber resources came under United States' control.

In the Western Hemisphere, American policy was a mixture of "Big Stick" interventionism and dollar diplomacy. In 1921, Harding took a small but welcome step toward improving relations with Latin America when he removed from Honduras the American troops that Wilson had sent there earlier. Unfortunately, Coolidge took a large step backward in 1924 by returning the troops to Honduras and sending others to Nicaragua, apparently because he feared that Mexico was trying to foment revolution in the two countries. He also became involved in a nasty new dispute with Mexico over the old question of who should control that nation's mineral resources— Mexicans or Americans.

This time, the argument between the two countries was complicated by Coolidge's assertion that Mexico meant to transform Central America into a Bolshevik base from which to harass the United States! The charge was patently ridiculous and totally lacking in substantiation; but it suggested that some American politicians were ready to equate *any* kind of revolutionary activity with Bolshevism. Pressure from progressives in Congress and businessmen with interests in Mexico forced Coolidge to back down from his extreme position. Ambassador Dwight Morrow, a skilled lawyer and diplomat, soon negotiated a settlement to the dispute that put Mexican-American relations on a relatively even keel once again.

Determined to find a better way of dealing with Latin America, Hoover pledged that instead of invading its sister republics, the United States henceforth would be their friend and partner. But again, Republican tariff policy undid the good work of diplomacy. Desperately in need of markets, the Latin Americans found that their "partner" to the North was not interested in buying their goods. Still, Hoover's change of course provided a foundation upon which Roosevelt was able to build the Good Neighbor Policy of his administration.

3 Roosevelt Attempts To Protect The Economy

1. What were the provisions of Roosevelt's foreign policy? How were they similar and how were they different from the foreign policy of the twenties?

2. What were the goals of the Good Neighbor Policy? How successful was Roosevelt in reaching these goals?

3. How did the depression affect international affairs?

4. What steps were taken by the United States to assure a neutral position in the world? How effective were these steps in securing neutrality?

Diplomacy during the early years of the New Deal consisted chiefly of protecting the American economy from the international effects of the Great Depression. Franklin D. Roosevelt was most assuredly not an isolationist. Indeed, his preparation for the Presidency and his entire background marked him as a man with a clear concept of America's position in the world and a sensitive ear to events abroad.

If Roosevelt's early program was one of economic nationalism, it was not because he wanted to make the United States a hermit nation, oblivious to the outside world. On the contrary, it was because he believed this country had to recover its economic strength as quickly as possible in order to reassert itself as a force for stability in international affairs. This purpose would best be accomplished, he concluded, by focusing temporarily on domestic recovery rather than on the world economic crisis.

In search of new markets. From the start of his administration, Roosevelt made rearmament and the expansion of foreign trade key elements in his recovery program. In 1933, he began a major naval building program, even as the nation's official policy was to seek naval disarmament among the powers; and never during his tenure did he find Congress reluctant to give him

money for the armed forces. The Reconstruction Finance Corporation loaned money to many nations to enable them to buy up American farm surpluses. In 1934, the Export-Import Bank was set up by executive order, and it took over much of this work. Not until after World War II did Eximbank, as it was called, become the powerful international credit agency it is today; but during the depression it was important in helping American exporters find markets abroad, even in the Soviet Union.

Indeed, it was pressure from farmers and businessmen that prompted Roosevelt finally to extend diplomatic recognition to the Soviet government. Many Americans were convinced that vast new markets for their goods existed in the Soviet Union and that trade between the two nations might be large enough to bring recovery at home. In the recognition treaty, the Soviet Union pledged not to spread propaganda or to agitate for revolution in the United States, a promise the Russians broke almost at once. Although recognition never brought the expected harvest of new markets for American business, at least it put relations between the two nations on a realistic basis.

Long an advocate of liberal tariff policies, Secretary of State Cordell Hull saw an old dream come true in 1934, with the passage of the Reciprocal Trade Agreements Act. This legislation gave the President great flexibility in negotiating trade agreements with such nations as would agree to a mutual reduction of tariffs. By no means a free-trade measure, it was nonetheless an immense improvement over the disastrous Hawley-Smoot Tariff. It opened new markets for American producers and eased some of the international tension that past trade policies had produced.

The Good Neighbor Policy. After a shaky start, Roosevelt's Good Neighbor Policy developed into one of the most successful endeavors in American diplomatic history. It had several aims, and to a marked degree it achieved each of them. First, Washington sought to preserve order in Latin America without using military force, chiefly as a means of guaranteeing the area as an expanding field for American investors and traders. Second, the United States transformed the Monroe Doctrine from a unilateral statement into a policy to which most of the other American republics could subscribe. And third, the Good Neighbor Policy promoted the concept of hemispheric solidarity against the rising threat of economic and military penetration of the hemisphere by the totalitarian powers of Europe and Asia.

In 1933, just as Washington was preparing to put the Good Neighbor Policy into effect, Cuba underwent a revolution in which the ruling dictatorship was replaced by a moderately leftist regime. Although the United States publicly asserted that Cubans had a right to choose their own rulers, the State Department feared that a "radical" regime might take over American holdings as Mexico had done in 1918 and 1927. Roosevelt was determined to bring down the leftist regime and, as historian Bryce Wood notes, he was prepared to use economic and diplomatic pressure, plus the threat of intervention, in order to achieve his purpose. Yet, the President had to move cautiously lest he jeopardize his long-range plan to become a "good neighbor" to Latin America.

No American troops went to Cuba in 1933, although units of the United States Navy appeared in Cuban waters as a reminder of American power. More important, Roosevelt withheld diplomatic recognition and economic assistance from the new government; and in those days, no Cuban government could hope to survive without the approval of Washington. The tactics worked, and when a government acceptable to the United States took power, Roosevelt promptly recognized it.

To soften the effect of his blunt tactics and to persuade Latin Americans that he genuinely meant to change this nation's relations with them, he also abrogated the Platt Amendment (page 481), a move all Cubans welcomed as a long overdue concession by the United States. Still, many Cubans bitterly resented the American interference in their affairs, and much of the violent anti-Americanism of the Castro revolution in the 1960's could be traced directly to the events of 1933–34.

In spite of the questionable dealings in Cuba, the Good Neighbor Policy made steady headway elsewhere. The United States continued to substitute economic and political pressure for military force in policing Central America and the Caribbean. In a series of conferences among the American republics, it was agreed that no nation had a right to interfere in the affairs of another (a move aimed chiefly at keeping the United States from interfering in Latin America), and provisions were fixed for mutual consultation between the United States and the Latin republics in the event of an outside threat to the hemisphere.

Finally, in the Act of Havana (1940), machinery was provided for the mutual defense of the Americas. The value of hemispheric solidarity proved itself during World War II, when the United States fought a two-front war in Asia and Europe, secure in the knowledge that the Western Hemisphere would remain relatively safe and stable during the conflict.

Depression and disillusionment. In dealing with other parts of the world, Roosevelt was severely restricted for a time by the impact of the depression. The economic collapse devastated the capitalist nations of Europe, reopened old international rivalries and suspicions, and produced precisely the disorder in the world that American policy had been designed to counter. The depression wrecked Germany's fledgling postwar democracy and led to the triumph of Nazism, the most disruptive political phenomenon of the twentieth century. Economic conflict among the great powers shattered whatever goodwill had been built up during the 1920's. Each nation retreated into its own shell, at least momentarily, to lick its wounds and nurse its grievances.

In this country, the depression understandably caused people to turn their attentions inward. Preoccupied with their own problems, few Americans had time to ponder the significance of Adolf Hitler's rise in Germany or of Japan's expansion in Asia. Moreover, the depression coincided with an intensive reexamination among scholars of America's participation in World War I. Some historians argued that Wilson had made a grave mistake in taking the country into the war, while others criticized him for misleading the people about the nature of the conflict.

Such so-called revisionist historians as Charles A. Beard and Walter Millis (scholars who rejected the majority viewpoint in favor of an unorthodox

DEVELOPMENT OF PAN-AMERICANISM DURING ROOSEVELT'S ADMINISTRATION

Conference or Meeting	Principles Established
Seventh International Conference of American States, Montevideo, 1933	**Convention on Rights and Duties of States.** Established the principle of non-intervention. "No state has the right to intervene in the internal or external affairs of another."
Inter-American Conference for the Maintenance of Peace, Buenos Aires, 1936	Reaffirmed the principle of non-intervention.
Eighth International Conference of American States, Lima, 1938	**Declaration of Lima.** Pledged the American republics to consult with one another for common action in case of a threat to the security of one, and provided for mutual consultation in the event of an outside threat to the hemisphere.
First Meeting of Consultation of Foreign Ministers, Panama City, 1939	**Declaration of Panama.** General declaration of neutrality. Established hemispheric zone within which the belligerents (of World War II) were to commit no hostile acts.
Second Meeting of Consultation of Foreign Ministers, Havana, 1940	**Act of Havana and Convention of Havana.** Declared any attempt by a non-American state against the sovereignty or independence of an American state would be considered an attack on all.
Third Meeting of Consultation of Foreign Ministers, Rio de Janeiro, 1942	Decided upon recommendations for the cooperation of the American states in measures for common defense against the Axis.
Inter-American Conference on Problems of War and Peace, Mexico City, 1945	**Act of Chapultepec.** Extended the principle of collective security insofar as it included aggression within the continent.

approach) were able champions of this new look at old policies, and they struck a responsive chord among their readers. Moreover, they appealed to the deep-rooted antiwar sentiments of the American people and to a genuine desire on the part of many to keep the nation out of any new world conflict.

Frightened by the depression and disillusioned because the war had not produced permanent peace and prosperity, millions of Americans became cynical about international affairs. A Gallup Poll in 1937 revealed that 70 percent of those questioned believed the country had erred in entering the war. The longer the depression persisted, the more pervasive the disillusion became. Roosevelt and his advisers found it exceedingly difficult to devise a foreign policy that would command the enthusiastic support of the people.

Neutrality legislation. As Japan, Germany, and Italy embarked upon a series of aggressions in Europe and Asia, the disillusionment showed itself politically in a rash of legislation, ostensibly designed to keep the United States from becoming involved in any new war. The Johnson Act (1934) prohibited American loans to any country that defaulted on payments of its past war debts.

A series of Neutrality Acts (1935–37) limited the President's power to act in dealing with belligerent nations. Americans were forbidden to travel on belligerent ships. American ships could not be used to carry war materials. The export of arms and munitions to all belligerents was prohibited. And the President was authorized to prohibit or curtail *all* trade with belligerents, when he deemed it wise do do so. In effect, the Neutrality Acts of the 1930's were admirably designed to keep the United States out of World War I.

But America's deep involvement in world affairs since the turn of the century made neutrality totally irrelevant as a foreign policy in the 1930's. Moreover, the Neutrality Acts did not set forth a policy of genuine neutrality. Such war materials as oil, steel, and copper were not covered. The acts did nothing to curtail the country's extensive commercial relations with the world. To most politicans who supported it, neutrality meant in essence that the United States should avoid any political commitments in world affairs, while maintaining and even extending its strong economic position internationally. No one advocated total neutrality as Jefferson had proposed in his Embargo of 1807 (page 114).

Neutrality legislation acted as a drag on New Deal diplomacy, but it did not cripple it. At base, Roosevelt's objectives were almost identical with those of the Republican leaders who preceded him: maintaining order and stability in the world; insuring the Open Door for American investors and traders; and countering the pressures for revolution and political extremism wherever they arose. He was, perhaps, more sympathetic to Wilson's dream of international order than most Republicans, but the difference was not crucial. In defending Wilson's policies, Secretary of State Hull could have been speaking for most American leaders in 1932 when he said:

America, thus exceptionally equipped to lead the world to heights of wealth and civilization undreamed of, had but to gird herself, yield to the law of manifest destiny, and go forward as the supreme world factor economically and morally.

A handful of true isolationists wanted the United States to withdraw entirely from Europe's affairs and focus its attention exclusively on the Western Hemisphere. But the great debate over foreign policy in the thirties was not between isolationists and interventionists. Rather it pitted those who wanted America to follow a *unilateral* course in world affairs, pursuing its own interests abroad with minimum concern for their effects on other nations, against those who sought some *collective* arrangement among several nations for mutual security.

Roosevelt switched from one position to the other as the demands of domestic politics and international events dictated. Generally, he adopted a unilateral approach in dealing with Japan and the Far East, in keeping with a widespread and old feeling among Americans that the Pacific was this country's special interest. In his policy toward Europe, he moved gradually (and often erratically) from unilateralism to collective security, especially as he began to estimate the military strength of Nazi Germany.

4 World Events Challenge American Foreign Policy

1. What were the historical and geographic characteristics of Japan, Italy, and Germany and what problems did they face in the thirties. How did they attempt to solve these problems?

2. How could the United States have intervened to halt or contain aggression by Japan, Italy, and Germany? Do you think it was realistic to expect that the United States would intervene?

3. How did Hitler come to be absolute master of Germany?

4. What were the advantages and disadvantages of following a course of appeasement to Hitler's demands at Munich?

In the Far East, Japan's dilemma dominated the international situation during the thirties. As Asia's largest industrial nation, Japan needed a constantly expanding market for its goods. Yet, tariff barriers all but closed the markets of the West to Japan. In Asia, the West's insistence upon either an Open Door policy or national spheres of influence and colonies severely limited Japan's access to the markets of China and the rich raw materials of Southeast Asia.

Japan's leaders, civilian and military, believed their country should enjoy a special position in the Far East, comparable to that which the United States commanded in the Americas. Indeed, they sometimes referred to their plan for Asia (the "Greater East Asia Co-Prosperity Sphere") as their Monroe Doctrine. Where the leaders in Tokyo disagreed among themselves was on how to gain the position they desired in Asia.

Most of Japan's civilian leaders wanted to resolve the dilemma without unduly antagonizing the Western powers. But the militarists argued that only a policy of conquest would give Japan the advantages it sought. Their position was weakened by the fact that Japan's economic resources were insufficient to sustain a prolonged modern war. With economic concessions and political support from the Western democracies, the civilians might have prevailed over the military. But neither the United States nor the European democracies were willing to concede Japan a special position in Asia. As elsewhere in the world, Washington relied upon moral and economic tactics to do a job requiring a skilled political touch.

Japanese aggression. Gradually, the Japanese militarists had their way. In 1931, they precipitated the Manchurian crisis (page 610), and then six years later they launched an all-out war against China. In the process, they confronted the United States with a direct challenge to the Open Door. As a War Department memorandum in 1935 observed, Japan's dominance of Asia's commerce would pose a "threat" to the Western powers, and especially the United States, if not immediately then certainly in the future.

Roosevelt's response to these developments was an ambiguous one. During the early thirties, the economic crisis at home restrained his hand. Later in the decade, the military threat in Europe forced him to move cautiously in Asia, lest he find himself in a two-front war. Before 1940, his most important move was to give limited aid to the Chinese, most of which was carried over the

American-built Burma Road from Burma into China. Volunteers from the United States (the "Flying Tigers") trained Chinese pilots and fought the Japanese in the skies of Asia.

Roosevelt also threatened Japan with an embargo, although he was careful not to carry the threat too far. If he had cut off oil and metals shipments to Japan, to be sure, the action might have crippled the Japanese Emperor Hirohito's war machine within a few months. Yet, such drastic action might have prompted the militarists to strike immediately at Southeast Asia to get the oil and other raw materials there. Although the Japanese applied steady pressure to achieve their goals, they too moved carefully to avoid a direct confrontation with the Americans.

But after war broke out in Europe, Japan became more aggressive, applying new pressures everywhere in Asia, stepping up the war in China, and slowly but steadily penetrating the Indochina peninsula. Moreover, Japan entered into a treaty of alliance with Germany and Italy.

The Tripartite Pact (1940), also known as the Axis Pact, was actually a defensive alliance, designed to keep the United States out of the war in Europe and dissuade this country from pressing Japan to the point of war in the Pacific. But by linking the crises in Asia and Europe, the alliance convinced the American people that the two crises had become one. Worse, it misled them into thinking of Japan as part of the Nazi-Fascist conspiracy against liberal democracy, an unfortunate oversimplification of the true situation. Japan was an imperialist power, often aggressive and warlike in its behavior; but it did not threaten the Far East with the kind of totalitarian political domination that the fascist powers represented in the West.

Italian and German fascism. In Europe, the challenge to democracy most assuredly came from fascism. It appeared first in Italy (in 1922), where the dictator Benito Mussolini tried to restore the ancient grandeur of Rome. But for all its gaudy trappings, Italian fascism was always limited by the country's chronic economic weakness. Although Il Duce ("The Leader"), as the pompous Mussolini called himself, was a noisy military aggressor several times in the 1930's, it was his alliance with the German dictator, Adolf Hitler, that made him genuinely dangerous.

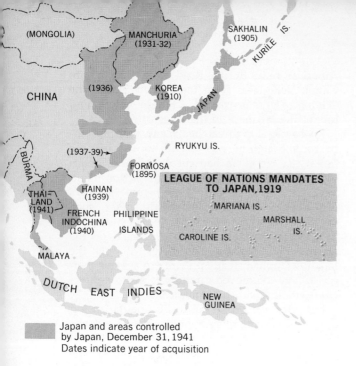

(MONGOLIA) MANCHURIA
(1931-32)
SAKHALIN IS.
(1905)
KURILE IS.

CHINA   (1936)   KOREA
(1910)   JAPAN

(1937-39) →   RYUKYU IS.

BURMA   FORMOSA
(1895)

**LEAGUE OF NATIONS MANDATES
TO JAPAN, 1919**

THAI-   HAINAN
LAND   (1939)
(1941)   FRENCH   PHILIPPINE
INDOCHINA   ISLANDS
(1940)

MARIANA IS.

MARSHALL
IS.

CAROLINE IS.

MALAYA

DUTCH EAST INDIES   NEW
GUINEA

Japan and areas controlled
by Japan, December 31, 1941
Dates indicate year of acquisition

SPREAD OF JAPANESE POWER
1895-1941

Germany was no Italy. It was a powerful nation with enormous economic potential, a tradition of militarism, and a strong—almost mystical—sense of history. When fascism came to Germany as National Socialism (or nazism), the entire world had reason to be alarmed. Moreover, Hitler was no Mussolini. He was a political adventurer of uncommon ability, a demagogue with magnetic appeal, and a totally ruthless fanatic.

The rise of Hitler. How did a social misfit come to be absolute master of a civilized, cultured people like the Germans? Chiefly, by shrewdly exploiting the disorder and political turmoil that afflicted Germany during the Great Depression. He appealed to all the people's fears and frustrations. He told them that Jews and Bolsheviks were responsible for their troubles. He promised to bring order, to repudiate the hated Treaty of Versailles, to make Germany the greatest nation in Europe.

Millions of Germans flocked to Hitler's swastika banner—disgruntled peasants, beleaguered shopkeepers and white-collar workers, intellectuals and professional men who blamed Jewish

competition for their own shortcomings, industrialists and bankers who saw in him a bulwark against the Communists and who naïvely thought they could control him once they put him in power.

Many Germans recognized Hitler as a menace from the start and tried to forestall his rise. But once the Nazis took power, they throttled all opposition and imposed an absolute dictatorship. Germany became a police state in which Gestapo (secret police) and Nazi party leaders enforced Hitler's will. Hitler proclaimed the Third Reich—the new German Empire—and armed it to the teeth, in violation of the Treaty of Versailles.

A vicious anti-Semite, he concocted a ridiculous theory of German racial superiority in which the world's "inferior peoples"—the Slavs, the Latins, and especially the Jews—were destined to serve the "master race" of Germans. Ultimately, he set out to exterminate the Jews, first in Germany, then in all of Europe. In all, the Nazis murdered some 6 million innocent men, women, and children—most of them Jews—to satisfy their *Führer* ("Leader") and his insane racial beliefs.

Bloated with ambition and egotism, Hitler took only six and a half years to plunge Europe into a new war. Germany had some legitimate grievances that deserved to be heard by the other powers and the League of Nations. Germany had been unfairly saddled with all the "guilt" and most of the cost of World War I. Some of its boundaries had been drawn with no regard for ethnic or political sense.

As a great industrial nation in the heart of Europe, it deserved political and economic influence on the Continent at least equal to that of the British and French. Probably any German government in the 1930's would have worked to restore Germany's power and change its relations with the former Allied nations. Hitler, however, wanted more. His goal was the total control of Europe under a system in which other nations would be vassal states to Germany. And he used military force and political arrogance to gain his objectives.

Along the way, he picked up Mussolini as a useful ally in his plans. While Germany rearmed, Italy tried to carve out an African empire by invading the nation of Ethiopia in 1935, subduing it only after a surprisingly difficult struggle against the all but defenseless Ethiopians. A year later, German troops marched into the Rhineland, in defiance of the Treaty of Versailles. When civil war erupted in Spain in 1936, Hitler came to the aid of the fascist leader, Francisco Franco, with tanks and dive-bombers, while Mussolini offered his Italian legions.

In 1938, the Nazis forced an *Anschluss*, or union, of Austria and Germany, proclaiming that all German-speaking peoples deserved to be part of the Third Reich. When Hitler demanded the Sudeten provinces of Czechoslovakia in that country's western region, because the people living there were Germans, he provoked a major European crisis.

The appeasement of Hitler. How did the other powers in Europe react to Hitler and his aggressive tactics? Preoccupied with their own economic problems, Britain and France displayed a striking indifference to the Nazi threat. Many people thought that Hitler would surely listen to reason, once he satisfied a few of his nationalistic ambitions. Given a reasonable amount of power, he might even become the guardian of the West against the Red hordes of communism—a role Hitler was determined to play in any case, although only on his own terms. As one historian has observed:

> The Nazi racist policy was indeed repugnant to many leaders in Western Europe and the United States, but if Hitler had concentrated on Eastern Europe and Soviet Russia, he probably could have avoided a war with these nations.

Wishful thinking that the Soviet Union and Germany might tear each other apart in a war of dictators also influenced Western estimations.

Where the democratic leaders went wrong was in underestimating Hitler's fanaticism and his determination to conquer all of Europe. In the face of his challenge, they did nothing. They ignored the desperate appeal of Ethiopian emperor Haile Selassie to save his country. They turned away as the fascists crushed the Spanish Republic.

When Hitler made his demands on the Czechs, Western leaders were almost eager to accept his assurance that the Sudeten provinces were his last territorial demand. Thus, at a fateful conference

Axis countries and Axis-controlled areas, September 1939
Dates indicate year of acquisition

SPREAD OF AXIS POWER
1935–1939

in Munich in September 1938, France and Britain gave Hitler what he wanted—a free hand in the Czech situation. In so doing, France betrayed its solemn treaty of alliance with the Czechs. Britain's Prime Minister Chamberlain returned to London from the meeting to announce that "it is peace in our time." Within a matter of months, Czechoslovakia ceased to exist, as Germany dismembered it into a number of puppet states.

The Munich settlement was made without consulting the Soviet Union, bringing on consequences that were disastrous to the West. Aware that Hitler someday intended to strike at the oil fields of the Caucasus and the rich granaries of the Ukraine, the Soviets had taken the lead in trying to generate some collective resistance to German expansion. Even after Munich, they offered to join the British in defending Poland, Hitler's next target. But Western fears of communism and distrust of the Soviet dictatorship wrecked every meaningful move toward cooperation. Poland, moreover, was ready to submit to Germany rather than become an ally of the hated Russians to the East.

The rising tide of fascist aggression began to threaten world peace in the mid-1930's. A harbinger of things to come was Italy's invasion of Ethiopia in October 1935. Italy had nursed hopes for a great African empire since the late nineteenth century, and the military "glory" won in this unequal contest helped Mussolini's campaign to build Italian pride. When Haile Selassie pleaded for help from the League of Nations in 1936, right, he received sympathy but no real aid. By 1938, the situation had deteriorated greatly. At a September meeting, when German dictator Hitler demanded the Sudetenland—a region of Czechoslovakia with a heavy German population—the British and French agreed. British Prime Minister Chamberlain returned to England, below left, proud of forestalling war. (Ever since, the word *Munich*, Chamberlain's name, and even the rolled umbrella he carried with him have symbolized appeasement to Americans.) In less than six months, Hitler took the rest of Czechoslovakia. When he was driven through Prague in March 1939, below right, a few pro-Nazis cheered, but most Czechs—and most Americans—felt little but anxiety about what lay ahead.

Left to his own resources, the Soviet dictator Josef Stalin then brought off what the West thought could never happen. On August 24, 1939, the two "natural enemies," Communist Russia and Nazi Germany signed a nonaggression pact in which each nation promised not to go to war against the other. It was a cynical move on the part of both dictators, but it bought time for Stalin to prepare against the inevitable German attack, and it assured Hitler that he need not fight a two-front war in case the West moved against him. A secret provision of the pact sealed the fate of Poland by providing for its partition between Germany and the Soviet Union.

Without hesitation, the Germans struck at Poland on September 1. Two days later, in accord with a belated commitment to aid the Poles, Britain and France declared war on Germany. After two decades of fragile peace, the long armistice came to a shattering end.

5 Americans Go To War Again

1. What were the steps of aggression taken by Germany on its road to European domination?

2. What forces were working against American intervention in Europe and the Far East?

3. At what point was the satisfactory settlement of differences between the United States and Germany and the United States and Japan no longer possible?

4. To what extent was Roosevelt a leader of public opinion, and to what extent did he cater to public sentiment?

Poland fell quickly, overwhelmed by the lightning-like thrust (*blitzkrieg*) of German tanks and bombers. The Red Army moved in to claim the eastern half of the country. Then the conflict settled into a brief period of relative inactivity, broken in the East by a brutal Soviet attack on Finland to secure certain strategic border areas.

The lull in the West came to a shocking end in April 1940, when Hitler's troops invaded Denmark and Norway. On May 10, the *blitzkrieg* swept into neutral Belgium and Holland, then stabbed into France. Paris fell on June 13. A week later, Hitler dictated terms to the stunned and broken French. Western Europe became Nazi-occupied territory, and only Great Britain remained to defy Hitler in the Old World.

Initial American reaction. By attacking Western Europe, Hitler made American involvement in the war inevitable. To be sure, the American people were reluctant to get into another war, and they delayed formal entry as long as they dared. But their cultural, political, and economic ties with Western Europe were too strong for them to look the other way as the Nazis rolled over the Continent. By 1940, it was too late to talk of what might have been done earlier to prevent the rise of a Hitler. The choices for the United States were down to two: either let Hitler have Europe, or come to Britain's rescue.

Roosevelt had no second thoughts in the matter. A Europe dominated by Hitler was out of the question for him, and most important business and political leaders agreed with him. It was not only the arrogant racism of the Nazis that disturbed them. From a strategic viewpoint, it was the threat Hitler posed to the rest of the world, including the United States.

They feared that a triumphant Germany would control the markets and colonies of the defeated Allied nations. It would export political extremism to such vulnerable areas as Latin America and the Middle East. Its fleet would assume the old role of the British Royal Navy as master of the North Atlantic and guardian of the world's shipping lanes. Everywhere in the world, including its own backyard, the United States would be thrown onto the defensive. Germany had to be stopped. If Britain fell, moreover, the task would become immeasurably more difficult than if it could be saved.

But it took time to convince a skeptical public that the situation was a desperate one. The cynicism and disillusion of the early thirties persisted stubbornly, even after the fall of France. Moreover, Roosevelt's own vacillation (some called it deviousness) in the past made it difficult for him to rally public opinion later.

In October 1937, the President had called for a "quarantine" by the law-abiding nations to isolate aggressor nations morally and diplomatically; but the public reaction to his remarks was unenthusiastic and he immediately retreated to a more cautious position. After the Munich Conference gave Hitler what he wanted, moreover, Roosevelt remarked that he was "not a bit upset over the final result." Political historian James MacGregor Burns perceptively describes Roosevelt's diplomacy during this period as more that of a "pussyfooting politician" than of a political leader.

To be sure, many obstacles stood in the way of developing a consistent policy toward Hitler. Until long after the war started in Europe, Roosevelt lacked the military power to back up a stiff policy. Probably he recognized the Nazis as a potential threat as soon as they came to power, and certainly he despised Hitler's brand of politics. Like the leaders of France and Britain, however, the American leaders assumed that the dictator was basically just another politician who could be reached by reason. Roosevelt was also too sensitive to domestic politics. Rather than take a firm, consistent lead in educating people about the Nazi menace, he tried to please everyone and consequently convinced no one.

The outbreak of war in 1939 stiffened his resolve. Although he proclaimed America's neutrality, he frankly admitted that genuine neutrality was neither possible nor necessarily desirable. He pressured Congress into repealing the arms embargo, a move which permitted Britain and France to buy war materials in the United States on a "cash and carry" basis.

When France fell in 1940, leaving Britain alone to face the Nazis, Roosevelt acted boldly. By executive decree, he transferred fifty overage destroyers to the British in exchange for long-term leases on strategic bases in British territories from Newfoundland in Canada to the Guianas in South America. In October 1940, Congress passed the first peacetime program of compulsory military service in American history. Clearly, the nation was moving toward full commitment to the Allied cause.

Opposition to Roosevelt's policies. Measures of this sort naturally aroused opposition. While denouncing nazism, responsible critics of Roosevelt's policy argued that America should build up its defenses in the Western Hemisphere and the Pacific. Fearful that a major war would undermine democracy and inspire new revolutions everywhere in the world, unilateralists wanted the United States to stand fast and be prepared to bring stability to the world once the conflict ended. They did not want Hitler to have the world, and they advocated a tough interventionist policy in Asia.

But they *were* willing to abandon Western Europe, for the time being at least, and this indifference to the fate of France and Britain weakened their entire argument. For, as Hitler's tyranny became increasingly evident, the emotional response in this country was of major importance in swinging public opinion to the side of those who advocated intervention in Europe on behalf of "freedom" and "democracy."

In July 1940, some opponents of Roosevelt's policy organized the America First Committee. Most America Firsters were moderate, sensible men who sincerely feared that involvement in another European war would damage the national interest. But a noisy minority were either Nazi sympathizers or genuine isolationists, whose opposition rested on disreputable or irrational grounds. On the other side of the fence, the "Committee to Defend America by Aiding the Allies" echoed Roosevelt's call for all-out aid to Britain short of war.

The unilateralists hoped that the election of 1940 would result in Roosevelt's defeat, or at least a massive show of opposition to his foreign policy. But the President outsmarted his political enemies. In June, he appointed two Republican interventionists to his cabinet, former Secretary of State Henry L. Stimson taking over the War Department and publisher Frank Knox becoming secretary of the navy. Thereafter, he claimed that his foreign policy was *bipartisan,* or supported by people in both parties.

At the Republican convention, the unilateralists suffered a crushing defeat when the Presidential nomination went to Wendell Willkie. A moderate in domestic affairs and an interventionist in diplomacy, the businessman from Indiana challenged Roosevelt effectively on only one point—the President's ability to keep the country out of the war while giving aid to the Allies. Roosevelt responded with a rash and opportunistic pledge that "your boys are not going to be sent into any foreign wars." Never during the campaign did he engage in a full-scale discussion of foreign policy, nor did he ever take the country entirely into his confidence regarding the world situation. Yet, so great was the people's trust in him that he won reelection handily, becoming the only President ever to serve a third term.

America—"arsenal of democracy." Any lingering doubts about America's commitment to the Allies were dispelled on March 11, 1941, when Congress passed the Lend-Lease Act, which empowered the President, at his discretion, to sell, transfer, or loan supplies to other countries. In Roosevelt's words, America now became a "great arsenal of democracy," supplying war material to its friends as fast as production allowed and giving little thought to the matter of payment. In August, Roosevelt and Britain's Prime Minister Winston Churchill met on a battleship off Newfoundland and proclaimed the Atlantic Charter. As a statement of war aims, it expressed the traditional American wish for an orderly, peaceful world, secured by international organization and attentive to the rights of all men. Perhaps more important at the time, the meeting cemented the Anglo-American alliance.

With Lend-Lease in effect, the problem was to transport arms and supplies to the Allies through waters in which German submarines were taking a frightful toll of Allied shipping. Accordingly, American forces occupied Greenland and Iceland, using the islands as bases from which to protect British convoys in the northwestern Atlantic. When a submarine attacked the United States destroyer *Greer* in September 1941, Roosevelt ordered the navy to "shoot on sight" any German craft found in American-patrolled waters. Several weeks later, the American destroyer *Reuben James* was torpedoed, and Congress authorized the arming of merchant ships. This undeclared naval war might have gone on for months had not events elsewhere transformed it into formal war between this country and the Axis powers.

In June 1941, Hitler had torn up his nonaggression pact with Stalin and opened the most titanic military struggle in modern history by attacking the Soviet Union. Immediately, Britain and the United States came to Russia's assistance.

AN ISOLATIONIST SPEAKS

One spokesman for American isolationism was Charles A. Lindbergh, the aviation hero of the 1920's. In a speech to the America First Committee in 1941, he expressed his views on America's involvement in foreign wars.

"War is not inevitable for this country. Such a claim is defeatism in the true sense. No one can make us fight abroad unless we ourselves are willing to do so. No one will attempt to fight us here if we arm ourselves as a great nation should be armed. Over a hundred million people in this nation are opposed to entering the war. If the principles of democracy mean anything at all, that is reason enough for us to stay out. If we are forced into a war against the wishes of an overwhelming majority of our people, we will have proved democracy such a failure at home that there will be little use fighting for it abroad. . . .

"We have been led toward war by a minority of our people. This minority has power. It has influence. It has a loud voice. But it does not represent the American people. . . .

"Most of these people have no influence or power. Most of them have no means of expressing their convictions, except by their vote which has always been against this war. They are the citizens who have had to work too hard at their daily jobs to organize political meetings. Hitherto, they have relied upon their vote to express their feelings; but now they find that it is hardly remembered except in the oratory of a political campaign. These people—the majority of hardworking American citizens, are with us. They are the true strength of our country. And they are beginning to realize, as you and I, that there are times when we must sacrifice our normal interests in life in order to insure the safety and the welfare of our nation.

"Such a time has come. Such a crisis is here. That is why the America First Committee has been formed—to give voice to the people. . . ."

By the fall of 1941, relations between the United States and Japan had reached a breaking point. The militarists who ruled Japan were committed to an attack on the Americans, but held off in part because Emperor Hirohito wanted to achieve a peaceful solution if possible. As late as November, Secretary of State Cordell Hull—at center in the photograph above—was negotiating with Japanese ambassador Kichisaburo Nomura, left, and special envoy Saburo Kurusu. Even as they met, Japanese pilots were being briefed for the coming attack, right. (This scene is from a Japanese newsreel that fell into American hands in 1943.) The actual attack on Pearl Harbor began at 7:55 on the morning of December 7, and resulted in the sinking or disabling of 19 American ships and the death of more than 2,300 soldiers and sailors. Below, warships burn at anchor.

The old fear of Bolshevism temporarily retreated. As Churchill noted at the time, he would accept the help of Satan himself in the battle against Hitler.

It was the lingering crisis in Asia that finally propelled the United States into war. As Japan prepared to move into the Southeast Asian holdings of the old colonial powers, Roosevelt made the fateful decision in July to stop exporting aviation fuel to Japan and to freeze all its assets in this country. Japan's dilemma now became clear and pressing: either it must accede to American demands to pull back throughout Asia and recognize the Open Door, or it must plunge ahead to consolidate its holdings before the Americans could check it.

In October, the militarists took over the government of Japan, naming General Hideki Tojo as premier. Before going to war, however, they acceded to civilian demands for a final try at negotiations. As Secretary Hull talked with their envoys at Washington in November, the Japanese prepared to launch a massive offensive throughout Asia. Fearing the power of the American navy, they also made secret plans to attack the Pacific Fleet in Hawaii.

In the talks at Washington, Japan promised to withdraw from Southeast Asia once the United States recognized its special position in Asia and agreed to a "just peace" in the area. Hull's response was simply to insist again upon the Open Door. As in the past, the American position was essentially a moral one, marked by nothing of political or economic substance.

The attack on Pearl Harbor. On December 7, 1941, the militarists resolved Japan's dilemma by sending their planes sweeping into Hawaii's Pearl Harbor from nearby carriers. In a brilliant surprise attack, they crippled most American naval and air facilities there. A day later, Congress declared war—whereupon Germany and Italy declared war on the United States. Global war became a reality.

Roosevelt's enemies accused him of leaving Pearl Harbor deliberately exposed, hoping to lure the Japanese into attacking. The charge has absolutely no basis in fact and does not deserve serious consideration. But some critics, then and later (including revisionist historians), argued that Washington deliberately maneuvered the Japanese into hostilities as a means of going to war against Germany.

Certainly, the Japanese attack solved the problem of those who wanted to intervene in Europe. Despite much circumstantial evidence in favor of the revisionist viewpoint, however, it cannot be proved with historical accuracy. It seems unlikely that Roosevelt deliberately chose to fight a difficult two-front war. As for entering the European war, events in the North Atlantic in 1941 were already leading the United States rapidly in that direction.

More important is the historical fact that Japan and the United States had been on a collision course for decades, not just in Roosevelt's time. American insistence on the Open Door simply was incompatible with Japan's position and ambitions in East Asia. As long as the United States ignored the *existing* realities in the area while pursuing a policy which was, actually, a holding action for the future, war between the two nations was always a danger.

CONCLUSION

Strangely enough, some historians describe the years between the two world wars as a time of American withdrawal into isolation from the world's affairs. In fact, this nation followed a vigorous course of unilateralism, not isolation, becoming involved in the affairs of the entire world under conditions which made it extremely difficult for other nations to control or influence its actions. The great objective of the diplomats and politicians was to establish a world order of harmonious, just societies, living together in peace and mutual respect—the perfect expression of the nineteenth-century liberal ideal in Western civilization. They failed in their pursuit, of course, and their goal was smothered in the chaos and violence of global depression and war.

But the failures of American diplomacy were failures of policy and execution, not of intent. As the historian William Appleman Williams asserts, "The widely accepted assumption that the United States was isolationist from 1920 through 1932 is no more than a legend." As such, it deserves to be buried and forgotten.

QUESTIONS

1. What was the intent of American foreign policy from 1920 to 1940? Was this a reasonable policy for America during this period? Justify your answer.

2. What is the difference between unilateralism, collectivism, and isolationism? Which term best describes American foreign policy in the period between the wars? Why?

3. How did the specter of communism in Russia influence American foreign relations?

4. How effective was Roosevelt in providing leadership for American foreign affairs?

5. To what extent was America a "good neighbor" in Latin America from 1920 to 1940? Explain your answer.

6. How did American foreign trade and tariff policy affect the nation's international relations?

7. How did the depression influence international relations?

8. To what extent did the treaty of Versailles cause World War II? Explain your answer?

9. Why was Hitler able to come to power in Germany?

10. What were the sources of friction between the United States and Japan in the Far East?

11. Were there any alternatives that would have had a reasonable chance of averting World War II and still maintained a peaceful, harmonious world of just nations? Explain your answers.

BIBLIOGRAPHY

ROBINSON, D. W., ED., *As Others See Us: International Views of American History*, Houghton Mifflin. This book provides an excellent selection of excerpts from foreign texts dealing with American history. The student should refer to this book at numerous times during the year, or he may browse through it for particular topics or time periods which interest him.

ORWELL, GEORGE, *Animal Farm*, New American Library (Signet Books). This is a brief, provocative fable describing the rise of totalitarian governments in the form of an animal uprising on a farm. The book could provoke many interesting discussions.

OVERSTREET, HARRY A. AND BONARO, *What We Must Know About Communism*, Simon & Schuster (Pocket Books). This book is a simple, well-balanced account of the nature of communism. Once the student has read the book, he should read examples of specific Communist literature and study its influence in specific historical cases.

KENNAN, GEORGE F., *Russia and the West Under Lenin and Stalin*, New American Library (Mentor Books). Kennan is a recognized authority on Russia, with credentials as historian and ambassador to Russia, and he does a fine job of surveying American relations with the Communists during the first half of the twentieth century. Although some of his opinions have been challenged, students may refer to this readable book for background on American foreign policy.

FRANK, ANNE, *The Diary of a Young Girl*, Simon & Schuster (Pocket Books). This diary of a young girl, hidden away from the Nazis during the early years of World War II, has been read by countless numbers of young people. It is a warm, human portrait of one girl and a sad commentary upon the devastations of war.

The Global War

At the time Pearl Harbor was attacked, World War II had already been raging for over two years. As in the years from 1914 to 1917, the American people had enjoyed the luxury of debating among themselves while the rest of the world fought. The Japanese attack abruptly ended the debate, and the United States suddenly found itself involved in a desperate military struggle on two far-flung fronts in Europe and in the Pacific. Before the attack, the Roosevelt administration had taken some steps to prepare the country for war; but a general mobilization of men and materiel did not begin in earnest until after Pearl Harbor. The problems of mobilization and of carrying the war to the enemy were enormous; yet, from the start, Americans exhibited a tough-minded determination to see the job through as quickly and efficiently as possible.

Total war put heavy strains on American democracy and in several notable instances caused a breakdown of the democratic process. Compared to their experiences in World War I, however, the American people fought the war against the Axis with a minimum of national hysteria and irrational behavior. As you read this chapter on World War II, consider these questions:

1. What were the key factors in the Allied victory in Europe? in the Pacific?
2. How did Americans at home contribute to the war effort?
3. What were the political objectives of wartime diplomacy?
4. What were the material, human, and social costs of the war?

1 The Grand Alliance Liberates Europe

1. Do you think there were any better alternatives to the American strategy of concentrating the war effort in Europe?

2. What were the conflicting war strategies of the three major allies, and how were they modified into acceptability? Do you think this compromise was in the best interests of the United States?

3. How did the concepts of "total war" and "unconditional surrender" affect the results of World War II?

4. How does war affect the participants?

Japan's attack on Pearl Harbor gravely damaged the Pacific fleet; yet it also proved to be a major strategic blunder on the enemy's part. Overnight, Americans rallied to the support of President Roosevelt in his determination to prosecute the war to total victory. The bitter debate over foreign policy ended. In his first wartime state of the Union message, the President expressed the national mood perfectly:

We cannot wage this war in a defensive spirit. As our power and our resources are fully mobilized, we shall carry the attack against the enemy—we shall hit him and hit him again wherever and whenever we can reach him.

The first few months after December 7 were grim ones for the American people, however, as the Japanese quickly overran Southeast Asia and much of the Pacific while the allies stood helplessly by. In the Philippines, American and Filipino troops under the command of General Douglas MacArthur fought bravely against hopeless odds, finally going down to defeat on the Bataan Peninsula and on Corregidor island in Manila Bay. Ordered out of the islands because the War Department knew that his skills would be needed later in the war, MacArthur established a new American headquarters in Australia, pledging to the Filipinos, "I shall return."

From the start, American strategy was to concentrate the main war effort in Europe. Not that the Pacific was abandoned or even really neglected; on the contrary, it was absolutely essential, in 1942, to stop the Japanese advance before it swallowed Australia and New Zealand or swept westward into India. Moreover, because the Japanese had attacked American soil, the war in the Pacific had great symbolic significance for the American people.

Nevertheless, Roosevelt reasoned correctly that Germany was a more powerful and ominous adversary than Japan. If Hitler defeated Great Britain and the Soviet Union, the United States would be thrown onto the lonely defensive throughout the Atlantic world. Accordingly, the war plan called for checking the Japanese and making whatever gains could be made with a minimum of forces in Asia while mounting a devastating offensive against the German citadel. With Hitler out of the way, the full weight of American power would then be brought against Japan to avenge Pearl Harbor.

The Grand Alliance. Several weeks after the United States entered the war, the representatives of twenty-six nations fighting the Axis powers gathered in Washington, D.C., and issued the Declaration of the United Nations. Pledging a war to total victory against the enemy, each nation agreed to abide by the principles of the Atlantic Charter (Chapter 24). The declaration, in effect, brought into existence a Grand Alliance against fascism.

The strongest members of the coalition were, of course, the great powers—the United States, Great Britain, and the Soviet Union. Ties between the two English-speaking nations, moreover, were probably the closest between any two great powers in history. The two belligerents agreed to merge their war strategies, their top staffs, and even their commands in the field.

The presence of the Soviet Union in the coalition, on the other hand, meant that the Grand Alliance was a shaky marriage of convenience, not a genuine covenant among trusted friends. By the time the United States entered the war, Soviet troops were engaging one hundred Nazi divisions and taking the brunt of Hitler's military might; American planners pragmatically decided that the Red Army had to be supported fully with arms and supplies. As for the Russians, they were equally pragmatic about accepting whatever goods came their way. Nothing was done to establish a unified command or to coordinate military operations in the field. For all practical purposes the Russians fought their own war in the East, the British and Americans fought their own war in the West.

The German war machine. The threat from Germany was indeed ominous at the time the United States entered the war. U-boats were taking a frightful toll of Allied shipping in the Atlantic. Throughout Europe, the Nazis were mobilizing the resources of a dozen nations on behalf of the Third Reich.

The German army was a tough, experienced force—doubtless, at the time, the most formidable military machine in the world. Under the leadership of General Erwin Rommel, the Afrika Korps (Germany's desert troops) was poised to overrun Egypt, seize the Suez Canal, deliver the vital oil of the Middle East to Hitler, and perhaps even link up with the Japanese somewhere in India. Moreover, although the Red Army was fighting a tough defensive war, it seemed only a matter of time before the Nazi legions knocked out the Russians and brought all of Eastern Europe and much of Asia under German control.

At the same time, there were cracks in the German armor that the Allies were able to exploit. Nazi air power had failed to bomb Britain into submission, and Hitler had given up his plan to cross the English Channel. In much of German-occupied Europe, guerrilla forces were harrassing the occupiers and forcing them to divert men from the Soviet front.

Although the Nazis were inflicting frightful damage on the Russians, they had not yet engaged the Red Army in decisive battle. Indeed, as the Soviet troops retreated, they sucked the Germans deeper and deeper into an inhospitable land, forcing the invaders to fight on Russian terms. Finally, for some unfathomable reason, Hitler had failed to mobilize German industry and society fully for total war. Despite the militaristic posture of the regime, many factories had not been geared to war production or even given adequate protection from aerial bombing.

Mindful of the inconclusive ending of World War I, Allied leaders were determined to bring the war home to Germany this time. Halfway measures would not suffice: the German army was to be crushed and humiliated; the German people were to experience the horrors of total war; the Nazi state was to be wiped out. Roosevelt, indeed, insisted that the war be fought until the "unconditional surrender" of the enemy nations. Although both Churchill and Stalin doubted the wisdom of such a policy, they accepted it as a war aim.

Devising a military strategy. In devising a strategy for defeating Hitler, Roosevelt and his military advisers (notably the chief of staff, General George C. Marshall, and the commander in Europe, General Dwight D. Eisenhower) concluded that only a massive invasion of Europe from the British Isles would do the job. They projected an operation that would liberate Western Europe, strike into the heart of enemy country, and end in a full-scale military occupation of Germany. To Stalin, an invasion of Western Europe was essential. Not only would it relieve the murderous German pressure on his armies; it would also keep British and American influence in Eastern Europe to a minimum, leaving him relatively free to influence events there after the war.

Churchill, of course, was eager to defeat Hitler. But he also hoped to reestablish British power in the Mediterranean and the Balkans, and he was apprehensive lest the Russians penetrate too deeply into central Europe. Accordingly, he held out stubbornly for a major British-American effort in the Mediterranean, to culminate in an invasion from the south, up through what he called Europe's "soft underbelly." Such an operation, he believed, could sweep rapidly into central Europe, ripping apart Hitler's empire while it also checked the Russian advance. As the subsequent campaign in Italy and the bitter guerrilla fighting in the Balkans proved, however, there was nothing at all soft about the "underbelly" of the Continent.

In the end, a compromise strategy was agreed upon. The cross-channel invasion became the major Anglo-American effort in the European war. But an operation of this sort was a very hazardous undertaking. Before it could be mounted, the Allies had to win absolute control of the Atlantic and of the skies over Western Europe, then amass huge numbers of well-trained troops, backed by enormous stores of supplies.

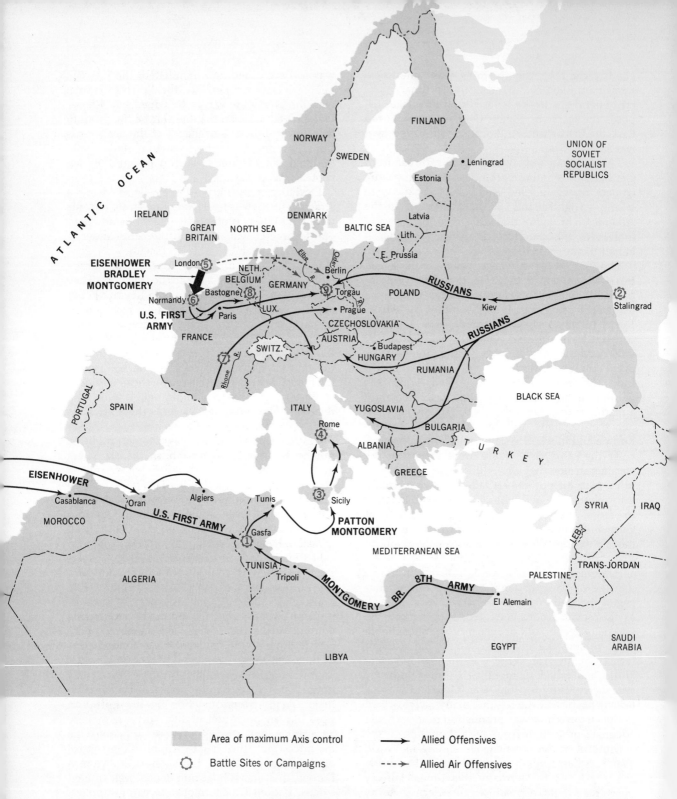

ATLANTIC OCEAN

IRELAND

GREAT BRITAIN

NORTH SEA

NORWAY

SWEDEN

FINLAND

DENMARK

Estonia

Leningrad

UNION OF SOVIET SOCIALIST REPUBLICS

BALTIC SEA

Latvia

Lith.

E. Prussia

EISENHOWER BRADLEY MONTGOMERY

London ⑤

NETH.

BELGIUM

Bastogne ⑧

GERMANY

Elbe R.

Oder R.

Berlin

Torgau ⑨

RUSSIANS

POLAND

Kiev

RUSSIANS

② Stalingrad

Normandy ⑥

U.S. FIRST ARMY

LUX.

Paris

Prague

CZECHOSLOVAKIA

AUSTRIA

RUSSIANS

FRANCE

⑦

Rhone R.

SWITZ.

Budapest

HUNGARY

RUMANIA

BLACK SEA

PORTUGAL

SPAIN

ITALY

Rome ④

YUGOSLAVIA

ALBANIA

GREECE

BULGARIA

T U R K E Y

EISENHOWER

Casablanca

Oran

Algiers

Tunis

③ Sicily

PATTON MONTGOMERY

SYRIA

IRAQ

MOROCCO

U.S. FIRST ARMY

Gasfa ①

TUNISIA

Tripoli

MONTGOMERY - BR. 8TH ARMY

El Alemain

MEDITERRANEAN SEA

LEB.

PALESTINE

TRANS-JORDAN

ALGERIA

LIBYA

EGYPT

SAUDI ARABIA

Area of maximum Axis control

Battle Sites or Campaigns

Allied Offensives

Allied Air Offensives

628

WORLD WAR II
Allied Victory in Europe and North Africa, 1942-1945

WORLD WAR II—ALLIED VICTORY IN EUROPE AND NORTH AFRICA, 1942–1945

① Nov. 8, 1942–May 13, 1943. North African Campaign. An invasion force under Eisenhower lands near Casablanca, Oran, and Algiers, and advances east to Tunisia. Meanwhile, British troops under Montgomery defeat the Germans at El Alemein and push them westward to Tunisia. On April 7, the Allied armies meet near Gasfa, encircling the Axis forces. The Axis forces surrender on May 13.

② Feb. 2, 1943–May 1944. Russian Counteroffensive. After retaking Stalingrad, the Russians begin to push the Germans out of Russia. Kiev is taken in November 1943; the Russians then drive into Poland, Rumania, Yugoslavia, and Bulgaria.

③ July 10–Aug. 17, 1943. Invasion of Sicily. Anglo-American forces under Montgomery and Patton overrun the island in five weeks.

④ Sept. 3, 1943–June 4, 1944. Invasion of Italy. Anglo-American forces invade Italy. After months of heavy fighting, the Allies gain control of central Italy and liberate Rome on June 4.

⑤ Jan.–May 1944. Air Offensive. The Allies launch a strategic air offensive from Britain, crippling German air power. Berlin is bombed.

⑥ June 6, 1944. Invasion of Normandy. Allied forces under Eisenhower storm the Normandy coast (Operation Overlord) and sweep across France. On August 25, Paris is liberated, and the Allies drive on to Belgium and Luxembourg.

⑦ Aug. 15, 1944. Invasion of Southern France. Allied forces land in southern France and move up the Rhone Valley to join the Normandy invaders at Paris. They then proceed to Austria and Germany.

⑧ Dec. 16–26, 1944. Battle of the Bulge. The Germans counterattack against U.S. troops in Belgium. After pushing 50 miles into Belgium, the Germans are checked at Bastogne.

⑨ March 7–May 8, 1945. Fall of Germany. From the west, Eisenhower's army pushes into Germany and overruns its industrial heartland. From the east, the Russian army takes Warsaw and crosses into Germany. On April 25, American and Russian troops meet at Torgau on the Elbe. Berlin falls on May 2, and on May 8 Germany surrenders (V–E day).

During the long months of preparation for Operation Overlord (the code name for the invasion), the Allies adopted a modified version of Churchill's Mediterranean strategy. On November 8, 1942, an Anglo-American force invaded Morocco and Algeria in North Africa. In six months of hard desert fighting, it drove the Afrika Korps into the sea and ended the Axis threat to the Middle East. Quickly following up their advantage, Allied forces next crossed the Mediterranean to invade Sicily and Italy. The effect of this move was to knock Italy out of the war in the summer of 1943.

As Mussolini's regime crumbled, however, the German army moved in to confront the liberators. In some of the war's fiercest fighting, the Allies painfully inched their way up the long peninsula. Rome fell to them in May 1944, but months of fighting ensued before all of Italy was secured. During the campaign, a young cartoonist with the Fifth Army, Bill Mauldin, made national heroes out of "Willie and Joe," his poignant caricatures of the weary, hard-bitten infantrymen of the war. As the equally famous war correspondent Ernie Pyle wrote of such men, they lived and fought in "almost inconceivable misery . . . like men in prehistoric times, and a club would have become them more than a machine gun."

Aerial warfare. Convinced that Germany could be bombed into submission without a long, grueling land war, American and British airmen mounted an awesome aerial offensive against the enemy. Fleets of long-range bombers struck repeated blows at submarine pens, aircraft facilities, communications lines, oil depots, and other strategic targets all over Europe. The air war was a hazardous operation, for Allied flyers encountered deadly screens of antiaircraft fire and a determined, skillful resistance from the *Luftwaffe* (German air force). Slowly but surely, however, they gained command of the skies, crippling enemy air power and leaving Germany's cities open to devastating bombing attacks.

By striking at the U-boats in their home bases, the air offensive contributed greatly to the Allied victory in the crucial battle of the Atlantic. And in all but wiping out the *Luftwaffe*, it was a vital factor in the ultimate success of the invasion. But the bombing of Germany did not significantly reduce the output of war materials in Hitler's factories. Indeed, production of enemy fighter planes actually increased steadily until very late in the war. It was the marksmanship and superior firepower of Allied gunners in the air, not the bombing of aircraft factories, that drove the *Luftwaffe* from the skies.

In late 1944, moreover, the Germans began to bombard Britain with terrifying new weapons against which Allied air power was helpless—the V-1, a pilotless flying bomb, and the V-2, a rocket-powered missile. Only when ground forces captured the European launching sites of these weapons did they cease to be a menace. If Hitler had put the V-2 into mass production earlier in the war, the success of an Allied landing in Western Europe would have been seriously threatened.

The turning of the tide. The great turning point in the European war came in February 1943, when the titanic Battle of Stalingrad, deep inside the Soviet Union, ended in a crushing German defeat. As the Red Army went over to the offensive, ponderously but steadily driving back the invaders, Western leaders stepped up their war plans. Under the command of Eisenhower, they finally launched the largest amphibious operation in history—the invasion of Western Europe.

On June 6, 1944 (D-Day), a spearhead of 176,000 Allied troops landed on the Normandy coast of France. Supported by 600 warships and 11,000 aircraft, the invaders secured the beaches under extremely dangerous conditions, taking heavy casualties. Immediately, a torrent of men and supplies poured onto the Continent, enabling the Allied soldiers to turn the blitzkrieg against its inventors. American, British, Canadian, and Free French troops raced toward Paris. New pressure was put on the Germans on August 15, when Allied forces invaded southern France and began to advance up the Rhone valley. Ten days later, General Charles deGaulle, the proud leader of the French government in exile, marched into Paris and proclaimed the liberation of his country.

By September, Eisenhower had two million troops on the continent. In the East, meanwhile, the Red Army crossed into Poland and opened a great offensive against the Germans along an eight-hundred-mile front. Two massive walls began to close in on the Reich that Hitler had boasted would last a thousand years.

In a desperate effort to stem the invasion from the West, German troops counterattacked against American positions in Belgium in December 1944. For a week or so, the Battle of the Bulge threatened to become a major Allied defeat. At Bastogne, the American commander responded to an enemy demand that he surrender with one pointed, defiant word: "Nuts!" As the Allied lines stiffened, the Germans fell back.

Thereafter, the initiative was all with the Grand Alliance. While Soviet troops crossed the Oder River and moved on Berlin, Eisenhower's armies pushed across the Rhine River and overran the industrial heartland of Germany. Early in May, the victorious forces met at the Elbe River, near Torgau, where Soviet and American soldiers toasted each other in an all-too-brief moment of genuine friendship and goodwill.

The Third Reich died a cataclysmic death. Soviet artillery and American bombers reduced the heart of Berlin to flaming rubble. Battering their way into the city, Soviet soldiers took fierce revenge for the carnage the Germans had left in their homeland. Deep in his bunker beneath the holocaust, the Nazi dictator finally put an end to his malignant career by shooting himself. On May 8, 1945, the once-haughty German generals ignominiously surrendered what was left of their armies and their battered country to the Allies.

2 Americans Fight The War In The Pacific

1. Why did Japan not fight a defensive war in the Pacific? What were the advantages and disadvantages of the Japanese military position in 1942?

2. What was the strategy of American military planners in the Far East?

3. Do you think the eventual American victory over Japan was more a result of superior American planning, supplying, and fighting or more a result of Japanese weaknesses and blunders?

4. Should the atomic bomb have been used against an enemy that was clearly defeated?

On the other side of the world, the initiative passed to the United States in an astonishingly brief time. After their initial spectacular successes, the Japanese might have dug in, gone over to the defensive, and forced the Americans to come to them. Such a strategy would have made it extremely difficult for the United States to gain control of the Pacific and root out the enemy from his heavily fortified positions.

At such places as Rabaul in New Britain, Truk in the Caroline Islands, and Saipan in the Marianas, the Japanese established formidable bases that were ideally suited to a defensive war. Their navy was a first-class fighting force and their air power was built around fast, easily maneuverable fighter planes (such as the Zero), skillfully piloted. As for their army, it was a tough, experienced force.

Japanese liabilities and losses. On the other side of the ledger, Japan's new empire encompassed far too much territory to be readily defended. Moreover, rather than rest on their laurels early in 1942, the Japanese militarists decided to further extend their holdings. In so doing, they inevitably encountered the weakened but still formidable United States Navy. Although the Japanese fought well and inflicted heavy damage on their opponents in these encounters, every ship and plane they lost seriously weakened their ability to defend their holdings.

Japan's greatest liability was its inability to replace the battle losses in its navy and air force. By the same token, the greatest advantage the United States had was the ability to absorb the early losses to the fleet, then to replace them ten times over. Moreover, by a great stroke of luck, the American aircraft carriers in the Pacific had all been on the high seas when the Japanese attacked Pearl Harbor. They survived to inflict heavy damage on the enemy in later engagements.

Japan's new objectives in the spring of 1942 were Port Moresby in southern New Guinea and Midway island at the western tip of the Hawaiian chain. Fearing an invasion of Australia, the Allies moved quickly to counter the New Guinea operation. In May, they intercepted the Japanese task force moving toward Moresby (see battle map, page 632). In the Battle of the Coral Sea, the enemy won a tactical victory by sinking the car-

rier *Lexington.* But the strategic victory went to the Allies, who turned back the invading force and ended the threat to Australia. The battle was noteworthy, too, for being the first naval action in history in which the ships of neither side fired a shot at those of the other. The entire action was fought by carrier-based planes.

An even more momentous victory—indeed, a major turning point in the war—came at the Battle of Midway in June 1942. As a part of this operation to extend their defense perimeter, the Japanese occupied several islands in the Aleutians, off Alaska. Whatever threat this move may have posed to the continental United States was quickly nullified with their defeat at Midway. In a fierce carrier battle, the Japanese lost 4 carriers, a cruiser, and 250 planes—a staggering blow, which reduced their carrier strength by half. The invading force was turned back, and the Japanese high command had its confidence badly shaken. American forces, on the other hand, regained the confidence that Pearl Harbor had shattered. From this point on, they assumed the offensive in the Pacific.

Events in the Solomon Islands in 1943 confirmed this optimism. In August, a small force of marines landed on Guadalcanal, where they seized the Japanese airfield and held it against repeated attempts to dislodge them. Seven major naval engagements took place in the Solomons area. In the decisive naval battle of Guadalcanal, in November, the American forces prevented the Japanese from landing reinforcements, thus making possible the conquest of Guadalcanal. Japan endured a great loss of planes and pilots in these actions. Moreover, it was clear that if Japan could not hold a position such as Guadalcanal—early in the war and against a relatively weak force—its chances of faring well later were slight.

American strategy. From start to finish, the war in the Pacific was an American war. To be sure, other nations (especially Australia and New Zealand) contributed men and ships to help defeat Japan; but the United States made little effort to enlist their assistance. Professional military and naval officers regarded the conflict almost in personal terms as a test of American fighting ability after the humiliating early defeats in the Philippines and elsewhere.

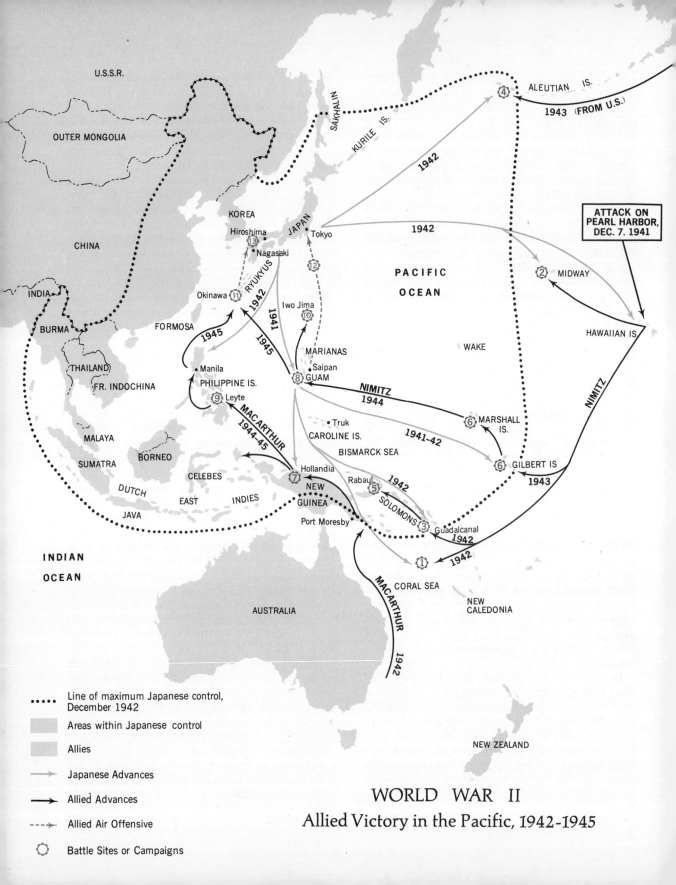

U.S.S.R.

OUTER MONGOLIA

CHINA

INDIA

BURMA

THAILAND

FR. INDOCHINA

MALAYA

SUMATRA

BORNEO

DUTCH
EAST INDIES

CELEBES

JAVA

INDIAN
OCEAN

SAKHALIN

KURILE IS.

KOREA

JAPAN

Hiroshima
⑬
• Nagasaki

Okinawa ⑪ RYUKYUS

FORMOSA

• Manila

PHILIPPINE IS.

⑨ Leyte

Iwo Jima
⑩

MARIANAS

• Saipan
⑧ GUAM

• Truk

CAROLINE IS.

Tokyo

⑫

1942

1941

1945

1945

1942

MACARTHUR
1944-45

Hollandia
⑦

NEW
GUINEA

Port Moresby

ALEUTIAN IS.

④
1943 (FROM U.S.)

1942

1942

PACIFIC
OCEAN

ATTACK ON
PEARL HARBOR,
DEC. 7, 1941

② MIDWAY

WAKE

HAWAIIAN IS.

NIMITZ
1944

NIMITZ

⑥ MARSHALL
IS.

1941-42

⑥ GILBERT IS

1943

Rabaul
⑤

1942

BISMARCK SEA

SOLOMONS

③ Guadalcanal

1942

①

1942

MACARTHUR

1942

CORAL SEA

NEW
CALEDONIA

AUSTRALIA

NEW ZEALAND

**•••• Line of maximum Japanese control,
December 1942**

Areas within Japanese control

Allies

⟶ Japanese Advances

⟶ Allied Advances

- - -▸ Allied Air Offensive

◯ Battle Sites or Campaigns

WORLD WAR II
Allied Victory in the Pacific, 1942-1945

WORLD WAR II—ALLIED VICTORY IN THE PACIFIC, 1942–1945

① **May 7–8, 1942. Battle of the Coral Sea.** U.S. pilots thwart a Japanese attempt to seize Port Moresby in southern New Guinea.

② **June 3–6, 1942. Battle of Midway.** Admiral Nimitz repels an enemy attempt to take Midway.

③ **Aug. 7, 1942–Feb. 9, 1943. Guadalcanal.** Marines land on Guadalcanal and seize the airport. Months of fighting follow. In the Battle of Guadalcanal (November 25), American forces prevent the Japanese from landing reinforcements, making possible the conquest of the island.

④ **March 24–Aug. 15, 1943. The Aleutians.** American troops force the Japanese from the Aleutians.

⑤ **July–Nov. 1943, Solomons Campaign.** American forces move up the Solomons from Guadalcanal and bombard Rabaul, the Japanese stronghold, cutting off all its supply lines.

⑥ **Nov. 1943–Feb. 1944. Central Pacific Campaign.** Nimitz successfully assaults the Gilbert and Marshall islands.

⑦ **Jan.–Sept. 1944. New Guinea Campaign.** MacArthur moves up the New Guinea coast from Port Moresby to take Hollandia. After months of fighting in Hollandia, Japanese resistance ends.

⑧ **June 15–July 21, 1944. Saipan and Guam.** Nimitz continues his Pacific advance, taking Saipan (July 9) and Guam (July 21) in the Marianas.

⑨ **Oct. 20, 1944–Feb. 23, 1945. Philippines.** Beginning his drive, MacArthur invades Leyte. In the Battle of Leyte Gulf, the Navy virtually wipes out the Japanese fleet. American forces retake Manila on February 23.

⑩ **Feb. 19–March 17, 1945. Iwo Jima.** Americans take the island, just 750 miles from Tokyo.

⑪ **April 1–June 21, 1945. Okinawa.** Americans seize Okinawa, main island of the Ryukyus.

⑫ **May–July 1945. U.S. Air Offensive.** The Air Force bombs the Japanese home islands.

⑬ **Aug. 6 and 9, 1945. Hiroshima and Nagasaki.** Americans drop an atomic bomb on Hiroshima. Three days later another bomb is dropped on Nagasaki.

To the public, the war was a grim crusade to avenge a "sneak attack" upon American soil. Even China, which had been at war with Japan for years, assumed a distinctly secondary position in the thinking of American strategists. To be sure, Chiang Kai-shek's forces were given what supplies could be transported to him, and he was encouraged to strike hard at the enemy. But the Chinese did little to affect the outcome of the war. Japan was defeated because of American decisions and American military power.

Moreover, the Pacific war was the navy's war. Because of his commanding personality and dramatic tactics, General MacArthur became a national hero and symbol of the war in the Far East. But the strategists who turned the tide in the Pacific were such men of the sea as Admirals Ernest J. King and Chester E. Nimitz. Shucking off the old naval theory that wars at sea are won by battleships, they used swift task forces of aircraft carriers protected by cruisers, destroyers, and submarines. Their objectives were to sweep the enemy's ships from the sea, capture or neutralize his bases throughout the Pacific, and finally subject his homeland to intense aerial and naval bombardment until he surrendered.

MacArthur differed with them chiefly in insisting that the United States liberate the Philippines before going on to attack Japan itself. Ultimately, both strategies were adopted in modified form, and MacArthur's command in the Southwest Pacific worked closely with Nimitz's forces in the Central Pacific to deal the enemy a series of crushing blows.

Campaigns in the Pacific. MacArthur's first big step on the road back to Manila was to establish a strong position in New Guinea from which his air forces could fan out to attack Japanese bases in the Bismarck Sea. He first defeated the enemy in southeastern New Guinea, then made a dramatic leapfrog jump up the coast of the huge island to take Hollandia. In the process, he bypassed thousands of Japanese soldiers, cutting them off from all hope of being evacuated or reinforced, and leaving them to their fate in the inhospitable jungle. Leapfrogging was a brilliant tactic, ideally suited to American strategy. It upset the enemy's strategy of wearing down the Americans by forcing them to pay a high cost for every island they contested. Indeed, General Tojo considered it the major cause of American victory in the war.

To the east, a joint army-navy command moved up the Solomons from Guadalcanal. From bases in New Guinea and the Solomons, planes of the 5th and 13th Air Forces battered the enemy stronghold at Rabaul into uselessness. Both the New Guinea and the Solomons campaigns were characterized by savage jungle warfare.

In addition to the enemy, American troops had to contend with a host of tropical ailments that sometimes baffled their doctors. They hacked their way through dense rain forests and sloshed through swamps that were often alive with leeches. Equatorial heat and steaming rains drained them of energy and spirit. An enemy that fought to the last man rather than surrender gave them no respite until he was wiped out. For thousands of young soldiers and marines, the islands of the exotic South Seas became a special kind of hell. In his novel *The Naked and The Dead* (1948), Norman Mailer came close to recording their feelings.

In the Central Pacific, Nimitz's forces cleared the Gilbert and Marshall Islands, neutralizing and bypassing the Japanese bastion at Truk. In July 1944, Americans returned to Guam and conquered the nearby Japanese base at Saipan. In a great air battle off Saipan—the "Marianas Turkey Shoot"—Japan lost 3 carriers and 475 planes.

By the fall of the year, MacArthur was ready to return to the Philippines. The campaign began with an invasion of Leyte in October and ended four months later when Manila fell. It was highlighted by the largest naval engagement in history, the decisive Battle of Leyte Gulf. Japan committed all of its major warships and lost nearly half of them. Deprived of its sea power, its most effective weapon thereafter was the *Kamikaze* ("Divine Wind"), an extraordinary force of suicide pilots who deliberately crashed their bomb-laden planes into American ships. Their attacks strengthened the American conviction that the Japanese would put up a fanatical and costly resistance to an invasion of their home islands.

Two outer islands off Japan, Iwo Jima and Okinawa, fell early in 1945, but only after a suicidal defense by the Japanese. Indeed, Okinawa was the costliest action of the war for the navy. Kamikaze attacks sank or damaged nearly eighty ships.

Already, however, American warships were beginning to shell the Japanese home islands, while the air force was mounting a fearsome bombardment. Flying from bases in the Marianas, B-29 Superfortresses pounded city after city, sparing only the beautiful religious center of Kyoto. The purpose was frankly to terrorize the civilian population and force the military leaders to realize that their cause was hopeless. On March 10, 1945, the full might of American air power fell on Tokyo. In the most destructive air raid in history, the city was turned into an inferno in which 130,000 people died.

The defeat of Japan. As early as February, Emperor Hirohito knew the war was lost. But the Japanese generals seemed intent on seeing their country utterly destroyed rather than acknowledge their failure. In Washington, the great question in early 1945 was whether or not to invade Japan itself. Military men warned that American casualties would reach a frightful figure in such an assault. On July 26, the United States and Britain issued an ultimatum to Japan demanding that it surrender or face total destruction.

At the time, an atomic bomb had just been successfully tested, and preparations were under way to use the fantastic new weapon against Japan. Moreover, keeping their promise to enter the Pacific war ninety days after Germany's surrender (page 630), the Russians were ready to strike Manchuria. The end was at hand.

On the fateful morning of August 6, the Superfortress *Enola Gay* dropped an atomic bomb on the city of Hiroshima. "My God!" was all the pilot could say as he looked down upon the scene that followed. In an explosion that cast a light "brighter than a thousand suns," the city simply vanished. In an instant, 70,000 people died, and 70,000 of the city's other 280,000 inhabitants were wounded, many of them suffering a lingering death from radiation many years later. At one stroke, the nature of warfare was revolutionized and the world entered a new era.

The atomic bomb controversy. Should the bomb have been used against an enemy that was already clearly defeated? The question was debated by scientists and military men at the time of Hiroshima, and it has been a subject of controversy ever since among historians. President Harry S. Truman, who made the fateful decision, had no doubts about the choice before him. In his view, the bomb saved thousands of American lives by forcing Japan out of the war before an invasion of the home islands became necessary. Only a dramatic demonstration of American power, he believed, would bring the Japanese militarists to their senses.

In the emotional heat of war, it would have been very difficult indeed for Truman to resist using the new weapon. Unfortunately, moreover, the Japanese reply to the Allied ultimatum was garbled in translation. Truman took it to be a defiant rejection, whereas the Japanese probably meant to leave the door open for further discussion.

Critics at the time argued that a demonstration explosion of the bomb in an isolated, sparsely populated area would be just as effective in bringing the war to an end as dropping it into a large city without warning. Others were persuaded that conventional bombing and blockade, plus the Soviet Union's entry into the Pacific war, would bring Japan to heel in a matter of weeks. They argued that the United States should not jeopardize its moral position in the world by becoming the first nation to use the terrifying new weapon, especially against civilians.

Historical hindsight suggests that the critics were probably right. In the light of developments since 1945, hindsight also hints that Truman may have wanted to impress the Soviet Union with the power of the new weapon and the willingness of the United States to use it. Perhaps he even hoped to end the war before Stalin could gain a commanding position in Asia. At the time the alliance between the great powers was coming unraveled, and the cold war that was to plague the world for years was appearing on the horizon.

In any case, events early in August combined to bring peace. Two days after Hiroshima—and precisely on schedule—the Soviet Union declared war. On August 9, a second atomic bomb was dropped, this one on Nagasaki, killing 38,000 people. Japan surrendered on August 15 (V-J Day), and immediately an occupation force under General MacArthur moved into the country. In a formal ceremony on September 2 aboard the battleship *Missouri* in Tokyo Bay, mankind's most destructive war officially ended.

HIROSHIMA

In the following excerpt, one of the survivors of Hiroshima, Yashiaki Sasai, who was in the sixth grade at the time the bomb was dropped, recalls her experience:

"... Just we [Yashiaki and her mother] were in the middle of the grade crossing at Yokogawa Station, a terrific flash raced across the sky and immediately afterward we were dashed to the ground by the explosion blast. When I opened my eyes and looked around, dust was enveloping everything, making it dark like twilight; through the dusk, scraps of boards and fragments of all sorts were raining down on my head. A big ox that a minute ago had been pulling a cart was now thrashing about in agony, and the houses that until now had stood in a line were squashed flat. When I looked toward the trolley tracks, blood-smeared passengers, fighting to be first, were trying to get out of a trolley car, and I could hear the cries of children and the groaning voices of adults.

"Suddenly both of us began to worry about the three we had left at home ... and we turned toward home and started to run. From under the collapsed houses the voices calling for help, echoing in the ears of the two of us who were thinking only of returning home, sounded as if they were chasing us. The warehouse of the government bus line was demolished, the two-story firehouse was flat on the ground, and the four fire engines were a pathetic sight. We were frantically impatient to reach home, but every street we came to was filled with collapsed houses or buildings on the verge of collapse, and there was no help for it but to scramble over the roofs of the collapsed houses. From beneath the roofs that we walked over came the cries of children and the voices of their parents calling for help; tormented by harrowing feelings we hurried on and finally arrived at our home."

3 Americans Wage War Behind The Battle Lines

1. If the American economy could be quickly and effectively geared for an effort like World War II, how do you think the nation would fare in future war experiences? What type of war would be the most difficult for the United States to fight?

2. If you were selecting the ideal leader to conduct the war, what would be his characteristics?

3. In what ways did business, labor, agriculture, and the general public contribute to the war effort, and in what ways did they take advantage of the war for private gains?

4. To what extent was Harry S. Truman prepared for the Presidency?

Although Pearl Harbor brought a rush of volunteers for military service, in the long run the draft furnished the manpower needed to win the war. Total mobilization ultimately put over 15 million men into uniform. Several hundred thousand women served in the new auxiliary branches of the armed forces such as the Women's Army Corps (WACS) and the navy's WAVES. Military bases sprang up all over the country, and the GI (as the soldier of World War II was called) became the nation's popular hero.

American and Allied forces fought brilliantly in the war and deserved the hard-earned victories they won. In the end, however, the Axis was defeated more by the superior technology of the United States than by military strategy and tactics. Because of its tremendous material resources and productive genius, the United States held a great strategic advantage over its adversaries. For World War II was a contest of machines, a test of organizational and technological skills, precisely the kind of war to which the American economy could be quickly and effectively geared. Industry, labor, and farming joined with the armed forces to put on a remarkable performance in the war years.

Production of war materials. Nowhere was a production miracle more needed than in merchant shipping, and nowhere was the challenge more decisively met. More than 5,000 vessels were built during the war, giving the merchant marine 50 million tons of shipping resources. New methods of construction cut the time needed to build a standard freighter from six months to seventeen days. By mid–1943, incredibly, the country was actually producing more ships than it could immediately use!

This merchant fleet carried war materials to every corner of the world. Great stores of arms, ammunition, food, and fuel poured across the oceans. In addition, the ships carried a fascinating variety of other cargoes—hospitals, portable movie theaters, dry docks, millions of tiny Atabrine pills (to combat malaria), laundry units, entire railroad lines, barrels of soft drinks, radio stations, athletic gear, suspension bridges, and vehicles of every size and description. Men of the merchant marine sailed in lightly protected hulls along the frigid, submarine-infested run to northern Russia. Many of them burned to death in fiery explosions, or suffocated in oil-covered waters, or went down trapped inside the ships they sailed. In all, the merchant marine suffered some 6,000 casualties during the war.

Equally great was the demand for airplanes with which to bring the war home to the enemy. When Roosevelt called for 50,000 planes a year in 1940, the figure seemed an utterly unreasonable one. By 1945, industry was easily producing double that number. Supplementing the expansion of plane production, the military air arm underwent a phenomenal growth and change. In 1943 alone, it trained 65,000 pilots, 14,000 bombardiers, 82,000 aerial gunners, and 530,000 technicians. Glider pilots, paratroops, and other airborne forces became regular units in the military establishment. So powerful did the air arm become that it was accorded semiautonomous status as the Army Air Force, a step which anticipated the establishment after the war of the independent United States Air Force.

The navy underwent an enormous expansion, too, adding 70,000 new craft in the fleet. The important expansion was made in aircraft carriers (including small attack carriers), submarines, cruisers, and a whole range of new craft designed to carry men and equipment in amphibious operations. To man and equip the carrier force, the navy air force underwent comparable growth.

Industry joins the war effort. Before Pearl Harbor, Roosevelt had difficulty persuading the leaders of industry to retool their plants for war production. In part, the fault was his own, for his cautious moves before the war did little to inspire a sense of emergency. Business leaders were to blame, too; many of them stubbornly refused to convert their factories until the government gave them large loans and promised them favorable tax benefits in the future.

To establish production priorities and otherwise prod industry into action, Roosevelt created an Office of Production Management (OPM) in late 1940. Under the unlikely joint direction of the president of General Motors and the head of the Amalgamated Clothing Workers of America, OPM made some headway, finally persuading the vital auto industry, for example, to devote a quarter of its output to military vehicles.

After December 7, industry rallied to support the war effort. Enormous government expenditures and American technological know-how combined to produce results. Production soared to record heights, and by late 1943, some industries had produced a surplus of war goods and were starting to think about conversion to peacetime production. Yet, the war effort at home did not really function efficiently until Roosevelt put former Senator and Supreme Court Justice James F. Byrnes in charge of a powerful new Office of War Mobilization in May 1943. An experienced politician, Byrnes became an "assistant President," acting as chief executive in many domestic matters while Roosevelt busied himself with diplomacy and the war overseas.

Mobilizing scientific resources. Perhaps the most successful mobilization effort was the organization of American science. It was a crucial effort, too, for Germany had a scientific potential which, conceivably, could have produced new weapons against which the Allies would have been defenseless (as was almost the case with the V-2 rocket).

Early in the war, the Office of Scientific Research and Development was established. Scientists and laboratories all over the nation went to work developing new weapons or improving old ones. A British invention, radar, was developed into a highly sophisticated defense mechanism. New navigational devices were of indispensable aid to flyers and submarine skippers. The proximity fuse, a tiny radio device that exploded a shell or bomb when it got close to target, was especially effective in antiaircraft warfare. In the field of medicine, advances were made in the development and use of new drugs (such as penicillin and the sulfonamides) and surgical techniques.

Overshadowing all other scientific achievements—and, indeed, all other results of the war—was the development of the atomic bomb. As early as 1939, the refugee scientist Albert Einstein had told Roosevelt that it was possible to create a weapon utilizing the energy of the atom. Fearful of German advances in the field of nuclear physics, Roosevelt instituted a crash program to overcome the incredibly complex technological problems involved in building such a weapon.

Between 1940 and 1945, the government spent over $2 billion in secret appropriations for work on the bomb. The Manhattan Project, as the effort was called, established secret plants at Oak Ridge, Tennessee, and Hanford, Washington, where the practical work of developing the bomb went on. At Los Alamos, New Mexico, a group of scientists under the brilliant direction of J. Robert Oppenheimer, finally accomplished the job. On the morning of July 16, 1945, they detonated the first atomic device in history.

Wartime economy measures. World War II put an end to the Great Depression in the United States. Massive government spending—$300 billion between 1940 and 1945—brought full employment and sustained economic growth once again. Gross national product rose 67 percent, a striking increase which enabled the nation to meet its war obligations and still put more hard cash in the hands of civilians than at any time during the depression. Families which had scraped by on a small income for years suddenly found themselves flush with the earnings of one, two, even three breadwinners. People were eager to buy anything at almost any price. Ironically, the threat of inflation—the most dangerous internal enemy of any nation at war—forced the government to put severe restrictions on civilian spending.

Under the Office of Price Administration (OPA), price controls were established early in the war and were remarkably successful, in the long run, in controlling inflation. Because so many industries had to be retooled to produce war materials, luxury goods and many of life's little conveniences were in short supply throughout the conflict. Rationing of such critical materials as fuel and rubber kept the family auto in the garage most of the time. As in all wars, too, "black markets" and profiteering enabled an unscrupulous few to thrive as parasites on the rest of society. But the necessities of life were never lacking in the United States, in marked contrast to conditions in the other belligerent nations. Indeed, even with the heavy demands of the military and the Allied nations, civilians at home consumed more food in 1944 than in any previous year in history.

At the outset of hostilities, the big labor unions pledged to support the war effort and promised not to strike for higher wages. But until prices were brought under effective control in 1943, heavy pressure built up among the workers to get a larger piece of the economic pie. Only one union, John L. Lewis's United Mine Workers, actually defied the government and broke the "no strike" pledge.

But organized labor as a whole was criticized by the politicians and much of the public, during and after the war, for allegedly hampering the war effort. In contrast, only a handful of critics pointed to the harmful effects of business's demands for favorable tax write-offs and other benefits from Washington. And no one condemned agricultural subsidies as contributing to inflation, even though net farm income rose during the war by more than 300 percent.

Determined to put the war on a pay-as-you-go basis, Roosevelt pressured a reluctant Congress into enacting far-reaching tax measures in 1942 and 1943. The number of income tax–payers increased from 13 million to 50 million, thus enlarging appreciably the ranks of people who had a direct stake in the government. Only about 40 percent of the war's cost was met by taxes, however, the remainder being raised by deficit financing. All told, the national debt rose from $49 billion at the start of the war to about $260 billion in 1945.

The election of 1944. In the midst of war, the American people were called upon to test their democratic institutions in a Presidential election. For the most part, Roosevelt had let partisan politics take second place to the war effort in his attentions. "Dr. Win-the-War," as he put it, had taken over from "Dr. New Deal." While strongly supporting the war effort, a conservative coalition in Congress was determined to block any extension of Roosevelt's old domestic reform program.

The Presidential election of 1944, thus, was a rather dull affair. About all the Republicans could do was to criticize the President for "inefficiency" and "confusion" in his conduct of the war and argue that they could do better. Some Republicans tried to start a national boom for General MacArthur, but the war hero wisely spurned their efforts and kept his mind on his job in the Pacific. After passing over their 1940 candidate, Wendell Willkie, the party picked Thomas E. Dewey, the vigorous young governor of New York, to run against the Democratic champion.

Possibly Roosevelt would have preferred to stay out of the race in 1944. He was tired of the immense burdens of the office and his health was failing, although no one at the time knew just how badly. But the logic of events and time forced him to run for a fourth term. As a dynamic world figure, in some sense a symbol of democracy's struggle against totalitarianism, he would have found it very difficult, indeed, to bow out of the picture at the moment when the initiative in the war was passing to the Allies. Ego and a sense of duty compelled him to stay on until the job was finished. Some historians suggest that Roosevelt hoped to win a fourth term, serve until the war ended and the peace was assured, then hand the reins of government to a successor.

Under these circumstances, his attitude toward the Vice Presidency in 1944 was a strange one, indeed. Passing over the incumbent, Henry A. Wallace, he told the party bosses to pick someone to their liking and seemed almost indifferent to their choice. The man they named was Harry S. Truman. An able but obscure senator from Missouri and a loyal, hard-working member of his party, Truman had absolutely no experience in foreign affairs. His only signal national service was as chairman of a Senate Committee to Investigate the National Defense Program, a task he performed with fair mind and solid competence. As usual, the voters paid little attention to the qualifications of Vice Presidential candidates. The Democratic ticket swept to a comfortable victory in the election.

The death of FDR. During the few brief weeks of his fourth term, Roosevelt was so preoccupied with diplomacy that he all but ignored his new Vice President. Truman was told nothing about the atomic bomb project, for example, and he had only the haziest notion of what weighty matters were being discussed among leaders of the Grand Alliance.

Then, on April 12, 1945, Roosevelt suddenly died of a massive cerebral hemorrhage. Harry S. Truman became the thirty-third President of the United States. Next morning he expressed his feelings in the blunt midwestern language that would become so familiar to his countrymen during the next eight years: "Did you ever have a bull or a load of hay fall on you? If you ever did, you know how I felt last night." It was an understandable reaction, for certainly no other man in American history has succeeded to the awesome office of the Presidency under more difficult circumstances.

4 American Diplomacy Seeks A Framework For Peace

1. What were the American objectives in fighting World War II? What do you consider to be the desired ends of the war? How would you accomplish these ends?

2. How did Roosevelt attempt to accomplish American diplomatic desires? To what extent did he rely upon the power of words to affect changes?

3. What were the vested interests of the great powers which made the formation of the United Nations so difficult? How effective do you think the United Nations has been in encouraging a politically stable and harmonious world?

4. Do you think Roosevelt was successful in achieving as much as could be expected at Yalta for American interests?

When the United States went to war in December 1941, the chief thought in the minds of most people, doubtless, was simply to defeat the enemy as quickly and decisively as possible. Little consideration was given to the political consequences of victory, or even to the certainty that the war would disrupt many old social and political patterns throughout the world. Beyond victory, the nation's war aims were perhaps best expressed in the Atlantic Charter, with its call for a new world organization and a "better future world."

As in World War I, so in the global conflict of the 1940's, the American people fought to pursue the ideals of liberal democracy as much as to attain any specific material objectives. Victory over the Axis was expected to bring mankind closer to realizing Wilson's dream of a politically stable and harmonious world. If it was a noble ideal, it was hardly attainable in the middle of history's most turbulent and revolutionary century.

Roosevelt's wartime diplomacy. Roosevelt was as caught up as any American in the Wilsonian vision of an international organization to preserve peace. But he was also pragmatic politician enough to understand that any collective-security arrangement would be only as effective as the great powers permitted it to be. His wartime diplomacy, accordingly, proceeded along two parallel tracks—one leading to the establishment of an organization to replace the League of Nations, the other seeking to continue and strengthen the wartime alliance of the great powers into the postwar period.

Roosevelt did not deceive himself into thinking that relations between the United States and the Soviet Union would be entirely smooth after the war. But he believed that the major issues could be handled in a reasonable manner by reasonable men, if not in the world organization, then by discussions among the leaders of the great powers. A major effort in his diplomacy, then, was to win the confidence of the Russians, particularly Josef Stalin.

He also sought to win the confidence and support of his political opponents at home. In 1943, Congress overwhelmingly approved a resolution proposed by Tom Connally of Texas and J. William Fulbright of Arkansas which called for full American participation in a new world organization. Foreign policy thereafter was conducted on a bipartisan basis; that is, the two major parties usually came to an agreement about a diplomatic move, then upheld it when it went into effect. It was an attempt to avoid the vicious political infighting that had wrecked Wilson's hopes in 1919.

The most important wartime convert to collective security was Michigan's Senator Arthur H. Vandenberg. A prewar unilateralist, Vandenberg was a tough Republican politician who had little use for Roosevelt or the New Deal. But after Pearl Harbor, he abandoned his earlier views on foreign policy, accepted the position of the interventionists, and worked closely with two Democratic Presidents. No man was more influential in the shaping of foreign policy during the late 1940's than Vandenberg.

In dealing with his fellow leaders of the Grand Alliance, Roosevelt alternately played the lion and the fox. Although he worked closely with Churchill, the President had little use for Britain's hopes to reestablish its colonial empire after the war. At times, he used Churchill as something of a scapegoat, especially when the two Western leaders conferred with Stalin. Intent upon winning over the Soviet dictator, he sometimes made it clear that Britain's position in the Grand Alliance was secondary to that of the United States and the Soviet Union. As for the French, Roosevelt supported their government in exile and gladly armed a Free French army of liberation. But he refused to accord them the status of a great power, thereby infuriating the proud General deGaulle.

On the other hand, Roosevelt tried his best to raise China to a position of world power. Unfortunately, the ingredients for such power were totally lacking in China at the time. Torn apart by internal strife, China tottered on the verge of disaster throughout the war (Japan actually held more Chinese territory in 1945 than 1941). Nonetheless, Roosevelt insisted upon treating Chiang Kai-shek as an equal partner with the Big Three in planning for the postwar world. Both Churchill and Stalin saw little sense in his demand, yet they acceded to it halfheartedly.

Relations between Roosevelt and Stalin were always severely qualified by the fact that the two men had nothing in common beyond a wish to see Germany defeated. Stalin was a despot, suspicious of even his closest advisers and unable to comprehend a simple, direct expression of goodwill. Like many Russian leaders in the past, he feared and distrusted the West.

Even the optimistic Roosevelt was bothered by a nagging doubt that the dictator ever understood anything that was said to him. In truth, when the two men talked, they spoke entirely different languages—figuratively as well as literally. To Roosevelt, the word *democracy* meant the liberal democracy of open discussion and free election so familiar to the American people. When Stalin used the word, it was in the context of a "people's democracy"—rule by the Communist party in the Soviet Union in the name of "the people." The wonder is that the two leaders came to agreement on anything.

Launching the United Nations. In a series of conferences in 1943 and 1944, the structure of the new United Nations organization was slowly and painfully hammered out by the diplomats of East and West. None of the great powers was really willing to part with its sovereignty or sacrifice what it considered its vital interests sufficiently to make the new body an effective peace-keeping force.

The United States, for example, refused to subordinate the Monroe Doctrine to the UN, insisting that the rest of the world acknowledge its regional interests in the Western Hemisphere. Russia demanded a veto for the great powers over any matter that might come before the organization, even a simple proposal to discuss a topic. Ultimately, Stalin modified his stand and accepted the veto in substantive matters only (matters on which the UN might take action). It should be noted that none of the powers, including the United States, would accept the UN charter without some provision for a veto.

On April 25, 1945, the representatives of fifty nations gathered at San Francisco and launched the United Nations. For all its weaknesses, the new organization was an improvement over the League of Nations. At least it provided a public forum in which such antagonists as the United States and the Soviet Union could air their differences and vie for the approval of the world. Roosevelt did not live to see the birth of the UN,

Victory Bond Poster, Norman Rockwell, *c.* 1943

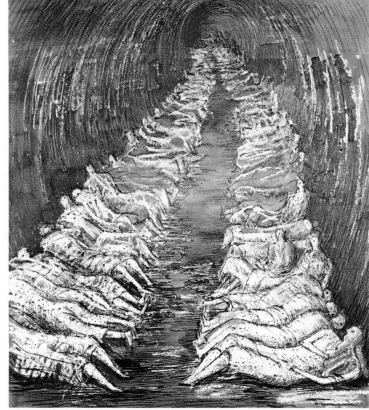

Tube Shelter Perspective, Henry Moore, 1941

Women at Work in Government Arsenal, 1942

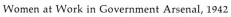

After the attack on Pearl Harbor, life in the United States took on an almost single-minded aspect—to do all that was necessary to win the war. Everyone was enlisted in the effort—men into the factories and onto the battlefield, women into the military and into the war plants, and children into drives to collect needed materials.

Signs saying "Closed for the Duration" appeared in store windows, showing either that the owner had joined the war effort or that his particular goods would not be available to civilians. "Don't you know there's a war on?" became the standard retort to any complaint about goods or service, and Americans came to expect shortages in food, clothing, and gasoline and to accept the idea of rationing.

Inconveniences that Americans had to accept were slight in comparison to those in other belligerent countries. Before the United States entered the war, Henry Moore had done a series of "shelter" drawings, showing Londoners undergoing bombing attacks. At the left he shows them herded into an underground station, a thousand at a time, to spend the night.

Scrap Drive in Chicago, 1942

American Troop Landing, D-Day, Robert Capa, 1944

American Marines on Torokina Island in the Pacific, 1943

American troops joined the British, and three years later landed with them on France's shore, to begin the long trek overland to Germany. Thousands of miles away, other American troops fought the Japanese on Pacific atolls, sustaining heavy casualties but seizing control of the Pacific islands one by one. At last the end came, and a jubilant American public celebrated the end of "the duration," while shocked and saddened Japanese citizens learned of their defeat from their emperor.

Japanese Citizens After the Surrender, 1945

THE UNITED NATIONS

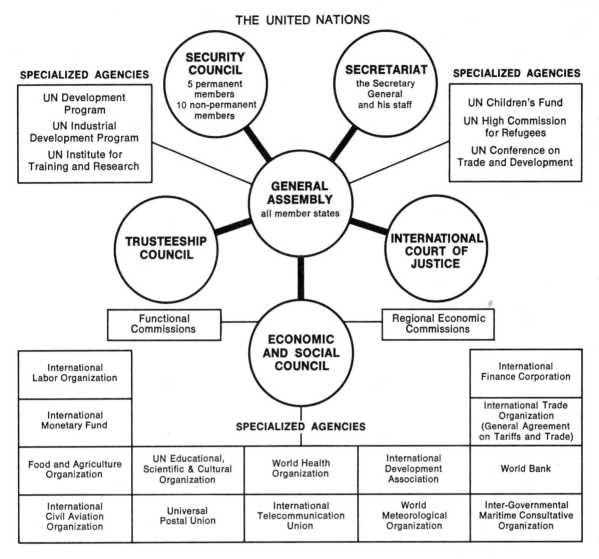

but it stands as his most enduring and constructive achievement in foreign policy.

But in one sense, the UN also pointed up Roosevelt's greatest failing as a diplomat. He had an American politician's trust in the power of words to effect change. Throughout the war, he avoided any discussion of specific political settlements to follow upon the "unconditional surrender" of the enemy. Establish a framework for peace and negotiation, he argued, and the political questions could then be considered by the statesmen of the world in an atmosphere of mutual respect and cooperation. In this respect, Roosevelt reflected the deep-seated American belief in the perfectibility of men and institutions. Given an international forum and a genuine accord among the victorious great powers, the future could be expected to take care of itself.

The Big Three meet. Neither Churchill nor Stalin shared Roosevelt's neglect of political questions. Churchill clearly intended to reassert British power in the Mediterranean as quickly as possible. But because his country was dependent upon American support, his diplomatic maneuvering was restricted by the reaction he might get from his great friend Roosevelt. This was not the case with Stalin. Very early in the war, the Russian indicated that he expected to control political events in Eastern Europe, and he never lost sight of this objective.

Nonetheless, some progress was made toward establishing an accord among the great powers that might outlast the war. Meeting in Moscow in October 1943, the Big Three foreign ministers agreed on the necessity for a second front in Europe, on the "unconditional surrender" of the Axis powers, and on the need for a new international organization. Moreover, the Soviets privately agreed to enter the war in Asia once Germany was defeated. This pledge was of great importance to the United States, for American military men looked upon Soviet help in Asia as the best means of bringing about Japan's defeat without an invasion of the home islands.

Later in 1943, Roosevelt and Churchill journeyed to Teheran, Iran, for their first meeting with Stalin. The very fact that these three leaders could sit down together, face-to-face, to discuss problems of mutual concern was a historic reversal of past relationships among their countries. Although the meeting was essentially only an exploratory session, Roosevelt considered it a useful exchange. They talked informally about operations against Germany and discussed the postwar fate of Poland and the colonial areas. Stalin again pledged his aid in the Pacific war.

Meanwhile, Roosevelt indulged his fixation to bring China into the high-level deliberations. On the way to Teheran, he and Churchill conferred at Cairo with Chiang Kai-shek. In a joint declaration, the three leaders announced plans for the postwar dismemberment of the Japanese Empire. Clearly, Roosevelt assumed that China could pull itself together under Chiang's leadership and muster sufficient power to fill the vacuum in Asia left by Japan's defeat. It was an assumption based on wishful thinking rather than on political realities.

The Yalta Conference. The great test of Roosevelt's pragmatic diplomacy came at the Yalta Conference in February 1945. Several months earlier, Churchill and Stalin had reached an agreement to chop up the Balkans area into Russian and British spheres of influence. Churchill considered the arrangement a great bargain, for Stalin was under no compulsion to

A CRITIC OF YALTA

A severe critic of the Yalta agreement was Patrick J. Hurley, American ambassador to China at the time of Yalta. In 1951, he testified before a Senate committee on the effects of the Yalta agreement in the Far East:

"... at the time of Yalta the United States had unquestionable power to make Russia respect her solemn agreements, but instead we surrendered them in secret. Russia did not have to break her agreements or commitments. All of them were surrendered to her by American diplomats at Yalta and subsequently.

"The postwar success of Russia is not due to Russia's strength but to the weakness of American foreign policy. Mr. Acheson has been telling you that all of the principles and objectives stated in the Atlantic Charter and the territorial integrity and political independence of our ally, China, were given away in secret because our State Department was convinced that Russia would not keep her commitments and was in the position to seize all of the properties that we gave her in secret.

"Rather than face this threat by Russia, American diplomats weakly surrendered the objectives to which Russia and 45 other nations had agreed. The American State Department, instead of demanding that Russia respect its commitment, secretly released her from those commitments. This weakness brought about the ruthless conquest of other people both in the east and in the west. Through the weakness of the Yalta secret agreement with Russia, we have lost 450,000,000 Chinese friends in Asia. . . .

"None of the property that we used to appease Russia belonged to the United States. As Mr. Acheson has ably said, we paid with the property of another to save American casualties. . . .

"I believe that the verdict of history on the Yalta agreement will mark it as both immoral and cowardly."

make any concessions in the Balkans, given his military power in Eastern Europe.

Roosevelt, however, refused to recognize the deal. At Yalta, he tried to loosen the Soviet Union's hold on Eastern Europe by securing a pledge from Stalin to let the people in the countries there determine their own political future by democratic means. Acknowledging that the military advantage all lay with Stalin, he could only hope that the Soviet leader would make concessions in the interests of future good relations. Stalin made the concessions, particularly with regard to Poland, and even joined in issuing a "Declaration on Liberated Europe," which vaguely called for democracy throughout the Continent.

Roosevelt's other objective at Yalta was to secure an ironclad agreement by Stalin to enter the war against Japan. In exchange for the Soviet Union's promise to make a treaty of friendship with Chiang Kai-shek, the Western leaders agreed that it should have certain territorial concessions in Asia in such areas that had long been in dispute with Japan as the Kurile Islands and Port Arthur.

Roosevelt's critics charged that he was "taken in" at Yalta and that he "appeased" Stalin by giving in to him on point after point. Quite the reverse was actually the case. As the war came to an end in Europe, the overwhelming political fact of life in Eastern Europe was the presence of the Red Army. Whatever political objectives the West had in Poland, Hungary, Rumania, Bulgaria, and (to a lesser extent) in Yugoslavia and Greece, could have been gained only in one of two ways: either by a military confrontation with the Soviet Union almost certain to bring on war; or by negotiations to secure some concessions from Stalin. Given the war-weariness in Europe and the United States, the first alternative was unthinkable. The second actually produced the desired results, for it was Stalin who made the significant concessions at Yalta, not Roosevelt and Churchill.

In Asia, the West made some territorial concessions to the Russians; but these had little effect on the subsequent course of events in that turbulent area. At the time of Yalta, Roosevelt and his military advisers were convinced that they were trading minor territorial concessions to Stalin for the lives of thousands of American servicemen who would die in an invasion of Japan. The fact that the Yalta Agreements broke down within a few months of the conference does not mean that the conference itself was a failure. Indeed, Yalta was the high-water mark in the success of the Grand Alliance, for the great powers actually reached agreement on their major differences.

Yet, in the long run, Roosevelt's personal diplomacy failed to achieve its great objective. For all his efforts, the wartime unity of the Grand Allies began to crumble even as victory became certain. There was something tragically symbolic about the death of Roosevelt in April 1945; for with the succession of Harry S. Truman and the end of hostilities in Europe a few weeks later, a new era in Soviet-American relations began.

5 The War Exacts A Great Price

1. Why were the Japanese living in America and Americans of Japanese ancestry placed in relocation centers?

2. Have civil rights always been restricted during war time? Do you think it is necessary to restrict citizens' rights in wartime?

3. To what extent were blacks the victims of discrimination during World War II? How did the war influence the search for racial equality?

4. What was the cost of the war in human misery and loss of lives?

Isolated geographically from the fighting and free—for the last time in history, incidentally—from fear that the enemy would destroy their homeland, the American people as a whole took the war in their stride. Theirs was a luxury not enjoyed by the British, the Russians, the French, the Chinese, the Germans, the Japanese, and the other belligerents, all of whom suffered the full effects of mankind's most destructive war. For great numbers of Americans, indeed, the war was actually a boon, bringing steady jobs and a degree of economic security not known for many years.

Even the emotional impact was less severe for most people than in several earlier American wars. Unless one was involved in the fighting himself or had a loved one in a combat zone, it was quite possible to view the war simply as one more challenge, albeit an enormous one, to the nation's productive and technological genius.

Yet, as with all man-made disasters, World War II exacted a terrible price in lives, property, human ideals, and social disruption. If the United States suffered less than the other belligerents, it did not escape the experience entirely unscathed.

Japanese internment. Barely two months after Pearl Harbor, for example, the government committed the worst single mass violation of civil liberties in American history. Yielding to racist pressures and war hysteria, the authorities forcibly removed *all* persons of Japanese ancestry from their homes on the Pacific coast and "relocated" them in the interior of the country.

Of the 117,000 men, women, and children affected, more than 71,000 were native-born Americans; yet, they suffered the same fate as their parents and friends who had come from Japan. Forced to sell their farms, their businesses, and their homes for whatever prices they could get, they were herded together in barbed wire stockades and subjected to indignities of the worst sort. Ultimately, they were removed to concentration camps (which the government called "relocation centers") in the Rocky Mountain area. Not since the days of slavery in the Old South had a group of Americans endured a more degrading experience.

Ostensibly, the relocation was made to protect the coast from possible acts of sabotage. In fact, it was the climax to half a century of vicious anti-Oriental prejudice in the western states. Perhaps the worst aspect of the affair was that so few people in positions of responsibility raised any objections to it.

Roosevelt officially authorized the action; and even the Supreme Court (in the case of *Korematsu v. United States*) tortuously found grounds to uphold it. As historian Arthur S. Link has observed:

The meaning of the decision was clear and foreboding: In future emergencies no American citizen would have any rights that the President and army were bound to respect when, *in their judgment,* the emergency justified drastic denial of civil rights.

Parenthetically, German-Americans and Italian-Americans entirely escaped the fate suffered by Japanese-Americans.

Racial discrimination. Racism showed itself in the wartime treatment of black Americans as well. To meet the demand for labor in the factories and shipyards of the North and West, nearly a million blacks migrated from the South. Racial clashes flared in many cities where the newcomers were thrown into contact with lower-class whites, many of whom were themselves only recently arrived in the burgeoning urban centers. New York narrowly averted a major race riot. Detroit was not so lucky, suffering an upheaval of tragic proportions in 1943. In Los Angeles, both blacks and Mexican-Americans were the subject of race-baiting and organized prejudice.

Led by A. Philip Randolph, president of the Brotherhood of Sleeping Car Porters, black spokesmen demanded an end to discrimination in the hiring of workers in defense industries. Putting heavy pressure on the government, they finally persuaded Roosevelt in June 1941 to yield to their demands and establish the Fair Employment Practices Committee (FEPC).

The most significant advance ever made, to that time, by organized black action, FEPC was only a partial success. Although it publicized the problem and exerted a certain moral influence on industry and organized labor to do away with discrimination, it lacked power to enforce its directives. Nearly two million blacks eventually found work in defense plants and made important contributions to the war effort. But the majority of them still suffered from being "the last hired, the first fired."

In a war against the Nazis, with their vicious racial theories, the persistence of discrimination in the armed forces was particularly galling to black Americans. Segregated units continued to be the norm in all the services. Ugly race riots broke out in a number of military camps and nearby army towns. Black soldiers suffered the intolerable indignity of being treated worse then enemy prisoners who were brought to this country for incarceration.

Roughly half a million blacks served in the military forces, probably half of them overseas. With some notable exceptions, they were confined to construction work, waiting on tables, and similar menial, noncombat duties. When given an opportunity to fight under the same conditions as whites, black soldiers did their job with distinction. Late in the war, the services responded to pressure from the black community and timidly experimented with a few semi-integrated combat units. The results were gratifying to all concerned, except perhaps the enemy forces these units confronted.

The black historian John Hope Franklin writes of the black soldiers:

The emotional conflicts and frustrations they went through as they sought to reconcile the doctrine of the Four Freedoms* with their own plight discouraged many of them. Neither the antidiscrimination orders of the War Department nor the concessions made in the commissioning of Negro officers in the Navy could compensate for the hurt which Negroes felt when rebuffed while wearing the uniform of their country. At the end of the war realists would admit that the morale of Negro soldiers could be substantially raised only by granting to them the Four Freedoms for which they were fighting.

Clearly, their experiences in the war strengthened the determination of black Americans to demand in fact the rights which were theirs in theory.

Aside from the manner in which racial minorities were treated, relative calm and reason prevailed on the homefront during the war. There was none of the wild-eyed hysteria of World War I, not, at least, after the incarceration of the Japanese-Americans. Government agencies such as the FBI went about the work of countering espionage and sabotage with quiet and notable efficiency. Even the propaganda was restrained in tone and content; and Elmer Davis, the able director of the Office of War Information, saw to it that war news reached the public as untouched by the censors as possible without endangering the war effort.

Destruction of life and property. For the rest of the world, the war was a nightmare of death and disruption on a scale unparalleled in history.

*Expressed by FDR in January 1941 as freedom from want, from fear, of speech and expression, and of worship.

Some 80 million men served in the armed forces of all the belligerent nations. At least 14 million of them died in the fighting. Another 25 million suffered war wounds. No one knows for certain how many civilians lost their lives. The Germans officially *ordered* the slaughter of 6 million innocent people, most of them Jews, but also many Slavs, gypsies, and other "inferior peoples." It has been estimated that upwards of 20 million Russians, civilians and soldiers, perished in the holocaust.

Millions of people were torn from their homes and became DP's (displaced persons), wandering over the face of the Continent in search of some sanctuary from the war. In monetary terms, the war cost more than a *trillion* dollars, about a third of which the United States paid. The figures defy the imagination of rational men.

So does the destruction that was visited upon Europe and Asia. The Germans devastated European Russia, reducing city after city to unrecognizable rubble. What the invaders spared, the Soviet troops themselves destroyed in a "scorched earth" policy as they retreated early in the war. On the North Atlantic, huge oil slicks and mile after mile of debris testified to the relentless destruction of ships and men.

Commencing in early 1943, the Allies struck massive aerial blows at the cities of Germany in a deliberate effort to terrorize the civilian population and undermine morale. In July, Hamburg experienced the first fire-storm of the war—an uncontrollable cyclone of fire produced by an enormous concentration of incendiary bombs. In the end, no German city escaped the holocaust.

To be sure, Hitler's airmen had themselves introduced the practice of saturation bombing of civilian centers, first in Spain, later in such cities as Warsaw, Rotterdam, Coventry, and London. But there is little evidence to suggest that the Allies gained any great advantage by imitating the Germans. Indeed, German morale stiffened rather than weakened under the pounding. And surely the wholesale destruction of the magnificent city of Dresden in 1945, when it was obvious Germany was finished, was a senseless act. In the fire-storm that destroyed this treasure-house of the world's art, between 100,000 and 250,000 people perished, most of them refugees from all over central Europe.

The cost of World War II in material devastation and human suffering is incalculable. Of the millions of inmates of concentration camps, only a handful survived. Many of those, like the men in the photograph at left in a barracks at Buchenwald, were barely alive when the Allies liberated them. Many of Europe's cities were almost completely destroyed by the massive aerial attacks of both the Axis and the Allies. The fire-bombing of the historic city of Dresden (below) left that city little more than a pile of rubble.

The ultimate horror of the war was revealed as Allied soldiers entered Germany. At Dachau, at Buchenwald, at Belsen, at Sachsenhausen, at a score of sites from one end of Germany to the other, they came upon the concentration camps of the Nazis. Incredulous young Americans saw with their own eyes the great stacks of withered bodies, the half-covered mass graves, the stark white gas chambers, the efficient cremation ovens, the grisly laboratories in which "scientists" had used human beings as guinea pigs—all the grim machinery of murder which the Germans had assembled and used to carry out the orders of their mad Führer.

Warsaw, London, Manila, Stalingrad, Normandy, Dresden, above all Dachau and Hiroshima: the cost of the World War II was great indeed. And the tragedy of it is that it brought not peace to the world, but a sword.

■ CONCLUSION

World War II was a global conflict of epic proportions. It engaged more men in combat than any other war in human history. It involved civilians in the actual horrors of conflict on a scale unprecedented in the human experience. It engulfed entire continents and vast expanses of the seven seas. Few people escaped its consequences, not even the primitive headhunter in New Guinea or the Bedouin tribesman in the lonely Sahara. It was truly one of history's great cataclysms.

For the American people, the war put an abrupt end to much of the provincialism in the national character. American forces fought on the continents of Europe, Africa, and Asia, and on hundreds of islands in the far Pacific. They fought on all the oceans and carried the goods of war to every corner of the globe. Soldiers and Marines invaded jungle-covered islands on the Equator and occupied vast expanses of dreary tundra in the Arctic. They fought on the fabled deserts of North Africa, along the Appian Way of the ancient Romans, in the exotic East Indies.

Young men from Sioux City and Wilkes-Barre found themselves flying regular runs over the mighty Himalayas or dropping by parachute onto the Kunai plains of New Guinea. Some shared the rough fare of guerrilla fighters in Yugoslavia, others waded up steaming rivers in Burma at the side of turbaned Sikhs, while still others charged onto beachheads alongside of fierce Fiji warriors. Men and women in the armed forces learned to work with Sicilian goatherds and Filipino rice farmers, with Eskimo fisherman and Arab camel drivers. For millions of Americans the war revealed the world in all its incredible variety.

The war also tested the fighting skill of Americans in all varieties of combat and put extraordinary demands on American industry and technology. Both men and machines gave a splendid account of themselves. Factories in the United States turned out arms and other war materials in prodigious quantities, supplying both the American armed forces and the armies of the allied nations—including the Soviet Union.

On the battlefield, Americans and their allies ultimately carried the war to the streets of Berlin and Rome and the bay of Tokyo, forcing the Axis powers to surrender unconditionally. Tragically, however, the brilliant victory of the Grand Alliance over fascism in Europe and Japanese imperialism in Asia did not produce the peace and security in the world that Americans hoped for. Almost at the moment of triumph, a new period of tension and turmoil began.

■ QUESTIONS

1. Were American war aims consistent with traditional American values and institutions? Were the most appropriate strategies used to attain those aims? Explain your answers.

2. What were the most important factors to account for American success in World War II? Justify your answer.

3. Should citizens enjoy the same rights during a war as they do during a time of peace? Why or why not?

4. To what extent did World War II and related events affect the quest for racial equality?

5. Why was there less national hysteria and irrational behavior among American citizens during World War II than during World War I?

6. What were the strategies of the Germans and Japanese? What were their weaknesses?

7. What were the consequences of a policy of total war and unconditional surrender?

8. What is war like as portrayed by Mauldin, Pyle, and the contemporary media?

9. Should the atomic bomb have been used against Japan in August of 1945? Justify your answer.

10. Why was America particularly adaptable to a war such as World War II? What types of war would cause more difficulties for the United States? Why?

11. How effective was Roosevelt as commander-in-chief, diplomat, and chief economic administrator during World War II?

12. Did Roosevelt follow a policy of appeasing Stalin at Yalta? Explain your answer.

13. What were the strengths and weaknesses of the United Nations at its inception? How effective has it been during its first quarter century?

14. Why are there wars?

■ BIBLIOGRAPHY

CHURCHILL, SIR WINSTON S., *The Second World War*, 6 vols., Bantam Books. Of all the personal accounts of World War II this is perhaps the best. Churchill represents one of the three major allied decision-makers, a first class historian, and a writer of considerable capability. His study is long and well worth the student's time, but he may feel the need to read the condensation or selected volumes.

EISENHOWER, DWIGHT D., *Crusade in Europe*, Doubleday (Dolphin Books). As American commander in Europe and leader of Allied forces, Eisenhower's account of the war is critical. The memoir is very well done to the student's greater gain.

MORISON, SAMUEL E., *The Two Ocean War: A Short History of the United States Navy in the Second World War*, Little, Brown. Students who have enjoyed Morison's other works will like this account of the American Navy in World War II. The same moving narrative style continues to show respect for the sea, men, and ships. This book is a condensation of Morison's official 15-volume history which he prepared during the war as officer-historian-participant.

SPEER, ALBERT, *Inside the Third Reich: Memoirs of Albert Speer*, Macmillan. Speer, who spent many years in prison as a war criminal, has recently written his memoirs of life with Hitler during World War II. It is particularly good for its insights into the character of Hitler.

MAULDIN, BILL, *Up Front*, Norton. World War II is remembered by many in the form of Mauldin's GI Joe and Willy. This collection of cartoons drawn during the campaigns of World War II represents war as the GI experienced it, a certain humor and spirit transcending dirt and fatigue.

PYLE, ERNIE, *Here is Your War*, Lancer Books. Ernie Pyle was able to translate the life of the common soldier for the people back home in the states. The student will be able to respond to this journalist who shared the foxholes and the dangers with the front-line soldier.

HERSEY, JOHN, *Hiroshima*, Bantam Books. *Hiroshima* is a moving account of the explosion of the atom bomb over Japan. The author looks at the event through the eyes of six witnesses. It is good reading for those who are not fully aware of the destructive power of atomic weapons in individual human terms.

FOGELMAN, EDWIN, ED., *Hiroshima: The Decision to Use the A-Bomb*, Research Anthology Series, Scribners. The editor has collected articles dealing with the moral, political, and scientific considerations surrounding the decision to drop the bomb. There is apt to be continual disagreement over the decision, but this book provides the student with information to use in making his own decision. This book is a good place for a student to begin in researching topics related to the atom bomb.

HOSOKAWA, BILL, *Nisei: The Quiet Americans*, William Morrow. Hosokawa is a Nisei himself, and he experienced the humiliation of relocation during the war. But this book is about more than the relocation. It considers racial discrimination against the Oriental in broader terms and fits well with current interest in racial understanding.

SOBUL, DE ANNE, *Encounters with America's History*, Holt, Rinehart & Winston. The internment of Japanese aliens and Japanese-Americans during World War II has become a subject of controversy in the years since it occurred. Why were they interned? The fourth problem in this book provides source material for the student to study so that he can try to answer this question.

Part 5

Facing The Challenges Of The Modern World

View of earth as seen from Apollo 8 spacecraft, 1968

The Cold War From Yalta To Korea

Alliances have a way of becoming obsolete almost at the moment they achieve the purposes which called them into being. The Grand Alliance between the Soviet Union and the West existed for one overriding purpose—the defeat of Nazi Germany. Once that task was finished, the national interests of the various members once again came to the fore and the Alliance fell apart. By 1947, the impasse between the Soviet Union and the United States had become so fixed and seemingly unbreakable that journalist Walter Lippmann coined a term for it—the cold war.

In essence, the cold war was a *series* of international crises, usually but not always pitting the Russians against the Americans. In many ways, the situation resembled periods of international tension in the past, when the balance of power had been unsettled by a war. For Europeans, and perhaps especially for Russians, the experience was an old and familiar one.

For the American people, on the other hand, the cold war was a new and decidedly unwelcome experience. It seemed to deny this country any of the fruits of victory, to make a mockery of the "crusade in Europe" (as Eisenhower called the war against Hitler), and even to make the war of revenge in the Pacific a futile undertaking. Accustomed to fighting their wars for great ideals, Americans have always expected more from war than they realistically should. For while wars may decide certain questions and make others irrelevant, inevitably they also spawn new disputes, often far more difficult to deal with than the old ones. In a modern war, thus, a victor does not "win" very much, especially if his conception of victory encompasses goals of a permanent or universal nature. As you read about the origins and effects of the cold war, keep these questions in mind:

1. What was the international political situation at the end of the war?
2. What events led to increased tension between the United States and the Soviet Union?
3. How did the rise of revolutionary movements in Asia affect American foreign policy?
4. How was Europe rebuilt economically and militarily?
5. Why did the United States go to war in Korea?

1 Hope And Despair Mark The Postwar World

1. How did World War II disrupt the old social and political patterns of European imperialism? What were some of the results of this disruption?

2. Why was revolutionary radicalism so popular? Why did the revolutionists turn to communism for inspiration rather than to American democracy?

3. What was the relative balance of power in the world between the United States and the Soviet Union after World War II?

4. What were the Soviet Union's postwar national goals? What do you think America's postwar national goals should have been?

Because it engulfed the entire globe, World War II inevitably disrupted old social and political patterns wherever it touched. Just as revolutionary communism had burst forth during World War I, so revolutionary nationalism, often strongly radical, boiled up and spilled over the old colonial world during the war against the Axis. The war wrote *finis* to the age of Western colonialism and toppled the white man from his position of dominance over the world's vast majority of colored peoples. In 1942, Winston Churchill could still solemnly vow that he had "not become the King's First Minister in order to preside over the liquidation of the British Empire." By 1945, the sun was setting all over the king's domains, and Churchill had no more success than the Biblical Joshua in commanding the sun to stand still in mid-sky.

Japan's easy conquest of the colonial areas in the Far East, for example, had an enormous impact on the thinking of native political leaders in Asia and Africa. A non-Western nation of yellow-skinned people had bested the white man at his own game, modern war, and had even humiliated the powerful United States. It mattered little that the Japanese behaved cruelly in areas they conquered or that they were ultimately humiliated themselves. Never again would Asians accept rule by a foreign power, especially a white, Western power. Colonial peoples in many parts of the world moved, even before the war was over, to take control of their own affairs, peaceably if possible, forcibly if necessary.

Revolution, nationalism, and communism. Revolution was another natural spawn of the war, and in some instances it was indistinguishable from nationalism. In Southeast Asia, a Communist leader, Ho Chi Minh, became the popular symbol of Vietnamese resistance to alien rule, whether of the Japanese or French variety. It was impossible to say which cause was uppermost in Ho's mind, communism or Vietnamese nationalism, for he and his followers simply identified the two as one. In China, the Communists under Mao Tse-tung had broken with the Nationalist Kuomintang government of Chiang Kai-shek in 1934. After the war, they probably claimed the patriotic allegiance of at least as many people as Chiang Kai-shek's Kuomintang. Moreover, Mao's highly disciplined, politically alert movement appealed to Chinese nationalist sentiments in a way that Chiang's regime never matched.

Revolutionary radicalism had great appeal in wartorn Europe, as well. Communists had been very active in the wartime anti-Nazi underground, often heading the partisan forces in resisting the German occupation. Their efforts earned them the gratitude of voters in many countries later. Communists emerged after the war as the strongest party in the French National Assembly, as Italy's third most important party, and as leaders of a coalition government in Czechoslovakia. A veteran Communist known as Tito performed so successfully (and ruthlessly) as leader of the resistance in Yugoslavia that he easily assumed control of that country when peace came.

Indeed, for a brief time after the war, many people throughout the world saw communism as a viable, legitimate political alternative, not as something beyond the pale of respectability. Even in the United States, the Soviet system had a great many honest, if uncritical, admirers, doubtless because of the Soviet Union's successful performance in the war against fascism.

Postwar economic assistance. Torn and battered by long years of conflict, both Europe and Asia desperately needed American economic assistance in the work of reconstruction. In August 1945, President Truman abruptly ended the Lend-Lease program, a move which dismayed

655

many Europeans (including the Russians). But by the end of the year, he was giving full support to UNRRA, the United Nations Relief and Rehabilitation Administration. In all, the United States funneled some $11 billion in aid through UNRRA to help Europe to build itself up again, but even this sum was inadequate for the task. Because the Russians and the Americans could not agree on the purposes to which aid of this sort should be put, UNRRA died in 1947, one of the earliest victims of the emerging cold war. Many Americans were glad to see it go, moreover, because they disliked the idea of an international organization dispensing American dollars abroad.

Ironically, the nation most in need of economic assistance was the victorious Soviet Union. Few nations in history have known such devastation as the Soviet Union absorbed from the German invaders. Every major city in the European part of Russia was destroyed or badly damaged, and perhaps seventy thousand villages suffered a similar fate. In Leningrad alone, a million and a half people perished.

This devastation of their homeland conditioned the entire outlook of the Russians after the war. Together with millions of other Europeans who had experienced the Nazi nightmare at first hand, they displayed a fear and hatred of everything German, which was entirely foreign to the American people. Soviet diplomacy had as its first and absolutely unshakable aim the protection of Russia's vulnerable western frontiers against any possible future threat, whether that threat came from the Germans or from any other source.

Stalin's postwar policy. To be sure, Stalin was ready to extend the Soviet Union's influence as far into Europe as possible. And the Kremlin knew that one sure way to protect Soviet borders was to ring the country with satellite nations under the control of friendly governments. But the stolid dictator was not a reckless military adventurer, willing to risk his forces in situations where the odds seemed to be against him. Indeed, as an official United States Army history concludes, he was actually overcautious about moving the Red Army into the heart of Europe in the waning months of the war, at a time when there was little that could have stopped him.

Nor was Stalin quite the Red messiah many Americans once thought him to be. He did not

RUSSIAN LOSSES IN WORLD WAR II	
Citizens killed	c.20,000,000
Civilians	12,500,000
Military	7,500,000
Homeless people	c.25,000,000
Buildings destroyed	6,000,000
Factories	32,000
Power stations	10,000
Steam plants	14,000
Collective farms	98,000
Highway and railroad mileage	c.107,000
Hospitals and medical centers	40,000
Livestock	181,000,000

come sweeping into Europe in 1945 as a zealous crusader for the hammer and sickle; he came as the saviour of Mother Russia and the conqueror of Germany. In a perceptive evaluation of Stalin's policy after the war, historian Charles O. Lerche, Jr., writes:

If we disregard the flamboyant rhetoric in which Moscow loves to clothe its pronouncements, the hard stuff of Soviet action is less Leninist than Bismarckian* in its objectives and maneuvers. The alleged goal may be communism, but the working criteria are Soviet security, prestige, and power.

Too often in the West, during the postwar years, Soviet rhetoric was taken for Soviet action.

Yet, the presence of Soviet power in central Europe was a tactical factor of great importance in the coming of the cold war. However cautious Stalin may have been about using his military forces, the Red Army was a *potential* threat to Western Europe that could not be ignored. Moreover, the political skill of those Communists in Europe who slavishly bent to Moscow's will made the shaky postwar governments of Western

* Nikolai Lenin had been a much revered Russian Communist leader, while Otto von Bismarck had been a powerful Prussian-German military leader and statesman.

Europe particularly vulnerable to subversion or revolution. Backed by the *threat* of military support from the Soviet Union, Europe's Communists for a time seemed capable of taking over most of the Continent. From the American point of view, an even greater danger was that Stalin might use his tactical advantage to gain control of Germany, a move which probably would have given him dominant influence in all of Europe.

American strategic supremacy. On the other hand, the strategic advantage after the war rested overwhelmingly with the United States. Rapid demobilization cut the size of the swollen military establishment to 13 percent of the wartime peak, leaving the armed forces with about a million and a half men. Some historians have suggested that this reduction seriously weakened American power in the world in the face of Soviet military dominance. They overlook the fact that the Soviet Union, too, rapidly demobilized in 1945 and 1946, cutting its forces to 2.9 million men, or about 25 percent of wartime strength. Actually, the cuts did not appreciably affect the power of either nation; for the Red Army remained in Europe and the United States continued to be the world's strongest military power.

Even in time of war, this country has never measured its military strength primarily in terms of sheer manpower. After demobilization, the United States Navy was still in absolute control of the seas, operating out of bases all over the world. American air power was still capable of sweeping any opposing air force from the skies and of inflicting appalling damage on an enemy's cities or armies in the field.

Above all, the United States (with Britain) claimed an absolute monopoly on nuclear weapons until late in 1949; and thereafter, for many years, it enjoyed overwhelming superiority. Hiroshima and Nagasaki, moreover, stood as grim evidence to any potential enemy that the Americans were willing to use the new weapons under certain circumstances. Until the Soviet leaders reached a position of nuclear equality with the United States, and until their devastated nation made substantial progress in rebuilding itself, their ability to challenge American strategic supremacy anywhere in the world, in either military or diplomatic terms, was severely limited.

American-Soviet accord. Despite mounting tension after the war, the two great powers managed to agree on some important matters. After a year of haggling, they reached accord on peace treaties for Italy, Hungary, Rumania, Bulgaria, and Finland, all of which had been members of the Axis. It took them ten years to do the same for Austria, but their joint occupation of that country was a relatively smooth affair. When the new state of Israel arose in the Holy Land and proclaimed its independence, both powers rushed to recognize it.

Each power tried to use the new United Nations for its own purpose, to be sure, and the Soviets often made use of the veto power; yet they both supported the organization sufficiently to insure its survival through the first crucial years. All of this suggests that the cold war was not ordained by fate. Perhaps it might even have been avoided, or at least minimized, if the politicians on both sides had kept cool heads and made a greater effort to understand the pragmatic requirements of each other's countries.

2 The Grand Alliance Comes To An End

1. How did the attitude of the Soviet Union vary toward Eastern European nations? What accounted for that variance?

2. Where did the United States and the Soviet Union come into conflict over the political settlement of postwar Europe? Do you think there were any reasonable alternatives to minimize the friction between the United States and the Soviet Union and eliminate the "iron curtain"?

3. Do you think Americans were inconsistent in opposing Soviet intervention in Eastern Europe while the United States occupied both Italy and Japan and established terms for the political settlement there?

4. To what extent were the Nuremberg trials indicative of impartial justice, and to what extent were they the imposition of the victors' justice?

"Whoever occupies a territory also imposes on it his own social system," Stalin remarked bluntly in 1945. It was a truism which American policy-makers were reluctant to accept in Europe, even as they were turning the words into deeds in Japan. Throughout the war, official United States policy was to avoid any specific discussion of political questions relating to Germany and Eastern Europe. Roosevelt hoped to avoid splitting the Big Three by keeping these questions open for settlement in the friendly, more relaxed atmosphere of victory. At the same time, it is clear that the United States wanted to see a postwar Europe in which all nations would choose their own governments (within a framework of liberal democracy, however) and move toward some form of political and economic integration of the Continent. For this reason, American policy was avowedly hostile to spheres of influence in Europe.

Soviet relations with Eastern Europe. From the Soviet point of view, the war had already divided Europe into spheres of influence. Stalin acknowledged the British presence in Greece, for example, and refused to help the Communists in that country come to power. In dealing with the rest of Eastern Europe and Germany, however, he insisted that the requirements of Soviet security take precedence over all other matters.

For a brief period after the war, he was willing to accept non-Communist governments along his borders, provided always that they maintain friendly relations with Moscow and resist manipulation by the West. Thus, his behavior toward the various nations in the area varied greatly. He clamped an iron hand on Rumania even before the war ended, perhaps because the Rumanians had been too eager to join Hitler in making war on Russia. In Bulgaria, his men rigged an election to bring in a Communist government. At the same time, he did not foist communism on the people in the Soviet zone of Austria; and in Hungary, he accepted for a time a duly-elected non-Communist government.

Most significant, perhaps, was his attitude toward Finland. That nation had fought a bloody border war with Russia in 1939–40, then had gone on to ally itself with Germany. Yet, once the Finns pledged themselves to a foreign policy of strict neutrality and a generally friendly relationship

with Moscow, they were permitted to determine their own form of government. Poised on one of Russia's vulnerable borders, Finland was in danger several times during the worst years of the cold war. But Finland weathered the difficulties and still manages to maintain both its neutrality and its sovereignty.

Settlement of the "Polish question." But Poland was quite another matter, and it was there the Grand Alliance received the blow that, for all practical purposes, shattered it beyond repair. As already noted, the Yalta Conference failed to bridge the gap between Western and Soviet thinking on the future of Eastern Europe and especially Poland. At the time, Roosevelt and Churchill hoped to convince Stalin that Soviet security interests would be best served through collective action in the United Nations and in a continuation of the Grand Alliance. It was a moment when Western goodwill toward the Soviets was at a peak.

Tragically, according to later revelations by high Russian officials, it may also have been a time when Stalin was succumbing to insanity. Crafty, suspicious of everyone around him, willing to believe the worst in any situation, he displayed a paranoic obsession with the notion that the Soviet Union could rely only on itself for protection.

Ignoring the protests of his allies, Stalin annexed eastern Poland, claiming that the area was essential to Soviet security. To compensate the Poles, he demanded that Germany give up all of its territory east of the Oder and Neisse rivers (see map, page 661). It was a territorial "adjustment" of epic proportions, involving the lives of millions of Germans and Poles. Of its effect, the historian Hans W. Gatzke concludes:

> Together with the redrawing of the territorial frontiers, these population shifts have greatly simplified the ethnic picture in Eastern Europe. But they have done so at a price of much human suffering and great injustice.

The Oder-Neisse line separating Germany and Poland remains today as a blunt reminder that Soviet power in Eastern Europe, not American wishes, dictated the territorial settlement there.

The same can be said about Poland's government. At Yalta, the Big Three agreed vaguely on the principle of self-determination for all peoples

By the war's end, Soviet troops, like those below passing through Krakow, Poland, had overrun much of Eastern and Central Europe. The presence of the Red Army helped consolidate Soviet power in such countries as Czechoslovakia, where in 1948 a Communist regime was set up. Above, in Prague, Communist leaders view a party rally whose slogan reads "Solidarity to the working people of the world."

in Europe. Roosevelt and Churchill called for free elections in Poland, leading to democratic government there. What they failed to realize, or at least to acknowledge frankly, was that truly free elections in Poland would have brought in a government hostile to the Soviet Union. Stalin made a few gestures toward including elements friendly to the West in the Polish government, but there was never the slightest chance that he would permit a Western-oriented regime in that country. "Poland borders on the Soviet Union, which cannot be said about Great Britain or the U.S.A.," he observed pointedly. That fact, above all else, settled the "Polish question."

Arriving at political settlements. At no time, it should be noted, did the United States and Britain consult the Russians about the political settlement of Western Europe. Indeed, they even excluded the Soviets from membership in a commission which supervised the occupation of Italy, an action Stalin cited later as a precedent for barring American participation in the Rumanian settlement.

Why, then, did the West try to influence political developments in the East? The answer lies in the firm belief, especially among the Americans, that self-determination in all the nations of Europe would best promote peace and stability on the Continent. In Western Europe, democratic traditions and the presence of a strong Anglo-American influence were sufficient to insure relatively free elections and return to some form of representative government. (Even Stalin understood this situation, for he advised Communist parties in the West to seek power through regular parliamentary channels rather than through revolutionary activity.)

Eastern Europe, on the other hand, had at best only a weak tradition of democracy and was occupied by the Red Army or immediately subject to Soviet influence. Thus, after the war the United States and Britain confronted a situation that was plainly beyond their power to control. All they could do was to demand "free elections," in the hope of putting moral pressure on Stalin and thereby salvaging something for Western ideals. But as long as the Soviet Union distrusted the West, there was no hope for "free elections" in Eastern Europe. Moreover, the more the West

clamored for political influence in the area, the more the Soviets tightened their control.

It is probable that the Soviet leaders originally hoped to settle matters along their western borders quickly, then turn to the immense task of rebuilding their own country. If so, they reckoned without the effect their tactics in Poland would have in the United States. As Harry Hopkins warned Stalin in May 1945, Poland had become a symbol of the ability of the wartime allies to work out their problems.

Within days after taking office, President Truman told Soviet Foreign Minister Molotov to his face that Russians were guilty of "bad faith" in Poland. When Molotov protested Truman's blunt, undiplomatic language, he was advised to "Carry out your agreements and you won't get talked to like that." Events in Eastern Europe convinced Senator Vandenberg that the United States must switch to a "hard line" in dealing with Stalin. Clearly, by the summer of 1945, the misunderstandings between the Soviet Union and the West were hardening into a serious conflict of interest and interpretations.

The fate of Germany. Still, the Grand Alliance managed to stagger on for six months or so. In July, the Big Three met at Potsdam, near Berlin, to decide the fate of Germany. They agreed to divide the country into four zones of occupation (France joining them as an occupying power) and to establish an Allied Control Council as an instrument for joint action. Germany was to be demilitarized, deindustrialized, decentralized, denazified, and democratized (the "five D's"). For a brief moment, it appeared that the highly explosive issue of Germany's future in Europe would be defused and settled peaceably.

But the moment was a fleeting one. Even in defeat, Germany—with its highly skilled labor force and huge industrial capacity—was the great prize of the war. Whoever controlled Germany controlled the balance of power in Europe. Realistically, neither the Soviets nor the Americans could have resisted the temptation to claim it.

After toying briefly with the odd notion that the country could be reduced to a cluster of weak, agricultural states, the Americans decided that a strong, democratized Germany was essential to the political and economic health of Europe. In

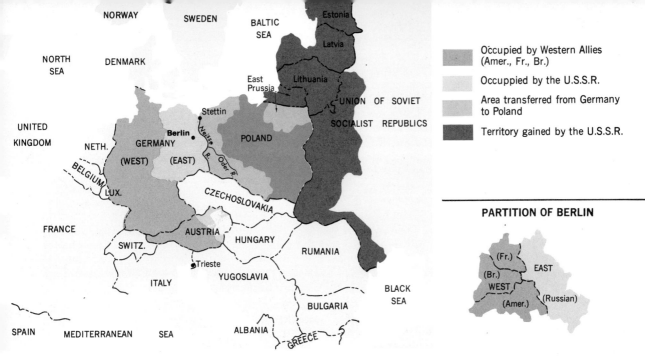

NORWAY   SWEDEN   BALTIC
SEA
NORTH
SEA   DENMARK
UNITED
KINGDOM   NETH.

Legend:

- Occupied by Western Allies (Amer., Fr., Br.)
- Occupied by the U.S.S.R.
- Area transferred from Germany to Poland
- Territory gained by the U.S.S.R.

PARTITION OF BERLIN

(Fr.) (Br.) WEST (Amer.) EAST (Russian)

EUROPE AFTER WORLD WAR II

the Soviet view, only a dismembered, economically crippled Germany—preferably controlled by Communists or elements friendly to Moscow—could be counted on not to threaten the peace and security of Eastern Europe in the future. The two views were clearly incompatible, and the great powers were soon at loggerheads over the issue.

Occupation and denazification. Joint occupation was a mirage from the start. Each occupying power decided for itself how to implement the "five D's" within its own zone. Although France had not participated in the wartime summit conferences and was not bound by their agreements, it exercised equal authority with the Big Three in the occupation. Even more than the Russians, the French wrecked every attempt at working out a joint policy for Germany in the early postwar years because of their deep fears of a resurgence of their old enemy.

The only display of unity came in the matter of denazification. In November 1945, a four-power military tribunal convened at Nuremberg to try the surviving Nazi leaders for "war crimes." The trials revealed the horrors of the Nazi tyranny in grisly detail. Moreover, they proceeded

on the assumption that a citizen has an ultimate *moral* responsibility not to obey orders which are clearly immoral. But, as historian Arthur S. Link observes, they also violated every tenet of Anglo-American justice and established the dubious principle that the victors, after a war, may "legally" try and execute the leaders of the defeated foe.

Determined to make Germany pay heavily for the war, the Russians stripped their zone of all industry and asked the other powers for a large share of the resources in their zones. For a time, the British and Americans agreed, although always reluctantly. As it became clear that joint occupation would not succeed, they stopped the practice and began building up German economic strength.

On the question of Germany's political future, again disagreement ran deep. The Western powers were against any permanent division of the country, hoping eventually to unite all the zones and create a democratic republic. Their goal was completely at odds with the Soviet intent to prevent unification in order to insure German weakness. Ironically, the cold war itself settled the whole matter by producing a *de facto* partition of Germany which remains in effect today.

In establishing their zones of occupation (see map, page 661), the powers chopped Berlin into four sectors and made it the nominal center of their joint control. But the former German capital lay deep within the Soviet zone, and the Western powers neglected to secure guaranteed right of access to the city. In time, Berlin became the focal point of the cold war, producing several major international crises. The Western presence in the city was, literally, a thorn in the Soviet Union's side, constantly reminding the Kremlin that American military and political power was in Europe to stay.

The Baruch Plan. Unable to agree on a political settlement in Europe, the two great powers clashed as well on the vital question of how to control newly discovered atomic energy. In the Baruch Plan, named after its sponsor, financier Bernard Baruch, the United States offered to share its atomic know-how with the entire world, provided an international control agency be established and empowered to carry out periodic inspections in all countries. Predictably, Moscow scorned the proposal as simply an American scheme to pry into the Soviet Union's internal affairs and prevent it from developing its own nuclear arsenal.

An iron curtain descends. As the Soviet Union's suspicion of the West increased, its control over the nations in Eastern Europe tightened. In February 1946, Stalin signaled the Soviet Union's intention to rely upon its own economic and ideological resources henceforth, shunning any formal cooperation with the capitalist nations. Several weeks later, on March 5, Winston Churchill proclaimed the existence of a divided Europe.

Speaking at Fulton, Missouri, with the evident approval of President Truman, Churchill declared that "From Stettin in the Baltic to Trieste in the Adriatic, an iron curtain has descended across the continent." Clearly, the Grand Alliance had become a thing of the past, while relations between the United States and the Soviet Union entered an entirely new phase. Events elsewhere in the world, moreover, helped to confirm the view that a cold war had indeed broken out between the two great powers.

3 Troubles In Asia Bring An End To An Illusion

1. What were the consequences of American occupation of Japan following the war?

2. How did United States policy toward Japan compare to its policy toward China and the countries of Southeast Asia?

3. Why did China fall to the forces of Mao Tse-tung? What errors did the United States make in relationship to the Kuomintang? What should the United States have done differently?

4. To what extent was Stalin influential in the Communist takeover of China?

In the Far East, the United States encountered the full force of revolutionary nationalism after the war. Roosevelt's dream of raising China to the status of a great world power became a nightmare, as civil conflict in that huge country quickly revealed the strength of Mao Tse-tung's Communists. Elsewhere, American foreign policy was caught in a dilemma—whether to back nationalist movements directed at overthrowing European rule throughout Asia, or to stand by its allies—Britain, France, and the Netherlands—as they sought to reassert their colonial authority. Only in Japan did the United States have an entirely free hand in dealing with postwar conditions.

American occupation of Japan. Just as the Pacific war had been an American war, the occupation of Japan became an American occupation. Japan was not divided into zones of occupation, nor were America's allies permitted more than an advisory voice in making the decisions which determined Japan's future. It was not only the Soviets who were shut out of the picture; even such a staunch wartime friend as Australia had little or no say in the occupation. Japan was to be reconstructed according to American dictates.

In his capacity as Supreme Commander for the Allied Powers (SCAP), General Douglas Mac-

THE FAR EAST AND SOUTHEAST ASIA, 1957

Arthur ruled Japan during the years of occupation. Theoretically, he was responsible to an eleven-nation Far Eastern Commission and to a four-power (United States, Britain, USSR, and China) Allied Council. In practice, he and a small, intimate group of advisers governed according to their own and the State Department's decisions. Japan was stripped of its empire and purged of militarism. Former Premier Tojo and other high-ranking wartime leaders were executed for "war crimes," after trials similar to those at Nuremberg.

An extensive program of agrarian reform broke up the old feudal holdings so successfully that by 1952, some 90 percent of the arable land was in the hands of former tenant farmers. Renouncing his historic claim to divine birth and rule, Emperor Hirohito told the nation that his power derived from "the sovereign will of the people." With astonishing submissiveness, the Japanese people accepted the new order imposed by the Americans. In 1946, a new constitution proclaimed Japan a democracy, forbade the country to have an army or navy, and even outlawed war as an instrument of Japanese policy.

At the start of the occupation, the American aim was to reduce Japan to second-rate status in Asia, well behind China. But as China slipped into the hands of the Communists, Washington decided to build up Japan as an antirevolutionary bastion in Asia. Economic recovery was slow until the Korean War (beginning in June 1950) turned the island nation into a bustling American military base. From that point on, Japan enjoyed a phenomenal economic growth.

Over the protests of the Soviet Union and with only the reluctant support of the other Pacific nations, the United States made formal peace with Japan in 1951. The treaty (signed at San Francisco on September 8) was a generous document, restoring full sovereignty to the former enemy nation. To bolster Japan's position in Asia, moreover, the United States entered into a mutual-security arrangement with it. On most counts, American policy in Japan was generally enlightened and successful.

American diplomacy in Asia. Elsewhere in Asia, Yankee diplomacy ran an obstacle course. In Korea, Soviet troops occupied the northern half of the country, while American forces took control of the south. As in the case of Germany, the division was a "temporary" one; but it quickly took on the look of permanence. Fulfilling an old promise to the Filipino people, the United States on July 4, 1946, granted independence to the Republic of the Philippines. Independence was not as complete as many Filipino nationalists wanted, however, as the Americans retained military bases throughout the islands and continued to control much of the Philippine economy. Almost at once, revolutionary ferment beset the new nation, most of it directed by a leftist group called the Hukbalahap or "Huks."

Southeast of the Philippines, the sprawling new nation of Indonesia painfully emerged in the postwar period. Successor to the Dutch empire in the East Indies, Indonesia contained 100 million people settled over 18,000 islands. For many years, the nation was synonymous with its brilliant but erratic leader, Achmed Sukarno.

Once the heart of the white man's empires in the Orient, Southeast Asia after 1945 became the arena in which old-fashioned colonialism met its match in revolutionary nationalism. Before 1945, the only independent nation in the area was Thailand. As the war came to a close, the demand for independence swept through Burma, the Malay Peninsula, and Indochina. Farther to the west, the great subcontinent of India rumbled with discontent at alien rule.

The struggle put United States foreign policy to a severe test. Although they were basically sympathetic to the anticolonial movement, American policy-makers disliked the radical economic and political orientation of many of its spokesmen. Moreover, as the United States and the Soviet Union moved into a major confrontation in Europe, Washington became reluctant to jeopardize its relations with London and Paris by siding with anti-British and anti-French elements in Asia. The unfortunate result was that the United States identified itself increasingly with European colonialism, thereby losing a great opportunity to influence the nationalist movements in the Far East.

Faced with a choice between a series of costly colonial wars they could not afford, or giving way to the nationalists as gracefully as possible, the British took the latter course. In 1947 and 1948,

they gave up the struggle to hold on to their Empire and released India, Ceylon, and Burma. India's large Muslim minority refused to be ruled by the Hindu majority and split off to form Pakistan. Malaya remained under Britain's wing until 1957, although a Communist-led insurgency wracked the colony for many years. The British Far East Empire did not die without a few loud whimpers, to be sure, but it expired with a minimum of embarrassment for the United States.

French defeat in Vietnam. The same was not true of the French empire. As soon as Japanese troops moved out of Indochina, France stepped in to reassert control over the rich colony. At once France was plunged into a drawn-out, bloody fight with the nationalists. During World War II, Ho Chi Minh had organized the League for the Independence of Vietnam (better known as the Vietminh) in which Communists played a leading part. In 1945, he proclaimed a provisional Republic of Vietnam and asked the great powers for recognition. Significantly, neither the United States nor the Soviet Union responded favorably. Washington did not want to risk losing France's support in Europe, while Moscow distrusted Ho's particular brand of national Communism.

The First Vietnam War (1946–1954) was an effort by France, backed by American dollars and arms, to crush the Vietminh. It was a futile undertaking, for the Vietminh gained steadily. After the French suffered a disastrous defeat at Dien Bien Phu in May 1954, they agreed to an armistice. At the Geneva Conference in July, the great powers (including Red China) and the belligerents agreed to separate the old French Indochina into three independent states—Cambodia, Laos, and Vietnam. Until it could be unified through free elections, Vietnam was temporarily divided into two provisional states, a pro-Communist north and a pro-French south. For the United States, unhappily, the Vietnam problem was far from settled.

The "loss" of China. By far the most significant events in Asia after the war against Japan occurred in China. Throughout the war, the United States had anticipated China's emergence as the dominant power in East Asia, firmly aligned with Washington. Within four years after the defeat of Japan, China had become Communist, and

With the defeat of the French forces at Dien Bien Phu, the French colonial empire in Southeast Asia was lost. On May 5, 1954, surrounded and outnumbered by the Vietminh, the embattled French troops were finally overcome. At right, two soldiers on the parade field at Dien Bien Phu have just taken down the French tricolor, the sign of final surrender. Even as France was fighting to maintain its empire, China became a Communist nation. On October 1, 1949, Mao-Tse-tung proclaimed the People's Republic of China. Below, Mao stands in the midst of several party dignitaries at the proclamation celebration in Peking.

American illusions had been shattered. Almost as though it had been theirs to dispose of, many Americans spoke of the "loss" of China; and the issue stirred up a furious storm in American domestic politics (Chapter 27). Indeed, the political repercussions crippled subsequent efforts by the diplomatists to forge a new foreign policy toward China that would accept the reality of the Communist revolution.

China fell to Mao Tse-tung's forces for several reasons. Long years of war against the Japanese had badly weakened the political and economic structure of China's government and drained away the spirit of the Kuomintang. Despite Chiang Kai-shek's good intentions, his regime had become increasingly corrupt, inefficient, and authoritarian. He and his warlords resisted every effort by American advisers to institute reforms. Finally, the Communists captured the imagination of millions of Chinese with their promises of reform. Their troops had such an advantage in morale and internal discipline that Chiang's forces proved hardly a match for them once they met in a military showdown.

Under the circumstances, there was little the United States could do to salvage the situation. More than $2 billion in American aid went to China after the war in an effort to bolster the faltering Nationalist cause. Perhaps a massive United States military effort could have saved the day for Chiang; but public opinion would hardly have supported a costly war on the Asian mainland so soon after V-J Day.

Instead, Truman put his faith in diplomacy. He sent General George C. Marshall to China with instructions to bring the two factions together, hopefully in a coalition government. The Marshall mission failed, and in August 1949, the United States cut off aid to Chiang, in effect giving him up as a hopeless cause. On October 1, the People's Republic of China was proclaimed at Peking. Chiang and the remnants of his Nationalist government fled to the island of Formosa. In mainland China, Mao Tse-tung reigned supreme, and American influence came to an abrupt end.

Why China went Communist. Most Americans assumed almost automatically in 1949 that the Soviet Union was responsible for the Red

THE CHINA QUESTION

The question of why China fell to communism continues to be debated. Historian Anthony Kubeck believes it was Soviet pressure and lack of American aid:

"In its campaign to conquer China, the Soviet Union took steps to cover up the Chinese Communists' direct subordination to Moscow. The International Communists and their fellow travelers no longer referred to the Chinese Communists in their propaganda as an ordinary Communist Party or an instrument of Soviet Russia, but as 'a democratic party' of Chinese farmers and 'agrarian reformers.' The strategy, both of Moscow and the Chinese Communists, was to launch political attacks against the Nationalist Government in order to destroy its effectiveness in the eyes of the world. . . .

"Both the Chinese people and their leaders had the will to resist the Communists, but what we gave them in the form of aid and moral support was the difference between a hopeless and effective resistance. What amount we did give them in terms of actual aid was 'too little and too late' to be of any real use. . . .

"Most important of all was the refusal to let our military mission in China give real advice and training to the Chinese armed forces at all levels. . . . And, still worse, the refusal to give one word of moral support and encouragement during those long, dreary years did much to bring about the defeat of the Nationalist Government. . . .

"The result—sovietization of China and Manchuria—could be the only logical outcome of postwar United States policy toward China. The utter consistency of our policy in serving Soviet ends leaves no conclusion other than that pro-Communist elements in our government and press 'planned it that way.' But top American officials who sought to buy Soviet cooperation at any price must bear the final responsibility."

victory in China. Indeed, some high-ranking diplomats at Washington were so caught up in the emotional fever of the cold war that they saw events in China simply as another example of Soviet aggression. According to Assistant Secretary of State for Far Eastern Affairs Dean Rusk, the new regime at Peking was not Chinese at all; rather it was a Soviet rule, conceived in Moscow and imposed upon the unwilling Chinese people by Stalin!

Rusk and others vastly oversimplified a complex chain of events and failed to make the essential historical distinctions between the Russian Revolution and the Chinese revolution. China became a Communist country because of conditions inside China, not because the Soviet dictator willed it.

When Soviet occupation troops evacuated Manchuria, in keeping with an agreement Stalin made with Chiang, they left behind a large number of Japanese small arms which Mao's troops grabbed. But that was the only material "aid" they gave Mao, for they carted off all the heavy weapons and industrial facilities for themselves. Indeed, in accordance with the Yalta Agreements, Stalin allied himself with Chiang in August 1945, and openly discouraged Mao's revolutionary efforts. It was precisely because Mao was *not* the servant of Moscow that Stalin was less than enthusiastic about the turnover in government in China, even though, doubtless, Stalin hoped to see communism prevail in that nation some day.

As both Moscow and Washington soon learned, each in its own way, the new mainland leaders were Chinese to the core. Immediately, radicals everywhere had a new revolutionary example to emulate; and the Chinese soon joined the United States and the Soviet Union in a three-way competition to exercise leadership in the world's underdeveloped nations and colonial areas.

Coming at a time when the cold war was heating up in Europe, the Chinese revolution could not help but worsen relations between the United States and the Soviet Union. To the American people, the "loss" of China to communism was a sign that the cold war had become a new global conflict.

4 Cold War Intensifies In The West

1. What were the similarities and what were the differences between the Truman Doctrine and the Marshall Plan? How would you evaluate the effectiveness of each plan?

2. What evidence is there of American idealism and American pragmatism in foreign policy after World War II?

3. Do you think the American instigation and participation in the North Atlantic Treaty Organization was a wise move?

4. How did the United States demonstrate a "hard line" against the potential spread of communism?

By the end of 1946, most Americans seemed to have concluded that peaceful cooperation with the Soviets was no longer possible. Truman had already indicated that he was "tired of babying the Soviets," and Churchill's "iron curtain" had become a catch phrase for referring to relations between East and West. In September, Secretary of State James Byrnes clearly implied that the United States was preparing to solve the German problem, with or without Soviet cooperation. When former Vice President Wallace spoke out in criticism of the administration's "hard line" policy toward the Soviet Union, he was fired from his position as secretary of commerce. In Turkey, Stalin attempted to reassert Russia's historic claims to joint control of the Dardanelles, the straits connecting the Mediterranean with the Black Sea. He met with no success, but the United States and Britain feared that the weak Turkish government might collapse under the pressure.

The Truman Doctrine. In Greece an even more serious situation developed in 1946–47. In reestablishing their old sphere of influence there, the British imposed a reactionary monarchy on the country and thereby provoked a bitter civil war. Led by Greek Communists and supplied by the Red governments of Yugoslavia and Bulgaria, nationalist elements waged a fierce guerrilla campaign in northern Greece, seriously jeopardizing the British position.

Unable to stand the financial drain of the effort, Britain informed the United States of its intention to withdraw from Greece by April 1, 1947. Without hesitation, Truman decided that this country must take over from the British as protector of the eastern Mediterranean. He reasoned that if the Communists won Greece, Turkey would be at the mercy of the Soviet Union. The balance of power in the Middle East, as well as in Europe, would be radically altered.

Aware that Congress would balk at the cost of a major military and economic effort in Greece, Truman relied on Senator Arthur Vandenberg to line up support for the venture. Vandenberg told him, "Mr. President, if that's what you want, there's only one way to get it. That is to make a personal appearance before Congress and scare hell out of the country." Truman did just that. On March 12, 1947, he enunciated the Truman Doctrine, the most far-reaching statement of American foreign policy since the promulgation of the Open Door in 1899.

To prevent Greece and Turkey from slipping into Stalin's bloc, Truman proposed a program of major economic and military assistance to the two countries. His objective was a concrete, attainable one, fully in keeping with Western Europe's historic effort to check Russian influence in the Mediterranean. American aid did the job it was designed to do in Greece and Turkey, and it was helped along when early in 1948 Tito broke his ties with Moscow and terminated Yugoslav support to the Greek rebels. In this respect, the Truman Doctrine was a highly successful policy.

But the Presidential statement also launched the United States on a holy crusade against revolution everywhere in the world. Henceforth, in Truman's words, it would be American policy "to support free peoples who are resisting attempted subjugation by armed minorities or by outside pressures." In seeking what historian Hans Morganthau has called "a world-embracing moral principle," Truman made no distinction between genuine military threats to American interests and spontaneous internal revolutions arising from local conditions.

Revolution was to be equated with Soviet armed aggression. It had to be checked, even suppressed, wherever it appeared, especially in the Third World—the underdeveloped areas in which emerging nationalism was usually tied to radical economic and social theories. In this respect, the Truman Doctrine was a pit of quicksand, drawing the United States ever deeper into situations over which American leaders had little or no real control.

The Truman Doctrine also reflected the belief in Washington that the One World of the war years had given way to two hostile and competing worlds. In the USSR the same assumption underlay the so-called "Zhdanov Doctrine," (proclaimed by Andrei Zhdanov of the Politburo) which divided the world into two irreconcilable camps, one socialist, one capitalist. "Two worlds" or "two camps"—the effect of the Truman and Zhdanov statements was to transform the cold war into a permanent, global institution.

Policy of containment. Aid to Greece and Turkey was the first practical application of George F. Kennan's theory of containment. As a member of the State Department policy-planning staff, Kennan reasoned that Soviet expansion could be "contained," or checked, if deterrent pressure was applied judiciously at selected points where it threatened to erupt. He considered containment an expedient only, to be used in specific situations where the odds were strongly in its favor, as in Europe. Thus, he welcomed its use in Greece. But he was appalled when the Truman administration embraced containment as the whole of American foreign policy.

For his part, Truman was only responding to the deep-rooted urge among Americans to seek permanent, universal solutions to complex problems. As Vandenberg remarked at the time: "We are at odds with communism on many fronts. We must have a total policy." Interpreting containment in its literal sense, the United States set out (over Kennan's vigorous protest) to ring the USSR with military bases. The move convinced Soviet leaders that the capitalist "camp" was intent upon encircling the socialist "camp," then subjecting the Soviet system to such intense pressure that it would collapse from within.

The Marshall Plan. A more positive side of American diplomacy was the Marshall Plan. On June 5, 1947, Secretary of State Marshall outlined a sweeping plan of economic assistance to the faltering countries of Europe. "Our policy is not directed against any country or doctrine," he explained, "but against hunger, poverty, desperation and chaos." The American aim was to revive Europe's economies, "so as to permit the emergence of political and social conditions in which free institutions can exist."

The Marshall Plan was a superb blend of ideals and self-interest in diplomacy. On the one hand, it reflected a humanitarian concern for people who desperately needed help, and it revived Western Europe's faith in liberal democracy. On the other hand, it bolstered this country's sagging postwar economy, while opening Europe to increased exploitation by American business. A prosperous Europe would be a democratic Europe, strong enough to resist subversion from within and aggression from without.

Thus, despite Marshall's disclaimer, the plan was a very effective weapon in the cold war. To be sure, the Soviet bloc was invited to participate in the Marshall Plan, and the Russians actually attended the first planning conference. But the "Open-Door" conditions under which the United States proposed to dispense its aid insured that the Soviet leaders would reject the offer and force the Eastern European nations to do the same.

For a time, Truman had difficulty persuading Congress to appropriate the huge sums needed for the Marshall Plan. Then, in February 1948, the powerful Communist party in Czechoslovakia seized control of that country and took it behind the "iron curtain." The effect in Washington was to dispel any lingering doubts that Western Europe was in danger of going the way of the Czechs. Within weeks, the Marshall Plan was in full operation.

Economic recovery in Europe. Four years of careful planning and international cooperation produced the desired results. Western Europe reconstructed itself chiefly with its own resources; but $13 billion in American aid speeded up the process and helped to produce spectacular results. ERP (the European Recovery Program, as the Marshall Plan was called in operation) raised living standards in some nations above prewar levels. It eliminated the danger of Czech-type coups in Italy and France. It established an important precedent for real economic and political integration in Europe. It also gave the United

States, as one cold war historian notes, "a position of political and economic primacy in Western Europe that remained until the late 1950s and was not seriously challenged until the 1960s."

Predictably, too, ERP provoked a vigorous Russian response. To coordinate the activities of Europe's Communist parties against "American imperialism," Moscow organized the Cominform, or Communist Information Bureau. Economic recovery and development in Eastern Europe was spurred by a Soviet counterpart to ERP, the Molotov Plan. Recovery was a slow and painful ordeal in the East; but, in the end, it produced material results almost as striking as those in the Marshall Plan countries. Unfortunately, recovery did little to benefit the people of Eastern Europe, who continued to live drab, difficult lives, with no political freedom.

The creation of two Germanies. West Germany not only enjoyed a *Wirtschaftswunder* (economic miracle), but also underwent a significant political transformation. In December 1946, the Americans and British (joined later by the French) merged their zones and undertook to revive the German economy. When they issued a new currency for their zones and circulated it in Berlin as well, they met fierce resistance from the Soviets, who feared that the new money would upset economic conditions in their zone.

In June 1948, the Soviets threw a blockade around Berlin, cutting the city off from all land access to the West. It was a determined effort to force the Western Allies out of Berlin, and it almost worked. The American response was to mount an airlift, flying the necessities of life into the city's beleaguered Western sectors. The airlift was a heroic gesture. But it was not the decisive factor in persuading Stalin, after nearly a year, to lift the blockade. Rather, the Soviet leader backed down as he began to realize that the United States would actually go to war, even nuclear war (Truman had sent atomic bombers to England), to maintain its position in Germany. For Stalin, the stakes in Berlin were high, but not *that* high. Thus, America's strategic advantages in the early years of the cold war—air power and the atomic monopoly—decided the issue in the Berlin crisis.

After the blockade, both sides took the steps which formally created two Germanies. Spon-

When the Russians blockaded Berlin, cutting the city off from all land access to the West, President Truman responded by ordering an immediate Allied airlift of supplies to the West Berliners (right). During the eleven months of the airlift, British and American planes flew more than 277,000 flights and brought in nearly 2,500,000 tons of food, in what the pilots called "Operation Vittles." Elsewhere, American aid in the form of the Marshall Plan was stimulating economic recovery in the non-Communist nations of Western and Southern Europe. Below, sacks of American food supplies, clearly marked with the Stars and Stripes, are unloaded in Athens for distribution throughout Greece.

sored chiefly by the Americans, the Federal Republic of Germany emerged in the West with a liberal democratic government. To the East, the Soviet authorities produced the German Democratic Republic, a totalitarian regime controlled by German Communists. As Stalin had predicted in 1945, each occupying power had imposed its own social system on the territory under its control.

A tough new foreign policy. In 1949–50, the Truman administration shifted from an economic offensive to a frank emphasis upon military power. As the Soviet Union exploded its first atom bomb in September 1949, Truman moved to strengthen the United States' tactical position everywhere, but especially in Europe. Accepting the two-world thesis and rejecting the possibility of "meaningful" negotiations with the Soviet Union, Washington assumed that an indefinite period of tension and danger lay ahead. Truman proposed massive expenditures for arms, estimating that as much as 20 percent of gross national product could be diverted to military spending.

The "new look" in foreign policy reflected the influence of Truman's new secretary of state, Dean Acheson. One of the strongest-willed men ever to head the State Department, Acheson was brilliant, arrogant, and conservative to the core. He thought of himself always as a tough-minded realist and dismissed those who disagreed with him as muddleheaded dreamers. One of the ironies of the cold war is that Acheson's political foes branded him an "appeaser" and charged him with being "soft on Communism." In fact, he was one of the toughest "Cold Warriors" in the West (Chapter 27).

Setting up NATO. Truman's new approach brought into existence the North Atlantic Treaty Organization (NATO). After heeding for 150 years George Washington's warning against "entangling alliances," the United States signed the North Atlantic Treaty on March 15, 1949. Binding this country together with Canada, Iceland, and the nations of Western Europe in a mutual defense system, the pact stipulated that a military attack on one signatory would be construed as an attack on all. It led naturally to the creation of a NATO defense force, to which all the signa-

tory nations contributed men and materiel. The Soviet Union immediately followed suit with the Warsaw Pact, setting up a comparable military system in Eastern Europe.

The logic of NATO required the rearming of West Germany. Against strenuous objections from the French and other Europeans, all of whom had good reason to fear any German in uniform, Acheson pressed relentlessly to bring the Federal Republic into NATO and to make German manpower the core of the NATO army. The goal was attained in 1955, after Acheson had left office. For good or for ill, however, the remilitarization of Germany was his personal triumph.

As George Kennan and others have observed, NATO was a military response to a nonexistent or grossly exaggerated threat. Russia had already been contained; the West had built up powerful economic and political defenses against Communism; and an acceptable balance existed on the Continent between two clearly defined spheres of influence. NATO was a system suited to the world of 1947, not the fast-changing world of the mid-1950's in which it functioned. Even as it got under way, ironically, some of its members began to question its usefulness.

5 Americans Go To War In Korea

1. To what extent was the outbreak of the Korean War a result of regional circumstances, and to what extent was it a result of international pressures between Communist countries and democratic countries?

2. What were the advantages and disadvantages of bombing Chinese air fields north of the Yalu River in support of United Nations forces? Do you think the air fields should have been bombed?

3. What were the lessons of the Korean War for American military and diplomatic experts?

Even with its enormous power, the United States had to establish certain defense priorities in the global cold war. Committed first to the well-being of Europe, the Truman administration sought to streamline its tactical position elsewhere in the world, particularly in the Far East. Momentarily recognizing that nationalism in Asia might be as powerful a force as Communism, Acheson even seemed willing to recognize the revolutionary government in China.

As a step in adjusting the American position in Asia, Acheson in January 1950, defined a new "defense perimeter" extending from the Aleutians in the north, down through Japan and the Ryukus to the Philippines in the south (see map, page 663). Although he implied that Korea's security would be a matter of concern to the United States, his remarks suggested that this country would not directly defend the peninsula. But Korea's proximity to Japan, the American military stronghold in Asia, made it highly unlikely that Washington would turn the other cheek if the entire peninsula seemed in danger of falling into hostile hands.

A divided Korea. In Korea itself, a tense situation had developed by 1950. Both the Soviet Union and the United States had stationed occupation forces in Korea following the war. When they withdrew them, they left behind two Koreas, separated by the 38th parallel and at deadly odds with each other. All efforts by the United Nations to reunite the two Koreas had failed; and as early as September 1949, observers on the scene were warning of imminent civil conflict.

To the north of the line, the People's Republic controlled the country's industrial resources and boasted a large, Soviet-trained and equipped army. Kim Il Sung's Communist government had shrewdly merged revolution with nationalism, initiating a sweeping program of agrarian land reform that won it many admirers on both sides of the 38th parallel. The Republic of Korea, to the south, lagged far behind in nationalist development. Its American-sponsored government was a conservative oligarchy headed by Syngman Rhee, an aged, quarrelsome authoritarian, who, before taking power in 1948, had lived in exile since the turn of the century. Ignoring the country's pressing domestic needs, Rhee spent most of his time and energy badgering the Americans

to support him in a personal crusade to reunify Korea. Fearing his aggressiveness, the United States deliberately kept his army weak so that he would not be tempted to attack the north.

Aggression by North Korea. In both Koreas, the urge for reunification was overpowering, however, and each side had repeatedly threatened to strike at the other. On June 25, 1950, the North Koreans acted, sending their army across the 38th parallel and routing Rhee's ragged forces. Just why Kim chose to attack at that particular moment is still something of a mystery. The military odds were heavily in his favor, to be sure, and he expected to win a quick, easy victory. And the political advantages were all on his side, too; that is, given the disparity in political vigor between the two sides, he had good reason to believe that the north would peaceably absorb the south in the relatively near future. Logic dictated that Kim bide his time; but then, logic seldom has much to do with the decisions of men to make war.

The immediate assumption in Washington was that the attack was a cold war offensive, set in motion at Moscow's direct orders. Indeed, Truman and Acheson concluded that Communism was on the move throughout Asia. One of the President's first moves, after he received news of the invasion, was to send the Seventh Fleet to the Formosa Straits off the southern coast of China, apparently because he feared a Communist attack on Chiang's retreat. He also stepped up American military aid to the French for their fight against the Vietminh in Indochina.

Communist China had repeatedly warned that it intended to drive Chiang from Formosa, and Mao's propaganda mill was always blustering about American "imperialism." But the Communists were too busy in 1950 consolidating their control over the mainland to engage in any reckless acts beyond their immediate borders. At the same time, they were acutely sensitive to political and military developments which might threaten those borders.

As for the Russians, they had little to gain and a good deal to lose by trying for a military solution to the Korean problem in 1950. Any aggressive move on their part was sure to arouse memories of Czechoslovakia throughout the West and to increase tensions in Europe. Inevitably, it would provoke the West into a new arms build-up, thereby tightening the encirclement of the Soviet Union which they feared so greatly. At the time of the attack, moreover, the Russians were boycotting the Security Council in protest against the exclusion of Communist China from the United Nations. Considering their concern with propaganda, it was at least questionable that they would instigate an act of raw aggression at a moment when they had no access to the world's primary forum of public opinion.

Stalin armed the North Koreans, doubtless expecting that they would one day assume control of the entire peninsula. But the probability is strong that the Koreans acted on their own initiative in 1950, catching the Soviets as well as the West by surprise (much of the world assumed that Rhee had invaded the north, when news of the attack first got out). As one authority suggested at the time, "Stalin may have loaded the gun, but it was Kim Il Sung who seized upon it and pulled the trigger!" Certainly, enough pressure had built up in Korea itself to provoke a war without any prodding from outside.

Truman responds. In any case, the American response was prompt and decisive. Recognizing the threat to Japan, Truman put United States forces in the field to aid the South Koreans. Taking full advantage of the Soviet Union's absence from the Security Council, he persuaded the council to condemn North Korea as an aggressor and to authorize a "police action" to "restore peace . . . and to restore the border." It was a landmark decision for the UN and a great diplomatic victory for the United States. Washington's unilateral initial action in Korea now became an act of "collective security." And even though the Korean War was always primarily an American operation, technically the United Nations fielded an international army charged with the duty to repel aggression.

Under General MacArthur's command, the UN forces checked the North Korean advance just in time to avoid disaster. Within a matter of weeks, they dealt the invaders a series of crushing blows that completely turned the tide in Korea. By the end of September, the battered remnants of the North Korean army had been thrown back across the 38th parallel. MacArthur had brilliantly fulfilled his assignment to repel aggression and re-

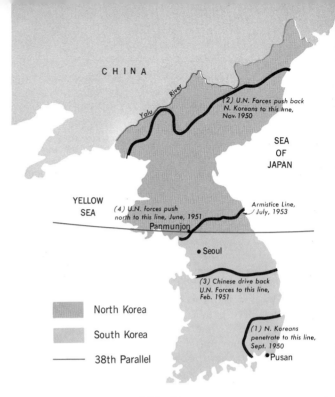

THE KOREAN WAR, 1950–1953

store the border. North Korea's attempt to solve a political problem by military means had led her to disaster.

Escalation and stalemate. At this point, the entire nature of the Korean "police action" changed. Instead of holding at the 38th parallel and restoring the *status quo ante bellum* (conditions as they existed before the war), the United States escalated its war aims. Repelling the aggressor was not enough; the Korean problem had to be "solved" permanently. Thus, the United Nations—at the behest of Washington—tried to do what the North Koreans had just failed to do: unify Korea by force. MacArthur was authorized to cross the parallel, mop up what was left of the enemy army, and advance to the Yalu River, Korea's border with China.

The decision was made in the face of strong evidence that the Chinese would enter the war rather than see North Korea occupied by American troops. Just as the North Korean sweep into the south had almost automatically brought the United States into the conflict, so the UN push to the Yalu and the border between Korea and

China triggered a predictable Chinese response. Oddly enough, neither MacArthur nor his superiors in Washington took the threat of Chinese intervention seriously. On November 24, 1950, the General assured Truman that his imminent "end the war" offensive would have American boys home by Christmas. The President took him at his word.

Two days later, the Chinese attacked in overwhelming numbers, sending the UN force reeling in retreat. American soldiers and marines fought gallantly to hold their ground, taking terrible losses. In the end, however, MacArthur's campaign in North Korea crumbled into one of the worst defeats in American military history. Within three weeks, the Chinese were south of the 38th parallel, ready to try their hand at unifying the country by force. They had no better luck than the North Koreans or the Americans before them. Rallying his forces, MacArthur slowly drove the enemy back to the parallel. The Korean War settled into a stalemate.

Truce talks, which began in July 1951, dragged on for two years. The fighting during that time was bloody and destructive, costing the Chinese a huge toll in human life and laying waste to all of North Korea. After thirty-seven months of fighting, the two sides signed an armistice on July 27, 1953. More than 54,000 Americans died in the Korean War and the cost to the taxpayers was over $22 billion. And the war ended where it began—at the 38th parallel.

Criticism of the war. The Korean War produced a political crisis in the United States, especially as it became a contest to see which side could most wear down the other. Accustomed to "winning" their wars, the American people found it hard to swallow the defeat at the Yalu and the ensuing stalemate. Truman was urged to carry the war to the Chinese—to bomb their cities and factories, even to use nuclear weapons against them. His more extreme critics wanted a showdown with the Russians, who were supposedly masterminding the Chinese effort in Korea.

The critics at home had a powerful ally in the field—General MacArthur himself. Yalu was a terrible blow to his pride and reputation; understandably, he wanted to avenge the defeat with an all-out onslaught against his enemy. Washington's restrictions on his movements caused

A DEFENSE OF MACARTHUR

President Truman's removal of MacArthur from command generated a storm of controversy. Many people shared MacArthur's view of the situation in the Far East and defended his actions. One who backed MacArthur was Major General Courtney Whitney, who served with the general in Korea:

"Final judgment upon Korean war decisions, although still awaiting events now in the making, has steadily crystallized toward an overwhelming conviction that MacArthur was right and Truman wrong. MacArthur's viewpoint was dictated by his professional judgment, well tested by historic lessons across the panorama of time; Truman's by his rejection of such judgment in the service of what he believed to be the political expediency of the time. MacArthur understood, what Truman did not, that the admixture of military strategy with political expediency can produce national disaster. And he sought to avoid it. He felt, as experience has long taught, that once the diplomats have failed to preserve the peace, it becomes a responsibility of military leadership to devise the strategy which will win the war. . . ."

him to criticize the President openly. Indeed, he became so insubordinate that Truman relieved him of command on April 11, 1951. For his action to uphold the Constitutional dictate that civilian authority shall always prevail over military, Truman was subjected to a storm of abuse. But as he later wrote of the incident, "I could do nothing else and still be President of the United States."

MacArthur believed that "in war there is no substitute for victory"—a simplistic concept that had no relevance to the Korean War. Stalemate had to be a substitute for victory, unless the conflict was to escalate into a general world war and probable nuclear catastrophe. Moreover, every move the United States made in the Far

East was conditioned by the effect it would have in Europe. Having carefully put together the North Atlantic Alliance, Truman dared not weaken or destroy it by overcommitting the United States in Asia. To have engaged China in an all-out war would have been to commit all of America's resources, human and material, to a conflict with no discernible end. NATO would have been the first victim of such a war.

After the failure of his attempt to unify Korea by force, Truman acted with admirable restraint in the war. So did the enemy. Each side enjoyed, in effect, a privileged sanctuary, in which no bombs fell and no lives were taken—mainland China for the enemy, Japan for the United States. The Korean War, thus, was a true limited war, in which both the United States and China learned the lesson all great nations in the past have had to learn: that there are limits to how much power even the most powerful of nations can use in any given situation.

CONCLUSION

Historically, both the United States and Russia were expansionist nations. During the nineteenth century, each had extended its control over vast undeveloped areas in imperial thrusts which had carried both nations to the Pacific—the United States westward across the Great Plains and Rockies, Russia eastward across the Urals and Siberia. As early as 1835, the shrewd French observer Alexis de Tocqueville had predicted that the two growing giants would one day dominate the entire world, and events after World War II seemed to bear out his prediction. At one level, thus, the cold war could be seen as a conventional clash of political, geographic, and economic ambitions between two great powers.

Complicating the picture, however, was a conflict of ideologies as well. Both powers were missionary nations, gripped by a sense of Manifest Destiny and driven by visions of the future that were poles apart, ideologically. Americans foresaw a world of democratic, free-enterprise nations, living in harmonious relationship with one another and looking to the United States for guidance. The leaders of the Soviet Union saw communism as the wave of the future, as the goal toward which history was inexorably moving all mankind.

When ideals clash and utopias are at cross-purposes, reason becomes the victim of passion. One great tragedy of the cold war was that it warped the perspective of men on both sides. Myth and reality merged in the minds of men; petty grievances were puffed up to the stature of world-shaking crises; common sense was scattered to the four winds by partisan fervor. Both sides claimed a monopoly on virtue and justness in the struggle. But as in all great conflicts in history, the responsibility for the cold war was shared by all the disputants.

QUESTIONS

1. What were the postwar goals of the Soviet Union? How successful was the Soviet Union in attaining these goals?

2. How influential was the Soviet Union in leading international communism after the war?

3. Where were some examples of revolutionary radicalism following the war? Why was communism more apt to be the political inclination of revolutionist than democratic liberalism?

4. What were the basic tenets of American foreign policy after World War II? To what extent was Russia a threat to American postwar goals? Were there any more appropriate goals for American policy? If so, explain.

5. How did the tension between Russia and the United States become reflected in the United Nations?

6. What were the advantages and disadvantages of the United Nations. What changes would need to be made to make a more effective U.N.?

7. Why did difficulties exist in solving the postwar problems of Poland and Germany?

8. Were the Axis countries fairly treated by the Allies in the postwar settlement? Explain your answer?

9. Why did the Cold War appear and become a permanent part of postwar international relations?

10. Why were the Communists successful in the Chinese civil war? What implications does Communist China hold for the rest of Asia today?

11. To what extent was American postwar policy based upon idealism and to what extent was it based upon pragmatism?

12. How did the limited war of Korea differ from the total war of World War II?

■ BIBLIOGRAPHY

GOLDMAN, ERIC F., *The Crucial Decade and After: America 1945–1960*, Random House (Vintage Books). This is an excellent summary of the postwar period, and the student will profit from the overview it provides. The author considers the period crucial because Americans had to decide whether to support the concepts of the welfare state and world leadership or seek other alternatives.

REISCHAUER, EDWIN O., *The United States and Japan*, Viking Press (Compass Books). Reischauer is one of the most respected American authorities on Japan. He has learned Japanese, studied the history and culture, married a Japanese woman, and served in Japan as American ambassador. This is an excellent book for the student to read to understand American relations with Japan.

TSOU, TANG, *America's Failure in China, 1941–1950*, 2 vols., U. of Chicago Press (Phoenix Books). Chinese relations with the rest of the world become increasingly important, and the student should try to understand the background for the Communist takeover. This book would be a good place to start the study.

LEDERER, WILLIAM J. AND EUGENE BURDICK, *The Ugly American*, Fawcett (Crest Books). This little novel was very influential in calling attention to the negative image of Americans abroad held by many foreigners. The story bears striking similarities to our involvement in Vietnam. Most students will find the book easy reading and quite provocative.

LECKIE, ROBERT, *Conflict: The History of the Korean War 1950–1953*, Avon Books. This book will help the student understand American involvement in the Korean War. Although the author relied primarily upon secondary sources, it is an accurate account which concentrates upon the first six months of the war.

MILLIS, WALTER, ET. AL., *Arms and the State: Civil-Military Elements in National Policy*, Twentieth Century Fund. This is an excellent collection of essays dealing with the military and democratic government. Millis is an outstanding military historian and provides useful insights into the operation of the military.

Target with Plaster Casts, Jasper Johns, 1955

Convergence, Jackson Pollock, 1952

That Gentlemen, Andrew Wyeth, 1960

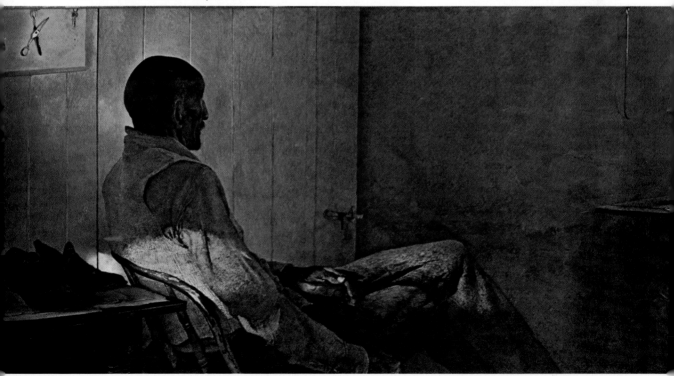

After World War II, the center of the art world moved from Paris to New York, and a group of American artists emerged as leaders of new trends. The social realism of the thirties and the cubism of the twenties was replaced by a new style—abstract expressionism.

Among these new leaders were Jasper Johns, who went beyond the limits of the canvas and used materials other than paint, like plaster and wood (page 677), and Jackson Pollock (top left). Although their individual techniques are vastly different, they nevertheless both reflect the abstract expressionist philosophy. Not all artists of the period adopted it completely however. Andrew Wyeth (bottom left) considers himself an abstractionist, yet he does not totally reject realism. He draws figures, but he seeks to go beyond mere portraiture and make a statement about man's mortality.

Sculpture, photography, and architecture took on

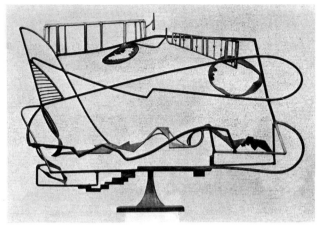

Hudson River Landscape, David Smith, 1951

Aspens, New Mexico, Ansel Adams, 1958

Lever House, New York, Skidmore, Owings and Merrill, 1952

new styles after the war. David Smith, an innovator using such materials as steel, created the "drawing-in-space construction" on the preceding page, in which he expresses his impressions of a landscape as he moved past it on a train. Ansel Adams relied on straight photography as his medium of expression; he records exact images, but makes of them a photographic composition (page 679). The Lever House (above) set a new style in skyscraper design. Gone is heavy masonry, so long a tradition in Western architecture, and in its place is bright and light glass and stainless steel.

The Postwar Years At Home

V-J Day in August 1945 was a day of thankful relief and wild celebration for the American people. Long years of war had ended in total mastery of the enemy, and the taste of victory was sweet. Many people had suffered hardship and personal loss during the war, but the country as a whole had come through the ordeal in good shape. Prosperity had returned, people had money in their pockets, the nation's prestige and power had never been greater, and the future looked bright. It seemed that a new era full of promise had begun.

Almost immediately, however, a host of problems arose to dampen the optimism and to tax the ingenuity and imagination of the nation's leaders. The United States faced new responsibilities as a world power as it expanded its political and military commitments around the world. It was a nation that was eager to demobilize, but it needed a large standing military force to meet these commitments. Millions of war veterans were returning home, and the society had to absorb them with a minimum of dislocation.

Americans, anxious to buy the consumer goods the war had made unavailable, clamored for the reconversion of the economy to peacetime production, and runaway inflation seemed sure to follow. During the war the demand for manpower had worked profound changes among black people, and many had become aware for the first time of their importance as productive members of society. They would probably not accept being pushed into the background again, as they had been after World War I.

The problems, clearly, were pressing and difficult. And the nation needed able political leadership to deal with them effectively. An inexperienced new President sat in the White House, and many people had serious doubts that he could respond to the nation's needs. As you read about the postwar domestic policies, these are some questions to consider:

1. What measures were taken to restore the nation to a peacetime economy?
2. How would you evaluate Truman's record as President?
3. How did the cold war affect domestic politics?
4. How would you evaluate Eisenhower's Presidency?
5. On what issues did the Supreme Court make landmark decisions?

1 Demobilization Is Followed By Remobilization

1. How did Truman go about converting the economy to a peacetime basis?

2. Why did such runaway inflation occur in the postwar years?

3. Why did so many strikes follow the war? What effect did they have on workers, public opinion, and congressional action?

4. What changes did Truman make in the organization and practices of the national defense organizations?

Demobilization came swiftly in the wake of victory, too swiftly in the opinion of the diplomats in Washington who were responsible for honoring the United States' new global commitments. Soldiers and civilians alike clamored for drastic reductions in the wartime armed forces, and President Truman had little choice but to do their bidding. By January 1947, the military had been cut to about a million and a half men. It was still a sizable force, but in order to staff the numerous American military bases abroad, the administration had to extend the wartime draft, temporarily most people assumed. At the same time, with its air and sea power and its monopoly of atomic weapons, the United States retained its strategic dominance in global military affairs.

The GI bill. Responding to pressure from the veterans' lobby, Congress enacted a "GI bill of rights" (the Servicemen's Readjustment Act of 1944), designed to ease the transition of servicemen to civilian life. The act provided veterans with substantial educational and employment benefits and was an enormously successful measure.

Almost overnight a population explosion took place in the schools and colleges, as millions of veterans enrolled to study everything from philosophy to basket-weaving. Younger students, just out of high school, found their older classmates to be disturbingly serious about getting an education. New standards of academic performance were established during the years of the GI bill, while new problems appeared that would become increasingly serious in years ahead—campus overpopulation, overemphasis on specialization among scholars, a widening gap between faculty and students, among others.

Reconverting the economy. For all their exuberance at the end of the war, many people harbored nagging memories of the Great Depression and wondered how long the war-induced prosperity would last. No one could be absolutely sure that the economy had fully recovered, and many voices warned that the nation was doomed to repeat the boom and bust experience of the twenties. Other prophets spoke of a coming "golden age," almost in utopian terms. Former Vice President Henry A. Wallace, for example, predicted in 1944 that the day was not distant when 60 million Americans would be gainfully employed in peacetime work. At the time, Wallace's critics thought he had taken leave of his senses.

But less than two years after the war, 60 million people *were* employed, and the United States was enjoying a remarkable economic boom. The transition of the economy from war to peace was not made without some difficulties; and, in one sense, the transition was never really completed. For with the onset of the cold war, the government began pumping new contracts and money into defense industries, giving the entire economy a big boost in the process.

Still, the country enjoyed a genuine boom after the war. Because of shortages in consumer goods, Americans had saved some $140 billion during the war, and they could hardly wait to start spending the money once peace came. Eager to satisfy these impatient consumers, industry demanded an abrupt end to all price and production controls.

Truman favored a speedy reconversion of the economy and put the resources of Washington at the disposal of the business community. Government-owned war industries were turned over to private operators at a fraction of their true value, while huge stockpiles of surplus war goods ranging from merchant ships to mosquito netting were sold off at ridiculously low prices. War agencies were abolished, taxes were cut, and controls on all but a few critically scarce items were lifted or eased. At the same time, the President moved to guarantee "full employment."

Although the Maximum Employment Act which Congress passed early in 1946 fell far short of his expectations, it established a Council of Economic Advisers to work with the White House in maintaining the nation's economic health.

The most serious threat to the economy after the war came from runaway inflation. Consumers wanted to buy, manufacturers and farmers wanted to sell, workers wanted high wages, investors wanted greater profits. From all sides, the administration was pressured to do away with all price and wage controls and to kill off the OPA. A growing black market in civilian goods indicated that price regulations really had lost their effectiveness.

For a time, Truman resisted the pressure, mindful that runaway inflation could wreck the entire economy. But he received little support in Congress, and in the end, he reluctantly gave in to the inflationists. By the end of 1946, the soaring wage-price spiral was evident everywhere in the economy. Prices leveled off in 1948 and 1949, then took off again to new highs as the Korean War added a new stimulus to the economy.

Postwar labor strikes. While professing to be a champion of the OPA, organized labor helped greatly to undermine the entire system of controls in 1946. During the war, workers had received substantial wage increases in the form of pay for overtime work. To compensate for the loss of these increases when peace came, unions demanded raises in regular pay. A series of strikes in the automobile, railroading, mining, and other heavy industries brought substantial raises to many workers, but the increases were immediately matched by price rises. In April 1946, John L. Lewis refused to call off a strike and defied a government injunction against his United Mine Workers. As a result, the union was subjected to a heavy fine by the courts, something entirely new in American labor history.

One of the first acts of the Eightieth Congress (elected in 1946 and controlled by the Republicans) was to pass the Taft-Hartley Law. Designed to make it more difficult for unions to call strikes, Taft-Hartley reorganized the National Labor Relations Board and made it a court for enforcing collective bargaining among both unions and industry. The new law reflected a postwar reaction and popular disenchantment with organized labor; but it was far from being the "slave-labor law" that the unions called it.

Control over atomic energy. A matter of the gravest urgency after the war was to decide who would control development and uses of atomic energy. Military leaders naturally wanted the question decided in their favor, and they were strongly backed by leading Republicans, including the influential Senator Arthur Vandenberg. But the President wanted strict civilian control, with emphasis upon the peaceful uses of the atom, and in the end his views prevailed.

In 1946, Congress passed the McMahon Act, establishing the Atomic Energy Commission as a civilian agency with complete jurisdiction in the matter. Although the United States continued to manufacture and deploy atomic bombs, the AEC also found other, more constructive uses for the atom in science and industry. But as already noted, the effort to achieve a similar rational control of nuclear energy throughout the world failed.

Providing for national defense. During the war, rivalry among the various military services had sometimes actually impaired military operations. Determined to streamline the military establishment and provide for more efficient national defense, President Truman hailed the passage of the National Security Act in 1947. A measure of far-reaching consequence, the act established a Department of Defense with jurisdiction over the army, the navy, and the new separate air force. The secretary of defense and a new Joint Chiefs of Staff became the President's chief advisers on military matters.

The act also created the National Security Council (NSC), an extremely high-level board of advisers in diplomatic and military matters, and established the Central Intelligence Agency (CIA) as the nation's chief center for gathering and evaluating intelligence. The new setup increased efficiency in the armed forces, but it also made it more difficult than ever for Congress and the public to influence the great decisions pertaining to war and peace.

Clearly, Washington was concerned in 1947 and 1948 about the military ramifications of the international situation. Remobilization of the nation was undertaken slowly and with little fanfare for a time, but the importance of the military increased steadily. The new Department of Defense soon became as much involved in the making of foreign policy as in the determination of military questions.

To meet the nation's manpower commitments around the globe, Truman asked Congress to establish a system of universal military training on a permanent basis. The President envisioned a system which, during peacetime, would "provide this country with a well-trained and effective organized citizen reserve to reinforce the professional armed forces in times of danger as decided upon by the Congress." Probably because the proposal smacked too much of *conscription*, a word most Americans identified with the old military despotisms of Europe, Congress balked at giving the President what he wanted. Instead, it authorized him to continue the wartime draft, or Selective Service System, indefinitely.

Desegregating the armed forces. In July 1948, Truman issued an executive order in connection with Selective Service which had far-reaching consequences. He decreed that there should be "equality of treatment and opportunity for all persons in the armed services without regard to race, color, religion or national origin." Doubtless, the order was intended to eliminate the inefficiency which segregation fostered in the armed forces. But it also reflected the rising demands of black America and the increasing awareness among most Americans that the old order was giving way to a new order.

2 Politics Moves To Dead Center

1. What qualities did Harry Truman possess which could have served to make him a great President or kept him from being one?

2. What were the components of the Fair Deal program proposed by Truman? How did it compare to Roosevelt's New Deal?

3. What divisions emerged in the Democratic party in 1948?

4. How do you account for Truman's upset victory over Thomas E. Dewey in the election of 1948?

After sixteen long years out of power in Washington, the Republicans finally made a comeback in 1946. "Had Enough? Vote Republican!" was their slogan in the off-year elections, and it worked well enough to win them control of both houses of the Eightieth Congress. Many people expected the Republicans to "repeal the New Deal," that is, to undo much of the social-welfare legislation enacted during the Roosevelt years. But they did no such thing; indeed, their "revenge" against the New Deal consisted of the Twenty-Second Amendment to the Constitution, limiting future Presidents to two terms in office, and an act to change the name of Boulder Dam on the Colorado River to Hoover Dam.

Truman's personality. Politics moved to dead center during the postwar period. Probably this was a natural development, coming after a long, intense period of reform and an exhausting global war. Both major parties floundered, badly split in their ranks. In the field of foreign affairs, bipartisanship worked well enough to give the President a strong voice. At home, Truman rapidly accumulated a host of enemies, even within his own party.

Some of his troubles were of his own making. A product of Kansas City's shoddy machine politics, Truman lacked the image of firm, imaginative leadership cast by his predecessor in the White House. While in the Senate, he had been known best as a faithful party wheelhorse, always ready to toe the party line and to do the conventional thing. He had an explosive temperament, and he could be inordinately stubborn. There was a touch of Warren G. Harding in Truman, too. Although he named strong and able men to high positions in his administration, too often he opened the doors of lesser offices to old friends and party hacks. As historian Eric Goldman notes:

Month after month the President permitted cronies to smirch the Administration with favor-selling, and when the criticisms came, he reacted with irascible statements that no friend of Harry Truman was a dishonorable man.

But the resemblance to Harding did not go far. Truman was a tough-minded, courageous President, who neither shirked his responsibilities nor hesitated to make important decisions. Cocky in manner, earthy in expression, he understood the nature of his office and the position of the United States in the world. One of his favorite sayings was: "If you can't stand the heat, get out of the kitchen." On his desk he kept a small sign reading: "The buck stops here." If greatness is to be measured solely in terms of strength, Truman was a great President. If wisdom ought to temper strength, on the other hand, he falls somewhat short of greatness.

The Fair Deal. In some respects, Truman was a southern Democrat, raised in the states' rights tradition and restrained in his approach to domestic reform. Certainly, his close advisers were generally conservative: Fred M. Vinson, his first secretary of the Treasury, whom he named Chief Justice in 1946; John M. Snyder, a thoroughly conventional banker who succeeded Vinson in the Cabinet; Tom Clark of Texas, his attorney general; Dean Acheson, the able, opinionated diplomatist.

Truman relied heavily on military men for advice in many areas. Indeed, the military always fascinated him, and he was fond of recalling his World War I experiences or his service with the National Guard. His hero was General George C. Marshall, who served successively as chief of staff, secretary of state, and secretary of defense in the administration.

Yet, Truman's program of domestic reforms—the Fair Deal—put him also squarely in the Progressive-New Deal tradition. In the area of civil rights, moreover, Truman completely belied his border-state background by making his administration one of the boldest in history. In 1946, a special Presidential commission on civil rights prepared a sweeping report on race relations in America entitled "To Secure These Rights." The President thereupon regularly asked Congress for legislation against lynching and the poll tax and for a permanent Fair Employment Practices Commission. When Congress turned him down, he implemented his liberal views through executive decrees, as when he began the desegregation of the military. In the context of the times, Truman's proposals on civil rights were the boldest measures in his domestic program.

As for the rest of the Fair Deal, it was chiefly an extension of the New Deal. Truman asked for a program of national health insurance, for federal aid to education, for a modest public housing program, for stronger social security, for a full employment guarantee, and for reform in the government's farm price-support program. He made some headway after 1948, but throughout his tenure he was hampered by conservatives in Congress. He was also inconsistent in pushing his own proposals, often settling for much less than most observers thought he could get.

Mild as the Fair Deal was, it aroused bitter opposition. National health insurance was labeled "socialism" by the American Medical Association, a powerful doctors' lobby. Conservatives attacked federal aid to education as a measure through which the government would "control" the minds of students. Southern Democrats viewed civil rights proposals as dangerous threats to the social order. Although the Eightieth Congress did little to turn back the clock to pre–New Deal days, it balked at enacting any new reforms. Only in foreign policy did it give Truman the things he wanted.

The divided Republicans. Republicans were divided as to what kind of image the party should project to the voters. Liberal Republicans were prepared to accept the New Deal intact and to carry on from there in a generally progressive manner. On the far right, a few diehards genuinely wanted to repeal the New Deal and return to the "good old days" of the 1920's.

In between, and probably representing most party members, were the moderate conservatives. In Congress, they were led by Robert A. Taft, senator from Ohio, son of the former President. Taft was a man of great intelligence and integrity, honestly conservative in that he wanted to hold the line on welfare legislation, but also enlightened enough to understand some of the country's pressing needs.

Taft always spoke bluntly and to the point, sometimes taking the unpopular side to the detriment of his ambitions. Thus, he condemned the Nuremberg War Crimes Tribunal as a travesty on Anglo-American concepts of justice. And he clung stubbornly to a unilateralist position in foreign affairs, while his party moved toward internationalism. Impatient and brusque, he often gave the impression of callous indifference to human and social problems. In answer to a question about how the poor could survive in an inflated economy, he once snapped, "Eat less!"

Taft was "Mr. Republican" to the party faithful, in Congress and out. Yet, the Republicans turned away from him in 1948 to nominate, once again, the governor of New York, Thomas E. Dewey. Dewey's views were similar to Taft's on many issues, but his public image was that of a young, dedicated crusader. Even though all Republicans thought that 1948 was to be their year, many had a hunch that Taft just might not win. Better to go with such a proven vote-getter as Dewey. To run with him, they chose the progressive California governor Earl Warren.

The divided Democrats. Indeed, it seemed absolutely certain to most Americans in the summer of 1948 that Truman would be toppled in the forthcoming Presidential election. The Democrats were even more badly divided than the Republicans, and the Truman record had not been one to inspire zeal among ordinary Democrats. To some observers, it appeared that Roosevelt's great coalition was about to fly apart in all directions. As Democrats gathered for their convention, there was much talk of abandoning Truman and nominating a "winner." But the President was leader of his party and he easily won nomination for a term in his own right. His running mate was a popular senator from Kentucky, Alben W. Barkley.

The split among Democrats ran in four directions. One line represented the orthodox party members, whose loyalty was always to the party leader. Another line represented the moderate liberals, most of whom had become Democrats because of Roosevelt and the New Deal. In 1947, they organized Americans for Democratic Action (ADA) as a strongly anti-Communist, liberal, political-action vehicle. Although they opposed Truman before the convention, they supported him in the election. Because of their efforts, the party adopted a very strong civil rights plank. A representative member of the ADA wing at the time was the vociferous young mayor of Minneapolis, Hubert H. Humphrey.

A third faction of Democrats represented a potentially fatal division of the party. Many liberals were strongly opposed to Truman's "hard line" policy in the cold war. They believed that the United States, as much as Russia, was to blame for the break-up of the wartime alliance.

Moreover, they accused the administration of dragging its feet on domestic reforms.

Former Vice President Henry A. Wallace thought along these lines. When Truman fired him as secretary of commerce for voicing foreign-policy views at odds with his own, Wallace opened a running battle with the administration. His followers ultimately formed a new Progressive party and nominated him for President. Glen Taylor, a guitar-playing senator from Idaho, was his running mate. The new party quickly attracted an odd conglomeration of leftists, including hard-core Communists. Gradually, those on the extreme left assumed control of the party, to the dismay of the alienated liberals. On paper, at least, the Progressives represented a sizable bloc of Democratic voters.

The fourth line represented the anti–civil rights Democrats of the Deep South. Angered by Truman's strong stand on the issue of racial justice, they formed the States Rights' Democratic party and nominated two ultra-conservatives, Strom Thurmond of South Carolina and Fielding Wright of Mississippi.

The election upset of 1948. Dewey's campaign was a model of quiet confidence. So sure were the Republicans of a sweeping victory that they simply avoided talking about the issues. President Truman, on the other hand, went onto the offensive with a vengeance. In a strenuous campaign, he canvassed the entire country by train, speaking to large crowds and small, always with the same message. The Republicans, he warned, would bring back the misery of the Great Depression. Their "do-nothing 80th Congress," as he labeled the current legislature, had already shown its utter indifference to the plight of the "little man." From his audiences came shouts of "Give 'em hell, Harry!" and Truman did just that.

It was an extraordinary campaign effort, but on election eve almost everyone in the country except Truman was ready to concede his defeat. As the first returns came in, showing Dewey taking a strong lead, the Chicago *Tribune* put out its early morning edition with a banner headline hailing Truman's ignominious defeat.

The *Tribune* and a great many other "experts" had to eat crow when the final returns came in, late on election night. For Truman scored a strik-

The favored candidate in the 1948 Presidential election was Republican Thomas E. Dewey, shown at top left as he acknowledges an ovation from a crowd in Madison Square Garden just before delivering his final campaign speech. Of the three other parties in the race, one of them, the new Progressive party was led by Henry A. Wallace. At top right Wallace waves to a group of workers on the United Auto Workers picket line at the Dodge Plant in Detroit. But it was the candidate everyone underestimated who won. Below, Harry Truman triumphantly displays the headline that prematurely announced his defeat.

ing victory. The threat from Wallace had faded away during the campaign, as liberals became disillusioned with the Communist element in the Progressive party. As for the Dixiecrats, as Thurmond's party was nicknamed, they won 38 electoral votes in the Deep South. In the main contest, Truman bested Dewey by about 2 million popular votes and won a decisive victory in the electoral college.

How did Truman bring off his great upset victory? Republicans had all sorts of explanations, ranging from rainy weather to the alienation of their party's conservatives. Their attitude was well expressed by Senator Taft, who reportedly grumbled: "I don't care how the thing is explained; it defies all common sense." But there was no mystery to the Truman victory. People simply were not ready to abandon the New Deal and trust the economy to FDR's old opponents. Farmers, workers, and minority groups put aside their separate grievances on election day, filed into the polling places, and voted their pocketbooks and their hearts. The victory belonged to Harry Truman, to be sure; but it was also a triumph for Franklin D. Roosevelt.

3 The Cold War Is Waged At Home

1. What were the roots of the popular fear of communism in the late forties and early fifties?

2. Why could the execution of Julius and Ethel Rosenberg be considered an example of the extremes to which fear could carry men?

3. How was the problem of internal security handled in the postwar years? How do you think internal security should have been handled?

4. In what ways was McCarthyism the worst symptom of the fear which gripped the United States.

Truman's second administration was dominated by the Korean War. Once he committed American troops in Asia, the President had to remobilize the economy for a major war effort. It was not an easy undertaking, for most people rebelled against the thought of enduring another time of controls and high taxes. Korea was a major American war. To many people at home, however, it did not seem so, especially when they compared it with the recent global conflict. Thus, the nation tried to behave normally in a situation that was not at all normal. Mobilization was spotty and inefficient, while inflation spiraled beyond all sensible limits.

The problem of internal security. The Korean War also brought into sharp focus a question that had been rankling in the public mind for several years. Was the United States internally secure against Communist infiltration and subversion? For some people, the exuberant mood of 1945 had changed, by 1948, to a mood of bitter frustration. Things were not going right in the world and, once again, it appeared that the United States had "lost the peace."

From 1948 on, moreover, the example of Czechoslovakia provided solid evidence that subversion could bring down a government. When China fell to the Communists early in 1950, many Americans reacted as though their own country had been attacked. It was difficult to believe that the turbulent events of the postwar years were not the result of a conspiracy—a conspiracy hatched in the Kremlin, no doubt, but likely aided by traitors in Washington.

Beneath the usually calm surface of American life there lies a streak of irrationalism and intolerance. Occasionally, it breaks through to overwhelm the common sense of the people and set off waves of public hysteria. Sometimes, it has led to vicious witch-hunts. The big Red scare of the twenties was such an instance, as were the outbursts of nativism and anti-Catholicism in the nineteenth century. As the cold war settled in, late in the 1940's, the country underwent one of its worst experiences of this sort. Before the witch-hunt ran its course, it did grave harm to the lives and reputations of innocent people and subjected the basic institutions of a free society to a painful wrench.

The hysteria was rooted deep in the popular fear of Communism. Even when the Soviet Union had been but a weak and half-formed experiment, in the 1920's and 1930's, some Americans saw Bolshevism as an imminent threat to the "American way of life." The more extreme and vociferous anti-Communists seemed to assume that American institutions were somehow peculiarly vulnerable to subversion by the agents of the Kremlin. Anti-Communists of a less extravagant nature, on the other hand, trusted in the strength of those institutions and the good sense of the people to resist the blandishments of the Communists.

Starting in 1946, a series of sensational spy cases touched off a wave of fear in the United States. All of them involved Soviet agents and local Communists, and they were made all the more sensational by the fact that the material transmitted to the agents had to do with atomic research. Federal authorities quickly moved to expose and prosecute the offenders, and Washington tightened up its security arrangements to prevent future espionage. But a number of politicians just as quickly seized upon the issue of "subversion in high places" to smear their opponents and further their own interests.

The spy ring was international in nature. In England, Dr. Klaus Fuchs, who had worked on the Manhattan Project during the war, confessed that he had been turning over classified material to the Russians for years. Ultimately, the case implicated a number of Americans. Several American spies were sentenced to long prison terms, but two of them—Julius Rosenberg and his wife Ethel—went to the electric chair.

That the Rosenbergs were guilty of espionage was one thing. That they should have been executed for high treason—the first peacetime executions in American history—suggested that the court itself was guilty of judicial vengeance. For in sentencing the pair to die, the trial judge held them responsible for "the Communist aggression in Korea, with the resultant casualties exceeding fifty thousand," and suggested that "millions more of innocent people may pay the price for your treason." Coming during the worst years of the cold war, the Rosenberg case was an example of the extremes to which fear could carry men.

The case also pointed up a popular misunderstanding about the nature of atomic technology. Russia, by then, had developed an atomic bomb. Because so many Americans believed that the backward Russians were incapable of producing such a weapon all by themselves, it was assumed that the men in the Kremlin stole the American "secret" of the bomb. In fact, as scientists tried to point out at the time, any modern industrial nation was capable of acquiring a nuclear arsenal of its own.

Loyalty investigations. Espionage and treason were one thing. Loyalty was quite another. It was extremely difficult to deal with the question of loyalty in America, precisely because diversity of opinion and criticism of established institutions were hallmarks of a free society. Yet, as the tensions of the cold war mounted, the entire machinery of government became involved in a tortuous preoccupation with loyalty investigations.

In 1947, Truman authorized a sweeping check into the backgrounds and beliefs of all government employees. No precise definition of loyalty was offered to guide the investigators, nor were the ordinary courtroom safeguards of individual rights provided to those being checked. Secret evidence was accepted and informers were encouraged to come forward with whatever "evidence" they had available. In one case, an informant told of hearing a strange language—Russian, she was sure—coming from the apartment of an Agriculture Department employee. As it turned out afterward the "Russian" that the employee heard was the gibberish produced when an ordinary tape is run backward through a tape recorder! Not all loyalty checks were run in so careless and frivolous a manner, but enough were to cast serious doubts on the value of the whole program.

By late 1952, security checks had been run on 6.6 million people, of whom about 500 had been dismissed from their jobs, while another 5,000 had resigned. How many of these people were actual security risks was impossible to determine. Long after he left the White House, Truman admitted that his loyalty order had been too sweeping and that innocent people had been victimized.

INTERNAL SECURITY MEASURES

Act	Provisions
Smith Act (Alien Registration Act), June, 1940	Made it unlawful for any person to advocate or teach the overthrow or destruction of any government in the United States by force or violence, or to organize or join any group dedicated to that aim. This provision was declared unconstitutional in 1957.

Strengthened existing laws governing the admission and deportation of aliens.

Required the fingerprinting of all aliens in the country. |
| McCarran Act (Internal Security Act of 1950), September, 1950 | Provided for registration of Communist and Communist-front organizations. This provision was declared unconstitutional in 1965.

Prohibited the employment of Communists in national defense work. This provision was declared unconstitutional in 1968.

Prohibited entry into the United States of anyone who had been a member of a totalitarian organization. In 1951 this provision was amended to exempt anyone who was under sixteen when forced to join a group or who had joined to maintain his livelihood.

Prohibited members of Communist organizations from applying for or using United States passports. This provision was declared unconstitutional in 1964.

Authorized the President, in a national emergency, to arrest and detain persons he believed might engage in espionage or sabotage. |

Prosecuting the Communists. The administration also moved against known leaders of the Communist party. Using the Smith Act of 1940, which prohibited groups from conspiring to overthrow the government, the Justice Department successfully prosecuted eleven top American Communists. On appeal to the Supreme Court, the convictions were upheld, with Chief Justice Vinson arguing for the majority that mere advocacy of revolution constitutes a clear and present danger to security. In a vigorous dissent, Justice Hugo Black warned against prosecuting people for their opinions rather than their acts.

Nothing showed the political appeal of indiscriminate anti-communism better than the McCarran-Nixon Internal Security Act of 1950 (see chart above). Truman vetoed the measure when it came before him, condemning the "cowering and foolish fear" of freedom it signified to him. But Congress overrode his veto.

The act established a Subversive Activities Control Board, whose job it was to check on all Communist activity in the country. It was a foolish measure in a number of ways, not least because it barred from entry into the United States any foreigner who had ever been connected with a totalitarian organization. To the chagrin of the State Department and the CIA, the act thus discouraged possible defections of former Communists from the Soviet bloc countries. Ultimately, the Supreme Court found much of the McCarran-Nixon Act to be blatantly unconstitutional.

The Alger Hiss case. One especially disturbing case of the late 1940's was that of Alger Hiss. A former State Department officer with a good public record, Hiss was accused of being a Communist spy. The accuser was Whitaker Chambers, himself a former spy who, more recently, had been an editor of *Time* magazine. Chambers charged that during the 1930's, Hiss had given him military secrets to be passed on to the Soviet Union.

Many people found it hard to believe that a man of Hiss's education and general background could ever have betrayed his country. But many others saw in him a symbol of an imagined "great betrayal" of America, which had started when the cocky young New Dealers, like Hiss, had flocked to Washington back in the thirties. Hiss was the perfect scapegoat for people who were certain there was a simple explanation for all the troubles that beset the country at home and abroad.

The full story of Hiss and Chambers continues to elude the historian even today. But Hiss trapped himself by telling a strange tale full of inconsistencies, and after two dramatic trials he was sent to prison for perjury. Several prominent men who had known Hiss earlier publicly testified to his good character, as they had known it. One of them was Secretary of State Dean Acheson. Thereafter, this tough, unrelenting anti-Communist diplomat was plagued with charges by his political foes that he was a Communist sympathizer.

The rise of "McCarthyism". A number of politicians unabashedly used the anti-Communist issue as a stepping-stone to higher office. But the man who turned the Red scare into a deadly political weapon and who became an international symbol of witch-hunting was Senator Joseph R. McCarthy of Wisconsin. Indeed, the term "McCarthyism" quickly came to denote the irresponsible Redbaiting, the character assassination, the abrasive demagoguery, that scarred so much of American politics in the early 1950's.

Probably the appearance of a McCarthy at that particular time was inevitable. The country was bewildered by the cold war, shocked to the heart by sordid tales of spying, disillusioned with the diplomats, frustrated by the "police action" in Korea. Any political medicine man with a clever pitch and an appealing panacea could have exploited the situation. The odd thing about Joe McCarthy was that he was a thoroughly nondescript person, with a record of ineffectiveness as a senator. Almost by accident, he stumbled upon the anti-Communist issue at a moment when many people were ready to believe almost any tale of treason and betrayal.

His favorite targets were diplomats and intellectuals. Asserting baldly that the State Department was riddled with known Reds (just who they were, or how many, he never specified), he accused Truman and Acheson of coddling the culprits. Here again was the easy explanation for the "loss" of China, the war in Korea, the spread of communism in Eastern Europe, the American "retreat" all over the world.

McCarthy was a master of the "big lie"; that is, his untruths and insinuations were so monstrous and repeated so often that he convinced many of his listeners that they must be hearing the truth. It was impossible to pin him down on anything. His charges shot off in all directions—smearing an innocent victim here, inferring some dastardly plot there, implying treason everywhere.

And he was audacious! He even struck out in the Senate, taking on the most conservative of his colleagues. In the end, his audacity proved his undoing; but he got away with it for a long time. Early in the game, the impeccably conservative senior senator from Maryland, Millard Tydings, let it be known that he considered McCarthy to be something of a fraud. Whereupon, McCarthy unleashed a vicious smear campaign against Tydings that helped to wreck the latter's bid for reelection in 1950. Tydings was a Democrat, and the lesson was not lost on McCarthy's fellow Republicans. Anti-communism was good politics, many of them concluded, and some Republicans were quite content thereafter to let McCarthy chop down as many Democrats as he could, by whatever means he chose to use.

McCarthyism was only the worst symptom of the political malaise that gripped the United States at the time. Internal security and international espionage were matters of the utmost seriousness, demanding calm, dispassionate attention, not indiscriminate accusation and sideshow dramatics. American institutions were sound, and the normal police and judicial processes were quite adequate to cope with the problem of subversion. Yet, reason gave way to unreason in politics, while hysteria overwhelmed common sense among large sections of the population. It was difficult to predict in the early 1950's when, or whether, the nation would shake off the malaise.

4 Eisenhower Creates The Businessman's Administration

1. What factors contributed to Eisenhower's election in 1952?

2. How would you characterize Eisenhower as a politician?

3. What were the fiscal policies of the Eisenhower administration? How successful were these policies?

4. Were there any substantial differences between the Eisenhower and Truman administrations?

"Communism in government" was not the only hot issue the Democratic party had to contend with as the election of 1952 approached. In Korea the war dragged on, promising nothing for the future but more casualties, more stalemate, more frustration. Within the Truman administration, corruption had become widespread.

Much of it was the petty chiseling of so-called five percenters, minor officials who took payoffs from persons seeking special privileges in Washington. But Senate investigators also uncovered cases of flagrant abuse of the public trust in the Bureau of Internal Revenue, the Reconstruction Finance Corporation, and the tax division of the Justice Department. Truman himself was completely honest; but some of his close associates were implicated in questionable activities, and his administration was the most corrupt since that of Harding.

To add insult to injury for the Democratic party, a crusading Democratic senator, Estes Kefauver of Tennessee, held public hearings on crime in America, which showed unsavory connections between the underworld and certain Democratic city machines. Kefauver was an able man and a likely candidate for the party's nomination in 1952; but the city bosses turned away from him in droves after his hearings embarrassed some of them.

The election of 1952. "Communism, Corruption, and Korea!" was a natural battlecry for the Republicans in 1952, and they made the most of it. Once again, the party was split: its heart belonged to Senator Taft, while its head went searching for a winner. It found one in General Dwight D. Eisenhower, the hero of Normandy and the war against Hitler.

The movement to nominate "Ike," as he was known familiarly, began with eastern liberal Republicans who were anxious to keep the party oriented toward internationalism. But even the die-hard Taftites had to acknowledge that, at last, the party really did have a winner in the enormously popular general. Eisenhower acknowledged their influence by naming a young conservative from California, Senator Richard M. Nixon, to run with him and by promising to campaign against the "creeping socialism" of the Democrats.

When Truman decided not to seek another term,* the race among the Democrats became wide open. Truman wanted Chief Justice Vinson to succeed him; but his old friend preferred to remain on the court. Among other possible candidates, the name of Adlai E. Stevenson was especially prominent. But Stevenson honestly did not want the nomination in 1952, for he was in his first term as governor of Illinois and wanted to finish his program there. His welcoming address to the Chicago convention, nonetheless, lit a fire of enthusiasm for him that got beyond his control. In the first genuine draft of a candidate since 1880, the delegates named Stevenson as their man. His running mate was a moderate southerner, Senator John Sparkman of Alabama.

Stevenson proved to be a most unusual candidate. At the outset, he promised to "talk sense to the American people." His speeches were eloquent and pointed, and many people delighted in his wit and introspective manner. Yet, the same qualities irritated many other voters. His enemies ridiculed him as an "egghead," a term his supporters considered a compliment to his intelligence. But Stevenson was not just dabbling in

---

*The Twenty-Second Amendment specifically exempted the incumbent from its two-term limitation.

692

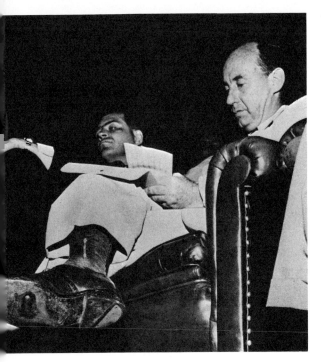

During the 1952 campaign, Democratic candidate Adlai Stevenson (top left) bares the worn sole of his shoe to the audience at a Labor Day rally in Flint, Michigan. The photographer who captured this shot won a Pulitzer Prize. Although Stevenson conducted a vigorous campaign, the witty and urbane candidate lost to his opponent's overwhelming popularity. At right, "Ike" is almost lost in the crowd that beseiged him at Manhasset, New York, during a campaign swing through Long Island. True to his campaign promise to go to Korea to try and arrange a truce, Eisenhower visited the troops there before he took office. Above right, the President-elect shares a meal with GI's of the battalion he had commanded twelve years earlier.

politics as an intellectual pastime. He was a tough professional in his own right, as his success in the rough-and-tumble politics of Illinois testified. Even in losing, he had a profound effect upon his party. As an eloquent spokesman for the new opposition, he inspired a generation of young Democrats to rebuild their party.

An Eisenhower victory. Eisenhower won the election handily, even taking parts of the once solidly Democratic South. The people genuinely "liked Ike," and with good reason. He epitomized the American success story, having risen from poverty and obscurity to become a world figure. His open face and broad grin captivated people everywhere, while his rambling, often awkward speeches said straightforward things the voters wanted to hear. Doubtless, he clinched his victory by pledging, late in the campaign, to "go to Korea" if elected. The implication was that he would end the unpopular war.

During his military career, "Ike" had been at his best as an administrator and reconciler of conflicting viewpoints. To the Presidency he brought his long experience as a staff officer, establishing a militarylike chain of command in the White House. Unfortunately, politics was not the Army, and while his system usually worked well enough, sometimes it failed dismally.

In Eisenhower, the voters chose not merely a Republican, but a Whiggish Republican. True to the tradition of the pre–Civil War Whigs, he deliberately underplayed the power of the Presidency. Styling himself a "caretaker" President, he wanted only to carry out the will of the people as expressed in Congress. Thus, he never became his party's leader in Congress in the way that Roosevelt and Truman had been for the Democrats. His way was to propose legislation, then to let the lawmakers handle things on their own. It was a concept of the Presidency that an earlier popular Republican, Theodore Roosevelt, would have scorned in favor of a vigorous, activist role.

Eisenhower as a politician. As a politician, Eisenhower was something of an enigma. It was fashionable among his critics, at the time, to dismiss him as a political babe in the woods, wandering aimlessly in the thickets of intricate party affairs. As the political analyst Samuel Lubell noted, however, he had a driving determi-

nation to win in politics as in war, and he was a master of public relations. His personal popularity never waned. Three times during his first term he was stricken with serious illness; yet, he easily defeated Stevenson with a huge majority in their 1956 rematch. But for the Twenty-Second Amendment, he could easily have had a third term in 1960. Moreover, he tried hard to heal the deep ideological split between ultraconservative and moderate Republicans.

Still, he failed to reshape his party or to build it into a national majority. His coattails were astonishingly short, for he was seldom able to transfer his own great popularity to other Republican candidates. In 1952, the Republicans barely captured control of Congress. Two years later they lost it again, and they never regained it during his tenure, not even in the Eisenhower landslide of 1956. The key man in Congress during the "Republican years" was not a Republican at all, but rather the powerful leader of the Democrats in the Senate, Lyndon Baines Johnson. Because both Eisenhower and Johnson were "practical men" who worked together well, the President did not find the situation a difficult one at all.

Eisenhower was a moderate conservative ("liberal conservative" was the undefinable term he used), and his approach to government was one of studied moderation. Keeping deliberately to the middle of the road, he set a comfortable, unexciting pace for his administration and avoided extremes of any sort. In this respect, he read the national temper perfectly. People were tired of activist Presidents, bewildered by difficult economic and diplomatic problems, anxious to tend to their own personal affairs. In the person of "Ike" Eisenhower, they saw a commanding figure who would shield them from the harsh realities of the larger world, while safeguarding the nation from its external and internal enemies.

Businessmen in government. In the armylike command and staff arrangement in the White House, several members of the cabinet came to exert very great influence. Most were former businessmen, and the administration undertook to govern in accordance with sound business principles. Secretary of State John Foster Dulles was a corporation lawyer, long active in international business dealings. The strong voice in domestic matters was that of Secretary of the Treasury George M. Humphrey, a steel executive whose hero was Andrew Mellon of the Harding-Coolidge era. Charles E. Wilson left General Motors to take over the Defense Department. Somehow, the president of the plumbers union, Martin Durkin, turned up briefly as secretary of labor, prompting wags to remark that the new Cabinet was composed of "eight millionaires and a plumber."

None of the businessmen saw any conflict of interest between their ties to the corporate world and their new roles as public servants. With Secretary of Defense Wilson, they sincerely felt that "what was good for our country was good for General Motors, and *vice versa.*" But not even Senator Taft was sure that it was such a good thing to put so many businessmen in positions of power. "I don't know of any reason why success in business should mean success in public service," he observed tartly.

Eisenhower clearly preferred to have businessmen at his side, rather than politicians. One of the few political types to have any real influence with him was his trusted "assistant president," Sherman Adams, a former governor of New Hampshire, and one of Adams's jobs was to shield him from other politicians.

Republican fiscal policies. In office, the Republicans made a valiant attempt to cut spending, reduce the national debt, lower taxes, and, above all, balance the budget. They met with only limited success, for the demands of the cold war and of an increasingly complex society at home made it difficult for them to pursue a consistent course.

Eisenhower began on an orthodox fiscal note, cutting back on credit and reducing spending in order to curb inflation and stabilize the dollar. But the country suffered three serious business recessions during his tenure (1953–54, 1957–58, 1960–61). On each occasion, rather than risk seeing a recession become a major depression, the President fell back on policies which were, in effect, modifications of Keynesian economics. He managed to balance the budget three times during his eight years in office, a feat he noted proudly in his memoirs as his most significant achievement as President. Yet, he also spent more than his predecessor and piled up the biggest peacetime budgetary deficit in history in 1959.

Taft Republicans were dismayed because Eisenhower did not achieve "real economy," but "real economy" could have been effected only through drastic, far-reaching slashes in spending for the military and for foreign aid, cuts which the President refused to consider. At the same time, his fiscal policies helped to slow down the economy by promoting a bewildering series of alternations between inflation and deflation. During the Eisenhower years, the country's rate of economic growth slipped from 4.3 percent annually to 2.5 percent.

Despite demands from the right wing for wholesale dismantling of the New and Fair Deals, the Republicans made no serious attempt to "repeal the past." But they did reduce the government's role in economic affairs. A tax reduction in 1954 helped to stimulate private investment, though it did little for the individual taxpayer. Private utilities won out over publicly financed efforts in developing such natural resources as electric power. In a particularly obtuse moment, moreover, the administration opposed government distribution of the long-awaited Salk antipolio vaccine for fear it might encourage "socialized medicine."

Nonetheless, the Eisenhower Republicans, at least, accepted the welfare measures of previous administrations as a permanent feature of American society. In 1953, they established a Department of Health, Education, and Welfare. They increased benefits under Social Security and extended its coverage to 10 million more people.

Historical perspective enables us to see that the differences between Eisenhower's administration and Truman's were mostly in style and rhetoric, rather than in substance. Doubtless, the Republicans wanted to break sharply with the Democratic past when they took over in 1953. But they learned quickly that the forces working for continuity in American politics are sometimes stronger than the forces working for change. Truman tried to move the nation forward in the Progressive manner. Eisenhower tried to slow the pace of government and restore something, at least, of pre–New Deal America. Both men ended up on political dead center.

5 The Warren Court Assumes An Activist Role

1. Why did the Supreme Court become so active during the Eisenhower years? To what extent did the Warren Court work within the traditional bounds of the Supreme Court, and to what extent did it stretch the Constitution by assuming greater authority and working in new areas?

2. What was done by the Warren Court to reconcile the rights of the individual with the security of the nation? How did the Supreme Court act to protect the rights of the accused?

3. How did judicial, legislative, and executive action during the 1950's attempt to provide equal civil rights for all American citizens?

4. How did the white South react to the desegregation orders?

In September 1953, Eisenhower made the single most important appointment of his tenure as President. To fill the vacancy caused by Fred M. Vinson's death, he named Earl Warren to be chief justice of the United States. Few observers at the time expected the California governor to be a particularly forceful member of the Supreme Court. His background was that of a very successful, though hardly dynamic, provincial politician, who had diligently climbed the political ladder in his home state. Warren was much more in the Bull Moose-Progressive tradition of his party than most Republicans in Washington. Eisenhower's advisers thought it would be "good politics" to appoint him to the Court.

The Court asserts itself. At times in history the Supreme Court has moved boldly into areas of public policy which, for one reason or another, elected officials have shunned. The Marshall Court (1800–35), early in the history of the republic, was such an activist court, as was the Taney Court (1836–64) in some of its major decisions.

During his first two years on the bench, Chief Justice Warren was restrained in his view of the Court's powers. But in 1955, he began to change, becoming increasingly assertive and libertarian. From then until he retired in 1969, he made the Court one of the most active in history, second only to the Marshall Court.

Why did the judiciary become so active at this particular moment? Chiefly because of weaknesses in the other elements of government. State and local governments showed a profound inability or unwillingness to keep pace with a rapidly changing American society. At the federal level, both Congress and the executive branch had floundered badly in dealing with issues of vital importance to the peace and tranquillity, as well as the general welfare, of the nation. Most of these issues concerned the rights and liberties of citizens in conflict with the power of government.

McCarthy's downfall. The Court, for example, had to deal with the problem of McCarthyism (though the politicians were finally to handle McCarthy himself). Far from fading away when the Republicans took over in Washington, the cloud of McCarthyism grew larger and more menacing after 1952. Eisenhower reinstituted loyalty checks, broadening the category of "security risk" to include persons suspected of "immoral conduct." Even J. Robert Oppenheimer, the "father of the atomic bomb," was denied security clearance because of past associations with "radicals."

At the State Department, McCarthyism inflicted lasting damage. Dulles put a zealous McCarthyite in charge of security and outdid himself in currying the senator's favor. Morale fell among young foreign-service officers, who saw that their superiors wanted reports which would feed the preconceptions of the politicians rather than present an honest, objective evaluation of conditions in the world. Indeed, the China service in the diplomatic corps simply fell apart. Seldom has an American government behaved more foolishly than when it penalized—and in some cases openly persecuted—the "old China hands," as the Asia experts were known, for accurately predicting the outcome of a revolution in China which many people in Washington wanted to believe had never occurred.

As for McCarthy himself, he became the hottest news item in Washington. But after badgering a number of lesser agencies and individuals, he finally overplayed his hand. Puffed up by his own ego and the fawning of his staff, he accused the army of deliberately harboring subversives. It became clear that McCarthy was quite willing to destroy the morale of the armed forces in his zeal to unravel such world-shaking mysteries as who had promoted an obscure army dentist suspected of left-wing sympathies. Moreover, McCarthy was so confident of his power that he began to attack Republicans, and that indiscretion sealed his fate. To protect itself and the GOP from his recklessness, the Eisenhower administration finally moved against him.

McCarthy's downfall took place before millions of people, as he did battle with the army and the administration in a dramatic televised hearing. The senator put on his usual show, and at last the public saw him for the bully and boor he was. As his popular support melted away, the Senate summoned up the courage to act. In December 1954, McCarthy's colleagues formally "condemned" him for improper conduct. Thereafter, he faded back into the obscurity from which he had come.

Individual rights and state security. McCarthyism long survived McCarthy. At every level of government (and in many private areas, as well), it showed itself in the form of laws, loyalty oaths, and administrative practices, all with a single purpose. They were designed to enforce a particular standard of political and intellectual conformity, a standard which was established in a wholly arbitrary manner. For the first time in American history, the government set limits on what people could think and advocate, who they could associate with, even how they could conduct themselves in the privacy of their homes. In this situation, the Supreme Court had little choice but to move assertively, if only to clarify the meaning of the Bill of Rights.

Do the rights of the individual citizen count for more than the security interests of the nation when the two are in conflict? The Court did not always speak unanimously or reason consistently in answering this difficult question. In most instances, the majority came to the side of the individual citizen. The Court ruled that it is not a crime to advocate overthrow of the government if the advocacy does not lead to direct action. It curbed the arbitrary behavior of congressional investigators in dealing with witnesses. One decision invalidated state subversion laws, many of which had been recklessly drawn. In other cases, the Court struck down some of the objectionable provisions of the Internal Security Act.

Still, the Court did not seriously curb the power of any duly constituted authority to investigate or prosecute where subversion was indicated. Its aim, simply, was to strike some reasonable balance between the citizen's rights and the power of the state.

Individual rights and criminal cases. In the same spirit the Court moved boldly to protect the rights of citizens accused of crimes. Its concern here was with insuring that police behavior was compatible with principles of human dignity. Aware that many persons taken into custody are ignorant of their legal rights, the Court laid down strict rules under which arrests and interrogations must be conducted.

Some Constitutional lawyers thought the Court acted, here, in an area in which it lacked jurisdiction. Less reasonable critics accused it of "coddling criminals" and hamstringing the police. Pointing to the words carved over the portal of the Supreme Court Building in Washington, the Court's defenders replied that the justices were only insuring that every individual receive "Equal Justice Under Law."

Civil rights rulings. Half a century after the case of *Plessy* v. *Ferguson* (page 432) had established the doctrine of "separate but equal" in race relations, it was painfully obvious that black Americans lived in conditions of "separate and unequal." Conditions were particularly disgraceful in education, where separate facilities for blacks lagged miserably behind those for whites. In the case of *Brown* v. *Topeka Board of Education* (May 17, 1954), the Supreme Court ruled that segregated public education was unconstitutional. Speaking for the entire Court, the Chief Justice ruled that separate schools were "inherently unequal," because of the psychological and social disadvantages they imposed on black children. Local school boards were ordered to desegregate "with all deliberate speed."

From that point on, the Supreme Court struck down law after law by which the states had segregated blacks from whites in public facilities.

McCarthyism and school integration were two of the major domestic issues in the 1950's. McCarthy's career finally ended in 1954 during a controversy with the army. Appearing before a Senate subcommittee, McCarthy (above) points to a huge map purporting to show Communist party organizations throughout the country. The dejected man at the center of the table is army counsel Joseph N. Welch, whose dignity in the face of McCarthy's attacks won him widespread admiration. When it became necessary to enforce integration in Little Rock, Arkansas, troops of the 101st Airborne Division escorted black children into the city's Central High School (below).

Legal discrimination in America at last came to a long overdue end. Unhappily, bigotry and prejudice did not die with the archaic laws.

In a nation calling itself a democracy, it was plainly intolerable that some people should be set aside as second-class citizens, to be systematically deprived of their rights, and otherwise exploited. Moreover, considering the objectives of United States' foreign policy and the revolutionary mood in much of the world, it was downright stupid. Among the emerging "Third World" nations of Asia and Africa, racism in the United States was taken as an insult to nonwhite peoples everywhere.

Whether because of moral principle or crude expedience, legalized racism had to go. Because the Supreme Court is an august body, deliberately placed by the Constitution above the winds of partisan politics and social change, it usually moves slowly, often ponderously in response to society's demonstrated needs. But in the civil rights cases of the 1950's, it was clearly in step with the changing times.

Black people themselves created the pressure for change within American society. Indeed, a civil rights revolution had been in the making for several decades, unseen or ignored by most whites. The court cases of the 1950's marked the climax of that revolution's "quiet" phase, preparing the way for the subsequent, more militant phase (Chapter 29). Such men of quiet dedication as Roy Wilkins and Thurgood Marshall of the National Association for the Advancement of Colored People worked tirelessly in courtrooms and legislative anterooms to pull down the legal walls confining black Americans.

Reaction to desegregation. Reaction in the white South to the desegregation order varied. Some extremists vowed never to obey it and went about stirring up the worst kind of public emotionalism. White Citizens' Councils popped up all over the Deep South, for the purpose of preventing school integration—by any means. Southern legislators outdid themselves in trying to find some way of circumventing the Court. Virginia, for example, resurrected John C. Calhoun's notion that a state can "interpose" itself between the Supreme Court and "the people." Men of goodwill and common sense, on the other hand, welcomed the decision. They saw it as an

A DISSENTING VIEW OF THE WARREN COURT

James F. Byrnes, secretary of state in the postwar years, also served on the Supreme Court from 1941 to 1942. He disagreed sharply with the Warren Court's desegregation decision and criticized it for usurping state powers:

"Two years ago, on May 17, 1954, the Supreme Court of the United States reversed what had been the law of the land for 75 years and declared unconstitutional the laws of 17 States under which segregated public-school systems were established.

"The Court did not interpret the Constitution—the Court amended it.

"We have a written Constitution. Under that Constitution the people of the United States have enjoyed great progress and freedom. The usurpation by the Court of the power to amend the Constitution and destroy State governments may impair our progress and take our freedom.

"An immediate consequence of the segregation decision is that much of the progress made in the last half century of steadily advancing racial amity has been undone. Confidence and trust have been supplanted by suspicion and distrust. The races are divided and the breach is widening. The truth is, there has not been such tension between the races in the South since the days of Reconstruction.

"One threatened consequence is the closing of public schools in many States of the South.

"A further consequence is the harm done to the entire country by the demonstrated willingness of the Supreme Court to disregard our written Constitution and its own decisions, invalidate the laws of States, and substitute for these a policy of its own, supported not by legal precedents but by the writings of sociologists.

"Today, this usurpation by the Court of the power of the States hurts the South. Tomorrow, it may hurt the North, East, and West. It may hurt *you*. . . ."

Brown v. Topeka Board of Education (1954). Ruled that racial segregation in public elementary schools is unconstitutional.

Griffen v. Illinois (1956). Held that a state's denial of a defendant's right of appeal is a violation of the due process clause of the Constitution.

Yates v. U.S. (1957). Ruled that advocating overthrow of the government as an abstract doctrine is not unlawful if it does not lead to direct action.

Watkins v. U.S. (1957). Limited the use of congressional investigation of individuals.

Jencks v. U.S. (1957). Held that a criminal defendant must have equal access to material used against him.

Mapp v. Ohio (1961). Ruled that evidence seized in an illegal search may not be introduced into court.

Baker v. Carr (1962). Held that discriminatory apportionment for voting districts for state legislatures is in violation of the equal protection clause of the Constitution. Also ruled that federal courts may intervene if state legislators do not correct malapportionment.

Engel v. Vitale (1962). Banned prayers in public schools.

Abingdon School District v. Schempp (1963). Banned devotional Bible reading in public schools.

Gideon v. Wainwright (1963). Held that a man accused of a felony is entitled to free counsel if he cannot afford a lawyer.

Escobedo v. Illinois (1964). Held that a criminal suspect may not be prevented from seeing his lawyer during police questioning.

Wesberry v. Sanders (1964). Ruled that congressional voting districts must be equal in population.

Reynolds v. Sims (1964). Ruled that voting districts for both houses of state legislatures must be equal in population.

Atlanta Motel v. U.S. (1964). Upheld the Civil Rights Act of 1964 prohibiting racial discrimination in public accommodations.

Aptheker v. Secretary of State (1964). Held that denial of passport privileges to Communists is a violation of the due process clause of the Constitution.

Albertson v. Subversive Activities Control Board (1965). Held that the Internal Security Act of 1950 providing that Communist-party members must register with the government was unconstitutional because it forced party members to incriminate themselves (a denial of the Fifth Amendment).

Miranda v. Arizona (1966). Held that a criminal suspect must be informed of his right to remain silent and to have a lawyer present before being questioned.

---

opportunity for the South to rid itself of the immense social and financial burden of a dual school system.

Tragically, the forces of moderation received little support from political leaders in Washington or their own states. In Congress, one hundred southern members issued a "manifesto," in which they approved of all "legal" efforts to resist integration, an action which invited defiance of the Court. Many politicians skillfully exploited old fears among white voters to advance themselves rapidly, and a new breed of demagogues descended upon many southern statehouses. Men

sworn to uphold the law became open and arrogant in their defiance of the law.

From the White House, the Supreme Court decision evoked only silence. With his great prestige and popularity, Eisenhower might have tipped the scales in favor of peaceful integration had he spoken out for compliance with the law. But he said nothing and did nothing until September 1957, when his hand was forced.

To prevent nine black children from enrolling in Little Rock's Central High School, the governor of Arkansas, Orval Faubus, surrounded the school with National Guardsmen. When a federal court enjoined him to cease and desist, Faubus withdrew the troops and, in effect, invited a mob to intimidate the children. Inevitably, a riot ensued. Eisenhower could not ignore this blatant challenge to the federal courts, and he ordered one thousand paratroopers to the scene. Order was restored and the black children were enrolled. But the damage was done, and it was many years before the wounds healed in Little Rock. Elsewhere in the South, meanwhile, new wounds were opened almost daily.

Civil rights legislation. Two Civil Rights Acts (1957 and 1960) during the Eisenhower years modestly advanced the legal position of black people. But the great thrust for justice and equality came from the Supreme Court. Judicial activism in civil rights, as on other issues, provoked loud and angry opposition. Some extremists wanted to destroy the Supreme Court. Others cried for the impeachment of the Chief Justice. Through all the turbulence and noisy breast-beating, Earl Warren remained a firm rock of judicial integrity. During his tenure on the bench, the Supreme Court spoke the will of the law and the conscience of the nation.

■ CONCLUSION

Life in the United States after World War II was a strange combination of exhilaration and anxiety, of high hopes and deep fears. Demobilization took place quickly and was followed by a period of rapid economic growth and general prosperity. But inevitably, the tensions of the cold war spread into domestic politics. Frustrated by supposed failures in foreign policy, shocked by the disclosures of a few Communists in their midst, many people succumbed to the temptation to seek scapegoats rather than understanding. And there were enough opportunistic politicians on hand to play upon the public's fears to a point where civil liberties were seriously damaged.

A striking feature of the times was the lack of dynamic political leadership. President Truman's Fair Deal was little more than a mild extension of the New Deal, and, as such, it aroused the hostility of conservatives. Even if it had been enacted intact, however, it would not have begun to meet the demand for action created by such staggering developments as the population explosion, the revolution in science and technology, the ugly tangle of racial difficulties, and the growing disparity between the prosperous and the poor, especially in the cities.

As for Truman's successor, General Eisenhower, he proved to be one of the most popular Presidents in history—and one of the least effective. After eight years in office, he left his party weak, divided, and still in the minority; while he bequeathed his successor a logjam of ignored or unresolved problems.

It was the Supreme Court which moved into the political vacuum and confronted many of the great issues of the day. Its landmark decisions in the areas of civil rights, education, political representation, individual liberty, and police powers aroused intense controversy; but they also dramatized the failure of the executive and legislative branches. In the end, the most dynamic and responsive political figure of the time was Chief Justice Earl Warren.

■ QUESTIONS

1. What pressing domestic problems did America face after World War II?

2. How did the government handle the internal security issue in the postwar years?

3. Why did the country undergo one of its worst periods of public hysteria during the period?

4. In what ways did Eisenhower and Truman differ as Presidents? In what ways were they similar?

5. Did Eisenhower and Truman end up on political dead center? Explain your answer.

6. Was Earl Warren the most dynamic and responsive political figure of the postwar period? Defend your answer.

7. How and why did the Warren Court extend the rights of the individual in American society?

8. What were the similarities and what were the differences between the post World War II period and the periods following the Civil War and World War I?

9. Which branch of the federal government has experienced the greatest amount of change in the last hundred years? Defend your answer.

■ BIBLIOGRAPHY

O'CONNOR, EDWIN, *The Last Hurrah*, Bantam Books. O'Connor's novel deals with the last campaign of an Irish political chieftain in a large eastern city. There is a contrast between the old style of politicians that is reminiscent of *Plunkitt of Tammany Hall* and the new modern campaign such as that discussed in *The Making of the President*. It is a good story to hold the student's interest while shedding light on city politics.

TRUMAN, HARRY S., *Memoirs by Harry S. Truman*, 2 vols., *Years of Decision, Years of Trial and Hope*, New American Library (Signet Books). In this two-volume memoir of his Presidency, Truman elucidates on the important issues and events which required Presidential reaction. This is a necessary source for the student who wants to understand the postwar period, particularly since there is a lack of biographical studies of Truman.

ALBERTSON, DEAN, ED., *Eisenhower as President*, Hill & Wang (American Century Series). The student should read Eisenhower's memoirs as well as this collection of essays which evaluates the practice and philosophy of his administration. Because of the fairly recent terms of Eisenhower, there is still much that can be found in the periodical literature on Eisenhower, and many of his own statements are still easily accessible. But this collection provides the student with a valuable summary perspective on the fifties by participants and observers of the Eisenhower administration.

ROVERE, RICHARD H., *Senator Joe McCarthy*, World (Meridian Books). Rovere is a critic of the controversial Joseph McCarthy, and he indicates the dangers of a demagogue in American society. The student may also consult the appropriate problem-series booklet for opposing interpretations of McCarthy. There is also a good film, *Point of Order*, which documents the hearings.

BICKEL, ALEXANDER M., *The Supreme Court and the Idea of Progress*, Harper & Row (Torchbooks). Bickel provides a sound analysis of the Warren Court. He devotes attention to the issues of civil rights, representation, police powers, individual rights, and desegregation.

LEWIS, ANTHONY, *Gideon's Trumpet*, Random House (Vintage Books). This is the story of the famous case which began with a simple breaking and entering trial and ended with the Supreme Court's important decision on the rights of the accused. It is both a personal story of one man's appeal for redress of grievances and also an excellent description of the operation of the American court system.

STROUT, CUSHING, ED., *Conscience, Science, and Security: The Case of Dr. J. Robert Oppenheimer*, Berkeley Series in American History, Rand McNally. This booklet does a good job of raising the issues surrounding the relationship between the scientist and his society. Oppenheimer, one of the key figures in the development of the atom bomb, was given a hearing concerning his security clearance in 1954, and the subsequent proceedings released many of the conflicting currents which were prevalent in America in the early fifties. The booklet is an edited version of Oppenheimer's hearing.

The Cold War In Transition

By 1952, the cold war had become almost a "way of life" for the American people. The continuing enmity between Washington and Moscow, the triumph of Mao Tse-tung in China, and above all, the agony of the Korean War all contributed to a general feeling that relations between the United States and the Communist nations were utterly irreconcilable. Indeed, many people were sure that a military showdown between this nation and the Soviet Union was inevitable and only a matter of time. At home, moreover, the domestic effects of the cold war became a dominant political issue. In 1953, the Republicans came to power, promising not only to "clean up the mess" in Washington, but also to "roll back" communism everywhere in the world. To some observers, it appeared that the expected international showdown was imminent.

Yet, while the cold war persisted throughout the 1950's and into the 1960's, its nature changed in subtle and important ways. Quickly, the Republicans learned of the limits of power, and so did the men in control of matters in Moscow. While the cold war flared up angrily on occasion and even spread into Africa and Latin America, somehow the United States and the Soviet Union managed to avoid open conflict. Indeed, they even began groping toward some basis for living together in relative peace. As you read about these years of transition, consider these questions:

1. How did internal changes in Communist countries affect American foreign policy?
2. How did America get involved in the politics of underdeveloped nations, and what were the consequences?
3. How successful was the policy of "peaceful coexistence" between the United States and the Soviet Union?
4. What policy did the United States follow toward Latin America?
5. What were President Kennedy's successes and failures in foreign policy?

1 A Changing World Stimulates Changes In Foreign Policy

1. What characteristics of the 1950's strongly affected American foreign policy?

2. What were the qualifications and the limitations of John Foster Dulles as Secretary of State? How did these affect his diplomacy?

3. How did Sputnik and related Soviet achievements affect American foreign policy? How would you expect it to affect American domestic policy?

4. What were the causes of friction between China and the Soviet Union? How did this friction influence international communism?

As the first Republican President in two decades, Eisenhower was under great pressure from elements in his party to effect major changes in foreign policy. Senator Robert Taft and his fellow conservatives distrusted the North Atlantic Treaty Organization, seeing it as a reckless intrusion of Americans in Europe's political jungles. They criticized foreign aid as an international "boondoggle" in which Americans would receive nothing in return for their generous gifts.

A few were authentic isolationists, who wanted the United States to entrench itself within a "Fortress America" of the Western Hemisphere. But most were the same people who, before Pearl Harbor, had stood for unilateralism in foreign policy. While they opposed Washington's getting itself politically involved abroad, they had no objection to an assertive expansion of American economic and moral power throughout the world.

Along with most other Americans, the conservative Republicans saw Asia as this country's great economic frontier of the future. Unlike the moderate wing of the GOP and the majority of Democrats, they were prepared to accept a weakening of the Atlantic community in order to extend American involvement in the Far East. Thus, they demanded a foreign policy which would somehow undo the Chinese revolution and restore the old conditions of the Open Door throughout Asia. The "loss" of China to the Communists, they tended to believe, could have been prevented if only the Roosevelt and Truman foreign policies had not favored Europe over the Far East. Echoing a sentiment of the past, they proclaimed that America's destiny lay to the west, over the vast Pacific, not with the decadent Old World of the Atlantic.

Eisenhower was well aware of the significance of the Open Door in American history, and he did not turn his back on the Far East (nor had Roosevelt or Truman, for that matter). But neither did he shift his primary attention away from the Atlantic community. It would have been strange if he had done so; for, to a large extent, he was himself a product of the Europe-oriented diplomacy of the war and postwar years. Indeed, he came to the campaign of 1952 directly from his post as commander of the NATO army in Europe, a position to which Truman had recalled him from retirement. Throughout his Presidency, he worked to strengthen NATO and to improve America's position in Western Europe.

John Foster Dulles. For a time, nonetheless, his administration appeared to take a new tack. It showed chiefly in the personality and rhetoric of Secretary of State John Foster Dulles. Descended from two earlier secretaries of state, Dulles had spent years preparing for the office he believed himself destined to occupy. During the long wait, he distinguished himself as an attorney and as a lay leader in the Presbyterian church. Both interests strongly affected his diplomacy when he finally gained the coveted position as head of the State Department.

Dulles remained ever the lawyer, ready to advocate or to arraign as the case might require, using his talent for courtroom dramatics both in conducting foreign affairs and in creating public support for his views. As Presidential aide Emmet John Hughes put it, Dulles always saw himself as "in effect, the prosecutor assigned to the historic labor of arraignment, condemnation, and punishment of the Soviet Union for crimes against freedom and peace."

Dulles found it all but impossible to view communism with an objective, even a pragmatic, eye. To him, all Marxists were so patently evil, so inherently immoral, that their system *must* soon crumble from internal decay. Decent men everywhere, he believed, had a moral duty not only to resist communism, but also to fight it actively. Dulles's moralistic-legalistic approach to the cold war left no room for neutralism (a policy favored by many emerging nations in Asia and Africa). Indeed, he alienated the leaders of such crucial nations as India and Indonesia by lecturing them on their moral responsibilities.

In private, the secretary often displayed an impressive grasp of history and sound sense of proportion, two qualities essential in a diplomatist. In public, he often behaved almost as though only he knew right from wrong. Few of his subordinates found him easy to work with, for he seldom gave them any major responsibilities of their own.

Dulles became a one-man traveling State Department. He was always on the go, making his impressive presence felt everywhere in the world except where it was most needed—in the State Department building itself, where the routine, daily work of protecting American interests abroad was conducted. His hustle and bustle had a confusing effect. Britain's Sir Anthony Eden probably spoke the private views of many foreign diplomats when he complained that one never knew just what the secretary meant or what he was really trying to do.

The policy of brinkmanship. Dulles added to the confusion by his rhetorical extravagance and addiction to slogans. Soon after he took office, he announced that Chiang Kai-shek was to be "unleashed" to attack mainland China. He pledged that the United States would "roll back" the Communists, rather than passively contain them. Mere containment meant abandoning the "captive peoples" of Eastern Europe to their Red masters, he argued; the United States should mount a moral offensive to bring about their "liberation."

Any new aggressive moves by Russia or China, Dulles warned, would be met with "massive retaliation," a term which implied that *any* disruption of peace would automatically trigger an American nuclear response. Faced with French opposition to the unrestricted rearming of Germany, Dulles warned that such obstructionism might well force an "agonizing reappraisal" of this nation's relations with its allies. After the secretary stated that he was willing to "go to the

brink" of war in dealing with his adversaries, critics dubbed his diplomacy "brinkmanship."

To support Dulles's unique style and rhetoric, the administration proposed a "New Look" in military affairs, as well. Military spending was cut, while administration spokesmen promised the taxpayers a more efficient defense establishment. Reflecting the prevailing disillusionment with the Korean "police action," the Republicans reduced the ground forces and put new emphasis upon air power and nuclear weapons. In effect, the military was stripped of its ability to fight small, limited wars. The threat of "massive nuclear retaliation" was relied upon to deter the Russians, or other potential aggressors.

Khrushchev assumes power. On March 5, 1953, only weeks after Eisenhower took office, the Kremlin announced the death of Stalin. In the struggle for succession, Nikita Khrushchev ultimately emerged as the strong man in Moscow. A shrewd, tough, professional politician, the new leader was a Communist version of Horatio Alger's self-made man. Born in poverty and poorly educated, he had pushed his way up the political ranks with ruthless determination, finally becoming head of the Communist party itself and, in 1958, premier of the Soviet Union as well.

Khrushchev took the Soviet Union, and the world, entirely by surprise in February 1956, when he bitterly denounced Stalin in an extraordinary speech to the Twentieth Congress of the Communist party. For a time thereafter, Russia was deliberately "de-Stalinized." History was rewritten to downgrade the old dictator, while even the heroic city of Stalingrad had its name changed to Volgograd. At the same time, the new regime eased up in its control over the Russian people. To be sure, the change brought nothing like American-style political and intellectual freedom; but the "liberalization" was a welcome relief to most Russians. To an extent, too, Khrushchev loosened Moscow's reins on the satellite countries of Eastern Europe, although events soon proved that the change here was a very restricted one.

The rest of the world found Khrushchev a distinct change from Stalin. Whereas the old dictator had left the Soviet Union only once during his long rule, the bouncy new premier traveled all over the globe on "goodwill missions." He

UNITED STATES LOANS AND GRANTS

Area	1949–52 Annual Average	1953–61 Annual Average	1962	1966	1970
Western Europe					
Economic aid	$ 3.8 billion	$ 395,500,000	$142,400,000	$165,800,000	$434,400,000
Military aid	$ 507,900,000	$ 1.22 billion	$425,800,000	$223,400,000	$169,500,000
Eastern Europe					
Economic aid	$ 83,000,000	$ 133,900,000	$124,100,000	$ 42,900,000	$ 19,100,000
Military aid	$ 15,000,000	$ 70,300,000	*	$ 300,000	*
Middle East and Southwest Asia					
Economic aid	$ 376,300,000	$ 884,900,000	$ 1.9 billion	$ 1.43 billion	$ 1.30 billion
Military aid	$ 144,000,000	$ 384,000,000	$ 265,100,000	$ 295,100,000	$369,800,000
Far East and Southeast Asia					
Economic aid	$ 792,100,000	$ 871,800,000	$ 632,200,000	$ 1.28 billion	$ 1.47 billion
Military aid	$ 101,400,000	$ 659,870,000	$ 739,800,000	**	**
Africa					
Economic aid	$ 12,800,000	$143,500,000	$475,800,000	$ 365,100,000	$ 294,300,000
Military aid	*	$ 5,900,000	$ 23,600,000	$ 21,900,000	$ 32,400,000
Latin America					
Economic aid	$148,400,000	$ 438,800,000	$ 1.01 billion	$ 1.22 billion	$ 1.06 billion
Military aid	*	$ 46,000,000	$132,800,000	$ 82,000,000	$ 61,500,000

* Less than $50,000.   ** Figures for direct military aid from 1966 on are not differentiated from overall military operations in Southeast Asia.

even came to the United States, where he both amused and irritated the American people. Adopting a new attitude toward old rivalries, Khrushchev denied that war between capitalism and communism was inevitable. While the two would remain foes, he announced, henceforth their arena would be the marketplace, their competition peaceful. In this new contest of production and technology, he boasted, "we will bury you!"

Soviet scientific achievements. Khrushchev's bumptious self-confidence reflected a surge of confidence within Russia itself. Having finally recovered from World War II, the Russians astonished the Western world with a series of spectacular developments in science and tech-

nology. In 1953, they exploded a hydrogen bomb, then quickly perfected an intercontinental delivery system for the awesome new weapon. Although the United States also soon developed a hydrogen warfare capability, American strategic supremacy in the world vanished, to be replaced by a global "balance of terror." Each side in the cold war was now capable of utterly destroying the other—and the world, in the bargain.

These Soviet scientific achievements stunned most Americans. Long years of wishful thinking had misled people into thinking of Russia as a backward, peasant land, saddled with an oppressive, unworkable political system. But science can be totally neutral where politics is concerned. Even in the worst years of the Stalin dictatorship, the Russians made notable advances in many fields of knowledge.*

New proof of their technical skill came in 1957, when they beat the United States into space with *Sputnik I*, the world's first artificial satellite. Two years later, they sent an unmanned rocket to the moon. In 1961, the Soviet "cosmonaut" Yuri Gagarin orbited the earth to become the first man in space. Coming at a time when America's space program, quite literally, was still stuck on the launching pad, these feats greatly enhanced Soviet prestige. Moreover, they suggested that the Russians were moving well ahead of the United States in military rocketry.

Conflict between China and Russia. Events in the other great center of communism, mainland China, also affected the diplomacy of the 1950's. The decade opened with China and Russia signing a treaty of alliance; it closed with the two Red giants moving apart in a momentous split over ideological and political questions. In a sense, they were victims of a "generation gap." Still fired by revolutionary zeal, the young Peking regime saw Russia's bid for "peaceful coexistence" with the West and its denunciation of Stalinism as evidence that the men in the Kremlin had grown old and given up the revolutionary struggle. Accusations that once had been reserved for "capitalist imperialists" began to flow freely between Moscow and Peking.

In the wake of its revolution, moreover, China experienced a wave of militant nationalism. History provided the chief stimulus here, as Mao Tse-tung sought to recover the borderlands which the Western powers had taken from the old Chinese empire. His armies first overran Tibet, a remote mountain land, which British colonialists had "separated" from China early in the century. Next, he turned to the complex problem of China's borders with India, a nation which was one of his few outspoken friends.

When Prime Minister Nehru of India balked at discussing a redrawing of the borders (which also had been drawn by British map-makers), Mao did not hesitate to put China's interests above any gratitude he may have felt for Nehru's

---

* They also made some incredible blunders, as when—to please Stalin—they adopted a spurious theory of heredity, thereby all but destroying the science of biology in Russia.

friendship. In a remarkable display of limited warfare, his troops routed the weak Indian border forces in 1962, took the territories in dispute, then halted their advance—even though all of northern India lay helpless before them and could have been conquered easily.

But the old territories which all Chinese nationalists most coveted were those which the czars had taken and which now were held by the Soviet Union. By 1960, the two Communist powers were entangled in an explosive, old-fashioned boundary dispute as well as an increasingly bitter ideological conflict. Just how serious their differences were became evident when the Chinese spurned Russia's half-hearted offer to help them develop a nuclear capability. Chinese talent and resources would do the job alone, they announced defiantly. They made good their boast in short order, successfully testing both atomic and hydrogen bombs in the mid-1960's. By then, the myth of monolithic communism—communism as a uniform, intractable, centrally directed entity—had been scattered to the four winds.

2 The United States Faces New Crises In Asia And Africa

1. Why was there so much international controversy over the two small islands of Quemoy and Matsu?

2. What is the domino theory? How effective is it in explaining the realities of international affairs?

3. How did Eisenhower's actions toward Indochina in the early 1950's affect the course of the Vietnam War? Do you think he had any reasonable alternatives? Was Eisenhower's policy toward Indochina consistent with American goals and values?

4. Why was the United States relatively unprepared to handle the emergence of the new African nations?

True to his campaign pledge, Eisenhower brought an end to the Korean War after taking office. The armistice agreement, signed on July 27, 1953, actually resolved none of the war's political questions. Korea remained divided into two hostile camps, and prospects for future stability in the peninsula were dim. Had Truman made the same settlement before leaving office, he probably would have been accused of "selling out" to the enemy. As it was, Eisenhower's great popularity and prestige as a military leader were enough to convince most people that he had salvaged all that he could from the stalemate—which was doubtless the case.

In making the settlement, Eisenhower apparently notified Peking that he would enlarge the war unless the truce talks produced peace. How far he might have gone if the Chinese had spurned an armistice, no one knows. Fortunately, Mao saw the futility of continued fighting and agreed to a settlement. Dulles later cited the negotiations as an instance of "going to the brink of war" to make the enemy back down. The example was not an apt one, for Americans and Chinese were already fighting each other. But it pointed up Dulles's determination to "get tough" with both China and the Soviet Union.

In practice, "getting tough" usually amounted to "talking tough." In "unleashing" Chiang Kai-shek in 1953, for example, presumably the administration freed him from the restraints Truman had imposed during the Korean War, when the Seventh Fleet moved into the Formosa Strait to prevent either of the Chinas from attacking the other. In reality, the announcement changed nothing. Indeed, Washington actually shortened the leash on Chiang in 1954, in a mutual security pact which pledged United States' support of his regime, while binding him to make no moves toward the mainland without Washington's approval.

Quemoy and Matsu. In a way, this pact restrained both Chinas. For while Peking railed against it and vowed to "liberate" Formosa, Mao knew that he could not invade the island against American naval and air power. Other islands in the strait, however, lay close to China and hundreds of miles from Formosa, and many mapmakers had already assumed that they were part of the People's Republic. When Mao moved to occupy Quemoy and Matsu (tiny islets lying off the coast of mainland China), Eisenhower's uncertainty as to their exact status helped to turn a minor incident into a serious international crisis. Peking's preoccupation with events elsewhere in Asia in 1954 prevented the situation from getting out of hand at that time.

But the crisis erupted anew in 1958. By then, Chiang had fortified the two little islands, plainly hoping to provoke a clash with Peking which would draw the United States to his side militarily. He almost succeeded. While Communist artillery pounded the islands, American warships convoyed Chiang's troops and supplies to them. War seemed a certainty; yet, aside from Chiang, no one really wanted war. To many Americans, it was unthinkable that a new major conflict should break out over these two tiny Asian islands. Public pressure forced Dulles to retreat from the brink and modify his "tough line" considerably. When he announced that the United States was not committed to helping Chiang retake the mainland, Peking reciprocated by easing the pressure on Quemoy and Matsu.

Dulles later confided that the "defense" of Quemoy was "the most brilliant thing I have done." Certainly, it was a forceful show of American power in Asia. It was also a reckless show, however, for it provoked a crisis for no good reason. Quemoy and Matsu were of no strategic or tactical value to the United States, and their fate was of no consequence to the balance of power in the Pacific. The main effect of the crisis was momentarily to raise Chiang's hopes of regaining the mainland. Even Dulles eventually acknowledged that these hopes were false.

The "domino theory." In Southeast Asia, too, Eisenhower and Dulles walked to the brink, then pulled back. Since 1950, the United States had supplied and financed the French forces fighting the Vietminh in Indochina (page 664). After the Korean armistice, China sent substantial aid to Ho Chi Minh. As the French position deteriorated, Eisenhower had to decide how big the stakes were in Indochina. He likened the situation to a row of dominoes. Knock over one domino (Indochina) in the row, he said, and the rest (the other nations of Southeast Asia) will fall, too.

The "domino theory" offered a simple explanation for the complex phenomenon of radical

AFRICA AND THE MIDDLE EAST, 1970 709

nationalism in the old colonial world. It was of dubious value in making foreign policy, however. It assumed that conditions in Burma and Thailand, for example, were identical to those in Indochina, which was not the case at all. Each nation had unique historical and cultural factors which gave it an identity and integrity all its own. Eisenhower also did not recognize the extent to which the Vietminh movement had the backing of the Vietnamese people, assuming incorrectly that it was simply an extension of Russian or Chinese communism.

Vietnam. As the crisis deepened, Dulles and Vice-President Nixon recommended sending American troops to help the French. Eisenhower's chief military adviser wanted to relieve the siege of Dien Bien Phu (page 664) with a nuclear air strike. Unable to get support from his European allies for such drastic moves, Eisenhower decided to pull back from the brink. Instead of sending troops to Indochina, he sent a reluctant Dulles to the Geneva Conference of 1954. As the fate of Indochina was decided, Secretary Dulles refused even to look at the Chinese foreign minister, Chou En-lai.

The Geneva agreements temporarily divided Vietnam into two sectors. Free elections were to be held throughout the land under international supervision in July 1956, to bring about reunification. But elections were never held, chiefly because the United States treated South Vietnam as an independent sovereign nation. Had the elections been held as scheduled, as even Eisenhower acknowledged, "possibly 80 percent of the population" would have voted to make Ho ruler of all Vietnam. Determined to maintain a pro-Western regime at Saigon, Washington began a military and economic buildup of South Vietnam.

The formation of SEATO. To forestall further erosion of the West's position in Southeast Asia, Dulles in 1954 persuaded two European nations (Britain and France), two white Pacific nations (Australia and New Zealand), and three Asian nations (Thailand, Pakistan, and the Philippines), to join the United States in a Southeast Asia Treaty Organization.

SEATO was a sterile undertaking, for it was a military pact, while the area's problems were social and economic. None of the big Asian nations joined it, and many Asians considered it a new instrument of Western imperialism. But the United States made SEATO the cornerstone of its Asian policy, even stretching the treaty's provisions to justify the Vietnam war after 1964. The pact proved to be a weak reed upon which to lean for support.

Afro-Asian neutralism. Most Asians preferred neutralism to alignment with either side in the cold war. Delegates from twenty-nine Asian and African nations met at Bandung, Indonesia, in April 1955, to denounce colonialism and to underscore their commitment to neutralism. Yet, Dulles continued to regard neutralism as immoral in international affairs.

Dulles died before the United States learned the power of the neutralist doctrine. Ironically, the lesson came in Japan, a nation he had cultivated as an Asian bulwark against communism. Anti-Americanism grew in Japan during the fifties, nourished by the continued American military presence and by Dulles's heavy-handed efforts to align the Japanese in the cold war. While on a goodwill tour of Asia in 1960, Eisenhower collided head-on with the bitter truth. Two days before he was to land at Tokyo for a state visit, he was forced to cancel his plans and return to Washington. Anti-American rioting had become so violent that Japanese authorities could not guarantee his personal safety. It was a humiliating experience for the American President.

Caught up in a revolution of rising expectations, the Afro-Asian peoples had no real interest in the quarrels of the great powers. They needed rapid economic development and social modernization, not involvement in exotic political adventures. As the situation in Europe settled into a stand-off, however, the cold war protagonists shifted their attention to the developing areas of the world. Russia and China both launched vigorous drives for influence in the new nations, while the former colonial powers tried to retain their hold. In most instances, the United States backed its European allies, sometimes because of expediency, sometimes to counter Russian or Chinese influence. Involvement in cold war rivalries complicated the already difficult problems in the new nations, particularly in the Middle East and Africa.

Black African nationalism. "Uhuru!"—the cry of freedom—brought a quick end to colonialism in much of black Africa.* Indeed, so many new nations emerged in the 1950's that the United States was caught without a clear-cut foreign policy for Africa. Torn between obligations to this country's allies and a historic commitment to self-determination, American leaders moved cautiously. Their problem was complicated by the fact that in Africa, as in Asia, many nationalists were social and economic radicals. Washington feared that unrestrained self-determination might produce a host of pro-Communist regimes in Africa.

Ghana, the former Gold Coast, became the first new African nation in 1957. Thereafter, the floodgates opened; and in 1960 alone, sixteen new African states entered the United Nations. Together with the new Asian states, they formed a huge neutralist Afro-Asian bloc in the UN's General Assembly. The United Nations took on an entirely new look, as the influence of the Security Council (dominated by the big powers) waned.

Bitter problems beset the new African states from the start. National boundaries usually followed artificial lines drawn by European empire-builders, often making no sense at all in ethnic or tribal terms. Nigeria, for example, included three tribal groups with a long and bloody history of mutual hatred. Kenya survived against tribal pressures for dismemberment only because of the strong personality and the skill of its leader Jomo Kenyatta. In Ghana, the career of President Kwame Nkrumah was tragic testimony to the problem of the new nations. For a time, Nkrumah led his country brilliantly; then, determined to unite all of black Africa, he played the dangerous game of courting both sides in the cold war. Nkrumah's own ambition and international intrigue finally overwhelmed him, and he ended by wrecking much of what he had built in Ghana.

In some African states, Communist influence became strong. In the Republic of Guinea, its leader Sekou Toure welcomed the support of both the Soviet Union and China, as did Julius Nyrerere in Tanzania. Nevertheless, both of these leaders showed on numerous occasions that they were African nationalists first and foremost, determined to maintain their nations' independence.

All of Africa's worst problems converged in the Belgian Congo to produce an episode of conflict and chaos. Belgium's rule had been a dismal failure, leaving the Congo miserably unprepared for the independence which came to it in 1960. At once, the new republic slid into a snakepit of tribal wars, personal rivalries, secessionist plots, and international intrigue. UN forces were called in to stabilize the situation; but bloody fighting erupted everywhere, and the security force had an extremely difficult time restoring order.

Dag Hammarskjöld, the courageous secretary-general of the UN who was working to restore peace, lost his life in a plane crash as he was on a peace mission to the Congo. And the murder by pro-Belgian terrorists of Patrice Lumumba, a young Congolese nationalist whose following crossed tribal lines, gave black people everywhere in the world a martyr.

North Africa and the Middle East. Despite the fact that millions of its citizens were of African descent, the American government paid little attention to black Africa until events forced it to. Not until 1958 did the State Department even establish a division to deal exclusively with African affairs. Indeed, it was the rise of black nationalism at home and the spread of Russian and Chinese influence abroad that finally moved Washington to take an active interest in all things African.

In the Moslem countries of North Africa, too, the fires of nationalism caught this nation unprepared. Young army officers in Egypt, led by Gamal Abdel Nasser, deposed their corrupt king in 1953 and proclaimed a fiercely nationalistic republic. In Algeria, guerrilla warfare against French colonial rule flared into a crisis for all the Western powers. Throughout North Africa and the Middle East, Washington suddenly had to wrestle with problems long familiar in Paris and London.

* Africa below the belt of nations touching on the Mediterranean; also known as Sub-Saharan Africa.

711

Before 1950, 80 percent of Africa's population was under European colonial rule. Within twenty years, almost all of Africa had emerged into new, independent countries. But independence was not easily won; it cost the blood of Europeans and Africans alike, that of Europeans when they were driven out, and that of Africans when they were fighting the Europeans and when they were fighting among themselves. Among the earliest nations to claim its independence was Ghana, formerly under British rule. In 1952, Kwame Nkrumah became prime minister (although the British still retained some power), and in 1957, the British departed for good. Nkrumah seemed at the time to be a force to unite all of black Africa, as his soldiers (bottom right) symbolize in 1960. Their signs call for both Ghana's unity and Africa's unity and their legs tied together show the unity they desire. Farther north, in Algeria, rebellion against European rule was also making itself felt, this time against the French. In perhaps one of the bitterest wars of African independence, the French finally withdrew from Algeria, where they had been in power for more than a century. In the picture below, young boys form a parade to celebrate the news that a referendum on Algerian independence has received the necessary "yes" votes to carry. The flags they hold are those of the *FLN*—the National Liberation Front—which had carried the long fight. At right is another triumphant African scene. In it, Jomo Kenyatta addresses a crowd in Nairobi, Kenya, a nation that gained its independence from Great Britain in 1963. Kenyatta had been convicted of leading a secret movement—the *KAU*, or *Mau Mau*—and was jailed until 1961. But by the time a constitution had been drawn up and accepted and independence was granted, he was powerful enough to become Kenya's first prime minister. The fly whisk that he waves is a traditional tribal symbol denoting a chief's power.

3 America And Russia Achieve A "Peaceful Coexistence"

1. Do you think the climate of the cold war significantly changed over the decade of the 1950's or at any one particular time during the decade?

2. What factors had to be considered before Eisenhower could decide on an American response to the Hungarian revolution? Do you think Eisenhower made the wisest decision?

3. What accounted for the hostilities in the Middle East in 1956?

4. How justifiable were U-2 reconnaisance flights by the United States?

As early as 1953, Winston Churchill detected enough evidence of change in Russian diplomacy to convince him that the time was ripe for putting an end to the cold war. As an experienced diplomat, he was willing to meet flexibility with flexibility; thus, he urged Eisenhower to join him in sitting down with the new men in the Kremlin to work out a formula for international understanding. Dulles adamantly opposed the idea, and the bitterness of past differences with Moscow could not be dispersed in Washington as easily and abruptly as Churchill hoped.

In search of lasting peace. Despite Dulles's gloomy pessimism, on the other hand, Eisenhower worked earnestly to bring lasting peace to the world. Often his efforts were roughly conceived or marked by a naïve faith in the good intentions of other men. But in his simple, direct manner, Eisenhower epitomized the old American belief that permanent universal peace is an attainable goal.

In December 1953, for example, the President proposed that all nations pool their atomic know-how for the benefit of mankind. The United States, he pledged, would "devote its entire heart and mind to find the way by which the miraculous inventiveness of man shall not be dedicated to his death, but consecrated to his life." Russian

skepticism and congressional stinginess almost smothered the "atoms-for-peace" plan at the outset. But the idea caught on; and in 1956, an International Atomic Energy Agency came into being, supported by both the United States and the USSR. Unfortunately, it was not able to check the spread of nuclear arms in the world.

The "spirit of Geneva." Russia's bid for "peaceful coexistence" aroused enough interest in Western Europe to persuade Eisenhower, in 1955, that a "summit" meeting would be worthwhile. In July, the leaders of the Big Four (the United States, the Soviet Union, Britain, and France) met at Geneva, Switzerland, in the first such high-level gathering since Potsdam, ten years earlier. As at Potsdam, the chief barrier to any real agreement was Germany. Neither side was willing to concede enough to make its proposals for Germany's future acceptable to the other side. Nothing of substance came from the Geneva Conference, although the participants met in a general atmosphere of friendliness.

The dramatic moment came when Eisenhower proposed that the Soviet Union and the United States put an end to traditional military secrecy. To bring about genuine disarmament, he asked the powers to open themselves to periodic aerial inspection of their war-making facilities. Khrushchev responded with a plan for immediate nuclear disarmament, but flatly rejected Eisenhower's bid for "open skies" inspection. Once again, the Russians could not overcome their suspicion that an ulterior motive lay behind a sincere, if somewhat naïve, American proposal.

For a few months, the "spirit of Geneva" softened relations between East and West. Then events in Eastern Europe and the Middle East converged to put an end to the first brief "thaw" in the cold war. Indeed, the world almost tumbled into a new hot war in 1956.

Uprisings in Poland and Hungary. Trouble erupted in Eastern Europe as the Kremlin's "liberal" policies toward the satellite nations unleashed the nationalistic feelings of the people. Serious revolts broke out in Poland and Hungary. The Polish revolt was quickly brought under control. But in Hungary, a mild revolt within the ruling hierarchy boiled up into full-scale popular revolution. Fully expecting United States help, Hungarian "freedom fighters" bravely defied their rulers and the Red Army. But Washington did nothing, tacitly acknowledging that Hungary belonged within the Russian sphere of influence. The Soviets correctly estimated the uprising as a challenge to their entire position in Eastern Europe. Soviet armor ruthlessly crushed the revolt.

These events in Eastern Europe revealed the hollowness of Dulles's promise to "roll back" communism. Clearly, the United States did not intend to "liberate" anyone at the risk of war with Russia. In any case, at the time of the Hungarian uprising, Washington had its hands so full in the Middle East that it could only cast a passing glance at Budapest's plight.

Trouble in the Middle East. Immensely rich in oil, the Middle East was a great prize in the cold war. As an area of political instability and social discontent, moreover, it was an ideal arena for international intrigue. Nationalism among the Arabs had been a seething force since World War I; after 1945, it welled up throughout the region. By the mid-1950's, it had broken the Anglo-French political hold in the Middle East, although it was still far short of its larger goal of uniting all Arabs under a single standard.

Further complicating the Middle East problem was the insistence of Arab extremists that Israel had no right to exist as a nation. In 1948 the Israelis routed an Arab invasion force, but Arab fanatics continued to call for the annihilation of the Jewish state. Egypt's strong man, Gamal Abdel Nasser, made himself the mortal enemy of Israel by exploiting the conflict in order to further his ambition to create a pan-Arab empire.

Aside from the importance of its oil, the Middle East most impressed Dulles as a battleground in the ideological cold war. To quarantine the region both from Russian penetration and from neutralism, he created the Baghdad Pact in 1955. This pale imitation of NATO aligned several weak Arab states with Britain in a security arrangement. Far from stabilizing anything, however, the pact precipitated a major crisis. Nasser denounced it as a deliberate effort to undermine him and split the Arab world. Predictably, he moved closer to the Soviet bloc, while making things uncomfortable for the Western powers (for example, by giving open support to the rebels in French Algeria). Moreover, he entered into a military alliance with Syria, Jordan, and Saudi Arabia, obviously aimed at destroying Israel.

The Suez crisis. At the same time, Nasser asked both Russia and the West for aid in building the Aswan Dam project on the Nile. At first, Dulles agreed to help finance the project. When he learned that Egypt was also accepting aid from Moscow, however, he humiliated Nasser by abruptly withdrawing the offer in July 1956. Dulles gambled on pressuring the Egyptians into relying totally on the West for assistance, but the gamble failed. A week later, on July 26, Nasser seized the Suez Canal from its British operators and nationalized it. He did so to recoup the prestige Dulles had stripped from him and to divert the canal's revenues to finance the Aswan project.

Britain and France wanted to move against Egypt at once, not only to retake the canal, but also to get rid of Nasser. They saw him chiefly as a threat to their oil interests, but also as a potential instrument by which Russian power could move into the Mediterranean. They failed to win Washington to their side, however. Dulles now believed that an attack on Nasser would drive all the Arabs into Moscow's arms. Moreover, he saw the crisis as an opportunity to dissociate this country temporarily from the old colonial powers and thereby impress the Third World nations. Thus, the United States jeopardized the NATO alliance by turning against its principal European allies. Indeed, Washington all but cut off communication with Paris and London during the crisis.

On October 29, 1956, the Israelis knifed into Gaza and the Sinai Peninsula and dealt Nasser's army a crushing blow. The attack was designed to thwart the invasion of Israel that Nasser had been promising. Britain and France also moved against Egypt, although with considerably less effectiveness. To their dismay, the United States thereupon joined Russia in sponsoring a UN resolution demanding that the three nations immediately withdraw from Egyptian soil. It was a humiliating moment for Britain and France, especially, but they had little choice except to comply.

The Suez crisis momentarily raised American prestige in the Third World. But it almost wrecked the European alliance, and relations among the Western allies were never quite the

Events in Eastern Europe and the Middle East seriously threatened the tenuous peace in the 1950's. During the Hungarian revolt, citizens of Budapest showed their defiance of Russia by not only fighting but also burning pictures of Stalin (below left). In the aftermath of the Suez crisis, a member of the UN emergency force (below right) stands guard in a desert outpost in the Sinai Peninsula following the withdrawal of Israeli forces. In Lebanon, where more than 6,000 U.S. marines were sent, the citizens of Beirut turned out to watch them as they entered the city (above).

same again. Nasser's prestige soared among the Arabs, despite the humiliating defeat Israel had handed him. For the Russians, Suez was an unmixed blessing. It diverted world attention from their own bloody actions in Hungary, created dissension within the Atlantic alliance, and opened new channels through which they could exert influence in the Middle East.

The election of 1956. Coming as they did during the Presidential campaign of 1956, the Middle East and Hungarian crises actually strengthened Eisenhower's political position. Adlai Stevenson ran again as the Democratic nominee, with Senator Kefauver on the ticket with him. Stevenson pointed out that Republican foreign policy had helped to create the crises. But the voters still liked "Ike," and the President swept to an overwhelming victory.

The Eisenhower doctrine. In the aftermath of Suez, Washington took new steps to curb Russian influence among the Arabs. In March 1957, Congress gave the President authority to send American aid, including troops, to any Middle East nation "threatened by aggression from any country controlled by international communism." The Eisenhower doctrine came into play most notably when the president of Lebanon asked for help in 1958. Lebanon actually was threatened by pro-Nasser Arab nationalists, not Communist aggressors, but Eisenhower sent 14,000 Marines to Beirut, where they remained for three months.

Disunity among cold war allies. Meanwhile, both the United States and Russia found it increasingly difficult to maintain unity among their cold war allies. In June 1958, Charles de Gaulle came to power in France and began to assert his independence of Washington. A proud nationalist, de Gaulle wanted to restore France to a position of authority in Europe. Moreover, Suez convinced him that the Continent could no longer rely on American promises of aid and protection. Europe had to develop a power and identity of its own. As if to add weight to his views, the flow of gold from the United States to the rest of the world deeply concerned Washington. Heavy expenditures in military and economic aid had created an unfavorable *balance of payments* (more money going out of the country than was coming in), a situation which bore directly on America's commitments to her allies.

In the Communist world, China's biting criticism of Khrushchev and his "peaceful coexistence" attitude put the Soviet premier on the defensive. While he wanted at least a temporary accommodation with the West, above all he had to maintain Russia's primacy among the Communist nations.

Another Berlin crisis. Later in 1958, Khrushchev touched off a new crisis over Berlin. Unless the German problem was solved within six months, he announced, the Soviet Union would sign a separate peace treaty with the East Germans and give them control over the access routes to Berlin. The threat did not intimidate Western leaders—whereupon Khrushchev changed tactics, became conciliatory, and talked of a new summit meeting.

By this time, Dulles had died, and Eisenhower turned again to personal diplomacy. He invited the Soviet premier to visit the United States in 1959, agreeing to return the call the following year. Khrushchev arrived in September, and his cordial talks with the President at Camp David produced a new easing of cold war tensions. They also opened the way to the abortive Paris summit meeting, a "non-event" that ranks as the cold war's most grotesque episode.

The U-2 incident. In May 1960, less than two weeks before the Paris conference was to open, Moscow announced the destruction of an American U-2 type reconnaissance plane over Russia. Washington claimed that the aircraft was a weather ship which had probably strayed off course. Khrushchev then produced both the plane and its pilot, who confessed that he had been flying an espionage mission for the Central Intelligence Agency. Caught in one lie, American spokesmen made matters worse by continuing to lie. In the end, Eisenhower assumed full responsibility for the affair, saying that Russia's passion for secrecy made such aerial reconnaissance necessary for Western security.

The U-2 incident wrecked the Paris meeting, but only because Khrushchev used it to that end. Weeks earlier, it had become apparent that neither side was willing to concede anything of substance on the German question. Moscow had become particularly belligerent about Berlin, doubtless because of heavy pressure from Peking to "get tough" with the Western powers. Moreover, Khrushchev now knew that U-2 flights in recent months had given Washington an accurate appraisal of Soviet military strength. Apparently, he felt obliged to cover his humiliation by rattling his verbal sabers. As the Paris meeting opened, he denounced Eisenhower in abusive terms, withdrawing the invitation to visit Russia and demanding an abject apology for the U-2 incident. The conference quickly broke up.

"Peaceful coexistence" continued after the Paris debacle, but it was badly strained by the events of May 1960. Matters became even more precarious because of events in an entirely new theater of cold war—the Caribbean.

4 The Cold War Reaches Latin America

1. Do you think the United States had a sphere of influence in Latin America which under any other nation's control would have been contrary to American policy?

2. What indications were there of hemispheric solidarity during and after World War II, and what indications were there of friction?

3. To what extent was the United States responsible for the overthrow of the Guatemalan government in 1954?

4. Why did Castro's Cuba split with the United States?

During World War II, the United States carefully cultivated the support of its "good neighbors" to the south. Although only Brazil took part in the fighting, all but Argentina broke relations with the Axis powers early in the war. As the conflict drew to a close, Washington moved to turn this support into a permanent hemispheric defense system.

A necessary first step was taken when Senator Arthur Vandenberg and Nelson Rockefeller, then a State Department aide, drafted Article 51 of the United Nations Charter. Article 51 specifically provided for regional defense organizations, permitting them to operate semi-independently of the world body. While the United States frowned on spheres of influence controlled by other powers, it insisted upon continuing its own "special relationship" with Latin America.

From an economic point of view, Washington took this "special relationship" for granted. During the war, the United States had greatly expanded its dominant economic position in Latin America. Most Latin American countries had willingly responded to Washington's wartime call for cheap raw materials. Government loans and private investments further strengthened the economic link. After the war, the Latin American nations expected the United States to begin a program of economic development to help them modernize their economies and relieve their pressing social needs.

To their dismay, American aid slowed to a trickle. Indeed, during the first five postwar years, Latin America received less than 2 percent of America's total foreign aid. Even when the percentage rose after 1950, the aid was usually in the form of military assistance, rather than economic help. Latin America needed a Marshall Plan of its own; instead, it received what was left after Europe and other global trouble spots claimed the lion's share. Thus, while the United States was busy shoring up the economies of its allies in Europe and Asia, its southern neighbors were slipping into conditions of economic disarray. Anti-American feelings and the danger of violent social upheaval mounted steadily.

Achieving hemispheric security. Washington's first concern in Latin America, after the war, was to achieve hemispheric defense solidarity. At Mexico City in March 1945, twenty nations adopted the Act of Chapultepec, accepting the principle that an attack on one American state was an attack on all. The one holdout, Argentina, belatedly declared war on the tottering Axis several weeks later, accepting the Chapultepec statement as well.

Openly sympathetic to Germany and Italy, Argentina had become a fascist military dictatorship in 1944. For a time, Washington viewed that nation and its strong man, Juan Peron, along with his powerful wife Evita, as the major threat in the hemisphere. Indeed, American diplomats interfered blatantly, and unsuccessfully, in the Argentine elections of 1946, hoping to bring down Peron. As the cold war mounted in Europe, however, the Truman administration came to terms with the Peronistas. Washington gave first priority, after 1946, to maintaining a solid hemispheric front against the Soviet Union.

A formal system of regional collective security emerged in 1947–48, first with the signing of the Inter-American Treaty of Reciprocal Assistance (known as the Rio Pact), then with the establishment of the Organization of American States (OAS). Two provisions of the OAS charter were especially significant: disputes among the American nations were to be settled by the OAS *before* being taken to the UN; and mutual consultation was to take place within the OAS *before* one member state took independent action against another.

Having created a defense system, the Truman administration indiscriminately pumped military aid into Latin America. Backed by local elements of reaction and repression, military dictatorships took power even in several of the more advanced countries. When Dulles became secretary of state, he noted the rapidly deteriorating situation. Obsessed with the "rollback" of communism elsewhere, however, he did little to remedy the problem. In 1953–54, a situation in Guatemala revealed the extent to which Washington had lost touch with conditions in its own sphere of influence.

U.S. involvement in Guatemala. After enduring years of right-wing dictatorship, Guatemalans had revolted in 1944 and installed a reform government. Pledged to genuine land reform, the new regime collided head-on with the United Fruit Company, an American corporation which was Guatemala's biggest landowner and employer.

Democratic elections in 1950 brought Jacobo Arbenz Guzmán to the presidency. Although a landowner and army officer himself, Arbenz moved to the left. He confiscated United Fruit's unused land and offered to compensate the owners at the low rates they themselves had set for tax purposes. With Washington's backing, United Fruit rejected the offer. When Arbenz refused to arbitrate the matter, Eisenhower laid it before the OAS. Dulles charged that Guatemala was a case of "international communism" subverting a free American republic. He secured a general condemnation of communism in the Americas by pushing through the Caracas Resolution (June 1954), calling for OAS consultation to consider "appropriate action" in case a member state came under Communist control.

Guatemala was never under the control of "international communism." Local Communists held a number of posts in the government and exerted some influence on Arbenz. But the government had no ties with Russia, and its program of land reform was patterned after Mexico's, not Marx's. Moreover, it was a constitutional government, democratically elected and prepared to go before the electorate again at the time Dulles condemned it. The United States simply would not tolerate a government even remotely tainted by communism so close to the Panama Canal, nor would it accept the kind of radical reform which the Arbenz regime contemplated. When Guatemala received a shipment of arms from Czechoslovakia, Washington acted to destroy Arbenz.

Inside Guatemala, the American ambassador conspired to align the army against the government. In Honduras and Nicaragua, CIA agents prepared an invasion force under a right-wing exile, Colonel Carlos Castello Armas. On June 18, 1954, the force invaded Guatemala. Lacking the support of his army and rather than subject the country to a bloodbath, Arbenz stepped down. Thus ended ten years of uninterrupted democratic rule in Guatemala.

When Arbenz tried to appeal his case to the UN, Dulles refused to let the Security Council hear his plea, insisting that the matter was of concern only to the OAS. The incident was "a new and glorious chapter" in the history of Pan-Americanism, he boasted later, for the Guatemalan people themselves had rid their country of communism.

Anti-American feeling. Seemingly, few Latin Americans agreed with him. The coup set off a wave of anti-American violence throughout the hemisphere. Contrary to the Caracas Resolution and the OAS charter, the United States had moved (albeit surreptitiously) against another American nation without the knowledge of the OAS. Britain's Prime Minister Clement Attlee told the House of Commons, "The fact is that this was a plain act of aggression, and one cannot take one line on aggression in Asia and another line in Central America."

The Eisenhower administration poured aid into Guatemala, but conditions there went from bad to worse. Arbenz's reforms were undone, United Fruit took back its land, democratic elections became a farce, and—most significantly—a strong, Communist-oriented guerrilla movement began to operate in the Guatemalan highlands.

Although the United States increased its aid to Latin America after 1954, the amount remained grossly inadequate to the need. Economic and social distress mounted steadily, feeding the forces of violent change in every country. In April 1958, Eisenhower sent Vice-President Nixon on a "goodwill tour" to try to improve relations with the major South American nations. Everywhere he went, Nixon encountered abusive mobs; a steady barrage of rocks, eggs, and spit finally drove him back to Washington. Stung by this display of ill will, the administration at last loosened its purse strings and began to funnel economic assistance to the area through a newly formed Inter-American Development Bank. But already it was too late to prevent a major disaster for American policy from developing in Cuba.

U.S. policy in Cuba. If any Latin American nation should have been a stable, reliable ally of the United States, it was Cuba. Of all the Latin American countries, it had received the most lavish attention from Washington. Since the Spanish-American War, the island had been developed by American capital, industrialized by American corporations, serviced by American businessmen, and governed by American-approved leaders. Americans thought of Cuba as a favored protectorate, blessed by stability and prosperity. Looking only at the glitter and bustle of Havana, they assumed that Washington's policies had given the island the most modern and progressive society in Latin America.

In reality, Washington's policies actually had created a terrible imbalance in the economy, providing great wealth to a fortunate few, while all but ignoring the peasants. Beyond the glamor of Havana existed misery and rural squalor to match the worst in any Latin American country. Millions of people lived in slums without sanitary

facilities; 40 percent of the population was illiterate; 95 percent of the rural children suffered from parasitic disease. Worse, past efforts by reformers to confront these problems, even with mild proposals for social change, had been blocked by the ruling class with Washington's direct or implicit support.

The Cuban revolution. Into this explosive situation stepped the young radical nationalist, Fidel Castro. During the late 1950's, Castro led a five-year guerrilla struggle against the brutal dictatorship of Fulgencio Batista. The United States kept Batista well supplied with arms and military advice, which he, in turn, used against the rebels. But he did so with steadily diminishing effect, for on January 1, 1959, the revolution triumphed.

Washington assumed that the upheaval, like most Latin American revolutions, would bring a change in leadership and little else. But Castro meant to effect a radical social revolution, akin to the Mexican revolution of 1910. Not only did he make sweeping changes within Cuba; he also cut the ties which had made Cuba an economic and political satellite of this country. Relations between Washington and Havana began to deteriorate early in 1959, when Castro implemented his far-reaching Agrarian Reform Law by taking possession of American property in Cuba. From that moment on, Washington viewed the Cuban revolution as a Communist-inspired plague in the hemisphere. It had to be isolated, then eliminated.

Cuba enters the Soviet orbit. Castro's closest advisers were Communists, and under his leadership Cuba was gradually transformed into a Marxist society. But Castro's brand of communism bore a distinctive Cuban imprint, substantially different from the communism of Europe or Asia. Early in the revolution, it is doubtful that Castro intended to take his country into the Soviet bloc of nations as an ally of Russia. By late 1960, however, a series of blunders and provocations by both Cuba and the United States settled the matter.

Russia naturally encouraged the Cuban revolution, even sending Deputy Premier Anastas I. Mikoyan to Havana, where he concluded a major economic agreement with the new regime. Eisenhower countered by embargoing Cuban sugar, prohibiting its importation by this country. The move was a crushing blow to the island's economy, to be sure; but it also drove Castro into further dependence upon the Russians.

As Washington moved to bring OAS pressure against Cuba, Castro announced defiantly that, henceforth, he would rely upon Soviet protection against "American aggression." He also stepped up efforts to spread revolution into other parts of Latin America. Tightening its squeeze on Cuba, the administration then laid down a sweeping embargo, covering all but a handful of items. Moreover, Eisenhower authorized the CIA to secretly prepare for an invasion of the island. American agents began training and arming a force of Cuban exiles in Central America.

Thus, as Eisenhower left office in January 1961, a major crisis was at hand only ninety miles from American shores. Alone among the American nations, Cuba had become a Communist state and now moved within the Soviet orbit. The United States was preparing to solve the problem by overthrowing the Castro regime through an undercover use of force. Together with Southeast Asia, the Middle East, and Berlin, Cuba was part of the explosive legacy Eisenhower left to his successor.

5 Kennedy's Policy Fails To Solve Major Problems

1. Why was Kennedy successful in the Presidential campaign against Nixon in 1960? What would you consider the most important factor in determining the outcome?

2. What are the merits and demerits of an American military intervention, an Alliance for Progress, and a Peace Corps as elements of a desirable American foreign policy?

3. How effective was President Kennedy as a foreign diplomat?

Youth, intelligence, driving ambition, a reputation as a war hero, and a winning record in politics—these were the evident qualifications John Fitzgerald Kennedy brought to the Presidential campaign of 1960. An able, though hardly outstanding, senator from Massachusetts, Kennedy captured the Democratic nomination because of hard work, a sizable expenditure of his family's fortune, and success in the primaries against such tough competition as Hubert H. Humphrey, Lyndon B. Johnson, and Adlai Stevenson. He had two major handicaps—his Roman Catholic religion (no Catholic had ever been elected President), and the South's indifference to his candidacy. The first he overcame himself, frankly discussing the issue with the people. The second he neutralized by naming Lyndon B. Johnson, a Texan, as his running mate.

The election of 1960. Richard Nixon easily won the Republican nomination, choosing Henry Cabot Lodge (Eisenhower's ambassador to the UN) as his running mate. The advantage was Nixon's as the campaign opened, for the Vice-President was well known, while Kennedy was a relative newcomer on the national scene. But Nixon lost his advantage in a series of televised debates with his opponent. Kennedy handled himself well, put Nixon on the defensive, and gained valuable national exposure. In a close election, Kennedy won a hairline victory.

The Kennedy administration begins. In his inaugural address, the youngest man ever to be elected President sounded a note both of challenge and of conciliation. He noted that a new generation had come to power in this country, a generation "born in this century, tempered by war, disciplined by a hard and bitter peace, proud of our ancient heritage ..." He called for a new beginning in international relations, "remembering on both sides that civility is not a sign of weakness, and sincerity is always subject to proof. Let us never negotiate out of fear. But let us never fear to negotiate."

Although Kennedy had thought much about world affairs, his views on foreign policy contained nothing particularly new or imaginative. To head the State Department he chose the deceptively bland Dean Rusk, a man whose cold war views had changed little since the days of the Truman Doctrine. Representing a conciliatory position, Adlai Stevenson became representative at the UN. But Kennedy became his own secretary of state, in effect, threading his way pragmatically between toughness and conciliation. In all things, his closest adviser and confidante was his younger brother Robert F. Kennedy, whom he named attorney general.

Eisenhower had gone to General Motors for a secretary of defense. Kennedy turned to Ford, taking Robert S. McNamara from his job as president of that company. McNamara de-emphasized "massive retaliation" and nuclear deterrence. Instead, he sought to give the President flexibility in diplomacy by developing a capacity for fighting limited wars—the kind of guerrilla warfare in which intercontinental missiles with atomic warheads were useless. He expanded the army's Special Forces Command (the Green Berets), making it an elite counter-insurgency force.

The Bay of Pigs fiasco. First on Kennedy's agenda of problems was the projected invasion of Cuba. His inclination was to kill the scheme outright. But his military and intelligence advisers persuaded him that the plan could not fail to bring down Castro. After ordering that no United States forces be used in the fighting, he let the operation proceed. On April 17, 1961, the CIA's army of Cuban exiles landed at Bahia de Cochinos (the Bay of Pigs), confident that the Cuban people would rally to their cause. But the whole operation was an unrelieved disaster. No popular uprising took place, and Castro's army routed the invaders. American intelligence had badly underestimated the strength of the Cuban revolution and its popularity among the *campesinos,* the rural peasants who were the majority of the Cuban people.

The Bay of Pigs was an inexcusable act of adventurism. It was planned and conducted in violation of international law and in contempt of the OAS's rules for handling disputes among American nations. American prestige everywhere in the world fell sharply, while the Communists took particular delight in Washington's embarrassment. Latin Americans almost universally condemned the action as a reversion to old-style Yankee imperialism. Ironically, the chief beneficiary of the invasion was Castro, who could now boast in truth that he had "saved Cuba" from overt United States aggression. Not surprisingly, Cuba moved deeper and all but irrevocably into the Soviet bloc.

Kennedy publicly assumed full blame for the disaster, a move which rallied the people to his side. In private, he expressed dismay at the advice the military and CIA had given him. "How could I have been so far off base?" he wondered to his aide, Theodore C. Sorensen. "All my life I've known better than to depend on the experts. How could I have been so stupid, to let them go ahead?" But the misadventure did not persuade Kennedy that perhaps the United States should accept the Cuban revolution as a fact and learn to live with it. On the contrary, he asked the military to prepare a new, "foolproof" invasion plan (which was never used). Over the strong protest of the principal Latin American states, he also managed to get Cuba expelled from the OAS.

Two Kennedy programs. To prevent the rest of Latin America from going the way of Cuba, Kennedy proposed an Alliance for Progress among the American nations. Adopted by the OAS in August 1961, the alliance was a ten-year, $20 billion cooperative effort to stimulate economic growth and social reforms. For a time, it succeeded in thwarting any new left-wing revolutions. In the long run, however, the alliance was a disappointment. While it brought some visible improvements and was a step in the right direction, it could not provide a rate of economic growth to match the incredibly high rate of population increase. Economic stability became ever more elusive in most countries. Moreover, reform was painfully slow, and Latin American nationalists were as impatient as those in other developing areas.

A more modest and successful program was the Peace Corps. This unique organization sent young volunteers—teachers, doctors, agricultural experts, and the like—into the developing nations to work with the people there.

The Berlin Wall. Meanwhile, a new crisis developed in Europe. Lured by the promise of freedom and opportunity in the West, thousands of refugees left East Germany, crossing into West Berlin. The drain threatened to leave East Germany critically short of skilled manpower. Once again, Khrushchev threatened to "solve" the German problem by making a separate peace with the East Germans.

Anxious to regain the prestige he had lost in the Cuban mess, Kennedy flew to Vienna for a confrontation with the Soviet premier on the issue. Khrushchev tried unsuccessfully to bully

In July 1963, President Kennedy visited West Berlin, where more than one million Berliners turned out to see and hear him. It was on this visit that he expressed the United States' position on the freedom of Berlin by declaring *"Ich bin ein Berliner"*—"I am a Berliner." At right, Kennedy, flanked on his right by Mayor Willy Brandt and Chancellor Konrad Adenauer of West Germany, views the Berlin Wall from a special podium. In front of Kennedy, but not seen in the photograph, is the famous Brandenburg Gate, over which the Communists had hung red draperies to cut off Kennedy's view of East Berlin. Less than a year before this visit, Kennedy had faced what was surely the most serious crisis of his administration when it was discovered that the Russians were setting up missile bases in Cuba, just ninety miles off the coast of Florida. The aerial photograph below, taken by the Air Force, is of the medium-range ballistic missile site number 3 at San Cristobal, Cuba. The various areas are labeled, including the launch site at upper right and the probable nuclear warhead bunker at upper left.

27 OCTOBER 1962

MRBM LAUNCH SITE 3
SAN CRISTOBAL, CUBA

LAUNCH AREA

PROB NUCLEAR WARHEAD BUNKER U C

OPEN STORAGE

TRENCH

him, and the meeting produced only a hardening of attitudes. To convince the Russians of his toughness, Kennedy reacted strongly to the crisis (too strongly, some said) by calling up the reserves, pouring troops into Berlin, and asking Congress for heavy new expenditures for arms. He also needlessly aroused public anxiety by pushing a bizarre scheme for people to build bomb shelters in their backyards.

East Germany finally "solved" the refugee problem by walling in its people behind an ugly barrier stretching along the border between the two Berlins. The Berlin Wall was a hideous monument to the oppressiveness of communism. But it eased tension in the city and brought the crisis to an end.

The Laotian problem. On the other side of the world, Kennedy found himself deep in the thickets of Southeast Asia's problems from the moment he took office. For a time, Laos was the focus of trouble. Eisenhower had lavished $400 million in aid on the little Indochinese kingdom, trying to align it with the West. The money was wasted. The Pathet Lao, a nationalist movement supported by the Communists, gained the political initiative and moved to take over the country.

Seeing that the Laotian people were indifferent to the West, Kennedy tried to neutralize the situation. At Vienna, he gained the support of Khrushchev, who feared China's growing influence in the area. Kennedy also sent units of the navy to the area and posted 5,000 American troops to nearby Thailand. Prolonged negotiations finally produced a coalition government in Laos. But the country remained torn by factionalism, and the Pathet Lao soon withdrew from the coalition to resume its struggle for complete control.

Military commitment in Vietnam. In neighboring Vietnam, the United States rejected neutralization in favor of a major military effort. As a senator in 1954, Kennedy had said:

I am frankly of the belief that no amount of American military assistance in Indo-China can conquer an enemy which is everywhere, and at the same time, nowhere, an enemy of the people which has the sympathy and covert support of the people.

As President, he put 18,000 American soldiers in Vietnam as "advisers" and involved them in that country's civil war.

In taking this crucial step, Kennedy followed the recommendations of two very influential men in his administration: General Maxwell Taylor, a proponent of conventional warfare, who was his personal adviser on military matters; and Walt Whitman Rostow, a distinguished historian who entered the State Department in 1961 and became a self-styled "expert" on guerrilla war.

Power in South Vietnam rested with the American-backed president, Ngo Dinh Diem. Ignoring the call of the 1954 Geneva Conference for elections in 1956, Diem imposed a right-wing dictatorship that matched the North Vietnamese in repressiveness, while falling far behind it in land and social reforms. By 1958, civil war had erupted.

Encouraged by Ho Chi Minh, radical nationalists and pro-Communists in the south formed the National Liberation Front (NLF), whose military arm was the Vietcong. With strong support in the peasantry, the NLF began a guerrilla campaign against the Saigon government. Diem's efforts to cope with the rebellion failed miserably. Not only did he lack popular support, but his army was riddled with corruption and his soldiers lacked the will to fight.

Choosing to regard the conflict as an instance of aggression by "international communism" rather than as a civil war among Vietnamese factions, Kennedy committed the United States to the defense of Saigon. Doubtless, he hoped to keep the military commitment as small as possible, for he realized that the conflict was more political than military in nature. "In the final analysis it's their war," he said in mid-1963. "They're the ones who have to win it or lose it." Again, however, he depended too much on the "experts"—Taylor, Rostow, McNamara, Rusk, and others—who repeatedly assured him that things were going well, when, in fact, things were getting progressively worse.

Early in November, a group of Saigon generals overthrew Diem, with American encouragement—then murdered him. The coup brought no improvement in the war, as the Vietcong grew in numbers. As Washington increased its commitment to Saigon, Ho stepped up aid to the NLF. Kennedy's options in Vietnam rapidly narrowed, until they were down to two—withdrawal or massive reinforcement.

The Cuban missile crisis. In October 1962, Khrushchev provoked the grimmest crisis of the cold war by recklessly challenging the Monroe Doctrine. United States reconnaissance flights over Cuba disclosed that Soviet technicians were setting up bases for intermediate-range missiles. Seeing the bases as a threat to Cuba's neighbors, as well as to America, Kennedy resolved to remove them—by whatever means was necessary.

Rather than bomb them immediately or send an invasion force to capture them, he proclaimed a naval blockade of Cuba and laid down an ultimatum to the Kremlin. If a single missile was fired from Cuba, he warned Khrushchev, the United States would retaliate with a missile attack on Russia. He demanded that the missiles be removed and that shipments of "offensive weapons" to Cuba be halted at once. The cold war had finally produced an "eyeball-to-eyeball" confrontation between the world's two great nuclear powers.

As mankind stood on the brink of catastrophe, Khrushchev backed down. Soviet ships carrying missiles to Cuba turned back without challenging the blockade. In an exchange of notes with Washington, the Kremlin agreed to remove the bases if the United States lifted the blockade and promised not to invade Cuba. Having achieved his main objective of forcing the Russians to retreat, Kennedy did not press his luck. As new reconnaissance flights satisfied him that the Soviet bases were actually being dismantled, he called off the blockade and the crisis subsided. When the chips were down and the stake was mutual destruction, the two powers came to their senses and acted with fortunate restraint.

The Test Ban Treaty. The Cuban missile crisis brought the postwar era in diplomacy to an end. Sobered by their nearly catastrophic confrontation, the United States and Russia began to seek an accommodation which would enable them to live together in relative peace, if not in harmony. On August 5, 1963, they signed a Test Ban Treaty, a long-sought agreement to discontinue the testing of nuclear weapons in the atmosphere. The treaty was Kennedy's greatest accomplishment, for it signaled an abandonment of many old assumptions about the cold war and marked the acceptance by the United States, at least, of diversity in the world community.

THE CUBAN MISSILE CRISIS

Robert F. Kennedy described the discussions that took place in October 1962 over whether to take military action or blockade Cuba:

". . . Secretary [of Defense] McNamara, by Wednesday, became the blockade's strongest advocate. He argued that it was limited pressure, which could be increased as the circumstances warranted. Further, it was dramatic and forceful pressure, which would be understood yet, most importantly, still leave us in control of events. Later he reinforced his position by reporting that a surprise air strike against the missile bases alone—a surgical air strike, as it came to be called—was militarily impractical in the view of the Joint Chiefs of Staff, that any such military action would have to include all military installations in Cuba, eventually leading to an invasion. . . .

"Those who argued for the military strike instead of a blockade pointed out that a blockade would not in fact remove the missiles and would not even stop the work from going ahead on the missile sites themselves. The missiles were already in Cuba, and all we would be doing with a blockade would be 'closing the door after the horse had left the barn.' Further, they argued, we would be bringing about a confrontation with the Soviet Union by stopping their ships, when we should be concentrating on Cuba and Castro.

"Their most forceful argument was that our installation of a blockade around Cuba invited the Russians to do the same to Berlin. If we demanded the removal of missiles from Cuba as the price for lifting our blockade, they would demand the removal of missiles surrounding the Soviet Union as the reciprocal act.

"And so we argued, and so we disagreed—all dedicated, intelligent men, disagreeing and fighting about the future of their country, and of mankind. Meanwhile, time was slowly running out."

■ CONCLUSION

As the Soviet Union gained nuclear parity with the United States, relations between the two powers underwent a subtle and important change. Gradually, unremitting hostility gave way to a tacit, sometimes grudging, acknowledgment that some form of "peaceful coexistence" was preferable to mutual annihilation. Peaceful coexistence was an irregular and imperfect condition, to be sure. As some of the familiar points at issue between East and West faded or were pushed into the background, new issues arose to bedevil the diplomats in both camps.

Most of the impetus for the change in the nature of the cold war came from events within the Communist world. Within Russia, the death of Stalin in 1953 set off a power struggle which ultimately brought a new generation of rulers to power. Both the struggle and its outcome profoundly affected the Kremlin's relations not only with the Western world, but with the other Communist nations, as well—especially mainland China. Indeed, the rift between Moscow and Peking late in the fifties had implications for the future of international politics that few in the West could guess at the time.

As in domestic affairs, so in diplomacy the Eisenhower administration generally followed a course laid out by its predecessor. Sometimes the tone of America's voice in world councils became more strident, especially when Secretary of State Dulles spoke. And Eisenhower always had difficulty restraining an "Asia first" element within the Republican party. But he remained committed to NATO and the goal of European unity, and he took the nation through several severe crises without either going to war or seriously altering the world balance of power. Unfortunately, at least two of these crises—Cuba and Vietnam—were handled with singular awkwardness and indecision. They became a burdensome and dangerous legacy for Eisenhower to pass on to his successor in the White House.

John F. Kennedy's first year in office was marred by an appalling clumsiness in foreign policy. After the near cataclysmic showdown with the Russians in 1962, however, he moved on to effect a noticeable reduction of tension between Washington and Moscow. Indeed, by 1963, the cold war—in the form the world had known since 1947—also passed from the scene. If the American people did not recognize its passing, their lack of perception was understandable. For already the United States was slipping deeper and deeper into the quagmire of the Vietnam war.

■ QUESTIONS

1. Was there a monolithic communism from 1952 to 1964 or simply a number of unique nationalistic Communist variations? Explain your answer.

2. How were the issues which separated the United States and the Soviet Union from 1952 to 1964 similar to the issues of the period from 1945 to 1952? How were they different?

3. How did the nuclear parity which came to exist between the Soviet Union and the United States affect each country's foreign relations?

4. Is "peaceful co-existence" possible between the United States and the Soviet Union? Explain.

5. What is a legalistic-moralistic approach to foreign affairs? How was this approach reflected in the policy of Eisenhower and Kennedy?

6. What are the dangers, real and imagined, of international communism, and what is the most effective means of eliminating those dangers?

7. What were the causes of Latin American radicalism from 1952 to 1964?

8. Compare and evaluate the Peace Corps and the Bay of Pigs invasion regarding their purposes and their implementations?

9. To what extent did American economic interests influence American foreign policy?

10. How did the United States demonstrate a collective security approach, and how did it demonstrate a unilateral approach to foreign affairs?

11. How did the United States become involved in Vietnam, and what might have been done to avoid a prolonged military commitment in South Vietnam?

12. What would be the proper military orientation for the United States to establish in confronting the international affairs of the 1970's and 1980's: a military establishment built around "massive retaliation," or a flexible force capable of countering insurgency, or some other model? Explain.

■ BIBLIOGRAPHY

SPANIER, JOHN, *American Foreign Policy Since World War II*, 3rd ed., Praeger. This study will provide the student with a fine summary of American foreign policy from Truman through Kennedy. It is a good analysis of the liberal response to foreign affairs.

WARD, BARBARA, *The Rich Nations and the Poor Nations*, Norton. The author has provided the student with an insightful commentary on the relationship between the emerging, generally poor nations and the wealthy, established nations. She raises some very important issues which need serious consideration.

WISE, DAVID AND THOMAS B. ROSS, *The U-2 Affair*, Bantam Books. The co-authors provide the necessary background for one of the major events of the Eisenhower administration, beginning with the development of the U-2 plane and ending with the final release of the pilot by the Soviet Union. Not only should the student consider the specific series of events, but he should study the general issue of air surveillance.

KENNEDY, ROBERT, *Thirteen Days: A Memoir of the Cuban Missile Crisis*, intros. by Robert S. McNamara and Harold Macmillan, New American Library (Signet Books). Robert Kennedy, brother and close adviser of the President, recounts the days of the missile crisis when the world held its breath. The author takes the reader behind the scenes to show how a critically important decision was made. The book also includes speeches, letters, and the Kennedy–Khrushchev correspondence.

SORENSEN, THEODORE, *Kennedy*, Harper & Row. It seems that everyone who knew John Kennedy has published a book on him, and the student may select according to personal inclination or dimension of the President being studied. This well-written book is by a very close friend, adviser, and speech writer of Kennedy. The author is obviously favorable toward Kennedy, but there is still a generally fair appraisal of his administration.

WHITE, THEODORE H., *The Making of the President, 1960*, New American Library (Signet Books). White's first recounting of a Presidential campaign has become a standard source, and none of his later studies have been able to match this initial success. The writing is easily intelligible to the general audience, which gains a clear understanding of the nature of Presidential campaigns. There is also an excellent movie based upon the book which is available to high school audiences.

SOBUL, DE ANNE, *Encounters with America's History*, Holt, Rinehart & Winston. The Cuban missile crisis necessitated momentous decision-making at the highest levels. How were these decisions made? Why did the United States act as it did in the face of the crisis? The fifth problem in this book deals with this tense moment in human history and provides source material for students to work with.

A Changing American Civilization

"The United States," writes sociologist Daniel Bell, "is probably the first large society in history to have change and innovation 'built into' its culture." Throughout their history, the American people have unhestitatingly welcomed growth and development, assuming almost automatically that change means progress. To an extraordinary degree, their optimism has been warranted; for the United States has developed into the most economically successful society in modern history, bringing at least a measure of security and well-being to great masses of people.

The quarter century from 1945 to 1970 was a period of astonishing growth and change in American life. In many ways, as anthropologist Margaret Mead observes, the gulf separating the two dates "is as deep as the gulf that separated the men who became builders of cities from Stone Age men." Many aspects of life in America after 1945 bore only slight resemblance to conditions earlier in the twentieth century or even in the immediate pre-World War II years; and some observers proclaimed the emergence of an entirely new American civilization.

Yet, postwar civilization in the United States was not really new, for it represented the maturing of trends, both positive and negative, that were deeply rooted in the American experience. What actually occurred was a "great mutation," to use historian Carl Bridenbaugh's phrase, in which growth came so rapidly and change spread so pervasively that neither the people nor their established institutions were prepared for the transformation. Few had any notion that the future would offer remarkable possibilities for advances in every area of human endeavor. And almost no one foresaw the building up of social and cultural problems so serious as to threaten the very survival of the American nation. Here are some questions to answer as you read about these changes:

1. What were the material benefits of unprecedented affluence?
2. What were the social consequences of affluence?
3. What problems were created by urbanization, industrialization, and affluence?
4. In what ways was the culture of affluence reflected in the arts?

1 Affluence Grows After The War

1. How did the United States reflect the characteristics of an affluent society during the 1950's and 1960's?

2. What accounted for the remarkable economic growth in the United States during the postwar years?

3. In what ways was the postwar period similar to the 1920's? In what ways was it different?

4. What were the characteristics of the labor force in America during this period? How did unionized labor reflect the classic pattern of social mobility?

"That's one small step for a man, one giant leap for mankind." With these words, American astronaut Neil Armstrong took man's historic first step on the moon on July 24, 1969. When World War II ended in 1945, mankind knew nothing about space travel, and the idea that a man would walk on the moon during the lifetime of people then living seemed pure fantasy. It remained an idle dream for most people as late as 1961, when President John F. Kennedy announced that the United States would try to put a man on the moon before the end of the decade. A prodigious effort by American science and technology, plus the expenditure of $25 billion, transformed the dream into reality just eight years later.

The epic flight of Apollo 11 was a triumph of the universal human will and a milestone for all mankind. It was also impressive evidence of fantastic changes in the United States since the grim days of the Great Depression. Three decades of almost uninterrupted prosperity and growth had provided a solid economic base for the world's most advanced technological society. Space travel was only the most dramatic manifestation of change during those years.

An economic "boom." Economic growth was nothing less then phenomenal. From a base of $100 billion in 1940, Gross National Product rose to $285 billion in 1950, then soared to $504 billion in 1960, and reached the incredible figure of $925 billion in 1969. Per capita personal income more than quadrupled, and not even high taxes and persistent inflation kept consumer expenditures from doing the same. Corporate profits grew as never before—$50.8 billion after taxes in 1969 as compared to a mere $7.2 billion in 1940.

Several factors accounted for this remarkable economic growth and for the persistence of prosperity throughout the postwar period. For one thing, an unexpected population explosion created a sustained demand for goods and services. History has a whimsical way of making prophets look foolish. In 1946, the Director of the Census predicted that the nation's population would not reach 160 million before the end of the century. In fact, the population soared past the 200 million mark by the end of the 1960's.

Contrary to expectations, the high birth rate of the immediate postwar years continued into the sixties and slackened only toward the end of that decade. At the peak, some four million babies joined the population each year. People married young and planned large families. They also lived longer, thanks to better health care and a declining death rate. Thus, the population bulged especially near the two ends of the life cycle, with both the young and the elderly showing dramatic numerical increases.

Of primary importance in sustaining the "boom" was the federal government. New Deal economic measures cushioned business from the effects of market fluctuations and helped to ward off serious recessions. Washington regulated the money supply and stock market, helped business expand overseas, and generally fostered conditions favorable to industrial expansion. Government subsidies sustained entire areas of the economy, such as the aircraft and aerospace industries. The Defense Department easily became industry's biggest customer, spending some $60 billion annually for arms and supplies. Over the years, a close relationship developed between the military establishment and those industries which thrived on defense contracts, and the line between public interest and private gain became increasingly blurred. As President Eisenhower warned in 1961, this "military-industrial complex" had enormous power to influence national affairs.

Consolidation accompanied expansion. Washington's complicated antitrust machinery sometimes checked the growth of monopoly (as when a federal court ordered the huge DuPont chemical firm to sell its holdings in General Motors); but little was done to curb the spread of *oligopoly*, a condition in which price competition disappeared in entire industries, such as automobiles and steel, because a handful of operators controlled the market. Consolidation later took the form of *conglomerates*, large corporate entities with controlling interests in such diverse activities as publishing, television, and professional baseball.

A transportation revolution. Some sectors of the economy literally underwent a revolution. In transportation, air travel all but drove the railroads out of passenger service, gobbling up nearly 70 percent of the total traffic by 1968. With the advent of fast, safe, and comfortable jet aircraft, the airlines also took over and greatly expanded the international passenger service, reducing ocean-going travel (except for luxury cruises) to a trickle. Tourism became a burgeoning industry, as air travel offered millions of ordinary people quick, relatively inexpensive transportation to vacation areas throughout the world.

Automobile production soared to nearly ten million units a year, compared to less than four million before the war. Together with its satellite industries, automobile manufacturing remained the mainstay of the economy. As people gained more money to spend, the demand for services connected with highway travel became insatiable. In the 1950's, the federal government undertook a huge program of building interstate superhighways; but within a decade, even this great system became inadequate in many parts of the country. Across America, motels, restaurants, drive-in theaters, giant shopping plazas, crisscrossing expressways, enormous traffic jams, and noxious fogs of exhaust fumes attested the popular infatuation with what one critic called the "insolent chariots."

Research and development. Chemistry gave much of the economy a new look by wrapping it in plastic. Industrial laboratories developed synthetic materials for almost every conceivable use, and by the 1960's the nation was using ten billion pounds of plastics annually. Power companies built nuclear reactors to generate the huge amounts of electricity needed in the expanding economy.

In the new technological age, research itself became a major industry, subsidized by both private and public funds. In 1950, Congress established the National Science Foundation to encourage theoretical and applied research. Such private institutions as the RAND Corporation worked on problems for industry and the military. Funds became available for wide-ranging research in all the sciences, with some exciting results.

Medical research produced vaccines for polio, all but eliminating the disease from the United States; "tranquillizer" drugs to aid the mentally ill; contraceptive pills; techniques for transplanting vital organs from one body to another; and new beneficial uses for atomic energy. Biologists broke the "genetic code," revealing the composition and organization of chromosomes and moving startlingly near the secret of life itself. In 1957–58, the United States participated with sixty-two other nations in the International Geophysical Year, a remarkable cooperative effort to explore every aspect of planet Earth.

Technological advances were especially dramatic in electronics. As tiny transistors replaced bulky vacuum tubes, television came into its own. Commercial telecasting started in New York in 1941, then became a major industry after the war. From one million sets in use in the United States in 1949, the number climbed to over eighty million in twenty years.

Revolutionary techniques for miniaturizing electronic components opened the age of computers. In industry, science, and education, these "mechanical brains" stored prodigious quantities of information for use in simplifying the most complex operations or "solving" the most difficult problems. Computers led to the automation of many industries. On an automated assembly line, operations were directed and effected by a few technicians at a control panel, rather than by hundreds of men working on the line itself.

Without transistors, computers, and miniaturization, the aerospace industry would have remained an infant. The gigantic interplanetary rockets, intricate control devices, and fragile space vehicles of the United States space program all evolved from the revolution in electronics. After

Mankind's knowledge of the universe was advanced by a small degree when astronauts Neil Armstrong and Edwin Aldrin landed on the moon on July 20, 1969. The picture at right was taken by the television camera set up on the moon. Astronaut Aldrin, whose footprints appear on the dusty surface of the moon, stands by the American flag; part of the lunar landing module, the LEM, is visible at the left. The historic moon landing was not the only witness to man's scientific achievements in the twentieth century. The tremendous advances in electronics are illustrated by the picture below of a printed circuit, in this case part of a computor. A printed circuit, which is actually printed, or etched, on brass or copper, is the form of circuitry which has replaced the old jumble of tubes and wires used in the first radios and other electric equipment. To illustrate the infinitesimal size of these circuits, this one has been photographed against granules of salt.

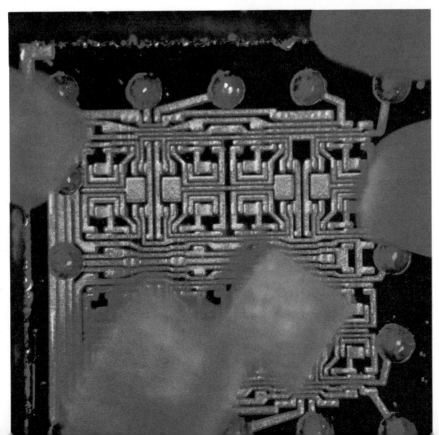

lagging behind the Soviet Union in space technology, the United States forged ahead in the sixties, as Washington undertook a massive program of subsidizing and encouraging the aerospace industry. By the end of the decade, not only had Americans walked on the moon; but NASA (the National Aeronautics and Space Administration) was laying plans to explore the planets beyond.

Consumer trends. Prosperity changed the consuming habits of the nation. Before the war, consumer credit had totalled barely $7 billion; by 1969, it was past the $122 billion mark. Millions of people used credit cards as a substitute for cash. New advertising techniques helped to shape public taste and fueled the demand for goods and services of every description.

People bought automobiles with garish, useless tailfins and other costly gimmickry. Youngsters walked about with tiny, cheap transistor radios glued to their ears, listening to pop music pumped out by windy "disc jockeys." Millions filled their stomachs with more rich food and drink than was good for them and readily indulged themselves in such luxuries as power lawnmowers, motorboats, mobile campers, color television, poodles and Siamese cats, and frequent trips to the beauty parlor, the race track, the golf links, and the bowling alley. Times were "good" after the war for vastly more people than in the "boom" of the 1920's, and big business thrived.

Agriculture and labor. Big agriculture and unionized labor also thrived. Agriculture became a highly specialized, heavily capitalized, corporate enterprise, with little room for the traditional individual subsistence farmer. Indeed, the number of farmers fell sharply after the war; while the "factories in the field" produced record crops and raised farm income to an all-time high.

In 1955, the AFL and CIO merged, giving seventeen million unionized workers a powerful voice in national affairs and collective bargaining. In most industries, the workweek shrank to forty hours or less, while wages steadily rose. Labor's increased share of the national income contributed to the economic stability of the times. Many unions were notably successful in gaining a wide range of benefits for their members, including pensions, welfare funds, and paid vacations.

As union labor prospered, its militancy faded. Affluence minimized class differences by putting goods and services at the disposal of great masses of people. Many blue-collar workers moved from the cities to the suburbs, where they joined country clubs, sent their children to good schools and colleges, and otherwise adopted the material trappings of the middle class. They also became increasingly conservative in matters of social and economic consequence to unorganized workers and ethnic minorities. In the classic pattern of social mobility, they resisted the upward thrust of those below them on the economic ladder for fear of losing their own hard-won gains.

As large numbers of workers moved into the service occupations—as clerks, salespeople, teachers, civil servants, laboratory assistants, and the like—the unions followed, albeit slowly, bringing a new element into the ranks of organized labor. Yet, union membership actually declined in the 1960's. Automated industries and an increasingly complex economy demanded fewer traditional craft and industrial workers and more white-collar technicians. Union leaders tried to protect their members by pressing for a guaranteed annual wage, job retraining programs, and other cushions against rapid change. But the work force of the future, it was clear, would be dominated by the highly trained experts and professional people.

A "mixed economy." In achieving an affluent economy after the war, the American people rejected both the total planning of state socialism and the traditional laissez faire capitalism of their past. Instead, they settled for the "mixed economy" which the New Deal had anticipated in its pragmatic economic and social reforms. Modified capitalism blended with social welfareism to provide for a measure of rational economic planning as well as for individual initiative. Government spending for military purposes clearly underwrote much of the postwar prosperity, although no one could say to what precise extent. In any event, the "mixed economy" gave the United States the world's highest standard of living by far. In 1967 alone, American consumers spent $500 billion, of which $110 billion went for food, $71 billion for housing, and $51 billion for clothing. Never in history had so many people been better fed, better sheltered, and better clothed.

2 Affluence Brings On Social Consequences

1. What were the characteristics of the poor in American society? Why did chronic poverty thrive in the midst of affluence? How did poverty and unemployment affect the overall health of American society?

2. To what extent have the roles within the American family been modified over the past forty years? What accounts for this change? Do you think any patterns have evolved over the years?

3. How has the population redistributed itself within the United States since the end of World War II? Why have these shifts occurred, and what have been some of the consequences?

In 1960, the Bureau of Labor Statistics revealed some startling information on the subject of affluence. One quarter of all American families, it reported, had incomes so low that they lived in poverty; while an additional 16.5 percent lived on the verge of poverty. Which is to say that 80 million Americans out of a total population of 180 million were classified as poor or near-poor by their own government. As the population grew to 200 million later in the sixties, the percentage of the poor declined somewhat. But chronic poverty persisted as a vexing national problem throughout the "age of affluence."

So did chronic unemployment. In the prosperous year of 1961, for example, employment reached a record high; yet 6.9 percent of the labor force was jobless. For an affluent economy, the percentage was a staggering one. (On the eve of the Great Depression in 1929, the rate had been only 3.1 percent.) Some economists argued that an unemployment rate of 6 percent was "acceptable" in terms of the overall health of the economy. Combined with widespread poverty, however, chronic unemployment meant wretched social insecurity and misery for millions of Americans.

Poverty and affluence. Who were the poor and what was their lot? Sociologist Michael Harring-ton provided a revealing answer in his influential study of poverty *The Other America* (1962). They were society's "less visible" members, he noted—people who, for one reason or another, were out of the social and economic mainstream and thus easily ignored by the rest of society. They were the unskilled, the uneducated, the underprivileged, the handicapped. They were young school drop-outs with no hope of finding jobs and retired oldsters scraping along on meager pensions. They were the cruelly neglected American Indians. They were sharecroppers in the South, black and white, and migrant farm workers in the West, many of them Mexican-Americans. They were mountain folk in the Appalachians and the Ozarks, unemployed miners in the dwindling coal fields of Pennsylvania and West Virginia, jobless textile workers in New England mill towns.

Above all, they were the racial minorities pressed together in the teeming ghettos of the cities, especially blacks and Puerto Ricans. Indeed, 90 percent of the people classified as poor by the government lived in city slums, and their poverty and social isolation was the single most serious problem of modern American cities.

Rejected by society and in many cases systematically deprived for generations, the poor developed what Harrington called a "culture of poverty." They became hopeless and indifferent, or bitterly resentful. Sensing their rejection, they in turn rejected society's institutions and laws, substituting a makeshift, primitive code of conduct all their own. Young people dropped out of schools that ignored their basic needs, turning to crime or vagrancy, living in the streets, joining gangs that terrorized each other and the surrounding community.

Disease and mental illness stalked the poor constantly, shortening their life span and driving thousands to suicide. In short, the poor had little to live for. They knew nothing of that "stake in society" which the Founding Fathers had recognized as the essential cement holding any society together.

Just how badly off the poor really were was revealed in a government survey late in the sixties. At a time when GNP was nearing the fantastic figure of $1 trillion, 14 million Americans were actually hungry and another 23.6 million were in danger of malnutrition. The brutal fact, as Margaret Mead told a Senate committee in 1969, was that "The American people are less well nourished as a whole, than they were 10 years ago." The social and economic disabilities of poverty itself were bad enough. To these, hunger added irreparable damage to the bodies and minds of its victims—usually little children in the ghetto—sapping their stamina and dulling their senses.

Poverty and its attendant misery was a blight the affluent society could ignore in the 1960's only at its own peril. For as the urban poor began to awaken to their plight, it became clear that unless society attended to their needs quickly and fully, it would suffer the consequences of mounting social upheaval.

Why did chronic poverty thrive in the midst of affluence? Chiefly because political and economic leaders in the United States—despite the lesson of boom and bust in the 1920's—had not yet learned to match gains in the production of national wealth with a rational distribution of that wealth. Despite the overall prosperity, no significant redistribution of national income took place. More people had more money, to be sure; but for most, their *relative* share of national income increased only slightly, and in many cases it actually declined as inflation took its toll. The only group to receive a steadily rising share of income was the upper middle class—perhaps two-fifths of the population.

Changing social attitudes. To the surprise of observers who had expected a continuation of prewar familial trends (Chapter 23), the American family showed remarkable stability during the postwar decades. The divorce rate was high, to be sure (about one in four marriages failed), but so was the marriage rate; and the old tradition of the large family came surging back, after an understandable decline during the lean depression years.

Moreover, children more than ever became the center of attention in most families. Parents who themselves had known hardship and want as children in the thirties, now overcompensated by shielding their own young from life's difficulties. In middle-class homes, the tendency was to indulge children their every whim and to plan the family's every activity in terms of whatever was "good for the kids." As historian John Brooks commented, "Children seem to be born believing that they enjoy full equal rights with their parents, and our society encourages—very nearly compels—them to retain that belief."

Children also grew up learning more about "life" from television than from reading books or talking with parents. Together with parental permissiveness, indeed, television helped to shape the social attitudes of the postwar young in ways profoundly significant for the future. On the one hand, in the wholly passive process of "receiving" whatever television offered them, many young people failed to develop a capacity for rational discourse or critical analysis. On the other hand, the medium's emphasis on action, often purely for its own sake, taught many young viewers the false notion that "instant gratification" of one's needs and desires was the normal condition of life.

For American women, the postwar decades did little to resolve the dilemma posed by the seeming conflict between motherhood and career. In the 1950's, the tendency was toward a revival of domesticity. Among middle-class women, the concern for social activism of the war and prewar years gave way to a conviction that motherhood was a woman's highest duty and most fulfilling role. Television, women's magazines, and the retail sales industry exploited this "feminine mystique." In a book of that title in 1964, Betty Friedan argued strongly that woman's place was not in the home, but rather in a career.

In fact, even as the marriage and birth rates soared, more and more women went to work. By 1960, they made up a third of the total labor force and held an impressively large share of the national wealth. Yet, as a group they were among the exploited workers in the economy. Paid less than men for comparable work and usually discriminated against in promotions, they were also confined largely to certain kinds of work, even when they were fully qualified by education for other duties.

In the general re-awakening of social consciousness in the 1960's, a "women's liberation movement" emerged, demanding full equality of women with men. Unfortunately, the leaders of "women's lib" differed sharply among themselves as to precise goals. Perhaps in its very nature,

734

WOMEN'S LIBERATION

Journalist Gloria Steinem speculates on what the world might be like if the feminist revolt is successful:

". . . Men assume that women want to imitate them. . . .

"That is not our goal. But we do want to change the economic system to one more based on merit. In Women's Lib Utopia, there will be free access to good jobs—and decent pay for the bad ones women have been performing all along, including housework. Increased skilled labor might lead to a four-hour workday, and higher wages would encourage further mechanization of repetitive jobs now kept alive by cheap labor.

"With women as half the country's elected representatives, and a woman President once in a while, the country's *machismo* [aggressive masculinity] problems would be greatly reduced. The old-fashioned idea that manhood depends on violence and victory is, after all, an important part of our troubles in the streets, and in Viet Nam. I'm not saying that women leaders would eliminate violence. We are not more moral than men; we are only uncorrupted by power so far. . . .

"As for the American child's classic problem— too much mother, too little father—that would be cured by an equalization of parental responsibility. Free nurseries, school lunches, family cafeterias built into every housing complex, service companies that will do household cleaning chores in a regular businesslike way, and more responsibility by the entire community for the children; all these will make it possible for both mother and father to work, and to have equal leisure time with the children at home. . . .

"The revolution would not take away the option of being a housewife. A woman who prefers to be her husband's housekeeper and/or hostess would receive a percentage of his pay determined by the domestic relations courts. If divorced, she might be eligible for a pension fund, and for a job-training allowance. . . ."

the dilemma of home versus career was an unresolvable one.

Population redistribution. As the population grew, it redistributed itself significantly throughout the country. Many areas once considered underpopulated or economically backward underwent striking changes, while older, more settled regions remained relatively static. New England, for example, showed growth characteristics much less dynamic than those of the South or the West.

Much of the South remained rural and poor, to be sure. But per capita income rose faster there than elsewhere, and southern cities grew rapidly in the midst of an increasingly diversified economy. Atlanta was a bustling, progressive metropolis, a center of culture and commerce to rival any of the great midwestern cities. Texas was a "boom state," prospering from the many electronic and aerospace industries that located there after the war, as well as from its older oil and ranching resources. Long a haven for the retired elderly, Florida took on a brisk young look as it became a center of tourism and light industry. Moreover, it boasted Cape Kennedy, the spaceport from which moon rockets were launched.

In the West and Southwest, a population explosion of unprecedented proportions turned once arid deserts into bustling cities and suburbs, teeming with migrants from the rest of the nation. The federal government stimulated the boom by locating many defense installations in the Southwest and by subsidizing defense-related industries throughout the West. It also literally made life possible in much of the region by building mammoth facilities for bringing precious water to parched land.

Early in the sixties, California supplanted New York as the nation's richest and most populous state. Everything about California was big—its birthrate, its per capita income, its schools and universities, the number of autos its people owned, and also its taxes, its public debt, its unemployment rate, its highway death figures. In the loose, restless, "outdoor" style many Californians adopted, some observers saw a portent of the future for the entire nation. Further evidence of the westward tilt of national growth was the admission of Alaska and Hawaii as states of the Union in 1959.

Some cities grew so large after the war that they overlapped each other, forming super-cities—or *megalopolises*—that sprawled with no regard for state boundaries. The "Northeastern Megalopolis," from the New Hampshire-Massachusetts line south through metropolitan Washington, contained 31 million people. Many cities also experienced an enormous influx of racial minorities. By 1960, New York City contained more Puerto Ricans than Puerto Rico's capital city of San Juan, and Washington, D.C., was over 50 percent black.

The expansion of suburbia. But the most striking aspect of urban growth was the exodus from the inner cities to the suburbs. While suburbia expanded by better than 100 percent, the inner cores grew by only 25 percent. By 1970, some 74.9 million people, nominally urban dwellers, lived in communities on the fringes of the cities, trying to find some semblance of a rural existence. Suburbia ranged from plush, exclusive enclaves for the very rich, to sprawling developments of monotonously similar houses, each a little box on its own tiny plot of land, for white-collar and blue-collar working people. Far from being rural, however, suburbia was only the outer ring of a sprawling urban complex to which it was tied by unbreakable economic and other bonds.

To the millions who flocked to the fringes, suburbia promised open spaces, uncrowded schools, safe streets and neighborhoods, and a "better life" generally than the inner cities offered. In a single decade, more than a million and a half people left New York City alone for the suburbs, a pattern of emigration repeated in cities across the country.

For most of the migrants, moreover, suburbia lived up to its promise. Author Max Lerner suggests that, in an institutional sense, the suburb filled "the vacuum of the American home place left by the decline of the small town and the decay of the city." It supplied a sense of community sought by millions. Rugged individualism had no place in suburbia. On the contrary, people who already shared the same social values and aspirations welcomed the security of suburbia's standardized, homogeneous environment. Their life style became pre-eminently the life style of middle-class America.

Most suburbs grew in unplanned haste, with little thought of future needs. In time, the population explosion caught up with them, swamping them with problems that had long beset the inner cities—overcrowded, inferior schools; polluted water; a rising crime rate; high taxes; deteriorating public services. Ironically, the rush to suburbia in many instances destroyed the very things people most wanted there—space and livability. Yet, few suburbanites chose to return to the inner cities.

3 Affluence Contributes To A Troubled Society

1. What are the problems of the modern American city? Why have they been allowed to develop? What can be done to alleviate the problems?

2. In what ways was the United States a polluted society in the 1950's and 1960's?

3. How did Americans "cope" with the anxieties of their polluted society?

By the 1960's, many cities were dying of slow rot. Plagued by problems that had been building for a century, the inner cities were desperately in need of a massive rescue operation that many thought could be financed and directed only by the federal government. Even then, it was by no means clear that they could be saved.

The breakdown of American cities. As one observer noted, American cities had become "the acme of discomfort—congested, traffic-stalled, smog-filled, shut out from sunlight, with scarcely space for breathing and no feel of soil beneath one's feet and no sense of the rhythm of the seasons." Urban housing was crowded, antiquated, and cheerless. Urban transport was clogged and outmoded. Human and industrial waste accumulated in mountainous quantities (a city of a million people produced a half million tons of sewage daily), taxing the ingenuity of those responsible for its disposal.

Water became increasingly befouled, and the air was thick with choking fumes. Public services were grossly inadequate to needs. Not only were schools crowded and frequently inferior, but in slum areas many were "blackboard jungles," rife with violence and moral squalor. Ghettos drained people of hope, while spawning crime, vice, and drug addiction. Parks built to beautify the city and give respite to people became enclaves of fear, unsafe to walk in at night.

In short, many inner cities were places of filth, violence, despair, and revolutionary ferment. The ability of municipalities to maintain essential services—to govern at all, that is—grew increasingly questionable. City governments were frequently clutters of conflicting, often corrupt, institutions. The mounting exodus to suburbia drained cities of young, vigorous people, and of sizable tax revenues. Yet, because the cities remained the vital center of economic life—for suburban dwellers as well as urbanites—the demands on their services grew steadily heavier.

The spread of blight. In many ways, the automobile was the curse of the cities. It clogged the streets and poisoned the air with carbon monoxide, then offered escape to the suburbs for the very people whose talents the cities needed. Tax monies that might have gone to improving public transportation instead fed the automobile's insatiable demands. A blight of parking lots and tangled expressways spread over the cities. By the 1960's, two-thirds of Los Angeles was paved in the service of the automobile.

Indeed, the automobile helped to turn much of America into what architect Peter Blake called "God's Own Junkyard." In 1965 alone, 16,000 cars went to the scrap heap. By then, probably 35 million scrapped autos already littered the countryside in rusty, grotesque profusion. America was a beautiful country; but often its beauty was hidden behind giant billboards blaring messages of every description to the motorist. Tasteless buildings and garish neon signs added to the pollution of the eye.

Motorists carried their garbage to the remotest unspoiled corners of the land. Each year industry produced 48 billion cans and 26 million bottles, uncounted millions of which ended up strewn over the landscape or at the bottom of lakes and rivers.

Pollution. The affluent society was truly an effluent society, befouling itself with an enormous outpouring of pollutants. Fifty million pounds of solid waste, much of it raw sewage, flowed into the nation's waterways each day. Pollution turned Lake Erie into a foul-smelling dead sea, and Lake Michigan seemed fated to become the same. Men pumped oil, chemicals, and sewage into the oceans, upsetting the biology of the seas with incalculable consequences for future generations. After crossing the South Atlantic on a reed raft in 1970, Norwegian explorer Thor Heyerdahl commented that the only evidence of man he had seen on the long, lonely voyage was his garbage—and that was everywhere.

Automobile exhaust fumes were the worst air pollutant, followed closely by industrial smoke. All told, some 360,000 tons of irritants poured into the atmosphere each day in the United States, plaguing vast areas with frequent smogs. The cost of air pollution alone ran to $11 billion a year, while the incidence of fatal or crippling respiratory disease soared.

Pollution took many forms. It was noise, sometimes so high in decibels as to have marked psychological effects on the people it assaulted. It was laundry detergents, flowing into the water supply as sudsy sewage, then returning to the home as sudsy drinking water. In *The Silent Spring* (1962), Rachel Carson warned about the indiscriminate use of poisonous chemicals to control pests in agriculture. Picked up by birds or leaked into the underground water supply, such insecticides as DDT not only killed off animal life, but also became part of the human diet in the foods people ate. Only when it became perfectly clear that man *was* poisoning himself with such agents were steps taken to control their use.

An ecological crisis. Pollution was part of an ecological crisis threatening life everywhere in the world. Ecology was a relatively new science, dealing with the biological interdependence of living things and the sociological effects of man's relationship to his environment. The crisis resulted from a misuse of technology, especially in such industrial societies as the United States. Men failed to consider the balance of life in nature, or the effects their economically desirable actions had on the environment. They dredged and filled in estuaries, giving no thought to what the de-

Americans in the 1960's were faced with seemingly insurmountable environmental problems—overcrowding, pollution, and increasing urban blight. A mere five miles from the White House, Washington's Kenilworth garbage dump (above left), located on land owned by the National Park Service, sends up a noxious cloud of smoke and grime. The buildings above right were once-fine residences in New York's South Bronx but have been abandoned to decay and vandalism. The unplanned sprawl of many American cities is illustrated by the famed Las Vegas Strip (below) with its haphazard mix of night clubs, motels, filling stations, and gambling casinos.

struction of these "nurseries of the seas" did to the chain of marine life. They built airports on swamps and marshes and paved vast areas of once-green land, destroying heedlessly the plant life whose chlorophyll produced the oxygen they breathed.

By the 1960's, the danger to life became so real that man began to take action. But science and technology were propelling the United States so fast that the task of catching up socially, culturally, and politically to their effects was an enormous one. Because the entire planet was an ecosystem, measures to check pollution and environmental destruction could succeed only if they were conducted on an international basis.

The rising crime rate. Other unpleasant aspects of modern civilization added to the growing concern about the quality of life. By 1965, the cost of crime in the United States ran close to $21 billion a year. Just as organized crime flourished during the prosperous twenties, so it shared lustily in the affluence of the postwar years. So pervasive and often subtle were the activities of the criminal syndicate that they touched the lives of everyone in urban America, directly or indirectly.

Individual crimes of violence also increased markedly, nearly half being committed by young people, eighteen or under. In part, the rising crime rate reflected the social disorganization in the cities, particularly the traumatic effect of ghetto life on young male members of the racial minorities. But the crime rate skyrocketed in white middle-class suburbs, too, where young vandals and delinquents sometimes committed senseless atrocities. Among all social groupings, moreover, the rate of increase was highest among teen-age girls.

Drug addiction. A very high percentage of crimes against property (theft, burglary, larceny) was the work of active drug addicts. In 1970, there were an estimated 200,000 active addicts in the United States. Addiction among the young mounted each year, in many instances entrapping children of elementary and high-school age. Once "hooked" on hard, habit-forming drugs, the typical addict often turned to crime or prostitution for money to support an insatiable, daily "habit."

The use of narcotics by relatively large numbers of people was a phenomenon entirely new to the American experience. Once confined to the dark corners of society, it now emerged starkly into the open. Many young people (although no one could say for sure how many) experimented with marijuana. Some used chemical compounds and other agents to induce hallucinatory effects—psychedelic "trips," as they were called.

But drug usage was by no means confined to the young. Millions of Americans daily consumed an enormous quantity of "legal" stimulants and tranquillizing drugs. Moreover, they drank a huge volume of alcoholic beverages—all, apparently, to ease the task of "coping" with modern life.

Attempts to cope with modern life. In the 1950's, the dominant pattern of life for most middle-class people was one of conformism and blandness. People wanted economic security above all and were quite prepared to temper their personalities to achieve it. The ideological struggle with the Soviet Union made them very careful of doing or saying anything that might be construed as a denigration of American values or the capitalist system.

Group harmony was the ideal sought in most situations, and individual initiative was actually discouraged. Bright young people in business were admonished to "play the game" and never to "rock the boat." The real worth of people, ideas, and products became less important than the "images" they projected. Television, advertising, and the news media all contributed to laying a facade of blandness over a society in reality teeming with unresolved problems and mounting tensions—race conflict, poverty, urban blight, unprecedented population growth, and the like.

A few rough spots showed on the bland facade, to be sure. In the black community, the decade was a time of mounting activity, but also smoldering alienation, a feeling that man is a stranger to himself and society (Chapter 30). Among young whites, members of the Beat Generation deliberately adopted a life style contrary to dominant American values. Rejecting materialism in favor of mysticism, they praised failure rather than success, affected long hair and exotic clothes, went dirty and used drugs. At the other extreme, right-wing fanatics organized the John Birch Society, to prevent what they were sure was the imminent takeover of the United States by communism. Nevertheless, only a small minority of the population was affected by activities of these sorts.

In the 1960's, the facade faded and the realities of modern life broke through. The very act of exposing these realities produced profound feelings of anxiety and alienation in the population as a whole.

For middle-class and working-class whites, alienation manifested itself in growing anxiety about the condition of American life. In the turmoil and tragedies of the sixties, millions of people became apprehensive that their values and the goals they had set for themselves were not, after all, invulnerable to change, perhaps even to destruction. The nation's problems suddenly loomed so large and various as to overwhelm certainty and dim optimism.

Merely "coping" became increasingly difficult, for the rapid pace of change befuddled the senses and made it easy to lose perspective. One observer captured the mood of anxiety when he noted that "Middle-class people look around and say, 'We've entered paradise and it looks like the place we just left. And if this is paradise why am I so miserable?'"

The answer to that question was simply that, as never before in American history, the problems facing society could no longer be escaped. Almost without exception, the great problems besetting the nation in the 1960's had been festering for years. In the past, the tendency had been to ignore them or somehow escape their effects. The problem of racism had been ignored by consigning black people to ghettos, rendering them "invisible" to the rest of society. Pollution and environmental destruction had been ignored by pretending that nature's gifts to the American people were unlimited. Urban blight and deterioration had been escaped by fleeing to the ever-growing suburbs.

In the sixties, the problems could no longer be ignored or escaped, for they threatened future national development. The American people were thrown into direct confrontation with their own history.

4 The Critics Examine The Affluent Society

1. According to writers of the fifties and sixties what were the weaknesses of traditional liberal democracy which handicapped its response to problems of modern society?

2. Do you think it would be accurate to identify some authors of the period as muckrakers similar to the muckrakers of the Progressive Era?

3. What were the religious and educational responses to the challenges of contemporary society? Has the United States continually emphasized religion and education to the same extent as during the fifties and sixties?

4. How did the Hippies reflect the strains upon American life?

Critical commentary on the affluent society and its values came from many quarters and took many forms. Many critics of the 1950's were concerned with the moral consequences of affluence. Sociologist David Riesman in *The Lonely Crowd* (1950) argued that the "inner-directed" nineteenth-century American with his fixed, certain set of values, had given way to a modern "other-directed" individual, whose conduct and values—indeed, whose very concepts of right and wrong—were dictated by the views of his peer group. This "organization man," as writer William H. Whyte, Jr., observed, willingly sacrificed his individual integrity in an almost pathetic eagerness to "belong." He became the perfect conformist—the bland, faceless "man in the gray flannel suit," as a popular expression put it.

Social thought. Looking more specifically at the problems of prosperity, economist John Kenneth Galbraith observed in *The Affluent Society* (1958) that, while the private sectors of society reaped enormous benefits from the outpouring of national wealth, the public sectors—housing, education, urban renewal, and so on—were desperately impoverished. Galbraith called for government action to divert funds to the public sector.

Other critics, however, warned against putting too much faith in government to right society's wrongs. In *The Death and Life of Great American Cities* (1961), urbanologist Jane Jacobs criticized city planners for casual disregard of human needs in their rush to tear down old familiar environments and replace them with "model" neighborhoods that offered the inhabitants nothing in the way of community or a sense of continuity. And economist Peter Drucker noted the alarming growth of frustration and cynicism among people who learned from experience that governments promise much but deliver little.

Some critics argued that the flaws in American society were too overwhelming to be solved by traditional liberal reform. Sociologist C. Wright Mills influenced the thinking of a generation of students with his book *The Power Elite* (1956), in which he asserted that an oligarchy of corporate, political, and military leaders made the important decisions affecting people's lives. Mills's thesis suffered from too-rigid determinism; yet, the growing power of the "military-industrial complex" in the 1960's tended to confirm his assumption that the decision-making process had undergone significant changes in modern times.

Equally influential was Paul Goodman, a free-ranging critic, whose book *Growing Up Absurd* (1960) was a searching indictment of modern America for wasting the humanity of its youth. To conform to the dominant society, Goodman argued, meant to become apathetic, cynical, bitter. A "conformist and ignoble system" could never hope to breed the "skillful and spirited men" needed by any vital, growing society. Goodman appealed for a revitalization of the "radical-liberal" tradition in America, and his influence was especially strong among middle-class student activists in the 1960's.

Much farther to the left was philosopher Herbert Marcuse, whose cumbersome, often incomprehensible book *One-Dimensional Man* (1965) "inspired" a small group of campus radicals during the sixties. Finding nothing of value in modern American civilization, Marcuse posited a utopian view of the future, in which "truth" was dictated by an immaculate majority, infinite in wisdom and moral purity. In his rejection of reason and his intolerance of opinions different from his own, Marcuse stood squarely in the tradition of revolutionary totalitarianism. In one particularly revealing passage, he wrote that the "restoration of freedom of thought may necessitate new and rigid restrictions on teachings and practices in the educational institutions." To Marcuse, the end (freedom) justified the means (the destruction of freedom)!

Concern for the quality of life in America stimulated a revival of the muckraking tradition. Michael Harrington's study of poverty was an effective work of muckraking, as was Rachel Carson's probing work on environmental destruction. Doubtless, the most spirited of the "new muckrakers" was Ralph Nader, an intense young crusader for the public interest against corporate and governmental bureaucracies. "Nader's Raiders," as he and his group of young followers were known, turned the spotlight of publicity on subjects ranging from inadequate standards of automobile safety to haphazard methods of testing new pharmaceutical products.

Journalistic criticism. In journalism, Walter Lippmann continued to play the role of "public philosopher," setting high standards of ruggedly independent commentary. Carl Rowan was the most effective of the black columnists, while Murray Kempton provided urbane commentary from the liberal side of the political spectrum to match William Buckley's contributions from the conservative side. Cartoonists Herbert Block ("Herblock") and Bill Mauldin reached huge audiences with their spirited visual commentaries on public figures and issues. More subtle were Jules Feiffer's mocking cartoon satires on the social foibles of the sixties.

Among the popular magazines, such old general favorites as *Collier's* and *The Saturday Evening Post* gave way to new periodicals having specific appeal to various social groups. *Playboy*, a glossy, vivid magazine aimed at young male readers, was a phenomenal commercial success. In its glorification of materialism and sex, *Playboy* epitomized the affluent society; yet, occasionally it offered responsible social criticism as well. *Ebony* was a successful magazine for black readers, although militant young blacks scorned its conventional, middle-class orientation.

For political commentary, the choice ranged from the left-wing, muckraking *Ramparts* to the decidedly conservative *National Review.* The most

741

© 1963 MAULDIN
Chicago Sun-Times

Cartoonists in the 1960's eloquently reflected the problems besetting American society. William Mauldin, twice winner of the Pulitzer Prize, gained fame as the creator of the indominatable GI's Willy and Joe during World War II, and he continued to comment on the American scene. His portrayal at left of a grieving Lincoln was a moving expression of the nation's feelings after the assassination of President Kennedy. Herbert Block, better known as Herblock, is perhaps the best-known living political cartoonist. At right, he succinctly presents the overwhelming problems of the nation's cities. Once described as "the best writer now cartooning," Jules Feiffer is a social commentator whose simply drawn cartoons are captioned by dialogues or soliloquies which probe American behavior and attitudes. Feiffer is a humorist who does not tell jokes or offer gags. Sometimes with scorn, often with compassion, as in the cartoon below, he examines the alienation that characterizes a part of contemporary American society.

from *The Herblock Gallery* (Simon & Schuster, 1968)

THE SILENT SPRING

Rachel Carson wrote eloquently of how man is destroying his environment. In *The Silent Spring*, she describes how the beauty and abundance of life in a small town died:

"... a strange blight crept over the area and everything began to change. Some evil spell had settled on the community: mysterious maladies swept the flocks of chickens; the cattle and sheep sickened and died. Everywhere was a shadow of death. The farmers spoke of much illness among their families. In the town the doctors had become more and more puzzled by new kinds of sickness appearing among their patients. There had been several sudden and unexplained deaths. . . .

"There was a strange stillness. The birds, for example—where had they gone? Many people spoke of them, puzzled and disturbed. . . . The few birds seen anywhere were moribund [dying]; they trembled violently and could not fly. It was a spring without voices. On the mornings that had once throbbed with the dawn chorus of robins, catbirds, doves, jays, wrens, and scores of other bird voices there was now no sound; only silence lay over the fields and woods and marsh. . . .

"The roadsides, once so attractive, were now lined with browned and withered vegetation as though swept by fire. These, too, were silent, deserted by all living things. Even the streams were now lifeless. Anglers no longer visited them, for all the fish had died.

"In the gutters under the eaves and between the shingles of the roofs, a white granular powder still showed a few patches; some weeks before it had fallen like snow upon the roofs and the lawns, the fields and streams.

"No witchcraft, no enemy action had silenced the rebirth of new life in this stricken world. The people had done it themselves."

"This town does not actually exist. . . . Yet every one of these disasters has actually happened somewhere. . . ."

effective voice of moderate liberalism in the 1950's was *The Reporter*, an intelligently edited journal which, however, succumbed to a general disillusionment with liberalism in the next decade. More in tune with the radical thought of many intellectuals in the 1960's was the *New York Review of Books*, a sophisticated, sometimes pretentious journal, often sharply critical of prevailing American values.

Changing religious thought. Among theologians, the mounting tensions of the postwar years served to confirm the earlier swing to "neo-orthodoxy" (Chapter 23). Swiss theologian Karl Barth remained a strong influence among Americans. In his "crisis theology," Barth argued that man had no choice but to substitute faith for reason, given the chaos surrounding him. In *Christian Realism and Political Problems* (1954), Reinhold Niebuhr reiterated criticism of the liberal faith in human reason.

Younger theologians carried their disillusion further, some suggesting that modern civilization had become so dehumanizing as to render God irrelevant or "dead." The "God is dead" movement was an extraordinary intellectual phenomenon, rousing controversy among people who understood its theological implications and stirring resentment among people who did not. Far from denigrating the religious experience, the "God is dead" theologians put stronger emphasis on Christ as an inspirational figure.

In Protestant churches, something of a religious revival took place. Membership in churches increased sharply and attendance figures set new records. Moreover, the Reverend Billy Graham, an evangelist in the rural, fundamentalist tradition, had a wide following, even among the urban masses. People of all classes and creeds flocked to Graham's revival meetings, although it was impossible to say how profoundly his messages affected them.

Indeed, as church historian Will Herberg observes, the religious revival was actually a revival of religiosity—a search for the appearance of religion rather than the substance. Doctrine counted for little among the church-going masses, who sought instead simple reassurance in the face of permanent crisis and comforting advice about social conduct. Norman Vincent Peale provided both in such works as *The Power of Positive Thinking*

ART IN CONTEMPORARY AMERICA

The Human Edge, Helen Frankenthaler, 1967

By 1960, the basic trend of the previous twenty years—abstract expressionism—had come to an end, and the art world splintered into a new series of styles—junk, assemblage, hard-edge, pop, op, and minimal were just a few of the names given to the new approaches.

Helen Frankenthaler continued to paint in an abstract expressionist style, not following any of the newer innovations. Andy Warhol, on the other hand, was a leader in the pop art style, which used as its subject matter such objects as comic strips, billboards, and food cans. In his picture left, he made a silk screen adaptation of a photograph on canvas. Another leader in pop art was Claes Oldenburg. An artist of wit and imagination, he created many "soft sculptures," objects that one expects to be hard but that collapse into malleability.

Minimal art is represented by Tony Smith's sculpture. It seems very simple and totally lacking in emotion. The painter Frank Stella uses elements of minimal, hard-edge (so-called because of its sharp definition), and op (so-called because of its primarily visual emphasis).

Paolo Solari created a totally new, visionary architecture, which he termed "arcology," combining architecture with ecology. He produces environmental designs to serve man and ecology. Richard Avedon's photographic compositions, like his picture of George Harrison, take photo technology to its most advanced extent.

Marilyn Monroe, Andy Warhol, 1962

Ctesiphon II, Frank Stella, 1968

Giant Soft Drum Set, Claes Oldenburg, 1967

Willy, Tony Smith, 1962

Arcvillage, Paolo Soleri, *c.* 1968

George Harrison, Richard Avedon, 1967

748

(1952), which became almost a textbook for people seeking religious justification for material success.

Partly because of the leveling influence of affluence, partly because of the general suppression of doctrine in the worldwide ecumenical (co-operative) movement among religious groups, the distinctions among Protestants, Catholics, and Jews faded. As Herberg notes: "By and large, the religion which actually prevails among Americans today has lost much of its authentic Christian (or Jewish) content." Evidence of this de-emphasis of doctrine could be seen in the marked increase of interfaith marriages, as well as in the election of a Catholic to the Presidency. In the 1960's, moreover, the clergy of all religions participated actively in the civil rights movement and in the protests against the Vietnam War, the draft, and the ghetto.

Education re-examined. Ironically, it was in education—the institution Americans believed as an article of faith was the key to worldly success—that the deficiencies of the affluent society ultimately came to focus. The years after 1945 saw a phenomenal expansion of the student population in every grade—an expansion resulting not only from the high birthrate, but also from a rising economic and social demand for "educated people." In 1968, 94 percent of children between the ages of fourteen and seventeen were in school—more than 57 million young people as compared to 25 million in 1940. At the college and university level, enrollments mushroomed from about 1.5 million in 1940 to over 7 million by 1970. This explosion of student population put an unprecedented burden on the entire educational system and taxed the willingness of society as a whole to provide the necessary physical plant, books, and competent teachers.

It also reopened the old debate about the quality and purpose of education in the United States. In 1957, the Soviet Union's space exploits shocked Americans into realizing that first-rate scientists and technicians were as easily produced by a Communist educational system as by schools in a democracy. In response to the "Sputnik crisis," Congress the following year passed the National Defense Education Act (NDEA), the first major federal law for higher education since the Morrill Act of 1863. But NDEA was really a cold war measure, little concerned with improving the intellectual quality of education. Rather, its purpose was to encourage American students to outdo their Russian counterparts in the study of foreign languages, engineering, mathematics, and the sciences.

A more profound critique of American education came well before the "Sputnik crisis." Historian Arthur Bestor in his book *Educational Wastelands* (1953) scathingly attacked the "life-oriented" education most children received and called for new emphasis upon intellectual discipline and rigorous training. Educator R. E. Flesch's provocative 1955 book explained *Why Johnny Can't Read* in terms of the failure of schools to teach even the fundamentals of learning. In 1959, former Harvard University president James B. Conant echoed these criticisms, charging that both the high schools and the teacher-training institutions catered to the mediocre middle in the student population, while neglecting the bright student and the less than average, both of whom needed special attention.

Despite these criticisms, most schools continued to function much as they had in the past. In the more affluent communities, on the other hand, some schools responded to the criticisms with imaginative and sometimes successful changes in educational theory and techniques. Methods of teaching mathematics and physics were completely overhauled, while new techniques were introduced to improve reading skills and comprehension. Automation moved into the classroom, "programmed instruction" in some learning instances doing away with the need for a teacher altogether. In a few schools, the entire traditional routine of classes and grading was thrown out in favor of programs that encouraged students to progress at their own rate in response to their own motivations.

In 1940, higher education had been a luxury reserved for the privileged few. After the war, it became increasingly a necessity for the great majority of people involved in the complex social and economic functions of modern civilization. California and New York pioneered in providing facilities of higher education for every level of competence and every purpose, ranging from two-year community technical colleges to great centers for scholarly research and contemplation.

For all their shortcomings, the colleges and universities of the United States by the 1960's provided more people with a richer, more varied range of educational experiences than could be found anywhere else in the world.

Youthful unrest and alienation. Yet, the American campuses were swept by a wave of student protest and alienation, the full consequences of which cannot yet be assessed. The first sign of disaffection came in 1963 at the huge Berkeley campus of the University of California, where a minor student demonstration suddenly exploded into a sweeping protest against the bureaucratic indifference and impersonality of the university.

Dissent spread quickly, and by 1968 it was a rare and isolated campus that had not experienced some manifestation of student unrest. In educational terms, student protest was directed at rigid academic requirements, the relevance of courses to modern life, ethnic studies, the education of the poor and racial minorities, and the role of the college in the private lives of students.

But rebellion on the campus was only symptomatic of a deeper, more pervasive mood of dissatisfaction that affected many members of the younger generation generally. Racism, the war in Vietnam, poverty, pollution, moral hypocrisy, the power of the military-industrial complex, the unresponsiveness of government to the felt needs of people, the failure of their elders to move decisively on behalf of just causes—these and other grievances stirred a sensitive and articulate minority of young people to action.

Youth has always been a time of idealism. As one authority observes, however, the young rebels of the sixties were "much more vociferous in stating their idealism, in protesting against inhumanity where they find it, and in trying to do something about changing the world, than were the youth of previous generations." They were also afflicted with profound feelings of alienation from the "normal" routines and values of society. Many cultivated an attitude of extreme individualism—of "doing one's thing"—while others turned to drugs as a means of coping with life.

Bohemianism flourished among the Hippies, young people who sought to live the "natural life" of pre-industrial peoples, or who practiced mass sharing and communal living. In their dress, their bare feet, their long hair, their psychedelic "acid rock" music, their sexual freedom, the Hippies expressed a longing to be open and honest and free in human relationships. Other young rebels turned to romantic revolution as the "salvation" of modern civilization, adopting the Marcusean philosophy that the end justifies the means.

Whatever its manifestations, the alienation of so many bright, sensitive young people was a cause of deep concern to many older Americans. As Senator Robert F. Kennedy once wrote:

> Self-assured societies, confident of their wisdom and purpose, are not afflicted with rebellions of the young. . . . If the young scorn conventional politics and mock our ideals, surely this mirrors our own sense that these ideals have too often and too easily been abandoned for the sake of comfort and convenience.

5 The Visual Arts Flourish In The Affluent Society

1. Why was there a culture explosion during the postwar years?

2. What were the trends in television, movies, painting, sculpture, and architecture during the postwar years? How did the visual arts of the period reflect conditions in America at that time?

3. What are the standards used to judge good and bad art? Do you think it is possible to make a reasonable judgment on the excellence of art at the time of its creation?

As at no other time in American history, the postwar years saw mass culture flourish. Indeed, a "culture explosion" took place—a burgeoning of art schools, museums, community theaters, symphony orchestras, and opera companies. Literature and the arts came within the reach of millions, to be gratefully received if not always aesthetically appreciated. Americans gobbled up books by the millions, claimed half the world's total number of symphony orchestras, spent more on concerts and phonograph records than on spectator sports, and crowded their museums and galleries to view the works of old masters and new aspirants with cordial impartiality.

Mass culture had its sordid side, to be sure. Millions of consumer dollars went for trash—cheap, sensational novels; comic books; magazines of sex and sadism; simple-minded music; and "art" calculated to debase the public taste rather than raise it. Moreover, the strong commercial orientation of American life frequently corrupted the integrity of both artist and patron of the arts. Nonetheless, a rise in the public's general educational level, plus the measurable affluence of the time, gave many people the opportunity and intellectual wherewithal to discriminate between shoddiness and quality.

The emergence of television. Nowhere did the best and worst in American culture conflict more openly than on television. Establishing itself almost overnight after the war as a part of everyday life, the new medium was hailed by some as the most exciting and promising cultural development since the invention of printing. As an art form, however, television never really had a chance. From the start, the national networks and local stations alike used it primarily to sell products, secondarily to entertain viewers, and only incidentally to cultivate and promote the arts. As a news medium, television often did superb work, as in the breathtaking live transmission of pictures from the moon by Apollo 11. Occasionally, it produced documentary material of genuine significance. For the most part, programming became what Newton Minow, Chairman of the Federal Communications Commission, called it in 1961—a "vast wasteland."

NET (the National Educational Television Network, a non-commercial enterprise) maintained cultural quality in much of its programming, but the commercial networks succumbed to a sterile competition among themselves to dominate the viewer ratings. In their greed to attract large "prime time" audiences, they pandered to the simplest, most banal elements of popular taste. Unlike television in western Europe, American television somehow never managed to strike a reasonable balance among quality information, entertainment, and enlightenment.

The changing film industry. Late-night viewers took comfort in watching televised reruns of movies from Hollywood's earlier Golden Age. As for the motion picture industry itself, it suffered badly from TV's rising competition. In the decade from 1948 to 1958, attendance figures dropped by half, and hundreds of movie theaters closed. In a frantic effort to recapture its fading audiences, Hollywood occasionally turned to themes it had once dismissed as "too controversial" for filming—race relations, anti-Semitism, the darker aspects of human nature, explicit sex. Studios also lavished enormous sums on "spectacles," of which the $42 million *Cleopatra* in 1963 was a prime, grotesque example. In the end, the industry came to uneasy terms with television, selling it old films for rerun and turning over old movie lots to TV producers.

Under the circumstances, the cinema as an art form endured rough going. A list of memorable films for the quarter century from 1945 to 1970 reveals numerous distinguished contributions from Italy, France, Japan, Poland, India, and England, but strikingly few from the United States. Plagued by high costs and the insistence of studios that profits take precedence over artistic integrity, American filmmakers nonetheless turned out some works of lasting quality.

In *Treasure of the Sierra Madre* (1948), director John Huston turned a derisive camera on human nature, disclosing the disintegration of people confronted with unexpected wealth. *The Man With the Golden Arm* (1956) took an unflinching look at the agony and sordidness of drug addiction. One of the first films to treat a black man as a purposeful, uninhibited human being, rather than a submissive underdog, was *Edge of the City* (1957). *Some Like It Hot* (1959) was Hollywood humor at its sardonic best, while *Shane* (1953) was one of the great Westerns of all time.

In the 1960's, imaginative directors in Hollywood and "underground" produced some films that broke with many past conventions. Stanley Kubrick's *Dr. Strangelove* (1964) was Black Humor brought to the screen, an antic vision of nuclear doomsday. In *Faces* (1969), John Cassavetes effectively employed the semidocumentary technique favored by many young "underground" producers to tell a simple story about very believable people. A wry tale of the "generation gap" in middle-class America was *The Graduate* (1967), while *Midnight Cowboy* (1969) was a disquieting look at the physical and moral squalor of the affluent society. Perhaps the representative film of the decade was *Bonnie and Clyde* (1967), an unabashed celebration of the public's fascination with action and violence.

The "American school" of painting. In painting, New York City after World War II became what Paris had been before the war—the focus of ferment and change, the Mecca to which young artists elsewhere looked for inspiration. Indeed, American painting largely freed itself from its European ancestry. To be sure, the new "American school" owed much to the example of Pablo Picasso and built on the work of such refugee artists as Hans Hoffman and Piet Mondrian. But a strong native American influence easily predominated, as in the crude western individualism evident in the work of Jackson Pollock.

The dominant movement was Abstract Expressionism—a free-swinging, warm, sensual style, involving a lavish, impetuous use of paint on large formats. It was a conscious rejection of conventional middle-class tastes in favor of a highly personalized art for art's sake. Unlike the realists of the 1930's, the new painters refused to use art for conscious social or political ends. As one of them insisted, "the Painting itself is the responsible Social Act of the Artist, and is one of the surest, most direct forms of Communication known to man."

Often called "action" painters or artists of "impulse and chance," the Abstract Expressionists worked intuitively, relying upon the finished painting itself to reveal their introspective, often unrealized, purpose. They splashed and hurled and dripped and squashed paint on their canvasses, letting the material flow and form as it would. Pollock laid canvas on the floor; then, as one observer described him, "raced around it with pails, hurling gushes of violent hues to splash and flow, to gut and congeal.... Hours went by before the pails were empty and the fury over. Pollock squatted on his heels in a corner, trembling and spent."

At its worst, as it became popular and commercial, Abstract Expressionism aimed only at shocking people in a tawdry, mindless way. At its best, it was an exciting expression of America's vitality and potential in the postwar years. Pollock's *Mural on Indian Red Ground* (1950) successfully achieved a total unity and coherence of image within a labyrinth of lines and movements. In *The Liver Is the Cock's Comb* (1944), Arshile Gorky merged his own freely invented forms into a brilliant, indissoluble arrangement.

By 1960, Abstract Expressionism dominated the galleries of modern art; yet, already younger painters were reacting against it. The new decade was one of the most extraordinary in the history of American art. Initially, the tendency was to become much cooler, precise, cleaner, and impersonal. Pop art reflected the disillusionment that settled over many artists; and its ironic, hard-edge style was a mocking response to the mass culture of television, advertising, comic books, and the movies.

Typical was Andy Warhol's art: he used soup cans and the like as subjects and painted them in a mechanical, silk-screening style that seemed untouched by human hands. Robert Rauschenberg and Jasper Johns incorporated objects from everyday life—tin cans, rags, stuffed animals, automobile tires—into paintings that almost merged with sculpture. Later and briefly came Op art, a rather juvenile style relying on optical illusions.

American sculpture. Sculpture followed the same trends as painting, exploring the subtleties and potentialities of materials and construction. Alexander Calder pioneered in testing the vitality of metals. His wind-propelled "mobiles" were, as he put it, "detached bodies floating in space, of different sizes and densities ... some at rest while others move in peculiar manners." Isamu Noguchi's deep respect for wood could be seen in the highly polished surfaces and pure, simple forms of his works.

David Smith towered above his contemporaries and brought American sculpture to full maturity. Descendant of a blacksmith, he used heavy metals and techniques of welding in a style close to Abstract Expressionism in painting. His masterpieces were *Blackburn—Song of An Irish Blacksmith* (1950), in which fanciful forms combine in complex interplay; and *Hudson River Landscape* (1951), called by critics a "drawing-in-space." Later he became less fanciful and more geometric, as in his "Cubi" series (1963-65), which balance great metal cubes in three-dimensional buoyancy. Rather than romanticize or reject the Machine Age, Smith cheerfully used its materials and themes.

"The medium is the message." By the end of the sixties, art in America was a fluid mixture of styles, some complex, some starkly simple. Technologically inspired forms further blurred the line between painting and sculpture, as artists worked with light, sound, liquids, machinery, kinetic energy, and electronic programming to create new and often weird effects. Essentially anti-art and anti-establishment, the new artistic mood expressed philosopher Marshall McLuhan's view that in the age of the masses, the individual counted for nothing; the medium itself was the message. Perhaps there was something symbolic of the 1960's in sculptor Claes Oldenburg's last work of the decade: a hole dug behind the Metropolitan Museum of Art in New York, then filled in again to create an "invisible underground sculpture."

American architecture. Economic growth, the population explosion, the rise of suburbia, and urban renewal all had profound effects on architecture. In New York City, the International Style had an overpowering effect, literally transforming the appearance of midtown Manhattan with its "glittering glass-box transparency." An American adaptation of the Bauhaus School (Chapter 23), it was coldly functional and rigorously disciplined in its use of rectangularity. Mies van der Rohe, its great exponent, called it "the only practical way to build today, because the functions of most buildings are continually changing, but economically the buildings cannot change."

New York's elegant Lever House (1952) and Seagram Building (1958) were masterpieces of the International Style. But the style was grossly overused by builders in New York and other cities, with the result that many imitations were often ugly, graceless structures. The great Bauhaus master himself, Walter Gropius, helped to design one of the worst offenders—the shapeless, monolithic Pan Am Building, which glowered down on New York's Park Avenue, utterly obliterating a once elegant vista. An "aesthetic pollutant!" one critic labeled Chicago's John Hancock Building, a giant smokestack of a structure. Perhaps the most disastrous effect of this overuse

of the International Style was its cruel distortion of San Francisco's magnificent skyline.

Shunning the "curtain wall" glass towers, other architects adopted new techniques of molding concrete to expand the idea of the shaped surface. Frank Lloyd Wright cast concrete in a great spiral for his last work, New York's Guggenheim Museum. Eero Saarinen's fluid sculpturing brought forth concrete buildings that seemed poised for flight. University architecture took on an emphatic, robust look in buildings by Paul Rudolph and Louis Kahn, especially. Buckminster Fuller's "geodesic domes" (*geodesic* refers to the shortest line between two points in space) pointed the way to a whole new concept in building. Demountable, reusable structures, the domes used materials in tension, each part pulling on the other parts to support the whole structure.

Mass construction, whether of individual homes for suburban residents or in city planning and urban renewal projects, reflected little in the way of imaginative innovation. Cities threw up stolid blocklike housing projects, paying minimal attention to the felt needs of people who lived in them. Express highways slashed through metropolitan areas, often becoming barriers to wall in people and to keep out light, air, and space. Philadelphia, New Haven, and a few other cities engaged in responsible, considerate city planning; but most municipalities "renewed" themselves in sterile disorder.

Much of suburbia fell victim to the bulldozers and quick-profit push of promoters, and only in high income areas did homes of architectural distinction appear. Areas of rapid growth suffered the worst depredations. Developers in California, for example, cut ugly gashes into the hills, then spread them with row after row of depressingly similar houses. As folksinger Malvina Reynolds described the scene, it was one of

> Little boxes on a hillside,
> Little boxes made out of ticky-tacky,
> Little boxes made out of ticky-tacky,
> And they're all built just the same.

Whatever their aesthetic limitations, however, to the people who lived in them the "little boxes"—mortgages and all—were infinitely preferable as homes to the "caves" of the city.

6 Literature, The Theater, And Music Reflect Changing Times

1. What were the themes of American novelists in the fifties and sixties? How were these themes repeated in poetry, drama, and music?

2. To what extent has commercialism permeated the arts in America?

3. Do you think it is possible to discern a mature black cultural expression in America during the 1960's?

4. How should one interpret the general health of the United States based upon an understanding of the artistic output of the United States in the last two decades?

American novelists after the Second World War did not attain the stature of the literary giants of the period between the great wars. But if the mid-century years produced no new Hemingways or Faulkners, they claimed a number of gifted literary craftsmen. Often deeply alienated from the society around them, these writers nonetheless showed unusual sensitivity to the changes taking place in American life. In their works they expressed the fears and aspirations of minority peoples, disdain for the materialistic values of the affluent, disillusion with politics and diplomacy, and a growing concern with the problem of individual identity in a mass society. Unlike the expatriates of the Jazz Age, they did not flee the sources of their alienation, but rather stayed to confront them as best they could.

The postwar novel. Understandably, the war was a theme of many novels in the 1940's and 1950's. Both Norman Mailer and James Jones were especially effective at evoking the crude human relationships of life in the military. In *Catch 22* (1961), Joseph Heller produced at once a comic masterpiece and a scathing denunciation of war. Although he wrote about the Second World War, his indictment of war's grotesque stupidity took on more pointed relevance, as Heller freely acknowledged, as the United States

drifted into the Vietnam War in the 1960's. A moving story of black soldiers at war was John Oliver Killens's *And Then We Heard the Thunder* (1963).

Black writers reached a growing and increasingly appreciative white audience after the war. Perhaps the most articulate interpreter of the black experience was James Baldwin, whose promise as a novelist showed brightly in *Go Tell It on the Mountain* (1953), then blurred as he turned to writing essays of powerful social criticism. Baldwin was a protege of Richard Wright (page 585), whom some critics hailed as the foremost black writer of the twentieth century.

Others assigned that honor to Ralph Ellison; indeed, many thought his *Invisible Man* (1947) the best American work of fiction in the postwar period. A soul-searching story of a young black's struggle to discover his true identity, the novel offered white readers profound insights into the nature of the black ordeal in America. But it also struck a note of universality in dissecting the problem of individual survival in an impersonal technological society. Eldridge Cleaver's remarkable *Soul on Ice* (1968) was not only a compelling denunciation of white society's exploitation of black men, but also a work of art in its revelation of the black American's new sense of selfhood.

Standing with Ellison in the front rank of novelists was Saul Bellow, whose theme was also the search for identity. *Henderson the Rain King* (1959) and *Herzog* (1964) both portrayed the struggle of the postwar Jew to achieve some inner reconciliation, if not fulfillment. Sophisticated, ironic, and blandly detached from a world he knows very well, Herzog makes his way without apology or deep reflection. "If I am out of my mind, it's all right with me," he says in the novel's opening line.

For readers apprehensive about what they saw as the mindless drift of postwar America, Ken Kesey's parable *One Flew Over the Cuckoo's Nest* (1962) foretold a grim future. Set in a mental ward where all individuality must be suppressed for the good of the group, the novel suggests a world ruled by a tyranny of conformity and compulsion. Young readers, especially, sympathized with the awkward rebellion of Holden Caulfield, the adolescent hero of J. D. Salinger's *Catcher in the*

Rye (1951), against just such a tyranny in his own small world. Through Holden, Salinger expresses the poignant lament that we all must shed our childhood innocence and come to grips with the harsh and often cruel realities of life.

"Black Humor." The best "school" of writing in the postwar years was Black Humor, a form which one critic noted was harder to define than "an elbow or a corned-beef sandwich." Black Humor had nothing to do with race. Rather, it assumed that the absurd reality of the world exceeded satire, that one could only laugh outright at the human condition while cynically accepting it. *Catch 22* was superb Black Humor, as were J. P. Donleavy's *The Ginger Man* (1955) and the works of Kurt Vonnegut and John Barth.

Going a step further, some writers found fiction irrelevant altogether. For Norman Mailer (after his early work), life was so grotesque and unreal that it could only be reported, not treated seriously in fiction. Mailer's *Miami and the Battle of Chicago* (1969) was brilliant, imaginative reporting of the election of 1968.

The poetic mood. As the Jazz Age produced the Lost Generation, so the Atomic Age spawned the Beat Generation. Such Beatnik writers as Jack Kerouac advertised their alienation in a body of chaotic, mostly third-rate literature. They self-consciously sought solace in mystical experiences, such as Zen Buddhism; but only a few Beat poets, notably Allen Ginsburg and Lawrence Ferlinghetti, managed to translate their mood into art. Alienation submerged in mysticism also characterized the work of the Hippie writers who succeeded the Beats in the sixties.

In general, poetry exhibited a vigor and experimental soundness lacking in much of the fiction of the time. Often it was obscure, after the fashion of Ezra Pound, whose influence remained strong. In the well-knit works of Robert Lowell and Theodore Roethke, the theme often was a carefully controlled exploration of human alienation. Wallace Stevens chose simpler themes about nature and man, although he experimented boldly with complex allusions and exotic language too.

Gwendolyn Brooks and Le Roi Jones were black poets, deeply concerned with the black experience. In her direct, natural style, Miss Brooks approached the subject with compassion, recognizing that some problems of black people are universal problems—intensified by experience, doubtless, but never set apart from the rest of the world. Jones's searing verse was of another breed, as were the unflinching plays he wrote mocking the white man and his institutions.

The theater. Although the theater flourished as a commercial venture, its very emphasis on commercialism seriously damaged its artistic integrity. Broadway increasingly presented plays remarkable for their lack of distinction; while much of the *avant garde* work in the smaller theaters was aimed as much at shocking audiences as at probing new artistic frontiers.

The best dramatists were beset by the same moods of disillusion and alienation that stalked the novelists and poets. Arthur Miller's *Death of a Salesman* (1949) and *The Crucible* (1953) were successful protests against conformity and materialism. In the work of Tennessee Williams, from *The Glass Menagerie* and *A Streetcar Named Desire* in the 1940's to *Night of the Iguana* in 1961, theater-goers found exciting drama, even though the subjects were invariably the deepest, ugliest aspects of human nature. Often obscure in meaning and imperfectly crafted, Edward Albee's works—of which the best were *The Zoo Story* (1958) and *Who's Afraid of Virginia Woolf?* (1961)— suggested a first-rate talent not really in control of its complex material.

New developments in music. In music, the electronics revolution produced exciting new developments. High-fidelity (hi-fi) and stereophonic improvements established high standards in the recording industry and led to a vast enlargement of the audience for good music. Electronics created new instruments, modified old stand-bys like the violin, and even made the computer into a musical instrument of sorts. Merging with the modernist influence of such European refugee composers as Arnold Schönberg and Igor Stravinsky, these technical advances opened revolutionary new areas for young American composers.

One of the more influential innovators was John Cage, who produced new sounds and rhythms on a wondrous variety of "instruments" including flowerpots and doorbells. Many composers abandoned the traditional eight-tone scale of the classics to infuse their work with an atonal Oriental quality and a dissonance strange to the

Rock is more than just music. As the young author of the following excerpt, who is herself a rock enthusiast, describes it, rock has generated a whole new life style:

"Rock 'n' roll is such friendly music. No wonder we love it. Simple and straightforward at its best, courageous and flamboyant in its most glorious moments, it has an eagerly faithful audience, the joyfully committed disciples. Rock has worked as a catalyst for this aroused and articulate young generation.

"The recognition of rock as a significant cultural entity is, by extension, the recognition of the young as a potent social force. The most auspicious aspect of the Technicolor bloom in the rock garden is not the music itself but the social dissatisfaction, political unrest, and the determination to remedy it through the romantic, freewheeling alternative life-style which rock has unleashed.

"Rock is the music of the technological children. Though protest music has ceased to be proper nomenclature for rock material, rock protests everything (including its own limitations) and seals its wistful spirituality with affirmation. . . . It has inspired a characteristic style of fashion, vernacular, journalism, and sexual behaviour as well as an idiosyncratic business community that generates millions of dollars. But rock's most important element transcends these. Rock 'n' roll, above all else, has made a community of its audience, a community that responds and reacts to every beat of the music and every nuance of the style. . . .

". . . As silly and as sassy as rock can be, it means what it says. That conviction and an aesthetic relying on emotional validity are what has rooted rock fans so solidly. Rock has generated a subculture with visible affectations, romantic visions, political inclinations. It both inspires and reflects the final frontiers of its audience, an actual youth movement, however unorganized. . . ."

unpracticed Western ear. Innovative, but also more familiar, were the compositions of Samuel Barber and Roger Sessions. Using traditional forms and modern themes, Gian-Carlo Menotti won critical acclaim for his operas *The Medium* and *The Saint of Bleecker Street.*

Linking the traditional serious music of the concert hall with the imaginative popular music of the American theater was the virtuoso conductor-composer Leonard Bernstein. As conductor of the New York Philharmonic from 1958 to 1969, Bernstein poured his talent and energy into musical efforts of every conceivable sort. His exciting score for *West Side Story* (1957) helped to make that musical drama an artistic success. Memorable music for Broadway also came from Richard Rodgers (*Oklahoma!* (1943), *South Pacific* (1949), *The King and I* (1951) and from Frederick Lowe (*Brigadoon* (1946), *My Fair Lady* (1956). In 1967, the folk-rock musical *Hair* proclaimed the "dawning of the Age of Aquarius," and was enthusiastically received, especially by young audiences, wherever it played in the world. Popular musical drama was a form at which Americans excelled.

New sounds. The big band sounds of swing lost favor after the war, as jazz took on new forms. "Bebop" was a looser, more harmonic version, exemplified in the work of saxophonist Charlie Parker and trumpeter Dizzy Gillespie. In the 1950's, "cool jazz" caught the public's fancy. Detached, lacking the uninhibited freedom of basic jazz, yet somehow expressing rebellion, it was an idiom well-suited to the Beat Generation. Other artists—composer-pianist Duke Ellington, saxophonist Ornette Coleman, the Modern Jazz Quartet, Dave Brubeck—developed jazz into a highly sophisticated music, as serious as any of the traditional classical forms.

Black people had long known an elemental form of jazz called "rhythm and blues." A sensual, pulsating music—sometimes plaintive, sometimes rollicking—it freely expressed the innermost feelings—the "soul"—of those who sang and played it. Among the black artists to give "rhythm and blues" a national audience were Chuck Berry, Aretha Franklin, and James Brown. White singer Elvis Presley was enormously successful with his own highly stylized version. But no one excelled Ray Charles as an exponent of "soul music." A black artist with a remarkable gift for phrasing, he conveyed the full range of joy and sorrow in the idiom.

"Rock-'n'-roll" developed as a popular version of "rhythm and blues" and became pre-eminently the music of the young in the 1960's. In the lyrics of "The Beatles," an English foursome who stormed the United States with their songs and style, young people found many of their views and aspirations expressed. Later, the influence of Hindu and other exotic forms gave some rock music a mystical, ethereal quality. "Acid rock" musicians sought to achieve psychedelic effects in their music, sometimes by using drugs themselves, sometimes by combining sound, light, and color to induce hallucinatory responses in their audiences.

The revival of folk music. Folk music enjoyed a phenomenal revival after the war. With its relatively simple tunes readily adaptable to spontaneous lyrics, it had always been a medium of protest and personal statement. Veteran folksingers like Woody Guthrie, Pete Seeger, and Leadbelly (Huddie Ledbetter) sang of social injustice and the plight of exploited workers and farmers. Younger guitar-strumming singers joined in with protests against war, racism, and the pressures of mass society. Bob Dylan was a gifted lyricist, whose folksongs were always perceptive and sometimes poetic. His "Blowin' In the Wind" spoke volumes about the rebellious mood of young blacks and whites:

> How many years can a mountain exist
> Before it's washed to the sea?
> How many years can some people exist
> Before they're allowed to be free?
> How many times can a man turn his head
> Pretending he just doesn't see?
> The answer, my friend, is blowin' in the wind,
> The answer is blowin' in the wind.

Many young artists, including Dylan, ultimately tried to combine folk music, "soul," and "acid rock," to develop a distinctive sound expressive of the political frustration, rebelliousness, and antimaterialist protest of much of the younger generation.

Vibrant and vigorous, the explosion of mass culture left a residue of uncertain over-all quality. Some of it surely ranks among the finest attainments of modern man; much of it deserves to be hastily forgotten. Barriers of artistic convention fell readily—as did those of moral restraint, as the courts struck down almost all censorship laws. The result was a raw new freedom, not yet disciplined in most of the arts as the 1960's drew to a close, not yet congealed into a clear form with an integrity and personality of its own.

CONCLUSION

Affluence and its effects reshaped the lives of all Americans, rich and poor, black and white, young and old, contented and restless. It blurred class distinctions and brought the "good life" to millions who once had been economically insecure. It altered traditional life styles in families and communities. It carved the landscape into new shapes, some exciting, others frightening. In the sciences and arts, it helped men break loose from conventional thinking and habits and to explore wild new territories of nature and the mind. It provided the means for sending men off to the trackless new frontier of outer space.

Ironically, as man set out to explore the moon and planets, he let his own Earth deteriorate to the point where its capacity to sustain life was endangered. Affluent America pumped so much poison into its waters and atmosphere that people died from breathing the air, and lakes turned into dead seas. Cities fell into decay, trapping millions of underprivileged people in concrete and asphalt jungles.

Affluent America neglected millions of its people, denying them even the means for subsistence, much less for prosperity or affluence. And while it gave affluence to others, often it left them also with a hollowness of heart, a sense of unease about the conduct and meaning of their lives. Many young people scorned the bounty of the affluent society and mocked its materialist values. But others sought to spread the bounty, realizing that efforts to change American values had little chance of succeeding until all Americans gained economic security.

The years since 1945 have been a time of startling contrasts—of promise and tragedy, of progress and regression, of boundless hopes and deadly fears. Man reached the moon and looked beyond it to the stars. But was he capable of solving the problems on Earth that threatened his very survival? Given the experiences of the past, there were reasons for the American people to view the future both with doubt and with optimism.

QUESTIONS

1. Was the United States a basically healthy country during the 1950's and 1960's? Explain your answer.

2. How effective was the American economic system in providing for the needs of the people?

3. What are the characteristics of poverty in America? Were there adequate opportunities for the poor or their children to achieve prosperity? Explain.

4. What accounted for population shifts in the United States during the 1950's and 1960's, and what were some of the consequences of these shifts?

5. What problems have confronted American cities continuously during the nation's history, and what problems are of recent origin?

6. In what ways has man become out of balance with his environment? What steps should be taken to correct the balance?

7. Were American problems of the 1950's and 1960's any worse than earlier eras? Were Americans able to make reasonable adjustments to the problems? Explain your answers.

8. How did traditional American institutions, such as the school and the church, respond to changing America?

9. What were the most important values of Americans at the middle of the twentieth century? Justify your choices.

10. Was the American cultural experience of the last two decades one of enlightenment or degeneration? Explain your answer.

11. To what extent have the writers and artists of the 1950's and 1960's accurately reflected American society?

12. In what ways were the 1950's and 1960's similar to the 1920's in America, and in what ways were they different?

13. How would you compare the relative influence of the automobile, radio, and television upon American history and life?

BIBLIOGRAPHY

GALBRAITH, JOHN K., *The Affluent Society,* New American Library (Mentor Books). This book has become a standard reference on affluence in America. The student can read the book and understand the important economic forces at work as well as the problems which arise as a result of affluence. The author makes several interesting suggestions to solve these problems.

BAGDIKIAN, BEN H., *In the Midst of Plenty: The Poor in America,* New American Library (Signet Books). Bagdikian's message is much the same as Michael Harrington's, but his approach is at a much more personal level. Students who have read the two books generally react more to the human dimension of this book.

RIESMAN, DAVID ET. AL., *The Lonely Crowd: A Study of the Changing American Character,* rev. ed., Yale University Press. Riesman's account documents the shift from individualism to conformity among Americans. It is a classic study of national character, and, although difficult reading at times, is an important resource for the student.

ROSENBERG, BERNARD AND D. M. WHITE EDS., *Mass Culture: The Popular Arts in America,* Free Press. This book provides a useful survey of mass culture in America. It surveys the impact of popular literature, radio, television, the movies, and advertising for their influence on American life. The contributors represent a wide range of fields, which results in a diversified, balanced account.

HERBERG, WILL, *Protestant, Catholic, Jew: An Essay in American Religious Sociology,* rev. ed., Doubleday (Anchor Books). Herberg surveys the three major religions of the United States and their interrelationships. He concludes with an excellent section on religion in American life.

SILBERMAN, CHARLES E., *Crisis in the Classroom: The Remaking of American Education,* Random House. There have been a large number of critical appraisals of American education as well as numerous proposals for dramatic overhaul. Silberman is one of the latest education critics, and he does a thorough job of investigating the subject and suggesting possible alternatives. The student will find this book particularly interesting since there seems to be a growing awareness among students of the strengths and weaknesses of their educational program.

SMITH, PAGE, *Daughters of the Promised Land: Women in American History,* Little, Brown. Because of the increasing interest in the role of women in American society, this book is necessary to trace the historical background. It is a general survey account, and the student may also want to read some of the recent women's liberation literature.

MADSEN, WILLIAM, *The Mexican-Americans of South Texas,* Case Studies in Cultural Anthropology, Holt, Rinehart & Winston.

STEINER, STAN, *La Raza: The Mexican-Americans,* Harper & Row (Colophon Books).
These two volumes are excellent companion studies in facilitating the understanding of the Mexican-American. The first is an anthropological study which emphasizes such topics as family and cultural patterns. The Steiner book deals more with the activist dimension of recent Mexican-American society. Both books are readable and attractive to high school students.

EDITORS OF FORTUNE, *The Exploding Metropolis,* Doubleday (Anchor Books). This collection of articles which originally appeared in *Fortune Magazine* provides the best survey of the problems facing our urban centers.

The articles provide excellent points of departure for more intense studies of the city.

GORO, HERB, *The Block,* Random House (Vintage Books). The author lived in the tenements he portrayed, interviewing and photographing his fellow inhabitants. The resulting book is an excellent portrayal of inner city life with the numerous photographs bound to move the student.

EDITORS OF FORTUNE, *The Environment: A National Mission for the Seventies,* Harper & Row (Perennial Library). In the same way that *Fortune* collected accounts on the city, it has provided an excellent collection of articles on the crisis facing the environment. The articles can be easily read by the student, and taken together they represent a balanced appraisal of the threats to man's environment.

SHEPARD, PAUL AND DANIEL MCKINLEY EDS., *The Subversive Science: Essay Toward an Ecology of Man,* Houghton-Mifflin. This is the best collection of essays available on the subject of ecology. Within that general topic many specific areas are discussed, including population, pollution, exploitation, and so forth. The articles are difficult reading, but worth the extra effort.

The Turbulent Sixties

Despite the logjam of neglected problems facing the nation's leaders, the new decade of the 1960's opened on a note of optimism and youthful exuberance. The new President was a young and vital man, eager to accept the challenges of his office. Young people generally seemed ready to work for the common good of society. Certainly, the nation had the resources and know-how with which to tackle the problems that beset it. If its will could be mobilized to the task, the future seemed bright and assured.

However, two major problems, one internal, the other external, hung as a shadow over the new administration and its youthful leaders. By the early sixties, the civil rights movement had moved into a position from which it was ready to launch an unrelenting attack on the whole structure and ideology of racism in America. Unless the white community responded fully and frankly to their demands, black leaders of a moderate persuasion might be forced by their followers to give way to more radical spokesmen. Abroad, the United States' involvement in Indochina threatened to mushroom at any moment into a major military commitment. Both problems—racism and Indochina—contained explosive social and political ingredients. The task of politicians was to solve the problems before they exploded. As you read about their attempts to deal with these problems, here are some questions to keep in mind:

1. Why did black Americans finally revolt, and to what extent did they succeed in achieving their goals?
2. How would you evaluate John F. Kennedy's achievements as President?
3. What was Lyndon Johnson's domestic program?
4. How did the United States become increasingly involved in the war in Vietnam?

1 Ethnic Minorities Revolt

1. What factors sparked the civil rights movement of the fifties and sixties?

2. How much actual progress had been made by black Americans to achieve equality by the end of the 1960's? What accounted for this change?

3. Do you think the nonviolence of Martin Luther King or the Black Power of Malcolm X, Stokely Carmichael, and H. Rap Brown was more effective in achieving racial equality and dignity for blacks?

4. What other American minority groups felt themselves discriminated against by the white American majority? Do you think their problems and goals were similar to those of black Americans?

Black scholar William E. B. DuBois once observed that the great problem facing twentieth-century man was "the problem of the color line—the relation of the darker to the lighter races of men in Asia and Africa, in America and the islands of the sea." After the Second World War, the people of the United States had to confront the problem of race directly. Led by a new breed of young activists, black Americans arose as a community to demand their full share of freedom, equal rights, and human dignity.

Contributing factors. Several factors coincided to spark the civil rights movement, including the war itself. Fighting against a Nazi ideology that included crude racial myths, the United States found itself embarrassed by its own race problem. After the war, the Soviet Union's challenge for influence among the emerging new nations of Asia and Africa forced Washington to take steps to eliminate *legalized* racism, at least, from the United States. As Secretary of State Dean Rusk remarked as late as 1961: "The biggest single burden that we carry on our backs in our foreign policy . . . is the problem of racial discrimination here at home. There is just no question about it."

Even more important was a new sense of self-importance within the black community itself. During World War II and the Korean War, black people moved out of the South in droves, seeking to enlarge their horizons and ambitions. They experienced a remarkable lift in racial pride when the self-governing black nations of Africa achieved independence in the 1950's. For the first time since the earliest days of slavery, great masses of black Americans throughout the country felt the magnetic pull of their ancestral past, of the African culture which centuries of slavery and white racism had stripped from them. As the term *black nationalism* came into use, it expressed not only their aspirations within this society, but also a profound sense of racial identity that transcended national boundaries.

Achievements and disappointments. Black Americans made significant gains in the postwar years, to be sure. The Supreme Court cut away legal discrimination in education and other social institutions (Chapter 27). Millions of blacks became new voters, while the number of blacks in college more than doubled. In government, business, sports, the military, and the entertainment world, individual black people achieved success and distinction. Jackie Robinson broke the color line in sports, becoming the first black player in major league baseball. Massachusetts sent Edward W. Brooke to the Senate, while several large cities elected black mayors. In Hollywood, Sidney Poitier became a leading star and Academy Award winner. Gwendolyn Brooks won the Pulitzer Prize for poetry in 1950. For some black people, at least, postwar America offered material rewards and recognition.

But these people were only a small minority of the black population. Poverty was the lot of the great majority—poverty perpetuated by chronic unemployment and rank discrimination against black workers; by menial jobs that neither fed a man's pride nor paid enough to support his family; by ghetto life with its substandard housing, inferior schools, high crime rate, and sometimes insensitive police. Mass advertising and the growing prosperity of white America raised the level of expectation for millions of black people. Yet, while the standard of living

A DREAM DEFERRED

Langston Hughes

What happens to a dream deferred?

Does it dry up
Like a raisin in the sun?
Or fester like a sore—
And then run?
Does it stink like rotten meat?
Or crust and sugar over—
Like a syrupy sweet?

Maybe it just sags
Like a heavy load.

Or does it explode?

for whites rose steadily from 1947 to 1966, blacks actually fell farther behind than ever on the economic ladder. The average annual income for a black family was only 59 percent that for a white family, while the unemployment rate in black ghettos was five times that of the white population.

Moreover, even the integration of public education proved to be a sad disappointment. By 1970, only 15 percent of black children in eleven southern states were attending integrated schools. In northern cities, where most black families were forced to live in ghettos, millions of children attended schools which were totally segregated.

Out of the misery of the ghetto, out of a profound sense of rights denied and hopes crushed among black people everywhere, arose the new militant movement. As it took shape, it developed a sense of purpose and staying power that earlier mass efforts had lacked. "Freedom Now!" the younger blacks cried; and their theme was echoed by the Reverend Martin Luther King, Jr., one of the movement's most inspired leaders: "We're through with tokenism and gradualism and see-how-far-you've-comeism. We're through with we've-done-more-for-your-people-than-anyone-elseism. We can't wait any longer. Now is the time."

King and nonviolent resistance. In leading the mass assault on racial barriers, King preached nonviolent resistance to unjust laws. It was a doctrine he derived from the teachings of Christianity and the historical examples of civil disobedience in Gandhi's struggle for India's independence and in Thoreau's protest against the Mexican War (page 208). King's tactics surfaced first in Montgomery, Alabama, where a black woman, Rosa Parks, was arrested in December 1955 for refusing to give up her seat in the white section of a bus. Led by King, the city's black people engaged in a massive bus boycott. After a year, the bus company agreed to desegregate its facilities. From Montgomery, the movement spread to Greensboro, North Carolina, where black college students staged a "sit-in" at a drugstore lunch counter to protest discrimination in places of public accommodation. This passive-resistance tactic caught on quickly, and subsequent "sit-ins" resulted in the desegregation of hundreds of public places throughout the South.

King's organization, the Southern Christian Leadership Conference (SCLC) was joined in peaceful resistance by the Congress of Racial Equality (CORE) and the Student Non-Violent Coordinating Committee (SNCC). The nonviolent phase of the civil rights drive reached a peak in the summer of 1964, when thousands of black and white students converged on the South from all over the nation to register prospective black voters and organize new biracial groups, such as the Mississippi Freedom Democratic Party. At this point, the goal of the movement was integration of black people into white society. Blacks and whites worked together, organized together, marched together, even died together, in pursuit of that goal.

Black Power. Within two years, however, the mood and goals of many blacks within the movement changed radically. Discouraged by the slow pace of integration, balked at every turn by die-hard segregationist politicians, too often brutally set upon by racist mobs, thousands of young blacks lost faith in King's tactics of peaceful resistance. In 1966, the newly elected chairman of SNCC, Stokely Carmichael, rejected the help of white students and called upon blacks to liberate themselves by cutting their ties to white society. Moreover, he insisted that black people assert their demands in the only terms white society understood—power. "We have to work for power, because this country does not function by morality, love, and nonviolence, but by power," he said. Before integration could take place, he maintained, black people by their own efforts had to attain full political and economic parity with whites.

Black Power was an outgrowth of black nationalism, which in turn reflected a growing sense of racial identity. Symbolic of the new mood, the aging scholar DuBois moved to Ghana, where he supervised the writing of an African encyclopedia until his death in 1963. Younger blacks sought in their African heritage some alternatives to the dominant ways of life in white America. They adopted African styles in dress and hairdo, rediscovered African cultures, and developed a self-conscious, highly assertive literature founded on Afro-American themes.

One group adopted the religion of Islam (out of disillusionment with Christianity as they saw it practiced), while also calling for the establishment of a separate "black nation" within the United States. Although few in number, these Black Muslims exerted a strong influence on the black community. The most remarkable member of the sect was Malcolm X, a young man of extraordinary personal magnetism, great oratorical power, and keen insight into the nature of the black-white relationship in the United States. A genuine leader of men, Malcolm was assassinated in 1965; but his example and writings continued to inspire young blacks long after his death.

Racial violence. To drive home the message of Black Power, orators like Carmichael and H. Rap Brown often used such fiery language that the only thing they communicated to whites was fear. Moreover, some groups undertook deliberate, planned acts of terrorism against the white power structure. But the wave of urban violence that swept the nation beginning in 1964 was simply an explosion of outrage in the ghetto—a blind, undirected protest against the conditions which white racism had imposed on black people. City after city suffered the agony of mass rioting. Most outbursts grew spontaneously from minor clashes between young blacks and a police establishment that sometimes behaved as their natural enemy. Detroit endured one of the worst ordeals in July 1966, when a week of rioting in the black ghetto produced an appalling toll: 40 dead; 2,000 injured; 5,000 burned out of their homes; property damage of half a billion dollars.

Nationalism and Black Power did not escape criticism from within the black community. Noting that blacks constituted only 15 percent of the nation's population, older civil rights leaders condemned separatism as a sterile, self-defeating concept. In a society overwhelmingly controlled by white economic and political power, they argued, blacks had little choice but to advance their interests in coalition with whites of good will. They deplored the extremist rhetoric and actions of some nationalists, warning that such tactics would only bring on new white repression against black people. At the same time, black nationalism also moved the moderate civil

CESAR CHAVEZ

Cesar Chavez, the leader and organizer of the migrant farm workers movement, tells in an interview what kind of society he would like to see in America and how he feels about nonviolence as a weapon:

"... Society is made up of groups, and so long as the smaller groups do not have the same rights and the same protection as others—I don't care whether you call it capitalism or communism—it is not going to work. Somehow, the guys in power have to be reached by counterpower, or through a change in their hearts and minds, or change will not come. . . .

"Non-violence is a very powerful weapon. Most people don't understand the power of non-violence and tend to be amazed by the whole idea. Those who have been involved in bringing about change and see the difference between violence and non-violence are firmly committed to a lifetime of non-violence, not because it's easy or because it is cowardly, but because it is an effective and very powerful way.

"Non-violence means people in action. People have to understand that with non-violence goes a hell of a lot of organization. We couldn't be non-violent in Salinas and win unless we had a lot of people organized around non-violence up and down the United States and Canada. We are organizers at heart. Most of us in the movement take great pride in being able to put things together."

rights leaders to adopt a more active, militant role themselves.

The crowning act of racial violence occurred on April 4, 1968, when a white sniper killed Martin Luther King, Jr., in Memphis, Tennessee. King had devoted his life to the principle of nonviolent reform, believing that the Christian ideal of brotherly love was indeed attainable in the United States. Awarded the Nobel Prize for Peace in 1964, he had become a symbol of faith in the ultimate reconciliation of the races for millions of blacks and whites. Not surprisingly, his senseless death touched off the worst rioting yet, as black ghettos in 125 cities exploded in fury.

"Our nation is moving toward two societies, one black, one white—separate and unequal." So reported the National Advisory Commission on Civil Disorders in 1968. White racism, it concluded, was the real cause of the riots. Systematically deprived of the things white Americans most cherished, young ghetto blacks endured lives of unrelieved economic exploitation, social degradation, police harassment, and spiritual despair. Like oppressed peoples everywhere, they struck at the society which victimized them with any weapon at hand.

Militancy among other minorities. The militant mood of black people spread to other minority groups, as well. American Indians, long the most oppressed and brutalized minority, began to assert themselves with a renewed sense of racial-tribal pride. Puerto Ricans copied the tactics of black militants in their struggle for liberation from racial oppression. Among Mexican-Americans, young spokesmen arose to lead a "Chicano" movement seeking cultural recognition as well as economic and political advances. Cesar Chavez appealed to ethnic pride in organizing California's seasonal agricultural workers, long exploited for their cheap, plentiful labor. Of New Mexico's colorful Chicano nationalist Reies Lopez Tijerina, it was said that he "made an oppressed people aware of themselves and their potential power."

White response. Confronted with the reality of racial crisis, white society responded in a variety of ways. Many businesses took steps to recruit and train black workers, often over the objection of labor unions, which remained strongly resistant to the "newcomers." Schools and colleges reformed their curricula to include courses in ethnic studies. Active efforts were made to bring minority peoples into the mainstream of American life. On the other hand, many white people reacted to the crisis in fear and resentment, and violent confrontations of blacks and whites inevitably occurred. No problem—not even the Vietnam War—tested the skill and good faith of America's political leaders in the 1960's more than the "problem of the color line."

2 Kennedy Explores The New Frontier

1. How would you characterize the Kennedy administration? What were some of the problems which faced Kennedy?

2. To what extent was the New Frontier of Kennedy influenced by the New Deal of Franklin Delano Roosevelt? How much similarity was there between the two administrations?

3. What were the strengths and weaknesses of a program of controlled inflation as implemented by the Kennedy administration?

4. How effective was John F. Kennedy as President?

During his campaign for the Presidency, John F. Kennedy evoked the vision of a New Frontier— "the frontier of the 1960's, a frontier of unknown opportunities and paths, a frontier of unfulfilled hopes and threats." Just as frontiers of the past had taxed the determination and ingenuity of the pioneers, so the New Frontier would test the mettle of modern Americans. As he took the oath of office, the new President enjoined his countrymen to "ask not what your country can do for you—ask what you can do for your country."

The Kennedy style. Kennedy's brief Presidency was a time of political inspiration to many people, particularly the young. Kennedy seemed to epitomize in his person and his style a readiness to accept the past for what it was and to move on eagerly to uncover the future. His style contrasted vividly with the amiable complacency of the Eisenhower era. *Vigor* was one of his favorite words ("vigah," he pronounced it, in his flat New England way), and Washington once again became the youthful, exciting city it had been in the early years of the New Deal and during World War II. Trim, handsome, and athletic in appearance, the President was full of restless energy fueled by an insatiable curiosity. Watching him in action, James Reston of the *New York Times* once wrote that "He did everything around here today but shimmy up the Washington Monument."

Kennedy was a well-educated and well-read President. His own book *Profiles in Courage* (1955) had won a Pulitzer Prize in 1957 and revealed in him a historian's fatalism and sense of perspective. He was entirely comfortable—and healthily skeptical—in the company of intellectuals. He and his wife Jacqueline made the White House a center of culture and a filter for new ideas, as well as a home of grace and elegance. Some of the best minds in the country went to work for him. Edwin O. Reischauer, a distinguished historian of Japan, became ambassador to that country. The economist John Kenneth Galbraith took a similar post in India. Arthur Goldberg, a brilliantly successful labor lawyer, became Secretary of Labor. McGeorge Bundy left the dean's chair at Harvard to become a White House aide. Also from Harvard came historian Arthur M. Schlesinger, Jr., to serve as an adviser and as "historian in residence."

Like most strong Presidents, Kennedy was both a conservative and a progressive. He had no desire to tamper with basic institutions, least of all with capitalism. He was contemptuous of theorists, whether of the left or of the right. At the same time, he stimulated inquiry into a host of ideas and institutions which had escaped healthy criticism for too long. Pragmatically, he tried to correct abuses where he could, or at least to rouse public awareness that certain things could be done better. As Schlesinger observed: "He saw history in its massive movements as shaped by forces beyond man's control. But he felt that there were still problems which man could resolve; and in any case, whether man could resolve these problems or not, the obligation was to carry on the struggle of existence." Kennedy's "cool" manner, his air of detachment, kept him alert to his own shortcomings, as well as sensitive to other people's problems and limitations.

His spotty record in foreign affairs and bare handful of legislative victories at home suggest that Kennedy was not a particularly successful President. Yet, he grew in popularity and public esteem, even in his moments of adversity. In 1962, the voters gave him a healthy Democratic majority in Congress. A year later, he was well on his way to winning another term. Moreover,

his growing hold on the public's imagination suggested that a second term might have been measurably more successful than the first. His record notwithstanding, Kennedy was one of the most interesting men ever to attain the Presidency.

New Frontier economic policies. When he took office, the economy was in a slump. Unemployment was high (six million), and the rate of economic growth had fallen off noticeably. To get the country "moving forward" again, he turned to Keynesian methods. Indeed, his administration set about educating the public in a "new economics." *Controlled inflation* was the key factor in this "new economics"—inflation carefully stimulated by tax reductions for individuals and corporations in order to put more money into circulation, supplemented by regulated fluctuations in government spending.* The aim was to keep consumer purchasing power high enough to absorb the enormous and growing output of industry.

At the same time, he was against *price inflation*—the spiraling inflation that comes when management and labor arbitrarily raise prices and wages without regard to increases in productivity. One of Kennedy's fears was that uncontrolled inflation would price American goods out of the world market, thereby turning the already serious balance-of-payments problem into an economic catastrophe. One of his major legislative victories was the Trade Expansion Act (1962), which gave the President unusual power to adjust tariffs to meet foreign competition. Kennedy hoped to use the act to stimulate economic growth at home by opening new markets abroad.

He also established "wage-price guidelines" as a help to business and labor in keeping increases within the limits of productivity gains. When the United Steelworkers union opened contract negotiations with the steel companies in 1961, Kennedy's men worked carefully with both sides to keep a lid on wage demands and thus not give the industry an excuse to raise prices. When the union accepted a non-inflationary agreement,

---

*Congress repeatedly refused to give him the tax reductions he asked for. In 1964, President Johnson pushed the measure through, and the tax cut provided the stimulus that Kennedy had predicted.

Kennedy assumed that management would reciprocate by holding the line on prices.

He assumed wrong. Without consulting the White House, the huge United States Steel corporation raised its prices six dollars a ton. Faced with this arbitrary challenge to his policy of controlled inflation, the President reacted with the forcefulness of a Teddy Roosevelt. Defense Department orders were shifted from U. S. Steel to companies which promised not to raise prices, while Justice Department officials hinted of possible antitrust action against the company. Within seventy-two hours, government pressure forced the corporation to roll back the increase.

Kennedy's tough stand in the steel situation prompted charges that he was antibusiness, but he was no such thing. His blunt action may have been highhanded, but it was a pragmatic response to a specific problem, not an ideological move against business. Indeed, the policy of controlled inflation brought unprecedented benefits to the business community. For while keeping a tight rein on price inflation, it touched off the longest period of sustained economic growth in American history.

Relations with Congress. In his dealings with Congress, Kennedy knew more frustration than satisfaction. Although his party nominally controlled both houses, a conservative coalition of southern Democrats and Old Guard Republicans in key committee positions actually determined the fate of his proposals. During his term, Congress raised the minimum wage, improved social security benefits, and authorized an urban housing program; but it denied him many other measures of social and economic importance. Knowing from his own personal experience as a senator how stubborn the lawmakers could be, the President often waited until the pressure of events created a crisis, then asked Congress for "emergency" legislation.

Poverty and racial strife. Late in his Presidency, Kennedy declared "unconditional war" on the chronic poverty that, paradoxically, still plagued millions of people in history's most affluent society. Doubtless, he was moved by a sincere determination to remedy an obvious social evil, and he recognized the potential explosiveness of a situation in which widespread poverty existed in the midst of burgeoning plenty. Perhaps, too, the work of the "new muckrakers" influenced him, especially Michael Harrington's *The Other America,* a searching inquiry into the plight of the poor.

But the stimulus that moved him to direct, forceful action was the rising tide of black militancy. Aware that poverty and racism fed each other, civil rights leaders increasingly worked to raise the black man's standard of living as well as to secure his rights as a citizen.

Early in his Presidency, Kennedy's relations with the black community were equivocal and marked by no sense of great urgency. Some of his appointments to federal judgeships in the South went to avowed segregationists. At the same time, he brought more blacks into important positions than any previous President. In the Justice Department, his brother expanded the Civil Rights Division, making it into an instrument of genuine law enforcement. Both Kennedy brothers became friends of Martin Luther King, Jr., a relationship that won them the support of millions of blacks. Most important, unlike Eisenhower before him, Kennedy moved swiftly and decisively to uphold the federal courts when governors defied the law.

In 1962, the courts ordered the University of Mississippi to end its policy of barring black students and to admit James Meredith, a black war veteran. Mississippi Governor Ross Barnett defied the order and personally intervened to prevent Meredith from enrolling. As the President issued an appeal for reason and respect for the law, the Attorney General sent federal marshals to escort Meredith onto the campus. Refusing even to maintain ordinary law and order, Barnett permitted a mob of white students and other hoodlums to attack the marshals. In the night of rioting that followed, two people were killed and hundreds were injured. Order was restored only when Kennedy rushed troops to the scene and took the Mississippi National Guard out of Barnett's hands by putting it under federal control. Showing extraordinary courage and determination, Meredith remained at the university to earn his degree.

Alabama, last of the "all white" state universities, was integrated the following year. The state's governor, George C. Wallace, had vowed to "stand in the schoolhouse door" to prevent integration, and in June 1963 he did just

Soon after taking office, Kennedy announced that one of the objectives of his administration was to commit the nation to putting a man on the moon by the end of the decade. Two years later, the program was well under way when Kennedy visited Cape Canaveral (now Cape Kennedy), where, at right, he is briefed in the Saturn control center. Kennedy never lived to see the completion of his goal, for less than two weeks after this visit, he was assassinated. Directly below, his funeral cortege, with the flag-draped coffin borne on a caisson, passes through Washington on its way to Arlington Cemetery. Kennedy's successor, Lyndon B. Johnson not only pushed on with the space program but also continued to work for other Kennedy goals, including racial equality. At bottom, Johnson exchanges a handshake with Martin Luther King, Jr. during ceremonies at the signing of the Civil Rights Act of 1964.

that. But his defiance ended quickly when Kennedy federalized the Alabama National Guard and moved it to the campus. Wallace behaved even more irresponsibly in Birmingham, when he interfered in local affairs to prevent the public schools from obeying a court order to integrate. Vicious riots in that city forced the President once again to send in troops to restore order and thwart the law-breaking governor.

Inevitably, the callous behavior of such officials as Barnett and Wallace inspired brutality at all levels in their states. In April 1963, Birmingham's Police Commissioner used barbarous tactics to rout peaceful civil rights demonstrators. In June, Medgar Evers, leader of the NAACP in Mississippi, fell dead from a white sniper's bullet. White racists shocked the nation in September by bombing a Birmingham church and killing four little black girls who were attending Sunday School. Not even this monstrous deed ended the bloodshed, however. As white violence mounted, so did black rage.

These events moved Kennedy to ask Congress for the most comprehensive civil rights legislation in history. In a televised appeal for racial justice, he asserted that America was in a great moral crisis. "It is time to act in the Congress, in your state and local legislative bodies, and, above all, in all of our daily lives." When a quarter of a million people—blacks and whites together—marched on Washington in September 1963 to demand "Freedom Now!" Kennedy welcomed them. But the mass plea for action failed to stir Congress.

The assassination of Kennedy. Three months later, John F. Kennedy was dead. As he rode through the streets of Dallas in the early afternoon of November 22, two bullets from an assassin's rifle struck his head. He died a half hour later, and a nation mourned.

The man charged with the crime was Lee Harvey Oswald, an unstable leftist with a disordered past. Oswald never stood trial for the murder, however, for he was himself shot to death while in police custody. His killer was a seedy night-club operator, who claimed to be avenging the dead President. The entire incredible episode took place before television cameras and was witnessed by an unbelieving audience of millions.

"This is a sad day for all peoples," the new President told a stunned and shaken nation. "I will do my best. That is all I can do. I ask for your help—and God's."

3 Johnson Works Toward "The Great Society"

1. What were Johnson's attributes and liabilities as a candidate for President of the United States? What were the similarities and what were the differences between the administrations of Kennedy and Johnson?

2. How successful was President Johnson in securing a domestic program to meet the needs of America in the sixties? What suggestions of future American difficulties can be perceived in the section?

3. Why was Goldwater beaten so badly in the election of 1964? Why did Goldwater follow the campaign strategy he did?

At the time he became President, Lyndon Baines Johnson was already one of the nation's most powerful and experienced politicians. He had first come to Washington from his native Texas in the heyday of the New Deal and had learned his politics from such masters of the art as Speaker of the House Sam Rayburn and FDR himself. After serving six terms in the House, he moved on to the Senate and in 1955 became Majority Leader of that body.

Johnson the man. Johnson served the oil and cattle interests of Texas well; but he was more than a mere sectional politician. He had a broad national outlook and an abiding interest in the problems of people everywhere. Although a thoroughly professional politician and loyal Democrat, he was capable of rising above partisanship to serve the national interest. He worked closely with Eisenhower, for example, especially in foreign policy.

His own political ideology was that of a New Deal liberal—progressive, pragmatic, fundamentally reasonable. He was enormously persuasive in dealing with individuals and small groups. And when "reasoning together" failed to produce what he wanted, he also knew how to twist arms—sometimes to the breaking point. Above all, he understood and relished power. As journalists Rowland Evans and Robert Novak wrote of him in 1966: "Johnson was born with the instinct of power, and . . . he knew exactly where it existed, how to obtain it, and, most important, how to exercise it—sometimes with restraint, sometimes without."

Johnson's personality, unfortunately, was also flawed in ways that markedly effected his public image. A man of massive ego, he was sensitive to the mildest criticism and quick to see personal slight where none was intended. He was also something of a prima donna, hungry for approval and always dominating the stage. President Kennedy once wryly remarked that writing a simple birthday greeting to Johnson took more care than drafting a state document.

Johnson seldom forgave those who disagreed with him publicly, and he could be ruthless in dealing with people, even his close associates. Yet, at times he became so unabashedly sentimental as to embarass those who worked with him. His most serious weakness was deviousness, especially in his dealings with the press. Ultimately, it led to an erosion of public confidence in him—to the opèning of a "credibility gap" between the White House and the people.

Johnson had few of Kennedy's problems with Congress. Wise to every rule and trick in the Congressional book, he exerted the kind of legislative leadership that Washington had not seen since FDR. In his first year in office, Congress passed more important legislation than in Kennedy's entire Presidency. To be sure, the tragedy of the assassination softened opposition to the Kennedy program. But Johnson deserved full credit for guiding the program through Congress. "Let us continue," he said, and the lawmakers responded. Moreover, his own program of reform and welfare legislation—the Great Society—went considerably beyond the New Frontier.

The war on poverty. After Johnson used his personal influence to break a Senate filibuster, Congress passed the sweeping Civil Rights Act of 1964, a measure which sought to protect women as well as ethnic minorities from various discriminatory practices. Another measure of immediate impact was the Economic Opportunity Act of the same year, the administration's biggest gun in the "war on poverty." Designed to give economically disadvantaged peoples an opportunity to share in the nation's affluence, the act also enabled the poor to participate directly in the administration of its activities. It assumed that much unemployment was due not so much to a lack of jobs as to a shortage of people with the necessary skills to fill existing jobs or jobs that the expanding economy would create. Thus, it established job training centers and a Job Corps for training young school dropouts. A domestic version of the Peace Corps, VISTA, sent volunteer workers into slums and ghettos, rural backwaters and Indian reservations to help disadvantaged peoples help themselves.

The act established the Office of Economic Opportunity (OEO). As head of OEO, R. Sargent Shriver commanded the "war on poverty." A brother-in-law of John Kennedy, Shriver had been director of the Peace Corps and was an able, dedicated administrator. Despite his best efforts, however, the whole antipoverty program became bogged down in political finagling and bureaucratic inefficiency. By the time Johnson left office in 1969, the "war on poverty" could claim several victories—but it was also clearly in need of reorganization and new battle plans.

For a time, Johnson succeeded admirably in creating a broad national consensus in support of his policies. Although Republican congressmen opposed his program, the leaders of Big Business generally applauded it. Ironically, the Republicans lost even the power to harass him after 1964. For in the election of that year, their party suffered one of the worst defeats in American political history.

The election of 1964. Naturally, the Democrats named Johnson as their Presidential candidate in 1964. At their convention, the President created the only real excitement by withholding the name of his choice for running mate until the last possible moment, then tapped Hubert H. Humphrey, the liberal senator from Minnesota. The Democratic platform pledged, in effect, to update the New Deal to meet the needs of the sixties.

In sharp contrast, the Republicans turned their backs on the future and reached into the past for a candidate and platform. Chiefly because the party's moderates had failed to build up a candidate of their own in the primaries, the Old Guard conservatives took control of the GOP convention. Demanding "a choice not an echo," they nominated for President a personable, outspoken senator from Arizona, Barry Goldwater. Moreover, they gave him a conservative running mate (William E. Miller, an obscure New York congressman) and a conservative platform, making no concessions whatever to the moderates. Indeed, when Governors George Romney of Michigan and Nelson Rockefeller of New York tried to speak for moderation, the Goldwater people shouted them down.

Many of Goldwater's views on social reform predated not only the New Deal, but Progressivism and even Populism as well. His conservatism was really nineteenth-century laissez-faire liberalism, laced with a commitment to states' rights reminiscent of the Old South. It was hardly surprising that he opposed most of the Kennedy-Johnson reform and welfare proposals. But Goldwater even spoke against Social Security, the TVA, and the progressive income tax, measures which most people in 1964 considered no more controversial than the Homestead Act or Sherman Antitrust Law. Goldwater was entirely sincere in his concern for individual liberty and his fear of big government. But he showed little understanding of the enormous social changes that had revolutionized life in America since the Civil War.

In foreign policy, moreover, Goldwater was an uncompromising cold warrior. He opposed the Test-Ban Treaty and all efforts to achieve an easing of tensions with the Soviet Union. He was contemptuous of the United Nations. He had a habit of carelessly tossing off opinions without giving thought to what he was actually saying, and this habit haunted him throughout the campaign. Indeed, he spent much of his time trying to erase his public image as a trigger-happy reactionary with a "shoot from the hip" mentality, an image he had done much to create himself. Naturally, the Democrats kept the image alive and vivid. Johnson's most telling campaign strategem was simply to remind people that a President's hand is always poised over a button capable of releasing nuclear destruction upon the world. Whose hand did they want there, his or Goldwater's?

The voters replied by burying Goldwater at the polls. In the worst showing of any serious candidate in history, he received 26 million votes to Johnson's 43 million, carrying only Arizona and five states in the Deep South—Alabama, Georgia, Louisiana, Mississippi, and South Carolina. Worse for his party's health, Goldwater carried down with him in defeat 47 Republican congressmen, 8 governors, and 500 state legislators across the land.

Legislation for the Great Society. With a new Congress in which liberal Democrats had replaced many conservative Republicans, Johnson had little trouble getting most of the legislation he wanted for the Great Society. Despite last-ditch opposition from the American Medical Association, Congress finally adopted "Medicare," a system of federally supervised medical care and health insurance for the aged. Responding to Johnson's call for an educational system that would insure every child "the fullest development of his mind and skills," Congress voted federal aid to students in both public and parochial schools. Congress also enacted a new immigration law, ending the old system of discriminating against prospective newcomers because of racial or ethnic origins.

Congress also showed that it was at last becoming aware of the urgent problem of the cities by approving a Department of Housing and Urban Development. Johnson appointed a black man, Robert C. Weaver, to head the new cabinet post. A Department of Transportation was also established. In a complex piece of legislation popularly known as the Model Cities Act, the government took an important first step toward improving the quality of housing (and, hence, of life itself) in the inner cities.

Southern born and bred though he was, Johnson was a vigorous champion of human rights. He named the first black men in history to the Cabinet (Weaver) and the Supreme Court (Thurgood Marshall). He tried to educate the country to accept the principle that black people are entitled to equality under the law and social justice in their everyday lives. Much of his antipoverty program was aimed at ending the economic disabilities under which so many blacks suffered. In 1965, he signed a tough Voting Rights Act, which empowered federal officials to supervise the registration of voters in areas where blacks had consistently been denied their Constitutional rights. Almost immediately, the percentage of black people participating in elections in the South climbed dramatically. For the first time since the days of Reconstruction, moreover, blacks were winning election to various offices in southern states.

The Voting Rights Act was passed in response to another violent confrontation between Washington and Governor Wallace. When civil rights workers in Selma, Alabama, tried to protest the denial of voting rights, Wallace's state troopers joined local authorities in first harassing them, then clubbing and gassing them. To dramatize their cause, the demonstrators marched to Montgomery, the state capital; but again Wallace's men attacked them along the way. Johnson took immediate action, federalizing the Alabama National Guard and ordering it to protect the marchers. Much as the President disliked mass demonstrations, he was determined to prevent the governor of Alabama from denying the protection of the law to citizens exercising their constitutional rights.

Breakdown of consensus. Johnson had sought a national *consensus*, or general agreement, for his policies, and by mid-1966, the Johnson administration could claim an impressive string of legislative victories. Moreover, the nation was riding a wave of unprecedented prosperity, and economic growth was setting new records. The consensus the President so desired had been shaken a bit since 1964, but it still held together remarkably well.

By the end of the year, however, the consensus was falling apart at the seams. Indeed, despite the outward signs of well-being, the United States had entered upon a period of severe social distress, marked by an alarming turn to extremism in politics and violence in the streets. Barely two years after his historic electoral triumph, both the President and the nation found themselves in deep trouble.

4 The War In Vietnam Becomes "Johnson's War"

1. What were Johnson's strengths and weaknesses in handling foreign affairs?

2. How did the United States become involved in an escalated Vietnamese war? Why did the United States increase its involvement? Do you think the United States was justified in its involvement?

3. What was the American strategy for victory in Vietnam? Do you think this was a reasonable plan of action? What happened to American expectations in Vietnam and why did this happen?

4. Why did the United States suffer increasing internal dissensions as a result of the war in Vietnam?

If Johnson had been able to focus his attention exclusively on domestic affairs, he might well have retained his mastery of the political situation. After 1964, however, events elsewhere in the world increasingly diverted him away from the Great Society. For all his skill in the politics of reason and compromise, moreover, the President showed a propensity to engage in "crisis diplomacy," often overreacting to events abroad and thereby magnifying their inherent significance as well as their impact on public opinion at home.

His diplomacy was by no means an unrelieved failure. In Europe, he handled himself well, especially when President de Gaulle of France tested his Texas patience by challenging American policies at every turn. Johnson also diligently sought better relations with the Soviet Union. In October 1964, Khrushchev was succeeded by Alexei Kosygin as Premier and Leonid Brezhnev as head of the Communist party. Hoping to improve relations between the two powers, Johnson met with Kosygin at Glassboro, New Jersey, in June 1967. But the meeting produced little of value. The Soviet Union's new leaders proved to be tough, unimaginative bureaucrats, who cracked down on intellectual freedom at home and brutally crushed a movement for political liberalization in Czechoslovakia in 1968.

Crisis diplomacy in Latin America. In this hemisphere, Johnson tried to reinvigorate the Alliance for Progress by channeling United States aid only to those Latin American nations which achieved political stability. Unhappily, this policy had the effect of encouraging military take-overs in a number of countries. A potentially explosive situation developed in Panama in 1964, moreover, when Panamanian nationalists demanded more say in the governing of the Canal Zone. For a time Johnson let the crisis deepen unnecessarily, then retrieved the situation by making concessions to the nationalists.

But a crisis in the Dominican Republic provoked him into a reaction that severely damaged America's image in the world. In April 1965, civil war broke out between the followers of former president Juan Bosch, a moderate reformer, and the forces of a conservative military oligarchy. Bosch's men tried unsuccessfully to enlist Washington's help in settling the conflict by arbitration. When the Bosch forces suddenly began to win the war, Johnson panicked. On flimsy evidence, he decided that the Bosch group was Communist-led and intent upon establishing another Cuba in the Americas. Without even consulting the OAS, he poured 24,000 Marines into the island and involved them in the civil conflict. His heavy-handed action ended Bosch's chances, to be sure. But the intervention also threatened, for a time, to turn the conflict into a prolonged guerrilla war. Fortunately, the two Dominican parties came to terms with each other and the fighting ended.

At home and abroad, Johnson was criticized for behaving in a manner the world had come to expect from Russia, but hardly from the United States. Added to mounting public dissatisfaction with the war in Vietnam, the outburst at home severely damaged his coveted consensus. In particular, he lost the support of J. William Fulbright, chairman of the prestigious Senate Foreign Relations Committee. Fulbright denounced the Dominican intervention in scathing terms, decrying the President's callous bypassing of the OAS.

Escalating the Vietnamese war. But it was Vietnam that put Johnson's diplomacy to the test and brought his administration to its knees. In

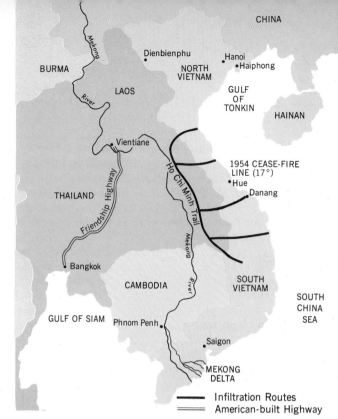

Infiltration Routes
American-built Highway

THE VIETNAM WAR

the campaign of 1964, Johnson assured the nation that American soldiers would never be used in Asia to do a job Asians had to do for themselves. Five years later, over half a million Americans were in Vietnam, fighting what had become, incredibly, the third largest war in American history.

The huge escalation of the conflict began in August 1964, when Johnson ordered an air strike against North Vietnam in retaliation for an alleged PT-boat attack on an American destroyer in the Gulf of Tonkin. Capitalizing on the air of crisis in Washington, he also persuaded Congress to authorize him to "take all necessary measures to repel any armed attack against the forces of the United States and to prevent future aggression." This Tonkin Gulf Resolution was an extraordinary surrender by Congress of power to the President—a blank check, in effect, which the White House construed as the "functional equivalent" of a declaration of war. Many members of Congress came to rue the day they voted for it, not least because a subsequent Senate inquiry cast doubt that the administration had told the whole truth about the Tonkin Gulf incident.

In February 1965, American planes began heavy, round-the-clock bombings of North Vietnam. Ostensibly, the air war was a response to guerrilla attacks on American bases in South Vietnam. But the evidence suggests that Johnson had been planning such an operation for some time and that the Vietcong actions gave him the excuse he needed to initiate it. Five months later, he committed the United States to a land war in Asia by ordering American troops into direct combat.

As Johnson escalated the war, so did the other side. National Liberation Front forces mushroomed in size, drawing from the peasant population, while Ho Chi Minh sent increasing numbers of his North Vietnamese regulars to help them. Both Russia and China furnished modern weapons, although their own escalating rivalry limited the amount of help each was willing to give the NLF. At the peak of fighting in 1968–69, some 600,000 Americans and 625,000 South Vietnamese faced a combined NLF-North Vietnamese force of approximately 281,000.

Why did Johnson take the fatal steps to involve the United States in Vietnam's complex civil war? Chiefly, because he believed in the "domino theory" that a victory for Ho Chi Minh in Vietnam would lead to a Communist take-over of all Southeast Asia. Still conditioned by conventional cold war thinking, he refused to concede that the conflict *was* a civil war. Moreover, he felt bound by the Eisenhower-Kennedy commitment to create a separate, sovereign nation of South Vietnam. By late 1964, it was clear that only direct American military intervention could save the Saigon forces from total collapse. Accordingly, Johnson sought the advice of experts who claimed to understand the problem—Secretaries Rusk and McNamara, White House aides Rostow and Mc-George Bundy, and General Taylor, all of whom, significantly, had been Kennedy advisers, too. They told the President that the situation could be salvaged with a minimal use of American military power.

The American strategy in Vietnam. On paper, their strategy was a simple one. American troops would hold off the Vietcong until a South Vietnamese army could be trained to do the fighting. At Saigon, American advisers would help create

a stable government, willing to make real democratic reforms and able to win the peasants away from the NLF. Meanwhile, the bombing of North Vietnam would prevent Hanoi from reinforcing the NLF, while also convincing Ho that he could never unite Vietnam on his terms.

In action, the strategy turned out to be far from a simple one. In effect, the United States tried to create in Vietnam a Western-style liberal democracy, then to make it into an anti-Communist bastion in Asia. Johnson always insisted that his purpose was only to bring the Vietnam question to the conference table, where reasonable men could settle it in a spirit of give-and-take.* But from 1964 on, he would bargain only from a position of overwhelming strength and only on terms that would insure the existence of a separate, pro-American South Vietnam.

The President and his advisers grossly underestimated the task they set for this nation in Vietnam. In the ground war, American soldiers fought a dogged, elusive enemy, who struck from ambush in brief bloody forays, then melted away into the general population. American commanders used every tactic in the book to check them, but still the men in the black pyjamas and straw hats of the Vietcong kept coming. Both sides used brutal, inhumane tactics against each other—and against the civilian population. For the young Americans who had to fight it, there was little ennobling about this bitter, dehumanizing war. Most of them fought only to stay alive for the day they could go home. With their superior firepower, they took a frightful toll of the enemy; but their own casualties mounted grimly, too. By the spring of 1971, American casualties totaled 340,000, including over 44,000 dead.

After President Diem's death, seven governments rose and fell at Saigon before a junta of military officers seized power in 1965. Lacking popular support, the generals ruled by stamping out all opposition, often with American help. Their strong men were Nguyen Van Thieu and Nguyen Cao Ky, both of whom had fought for the French against the Vietminh after World War II. In 1967, the junta yielded to American pressure

*In the eyes of much of the world, the problem had already been settled in precisely that manner by the Geneva Conference of 1954.

774

The following excerpt is from the diary of a soldier who served in Vietnam.

February 19—You are always frightened here. The other day, when bullets were flying over my head, I was one scared soldier. But I somehow kept my senses. Only once did I expose myself unnecessarily. Luckily, Charlie [the Viet Cong] wasn't waiting. That won't happen again if I can help it.

February 22—Charlie hit a village several miles from base camp about two o'clock this morning. He kept pouring it on, even though we were 30 tracks [armored personnel carriers] strong. Civilians were running, screaming and falling to the ground to protect their children. White, our gunner, got it in the arm, and I took his place and blasted a round at a tree holding two snipers. I must have got them; there was no more firing from that position. It left me feeling sort of funny, but not until the firing was over. All this only took half an hour. But it seemed like a year.

February 24—I can't wait until this bloody mess is over. Time can't go fast enough. Every day, you go out looking for someone to kill. And you're disappointed if you don't find a victim. . . .

and "legitimized" itself by holding elections for a constituent assembly in those parts of Vietnam it controlled. But the new assembly lacked the power and will to do anything beyond the bidding of the generals. Without American military backing, the Thieu-Ky regime could not have survived.

In North Vietnam, U.S. planes dropped more bombs than fell on all of Europe and Asia during World War II. Inevitably, the bombing produced widespread, indiscriminate destruction, even though the attacks were meant for military targets. Whole towns and villages were wiped out, while conventional transport and communications came to a standstill. But the pounding from the air, far from weakening morale or diverting Hanoi from its war aims, seemed to strengthen the North Vietnamese resolve. Ho proved able to rally his people to a remarkable common effort. Although the bombing often forced reinforcements to use dense jungle trails in nearby Laos and Cambodia, it never halted the steady flow of men and supplies southward.

Faced with a protracted major war when he had anticipated a brief, relatively painless one, Johnson floundered badly. Too often, his field commanders talked him into sending more troops to "turn the tide." Too often, his civilian advisers dashed off to Saigon for a quick look at things, then returned to assure him—and the country—that things were improving.

The Great Society falters. Eager to spare the country bad news, Johnson at first publicly misrepresented the seriousness of the war and the reasons for United States involvement. As the fighting mounted, however, so did opposition to the war—in Congress, in the general public, and especially among young people. In response, the administration became increasingly defensive about its commitment in Vietnam, while the rhetoric of government spokesmen became more extravagant. As historian Walter LaFeber observes:

> By constantly repeating the totality of that commitment, that upon it rested American credibility everywhere in the world, and that the Vietnamese struggle would decide whether Communists would conquer the other newly emerging nations through "wars of liberation," the Administration staked its reputation and power at home and abroad upon the conflict.

Johnson neither asked Congress for a formal declaration of war nor put the nation on an emergency wartime footing. Instead, he tried to provide both "guns and butter." With one hand, he fought the war, while with the other he tried to build his Great Society. But the effort to do both failed. Controlled inflation gave way to the steady, creeping price inflation that economists dread. Domestic needs gave way to the demands of war, usually at the expense of people who had stood to benefit most from the Great Society's programs.

In 1964, few Americans had been more than vaguely aware of a war in Vietnam. Four years later, with the monetary cost of the conflict standing well above $100 billion, the war touched the pocketbook, at least, of every American. For millions of people, moreover, it had become a matter of heart and conscience as well.

5 1968 Becomes A Year Of Turmoil And Tragedy

1. Why did President Johnson decline to run again in 1968? Do you think these reasons were justifiable?

2. To what extent was the country split over domestic and foreign issues in 1968? Do you think this was healthy disagreement or a serious erosion of national morale?

3. How did the Tet Offensive affect the war in Vietnam and American attitudes toward the war?

4. Do you think it is still possible for a grass roots political movement to significantly influence national policies?

Christmas 1967 brought a lull in the fighting in Vietnam, and for a moment it appeared that the war might be winding down. Then in January, the enemy launched a series of assaults throughout South Vietnam. Timed to coincide with Tet, the Chinese lunar new year, the attacks hit every city, plus hundreds of towns and villages, disrupting the American program of "democratization" in the Vietnamese countryside. In ten days of bloody fighting, thousands of civilians died, while half a million became refugees.

The Vietcong expected the Tet Offensive to trigger an uprising of the South Vietnamese people against the Thieu-Ky government. But while the attacks received substantial popular support, especially in the cities, the Saigon regime survived. Moreover, although the attackers badly mauled defending United States and South Vietnamese forces, they paid an enormous and perhaps crippling price in casualties themselves for a venture that gained them only a temporary success.

Opposition to the war grows. Ironically, the Tet Offensive had its greatest impact far from the battlefield—in American politics. Millions of Americans began to question the wisdom of continuing what now seemed an endless war. In the words of one historian:

> The destructive costs of the war, the credibility and competence of the American effort, and the complicity of the Vietnamese population in the preparations for the Viet Cong's offensive now became an embarrassment to the Administration's case for 'seeing the war through.'

Senator Fulbright's Foreign Relations Committee opened a full-scale investigation of the war. On campuses everywhere, students and faculty joined in "teach-ins," informal gatherings to protest the war and propose changes in foreign policy.

Protest against the war had been mounting for months, dividing public opinion into two sharply opposed camps. On the one hand, "hawks" vigorously defended Johnson's policies, arguing that the nation's vital security interests were at stake in Vietnam. Some called for all-out, total war against the Communists there. "Doves," on the other hand, condemned the war as a political and moral disaster—a conflict in which American lives, money, and power were being squandered in an effort that had little bearing on national security. Many young men faced a profound moral dilemma in their opposition to the war. Should they consent to be drafted, knowing that they might be sent to fight in a war their consciences condemned? Or should they refuse induction, thereby breaking the law of the land?

To test the strength of antiwar sentiment, Senator Eugene McCarthy of Minnesota set out to challenge President Johnson for the Democratic nomination in 1968. A contemplative man with a cool, clean style—as much a poet as a politician—McCarthy seemed an unlikely leader of a grass-roots political movement. Yet, in the New Hampshire primary election in March, he defeated Johnson and immediately became the hero of the antiwar movement. Thousands of young volunteers flocked to his standard, prompting some observers to dub his campaign "the children's crusade." Shortly thereafter, Senator Robert F. Kennedy of New York also entered the race as an opponent of the war. Wistful, pugnacious, and enormously energetic, Kennedy sought to revive the policies of his brother, the assassinated President.

Johnson's stature declines. The most astonishing development that spring, however, was the President's announcement on March 31 that he would not be a candidate for another term. As an incumbent, Johnson could have fought off the McCarthy-Kennedy challenges to win the nomination again. Why, then, did he withdraw? Certainly, McCarthy's showing in New Hampshire and Johnson's low standing in the public opinion polls had much to do with the decision. But Johnson also hoped that by withdrawing he would rally bipartisan support for his Vietnam policy and, in effect, "buy time" enough to press it to a successful conclusion. In withdrawing, he announced that the United States would begin peace talks with the "other side" at Paris.

What had caused Johnson's stature to decline so sharply since his great victory in 1964? For one thing, his popularity was never really as high as that triumph had suggested. Moderate Republicans by the thousands had voted *against* Goldwater more than *for* Johnson, and after the election they returned to the GOP fold. For another, Johnson had allowed the Democratic party to fall into disarray. When he came to need its support, it was sorely rent by factionalism and unable to unite behind him.

"White backlash." Johnson was also the chief political victim of a "white backlash"—a mounting reaction among hostile whites to black activism. As the civil rights movement spread into northern cities and suburbs, it encountered resistance as fierce as any it had met in the South. Fearful of losing their own recently won economic and social gains, white ethnic minorities bitterly resisted efforts by blacks to move out of the ghettos into *their* neighborhoods or to compete for *their* jobs. Racial tensions that had been building up for years among people who were themselves often victims of exploitation boiled out in ugly displays of fear and hatred. In Chicago's all-white suburb of Cicero, for example, a mob shouting Nazi slogans broke up a peaceful civil rights march with shocking brutality, while police looked the other way.

Although racism was its most virulent manifestation, the "backlash" also reflected a more general sense of distress in the population. Urban riots, crime in the streets, campus upheavals, the rising cost of living, the frustrating war—taken together, symptoms of this sort gave millions of people a feeling that the social order was breaking down. Many voters who had always thought of themselves as liberal Democrats began to flirt with Republicanism, while others gave themselves over to right-wing extremist politics.

One beneficiary of this rightward swing was Governor Wallace of Alabama. Carrying his attacks on integration and the federal government into the cities of the North, Wallace pieced together a national political organization and set out to challenge the two major parties for the Presidency. Wallace promised to bring "law and order" to America, and his rhetoric fed the fears of many frustrated, confused whites.

Nixon's comeback. Unrest in the land also helped to account for the astonishing comeback of a more conventional politician, Richard M. Nixon. After losing to Kennedy in 1960, the former Vice President made an unsuccessful try for the governorship of California, then faded into obscurity. But he re-emerged in 1965 to begin a carefully executed campaign to win the support of Republican party leaders throughout the country. At the GOP convention in 1968, Nixon controlled a huge block of delegates and easily won the Presidential nomination. In a bid to woo southern voters from both the Democrats and Wallace, he chose as his running mate a little-known conservative from below the Mason-Dixon Line, Governor Spiro T. Agnew of Maryland. Agnew was the first American of Greek descent to become a national political figure.

Turmoil and tragedy. For the Democrats, 1968 became a year of turmoil and tragedy. The murder of Martin Luther King, Jr., in April cast a pall over the liberal wing of the party, for the civil rights leader had been a strong voice for racial justice and against the war. After Johnson's withdrawal, Vice President Hubert H. Humphrey inherited much of the President's support. As an outspoken supporter of the war, Humphrey was anathema to many liberals, even though his record in domestic affairs was one of almost unblemished liberalism. Humphrey ignored the primaries, concentrating instead on gaining control of the party machinery to assure himself the nomination.

McCarthy and Kennedy, meanwhile, battled each other in the primaries. Kennedy won in Indiana, then lost to McCarthy in Oregon. California's primary was the crucial test for both men, and after a strenuous effort Kennedy won a decisive victory. But at the very moment of triumph, he was assassinated in his Los Angeles hotel. As his body joined that of his brother in Arlington National Cemetery, a wave of fear and despair swept the land. John and Robert Kennedy were perhaps the most imaginative leaders in American politics during the 1960's, and the senseless murders of the two brothers in the prime of their lives was an enormity almost too great for rational men to comprehend.

McCarthy stayed in the race to the end, although the tragedy plainly demoralized his campaign. At the Democratic convention in Chicago that August, Humphrey was the sure winner. But as one observer noted wryly, the Vice President "could have got a better deal in a court of bankruptcy." For the convention itself was a public relations disaster for the Democrats. Inside the hall, "dovish" delegates rebelled against the old-line professionals who controlled the proceedings. Demanding adoption of a strong antiwar resolution, they also insisted that the party open itself to greater participation by minority groups and young people in its affairs. Bitter floor fights left the party a shambles.

Outside convention hall, the scene was even more chaotic. Thousands of young people had converged on Chicago to protest the war and press their views on the delegates. Instead of

The dissent and unrest of the 1960's seemed to crystalize in the election year of 1968, turning it into perhaps the most turbulent year of the decade. The Democrats, torn by factionalism, their party all but leaderless, and demoralized by the assassination of a promising candidate, Robert F. Kennedy, held a stormy convention in Chicago. As the convention met, television viewers across the nation watched in horror as police and protesters clashed in the streets. Many of the demonstrators were followers of Eugene McCarthy and had come to Chicago to support his candidacy. At one point they gathered outside the Conrad Hilton Hotel (above left) as McCarthy addressed them. Inside Convention Hall, after a session of bitter debate over their platform, the Democrats nominated Hubert Humphrey, who chose as his running mate Senator Edmund Muskie of Maine. At right above, Humphrey and Muskie and their wives receive the ovation of the delegates. The Republicans, in a convention notable for its lack of excitement, nominated Richard M. Nixon (at right). Making considerable use of the mass media, the Republican candidate conducted a vigorous campaign. In an increasing atmosphere of polarization, Nixon won a narrow victory. As President he faced the formidable task of bringing the nation together.

accomodating them and taking reasonable steps to insure that their demonstrations would be peaceable, Mayor Richard J. Daley permitted a violent confrontation to take place in the streets between his police force and the youthful protestors. Deliberate provocation was evident on both sides in the melee; but, as the chief counsel for a Presidential investigating commission later concluded, the disorder was primarily a "police riot." Hundreds of persons were injured, and downtown Chicago resembled an armed camp for days.

The election of 1968. The election of 1968 was a traumatic experience for many Americans. Senseless killings and mindless disorder overwhelmed all other issues in politics, and few contests have been so fraught with emotionalism. Nixon's promise to restore "law and order" and his appeal for a general lowering of voices struck a responsive chord among the older generation, in particular. For many young people, the election seemed to prove that the established system was no longer responsive to popular appeals. How could it be otherwise, they asked themselves, when none of the major candidates in the November election had the courage to decry the American presence in Vietnam? Events at Chicago and after helped to "radicalize" many young people, making them impatient with the normal processes of democracy.

Nixon won in November, but with only 43 percent of the popular vote. Surprisingly, Humphrey managed to rally his demoralized party sufficiently to come within a hair's breadth of victory. One of his great assets was his running mate, Edmund Muskie of Maine, a soft-spoken senator of Polish ancestry, whose Lincolnesque bearing and calm, measured words helped to erase the unfavorable public image of the Democrats. As for Wallace, his appeal proved effective only in the Deep South. Although the combined vote for Nixon and Wallace suggested a national trend to the right, the electorate remained about evenly divided between liberals and conservatives.

For all its turmoil, the election produced several interesting and seemingly positive developments. For one thing, both the McCarthy and the Wallace campaigns—each in its own way—proved that grass-roots politics was far from dead. Al-though the McCarthy effort never attained its great objective of forcing an end to the war, it helped to bring about the retirement of an unpopular President and enlisted millions of young idealists in active politics. Moreover, pressure from antiwar Democrats moved Humphrey to demand of Johnson that he halt the bombing of North Vietnam. Whether because of Humphrey's plea or for other reasons, the President ended the bombing just before the election.

Finally, the changing temper of the times had an effect on Nixon. Retreating noticeably from the hard-line cold war stance of his past, he not only assured the voters that he had "a plan to end the war," but also promised a major overhaul of United States foreign policy in general.

6 America Moves Into The Seventies

1. Why was Nixon successful in the election of 1968?

2. What alternatives were available to Nixon at the start of his term in office concerning American involvement in Vietnam? Do you think Nixon made the best choice of alternatives?

3. Who or what is the "silent majority," and what is its role in American society?

Nixon's first task as President was to cool off the raging controversy over Vietnam and somehow heal the divisiveness besetting the country. Ironically, he himself had long been a sharply controversial figure. An unknown congressman in 1947, he had risen rapidly in politics, moving to the Senate in 1950, then to the Vice Presidency under Eisenhower in 1953. Along the way, he made a host of enemies, largely because of his rough, sometimes unprincipled, campaign tactics. In the heyday of McCarthyism (page 691), Nixon had recklessly impugned the loyalty of such Democratic leaders as Adlai Stevenson, Dean Acheson, and even President Truman.

LIFE IN CONTEMPORARY AMERICA

Woodstock Rock Music Festival, 1969

Buttons: Slogans of the Sixties

War Protest March on Washington, 1969

American life in the sixties had an almost schizo-phrenic aspect to it. The decade began on a note of hope, but after years of vast change, deep tragedy, and occasional triumph, it ended in what seemed a desperate search, sometimes highly individual and sometimes broadly organized—a search for an end to racial discord throughout the nation. For a way to counteract the dehumanizing forces that seem to reduce names and personalities to numbers and codes. For ways to save the earth from pollution and ecological disaster. For an end to war as the way to serve national self-interest. For life styles that enhance man's humanity rather than repress it.

Where the search would lead or with what success it would meet was in the hands of the Americans of the seventies.

782

Sensory Awareness at Esalen Institute, California, 1970

T.V. Commercials, Gerald Scarfe, 1968

Camping at Yellowstone National Park, 1965

Street Mural, Bronx, New York, 1971

Suburbia, Southern San Francisco, California, 1965

The "Nixon Doctrine." Once in the White House, however, he sought to project an image of reason and moderation. Having criticized Johnson for making promises that could not be kept, he deliberately softened his own voice. No longer did Washington ring with optimistic predictions about the war. Instead, Nixon appealed for time to work out a strategy for ending the war and gaining a "just and lasting peace."

Nixon had always been "hawkish" about the United States's position in Asia*; thus, his approach to Vietnam differed from Johnson's more in style and tactics than in substance or basic objectives. In June 1969, he declared that, henceforth, the United States would not involve itself in Asia's wars. Rather, we would arm and train the forces of friendly nations, then expect them to defend themselves against aggression and revolution. This so-called "Nixon Doctrine" was really only a reiteration of the fundamental policy pursued in Asia by the Eisenhower, Kennedy, and Johnson administrations—namely, to contain Communist China with a chain of well-armed, pro-American states, similar to NATO in Europe. The long-range objective was to maintain a strong American presence in Asia in anticipation of the day when the Chinese overthrew communism or otherwise returned to "normal," Open Door relations with this country.

"Vietnamization" of the war. But whereas Kennedy and Johnson had let the United States slip into the actual fighting in Asia, Nixon sought to "Vietnamize" the war. American ground forces would be withdrawn as rapidly as possible, leaving the fighting entirely in the hands of the South Vietnamese. Nothing was said about reducing U.S. air and naval power in Vietnam, nor did Nixon propose to dismantle the sprawling, permanent American bases in Southeast Asia. His immediate purpose, doubtless, was to reduce casualties to a level "acceptable" to public opinion at home, thus keeping his critics off balance and gaining time to pressure Hanoi into a settlement. Withdrawal was a slow and uncertain process, marked by continued fighting and casualties. But most Americans gave the President the

*During the siege of Dien Bien Phu in 1954, Nixon had favored sending American troops to help the French against the Vietminh.

benefit of the doubt, and he enjoyed a "honeymoon" on the war issue for nearly a year and a half.

Trouble in the Middle East. Nixon tried to enlist the Soviet Union's aid in pressuring Hanoi to end the war, promising in exchange improved relations between Washington and Moscow. But the Kremlin showed little interest, preferring to let the United States wallow in the Asian quagmire. Indeed, the Soviets took advantage of the situation to mount a bold thrust into the Middle East, by aiding the Arabs in their running conflict with Israel. In 1967, the "Six Days' War" between Israel and her Arab neighbors had resulted in a sweeping Israeli victory and the destruction of Egypt's Soviet-equipped armies. By 1970, the Soviets had rebuilt the Egyptian forces. Moreover, Russian pilots were themselves guarding the skies over the Nile, while Russian ships freely plied the Mediterranean.

Critics of the Vietnam war warned that Soviet penetration of the Mediterranean was a far greater threat to the United States' vital interest than the endless, pointless conflict in Asia. In the Middle East, they noted, the stakes could escalate rapidly to include not only Israel's very existence and the destiny of the Arabs, but even the security of Europe's southern flank. American policy had been to maintain a relatively even balance militarily between Israel and the Arab states, and Moscow's thrust threatened to destroy that balance. The new administration achieved a temporary cease-fire agreement between the Israelis and most of the Arab nations in 1970. But the situation in the Middle East remained highly unstable, threatening at any time to produce a grave confrontation with the Soviet Union.

Appealing to the silent majority. In domestic affairs, the administration veered firmly to the right. As a pragmatic politician, to be sure, Nixon for a time kept lines open to the more liberal element in his party. Robert H. Finch brought a modestly liberal view to Washington as secretary of Health, Education, and Welfare. And a liberal Democrat and former Kennedy adviser, Daniel P. Moynihan, counseled Nixon on urban matters. The President genuinely shocked conservative Republicans with a plan to overhaul the welfare system by establishing a minimum standard of aid for every needy family with children, thereby doubling the number of people eligible for public assistance.

But Nixon's instincts were conservative and on most issues he acted accordingly. His closest adviser on all matters, foreign and domestic, was his conservative Attorney General and former law partner John N. Mitchell. Strom Thurmond, senator from South Carolina and the former "Dixiecrat" Presidential candidate, exerted important influence in court appointments and civil rights matters. Increasingly, too, Vice President Agnew spoke the administration's conservative views on matters ranging from the right of dissent to the function of education. Agnew lambasted critics of the war, "liberal" newspapers and telecasters, black activists, youthful nonconformists, and other critics of administration policy.

Agnew's rhetorical bombast struck a responsive chord among people of all classes who were confused by the war and fearful of rapid social change. Indeed, it was part of a deliberate Republican appeal to the so-called "silent majority" of Americans, who supposedly wanted someone like Agnew to speak up for traditional values and conventional patriotism in opposition to the protesters and dissenters. Doubtless, the appeal was good politics in that it rallied support to Nixon, even from traditionally Democratic labor. Far from healing the divisions within American society, however, it tended further to polarize public opinion into two hostile camps, leaving little middle ground.

In the South, the administration's strategy for winning over conservative whites was to slow the pace of school integration, de-emphasize civil rights, and seek conservative southern representation on the Supreme Court. On this last point, Nixon ran into unexpected opposition in the Senate, where twice in succession he had southern nominees to the Court rejected. Neither man was rebuffed because of his southern background, however. In one case, the allegation was conflict of interest; in the other, incompetence and racism. The Senate gave quick approval to Nixon's other appointees, including the new Chief Justice, Warren E. Burger.

The Nixon administration made no special efforts on behalf of ethnic and racial minorities. Pursuing what one Presidential aide called a policy of "benign neglect," indeed, it steadily cut back the resources available to blacks and other disadvantaged peoples. In the Republican view, the President's efforts to curb inflation and put the economy on a sound peacetime basis would ultimately work to the benefit of everyone, including the very poor.

Nixon's economic policies. Nixon's economic policies were in the traditional Republican mold. To combat inflation, he cut government spending, tightened up the money supply, asked labor and management to forego wage and price increases, and settled back to await a slowing down of demand and "cooling off" of the economy. Interest rates soared, making it difficult for industries dependent on credit facilities—construction and utilities, for example—to borrow money for ordinary operations, much less for expansion.

Nixon assumed that highly competitive free market conditions prevailed generally in the American economy. In fact, entire sectors of industry were not competitive at all, but rather were dominated by oligopoly (page 730). Industries of this sort had amassed huge capital surpluses, which enabled them to ignore the high cost of money and to continue fueling the inflation. Moreover, Nixon's appeal for voluntary wage-price controls accomplished little in the way of holding down price increases or of preventing strikes for higher wages in key industries during 1969 and 1970. Like Johnson, Nixon refused to acknowledge that the nation was really at war and in need of some wartime controls, at least, on the economy.

By the fall of 1970, the nation was experiencing simultaneous inflation and recession. While the cost of living continued to rise, GNP dropped off and the stock market suffered its worst decline in decades. Unemployment neared the 6 percent mark and threatened to go higher. Gambling that its hands-off policies would put the economy on a sounder basis in the future, the administration predicted an upturn in conditions by the end of the year.

The invasion of Cambodia. In Asia, meanwhile, Nixon's policies were put to a severe test. Implicit in the policy of "Vietnamization" was an assumption that the United States, while pulling out of the ground fighting, could continue to control the direction of political and military developments. But early in 1970, a deteriorating situation in Laos led Nixon to escalate American military operations there. In March, the neutralist government of Prince Sihanouk in Cambodia fell to a military coup. For years, Vietcong and North Vietnamese forces had used jungle areas in western Cambodia as "sanctuaries" from which to strike into South Vietnam and return, safe from counterattack. Seizing the opportunity presented by the coup, Nixon ordered a combined U.S.-South Vietnamese attack on the "sanctuaries," an operation which involved the invasion of Cambodian territory.

"We take this action not for the purpose of expanding the war into Cambodia," the President stated, "but for the purpose of ending the war in Vietnam." Promising to clear the enemy from the sanctuaries and pull American forces out of Cambodia by the end of June, Nixon argued that the action would hasten the "Vietnamization" process. From the narrow military viewpoint, the Cambodian operation made sense. But the President underestimated the political, diplomatic, and psychological repercussions that were bound to occur in Asia and at home. For regardless of its intent, the operation expanded the war to all of Cambodia. Senator George McGovern of South Dakota, a sharp critic of the operation, noted its effect:

As I look at the situation, at the time we went in there, there were Communist forces scattered along the border of Cambodia, but the rest of the country was largely free from military operations. Today, virtually half the country has fallen to Communist control. I think what we did was to . . . dump over a beehive, and the bees have spread out all over the country.

Confrontation and crisis. At home, the Cambodian operation triggered an explosion of protest that took the administration aback. Instantly, the antiwar movement revived, its ranks swelled by thousands of formerly passive individuals who now joined in demanding an end to American interference in Southeast Asia's affairs. Administration spokesmen rallied the "silent majority" with appeals for support of the President in his effort to "save American lives."

Predictably, violent confrontations marked the crisis. At Kent State University in Ohio, National Guardsmen fired indiscriminately into a group of student protesters, killing four. Mississippi state police sent a hail of murderous fire into a dormitory at Jackson State College, killing two black students and wounding nine others. The two tragedies underscored the deep and dangerous divisions in American society; for while millions of people mourned the dead students, others took satisfaction from the gunning down of "radicals."

Spurred by the crisis at home, Nixon withdrew U.S. ground forces from Cambodia on schedule. But American planes continued to operate over the entire country, while South Vietnamese spokesmen indicated that they intended to keep their forces in Cambodia indefinitely. By mid-1970, the Vietnam war had become the Indochina war, and the only sure prediction that could be made was that the end was not yet in sight.

■ CONCLUSION

Historians in recent years have debated whether the American experience has been primarily one of consensus or of conflict. Scholars who experienced the traumas of the Great Depression and the Second World War noted the relative ease with which the nation weathered those great crises; and they tend to conclude that, for all the tension and potential conflict in their midst, the American people generally agree on the values and goals of their society.

Younger historians, on the other hand, see in the turmoil of the 1960's proof that society is racked by constant conflict among various social and interest groups. For them, the American experience is not so much unique as self-deceptive. Geographically isolated from the Old World throughout its period of national development, the United States seemed to have escaped the disruptive class conflict and other historical disturbances known to older societies. But the escape was only apparent. By the 1960's, they argued, history had caught up with the United States and there was no escaping its demands.

Certainly there was much in the years from 1960 to 1970 to confirm their judgment. Black people rose up in defiant protest against conditions which had long been intolerable. Urban rot and environmental destruction became evident to all but the willfully blind, and who could say whether or not society would respond quickly enough to their effects to prevent its own destruction? Poverty in the midst of affluence mocked the American dream. Government moved sluggishly or not at all to meet the needs of the people, yet plunged ahead eagerly to satisfy the demands of the dominant power structure, epitomized by the military-industrial complex. The war in Indochina laid waste to a weak and alien society, while it drained the powerful American nation of humanity, resources, and morale. Imaginative politics succumbed either to the assassin's bullets or to the cynicism of entrenched privilege and the indifference of bureaucracy. As journalist Richard Rovere concluded, the 1960's was indeed a "slum of a decade."

Yet Rovere also noted that the decade could be a great turning point in the American experience. At least it marked the time when men perceived the threats to their environment and took steps to eliminate them. Conceivably, too, it was the time in which the war in Indochina taught Americans that political problems are rarely solved by armed force; the time when racial violence and campus unrest led men to seek a redress of the grievances that spawned violence; the time in which "science made the greatest and most life-serving advances in human history." The evidence was abundant by 1970, certainly, that the United States was at a great turning point in its history. What the future held for the American experience no man could say.

■ QUESTIONS

1. Did the United States government pursue a reasonable course of action regarding American involvement in Vietnam during the sixties? Defend your answer.

2. What is there in American history which helps to explain black disadvantages and white discrimination?

3. To what extent is it true that "this country does not function by morality, love and nonviolence, but by Power"?

4. How effective is the use of planned programs of nonviolence as compared to organized strategies of violent confrontation in achieving goals of racial equality?

5. Compare the efforts and achievements of Kennedy, Johnson, and Nixon in bringing about a better society for all Americans.

6. How sound was the American economy in the sixties? Explain your answer.

7. What is the historical lineage of Goldwater's conservatism and Johnson's liberalism?

8. What were the basic principles behind American foreign policy in the sixties, and how similar were they to American principles in earlier decades?

9. What were the relative strengths of the legislative, executive, and judicial branches of the federal government in 1970? To what extent was this a change from earlier years?

10. What is American history, and of what relevance is it to the contemporary student? Explain your answer.

■ BIBLIOGRAPHY

MALCOLM X AND ALEX HALEY, *Autobiography of Malcolm X*, Grove Press. The *Autobiography of Malcolm X* reflects much of the truth in the life of black Americans. The student thus learns of the harsh realities of ghetto life and of the man who was able to rise above ghetto miseries and try to make a better life for other blacks.

GRIFFIN, JOHN HOWARD, *Black Like Me*, New American Library (Signet Books). In response to the challenge that whites did not know what it meant to be black, the author dyed his skin black and traveled through the South, experiencing the life of Jim Crowism. His accounting of this experiment is bound to move the student and provide a better understanding of the barriers facing blacks.

GOLDWATER, BARRY, *Conscience of a Conservative*, Macfadden. This book summarizes Goldwater's political philosophy. It gives the student a greater understanding of Goldwater, and more importantly, it provides some insight into the dimensions of conservatism in America during the sixties.

DUNCAN, DAVID DOUGLAS, *War Without Heroes*, Harper & Row. This book is primarily a collection of photographs depicting the war in Vietnam. The author is a veteran of World War II, the Korean War, and now Vietnam. The photographs in this book are particularly good in giving the student another dimension for understanding the nature of war.

FORTAS, ABE, *Concerning Dissent and Civil Disobedience,* New American Library (Signet Books). In a very brief readable account by a highly qualified legal authority, the reader will find a definition of the limits and scope of civil disobedience. This is an important book to read before discussing dissent in America during the sixties.

FULBRIGHT, J. WILLIAM, *The Arrogance of Power,* Random House (Vintage Books). The author is a recognized critic of American foreign policy during the sixties, and as chairman of the Senate Foreign Relations Committee, he was frequently in the forefront of disputes over Vietnam. He provides some interesting opinions on foreign policy which should be weighed carefully by the student.

Acknowledgments

AMERICAN HERITAGE PUBLISHING CO., INC., for excerpt from *Brother Against Brother* by Bruce Catton. Copyright © 1961 by American Heritage Publishing Co., Inc.

APPLETON-CENTURY-CROFTS, for excerpt from *Cases in Constitutional Law*, edited by Robert E. and Robert F. Cushman. Copyright © 1968.

BRANDT AND BRANDT, for excerpt from *Western Star* by Stephen Vincent Benet. Copyright 1943 by Rosemary Carr Benet.

GEORGE M. COHAN MUSIC PUBLISHING CO., for words from "Over There" by George M. Cohan. Copyright 1915. U.S. copyright renewed.

COLUMBIA UNIVERSITY PRESS AND KENNIKAT PRESS, for *The Negro in Colonial New England*, edited by Lorenzo Greene.

CONSTABLE & CO. LTD., for excerpt from *When I Was A Child* by Markino Yoshio. Copyright 1913 by Houghton Mifflin Company. Copyright renewed.

CREST BOOKS, DIVISION OF FAWCETT WORLD LIBRARY, for excerpt from *All Quiet on the Western Front* by Erich Maria Remarque. Copyright 1929, 1930, by Little, Brown & Company. Copyright © 1956 by Erich Maria Remarque.

DOUBLEDAY & COMPANY, INC., for excerpt from *Leaves of Grass* by Walt Whitman.

E. P. DUTTON & CO., INC., for excerpt from *Seventy Years of Life and Labor* by Samuel Gompers.

HARPER & ROW, INC., for excerpt from *G.I. Diary* by David Parks. Copyright © 1968 by David Parks. Excerpt from *The God That Failed* by Louis Fischer. Copyright 1949 by Louis Fisher.

D. C. HEATH & COMPANY, for excerpt from *The Yalta Conference*, edited by Richard F. Fenno, Jr. *Problems in America-Civilization Series*. Copyright © 1955 by D. C. Heath & Company.

HOLT, RINEHART AND WINSTON, INC., for excerpt from *Selected Speeches, Messages, Press Conferences, and Letters of F. D. Roosevelt*, edited by B. Rauch. Copyright © 1961. Excerpt from *Life Under The "Peculiar Institution"* by Norman R. Yetman. Copyright © 1970 by Holt, Rinehart and Winston, Inc.

HOUGHTON MIFFLIN COMPANY AND MARIE RODELL, for adaptation of selection from *The Silent Spring* by Rachel Carson. Copyright © 1962 by Houghton Mifflin Company. Words from "Unguarded Gates" by Thomas Bailey Aldrich from *An Anthology of New England Poets*, edited by Louis Untermeyer. Copyright 1948.

ALFRED A. KNOPF, INC., for "A Dream Deferred" from *The Panther and the Lash* by Langston Hughes. Copyright 1951 by Langston Hughes. Excerpt from *MacArthur, His Rendevous With History* by Courtney Whitney. Copyright © 1956.

THE MACMILLAN COMPANY, for excerpt from *Memoirs of Herbert Hoover* by Herbert Hoover. Copyright 1952. Excerpt from speech by Robert LaFollette from *Imperialism to Isolationism 1898–1919*. Copyright © 1964. Excerpt from *The Triumph of Conservatism* by Gabriel Kolko. Copyright by the Free Press of the Glencoe Division of the Macmillan Company © 1963.

Art Acknowledgments

p. ii (detail), Courtesy City Art Museum of St. Louis, Arthur B. Ziern, Jr. Collection. p. 11 (detail) Courtesy New York State Historical Association, Cooperstown. p. 16 Library of Congress. p. 24 (top) *Reasons for Establishing the Colony of Georgia,* The New York Public Library; (middle) The New York Public Library, Picture Collection; (bottom, detail) Courtesy The Virginia State Library. p. 25 (top) The New York Public Library, Stokes Collection; (middle) Courtesy John Street United Methodist Church, New York; (bottom) Courtesy The Metropolitan Museum of Art, New York; Gift of Edgar William and Bernice Chrysler Garbisch, 1963. p. 33 Courtesy Worcester Art Museum. p. 34 (top) Courtesy City Art Museum of St. Louis; (bottom) Courtesy Harvard University, Law School Collection. p. 35 Courtesy Massachusetts Historical Society. p. 36 (top) Mark Sexton; (bottom) Courtesy Massachusetts Historical Society. p. 56 Library of Congress. p. 57 (top left) Courtesy The John Carter Brown Library, Brown University; (top right) Library of Congress; (bottom) Sy Seidman. p. 69 Courtesy Kennedy Galleries. p. 70 Library of Congress. p. 71 (top) Courtesy The Historical Society of Pennsylvania; (bottom) The New York Public Library. p. 72 Courtesy Yale University Art Gallery: Gift of the Associates of Mr. Veblen. p. 115 (both) Courtesy The New York Historical Society. p. 121 Courtesy The Historical Society of Pennsylvania. p. 122 Courtesy Pennsylvania Academy of the Fine Arts. p. 123 (top left) Courtesy Bowdoin College Museum of Art, Brunswick, Maine; (top right) Courtesy The Metropolitan Museum of Art, New York: Gift of Henry G. Marquand, 1881; (bottom) Courtesy The Henry Francis du Pont Winterthur Museum. p. 124 (top) Courtesy Pennsylvania Academy of the Fine Arts; (bottom) Courtesy Museum of Fine Arts, Boston: Gift of Mrs. Samuel Hooper and Miss Alice Hooper. pp. 127, 130–31 Courtesy The Historical Society of Pennsylvania. p. 136 (top) Courtesy Philbrook Art Center, Oklahoma; (bottom) Courtesy Woolaroc Museum, Bartlesville, Oklahoma. p. 144 (both) Culver Pictures. p. 157 Courtesy Museum of the City of New York, Clarence J. Davies Collection. p. 158 (top) Courtesy State of Illinois, Department of Conservation, Division of Parks and Memorials; (bottom) Courtesy Abby Aldrich Rockefeller Folk Art Collection, Williamsburg, Virginia. p. 159 (top) Painting in the Savings Bank of New London Collection, on exhibit at Mystic Seaport, Mystic, Connecticut. p. 159 (bottom) Courtesy City Art Museum of St. Louis, Arthur B. Ziern Jr. Collection. p. 160 (top) Courtesy Chicago Historical Society; (bottom) Giraudon, Musee des Beaux-Arts, Pau. p. 162 (top) Courtesy The Virginia State Library; (bottom) Courtesy The New York Historical Society. p. 163 (top) Courtesy Columbia University Libraries; (bottom) Library of Congress. p. 175 (top) Courtesy The Houghton Library, Harvard University; (bottom) Sy Seidman. p. 177 Courtesy Lee B. Anderson (Photo, courtesy of *Time* Magazine). p. 178 (top) Courtesy Collection, Mr. and Mrs. Paul Mellon (Photo, courtesy American Heritage Publishing Company); (bottom) Courtesy Collection The Boatmen's National Bank of St. Louis. p. 179 Courtesy New York State Historical Association, Cooperstown. p. 180 (top) Courtesy Museum of Fine Arts, Boston: Bequest of Miss Caroline H. Rimmer; (bottom) Courtesy Museum of the City of New York, Clarence J. Davies Collection. p. 184 Courtesy Whaling Museum, New Bedford, Massachusetts. p. 193 (top, both) *Anti Slavery Almanac,* The New York Public Library; (bottom) *Anti Slavery Offering and Picknick,* The New York Public Library. p. 200 Courtesy M. H. De Young Memorial Museum, San Francisco: Gift of Mrs. Eleanor Martin. p. 201 (top) Courtesy Bexar County: On loan to Witte Memorial Museum, San Antonio, Texas; (bottom) Courtesy Utah State Historical Society. p. 206 (top) Herb Orth, *Life* Magazine © Time Inc; (bottom) Library of Congress. p. 214 Library of Congress. p. 224 (top) Courtesy Smithsonian Institution; (bottom) The New York Public Library. p. 231 (top left) Library of Congress; (top right) Courtesy Chicago Historical Society; (bottom) Library of Congress. p. 242 (top) Courtesy Valentine Museum, Richmond, Virginia; (bottom) Courtesy The West Point Museum, United States Military Academy, Alexander McCook Craighead Collection. p. 249 (all) Library of Congress. p. 261 Courtesy The Museum of the Confederacy, Richmond, Virginia. p. 262 (top) Courtesy The Historical Society of Pennsylvania; (bottom) Courtesy The Free Library of Philadelphia; p. 263 (top) Courtesy The Virginia State Library; (bottom) Culver Pictures. p. 264 (top) Library of Congress; (bottom) Courtesy The Metropolitan Museum of Art, New York: Gift of Mrs. Frank B. Porter, 1922. p. 268 (top) National Archives; (bottom) Library of Congress. p. 274 The Granger Collection. p. 275 (top left) Library of Congress; (top right) The New York Public Library; (bottom) Courtesy The New York Historical Society. p. 287 The New York Public Library, Prints Division. p. 297 Courtesy The Metropolitan Museum of Art, New York, Rogers Fund,

1907. p. 298 (top) Courtesy City Art Museum of St. Louis: Gift of Mrs. John T. Davis; (bottom) Courtesy The American Museum of Natural History. p. 299 (top) Courtesy Kansas State Historical Society; (bottom) Courtesy Southwest Museum, Los Angeles. p. 300 (top) Courtesy Denver Public Library; (bottom) Library of Congress. p. 302 (top) Courtesy Nebraska State Historical Society; (bottom) Courtesy Denver Public Library. p. 303 (top) Courtesy Denver Public Library; (bottom) Library of Congress. p. 311 (top) Courtesy Nebraska State Historical Society, S. D. Butcher Collection; (bottom) Courtesy International Harvestor Company. p. 321 (top) Courtesy Minnesota Historical Society; (bottom) Courtesy Collection, Union Pacific Railroad Museum. p. 328 (top) *The Rising of the Usurpers*, The New York Public Library; (bottom) Culver Pictures. p. 330 Courtesy Edward Steichen (Photo, courtesy The Museum of Modern Art, New York). p. 332 (top) Photo © Arnold Newman, (bottom) Courtesy Museum of the City of New York. p. 338 The Granger Collection. p. 339 (top) Courtesy Collection, George Eastman House; (bottom) Courtesy The National Child Labor Committee. p. 347 (top) Courtesy Warren Harder Collection; (bottom) Courtesy The Virginia State Library. p. 354 (top) The Granger Collection; (bottom) Library of Congress. p. 365 Courtesy Chicago Historical Society. p. 366 (top) Courtesy Museum of Fine Arts, Boston, Charles Henry Hayden Fund; (bottom) Courtesy Collection, Whitney Museum of American Art, New York. p. 367 (top) Courtesy Collection, George Eastman House; (bottom) Courtesy The Metropolitan Museum of Art, New York: Gift of Frederic H. Hatch, 1926. p. 368 (top) Courtesy Museum of the City of New York; (bottom) Courtesy The New York Historical Society. p. 370 (top) Sy Seidman; (bottom) The Bettmann Archive. p. 378 (top) Brown Brothers; (bottom) Sy Seidman. p. 379 (top) Courtesy Collection, The Museum of Modern Art, New York; (bottom) Courtesy The New York Historical Society. p. 387 (top left) Courtesy Minnesota Historical Society; (top right) Courtesy The State Historical Society of Wisconsin; (bottom) Courtesy Collection, The Museum of Modern Art, New York: Gift of Lincoln Kirstein. p. 391 Courtesy Yale University Art Gallery: Gift of the Associates of Mr. Veblen. p. 401 Courtesy Glasgow Art Gallery and Museum. p. 402 Courtesy Museum of Fine Arts, Boston, Otis Norcross Fund. p. 403 (top) Courtesy The Metropolitan Museum of Art, New York, Alfred N. Punnett Fund and Gift of George D. Pratt, 1934; (bottom) Courtesy The Cleveland Museum of Art: Purchase, J. H. Wade Fund. p. 404 (top) Courtesy Addison Gallery of American Art, Phillips Academy, Andover, Massachusetts; (bottom left) Courtesy The Metropolitan Museum of Art, New York: Gift of Alfred Stieglitz; (bottom right) Sandak. p. 406 (left, top right) Sy Seidman; (bottom right) Courtesy The New York Historical Society. p. 407 Sy Seidman. p. 413 (top) Culver Pictures; (bottom) Library of Congress. p. 420 (both) Sy Seidman. p. 429 (top) Becker Collection, Smithsonian Institution; (bottom) The Granger Collection. p. 439 (top left) *The Silent War*, The New York Public Library; (bottom) Culver Pictures. p. 446 (top left) Library of Congress; (top right) Culver Pictures; (bottom) Sy Seidman. p. 450 Smithsonian Institution. p. 469 The Bettmann Archive. p. 470 (top, bottom right) Sy Seidman; (bottom left) Courtesy American Telephone and Telegraph Company. p. 471 Courtesy Ringling Brothers-Barnum and Bailey Circus. p. 472 (top) Courtesy University of Kansas, Pennell Collection; (bottom) Courtesy Sears, Roebuck and Company. p. 474 Courtesy Mrs. Charles Johnson Post and Miss Phyllis B. Post (Photo, Herb orth, *Life* Magazine © Time Inc.). p. 478 (top) Culver Pictures; (bottom left) The New York Public Library; (bottom right) p. 484 Library of Congress. p. 491 (top left) *New York World*, The New York Public Library; (top right) Library of Congress; (bottom) Photoworld. p. 494 (top) National Archives; (bottom) Sy Seidman. p. 500 (top) Courtesy Imperial War Museum, London; (bottom) National Archives. p. 501 National Archives. p. 509 Courtesy Collection, New Britain Museum of American Art, Harriet Russell Stanley Fund. p. 514 (top, bottom left) Brown Brothers; (bottom right) Wide World Photos. p. 521 The New York Public Library, Picture Collection. pp. 524, 525 (top) Wide World Photos. p. 525 (bottom) Culver Pictures. p. 533 (top) The New York Public Library, Picture Collection; (bottom) The Granger Collection. p. 537 Courtesy Collection, Whitney Museum of American Art, New York. pp. 538–539 Courtesy The Phillips Collection. p. 540 (left) Courtesy Collection, Arnold H. Crane; (right) Courtesy Collection, Whitney Museum of American Art, New York. p. 544 (top left) The Granger Collection; (top right, bottom) The New York Public Library, Picture Collection. p. 552 (top) Brown Brothers; (bottom left) Copyright 1921 by Famous Players-Lasky Corporation, Copyright renewed (Photo, courtesy The Museum of Modern Art/Film Stills Archive); (bottom right) Photo, courtesy The Museum of Modern Art/Film Stills Archive. p. 559 (top) Courtesy Franklin D. Roosevelt Library; (bottom left) UPI (Photo, courtesy Franklin D. Roosevelt Library); (bottom right) National Archives. p. 567 (top) Wide World Photos; (bottom) Courtesy Wayne State University, Labor History Archives. p. 571 (top, bottom left) Library of Congress; (bottom right) Courtesy *The News*, New York. pp. 578, 579 (top) Courtesy Dorothea Lange, The Oakland Museum Collection. p. 579 (bottom) Library of Congress. p. 587 (top) Theatre Collection, The New York Public Library at Lincoln Center, Astor, Lenox and Tilden Foundations; (bottom) Penguin Photo. p. 589 Courtesy Collection, The Museum of Modern Art, New York: Gift of the Advisory Committee. p. 590 (top, detail) Courtesy Collection, Whitney Museum of American Art, New York; (bottom) Courtesy The Art Institute of Chicago. p. 591 (top) Courtesy Collection, The Museum of Modern Art, New York: Gift of Mrs. David M. Levy; (bottom) Courtesy Collection, Whitney Museum of American Art, New York. p. 592 (top) Library of Congress; (bottom) Hedrich-Blessing. p. 598 (top) Courtesy Universal Pictures (Photo, courtesy The Museum of Modern Art/Film Stills Archives); (bottom) Brown Brothers. p. 605 (top) Tass (Photo, Sovfoto); (bottom) Culver Pictures. pp. 618, 622 Wide World Photos. p. 641 Library of Congress. p. 642 (top) Courtesy The Tate Gallery, London; (bottom) UPI. p. 643 (top) Library of Congress; (bottom) Cornell Capa, Magnum Photos. p. 644 (top) U.S. Department of Defense, Marine Corps; (bottom) Courtesy Mainichi (Photo, courtesy Random House). p. 651 (top) Wide World Photos; (bottom) UPI. p. 653 Wide World Photos. p. 659 (top) Photoworld; (bottom) Eastfoto. p. 665 (top) *Paris Match* (Photo, Pictorial Parade, Inc.). p. 670 (top) Fenno Jacobs, Black Star. p. 671 (bottom) UPI. p. 677 Courtesy Collection, Mr. and Mrs. Leo Castelli, New York. p. 678 (top) Courtesy Albright-Knox Art Gallery, Buffalo, New York: Gift of Seymour H. Knox; (bottom) Courtesy Dallas Museum of Fine Arts. p. 679 (top) Courtesy Collection, Whitney Museum of American Art, New York; (bottom) Courtesy Ansel Adams. p. 680 Courtesy Lever House. p. 687 (top, both) Wide World Photos; (bottom) UPI. p. 693 (top left) Wide World Photos; (top right) Michael Rougier, *Life* Magazine ⓒ Time Inc.; (bottom) UPI. p. 698 (top) UPI; (bottom) Burt Glinn, Magnum Photos, Inc. p. 712 Marc Riboud, Magnum Photos, Inc. p. 713 (top) Wide World Photos; (bottom) Marc Riboud, Magnum Photos, Inc. p. 716 (top) UPI; (bottom left) Erich Lessing, Magnum Photos; (bottom right) Courtesy United Nations. p. 723 (top) *Paris Match* (Photo, Pictorial Parade); (bottom) U.S. Department of Defense. p. 731 (top) National Aeronautics Space Administration; (bottom) Phillip Harrington, Nancy Palmer Photo Agency. p. 738 (top left) Don Carl Steffen ⓒ Time Inc. 1967; (top right) Joan Menschenfreund; (bottom) Courtesy Las Vegas New Bureau (Photo, J. Anthony Cook). p. 742 Copyright 1963 *The Chicago Sun Times*, Courtesy Wil-Jo Associates and Bill Mauldin. p. 743 (top) Copyright 1966 *Herblock in the Washington Post*; (bottom) ⓒ 1969 Jules Feiffer. p. 745 Courtesy Everson Museum of Art, Syracuse, New York. p. 746 (top) Courtesy Collection, Mr. and Mrs. Leo Castelli, New York; (bottom) Courtesy Collection, Myron Orlofsky (Photo, courtesy Leo Castelli Gallery). p. 747 (top) Courtesy Collection, John and Kimiko Powers, Aspen, Colorado (Photo, courtesy Sidney Janis Gallery, New York); (bottom) Courtesy Collection, University of Nebraska, Sheldon Bequest (Photo, courtesy M. Knoedler and Company). p. 748 (top) Bill Bridges; (bottom) Courtesy Richard Avedon and Cowles Book Company, Inc. p. 762 *London Daily Express* (Photo, Pictorial Parade). p. 768 (top) Wide World Photos; (middle) Fred Ward, Black Star; (bottom) UPI. p. 775 D. McCullin, Magnum Photos. p. 779 (top left Roger Malloch, Magnum Photos, Inc.; (top right) Wide World Photos; (bottom) Burt Glinn, Magnum Photos. p. 781 Shelly Rusten. p. 782 (bottom) Ron Sherman, Nancy Palmer Photo Agency. p. 783 (top left) Arthur Schatz, *Time* Magazine ⓒ Time Inc. 1971; (top right) Robert Crandall, Time Magazine; (bottom) Gene Daniels, Black Star. p. 784 (top) Joan Menschenfreund; (bottom) Bruce Davidson, Magnum Photos. p. 802 (bottom left) Courtesy Museum of Fine Arts, Boston; (bottom right) the Granger Collection. p. 803 (top left) The Granger Collection; (top right) Courtesy Bowdoin College Museum of Art, Brunswick, Maine; (bottom left) Courtesy New York City Hall Gallery; (bottom right) Courtesy The Historical Society of Pennsylvania. p. 804 (top left) Courtesy The Corcoran Gallery of Art; (top right) Courtesy New York City Hall Gallery; (bottom left) Courtesy The Metropolitan Museum of Art, New York; (bottom right) Library of Congress. p. 805 (top, both) Library of Congress; (bottom left) Courtesy Chicago Historical Society; (bottom right) Library of Congress. pp. 806, 807, 808 (top, both) Library of Congress. p. 808 (bottom left) The Granger Collection; (bottom right) Library of Congress. p. 809 (top left) Library of Congress; (top right) The Granger Collection; (bottom, both) Library of Congress. p. 810 (top left) Library of Congress; (top right) The Granger Collection; (bottom left) Courtesy Harry S. Truman Library (Photo, U.S. Army); (bottom right) General Services Administration; (top right) Courtesy Lyndon B. Johnson Library; (bottom) HRW photo.

Reference

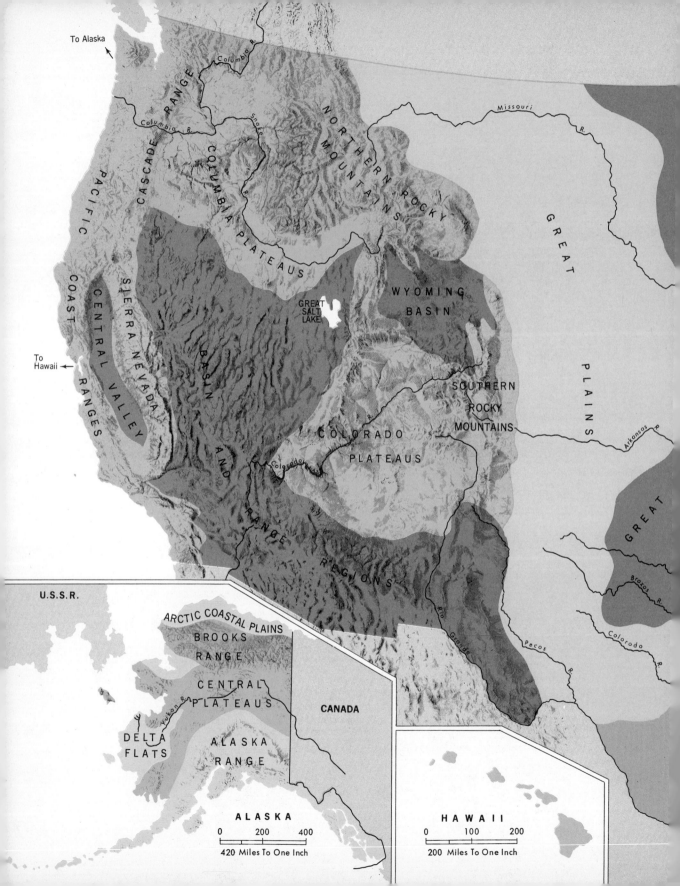

To Alaska

Columbia R.

PACIFIC

CASCADE RANGE

COLUMBIA PLATEAUS

Columbia R.

Snake R.

NORTHERN ROCKY MOUNTAINS

Missouri R.

GREAT

COAST

To Hawaii

SIERRA NEVADA

CENTRAL VALLEY

RANGES

GREAT SALT LAKE

WYOMING BASIN

BASIN

AND

SOUTHERN ROCKY MOUNTAINS

PLAINS

COLORADO PLATEAUS

Colorado R.

RANGE

REGIONS

Arkansas R.

GREAT

Rio Grande

Pecos R.

Brazos R.

Colorado R.

U.S.S.R.

ARCTIC COASTAL PLAINS

BROOKS RANGE

CENTRAL

PLATEAUS

Yukon R.

CANADA

DELTA FLATS

ALASKA

RANGE

ALASKA

0   200   400

420 Miles To One Inch

HAWAII

0   100   200

200 Miles To One Inch

PHYSICAL FEATURES OF THE UNITED STATES

797

0   200   400

208 Miles To One Inch

BASE MAP © 1958, JEPPESEN & CO. DENVER, COLO., U.S.A.

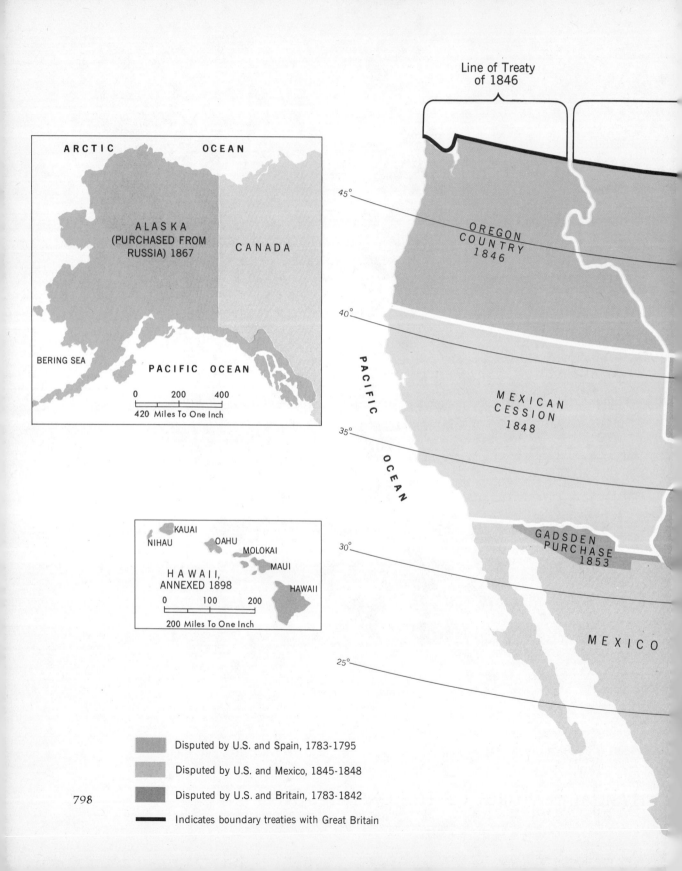

ARCTIC OCEAN

ALASKA
(PURCHASED FROM
RUSSIA) 1867

CANADA

BERING SEA

PACIFIC OCEAN

0   200   400

420 Miles To One Inch

KAUAI
NIHAU   OAHU
          MOLOKAI
             MAUI
HAWAII,   HAWAII
ANNEXED 1898

0   100   200

200 Miles To One Inch

Line of Treaty
of 1846

45°

OREGON
COUNTRY
1846

40°

PACIFIC

35°

MEXICAN
CESSION
1848

OCEAN

30°

GADSDEN
PURCHASE
1853

MEXICO

25°

798

Disputed by U.S. and Spain, 1783-1795

Disputed by U.S. and Mexico, 1845-1848

Disputed by U.S. and Britain, 1783-1842

Indicates boundary treaties with Great Britain

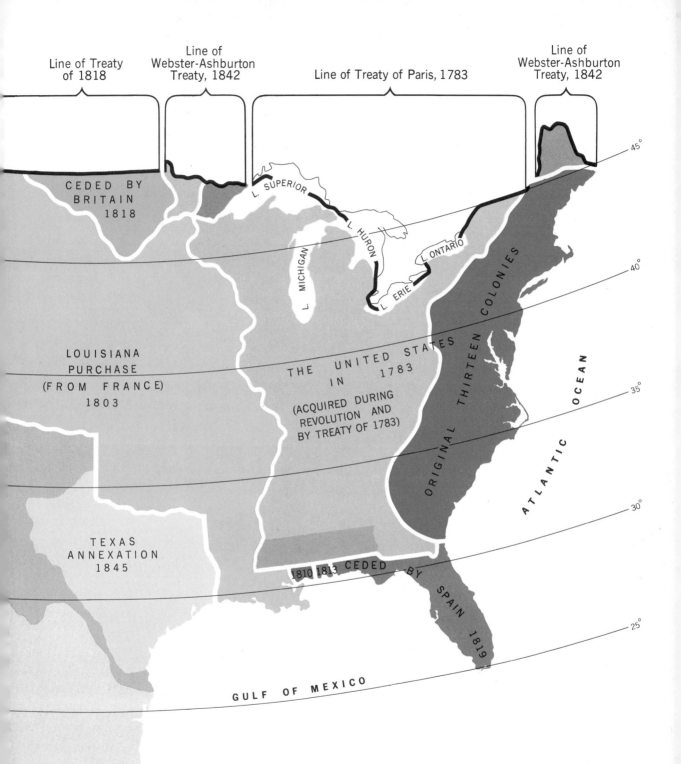

Line of Treaty
of 1818

Line of
Webster-Ashburton
Treaty, 1842

Line of Treaty of Paris, 1783

Line of
Webster-Ashburton
Treaty, 1842

45°

CEDED BY
BRITAIN
1818

L. SUPERIOR

L. HURON

L. MICHIGAN

L. ONTARIO

ORIGINAL THIRTEEN COLONIES

40°

L. ERIE

LOUISIANA
PURCHASE
(FROM FRANCE)
1803

THE UNITED STATES
IN 1783
(ACQUIRED DURING
REVOLUTION AND
BY TREATY OF 1783)

35°

ATLANTIC OCEAN

30°

TEXAS
ANNEXATION
1845

1810 1813 CEDED BY SPAIN 1819

25°

GULF OF MEXICO

TERRITORIAL GROWTH OF THE UNITED STATES

0   300   600

300 Miles To One Inch

POLITICAL MAP OF THE UNITED STATES

National Capital
State Capital
Other Cities
Dates indicate year state
was admitted to Union

0   200   400
208 Miles To One Inch

801

1 **George Washington** (1732–1799)
Virginia
In Office: 1789–1797
    Commander-in-Chief of the
      Continental Army, 1775–1783

2 **John Adams** (1735–1826)
Massachusetts—Federalist
In Office: 1797–1801
    Vice President, 1789–1797
    Minister to Great Britain, 1785–1788

3 **Thomas Jefferson** (1743–1826)
Virginia—Democratic-Republican
In Office: 1801–1809
  Vice President, 1797–1801
  Secretary of State, 1789–1793
  Minister to France, 1785–1789

4 **James Madison** (1751–1836)
Virginia—Democratic-Republican
In Office: 1809–1817
  Secretary of State, 1801–1809

5 **James Monroe** (1758–1831)
Virginia—Democratic-Republican
In Office: 1817–1825
  Secretary of State, 1811–1817
  Minister to Great Britain, 1803–1806
  Governor of Virginia, 1799–1802, 1811

6 **John Quincy Adams** (1767–1848)
Massachusetts—National Republican
In Office: 1825–1829
  Congressman, 1831–1848
  Secretary of State, 1817–1825
  Minister to Great Britain, 1815–1817

7 Andrew Jackson (1767–1845)
Tennessee—Democrat
In Office: 1829–1837
 Senator, 1797–1798, 1823–1825
 Major-General, United States Army,
  1814–1821
 Congressman, 1796

8 Martin Van Buren (1782–1862)
New York—Democrat
In Office: 1837–1841
 Vice President, 1833–1837
 Secretary of State, 1829–1831
 Senator, 1812–1820

9 William Henry Harrison (1773–1841)
Ohio—Whig
In Office: March 4–April 4, 1841
 Senator, 1825–1828
 Congressman, 1816–1819

10 John Tyler (1790–1862)
Virginia—Whig
In Office: 1841–1845
 Vice President, 1841
 Senator, 1827–1836

11 James K. Polk (1795–1849)
Tennessee—Democrat
In Office: 1845–1849
　　Governor of Tennessee, 1839–1841
　　Speaker of the House of Representatives,
　　　1835–1839
　　Congressman, 1825–1839

12 Zachary Taylor (1784–1850)
Louisiana—Whig
In Office: 1849–1850
　　Major-General in the Mexican War,
　　　1846–1847

13 Millard Fillmore (1800–1874)
New York—Whig
In Office: 1850–1853
　　Vice President, 1849–1850
　　Congressman, 1833–1835, 1837–1843

14 Franklin Pierce (1804–1869)
New Hampshire—Democrat
In Office: 1853–1857
　　Senator, 1837–1842
　　Congressman, 1833–1837

15 James Buchanan (1791–1868)
Pennsylvania—Democrat
In Office: 1857–1861
    Minister to Great Britain, 1853–1856
    Secretary of State, 1845–1849
    Senator, 1835–1845

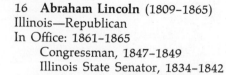

16 Abraham Lincoln (1809–1865)
Illinois—Republican
In Office: 1861–1865
    Congressman, 1847–1849
    Illinois State Senator, 1834–1842

17 Andrew Johnson (1808–1875)
Tennessee—Democrat*
In Office: 1865–1869
    Vice President, 1864–1865
    Senator, 1857–1862
    Governor of Tennessee, 1853–1857

18 Ulysses S. Grant (1822–1885)
Illinois—Republican
In Office: 1869–1877
    Commander of the United States Army,
    1863–1866

    *Johnson ran with Lincoln on the Union party ticket, as the
Republicans called themselves in the election of 1864.

19 **Rutherford B. Hayes** (1822–1893)
Ohio—Republican
In Office: 1877–1881
    Governor of Ohio, 1868–1872, 1875–1876

20 **James A. Garfield** (1831–1881)
Ohio—Republican
In Office: March 4–September 19, 1881
    Congressman, 1863–1881

21 **Chester A. Arthur** (1830–1886)
New York—Republican
In Office: 1881–1885
    Vice President, 1881

22 **Grover Cleveland** (1837–1908)
New York—Democrat
In Office: 1885–1889
    Governor of New York, 1882–1884

23 Benjamin Harrison (1833–1901)
Indiana—Republican
In Office: 1889–1893
    Senator, 1881–1887

24 Grover Cleveland (1837–1908)
New York—Democrat
In Office: 1893–1897
    President, 1885–1889
    Governor of New York, 1882–1884

25 William McKinley (1843–1901)
Ohio—Republican
In Office: 1897–1901
    Governor of Ohio, 1891–1896
    Congressman, 1876–1890

26 Theodore Roosevelt (1858–1919)
New York—Republican
In Office: 1901–1909
    Vice President, 1901
    Governor of New York, 1898–1900
    Assistant Secretary of the Navy, 1897–1898

27 **William Howard Taft** (1857–1930)
Ohio—Republican
In Office: 1909–1913
    Chief Justice of the Supreme Court,
      1921–1930
    Secretary of War, 1904–1908
    Governor of the Phillipines, 1901–1904

28 **Woodrow Wilson** (1856–1924)
New Jersey—Democrat
In Office: 1913–1921
    Governor of New Jersey, 1911–1912

29 **Warren G. Harding** (1865–1923)
Ohio—Republican
In Office: 1921–1923
    Senator, 1915–1921

30 **Calvin Coolidge** (1872–1933)
Massachusetts—Republican
In Office: 1923–1929
    Vice President, 1921–1923
    Governor of Massachusetts, 1919–1920

31 Herbert Hoover (1874–1964)
California—Republican
In Office: 1929–1933
    Secretary of Commerce, 1921–1928

32 Franklin Delano Roosevelt (1882–1945)
New York—Democrat
In Office: 1933–1945
    Governor of New York, 1928–1932
    Assistant Secretary of the Navy,
      1913–1920

33 Harry S. Truman (1884–   )
Missouri—Democrat
In Office: 1945–1953
    Vice President, 1945
    Senator, 1934–1944

34 Dwight D. Eisenhower (1890–1969)
Pennsylvania, New York*—Republican
In Office: 1953–1961
    Supreme Commander, Allied Forces in
      Europe, 1944–1945

*State residing in when elected President.

35 John F. Kennedy (1917–1963)
Massachusetts—Democrat
In Office: 1961–1963
    Senator, 1952–1960
    Congressman, 1946–1952

36 Lyndon B. Johnson (1908–
Texas—Democrat
In Office: 1963–1969
    Vice President, 1961–1963
    Senator, 1948–1960

37 Richard M. Nixon (1913–   )
California, New York*—Republican
In Office: 1969–
    Vice President, 1953–1961
    Senator from California, 1950–1953
    Congressman from California, 1946–1950
*State residing in when elected President.

INDEX

Italicized page numbers preceded by c, f, m, or p refer to a chart (c), feature (f), map (m), or picture (p) on the page. **Boldface** page numbers are pages on which a definition or explanation is given.

A

Abercromby, James, 32
Aberdeen, Lord, 199
Abilene, Kans., 301
Abolitionists, 73–74, 173, 190–194, *p 193,* 199, 208, 213, 227–228, 252, 267
Acheson, Dean, 561, 671–672, 685, 691, 780
Act of Chapultepec, 718
Act of Havana, 612
Act of Religious Toleration of 1649, 26
Adams, Ansel, 679
Adams, Henry, 317, 383, 391, 399, 412, 542
Adams, John, *p 802;* American minister to Britain, 81; appoints "Midnight Judges," 113; Federalist candidate for President, 111–112; nominates Washington commander-in-chief, 54; peace commissioner, 68; as President, 110; revolutionary leader, 39, 51–52, 55–58, 68; writes Massachusetts constitution, 75; writing of Declaration of Independence, 58
Adams, John Quincy, 391, *p 803;* acquires Florida for U.S., 119; favored for President by New England, 125; nominated for President, 125; as President, 133–134; as Secretary of State, 119–120
Adams-Onis Treaty of 1819, 119, 197
Adams, Samuel: anti-Federalist, 84; denounces British army, 48; organizes Boston Tea Party, 51; revolutionary leader, 50–53, 55, 68
Adams, Sherman, 695
Adamson Act, 454
Addams, Jane, 374, 456
Adenauer, Konrad, *p 723*
Administration of Justice Act, *c 52*
Advertising, 519, *p 521,* 732, 739, 751; finances newspapers, 405; radio and, 532
AFL. See American Federation of Labor.
Africa: cold war in, 703; colonialism in, 461; nationalist movement in, 655, 699, 710–711, 715, 761; neu-
tralism in, 705; newly independent, *p 712–713;* slave trade from, 12, 15–17, *f 16;* Third World nations emerge, 699, *p 712–713;* U.S. blacks and, 185, 191, 534, 761–765; U.S. investments in, 610; U.S. relations with, 711, 715–717, 761; World War II in, 617–619, 627, 629
Africans: enslavement of, 6, 15–17, 38. *See also* Blacks, Slavery.
Afrika Korps, 627, 629
Agee, James, 580
Agnew, Spiro T., 778, 786
Agricultural Adjustment Act, 561
Agricultural Adjustment Administration, 562
Agriculture: cities depend on, 361; colleges of, 386; colonial, 14; cooperatives, 517; crisis in 1920's, 517–518; crisis after World War I, 511, 517; "dust bowls," 526; European, 351; New Deal policies and, 562, 573; nineteenth century, 137–138, 152; of 1930's, 580; opposes protectionism, 419, 421, 422; organizations, 349, 424, 517; political parties and, 414–415, 515, 517–518; problems of, 411–416, 421–424, 430; produce transportation, 318; post-World War II, 732; sharecropping, 430–431, 456; slavery and, 165–167; southern, 165–166, 225; surpluses, 461; western, 156, 164, 225, 309–310; World War I profits from, 638. *See also* Cattle industry, Cotton, Great Plains, Populist party, Tobacco industry.
Agriculture, Department of, 447
Agricultural Revolution, 164, 308–312, 361
Aguinaldo, Emilio, 477
Alabama: cotton mills in, 431; early settlers, 156; enters Union, 120; land rush, 165; National Guard federalized, 769; secedes, 230; states rights in, 230, 767–769; Tuskegee Institute, 388
"Alabama," 253, 254
Alamo, the, 198
Alaska, 196; admitted to Union, 735; coal fields of, 448; purchased from Russia, 461, 464; Russia claims, 120
Albany, N.Y.: fur trading post, 29; Howe attempts march to, 63, 65; site of Albany Congress, 30
Albany Congress, 30

Albany Plan of Union, 30–31, 52–53
Albee, Edward, 409, 755
Alcorn, James L., 279
Aldrich, Thomas Bailey, 355
Aldrin, Edwin, *p 731*
Aleutian Islands, 631, 633
Alger, Horatio, 331, 400, 513, 515, 575
Algeria, 629, 711, *p 712,* 715
Alien Act, 111, 113
Alien Registration Act, *c 690*
Alienation, 739–740, 750, 754–755
All Quiet on the Western Front, *f 499*
Allegheny River, 29
Allen, Fred, 596, *f 597*
Allen, Frederick Lewis, 329, 523
Alliance for Progress, 722, 773
Allied Powers: aid Russian empire, 606; ask Japanese surrender, 634; force Germany to pay World War I debts, 607–608; in World War I, 488–490, 496–502; in World War II, 626–635. *See also* Grand Alliance, World War II.
Altgeld, John P., 346–348, 427, 467
Alton, Ill. 192
Amalgamated Association of Iron, Steel and Tin Workers, 346
Amalgamated Clothing Workers of America, 637
Amendments. See Constitution.
America First Committee, 620
American Anti-Slavery Society, 191–192, 194
American Art Union, 176
American Baseball League, 405
American Bible Society, 186
American Board of Commissioners of the Foreign Missions, 185
American Colonization Society, 185
American Educational Society, 185
American Expeditionary Force, 505
American Federation of Labor, 343–345, *f 344,* 518; merged with CIO, 732; no-strike agreement, 492
American Home Missions Society, 185
American Medical Association, 685
American Newspaper Guild, 599
American party ("Know-Nothing" party), 218, *p 224*
American Protective Association, 355
American Railway Union, 346
American Revolution: battles of, 62–68, *m 64,* 518; beginnings of, 53–54; catalyst toward democracy, 129;

colonial assemblies, 42–43, 48–53; conflicts leading to, 45–53; domestic debt, 81–82; end of, 67–68; financing of, *f 66;* fought under Confederation, 82; France joins, 63; leaders of, 39, 51–58; life during, *p 69–72;* in literature, 172; peace negotiated, 68; produces opposition to slavery, 73, 191; results of, 68–75; unifies colonists, 42, 48, 51
American School of Art, 595, 752
American Socialist-Labor party, 340
American Steel and Wire Company, 329
American Student Union, 583
American Sunday School Union, 186
American Telephone and Telegraph Company, 324
American Temperance Union, 187
American Tobacco Company, 445
American Tract Society, 186
American Youth Congress, 583
Americans for Democratic Action, 686
Ames, Oakes, 307
Amherst, Geoffrey, 32
Anaconda Plan, 244
Anacostia Flats, 527
Anarchism, 340, 343, 506
Anderson, Sherwood, 547–548
Andrews, Eliza Francis, *f 279*
Andrews, Sidney, 324
Andros, Edmund, 21, 26
Annapolis, Md., 83, 230
Annapolis Convention, 83
Antietam Creek, battle of, 246, 248, 251
Anti-Federalists, 84–85
Antioch College, 388
Anti-Saloon League, 536
Anti-Semitism, 325, 535; in Germany, 616, 649; in Russia, 352; in United States, 577, 582
Antitrust legislation, 327–329; against labor unions, 517–518; enforced, 445, 454–455, 560–561, 565, 730, 767
Antoine, C. C., 279
"Apollo 11," 729
Appalachian Mountains: migration across, 155–156; poverty in, 733
Appomattox, Va., 246, 259
Architecture, *p 378–381;* colonial, 35, *p 35;* early American, 181–182; of the 1920's, 550; of the 1930's, 580, 595; post-World War II, 753; urban, 369, 376, 381, 519, 580, 595

C

Y

Z